FOUNDATIONS

READINGS IN PRE-CONFEDERATION CANADIAN HISTORY

VOLUME 1

FOUNDATIONS

READINGS IN PRE-CONFEDERATION CANADIAN HISTORY

VOLUME 1

SECOND EDITION

MARGARET CONRAD
University of New Brunswick

ALVIN FINKEL
Athabasca University

PEARSON
Longman

Toronto

Library and Archives Canada Cataloguing in Publication

Foundations : readings in pre-Confederation Canadian history / [edited by] Margaret Conrad, Alvin Finkel.—2nd ed.

Volume 1
Includes bibliographical references and index.
ISBN-13: 978-0-321-49110-7
ISBN-10: 0-321-49110-6

1. Canada—History—To 1763 (New France)—Textbooks. 2. Canada—History—1763–1867—Textbooks. I. Conrad, Margaret II. Finkel, Alvin, 1949–

FC161.F66 2008   971   C2006-906985-9

ISBN-13: 978-0-321-49110-7
ISBN-10: 0-321-49110-6

Editor-in-Chief, Vice-President of Sales: Kelly Shaw
Senior Acquisitions Editors: Christine Cozens, Laura Forbes
Marketing Manager: Leigh-Anne Graham
Supervising Developmental Editor: Suzanne Schaan
Production Editor: Richard di Santo
Copy Editor: Anne Borden
Proofreader: Claudia Forgas
Permissions Research: Beth McAuley
Production Coordinator: Avinash Chandra
Composition: Laserwords
Art Direction and Cover Design: Julia Hall
Cover Image: Anglican Church of Canada, General Synod Archives (GS-75-103-S3-113)

Additional credits for this edition appear on pages viii–x, which constitute a continuation of the copyright page.

1 2 3 4 5   2007

Printed and bound in the United States of America.

PEARSON
Longman

Contents

PART V | Industrializing Canada, 1840–1867   417

List of Sources

PART I

Toby Morantz, "Plunder or Harmony? On Merging European and Native Views of Early Contact," in Germain Warkentin and Carolyn Podruchny, eds., *Decentering the Renaissance: Canada and Europe in Multidisciplinary Perspective,* pages 48–67. Copyright © 2001 University of Toronto Press Incorporated. Reprinted with permission of the publisher.

Winona Wheeler, "Reflections on the Social Relations of Indigenous Oral Histories," in Ute Lischke and David T. McNab, eds., *Walking a Tightrope: Aboriginal People and Their Representations* (Waterloo: Wilfrid Laurier University Press, 2005), 189–213. Reprinted with permission of the publisher.

Shelagh D. Grant, "North Baffin Prior to 1905," in Shelagh D. Grant, *Arctic Justice: On Trial for Murder, Pond Inlet, 1923,* 7–23. Copyright © 2002 McGill-Queen's University Press. Reprinted with permission of the publisher.

Excerpt from Ramsay Cook, "1492 and All That: Making a Garden Out of a Wilderness," from Ramsay Cook, *Canada, Quebec and the Uses of Nationalism,* Second Edition (Toronto: McClelland and Stewart, 1995), 51–72, 259–262. Used by permission, McClelland & Stewart Ltd. The Canadian Publishers.

PART II

Yves Landry, "Gender Imbalance, *Les Filles du Roi,* and Choice of Spouse in New France," translated by Jane Parniak, in Bettina Bradbury, ed., *Canadian Family History: Selected Readings* (Irwin, 2000), 14–32. Reprinted with permission of the author.

Gilles Havard, "1701: A New Situation," in Gilles Havard, *The Great Peace of Montreal of 1701: French-Native Diplomacy in the Seventeenth Century,* trans. Phyllis Aronoff and Howard Scott, pages, 160–78. Copyright © 2001 McGill-Queen's University Press. Reprinted with permission of the publisher.

Kenneth J. Banks, "Proclaiming Peace in 1713: A Case Study," in Kenneth J. Banks, ed., *Chasing Empire across the Sea: Communications and the State in the French Atlantic, 1713–1763,* pages 43–64. Copyright © 2002 McGill-Queen's University Press. Reprinted with permission of the publisher.

William Wicken, "Mi'kmaq Decisions: Antoine Tecouenemac, the Conquest, and the Treaty of Utrecht," in John Reid et al., *The Conquest of Acadia, 1710: Imperial Colonial and Aboriginal Constructs,* pages 86–100. Copyright © 2004 University of Toronto Press Incorporated. Reprinted with permission of the publisher.

Naomi E.S. Griffiths, "1755–1784: Exile Surmounted," in *The Contexts of Acadian History, 1686–1784* (Montreal: McGill-Queen's University Press, 1992), 95–127.

PART III

John Reid, "*Pax Britannica* or *Pax Indigena*? Planter Nova Scotia (1760–1782) and Competing Strategies of Pacification," *Canadian Historical Review* 85, 4 (December 2004): 669–692. Reprinted with permission of the University of Toronto Press Incorporated (www.utp.journals.com).

Ann Gorman Condon, "The Family in Exile: Loyalist Social Values after the Revolution," in Margaret Conrad, ed., *Intimate Relations: Family and Community in Planter Nova Scotia* (Fredericton: Acadiensis Press, 1995), 42–53.

F. Murray Greenwood, "The Security Danger, 1793–1798," in F. Murray Greenwood, *Legacies of Fear: Law and Politics in Quebec in the Era of the French Revolution* (Toronto: The Osgoode Society, 1993), 76–103. Reprinted with permission of the publisher.

George Sheppard, "'Cool Calculators': Brock's Militia," in *Plunder, Profit, and Paroles: A Social History of the War of 1812 in Upper Canada* (Montreal: McGill-Queen's University Press, 1994), 40–67.

Carolyn Podruchny, "Unfair Masters and Rascally Servants? Labour Relations among Bourgeois, Clerks and Voyageurs in the Montreal Fur Trade, 1780–1821," *Labour/Le Travail* 43 (Spring 1999): 43–70. © Canadian Committee on Labour History. Reprinted with the permission of CCLH.

Cole Harris, "Voices of Smallpox around the Strait of Georgia," *Ethnohistory* 41, 4 (Fall 1994): 593–626. Copyright 1994, the American Society for Ethnohistory. All rights reserved. Used by permission of the publisher.

PART IV

Rusty Bittermann and Margaret McCallum, "When Private Rights Become Public Wrongs: Property and the State in Prince Edward Island in the 1830s." Reprinted with permission of the Publisher from *Despotic Dominion: Property Rights in British Settler Societies* by McLaren, John, A.R. Buck, and Nancy E. Wright, eds. © University of British Columbia Press 2005. All rights reserved by the Publisher.

Jerry Bannister, "The Campaign for Representative Government in Newfoundland," *Journal of the Canadian Historical Association*, New Series, 5 (1999): 19–40.

Jean-Marie Fecteau, "'This Ultimate Resource': Martial Law and State Repression in Lower Canada, 1837–8," in F. Murray Greenwood and Barry Wright, eds., *Canadian State Trials*, vol. 2, pages 207–47. Copyright © 2002 University of Toronto Press Incorporated. Reprinted with permission of the publisher.

Mary Anne Poutanen, "Bonds of Friendship, Kinship, and Community: Gender, Homelessness, and Mutual Aid in Early Nineteenth-Century Montreal." Reprinted with permission of the Publisher from *Negotiating Identities in 19th and 20th Century Montreal* by Bradbury, Bettina and Tamara Myers, eds. © University of British Columbia Press 2006. All rights reserved by the Publisher.

Catharine Anne Wilson, "Reciprocal Work Bees and the Meaning of Neighbourhood," *Canadian Historical Review* 82, 3 (September 2001): 431–64. Reprinted with permission of the University of Toronto Press Incorporated (www.utp.journals.com).

Adele Perry, "Hardy Backwoodsmen, Wholesome Women, and Steady Families: Immigration and the Construction of a White Society in Colonial British Columbia, 1849–1871" in *Histoire sociale/Social History*, Vol. 33, no. 66 (November 2000): 343–360.

Lorne Hammond, "Marketing Wildlife: The Hudson's Bay Company and the Pacific Northwest, 1821–49," *Forest and Conservation History* 37, 1 (January 1993): 14–25. Reprinted by permission of the Forest History Society, Inc., Durham, NC (www.forest.history.org).

PART V

Claudette Knight, "Black Parents Speak: Education in Mid-Nineteenth-Century Canada West," *Ontario History* 89, 4 (December 1997): 269–284.

Cecilia Morgan, "'Better Than Diamonds' Sentimental Strategies and Middle-Class Culture in Canada West," *Journal of Canadian Studies* 32, 4 (1998): 125–148. Reprinted with permission of the University of Toronto Press Incorporated (www.utp.journals.com).

Lesley Erickson, "Constructed and Contested Truths: Aboriginal Suicide, Law, and Colonialism in the Canadian West(s), 1823–1927," *Canadian Historical Review* 86, 4 (December 2005): 595–618. Reprinted with permission of the University of Toronto Press Incorporated (www.utp.journals.com).

Bruce Curtis, "Social Investment in Medical Forms: The 1866 Cholera Scare and Beyond," *Canadian Historical Review* 81, 3 (2000): 347–379. Reprinted with permission of the University of Toronto Press Incorporated (www.utp.journals.com).

Ged Martin, "The Case Against Canadian Confederation, 1864–1867," in Ged Martin, ed., *The Causes of Canadian Confederation* (Fredericton: Acadiensis Press, 1990), 19–49.

Preface

The second edition of *Foundations: Readings in Pre-Confederation Canadian History* offers students a sample of some of the best scholarship on the history of Canada before Confederation. Although designed to accompany our two-volume *History of the Canadian Peoples* and our one-volume *Canada: A National History*, this anthology can supplement any survey of Canadian history or serve as a stand-alone text. The readings are grouped in overlapping time periods that have become more-or-less conventional for the study of pre-Confederation history: Beginnings to 1663; France in America, 1663–1763; The Origins of British North America, 1749–1821; Maturing Colonial Societies, 1815–1867; and Industrializing Canada, 1840–1867.

Our main goal in selecting which articles to publish was to ensure a balance of social, political, and economic topics as well as a balanced coverage of Canadian regions. Given the size of Canada and the explosion of historical research in recent years, this proved to be a difficult task.

The scholarly articles in this book are what historians call *secondary* sources. They offer a historian's interpretation of events in the past. To experience some of the excitement of coming face-to-face with the raw material of historical inquiry, we suggest that students consult the *primary* sources found in Cornelius Jaenen and Cecilia Morgan, *Material Memory: Documents in Pre-Confederation History* (Toronto: Pearson Education Canada, 1998). *Material Memory* includes such classic documents as the first recorded European encounter with Native North Americans, A Mi'kmaq Declaration of War in 1749, the Articles of Capitulation of New France in 1760, William Lyon Mackenzie's Draft Constitution, 1837, and excerpts from diaries and letters written by fur traders in the Northwest Territories. In such sources, voices from the past speak directly to us without being compromised by the interpretations of historians.

Many of the articles published here are less concerned with what happened in the past than with the different perspectives that historians bring to the study of history. For example, Winona Wheeler argues that most of the historical accounts dealing with European–Native encounters obscure the Native perspective because historians tend to privilege written documents over oral history. While these historians may believe that the written evidence produced at the time of an event is a superior source to interviews with First Nations individuals many years later, she suggests that the written evidence was produced almost exclusively by the European side and is riddled with misunderstandings of Native goals and Native character. Oral history, Wheeler argues, should be included among the sources consulted by historians because it offers a perspective from those who have preserved the historical memory of First Nations peoples.

The study of how history has been constructed and its changing interpretations over time and across cultural divides is called *historiography*. In recent years the lines between history—what happened in the past—and historiography—the study of how history has been written—have blurred somewhat. Most professional historians recognize that their interpretations, like those of their predecessors, are shaped by present biases and interests. With this understanding, they are more modest in their claims to objectivity and, instead, strive to examine their own motivations and explore a variety of perspectives on the topics they analyze.

The bias of this reader is toward articles in social history, a field of study that has gained prominence since the 1960s. As a result, many of the readings in this text deal with issues of class, culture, gender, race, and region—the mantra of social historians. These categories of analysis have opened new avenues of inquiry and changed the way Canadian history has been researched and written. Social history has also changed the way that older fields, such as economic history, have been understood. For instance, feminist theory and methodology have enabled Catharine Wilson, in her article published here, to explore how the gendered division of labour operated in mid-nineteenth-century rural families and communities. Even political history has been transformed by social history approaches, as the article by Jean-Marie Fecteau on martial law and state repression during the Lower Canada Rebellion of 1837 attests.

In this edition, we have also included more articles on environmental history. The current interest in our rapidly changing environment has prompted historians to ask new questions about the past. As is often the case in any line of historical inquiry, environmental history reveals that the problems concerning us today, such as resource depletion, species extinction, and pandemics, were also ones that preoccupied our ancestors.

In approaching secondary historical sources, students will need to apply their own critical reading skills. Some readings are more accessible than others, and a few can be downright challenging, even to the highly trained professional historian. Whatever the style of historical writing, students must engage the material. It is often best to read quickly, jotting down arguments and themes that seem most apparent. In

particular, it is important to establish the thesis, or the controlling argument, of the reading. Ideally, the thesis will be stated in a sentence or two. In a well-written essay, the thesis is usually clearly stated at the beginning and elaborated upon throughout the rest of the piece.

Once the arguments and themes have been determined, it is important to evaluate them. Are the arguments sound and well supported? One way of making such an assessment is to check the endnotes to see if the author has consulted primary and secondary sources relevant to the topic. Evaluating sources is a fundamental exercise for students of history. Another approach is to consult additional publications on the topic to see if they corroborate the author's claims or at least do not contradict them.

It is also important to evaluate the author's point of view, which often has an impact on how source materials are selected and interpreted. All of the articles in this reader have been written by trained scholars so it can be assumed that they know the nuts and bolts of their craft. Nevertheless, we must also remember that they write in a context that may slant their interpretations. For example, a historian may be eager to prove that a political policy has been damaging to a particular group and offer only evidence to support such a claim, ignoring all counter-evidence. Students often have not read broadly enough to detect such bias, but there are shortcuts to help them in their efforts. By finding out what else the author has published, it may be possible to discover that the article has been written by someone who has produced one or more books on the topic that have been reviewed by other scholars. These reviews usually highlight the positive and negative aspects of the author's approach.

The tone of the article also reveals something about the author. While some scholars strive for a detached, impersonal style, others bring passion and political commitment to the work; still others may be ironic or even sarcastic. History is written by people with their own special character traits and it is useful to reflect on how these find expression in their publications.

We hope that students will find these readings both challenging and enlightening. By helping students understand that history as represented in textbooks is constructed from sources such as the ones published here, we hope to open a window not only on developments in Canada's past but also on the discipline of history, which is ever evolving.

We would like to thank the following people who were instrumental in the production of this volume: Christine Cozens, Rachel Stuckey, Suzanne Schaan, and Richard di Santo from Pearson Education Canada; our proofreaders, Anne Borden and Claudia Forgas; and the reviewers whose comments helped shape this new edition, including Willeen G. Keough of Simon Fraser University, Peter McInnis of St Francis Xavier University, and others who choose to remain anonymous.

Beginnings to 1663

The human history of today's Canada traces back many millennia. Before Europeans began to fish, trade furs, and finally settle in the lands of the First Nations in the 1500s and 1600s, Natives had created a variety of societies that were adapted to the environmental conditions of the various regions of Canada. The European newcomers, having their own cultural inheritance, tended to dismiss the achievements of the First Nations even as they depended upon them to make settlement possible and the fur trade profitable.

Our readings in Part 1 provide critical perspectives on the efforts of historians to study both the character of Native societies and the dynamics of the early encounters between Natives and Europeans. Articles in this section examine three major themes: the differences in social values between Canada's Indigenous peoples and the European newcomers and the ways in which these differences have biased historical writing about both pre-contact societies and early Native–European relations; the justifications that the Europeans used in their efforts to impose their own social values on the long-established inhabitants of North America; and the ways that Natives resisted efforts to change them into Europeans.

Although Canada's First Peoples experienced many changes over time in the pre-contact period, they developed time-honoured seasonal rhythms, a cycle of work and leisure that was repeated annually. Europeans also worked to seasonal rhythms but were increasingly motivated by ideas of improvement, profit, and progress. When they encountered the First Nations, Europeans looked at them through their own cultural prism and often judged them to be backwards and in need of European help and therefore European domination. In her article "Plunder or Harmony? On Merging European and Native Views of Early Contact," anthropologist Toby Morantz takes the position that Europeans and Natives viewed the world so differently that the accounts from the two groups about the character of early encounters and much else bear no resemblance to each other and cannot be reconciled. Although this article focuses on the Cree of northern Quebec, it clearly has implications for scholarly work on Native-European relations generally. After analyzing scholarly accounts of initial Native–European dealings, Morantz is so sceptical of their utility in establishing a narrative that makes sense to the two sides that she comes to a radical conclusion: "To write a history that tries to find a correspondence between the full body of oral tradition and the archival records would only destroy what is left of the Cree notions of their past. It would be the last act of the almost completed assimilation process, a dismantling of the last bastion of a unique Cree outlook." While she believes that historians cannot justify simply plucking materials from oral history interviews that coincide with the archival record, she concludes: "I am not sure historians can do anything else."

Winona Wheeler, a historian of Plains Cree ancestry, has a very different outlook on the same set of issues. Although she is as critical as Morantz of much of the historical work on First Nations and their relations with foreigners who began landing on their shores about 500 years ago, she is far more hopeful that oral accounts can be given a similar pride of place in historical work to written documentary sources. She makes it clear, however, that credible oral history of Native peoples cannot occur when historians simply waltz into Native communities and begin recording what people are prepared to tell them. Native peoples will only speak freely to those who gain their trust and who understand Native notions of the ownership of stories belonging to their tellers. Such trust is only given to those who make a genuine effort to become part of the community whose members they wish to interview and who gradually begin to grasp the values of the community. "Learning how to learn from another people's point of view is not a revolutionary concept, but it is hard work," she concludes.

The gap between Native peoples' and Europeans' points of view is explored in Shelagh D. Grant's "North Baffin Prior to 1905." After analyzing the seasonal cycle and cultural values of the Inuit in the pre-contact period, Grant explores the conflicts that occurred between the Inuit and Europeans as a result of cultural misunderstandings. She observes that Inuit understandings of how to deal collectively with individuals whose behaviour represented a threat to small, unpoliced communities were often translated by the European authorities into premeditated murder.

On the whole, the Europeans who came to the Americas from the 1500s onward dismissed Native attitudes and behaviours as "savage." They regarded the "New World" through lenses shaped by their experiences in Europe rather than through Native eyes. While First Nations religious beliefs emphasized harmony among all elements of nature, including humans, Christian Europeans believed fervently that humans were God's special creation, and that the natural world must be subordinated to humans' needs. Ramsay Cook's article, "1492 and All That: Making a Garden Out of a Wilderness," assesses critically the language that Europeans used to describe both the state of the Americas and their intentions to transform its character.

As Cook observes, the European conquerors not only aimed to transform the natural environment of the Americas, but also wished to dispossess the original inhabitants. Their insistence that Natives had left their lands in a "wilderness" state, failing to establish either European-model agriculture or European-style social relations, provided, they argued, a moral justification for ignoring the rights of Indigenous peoples to the enjoyment of their territories. The lands collectively shared by various First Nations groups were parcelled out as "property" for Europeans, who intended to use them in ways reminiscent of Old-Country practices.

Plunder or Harmony? On Merging European and Native Views of Early Contact

Toby Morantz

Contact, direct face-to-face contact, between the Cree of James Bay and Europeans happened in the spring of 1611 somewhere near the mouth of the Rupert River. This was during Henry Hudson's voyage of discovery from England, which had begun the previous summer. A Cree man visited the ship while it was ice-bound. On their return voyage, the crew mutinied, and Hudson, his son, and others were set adrift in a small boat to perish. Nevertheless, an account of this first recorded meeting was left by a member of the crew, Abacuk Pricket. In Pricket's version, the Cree visitor to the ship gratefully ("thankefully") receives from Hudson "a knife, a looking-glass and buttons," returning the next day with two caribou skins and two beaver skins. The Cree man presented Hudson with the beaver skins in exchange for the items he had received the previous day. Pricket relates, "then the master shewed him an hatchet, for which hee would have given the master one of his deere skinnes, but our master would have them both, and so hee had, although not willingly" (Asher 1860, 114).

The Cree oral account provides us with a different view of this meeting. Rather than the Native visitors to the ship (in this account, a husband and wife) being grateful or delighted with the exchange (or greedy), it is the English who sound thrilled (or greedy) and the Cree amused. This story was originally told to anthropologist Colin Scott in 1979 at Wemindji, James Bay, by Geordie Georgekish:

> Their jackets were made of fur from animals that he trapped. So people on the ship gave them some other clothes to wear. "Take your clothes off" they were told, and they understood what they were told. "Put these clothes on" they were told. (Narrator's aside: I guess they took their clothes off where nobody could see them. There must have been a small room where they could undress.) So the woman, whose pants were made of muskrat fur, removed her pants. And they went home wearing the clothes that the people from the ship had given them. (Scott 1983, 230)[1]

Although these two versions of first contact in James Bay are recognizable as describing the same encounter, it is apparent each brings to the fore a different perspective.

The English account emphasizes the Cree's delight with things the English would consider trifling items, while the Cree narration mentions nothing of such goods. Instead, it highlights their amusement with the English desire for

Toby Morantz, "Plunder or Harmony? On Merging European and Native Views of Early Contact," in Germain Warkentin and Carolyn Podruchny, eds., *Decentering the Renaissance: Canada and Europe in Multidisciplinary Perspective,* pages 48–67. Copyright © 2001 University of Toronto Press Incorporated. Reprinted with permission of the publisher.

their clothes, no doubt trifling items, as well, for the Cree. On the surface, then, there is a paradoxical concordance between these western and non-western versions of an event that is important in North American history. However, much like the icebergs that Hudson must have encountered, only a small fraction of the Cree story is apparent to the western-trained mind; most of the messages and lessons to be conveyed remain submerged, and consequently out of our view.

The Cree of eastern James Bay are Algonquian speakers who have occupied this territory for several thousand years. Upon its creation in 1670, the Hudson's Bay Company began to establish fur trade posts in Cree territory, locating them at favoured Native meeting places. Today, the Cree are settled in nine villages on these same meeting sites. Before adopting village life, the Cree lived in small extended family groups, hunting, trapping, and fishing (Francis and Morantz 1983). It was within these family settings, around the campfire, that the elders would tell stories that encompassed their knowledge of Cree cosmology, history, and values. Can this oral tradition be used to construct a unified history of the relations of these two groups? Will academic historians ever be able to write the history of the first encounters (or any other encounters) between the Cree and the new arrivals that conveys, in the telling of such events, the intent, substance, and lessons intrinsic to both the Cree and Euro-Canadians? Can there be a single history that reflects both perspectives? The one draws on a rich, ancient oral tradition, and the other on an equally rich, relatively ancient recorded one, but each is embedded in radically different cultural contexts. This paper explores whether there is enough common ground between the two to create a single narrative that adequately reflects the actions, judgments, feelings, convictions, values, and ideas of both sets of actors. History, we are told, has become more democratic, more

challenging of single narratives, and more receptive to including diverse accounts (Appleby, Hunt, and Jacob 1994, 293). The interest of such historians in integrating oral text with the written stems from the expectation that histories and or ethnohistories produced today will call on all sources, with some privileging of the Native views of history (Trigger 1982, 7).

Yet whereas most of the papers in this volume celebrate new insights and new perspectives on the early encounters—as well they should—this one, alas, sounds a note of caution about how self-congratulatory academic historians can be in believing they have the means to unravel the Native past. I do not mean to suggest that historians discard oral tradition, but rather that historians need to think carefully of what distortions they might be creating in absorbing oral text into a new written historical narrative.

The concern with the "Native voice" is relatively recent in the field of ethnohistory. This subfield, wed of anthropology and history in the late 1950s, pioneered the rescuing of Native peoples from their place in the background, restoring them to centre stage in the unfolding histories of Canada and the United States. Histories of the fur trade began to locate the Native hunters and their families exactly where they were in the seventeenth- and eighteenth-century developments of the trade: squarely in the forefront, making decisions about alliances, the standard of exchange, the location of posts, the routes that were used, the commodities that were traded, and so on (Ray 1974; Bishop 1974; Francis and Morantz 1983). Important as this contribution to history was, it began to occur to ethnohistorians that this writing-*in* of Native actors was not sufficient. The changing focus highlighted the fact that these ethnohistories did not account for the motivations behind the actions of Native peoples or for these people's values or perceptions of events. Native peoples were totally submerged in the western narrative, form, and themes.

Writing in 1974, Raymond Fogelson drew attention to the ethnocentrism in ethnohistoric writings, and remarked that "native interpretation of critical events and significant historical personages are un- or under-represented in ethnohistorical research" (Fogelson 1974, 106). Such concerns obviously were fundamental to Bruce Trigger's thinking. In his *Children of Aataentsic: A History of the Huron People to 1660*, first published in 1976, he presented a Huron-centred history based on chronicles left by the Jesuits and early French explorers, and on the archaeological record. Such an ethnohistory was far ahead of its time in its attempt to impute motive and explain action. Using an interpretive framework predicated on rationalism and an analysis based on decision-making by interest groups, Trigger crafted a highly credible, fascinating, and elegant narrative, depicting not only seventeenth-century Huron life but the choices and strategies the Huron forged in turbulent times as they confronted the French and the Huron's Iroquois adversaries. Nevertheless, even though Trigger's study, in directing his interest and analysis to individual Huron and French actors, was light years ahead of Eric Wolf's *Europe and the People without History* (1982), today it would likely fall prey to Stephen Hugh-Jones's criticism of the latter, more global history. Hugh-Jones commented that Wolf "aims to give back history to those who have been denied it but the history he provides is doubly our own; not only is it dominated by our European world, it is also seen through our western eyes" (Hugh-Jones 1989, 53). Trigger anticipated such criticisms in his preface to the 1987 second edition of *The Children of Aataentsic* and welcomed the new insights that would add to an understanding of Huron culture (Trigger [1976] 1987, xxx). He accepted that there were costs as well as benefits in privileging the rationalist approach and that he might have downplayed "the culturally specific factors that shaped the Huron way of life" (xxii). Others, working with societies not caught up in events as cataclysmic as those facing the Huron, discovered a rich and substantial extant oral tradition that they hoped would provide these "culturally specific factors." The value of oral tradition for African history had already been strikingly demonstrated by Jan Vansina in 1965, and anthropologists working in North America began exploring its use and applicability to the ethnohistories they were developing.

My introduction to Cree oral tradition came originally from "Cree Way,"[2] a curriculum development project at Rupert House (Waskaganish), and later from the field notes of a number of anthropologists whose reports were on deposit at the former Museum of Man (now the Canadian Museum of Civilization). The stories collected by this project cover a variety of themes, from hardships on the land to the Natives of long ago, from confrontations with enemies to the mountainous land of the caribou, but mostly they are of a mix of human and non-human characters, of trickster figures, of malevolent spirits or beings. These stories often contain detailed portrayals of the social setting, often mirroring contemporary Cree life and a recurring theme of supernatural power—or "medicine," as it is sometimes called—that could be used to good or evil ends (see Bauer 1973, 1).

With this collection from the Cree Way project on hand, I was certain I would be able to correct, partially, the European biases of my earlier histories, based, as they were, only on the journals and correspondence books of the Hudson's Bay Company. I published a paper in 1984 on the blending of oral and recorded history (Morantz 1984), full of hope that the evidence from the two types of histories could be merged to produce a history informed by both English and Cree perceptions. I have never written such a volume. Moreover, I know I never can.

I am now sceptical about ever achieving a kind of blended, universal history that does justice to both cultural traditions. I question whether using both the written texts of the Europeans and the oral texts of Native peoples will yield anything but a low-level understanding. Will it ever approximate for the Native peoples the quality of insights into perception, motivation, and interests that Canadian historians can generate for the European conduct in a given Native territory? I question our ability to turn oral tradition into historical text, as we know it, and at the same time capture the Native perception of events and their significance. Instead, I suggest that the production of histories, such as those attempting to reflect first meetings and early contact, can adequately be met only by not wrenching each history from its cultural habitat; the alternative, as I see it, is to produce different accounts according to the cultural expertise of the writers.

Different Histories

Western history today is undergoing change as historians attempt to find some acceptable balance between postmodern critiques, which are based on the concept of relativism, and the more traditional western science-based model of objective truth or knowledge, an issue that took hold in the 1970s and 1980s. The latter model is criticized by Joyce Appleby, Lynn Hunt, and Margaret Jacob, authors of *Telling the Truth about History* (1994, 217), for producing histories that always involve power, are exclusionary, and portray only partial points of view (11). In contrast, the concept of relativism holds that the "truth of a statement is relative to the position of the person making the statement" (6). Thus, this concept raises doubts about the ideal of objectivity in history. The position of Appleby, Hunt, and Jacob is that the creation of knowledge today requires "a different, more nuanced, less absolutist kind of realism... [a] practical realism"(247) that perforce requires historians to accept the impossibility of any research being neutral or any interpretation being other than tentative and imperfect (254). The authors champion the cause of writing multicultural history, whether "cacophonous or harmonic" (301).

Nonetheless, they maintain that some principles must be preserved. These principles seem to reflect the "traditional" core of western historical knowledge that persists despite its state of flux. I want to examine them here in order to develop a comparison between western historiography and Cree and other non-western histories.

Appleby and her co-authors expect that historians will adhere to the rigorous search for truth through commonly accepted standards of inquiry, scrutiny, and verification. As well, they see the continuation of the nineteenth-century development of a so-called universal, real, and sequential temporal dimension in which the past informs the present (53, 59, 265). For them, narratives, although attacked by postmodernists as "fictitious," are essential both to individual and social identity (235), and they favour a style of narrative, recognizing that, like lives, there is a beginning, middle, and end (263). Furthermore, history must be based on a qualified objectivity, one that draws in the undeniable elements of subjectivity through which historians should seek to understand "the internal dispositions of historical actors"—their motivations, their responses to events, and the ideas that shaped their social world (259).

These are not the principal constraints or requirements of Cree oral histories, though there are some convergences. The Cree, as other Algonquian- and non-Algonquian-speaking Native peoples, distinguish between two types of oral tradition, which they term *atiukan* and *tipachiman,*[3] though Richard Preston sees this distinction more as a gradation than a dichotomy (R. Preston 1975, 292; and see Vincent 1981, 11, and Scott 1983, 21). The former refers to myths, stories concerning the creation of the world when people and animals were not differentiated. Sylvie Vincent refers to these as "foundation stories" that explain putting the world in order (1992, 20).[4] The *tipachiman* are about real people—living, or their ancestors—but not necessarily without reference to what western thinking would label the supernatural. For example, the narrative of the first meeting with the white man begins with a Cree man conjuring in a shaking tent in which his *mistabeo,* his guardian spirit, foretells the arrival of the visitors and reassures the Cree before they encounter the ship and strange men (Scott 1983, 230). Despite its supernatural elements, the *tipachiman* is more closely aligned with our notions of history than is the *atiukan,* since the former describes actual events involving human actors, rather than what Richard Preston calls the "epic stories."[5] A Cree storyteller usually makes it clear which type of story—*tipachiman* or *atiukan*—he or she is telling, but Preston does not believe a storyteller would see the line between the two as clearly as he does. Stan Cuthand, a Cree linguist from Saskatchewan, would agree. He notes a very strong relationship between Cree myths and Cree society: "The stories of the mythical beings reinforced socially beneficial behaviour" (Cuthand 1988, 195).

In Preston's analysis of both types of Cree narratives, he found five concepts that he suggests convey, to the Crees, notions of their past or history—that is, the foundations of their historical consciousness. Cree narratives convey local knowledge that presents a record of the recent past. They also impart a sense of continuity, of how the Cree people, through their competency, have been able to maintain their way of life. Two other functions of their narratives are to present their cosmology—which describes their environment and their place within it—and their moral teachings. Lastly, he sees the notion of evolution or change also embodied in the *atiukan* stories, though this focus is reserved for explaining how, in terms of the relationship between humans and animals, the world of very long ago changed into what it presently is. One story alone would not suffice to teach all these elements, but a number heard over time would.

Some of these features are shared with the Western historical tradition, but not all, as we can see in the differences Preston emphasizes. The reckoning of time is often a concept that distinguishes western history from other histories (Appleby, Hunt, and Jacob 1994, 71–2). The western tradition is represented as having a linear concept of time, and other peoples represented as having a circular or cyclical concept, though Preston suspects that all societies combine elements of both, as even ours recognizes seasonal and life cycles. He has identified in the Cree *tipachiman* stories this dual reckoning of time, for the telling of the stories is situated as occurring "long ago" or "when I was a boy," but their content is more cyclical, recounting perhaps what people were doing in a certain winter season. However, as must be evident, the Cree stories do not mark the linear progression of time as starkly as in western history. The role of the individual in the narrative also differs in the Cree historical tradition. Preston comments that western values make much of some individuals, but Cree stories "are not so concerned with prominence as with the action and what happened as a consequence of the action."[6]

Another dimension to "reading" time differently is the categorization of time, so necessary to locating events in time. In a combined history, whose categorization is used? The standard western one has been based on ethnocentric classifications: "prehistory" and "history," or "precontact" and "contact." In the subdiscipline of ethnohistory, focus has been on change from the time of contact. Implicit in these ethnohistories (see Francis and Morantz 1983, as one example) is the notion that change begins with the coming of the Europeans and is framed in terms of the trade in metal tools, often guns. Native peoples can and do view the significant markers differently, emphasizing what is important to them. Thus, in her work with the Innu of the lower north shore of Quebec, Sylvie Vincent discovered that the white man's presence per se is not the important factor in delineating meaningful periods of history. Instead, the Innu divide history into periods where there was "only game" (no flour) or "only hides" (no cloth). In fact, they recount stories according to whether something happened "before flour" or "after flour,"[7] a more meaningful designation than the usual ones of "postcontact" or "the post-1821 merger" or "post-Confederation," all meaningless designations in the life of the subarctic hunter. Thus, standard Canadian history and Innu history (and likely others) do not share the same objectives, the same notions of what periods are worth designating.

The differences Preston notes between Cree notions of history and the western variety are not, I contend, obstacles to writing a single history of the first encounters between seventeenth-century Cree and Englishmen. The themes may be different, as may the interpretation of the events, but these discrepancies or contradictions can be incorporated in a single history that, as I believe all histories should, reflects the voices of the different actors.

Complexities and Conventions in Oral Narratives

What complicates turning Cree oral tradition into a form of narrative that is combinable with Euro-Canadian historical writing is the oral tradition's representation of the past and its narrative conventions. Representation of past states is more difficult to retrieve, I contend, from oral accounts than from recorded ones. In addition, there are stylistic forms in both types of Cree narrative that do not have counterparts in western history and, even if they did, their representations are still culturally embedded and not readily apparent.

Writing in 1984, I assumed that *tipachiman* stories were the sole equivalents of the western historical tradition and that the *atiukan* stories could be ignored. This was short-sighted; the writings of Richard Preston, Stan Cuthand, and Sylvie Vincent,[8] and of Julie Cruikshank on Yukon peoples (1990, 1991, 1992, 1996), have demonstrated that both types of oral tradition constitute the historical consciousness of the Cree and other Native peoples.

How, then, are historians to use myth or mythic structures when, although there is often a strong resemblance, mythic narratives recounted today are not identical to the ones told centuries ago? Writes Terence Turner in his study of South American Native mythology: "history and myth are both primarily to be understood as modes of consciousness of the social present, expressed in terms of the relation of that present to its past (and future)" (Turner 1988b, 279). Thus, in a mythic story one is confronted with the present and the past at the same time, not in chronological sequence.

Europeans recorded their narratives, such as that of Abacuk Pricket, and, in doing so, documented the events and explanations of interest at the time. Nevertheless, each new generation of historians reinterprets these narratives in the light of new issues in the present that impose questions on the events of the past. However, these reinterpretations of documents are more constrained than those of oral traditions because more of the original account is preserved. Many factors affect the status of oral narratives as western-style "evidence." Although Preston informs us that a good storyteller is careful to tell the story just as he or she heard it,[9] these stories are hundreds, even thousands, of years old and must have been modified by storytellers along the way. Even in one community there are several versions, differing factually, of the "first white man" story.[10] Recorded history, on the other hand, generally preserves the rendition of the story that is in the documents.

The performance of the stories adds another dimension to Cree oral tradition that does not have its counterpart in written history. Each time the story is told, the elder is drawing from the past to inform the present (see Tonkin 1992, 89). A Cree storyteller might be prompted to choose to tell a specific story to make a point, perhaps about the behaviour of a young person or the events of the day. He or she has a body of stories from which to select the one he or she believes relates to the present situation.[11] In making the point, the story is told in a way that adds, deletes, or embellishes certain elements, altering the emphasis or even the interpretation. The lessons of the past become altered; simultaneously the story that is handed down to be told and retold also becomes changed over time, or takes on new significance. Besides being reinterpreted or changed, stories are dropped if they no longer serve the needs of the society (Tonkin 1992, 11). We know, here in the northeast, that stories have also become forgotten or "forcibly" abandoned. John T. MacPherson collected myths from the Algonquins at Abitibi in 1930. He observed that the missionaries were horrified to find explicit sexual references in many of the myths and thus made Native raconteurs ashamed "of their ware."[12]

Oral tradition is no less valuable because the present *may* impinge more on the past through such revisions, embellishments, and deletions. Indeed, studies of oral tradition such as Tonkin's argue for this genre's importance not only for gaining representations of the past but for understanding the present and future as well. Most importantly, she demonstrates that the purposes of historical references are multiple as are the expectations of its nature (Tonkin 1992, 121).

A second factor in attempting to turn Cree oral texts into historical representations of past Cree life is that anthropologists or historians have not considered how the collection of stories was made. *Tipachiman* are stories that Cree storytellers tell and retell;[13] as "true stories of real

people," they constitute specialized knowledge about the past. However, this type of story has not been effectively distinguished from those stories simply collected from informants in an interview setting where the anthropologist determines the topics. Life histories based on interviews form the largest part of the collection of Cree oral tradition held by the Canadian Museum of Civilization under its "urgent ethnology" program of the 1970s. These are personal reminiscences, which Jan Vansina labels as "oral history" or "bits of life history," and should not be considered "oral tradition," which has passed from "mouth to mouth, for a period beyond the lifetime of the informants." Vansina regards these as messages transmitted beyond the generation that gave rise to them (Vansina 1985, 8, 12–13). I would alter the terminology, using "oral history" for *tipachiman* stories and reserving "oral tradition" for *atiukan* stories, to emphasize the differences between the two types of narratives. However, I agree with Vansina that personal reminiscences or anecdotal accounts are not the material of a society's history. There is much value in them, and I use them freely, but they do not necessarily represent a community's sense of its history, of what is to be remembered or passed on, of what represents them.

The use of an interview format to develop oral accounts can lead to incorporating the biases of the interviewer rather than those of the Crees.[14] The transcription of oral accounts from Whapmagoostui (Great Whale River), on deposit at the Canadian Museum of Civilization, provides a striking example of this. An anthropologist, working in 1974, was questioning one of the hunters about the use of alcohol, and in doing so she asked the translator to inform the hunter that "in the West 200 years ago, the fur trader would make the Indians drunk so that they would steal some of the furs." The hunter rejected this version, but went on to explain that the Reverend Walton (the Anglican priest in the area from 1892 to 1924) had told them that the people in the south got rich from "the Indians' furs." Once again he was presented with the visiting anthropologist's version: "it's not the government that got rich, it was the Hudson [sic] Bay Company."[15] Thus, attention must also be paid to how the narratives were collected, whether the stories were ones the elders wanted to tell or were responses to structured questions formulated by the anthropologist. These two methods of collection result in essentially different sources, of varying interest to historians; they are what Tonkin labels "popular memory" (an individual's recall) and "collective memory" (the community's version) (1992, 132).

Yet even this distinction is clouded. Interviewer bias in the accounts collected at Whapmagoostui is quite evident, but in Regina Flannery's life history of the Cree woman Ellen Smallboy is seemingly much less so. Flannery's methodological approach was to approach her subject by "introducing a topic and letting her proceed with as few interruptions as possible" (Flannery 1995, 7). Ellen Smallboy told the stories she deemed important, but the general subject matter was still generated to satisfy academic interests. Similarly, in a life history that Sarah Preston wrote down for Alice Jacob, a Cree woman from Waskaganish, Preston remarked that she drew counsel from the observation of Paul Radin (S. Preston 1986, 14) that "the ideal collectors of [ethnological] data are the natives themselves and that the more the [ethnologist] keeps in the background, the more accurate and authentic will the archives of Aboriginal culture ultimately become" (Radin 1933, 70–1).

Translation from the indigenous language to English significantly lessens the accuracy and authenticity of the original account. Cruikshank (1991, 19) demonstrates how the structure of language introduces notions in one tongue that cannot be easily expressed in another; in my experience the absence of trained translators for

much of the work done on oral tradition in James Bay has made problematic the English versions of Cree oral tradition.

Yet another problem is that historians and anthropologists, in their respective fields, class some pieces of information as "better" than others (Tonkin 1992, 54). Accordingly, one has to weigh the use of a popular western historical genre, such as autobiography, which, in the interests of representation, gives prominence to the story of one individual in Cree society rather than the collectivity. Autobiography, which privileges the story of one individual, can be highly self-indulgent; this is anathema in a society that values collective action. Sylvie Vincent, however, suggests that one should not rely on a single person's autobiography as historical material, but rather should use several recorded autobiographies. Personal accounts are told, she suggests, principally from the perspective of the social group rather than the perspective of the narrator. Most of all, she sees value in autobiographies as furnishing a Native perspective, not only on the occasion, but also as a lesson in what memories are recalled, in what is important to the community (Vincent, personal communication, May 1997). Here she differs from Vansina, who holds that important historical information is determined only after it is transmitted beyond the generation that gave rise to the stories (Vansina 1985, 28), and with Sarah Preston, who downplays the importance of the individual in Cree narratives (S. Preston 1986, 6).

There is also the consideration of the time depth in Cree oral histories. *Tipachiman* stories, as "eyewitness" stories, cannot refer to a period more than several generations old, for the Cree expect "maximum precision in narration" (R. Preston 1975, 290).[16] Thus, in the oral histories of the Cree Way Project there are the relatively recent stories dating back to the later 1800s and into the 1930s, of the starvation period, sightings of the disappearing caribou, work for the Hudson's Bay Company, missionaries, raids on the Inuit, construction of birch bark canoes, rivalry between the coasters and inlanders, to name but a few.[17] But the English fur traders arrived in James Bay several hundred years earlier, in 1668. From where do we derive our interpretations of what this early contact meant to the Cree, psychologically and sociologically? What social adaptations or restructuring, if any, were necessitated by their engagement in the European fur trade, and how did they perceive them? If we turn to the Hudson's Bay Company archival records for answers to these questions, we find that they record only the Europeans' observations, made to satisfy the economic interests of the company bosses back in England.

In the introduction to this essay, I quoted a Cree *tipachiman*[18] account of the first meeting with the white man. Surely this is an old Cree story that does confront these issues. It is the oldest story with a *tipachiman* structure, more like an "eyewitness account," and quite similar to the English version in the construction of the narrative. Yet, as we shall see, other stories of a slightly later period, such as the Cree conflicts with the Iroquois in the mid-seventeenth century, incorporate more metaphoric conventions and have few similarities to the published accounts. Is it possible this first contact story did not originate with the Cree but was told to them by a white man? Such is Pierre Trudel's attribution of a very similar story relating the first Cree–English contact, one told to him at Whapmagoostui, which is on the eastern coast of Hudson Bay, north of Wemindji, where the first contact occurred. John Kawapit, the Cree elder who narrated this story, told Trudel he had heard it from Harold Udgarden, a "mixed blood" who worked at Whapmagoostui as a clerk for about fifty years, beginning in the late 1800s (P. Trudel 1992, 68).

An initial comparison of the Georgekish and Pricket accounts of the "first meeting" provides highly important, culturally embedded understandings of process that inform us, not only about the contrasting views of the Cree and the English, but also about the value in demonstrating both these perspectives in any historical account. Yet we would be deceived if we thought that the *tipachiman* story informs us of anything but early-twentieth-century Cree representations of the encounter.

In most cases of first or early contact, the Native side of the story has been lost to history because their understanding of the events was never recorded. This is a loss we must accept in probably all encounters, because preserving the Native response was not a seventeenth-century European concern. In 1668 and 1670 Captain Zachariah Gillam, captain of the trading ship the *Nonsuch,* responded to a questionnaire from the newly formed Royal Society of London, which had been distributed to all "seamen bound for far voyages." His testimony was read to Royal Society members on 19 May 1670 (Birch 1756–7, 2: 436, cited in Morantz 1992, 172). The account is important because it provides details about Cree religion, government, subsistence, trade, and numbers (Morantz 1992, 188–93). However, of the twenty-two questions to which Gillam was responding, nineteen were about the land and the voyage; only three gave him scope to comment on the local inhabitants. Not one of these three questions inquired about the views of the Natives they encountered or about the English reactions to them. By contrast, what interests us today are not the events themselves, but the way "Natives" think, feel, and perceive, to paraphrase Clifford Geertz (1983, 56). If, by some stroke of luck, Gillam had thought to reflect on what his voyages meant to the Cree he met at Charles Fort (Rupert House or Waskaganish), these views still would not be entirely acceptable today, having been filtered through late-seventeenth-century European thinking.

The conventions used in Cree narrative also pose special problems in consolidating the two kinds of history. As was mentioned earlier, the story of the first meeting with the white man contains reference to the conjuring that predicted his arrival. Perhaps this is a convention that offers reassurance to the Cree listener or indicates that this was preordained knowledge, that the Cree were in control of the events that were to transpire in their country. It is not, however, a convention that is used today in western history.

Other conventions, in the form of metaphors, also have symbolic significance for Cree who have been raised on these stories from childhood and in their own language. The repetition of these metaphors and the way they are used provide multiple messages for the Cree listener. One example is the collection of six Cree narratives on the theme of the "Nottoways." These are the stories that recount another event in James Bay, the Iroquois raids, presumably in the mid-1600s. Although the Jesuits were not eyewitnesses to these attacks, they did hear about them and recorded details of the year, place, and numbers killed or taken captive by the Iroquois (*Jesuit Relations* [1610–1791] 1896–1901 [hereafter *JR*] 47: 150–3). In the Nottoway stories,[19] the Cree are the victors; the Iroquois are vanquished not through fighting but through the medium of either an old man or an old woman who, taken captive by the Iroquois to serve as a guide, outsmarts them by leading them over cliffs or into rapids. Similar narratives recounting the supremacy of the elderly man or woman have been recorded for other Algonquian-speaking peoples, such as the Penobscots (N. Smith 1983) and Pasmaquoddy (Erikson 1983) on the Atlantic coast.

In Julie Cruikshank's major work on Dene oral history, she refers to these constructions as "recognizable formulaic narratives" (Cruikshank 1990, 339), remarking on their persistence over time, despite considerable changes in every aspect of the lives of the storytellers. These formulaic narratives are allegorical in nature, depicting cultural ideals in social interaction or confronting difficult issues. Furthermore, she comments that use of such customary cognitive models helps make unfamiliar events seem comprehensible; the conjuring in the "first white man" story is likely a good example of this. She suggests, needless to say, that the formulae or cognitive models, ideological and symbolic, must be understood in the context of the distinct cultural understandings and social relationships in place at the time (343–5). Cruikshank, as other writers, draws our attention to these historical narratives as focusing the listener more on process than event (Cruikshank 1991, 19, 135; 1992, 35). To this end, Vincent (personal communication, May 1997) suggests that the Nottoway stories are not intended to focus on the event so much as on the behaviour one should display towards the enemy. Similarly, both authors find the different versions informative for the different cultural values they reveal. Thus, the "first white man" story is told differently among the Algonquins living south of the James Bay area in the Abitibi region of Quebec. John T. MacPherson recorded a story that began in a similar way but then tells how the white sailors thought they would have some fun with the lone Native who greeted them. They gave him some firewater and left him in a drunken stupor. As his companions were about to bury him, he came to, much to everyone's surprise. Following this episode, the Natives thought the white men were gods "because they had a juice that would cause one to die and come to life again."[20] This version offers its listeners a different lesson than the Nottoway stories and is a good example of the focus on process rather than event, on the relationships rather than the objects. But how, then, does one bridge the gap between process and event in a combined history?

Precedents in Writing Blended Histories

We have much more to learn about Native societies, now that oral tradition has been drawn in as a valued source. However, my objective here is not to champion the cause of oral tradition, for Julie Cruikshank has ably done that in her studies of oral tradition in Athapaskan and Tlinglit-speaking societies (Cruikshank 1990, 1996). Rather, I have tried to examine the possibility of a history that serves, in one text, the various functions each society, Native and non-Native, expects from its own history. In the process, I looked for histories written by non-Native academics that bring together archival and oral records. Two of the most innovative are by the anthropologists Richard Price on the Saramaka of Surinam (1983), and Joanne Rappaport on the Cumbe of Colombia (1994). Each work provides striking insights into a period in a people's history and how that history is transformed and viewed. In Price's study of the Saramaka he alternates oral texts, as given him, with the documentary history he unearthed in the archives and with his commentary, often on the same page. The texts and commentary provide very rich insights into Saramaka thinking, which is framed by the details found in the archival records. Rappaport's history is similar, although in this study the Cumbe people themselves have consulted the documents and absorbed some of their contents into the oral history. It, too, provides fascinating insights into the interpretations the Cumbe give to specific historic conditions as well as how they "resisted, capitulated, and accommodated to the state" (Rappaport 1994, 8).

Yet as fascinating and informative as these blended histories are, what they have achieved is very *limited*. The writers have managed to weave what seem like well-blended histories, but have done so within very narrow parameters. Both are histories of specific events. Both pit the Saramaka or Cumbe peoples against the larger (colonial) society. The Saramaka were runaway slaves whose history speaks to their formative years and is referred to as "First-Time" (Price 1983, 5–7). A similar historical consciousness is expressed in the Cumbe history, for it recounts the loss of their aboriginal lands and preserves the dream of recovering it (Rappaport 1994, 2–4). Both accounts are of specific events and directed to establishing each group's identity. For reasons of identity and to assert claims to the land, these historical narratives are told and retold. So vivid and pronounced are they in the people's historical consciousness that they become accessible to ethnohistorians and pliant to blending with the documentary record, contributing to a history that is recognizable within the parameters of western history. Yet, they remain limited histories, because they address themselves only to specific issues. One could achieve such a limited, combined history in the case of the Cree. In fact, such history is probably sitting in the extensive records of the court battle of the mid-1970s when the Cree engaged with the government of Quebec over the building of the James Bay hydroelectric dam on the La Grande River. At that time, the Cree gave testimony that was directed to proving their age-old ownership of the land, and although they used metaphors such as "Job's Garden"[21] to represent that they too harvested their lands, these were metaphors that were understood by non-Cree society.

Nonetheless, there is far more to Cree history than their recent fight over their territory. It is this history, one that reflects their own ideals and aspirations, that should be told, a history important to them without necessarily being oriented to the conflicts and issues over land or identity imposed on them by the larger Canadian society. One would like to do greater justice to the broader themes in Cree history, to produce the grand narrative merited by their long and complex history. In Canada there is rich archival documentation and an even more extensive and richer oral tradition. How do we combine them without losing or distorting the Cree's particular view of their past?

The Distinctiveness of Oral Tradition

In this exploration of Cree oral tradition, the characteristics that make it distinctive, as a historical tradition, have been made quite explicit. There are cognitive models embedded in the oral tradition that do not have their counterparts in mainstream history; these cognitive models themselves reveal to the listener understandings that are not easily decoded by the non-Native. As well, beasts and spirits and man-animals float in and out of the narratives. These structures and beings are intrinsic to the telling of the story. If they are dislodged from their context or ignored, the story cannot impart the same meaning. This was evident almost thirty years ago to the anthropologist Catharine McClellan, who, Cruikshank tells us, argued convincingly "that such narratives cannot be pulled out of context and have to be understood in relation to the total bodies of oral literature in which they appear" (McClellan 1970 in Cruikshank 1996, 443). This position is endorsed today by Cruikshank (and see Cohen 1989), who warns that, however well intentioned, the "uncritical use of oral traditions developed in one cultural context as though they can be equated with tangible historical evidence may lead to misinterpretation of more complex messages in narrative" (Cruikshank 1990, 346).

Sylvie Vincent, whose research on Innu oral tradition also goes back almost three decades and who has recently been writing texts on Native history, has similarly concluded in a paper presented at a 1996 conference precisely addressed to this issue that it is impossible to harmonize the two traditions of history.[22] She argues that the obstacles are not the contradictory, irreconcilable interpretations, for those could be presented in the same text, but rather the differing conceptual and methodological frameworks. In the Innu stories she studies, both time and story (process rather than event) are fluid and based in analogy, compared to the precision and factuality of western history. How does one draw into a combined history the Native people's relations with non-human inhabitants so fundamental to their understanding of their past? Similar epistemological concerns are expressed by Homi Bhabha, who writes that "cultural translation is not simply appropriation or adaptation; it is a process through which cultures are required to revise their own systems of reference, norms and values, by departing from their habitual or 'inbred' rules of transformation" (Bhabha 1997, 14).

Conclusions

Having devoted a significant effort to writing a multicultural history in tune with both Innu/Cree and Euro-Canadian perceptions of history, Vincent and I have independently resolved that it is impossible. What is possible are histories, such as Price's or Rappaport's, that revolve around a single issue that has cast the local people into a confrontation with the larger society and thus produces histories more amenable to types of narrative that confirm the conventions of western discourse. To write a history that tries to find a correspondence between the full body of oral tradition and the archival records would only destroy what is left of the Cree notions of their past. It would be the last act of the almost completed assimilation process, a dismantling of the last bastion of a unique Cree outlook. It needs no belabouring of the point to argue that such a history, written by western-trained academics for an essentially western-trained readership, would distort and destroy the depiction of the relationships, the symbolism, the patterning, and the integrity of the Cree oral tradition. As for the interpretation of the oral tradition's coded messages—revealed as they are through the performance of a number of stories—the western historian's method of producing representation through selecting a few examples would undermine the interpretation and additionally lose for the Cree much of their oral tradition.

There is a political dimension to the use of oral tradition. Writing in the *University of British Columbia Law Review,* Cynthia Callison argues for restitution for and the protection of the oral tradition of Native peoples through copyright. Her desire is to protect the oral tradition and prevent its appropriation, for she sees cultural appropriation as the exercising of the power to dominate possessed by the larger society. Such an act threatens the distinct identity of aboriginal peoples and, along with it, their integrity and dignity (Callison 1995, 170, 165).

This is not a call for Canadian history to abandon the views and lessons learned from analysing the oral tradition. Far from it. Rather, it is a call to recognize that Canadian historians' use of oral tradition, though important, is limited. Oral tradition can be put to use, invaluably so, but this use is inevitably a form of "plunder," taking from the oral tradition what is needed to fit the Euro-Canadian view that history is structured, chronological, and progressive. Although Tonkin cautions that professional historians who use the recollections of others "cannot just scan them for useful facts to pick out, like currants from a cake" (Tonkin 1992, 6), I am not sure historians can do anything else. Historians have to abandon all notions of writing a truly multicultural history that includes Indian or Native history, and be content to ransack the oral tradition for what suits their conceptual needs. Those of us writing ethnohistories can have only the currants, not the cake. The different interpretations of the exchange of trade items in the first meeting of the Cree and English may not faithfully reflect the seventeenth-century Cree view, but their version's demonstration of the white man's exuberant materialism may well suit our time's postmodern views that history functions as "cultural myth" (Appleby, Hunt, and Jacob 1994, 216).[23]

Notes

1 A French translation of the various versions of this story appears in Scott (1992, 50). Frank Sun also collected several such stories at Wemindji in 1979; see Appendix A: "Stories" in Report of Wemindji Cree Views of Religion. On deposit in Ottawa at the National Ethnology Service, National Museum of Man.

2 Cree Way was a project initiated in the mid-1970s by the principal of the Waskaganish School, John Murdoch, and aided primarily by Mrs Annie Whiskeychan. Some of the narratives they collected and used in school texts were originally recorded by Richard J. Preston.

3 These terms are in the Waskaganish (Rupert House) dialect. See Richard J. Preston, "Notions of History Implicit in East Cree Narratives of the Past," unpublished report prepared for the Cree Regional Authority and la Société de l'énergie de la Baie James (1986), 3. Other Native peoples such as the Dene (McClellan 1975, 67) and the Innu (Vincent 1981, 11) also make similar distinctions in telling their stories.

4 Sylvie Vincent emphasizes that both types of oral tradition are *true* stories, the difference being that the *tipachiman* stories relate events that have been seen or heard about (Vincent, personal communication, May 1997).

5 Preston, "Notions of History," 4.

6 Ibid., 8, 9.

7 Sylvie Vincent, "Histoire du Québec: Fragments de la version 'Montagnaise,'" report presented to the Ethnology Service (Ottawa: National Museum of Man, 1976), 67.

8 Sylvie Vincent, "Compatibilité apparente, incompatibilité réelle des versions autochtones et des versions occidentales de l'histoire. L'exemple innu," unpublished paper presented to the conference "Les

obstacles ontologiques dans les relations interculturelles," Université Laval, 7–10 October 1996, 10–11.

9   Preston, "Notions of History," 3.

10 See Sun, Appendix A: "Stories." See also Scott 1983.

11 Vincent, "Compatibilité apparente," 11.

12 John T. MacPherson, "An Ethnological Study of the Abitibi Indians" (report prepared for the Division of Anthropology, National Museums of Canada, 1930), 103.

13 Preston, "Notions of History," 3.

14 For a more complete discussion of the problems inherent in recording narratives, see Julie Cruikshank (1990) and Regina Flannery (1995).

15 Ottawa, Museum of Civilization, Great Whale River Collection 1974, Tape III-D-20–T, Side B.

16 Again, Sylvie Vincent finds this contradicted by her research on Innu oral history, commenting that *tipachiman* stories need not only be those of a relatively recent period.

17 One of the oldest of these stories is of the 1832 Hannah Bay "massacre," when four Cree men, all related, attacked this small outpost, killing the postmaster, his Cree wife, and seven other Cree people (see Francis and Morantz 1983, 158). That this relatively old *tipachiman* story is still extant is not surprising: it was a terrifying occurrence and continues to be told in the region in details that are very consistent with the Hudson's Bay Company's record of 1832 (Morantz 1984, 181–2).

18 So designated by Colin Scott (1992, 50) in his rendition.

19 The Nottoway stories in the collection of Cree Way are not identified as either *atiukan* or *tipachiman* stories, but Vincent, commenting on similar stories among the Innu, refers to them as *tipachiman* stories (personal communication, May 1997).

20 MacPherson, "Ethnological Study of the Abitibi," 156–7.

21 *Job's Garden* is the title of a film produced by Boyce Richardson in 1975 to demonstrate what the land meant to the Cree. He may have derived the title from Job's wife, Mary, who told him, "We love our garden. We love the animals in it and everything that grows in it" (Richardson 1975, 146).

22 Vincent, "Compatibilité apparente."

23 Only after this paper had gone to press did I discover the article by Marianne Ignace, "Haida Public Discourse," in which she similarly raises the problem of translating Haida rhetorical devices to western conventions. See Ignace 1991.

Reflections on the Social Relations of Indigenous Oral Histories[1]

Winona Wheeler

Our annals, all happenings of human import, were stored in our song and dance rituals, our history differing in that it was not stored in books, but in the living memory. So, while the white people had much to teach us, we had much to teach them, and what a school could have been established upon that idea!

—Luther Standing Bear, Lakota

Returning home to Saskatchewan from graduate studies in Berkeley required mental readjustments and spiritual recentring. At the wîhkôhtowin ceremony that first summer, my mind drifted off to all the unfinished papers, unmarked exams, and phone messages waiting back at the office. Here it was, the beginning of the fall semester—could I really afford to spend twenty hours in the truck and twenty-four hours cooking and doing ceremony? Always so much to do. My poor command of Cree made it hard to follow the prayer songs, and I got tired of taxing my neighbours for translations. Very gently Maria leaned over and whispered "pê-atik nâtohta," listen gently, softly, with care. Reeled back in, I was calmed and refocused by the fires and the shadows of dancing feet, and I heard the songs again. They were talking to the spirits of the land, the animals, deceased relatives and ancestors, and they were asking for blessings, for guidance to help us live a good life. Wîtaskiwin, to live together on the land in harmony. Harmony and balance is a good thing to pray for, and my mind wandered off again—urban/bush, Cree/English, academic/nêhiyapwat, oral/written.

Wîhkôhtowin is a celebration of thanksgiving for life and renewal. We feast and dance with our ancestors and other good spirits in thanks for their sacrifices and teachings. Gazing into the fire that night I was comforted, and I remembered why I am a historian and why I am here. Nêhiyawîhckikêwin, *the Cree way/culture,* is an oral culture, a listening culture. We are a people to whom understanding and knowledge comes by way of relationships—with the Creator, the past, the present, the future, life around us, each other, and within ourselves. And, like my ancestors, I am here on this earth to learn.

By no means am I an expert in Indigenous oral histories. By Cree standards I am a fledgling, as my learning will take a lifetime and I have only just begun. What I understand so far comes from many places. It comes from being raised in a family that instilled in my generation a strong Cree identity, connection to homeland, and appreciation for oral traditions. It comes from living as a guest among many different Indigenous peoples, urban and rural,

Winona Wheeler, "Reflections on the Social Relations of Indigenous Oral Histories," in Ute Lischke and David T. McNab, eds., *Walking a Tightrope: Aboriginal People and Their Representations* (Waterloo: Wilfrid Laurier University Press, 2005), 189–213. Reprinted with permission of the publisher.

at home and abroad, and from close friends and teachers. My understanding of the intersections between Indigenous oral histories and Western historiography has also been as influenced by critical and post-colonial theorists and ethno-historians, as it has by our own Indigenous scholars and literary greats—Maria Campbell, Gerald Vizenor, N. Scott Momaday, John Joseph Mathews, Edward Ahenakew, Luther Standing Bear, and others—who have been writing in the oral tradition for a very long time. They teach by "doing" how oral traditions can inform our scholarship, and have paved the way for people of my generation to return home, relearn, and find new ways to write from our own places.

> When our grandfather was alive, when he was here, he was called Wapihesew (White Bird); that was his nickname. This is his story that he told. Keep this story, do not forget this story. In the future when you relate this story to your children you will keep it alive a long time if you remember it. Before he would start a story he used to pray first, then he would start his story. He gave thanks for his life.
>
> I am starting this story in the same fashion. I have finished my prayer so that I will not relate this old story in a different way than the way it is told. So I will also not slander the characters in the story. [So] If I make a mistake the Great Spirit will make it right.
>
> "Ah, grandchildren, I will tell you a story about myself."[2]

Memory is a beautiful gift. For those who grew up hearing stories about the distant past, the memories we hold of those times are more than mere mental exercises. Memories are also experienced at the somatic level and in the soul. To remember those times spent listening to old people tell histories at the kitchen table, on a road trip, or in the warm glow of a campfire, is to relive them. Memory, in the context of Indigenous oral traditions, is a resonance of senses—it evokes the relationship the listener had with the storyteller, and it evokes the emotional responses and the feeling of total absorption experienced at the time. The smells, nuances, facial expressions, body language, and range of audience response are as much a part of the memory of the story as the story itself. Very few historians recognize the deep effect that the oral transmission of knowledge has on the individual. Among them is Morris Berman, who tells us that "participation, or identification, is highly sensuous in nature, and it is a mode of knowing that cannot be intellectually refuted because of its immediate, visceral quality."[3]

For some time now, Indigenous and a handful of other scholars have stressed the importance of Indigenous oral history in the research, writing, and teaching of Indigenous histories. Studies galore have demonstrated that the exclusive dependence on documented records left by non-Indigenous people reinforces the colonialist notion that Western historical canons and conventions are superior—that their way of doing and writing history is the standard, and that Indigenous peoples have no intellectual traditions worth learning.[4] Slowly, historians are recognizing that Indigenous oral histories offer fresh insights and valuable information on significant historical events and outstanding personalities.[5] Following the lead of cutting-edge anthropology, ethno-history, the oral history movement, and especially Native/Indian studies, they are becoming increasingly aware that the conventional, modern, academic, document-driven approach to studying the Indigenous past is passé at best, and elitist and colonialist at worst.[6]

Given the wealth of oral histories alive and well in Indian country throughout Canada, one would expect to find Indigenous voices in every book or article written on any aspect of the Indigenous past. To what degree, then, have all these new insights and the wealth of oral histories influenced historians writing Indigenous histories? A brief look at a few of the more recent and notable texts emerging in Saskatchewan is revealing.

J. R. Miller's historical biography of Chief Big Bear, published in the Canadian Biography Series of ECW Press, does not contain a single oral history interview, nor does it make reference to any oral history archival collections.[7] In light of a much earlier biography of Big Bear that was inspired by oral history, and considering that interviewing is one of the prescribed methods of modern biography (for subjects living and deceased), Miller's treatment of Big Bear is anemic.[8] From a Cree perspective, it is also disrespectful, given the substantial recorded (and archived) as well as living oral history on the life and times of this prominent and revered nêhiyaw leader.[9]

Miller's treatment of Mistahi Muskwa is surprising, considering that it was published the same year as *Shingwauk's Vision,* the most thorough and comprehensive study of Indian residential schools in Canada to date, and most noted for its good use of a wide range of Indigenous life histories and personal reminiscences.[10] Had Miller expended an iota of the energy seeking Native voices for *Big Bear* that he spent on *Shingwauk's Vision,* the resulting treatment would have been much more balanced.

The late F. Laurie Barron's study of the CCF's Native policies is recent history.[11] The events he focused on occurred during the lifetimes of thousands of Aboriginal peoples in this province, but their voices are barely detectable. *Walking in Indian Moccasins* makes great tribute to the "significant contribution...made by the people who willingly participated in interviews recounting their personal experience and insights about the CCF," but there is little tangible evidence anywhere in the book to support the author's claim that the "views expressed by informants often shaped the content of the manuscript at critical

points and provided a richness in detail unavailable in archival sources."[12] Barron did little beyond the confines of archives and classroom. Of the four Native "informants" praised in the acknowledgements, only two were cited in the text, for one sentence each.[13] Data from two additional Native informants, previously interviewed by his students, were also used a few times.[14] Given that many of us growing up in the 1960s and earlier heard stories from our grandfathers about Tommy Douglas (some of us have cousins named Tommy), it is disheartening that the man our grandfathers personally knew, argued with, strategized with, bartered with, ate with, and laughed with, barely peeks through.

Blair Stonechild and Bill Waiser's *Loyal till Death* is the only Indian–white relations history text from Saskatchewan that relied on oral histories of distant historical events for its primary thesis.[15] Two sets of oral history interviews were conducted. The first set was collected by Wilfred Tootoosis in 1984–85 for the Saskatchewan Indian Federated College and served as the basis for Stonechild's *Saskatchewan Indians and the Resistance of 1885: Two Case Studies.*[16] The second set of interviews was conducted by local research assistants from ten reserves in 1992–94. In the first project Stonechild participated in a few of the oral history interviews, and fully translated transcriptions were made. In the second project, neither Stonechild nor Waiser participated in the oral history recording except for their initial reserve visits to secure cooperation and endorsement from chief and/or council.[17] The instructions they gave to researchers in this instance were to provide one-page interview summaries.[18]

Some of the most substantial criticisms of *Loyal till Death* have already been addressed in Margaret L. Clarke's review article.[19] Clarke's primary criticism is that, despite its promise to provide an Indian view, it relies too heavily on published secondary sources.[20] This is most evident in their descriptions of spiritual and ceremonial occurrences. Instead of going to local elders for accounts on the Treaty Pipe ceremony or Thirst Dance, they relied on Euro-Canadian secondary authorities.[21] Clarke is also dismayed that they used only one-third of the oral histories collected in the second project, and that there is no analysis of the interviews, or the interview and oral data selection.[22] Clarke expresses disappointment that the "freshness and the use of first-person narrative" found in Stonechild's earlier work are sadly lacking here.[23] Because it is missing the emphases, nuances, and humanity inherent in the voices of Indigenous oral historians—the inside point of view—it reads like most other conventional histories.[24]

How did the Cree, Assiniboine, and Saulteaux voices disappear from this text? The authors offer some insight: "Although the oral history accounts were often lacking in specific detail and therefore of limited use, the interviews provided invaluable insight into Indian attitudes and motivation in 1885."[25] Had the historians actively participated in the interviews they might have heard details about events considered significant from the "Indian perspective" rather than the official record. They might have heard about the spiritual occurrences and the "inside the Indian camps" stories, some of which were so significant from the Indian point of view that the oral historians prayed before they related them on tape.[26] Back in 1984, John B. Tootoosis described the magnitude of the promises made at Treaty Six and how being bound to those promises affected Indian actions during 1885. Even brief mention of the treaty prompted Tootoosis to exclaim, "I should have taken my pipe along with this. We should have a pipe here."[27] The voices disappeared in the written text because the authors did not hear them or they missed them.

While each of these studies is a valuable contribution to Indigenous history—historical biography, Native policy, Indian–white relations—they share varying degrees of the same problem: they treat and use Indigenous memories as they would any other documentary source, and in doing so, undervalue their potential. Miller in *Big Bear* simply ignores oral history; Barron gives it lip service; Stonechild and Waiser de-spiritualize/sanitize and distance themselves from it. While any number of factors could account for the choices these historians made, it is fair to say that most historians lack the understanding and skill to "do" Indigenous oral history within its own context. It is a methodological problem faced by many historians with no training in oral history methods, or more specifically, in traditional Indigenous oral history methods.

The tendency to treat oral history like any other documentary source comes from the conventional university training historians receive. Academic oral historians define that oral history as "a primary source material obtained by recording the spoken words—generally by means of planned, tape-recorded interviews—of persons deemed to harbor hitherto unavailable information worth preserving."[28] Oral historian William Moss speaks for most academics when he explains that once captured on tape, oral history becomes a document:

> In a sense it is no longer alive but rather like a slice of tissue on a slide under the microscope of history. Like other documents, it is but a representation of a moment in time, an abstraction from the continuum of human experience, a suggestive benchmark.[29]

Such a perception is diametrically opposite to how most Indigenous peoples relate to recorded voices. The fear that traditional knowledge and languages would be lost in this modern age of literacy, television, and socio-cultural alienation prompted a series of elder workshops throughout the 1970s in Saskatchewan. From 1970 to 1978 approximately 414 elders from fifty-five Cree, Assiniboine, Saulteaux, Dakota, and Dene communities participated in workshops coordinated by the Saskatchewan Indian Cultural Centre.[30] At first many were hesitant and worried about recording their oral histories, sacred songs, and ceremonial information, but fear that all could be lost convinced them that recording might be the only way to retain them for future generations. As Cree/Assiniboine oral historian Tyrone Tootoosis explained, "They came to the conclusion that they would have to make some compromise and concession regarding the laws of access and the custom of traditional protocol."[31]

Cree elder Jim Kâ-Nîpitêhtêw shared his teachings about the Treaty Six Pipestem at one of these workshops, and expressed his thanks that the teachings were being recorded "so that our relatives might learn by hearing about it in this way...that the young might thereby remind each other."[32] Alex Bonais also agreed to record his stories, knowledge, and songs in the early 1970s because he also feared that all might be lost, and then "where will the people take their children?... Only the white man's world will remain." As Tyrone and I listened to this old man's lament on the cassette deck, a sudden surge of hope broke through. He moved closer, more directly into the microphone, and raising his gentle voice slightly, he called out, "In the future you youth try to educate each other with this information!"[33] Thirty-five years later that old man spoke directly to us.

Vivid images of the old man talking into the tape recorder with so much hope and faith in future generations were overwhelming. We felt his urgent plea and were humbled by his compassion—his voice and messages reached into the very depths of our hearts and souls. The voice on that tape was not dead to us, it was êpimatciw akitêmaka, *something that has a spirit, something that can give life.* It was left for us to build on, to draw strength from, to empower ourselves with, so our people would live on, so that it could live on and *not die.*

In the Cree world, everyone's personal, family, and regional histories interconnect and overlap; all are extensions of the past, and all are grounded in wahkôtowin, *kinship/relations.* According to Nêhiyawiwîhtamawâkan, *Cree teaching, etymology,* we inherit relationships and obligations from and to the generations behind, among, and before us, to life on this earth as we know it, and to our homelands. Our histories are infused in our daily lives—they are lived experiences. So it is that the memories of our forefathers and foremothers become our own. And we are burdened with the obligation to keep them alive.

It is hard to avoid the language of essentialism, or even racialism some would charge, when trying to explain the nature of these generational memories. However, a few scholars of memory have found that "just as cultural memories may be imbedded in material artifacts, so too the memories of personal experiences leave permanent physical traces within our bodies."[34] Precisely how those traces are transmitted across the generations is hard to articulate. We carry inside us the stories we are personally given, but it is also true that we carry memories that we can't remember being given, and when we hear the voices of elders long gone on a tape, the body and spirit responds as if we were actually there, as if they were speaking directly to us. The only explanation I can give is wahkôtowin, *relations.*

So when historians have no relationship with the storyteller, or lack the lived experience, or have no personal investment in the histories they study, or do not understand the nature, quality, and role of Indigenous oral histories, it is no surprise that our oral histories become de-spiritualized, sanitized, amputated. The stories and teachings do not die when they are recorded on tape; rather, it is the way they are treated by historians that kills them. Undeniably, historians are most comfortable working in isolation with documents:

> Historians are literate people, *par excellence,* and for them the written word is paramount. It sets their standards and methods. It downgrades spoken words which are rendered utilitarian

and flat compared to the concentrated meaning of text. The nuances and types of oral data are not seen.[35]

Perhaps this accounts for their apparent preference for transcripts over the experience of the actual tellings. Perhaps they believe that discursively transforming oral history into a document elevates its value and status. Then again, there is the ingrained precept that personal experiences, and above all personal relationships, undermine "psychic distance" and "scientific" objectivity. In addition to all that baggage, the "problem" historians confront when faced with embedded mystical or spiritual elements makes it perfectly clear how ill equipped conventionally trained historians are to work with Indigenous oral histories.

In most Indigenous societies there is little distinction between the physical and metaphysical realms, nor is there any fragmentation of knowledge into discipline-like categories. The tendency of conventional historians to "demythologize" oral history to give it "greater validity" in the Western sense of history, "is a clear violation of its principles and practices."[36] Mainstream historians are not ignorant of the ethnocentrism inherent in the act of fragmenting Indigenous knowledge, but very few actually admit to the difficulties of transcending their own cultural norms. Richard White omitted significant supernatural events in Winnebago history because "I do not believe that the Winnebagos walked above the earth, nor that the prophet [Tenskwatawa] (Shawnee)] turned his belt into a snake." White admits that in "making this narrative decision, I failed to convey a full Winnebago understanding of significant events.... It is precisely this kind of narrative conundrum that writing Native American history forces historians to face."[37]

From a mainstream perspective, once a story is shared and recorded, "facts" are extracted and the remaining "superfluous" data set aside. The bundle is plundered, the voice silenced, and bits are extracted to meet empirical academic needs. It is then that the story dies because the teachings, responsibilities, and shared experience inherent in the social relations of the story are absent, dismissed, or forgotten.

In the past few decades a handful of scholars acknowledge that "history," historical consciousness, even "significant events" are socio-cultural constructs—that there are many more kinds and forms of "history" than the conventional/modernist template propagated in universities.[38] These few increasingly stress the need to "take seriously native theories of history as embedded in cosmology, in narratives, in rituals and ceremonies, and more generally in native philosophies and worldviews."[39] They have also agreed that historians' approaches, methods, values, and responsibilities derive from their own socio-cultural foundations, and these need to be seriously reconsidered. Anthropologist Julie Cruikshank came to understand that the elders she worked with had to provide "a kind of cultural scaffolding, the broad framework" that she needed to learn before she could even begin to ask intelligent questions about the past.[40] In a similar vein, Elizabeth Tonkins stresses that "Oralcy implies skilled production, and its messages are transmitted through artistic means. An oral testimony cannot be treated only as a repository of facts and errors of fact."[41]

Despite these and other new insights, few mainstream historians bother to go beyond the constructs of their academic training. Voicing the lament of most Native American scholars, Donald Grinde (Yamasee) explains, "Native Americans are painfully aware that our history is perhaps the only branch of the discipline in which one does not need a thorough knowledge of the language, culture, traditions, and philosophies of the people being studied."[42] How could one possibly study French or German social history, at the graduate level, without some working knowledge of their languages and cultures? History professors would consider such a proposition preposterous.

In Cree terms, education is understood as a lifelong process that emphasizes the whole person.

It strives for spiritual, mental, and physical balance, and emotional well-being within the context of family and community. Unlike the Western pedagogical model, Cree education is relational. Solomon Ratt explains that in Cree terms, education does not come in compartmentalized institutional stages. Cree education, kiskinohamatowin, refers to a reciprocal and interactive teaching relationship between student and teacher, a "community activity."[43] Thus, seeking Cree knowledge requires an entirely different kind of relationship based on long-term commitment, reciprocity, and respect. Willie Ermine explains further that interpersonal relationships facilitate dialogue, an important "instrument in Aboriginal pedagogy and protocol."[44]

Given the current political climate, most scholars are careful to keep their skepticism and criticisms of Indigenous oral histories private, but the argument still whispered is that Indigenous oral histories do not stand up to the tests of academic scholarship, that they are hearsay or anecdotal, that they are useful only insofar as they provide insight into Indigenous attitudes and motives. Some historians rationalize that they do not want to be charged with appropriation, and others are content simply to know the past from their ivory towers. Let's face it, doing oral history the "Indian way" is hard work. Traipsing around Indian country, chauffeuring old people, picking berries, hauling wood, smoking meat, digging wild turnips, hoeing potatoes, or taking them to and from the grocery store or bingo is a lot of work. Our finely tuned grey matter has difficulty equating chopping wood with intellectual pursuits, because it is a totally different kind of pedagogy that requires us to learn a new way of learning. And why should we? Our academic training indoctrinates us into what Hayden White calls the "ironic perspective."[45] Consciously or unconsciously, many historians hold the elitist and ironic view that people generally lack the perspective in their own time to view their experiences as clearly as outside historians can see it in retrospect.

The study of kayâs âcimowina, *stories of long ago*, has taken me moose-hunting and taught me to clean and prepare such fine feast food delicacies as moose-nose and smoked-intestine soup. Traditional copyright teachings came in the wee hours of the morning over cold Tim Horton's coffee in a 4x4 truck heading down the Peace River highway. One of my teachers has a propensity for second-hand store shopping—entire days have been spent mining sale bins for gold. Once it took us almost two days to make a ten-hour road trip because we stopped at every second-hand store and garage sale along the highway. Cree education is based on interactive and reciprocal relations, and all knowledge comes with some degree of personal sacrifice.

A conventional historian has little responsibility to his or her sources other than to treat them with integrity and critically engage them with methods appropriate to their nature. While oral histories are also critically engaged with a range of appropriate methods, they require far more from the researcher than documents command. In the Cree world, our sources are our teachers, and the student–teacher relationship prescribes life-long obligations, responsibilities, respect, and trust.

The social relations between a teacher and student, more specifically the degree of commitment on the part of the student, determine to a very large degree the quality and depth of knowledge the student receives. Back in the early 1970s, Catherine Littlejohn promoted the use of oral history in education curricula.[46] Applying conventional oral history techniques, she interviewed Mrs. Peemee—widow of Horse Child, the youngest son of Big Bear. Ms. Littlejohn went to Mrs. Peemee for the "Frog Lake Massacre" story, but instead of getting a narrative account was referred to a version translated and published by Maria Campbell in *Maclean's*.[47] While Mrs. Peemee elaborated on a few points, she refused to tell the whole story since the published version told it "as she wanted it told."[48] The researcher reasoned that Mrs. Peemee's account was "shorter and in less detail" because it was "more personal and apparently more painful to relate":

> Mrs. Peemee's traditionalism, her closeness to her husband and to the physical reminders of those troubled times—i.e., Cutknife Hill—may have kept the pain and sorrow more intimately with her. Therefore, in telling the story, Mrs. Peemee was concerned that her grandchild be present, for it was difficult to reveal the depths of her feelings to a stranger, especially one obviously outside her cultural background.[49]

The reader cannot ascertain whether Mrs. Peemee articulated these reasons herself or whether they were conjecture. "Pain and sorrow" may have been prohibiting factors behind Mrs. Peemee's reluctance to retell the story, but Ms. Littlejohn also identified "that the researcher must be accepted as from within the Cree worldview as well."[50] It may have helped the researcher to understand the impact of history on Poundmaker's people because it would have highlighted the depths of distrust the people had for strangers. They were justifiably suspicious of outsiders asking any questions about incidents associated with the 1885 resistance because both Poundmaker and Big Bear were wrongfully incarcerated, a number of men were hanged, many more were incarcerated, and the federal government penalized the entire band by denying them their treaty annuities and the right to select their own chief and council until the 1920s. As old as Mrs. Peemee was, she directly experienced the retribution inflicted on her family and community for their alleged role in the "massacre," and so, like other band members, she was extremely cautious of outsiders asking direct questions.

Maria Campbell, on the other hand, spent considerable time with Mrs. Peemee over a number of years during which strong and respectful student–teacher bonds were established. Maria chopped wood, carried water, drove Mrs. Peemee to town for shopping. In short, she was friend and apprentice. She not only received the full story—complete with biographical details on well- and lesser-known individuals, stories of spiritual occurrences, and humorous anecdotes—she and Mrs. Peemee collaboratively edited the story for publication; they agreed on an edited and somewhat softened version that respected Mrs. Peemee's caution and protected spiritual elements from outside judgments. Maria Campbell recalls that at no time did Mrs. Peemee express personal pain or sorrow when telling the stories: In fact, "she had a great sense of humor, laughing and talking the whole time."[51]

Two different research methods, two different results. Maria Campbell's research methods were grounded in nêhiyawîhcikêwin, *Cree ways/culture.* Clearly, conventional oral history interview methods do not meet Cree standards. Clearly there is a direct correlation between the depth and quality of knowledge a student acquires and the level of reciprocal trust and respect cultivated between the teacher and student. This is why the practice of racing into Indian country with tape recorder in hand and taking data meets with little success. This is also why historians who read interview summaries in distant offices are deaf to significant events from Indigenous perspectives.

Books or papers do not mediate the Cree relationship to the past. It is a lived experience embodied in everyday social interaction. The teaching and learning of history—historical study—is a social process based entirely on human relationships, and relations between human beings and the creation around them.

A conscientious historian, one who would take the time to learn about Cree ways of knowing (or Anishnabe, Nakoda, Dene, Metis, Dakota) would learn that there are many different kinds of stories in Cree oral traditions. They would learn that in Cree, as in Dakota and many other Indigenous worlds, there is no word for *history* in the Western sense.[52] They would learn that Cree histories consist of many different kinds of overlapping and related stories. That âtayôhkêwina are *sacred stories* of the mystical past when the earth was shaped, animal peoples conversed, and Wisakejac transformed the earth and its inhabitants through misadventure, mischief, and love into the world we presently know. Âtayôhkêwina are the foundations of Cree spirituality/religion, philosophy, and world view, and contain the laws given to the people to live by. They would learn that âcimowina are *stories* of events that have come to pass since Wisakejac's corporeal beingness transformed into spirit presence, that there are many different kinds of overlapping and related kayâs âcimowina, *stories about long ago,* that are often infused with the sacred. Because in our traditions, experience and knowledge are not compartmentalized; they do not adhere to modernist fact/fiction, truth/myth binaries. Academic scholars would do well to take heed of Harvey Knight's caution:

> Because Indian oral tradition blends the material, spiritual, and philosophical together into one historical entity, it would be a clear violation of the culture from which it is derived if well-meaning scholars were to try to demythologize it, in order to give it greater validity in the Western sense of historiography. It would be equally unjust and inappropriate to place this history into the category of mythology or folklore, thereby stripping it of its significance as authentic historical documentation.[53]

Students of Cree history would also learn that some old and great stories handed down through the generations are formally governed by sacred protocols—for example, stories of the treaties and some stories concerning the 1885 resistance—while others are not, that personal life histories or reminiscences are not bound by the same rules of transmission as the sacred and historical narratives, but they may be infused with some of those elements. A conscientious historian would also learn how best to use the material his or her teacher gives because active engagement in the oral history teaches one to discern what the significant events are from an Indigenous perspective, what can and cannot become public knowledge, and what narrative style would be most appropriate for its textual transformation.

Academics also need to respect the fact that Cree copyright laws and protocols exist and need to be adhered to if trust is going to be established and maintained. One of the major tenets of Western erudition is the belief that all knowledge is knowable, that "knowledge is and should be essentially 'free' and open; this notion remains a cornerstone of many of the professional attitudes, training, and ethics maintained by scholarly societies."[54] In the Cree world, not all knowledge is unknowable. Some knowledge is kept in the family lines; other kinds have to be earned. While all knowledge is intended for community well-being and welfare, to acquire certain kinds one is obligated to adhere to the rules of its acquisition. Access to knowledge requires long-term commitment, apprenticeship, and payment in various forms. Maria Campbell earned the stories published in *Stories of the Road Allowance People* by being helper or servant to her teachers in addition to paying for them with "gifts of blankets, tobacco and even a prize Arabian stallion."[55] In some instances tobacco and a gift are all that is required, in other instances tobacco and a gift are the means to receive instruction on the appropriate protocol. Harold Cardinal and others refer to these rules as traditional copyright.[56]

Harold Cardinal explains that there are not many things in Cree life where the right of ownership—the concept of exclusive ownership—is recognized. The one area where it does apply is for stories and ceremonies. Maria

Campbell explains further that while the English language has many words for various types of theft, some considered less horrendous or significant than others under law, in Cree there is only one word for *stealing:* kimotiwin. In Cree, any and all theft is considered unconscionable. To take a story and claim ownership without permission when it was only shared with you is stealing. Indigenous copyright systems are built on trust, and breach of that trust constitutes theft.[57]

Sadly, conventional copyright and intellectual property rights laws do not adequately protect Indigenous intellectual or "esoteric" knowledge from researchers.[58] This issue needs a more thorough treatment than space allows here. For now, it is vital to stress that signed consent forms do not mean that researchers have copyright over the stories. It means that the orator is willing to share them. Unlike Canadian copyright law, in the Cree world just because you acquired a set of cassette-recordings does not mean you own the content.

Since the issue of appropriation will be encountered by anyone doing oral history, it is vital that researchers become fully informed about their roles, responsibilities, and limits according to local standards and protocols.[59] Clearly, historians willing to engage in oral history research must take the time to learn how to learn. Learning how to learn from another people's point of view is not a revolutionary concept, but it is hard work. Learning in the oral tradition is not about racing into Indian country with tape recorder in hand and taking data. Neither is it about hiring locals to interview old people and supply transcripts for detached academic reflection in the isolated confines of distant offices. If historians take the time to question their motives and goals in doing historical research on the Indigenous past, great strides will be made.

When I think about the potential in my discipline—Native/Indian studies—for the development of a truly Indigenous oral traditions-based history, the voices of many long-gone old people fill my mind. They had dreams for us. They envisioned an education system where traditional knowledge and the "cunning of the white man" would be taught side-by-side. Neal McLeod accords that the biggest challenge in Indigenous studies today concerns "the transmission and translation of knowledge from traditional tribal environments to academic settings" as well as the "format and modes of articulation."[60] Like most scholars in the discipline, we see our tasks and our obligations differently from those in history, anthropology, and other disciplines. McLeod reminds us:

> The project of Indigenous Studies is an extension of collective memory which has existed since time immemorial...if we are to have genuine Indigenous Studies, we really need to use techniques of ways of knowing that stretch back deep within our tribal memories. The failure to utilize such techniques will amount, not to liberation through education, but rather assimilation through education.[61]

The challenge is not taken lightly. Luckily for us, our literary elders are in the forefront, guiding and encouraging us, with so much confidence in our abilities to meet the obligations we bear with mainstream tools. As Cree Metis elder Maria Campbell has noted:

> Our new storytellers have a big job. They must understand their sacred place and they must also understand the new language and use it to express their stories without losing the thoughts and images that are culturally unique to them. This new storyteller must also be a translator of the old way, so that it will not be lost to a new generation. And all this must be done on paper, for that is the new way.[62]

Notes

Special thanks to Maria Campbell and Tyrone Tootoosis for all the teachings, guidance, and support they continue to give on this learning journey. I thank them also for reading and commenting on earlier drafts and for food and shelter.

1 This paper derives from research conducted for my PhD dissertation, "Decolonizing Tribal Histories" (University of California, Berkeley, 2000), portions of which were published in "The Social Relations of Oral History," *Saskatchewan History* 51, 1 (1999): 29–35, and "The Othering of Indigenous History," *Saskatchewan History* 50, 2 (1999): 24–27.

2 Andrew Kay, "An Old Cree Indian Named Old Worm (Amiskosese)," March 18, 1972 (audio tape). Kawakatoose (Poor Man) Oral History Project, Registration No. AH 71.67.1, Provincial Museum of Alberta.

3 Morris Berman, *Coming to Our Senses: Body and Spirit in the Hidden History of the West* (New York: Simon and Schuster, 1989), 112.

4 See, for example, Angela Cavender Wilson, "Power of the Spoken Word: Native Oral Traditions in American Indian History," in *Rethinking American Indian History,* ed. Donald Fixico, 101–16 (Albuquerque: University of New Mexico, 1997); and Angela Cavender Wilson, "American Indian History or Non-Indian Perceptions of American Indian History?" *American Indian Quarterly* 20, 1 (1996): 3–5; Devon A. Mihesuah, "Voices, Interpretations, and the 'New Indian History': Comment on the *AIQ* Special Issue on Writing about American Indians," *American Indian Quarterly* 20, 1 (1996): 91–105; Calvin Martin, *The American Indian and the Problem of History* (New York: Oxford University Press, 1987); Gordon M. Day, "Roger's Raid in Indian Tradition," *Historical New Hampshire* 17 (June 1962): 3–17; Julie Cruikshank, "Discovery of Gold on the Klondike: Perspectives from Oral Tradition," in *Reading beyond Words: Contexts for Native History,* ed. Jennifer S.H. Brown and Elizabeth Vibert (Peterborough: Broadview Press, (1996), 433–53.

5 See for example, Calvin Martin, "The Metaphysics of Writing Indian–White History," in *The American Indian and the Problem of History,* ed. Calvin Martin (New York: Oxford University Press, 1987), 6, 9; Ken S. Coates and Robin Fisher, eds., *Out of the Background: Readings on Canadian Native History,* 2nd ed. (Toronto: Copp Clark, 1996), 3; Donald L. Fixico, ed., *Rethinking American Indian*

History (Albuquerque: University of New Mexico Press, 1997), 7.

6 Martin, "The Metaphysics," 6, 9.

7 J.R. Miller, *Big Bear [Mistahimusqua]: A Biography* (Toronto: ECW Press, 1996).

8 Hugh Dempsey, *Big Bear: The End of Freedom* (Vancouver: Greystone, 1984).

9 Dr. Miller's biography would have been greatly enhanced had he consulted the oral history collections at the Saskatchewan Indian Federated College and the Saskatchewan Indian Cultural Centre. The work of his colleague Dr. Bill Waiser, on the Indian involvement in 1885, with Blair Stonechild, also located oral history on Big Bear, which if not specifically helpful, could have steered Dr. Miller to living memories.

Granted, Dr. Miller was writing for the general public rather than his academic peers, or, apparently, Aboriginal people. Miller's exclusion of Cree voices, and the fact that not a single Aboriginal person is mentioned in his acknowledgements, maintains colonialist intellectual hegemony and promotes the notion that Cree people have no historical traditions worth consulting. A tone of condescension is also evident in his narrative: "Big Bear, of course, showed little or no awareness..." (25), "Big Bear would have hated..." (120). How does he know? This lack of Indigenous voice is especially offensive when coupled with Miller's literary strategy. He uses the voice of an extradiegetic omniscient narrator who tells the story in the third person, uses commentorial discourse, and is not accountable for his information. Through "psycho-narration," he implies personal knowledge of Big Bear and suggests the power to reach into his mind to know his thoughts and feelings, all of which is offensive to those who know the oral histories of Big Bear's life. For a more thorough description of this literary strategy, see Wallace Martin, *Recent Theories of Narrative* (Ithaca: Cornell University Press, 1991).

10 J.R. Miller, *Shingwauk's Vision: A History of Native Residential Schools* (Toronto: University of Toronto Press, 1996). Dr. Miller clearly expended considerable energies in search of Native voices, which he collected through interviews (conducted by himself

and research assistants) and from attending conferences. He also searched out oral history collections.

11 F Laurie Barron, *Walking in Indian Moccasins: The Native Policies of Tommy Douglas and the CCF* (Vancouver: University of British Columbia Press, 1997).

12 Barron, *Walking in Indian Moccasins,* xi–xii.

13 Ibid., 105n39; 132n148.

14 "Respondent A, Interviewed on James Smith Reserve as Part of a Native Studies 404.6 course project, March 1987," Ibid., 2.17n40; and two apparently separate interviews with John B. Tootoosis, one conducted by Murray Dobbin, November 9, 1977, housed in the SAB Oral History Project 21, Ibid., 68n39; the other (Ibid., 131n146) cited in James M. Pitsula, "The Saskatchewan CCF Government and Treaty Indians, 1944–64," *Canadian Historical Review* 75, 1 (1989): 34n56, n58. Ibid., 234.

15 Blair Stonechild and Bill Waiser, *Loyal till Death: Indians and the North-West Rebellion* (Calgary: Fifth House, 1997).

16 Blair Stonechild, *Saskatchewan Indians and the Resistance of 1885: Two Case Studies* (Regina: Saskatchewan Education, 1986).

17 Stonechild and Waiser, *Loyal,* viii.

18 Tyrone Tootoosis, personal communication, August 1999.

19 Margaret L. Clarke, "Review Article," *Prairie Forum* 23, 2 (1998): 267–73.

20 Clarke, "Review Article," 270.

21 Why go to Euro-Canadian secondary "authorities" for matters of Cree spirituality when living elders could give "authentic" accounts, and when a more thorough account, for example of the Calumet Dance, has been written by Joseph Dion? (See Joseph F. Dion, *My Tribe the Crees,* ed. Hugh Dempsey [Calgary: Glenbow, 1993, reprint].) See Stonechild and Waiser, *Loyal,* 269n18, 292n50. While David C. Mandelbaum gives a brief description of the Pipestem Bundle Dance on pages 210–11 in *The Plains Cree: An Ethnographic, Historical and Comparative Study* (Regina: Canadian Plains Research Centre, 1979), Joseph Dion's account on pages 52–53 describes it in relation to peace talks between nations. Katherine Pettipas's description of the Thirst Dance can be found on pages 56–61 in *Severing the Ties that Bind: Government Repression of Indigenous Religious Ceremonies on the Prairies* (Winnipeg: University of Manitoba Press, 1994), which is based almost entirely on published anthropological accounts except for snippets from Able Watetch, *Payepot and His People*

(Saskatoon: Modern Press, 1959) and Edward Ahenakew, *Voices of the Plains Cree,* ed. Ruth Buck (Toronto: McClelland and Stewart, 1973).

22 Clarke, "Review Article," 268, 271–72.

23 Ibid., 267.

24 Oral historians are increasingly turning their attention to how oral histories, especially cross-cultural ones, can and perhaps should be represented in textual form. For example see Peter Burke, "History of Events and the Revival of Narrative," in *New Perspectives on Historical Writing* (University Park: Pennsylvania University Press, 1992); Raphael Samuel, "Perils of the Transcript," in *The Oral History Reader,* ed. Robert Perks and Alistair Thomson (London: Routledge, 1998); Ruth Finnegan, *Oral Traditions and the Verbal Arts: A Guide to Research Practices* (London: Routledge, 1992); Dennis Tedlock, *The Spoken Word and the Art of Interpretation* (Philadelphia: University of Pennsylvania Press, 1983).

25 Stonechild and Waiser, *Loyal,* 264.

26 Tootoosis, personal communication, 1999.

27 Saskatchewan Indian Federated College, 1885 Indian Oral History Project. John B. Tootoosis, Poundmaker First Nations, interviewed by A. Blair Stonechild and Wilfred Tootoosis. Cutknife, Saskatchewan, 30 November 1984 (transcript).

28 Louis M. Star, "Oral History" *Encyclopedia of Library and Information Science* (New York: Marcel Dekker, 1978), 440.

29 William Moss, "Oral History: What Is It and Where Did It Come From?" in *The Past Meets the Present,* ed. David Strickland and Rebecca Sharpless (New York: University Press of America, 1988), 10.

30 Tyrone Tootoosis, "Our Legacy: Ka ke pesi nakata-makiawiyak," *Eagle Feather News* 1, 10 (1999), 21.

31 Ibid.

32 Jim Kâ-Nîpitêhtêw quoted in Freda Ahenakew and H.C. Wolfart, eds., *Ana kâ-pimwêwêhahk okakêskihkêmowina: The Counselling Speeches of Jim Kâ-Nîpitêhtêw* (Winnipeg: University of Manitoba Press, 1998), 105, 65.

33 Alex Bonais, Plains Cree, Little Pine First Nation. Interviewed by Wilfred Tootoosis, Poundmaker First Nations, ca. 1974. Audiotape in possession of Tyrone Wilfred Tootoosis,

34 Patricia Fara and Karalyn Patterson, eds., "Introduction," in *Memory* (New York: Cambridge University Press, 1998), 3.

35 Gwyn Prins, "Oral History" in *New Perspectives on Historical Writing,* ed. Peter Burke (University Park: Pennsylvania University Press, 1992), 118.

36 Harvey Knight, "Preface," in Alexander Wolfe, *Earth Elder Stories: The Pinayzitt Path* (Saskatoon: Fifth House, 1988), ix.

37 Richard White, "Using the Past: History and Native American Studies," in *Studying Native America: Problems and Prospects,* ed. Russell Thornton (Madison: University of Wisconsin Press, 1998), 227, 228.

38 See for example, Renato Rosaldo, *Ilongot Headhunting 1883–1974: A Study in Society and History* (Stanford: Stanford University Press, 1980), 54–55; Marshall Sahlins, "Other Times, Other Customs: The Anthropology of History," *American Anthropologist* 85 (1983), 517; Kirsten Hastrup, ed., *Other Histories* (New York: Routledge, 1992).

39 Raymond D. Fogelson, "The Ethnohistory of Events and Nonevents," *Ethnohistory* 36, 2 (1989): 134–35.

40 Julie Cruikshank, *The Social Life of Stories: Narrative and Knowledge in the Yukon Territory* (Lincoln: University of Nebraska Press, 1998), 27.

41 Quoted in Mary Chamberlain and Paul Thompson, eds., "Introduction: Genre and Narrative in Life Stories," in *Narrative and Genre* (London: Routledge, 1998), 10.

42 Donald A. Grinde Jr., "Teaching American Indian History: A Native American Voice," *Perspectives: American Historical Society Newsletter* 32, 6 (1994): 1.

43 Solomon Ratt, Testimony, *Office of the Treaty Commissioner Mock Trial* (14 September 1992), video.

44 Willie Ermine; "Pedagogy from the Ethos: An Interview with Elder Ermine on Language," in *As We See...Aboriginal Pedagogy,* ed. Lenore A. Stiffarm, (Saskatoon: University of Saskatchewan Extension Press, 1998), 10.

45 For a discussion on Hayden White's theory that modern historians are "locked within art ironic perspective" see Lloyd S. Kramer, "Literature, Criticism, and Historical Imagination: The Literary Challenges of Hayden White and Dominick LaCapra," in *The New Cultural History,* ed. Lynn Hunt (Berkeley: University of California Press, 1989), 104.

46 Catherine Isabel Littlejohn, "The Indian Oral Tradition: A Model for Teachers," M.Ed. Thesis: University of Saskatchewan College of Education, 1975.

47 Maria Campbell, "She Who Knows the Truth of Big Bear: History Calls Him Traitor, but History Sometimes Lies," *Maclean's* 88, 9 (1975), 46.

48 Ibid.

49 Ibid., 56.

50 Ibid., 58.

51 Maria Campbell, personal communication, August 1999.

52 See for example, Angela Cavender-Wilson, "Ehanna Woyakapi: History and the Language of Dakota Narration," paper presented at the Western History Association Conference, Sacramento, CA, October 15, 1998, 4.

53 Knight, "Preface," ix.

54 James D. Nason, "Native American Intellectual Property Rights: Issues in the Control of Esoteric Knowledge," in *Borrowed Power Essays on Cultural Appropriation,* ed. Bruce Ziff and Pratima V. Rao (New Brunswick, NJ: Rutgers University Press, 1997), 245.

55 Maria Campbell, *Stories of the Road Allowance People* (Penticton: Theytus, 1995), 2.

56 Harold Cardinal, personal communication, August 1997.

57 Alexander Wolf, "Introduction," in *Earth Elder Stories: The Pinayzitt Path* (Saskatoon: Fifth House, 1988), xv.

58 *Esoteric knowledge* is defined as "traditional, valued knowledge that is intended for and is to be used by the specially initiated or trained and that is most often owned or held in trust and treated as private property or secret by an individual, by a group within the community (such as a clan or society), or by the community as a whole." Nason, "Intellectual Property Rights," 242. See also, Gordon Christie, "Aboriginal Rights, Aboriginal Culture, and Protection," *Osgoode Hall Law Journal* 36, 3 (1998): 447–84; Jill Jarvis-Tonus, "Legal Issues Regarding Oral Histories," *Canadian Oral History Association Journal* 12 (1992): 18–24.

59 See for example, Bruce Ziff and Pratima V. Rao, eds., *Borrowed Power: Essays on Cultural Appropriation* (New Brunswick, NJ: Rutgers University Press, 1997).

60 Neal McLeod, "What is *indigenous* about Indigenous Studies?" *SIFC Magazine* (1998–99), 52.

61 Ibid.

62 Maria Campbell, "Introduction," *Acimoona* (Saskatoon: Fifth House, 1985), n.p.

North Baffin Prior to 1905

SHELAGH D. GRANT

The Arctic environment—its weather extremes and unique landforms—exerted a dominant influence on the lives of its indigenous peoples to produce a culture distinct from other hunters and gatherers in North America.[1] Over time, regional differences in wildlife resources created more subtle variations, as did migration patterns and climate change. The nature and timing of early contact with the Europeans would generate further distinctions. Yet with the exception of climate-induced changes during the Little Ice Age, the physical environment of the Arctic has remained relatively unchanged since the arrival of the first migrants from Siberia over four thousand years ago.

In sharp contrast to the lowlands in the south, the highland rim of the Canadian Shield along the northeastern coast of Baffin Island is characterized by peaked mountains, active glaciers, trough valleys, broad peninsulas, and deep fiords carved out of sedimentary rock by glacial erosion. Bylot Island, lying to the northeast, is separated from the larger island by Eclipse Sound, with access from Davis Strait by way of Pond's Inlet and from Lancaster Sound through Navy Board Inlet. The domed icecap on Bylot Island rises approximately six thousand feet above sea level, surrounded by snow-capped peaks and glaciers—an impressive site when viewed from across the sound. To the southwest lie the Tununiq Mountains at the head of Milne Inlet with the highest peak rising four thousand feet above sea level.[2]

For millennia the protected waters of Eclipse Sound and surrounding lands provided Inuit with an abundance of wildlife resources, including narwhal, seal, walrus, polar bear, fish, and a variety of migratory birds. Caribou, although at one time more numerous, can still be found feeding on the lichen-covered rocks of nearby hills.[3] There were other advantages. From August to October, icebergs frequently drift into Eclipse Sound, carried by the prevailing current from Greenland until caught in the winter freeze-up. Grounded each year on the shallow sand bars near the present-day settlement of Pond Inlet, they provided, and continue to provide, a ready source of fresh drinking water, a factor that may explain the number of ancient campsites at Mittimatalik and further west along the beach at Qilalukkan.[4] In summer the melting snow uncovers a profusion of vegetation ranging from the Arctic willow, only a few inches high, to a colourful array of tundra plants and perennial wildflowers. The season is short, but the intensity of the summer sun accelerates growth at a much faster rate than in southern climes, allowing the hardy vegetation to play a key role in the food chain of the precariously balanced high Arctic ecosystem.

Moving westward across the top of North Baffin, the jagged peaks give way to a more rounded landscape of undulating plateaus dissected by dried-up river valleys leading into Admiralty Inlet. On the east side, several bays probe inland like long fingers, the largest being Strathcona Sound to the north, then Adams Sound and Moffat Inlet to the south. At various points, glacial erosion created high cliffs marked horizontally with red and orange layers of rock stained by iron oxide. The other side of the Brodeur Peninsula slopes gradually to the shores of Prince Regent Inlet.[5] The height of land also diminishes southward towards the head of Admiralty Inlet until reaching the Foxe Basin lowlands and the camps of the Igloolik Inuit.

Since many Iglulingmiut are central to this story, the North Baffin region is defined here to include their camps in the vicinity of Aggu on Baffin Island and Igloolik Island. As was the case in Eclipse Sound, the abundance of wildlife resources in this area sustained a relatively large population over a very long period of time.

Migrants from the shores of Siberia by way of Alaska—the Palaeo-Eskimos—occupied sites in the vicinity of both Eclipse Sound and Igloolik, dating back to around 2000 BC. Today, Inuit elders refer to these Inuit as Tuniit* to distinguish them from their own ancestors, the Thule people or Tunijjuat, who arrived at North Baffin around 900 AD. The latter were smaller in stature but possessed more sophisticated tools and weapons.[6] The Tuniit were displaced from their traditional hunting grounds and eventually disappeared. That the two cultures actually lived together or adjacent to each other at any time is considered unlikely by most archaeologists, but elders' stories about Tuniit around Eclipse Sound suggest there was contact and that it was somewhat more than fleeting.[7] While in some areas the Little Ice Age caused the Thule people to migrate southward, archaeological evidence uncovered by the Danish Fifth Thule Expedition (1921–24) suggested that many living in the vicinity of Igloolik and Eclipse Sound did not leave the area but instead underwent a more gradual transition from the Thule culture to the present day.[8]

The Inuit living on Eclipse Sound call themselves Tununirmiut, meaning the people of Tununiq, "the land that faces away from the sun" or the "shaded place," in reference to the mountains at the head of Milne Inlet off Eclipse Sound. By similar definition, Tununirusiq, meaning the "lesser shaded place," refers to an area with smaller mountains in the vicinity of Arctic Bay off Admiralty Inlet, and the Tununirusirmiut as the people living there.[9] The leader of the Fifth Thule Expedition, Knud Rasmussen, suggested that these people belonged to a larger cultural grouping that included those residing in the vicinity of Igloolik Island. Father Guy Mary-Rousselière, an amateur archaeologist and long-time resident at Pond Inlet, believed the Tununirmiut were also closely related to the Adkudnirmiut of the Clyde River area because of similarities in their language and clothing.[10] How much interaction took place in the years prior to contact with Europeans is unknown, but trade with the whalers undoubtedly created closer ties between Inuit groups throughout North Baffin.

Cultural adaptations to the environment continued long after Inuit contact with the Europeans.[11] The sun, or its absence, for example, dictated a seasonal routine in their lives, differing in some regions according to the length of time without sunlight during the winter months and to the availability of certain species of wildlife. In North Baffin, located well above the Arctic Circle, the sun slipped below the horizon around mid-November and did not return until mid-February. As a consequence, Inuit would spend the winter months of darkness in quasi-hibernation, moving out of their insulated winter homes only to obtain seal oil for their lamps and food from their caches. The return of sunlight in late February was understandably cause for celebration. Children ventured outdoors to play, their laughter filling the air, while hunters headed out on the sea ice in search of seal (*nattiq*) and polar bear (*nanuq*). Later, they moved their entire families to spring hunting camps on

---

* Tuniit is the Inuktitut name used by Inuit elders for the people who occupied their lands before the arrival of their ancestors, the Tunijjuat—or in anthropological terms, the late Dorset culture and Thule people, respectively.

the ice or near the floe edge. As the sun's warmth began to melt the snow and ice around Eclipse Sound, the Inuit moved again, this time to fish at the mouths of rivers, and later to climb the well-worn paths along the banks to harvest those caught in shallow pools or man-made dams. In the Igloolik area the sea ice melted earlier, allowing the men to head out in their kayaks (*qajait*) in search of walrus (*aiviq*) or narwhal (*qilalugaq*). Once the snow disappeared from the hills, the hunters headed inland in search of caribou (*tuktuit*). Women and children, meanwhile, collected eggs and picked berries.

Inuit travelled great distances in the spring to visit friends and trade, but by late summer and early fall, activities were geared to preparing for winter. Hunters filled their food caches and the women sewed warmer outfits for the months ahead. Gradually families drifted back to their winter camps, where they rebuilt the stone foundations that were sunk into the ground for warmth. Skins were placed over whale ribs to form the roof, followed by a layer of heather for insulation, then a second layer of skins. A skin tent was attached on the inside to protect against frost build-up, and snow was packed around the outside for warmth. The pace of physical activities slowed dramatically as the sun slid below the horizon and once again everyone waited for spring.[12] During the winter months Inuit families were more vulnerable to hunger and disease, especially if there was a shortage of food or insufficient seal oil to keep the stone lamps (*qulliit*) lit for heat and light. For the more fortunate, it was just a matter of awaiting the return of the sun. Patience was not a virtue—it was a necessity.

The climate also dictated the mode for long-distance travel. For carrying heavy loads, the obvious choice was by *qamutiik* over hard-packed snow or sea ice. In summer, hunters might travel overland on foot for short distances, with their dogs carrying packs on their backs. Once the sea ice had melted, an *umiaq* (a large boat made of skins stretched over whale bone and rowed by the women) might be used to move families to a new campsite. Whatever the season, their dogs were critical to the hunters' ability to travel in search of food.

Sudden changes in the weather could be disastrous. An unusually early breakup of sea ice could strand entire families on the wrong side of a large body of water. Similarly, an unexpected warm spell in spring could turn hard snow into heavy wet mush, making travel overland difficult, sometimes impossible. The cold air could be brutal if accompanied by strong winds. At Pond Inlet the average low temperature in February is roughly –37 degrees Celsius, but known to fall as low as –59°C. Although the accumulation of snow is less than in more southerly regions, blizzard conditions are frequent.[13] There are many stories of hunters who became disoriented during intense storms and were later found frozen to death not far from their camp. Some elders maintain that the Inuktitut name for Pond Inlet—Mittimatalik, meaning the place where Mittima died—is derived from just such a story.[14]

According to history texts, the first European ship to reach Lancaster Sound was the British ship *Discovery* in 1616, commanded by Captain Robert Bylot. A recent discovery of handspun Viking yarn suggests that they may have been preceded in the early fourteenth century by Norsemen, sailing from their colony on southwest Greenland.[15] Nonetheless, the names of Bylot Island and the larger island called after his pilot, William Baffin, remain as a testament to the first British expedition to reach the northern-most tip of Baffin Island.[16] Owing to impenetrable ice in Davis Strait during the Little Ice Age, another two hundred years passed before explorers again ventured as far north as Lancaster Sound. The first was a British Admiralty Expedition in 1818, led by Captain John Ross. He landed briefly on Bylot Island and named the entrance to what appeared to be a large bay Pond's Inlet, after

John Pond, the Astronomer Royal. The following year Captain William Edward Parry led yet another expedition into Lancaster Sound, this time naming Devon and Somerset Islands, as well as Admiralty and Navy Board Inlets. Parry was the first to provide a detailed description of Inuit from this region after visiting a small camp near Clyde River just south of the entrance to Pond's Inlet.[17]

That same year several whalers from Scotland and England reached the shores of North Baffin, and reports of their success brought many more. Over the next decade roughly 750 vessels were reported to have fished the waters, with the average catch amounting to more than ten whales per ship.[18] Meanwhile the whaling captains mapped the coast and gave names to every unnamed landmark. More were added as they penetrated into Lancaster Sound and Hudson Bay. Eclipse Sound, as an example, was named by Captain John Gray after his ship. Likewise, Adams Sound and Arctic Bay were named after Captain William Adams Sr. and his ship *Arctic I*, the first to anchor in the sheltered bay off Admiralty Inlet.

By mid-century, whale stocks in the northern waters had declined from over-fishing, causing most ships to move southward to Cumberland Sound and later into Hudson Bay. At both locations, American and Scottish whalers began to winter over, utilizing Inuit to man the small whale boats, assist in rendering the whale blubber, and provide the ship's crew with country food and skin clothing. Intense social interaction was inevitable and resulted in a proliferation of children with mixed blood, all of whom were proudly raised as Inuit, either by their natural mother or adoptive families. Whalers were quite willing to take advantage of the fact that a husband, instead of expressing jealousy, often seemed pleased that his wife was appreciated.[19]

By the late 1800s most sailing ships were fitted with auxiliary steam engines, allowing them to arrive earlier, penetrate deeper into ice-strewn waters, and depart later in the season. A few whalers continued to fish off the North Baffin coast, nearly all from Peterhead, Aberdeen, or Dundee, Scotland. The technique they employed was called "rock-nosing," whereby a ship would anchor in a protected harbour or just off-shore, while its small whale boats searched for whales migrating to winter quarters off southern Greenland and Labrador. The ships were self-sufficient, carrying crews of forty or more to man the boats that brought the carcass alongside the ship. Here they removed the baleen and flensed the blubber. The baleen was tied into bundles and the whale blubber stored in large wooden casks for rendering back in Scotland. Although Inuit assistance was not required by the "rock-nose whalers," they were nevertheless welcomed aboard to trade their ivory and furs for European goods.[20]

Although a few ships were reported to have ventured into Prince Regent Inlet, the Iglulingmiut generally travelled to Eclipse Sound or Repulse Bay to trade with the whalers. Some reportedly were hired to work on the whaling ships in Hudson Bay. The trading sessions developed into social occasions that included tea and biscuits, musical entertainment, and square dances.[21] Inevitably the Inuit of North Baffin became dependent upon a trade economy over which they had little control, apart from their ability to negotiate. Favoured items were tobacco, guns, and ammunition, but the Inuit also valued knives, fox traps, saws, hatchets, clothing items, telescopes, tea, kettles, pots, and later, musical instruments and sewing machines.[22] Over time Inuit culture underwent subtle changes that included addiction to tobacco, new dietary preferences, use of *qallunaat* clothing, and loss of traditional hunting techniques. In addition to trade goods, the Europeans also brought infectious diseases such as measles, influenza, and venereal disease, all of which took their toll in deaths and disabilities.[23]

For the most part, relations between the Inuit of North Baffin and the whalers were peaceful—with a notable exception occurring in the late nineteenth century. According to elders' stories told to Father Guy Mary-Rousselière, several Inuit families had crossed over Lancaster Sound to hunt polar bears on Devon Island. When a whaling ship anchored near their camp, several hunters boarded the ship to trade. One Inuk, known to be a thief, stole a telescope and other items. In anger the ship's crew suddenly opened fire, killing all Inuit on board save one who was thought to have been taken a prisoner.[24] Those who witnessed the incident from the shore fled in fear that the whalers would come ashore and kill them as well. The fact that three elders were able to recall the story of the massacre almost a hundred years later reflects a deep and lasting impression.

With whale stocks almost depleted at the end of the nineteenth century, some shipowners maintained their former whaling stations in Cumberland Sound as trading centres for ivory, sealskin, furs, and fish, thus moderating the disruption in Inuit lives during the transition to a fur-trapping economy. At least two companies attempted to set up trading stations along the Baffin coast, but the supply system proved unstable. The Hudson's Bay Company (HBC), which began establishing posts in the Ungava region in mid-nineteenth century, moved slowly northward, to Lake Harbour in 1911, Cape Dorset in 1913, and as far as Repulse Bay in 1916. Further expansion halted during the Great War and did not resume until 1920.[25] Although the Iglulingmiut continued to trade at the HBC post at Repulse Bay, the Tununirmiut would have been without ammunition had it not been for the arrival of free traders at Eclipse Sound.[26]

There were inherent risks as Inuit moved further afield in search of whalers and trade goods. Family groups travelling through unfamiliar territory were sometimes caught by bad weather and lost their way. Some died of starvation, a fate feared worse than death itself. One story tells of thirteen Inuit in the 1870s who were beset by bad weather en route from Igloolik to Pond Inlet. Only two survived by eating the deceased and managed to make their way on foot to Eclipse Sound.[27] Around 1893 a group from a camp on Admiralty Inlet went over to Elwyn Bay on Somerset Island, apparently looking for whales or possibly whalers who sometimes visited that location. When the whaling ship *Baleana* arrived the next summer, they found their corpses, victims of starvation. It was reported that they had first eaten their dogs, then the dead, until the last succumbed sometime during the winter. Given the valuables left behind, it was believed that there had been no survivors.[28] Eating the flesh of a deceased human was a taboo in Inuit culture, just as in western societies, but acute starvation was claimed to cause one to lose all reason.

Unlike the Indian policies that evolved in British North America after the Royal Proclamation of 1763, no official Inuit policy—neither British nor later Canadian—existed until after the Second World War. Although recognized as "Natives," the Inuit were not included in the Indian Act, nor was legislation passed making them wards of the federal government.[29] As a consequence, they were technically full-fledged Canadian citizens without any privileges—no access to health or educational services, and no vote. As residents of the Northwest Territories, they fell under the general authority of the Department of the Interior until 1924, when the responsibility for Inuit policy was temporarily transferred to the Department of Indian Affairs by an amendment to a sub-section of the Indian Act. The RCMP were mandated to supervise their health and welfare in the field.[30]

Without a permanent government or police presence on Baffin Island, a mutually acceptable form of "frontier justice" prevailed in the nineteenth century, allowing for relatively easy coexistence between whalers and the Inuit. If a *qallunaaq* became angry, an Inuk might go out of his way to appease him,[31] a reaction that was likely responsible for the image of the Inuit as "a friendly, peaceful race." Most Inuit relationships with the *qallunaat* were influenced by a response knows as *ilira*, which resulted in a show of deference or subservience to frightening or intimidating individuals. By Hugh Brody's interpretation, that response was at the core of all early contact relationships: "The word *ilira* goes to the heart of colonial relationships, and it helps to explain the many times that Inuit, and so many other peoples, say yes when they want to say no, or say yes and reveal, later, that they never meant it at all. *Ilira* is a word that speaks to the subtle but pervasive result of inequality. Through the inequality it reveals, the word shapes the whole tenor of interpersonal behaviour, creating many forms of misunderstanding, mistrust, and bad faith. It is the fear that colonialism instils and evokes, which then distorts meanings, social life and politics."[32]

Inuit/whaler relationships also involved a natural co-dependency. Just as an Inuk would not wish to alienate those who supplied European goods, a ship's captain would not want to cut off his access to furs and ivory, particularly in light of the declining whale fishery. Even so, certain ground rules were established. According to one elder from Arctic Bay, it was understood that trouble would follow if they killed a white man.[33] Apparently such views were not understood in terms of "right or wrong" or Canadian laws but in terms of their own cultural traditions that allowed the family of a murdered man to take revenge on his killer.[34]

Similarly, most Europeans were mindful that it was not in their best interests to alienate the Inuit. As an example, the story of how shipwrecked sailors on Akpatok Island were killed by their Inuit hosts—because of food shortages and their unreasonable demands—was well known in the whaling fraternity.[35] As Commander A.P. Low of Canada's 1903–04

expedition to the Arctic explained, the Inuit as a people were "very hospitable and kind; but like other savages would probably soon tire of continuous efforts to support helpless whites cast upon them, especially when the guests assume a superiority over their hosts."[36]

In the nineteenth century, reports of violence among the Inuit were generally ignored. Whalers preferred not to get involved. This was not necessarily the case with the Hudson's Bay Company, as outbreaks of violence tended to have an adverse effect on their trade. In the Ungava region, for instance, it was reported that HBC traders supported the Inuit custom of execution as it was in their interest to be rid of a potential menace in their midst.[37] Yet prior to 1911 there were no HBC posts on Baffin Island. Nor was there a police presence before 1921, except for a very brief visit by the North West Mounted Police (NWMP) who had accompanied the 1897 and 1903 expeditions to Cumberland Sound. Significantly there were no police officers on board in 1904 when the A.P. Low expedition first visited Eclipse Sound. Nor were there any on the expeditions led by Captain Bernier from 1906 to 1911. Thus, while there was a fleeting government presence of sorts on Baffin Island between 1897 and 1911, there was no effective means of enforcing law and order in the region during the forty years following Britain's transfer of the territory to Canada. Likewise, except for a visit to Cumberland Sound by a Moravian brother in 1856, Baffin Island had no permanent missionary presence until 1894.[38] As a result, the Inuit were portrayed in nineteenth-century literature and art as an uncivilized pagan race who dressed in animal skins and carried Stone Age weapons but somehow managed to survive the most inhospitable environment known to western man. This stereotype prevailed well into the twentieth century.

The advance of Christianity in the eastern Arctic that began with the Moravians in

Labrador in 1776 continued into the mid-nineteenth century with the establishment of an Anglican mission at Moose River on James Bay and later at Great Whale River on the east coast of Hudson Bay, In 1876 Reverend Edmund Peck founded a mission at Little Whale River on Ungava Bay, where he began working on a syllabic alphabet to represent Inuktitut, based on one created by Reverend James Evans for use with the Cree Indians. In 1894, armed with syllabic prayer books and Bibles, Peck established the first Christian mission on Baffin Island, at a whaling station on Blacklead Island in Cumberland Sound. A rudimentary school was set up as well as a one-room mission hospital.[39]

Peck's travels and those of his assistants were generally limited to nearby camps, although one year he visited camps along the coast as far north as Qivittuuq while returning home to England on a whaling ship. A number of lay preachers travelled further afield, distributing Bibles and spreading word about the new religion.[40] Several families from Cumberland Sound were reported to have migrated to Igloolik with their Bibles. In this manner, many Iglulingmiut learned to read and write in syllabics without ever having met a *qallunaat* missionary.[41] Understanding the biblical passages was more difficult.

Literacy grew at an astonishing rate, but the meaning of the words was not always understood. This gave rise to a number of "syncretic movements" that combined traditional spiritual beliefs of shamanism with those of Christianity. Occasionally there were bouts of religious frenzy and in a few cases tragic deaths. Peter Pitseolak described two such occasions near Lake Harbour which he described as "overdoing religion." There were similar incidents reported near Sugluk in the Ungava region of Quebec and near Pangnirtung.[42] Although another Anglican mission opened at Lake Harbour in 1909, it was not until 1928 that a

European missionary visited Pond Inlet, and then only briefly during a stop by the HBC supply ship. In other words, there was no supervised teaching of Christianity north of Cumberland Sound until 1928.[43]

Inuit of North Baffin, like those elsewhere in the Arctic, had their own spiritual convictions as set out in the legends and teachings of the shamans. These beliefs were largely driven by fear and maintained by an elaborate network of taboos that governed their everyday life. There was no "one supreme being," although Sedna, the sea goddess, also known as Nuliajuk or Sanna, was considered to be the giver or taker of life because of her powerful influence over the fish and mammals. A number of lesser spirits were thought to have control over such things as the weather, health, fertility, and even one's happiness. Only the shamans possessed the ability to communicate with the spirits. Some had "great powers" to travel to the moon or to the depths of the sea. Some had special healing powers, while others were skilled at knowing where to look for caribou or marine mammals. Disease and starvation were believed to be caused by someone having broken a taboo. If anyone behaved badly, a shaman might encourage a public confession to help that person overcome the problem. There were good shamans and bad, the latter greatly feared because of their power to do evil.[44]

Commander A.P. Low appeared knowledgeable about Inuit spiritual beliefs and shamanism when he visited North Baffin in the summer of 1904.[45] In his book describing the expedition, he referred to Inuit rules governing social behaviour, including the criteria for executing an individual. By his understanding, "if an individual becomes dangerously obnoxious, or insane, a consultation of the men of the band is held, and one or more of them are deputed to remove the criminal or lunatic; in such a case the individuals acting are held blameless in the matter."[46]

Yet some government officials would argue that because the Inuit travelled in small groups, they did not possess a formal system of justice or governance. Zebedee Nungak, speaking as chairman of the Inuit Justice Task Force in Nunavik, strongly disagreed, claiming that not only did Inuit know right from wrong by their own standards but they also had a system to deal with serious offenders: "The overriding concern was the sustenance of the collective. Any dispute among the people was settled by the elders and/or leaders, who always had the respect and high regard of the group."[47] Inuit also employed various means such as counselling, derision, gossip, and public confession to modify unacceptable behaviour. Granted, there were regional differences, but only as a last resort did elders advise banishment or execution.[48] In spite of the many cultural differences, the tradition of consensual agreement and the goal of restoring harmony in the community were two traits Inuit shared with the Dogrib Indians of the Dene Nation.[49]

If an Inuk's actions became deviant and menaced others, and if that individual did not respond to other means of control, then he or she was considered to be insane, providing just cause that his or her life be terminated.[50] In such cases execution required careful planning to catch the victim when most vulnerable. By British standards such actions were clear evidence of premeditated murder, yet by Inuit customary law, consensual agreement legitimized the action. Equally at odds with British justice was the Inuit belief that "insanity" provided a justifiable reason for killing a person, compared to the *qallunaat* practice of pleading insanity to avoid responsibility for one's crime. Even the objectives of social control differed in the two societies. When Inuit were confronted with a serious crime such as persistent thieving, assault, or murder, the aim was to resolve the conflict, if possible, so as not to lose an able-bodied hunter. By British tradition a criminal was severely punished to deter others from contemplating similar acts.

Although the Inuit traditions in dealing with violence appear to have been understood by an informed white elite at the turn of the century, few were aware of the subtle regional differences in process.[51] In the southwest corner of Baffin Island, for example, discussion about a criminal act was formalized and involved a gathering of leaders and shamans in what Norman Hallendy describes as a "Great Council," which "questioned witnesses and the accused, heard confessions, listened to pleas, attempted to resolve conflicts, and decided punishments."[52] In North Baffin the procedure was far less formal and required only the consent of elders or camp leaders.[53]

Not all Inuit killings were planned in advance. As historian William R. Morrison explains, "in aboriginal Inuit groups, even temper was prized, and bad temper was regarded as a serious threat, not only to the individual, but to the whole band." In this context, "if a man spoke harshly to you, he had it in his mind to kill you, and it was thus entirely reasonable to defend yourself by killing him first."[54] In North Baffin an adult was expected to refrain from showing anger and instead show *isuma,* meaning "the capacity for a sense of reason." The loss of *isuma,* which might be evidenced by a flushed face or aggressive gestures, was equated with the loss of reason or insanity.[55] When the death of an Inuk was the result of an impulsive act without consensual agreement, a member of the victim's family possessed the right to retaliate and seek revenge. This often led to "blood feuds" if a killer was unable to convince the victim's family of the necessity of his act.[56]

Taking another's life without prior consent or provocation—*inuaqsiniq*—was considered the worst of all crimes because of the adverse effect it would have on a group with close kinship ties. But self-defence was an exception, according to Emile Imaruittuq, an elder from Igloolik. "If someone was attacking you, trying to kill you, you would be justified in defending yourself. If you killed the person before he killed you, that would be justified. But if a killing was committed without a provocation, that was terrible. We are on this Earth to try to live. We have to protect ourselves, if someone is trying to kill us."[57] In other words, self-defence was an acceptable motive.

In some cases murderers might be forgiven if they regretted their actions and showed a willingness to change. Even then, they tended to be feared, as it was thought that "once an individual has killed someone, the desire to kill again would return." Those most feared were individuals who claimed that they "heard voices" or were thought to be losing their minds.[58] Prior to 1912 there had been no reports of an Inuk killing a white man, and thus no attempts to interfere in what were perceived as domestic matters. Moreover, on Baffin Island, there were no police to receive such a report.

After 1904, trade improved for the Tununirmiut because of a new land-based whaling station established on Eclipse Sound by the Dundee Whaling Company. Captain James Mutch, a veteran whaler, accompanied by William Duval and several Inuit families from Cumberland Sound, was sent to establish a post in the vicinity of Pond Inlet.

According to Mutch, he had been unable to encourage families from Qivittuuq to join him because "they were afraid of the Ponds Bay Eskimos, as there were so many murders up there." John Matthiasson, an anthropologist who lived at Pond Inlet during the 1960s, was also told about "a very bad man" who had lived there many years ago, and who began to kill all the people who lived with him.[59] The Inuk in question may have been Qillaq, the leader of the Qitdlarssuaq migration to Greenland. According to several stories told by Inuit elders, this group appeared to be the primary cause of violence in the region.[60]

After spending one winter at Erik Harbour in the winter of 1903–04, Mutch moved to a permanent location at Igarjuaq in Albert Harbour, several miles east of the present-day site of Pond Inlet. Although the station was equipped to render whale blubber, it primarily operated as a trading post. Here Mutch employed a number of hunters to assist in harvesting seals and narwhals, and women to render the fat into oil. In summer the families lived in skin tents surrounding the main building. In the winter months they were paid "a scant weekly allowance of biscuits, tea, molasses and tobacco...to keep them on hand until the spring arrived," at which time, the small whale boats were pulled to floe edge to hunt seals, whales, narwhals, and polar bears.[61] Occasionally these boats were given to Inuit as payment for services or goods and were considered prize possessions.

Duval, a German-born American called Sivutiksaq, meaning "the harpooner," remained at the station for three years along with his Inuit wife and two daughters.[62] In 1923 he would return to Pond Inlet as the interpreter for the first jury trial held in the eastern Arctic.

Inuit living in vicinity of the whaling station enjoyed a few years of relative prosperity, as did those who came from Arctic Bay and Igloolik to trade. As Mutch (known to the Inuit as Jimmi Mutchie) observed, the Tununirmiut had become shrewd bargainers after eighty-five years of trade with the whalers: "The real Ponds Bay Eskimo had been coming and going all winter, trading a fox-skin when they had one, but always wanting nearly home value for it or for anything they might bring... When a bearskin was brought, though it was small, a telescope or a gun was asked for it. They are much like those who said, 'If one never asks, one never gets.' They all charged well for their goods, and had been accustomed to getting full value for seal-skins or for any other skins they ever took on board the whalers when they were there."[63]

Over the years, it appears, the Tununirmiut had learned the fair value of their trade items. Although increasingly dependent upon European goods, they were not easily intimidated or duped into handing over their furs and ivory for less than their worth. Inuit from Admiralty Inlet and Clyde River also travelled more often to Igarjuaq to trade. The Iglulingmiut, on the other hand, tended to alternate their travels between Eclipse Sound and Repulse Bay.[64] Social contact increased, and literacy also spread as a result of the syllabic Bibles brought to Igarjuaq by the Inuit families from Cumberland Sound.[65]

Although the physical environment was once the dominant influence on the culture and activities of the North Baffin Inuit, contact with the Scottish whalers caused many changes in food preferences, clothing, and hunting techniques. These would become even more pronounced in the twentieth century, but because the transition from a whaling economy to a fur trading economy took place gradually over a period of many years, the Inuit neither noticed nor feared it. Likely their greatest concern was that some day the ships might disappear altogether. Since many of the ancient hunting skills were abandoned after the introduction of rifles, such an event could have been disastrous.

Notes

1 Brody, *The Other Side of Eden,* 119.

2 Stager and Swain, *Canada North,* 90.

3 Ibid., 88–93.

4 As noted by Mathiassen in 1923. See Therkel Mathiassen, *Archaeology of the Central Eskimos,* 136.

5 Stager and Swain, *Canada North,* 95–8.

6 For more detailed descriptions, see McGhee, *Ancient People of the Arctic and Canadian Arctic Prehistory;* Mary-Rousselière, "Factors Affecting Human Occupation of the Land in the Pond Inlet Region from Prehistorical to Contemporary Times," and "Iglulik" in David Damas, ed., *Handbook of North American Indians,* and in the same volume, McGhee, "Thule Prehistory of Canada," and Maureau Maxwell, "Pre-Dorset and Dorset Prehistory of Canada."

7 A new study underway in the summer of 2001, under the supervision of Robert McGhee of the Canadian Museum of Civilization and Douglas Stenton, chief archaeologist with the Nunavut government, will be using new techniques to carbon date previously collected artifacts of both cultures to determine whether the dates overlap. Father Guy Mary-Rousselière, an amateur archaeologist who collected Inuit stories and studied artifacts from camps around Eclipse Sound, was convinced that they did.

8 Mathiassen (1927), 221. His comments were based on thousands of artifacts collected from the Eclipse Sound and Igloolik areas and compared to those collected at Repulse Bay and further south.

9 Mary-Rousselière, "Eskimo Toponymy of Pond Inlet."

10 Mary-Rousselière, "Iglulik," 442.

11 Personal communication, Douglas Stenton, 28 February 2001.

12 Information about the seasonal cycles in Inuit lives was derived from stories told by the elders at Pond Inlet, notably Timothy Kadloo, Ningiuk Killiktee, and Letia Kyak. Anthropologist Richard Condon also described these cycles in *Inuit Behaviour and Seasonal Change.*

13 Stager and Swain, *Canada North,* 90.

14 Letia Kyak and others affirm that as children they had been told that Mittima's grave was in the vicinity of a large rock on the beach. This story appears in an article by Father Guy Mary-Rousselière, "Mittima's Grave." Others accept the explanation by Danish explorer Peter Freuchen that Mittimatalik meant "where the bird lights," possibly referring to a sandbar that at one time extended some distance from the shore. See Freuchen, *Arctic Adventure,* 460.

15 Sutherland, "Strands of Culture Contact." Additional findings suggest the Norsemen may have travelled more widely than first suspected.

16 Cooke and Holland, *The Exploration of Northern Canada, 500 to 1920,* 22–4, 28.

17 Ibid., 138 and 142; also Parry, *Journal of a Voyage for the Discovery of a North-West Passage from the Atlantic to the Pacific,* 275–88.

18 Ross, "Whaling, Inuit, and the Arctic Islands," 239.

19 A.P. Low, *Report on the Dominion Government Expedition,* 164.

20 Ross, *Arctic Whalers, Icy Seas,* 49. See also Low, *Report on the Dominion Government Expedition,* 267–71.

21 This tradition continued with the government expeditions led by Captain Bernier on the CGS *Arctic* as seen in the National Film Board's silent movie takes of the CGS *Arctic* on the Eastern Arctic Patrol from 1922 to 1925. Also, *The Arctic Patrol,* Canadian Government Motion Picture Bureau, 1929, ISN 61875.

22 Goldring, "Inuit Economic Responses."

23 Ross, "Whaling, Inuit, and the Arctic Islands," 242–6; also Low, *Report on the Dominion Government Expedition,* 271–2.

24 Mary-Rousselière, *Qidtlarssuaq,* 141, and appendix 6, story by Inuguk, and appendix 7, story by Qanguq.

25 Goldring, "Inuit Economic Responses," 264–6.

26 Ross, ed., *An Arctic Whaling Diary,* 14–22.

27 Tremblay, *Cruise of the Minnie Maud,* 236.

28 Mary-Rousselière, *Qidtlarssuaq,* 144–6.

29 Backhouse, *A Legal History of Racism in Canada, 1900–1950,* 27–8. Although there was a debate in 1924 on whether Inuit should be brought under the Indian Act, it was rejected. Their status was again under debate in the 1930s, this time with regard to whether responsibility for welfare payments lay with federal or provincial governments. In April 1939 a decision of the Supreme Court of Canada established that the Inuit were Indians within the meaning of "aboriginal" in Section 91(24) of the British North America Act, and should be considered wards of the federal government. This decision was never supported by legislation with the result that the official status of the Inuit as full-fledged Canadian citizens remained intact.

30 Diubaldo, *The Government of Canada and the Inuit, 1900–1967,* 45.

31 Brody, *The Other Side of Eden,* 43–4; Stevenson, *Inuit, Whalers, and Cultural Persistence,* 117–20.

32 Brody, *The Other Side of Eden,* 43.

33 Cowan, ed., *We Don't Live in Snow Houses Now,* 25. "Ahlooloo" recalls how his father admonished his nephew for having killed the white trader Robert Janes, saying "You should not have killed a *qallunaaq.* Now you are going to see another one."

34 According to Noah Piuggttuk's explanation, the Inuit living at the Igarjuaq whaling station near Pond Inlet feared that "some white people might take revenge" for the death of a white fur trader (Interview IE-041, 16 January 1989, courtesy the Igloolik Inullariit Society, Igloolik Research Centre). In the Inuit statements taken for the preliminary trial, others also feared revenge.

35 Wakeham, *Report of the Expedition to Hudson Bay and Cumberland Gulf,* 44.

36 Low, *Report on the Dominion Government Expedition,* 182.

37 NAC, RG 18, vol. 3284, file 1920 HQ-1034-C-1, report from Port Harrison, 12 October 1921; RG 18, vol. 3313, file 1925 HQ-118-C-2. Governor C. Sale of the Hudson's Bay Company to W.S. Edwards, deputy minister of Justice, 12 October 1926; See also Hudson's Bay Archives, signed statement by the post manager, S.J. Stewart, dated 13 May 1927, at Port Harrison.

38 A Moravian, John Warmow, had accompanied the whaling ship captained by William Penny Junior that wintered over in 1857–58. See Ross, *This Distant and Unsurveyed Country.*

39 Trott, "The Rapture and the Rupture," 212.

40 Harper, "Writing in Inuktitut," 6–7.

41 Ibid. Therkel Mathiassen of the Danish Fifth Thule Expedition was surprised to find that most Inuit near Igloolik could both read and write in syllabics.

42 Pitseolak and Eber, *People from Our Side,* 40–4, 68–9; see also Grant, "Religious Fanaticism at Leaf Bay, Ungava," 163–5.

43 We know by his own report that Bernier had delivered Bibles in 1911 to the mission at Blacklead Island on instructions from Reverend Peck. See Canada, Department of Marine and Fisheries, *Report on the Dominion Government Expedition to the Northern Waters and Arctic Archipelago,* 80. According to Stéphane Cloutier, who has been compiling a collection of photographs and documents related to the life of Captain Bernier, one of his men also distributed some of Peck's Bibles to the Iglulingmiut in the winter of 1910–11.

44 Many sources explain Inuit spirituality and shamanism. A more sophisticated analysis is found in Brody's *The Other Side of Eden,* 229–49; for description based on Inuit oral history, see Laugrand et al., *Memory and History in Nunavut.*

45 Low, *Report on the Dominion Government Expedition,* 162–74. His knowledge was reportedly derived from the narratives of polar explorers and an ethnographic study of Cumberland Sound by Franz Boas.

46 Ibid., 165.

47 Nungak, "Fundamental Values, Norms and Concepts of Justice," 86. The concept that Inuit customary law was based on the objective of keeping peace in the community was recognized by anthropologists in the 1930s. See Birket-Smith, *The Eskimos,* 164.

48 Rasing, "Too Many People," 116–32; Nungak, "Fundamental Values," 86–104; Finkler, *Inuit and the Administration of Justice in the Northwest Territories;* Graburn, "Eskimo Law in Light of Self- and Group-Interest"; Patenaude, "Whose Law? Whose Justice?" Of the many sources on this general topic, only a few are recent and pertinent to Baffin Island. Most studies on traditional laws of indigenous peoples are either outdated or relate only to the North American Indian or to Inuit from other regions of the Arctic.

49 Ryan, *Doing Things the Right Way,* 101.

50 Brody, *Living Arctic,* 126–7.

51 Possibly the first anthropologist, or at least one of the first, to recognize the subtle differences in Inuit customary laws according to subgroups within the culture was Leopold J. Pospisil. See his *Anthropology of Law,* 106–97, 124–5.

52 Hallendy et al., "The Last Known Traditional Inuit Trial on Southwest Baffin Island in the Canadian Arctic," 7.

53 Tremblay, *Cruise of the Minnie Maud,* 121; see also Oosten, Laugrand, and Rasing, eds., *Perspectives on Traditional Law.*

54 Morrison, *Showing the Flag,* 148.

55 Brody, *The Other Side of Eden,* 46–7.

56 Stevenson, *Inuit, Whalers, and Cultural Persistance,* 54–8; Boas, *The Central Eskimo,* 174. Boas believed that "blood feuds" were more prevalent in Canada's eastern and central Arctic. In a more recent study of the Cumberland Sound area, Marc Stevenson argues that these feuds declined with greater exposure to the *qallunaat.*

57 Emile Imaruittuq in Oosten et al., *Perspectives on Traditional Law,* 160–1.

58 Ibid., 164–71.

59 Matthiasson, *Living on the Land,* 31; citing Mutch, "Whaling in Ponds Bay." 485.

60 Mary-Rousselière, *Qitdlarssuaq,* 30–40. This book tells of a group led by Qillaq who were thought to have arrived in Eclipse Sound in the mid-nineteenth century, retreating from possible attackers who might wish to avenge Qillaq for a murder in the Cumberland Sound area. Qillaq and his group were known to have attacked others at Eclipse Sound before heading off towards Admiralty Inlet and the Igloolik area.

61 Tremblay, *Cruise of the Minnie Maud,* 30–1; see also Mary-Rousselière, "Igarjuaq."

62 Mary-Rousselière, "Igarjuaq." Also see Harper, "William Duval (1858–1931)," in Davis, ed., *Lobsticks and Stone Cairns,* 263–4.

63 Matthiasson, *Living on the Land,* 32, citing Mutch, "Whaling in Ponds Bay," 488.

64 Wachowich, *Saqiyuq,* 19 and 71.

65 Harper, "Writing in Inuktitut," 7.

1492 and All That: Making a Garden Out of a Wilderness

RAMSAY COOK

"The Land is a Garden of Eden before them, and behind them a desolate wilderness."

Joel 2:3

"Is not America," Fernand Braudel asks in *The Perspective of the World,* the third volume of his magisterial *Civilization and Capitalism,* "perhaps the true explanation of Europe's greatness? Did not Europe discover or indeed 'invent' America, and has Europe not always celebrated Columbus's voyages as the greatest event in history 'since the creation?'" And then the great French historian concludes that "America was...the achievement by which Europe most truly revealed her own nature."[1] Braudel wrote without any intended irony, but that final remark about Europe truly revealing "her own nature" is perhaps what is really at issue in the current reassessment of the implications of Columbus's landfall at Guanahari, or San Salvador, as he named it in his first act of semiotic imperialism. ("Each received a new name from me,"[2] he recorded.)

That "nature" is captured by Marc Lescarbot in a sentence from his remarkable *History of New France,* published in 1609, which goes right to the heart of what we have apparently decided to call the "encounter" between the Old World and the New that Columbus symbolizes. Acadia, he wrote, "having two kinds of soil that God has given unto man as his possession, who can doubt that when it shall be cultivated it will be a land of promise?"[3] I hardly need to explain why I think

that sentence is so revealing of the European "nature," but I will. It forthrightly articulates the renaissance European's conviction that man was chosen by the Creator to possess and dominate the rest of creation. And it further assumes that, for the land to be fully possessed, it must be cultivated: tilled, improved, developed. The result: a promised land, a paradise, a garden of delights. Lescarbot's observations seemed so axiomatic then, and for nearly five centuries afterward, that almost no one questioned his vision of a promised land—at least almost no European. But that has begun to change. Contemporary Europe, as much in its western as in its eastern portions, struggles to redefine itself. Consequently Europe overseas, as J.G.A. Pocock recently argued in a brilliant essay,[4] is being forced to look again at the meaning of what Gómara in his *General History of the Indies* (1552) called "the greatest event since the creation of the world"[5]—the meaning of the "discovery of America." [...]

The process whereby a way of life—the European one—triumphed over the Amerindian one was fairly rapid in New England, being virtually completed by 1800. Since the colonization of Acadia, a vast area that included present-day Nova Scotia, New Brunswick, Prince Edward Island, part of Quebec (Gaspesia), and a portion of Maine, advanced at a slower pace, the two ways of life existed side by side, interacting with one another, for a longer period of time. Leslie Upton's study, *Micmacs and Colonists,* noted that

---

Excerpt from Ramsay Cook, "1492 and All That: Making a Garden Out of a Wilderness," from Ramsay Cook, *Canada, Quebec and the Uses of Nationalism,* Second Edition (Toronto: McClelland and Stewart, 1995), 51–72, 259–262. Used by permission, McClelland & Stewart Ltd. The Canadian Publishers.

at the beginning of this period, the Treaty of Utrecht of 1713, the number of Micmac people of Acadia still roughly equalled European settlers even though the Native population had declined drastically. In the seventeenth century Acadia had been the scene of imperial competition and war between France and Britain and that had hardly been conducive to extensive settlement. By 1650 there were some fifty households at Port Royal and Le Have; that population had grown to about 900 souls by the 1680s. So, too, population was spreading from Port Royal to the Minas Basin, to Beaubassin and scattered along the north shore of the Bay of Fundy. "When the British took control for the third and last time," Upton writes, "capturing Port Royal in 1710, there were just over 1,500 native born Acadians with roots going back from two to four generations. The Micmac population stood at about the same number having declined from 3,000 or so at the beginning of the seventeenth century. In one hundred years the French had been able to establish a white population only half the size of the Micmacs' at their first arrival."[6] It is the very slowness of the process, and the richness of the documentation for the seventeenth century, that makes the study of the ecology of contact in Acadia so fascinating.

Between 1604 and 1708 six major writers— of varied background—composed accounts of what Nicolas Denys called "the natural history" of Acadia (and this leaves out Jacques Cartier's sixteenth-century account). Now I think it is highly significant that Denys believed that "natural history" included not just geography, geology, climate, and the flora and fauna, but also the inhabitants of the new land. The model, of course, was Pliny's *Natural History*, a work that played such a large part in determining what was discovered in America that the Roman almost deserves to be ranked with Columbus.[7] Nor was Denys in anyway unique: Champlain, Lescarbot, Biard, Le Clercq, and Dièreville, the authors of the other five major contemporary accounts of seventeenth-century Acadia, all followed a similar recipe

though varying the amounts of the ingredients somewhat. Each of these writers approached Acadia from an ecological perspective, setting people squarely in their environment and noting the contrast between European and Amerindian ways of living in, and belonging to, their environment.

Each of these seventeenth-century writers devoted a substantial portion of his book to descriptions of the natural world. There was a certain awesomeness about this wilderness and its abundance of birds, beasts, fish, and flowers. In 1604, at Seal Island, Champlain's keen eye identified firs, pines, larches, and poplars, and more than a dozen species of birds, not all of which he recognized. At nearly every landing he made similar observations.[8] He identified the skimmer with its extended lower bill, while Denys described the majestic bald eagle carrying off a rabbit in its talons. Marc Lescarbot provided comparable descriptions. His famous poem "Adieu à la Nouvelle France" is a versified catalogue of the environment, including that indigenous marvel, *"un oiselet semblable au papillon,"* the hummingbird. This ornithological marvel, sometimes called the Bird of Heaven, provided the same sense of admiration in early visitors to North America that the flamboyant parrot produced in explorers of South America, beginning with Columbus. The parrot, captured and transported, quickly became the symbol of America in post-Columbian art. The hummingbird, impossible to rear in captivity, remained in the Americas. Among insects the firefly was highly appealing, the mosquito detested.[9]

Of the creatures of the animal world none attracted more curiosity than the beaver. It became an animal more marvellous in the Plinean imaginations of Le Clercq and Denys than in reality. It performed as architect, mason, carpenter, even hod carrier, walking upright with a load of mud piled on its broad tail. A natural rear end loader! "Its flesh is delicate," Father Le Clercq reported, "and very much like that of mutton. The kidneys are sought by apothecaries, and are used with effect in easing women in childbirth, and in mitigating hysterics."[10] The value of beaver pelts hardly needed comment.

Then there was the moose that cured itself of epilepsy by scratching its ear with its own cloven hoof. At least the flying squirrel was the real thing. Denys's description of the cod fishery, not surprisingly since he was a merchant, was accurate and detailed. On the southeast coast of St. Mary's Bay, when the tide dropped, Champlain found mussels, clams, and sea snails, while elsewhere oysters abounded. The swarms of fish that swam in the waterways filled these men with excitement. On the Miramichi, Denys claimed that he had been kept awake all night by the loud sounds of salmon splashing. The fertility and agricultural potential of the new land were naturally a constant preoccupation. "The entire country is covered with very dense forests," Champlain wrote of the site that would become Annapolis Royal, "...except a point a league and a half up the river, where there are some oaks which are very scattered and a number of wild vines. These could be easily cleared and the place brought under cultivation." Nor did Champlain miss the minerals and metals—silver at Mink Cove, iron further north on Digby Neck.[11]

Moreover, it is from these writers that at least a partial sketch of the lives and customs of the Northeastern Algonquian peoples can be reconstructed. Champlain recorded the practice of swidden agriculture among the Abenaki—corn, beans, and squash—and even noted the use of horseshoe crab shells, probably as fertilizer.[12] Hunting and fishing methods were remarked upon, though the lack of details is somewhat surprising, particularly when contrasted with the lengthy accounts of religious beliefs—or supposed lack of them—of the various inhabitants of Acadia. "Jugglery," or shamanism, and also medical practices were of particular interest—indeed, Dièreville even convinced himself of the efficacy of some shamanistic cures. So, too, dress, hairstyles, courtship and marriage customs, and cere-monies surrounding childbirth and death were carefully recorded and sometimes compared to classical and contemporary European practices. Lescarbot, for example, concluded that the Jesuits were quite mistaken in attempting to force Christian monogamy on the Micmacs, arguing that indigenous marriage customs would best be "left in the state in which they were found." In contrast to some Jesuit writers—and Brian Moore—Lescarbot judged the Aboriginal people very modest in sexual matters. This he attributed partly to their familiarity with nakedness but chiefly "to their keeping bared the head, where lies the fountain of the spirits which excite to procreation, partly to the lack of salt, of hot spices, of wine, of meats which provoke desire, and partly to their frequent use of tobacco, the smoke of which dulls the senses, and mounting up to the brain hinders the functions of Venus." On the other hand, he believed that one romantic innovation introduced by the French actually contributed to the improvement of Aboriginal life: the kiss. Though Professor Karen Anderson has followed up Lescarbot's insight about the impact of the missionaries on marriage among the Native people of New France, no one, as far as I know, has advanced our knowledge of the relationship between civilization and osculation.[13]

Virtually all male European visitors to Acadia were struck by the division of labour in Aboriginal communities. Women, it was agreed, "work harder than the men, who play the gentleman, and care only for hunting or for war." Despite this, Lescarbot wrote approvingly, "they love their husbands more than women of our parts." It is interesting that in his discussion of the ease with which Micmac marriages could be dissolved, Father Le Clercq remained detached and uncensorious. "In a word," he remarked laconically, "they hold it as a maxim that each one is free; that one can do whatever he wishes: and that it is not sensible to put constraint upon men." And the priest understood that the maxim applied to both men and women.[14]

Games and the Native peoples' apparent penchant for gambling were described though not always understood. Then there were science and technology. Father Le Clercq, perhaps the most ethnologically astute of seventeenth-century observers, provided an intriguing account of the ways the Gaspesians read the natural world: their interpretation of the stars and the winds, how they reckoned distance and recognized the changing seasons. The usefulness and limitations of indigenous technology were also commented upon. The efficiency of the birchbark canoe won widespread admiration. "The Savages of Port Royal can go to Kebec in ten or twelve days by means of the rivers which they navigate almost up to their sources," Lescarbot discovered, "and thence carrying their little bark canoes through the woods they reach another stream which flows into the river of Canada and thus greatly expedite their long voyages." While household utensils, manufactured from bark, roots, and stumps, were ingenious, the French realized that the Aboriginals were happy to replace them with metal wares. War and its weaponry drew the somewhat surprised comment that "neither profit nor the desire to extend boundaries, but rather vengeance, caused fairly frequent hostilities between native groups." Torture was graphically described, and condemned, though it was recognized—and judged a sign of savagery—that "to die in this manner is, among the savages, to die as a great captain and as a man of great courage."[15]

Much else also caught the attention of these ethnologists: the commonality of property, the importance of gift exchange, the practice of setting aside weapons before entering into discussions with strangers, and the expectation that strangers should do the same. And even though the Natives were "crafty, thievish and treacherous," Lescarbot admitted somewhat superciliously that "they do not lack wit, and might come to something if they were civilized, and knew the various trades."[16]

Though observations and judgements were made with great confidence, indeed, often rather cavalierly, these Europeans were aware that there often existed an unbridgeable communications chasm between the observers and the observed. Like every explorer before them, the French in Acadia attempted to resolve the problem in two ways. The first was to take young Natives back to France for an immersion course in French. ("We had on board a savage," Lescarbot noted in 1608, "who was much astonished to see the buildings, spires and windmills of France, but more the women, whom he had never seen dressed after our manner.") While these interpreters were doubtless helpful in breaking down the "effect of the confusion of Babel," it was hardly a permanent resolution to what Father Biard realized was a fundamental problem. Yet for the French to learn the local languages was time-consuming and the results often frustrating. Learning words was not the same as learning to communicate. "As these Savages have no formulated Religion, government, towns, nor trade," Biard recorded in exasperation, "so the words and proper phrases for all of these things are lacking." The confusion of words with things, of the sign with the referent, was, as Todorov has brilliantly shown, endemic to the European attempt to comprehend America. Acadia was no exception, though I have, unfortunately, not found any example quite so delicious as the linguistic dilemma encountered by Protestant missionaries in Hawaii. There the Islanders reportedly practised some twenty forms of sexual activity judged illicit—perhaps better, non-missionary. Each had a separate name in the native language, thus making translation of the Seventh Commandment virtually impossible without condoning the other nineteen forms of the joy of sex! The Native peoples of Acadia were apparently much less resourceful—or the celibate Jesuits less well trained as participant-observers.[17]

The natural, ethnographic, and linguistic accounts were not, of course, the work of biological scientists or cultural anthropologists—even taking into account our contemporary scepticism about the objectivity of anthropologists. Rather, they were the observations of seventeenth-century Frenchmen taking inventory of a new land they intended to explore, settle, develop, and Christianize—in brief, to colonize. It is in their works that much of what Braudel called Europe's "own nature" is "most truly revealed." In differing ways it is made emphatically plain by each of these authors that the French objective in Acadia, in the words of Father Biard, was "to make a Garden out of the wilderness." Nor should this be read narrowly as simply meaning the evangelization of the people who lived in Acadia.[18]

In the revealing introduction to his rich and thoughtful *Relation* of 1616, Biard wrote: "For verily all of this region, though capable of the same prosperity as ours, nevertheless through Satan's malevolence, which reigns there, is a horrible wilderness, scarcely less miserable on account of the scarcity of bodily comforts than for that which renders man absolutely miserable, the complete lack of the ornaments and riches of the soul." The missionary continues, offering his scientific conviction that "neither the sun, nor malice of the soil, neither the air nor the water, neither the men nor their caprices, are to be blamed for this. We are all created by and dependent upon the same principles: We breathe under the same sky; the same constellations influence us; and I do not believe that the land, which produces trees as tall and beautiful as ours, will not produce as fine harvests, *if it be cultivated*." Wilderness the expanses of Acadia might be, but a garden it could become, if cultivated. For Father Biard and his contemporaries, "subjugating Satanic monsters" and establishing "the order and discipline of heaven upon earth"[19] combined spiritual and worldly dimensions. Champlain, for whom the Devil and his agents were as real as for Biard, expressed the same objective in a more secular way when he told the local people he met in the region of the Penobscot River that the French "desired to settle in their country and show them how to cultivate it, in order that they might no longer live so miserable an existence as they are doing." The comment is made the more striking when we remember that Champlain knew that some of the inhabitants of Acadia did practise agriculture—though he never suggested that they "cultivated" the land.[20]

It is perhaps not too much to suggest that "cultivation" was a distinctly European concept. "For before everything else," Marc Lescarbot maintained, "one must set before oneself the tillage of the soil." At the first French settlement in Ste. Croix gardens were sown and some wheat "came up very fine and ripened." The poor quality of the soil was one reason for the move across the Bay of Fundy to establish Port Royal, "where the soil was ample to produce the necessities of life." But there was more to cultivation than the production of simple foodstuffs. For Lescarbot, at least, the powerful symbolism of planting a European garden in what had been a wilderness was manifest. He wrote on his departure from Port Royal to return to France in July, 1607:

> I have cause to rejoice that I was one of the party, and among the first tillers of this land. And herein I took the more pleasure in that I put before my eyes our ancient Father Noah, a great king, a great priest and a great prophet whose vocation was the plough and the vineyard; and the old Roman captain Serranus, who was found sowing his field when he was sent to lead the Roman army, and Quintus Cinncinnatus, who, all crowned with dust, bareheaded and ungirt, was ploughing four acres of land when the herald of the Senate brought him the letters of dictatorship.... Inasmuch as I took pleasure in this work, God blessed my poor labour, and I had in my garden as good wheat as could be grown in France.

While Lescarbot might be dismissed as suffering from an overdose of renaissance humanism, it seems more sensible to take him seriously. His florid rhetoric should be seen for what it really was: the ideology of what Alfred J. Crosby has called "ecological imperialism"— the biological expansion of Europe. What Lescarbot, and less literary Europeans, brought to bear on the Acadian landscape was the heavy freight of the European agricultural tradition with its long-established distinction between garden and wilderness. In that tradition God's "garden of delight" contrasted with the "desolate wilderness" of Satan. Though the concept of "garden" varies widely, as Hugh Johnson notes in his *Principles of Gardening,* "control of nature by man" is the single common denominator.[21]

The transformation of the wilderness into a garden is a constant theme in the early writings about Acadia. Father Biard had brought European seeds with him when he arrived in 1611 and at St. Saveur "in the middle of June, we planted some grains [wheat and barley], fruit, seeds, peas, beans and all kinds of garden plants." On Miscou Island (Shippegan Island) Denys discovered that although the soil was sandy, herbs of all sorts as well as "Peaches, Nectarines, Clingstones" and what the French always called "the Vine"—grapes—could be grown. But, as so often is the case, Lescarbot provides the most striking account of what gardening meant. At Port Royal, he "took pleasure in laying out and cultivating my gardens, in enclosing them to keep out the pigs, in making flower beds, staking out alleys, building summer houses, sowing wheat, rye, barley, oats, beans, peas and garden plants, and in watering them." European seeds, domestic animals—chickens and pigeons, too—fences—mine and thine.[22]

Of course, before a garden could be planted, the land had to be cleared. Denys described the work—and its by-product: squared oak timber that could fill the holds of vessels that would otherwise have returned empty to France. If clearing the land did not produce enough space for the garden, then the sea could be tamed, too. In the Minas Basin, where the settlers apparently found cultivating the land too difficult, Dièreville recounted the construction of a remarkable piece of European technology:

> Five or six rows of large logs are driven whole into the ground at the points where the Tide enters the Marsh, & between each row, other logs are laid, one on top of the other, & all the spaces between them are so carefully filled with well pounded clay, that the water can no longer get through. In the centre of this construction a Sluice is contrived in such a manner that the water on the Marshes flows out of its own accord, while that of the Sea is prevented from coming in.

Thus the tidal marshes were dyked for cultivation.[23]

Pushing back the forest, holding back the water, fencing a garden in the wilderness. The rewards would be great—"better worth than the treasures of Atahulpa [*sic*]," Lescarbot claimed. Was the symbolism intentional? Atahualpa, the defeated ruler of Peru, offered his Spanish captors led by Francisco Pizarro a room full of gold and silver in return for his freedom. The Spaniards accepted a ransom and then garrotted the Inca. Hardly a scene from a garden of delights.[24]

The French in Acadia were certainly not the Spanish in Peru. Still, the garden they planned was intended to produce a greater harvest than just sustenance for anticipated settlers. It was to be a garden for the civilization of the indigenous peoples. "In the course of time," Champlain observed on his initial meeting with the people he called Etechemins (Maliseet), "we hope to pacify them, and put an end to the wars which they wage against each other, in order that in the future we might derive service from them, and convert them to the Christian faith." The words were almost exactly those attributed to Columbus at his first sighting of the people of the "Indies": "they would be good servants... [and] would easily be made Christians." Even the most sympathetic observers of the Native peoples of Acadia were appalled by their apparent failure to make for themselves a better life, a failing that was often attributed to their unwillingness to plan for the future. For Father Biard, Christianity and husbandry obviously went hand in hand. Living the nomadic life of hunters, fishers, and gatherers resulted in permanent material and spiritual backwardness. "For in truth, this people," he claimed, "who, through the progress and experience of centuries, ought to have come to some perfections in the arts, sciences and philosophy, is like a great field of stunted and ill-begotten wild plants...[they] ought to be already prepared for the completeness of the Holy Gospel...Yet beholden [them] wretched and dispersed, given up to ravens, owls and infernal cuckoos, and to be the cursed prey of spiritual foxes, bears, boars and dragons." In Father Le Clercq's view the "wandering and vagabond life" had to be ended and a place "suitable for the cultivation of the soil" found so that he could "render the savages sedentary, settle them down, and civilize them among us." Though Lescarbot's outlook was more secular, he shared these sentiments completely and expressed them in verse:

This people are neither brutal, barbarous
    nor savage,
If you do not describe men of old that way,
His is subtle, capable, and full of good sense,
And not known to lack judgement,
All he asks is a father to teach him
To cultivate the earth, to work the grape vines,
And to live by laws, to be thrifty,
And under the sturdy roofs hereafter to shelter.

The leitmotif of the rhetoric is obvious: the images of the Christian garden and the satanic wilderness, summed up in the verse from the Book of Joel, quoted by Father Biard: "The Land is a Garden of Eden before them, and behind them a desolate wilderness."[25]

Yet it would be quite wrong to assume that these seventeenth-century French visitors to the New World were blind to the potential costs of gardening in the Acadian wilderness. Indeed, there is considerable evidence of nagging suspicions that the very abundance of nature provoked reckless exploitation. Denys witnessed an assault on a bird colony that is reminiscent of the profligacy of Cartier's crew among the birds at Funk Island in 1534. Denys's men "clubbed so great a number, as well of young as of their fathers and mothers...that we were unable to carry them all away." And Dièreville captured all too accurately the spirit of the uncontrolled hunt when he wrote that:

..., Wild Geese
And Cormorants, aroused in me
The wish to war on them....

He used the same militant language in his admiring account of the "Bloody Deeds" of the seal hunt, and also provided a sketch of another common pursuit: the theft of massive quantities of birds' eggs. "They collect all they can find," he remarked, "fill their canoes & take them away." Scenes like these presaged the fate of the Great Auk, the passenger pigeon, and many other species.[26]

These were the actions of men whose attitude toward the bounty of nature contrasted markedly with that of the indigenous inhabitants of North America. In Europe the slaughter of birds and animals was commonplace, indeed it was often encouraged by law. As Keith Thomas remarks in his study of *Man in the Natural World*—which is largely restricted to Great Britain—"It is easy to forget just how much human effort went into warring against species which competed with man for the earth's resources." Without succumbing to the temptation to romanticize the attitude of North American Native people toward their environment—they hunted, they fished, some practised slash and burn agriculture—there is no doubt that their sense of the natural world was based on a distinctive set of beliefs, a cosmology that placed them in nature rather than dominant over it. Animistic religion—"everything is animated," Father Le Clercq discovered—a simple technology, a relatively small population, and what Marshall Sahlins has termed "stone age economics" made "war" on nature unnecessary, even unacceptable. "They did not lack animals," Nicolas Denys noted, "which they killed only in proportion as they had need of them." By contrast, the Europeans who arrived in Acadia at the beginning of the seventeenth century belonged to a culture where, in Clarence Glacken's words, "roughly from the end of the fifteenth to the end of the seventeenth century one sees ideas of men as controllers of nature beginning to crystalize." Or, as Marc Lescarbot put it, articulating as he so often did the unstated assumptions of his fellow Frenchmen, "Man was placed in this world to command all that's here below."[27]

The distinction between the "wilderness" and the "garden," between "savagery" and "civilization," between "wandering about" and commanding "all that is here below," is more than a philosophical one, important as that is. It is also, both implicitly and explicitly, a question of ownership and possession. In what has been called "enlightenment anthropology"—though I think that places the development too late—the function of the term "savage" was to assert the existence of a state of nature where neither "heavy-plough agriculture nor monetarized exchange" was practised and from which, therefore, civil government was absent. Moreover, civil government, agriculture, and commerce

were assumed to exist only where land had been appropriated, where "possessive individualism" had taken root. Thus the wilderness was inhabited by nomadic savages, without agriculture or laws, where the land had never been appropriated. Consequently, when Europeans set about transforming the wilderness into a garden, they were engaged in taking possession of the land. "The ideology of agriculture and savagery," in the words of J.G.A. Pocock, "was formed to justify this expropriation."[28]

As European gardeners began slowly to transform the wilderness of Acadia, so, too, as was their intent, they began the remaking of its indigenous inhabitants. And once again, though they rarely expressed doubts about the ultimate value of the enterprise, some Europeans did recognize that a price was being exacted. First there was the puzzling evidence of population decline. In a letter to his superior in Paris in 1611, Father Biard wrote that the Micmac leader Membertou (who himself claimed to be old enough to remember Cartier's 1534 visit) had informed him that in his youth people were "as thickly planted there as the hairs upon his head." The priest continued, making a remarkably revealing comparison:

> It is maintained that they have thus diminished since the French have begun to frequent their country; for, since they do nothing all summer but eat; and the result is that, adopting an entirely different custom and thus breeding new diseases, they pay for their indulgence during the autumn and winter by pleurisy, quinsy and dysentery which kills them off. During this year alone sixty have died at Cape de la Hève, which is the greater part of those who lived there; yet not one of all of M. de Poutrincourt's little colony has ever been sick, notwithstanding all the privations they have suffered; which has caused the Savages to apprehend that God protects and defends us as his favorite and well-beloved people.[29]

The reality, of course, was more complex than this assertion that God was on the side of the immunized. Though the French were unaware of it, Acadia, like the rest of the Americas, was a "virgin land" for European pathogens. Denys hinted at this when he wrote that "in old times...they [the Natives] were not subject to diseases, and knew nothing of fevers." Certainly they had not been exposed to the common European maladies—measles, chickenpox, influenza, tuberculosis, and, worst of all, smallpox. (The "pox"—syphilis—Lescarbot believed was God's punishment of European men for their promiscuous sexual behaviour in the Indies.) The immune systems of the indigenous peoples of Acadia were unprepared for the introduction of these new diseases, which were consequently lethal in their impact. Father Le Clercq, at the end of the century, reported that "the gaspesian nation...has been wholly destroyed...in three or four visitations" of unidentified "Maladies." Marc Lescarbot probably identified one important carrier of European infections when he stated that "the savages had no knowledge of [rats] before our coming; but in our time they have been beset by them, since from our fort they went over to their lodges."[30]

Disease, radical alternations in diet—the substitution of dried peas and beans and hardtack for moosemeat and other country foods—and perhaps even the replacement of polygamy by monogamy with a consequent reduction in the birth rate all contributed to population decline. Then there was the debilitating scourge of alcohol, another European import for which Native people had little, if any, tolerance. Just as they sometimes gorged themselves during "eat all" feasts, so they seemed to drink like undergraduates with the simple goal of getting drunk. Even discounting Father Le Clercq's pious outlook, his description of the impact of brandy on the Gaspesians was probably not exaggerated. The fur traders, he charged, "make them drunk quite on purpose, in order to deprive these poor barbarians of the use of reason." That meant quick profits for the merchants, debauchery, destruction, murder, and, eventually, addiction for the Amerindians. Though less censorious, or less concerned, than the priest, Dièreville remarked that the Micmacs "drank Brandy with relish & less moderation than we do; they have a craving for it."[31]

Estimating population declines among Native peoples is at best controversial, at worst impossible. Nevertheless, there seems no reason to doubt that Acadia, like the rest of the Americas, underwent substantial reduction in numbers of inhabitants as a result of European contact. Jacques Cartier and his successors, who fished and traded along the coasts of Acadia, likely introduced many of the influences that undermined the health of the local people. Therefore Pierre Biard's 1616 estimate of a population of about 3,500 Micmacs is doubtless well below pre-contact numbers, as Membertou claimed. Since it has been estimated that neighbouring Maliseet, Pasamaquoddy, and Abenaki communities experienced reductions ranging from 67 to 98 per cent during the epidemics of 1616 and 1633 alone, Virginia Miller's calculation that the pre-contact Micmac population stood somewhere between 26,000 and 35,000 seems reasonable.[32] That was one of the costs of transforming the wilderness into a garden.

If the effects of disease and alcohol were apparent, though misunderstood, then another aspect of the civilizing process was more subtle. That process combined Christian proselytizing, which eroded traditional beliefs, with the fur trade, which undermined many aspects of the Native peoples' way of life. There is among contemporary historians of European–Amerindian relations a tendency to view the trading relationship, which was so central to the early years of contact, as almost benign, a relation between equals. Missionaries, politicians, and land-hungry settlers are credited with upsetting the balance that once existed between "Natives and newcomers" in the fur trade. There can be no doubt that recent scholarship has demonstrated that the Natives were certainly not passive participants in the trade. Far from being naive innocents who gave up valuable furs for a few baubles, they traded shrewdly and demanded good measure.[33]

Nevertheless, it is impossible to read seventeenth-century accounts of the trade and still accept the whole of this revisionist account. These were eyewitness testimonies to the devastating impact of alcohol on the Native traders and their families: murder of fellow Natives, maiming of women and abuse of children, the destruction of canoes and household goods. Beyond this, brandy, often adulterated with water, was used by Europeans "in order to abuse the savage women, who yield themselves readily during drunkenness to all kinds of indecency, although at other times...they would be more like to give a box on the ears rather than a kiss to whomsoever wished to engage them in evil, if they were in their right minds." The words come from the priest, Father Le Clercq, but the merchant, Nicolas Denys, concurred. That, too, was part of the fur trade.[34]

Moreover, the trade cannot be separated from other aspects of contact that contributed to the weakening of Micmac culture. Fur traders carrying disease and trade goods unintentionally contributed to the decline of both traditional skills and indigenous religious belief. Nicolas Denys's discussion of Micmac burial customs illustrates this point neatly. Like other Native people, the Micmacs buried many personal articles in graves so that the deceased would have use of them when they disembarked in the Land of the Dead. The French judged this practice both superstitious and wasteful—especially when the burial goods included thousands of pounds of valuable furs. They attempted to disabuse the Native of the efficacy of this practice by demonstrating that the goods did not leave the grave but rather remained in the ground, rotting. To this the Natives replied that it was the "souls" of these goods that accompanied the "souls" of the dead,

not the material goods themselves. Despite this failure Denys was able to report that the practice was in decline. The reason is significant and it was only marginally the result of conversion to Christianity. As trade between the French and the Micmacs developed, European goods—metal pots, knives, axes, firearms—gradually replaced traditional utensils and weapons that had once been included in burial pits. The use of European commodities as burial goods proved prohibitively expensive. Denys wrote that "since they cannot obtain from us with such ease as they had in retaining robes of Marten, of Otter, of Beaver, [or] bows and arrows, and since they have realized that guns and other things were not found in their woods or their rivers, *they have become less devout.*" Technological change brought religious change. It also led to dependence.[35]

No doubt the exchange of light, transportable copper pots for awkward, stationary wooden pots was a convenient, even revolutionary change in the lives of Micmacs. But convenience was purchased at a price, and the Native people knew it. Father Le Clercq was vastly amused when an old man told him that "the Beaver does everything to perfection. He makes us kettles, axes, swords, knives and gives us drink and food without the trouble of cultivating the ground." It was no laughing matter. If, at the outset of European contact, the Native people of Acadia had adapted to the trade with Europeans rather successfully, they gradually lost ground, their role of middlemen undermined by overseas traders who came to stay. While Nicolas Denys deplored the destructive impact of itinerant traders and fishermen on the Native people, his only solution was to advocate European settlement and the enforcement of French authority. "Above all," he concluded his assessment of the changes that had taken place in Native society during his time, "I hope that God may inspire in those who have part in the government of the State, all the discretion which can lead them to the consummation of an enterprise as glorious for the King as it can be useful and advantageous to those who will take interest therein." In that scheme, when it eventually came to pass, the Micmacs and their neighbours found themselves on the margin.[36]

To these signs that the work of cultivation produced ugly, unanticipated side effects must be added the evidence of near crop failure in the spiritual garden of Acadia. In 1613 a disgusted Father Biard reported meeting a St. John River sagamore (Cacagous) who, despite being "baptized in Bayonne," France, remained a "shrewd and cunning" polygamist. "There is scarcely any change in them after baptism," he admitted. Their traditional "vices" had not been replaced by Christian "virtues." Even Membertou, often held up as the exemplary convert, had difficulty grasping the subtleties of the new religion. He surely revealed something more than a quick wit in an exchange that amused the Jesuit. Attempting to teach him the Pater Noster, Biard asked Membertou to repeat in his own language, "Give us this day our daily bread." The old sagamore replied: "If I did not ask him for anything but bread, I would be without moose-meat or fish." Near the end of the century, Father Le Clercq's reflections on the results of his Gaspé mission were no more optimistic. Only a small number of the people lived like Christians; most "fell back into the irregularities of a brutal and wild life." Such, the somewhat depressed Recollet missionary concluded, was the meagre harvest among "the most docile of all the Savages of New France...the most susceptible to the instruction of Christianity."[37]

It was not just these weeds—disease, alcohol, dependence, and spiritual backsliding—in the European garden in Acadia that occasionally led the gardeners to pause and reflect. Possibly there was a more basic question: was the wilderness truly the Devil's domain? The Northeastern Algonquian people were admittedly "superstitious," even "barbarian," but certainly not the "wild men" of medieval imaginings, indistinguishable from the

beasts. If they enjoyed "neither faith, nor king, nor laws," living out "their unhappy Destiny," there was something distinctly noble about them, too. Despite the steady, evangelical light that burned in Biard's soul, he could not help wondering if the Micmac resistance to the proffered European garden of delights was not without foundation. "If we come to sum up the whole and compare their good and ill with ours," he mused briefly in the middle of his *Relation* of 1616, "I do not know but that they, in truth, have some reason to prefer (as they do) their own kind of happiness to ours, at least if we speak of the temporal happiness, which the rich and worldly seek in this life." Of course, these doubts quickly passed as he turned to consider "the means available to aid these nations to their eternal salvation."

Marc Lescarbot, for whom classicism and Christianity seemed to have reached their apogee in the France of his day, and whose fervour for cultivating the wilderness was unlimited, found much to admire in the peoples of Acadia. They lived "after the ancient fashion, without display": uncompetitive, unimpressed by material goods, temperate, free of corruption and of lawyers! "They have not that ambition, which in these parts gnaws men's minds, and fills them with cares, bringing blinded men to the grave in the very flower of their age and sometimes to the shameful spectacle of a public death." Here surely was "the noble savage," a Frenchman without warts—"a European dream," as J.H. Elliott remarks of the humanists' image of the New World, "which had little to do with American reality."[38]

There was yet another reason for self-doubts about the superiority of European ways over Amerindian ways; the Native people struggled to preserve their wilderness, refusing the supposed superiority of the garden. Even those who had become "philosophers and pretty good theologians," one missionary concluded, preferred "on the basis of foolish reasoning, the savage to the French life." And Father Le Clercq found that some of the people of Gaspesia stubbornly preferred their movable wigwams to stationary European houses. And that was not all. "Thou reproachest us, very inappropriately," their leader told a group of visiting Frenchmen, "that our country is a very little hell in contrast with France, which thou comparest to a terrestrial paradise, inasmuch as it yields thee, so thou sayest, every provision in abundance...I beg thee to believe, all miserable as we may seem in thine eyes, we consider ourselves nevertheless much happier than thou in this, that we are contented with the little that we have." Thus having demonstrated, 300 years before its discovery by modern anthropology, that having only a few possessions is not the same as being poor, the Algonquian leader then posed a devastating question: "If France, as thou sayest, is a little terrestrial paradise, are thou sensible to leave it?" No reply is recorded.[39]

It is simple enough to imagine one. Even those who could describe as "truly noble" the Aboriginal people of Acadia remained convinced that civilization meant cultivation. "In New France," Lescarbot proclaimed, "the golden age must be brought in again, the ancient crowns of ears of corn must be renewed, and the highest glory made that which the ancient Romans called *gloria adorea,* a glory of wheat, in order to invite everyone to till well his field, seeing that the land presents itself liberally to them that have none." The state of nature, a Hobbesian state of nature without laws or kings or religion, would be tamed, "civilized," when men "formed commonwealths to live under certain laws, rule, and police." Here, in Braudel's phrase, Europe's "own nature" was revealed.[40]

Perhaps such thoughts as these filled the heads of the Frenchmen who, according to Micmac tradition, gathered to enjoy one of the "curious adventures" of Silmoodawa, an Aboriginal hunter carried off to France "as a curiosity" by Champlain or some other "discoverer." On this occasion the Micmac was to give a command performance of hunting and curing techniques. The "savage" was placed in a ring with "a fat ox or deer...brought in from a beautiful park." (One definition of "paradise," the *OED* reports, is "an Oriental park or pleasure ground, especially one enclosing wild beasts for the chase.") The story, collected in 1870 by the Reverend Silas Tertius Rand, a Baptist missionary and amateur ethnologist, continues: "He shot the animal with a bow, bled him, skinned and dressed him, sliced up the meat and spread it out on flakes to dry; he then cooked a portion and ate it, and in order to exhibit the whole process, and to take a mischievous revenge upon them for making an exhibition of him, he went into a corner of the yard and eased himself before them all."[41]

If, as Lescarbot's contemporaries believed, the wilderness could be made into a garden, then the unscripted denouncement of Silmoodawa's performance revealed that a garden could also become a wilderness. Or was he acting out the Micmac version of Michel de Montaigne's often quoted remark about barbarians: we all call wilderness anything that is not *our* idea of a garden?

Notes

1 Fernand Braudel, *The Perspective of the World* (London, 1985), pp. 387, 388.

2 Cecil Jane, ed., *The Journal of Christopher Columbus* (New York, 1989), p. 191; Patricia Seed, "Taking Possession and Reading Texts: Establishing the Authority of Overseas Empires," *William and Mary Quarterly,* XLIX, 2 (April, 1992), p. 199.

3 Marc Lescarbot, *History of New France* (Toronto, 1914), III, p. 246. The theme of my lecture might have benefited had I been able to substantiate the claim, sometimes made, that "Acadie" is a corruption of "Arcadie"—an ideal, rural paradise. Unfortunately

the claim, sometimes made on the basis of Verrazzano's 1524 voyage when he described the coast of present-day Virginia as "Arcadie," is unfounded. "Acadie" likely is derived from the Micmac word "Quoddy" or "Cadie," meaning a piece of land. The French version became "la Cadie" or "l'Acadie," even though the French sometimes thought of the area as a potential "Arcadie." See Andrew Hill Clark, *Acadia: The Geography of Early Nova Scotia* (Madison, Wisconsin, 1968), p. 71.

4 J.G.A. Pocock, "Deconstructing Europe," *London Review of Books*, 19 December 1991, pp. 6–10.

5 J.H. Elliott, *The Old World and the New, 1492–1650* (Cambridge, 1989), p. 10.

6 Leslie Upton, *Micmacs and Colonists: Indian-White Relations in the Maritimes, 1713–1867* (Vancouver, 1979), p. 25.

7 Peter Mason, *Deconstructing America: Representations of the Other* (London, 1990); Antonello Gerbi, *Nature in the New World* (Pittsburgh, 1985).

8 *The Works of Samuel D. Champlain* (Toronto, 1922), I, p. 243 (hereafter Champlain).

9 Lescarbot, III, pp. 484–85; Nicolas Denys, *Description and Natural History of the Coasts of North America (Acadia)* (Toronto, 1908), pp. 393, 390; Hugh Honour, *The New Golden Land: European Images of America from the Discovery to the Present Time* (New York, 1975), pp. 36–37.

10 Denys, pp. 362–69; Le Clercq, *New Relations of Gaspesia* (Toronto, 1910), p. 279.

11 Le Clercq, p. 275; Denys, pp. 257–340; Champlain, pp. 368, 247; Denys, p. 199.

12 Champlain, p. 327. For a discussion of the distribution of Native peoples, see Bruce J. Bourque, "Ethnicity in the Maritime Peninsula, 1600–1759," *Ethnohistory*, 36 (1989), pp. 257–84.

13 Sieur de Dièreville, *Relation of the Voyage to Port Royal in Acadia* (Toronto, 1933), pp. 130–41; Lescarbot, III, pp. 54, 205, 164; Karen Anderson, *Chain Her by One Foot* (London, 1990).

14 Lescarbot, III, pp. 200–02; Le Clercq, p. 243.

15 Le Clercq, pp. 135–39; Denys, p. 420; Marc Lescarbot, *The Conversion of the Savages*, in Reuben Gold Thwaites, ed., *The Jesuit Relations and Allied Documents* (New York, 1959), I, p. 101; *Jesuit Relations*, III, p. 83; Le Clercq, pp. 265, 273.

16 Le Clercq, p. 243; Lescarbot, III, p. 333.

17 Lescarbot, III, pp. 365, 27, 113; *Jesuit Relations*, III, p. 21; Todorov, *Conquest*, pp. 27–33; Marshall Sahlins, *Islands of History* (Chicago, 1985), p. 10.

18 *Jesuit Relations*, III, pp. 33–35.

19 *Ibid.*, p. 33.

20 Champlain, p. 295.

21 Clarence J. Glacken, "Changing Ideas of the Habitable World," in William L. Thomas, ed., *Man's Role in Changing the Face of the Earth* (Chicago, 1956), pp. 70–92; Lescarbot, III, pp. 241, 351, 363–64; Alfred W. Crosby, Jr., *Ecological Imperialism: The Biological Expansion of Europe, 900–1900* (Cambridge, 1986); A. Barlett Giamatti, *The Early Paradise of the Renaissance Epic* (Princeton, N.J., 1969); Hugh Johnson, *The Principles of Gardening* (London, 1979), p. 8.

22 *Jesuit Relations*, III, p. 63; Denys, p. 303; Lescarbot, I, p. xii.

23 Denys, pp. 149–50; Dièreville, pp. 94–95. See Clark, *Acadia*, pp. 24–31.

24 Lescarbot, II, p. 317; John Hemming, *The Conquest of the Incas* (London, 1983), pp. 77–88.

25 Champlain, p. 272; Jane, ed., *Columbus*, p. 24; Le Clercq, p. 115; *Jesuit Relations*, III, p. III; Le Clercq, p. 205; Lescarbot, III, p. 487.

26 Denys, p. 156; Dièreville, pp. 75–77, 102, 122–23.

27 William M. Denevan, "The Pristine Myth: the Landscape of the Americas in 1492," *Annals of the Association of American Geographers*, 82, 3 (1992), pp. 369–85; Keith Thomas, *Man and the Natural World* (New York, 1983), p. 274; Le Clercq, p. 331; Marshall Sahlins, *Stone Age Economics* (Chicago, 1972); Denys, p. 403; Clarence J. Glacken, *Traces on the Rhodian Shore: Nature and Culture in Western Thought from Ancient Times until the End of the Eighteenth Century* (Berkeley, 1967), p. 494; Lescarbot, III, p. 137. See also Richard White, "Native Americans and the Environment," in W.E. Swagerty, ed., *Scholars and the Indian Experience* (Bloomington, Indiana, 1984), pp. 179–204; Lescarbot, III, p. 137.

28 Lescarbot, III, pp. 94, 127; J.G.A. Pocock, "Tangata Whenua and Enlightenment Anthropology," *New Zealand Journal of History*, 26, I (April, 1992), pp. 35, 36, 41. Pocock bases much of his intricate argument on late seventeenth-century and eighteenth-century sources, yet Marc Lescarbot's *History of New France*, first published in 1609, already articulates and assumes, though in a somewhat unsystematic way, a fairly full-blown version of the theory. See also John Locke's chapter "Of Property" in his *Essay*

Concerning the True Original Extent of Civil Government (1640).

29 Lescarbot, III, p. 254; *Jesuit Relations,* I, p. 177.

30 Denys, p. 415; Lescarbot, III, p. 163; Le Clercq, p. 151; Lescarbot, III, p. 227. Professor John Marshall has pointed to the importance of domestic animal imports as disease carriers by drawing my attention to Jared Diamond, "The Arrow of Disease," *Discover* (October, 1992), pp. 64–73.

31 Le Clercq, pp. 254–55; Dièreville, p. 77.

32 Dean R. Snow and Kim M. Lamphear, "European Contact and Indian Depopulation in the Northeast," *Ethnohistory,* 35 (1988), pp. 15–33; Virginia P. Miller, "Aboriginal Micmac Population: A Review of Evidence," *Ethnohistory,* 23 (1976), pp. 117–27, and "The Decline of Nova Scotia Micmac Population, A.D. 1600–1850," *Culture,* 3 (1982), pp. 107–20; John D. Daniels, "The Indian Population of North America in 1492," *William and Mary Quarterly,* XLIX, 2 (April, 1991), pp. 298–320.

33 Bruce G. Trigger, *Natives and Newcomers* (Montreal, 1985), pp. 183–94.

34 Le Clercq, p. 255; Denys, pp. 449–50.

35 Denys, p. 442.

36 Calvin Martin, "Four Lives of a Micmac Copper Pot," *Ethnohistory,* 22 (1975), pp. 111–33; Le Clercq, p. 277; Denys, p. 452. See also Wilson D. Wallis and Ruth S. Wallis, *The Micmac Indians of Eastern Canada* (Minneapolis, 1945); Bruce J. Bourque and Ruth Holmes Whitehead, "Tarrentines and the Introduction of European Trade Goods in the Gulf of Maine," *Ethnohistory,* 32 (1985), pp. 327–41.

37 *Jesuit Relations,* I, pp. 166–67; Le Clercq, pp. 193–94.

38 Denys, p. 437; *Jesuit Relations,* III, p. 135; Lescarbot, III, p. 189; Elliott, *The Old World,* p. 27.

39 Le Clercq, pp. 125, 104.

40 Lescarbot, III, pp. 256–57, 229.

41 Rev. Silas Tertius Rand, *Legends of the Micmacs* (London, 1894), 279.

Canadienne

Canadien

France in America, 1663–1763

In 1661 Louis XIV, king of France (1643–1715), decided to assert personal control over the affairs of state. One of his main goals was to establish a French overseas empire that would reflect positively on his wealth and power. As a result, New France became the focus of an intense, if brief, period of colony building. The French empire in North America at its height in the early eighteenth century included Newfoundland and Acadia, extended along the St. Lawrence and Great Lakes (the region called *Canada*), into the Prairies, and down the Mississippi. Though valued for the primary resources (mostly fish and fur), military potential, and prestige that they brought to the Crown, France's North American colonies attracted few permanent settlers and were ceded to Great Britain in the treaties ending the War of the Spanish Succession (1702–1713) and the Seven Years' War (1756–1763). Nevertheless, the legacy of French settlement in North America endures and prompts historians to continue to explore the characteristics of societies that proved so durable and adaptable.

The readings in this section reflect the rich historiography that has developed around questions relating to colonial societies in New France. For many historians, the French regime in North America offers clues to Quebec's distinctiveness as a province of Canada—though historians have rarely been in agreement about the nature of that distinctiveness. The jury is still out, for example, on whether the average Canadian peasant was liberated by the fur trade frontier and its Native inhabitants or increasingly shaped by institutions and values imposed by France. What is clear is that New France represented a way of life that has been greatly transformed since the eighteenth century by the institutions and values associated with the Industrial Revolution and the Information Age.

Scholars have focused on the autocratic state, Roman Catholic Church, military, fur trade, and seigneurial land holding system as the defining institutions of colonial society during the French regime. In recent years more attention has been paid to families, who, it can be argued, were essential to the very survival of the French colonies in North America.

Pre-industrial societies depended most fundamentally on the household economy for production and reproduction. Louis XIV and his ministers understood the importance of the family to colonial development and to that end shipped over 700 unmarried women to Canada between 1663 and 1673. Known as the *filles du roi* (daughters of the king), they were eagerly sought as marriage partners in a colony where bachelors outnumbered spinsters by a ratio of six to one. Yves Landry's article provides a detailed statistical profile of the *filles du roi* based primarily on evidence found in parish registers. This is an excellent example of the kind of information that demographers— social scientists who study population trends relating to births, marriage, literacy, death, and migrations— can tease out of seemingly "thin" documentary sources.

The Five Nations Iroquois Confederacy (Cayuga, Mohawk, Oneida, Onondaga, Seneca) proved to be a formidable foe to French imperial designs in the seventeenth century. As early as 1609 Samuel de Champlain joined the Algonquin in their ongoing war with the Confederacy. The French alliance with the Huron so provoked the Five Nation Confederacy that it destroyed the Huron villages in what is now southern Ontario in the late 1640s and paralyzed the fur trade. In the 1660s the Five Nations capped their military successes by establishing an alliance with the English, whose colonies along the Atlantic seaboard were rapidly increasing in numbers and economic strength. Wars between England and France inevitably engulfed their respective colonies and involved a growing number of Native nations caught up in a complicated skein of fur trade–military alliances.

After almost a century of intermittent warfare between and among Natives and newcomers, all sides were ready to compromise. In July 1701, 1300 Natives, representing nearly 40 nations from the Atlantic Ocean to the Mississippi Valley and beyond, assembled outside Montreal to make peace among themselves and to renew their alliances with the French. The Treaty of Montreal along with negotiations in Albany, New York, that took place at the same time between the English and the Iroquois, ushered in a new balance of power in northeastern North America. In his assessment of the diplomatic situation at the beginning of the eighteenth century, Gilles Havard questions assumptions of earlier historians with respect to the "Great Peace" of 1701 and concedes that it had major limitations—for the English, for the French and, above all for the Aboriginal nations—but that it was a powerful illustration of the success of the French in forging alliances that helped them extend their influence, at least for another half century, over a large part of the North American continent.

French power in North America was not only dependent upon good relations with Aboriginal peoples. It also often hinged on the tenuous nature of communications between France and its colonies. This was most obvious in wartime when the British navy could prevent French shipping from reaching New France with much-needed supplies and information, but peacetime communications were also often unreliable. Storms could delay travel by weeks and even months while shipwrecks took official despatches to a watery grave. As Kenneth J. Banks reveals in his careful mapping of the process by which news of the Treaty of Utrecht reached France's North American colonies, the complicated infrastructure and coordination required to send the king's word overseas was often the biggest obstacle to the timely arrival of imperial dispatches. Colonial administrators were thus left to their own devices in determining how to handle crises as they arose.

Within the colonies, the reach of imperial power also had its limits. In his article, William Wicken argues that the capture of Port Royal in 1710 initially had little impact on the Mi'kmaq, who continued to dominate the landscape of Mi'kma'ki. Even after the colony of Acadia was ceded to the British by the Treaty of Utrecht in 1713 and the French began building their fortified base at Louisbourg, the Mi'kmaq, Wicken suggests, "continued to live in their world outside of the sight of European officials and unrecorded by their

pens." It was not until the early 1720s that the Mi'kmaq and their allies in the Wabanaki Confederacy tried to halt the expansion of British influence in northeastern North America. Between 1722 and 1725, in response to the spread of New England settlement into what is now Maine and the arrival of New England fishermen in waters off Nova Scotia, the Confederacy waged war against the new claimants to their territories and resources. The treaties of 1725 and 1726 ending the war brought home to the Mi'kmaq the impact of the earlier conquest and ushered in a new era of conflict and accommodation.

The Treaty of Paris (1763) following the Seven Years' War marked the end of the French regime in northern North America. Although the British introduced political changes to their new colony of Quebec, continuity in social and institutional life was perhaps the most remarkable feature of the post-conquest period. The Acadians were less successful in their efforts to negotiate a satisfactory relationship with their conquerors. Unable to convince the British that they would remain neutral in the event of war with France, the Acadians faced the ultimate penalty—deportation. Despite being shipped from the British colony of Nova Scotia beginning in 1755, and later from Île Saint-Jean (Prince Edward Island) and Île Royale, they retained their attachment to a place called Acadia and nurtured a distinct sense of identity without the benefit of political autonomy. In her article, Naomi Griffiths tackles the difficult task of determining what happened to the Acadians after their initial deportation. From the fragments of information on the Acadian diaspora that she has been able to glean, Griffiths concludes that the strong ties of family and community developed in Acadie/Nova Scotia served the Acadians well during their difficult ordeal. The deportation, she argues, "destroyed Acadian power but not Acadian identity." That identity continues to thrive today in the Atlantic Provinces of Canada, Louisiana, and many other areas of the world where people can trace their genealogy back to "le grand dérangement."

Gender Imbalance, *les Filles du Roi*, and Choice of Spouse in New France

YVES LANDRY

The early European settlement of New France is an important period for family history. The vast majority of immigrants in the early years of settlement were men. The gender imbalance in the marriage market prior to 1680 created an unusual situation that led to variations in customary marriage practices.[1] These can be studied thanks to the historical and demographic data reconstructed from seventeenth- and eighteenth-century parish registers that are contained in the Population Register of Old Quebec.[2]

Over 700 women, known as the *filles du roi,* were sent to populate the St. Lawrence valley between 1663 and 1673. The mechanisms of Canadian family formation in the seventeenth century cannot be discussed without examining their role. In only eleven years, the number of *filles du roi* crossing the Atlantic represented almost half the total number of women immigrants arriving in the 150 years between the earliest settlement and the Conquest. Yet, because men dominated among immigrants, the *filles du roi* represented only 8 percent of all immigrants who settled in Canada under the French Regime. Their arrival got the young colony started demographically and socially. In less than ten years following their arrival, average annual population growth almost doubled, increasing from 5 to 9 percent, while the total

population almost tripled to approximately 8500 people in 1673. But most importantly, between 1660 and 1670, the natural growth rate rose sharply from less than one-third to more than three-quarters of the total growth rate. This dramatic demographic shift was entirely contingent on the rapid marriage rate of the *filles du roi*. Analysis of how these women chose their husbands helps to illustrate the atmosphere of urgency and haste that characterized marital matters in the colony at the time. It also shows how these women acted in a situation where the gender balance was decidedly in their favour. First, however, it is important to look at their background and the state of the marriage market prior to 1680.

The Background of the *Filles du Roi*

The life of most of the *filles du roi* had been marked by both economic and cultural poverty before leaving France. More than a third of them came from the Hôpital général de Paris, where the diet was meagre enough to cause stunted growth. Only 36 percent were able to sign their name on their marriage act, despite the fact that writing was

Yves Landry, "Gender Imbalance, *Les Filles du Roi*, and Choice of Spouse in New France," translated by Jane Parniak, in Bettina Bradbury, ed., *Canadian Family History: Selected Readings* (Irwin, 2000), 14–32. Reprinted with permission of the author.

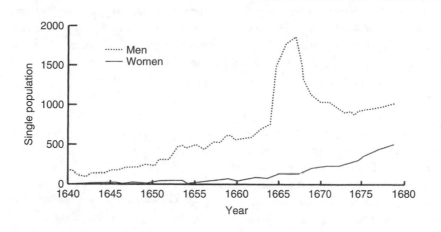

supposed to have been taught at the Hôpital général and that they came from Paris, a city that was intellectually far ahead of the rest of France, and where the literacy rate has been reported at 75 percent. Even among the *filles du roi* who came from noble or bourgeois background, only half could write their names, although historians suggest that the upper classes were 100 percent literate in France by the end of the seventeenth century.[3]

The lot of these women was undoubtedly tied to their tragic family lives. Declarations on their marriage certificates and contracts suggest that close to 65 percent of them had lost their fathers before they reached adulthood. This percentage indicates a paternal mortality rate almost 20 percent higher than the French averages during this period. Orphaned, usually illiterate, and often having spent years within the Hôpital général du Paris, the *filles du roi* clearly bore the scars of past misfortune when they left their native land.

The Marriage Market

A thorough reconstruction of the marriage market in New France prior to 1680 would require

knowing the exact annual numbers of men and women in the colony as well as their age and marital status. These conditions are satisfactorily fulfilled for the women, very few of whom escaped observation, but the situation is less clearcut for the men, many of whom were casual immigrants with demographically indeterminate profiles. However, current research, combined with some hypotheses allows for annual estimates of the numbers of marriageable men and women.[4] Comparison of the numbers in figure 1 with the historical censuses of 1666 and 1667, and with Marcel Trudel's reconstitution of the 1663, 1666, and 1667 censuses,[5] suggests that my estimates of the single male population are low, so that the discrepancy between marriageable men and women would in fact have been even greater than the figures suggest.

Despite the gaps in the data, figure 1 clearly depicts the predominance of male immigrants and, by implication, the tremendous value of women in the Canadian marriage market prior to 1680. There were always far more single men than women, particularly between 1665 and 1668, when the troops from the Carignan regiment were stationed in the colony. Until the beginning of the

1670s, there were between six and fourteen times more eligible men than women (figure 2). Analysis of the workings of the marriage market suggests that approximately nine out of ten of the marriageable men in New France during this period were immigrants. Many returned to France precisely because of the shortage of women. Women also entered the marriage market of New France by immigrating. In contrast to men, however, they left it by marrying.

As female immigration ceased at the beginning of the 1670s, this pattern changed radically. More and more young men and women who had been born in the colony began to enter the marriage market. The proportion entering through immigration fell proportionately. As more men were able to find spouses, the numbers returning to France fell off and some of the pressure on women to marry rapidly gradually eased. By 1680, the ratio of marriageable women to men had dropped to approximately two to one.

The *filles du roi* clearly played a fundamental role at a time when first-generation *Canadiennes* were still scarce and hundreds of men were obliged either to take work in the fur trade or to return to France. It would clearly have been in the interest of the authorities to continue the

immigration of the *filles du roi* for several more years to produce a more balanced number of men and women within the colony. This would have reduced the surplus of single males, of whom there were still at least five hundred in 1679. Furthermore, immigrant women would have provided spouses of a more appropriate age than the *Canadiennes,* many of whom were barely pubescent when they married.

Marriage Rates among the *Filles du Roi*

The *filles du roi* were sent to New France primarily to satisfy the colony's need for marriageable women. Did they fulfil these expectations? To answer this question we must look at how many married and how quickly they married as well as at the numbers who either died or returned to France without marrying.

Without thorough immigration records, a list of the *filles du roi* has to be culled from other references to women who arrived between 1663 and 1673. Single persons were less conspicuous than those who lived in families and appeared regularly in parish registers, so it is impossible to make a precise

---

FIGURE 2 | PERCENTAGE OF MEN IN THE MARRIAGE MARKET, NEW FRANCE, 1640-79

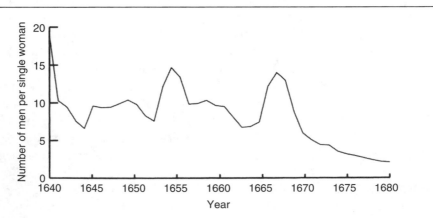

count of single women and widows who did not marry. However, genealogical research reveals that at least thirty-two *filles du roi* came to Canada but did not marry. Most of them are mentioned either as witnesses at the marriages of their fellow immigrants or as parties in marriage contracts that were subsequently annulled. There are no further references in the archives, so we assume that the vast majority returned to France, most of them during the first year of their arrival, some after three or even four years. Only one, Madeleine de Roybon d'Alonne, a lady of minor nobility and a famous adventurer, remained in Canada until she was elderly; she was still single when she died in Montreal in 1718 at the age of seventy-two.

The estimate that thirty-two *filles du roi,* or 4 percent of the total, did not marry in New France, is definitely conservative, since other immigrants could have lived for a short time in the colony without appearing in official documents. Nevertheless, this figure does signify that the marriage market exerted a strong pull on single women during this period of marked imbalance of the sexes. The full significance of the calculation becomes apparent if we consider only the *filles du roi* who settled in the colony. Only one out of 738, or 0.14 percent, died single at age fifty or over, compared to close to 10 percent of *Canadiennes* born at the end of the seventeenth and beginning of the eighteenth centuries or to approximately 7 percent of French women born between 1660 and 1664.[6] It is quite likely, moreover, that the pressures of the marriage market compelled the *filles du roi* not only to marry in great numbers, but also to marry soon after their arrival.

Marriage Schedule

Investigation of the schedule of first Canadian marriages of the *filles du roi* requires precise calculation of the interval between their arrival in the country and the celebration of their first marriage.

We first had to determine, for each year between 1663 and 1673, the exact arrival date of the first ships transporting these immigrants or, failing that, of the first ship that anchored outside of Quebec. This procedure is not ideal, as some women may have travelled on other ships that arrived later in the season. Comparison of the intervals calculated for each annual arrival with the observations of contemporaries does, however, substantiate our overall results. The *filles du roi* waited an average of five months to marry, and more than 80 percent of them married within the first six months. These figures may be surprising at first glance since the marriages of these women are notorious in historiography and folklore for being extremely hasty. The King's orders were in fact formal: courtships were to be kept to a strict minimum. A ruling handed down in 1670 and repeated the following year enjoined "all Voluntary Companions and other persons old enough to enter into marriage to marry within fifteen days of the arrival of the ships carrying the *filles* under Pain of being deprived of the rights to any kind of fishing, hunting, and trading with the natives."[7] Writing in 1703, the Baron de Lahontan is responsible for spreading the idea that all *filles du roi* married within fifteen days of their arrival.[8] Our analysis shows that this was not the case, even though they married much more quickly than the women who immigrated between 1632 and 1656, who waited roughly one year before marrying.[9]

The first official act publicizing a promise of marriage between a man and a woman was usually the betrothal, "carried out in the Church, in the presence of the Priest and Witnesses."[10] Before this custom was practically prohibited at the end of the seventeenth century,[11] most future spouses apparently used it to formalize their intentions for close to 60 percent of the marriage certificates registered in the parish of Notre-Dame-de-Québec from July 1659 until the end of 1662 mention the betrothal ceremony.[12] A random one-fifth sampling of all the 565 acts for first marriages of the *filles du roi* in the colony shows that the betrothal was mentioned in more than 65 percent of the cases, increasing to 92 percent in certificates of the Quebec register alone. Despite, or perhaps because of, the brevity of courtships, future spouses were anxious to formalize their relationship in an attempt to reinforce the tenuous bonds between them.

Alongside this ritual verbal promise, the couples could also make a written promise and stipulate the material terms of their union in a marriage contract. This procedure was not strictly necessary, since the *Coutume de Paris* made provisions for its absence, but most of the future spouses went to a notary in a gesture that betokened both social conformity and goodwill.[13] The data compiled by Marcel Trudel for the period from 1632 to 1662 suggest that marriage contracts were drawn up for more than 65 percent of marriages.[14] This percentage is consistent with Hubert Charbonneau's calculation for the seventeenth century as a whole.[15] In the following century, roughly 80 percent of couples signed a marriage contract, a rate comparable with those observed in France during the same era.[16] Among the *filles du roi,* 82 percent signed a contract for their first marriage, while 62 percent did so for subsequent marriages. The last figure may seem normal for the time, but the first is definitely high and, like the betrothal ceremony, could reflect a desire to create a bond between two people who hardly knew each other and to confirm a decision that the vagaries of time and chance might alter.

Almost all the marriage contracts were signed prior to the religious ceremony. Roughly half were concluded in the ten days preceding the wedding; in almost nine cases out of ten, the interval was one month or less. These results corroborate Charbonneau's results for the entire seventeenth century, but the average interval of nineteen days calculated for unions in which a contract preceded the marriage represents less than half of the forty-one-day interval calculated by Trudel for the period from 1632 to 1662.[17] The discrepancy could be explained in two ways. Firstly, Trudel looked at both rural and urban marriages, while 83 percent of the *filles du roi* had their first marriage entered in an urban register. Secondly, there was intense pressure on the *filles du roi* when they arrived in Canada, which reduced the interval between the marriage contract and the wedding to an average of seventeen days, or one week less than for subsequent marriages. Once the marriage agreements were signed, the *filles du roi* and their future husbands had literally promised to solemnize the eagerly awaited marriage before the Church "as soon as possible."

Before they could be blessed in marriage, the couple had to wait for the publication of the banns, to take place three times as stipulated by the Council of Trent. Table 1 shows that here again, the *filles du roi* clearly diverged, from common practice. Prior to 1663, only one out of four cases were granted a dispensation from publishing their banns, but the ratio rose to more than half for the wards of the King. This was most likely due to the relative isolation of the *filles du roi:* their lack of connections with other immigrants meant there were no potential objections regarding their liberty to marry, often making it futile to go through the long process of publishing the banns.

A quarter of the marriage certificates in our sampling specify the exact dates of publication of the banns. This information, coupled with the dates of marriage contracts, makes it possible to establish the typical chronology of the days preceding the wedding. In almost every case (26 of 27), the banns were published only after the marriage contract was signed. The publications then followed in quick succession (table 2), sometimes (in 8 out of 36 cases) even in violation of the rule "that there shall be at least two or three clear days between each, by three Sundays or Holidays."[18]

TABLE 1 | PUBLICATION OF BANNS FOR A SAMPLE OF FIRST MARRIAGES OF *FILLES DU ROI*, 1632–62

| | 1632–62 | | *Filles du roi* | |
	Number	Percentage	Number	Percentage
Publication of 3 banns	278	76	48	47
Publication of 2 banns	51	14	22	21
Publication of 1 bann	27	7	28	27
Dispensation from 3 banns	9	3	5	5
Total	365	100	103	100
Undetermined	41		10	
Combined	406		113	

Sources: 1632–62: Trudel, *Histoire de la Nouvelle-France*, 538. *Filles du roi:* random one-fifth sample.

TABLE 2 | INTERVAL BETWEEN MARRIAGE CONTRACT, BANNS, AND WEDDING FOR FIRST MARRIAGES OF *FILLES DU ROI*

| | Interval in days | | | |
Interval	Between contract and first bann	Between first and second bann	Between second and third bann	Between third bann and marriage
Average	16	5	5	5
Median	2	6	4	2
Modal	1	1	3	1
Number	26	20	16	28

Source: random one-fifth sample.

Given the hastiness with which they chose partners when they arrived in Canada, it is hardly surprising that many of the *filles du roi* regretted their decision before it had been made official by the priest. Figure 3 illustrates the complicated path followed by many immigrant women prior to their first marriage in the St. Lawrence valley. If all *filles du roi*, including those who returned to France or died without marrying, are considered, it can be seen that more than 15 percent of the women who concluded a first marriage contract (96 of 621) did not ultimately marry their fiancé. If only the immigrants who settled in the colony are considered, the rate of first marriages preceded by at least one cancellation of the marriage contract comes to 1.1 percent (79 of 737), which is double the rate for subsequent marriages (11 of 218, or 5 percent) and triple the rate calculated

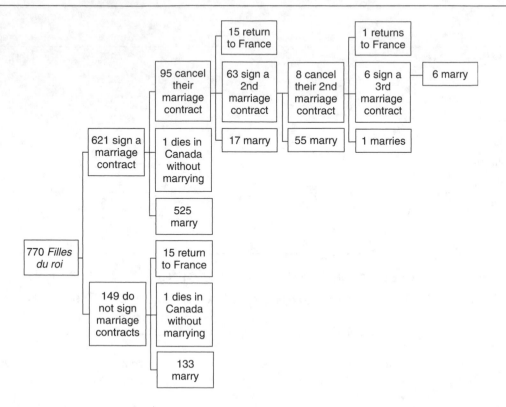

from Trudel's data for 1632 to 1662 (15 of 449, or 3.3 percent).[19] These results, which highlight the instability of the prenuptial relations of the *filles du roi,* are all the more striking in that, even after a first rupture, close to 13 percent of the women who concluded a second marriage contract (8 of 63) quickly cancelled it.[20] The time taken in choosing a candidate was a decisive factor in the outcome of the relationship. After a first marriage contract was cancelled, a second contract was concluded after an average interval of only twenty-two days (N = 7) if the second contract was also cancelled. By contrast, there was an average interval of more than 111 days (N = 62)[21] if the two parties ended up getting married.

Given the demand for women on the marriage market, it might be supposed that, if the first relationship failed, it would have been easier for the *filles du roi* than for the men to find a new partner. The results presented in table 3 substantiate this hypothesis. Once freed from an earlier promise, the women were back before the notary or priest seven times faster than were the men. From this it seems plausible that the women were primarily responsible for revoking marriage promises, since they had little to risk in looking for a better partner.[22] However, the archives have little to say on this point.

The Diocesan Tribunal had sole legal jurisdiction for dissolving marriage promises, whether it was a matter of amicable settlement or an actual trial in case of disagreement.[23] Since freedom of consent was required for the marriage to be valid, the official could not force

TABLE 3 | DISTRIBUTION OF CANCELLED MARRIAGE CONTRACTS ACCORDING TO FATE OF THE PARTIES

Fate	Women	Men
Signs a new marriage contract (or marries without a contract) after waiting:		
0–30 days	48	31
31–90 days	15	5
91–365 days	11	10
more than 365 days	4	29
Total	78	75
Average wait	108 days	741 days
Marries at an undetermined date	9	3
Dies in Canada (without marrying)	1	6
Returns to France	16	20
Combined	104	104

recalcitrant partners to make good their promises if there was disagreement between the parties.[24] However, the civil judge could order a man who backed out of his commitment to pay the woman a sum of money for damages and interest. The recalcitrant woman usually escaped this sanction but, in return, had to give back to the man the deposit he had made as security on his promise.[25] It's not surprising that nothing is found in the religious archives of New France about cancelled engagements and marriage contracts, since the Diocesan Tribunal was established around 1685 and the first preserved marriage files date back only to the nineteenth century. Yet even the legal archives yield practically no information about possible disagreements between the *filles du roi* and their rejected or fickle fiancés.[26] This suggests that the rejected partner usually agreed to the breakup, which would only be normal after such brief courtships that hardly gave two people a chance to become attached to each other.

The guilty party could not have made much restitution in any case; the man was often so poor that he would have been unable to pay any monetary compensation whatsoever, and a woman who had received no deposit had nothing to return. In forty-two out of 104 cancelled contracts, the notary added a footnote to the agreement, usually stating that the two partners "were voluntarily released from and acquitted of any claims they might have had with respect to each other," all without "any expenses for damages and interest."[27]

We know nothing about why these promises of marriage were broken. Jean-Louis Flandrin simply imputes it to lack of love.[28] This is a reasonable hypothesis, given the hastiness with which most relationships were formed and sometimes dissolved, but it would be risky to assume that every couple who ultimately sanctioned their promise by marrying did so out of love, especially in view of the cultural, social, and age differences between many spouses.

Cultural Differences

As they crossed the Atlantic, the *filles du roi* might have thought that, in adopting a new country, they would have to choose a husband from among the men born in the colony. In fact only 3 percent of the women married men born in New France; more than 95 percent married French immigrants like themselves. This situation apparently reflects the composition of the male marriage market, which largely consisted of single male immigrants.

The marriage of spouses who were both born in France is significant only in light of their regional and environmental background. Table 4 gives a breakdown of first marriages of French spouses according to their regions of origin. There is a relatively low rate of endogamy, which can be traced to differences in the areas of origin of male and female immigrants. Among individuals whose regional background is known, close to half of the women came from the Paris region and less than 15 percent came from the west of France, whereas almost 43 percent of the men were born in the west and only 8 percent came from the Paris region. The endogamy rate is only 18.7 percent compared to 33 percent for other pioneer couples who settled before 1680.[29] Marcel Trudel did a similar calculation for marriages that took place between 1632 and 1662; based on smaller geographical units: the provinces of France. He found that only 12.7 percent of marriages (52 of 408) brought together spouses who came from the same province or who were born in Canada.[30]

Shared regional background bore little weight when the *filles du roi* chose their marriage partners. If cases of indeterminate regional origins are excluded, the rate of homogamy, or marriage to those of similar origins, is low (0.116).[31] It is less than half that observed in the marriages of other pioneers who settled before 1680.[32] Heterogeneity of background does not seem to have been an obstacle in choosing a spouse. In this the marriages of these women do not seem very different from those observed by Jean Quéniart in the eighteenth and nineteenth centuries in coastal regions of Brittany, Normandy, Maine, and Anjou. He did not find that provincial boundaries in and of themselves defined limits when it came to choosing a spouse. Rather, he argued, they "played a role only insofar as provincial identity helped in constructing a network of relationships that went beyond the bonds of proximity."[33]

Nor did whether the partners came from a rural or an urban background make much difference. Given the predominantly urban background of the *filles du roi,* and the largely rural origins of the men, it is not surprising that in more than half of the marriages (348 of 626, or 55.6 percent) the spouses came from different backgrounds. After their marriage, nearly one in five couples would lead an essentially rural life, despite their lack of experience in such an environment.

Literacy was a slightly more important factor than region of origin or rural or urban background in determining who would marry whom. Still, the level of homogamy (0.258) was much lower among these couples than those found in seventeenth- and eighteenth-century European populations. Overall roughly one quarter of men and women were able to write their names on their marriage acts or contracts. While this figure seems low for the women given their largely urban backgrounds, it does seem to correspond with the data pertaining to the overall French male population during the same period.[34]

Social Differences

Chance, rather than shared literacy, illiteracy, or geographical origin, thus seems to have dictated these women's choice of husband. Or was a shared class background important? The

TABLE 4 | DISTRIBUTION OF MARRIAGES OF *FILLES DU ROI* BASED ON REGION OF ORIGIN OF SPOUSES

Man's region of origin	Women's region of origin										Undetermined	Combined	%
	Brittany	Normandy	Paris	Loire	North	East	West	Centre	South	Total			
Brittany	0	2	16	0	0	3	1	1	0	23	3	26	3.9
Normandy	3	32	46	11	5	9	12	1	0	119	7	126	19.0
Paris	0	15	28	1	2	3	5	0	0	54	0	54	8.2
Loire	2	4	35	4	2	5	4	0	1	57	2	59	8.9
North	0	5	12	2	1	1	4	0	0	25	1	26	3.9
East	0	5	5	1	1	0	3	2	0	17	0	17	2.6
West	6	44	123	14	5	22	54	1	3	272	11	283	42.8
Centre	1	3	9	2	0	1	2	0	0	18	0	18	2.7
South	1	9	23	3	0	8	6	1	0	51	2	53	8.0
Total	13	119	297	38	16	52	91	6	4	636	26	662	100.0
Undetermined	0	5	6	1	1	1	4	0	0	18	19	37	
Combined	13	124	303	39	17	53	95	6	4	654	45	699	
%	2.0	19.0	46.3	6.0	2.6	8.1	14.5	0.9	0.6	100.0			

TABLE 5 | DISTRIBUTION OF FIRST MARRIAGES OF *FILLES DU ROI* BASED ON RURAL OR URBAN BACKGROUND OF FRENCH SPOUSES

Man's background	Woman's background						Undeter-mined	Com-bined
	Urban		Rural		Total			
	N	%	N	%	N	%	N	N
Urban	140	22.4	57	9.1	197	31.5	9	206
Rural	291	46.5	138	22.0	429	68.5	11	440
Total	431	68.9	195	31.1	626	100.0	20	646
Undetermined	15		7		22		31	53
Combined	446		202		648		51	699

TABLE 6 | DISTRIBUTION OF FIRST MARRIAGES OF *FILLES DU ROI* BASED ON SPOUSE'S SIGNING ABILITY

Men	Women						Undeter-mined	Combined
	Able to sign		Unable to sign		Total			
	N	%	N	%	N	%	N	N
Able to sign	58	9.7	107	18.0	165	27.7	4	169
Unable to sign	67	11.3	363	61.0	430	72.3	13	443
Total	125	21.0	470	79.0	595	100.0	17	612
Undetermined	34		65		99		26	125
Combined	159		535		694		43	737

abundance of sources generated by these first Canadians (especially parish registers, censuses, and notarial acts) makes it possible to determine the social origins of 95 percent (700 of 737) of the first husbands of the *filles du roi*. In contrast, because so many of these women were orphans and far from their families of origin, it is only possible to identify the occupation of 23 percent of their fathers. As a result, the occupations of a woman's spouse and father are known for less than 22 percent of the marriages (164 of 737).

Despite these shortcomings in the data, the figures in table 7 do suggest several conclusions. Similarity of social background was not much more important than the other factors already considered. Only 25 percent of the *filles du roi* (42 of 164) married husbands of similar social background to their fathers. This compares with Marcel Trudel's finding that 60 percent of all marriages celebrated in the colony in the years before their arrival (between 1632 and 1662) were among couples of similar standing.[35] In France, historians have found 44 percent homogamy at Tourouvre-au-Perche between 1665 and 1770,[36] 57 percent at Vraiville, a small Normandy parish in the eighteenth century,[37] and 52 percent in the Basse-Meuse of Liège in the nineteenth century.[38] Clearly this high incidence of social intermingling was quite unusual during the Ancien Régime, a product of the arrival of the *filles du roi* into the particular frontier conditions and demographic imbalance of New France. Over a longer period, people were more likely to marry those of similar origins. A study of Quebec City in the period leading up to 1760, for instance, shows that occupational endogamy was a widespread practice, particularly among the children of military officers, civil officials, and merchants.[39]

Age Differences

Large age gaps between most *filles du roi* and their husbands added to the differences of social, economic, and geographical background that distinguished their marriages from those of other settlers or from their French compatriots. Six out of ten of the *filles du roi* were between the ages of fifteen and twenty-four when they married for the first time in Canada. A similar proportion of husbands was between twenty and twenty-nine years old. The average age at which women married was twenty-four, whereas for men it was twenty-eight, a difference of four and a half years. There was little difference in the age of men and women at the time of migration. This dif-

ference, then, is essentially a function of the time these men, who were mostly hired civilians or soldiers, had to wait before marrying, either because there were few available women or because they had not yet acquired the material basis necessary for marriage. Obtaining a land grant or buying a piece of land, clearing it, and constructing the necessary buildings all took time.

The resulting age gap between these women and their husbands is greater than that observed in seventeenth-century France, but is less than that estimated for all first marriages occuring in New France either between 1640 and 1679 or 1680 and 1699.[40]

Some of the age gaps between the *filles du roi* and their husbands were extremely large. In almost one-fifth of the unions more than ten years separated the spouses. In over half the cases the disparity was greater than five years. Some of the gaps were closer to what would have been expected among the first generation of native born *canadiennes* who married in a period of extreme imbalance between the sexes. One *fille du roi* for instance, married an immigrant thirty-two years her senior.[41] Marguerite Charpentier, in contrast, was nearly sixty when she married a man thirty-six years younger than herself.[42]

Conclusion

This study of the first marriages of the women known as the *filles du roi,* who arrived in the New World between 1663 and 1673, shows that their marriage practices diverged in a number of ways from nuptial behaviour observed throughout the seventeenth century, both in France and in New France. Cultural and social endogamy, whether measured by region of origin, rural or urban background, literacy, or socio-economic status was unusually low. The intense intermixing that characterized these

TABLE 7 | SOCIO-ECONOMIC CATEGORY OF HUSBAND

Socio-economic category of father	Socio-economic category of husband											Undetermined	Combined
	Aristocracy		Professionals		Farmers		Tradesmen		Total				
	N	%	N	%	N	%	N	%	N	%			
Aristocracy	26	15.9	17	10.4	42	25.6	3	1.8	88	53.7		5	93
Professionals	5	3.1	12	7.3	37	22.6	2	1.2	56	34.2		2	58
Farmers	1	0.6	2	1.2	4	2.4	1	0.6	8	4.8		0	8
Tradesmen	0	0.0	2	1.2	10	6.1	0	0.0	12	7.3		1	13
Total	32	19.6	33	20.1	93	56.7	6	3.6	164	100.0		8	172
Undetermined	21		94		398		23		536			29	565
Combined	53		127		491		29		700			37	737

TABLE 8 | DISTRIBUTION OF AGE DIFFERENCES BETWEEN PREVIOUSLY UNMARRIED SPOUSES FOR FIRST MARRIAGES OF *FILLES DU ROI*

Age difference in years*	Number	Percentage
⁻11 or less	8	1.6
⁻6–⁻10	27	5.4
⁻1–⁻5	86	17.1
0	26	5.2
1–5	131	26.1
6–10	140	27.9
11–15	52	10.3
16–20	22	4.4
21–25	6	1.2
26 or more	4	0.8
Combined	502	100.0
Average difference	4.5 years	
Median difference	4.2 years	

* Age of husband minus age of wife

marriages is inextricably tied to the sexual imbalance in the colony and the related atmosphere of urgency that accompanied the arrival of the women. The short interval between their arrival in Canada and the religious ceremony, and the frequency of dispensation from banns point to the precipitous nature of these marriages. The fact that spouses were chosen in haste highlights the state of expectancy of the male population—many of whom had long been deprived of women—and the women's apparent acceptance of their mission as future wives. On the other hand, lacking both kinship ties in the colony and experience in a frontier-type situation, it would have been difficult for most of these women to survive for long without a spouse. The large number of cancelled marriage contracts suggests that they could take some advantage from their situation and not necessarily accept just any partner. It would be interesting to know whether the haste of marriage meant that more ended up separating from their husbands than other immigrant or locally born women. Research currently underway using judicial archives and notarial minutes should soon provide us with answers to this question.[43]

The *filles du roi* were clearly instrumental in establishing a more equal balance of the sexes in the marriageable population of mid- to late seventeenth-century New France. Had they not been sent to the colony, the marriage rate could not have increased as it did during the early years of royal government.[44] The scarcity of wives, far more than the Iroquois threat, would have kept the population as low as it had been at the beginning of the century.

Notes

This work was produced within the Programme de recherche en démographie historique de l'Université Montréal which is subsidized by the Social Sciences and Humanities Research Council of Canada, the Fonds FCAR, and the Université de Montréal.

1 Hubert Charbonneau, Bertrand Desjardins, André Guillemette, Yves Landry, Jacques Légaré, and François Nault, *Birth of a Population: The French who Settled in the St. Lawrence Valley in the XVIIth Century* (Newark: University of Delaware Press, 1991) Raymond Roy and Hubert Charbonneau, "La nuptialité en situation de déséquilibre des sexes: le Canada du XVIIe siècle," *Annales de démographie historique* (1978): 285–94.

2 Jacques Légaré, "A Population Register for Canada Under the French Regime: Context, Scope, Content and Applications," *Canadian Studies in Population* 15, 1 (1988): 1–16. Yves Landry, "Le registre de population de la Nouvelle-France: un outil pratique au service de la démographie historique et de l'histoire sociale," *Revue d'histoire de l'Amérique française* (hereinafter *RHAF*) 38, 3 (Winter 1985), 423–26.

3 Alain Blum and Jacques Houdaille, "L'alphabétisation aux XVIIIe et XIXe siècles: l'illusion parisienne?" *Population,* 40th year, no. 6 (Nov.–Dec. 1985), 951.

4 For each year, boys and girls living in the country (born in Canada or not) who had reached the ages of 14 and 12, respectively, unmarried immigrants at least 14 and 12 years old when they arrived in Québec, and widowed persons enter the marriage market. Single persons who marry, enter a religious institution, die, or emigrate during that year withdraw from the market. For a discussion of methodological problems related to the statistical estimate of the number of single immigrants (unmentioned in the population register), see Landry, *Orphelines en France.*

5 Hubert Charbonneau and Jacques Légaré, "La population du Canada aux recensements de 1666 et 1667," *Population,* 22nd year, no. 6 (Nov.–Dec. 1967): 1047–54. Marcel Trudel, "Le recensement de 1666 et l'absence du quart de la population civile," *Mémoires de la Société généalogique canadienne-française* 40, 4 (Winter 1989): 258–69.

6 Hubert Charbonneau, *Vie et mort de nos ancêtres. Etude démographique* (Montreal: Les Presses de l'Université de Montréal, 1975) 154–58. Lorraine Gadoury, Yves Landry, and Hubert Charbonneau, "Démographie différentielle en Nouvelle-France: villes et campagnes," *RHAF* 38, 3 (Winter 1985), 366. Louis Henry and Jacques Houdaille, "Célibat et âge au mariage aux XVIIIe et XIXe siècles en France. I.—Célibat définitif," *Population,* 33rd year, no. 1 (Jan.–Feb. 1978), 50.

7 Ruling to force single men to marry the women who arrive from France..., Quebec, 20 Oct. 1671, in Pierre-Georges Roy, *Inventaire des ordonnances des intendants de la Nouvelle-France conservées aux Archives provinciales de Québec,* vol. III, (Beauceville: L'Eclaireur, 1919), 266. See also Mémoire de Talon sur le Canada au ministre Colbert, Quebec, 10 Nov. 1670, in *Rapport de l'Archiviste de la province du Québec pour 1930–1931* (Quebec: Paradis, 1931), 132, and lettre du ministre Colbert à Talon, 11 Feb. 1671, ibid., 145.

8 "There wasn't even one left after 15 days." *Nouveaux Voyages de M. le Baron de Lahontan, in l'Amérique Septentrionale,* vol. 1, La Haye, Frères l'Honoré, 1703, p. 11 (Lahontan, *Oeuvres complètes,* annotated ed. by Réal Ouellet and Alain Beaulieu [Montreal: Les Presses de l'Université de Montréal, 1990], 1: 266).

9 Marcel Trudel, *Histoire de la Nouvelle-France,* vol. 3; *La seigneurie des Cent-Associés (1627–1663),* tome 2; *La société* (Montreal, Fides, 1983), 78.

10 *Rituel du diocèse de Québec publié par l'ordre de Monseigneur l'evêque de Québec* (Paris: Simon Langlois, 1703), 339.

11 Following, it seems, infringements of the rule prohibiting "fiancés to live in the same house [and] to consort familiarly with each other." Ibid. Additions to the Synodal Statutes, settled in the third meeting of the synod held in Quebec on 27 Feb. 1698, in *Mandements, lettres pastorales et circulaires des evêques de Québec,* edited by H. Têtu and C.-O. Gagnon (Quebec: Coté, 1887), 376.

12 Trudel, *Histoire de la Nouvelle-France,* 537.

13 Louise Dechêne, *Habitants et marchands de Montréal au XVIIe siècle* (Paris: Plon, 1974), 418–19. Trudel, *Histoire de la Nouvelle-France,* 517–34.

14 Trudel, ibid., 518.

15 Charbonneau, *Vie et mort de nos ancêtres,* 151–52.

16 Louis Lavallée, "Les archives notariales et l'histoire sociale de la Nouvelle-France" *RHAF* 28, 3 (Dec. 1974), 388–89, Louis Lemoine, *Longueuil en Nouvelle-France* (Longueuil: Société d'histoire de Longueuil, 1975), 47. Yves Landry, *Quelques aspects du comportement démographique des troupes de terre envoyées au Canada pendant la guerre de Sept Ans* (M.A. thesis, Université de Montréal, 1977), 99.

17 Trudel, *Histoire de la Nouvelle-France,* 535.

18 *Rituel du diocese de Quebec,* 340.

19 Trudel, *Histoire de la Nouvelle-France,* 518.

20 Take, for instance, the inordinate case of Marie Ducoudray, who on 25 Aug. 1670, concluded a marriage contract with Jean Jouanne (notary Romain Becquet); the fact that neither signature appears on the document would seem to indicate that the parties immediately revoked their decision. Three days later, before the same notary, Marie Ducoudray got engaged to Robert Galien, but once again the relationship was shortlived: before the end of the day, the notary added a footnote to the contract rendering it "null and void." The next day, Ducoudray came to an agreement with François Grenet and ended up marrying him 17 days later.

21 This result incorporates the period of almost six years that Marguerite Jasselin waited to marry after breaking off an earlier engagement with Robert Gaumond (notary Romain Becquet, 8 Nov. 1670). Before marrying Mathurin Lelièvre in Oct. 1674, she gave birth in March 1674 to an illegitimate child whose fate was not settled until January 1676 by the Sovereign Council. If this long interval had not been retained, the average waiting period would have been 78 days.

22 The converse was observed in trials for breach of contract in the Cambrai diocese in the seventeenth and eighteenth centuries: "Who initiates the suit in rupture petitions? We cannot proffer an exact percentage, but clearly the man takes the initiative in petitions for breakups," A. Lottin and K. Pasquier, "Les fiançailles rompues ou empêchées," in *La désunion du couple sous l'Ancien Régime: L'exemple du Nord,* ed. Alain Lottin (Villeneuve d'Ascq and Paris: Université de Lille III and Editions universitaires, 1975), 58.

23 Jean Gaudemet, *Le mariage en Occident: Les moeurs et le droit* (Paris: Cerf, 1987), 362.

24 Although in the fifteenth and sixteenth centuries judges ordered the fiancés to marry, they revised this procedure in the following century in compliance with the Tametsi decree of the Council of Trent except, in rare cases, to force a man to marry a woman if he had had sexual relations with her, Claude-Joseph de Ferrière, *Dictionnaire de droit et de practique, contenant l'explication des termes de croit, d'ordonnances, de coutumes & de practique. Avec les jurisdictions de France* (Paris: Barrois, 1771), tome 2, pp. 447–48. Jean-Louis Flandrin, *Le sexe et l'Occident: Evolution des attitudes et des comportements* (Paris: Seuil, 1981), 75–78. Gaudemet, *Le mariage en Occident,* 363.

25 Ferrière, *Dictionnaire de droit,* 447–48. F.B. de Visme, *La science parfaite des notaires, ou le parfait notaire, contenant les ordonnances, arrêts & Réglemens rendus touchant la Fonction des Notaires, tant Royaux qu'Apostoliques...*(Paris: Desaint, 1771), tome 1, pp. 316–17. Flandrin, *Le sexe et l'Occident,* 72–74.

26 The only case we came across was that of Madeleine Plouard and Jean Cosset, who cancelled their marriage contract subsequent to a trial before the Provostship of Québec. Silvio Dumas, *Les filles du roi en Nouvelle-France. Etude historique avec repertoire biographique* (Quebec: Société historique de Québec, 1972), 314.

27 Marriage contract between Adrien Lacroix and Marie Hué, 18 Oct. 1667, notary Romain Becquet.

28 "Whereas in the fifteenth and sixteenth centuries [promises of marriage] were usually not dissolved except for serious and canonical reasons, in this second half of the seventeenth century the causes of dissolution are far more numerous, sometimes futile, or even unexpressed.... Whereas in the fifteenth and sixteenth centuries fiancés who did not love each other were forced to marry, the judges in the seventeenth century recognize the impossibility of marrying without love." Flandrin, *Le sexe et l'Occident,* 75–78.

29 Charbonneau et al., *Birth of a Population.* Unions of single pioneers excluding single *filles du roi* are 118 of 353, or 33.4 percent.

30 Trudel, *Histoire de la Nouvelle-France,* 511.

31 The homogamy index is based on the general formula devised by Albert Jacquard and Martine Segalen. The method consists of comparing marriages in the target population to marriages that would have taken place in a completely intermixed population and to marriages that would have taken place in a completely homogeneous population. The index summarizes the comparison so that 1 equals total homogamy and 0 complete intermixing. Martine Segalen and Albert Jacquard, "Choix du conjoint et homogamie," *Population,* 26th year, no. 3

(May–June 1971): 487–98. For a critique of this index, see Mark Lathrop and Gilles Pison, "Méthode statistique d'étude de l'endogamie: Application a l'étude du choix du conjoint chez les Peul Bandé," *Population,* 37th year, no. 3 (May–June, 1982), 522.

32 For unions of single pioneers excluding the *filles du roi:* = 0.272.

33 Jean Quéniart, "Le choix du conjoint dans une région de frontiére provinciale," in *La France d'Ancien Régime. Etudes réunies en l'honneur de Pierre Goubert* (Paris: Société de démographie historique et Privat, 1984), tome 2, p. 613.

34 Jacques Houdaille, "Les signatures au mariage, 1670–1739," *Population,* 43rd year, no. 1 (Jan–Feb. 1988), 209.

35 Trudel, *Histoire de la Nouvelle-France,* 512–13.

36 Hubert Charbonneau, *Tourouvre-au-Perche aux XVIIe et XVIIIe siècles: Etude de démographie historique* (Paris: PUF, 1970), 283.

37 Martine Segalen, *Nuptialité et alliance: Le choix du conjoint dans une commune de l'Eure* (Paris: Maisonneuve et Larose, 1972), 133.

38 Leboutte and Hélin, "Le choix du conjoint," 449.

39 Danielle Gauvreau, "Nuptialité et catégories professionelles à Québec pendant La régime français," *Sociologie et sociétés* 19, 1 (April 1987), 33–34.

40 Age difference in the countryside of the Bassin parisien, according to Dupâquier's estimates: 2.1 years. In Canada, according to Charbonneau's estimates: generations 1640 to 1679, 7.9 years; generations 1680 to 1699, 5.3 years; generations 1700 to 1729, 3.8 years; together, 5.7 years. Jacques Dupâquier, ed., *Histoire de la population française,* vol. 2, *De la Renaissance* à *1789* (Paris: PUF, 1988), 305. Charbonneau, *Vie et mort de nos ancêtres,* 165.

41 Barbe Duchesne was 23 and André Badel (known as Lamarche) 55 years old. The advanced age of the husband, who apparently had not been married before, did not stop the couple from having eight children, and the husband even outlived his wife. The fact that the couple were both of Swiss background might explain this somewhat unusual match.

42 Marguerite Charpentier was 59 and Toussaint Lucas 23 years old. The marriage apparently produced no offspring and the woman outlived her husband.

43 Sylvie Savoie, *Les couples en difficulté aux XVIIe et XVIIIe siècles: les demandes de séparation en Nouvelle-France* (M.A. thesis, Sherbrooke University, 1986). Hélène Lafortune and Normand Robert: "Parchemin: une banque de données notariales du Québec ancien (1635–1885)," *Archives* 20, 4 (Spring 1989): 51–58. France Parent, *Entre le juridique et le social: Le pouvoir des femmes à Québec an XVIIe siècle* Cahier 42, Les cahiers de recherche multidisciplinaire feministe, Université Laval, 1991.

44 Hubert Charbonneau and R. Cole Harris, "Resettling the St. Lawrence Valley," in *Historical Atlas of Canada,* vol. 1, *From the Beginning to 1800,* ed R. Cole Harris (Toronto: University of Toronto Press, 1987), plate 46.

1701: A New Situation

GILLES HAVARD

The Treaty of Montreal of 1701 involved the French, their Amerindian allies, and the Five Nations directly, and the English in New York indirectly. The Montreal agreements, along with those negotiated in Albany at the same time among the members of the Covenant Chain (the English and the Iroquois), are sometimes referred to as "the Grand Settlement of 1701."[1] It is important to analyse the balance of power in the diplomatic arena of northeastern North America at this time, and to determine how the Treaty of Montreal and the Albany Agreements affected it. We need to assess the situation of the various actors, taking care to consider the limits of the peace, since the Montreal treaty, as important as it is, certainly did not end the Amerindian wars in New France.

The Albany Agreements of July 1701: A Controversial Deed

Thirty-three sachems from the Five Nations (nine Mohawks, five Oneidas, twelve Onondagas, four Cayugas, and three Senecas) went to Albany to meet with John Nanfan, the new governor of New York, from 12 to 21 July 1701. These were the pro-English leaders, but like those who went to Montreal, they were motivated by the neutralist principles of Teganissorens. Their goal was to clarify the terms of the Covenant Chain in light of the treaty being signed that same summer in

Montreal. The Iroquois thus had to strike a delicate balance, confirming the alliance with the English in spite of their peace treaty with the French. Nanfan, who was backed by Robert Livingston, the secretary for Indian affairs, intended to obtain an explanation concerning the French-Iroquois negotiations in June in Onondaga, to settle the missionary issue in his favour, and to counter French plans to establish a post at Detroit.[2]

When the English governor complained that the Iroquois were negotiating separately with the French and were about to sign a peace treaty in Montreal, as Teganissorens had stated in Onondaga the previous month, the Mohawk orator Onucheranorum replied in a manner that was both defiant and evasive: "We have made strict enquiry among all our people and can learn nothing but what the people you sent thither are privy to, and what the[y] entred down in writing, if you know of anything else then what they have given you an account of, pray tell us, wee shall be glad to be informed."[3] The Iroquois managed to preserve the principle of their neutrality while notifying the English repeatedly that they were counting on their protection in the event of war with the French: "if a warr should break out between us and the French, wee desire you to come and stay here in this place [Albany], that you may be ready to assist and defend us."[4] Similarly, the delegates from the League clearly intended to use the British to counter French activities in the west. They asked that Livingston be sent "to Corakhoo the great King

Gilles Havard, "1701: A New Situation," in Gilles Havard, *The Great Peace of Montreal of 1701: French-Native Diplomacy in the Seventeenth Century*, trans. Phyllis Aronoff and Howard Scott, pages, 160–78. Copyright © 2001 McGill-Queen's University Press. Reprinted with permission of the publisher.

of England to acquaint how that the French of Canada encroach upon our territories by building a Forte att Tjughsaghrondie [Detroit] and to pray that our great King will use all means to prevent itt."[5] Cadillac's post could represent a threat to the Iroquois, but even more so to the English. Onucheranorum is said to have then made the offer to Nanfan and Livingston to "give and render up all that land where the Beaver hunting is which wee won with the sword eighty years ago to Coraghkoo our great King and pray that he may be our protector and defender there." Thus, on 19 July 1701, the well-known "Deed from the Five Nations to the King of their Beaver Hunting Ground" was signed (by Nanfan and twenty Iroquois headmen). Through this deed, the Iroquois placed under the protection of the English a huge territory situated approximately, from east to west, from Lake Ontario to Lake Michigan and, from north to south, from Lake Erie to Lake Superior (Detroit and Michilimackinac, for example, were within this territory).[6]

The interpretation of this deed is controversial. According to many authors, it was a challenge issued by the Five Nations to their English allies, forcing them to respect the military dimension of the Covenant Chain and protect the Iroquois' activities in the Great Lakes region. Brandão and Starna, for example, write: "This was a bold move made to draw out and compel the English to protect them against the French and their Indian allies, thus guaranteeing the Iroquois continued and unimpeded access to their vital hunting territories." For D.K. Richter, similarly, the deed "seems to have been the Five Nations' idea."[7] F. Jennings, following A. Trelease, has particularly emphasized the symbolic and even fictitious nature of this agreement. The territory in question, far from being under Iroquois sovereignty, was in fact under the control of the Amerindians of the Great Lakes and their French allies. "This 'deed' was a worthless piece of paper," writes Jennings.

"It purported to set forth the rights of the Iroquois to vast hunting territories in the west by rights of conquest over the Hurons and other Indians during the beaver wars, and it conveyed those asserted rights to the English Crown. But the conveyance was made precisely because the Iroquois had been driven out of those supposedly conquered lands." For the English, Jennings explains further, this deed was a document for the future: "The Iroquois gave a 'deed'...absurd on its face but taken seriously because it was later to be advanced in diplomacy to justify England's claims against France."[8]

The Canadian historian W.J. Eccles goes further. He suspects the New York authorities of fabricating this deed behind the backs of the Iroquois chiefs: "The 'Deed' is a spurious document contrived by Lieutenant Governor Nanfan and his Albany Officials without the participation or sanction of the Five Nations." And he continues: "The totems marks of the Iroquois sachems...bear no resemblance to those of the sachems on the Montreal Treaty, which I incline to think are authentic. I suspect that the Iroquois totems on the 'deed,' like the burden of the text, were contrived by an Albany official." The document, according to Eccles, is so contaminated with English legal language (for example, "To all Christian and Indian People in this part of the World and in Europe..."; "wee...have freely and voluntary surrendered delivered up and for ever quit claim, and by these presents doe for us our heires and successors absolutely surrender, deliver up and for ever quit claime unto our great Lord and Master the King of England...") that it loses all credibility. He also points out several examples of geographical errors, observes that the Amerindians did not measure distances in miles but in time, and, like Jennings, mentions the fact that the Iroquois no longer had control over their so-called Beaver Hunting Ground.[9]

Whether or not this deed was understood by the Iroquois, it was deceptive in that it was based on an extremely distorted representation of the balance of power in the Great Lakes region. How could the English guarantee to the Iroquois the possession of territories that no longer belonged to them? However, the idea of the Five Nations placing themselves under the protective wing of the English is not entirely lacking in credibility,[10] since the League had been weakened and such an agreement was in keeping with the logic of European-Native relations in colonial North America. It is not impossible that the original document recording the Iroquois orations had been rewritten by the New York authorities in "British" language before being sent to London.[11] It could also be that the Iroquois had adopted into their own discourse the rules of colonial politics, in particular the European rhetoric on the right of conquest. They would then have used the English imperial desire for expansion to win back a little of what they had lost.

During the Albany conference, the Iroquois sachems also renewed the economic alliance and took a conciliatory stance on the missionaries. In fact, Onucheranorum stated that the Iroquois had decided not to allow any Jesuits among them.[12] He did not, however, make any commitment to accept Protestant ministers.[13]

A Diplomatic Failure for New York

"Only New York was a loser by the treaty [of Montreal]," states F. Jennings. Governor Bellomont and his successor, Nanfan, were not able to prevent the Iroquois from making peace under the aegis of the French and they were forced to accept the principle of Iroquois neutrality between the empires. On the eve of a new war with New France, the treaty of 1707 thus deprived New York of an ally that had been very valuable to it in the previous war, the Iroquois having essentially fought on its behalf. In addition, by getting the Five Nations to accept the French fort at Detroit, the treaty in the short term destroyed English hopes of expansion towards the Great Lakes.[14] While New York seemed highly satisfied with the Albany Deed of July 1701,[15] it actually had little reason to be. The territorial cession they claimed to have won in the west was fictitious and at the very most could only be used as a diplomatic argument in negotiations with the French.[16]

There were, however, positive aspects for the British. As Starna writes, "the peace with the western Indians could only increase the flow of furs to Albany."[17] Moreover, the neutrality of the Five Nations prevented the French from making expeditions through Iroquoia. A buffer had been created between New France and New York, and when war again broke out between the two empires, New York was able to escape the horrors of guerrilla warfare from Canada. New England was not so lucky; starting in 1702, it suffered a great deal from border raids by the French and Abenakis.[18] Finally, in spite of the Montreal treaty, Nanfan was able to reconfirm the Covenant Chain with the Iroquois.

Were the Iroquois the Winners or the Losers?

Scholars have always agreed that the Grand Settlement of 1701 was a turning point in the history of the Five Nations. However, when it comes to analysing this turning point and assessing the diplomatic and military situation of the League at this time, their interpretations are widely divergent. There are two opposing positions. W.J. Eccles takes the view that the Iroquois were forced to capitulate in 1701 in Montreal, and that this admission of failure was the prelude to their irreversible decline. In this view, they were so weakened over the course of the eighteenth century that they were unable to pursue any ambitious objectives.[19] Brandão and Starna have a completely different analysis. According to them, the agreements of 1701 represent not a military defeat for the Five Nations but "the triumph of Iroquois diplomacy."[20]

Both positions have their flaws—but especially the latter. Let us start with that of Eccles, however. He fails to take into account the positive aspects of the Great Peace for the Iroquois, aspects that have been brought out by the historian Wallace and then by other scholars following him, such as Haan and Richter—in addition to Brandão and Starna.[21] The Iroquois' prospects for the future were in fact quite favourable, and they were not limited to the advantages of neutrality. Trade links with Albany were maintained, and now the Iroquois also had access to French sources of supplies—Fort Frontenac, Detroit, and also Montreal.[22] The peace of 1701 also led to the success of the Iroquois diplomatic and commercial overtures in the west.[23] Finally—something that has barely been mentioned by historians—the Iroquois recovered some thirty prisoners, which was one of their objectives. As well, according to D.K. Richter, the most important result obtained by the Five Nations in the negotiations of 1700–1701 was a partial solution to the internal quarrels that had divided the League for a decade and threatened to destroy it. In spite of enormous internal tensions, the Iroquois had reached a new consensus based on a kind of compromise, and they owed this in large part to the political genius of the Onondaga chief Teganissorens, who had been able to make the French strategy of neutralization of the Five Nations part of his program in order to resolve the internal struggles of the confederacy.[24] By thus preserving the League's unity and its autonomy vis-à-vis colonial powers, he established the conditions for a new Iroquois offensive, this time a diplomatic one.

It is Starna and Brandão who are the most emphatic about the "singularly positive" results achieved by the Five Nations in 1701.[25] In their view, the League had sufficient manoeuvring room to negotiate a favourable agreement with the two European colonies. This view is shared by O.P. Dickason, who sees the Iroquois as deceiving both the English and the French. She says, for example, that in Albany they hid from the English their neutrality and the fact that they no longer controlled the territories covered in the deed. They "were playing both ends against the middle with great skill," she writes, in my view overestimating their ability to escape colonial pressures.[26] According to Starna and Brandão as well, the Iroquois did not have their backs against the wall in 1701: "They had not been defeated. And they did not come on their knees."[27] However, the French and New York sources, as we have seen, taken together with several Amerindian oral accounts, show that the Iroquois had suffered many defeats in the 1690s. Starna, contradicting himself somewhat, actually acknowledges this fact: "Several Onondaga and Oneida headmen brought their complaints of continued raids and the killing of their people to Governor Callière."[28] Of course, F. Jennings may have overstated the case in his harsh verdict that "the Iroquois sued for peace because they had no alternative but complete collapse and disintegration."[29] The Five Nations had not lost all military capacity, and although they were in a position of weakness, they negotiated as equals with the French and their allies, obtaining the best terms possible. One fact clearly shows that the Iroquois were not totally defeated: they managed to obtain a peace agreement and, without returning their captives from the nations of the west, recovered their own prisoners, even though reciprocal exchange had been a central issue in the negotiations. However, as already stated, neutrality was more a French idea than an Iroquois one, and it was imposed on them. Had the Iroquois wanted to oppose it, would they have had the means to do so? What is certain is that the peace of 1701 consolidated the military victory of the French-Amerindian alliance—it was the military raids of the western nations that induced the Five Nations to accept peace—just as the dispersion of the Hurons and their neighbours in the years 1640 to 1660 had represented a victory for the Iroquois.

I therefore do not share the conclusion of O.P. Dickason, who writes: "What had been achieved by the century of war? It had shifted the balance of Amerindian regional power from Huronia to Iroquoia." This historian seems to be confusing the 1660s with the 1690s. She continues: "The Five Nations emerged with expanded territory, although not so much as they claimed." In the same vein, Starna, who is clearly obsessed with the issue of territory, goes so far as to assert: "Therefore, practically speaking, it was the Five Nations who were in the best overall position to exercise control over the lands described in the 1701 [Albany] deed."[30] This is completely false. How could the Iroquois control territories dominated by the allies of the French-Amerindian diplomatic network? The Iroquois, of course, were in a much more favourable situation in 1701 than they had been between 1697 and 1700—the Grand Settlement of 1701, as we have seen, was advantageous to them in many ways—but it would be an exaggeration to speak of a triumph. If there was a triumph for anyone, it was for the French. The Tree of Peace had been planted in Montreal, not in Onondaga.

New France: A Cornerstone in the Construction of the Empire

Shortly after the signing of the Montreal treaty, Callière explained to Minister of Marine Pontchartrain that "the separate peace made with the Iroquois in 1700, and which was made common in 1701 to all the known savage Nations, achieved for the King a certain, indisputable superiority in Canada over all New England."[31] While attributing the glory of this treaty to the king, the governor was obviously eager to take credit for its success, which was all the greater given that a new war was brewing across the Atlantic. Callière's judgment was too optimistic, however, because, in spite of the diplomatic defeat suffered by New York, the English colonies still had the advantage of their enormous demographic superiority. But the French governor was not wrong about the importance of the peace settlement with the Iroquois or about the vitality of all the alliances with the Amerindians, which provided support to New France. While the treaty of 1701 did not deal with the structural weaknesses of the colony or resolve the question of withdrawal from the Great Lakes region, it was nevertheless an undeniable political success for the French in that it furthered their hegemonic ambitions in North America.

The primary achievement, peace, was the result of a long diplomatic process initiated by Frontenac in the final years of his administration and completed brilliantly by Callière. The Iroquois, long a scourge of the colony on the St Lawrence, seemed to have been eliminated forever. This was an enormous relief for all the colonists, especially those in Montreal, who had been living under constant threat of attack by the Iroquois since the Lachine raid in 1689. Iroquois neutrality provided an additional guarantee in this regard. Callière knew that the British would still urge the Five Nations to fight on their side in the event of war; if the Iroquois maintained their neutrality, New York would be deprived of its first line of attack and the Iroquois would serve as a valuable buffer against the British. Moreover, the imperial rivalry with New York over the status of Iroquoia had turned in favour of the French, since the Treaty of Montreal denied any English sovereignty over the Five Nations.[32] It was the governor's hope that Jesuit missionaries might help to preserve the peace and even separate the Iroquois from the British alliance: "I hope...that through the familiarity that peace will bring about between us [French and Iroquois] more and more, the time will become favourable so that they will propose to me themselves that I send them Jesuits because in that case they will be obliged to defend them against the insults that the English could make to them through drunkards and other people connected to them." Callière was right: at the instigation of the pro-French factions, Jesuit missionaries began to settle in Iroquoia the following year.[33]

During the War of the Spanish Succession (1702–13), the priority for Governor Vaudreuil, Callière's successor (Callière died in 1703), was to preserve the peace with the Iroquois that had been won at such great cost, even if this meant to some extent neglecting the allies of the Great Lakes region. Vaudreuil went so far as to give the new alliance with the Iroquois precedence over the one with the Odawas (the main partner of the French in the west); in the event of "war between [these] two nations...we would be obliged to take the side of the Iroquois," he stated in 1706.[34] The fear felt by the Native people of the Pays d'en Haut, in particular Kondiaronk during the 1680s, of a French-Iroquois alliance at their expense was not unfounded. Vaudreuil gave clear expression to the temptation to make a shift of alliances, a temptation that had been a constant in French policy since the defeat of the Hurons in 1650. In 1656, for example, dozens of Huron refugees had been captured on Île d'Orléans by the Mohawks with the apparent blessing of the French authorities, who were more concerned about their relations with the Five Nations than about the fate of their defeated allies.[35] The governor's statement also confirmed that the Iroquois, although defeated, were still feared and respected by the French at the beginning of the eighteenth century.

It was not in the interest of New France to weaken the Five Nations too much, although not everyone accepted this view. Father Carheil, in 1702, wrote from Michilimackinac with respect to the Iroquois nations: "It is the only enemy that we have to fear and that fights with us over trade with our savages whom they want to attach to the English; what reason did we have not to want to destroy them in the war that we had undertaken against them, why did we want to preserve them? What would we lose in destroying them as few as they are now? Their destruction and the possession of their lands would assure us of the trade with all the savage nations up here."[36] While these remarks revealed the weakening of the Iroquois and the existence of trade between the nations of the west and Albany, they were still faulty in terms of strategy. The French, with the assistance of their Native allies, were probably in a position to further weaken the Iroquois (Onontio had demonstrated that he was capable of invading Iroquoia, and he had taken the hatchet away from many of his allies in 1700), but as noted above, it was not in their interest to do so. As Lahontan wrote:

> Those who alledge that the destruction of the *Iroquese*, would promote the interest of the Colonies of *New-France*, are strangers to the true interest of that Country; for if that were once accomplish'd, the Savages who are now the *French* Allies, would turn their greatest Enemies, as being then rid of their other fears. They would not fail to call in the *English*, by reason that their Commodities are at once cheaper; and more esteem'd then ours; and by that means the whole Commerce of that wide Country would he wrested out of our hands. I conclude therefore, that 'tis the interest of the *French* to weaken the *Iroquese*, but not to see 'em intirely defeated.[37]

Since the time of Champlain, the Iroquois had served for New France as a barrier between its Native allies and the English or Dutch merchants,[38] and there was no question of the French renouncing this time-honoured principle.[39] Maintaining the Iroquois as a secondary force allowed the French to preserve a geostrategic buffer separating its English enemies from its allies in the west; the loss of that buffer could lead to the commercial and political ruin of New France. In short, as B.G. Trigger writes, "if the hostile Iroquois had not existed, the French would have had to invent them."[40] Contrary to Jennings's view, however, it was not solely for this reason that "the French refrained from demanding Iroquois subjection in the great treaty settlement";[41] it was also because, despite a certain superiority,[42] the French were not really in a position to do so, and they may have feared the effects of a resurgence of Iroquois guerrilla warfare, which would have hindered the development of the colony.[43]

"This Peace [of 1701] engages all the savages in the interests of France," wrote Callière in his report to the minister.[44] These "savages" of course included the Iroquois—who seemed at the very least to have been neutralized—but he was referring above all to the nations of the Pays d'en Haut and of the St Lawrence and Acadia,[45] "peoples who are the support of Canada" according to La Potherie.[46] Onontio thus had good reason to be satisfied; the multilateral alliance with his "children," which had been shaky in the west in the previous decade, was consecrated by the treaty of 1701, in accordance with the very wishes of its members.[47] As host for the peace negotiations and intermediary between the allies of the west and the Iroquois, the governor made official the strategy of arbitration and mediation that he had applied in the Pays d'en Haut. The 1701 conference demonstrated in a most impressive way the central, influential place of

Onontio in the alliance. The chief Chichicatalo acknowledged Callière's right to act in Native affairs when he asked him to speak to the other Miamis in support of his decision to migrate to the St Joseph River.[48] Similarly, if the allies in the west agreed to make peace with the Iroquois, it was in part because of Callière's entreaties, with gifts to back them up, during Courtemanche and Father Enjalran's diplomatic mission in the winter of 1700–1701.[49] In 1701 Onontio wanted to appear as the master of war and peace, and in this case he managed to do so quite well.

Certainly the Pax Gallica had its limits; the impossibility of ending the conflict between the nations of the west and the Sioux attests to this. In addition, in spite of the establishment of Detroit, the Treaty of Montreal had not provided any solution to the interruption in trade resulting from the edict of 1696, which in the long term could result in the peoples of the Great Lakes trading their pelts in the English markets, thus weakening the alliance. But the Great Peace nonetheless constituted a success for New France. Versailles was particularly pleased, for the treaty was signed at a time when Louis XIV was giving new impetus to French imperial policy in North America with the decision (demonstrated in the founding of Detroit and, especially, Louisiana) to consolidate his control of the area west of the Appalachians from the Great Lakes to the Gulf of Mexico in order to prevent English expansion beyond the Appalachians.[50] Thus, 1701 must be seen as a pivotal time in the building of the French empire in America. According to W.A. Starna, "None of the parties to the 1701 treaties, whether France, England or the Five Nations, could reasonably exercise control over all or part of the territory described in the 1701 deed and treaties." Eccles, disagreeing with Starna, replies, "The French did." And they did, by means of their posts on both sides of Iroquoia (Fort Frontenac and Detroit) and the indispensable support of their allies.[51]

The Allied Nations in a Position of Strength

The delegations from the Great Lakes did not go to Montreal only because Onontio had asked them to. They came to defend their own interests, as demonstrated by their determination to make the voyage in spite of the rumours—which were well founded—of an epidemic. Each group had its own motives, which depended on their relations with the Iroquois and the Sioux and on their place in the network of French-Amerindian alliances (the Odawas, Huron-Petuns, and Potawatomis, as we have seen, occupied a more central position than for example, the Foxes, the Mascoutens, or the Gens des Terres). Certain nations—and sometimes mere bands or factions—were already negotiating peace with the Iroquois independently of Onontio. But the majority accepted his request to bury the hatchet in 1700–1701.

The Huron-Petun chief Kondiaronk is the best illustration of the key role played by the Great Lakes nations in building the Great Peace of Montreal. He contributed through his raids (the battle on Lake Erie in 1697, for example) to the weakening of the Iroquois, and he was, with Onontio, one of the leaders of the faction in favour of a general peace in 1700–1701. On many occasions, Kondiaronk showed himself to be a man of compromise and conciliation, able to overcome the various obstacles on the path to peace. At least twice he played a decisive role in winning over the Amerindians of the west, first, at the Michilimackinac conference in May 1701 (where all the nations of the alliance were represented), when he managed to achieve a precarious but functional consensus; then, in Montreal in August of that same year, when, to the great relief of Callière,

he settled the question of prisoners. It must also be noted that, in Montreal in September 1700 and August 1701, and also in separate meetings in the west in the absence of the French, Kondiaronk had the opportunity to talk directly with delegates from the Five Nations to persuade them to accept the terms of the general peace.[52] Thus, Kondiaronk was, with Onontio, one of the main artisans of the peace of 1701. He was probably also one of its initiators, but on this point the sources focus almost exclusively on the role of New France.

On the whole, we see in the year 1701 a reinforcement of the position of the nations of the Great Lakes. In fact, the peace settlement seems to have given them increased room to manoeuvre. The priority for most of the delegations, in addition to the recovery of prisoners, was to maintain the alliance with the French. As the governor and the intendant wrote, "permanent posts would do a great deal to satisfy our allied savages, who urgently asked Sieur Chevalier de Callières, when they were in Montreal for the peace negotiations, to be given Frenchmen among them."[53] The minutes of the treaty confirm that the allied chiefs asked repeatedly that officers, blacksmiths, and missionaries be sent to the Great Lakes region. In the following years, the Odawas would ask again and again for the reestablishment of a garrisoned post at Michilimackinac. Wanting to consolidate the alliance, these nations thus played on French imperial ambitions. Offering the French hospitality in the west, they intended to take advantage of their merchandise (in particular their weapons) and their power to mediate.[54]

The allies were in a favourable position in 1701 because through the peace settlement they had been reconciled with the Iroquois, and if the Five Nations gave them free passage through their territory, they might also have closer relations with Albany. The French strategy of maintaining the Iroquois as a buffer between the Native peoples of the west and the English was therefore not without its weak points. The general peace did in fact create the conditions for an alliance between the Great Lakes nations and the Iroquois.[55] It even opened the door to a shift of alliances in favour of the Covenant Chain, which was the policy favoured by the Huron chief Le Baron in the 1690s. In 1703 an administrator expressed his concern over this possibility: "It is not appropriate to bring together so closely the Iroquois with the Outaouais [Odawas], the Hurons and the other savages, we must use our skill to try to see that they are never too friendly."[56] Alliance with the English, which was likely to weaken their links with Onontio, was certainly not the plan of all the Amerindians of the Great Lakes region. As we have already seen, it is hardly possible, given the factional manoeuvring, to speak of common strategies, and the Amerindians' propensity for war could hinder plans of alliance. But it was an option that several groups would take advantage of in the ensuing years. As shown by the words of the Amikwa delegate at the Montreal conference, the intention of the nations of the west was not to leave the comfortable bosom of the French alliance, but rather to put pressure on Onontio to be more generous in trade, and to take advantage on occasion of the attractive New York market. In this sense, the nations of Great Lakes came out of the 1701 peace settlement more powerful, as they had become potentially less dependent on the French.

Onontio's influence on the Christian Iroquois was also declining somewhat at the turn of the eighteenth century. After 1701, Delâge notes, the settled Iroquois "were distancing themselves from the French." They shared the geopolitical analysis of the leaders of the League, that of Teganissorens in particular, who recognized the threat that the colonial societies represented to their security and who favoured a strategy aimed at intensifying competition between the colonial powers in order to neutralize their negative impact as much as possible. Breaking with the rules of the French-Amerindian

alliance, according to which the enemies of one were the enemies of all, they refused to regard the British as enemies simply because they were the enemies of Onontio."[57] The peace settlement of 1701, to which the agreement concluded in 1696 between the Iroquois of the League and the Iroquois in the réductions contributed, did even more to bring these two Amerindian groups together. Thanks to the Five Nations, in fact, the settled Iroquois obtained the freedom to trade with New York, which, unbeknownst to the French, consolidated their union with the Iroquois of the League.[58] The Iroquois settled in Montreal would thus act as middlemen in the "contraband" trading that was beginning and would soon flourish between Albany and Montreal.[59] The "great alliance,"[60] born of the Treaty of Montreal, that brought together the French, their allies, and the Five Nations was indeed a double-edged political weapon for New France.

The Limits of the Peace

"From then [1701] on," writes W.J. Eccles, "peace reigned in the west, until the resumption of Anglo-French hostilities in 1754."[61] This judgment needs to be qualified. Let us begin by looking at what La Potherie wrote shortly after the treaty of 1701: "So here is the peace made with the Iroquois, but I can assure you, Monseigneur, that our allies who have their people [prisoners] among the Iroquois will not fail to take revenge on the former if they meet them in their hunting parties."[62] La Potherie, who was not on good terms with Governor Callière, wanted to play down the diplomatic success of the treaty. But he was right about the importance of the problem of prisoners and the danger of a resumption of war. It should be pointed out that while the Great Peace of Montreal put an end to the open warfare of the preceding decades, it was not scrupulously respected in the Great Lakes region. The skirmishing of previous years between the Iroquois and the nations of the west continued sporadically at the instigation of certain groups or individuals. "[They] have uprooted the tree of peace," some Senecas complained to Vaudreuil in 1704. Attacked by Miami, Ouiatenon, Illinois, and Mascouten warriors in spite of the peace treaty of 1701 and the diplomatic voyage of Chief Aouenano to the Miamis at the beginning of 1702, these Iroquois appealed for the protection and arbitration of the French.[63] The Odawas of Michilimackinac—those, that is, who had not migrated to Detroit—also continued to make war with the Iroquois regardless of the general peace. In 1704 they attacked some Iroquois living "on the doorstep of Fort Frontenac" and captured forty of them. According to D.K. Richter, "the majority of the victims were dedicated francophiles who had placed their trust in French promises to keep the peace."[64]

These clashes did not prevent other western bands from forming trading relationships with the Iroquois and the English,[65] but they indicate how difficult it was to establish a lasting general peace. "My Father, all the men disobey you, they are all making war with each other and killing each other," exclaimed a Menominee chief in 1708.[66] For many Native people in the west, the peace of Montreal was a mere truce. In 1709 Governor Vaudreuil reminded the allies in the Pays d'en Haut of the agreements of 1701: "You have all forgotten the promise you made at the general peace; you all promised not to take revenge if someone attacked, but to rely on me to get satisfaction for it. You have not, however, done this and that is what today is causing your misfortunes."[67] The following year, some Onondaga and Seneca delegates complained to Vaudreuil under the terms of this arbitration clause: "Until now we have done as you wished. The Outaouais [Odawas] have not done the same, they have attacked us many times since the general peace.

We have been struck almost everywhere on our bodies, we are now completely fed up, but we have not taken revenge because you have until now always prevented it. Without that, our father, the Odawas would be no more, they must be persuaded that we do not fear them. They know like many others that when we go to war, it is not to kill two or three men, but to take an entire village."[68] The orator was anxious to affirm the power of his people, and his words to this effect were not without foundation. The Iroquois had since 1701 captured many enemies in attacks on southern tribes. This was not just a *petite guerre* but open warfare involving the capture of villages, like that waged against the western nations from 1640 to 1670, though certainly on a smaller scale.[69] The ambassador's main objective was to take advantage of French mediation to solve the League's problems with the Great Lakes nations. This remedy, incidentally, would have been unthinkable in 1690, evidence that the Iroquois had truly been defeated by the end of the century.[70]

Throughout the eighteenth century, then, when it was in their interest, the Iroquois reaffirmed the general peace agreement concluded in 1701. In 1757, for example, at a conference held in Montreal, the orator for the Five Nations reminded the French, "We can't write but know all that has past between us having good memories." He continued: "After the Warrs and troubles we together met you at this place [Montreal] where every trouble was buried and a fire kindled here. Where was to meet and Treat peaceably; you are daily now working disturbances and Seem to forget the old agreement... The Tree Seems to be falling, let it be now put up the Roots spread and the leaves flowrish as before."[71]

In addition to the tensions between the Great Lakes nations and the Iroquois, there were also occasional conflicts among the nations of the French-Amerindian alliance. For example, the peace negotiated between the Foxes and Ojibwas under Callière's auspices did not last. The Ojibwas were related both to the Sioux and to other Algonquian groups (Odawas, etc.), which created conflicts within the league of the Pays d'en Haut. There were recurring tensions between the Ojibwas, on one side, and the Foxes, Menominees, Potawatomis, and Sauks, on the other.[72] There were also tensions between the Odawas and the Hurons and Miamis, which degenerated into open warfare at Detroit in 1706.[73] It was also at Detroit, in 1712, that the French became involved in a terrible battle between the Foxes and several allied groups, including the Odawas and Potawatomis. This battle was the prelude to a long war that pitted the French and their allies against the Foxes, Mascoutens, and Kickapoos, a war that continued until 1738.[74] Callière had hoped to arrange a truce with the Sioux, but this had proved impossible because the Sioux had not been present in Montreal in 1701.[75]

While it essentially ended the Iroquois Wars, the treaty of 1701 did not stop the "Indian wars" in Canada. This was, first of all, because the French did not have the means to impose peace on all the groups as they would have liked to and, secondly—and especially—because of the inherently military nature of the Aboriginal societies.[76] It is important to understand the significance of the Amerindians' concepts of war and peace. "Wars are eternal among the savages," stated Charlevoix. War was a permanent condition, and peace, tactical and temporary, was often intended only to recover prisoners. Nicolas Perrot expressed the view that "there is no savage nation that does not have a grudge against another. The Miamis and the Illinois hate each other, the Iroquois detest the Outaouais [Odawas] and Saulteurs [Ojibwas], and so forth. There is none of these nations that does not say it is justified in making war with others." Perrot was describing the prevalence of war and the unstable nature of alliances, which constantly had to be reactivated if they were to last. Alliances were not by nature inviolable contracts, and intertribal relations were

thus marked by a structural alternation between phases of war and phases of peace. From one period to another, the cycle went from the violence of war to the exchange of gifts or women (or prisoners). Peace was even more fragile because war making was often an individual undertaking, carried out by reckless young men in defiance of the wisdom of the elders. Even the Iroquois, who in 1701 longed for peace with the nations of the west, were subject to this structural aspect of war, which hampered their strategy of rapprochement with the nations in the Great Lakes. As Richter explains, "When women mourned their dead kin and called on young men to bring them captives or scalps to ease their grief, and especially when warriors with no other foes at hand were in their cups, western Indians on their way to Albany made tempting targets."[77]

If the Amerindians of the west and the Iroquois were at war less after 1701 than during the seventeenth century, it is because they had opportunities to express their warrior ethos in other places and against other enemies. The concept of "universal peace" was unknown to the Natives, who, while they valued the military support or neutrality of allies, always had an adversary to fight and prisoners to be adopted or tortured. La Potherie observed that the Iroquois "never made Peace with any Nation without planning to make War elsewhere" And Intendant Raudot, speaking of Amerindians in general, said, "When they are not at war against any of their neighbours, they usually go to the lands of very distant nations."[78] This is exactly what the Iroquois did after 1701. Once the peace agreement was concluded with the allies of the French, they resumed and intensified their raids against the "Flatheads" (Catawbas, Choctaws, and various other southern peoples) in the Carolinas and Virginia, ending a truce that had lasted from 1692 to 1701,[79] the period when they had been on the defensive vis-à-vis the Great Lakes nations. These raids do not seem to have had an economic basis. They were part of the tradition of wars of capture, as an

Iroquois orator stated in 1719: "It seems that God in a particular manner is pleasd to Strengthen us by Severall prisoners which we do take from those people."[80] As for the western allies, they had no intention of making peace with both the Iroquois and the Sioux. As some Hurons told Vaudreuil in 1703, "You make war against the English, so let us go against the Sioux."[81] They continued to fight the Sioux and increased their raids against various groups in the Mississippi Valley, such as the Akansas, as well as the Flatheads, which brought them closer to Iroquoia.[82]

The French-Iroquois peace depended on the Five Nations maintaining their neutrality, in particular in the event of a war between the French and the English, and on New France's attitude to the trading relationships its allies in the west and the Five Nations might form. Vaudreuil endeavoured to discourage the development of trade cooperation between the two groups, even arranging the murder in 1709, of the Métis Alexander Montour—the son of a French officer and a Mohawk woman—who was acting as a guide in Iroquoia for Mississaugas, Ojibwas, Odawas, Huron-Petuns, and Miamis on their way to Albany. This did not help maintain the peace of 1701. It also explains in part why the Iroquois broke their promise of neutrality in 1709 and 1711.[83]

Because of factional manoeuvring, it was difficult for the Iroquois League to maintain neutrality when the French and the British were at war, as between 1702 and 1713. An Onondaga orator in 1710 expressed the reservations of the League to Vaudreuil: "Today I am on my mat and it is with sorrow that I see that you are fighting with the English. Are you both drunk...?"[84] As R. Haan has shown, the policy of balance between the empires was not always as successful during the eighteenth century as Wallace has asserted. Richter, in the same vein, writes, "[T]he diplomatic balancing act never seems to have worked very well in periods when the imperial powers pressed the Five Nations to choose sides." At least until 1720, Richter goes on, "anglophile, francophile, and neutralist factions continued to disagree." Neutrality, in 1701, was one option for the Iroquois; it did not necessarily have their unanimous support.[85]

During two attempts by the British to invade Canada—both unsuccessful—the Iroquois departed from the principle of neutrality, joining the English camp. In 1709 only the Senecas remained neutral. In 1711 warriors from all of the Five Nations (a total of 656 men) went to Albany to join an expedition that was planned against New France. But in subsequent years the League returned to a strict policy of neutrality. The policy would again be put to the test, however, during the War of the Austrian Succession (1744–48) and after 1754, during the Seven Years' War.[86]

Notes

1 As D.K. Richter explains (*Ordeal of the Longhouse*, 362), "The term 'Grand Settlement' was coined by Anthony F.C. Wallace, who first noted the connections between the Albany and Montreal Treaties." See Wallace, "Origins of Iroquois Neutrality."

2 Richter, "*Ordeal of the Longhouse*," 418; Richter, *Ordeal of the Longhouse*, 211; Brandão and Starna, "Treaties," 223.

3 *NYCD*, 4:899, Conference of Nanfan with the Indians, July 1701; Brandão and Starna, "Treaties."

4 And also: "if the French make any attempts or come into our country to delude us, wee desire you to send men of wisdom and understanding to countermine them, for they [are] to subtile and cunning for us"; "wee have not power to resist such a Christian enemy, therefore wee must depend upon you Brother Corlaer to take this case in hand" (*NYCD*, 4:905–6; Richter, *Ordeal of the Longhouse*, 212; Brandão and Starna, "Treaties," 225–7).

5 *NYCD*, 4:905; Richter, *Ordeal of the Longhouse*, 212.

6 *NYCD*, 4:905, 908–11; Brandão and Starna, "Treaties," 225–7.

7   Brandão and Starna, "Treaties," 228, 232; Richter, *Ordeal of the Longhouse,* 362. See also Wallace, "Origins of Iroquois Neutrality," 233–5; Haan, "Covenant Chain," 135.

8   Jennings, *Ambiguous Iroquois Empire,* 212 (see also 10–24). Trelease (*Indian Affairs,* 362) explains that the deed "was symbolic...The French naturally refused to recognize it, and the English were no more able to exercise control in that vast area than before the deed was executed. The Indians, moreover, had no intention of opening it to English settlement or of surrendering their hunting rights there—far from it. They merely offered the king the dubious privilege of protecting it." See also Kent, *Historical Report,* 42–3. Richter (*Ordeal of the Longhouse,* 362) disagrees with Jennings's analysis: "the thrust of his argument is correct, but it is placed a quarter century too early...[B]y 1726 no copy of it [the deed] could be found in the province."

9   Eccles, "Report," 35–40.

10 Even if, as Richter writes, "the previous decade of experience had disabused them of any illusions about New York martial value" (Richter, *Ordeal of the Longhouse,* 212).

11 In the autumn of 1703, the Seneca chief Oronyatez asked for the protection of the French governor: "We make you master of our land and this is something we have never done but for you; therefore my father if any accident happens to us look upon us as your children and give us your help." This speech calls for several observations. First of all, it contradicts the Albany Deed of 1701; thus—if the deed has an Iroquois origin—it reveals the divisions within the League (Oronyatez was a pro-French leader, while Onucheranorum represented the pro-English faction in Albany in 1701). It also shows that the Iroquois regularly called on the protection of the European colonies: Oronyatez did not want to surrender Seneca territory to the French colonists, but rather preferred to consolidate the alliance with Onontio—hence the Treaty of Montreal of 1701 (ANF, Col., C11A, vol. 21, f. 60, Parolles [...] Oronyatez [...] 26 octobre 1703 [TN: our translation]).

12 *NYCD,* 4905. The issue of missionaries was not raised at the Montreal conference (Charlevoix, *Histoire,* 2:284).

13 Richter, "Ordeal of the Longhouse," 419.

14 Jennings, *Ambiguous Iroquois Empire,* 211–12.

15 Trelease, *Indian Affairs,* 362–3.

16 *NYCD,* 4:1068, Memorial from Mr Livingston about New York, 1703.

17 Starna, "Concerning the Extent," 63.

18 Jennings, *Ambiguous Iroquois Empire,* 211; Charlevoix, *Histoire,* 2:303, 313, 328; ANF, Col., C11A, vol. 21, f. 73, Reponse de monsieur de vaudreuil aux parolles de Teganissorens a Quebec le 31 octobre 1703.

19 Eccles, *Frontenac,* 332–3; Eccles, "Teganissorens," *DCB,* 2:619–23; Eccles, *Canada under Louis XIV,* 244; Eccles, *France in America,* 100–1; Eccles, "Report," 17–19; see also Trelease, *Indian Affairs,* 363.

20 Brandão and Starna, "Treaties"; Starna, "Concerning the Extent of 'Free Hunting' Territory."

21 Wallace, "Origins of Iroquois Neutrality"; Haan, "Covenant Chain"; Richter, *Ordeal of the Longhouse.*

22 *NYCD,* 5:724.

23 Haan, "Covenant Chain," 102–3.

24 Richter, *Ordeal of the Longhouse,* 427–31.

25 Starna, "Concerning the Extent of 'Free Hunting' Territory," 61–2; Brandão and Starna, "Treaties," 232.

26 Dickason, *Canada's First Nations,* 155.

27 Brandão and Starna, "Treaties," 217; Starna, "Concerning the Extent of 'Free Hunting' Territory," 20; see also Brown, ed., *The Illustrated History of Canada,* 145–6.

28 Starna, "Concerning the Extent of 'Free Hunting' Territory," 26.

29 Jennings, *Ambiguous Iroquois Empire,* 210; Jennings, ed., *Iroquois Diplomacy,* 39.

30 Dickason, *Canada's First Nations,* 155; Starna, "Concerning the Extent of 'Free Hunting' Territory," 72; see also Brandão and Starna, "Treaties," 232, 209.

31 ANF, Col., C11A, vol. 19, f. 232, Calière, 1701 (TN: our translation); see also ANF, Col., C11A, vol. 19, f. 3, Callière et Champigny au ministre, Québec, 5 octobre 1701; ANF, Col., C11A, vol. 19, f. 232, Callière au ministre, Canada, Projets sur la Nouvelle Angleterre, 1701.

32 ANF, Col., C11A, vol. 20, f. 159, Callière au ministre, Québec, 4 novembre 1702; ANF, Col. B, vol. 23.1, p. 116, Le ministre à Callière, Versailles, 6 mai 1702; ANF, Col., B, vol. 23.2, p. 41, Le Roy à Callière et Beauharnois, 1703; ANF, Col., C11A, vol. 19, f. 232, Callière au ministre, Canada, Projets sur la Nouvelle Angleterre, 1701; Haan, "The Problem of Iroquois Neutrality," 319–20; Jennings, ed., *Iroquois Diplomacy,* 39;

Zoltvany, *Vaudreuil,* 34. The diplomats back in France even suggested, rather unrealistically, a military alliance with the Iroquois against the British.

33 ANF, Col., C11A, vol. 19, f. 118 (TN: our translation); Zoltvany, *Vaudreuil,* 35; Richter, *Ordeal of the Longhouse,* 217.

34 ANF, Col., C11A, vol. 24, f. IIV, Vaudreuil au ministre, Québec, 30 avril 1706; ANF, C11A, vol. 22, f. 238, Vaudreuil au ministre, Québec, 5 mai 1705 ("the Iroquois whom I regard as the only nation that it is important for me to conserve" [TN: our translation]); ANF, Col., C11A, vol. 24, f. 3, Vaudreuil au ministre, Québec, 28 avril 1706; ANF, Col., C11A, vol. 24, f. 14, Vaudreuil au ministre, Québec, 4 novembre 1706; ANF, Col., C11A, vol. 22, f. 8–9, Vaudreuil et Beauharnois au ministre, 17 novembre 1704; ANF, Col., C11A, vol. 22, f. 235v, Vaudreuil au ministre, Québec, 19 octobre 1705; ANF, Col., C11A, vol. 28, f. 104v, Vaudreuil au ministre, Québec, 5 novembre 1708; ANF, Col., C11A, vol. 28, f. 8v, 36v, Vaudreuil et Raudot au ministre, Québec, 14 novembre 1708. See also White, *The Middle Ground,* 150–1; Miquelon, *New France,* 38–9.

35 See Vaugeois, ed., *Les Hurons de Lorette,* 180–1, 264.

36 *JR,* 65:222. (TN: our translation.)

37 Lahontan, *New Voyages,* 1:394.

38 Trigger, "Mohawk-Mahican War," 285–6.

39 ANF, Col., B, vol. 19.1, pp. 111, 116, Le Roy à Frontenac et Champigny, Versailles, 26 may 1696; Jennings, *Ambiguous Iroquois Empire,* 211; Jennings, ed., *Iroquois Diplomacy,* 39.

40 Trigger, "Mohawk-Mahican War," 286.

41 Jennings, *Ambiguous Iroquois Empire,* 211.

42 Callière showed a great deal of confidence in his military possibilities: "This Peace," he wrote, "... prevents the Iroquois from joining with the English in the event of a break [with the French] if they did otherwise, all the other savages would join together to make war on the Iroquois who would soon be destroyed by the multitude. The Five Iroquois nations cannot assemble more than twelve hundred warriors at the most, it would be easy to make a corps of six thousand men of the other savages which joined with a detachment of five hundred men from our troops would annihilate the Iroquois for ever" (ANF, Col., C11A, vol. 19, F. 232v, Callière, 1701 [TN: our translation]).

43 See ANF, Col., C11A, vol. 21, f. 6v–7r, Beauharnois et Vaudreuil au ministre, Québec, 15 novembre 1703.

44 ANF, Col., C11A, vol. 19, f. 232v, Callières, 1701. (TN: our translation.)

45 The Abenakis of Acadia, who had economic links with New England, in 1701 reaffirmed their alliance with New France. In the War of the Spanish Succession, Callière and his successor, Vaudreuil, urged them to fight the British. See ANF, Col., C11A, vol. 21, f. 13–14, Beauharnois et Vaudreuil au ministre, Québec, 15 novembre 1703; ANF, Col., C11A, vol. 21, f. 51v, Vaudreuil au ministre, Québec, 14 novembre 1703; Zoltavany, *Vaudreuil,* 41–2, 45–6, 48–51; Miquelon, *New France,* 25–31, 40–1.

46 ANF, Col., F3, vol. 2, f. 267v. (TN: our translation.)

47 Charlevoix, *Histoire,* 2:267.

48 ANF, Col., F3, vol. 8, f. 263, Pourparlez [...] pour parvenir a la rattiffication de la paix, 29 juillet 1701.

49 ANF; Col., F3, vol. 8, f. 267, Pourparlez entre mr le chevalier de callière et les sauvages [...] 2ᵉ aoust 1701.

50 Louisiana was formed in 1699 by Le Moyne d'Iberville. It was dynastic rivalries that induced Louis XIV to sanction this new colony. The king of Spain, Charles II, who died in November 1700 without an heir, had bequeathed all his Spanish possessions to Philip of Anjou, the grandson of Louis XIV. The Sun King accepted the will of his brother-in-law Charles II, thus incurring the wrath of the Austrian monarchy and the maritime powers; by colonizing Louisiana, he wanted to create a protective bond between New France and New Spain. See Lebrun, Le *XVIIᵉ siècle,* 249, 317–20; Y.F. Zoltvany, "Callière," *DCB,* 2:116; Eccles, *Canadian Frontier,* 130.

51 Starna, "Concerning the Extent of 'Free Hunting' Territory," 72; Eccles, "Report," 26.

52 La Potherie, *Histoires,* 4:224; Charlevoix, *Histoire,* 2:273, 276, 279.

53 ANF, Col., C11A, vol. 19, f. 9r, Callière et Champigny au ministre, Québec, 5 octobre 1701. (TN: our translation.)

54 Havard, "Empire et métissages," 232–6.

55 ANF, Col., B, vol. 19.3, p. 37, Le Roy à Frontenac et Champigny, Versailles, 27 avril 1697.

56 ANF, Col., C11A, vol. 21, f. 81 (remarques de Champigny). (TN: our translation.)

57 Delâge, "Les Iroquois chrétiens, II," 43. (TN: our translation.)

58 Ibid., 41–2.

59 This "contraband" for fiscal reasons was against the interests of the colony (ANF, Col., B, vol. 23.1, p. 134, Mémoirc pour scrvir d'instruction au Sicur Beauharnois intendant, 6 may 1702), but it benefited the Montreal merchants, who in exchange for the furs from the Great Lakes received English textile products at an excellent price, which they used in trade with the Amerindians of the west: "More furs therefore came down from the Great Lakes to Montreal; consequently, fewer had to go through Iroquoia" (Delâge, "Les Iroquois chrétiens, II," 43 [TN: our translation]; see also Richter, "Ordeal of the Longhouse," 433–4).

60 The expression "la grande alliance" is used by La Potherie, *Histoire,* 4:252.

61 Eccles, "Report," 44.

62 ANF, Col., F3, vol. 2, f. 267v. (TN: our translation.)

63 ANF, Col., C11A, vol. 22, f. 54, Parolles des Sonnontouans [...] 30 may 1704 (TN: our translation); Richter (*Ordeal of the Longhouse,* 218) also speaks of the death in 1704 of five Oneidas during a skirmish.

64 ANF, Col., C11E, vol. 14, f. 188, mémoire de m. de la mothe Cadillac tonchant l'établissement du Détroit [avec les remarques de Pontchartrain], Québec, 14 novembre 1704 (TN: our translation); Richter, *Ordeal of the Longhouse,* 219.

65 Richter, *Ordeal of the Longhouse,* 214–16, 223. The strategy of attracting the nations of the west to the Albany market did not always win unanimous support from the League in the short term. In 1702, for example, some Senecas barred the way to a group of Amerindians from Detroit who had gone to trade with the English (ANF, Col., C11A vol. 20, f. 65, Callière, Champigny et Beauharnois au ministre, Québec, 3 novembre 1702).

66 ANF, Col., C11A, vol. 28, f. 211, Parolles des folles avoines a mr le gouverneur general [...] 23 juillet 1708. (TN: our translation.)

67 ANF, Col., C11A, vol. 30, f. 86v, Reponse de mr de Vaudreuil aux sauvages outtaois [...] 29 juillet 1709. (TN: our translation.)

68 ANF, Col., C11A, vol. 31, f. 99–100, Parolles des Iroquois sonnontouans et onnontaguez a mr le marquis de Vaudreuil 8 aout 1710. (TN: our translation.)

69 Richter, *Ordeal of the Longhouse,* 237.

70 See also ANF, Col., C11A, vol. 21, f. 62v, Parolles des Sonnontouans et onontaguez a monsieur de Vaudreuil le 12 juin 1703.

71 Quoted by Lytwyn, "Historical Research Report," 44.

72 ANF, Col., C11A,. vol. 20, f. 100v, Callière au ministre, Québec, 4 novembre 1702 (on the Sauks-Foxes against the Ojibwas); Margry, *Découvertes,* 5:327, Lamothe Cadillac à Pontchartrain, 31 aoust 1703 (on war between the Ojibwas and the Sauks-Menominees); ANF, Col., C11A, vol. 30, f. 86, 89–92, Reponse de mr de Vaudreuil aux sauvages outtaois [...] 29 juillet 1709 (mediation of the Sauks between the Foxes and Ojibwas); ANF, Col., C11A, vol. 31, f. 26–7, Vaudreuil et Raudot au ministre, Québec, 2 novembre 1710 (the Ojibwas against the Potawatomis); Havard, "Empire et métissages," 466.

73 Zoltvany, *Vaudreuil,* 81–4; White, *The Middle Ground,* 82–90.

74 White, *The Middle Ground,* 150–75; C. Callender, "Fox," *HNAI,* 15:643; Havard, "Empire et métissages," 473–6; Edmunds and Peyser, *Fox Wars.*

75 See ANF, Col., C11A, vol. 2o, f. 100, 156, Callière au ministre, Québec, 4 novembre 1702.

76 The Aboriginal societies of Canada were "stateless" societies and inherently military in the sense that "the role of war in the reproduction of social relationships and the value system [was] predominant... [in them]" ("Guerre," in Bonte, Izard, *Dictionnaire de l'ethnologie,* 315 [TN: our translation]).

77 Charlevoix, *Journal,* 528–9, 475; Perrot, Mémoire, 147 (TN: our translation); Havard, "Empire et métissages," 152–6; Richter, *Ordeal of the Longhouse,* 224.

78 La Potherie, *Histoire,* 1:303; ANF, Col., C11A, vol. 22, f. 207, mémoire de Raudot. (TN: our translations.)

79 This did not perhaps have unanimous support among the Iroquois, but apart from the fact that it was objectively necessary for them, they could not really avoid it.

80 Quotation in Richter, *Ordeal of the Longhouse,* 237–9 (quotation on p. 237); Aquila, *Iroquois Restoration,* 205–32. Richter (*Ordeal of the Longhouse,* 237) quotes another document from 1707, written by an English interpreter: "Most of the [young men of the] five Nations were out against the Flatheads[...]they brought in a great many prisoners."

81 ANF, Col., C11A, vol. 21, f. 74, Parolles des sauvages hurons a monsieur de Vaudreuil le 14 juillet 1703. (TN: our translation.)

82 ANF, Col., F3, vol. 87, F. 271 (on the Quapaw); ANF, Col., C11A, vol. 21, f. 75v, reponse de mr de Vaudreuil aux sauvages hurons; Richter, *Ordeal of the Longhouse,* 237–8.

83 Haan, "The Problem of Iroquois Neutrality," 323–4; Richter, *Ordeal of the Longhouse,* 224–30.

84 ANF, Col., C11A, vol. 31, f. 90, Parolles des sauvages onontaguez a mr le marquis de Vaudreuil a Montreal, 28 janvier 1710 (TN: our translation); see also ANF, Col., C11A, vol. 21, f. 72–3, Parolles du chef nommé Teganissorens au nom des Cinq Nations a Montreal le 24 octobre 1703.

85 For the traditional interpretation, see Wallace, "Origins of Iroquois Neutrality," 223–35; E. Tooker, "The League of the Iroquois: Its History, Politics, and Rituals," HNAI, 15:432–4. For the revisionist perspective, see Haan, "The Problem of Iroquois Neutrality," 317–27; Richter, *Ordeal of the Longhouse,* 362 (first quotation), 215 (second quotation); Aquila, *Iroquois Restoration,* 68–9.

86 During the War of the Austrian Succession, except for the Mohawks, the League remained neutral. During the Seven Years' War (1756–63), which the English colonists called the "French and Indian War" (1754–60), the Iroquois were split between the two camps: the Mohawks sided with the English, while the Senecas remained pro-French. See Haan, "The Problem of Iroquois Neutrality"; Richter, *Ordeal of the Longhouse,* 225–30; Aquila, *Iroquois Restoration,* 85–128; Tooker, "The League of the Iroquois," 433–4.

Proclaiming Peace in 1713:
A Case Study

KENNETH J. BANKS

On the morning of May 22, 1713, a Monday, thousands of Parisians thronged the Place de la Grève with tears in their eyes and joyous cries in their throats. After eleven long and brutal years, the War of the Spanish Succession had finally ended. A rumour had spread speculating that Louis XIV would announce the signing of a peace treaty at the Dutch city of Utrecht. The informed elite of Paris—royal officials, well-connected financiers, and bourgeois subscribers to one of the foreign *Gazettes* from Holland or Switzerland—already knew that the treaty had been signed more than a month before, on April 11th.[1] The celebrations were not for them, but for the illiterate mass of poorer Parisians, a reward for years of suffering and sacrifice.

According to an official report, the festivities began with the arrival at the Hôtel de Ville of seven royal heralds accompanied by a small musical battalion, composed of thirty-seven trumpeters, drummers, and pipers, and several companies of soldiers to keep exuberant merry-makers in check.[2] The royal officers were greeted at precisely 10 a.m. by city officials dressed in their traditional long, red robes. The municipal officials ushered the royal officers inside, where they gracefully received the proclamation from the king into their hands. Afterwards, the two sets of officials dined together on fresh fish and oysters, drank wine (white and red), and toasted the peace with shouts of "Long live the

king!" The soldiers stayed outside, watching the celebrating crowds. At the end of the feast, civic officials and their heralds reassembled outside the Hôtel de Ville and marched in an order prescribed by tradition through the streets of Paris to announce the signing of the treaty to the people. The king's word passed ceremoniously from him through his intermediaries, to the city officials, and finally to his subjects. The procession stopped fourteen times; including at the Tuilleries, Grand Chastelet, Les Halles, the Pilory, Place Louis le Grand, Pont Neuf, before the equestrian statue of Henri IV, and before the equestrian statue of Louis XIII at Place Royale, all places of social exchange or before landmarks of august royal authority.[3] At each stop, the officials made the same speech and read the proclamation to crowds of presumably cheering Parisians, although the account does not record any response from the people. As the cool of evening descended in shades of ever-darkening purple, the poor of Paris—apprentices, labourers, shopkeepers' wives, servants with some time off—wandered through the streets, drinking and singing, stopping to gather before noble *hôtels,* where they scooped up coins flung from the balconies above. The celebrations continued for three days, culminating in the singing of the traditional Te Deum at Notre-Dame Cathedral. Later that night, fireworks split the sky as noble revellers gathered at the home of the Duc de Tresmes, where an orchestra, the famed Vingt-Quatre Violons du Roi, played for the guests.[4] Although we have no accounts of the celebrations for the crowd, they may have helped themselves to free wine and bread provided in the city's main squares, as was the case during other similar state-sponsored celebrations.[5]

Three months to the day after the ceremonies in Paris, officials on the French island of Martinique sponsored celebrations in the two principal towns of the island, Saint Pierre and Fort Royal.[6] The governor general, Raymond-Balthazar de Phélypeaux du Verger, a cousin of Secretary of State for the Marine Jérôme Phélypeaux, Comte de Pontchartrain, had received the proclamation of peace from the king at least a month earlier, as well as letters from Pontchartrain instructing him to hold the "customary rejoicings."[7] Like the Parisian officials, Phélypeaux prepared the celebrations well in advance. In Fort Royal, the only town for which a detailed account still exists, the members of the colony's Superior Council, acting on behalf of the island's colonists, acknowledged receipt of the proclamation at the governor general's residence. Afterwards they marched with colonial officials in a solemn public procession to the parish church, stopping to read the proclamation aloud to those gathered in the town's square. Immediately after a performance of the Te Deum, the dignitaries and townsfolk, swelled to nearly two thousand with planters who had come from all over, the island, gathered in the small town square to watch a fireworks display, managed by the king's soldiers, on the beach. The night ended with a round of parties thrown in the rented homes of planters, often a few rooms in boarding houses or above a tavern. Although aping Paris, the king's officials controlled the entire round of celebrations in the Îles du Vent.

The exact same proclamations and instructions for celebrations that were sent to Martinique were also drawn up at Versailles and sent to Louisiana and Canada on the very same day. But the intended celebrations never took place in either colony.[8] Louisiana, the most recent and most promising of the Sun King's colonial projects, received the news only in early 1714. Although Governor Antoine Laumet de Lamothe Cadillac ordered the soldiers of the garrison of Fort Louis (near present-day Mobile, Alabama) to sing the Te Deum in the fort's small chapel, he lamented that "it is scarcely an occasion to celebrate because of the many hardships, for nearly everything is lacking."[9] In fact, he and the other colonists were facing starvation.

In Canada, no official celebrations were held at all. When the first merchant vessels anchored before Quebec in late June, Governor General Philippe de Rigaud, Marquis de Vaudreuil, learned along with the rest of the town that a peace treaty had been signed in April.[10] He waited for the king's ship to bring the official proclamation, but the ship never arrived.[11] The representation of royal power and the display of aristocratic grace and generosity of the Paris celebrants, so easily replicated three months later in Martinique, failed to be reproduced in Canada and Louisiana. Why did they not take place, and does their absence tell us something about the relative strength of royal authority in each colony? Did the lapse occur as a result of a unique combination of trying circumstances, or were such gaps in the expedition of royal orders endemic in the French system of colonial communications? Only the continual crossing of ships carrying the king's word guaranteed the presence of royal authority in the colonies. Should the flow be interrupted, colonial leaders found themselves isolated. Following the path of a single piece of news allows us to chart the problems of how the French state projected royal authority at the start of a spectacular period of French economic growth and colonial development. It can also help us appreciate the human labour and material cost of circulating information in the eighteenth century.

The infrastructure and coordination required to send the king's word overseas could be extraordinarily complicated. The treaties signed in 1713–14 and collectively known as the Peace of Utrecht (the companion Treaty of Radstadt was signed in 1714) are ideal for a case study of news dissemination for several reasons. The French proclamation was a single document, which called for a response. Tracking its progress through the French bureaucracy and over the ocean to each colony is relatively easy. Both the state and colonial officials understood the importance of the news for a variety of reasons: privateers had to be called back, merchant ships reloaded, militias disbanded. The news also provided an opportunity to display the king's concern for his overseas subjects (by giving them peace), and it supplied an occasion for colonial elites to publicly display their closeness to the sovereign. Also, the treaties and the accompanying king's instructions travelled on both land and sea, allowing a comparison of the relative efficiency of communications between the land-based royal postal system and the use of king's ships on transatlantic routes. By identifying the opportunities as well as the limitations of a single piece of information, we can better judge the efficiency of transatlantic information within an emerging imperial, and authoritarian, system.

A New Order

Peace negotiations to end the War of the Spanish Succession lasted nearly as long as the war itself.[12] By 1704, France had already lost effective use of its Navy and was halted on land at the battle of Blenheim. Secret peace overtures began in 1705, but England and Holland did not respond with any serious counter-proposals until the fall of the Duke of Marlborough in 1711. The articles for a possible ceasefire between France and Great Britain were agreed to in April 1711, and preliminary negotiations opened in July of that year. General peace negotiations began in Utrecht the following March. These discussions led to a ceasefire in Flanders in June 1712 and a four-month general ceasefire in August. The principal combatants prolonged this ceasefire for another four months in November. The Treaty of Utrecht, therefore, was not signed with a sudden gasp of exhaustion by each side. Instead, nearly two years of proposal and counter-proposal preceded the signing of the treaty early on the morning of 12 April 1713.

Throughout the later stages of the war, Pontchartrain informed French colonial leaders of the progress of negotiations. In August 1712 he sent word to all American colonies that a peace treaty would be signed shortly and ordered an immediate halt to all raids and privateer operations.[13] He sent the same letter to the governor and *commissaire ordonnateur* in Saint Domingue via Martinique, since this colony remained under Martinique's jurisdiction until 1714. The orders reached Martinique by a merchant vessel that arrived in early December 1712. Accompanying this letter of peace was another containing instructions to celebrate France's latest victories in Flanders.[14] At least two months prior to the letter from France, however, Phélypeaux had already received word from his counterpart in Barbados that a treaty would probably be signed within months. Between them, they agreed to extend the ceasefire then in effect in the Caribbean for six weeks longer than the date set in Europe, an example of how colonial leaders set their own agendas "beyond the line." In Canada, Pontchartrain's letter reached wily Governor General Vaudreuil overland via Boston, probably carried through the winter forests by Abenaki warriors or hunters.[15] Vaudreuil withdrew his forces slowly in order to wreak as much damage as possible on New England's outlying settlements, violating the spirit, if not the directives, of Pontchartrain's letter.

As for the newly commissioned governor of Louisiana, Cadillac spent the fall and winter of 1712–13 overseeing the loading of cargoes in several French Ponant ports. While in port, he wrote Pontchartrain several times, outlining his future plans for the colony.[16] Although his ship, *Le Baron de la Fauche,* was only the fourth to sail for the colony in nine years, a new commercial monopoly seemed to promise invigorated efforts at developing Louisiana through regular trade and contact.[17] Cadillac clearly understood that the court would reach a peace with Great Britain. By the end of March 1713, all three colonial leaders were therefore well aware of the definitive move toward a treaty. When the announcement of the treaty's signing arrived in their colonies later in the year, it did not have any value as news; the letters, if they received them, merely confirmed what most colonists already knew. Within the broad framework of an impending peace, colonial officers made their decisions by sifting through a variety of news sources and acted according to intuition and local circumstances. Pontchartrain's letters contained legitimating, rather than urgent, information. All news has a variety of uses, and official pronouncements may not be the most critical.

Immediately upon the signing of the treaty at Utrecht, clerks for the negotiators set to work to copy the document and brief reports; messengers awaited to take them. The news reached the king at Versailles on the evening of the 14th, brought by the Marquis de Torcy's own messenger.[18] De Torcy, the chief French negotiator, found the event so anticlimactic that he did not preside over the final signing of the treaty and passed over any description of the occasion in his memoirs.[19] Within days of receiving word, Pontchartrain's own secretaries began to copy out the proclamation and letters that notified colonial leaders of the substantial rearrangement of France's American colonies.

Clerks and Correspondence

As in all other aspects of *ancien régime* political life, the form of the peace proclamation reflected the king's role as sole lawgiver and final judge of his subjects, for all announcements were essentially pronouncements of law. A bewildering hierarchy of letters existed for official documents during the *ancien régime,* and the nuances of each still elude current scholarship. However, some basic characteristics are understood.[20] The vast majority of orders and judgments were issued in two ways: through general and specific sealed letters (*grandes* and *petites lettres patentes*)[21] issued by the King's Chancellery, which included ordinances and edicts applicable to the entire kingdom, or more commonly, through direct royal orders, called *lettres closes.*[22] The colonial proclamations of peace issued to the governors and intendants on May 22, 1713, follow the format of the *lettre close.*[23] Only a few of these were actually written and sealed in the king's presence. The vast majority were countersigned by one of the king's secretaries of state, and were used mainly for urgent notices, passports, ordering of payments, or circular letters concerning routine administrative practices. Secretaries specially skilled in copying the king's signature signed them, and secretaries of state such as Pontchartrain kept several hundred blank letters in their offices for use within their departments. In all probability, royal clerks drafted the proclamation according to a traditional format and presented it to Louis XIV for his approval. A second set of royal letters, destined for the governors and intendants of Canada, Louisiana, and Martinique, accompanied the proclamations. These were written nine days later, on May 31, 1713, and again the king likely did not see them, though they were issued in his name. Since these were addressed to specific persons and struck a more personal tone, they resembled the form of a *lettre de cachet*.[24] In each, Louis XIV notified the recipient that, after he had asked "our Lord for the grace to halt a war so long, so terrible, and so bloody," God had allowed the other princes to re-establish "a perfect understanding" with him. So that no mistake might be made, the document listed the nations signing the treaty and ended with orders for the official addressed to publicly attend the singing of the Te Deum of thanksgiving in the principal church of each colony, along with the "customary rejoicings."[25] Letters to the governors contained additional instructions to proclaim the peace to all French subjects and to halt all hostile actions.

Pontchartrain prefaced each of these letters with yet a third letter. He emphasized the importance of proclaiming peace promptly and asked the governors to ensure that the proclamation be made the day before the celebrations. He also wanted to know "in which manner the common people of your jurisdiction have received this agreeable announcement." Letters to the intendants included orders to make powder (for fireworks) and "other supplies" available for the necessary celebrations.[26] The most striking aspect of these letters is the concern with public presentation. A proclamation of peace did not merely inform the colonists of a cessation of war; it was a staged event, similar in function and even style to contemporary press conferences or photo opportunities. It is not clear if Pontchartrain stipulated the timing of celebrations because traditional practices in France were not followed in the colonies, or because he was concerned that governors, such as Vaudreuil in Canada, might drag out hostilities for their own purposes. But it is clear that the state had a keen interest in orchestrating the reaction of its overseas populations.

The task of actually composing and writing each of the proclamations and accompanying instructions fell to the clerks of the newly created Bureau of Colonies, established by Jérôme de Pontchartrain on January 1, 1710.[27] For reasons that remain unclear, but probably were a response to war, the younger Pontchartrain drastically remodelled the Marine bureaucracy inherited from his father. Gone was the old and cumbersome division between Ponant and Levant; instead, he created individual bureaus organized by function and appointed knowledgeable staffs of clerks to run them. Like many early modern institutions, it had one foot in the past and one in the future. For example, while all the colonies came under one agency, certain aspects, especially import tariffs and direction of state-supported companies, still remained in the hands of the controller general of France, and the French Council of Commerce (one of the king's councils) acted as a kind of pressure group for French ports involved in overseas commerce.[28]

Pontchartrain placed the bureau in the hands of a career administrator with the understated title of chief clerk (*premier commis*). During the eighteenth century, these *premier commis* and the common clerks who worked under them emerged as powerful men with extensive connections at court, specialized knowledge of maritime issues, and financial interests in the colonies, although the extent of these last remains poorly known.[29] The court valued their expertise because they could act as advisers and because of the administrative continuity they provided during periods when the secretaries of state were increasingly enmeshed in court intrigues. Although the first *premier commis* for the Colonies, Moïse-Augustin Fontanieu, had occupied his post only since November of 1710, he had long been a client of Pontchartrain's, having served as treasurer for the Marine since 1701.[30] He retained at least these two posts until his death in 1725.[31] Fontanieu's extensive knowledge of naval affairs, the more important merchants, and Parisian financiers allowed Pontchartrain to delegate lesser chores to him, such as the appointment of minor officials and the arrangement of the details for financing at least some of the voyages of the king's ships.[32] How many ordinary *commis* staffed the bureau at this early stage of its development is unknown. However, it was undoubtedly lower than the approximately five main clerks in each of the Marine's offices (including the Bureau of the Colonies) by the mid-eighteenth century.[33] Members of this small group occupied an extremely crucial position in colonial affairs, since they dictated what information and projects the secretary of state and the king would see and how these would be presented, and relayed back to colonial officials how the ideas were received.

The year 1713 appears to have been only slightly busier than others in Louis XIV's later reign for the Bureau of Colonies. In this year its clerks wrote out a total of 760 letters on 606 legal-size folios (1,212 pages) to the colonies and to French ports, principally the king's naval arsenal at Rochefort. However, this number represents only those letters actually copied into the bureau's register. The original letters were written twice and sent as duplicates to ensure that at least one arrived at its destination. Urgent news was sent as many as four times, all by different routes.[34] If it is conservatively estimated that each letter to Rochefort was written out twice (one to be kept, one to be sent) and those for the colonies three times, then the Bureau of Colonies produced a minimum of about 3,170 handwritten pages of recorded correspondence in 1713 (see table 1). The number is probably much higher for two reasons, First, a quick comparison of the bureau's letter register with the one kept at Rochefort reveals that Intendant François Beauharnais in fact received 568 letters from Pontchartrain over the course of the year, not the 280 recorded in the bureau's register. While many of these dealt with issues such as ordinances on coastal fishing and the impressment of sailors which were not under the jurisdiction of the Bureau of Colonies, these letters often included one or two paragraphs discussing the outfitting of colonial-bound ships.[35] Second, the recorded letters also refer to private letters not bound in the register, and many of these were copied and sent by Pontchartrain's clerks as well. The total volume of correspondence from this one bureau could conceivably mount to between six and seven thousand pages. The writing style of the recorded letters indicates that at least two clerks scribbled on colonial matters, one with a very refined hand, the other with a rougher script, perhaps a junior clerk. Even if a third clerk existed, these numbers indicate that each clerk copied out just over one thousand pages, and possibly double that amount, over the course of the year.

The volume for each destination indicates the priorities placed on maintaining overseas contact. The letters to Rochefort and other French points concerned with outfitting the king's ships collectively accounted for the largest share of the correspondence, comprising 225 (37.1 per cent) of the 606 folio pages and 440 (57.9 per cent) of the 760 letters. Of the French-bound letters, two-thirds were destined for Intendant Beauharnais at Rochefort. These letters were short and contained specific instructions for outfitting and cargo purchases or, less often, were concerned with buildings and personnel problems in Rochefort. Most of the other letters were sent to various nobles, clerics, and financiers in and around Paris. The efforts to coordinate money, people, and cargoes proved to be a very complicated undertaking and required constant attention to resolve an interminable number of problems: freight rates, objections by merchants, passage for clerics, poor cordage or tar, clarifications about fund allocations. The size of this correspondence points to two contradictory trends: the relative ease of contact with Rochefort allowed Pontchartrain, in contemporary parlance, to micromanage certain operations; but at the same time, the marshalling of money and goods to repair, man, and supply the king's ships on a schedule, even during peace, proved in many respects more complicated than attempts to direct colonial life.

Letters to French colonial officials were longer and mixed specific requests or orders with more general guidelines or observations. Of the 321 letters written, Canada led with 126 (16.6 per cent), compared to 81 for Martinique (10.7 per cent), 73 for Saint Domingue (9.6 per cent), 21 for Cayenne, and only 15 for Louisiana. The number of folio pages, however, demonstrates a more even distribution: 122 folios (20.1 per cent) were sent to Martinique compared to 118 folio pages (19.5 per cent) to Canada. While the discrepancy between the numbers of letters and folios may simply reflect a difference of form rather than substance, it also appears that Pontchartrain addressed a larger number of different correspondents in Canada. This volume of correspondence far outstrips England's contact with its colonies. As Ian K. Steele has shown, an estimated 3,720 letters were written by both American colonial governors and the Lords of Trade between 1675 and 1737, an average of just 52 per year.[36] The Bureau of Colonies clearly kept a more wary eye on colonial affairs than did its English counterpart.

The rhythm of correspondence indicates how closely metropolitan communication followed colonial needs. The imminent departure of a ship threw the Bureau of Colonies into a frenzy of letter-writing. Of the 126 destined for Canada, nearly two-thirds of the total (78) were written in the two weeks prior to the anticipated departure of its ship in late June. Since communications with the French Antilles could be maintained year-round, clerks could space copying out accordingly: 40 per cent (34 letters) were written in the two weeks prior to an April departure, and just 14 per cent (11 letters) before a September departure. These optimum departure times were in turn dictated by colonial seasons, a reminder that

TABLE 1 | VOLUME OF CORRESPONDENCE OF THE BUREAU OF COLONIES, 1713

Destination	No. of Folios	Percent	No. of Letters	Percent
Îles français de l'Amérique*	225	37.1	440	57.9
New France (Canada)	118	19.5	126	16.6
Louisiana	10	1.7	15	2.0
St. Domingue	114	18.8	73	9.6
Martinique and the Îles du Vent	122	20.1	81	10.7
Cayenne	10	1.7	21	2.8
Indes Orientales	7	1.2	4	0.5
Total	606	100.0	760	100.0

*Correspondence pertaining to the Marine's shipping to colonial ports.

Source: AC, B, vol. 35, [1713]. In addition, a single letter was written to the "Indes d'Espagne" (presumably the Spanish Main), but not included in the microfilmed set analyzed at the National Archives of Canada in Ottawa.

royal bureaucracies adjusted to nature, and not the reverse.

This brief outline of the correspondence of the Bureau of Colonies in 1713 underscores the efficiency with which a small office managed colonial affairs for France. Only a few people were required to handle a broad range of concerns; whenever problems arose, they could be dispatched surprisingly quickly. More importantly, the coordination of shipping, not the management of the colonies, consumed the largest single amount of time, energy, capital, and paper. This is the first indication of a dilemma for the strict management of an overseas imperial domain: the volume of correspondence within France was high because outfitting royal ships was a collective endeavour that drew upon a diverse range of people and resources: merchants from La Rochelle, Bordeaux, Saint Malo, and other ports; Rochefort's own intendant and port officials; a wide number of naval officers; Parisian financiers; and religious authorities from dioceses across France. The bureau's correspondence system, which coordinated and arbitrated between different groups within the kingdom to ensure orderly contact with the colonies, thus served as a microcosm for the coordination and arbitration functions of the king for the kingdom.

Messengers and Mail

Once written in the bureau's rooms at Marly, where Louis XIV spent the spring of 1713, the letters were either entrusted to confidants and special messengers or carried by regular post.[37] Historians often envision land travel as a slow and arduous process at the mercy of the seasons, serving only as a supplement to river transport until the "great restructuring of roads" inaugurated in the mid-nineteenth century.[38] It is true that in the spring of 1713, heavy rains had turned all roads leading from Paris and Versailles into ribbons of mud. However, the condition of roads did not appear to hinder messengers or France's well organized (and highly profitable) postal system. Correspondence between the Bureau of Colonies and Rochefort suggests that, as frightful as roads undoubtedly were by current standards in the West, the king's correspondence galloped with impressive regularity across *ancien régime* France. Exactly how the proclamations travelled from Marly to Rochefort remains a mystery. We do know that the bureau had three potential methods of sending mail. The first relied on personal contacts between Pontchartrain and colonial officials to carry dispatches. For example, when the king's lieutenant on Guadeloupe, Louis-Gaston de Cacqueray de Valminière, was about to leave Paris in January of 1713, he informed Pontchartrain of his imminent return to the colony and asked several favours. Pontchartrain thanked him for his courtesy, promised to make solicitations on Valminière's behalf, and forwarded several dispatches to him to carry on to Rochefort, where he was to take ship for Martinique.[39] Information exchange could thus be closely bound with clientage.

The other two options for carrying correspondence relied on less personal connections: the French postal system and the extensive network of king's roads. Under Louis XIV's secretary of state for War, François Le Tellier, Marquis de Louvois, the postal system had been expanded to help coordinate the movements and supplies of increasingly larger and larger French armies. Louvois reorganized the old postal system in 1691, and by 1713 it had emerged as a highly profitable venture. According to Eugène Vaillé, the postal service operated as a semi-autonomous department within the royal bureaucracy, employing its own inspectors and messengers and settling disputes in its own court system, an arrangement not unusual for *ancien régime* monopolies and institutions. Rates for mail carriage based on travel to and from Paris were published annually from 1708. Some twenty-two great roads, or *grands chemins,* radiated from Paris to connect the whole country, and along both these and the secondary roads, postmasters spaced about five kilometres apart provided the necessary change of horses for carriers and messengers.[40] This system, with slight modifications, remained intact until the Revolution.

In 1713 the *Almanach royal* listed daily connections for mail to each of the royal palaces and two departures per week from Paris to La Rochelle and Rochefort. Messengers also arrived in Paris twice a week from Bordeaux and most parts of Guyenne. We know, as well, that the distance between Paris and La Rochelle was ten days by carriage in 1765, when improvement of the great roads had begun. Messengers travelled an average of about forty-seven kilometres per day, an impressive distance for eighteenth-century land travel.[41] Two types of letter carriers used these roads: the *chevaucheurs de l'écurie du roi* (literally, "riders from the king's stables") and the routine couriers employed by the postal service. The king's messengers (a non-venal post reserved for nobles) formed an elite corps of just eleven men, and each minister of state claimed at least one. In 1713 Sauveur Jussau served as Pontchartrain's messenger.[42] However, Pontchartrain dispatched a special courier only twice (in February and again in July), both times at critical periods prior to ship departures. The first was too early for the proclamation to be sent, and the second too late.[43] It appears that these important proclamations were sent via ordinary post.

Knowing that the letters were carried by the postal service does not tell us how frequently or easily correspondence flowed between Versailles/Marly and Rochefort. We know from René Mémain's work that, in the year 1680, couriers lugged mail three times per week between Paris and Rochefort in each direction, taking four to six days to complete the journey each way; express messengers accomplished the trip in two to three days.[44] However, knowing the frequency and length of time of postal trips does not tell us how quickly mail was actually answered; it only indicates how fast a letter could theoretically reach its intended recipient, if written and posted on the same day, if read on the day it arrived, and if acted upon on the same day.

The Marine's correspondence between Pontchartrain's clerks and Beauharnais's clerks at Rochefort indicates that this theoretical rate of exchange rarely occurred. Letters might be held up in a postal bureau, stopped at an inn until roads became passable, or simply sit upon arrival for days—or in a few cases, weeks—before the recipient returned from a voyage or simply found time to read them. The problem is important, for by assuming that eighteenth-century correspondents could and always did act immediately within the potential speed of news distorts the actual pace of human interactions. A more accurate method is to track what is termed here the "response time" of a given piece of correspondence. In official correspondence, and in most private correspondence, often the first item mentioned is the date when the preceding communication was penned to the recipient. "Response time," refers to the time between the writing of the initial letter and the action of responding to it by the recipient. While the empirical base is small in this case, this method has the advantage of being precise, is applicable to any exchange in which dates of correspondence are known, and most important of all, demonstrates the wide variability possible for acting on discrete pieces of information. Tracking the flow of letters over the course of a year also indicates periods of seasonal disruptions or intense shipping activity.

The results suggest a smoothly run communications system, despite the bankruptcy of the treasury and the poverty of France at the end of a long war (see table 2). Beauharnais's clerks in Rochefort consistently acted on orders within

TABLE 2 | RESPONSE TIME BETWEEN THE COURT AND
ROCHEFORT, 1713

Month	Court to Rochefort			Rochefort to court		
	No.	Var. (days)	Ave. time	No.	Var. (days)	Ave. time
Jan.	3	11–20	15	5	10–27	15
Feb.	4	8–14	11½	5	7–38	15
March	4	8–24	12½	4	8–12	10
April	8	5–14	10	6	5–17	10½
May	4	10–13	12	4	8–15	11
June	4	8–24	11½	5	4–25	12½
July	3	8–23	13½	4	3–13	6
Aug.	4	4–35	18	5	10–15	13½
Sept.	1	8	8	3	10–16	15½
Oct.	1	31	31	4	8–27	14½
Nov.	4	9–62	26	—	—	—
Dec.	1	12	12	3	9–15	12

Key: No. = number of dated letters; var. = variation between slowest and fastest response time in days; ave. time = average response time, rounded to nearest half-day.

Sources: Rochefort IE, vols. 81–3, Dispatches from the court to the intendants; ibid., vols. 342–3, Letters from the intendants to the court; and AC, B, vol. 35, [1713].

two weeks after the Bureau of Colonies sent them. On the two known occasions that Pontchartrain sent his own courier, the response time was cut to a mere four days. In the opposite direction, the bureau could rely on receiving reports from Rochefort within two weeks. More importantly, while great variations in individual response times exist, ranging from between three and sixty-two days, the average response times for each month, and in both directions, are strikingly consistent. These conclusions suggest that some issues received priority, while others could be placed aside for periods of slower activity. Less obviously, the figures provide a measuring stick by contemporaries for acceptable communications: the Bureau of Colonies and the intendant at Rochefort could be assured that most issues would be handled between one to two weeks; any time beyond that suggested a problem, or that the recipient had become sloppy or preoccupied, and called for a prompt. The very consistency of contact is noteworthy. Road conditions apparently had little, if any, influence on the flow of official correspondence, although the wet months of early fall and winter tended to increase time. This impression is reinforced by the fact that, although Pontchartrain often stated his impatience for news, none of the letters examined ever mentioned poor road conditions or confusion in the posts as problems. The Bureau of Colonies–Rochefort contact is consistent with other examples. For example, William Beik showed that the response time between Jean-Baptiste Colbert and the intendant of Languedoc in 1675 took between two and three weeks.[45] From the Bureau of Colonies to the Ponant, the state demonstrated an assured grip on internal communications, despite the bleak year of 1713.

Rochefort and the French Atlantic

The real complications in information exchange began after the dispatches reached the king's naval arsenal at Rochefort. Fifty years before, this slumbering town had occupied a patch of muddy terrain between the Charente River and a wide expanse of wild and dreary marshland. In 1666 Colbert selected the site for a new base.[46] It lay only twenty-five kilometres from the spacious and sheltered stretch of the coast known as the Basque Roads, where warships by the dozens might drop anchor safe from attack and secure from storms. The bustling commercial port of La Rochelle lay only thirty kilometres away to the northwest; upriver to the east was the city of Angoulême, famous for its iron and cannon foundries. Construction of Rochefort's dry docks, rope works, king's storehouses, and officials' homes began in 1669. The town had grown to the respectable size of 15,000 by 1713, yet Marine officials in Versailles fretted that Rochefort would never fulfill its vital role. Groundwater rotted walls, river mud clogged dry docks, and fevers from the swamps surrounding the town earned it the title of the "graveyard of the Navy" among officers and sailors alike.[47] Rochefort's buildings always appeared to be dilapidated, and the periodic cramming of tons upon tons of ships' supplies into the already crowded warehouses gave rise to storage congestion and easy theft. In the mid-eighteenth century, one intendant characterized Rochefort as little more than a chaotic farmyard."[48]

There is no reason to believe this description was any less applicable in 1713. Maintenance of royal buildings and docks had ceased since 1704 because of a lack of money, and fire destroyed part of the town in 1706. The Marine's credit had sunk so low that merchants began refusing its bills, and port labourers balked at loading ships when their pay was slow in coming. In addition, a series of poor harvests had struck the region during the war and diminished food supplies.[49] It was against these harsh conditions that the officials and labourers of the port struggled to outfit royal ships for the colonies in 1713.

The end of war brought increased demands to resupply the colonies. Canada, Louisiana, Cayenne, Saint Domingue, and Martinique (along with its dependent islands) were all to be sent new troop detachments, uniforms, muskets, shot, and thousands of barrels of flour in case the ceasefire broke down. A new crop of colonial officials sprang up to replace those worn down by the war, and they began arriving in Rochefort to await the ships that would carry them to their new assignments. Contracts had to be negotiated with merchants in La Rochelle, Bordeaux, and other ports for return cargoes of colonial sugar, cocoa, and furs to help defray the cost of voyages. When it became clear by February that a treaty would be signed, other pressing matters arose. The bureau knew that the British would probably receive title to Saint Christophe in the Caribbean and to Acadia and Terre-Neuve in North America. The governor general of the Îles-du-Vent, Phélypeaux, would need time to arrange the transfer of the French settlers from Saint Christophe to a new home, as well as call back Martinique's highly successful privateers.[50] Terre-Neuve's situation caused great anxiety in the bureau because the French post of Plaisance (Placentia), which provided some protection to the invaluable cod fisheries of the Grand Banks, would have to be abandoned. The small community and its tiny garrison would have to be evacuated to a new port somewhere on Cape Breton Island (now renamed Île Royale), all at the king's expense. As 1713 progressed, the search for a new and strategically situated port, and the ship to carry the refugees, supplies, and soldiers to build it, increasingly taxed Pontchartrain's time and patience.

Readying the ships for the colonies followed a routine arrived at by trial and error over the previous forty years. Colonial seasons dictated the ideal departure dates, and these in turn determined the pace of careening, refitting, victualling, manning, and loading. Ships left for Martinique and Saint Domingue twice yearly, once in mid- or late March and again in early to mid-September. The March departures allowed them time to cross the Atlantic, unload supplies and load a new crop of colonial sugar and then depart the Antilles before the *mauvais temps* (hurricane season) began in mid-July. The September departures allowed ships to arrive in the Antilles shortly after the hurricane season ended by mid-October.[51] Sailing to Louisiana imposed a similar regimen, since the same violent storms that struck Martinique also lashed the northern Gulf coast.[52] Canadian-bound ships followed a very different schedule. By 1713, officials strove to ready ships for departure by late May in order to allow plenty of time to cross the Atlantic, unload supplies and load furs, and depart before ice formed on the St Lawrence River and the sharp northeast gales slashed sailors and sails by late October.[53] However, the Marine usually found it impossible to ready a ship for the Canada run so early. These departure dates served more as theoretical statements of ideal goals than as rigid guidelines. Imperial designs and colonial shipping demands seldom complemented each other in reality.

Outfitting the News

By December 1712 the colonial intendants had sent Pontchartrain reports listing the supplies needed for each colony, along with cost estimates. In addition, Intendant Beauharnais at Rochefort provided appraisals of the seaworthiness and cost of repairing each ship, along with his recommendations for that year's itinerary. On January 20, 1713, Pontchartrain wrote to Beauharnais with his assignments. He switched *L'Héros*, which had supplied Quebec the year previously, to the Martinique run and designated *L'Afriquain* to sail for both Quebec and Plaisance. But the secretary of state allowed only the paltry sum of 35,000 livres for careening, repairing, and outfitting both ships, with *L'Héros* to receive the major part of the money and priority in outfitting. Beauharnais also received orders to draw up contracts with Rochellais merchants to provide ships' supplies. Finally, Pontchartrain notified Beauharnais that the Louisiana-bound *Le Baron de la Fauche* had left its home port of Saint Malo and was slowly fighting through winter storms off Brittany's Cape Finisterre to reach La Rochelle. There it would load its main cargo of uniforms, muskets, and Native trade goods.[54]

Problems over cargoes, repairs, and ship assignments arose immediately. A messy lawsuit had developed over *L'Héros*'s previous shipment, and the creditors had sent a complaint to the king, effectively placing the ship's destination temporarily in doubt.[55] Worse, poor weather had slowed the ship's careening. Pontchartrain nevertheless pressed Beauharnais to finish the work quickly, for he wished to send Governor-General Phélypeaux of Martinique the news of the extension of a ceasefire with Portugal.[56] News that port officials at La Rochelle had detained the ship for Louisiana to unload several tons of the new *commissaire-ordonnateur* Jean-Baptiste Duclos's private freight allotment, apparently including several kinds of trade items, forced Beauharnais to visit the town and investigate.[57] The imminent signing of the peace treaty sent Pontchartrain scrambling to find a new port to replace Plaisance sooner than expected. Instead of the original single ship for Canada, he decided to send two, one to supply Canada and another, *Le Samslack,* to evacuate Plaisance and transport its inhabitants and a contingent of workers to a yet to be determined harbour on Île Royale. In conjunction with this project, he also ordered Beauharnais to contact key Rochellais merchants for their ideas on the best site for a new port.[58] On the basis of these discussions, Beauharnais wrote back and recommended Baie des Espagnols, but noted that several other harbours, including Baie des Anglais (more commonly referred to as "Havre des Anglais") the future site of Louisbourg, would be suitable alternatives. By late February, Pontchartrain began urging Beauharnais to speed up repairs to *Le Samslack,* using what soon became a familiar refrain: "Time is extremely pressing!"[59]

A bleak winter turned into a more promising spring. Although Beauharnais had not told Pontchartrain of *L'Héros's* progress, by early April the latter guessed that it was ready to hoist sail. On April 9 Pontchartrain sent all the Antilles dispatches to Rochefort by his own courier. Beauharnais's confirmation that workers had completed *L'Héros's* outfit crossed in the mail. Rough seas and stiff contrary winds kept the ship in port another week, but it finally sailed from the Basque Roads on April 17, a month later than the anticipated departure date.[60] However, Pontchartrain only wrote of the treaty's signing to Beauharnais on April 22, and the proclamations destined for the colonies were not penned until May 22.[61] Even though Pontchartrain's guess for the departure of *L'Héros* had been accurate, his latest dispatches

were dated April 6th.[62] The peace proclamations and Pontchartrain's orders regarding Saint Christophe would have to travel on a merchant ship, since the next royal vessel would sail only in September.

How then did the announcements arrive in the Îles du Vent? There is some evidence that they were rerouted back through France to be placed on board another merchant vessel. Pontchartrain sent a letter of introduction to Governor-General Phélypeaux for one Sieur de La Mothe (not related to Lamothe Cadillac). Phélypeaux responded on August 12, announcing that La Mothe had indeed arrived, as had several letters, including the peace treaty.[63] At about the same date, Intendant Vaucresson reported that several of Pontchartrain's winter dispatches had reached Martinique on July 14 by a merchant vessel from Le Havre. It is quite possible that La Mothe carried the dispatches. Another set of dispatches, including instructions on the transfer of Saint Christophe and new regulations on Anglo-French trade, were carried by the captain of a Marseille merchant vessel that dropped anchor at Saint Pierre in early September.[64] Clearly, the Marine depended on merchant vessels leaving from ports throughout France to carry official mail, especially to a colony as readily accessible as Martinique. While it is not clear whether the Marine paid for the service or whether merchants, as dutiful subjects, were expected to provide it at no charge, this example underscores the interpenetration of royal and mercantile interests in maintaining colonial contact. However, though the state needed merchant ships in times of peace, merchants did not need those of the state.

Throughout February and early March, the Louisiana-bound *Le Baron de la Fauche* remained tied up in La Rochelle, where presumably Duclos fumed over the removal of his goods. The ship finally made a last call back north at Brest; it then began its Atlantic crossing on March 18, bound first for Le Cap Français on Saint Domingue. Like *L'Héros*, this ship left too early to take the proclamations. However, Crozat already had another ship, *La Louisiane,* scheduled to leave Port Louis in June. The records on this second ship have thus far proved elusive, but it was the only vessel scheduled to call at Louisiana that left late enough to carry the proclamations. Either it or another merchant vessel may have halted at Le Cap and transferred the dispatches to a smaller vessel.[65] Despite the new Cadillac-Crozat company, regular and consistent contact with Louisiana was already beginning to prove just as difficult as under royal auspices.

Meanwhile, the preparations for the Canadian-bound ships continued. Difficulties in rounding up reluctant sailors and contrary winds hampered the ship destined for Île Royale, *Le Samslack*. It finally sailed for Plaisance in mid-June, two and a half months behind schedule.[66] Pontchartrain would not know of its fate, nor of Île Royale's, until late October, when a fishing boat brought news of the successful removal of the settlement.[67] As for Quebec's ship, *L'Afriquain,* financial problems dogged its preparations from the start. The refit of *L'Héros* had been somewhat cheaper than expected (perhaps because it was not completed), and Pontchartrain directed Beauharnais to use the remaining 10,000 livres for *L'Afriquain*'s outfitting. But the intendant reported that the money could only cover the ship's repairs and not the cost of supplies. Pontchartrain briefly considered changing *Le Samslack*'s itinerary so that it would anchor at Quebec first in order to embark a detachment of *troupes de la Marine* for the new post. But he changed his mind two days later and ordered Beauharnais to round up private cargoes to underwrite *L'Afriquain*'s cost. They exchanged a flurry of letters on contract options, but the ship's designated captain complained of the "exorbitant" demands of La Rochelle's merchants. Pontchartrain again ordered Beauharnais to use the leftover *L'Héros* funds. In late April, Beauharnais repeated that the funds were insufficient. For the next two weeks Pontchartrain sought in vain to interest other parties in *L'Afriquain,* including return cargoes for the monopoly Compagnie du Castor. Meanwhile, he still pressed the intendant to ready the ship for departure by mid-June.[68] During this period, Pontchartrain wrote letters to Canadian officials, to be sent on private ships, informing them of events at Utrecht and indicating that the year's supplies and dispatches would arrive on *L'Afriquain*.[69] However, on the last day of May, Beauharnais received word from Pontchartrain that the king had cancelled plans to send a ship to Canada for that year. Although he did not provide the king's reasons, clearly the Marine's credit had run too low to finance a separate voyage; Pontchartrain, we may assume, actually cancelled the voyage. Instead, he ordered Beauharnais to contract with two solid Rochelais merchants long familiar with the Canada trade, Fleury and Pagés, to take most of the supplies and the dispatches.[70]

Unknown to the secretary of state, Beauharnais had taken the initiative and had already negotiated a contract on June 2nd with a Rochelais merchant named Faures de la Grivolière, owner of *Le Prince*. The terms of the deal were better than the usual ones offered by Fleury and Pagés, Beauharnais explained, and the ship awaited only the royal cargo to sail. Pontchartrain quickly approved this *fait accompli*.[71] In late June and early July, he forwarded the dispatches for Canada to Rochefort. Included were copies of the peace treaty itself, so that the colony's officials could study the clauses on the cession of Acadia to Great Britain; *Le Prince* finally departed La Rochelle in mid-July, a full six weeks behind its original sailing date.[72] By mid-July all the three sets of proclamations were on ships headed across the Atlantic for the Caribbean and North America.

Mixed Results

The first batch, as we have seen, reached Martinique sometime between mid-July and the first days of August, in the middle of the hurricane season. Governor General Phélypeaux immediately set to work to ensure that the celebrations were as carefully orchestrated as those held in Paris.[73] He appointed the date for festivities to coincide with the feast of Saint Louis on August 25th, one of the most important feast days in France. Copies of the proclamation were sent ahead of time to Guadeloupe and Grenada, so that all three governors would announce the celebrations at the same time for the same day. The one-day gap between the announcement and the commencement of festivities remains puzzling; it is the only order to do so in colonial dispatches until at least 1763. Officials in both France and the colonies had ample time to prepare festivities. One might speculate that by announcing the treaty and the orchestrated celebrations at the same time, Pontchartrain hoped to dissuade rowdy colonists from launching their own impromptu gatherings.

On the morning of August 25th, the main festivities began at the capital of Fort Royal and in the main port of Saint Pierre. The members of the Superior Council assembled at their usual meeting place at four o'clock in the afternoon and then marched to the governor's residence, located inside the fort itself. There Governor General Phélypeaux first formally read them the proclamation, after which the king's prosecutor agreed to abide by the terms on behalf of the council members and the colonists. The councillors reassembled outside the fort and then marched in procession to the Capuchin church of Saint Louis to the sound of seven cannon salvos. There the governor general and Intendant Vaucresson joined them, and together with nobles drawn from across the islands, they sang the Te Deum of thanksgiving as ordered. After services, a final procession marched the short distance to the central

place d'armes. At eight o'clock in the evening, the governor general, intendant, and Capuchin superior together ignited the traditional bonfire, while the fort's garrison and the local militia unit fired several musket volleys into the air. As the smoke lingered on the darkened beach, guns from some forty merchant vessels anchored in Fort Royal Bay answered with their own salutes. Because the celebrations were held during hurricane season, Fort Royal's harbour was unusually crowded, although no king's vessel lay at anchor: *L'Héros* had already departed for Saint Domingue. A fireworks display followed, fired from a "structure" (a triumphal arch?) adorned on four sides with symbols and inscriptions in Latin attesting to the new amity between the kings of France and Great Britain and the return of wealth and prosperity to the king's loyal subjects. A figure representing Public Order stamping out Discord decorated the top of the structure. Although no lavish official dinners were reported, Phélypeaux and Vaucresson both related that celebrations had ended by two o'clock in the morning. Similar celebrations took place on the same day in Saint Pierre. Phélypeaux reported back to Pontchartrain that he was pleased with the display of fidelity and honour shown the king, although he noted with his usual candour that "people here have displayed their great joy for the increase in the selling price of their sugar, cocoa, and indigo, and the decrease in the price of food; they have no other concerns save these."[74]

In a later letter, Phélypeaux reported his displeasure over only one thing. He had not received a copy of the treaty itself, as had his counterpart on Antigua, Lieutenant-Governor Matthew Douglas. Not only had Douglas obtained the treaty in early July, but he received copies in both English and Latin. Most important of all, he had also received a copy of the commercial treaty, which appeared to proclaim freer trade between the French and British islands.[75] This was not at all Louis XIV's intention, and the prior restrictions were quickly reimposed for the colonies within two years. The new ordinances became the tinder that eventually ignited the planter revolt on Martinique known as the Gaoulé of 1717.[76]

In stark contrast to Martinique's lively events, the proclamation of peace produced barely a ripple of relief in Louisiana and Canada. As we have seen, settlers in Louisiana greeted the news with little joy in the rough-hewn post of Fort Saint Louis, which Cadillac and Duclos had proclaimed the seat of government: Governor and *commissaire ordonnateur* had begun bickering on the Atlantic crossing, add their relations worsened upon arrival, forcing colonists to publicly choose loyalties.[77] The display of elite unity that the celebrations were supposed to help reinforce were impossible under such conditions.

No celebration took place in Canada at all, for *Le Prince* never reached North American waters. On August 26th, Intendant Beauharnais reported to Pontchartrain that the ship had put into Brest a few days previously, partially flooded. Its captain, one Sieur Raudouin, reported that after the ship had fought stormy seas for two months, a series of great waves had smashed the mainmast, and the crew had barely managed to bring the stricken vessel back to port.[78] Beauharnais urged that another royal ship then at Brest, *Le Milfort,* be quickly loaded so as to arrive at Quebec before winter. But at that moment, shipwrights and labourers were preparing it for a second voyage to Martinique and Saint Domingue, and its itinerary could not be changed.[79]

In Quebec, Canadian officials still expected the arrival of *Le Prince* in the fall. Since *Le Samslack* reached Plaisance in late July, it is probable that Governor Philippe Pasteur de Costebelle at Plaisance (who did receive an official proclamation) sent a copy via a small coasting vessel to the capital.[80] But Quebec's officials received no further word. Governor General Vaudreuil and Intendant Bégon wrote Pontchartrain on November 15

by the last ship to leave the harbour that they had given up hope of seeing *Le Prince*. What had happened? they asked. Without the official proclamations, no royal celebrations took place, although officials clearly knew that peace had been signed. It was not until the following year, on March 22, 1714, that Pontchartrain explained the fate of *Le Prince* to Bégon, promised him that copies of all the 1713 dispatches would accompany those of 1714, and pledged that the ship for Canada (*L'Afriquain* again) would depart France much earlier. He tried to correct the situation by sending orders to sing another Te Deum, this time to celebrate the peace of Radstadt with Austria, the final peace treaty signed at the end of the War of the Spanish Succession. These dispatches did reach Quebec, but in September 1714, seventeen months after the Utrecht treaty had been signed.[81]

While we may be reasonably sure that Canadians held their own private celebrations upon the first receipt of the news, the official correspondence is strangely quiet on the issue.

It is highly significant that Quebec's officials did not bemoan the fact that royal ships could make only one voyage per year. Storms, shipwreck, and hazardous coastlines were simply part of the challenges and sorrows of life. What did upset them was the too often tardy arrival of the king's ship late in the navigation season, a situation that they knew could be remedied by more careful attention to outfitting and coordination on the part of the secretary of state and the intendant at Rochefort. Much the same could be said for Louisiana, even at this early date. But Saint Pierre's situation was entirely different. Even in the event that the king's ship missed important freight or news, the Bureau of Colonies could forward these on another vessel within six months. Moreover, a wide variety of merchant vessels sailed throughout the year to the Îles du Vent. The ability to send information and supervise the colonies depended on the regularity and consistency of contact, nor upon the distance or length of sailing time between France and its colonies.

The snapshot of communications efficiency provided in this case study indicates important differences in information flows between the home country and its colonies. Exchanges between French and British colonies showed that royal news openly competed with foreign sources, a situation absent in most of France itself. There the court, whether at Versailles, Marly, or elsewhere, supervised and coordinated symbolic displays in most parts of the nation, thanks to a productive and increasingly centralized bureaucracy and by relying on relatively efficient courier and postal systems. This organizational finesse stopped at France's shores. Beyond, bourgeois merchants provided the only consistently reliable method for transporting and distributing news. The crown could only establish an effective presence when its own ships and officials could travel to the colonies and back fast enough to keep the court's attention focused on specific issues for long periods of time. A six-to-eight-month gap between the issuing of orders and receipt of feedback seems to have been the limit for effective counteraction. Only with the Îles du Vent and Saint Domingue would such close contact operate, and it should not surprise us that instructions were followed the most closely in the Îles du Vent. Louisiana and Canada, progressively further away and more difficult to reach, were the only two French colonies in the Americas that could not receive, react to, and have confirmation of orders within a six-to-eight-month period. The state could be only as strong as its most recent dispatches.

Notes

1 Saint-Simon, *Mémoires*, 4: 628, 1347.

2 AN, K 1719/11, "Report on the proclamation of peace by the king," May 22, 1713 [signed Montjoye St. Denis].

3 Ibid.

4 Isherwood, *Music in the Service of the King*, 89, 250–1.

5 Saint-Simon, *Mémoires,* 4: 628. For other occasions, see AN, K 1719, 30/8, "Birth of Monseigneur le Dauphin" [September 9, 1729]; ibid., 15/12, *Relations des Cérémonies de la Paix qui doivent s'observer à la publication qui se sera à Paris le 12 février 1749...*[printed January 30, 1749].

6 AC, C8A 19, ff. 217–18, Phélypeaux to Pontchartrain, September 10, 1713. See also chapter 4.

7 AC, B 35, ff. 524, Pontchartrain to Phélypeaux, April 21, 1713; ibid., ff. 526–6v., King's orders, May 22, 1713.

8 Ibid., ff. 270–70v., King's orders [New France], May 22, 1713; ibid., ff. 354–4v., King's orders [Louisiana], May 22, 1713.

9 AC, C13A 3, ff. 437v.–38, Cadillac to Pontchartrain, February 20, 1714.

10 Juchereau, *Histoire de l'Hôtel-Dieu de Québec,* 503–4.

11 AC, C11A 34, f. 41, Vaudreuil to Pontchartrain, September 8, 1713; ibid., f. 4v., same to same, November 15, 1713.

12 Savelle, *Origins of American Diplomacy,* 125–44; McKay and Scott, *Rise of the Great Powers, 1648–1815,* 58–66; and Vries, *Economy of Europe in an Age of Crisis, 1600–1750,* 125–44. For Canada, see Miquelon, *New France, 1701–1744,* chapter 3. For Louisiana, see Giraud, *History of French Louisiana,* I: chaps 6 and 7.

13 AC, B 34, ff. 185v.–6, Pontchartrain to Vaudreuil, August 9, 1712; ibid., ff. 186v.–7, same to same, August 31, 1712.

14 AC, C8A 19, ff. 2, 16v.–17v., Phélypeaux to Pontchartrain, January 10, 1713.

15 Ibid., C11A 34, ff. 34–5v., Vaudreuil to Pontchartrain, February 11, 1713.

16 Ibid., B 35, f. 353, Pontchartrain to Cadillac, March 12, 1713.

17 See Giraud, *History of French Louisiana,* I: 249–54.

18 Saint-Simon, *Mémoires,* 4: 628 and 1347n3.

19 Petitot and Monmerqué, *Collection des mémoires*, 224.

20 Tessier, *Diplomatie royale française;* Antoine, *Conseil du roi*, 543; Mousnier, *Institutions of France under the Absolute Monarchy*, 2: 235–44; Boshe, *French Finances, 1770–1795*, 346.

21 Mousnier, *Institutions of France under the Absolute Monarchy*, 2: 235–39; Antoine, *Conseil du roi*, 544–56; Frégault, *XVIIIe siècle canadien*, 168.

22 Bosher, *French Finances, 1770–1795*, 36.

23 Mousnier, *Institutions of France under the Absolute Monarchy*, 2: 240–2; Tessier, *Diplomatie royale française*, 298–303.

24 Term used in AC, C8A 19, f. 205, Phélypeaux to Pontchartrain, August 12, 1713; see also Strayer, *Lettres de Cachet and Social Control*, 1–3.

25 AC, B 35, ff. 44–5, Louis to M. l'Evésque de Québec, May 31, 1713.

26 Ibid., f. 271, Pontchartrain to Vaudreuil, May 31, 1713; ibid., ff. 271v.–2, Pontchartrain to Bégon, May 31, 1713; ibid., ff. 272–3, Louis to M. l'Evésque de Québec, May 31, 1713; ibid., ff. 273–3v., Louis to Bégon, May 31, 1713. See also for Plaisance (Placentia), ibid., ff. 273–3v; Louisiana, ibid., ff. 354–5; and the Îles du Vent, ibid., ff. 526–7.

27 Boulle, "French Colonies and the Reform," 28–50; Deschamps, *Méthodes et les doctrines coloniales*, 35–7; Duchêne, *Politique coloniale de La France* 30–9; Rule, "Colbert de Torcy"; Symcox, "Navy of Louis XIV," 132–5.

28 Schaeper, *French Council of Commerce*, 242–6.

29 Meyer, "Decideurs," 81–97.

30 Bosher, "Treasurers of the Navy and Colonies," 327–48; Mousnier, *Institutions of France under the Absolute Monarchy*, 2: 144–5, 172–9; Duchêne, *Politique coloniale de la France*, 37; Frégault, *XVIIIe siècle canadien*, 165–7.

31 Duchêne, *Politique coloniale de la France*, 39–42.

32 AC, B 35, f. 225, Pontchartrain to Fontanieu, August 2, 1713.

33 Pritchard, *Louis XV's Navy*, 22.

34 AC, B 35, f. 254, Pontchartrain to Vaudreuil, March 29, 1713.

35 Figures based on Rochefort 1E, vols. 81–3, 1713.

36 Steele, "Moat Theories and the English Atlantic," 25 and note 38 (note computational error); also *Politics of Colonial Policy*, 7–9, 142–3; and Baugh, *British Naval Administration*, 35, 61–3.

37 Memain, *Marine de guerre sous Louis XIV*, 287–91.

38 Arbellot, "Grande mutation des routes," 765–6; Livet, "Route royale et la civilisation française," 63–5; Trénard, "De la route royale à l'âge d'or des diligences," 102–3; Lepetit, *Chemins de terre et voies d'eau*, chap. 1; Beik, *Absolutism and Society*, 99–100.

39 AC, B 35, ff. 30v.–31, Pontchartrain to Valminière, February 8, 1713.

40 Vaillé, *Histoire générale des postes françaises*, 4: 83–92; 5: 8–29, 231–8, 292–300.

41 *Almanach royal*, 176, 180, 182; Arbellot, "Grande mutation des routes," 765, 790.

42 Vaillé, *Histoire générale des postes françaises*, 5: 227–32.

43 AC, B 35, f. 125v., Pontchartrain to Beauharnais, July 8, 1713.

44 Mémain, *Marine de guerre sous Louis XIV*, 287.

45 Beik, *Absolutism and Society*, 100.

46 Mémain, *Marine de guerre sous Louis XIV*, chap. 1; Accera, "Rochefort: l'arsenal, l'eau, et les vaisseaux"; Lavedan, *Histoire de l'urbanisme*, 2: 213–16.

47 Accera, "Rochefort: l'arsénal, l'eau, et les vaisseaux," 55.

48 Quoted in Pritchard, *Louis XV's Navy*, 91.

49 Accera, "Rochefort: l'arsenal, l'eau, et les vaisseaux," 52–3; Giraud, "France and Louisiana in the Early Eighteenth Century," 659; and Bosher, *Business and Religion*, 294–5.

50 AC, B 35, f. 524, Pontchartrain to Phélypeaux, April 21, 1713; ibid., ff. 524–5v., same to same, April 26, 1713.

51 Ibid., C8A 10, ff. 239–49, d'Amblimont to Pontchartrain, July 10, 1698; ibid., 13, ff. 305–6v., Observations of America made by the Sieur Lainé royal pilot..., February 1701; also Stein, *French Sugar Business*, 60–4.

52 Giraud, *History of French Louisiana*, 1: 62–5.

53 Pritchard, "Ships, Men, and Commerce," 39.

54 AC, B 35, ff. 4–5v., Pontchartrain to Beauharnais, January 20, 1713 [marked January 30 in inventory].

55 Rochefort 1E/81, 46–9, La Maignière to Pontchartrain [sent February 1713]; AC, B 35, f. 30v., Pontchartrain to Beauharnais, February 7, 1713. On the lawsuit, see Bosher, *Business and Religion*, 296–302.

56 Rochefort 1E/342, 23–5, Beauharnais to Pontchartrain, February 14, 1713; AC, B 35, ff. 39v.–40v., Pontchartrain to Beauharnais; February 22, 1713.

57 Rochefort 1E/342, Beauharnais to Pontchartrain, February 9, 1713; AC, B 35, ff. 39v–40v, Pontchartrain to Beauharnais, February 22, 1713.

58 Ibid, f. 34, Pontchartrain to Beauharnais, February 10, 1713; Rochefort 1E/342 35–41, Beauharnais to Pontchartrain, February 25, 1713.

59 AC, B 35, f. 40v., Pontchartrain to Beauharnais, February 22, 1713.

60 Rochefort 1E/81, 137, Pontchartrain to Beauharnais, April 19, 1713; AC, C8A 19, ff. 151–1v., Phélypeaux to Pontchartrain, June 20, 1713.

61 Rochefort 1E/81, 139–40, Pontchartrain to Beauharnais, April 22, 1713.

62 AC, C8A 19, Phélypeaux to Pontchartrain, June 20, 1713.

63 Ibid., B 35, f. 525v., Pontchartrain to Phélypeaux, May 8, 1713; ibid., C8A 19, f. 204v., Phélypeaux to Pontchartrain, August 12, 1713.

64 Ibid., C8A 19, ff. 416–16v., Vaucresson to Pontchartrain, September 1, 1713; ibid., f. 217, Phélypeaux to Pontchartrain, September 10, 1713.

65 Ibid., B 35, vol. ff. 7–7v., Pontchartrain to Duclos, January 27, 1713; Ibid., ff. 39v.–40v., same to Beauharnais, February 22, 1713; ibid., C13A 3, ff. 319–20, Beauvais to Crozat, January 18, 1713; and ibid., ff. 343–5, Crozat to Pontchartrain, May 18, 1713.

66 Rochefort 1E/342, 93–6, Beauharnais to Pontchartrain, June 12, 1713; ibid., 109–13, same to same, August 31, 1713.

67 AC, B 35, ff. 153–3v., Pontchartrain to Desmarest, September 8, 1713; ibid., f. 178v., same to Laudreau, October 25, 1713.

68 Ibid., ff. 70–1, Pontchartrain to Beauharnais, March 22, 1713; ibid., f. 86v., same to Besnard, April 10, 1713; ibid, ff. 86–6v., same to Beauharnais, April 10, 1713, ibid., ff. 95v.–6, same to same, May 10, 1713.

69 Ibid., ff. 254–8, Pontchartrain to Vaudreuil, March 29, 1713; ibid., ff. 265v.–6, same to same, April 18, 1713; ibid., ff. 320v.–7v., same to same, July 4, 1713.

70 Ibid., ff. 107v.–8v., Pontchartrain to Beauharnais, May 31, 1713.

71 Rochefort 1E/342, 91–2, Beauharnais to Pontchartrain, June 6, 1713; AC, B 35, ff. 120v.–1, Pontchartrain to Beauharnais, June 14, 1713; ibid., C11A 36, ff. 198–9, Sieur Faures Grivollière [sic], 1716.

72 Ibid., 35, ff. 275v.–86, Memorandum from the king to Vaudreuil and Bégon, June 25, 1713; ibid., ff. 320v.–7v., Pontchartrain to Vaudreuil, July 4, 1713; ibid., f. 125v., same to Beauharnais, July 8, 1713.

73 AC, C8A 19, ff. 217–20, Phélypeaux to Pontchartrain, September 10, 1713; and ibid., ff. 416–18v., Vaucresson to Pontchartrain, September 1, 1713; Dessalles, *Histoire générale des Antilles,* 3: 406–8.

74 AC, C8A 19, f. 205, Phélypeaux to Pontchartrain, August 12, 1713.

75 Ibid., ff. 204–5v.

76 Petitjean Roget, *Gaoulé,* 199–200.

77 AC, C13A 3, ff. 437v.–8, Cadillac to Pontchartrain, February 20, 1714; also RSC 16: 305–7, Duclos to Pontchartrain, October 25, 1713, 17: 282–3, 287, Memorandum of M. Duclos, October 1713.

78 AC, C11A 36, ff. 198–9, Sieur Faures [de la] Grivollière [sic], 1716; ADCM, C 157/62, Marine Council to Beauharnais, June 10, 1716.

79 Rochefort 1E/342, 107, Beauharnais to Pontchartrain, August 26, 1713; AC, B 35, ff. 128v.–9, Pontchartrain to Buisson, July 19, 1713; ibid., ff. 156–8v., same to Beaumanoir, September 19, 1713.

80 AC, C11B 1, ff. 30–7, Costebelle to Pontchartrain, August 10, 1713.

81 Ibid., B 36, ff. 362–2v. 375, Pontchartrain to Bégon, March 22, 1714; ibid., ff. 375–5v., king's Letter for singing the Te Deum, April 19, 1714; and ibid., ff. 376–76v., Letter of the king for singing the Te Deum for the Peace of Rastatt [sic], April 19, 1714.

Mi'kmaq Decisions: Antoine Tecouenemac, the Conquest, and the Treaty of Utrecht

WILLIAM WICKEN

The conquest of 1710, at the time, was not a significant event for the Mi'kmaq. It only became so afterwards, as the British attempted to extend their economic and political control over the region. This is because the Mi'kmaq, unlike the Acadians, were not farmers. They did not keep livestock, they did not enclose their land, and they did not live along the major river systems which flowed into the Bay of Fundy; for these reasons they were less vulnerable to British attack than were the Acadians, whose fields and livestock had been ravaged by New England raiders in earlier conflicts.[1] The Mi'kmaq were a nomadic people, living in coastal areas during spring and summer and moving inland during the winter. However, as the British presence along the eastern coast of Nova Scotia expanded after 1713, many Mi'kmaq communities were forced to deal with the changed political situation precipitated by the Treaty of Utrecht, eventually resulting in the signing of a treaty with British authorities in 1726.

This change can be illustrated through the life of Antoine Tecouenemac, who at the time of the siege was sixteen years of age. His story reveals something about those Mi'kmaq who chose not to be present at the siege but whose lives would become infected by the narrative it set in motion. Indeed, it is precisely because the narrative's tempo quickened after 1710 that we know more about Antoine than about his father, Paul Tecouenemac.

This is the paradox in which Antoine would live his life—that his existence as a historical figure resulted from the intensification of French–English rivalry but that colonization would gradually restrict his ability to act upon his world independently of the forces arrayed against him.

Antoine Tecouenemac was the son of Paul and Marie Agathe Tecouenemac. In 1708, Antoine had four siblings—two brothers and two sisters—a household size not unlike others of his generation. Antoine was fourteen. His brother Guillaume was seventeen, Philippe eight, Marie twelve, and Cecile only one year old. Remarkably, Antoine's mother was fifty years of age in 1708, suggesting perhaps that Cecile was a relative's child, not her own.[2]

The reason so much is known about Antoine's family is because of the nominal census made of seven Mi'kmaq villages in 1708. The author of the census was the abbé Antoine Gaulin, a young and enterprising French Catholic missionary who had laboured among the Mi'kmaq from about 1704. Gaulin was no impartial census-taker, but an individual whose salary was paid by the French crown in recognition of his services, though such monies were never enough to subsidize all of his work.[3] The Mi'kmaq were his charges and the service he performed was instruction in the Catholic faith, which in turn rendered the Mi'kmaq better candidates for defending New France from the New England hordes. Though Gaulin was not likely to perceive his work in such a fashion, he believed that it was better for the Mi'kmaq to live in a world where French Catholics held sway than one where they did not. For these reasons, Gaulin's 1708 census illustrates French colonial perceptions of the Mi'kmaq, providing a means to evaluate the importance that French officials placed upon their Aboriginal allies for defending Port Royal.

In 1706 and 1707, Gaulin had journeyed to each of the seven Mi'kmaq villages in what is now mainland Nova Scotia and Cape Breton. At each place, the good father had recorded the names and ages of every village member. Each individual was listed relative to village and family membership. However, the way Gaulin divided the population at the end of the census was significant. Females were divided according to their marital status: women, girls, and widows. Men, however, were divided differently. Though married men were listed separately, the rest of the male population was divided according to age: those fifteen years of age and older, and those who were younger than fifteen. It was this information regarding the male population that commanded both Gaulin's attention and that of his superiors at Port Royal and Versailles. This is suggested in the last column of the table at the end of the census in which Gaulin tallied the total number of warriors, that is, men and boys fifteen years and older. No doubt, the figures regarding the size of the population formed an important part of Gaulin's census-taking. More critical for French military and political officials was the total number of Mi'kmaq warriors who might be recruited to defend Port Royal from British attack.

Gaulin's census recorded 842 Mi'kmaq, a total that could not have incorporated all Mi'kmaq living in the Atlantic region in 1708. There are two problems with the census. First, Gaulin's total only encompassed those communities located on mainland Nova Scotia and Cape Breton Island and therefore did not include other villages, namely those situated along the eastern coast of present-day New Brunswick and the Gaspé coast. For instance, we know from a census made later, in 1735, that these other villages might comprise as much as 35 per cent of the total Mi'kmaq population living in the Atlantic region.[4] More difficult to gauge is the number of people who lived within Gaulin's catchment area but were not enumerated. The size of this group is unknown. However, it only stands to reason that the timing of Gaulin's visit to communities—during summer—and the large areas he canvassed, must have resulted in inadvertent omissions from his census.

Regardless of the problems with the census, Gaulin's efforts were much appreciated by French officialdom, as the Mi'kmaq were integral to securing the region from the English. Versailles was unwilling to expend much to shore up Port Royal's defences. To be sure, the fort at Port Royal had been rebuilt in 1704, more soldiers assigned to guard its walls, and the Acadians organized into militia companies.[5] Still, there were only slightly more than 200 French regular soldiers and 180 Acadian militiamen who comprised the potential fighting force arrayed against the 1900 British and New Englanders sailing towards the head of the Annapolis Basin in September 1710. Therefore, the 240 Mi'kmaq warriors (out of the overall population of 842) whom Gaulin recorded in his census in 1708 provided French officials with some sense of the number of Mi'kmaq who might, they hoped, be rallied to withstand a British assault.

Indeed, Gaulin's census of 1708 can be understood as part of a broader policy initiated by French military and religious officials to employ the Mi'kmaq as a military force against New England. This strategy dated at least from the late seventeenth century, when proposals were made that the Mi'kmaq be relocated to an area where they might serve French military interests more satisfactorily. Such a proposal had first been made in 1698 by Gaulin's predecessor, Louis-Pierre Thury. In a letter to the minister of the Marine in Versailles, Thury proposed that the entire Mi'kmaq mainland population be resettled along the Piziquit (Avon) River.[6] According to Thury, by placing the mission between eastern and western regions of the mainland, French Acadia would be made more secure from enemy attacks as the Mi'kmaq could then be easily deployed. The plan would also assist in bringing the faith to the Mi'kmaq, as their settlement at one location would render their Christianization much easier in teaching them not only the precepts of the Catholic faith but also the rudiments of agriculture. Thury, of course, realized that any effort would be foolhardy without providing the Mi'kmaq with the skills they would need to live year-round at the mission. For this task, he requested the financial support of the crown in the form of provisions to feed the Mi'kmaq initially, as well as the materials needed to build a self-sustaining economy. This material support included 400 tools to clear the land, 50 fishing lines, 200 codfish hooks, 200 to 300 hatchets, and two large shallops.[7] Thury's proposal was approved by the minister of the Marine, who in April 1699 expressed the King's approval for establishing a permanent mission, though providing only 2,000 of the 6,000 livres requested.[8]

Despite royal approval, the plan went nowhere, probably because of Thury's death in 1699 and the resumption of conflict between France and England two years later. Thury's successor, Gaulin, later resuscitated the idea as did Jacques-François de Mombeton de Brouillan, governor of Acadia from 1701 to 1705.[9] Two years later, their plans led to the building of a mission, but at Chebuctou and not at Piziquit as Thury had originally envisioned.[10] The mission's location was derided by some Mi'kmaq, who complained to Gaulin that Chebuctou was too distant from their hunting areas and "too exposed to the English who come there every day." As a result, the mission was relocated to

the Rivière Sainte-Marie in the centre of the Bay of Islands, an area renowned for its abundance of moose, beaver, and other wild game.[11]

Though the size of Gaulin's mission is not known, it likely consisted of the local Mi'kmaq as well as families from outlying areas. People from other regions did not relocate there, as indicated by Gaulin's complaint in 1708 that he was "continually occupied in going to all the places where the Mi'kmaq live to instruct and hold them in obedience."[12] It is probable therefore that the mission Gaulin established along the Rivière Sainte-Marie existed in name only, populated by families who normally lived there.

Gaulin's lack of success was also symptomatic of French difficulties in recruiting the Mi'kmaq to assist in defending Port Royal. The Mi'kmaq refused to cooperate, resisting suggestions that they abandon their community interests in order to protect the King's need to protect his sovereign power over Acadia from English usurpation. Indeed, it is likely that some Mi'kmaq tended not to see their own interest to be irrevocably submerged with French imperial interests, but more pragmatically grounded on their allies' ability—or inability—to provide them with guns, powder, shot, and other manufactured goods.[13] And so, we may surmise that individual communities chose either to not answer Governor Subercase's plea for assistance in defending Port Royal, or to abandon their French allies when the victory of the New Englanders had become clear. Indeed, this may have been the Tecouenemac family's response to the siege, reflecting a closer identification with their familial and societal interests than with France's imperial ambitions. If Antoine Tecouenemac was not at Port Royal on 2 October 1710 when Subercase formally surrendered to Colonel Francis Nicholson, then where was he?

Some historians would have us believe that Antoine Tecouenemac lived in Acadia up until 1713, and afterwards in Nova Scotia. Stephen Patterson, for instance, writes of the "Nova Scotia Indians."[14] Such linguistic turns of phrase subsume

Antoine into a European world order, as though his identity would henceforth be closely associated with the world that French and later British settlers and their governments would create. Such toponymical inventions belie the realities of the eighteenth-century world that Antoine inhabited. After all, the Acadian population in 1710 was settled mostly in small communities along rivers flowing into the Bay of Fundy, while a small number of families lived scattered along the eastern coast of the mainland. And in the period after 1710, the British presence in the region was minuscule, confined until 1749 to Annapolis Royal and a small garrison at Canso. The rest of the mainland was inhabited by the Mi'kmaq, and rarely, if at all, did either the British or the Acadians venture onto their lands. These areas, which comprise the bulk of the landmass of what we know today as mainland Nova Scotia, cannot be so easily called "Acadia" or "Nova Scotia," as those terms were legal fictions used by France and Great Britain to justify the exclusion of other European nations from the region. This land was not Acadia, or Nova Scotia, but Mi'kma'ki, the land of the Mi'kmaq, and it was in this fashion that Antoine Tecouenemac and his family conceptualized their world.

But while Antoine Tecouenemac lived in Mi'kma'ki, he was also closely identified with a specific geographical landscape. According to the 1708 census, Antoine lived at a place called "Cap de Sable,"[15] though Antoine himself more likely thought of this place as Kesputkwitk. In later censuses compiled first by the abbé Gaulin and then by other missionaries, the term "Cap de Sable" would be used to locate a community of Mi'kmaq living on the southwestern mainland. In 1708, their population was given as 97, in 1721, 94, and in 1735, 167.[16] This pattern of persistent residency by distinct communities of Mi'kmaq families was repeated in the censuses made of other Mi'kmaq communities living on mainland Mi'kma'ki and Unamaki (Cape Breton) in the 1700s, showing that areas where

the Mi'kmaq lived remained constant from the 1600s to 1735. The censuses show that succeeding generations of families continued to reside in areas inhabited by their parents and grandparents. In this sense, Antoine's identity was merged with a specific landscape, not several, much in the same way that other Mi'kmaq of his generation were associated with other geographical areas of Mi'kma'ki.

The Tecouenemac family lived in coastal areas during spring, summer, and fall. This conclusion is suggested in scattered reports made by New England fishermen and colonial officials regarding their encounters with Mi'kmaq people. In March 1706, for instance, John Curtiss from Marblehead stated that he was aboard a vessel which put into Pubnico, "where came on board us several French and Indians to whom we sold sundry Goods, particularly Shott."[17] On 4 November 1715, Peter Capon, under orders from the Massachusetts General Court to recover fishing vessels hijacked by some local Mi'kmaq, met some families at the Pubnico River, though he had also been there on 31 August and only encountered Acadians.[18] Six years later, Captain Paul Mascarene, an officer from the British fort at Annapolis Royal, reported that the Mi'kmaq "happened to be in some number about" Pubnico during the early part of September and as a result had likely taken provisions from a vessel shipwrecked there.[19]

While this evidence gives a strong indication of the presence of Mi'kmaq along the southwestern coastal mainland during the summer months, it does not tell us the size of Antoine Tecouenemac's community or its location. We might ask, for instance, if the 97 people enumerated as residents of "Cap de Sable" in 1708 lived continuously together between March and November or if they divided into smaller family groupings. After all, the work of various researchers has concluded that the Mi'kmaq in the early eighteenth century were a semi-nomadic people who were for the most part dependent upon fish and animal populations for their subsistence.[20] Were there sufficient resources along the coastline to sustain a population of this size over the spring, summer, and fall?

On this question, there are no definitive answers, though most researchers have suggested that families tended to live in at least two different sites between March and November. During the early spring, families lived along river systems, near to favoured fishing sites. At some time during the late spring they moved towards coastal areas, living as members of a larger community. For this reason, it is fair to assume that abbé Gaulin's 1708 census, which records 97 Mi'kmaq living at "Cap de Sable," reflects this summer congregation of families. However, sometime during the late summer or early fall, families began moving inland, often settling near favoured fish runs that had been temporarily vacated during the late spring.

Antoine Tecouenemac's family appears to have engaged in this kind of movement. They lived at least from March to May at a village called "Ouikmakanan." The identity of the Tecouenemac family's spring village is suggested in the deposition of a Joseph Vigé, who recounted meeting Antoine Tecouenemac in early April 1736, at an Indian village where Vigé happened "to be...fishing for Eels."[21] A memorial written by French officials earlier in the century recounted that between the Chebogue and Pubnico Rivers was a place where "can be fished a prodigious quantity of eels in the months of April and May."[22] Half a century later this spot was said to be the location of a Mi'kmaq village called "Ouikmakanan" or "place of eels."[23] However, none of these documents precisely determines the village's location. There is little reason to doubt that the French writers had visited the village, but they had no incentive to explain further as it held no importance for either the French or the British.

Evidence from later documents suggests that the village where Antoine Tecouenemac and his family lived was situated on or near Robert's

Island, which lies southwest of the Argyle River. The first document dates from 1771 and is a commission given by the governor of Nova Scotia, Lord William Campbell, to Francis Alexis to "Fish, Hunt and Improve lands...in the Creek—called Ell [sic] Creek."[24] This allotment of land stemmed from a petition to the government by Alexis and his people, suggesting the importance of the area to the Mi'kmaq. Though the location of this site is not specified, a report issued by the government surveyor Charles Morris in 1820 provides more details. In this area, wrote Morris, "are places of resort for the Indians particularly at Eel Bay near the Tusket River where they take Eels in great quantities."[25] Finally, there is the information recorded by a local historian, Jackson Ricker, who in a 1941 book recounted the oral history of the region as related by his father. In one of these stories Ricker wrote that during the 1870s, every spring nine or ten canoes of Mi'kmaq camped on Robert's Island, located adjacent to the Argyle River northeast of Pubnico. "One of the attractions of Roberts Island," he writes, "was the eel fishing at Goose Bay."[26] From all of the preceding information Robert's Island seems to have been the most likely location of Ouikmakanan.

The village itself appears to have been situated on agriculturally useful land—a 1701 memorial indicated that the soil was "of a black colour" and very admirable. Suggestive of the land's fertility was the presence of four arpents of chicabens,[27] a vine which grows throughout the southern and middle regions of Nova Scotia. In 1692, Antoine Laumet dit de Lamothe Cadillac had noted that chicaben "was a root that one found in the earth like truffles and which is very good to eat."[28] In English this plant is known as the groundnut and in Latin, *Apios tuberosa*. Attached to the roots of the groundnut are anywhere from five to fifty tubers which resemble sweet potatoes in appearance. Two to five centimetres in length, these tubers can be boiled and eaten. According to a twentieth-century commentator, they are rich in vitamins and can be gathered at any time of the year.[29] The vine appears to have been plentiful throughout the region as it also grew in abundance at Cap Fourchu situated three and a half leagues to the northeast.

As the name of the village suggests, Ouimakanan was a "place of eels," a place in close proximity to river systems frequented by eels migrating to and from the sea. Eels are a catadromous fish, meaning that they spawn in the ocean. There is only one place, however, where they are known to spawn: the Sargasso Sea, located east of Florida and south of Bermuda. The eggs deposited in the sea by female adults gradually drift north-eastward towards the coast of North America, and arrive in eastern Canadian waters a year after hatching, sometime between April and June. The hatched elvers then move into freshwater as well as into tidal and estuarine waters, and remain there anywhere from five to twenty years. In the fall, mature adults move down river systems to begin their migration to the Sargasso Sea to spawn.[30]

The eel migrations in the spring and fall provided Antoine Tecouenemac's family with a reliable and productive food source during two crucial periods of the year. In the early spring, the migration of elvers upriver provided his family with a plentiful resource at the end of winter, when they would have migrated inland to hunt for moose, woodland caribou, and beaver. Winter was a potentially difficult time of the year, not only because of the cold weather, but also because of the scarcity of dependable wildlife. For this reason, the knowledge that eels could be caught in great numbers at Ouikmakanan early in the spring must have acted as a physical and psychological marker within Antoine's conception of the world.

Eels were also harvested in the fall, but instead of the small elvers which had been caught in the spring, families fished for the larger mature adult eels migrating to the sea to spawn. Their migration provided the Mi'kmaq of Ouikmakanan with a plentiful food supply which could be smoked and later eaten during the winter months when food was less readily available.

Catching and cleaning the eels during the fall was a labour-intensive process which would have involved the assistance of all able-bodied adults and mature, single women and men. In 1801, Titus Smith, who surveyed Nova Scotia for its government, wrote that the best place to catch eels was where a stream emptied into a lake. There, the Mi'kmaq would build a dam of stones interspliced with spruce or fir boughs. If the stream had a muddy bottom, a weir was constructed "by driving stakes so close together that the Eels cannot pass between them."[31] After the eels were caught, they were deboned and then cut into thin shreds before being smoked.

The labour involved in the catching and drying of eels likely meant that Antoine, his older brother, and his father, would not have abandoned their family during the fall to defend Port Royal from the New Englanders. By doing so, the Tecouenemac men would have placed their own personal and familial survival in jeopardy. Their world was not governed by French–British rivalry for control of the northeastern mainland, nor indeed by any necessity of defending Acadian farms from the depredations of New England privateers. Rather, Antoine Tecouenemac's world was governed by a different way of life, regulated by the migrations of the fish and wildlife upon which he and his family depended. That life cycle did not exist in a vacuum, but rather was identified with a specific geographical area and with a world far different from that inhabited by the soldiers and militiamen who confronted each other at the head of the Annapolis Basin during the latter days of September 1710.

This suggests that in 1710 Antoine and his family lived their lives outside the events and the documents which form the basis for understanding the history of "Acadia" and "Nova Scotia." The siege of Port Royal by New

England forces offers a revealing example. The story told of the siege, and the relative importance that historians place on that event, reflects a narrative pitting Great Britain against France. Significantly, the demise of one colony, Acadia, and the creation of another, Nova Scotia, occurs within the land where the Mi'kmaq had lived from before the arrival of either British or French people into their midst. Despite the presence of French and British, the Mi'kmaq continued to live in their world, outside the sight of European officials and unrecorded by their pens. The "silences" of history represent their past and one that is sometimes ignored.

That being said, it is also true that the British conquest of Port Royal and the subsequent signing of the Treaty of Utrecht had momentous consequences for Antoine Tecouenemac and for the Mi'kmaq generally, in that after 1713 their lives intersected with British and French settlers to a greater extent than before. The consequences are most readily apparent in the treaty signed between the British and the Mi'kmaq during the summer of 1726. Among those Mi'kmaq signing the treaty were Antoine, his father Paul, his brother Philippe, and other prominent male members of the Cape Sable community. The treaty's signing was a direct result of Utrecht.

The Treaty of Utrecht ushered in a new political configuration in the history of the Mi'kmaq and in their relationships with France and Great Britain. First, the treaty formalized the British garrison's occupation of Annapolis Royal. In succeeding years, the British would attempt to secure political control over lands occupied and used by Mi'kmaq communities. Second, British attempts to do so would occur within the context of an Abenaki–Massachusetts conflict which had been escalating since King Philip's War of 1675–6, as New Englanders pushed further and further eastward.[32] And finally, this conflict would itself be subsumed by an international struggle for control over North Atlantic trade, pitting Europe's two most powerful trading states, Great Britain and France, against each other.

At the edges of this emerging conflict stood the Mi'kmaq and their Wulstukwiuk and Abenaki allies. After 1713, the region inhabited by these communities became strategically important to France and Great Britain for two reasons. First, the area was located adjacent to the North Atlantic fish stocks, a plentiful and valuable commodity traded on the open market in Europe but also used as a cheap food source to feed enslaved Africans working on British and French sugar plantations in the Caribbean. Second, the maritime region's geography added to its strategic value, as it lay directly between New England and access to the St Lawrence River, which cut deeply into Canada's hinterland and led directly to Quebec and Montreal. Both factors were influential in animating French relations with the Mi'kmaq, Wulstukwiuk, and Abenaki after 1713.

Indeed, beginning in 1719, the French governor of Île Royale, Joseph de Saint-Ovide, would meet annually with Mi'kmaq elders and sakamows to discuss their common economic, and political interests. Such meetings were consistent with a general French strategy of forging direct relationships with neighbouring Aboriginal peoples to enlist and solidify their support in France's conflict with Great Britain. Though this strategy had long been employed with the Abenaki, Huron, and Mohawk, the period after 1713 witnessed its intensification as France's own economic and political interest in the North Atlantic expanded. Saint-Ovide's yearly meetings with the Mi'kmaq reflected this new conjuncture in French–British relations. What had been a local conflict between struggling planter colonies escalated towards an international war engulfing many Aboriginal communities, including the Mi'kmaq, the Wulstukwiuk, and the Abenaki. And so, the colonial officials of New France had an abiding interest not only in encouraging political and military cooperation among northeastern

Aboriginal people but also in ensuring that their political interests were firmly defined to include opposing New England's economic expansion into Abenaki and Mi'kmaq territory.

Yet the Mi'kmaq and their allies were no mere pawns of the French king, moving as they were told to protect the King's interests. To the contrary. They at times ignored the King's advice. This suggests that the Mi'kmaq and their allies were more than just an unruly group of "savages," and that they themselves decided how to react to the British claims of sovereignty in the Atlantic northeast after 1713. This independence of action is shown by the events of the 1720s, which would eventually result in the signing of the 1726 treaty.

The 1720s brought fundamental change in the military and political history of the Mi'kmaq and their Wabanaki neighbours. For the first and only time, they would fight the three northernmost British colonies—Massachusetts, New Hampshire, and Nova Scotia—on their own terms and for their own reasons and not principally to defend French imperial interests. The war lasted about three years, from 1722 to 1725, and occurred as a result of an expansion of New England settlements along the Kennebec River and of the movement of more New England fishermen into Nova Scotia waters. The Treaty of Utrecht had facilitated this expansion by giving more security to British settlers and fishermen. Utrecht, however, had been signed in Europe and had not involved either the Mi'kmaq or the Wabanaki. Neither had been consulted. Neither was amused. And neither reacted passively to New England's aggression.

The Wabanaki expressed their opposition to New England's expansion in a letter they sent to Governor Samuel Shute of Massachusetts in late July 1721.[33] The letter, written by the Jesuit missionary Pierre de La Chasse, expressed Wabanaki anger to New Englanders settling lands at the mouth of the Kennebec in violation of previous treaties signed between Massachusetts and the Abenaki in 1693, 1699, and 1713. The letter is significant not so much for what it said but for who signed it and how they did so. In the 1693, 1699, and 1713 treaties, the Abenaki had been represented by individual chiefs who had signed on behalf of their communities. Not so with the letter sent to Shute. In this case, individual villages and tribes identified themselves by their collective names and signed by affixing an animal totem. The letter was signed by eleven Wabanaki communities and seven allied peoples. The Wabanaki communities were Narantsouak (Norridgewock), Pentugouet (Penobscot), Naurakamig (upper reaches of the Androscoggin), Anmesokkanti (on the Kennebec River), Muanbissek (along the Merrimac River), Pegouaki (on the upper reaches of the Saco River), Medoctec (St John River, below Woodstock), Aukpaque (St John River, near Fredericton), Pesmonkanti (Passamaquoddy), Arsikanteg (lower reaches of the Androscoggin), and the 8an8inak (unknown).[34] These villages encompassed the major river systems stretching from the Merrimac River in present-day New Hampshire to the St John River in central New Brunswick. The seven allied people signing the letter were the "Iroquois du Saute" (Kahnewake), the "Iroquois de la Montagne" (Kahnesetake), the Algonquins, the Hurons, the "Mikemakes," the "Montagnes du costé du nord," and the "papinichois & autres nations voisines."

Although the letter did not bring a halt to the Abenaki–British confrontation in the Kennebec region, it had a profound and threefold significance. First, it shows that by at least 1721, the political ramifications stemming from an extension of British sovereignty in the northeast had precipitated a coordinated political response from the region's principal Aboriginal inhabitants, namely the Wabanaki and the Mi'kmaq. Second, the letter shows the close political relationship linking the Wabanaki and the Mi'kmaq with other aboriginal people living along the St Lawrence River.

And finally, the letter suggests that this political confederacy, linking the region's main aboriginal communities, operated to a large degree independently of French political authorities. In sum, the letter indicates the degree to which the Mi'kmaq had become entangled in French–British rivalry but still resisted French political manipulation.

This tension found further expression in the treaty of 1726, signed by the Tecouenemacs along with other Mi'kmaq. A total of seventy-seven aboriginal individuals signed the treaty.[35] Fifty of these people were Mi'kmaq, twenty-five were Wulstukwiuk (including Passamaquoddy delegates), and three others were from the Penobscot River. Signing on behalf of the British crown was the lieutenant-governor of Nova Scotia, Lawrence Armstrong.

The treaty ended the 1722–5 war and established some general laws regarding the relationship of "Nova Scotia's" aboriginal inhabitants—namely the Mi'kmaq and Wulstukwiuk—with Great Britain. The terms of the agreement were first set down in written form in November and December of 1725, when four Abenaki delegates from the Penobscot River, acting on behalf of Wabanaki and Mi'kmaq communities, negotiated terms with Massachusetts officials.[36] Two separate treaties were negotiated at this time: one with those Abenaki communities living between the Saco and Penobscot rivers and another with the Wulstukwiuk and Mi'kmaq.[37] Both treaties were later ratified by each individual community: by the Abenaki during the summers of 1726 and 1727 at Casco Bay, and by the Mi'kmaq and Wulstukwiuk at Annapolis Royal between 1726 and 1728.

One important difference between the two treaties is that the Abenaki treaty made no mention of the Treaty of Utrecht but rather referred to past agreements made with the colony of Massachusetts. In contrast, the Mi'kmaq/Wulstukwiuk treaty referred to Utrecht:

Whereas His Majesty King George by the Concession of the Most Christian King made att the Treaty of Utrecht is become ye Rightfull Possessor of the Province of Nova Scotia or Acadia According it its ancient Boundaries, wee the Said Chiefs & Representatives of ye Penobscott, Norridgewalk, St. Johns, Cape Sables & of the Other Indian Tribes Belonging to & Inhabiting within This His Majesties Province of Nova scotia Or Acadia & New England do for our Selves & the said Tribes Wee represent acknowledge His Said Majesty King George's Jurisdiction & Dominion Over The Territories of the said Province of Nova Scotia or Acadia & make our Submission to His said Majesty in as Ample a Manner as wee have formerly done to the Most Christian King.[38]

The difference between the two treaties is significant for two reasons. First, it suggests that prior to the signing of the treaty, Great Britain had not established a formal relationship with either the Mi'kmaq or the Wulstukwiuk. Informal talks had occurred between individual communities and British officials at Annapolis Royal, though without result, as had been true of discussions with Abenaki communities.[39] Second, and more important, the effort to get the Mi'kmaq and the Wulstukwiuk to sign a treaty in which they recognized British sovereignty over Nova Scotia "according to its ancient limits" suggests British recognition that occupation of the region could only be accomplished with the acquiescence of the indigenous inhabitants. Indeed, the war of 1722–5 had demonstrated the difficulties Great Britain would encounter in the region if it did not treat with the Mi'kmaq and Wulstukwiuk.

Through their signatures on the treaty, Antoine, Paul, and Philippe Tecouenemac recognized the irrevocable manner in which their lives had changed since the British had conquered Port Royal almost sixteen years before. In 1710, the British presence at Port Royal had not significantly affected Antoine and his family, and therefore the conquest probably meant little to them at the time. By the mid-1720s, however, things had changed. Though there were still few British soldiers at Annapolis, a small fort had been built at Canso and the size of the New England fishery had increased substantially. With that increase had also come the threat of retaliation from Massachusetts in the event of conflict with local Mi'kmaq communities. On the other hand, the French presence in the region had also increased since 1710. Witness, for example, the decision to build a fortress at Louisbourg and Governor Saint-Ovide's decision to meet with community elders yearly. For Antoine and his family, disinterest in what either the French or the British were doing in Mi'kma'ki was no longer possible. Indeed, British–French rivalry forced them to choose how their community would interact with both nations.

The particular issues elaborated by the Treaty of 1726 have been extensively discussed elsewhere and therefore do not require elaboration here. However, in terms of evaluating the long-term consequences of Utrecht for the Mi'kmaq, it is important to note that by signing the 1726 treaty, Antoine, his family, and his community were explicitly accepting the fact that the Treaty of Utrecht had altered their world. Henceforth, the British, not the French, would have jurisdiction over Europeans who entered Nova Scotia. Equally important, Antoine and his family accepted—as did other Mi'kmaq—that this new political conjuncture necessitated certain limitations on their own actions. For instance, the sixth clause of the treaty stated that in cases of dispute or misunderstanding between the Mi'kmaq and subjects of the British crown, the Mi'kmaq would not unilaterally take action but rather would apply to the crown's servants at Annapolis for redress. Similarly, Antoine and his family agreed that they would neither assist nor harbour British soldiers attempting to desert from their regiment but rather would do their utmost to return them to Annapolis.[40] However, the agreement was not entirely one-sided, The British also made promises to the Mi'kmaq, the most significant of which was that communities would not be molested in their hunting, fishing, gathering or other lawful activities.[41]

We can interpret the 1726 treaty as a conscious attempt by the Mi'kmaq and the Wulstukwiuk to negotiate the terms of an agreement with the British that would allow them to live side by side with each other by providing some guidelines for mediating their disputes. This attempt—though ultimately unsuccessful in avoiding future conflicts—marked a significant departure from the fall of 1710, when the British conquest of Port Royal seemed to have little impact on many Mi'kmaq communities. In 1710 Antoine Tecouenemac and his family had chosen—for familial reasons—not to assist the French in defending Port Royal. In 1726 the Tecouenemac family chose to sign a treaty with the British, and in so doing they signified their conscious understanding of how their world had changed since 1710.

Notes

1 For instance, Expedition faites par les anglois de la Nouvelle Angleterre au Port Royal, Les Mines et Beaubassin à L'accadie, AC, C11D, 5, ff. 27–9.

2 Recensement générale fait au mois de novembre mille Sept cent huit de tous les sauvages de l'Acadie, 1708 (hereafter 1708 census), Newberry Library, Edward E. Ayer MSS, IV, no. 751.

3 Subercase au ministre, 20 décembre 1708, AC, C11D, 6, f. 184.

4 Recensement fait cette presente année du nombre des sauvages, 1735, AC, G1466, no. 71.

5 M. Delabat to M. De Villermont, 20 Nov. 1703, in Morse, ed. Acadiensa Nova, II, 1–12.

6 Mémoire concernant l'acadie, 9 décembre 1698, AC, C11D, 3, ff. 320, 324.

7 Thury au ministre, 11 octobre 1698, AC, C11D, 3, f. 309.

8   Ministre à Thury, 15 avril 1699, AC, B, 20, ff. 167–8.

9   Brouillan au ministre, 25 novembre 1703, AC, C11D, 4, f. 277; Mémoire de M. de Brouillan qui concerne le Fort Royal de l'Acadie, 5 mars 1705, AC, C11D, 5, f. 71.

10 Conseil de la Marine, 3 mai 1718, AC, C11B, 3, f. 42. In the correspondence regarding the mission, it is called "Chedabouctou," which is located adjacent to the Strait of Fronsac and separates the Acadian peninsula from Cape Breton. However, in discussing the proposed mission in 1705, Subercase said that it was at the head of "Naspatagan Bay." He stated that the mission was located only three to four hours from La Hève. Mémoire de M. de Brouillan qui concerne le Fort Royal de l'Acadie, 5 mars 1705, AC, C11D, 5, f. 71. According to a survey of Nova Scotia completed in 1764, "Aspotagoen" refers to the high land which separates Saint Margaret's and Mahone Bay. See "Miscellaneous Remarks and Observations on Nova Scotia, New Brunswick and Cape Breton," in *Collections of the Massachusetts Historical Society for the Year 1794*, First Series, vol. III (New York, Johnson Reprint Company), 96. This would suggest that in transcribing correspondence, French officials in Versailles had written "Chedabouctou" instead of "Chebouctou." Royal approval for the change of location is in Ministre à Subercase, 24 août 1707, AC, B, 29, f. 47.

11 Gaulin au ministre, 20 décembre 1708, AC, C11D, 6, ff. 250–1.

12 Gaulin au ministre, 23 décembre 1708, AC, C11D, 6, f. 263.

13 Bonaventure au ministre, 24 septembre 1706, AC, C11D, 5, f. 246.

14 Patterson, "Indian–White Relations in Nova Scotia," 24–6.

15 "Cap de Sable" is the term used by Gaulin in the 1708 census. This region was called Cape Sable by the British during the same time period.

16 Recensement générale, 1708 census, Newberry Library, Ayer MSS, IV, no. 751; Recensement des sauvages, 27 décembre 1721, AC, C11B, 6, f. 74; Recensement fait cette presente année du nombre des sauvages, 1735, AC, G1466, no. 71.

17 Deposition of John Curtiss Senior of Marblehead, 14 June 1706, PRO, CO5/864, 160.

18 "A Journal of a Voyage to Cape Briton on the King's Acct. by Mr. Peter Capoon," 1715, MA, 38A, 11, 15.

19 Paul Mascarene, "Journal of a Voyage from Annapolis Royal to Canso, 1721," NSARM, RG1, 9, 113.

20 The following analysis relies upon Miller, "The Micmac: A Maritime Woodland Group," 326–31; Nietfeld, "Determinants of Aboriginal Micmac Political Organization," 306–84.

21 The Examination of Charles D'Entremont of Pobomcoup in his Majesty's Province of Nova Scotia, 11 May 1736, PRO, CO217/7, ff. 182–5.

22 Mémoire des costes de L'acadie, 12 octobre 1701, AC, C11D, 4, f. 85.

23 Sur L'Acadie, 1748, AC, C11D, 10, n.p.; J.R. Campbell, *A History of the County of Yarmouth*, 20.

24 Commission of Governor William Campbell to Francis Alexis, Chief of the Tribe of Cape Sable Indians, 22 June 1771, NSARM, RG1, 168, 155.

25 Report of the Reservations for the Indians by the Surveyor General, 7 May 1820, NSARM, Miscellaneous: Indians, Land Documents.

26 Ricker, *Historical Sketches of Glenwood and the Argyles*, 4.

27 Mémoire de Bonaventure, 1701, AC, C11D, 4, f. 85.

28 Mémoire et Description de l'Acadie par de Cadillac, 1692, AC, C11D, 2, f. 195.

29 Prest, "Edible Wild Plants of Nova Scotia," 404–5.

30 Eales, *The Eel Fisheries of Eastern Canada*, 3–5.

31 Smith, "Survey of Western Nova Scotia," 1801, NSARM, RG1, 380A.

32 Morrison, "The Bias of Colonial Law"; Baker and Reid, *The New England Knight*, 156–177.

33 Eastern Indians' Letter to the Governour, 27–8 July 1721, in *Collections of the Massachusetts Historical Society*, ser. 2, VIII, 259–63. The letter has been translated into English, in *Maine Historical Society Quarterly*, 13:3 (1974), 179–84.

34 The location of individual villages is given in Sévigny, *Les Abénaquis*.

35 The 1726 treaty is examined in detail in Wicken, *Mi'kmaq Treaties on Trial*, 25–159.

36 For a summary of the discussions, see PRO, CO5/898, ff. 178–188.

37 Submission and Agreement of the Delegates of the Eastern Indians, 15 December 1725, PRO, CO5/898, ff. 173–4.

38 Articles of Peace and Agreement, 4 June 1726, PRO, CO217/5, f. 3.

39 These talks are discussed in Wicken, *Mi'kmaq Treaties on Trial*, 107–9.

40 Articles of Peace and Agreement, 4 June 1726, PRO, CO217/5, f. 3.

41 Promises of John Doucett, 4 June 1726, PRO, CO217/4, f. 321.

1755–1784:
Exile Surmounted

Naomi E.S. Griffiths

The years of proscription, from 1755–64, were years of bitter trauma for the Acadian community. They were the years during which the authorities at Halifax attempted to enforce a policy of banishment and exile on all members of the Acadian community. They were the years when the Acadians were dispossessed of all rights to own land within Nova Scotia. The events of these years, whether labelled as "the deportation," "the time of exile," or "le grand dérangement," have become so central to the self-definition of later generations of Acadians that the reality of what actually happened has often been overlooked.[1] Yet the broad outlines of the cataclysm are clear enough. For more than a hundred years, the Acadians had been the dominant society of European descent within the territory covered by the present-day provinces of Nova Scotia, New Brunswick, and Prince Edward Island. In 1755 this pre-eminence was ended, never to be regained. It took more than seventy years for the Acadian population within the Maritimes to reach the level that it had been in the summer months before the boats left. When the numbers once more reached the pre-deportation level of some 20,000 people, the Acadian communities were to be found, geographically, politically and economically, in a very different situation than they had been in 1755. The policy carried out by Lawrence had both succeeded and failed. It had destroyed Acadian power but not Acadian identity.

Politically after 1755, the Acadian communities would be marginal, if not peripheral, to a majority made up of several collectivities of newcomers: above all to the Planters and the Scots in Nova Scotia, Cape Breton and Prince Edward Island, and to the Loyalists in New Brunswick. Economically, in the 1780s, the Acadian communities were primarily dependent on subsistence farming, fishing, and the lumber trade. Acadians never regained control of the rich lands of the Annapolis Valley, the Minas Basin, and the largest salt-marsh lands in the world, the Tantramar. Instead, significant Acadian communities were to be found much where they are now: on the northern sea shores of New Brunswick, in the upper Saint John River Valley, around the Petitcodiac and the Memramcook valleys, with a bare scattering of settlements around Cape Breton Island and St Mary's Bay in Nova Scotia, and on the northern shores of Prince Edward Island.[2] From 1755 onwards, the Acadians were a minority where they had once been a majority. They were a community often excluded from the norms of the political life of a broader polity of which they formed part,[3] and their legal rights to establish themselves in certain areas were often successfully challenged.[4] But from 1755 onwards, as in the years leading up to that date, the Acadians lived as a collectivity, as a people with a sense of their distinctiveness, as members of communities with specific and deeply held beliefs in their unique identity. Even when the sense of identity is despairing, a

Naomi E.S. Griffiths, "1755–1784: Exile Surmounted," in *The Contexts of Acadian History, 1686–1784* (Montreal: McGill-Queen's University Press, 1992), 95–127.

bitter cry of defeat and powerlessness in the face of an uncomprehending majority,[5] an Acadian sense of self endured.

But how did the Acadians survive as a distinct people? What are the connections, other than the purely genealogical, between the pre-deportation Acadian community and later manifestations of Acadian distinctiveness? What is the relationship between the Acadians who returned from exile after 1764 and the shattered remnants of the Acadian society that continued in the Maritimes after 1755, despite every effort of the authorities to complete the banishment of the Acadians. Many of the answers to these questions are to be found in the complexities of what exactly occurred between 1755 and 1763. First and foremost, the Acadian reaction to exile has to be understood. How was it that they did not disappear as a distinct people, that they did not end up by being assimilated into the societies of other British North American colonies or in France? How was it that a significant and important number of them, if by no means the majority, made their way back to Nova Scotia?

But the history of what actually occurred provides only part of the answer to questions of Acadian identity after 1755. A second part of the answer lies in the Acadians' interpretation of the deportation and its aftermath. By the end of the eighteenth century, a shared Acadian belief had evolved about why the deportation had occurred and what it had meant for the Acadian community. This belief was and is crucial for their continued existence as a separate people within New Brunswick, Nova Scotia, and Prince Edward Island. The Acadian history of the exile, as much as the history of the exile itself, needs to be examined. The Acadian interpretation of the deportation became the framework for the development of a rich and distinct identity in the nineteenth and twentieth century.

In the first instance, exile scattered the Acadians into the other British North American colonies from Massachusetts to Georgia. But this was only in the first instance. One of the most important factors which influenced the fate of the Acadians during their exile is that these were years of war. The places of exile were themselves embroiled, to a greater or lesser extent, in the Anglo-French battle for dominance of North America. What happened to the Acadians immediately on arrival in new lands was often only the beginning of their travails. The Acadians would nowhere find the conditions of their exile stable and unchanging. For many Acadians the deportation meant far-ranging voyages, quite beyond anything imagined by those who had supervised their embarkation in Nova Scotia.

For example, a number of those sent to Maryland, South Carolina, and Georgia went on to Santo Domingo and some of these journeyed to either Louisiana or British Honduras. Others first landed in Massachusetts but after 1763 went to the banks of the St Lawrence. Some voyaged to the Channel Islands and then to the islands of St Pierre and Miquelon. Most of those who were first landed in Virginia were sent on to England and then to France. Many of those who survived this trek sailed from Nantes in 1785 for Louisiana at the expense of Spain, whose territory Louisiana then was.

There is as yet no single-volume history of the Acadian experiences in exile during the years 1755–84, from the deportation to a time when an Acadian community can be considered to have achieved, once more, a legitimacy in the territory, if not on the actual lands, previously settled by their ancestors. There are a considerable number of works which either relate the whole story of some particular group of Acadians or some part of the experiences of most of the exiles. Works such as Emile Lauvrière's *La tragédie d'un peuple*[6] give an overview of what occurred. Others, such as O.W. Winzerling's *Acadian Odyssey,*[7] and the more recent work by William Faulkner Rushton,[8] both of which are concerned with the history of how the majority of Acadians that reached Louisiana did so, concentrate on events that only some of the Acadian exiles experienced.[9] Few works have attempted to discuss the available information in order to answer wide-ranging questions about how various jurisdictions dealt with the Acadians on their arrival or what impact exile had on the Acadian sense of identity. The widely scattered nature of the sources available, both for the North American narrative and for the more far-ranging paths of exile (resources which include the Vatican archives[10] and the graveyards of British Honduras[11]), has understandably tended to encourage the writing of the more restricted accounts of a particular local group. Even the magnificent work of collection which has been undertaken by the Centre d'études acadiennes, at the Université de Moncton, has not yet gathered all known archival deposits. In sum, the history of the Acadians during exile has been recorded either in broad but shallow overviews or narrow but detailed accounts.

The very strength of those incidents of the exile that have entered public knowledge has overshadowed the intricate reality of the exile as a whole, in much the same way as the episode of the deportation itself has thrown so very much of Acadian experience into shadow. Longfellow's poem *Evangeline,* for example, has led many to believe that the deportation of the Acadians entailed the wholesale and deliberate separation of close-knit families, as well as the removal of the whole community directly to Louisiana.[12] The incompatibility of these two ideas is not often noticed. Both remain powerful images of the deportation and both have enough connection with reality to make them enduring myths.

In fact, no one was deported *directly* from Nova Scotia to Louisiana, for, in 1755 Louisiana was French territory and the Acadians were destined for the British North American colonies from Massachusetts to Georgia.[13] As noted already, the majority of those Acadians who did reach Louisiana were those who had initially landed in Virginia.[14] There were some Acadians who, having been landed in South Carolina, made their way by land to the mouth of Mississippi, although the most used "other route" was via Santo Domingo.[15] The essential plot of Longfellow's poem could have happened and perhaps did. Longfellow heard of the story from an Acadian who was a serving maid, and the legend of lovers parted by the deportation to meet only as death strikes one of them is found in varying forms among several groups of people whose ancestors were Acadian. As suggested already, the years of exile were years of wandering, not years of stability. However inaccurate the detail of incident in the work of this American poet, there is an essential element of truth: the deportation meant the end of a way of life and, for many, the need to construct the pattern of the days in a foreign land.

Similarly, the popular image of the separation of loved ones is both true and false. The break-up of communities was a calculated part of the deportation but, as will be seen in a moment, the separation of closely connected groups was not part of the original plan and was rarely deliberate. As has been noted, when the decision was made to deport, Colonel Lawrence and those associated with him were well aware of the danger of adding to the strength of France in North America. It was for this reason above all that it was decided to split up the various settlements and divide them among the British colonies in North America. To repeat the words of Lawrence again, it was agreed "to divide them [the Acadians] among the Colonies…and as they cannot easily collect themselves together again it will be out of their power to do any mischief."[16]

Very detailed plans were drawn up to organise the deportation, based largely on the work of surveyor Charles Morris, elaborated by the lieutenant-governor and other members of council.[17] Each major collection of Acadian villages was to be divided up among several colonies. It bears repeating that the Acadians deported from Nova Scotia in

1755, who constituted the vast majority of those sent into exile between 1755 and 1763, *without exception* had as their appointed destination one of the British colonies in North America. The instructions sent to Lieutenant-Colonel Winslow, who would be in charge of the removal of the Acadians from the Grand-Pré, instructed him to ship "To North Carolina... Five hundred persons or thereabouts...to Virginia... one thousand persons;... To Maryland... Five hundred persons."[18] Major Handfield, who was in charge of deporting those who were to be removed from the Annapolis Valley, was ordered that the community was to be divided approximately as follows: 300 persons to Philadelphia; 200 persons to New York; 300 to Connecticut; 200 to Boston.[19] The instructions to Colonel Moncton, who was in charge of the Chignecto Isthmus, were to divide those deported as follows: "528 [persons] to Georgia; 1020 to South Carolina and 392 to Philadelphia."[20]

This division of the Acadians can be seen as characteristic of the deportation: it was conceived as a military tactic and designed to mean the end of the Acadian community. It was an act of war. It was not, however, a policy aimed at the extermination of the individual; it was not a "Final Solution" bred out of the madness of racial hatred. It was an action comparable to the Highland Clearances. There was no deliberate intention in the plan itself to separate nuclear families, to divide husband and wife, parents and children. In fact, during most of the embarkation proceedings, special efforts were made by Winslow and some of the other officers to bring parents and children together.[21] At the same time, however, there was no attempt to keep the extended family together, as can be seen from cases such as that of René Leblanc, the notary who was landed with his wife and two of his youngest children in New York, with the rest of the family being sent on to Philadelphia.[22]

But it is important to remark that the plan sketched above was only a plan. It was carried out

with all the mishaps and bungling which attend most large-scale human endeavours. Those carrying it out found that it was subject to modification in many details. Most of the changes increased the distress of the Acadians. Some changes were made because certain of the Acadians proved much more recalcitrant than had been expected. For example, some eighty-six men who had been held in Fort Lawrence awaiting the arrival of the ships, "got away...by making a Hole under ground from the Barrack through the South Curtain above thirty feet."[23] Further, as the months passed, Lawrence became impatient and ordered his officers to be more zealous in getting the ships away, and hence to take less account of embarking the men with their families.[24] Yet other changes came about because of the difficulty of organizing and provisioning the transports.[25] Perhaps the most devastating changes came because of the weather, which delayed embarkations and then blew many ships from their approved destinations.[26]

The deportation destroyed a way of life and broke a close-knit kin group into fragments, but it was no massacre. Yet limited horror and controlled disaster are horror and disaster nonetheless. Those who survived the voyage often found on disembarkation that their distress had only just begun. The initial separation from neighbours and the break-up of the extended family was often immediately compounded once disembarked. The authorities frequently then split the Acadians into their nuclear families of five to eleven persons in order to ensure that the newcomers would constitute no danger to public order, and to provide for the support of the Acadians according to the norms these polities had evolved for the sustenance of their own sick and poor.

These policies towards the Acadians were adopted in haste by the various colonies. In most cases, the first the new hosts of the Acadians knew about the deportation was on the delivery of a letter when a shipload of exiles arrived in the major colonial port, whether that was Boston, Massachusetts; Annapolis, Maryland; Columbia, South Carolina; Savannah, Georgia; or some other port. The captains of the ships on which the exiles left carried a copy of the circular from Lawrence to the "Governors on the continent," dated 11 August 1755. None of the colonies had received any previous official notification, let alone been consulted, about the deportation. Thus, the general pattern of the Acadians' reception was that of an administration having to make some immediate provisions to house and feed unexpected and unwelcome newcomers.

On arrival, therefore, the Acadians were the subject of extensive official discussions and much public scrutiny. They were immediately recognized everywhere as a distinct people: they were unexpected refugees, they spoke French, they were Catholic, and they were in desperate need of succour after the long sea voyage. None of the authorities, whose charge they now were, knew whether to greet them as fellow subjects of the British Crown, removed from a battle zone, prisoners-of-war, "neutrals," or—as Governor Dinwiddie of Virginia wrote to Governor Shirley of Massachusetts—"intestine Enemies."[27] In Pennsylvania the Acadians were considered, and accorded treatment, as "Subjects of Great Britain,"[28] while in South Carolina their treatment wavered between that accorded prisoners-of-war and that which would be given to "natural-born subjects of the Crown" who were yet in need of surveillance.[29] The Acadians were certainly seen as different from those among whom they had been sent to live. And this distinctiveness was further emphasized at the outset by the poor physical condition of the Acadians on arrival. The ill-health of the Acadians meant that the authorities had to intervene decisively and immediately on their behalf. Without exception, all colonies had to set about provisioning the exiles, coping with the impact on them of typhoid and smallpox, and deciding whether they permitted them to land, as did Massachusetts, or to keep them temporarily on board ship, as did Pennsylvania, Virginia, and Georgia.[30]

The debate about what should happen next to the exiles was considerably influenced by how sharply the colony felt the threat of the coming hostilities, for by the fall of 1755 there was no longer any question that a formal declaration of war would very soon regularize the fighting of England and France. If Nova Scotia saw danger in the presence of French-speaking Catholics, the other colonies were equally as aware of the possibility of the Acadians giving aid and comfort to the French cause. The Governors of the differing jurisdictions wrote to one another in great perturbation. Governor Belcher[31] of New Jersey expressed a common view in his letter to Governor Morris of Pennsylvania dated 25 November 1755. "I am, Sir," he wrote, "truly surprised how it would ever enter into the thoughts of those, who had the ordering of the French Neutrals, or rather Traitors and Rebels to the Crown of Great Britain, to direct any of them into these Provinces where we have already too great a number of foreigners for our own good and safety." He was of the opinion that the Acadians "should have been transported already to old France."[32] In Massachusetts, a petition to the governor in February of 1756 complained that about 1,000 Acadians had been landed in the Commonwealth, all in great want and distress, and that "the receiving among us so great a Number of Persons whose gross Bigotry to the Roman Catholick Religion is notorious and whose Loyalty to His Majesty Louis XV is a thing very disagreeable to us."[33] Even in colonies where there was an immediate expression of sympathy for the bereft, there was also wariness and fear. *The Maryland Gazette* of December 1755 remarked: "Sunday Last [Nov 30th] arrived here the last of the vessels from Nova Scotia with French neutrals for this place, which make four within this fortnight who have brought upwards of 900 of them. As the poor people have been deprived of their settlements in Nova Scotia, and sent here for some very political reason bare and destitute Christian charity, nay common humanity, calls upon everyone according to their ability to lend their help and assistance to these objects of compassion."[34] Considerable concern was also expressed, however, that the Acadians would prove to be spies. The first act which Maryland passed on their account was one in May 1756 to keep them from witnessing any training manoeuvres.[35]

There were some common characteristics in the reception of the Acadians by the governments of the varying colonies on arrival, although the provisions then made for the exiles varied. In general, the exiles were put in the charge of those responsible for the poor of the colony, and distributed, in small groups, throughout the colony in question. As might be expected, colonies north of, and including, Pennsylvania took greater pains to circumscribe the exiles than did the colonies to the south, Maryland, for example, or the Carolinas and Georgia. The actions of the Commonwealth of Massachusetts were followed, to a greater or lesser extent, by Connecticut, New York, and Pennsylvania. A first step taken by the commonwealth was not followed by any other jurisdiction, however. Lawrence was advised, in November 1755, that Massachusetts expected to be reimbursed for any money spent on the Acadians.[36] No other jurisdiction, to my knowledge, took this path. As a second step, the commonwealth passed an act on 16 December 1755 to cope "with divers of the Inhabitants and Families in Nova Scotia...sent by the Government...to prevent their suffering by sickness and Famine."[37] By its provisions, a committee was brought into being to organize the immediate supply of food and shelter to the Acadians. Once the immediate needs of the Acadians were met, the commonwealth endeavoured to disperse them among various towns and villages of the

colony in order that no danger could arise from the exiles gathering together and threatening public safety. Thus, on 27 December 1755, another act was passed which provided for the dispersal of the Acadian families among "several towns" and the binding out of children as servants and apprentices.[38]

There was an immediate outcry against this practice from the Acadians. They organized petitions to Governor Hutchinson, one of which reads in part: "La prève que nous avons souffrir de nos habitations et a mene ici et Nos Separations les Uns les autres n'est Rien a compare a Cell que de prendre Nos Enfans devant nos yex: La Nature meme ne peut souffrir cela."[39] As a result of this and similar petitions,[40] a committee was appointed by the Council of Massachusetts to look into the matter. The report, which they made within two days, and which was concurred in by Council on the day it was presented, recommended that "Selectmen or Overseers should desist binding them out."[41]

The people of Massachusetts, in the words of Doughty, "Loved not Catholics and Frenchmen,"[42] but they were affected by the distress of the Acadians, even though they feared both the expense they would incur on their behalf and the danger that the Acadians might prove to the commonwealth. By June 1756 the roaming of Acadians about Massachusetts, in search of relatives and friends, led to an investigation.[43] On 11 August 1756 an act was proposed "for the better ordering of the late inhabitants of Nova Scotia," which made the penalty for such wanderings "imprisonment and return to their district."[44]

The more time passed the more complicated the problem became. By mid-summer 1756, Massachusetts had not only to cope with those Acadians who had been directly sent to her shores but also had news that "ninety of the French inhabitants of Nova Scotia having coasted along shore from Georgia and South Carolina...had put into harbour in the southern part of this province."[45] An attempt was made to put an end to such voyagings, as well as to the comings and goings of Acadians within the commonwealth. The records show remarkably little success. Repeated acts and resolutions of the colony's administration reveal a continuing problem, part of it caused by humanitarian reactions. Some voyagings were permitted as Acadian petitions to be allowed to join with relatives were granted.[46] In January, Dedham's answer to a request as to the whereabouts of the Acadians ends with the sentence: "There is another girl who is sometimes here and sometimes not."[47]

On 13 August 1757 the commonwealth made yet another effort to deal directly with the security problem posed by the Acadians who wandered their towns and villages. A circular was issued to all sheriffs, under-sheriffs or deputies, pointing out that "there may be great Danger in allowing the French people, late Inhabitants of Nova Scotia, too great a Liberty at this critical Juncture."[48] But nothing really changed. In 1759, General Wolfe was complaining that "some of the said Nova Scotians have deserted the Province and gone to Canada,"[49] and he demanded a closer surveillance of them. As a result, one more survey was undertaken which reported as follows:[50]

January 25th, 1760:	
Acadians able to Labour	304
Incapable by reasons of old age, 50 and up	61
Incapable by reasons of Sickness	107
Children under 7	240
Children capable of being put out from 7 to 14	187
Employed in attending and nursing sick	28
	947 [sic]

As was to be expected, considering the resolution that had been made when the Acadians first arrived, Massachusetts kept accounts of the cost of their support. For the year 1759 it was calculated as £1478 2s. 9d. Over the years more than one community complained, as did Salem, that "by reason of this addition of Neutrals, the poor of our Town are kept out of the almshouse."[51] The sort of support that the Acadians received is typified by the records of Medway, which spent £7 11s. 3d. to support nine people from 28 October 1756 to 7 March 1757. The full report reads as follows:[52]

	£	s	d
To House Rent for One Family from October 28th, 1756 to March 7th, 1757		2	8
To nine Bushels of rye meal	1	10	
To nine Bushels and one half of Indian mealand corn	1	2	9½
To 286 pounds of Beef	1	18	1½
To 64 pounds of Pork		8	6½
To 32 pounds of cheese		5	9
To 3 pounds of Butter		1	10
To 8 pounds of Mutton		1	1
To 10 gallons of milk		4	6
To 13 loads of wood		13	
To half a bushel and a peck of Salt		1	9
To Bread		4	
To five gallons of Cyder		1	2½
To 2 pounds of wool		4	8
To mending a pot		8	
To a wheel and an Axe		16	8
To Mr. John Thibault for Trouble as an Interpreter			8
	7	11	3
		[sic]	

The nine persons above mentioned the head of the family...aged 53, his wife 48, they are not well and healthy, not capable of constant labour; their eldest son aged 28, his wife, 23, well and healthy, the next son aged 20 and healthy, the next son aged 16 has been poor and weakly, the next aged 13, next aged 9, the youngest son aged 6, the four last mentioned are small and not capable of doing much for their support. The men are all fishermen. They can handle an axe But do not understand our common husbandry; By reason thereof we can't find 'em Constant Labour.

The final bill for the monies spent by Massachusetts for the support of the Acadians was computed in September of 1762 as £6,000 and by August of 1763 as £9,563 9s. 10d.[53] As far as I know, these accounts were never paid.

But while the archives of Massachusetts are full of evidence concerning the expenditures of the commonwealth on the Acadians, that is really the least part of the matter. The decision to deport the Acadians might have seemed a swift and simple solution to a long-standing and thorny problem to the Governor's Council in Halifax in 1755, but its outcome was an exacerbation of difficulties for other British colonial administrations in North America and a calvary for the Acadians. In truth, the deportation was a matter of perplexity and confusion for the officials of the colonies to which they were sent, as much as for the Acadians themselves. Further, all involved would find that the repercussions of the policy did not end with Peace of Paris in 1763. In January 1764, Bernard, then Governor of Massachusetts, wrote to the House of Representatives, on the occasion of an epidemic of small-pox in the colony:[54] "The case of these people [the Acadians] is truly deplorable. They have none of them had the small-pox and they depend upon their daily labour for their bread. If they don't go about town they must starve; if they do go about they contract the distemper, and as they are crowded in small apartments and wanting the necessaries of life, they must have a common chance to escape perishing.... I am therefore obliged to apply to you to help to save these

people." Some measures were taken to lessen the misery of the Acadians, but their circumstances continued to be pitiable.[55]

In the summer of 1764 there seemed to be a possibility for a new and better life for the exiles, albeit in very foreign circumstances. An invitation was made "to all the Acadians residing in New England" to go to Santo Domingo where they "shall have grants of land made to them and they shall be maintained by the King [Louis XVI] during the first months of their abode."[56] Bernard was much against this. In January of 1765, he sent a message to the House of Representatives that he had been informed that "the Acadians belonging to this province were going hence in large numbers to form a settlement in French Hispaniola." He continued: "Their case is truly pitiable; if they go to Hispaniola they run into certain destruction very few escaping with life, the Effects of the bad climate there and yet they have no Encouragement in this Country; Humanity more than Policy makes me desirous to prevent the remainder of them taking this fateful voyage; I want not so much to make them British subjects as to keep them from perishing."[57]

At least some Acadians reacted bitterly to this well-meant paternalism. They informed the governor that "for nine years we have lived in hopes of joining our Country men and it seems to us that you have caused a door which was open to be shut upon us. We have always understood that in times of Peace and in all countries the prison doors are open to Prisoners. It is therefore astonishing to us, Sir, to be detained here.... This is very hard upon us. It is hard to reflect upon our Present situation, to see ourselves by one sudden blow rendered incapable of affording ourselves relief."[58] The governor's desires, however, prevented them leaving.

One scheme might have been thwarted, but another avenue opened. In the spring of 1766 Governor Murray of Quebec wrote to Governor Bernard suggesting that under certain circumstances the Acadians might be settled in his province "for the Good of the British Empire."[59] By 2 June, some 890 Acadians had agreed to be transported to the banks of the St Lawrence. The *Quebec Gazette* of 1 September 1766 reported the arrival of a sloop from Boston with "forty Acadians who, for the Benefit of their Religion, are come here to settle." On Monday 8 September, 1766 "At the Council Chamber in the Castle of St. Louis in the City of Quebec"[60] an order was given to provide one month's supplies to some ninety Acadians, men, women and children.

After this date, information in Massachusetts archives about the Acadians dwindles. In 1766, eleven years after the first Acadian exiles arrive in Boston harbour, noticeable numbers begin to depart. How many made their way back to Nova Scotia is debatable and will be considered later in this chapter. For present purposes, suffice it to say that the Acadians who were sent to Massachusetts were treated as some peculiar form of prisoners-of-war, although such a status was never officially accorded them. Since the majority of the Acadians had been born since 1713, on British territory, there was grave doubt as to what their legal rights might be. The question of subjecthood and citizenship is complex enough in the eighteenth century, whether the state be France, England, or a British North American colony. The rights of non-juring, native-born subjects posed a sufficient conundrum to colonial officials to make them cautious in their treatment of the Acadians. The Acadians were convinced that, if they were prisoners-of-war, then they should be treated as such: confined as a group, provided for by their enemy. If they were other than prisoners-of-war, then the limits placed on their freedom were utterly without justification. In either case, in Acadian eyes, forced separation of parents and children was monstrous. Massachusetts avoided any final pronouncement on the matter of Acadian legal status, referring to Acadians whenever possible as "inhabitants of Nova Scotia" or "exiles from Nova

Scotia." The binding out of children, however, was halted. In the final analysis, however, whatever rights the Acadians might have had, their situation in Massachusetts was one of poverty, sickness, and limited freedom of movement. Their final disposition was as arbitrary as much of their treatment had been: a gradual and relatively unrecorded dispersal to destinations out of province.

From Massachusetts to Pennsylvania the governors, councils, and assemblies received the Acadians with considerable displeasure but made some sort of provision for their subsistence and something of an effort to keep them under surveillance until 1763. All these more northerly colonies attempted a distribution of the exiles among different towns and villages in order both to minimise the impact of the exiles on the public purse of any particular settlement and to prevent any conspiracy of the Acadians against their hosts. New York received some five hundred of the exiles and by 9 July 1756, had passed an act empowering the justices "to bind out such of his Majesty's Subjects, commonly called Neutral French...to the End that they may not continue, as they now really are, useless to his Majesty, themselves and a burden on the Colony."[61] The justices were further urged to treat "the said people committed to their Care, with all the Justice in their Power, observing to make the most favourable contracts for them."[62]

Connecticut received perhaps 400.[63] They were divided into groups of no more than seventeen persons, and usually of only six or seven, and the groups were distributed among fifty different settlements throughout that colony.[64] In 1760 there is a report that about twenty-two vessels arrived in Boston from Connecticut and were refused permission to land the Acadians they had on board.[65] The next destination of these Acadians would almost certainly have been Santo Domingo.

The history of the Acadians who went to the Caribbean is difficult to piece together.

What is known at present can be summarized as follows. The Caribbean was, in every case, the exiles' second destination. In some cases, it was their third or fourth halt.[66] According to present knowledge, some 418 left from New York for Santo Domingo in 1764 and of these, 231 left in 1765 for Louisiana. In 1765, another 600 are reported as arriving in the Caribbean from "Acadie." It was thought they had been encouraged to do so by the English.[67] Parish registers indicate that the "Acadians were decimated by disease during the first months following their arrival."[68] What happened to them after that is a matter of debate. A large number went on to Louisiana, with either French or Spanish government aid. But there is no doubt that others remained, and in 1770 Acadians are still recorded in the records of Martinique, Guadaloupe, and Santo Domingo. In the mid-1820s a French government enquiry was undertaken for purposes of indemnifying former planters of Santo Domingo who had suffered losses during the Revolutionary year.[69]

Only six Acadian names appear on this list.[70] In sum, the Acadians can be distinguished in the records of Santo Domingo from 1764 until 1790. After that date, information about them is sparse indeed.

To return to the experiences of the exiles in their places of first landing, the number sent directly to Pennsylvania does not seem to have been much more than that sent to New York and Connecticut. But the plight of the exiles seems to have produced much more concern among the legislators and leading men there than anywhere else except France. Approximately 400 Acadians were landed in Pennsylvania on December 1755.[71] The governor requested an immediate opinion of his council as to what should be done with them.[72] It was not until the spring of 1756 that Benjamin Franklin received the commission as the printer of the act for "dispersing the Inhabitants of Nova Scotia, imported into this Province, into the several Counties of Philadelphia."[73] The act made provisions much like those of Massachusetts, placing the Acadians in the hands of the overseers of the poor, but it added to the powers the command to settle the Acadians on farming families.[74] By January 1757, Pennsylvania had decided to follow the procedure of Massachusetts and bind out children, while continuing to make provision for the "aged, sick and maimed at the charge of the province."[75] The Acadians reacted as they had in Massachusetts: they wrote petitions saying that the law should be revoked. In one petition it was stated that "to separate innocent Children who have committed no Crime from their Parents appears contrary to the Precept of Jesus Christ."[76] This particular petition ended with the point that the Acadians should be permitted to depart as soon as they were able if they would give assurance that they would not join the French. "If we had inclined to War," they claimed, "we should have been still perhaps in our own Country."[77]

The records of the province show that binding out was halted and that the Acadians were supported "in great Measure by private Charities, whence they are become extremely burdensome to the well-disposed Inhabitants."[78] In 1760 an Acadian petition was sent to the Penn brothers in London, accompanied by a covering letter signed by several of Philadelphia's leading men. Pemberton, Hantin, Emton, and others wrote that the Acadians had been struck by all manner of diseases, but above all by smallpox. "Those who have survived," the letter continued, "have flattered themselves with a hope that at the End of the Warr, they should be restored to their former Possessions, which we conceive, arises in part from a Consciousness that they were dispossessed out of Political Considerations rather than by way of Punishment for any Offence."[79]

Pennsylvania records fall silent after this point until 1771 when an account was made of some twenty-two families still in Philadelphia, most of them burdened with sickness of one kind or another.[80] This account is very different from the contemporary accounts of the Acadians in Massachusetts during the 1760s, or from the comparable reports from France at the opening of the 1770s, when officials in both places counted up to ten children a family. The Philadelphia list is filled with details of the blind, of sick children, of children that were "Foolish." In general a picture is painted of the very depths of misery. Apart from the records of death, there is no clear indication in the archives of Pennsylvania whether the fate of those Acadians sent there led back to Nova Scotia or southward to the Caribbean and to Louisiana.

Maryland and colonies further south did not allow the Acadians complete freedom of movement, but the attempts of these colonies to circumscribe Acadian activities were less efficient and less long-lasting than the efforts of the more northerly colonies. As has been noted, the immediate response of Maryland to the Acadians was a mixture of fear and compassion, with fear predominating. The Act already cited, which banned them from witnessing any training manoeuvres, was followed five days later by an act to empower the justices of the county courts to make provision for the Acadians, who were to be dispersed through various settlements.[81] By 1757 various county supervisors were asking for help from the authorities at Annapolis. Talbot County commissioners reported that the Acadians "are become a grievance; inasmuch as we are not at present in a Situation and in a Circumstance capable of seconding their own Fruitless Endeavours to support their numerous families, as a People Plunder'd of their Effects: for tho' perhaps our Magistrates have taxed us, perhaps sufficient to feed such of them as cannot feed themselves, they cannot find Houses, Cloathing and other Comforts, in their Condition needful, without going from House to House Begging."[82]

By 1763 Maryland records show that about one-third of those landed in 1755 had died or emigrated.[83] In 1765 a petition by the Acadians was presented to the Justices of the Peace of Cecil County, asking for help to leave for the Mississippi.[84] Some ships did leave for this destination two years later. The *Maryland Gazette* reported that the schooner *Virgin* with some Acadians aboard cleared Annapolis in 1767.[85] But reports show that the passengers of this ship almost certainly ended up in Sante Fe.[86] The story of the Acadians sent to Maryland dwindles into the occasional genealogical detail and the fate of the majority becomes, once more, a matter for conjecture.

Once south of Maryland, the treatment meted out to the Acadians becomes even less uniform. As has been noted, Virginia exported the problem one more time. This colony introduced a bill into its House of Burgesses on 1 April 1756 to "enable certain persons to contract for the Transportation of the Neutral French to Great Britain."[87] The cost was about £5000.[88] North and South Carolina and Georgia kept less than total control of the exiles that came their way. North Carolina, in fact, had no Acadians actually destined for her shores. However, in Cape Few, on 22 April 1756, one Jacques Morris appeared: "on behalf of himself and one hundred French, being part of the French Neutrals sent to Georgia and come coastwise in small boats, having a pass for himself from Governor Reynolds [Georgia] and Governor Glen [South Carolina]."[89]

The exiles were allowed to continue north. There is considerable debate about whether any particular group that left a southern colony was the one which is reported as being held in custody in a more northerly jurisdiction. It is, however, probable that this group made it as far as New York.[90]

South Carolina received more than 1,000 Acadians.[91] The policy evolved in Charleston was a combination of the actions of

Massachusetts, but with occasional forced labour, and the dispatch of a few families to England.[92] In general, however, exiles to this colony had their lives regulated by the legislation of 6 July 1756; this was entitled "An Act for disposing of the Acadians now in Charleston, by settling some fifth part of their number in the parishes of St. Philip and St. Michele and the four other parts of them in the other Parishes within this Province."[93] On 14 November 1755, Georgia received notice that Acadians had arrived. There was "great Confusion and Consternation"[94] and no coherent policy of any sort emerged from the discussions of governor and council. There were perhaps 600 to 700 Acadians in Savannah at any one time, and some of them were provided with boats and allowed to attempt the journey back. Lawrence was writing indignantly to the Board of Trade in August 1756 that "French Inhabitants sent to Ga...have been assisted at the Public Expense and are making for Nova Scotia."[95] Georgia did not manage to draft an act for "providing and disposing of the Acadians now in this province" until February 1757. At that point the provisions were similar to those of Massachusetts: the Acadians were divided among the townships and power was given to the Justices of the Peace to bind out the healthy into labour.[96]

The general impression one has of the deportation and years of exile is of the misery and distress of the Acadians. The entry for 8 October 1755 in Capt. Winslow's diary reads, "began to Embark the Inhabitants who went off Very Solentarily and unwillingly, the women in Great Distress Carrying off their children in their Arms, Others Carrying their Decript Parents in their Carts and all their Goods moving in Great Confusion and it appeared a scene of Woe and Distress."[97] His words are vivid and he is reporting a scene of human suffering accurately. But these words are utterly inadequate as a summary of Acadian reaction to what occurred. After all, the Acadians *survived* deportation and exile. Not only do some descendants

of those loaded on the ships live as a coherent group in the Maritimes today, but others live as part of a coherent community which was established some 2,000 miles south. A 1930s survey of French-speaking peoples in the southern part of the state of Louisiana noted that "out of 120 families...[there were] 108 reporting lines of descent on both sides as French...11 families reporting the use of both French and English in the home but French was the language stated to be most commonly used...solidly Catholic in religion, not a single exception to be found... [further] 72 of the families have as their nearest neighbour...the family of a some relative...[and this report] takes no account of relationships more remote than first cousin."[98]

The Acadians were nowhere merely passive recipients of the policies imposed on them by others. Even during the process of embarkation, some Acadian communities were able successfully to resist the plans for their exile. Once disembarked in new lands, the exiles continued to behave as if they were much more than just a body of refugees, or victims of war, and began to act with considerable political acumen. As soon as the Acadians had made even a minimal adaption to their new situation, they gathered their wits and wrote, or employed the local legal talent to write, petitions which set forth the totally unjustified nature of the punishment they had suffered and requested a variety of alterations in their situation.[99] This motif, that the deportation was basically unjust, is present no matter where the petitioners were and irrespective of whether the petition in question was made by an individual asking for consideration of a specific wrong, or by a group aimed at righting a more general wrong. Whether the petitions were written to the authorities of the British colonies in North America, to the British authorities in London by those Acadians sent abroad by Virginia, to the French authorities by the Acadians who arrived there between 1758 and 1764, or to the Spanish authorities at the time of the removal of Acadians from France to Louisiana in 1785, the tenor of the petitions is similar: for various and particular reasons, the deportation was unjustified and the authorities were asked to do something about the unfortunate situation in which the Acadians now found themselves.[100]

It is fascinating to compare the way in which this belief—that the deportation was a matter of singular injustice—was expressed to the different jurisdictions. In North America, of course, such petitions often contained assertions of past loyalty to British interests. For example, Joseph Michelle, in a protest sent to Governor Shirley of Massachusetts about the way in which his son was treated, remarked that he and his family had "been employed in repairing the forts at Annapolis, as an overseer of all Carts in bringing up Timber which I was obliged to do in the Night Time for fear of the Indians where I and my family run the risk of our Lives."[101] Similarly, in a handbill circulated in Philadelphia in 1758, the Acadians asserted "Almost numberless are the Instances which might be given to the Abuses and Losses we have undergone from the French and the Indians, only on account of our adherence to our Oath of Fidelity."[102]

Those Acadians whose exile took them to England and to France also petitioned about the conditions under which they lived and the payment of the government support which both countries accorded them. In neither country were the Acadians over-awed by the status of those whose business it was to oversee their lives. The Acadians who arrived in England did so in early summer 1756. They are reported as numbering over 1,044.[103] They remained in England for nearly seven years and never hesitated to dispute measures that the British government took towards them. As peace approached in 1763, steps were taken to ask those Acadians then living in Liverpool, Southampton, Penryn, Falmouth, and Bristol what they hoped for. In no uncertain terms, the Acadians demanded that they be returned to Acadia. "We hope We shall be sent into Our Countries," their petition noted, "and that our Effects etc., which We have been dispossessed of (notwithstanding the faithful neutrality which We have always observed) will be restored to Us."[104] That these views were ignored does not alter the fact that those who expressed them had a clear idea of what their future should be. The immediate fate of these particular Acadians was to be shipped to France in the summer of 1763. They were fewer than the number that had arrived from Virginia, being in total no more than 866.[105]

These were by no means the first Acadians to arrive in France.[106] As early as 1749 an English vessel was reported as arriving at Nantes with "Acadians" from Louisbourg.[107] Almost ten years later, in 1758, separate arrivals were reported at Boulogne, Brest, Cherbourg, and St Malo; in 1759, further listings are given for ships arriving at Boulogne, Dunkerque, and St Malo; in 1760 there is a listing for Cherbourg; in 1761 for Rochefort; and in 1763 for Marlaix.[108] The numbers are difficult to establish. I would estimate that, including those sent on from England, there were some 3,000 Acadians in France at the end of 1763.

Their attitude towards French officialdom was as trenchant as it had been to English bureaucracy. The first reply of the exiles to French proposals for their settlement in Belle-Île-en-Mer, a small island off the south coast of Brittany, was less than grateful. In the Acadians' view, the land was poor, and the island far too near English power for comfort.[109] This response set the tone for much of the future interaction between the Acadians and French authorities. The two major attempts at resettlement, at Belle Île and at "La ligne acadienne" in Poitou, both failed.[110] The majority of the Acadians left France in 1785 for Louisiana.[111]

At first sight, this seems surprising. Acadians were, after all, French-speaking Catholics: there was at least a supposition of commonalty of interest with the French nation, and one of the proposed sites for their resettlement was in a part of France from which many of their ancestors had emigrated. Superficially, having been given considerable aid from the French government and having had the experience of exile in British communities, assimilation into eighteenth-century France would appear a distinct possibility. But this did not happen: the Acadians were French-speaking and Catholic, but they were also North American. The norms of the Acadians during the twenty years they spent in France were dominated by the Acadian identity that had been forged in "Acadia or Nova Scotia." They did not prove malleable to French influence. Some reasons for this are suggested in a letter by a lawyer of Dinan in 1759 to the naval commissioner at St Malo, asking help for the twenty-two Acadians he had established on his own farm.[112] He wrote in part as follows: "Premierement ses peuples sont elévés dans un pays d'abondance, de terres a discretion, par consequent moins difficile a cultiver...de plus les hommes...ressentent déjà les chaleurs quoy aye point encore sensibles pour nous, ils mannient un peu la hache pour logement et assez mal quelques chose a leurs usages, ce qu'on n'appeller que hacheur des bois, les femmes filent un peu des bas." According to this same source, the Acadians wanted a great deal of bread, demanded milk and butter, and would not be weaned to cider: the desire for North American foodstuffs had replaced an appetite for French staples.

But material customs, however, are only a part—if an important part—of the life of a distinct community. The Acadians confronted not merely a different agricultural environment but a fundamentally different social and political context. As was shown very early on in the Belle Île experiment, the Acadians were not used to the structured organization of eighteenth-century French bureaucracy.[113] Acadians did not like tithes, bitterly resented the idea that they should stay in one place, and found little in common with their new

neighbours, the original inhabitants of Belle Île. Similarly, the efforts made in the 1770s to establish the Acadians on the estates of the Marquis de Perusse des Cars came to naught.[114] Although one can find traces that record the treatment of Acadians as a distinct group in France as late as 1828, after 1785 their history there is once again a matter of genealogical interest in individuals rather than a question of the survival of a community.

The reactions of a group in exile are influenced not only by conditions existing within the group but also by their new external environment. The binding nature of Acadian kinship ties was reinforced by their total lack of such ties, at least during the early years, with the people among whom they were exiled. The Acadians retained their identity in exile partly because of official policies that designated them a group. Thus, the ways in which governments organized the exiles, paid them pensions, or settled them in areas reserved exclusively for them all helped preserve the Acadian sense of their unique identity. But when all is said and done, the Acadians remained a coherent group in exile because they were a coherent people before they went into exile. It is the sense of community that was part and parcel of the Acadians as individuals that led to behaviour which caused a Georgia official to comment, "such is the Bigotry and Obstinacy of these People that they have chosen rather to live miserably than to separate and live comfortably."[115]

The most important resources that the Acadians took with them into exile were social and political strengths. Acadian society was really built on the extended family. Thus, while brutal family separations did take place during the exile, there always remained a web of family linkages which supported the individuals in the strange new lands. The network of inter-marriages, which brought together people from different settlements as well as from within the same village, is documented in the registers compiled by the French government for Belle Île.[116] The psychological impact of the trauma, the impact of death and sickness, would be somewhat mitigated by the presence of people who were obviously kin. The political experience of the Acadians before 1755 gave the exiles not only a known pattern of leadership, but forged a people accustomed to arguing with an authority that, in its own eyes, was stronger and more righteous.

There was a third factor which not only sustained the Acadians who went into exile but was also a significant factor in the continuance of the Acadians in Nova Scotia. This was the belief, held by the community as a whole, that the Acadians were a people distinct from others. Their legitimate country was "Acadia or Nova Scotia." The eighteenth century Acadians were not a nation, but they were a distinct culture. The Acadian sense that the lands surrounding their villages were theirs to exploit, coupled with a clear sense of the family connections which ran from village to village and a distinctive life-style, was by 1755 the fundamental background for Acadian political action. The Acadians considered that they had developed a political culture which fitted the needs of the society that they had built between two empires. In the Acadian view, a view that is repeated over and over again in the petitions they presented in exile, they had done nothing, nothing at all, to deserve deportation. It is the sense of being a society, of possessing both a group identity and the right to live in a particular place, that allowed the Acadians to surmount the exile and later rebuild their community in the Maritimes, as well as establishing another in Louisiana.

The deportation was not an incident which took place in a single year, but a policy pursued until 1763. Despite the zeal with which the policy was prosecuted, however, the colony was never entirely without Acadians.[117] On 26 July 1764, the Lords of Trade informed the governor of Nova Scotia that he should allow the Acadians to settle in Nova Scotia, provided they took the oath of allegiance, in spite of their "having taken up Arms in support of France during the late war."[118] Nine years after the transports first left, the Acadians were admitted once more as subjects with legal status in the colony. There were at that time about 1,500 of them actually within Nova Scotia.[119]

From the moment they left the coast of Nova Scotia, the Acadians had made every effort to return. Even those who escaped to Quebec did not find that society to their liking. Bishop Pontbriand wrote in 1756 that "le sort des Acadiens m'afflige; a en juger par ceux qui sont ici, ils ne veulent par demeurer parmi nous."[120] They returned from all points of the globe, Massachusetts as well as France. On arrival in Nova Scotia they found their former lands occupied, their villages truly conquered territory. They found that those who had escaped deportation had relocated in new settlements, some within the peninsula, but most on the very boundaries of the territory once called "Acadia or Nova Scotia." They had some choice. They could attach themselves to the Acadian communities within Nova Scotia on the lands which had been specifically assigned to them: in particular, they could join those living along Baie St Marie, district of Clare.[121] They could elect to join the tiny communities on Cape Breton Island or to join those established in what after 1798 would be called Prince Edward Island. They could go to the Acadian communities that existed in what would become New Brunswick in 1784, either to those of the St John River Valley or to those on its coast between the Baie de Chaleurs and Baie Verte.

Wherever the Acadians were established after 1764, one thing became clear: their sense of themselves as a people was undiminished. As far as it lay in their power, they attempted to recreate the same self-contained and independent life they had had before 1755. The circumstances were very different. They were no longer a border people but were now merely one group within a large empire. By the end of the 1780s, the Acadians had recovered some of their former demographic strength, but they were still a minority in the three Maritime colonies and would remain so over the ensuing decades. Yet the reports sent by Quebec missionaries to the Archbishop of Quebec in the late 1780s still characterize the Acadians as stubborn, argumentative, and clearly determined to assert their right to argue the politics of their lives with all those who considered them subject to their authority.[122] The subsequent growth and development of the identity of this Acadian society is as complex as the history of its genesis. It was an identity that included not only the experience of the cataclysmic events of the Deportation but also beliefs about the pre-deportation Acadian society. It was an identity that would be built not only on a common language and religion, and on a common culture, but on a common interpretation of the history of the Deportation. The Acadians of the nineteenth century would find an extraordinary force for unity in their adherence to a particular interpretation of the events of 1755. One thing is clear, the policy initiated by Colonel Lawrence at mid-century failed to destroy the Acadian community. Further, in the very circumstances of its failure, it provided the Acadians with one of the foundations of their unique identity in the centuries to come.

Notes

1 Michel Roy, in his work *L'Acadie Perdue* (Quebec, 1978), 39, considers that the task is both the historian's challenge and the historian's inevitable defeat. Both he and Leon Theriault, the latter in a work entitled *La question du pouvoir en Acadie* (Ottawa, 1982), struggle with what the dominance of the idea of the deportation means to Acadian identity today.

2 In 1981, Statistics Canada reported that those with French as a mother tongue made up 5 percent of the population of Prince Edward Island, 4 percent of the population of Nova Scotia, and 34 percent of the population of New Brunswick. Recognition of the Acadians as a French-speaking people with a recognizable community identity encapsulated by the word "Acadian" has not yet been accorded them by the Canadian federal government.

3 N.E.S. Griffiths, "The Acadians," *DCB* 4: xxvii–xxxi.

4 The organization of Acadian settlements after 1764 was controlled by the authorities at Halifax and, later, by those in Fredericton and Charlottetown. There is no question that an Acadian's absolute title to land was often abrogated. On the question of Acadian holdings in the Saint John River Valley see E.C. Wright, *The Loyalists of New Brunswick* (Moncton, 1955).

5 The poems of Hermenegilde Chiasson are a riveting expression of such emotion, especially those collected in the volume *Mourir à Scoudouc* (Moncton, 1979). It is in his works that one reads: "Comment faire comprendre, faire sentir, faire vivre que l'Acadie ce n'est pas le lèpre que nous ne voulons plus qu'on vienne faire ses bonnes oeuvres parmi nous," 33.

6 Emile Louvrière, *La Tragédie d'un peuple,* subtitled: *Histoire du peuple acadien de ses origines à nos jours* (Paris, 1923).

7 O.W. Winzerling, *Acadian Odyssey* (Lafayette, 1955).

8 William Faulkner Rushton, *The Cajuns From Acadia to Louisiana* (New York, 1987).

9 The best bibliographic references for this subject are the relevant pages of *Bibliographie acadienne: Liste des Volumes, Brochures et Thèses concernant l'Acadie et les Acadiens des debuts à 1975* (Moncton, n.d.); and Helene Harbec and Paulette Leversque, eds., *Guide bibliographique de l'Acadie, 1976–1987* (Moncton, 1988).

10 Archivo Segreto Vaticano, Collegione Nunziatura de Fiandra, 22 November 1763, Leg. 135, which was used by O.W. Winzerling, *Acadian Odyssey: Exile Without End* (Louisiana, 1955).

11 Winzerling notes that he spent several years in the colony where there "were graves of scores of Acadians who had once sought refuge on the shores between Monkey River and Point Diable." Ibid., 70.

12 For a survey of the historical roots of this poem and of the circumstances in which it was written, see N.E.S. Griffiths: "Longfellow's Evangeline: The Birth and Acceptance of a Legend," *Acadiensis* 11 (1982): 28–41.

13 R. Cole Harris, ed., *Historical Atlas of Canada: From the Beginning to 1800* (Toronto, 1987), 1: Plate 24.

14 Winzerling, *Acadian Odyssey.*

15 The best collection of essays on the way in which the Acadians arrived and settled in Louisiana is that edited

by Glenn R. Conrad, *The Cajuns: Essays on their history and culture,* The University of Southwestern Louisiana History series no. 11, (Lafayette, LA, 1978).

16 "Circular from Governor Lawrence to the Governors on the continent, Halifax, August 11th, 1755," in *Report Concerning Canadian Archives for the Year 1905,* 3 vols. (Ottawa: Public Archives of Canada, 1906), 2: App. 3, 15–16.

17 Brown Manuscripts, Add. Mss. 1907, 11–73, British Museum. Lawrence's letter of instructions are in *Northcliffe Collection Reports* (Ottawa: Public Archives of Canada, 1926), 80–3.

18 "Instructions for Lieut. Colonel Winslow, Halifax, August 11th, 1755," in T.B. Akins, *Selections from the Public Documents of the Province of Nova Scotia* (Halifax, 1869), 271–4.

19 Ibid., "Instructions to Major Handfield, Halifax, 11th August," 275.

20 "Instructions to Moncton, August 11th, 1755," in *Northcliffe Collection,* 65–7.

21 "Winslow's Journal," *Collections of the Nova Scotia Historical Society* 3 (1883): 97 ff.

22 "Petition to the King of Great Britain, c. 1760," in L. Smith, *Acadia: A Lost Chapter in American History* (Boston, 1884).

23 "Moncton to Winslow, October 7th, 1755," *Report for 1905,* 2: App. B, 30.

24 "Lawrence to Moncton, September 1755," Vernon-Wager Mss., Library of Congress (Washington, DC).

25 See "Winslow's Journal," vol. 3.

26 The first Acadians to be landed in Boston arrived there as a result of stormy weather. *Report for 1905,* 2: App. E, 81.

27 "Dinwiddie to Shirley, 28th April, 1756," in R. Brooks, ed., "Dinwiddie Papers," *Virginia Historical Society Collections* (Richmond, 1899), 2: 394.

28 "Minutes of the Provincial Council, September 1756," *Colonial Records: Minutes of the Provincial Council of Pennsylvania from the Organization of the Termination of the Proprietary Government,* 16 vols., (Harrisburg, Pa., 1852–3), 7: 239–41.

29 28 November 1755: *Extracts from the Journals of the Provincial Congress of South Carolina* (Charlestown, 1775–6), 513.

30 Massachusetts: 7 November 1755, Boston State House, Hutchinson Papers, vol. 23; Pennsylvania: "Minutes of the Provincial Council," 6: 712–3; Georgia: George C. Candler, ed., *The Colonial Records of the State of Georgia,* 26 vols. (1904–13), 7:

301 ff.; Virginia: Robert Dinwiddie, *The Official Records of Robert Dinwiddie, Lieutenant-Governor of the Colony of Virginia, 1751–1758,* ed. Robert A. Brock, 2 vols. (Richmond, VA, 1883–84), 2: 269 ff.

31 He was the father of Jonathon Belcher, at that time Chief Justice of Nova Scotia and much involved in the organization of the deportation.

32 Pennsylvania Archives, First Series, 1748–56, 2: 514.

33 Massachusetts State Archives, Council Records, Commonwealth of Massachusetts, 21: 80.

34 Cited in Placide Gaudet, "Acadian Genealogy and Notes," *Report for 1905,* 2: v.

35 Proceedings and Acts of the General Assembly of Maryland (Baltimore, 1930), 24: 461.

36 *Report for 1905,* 2: App. E, 81. Massachusetts nagged at this question throughout the years that Acadians remained a public charge; the final account of £9563 9 shillings and 10 pence was submitted in August 1763, ibid., App. F, 133.

37 *The Acts and Resolves, Public and Private of... Massachusetts Bay to which are Prefixed the Charters of the Province,* 21 vols. (Boston, 1869–1922), 3: 951.

38 Ibid., 887.

39 Boston State House, *Hutchinson Papers,* vol. 23. This petition is translated and printed in *Report for 1905,* 2: App. E, 88. It is important to consider the original, in which the spelling and grammar indicate that it was most probably written by the Acadians themselves.

40 *Report for 1905,* 2: App. E, 100 ff.

41 13 April 1756, Boston State House, *Hutchinson Papers,* vol. 23. See also Massachusetts State Archives, Council Records, Commonwealth of Massachusetts, 21: passim.

42 A.G. Doughty, *The Acadian Exiles: A Chronicle of the Land of Evangeline* (Toronto, 1916), 184.

43 10 June 1756, Boston State House, *Hutchinson Papers,* vol. 23.

44 Boston State House, *Hutchinson Papers,* vol. 23. Gaudet, "Acadian Genealogy," *Report for 1905,* 2: 89 has the Act as 28–30 August 1756. *Acts and Resolves...Massachusetts Bay,* 3: 986.

45 23 July 1756, Boston State House, *Hutchinson Papers,* vol. 23. Much of the documentation of this episode is printed in Akins, *Nova Scotia Documents,* 302 ff.

46 A good collection of these can be found in *Report for 1905,* 2: 104 ff.

47 Boston State House, *Hutchinson Papers,* vol. 23.

48 *Report for 1905,* 2: 114.

49 5 October 1759, *Acts and Resolves...Massachusetts Bay,* 4: 102.

50 Massachusetts State Archives, Council Records, Commonwealth of Massachusetts, 23: 210.

51 15 January 1757, Boston State House, *Hutchinson Papers,* vol. 23.

52 (no day given) March 1757, ibid.

53 6 September 1762, *Acts and Resolves...Massachusetts Bay,* 5: 104; and *Report for 1905,* 2: App. F, 133–4.

54 18 January 1764, *Report for 1905,* 2: App. E, 90.

55 A somewhat muddled, but exhaustive account of this can be found in Pierre Belliveau, *French Neutrals in Massachusetts* (Boston, 1972), 22 ff.

56 *Report for 1905,* 2: App. E, 90.

57 24 January 1765, *Acts and Resolves...Massachusetts Bay,* 6: 105.

58 "Jean Trahant, Castin Thibodet, Jean Hebaire, Charles Landry, Allexis Braux to the Governor and Commander in Chief of Massachusetts Bay, Boston 1st Jan. 1765," in *Report for 1905,* 2: App. E, 92–3.

59 Ibid., 96–9. See also *Acts and Resolves...Massachusetts Bay,* 4: 911.

60 Account published in Gaudet, "Acadian Genealogy," 100.

61 W. Livingstone and W. Smith, eds., *Laws of New York from the 11th November, 1752 to 22nd of May, 1762,* 2 vols. (New York, 1762), 2: 103–4.

62 Ibid.

63 Trumbell, James Hammond, and C.J. Hoadley, eds., *Public Records of the Colony of Connecticut, May, 1751–February, 1757,* 15 vols. (New Haven, 1850–90), vol. 10.

64 "An Act for distributing and well-ordering the French people sent into this colony from Nova Scotia, January 1756," *Report for 1905,* 2: App. K, 254.

65 L.W. Cross, *The Acadians and the New England Planters* (Cambridge, NS, 1962).

66 J.T. Vocelle, *The Triumph of the Acadians* (1930), is the best short account but see also Gabriel Debien, "The Acadians in Santo Domingo," in Conrad, *The Cajuns,* 21–96.

67 Archives Colonial de Commerce de Guyenne, c. 4328, 1765, in 1F2161, AD, Ille-et-Vilaine (Rennes).

68 Debien, "The Acadians in Santo Domingo," in Conrad, *The Cajun,* 87.

69 *The Detailed List of Indemnities, Drawn up by the Commission Charged with Indemnifying the Former Planters of Santo Domingo, According to the Law of April 10th, 1826,* 6 vols. (Paris, 1827–33), cited in Conrad, *The Cajuns,* 90.

70 A. Therior, Jacques Genton, Victoire Jourdain, Joseph Giroir, Michael Poirier, and Marie-Madeleine Poirier.

71 Samuel Hazard et al., eds., *Pennsylvania Archives: Selected and Arranged from the original documents in the Office of the Secretary of State of the Commonwealth...* 138 vols. (Harrisburg and Philadelphia 3 PA, 1852–1935). Eight Series, 1931, 6: 4159.

72 9th of December, 1755, Minutes of the Provincial Council, *Colonial Records, Pennsylvania,* 6: 751.

73 J.T. Mitchell and H. Flanders, eds., *Statutes at Large of Pennsylvania from 1682 to 1801,* 17 vols. (1896–1915), 5: 215–19.

74 Hazard et al., *Pennsylvania Archives,* 6: 4408.

75 Mitchell and Flanders, *Statutes at Large of Pennsylvania,* 278–80.

76 Public Archives of Pennsylvania, Votes of Assembly, 4509–12.

77 Ibid., 4512.

78 Hazard et al., *Pennsylvania Archives,* 6: 4901.

79 *"Pemberton Papers"* (Harrisburg, n.d.), 1: 99.

80 2 November 1771, Pennsylvania Historical Society Collections, printed in *American Catholic Historical Review* 18 (1901): 140–2.

81 27 May, 1756, *Proceedings and Acts of the General Assembly of Maryland* (Baltimore, 1930), 24: 542 ff.

82 Cited in B. Sollers, "The Acadians (French Neutrals) Transported to Maryland," *Maryland Historical Magazine* 3 (1907): 18.

83 Census of Acadians, July 1763, photostat in Hall of Records, Annapolis, Maryland. The original is in the Archives Nationales (Paris), Affaires Etrangères, Politique Angleterre, vol. 451, f. 438.

84 Printed in J. Johnston, *History of Cecil County, Maryland* (Elkton, 1881), 263.

85 9 April 1767 (Annapolis).

86 B. Sollers, "Report on Smyth, *A Tour of U.S.A.* (London, 1784)," *Maryland Historical Magazine* 4 (1909): 279.

87 McIlwaine, ed., *Journals of the Houses of Burgesses of Virginia* (Charlottesville, 1909), 353. The bill was given assent by the Governor on 15 April 1756.

88 "Governor Dinwiddie to Dobbs, June 11th, 1756," in Dinwiddie, *The Official Records,* 2: 442–3.

89 W. Saunders, *Colonial Records of North Carolina, 1752–59,* 5: 655.

90 Doughty, *The Acadian Exiles,* 147.

91 Figures derived from the reports of the arrival of various ships in *Carolina Gazette,* 13–20 November, 20–27 November, and 4–11 December 1755. See also C.J. Milling, *Exile without End* (Columbia, SC, 1945).

92 The best short account of this episode is Milling, *Exile without End.*

93 T. Cooper and David James MacCord, eds., *The Statutes at Large of South Carolina, 1682–1838.* 10 vols. (S. Carolina, 1836–41), 3: 31.

94 "Letter of Council to the Board of Trade, 5th January 1756," in Allan D. Candler, ed., *Colonial Records of the State of Georgia,* 7: 207.

95 Akins, *Nova Scotia Documents,* 302–3.

96 *Statutes enacted by the Royal Legislature, Georgia* (1757), 18: 188.

97 "Winslow's Journals," *Collections of the Nova Scotia Historical Society,* 3: 166.

98 T.L. Smith, "An Analysis of Rural Social Organization Among the French Speaking People of Southern Louisiana," *Journal of Farm Economics* 16 (1937): 682–4.

99 N.E.S. Griffiths, "Petitions of Acadian Exiles, 1755–1785. A Neglected Source," *Histoire Sociale / Social History 11,* no. 21 (mai–May 1978): 215–23 presents a summary of many of these.

100 A selection of these petitions has been printed in *Report for 1905,* vol. 2; and L.H. Gipson, *The British Empire Before the American Revolution,* 6: chapter 6.

101 *Report for 1905,* 2: App. E, 100.

102 Hazard et al., *Pennsylvania Archives, First Series, 1752–1756,* 3: 566.

103 N.E.S. Griffiths, "Acadians in Exile," *Acadiensis* 4 (1974): 70.

104 "L.G. and J.B. to John Cleveland, 4th January, 1763, Admiralty Records 98/9," partially printed in ibid., 74.

105 *Report for 1905,* 2: 150.

106 For a general survey of Acadian experience in France see N.E.S. Griffiths, "The Acadians Who Returned to France," *Natural History* 90 (1981): 48–57.

107 There is not much information about these people, save that they are called Acadian in the port listings of arrival, 1F2160, Archives d'Ille-et-Vilaine (Rennes).

108 Ibid.

109 Petition dated Morlaix, 31st octobre 1763, c. 5058, AD, Ille-et-Vilaine (Rennes).

110 Winzerling, *Acadian Odyssey,* describes the arrival in France of those who had been sent to England. The works of Milton P. Rieder and Norma Gaudet Rieder, including *The Acadians in France,* 3 vols. (Lafayette, 1973), are most useful. Ernest Martin, *Les exiles Acadiens en France au XVIII siècle et leur établissement en Poitou* (Brissard, 1979) gives a solid narrative of Acadian experience in one area of France from 1763 to 1785.

111 N.E.S. Griffiths, "Les Acadiens et leur établissement en Louisiane," *France-Amérique* 35 (1983): 1–4.

112 "Dinan, l'avocat de la Crochais to Guilot, St. Malo, 10 mai 1750," IF2159, Archives d'Ille-et-Vilaine, Rennes.

113 Griffiths, "The Acadians Who Returned to France," 53 ff.

114 On this see Martin, *Les exiles Acadiens.*

115 "Report of the Committee...12th July, 1760" in the Journals of the House of Assembly, State Archives, Columbia, South Carolina. These records are now part of a publication series, viz: Easterby, J.H., ed., *The Journal of the Commons House of Assembly of South Carolina, South Carolina Colonial Records.*

116 Rieder and Rieder, eds., *The Acadians in France,* vol. 2.

117 *Censuses of Canada, 1665–1871* (Ottawa, 1876), 4: xxviii.

118 "Lords of Trade to Wilmot, July 16th, 1764," NA, CO218/6, B 1115.

119 PANS, "Early Descriptions of Nova Scotia," *Reports* (Halifax, 1943), App. B, part 2, 32.

120 "Pontbriand a Belair, 23rd juillet, 1756," Archives Archévêque de Québec (Quebec), 2: 620.

121 M.A. Tremblay, "Les Acadiens de la Baie Francaise: L'histoire d'une survivance," *Revue de l'histoire de l'Amerique française* 20 (1962).

122 "Etat de la Mission de l'Acadie," Archives Archévêque de Québec NE/1–12, 1786.

PART III

The Origins of British North America, 1749–1821

Imperial rivalries did not end with the Seven Years War. In 1776, thirteen of Great Britain's colonies along the Atlantic seaboard declared independence. France took advantage of the war between Great Britain and the newly declared United States to hit back at its old enemy. When the American Revolution ended in 1783, only colonies that had once been claimed by France remained under British control. They became the foundation upon which the future nation of Canada would be built, but the building occurred in a difficult context. In 1789, the French Revolution erupted, drawing most of Europe and, for a brief time, the United States into a long struggle known as the French and Napoleonic Wars (1793–1815). Despite the embarrassing loss of the Thirteen Colonies, Great Britain emerged as the dominant power in the new world order that emerged early in the nineteenth century.

In addition to seeking territorial gains, the combatants in these wars fought over political ideas. The American and French revolutions signalled the birth of a new era characterized by liberal democratic political systems, capitalist commercial relations, and new social values focused on individualism and secularism. In this period Great Britain fought a rearguard action against the more advanced tenets of liberalism, which called for separation of church and state, abolition of monarchies, and universal manhood suffrage. Such a position in part explains the policies adopted toward Quebec, the name given to its newly conquered colony in 1763. While designed to placate their new subjects in the context of impending wars, both the Quebec Act of 1774 and the Constitutional Act of 1791 were also crafted to preserve and even strengthen conservative elements in colonial governance.

The arrival of 35 000 Loyalists in the Maritime colonies and another 15 000 in Quebec following the American Revolution further strengthened the bias toward conservatism. While in no way a uniform group in their cultural or political values, many Loyalists were initially reluctant, because of their experience in the United States, to champion the republican cause. Moreover, British authorities kept a watchful eye on their remaining North American colonies, especially the new ones designed to accommodate the Loyalists: New Brunswick and Upper Canada (now Ontario). The War of 1812, which found the British North American colonies caught in another war between Great Britain and the United States, served to harden political lines, especially in Upper Canada, where the bulk of the fighting occurred. Following the war, a conservative backlash helped to maintain a hierarchical, class-structured society in Upper Canada that many hoped would preserve British institutions in the face of American republicanism and territorial expansion.

The readings in this section focus on the social adjustments that accompanied the warfare and political turmoil of the late eighteenth and early nineteenth centuries. Foremost among those making adjustments were the Aboriginal peoples, whose lands were increasingly being claimed and occupied by European settlers. In the years immediately following the fall of New France, the Natives along the Anglo-American frontier attacked British-occupied trading posts and secured, in the Royal Proclamation of 1763, a guarantee of land rights in areas of North America not previously ceded or purchased by European powers. In the Maritime colonies, the story was more complicated. Immigrants from Great Britain, Europe, and New England had been "planted" in the region following the founding of Halifax and the Acadian deportation. As John Reid explains in his article on Planter Nova Scotia, the Mi'kmaq, Maliseet, and Passamaquoddy had signed treaties with the British in 1760–61, but their land rights remained unacknowledged. This set the stage, Reid notes, for a brief period in which Aboriginal and British pacification strategies competed, followed by a partial reconciliation, which was swept away by the Loyalist migration.

While most Loyalists were drawn from the farming and artisan classes, and left few personal records to describe their experience of exile, the minority who became office holders and professionals produced a wealth of documentary evidence. Ann Gorman Condon uses personal letters written by these elite Loyalists to explore how families coped with the migration to what would become the province of New Brunswick. The family letters, she notes, are "delicate, witty, warmly demonstrative," suggesting that close family relationships for Loyalist refugees, as for the Acadians, played an important role in accommodating the difficulties posed by being uprooted. Interestingly, the elegance, the exclusivity, and the intensity reflected in the Loyalist letters were transferred to their children but not to their grandchildren. For the latter, oral histories transmitted by families were giving way to written accounts of the Loyalist experience that were prompted more by public motives than a desire to preserve family lore.

During the period that Lower Canada was adjusting to its new status as a British colony with a representative assembly, the French Revolution was introducing more radical notions of political rights. How did ordinary Canadiens respond to ideas of liberty, equality, and fraternity that might serve to release them not only from the yoke of the conquest but also from colonial elites who wanted to conscript them into militia duty and road work? In his article, F. Murray Greenwood explores threats to the security of Lower Canada between 1793 and 1798, including plans by Revolutionary France to invade the colony and, on two occasions, province-wide rioting. For the most part, Greenwood concludes, the external threat was imaginary and the provocation for rioting locally generated. He further surmises that neither urban workers nor habitant farmers would have been likely to support French forces had they managed to invade the colony. Quick to resist oppression when it bore down upon them, Canadiens had little understanding of revolutionary ideals and few educated leaders to enlist them in the revolutionary cause.

Most people in Upper Canada during the War of 1812 were equally reluctant to fight for political ideals. After the fact, Upper Canadians often boasted about their loyalty to the British Crown and their commitment to militia duty. Their historical memory, it appears, quickly became distorted. As George Sheppard argues, most Upper Canadians were "cool calculators," hoping, like so many ordinary people trapped in a war zone, that they would not lose everything by backing the wrong side. Indeed, he concludes, "avoidance of militia duty was the norm for Upper Canadian males throughout the struggle."

As Carolyn Podruchny shows, men working on the fur trade frontier between 1780 and 1821 reluctantly conformed to the ideals laid down for them in labour contracts. Both masters and servants constantly renegotiated their relationships, with labour disputes and power struggles punctuating the process. While Podruchny is unable to determine whether accommodation or confrontation predominated as a means of settling disputes, she is certain that what she calls the "social contract" had more impact than the legal one in a world where employers sustained their authority by controlling European necessities, carefully dispensing perks, and keeping their employees in indebtedness.

For Aboriginal peoples on the Pacific coast and elsewhere in the Northwest, the impact of disease was undoubtedly the most significant historical event in this period. Geographer Cole Harris uses Coast Salish oral accounts of the devastation wrought by the arrival of smallpox in 1782 to help piece together the extent of the tragedy that accounted for the deserted beaches that greeted George Vancouver when he arrived in the early 1790s. A pandemic that began in Mexico in 1779, smallpox spread quickly throughout North and South America, killing as many as 90 percent of the people in its path. In the past this event has largely been ignored by scholars who, Harris points out, clung to the European belief that they brought only "enlightenment and civilization to savage peoples." With new attitudes toward Native peoples and new approaches to researching the past, such silences, we hope, no longer prevail in the writing of Canadian history.

Pax Britannica or Pax Indigena? Planter Nova Scotia (1760–1782) and Competing Strategies of Pacification

JOHN G. REID

Planter Nova Scotia spanned the years from the start of the New England migration into the province in 1760 to the Loyalist influx, which began on a large scale in 1782. For many years, historians of this era concentrated their efforts on two principal questions: Why did the New England Planters fail to join the American Revolution in significant numbers? What differentiated the Planters from the later Loyalist migrants?[1] These remain significant issues, and yet the historiographical context for considering them has shifted markedly in recent years. The change is owed in part to the publication since 1987 of four major collections of essays bearing specifically on the Planter era. The Planter Studies Conferences at Acadia University, and the published volumes drawn from them, have accomplished much more than their original modest aim of rescuing the Planters from historical obscurity.[2] The series has provided the motive power for a fundamental re-engineering of our understanding of the Maritime colonies in the eighteenth century. Planter Studies, from the beginning, was broadly and inclusively designed so that not only could a wide variety of disciplinary approaches be accommodated but

studies of Acadians, Mi'kmaq and Wulstukwiuk (Maliseet), Halifax and Lunenberg settlers, and even Loyalists, were also included, along with those dealing more strictly with New England Planters. Taking the four Planter Studies volumes together, the result has been to underline the socio-ethnic diversity of Planter Nova Scotia.

Yet one area considered only peripherally in the Planter Studies volumes is the interaction of Planters with Aboriginal inhabitants. While the Mi'kmaq and the Wulstukwiuk, as noted above, are far from being ignored, the only essay dealing centrally with Aboriginal history is William Wicken's "Mi'kmaq Land in Southwestern Nova Scotia, 1771–1823," which explores a specific aspect of the Mi'kmaq experience over a period that extends chronologically far beyond the Planter era.[3] The absence of other essays on Aboriginal themes reflects a broader historiographical reality: The role of Aboriginal nations in the region during the 1760s and 1770s has hitherto lacked comprehensive study (especially by comparison with the attention historians have given to earlier decades), and the integration of the Aboriginal with the non-Aboriginal

John Reid, "*Pax Britannica* or *Pax Indigena*? Planter Nova Scotia (1760–1782) and Competing Strategies of Pacification," *Canadian Historical Review* 85, 4 (December 2004): 669–692. Reprinted with permission of the University of Toronto Press Incorporated (www.utp.journals.com).

history of the era has been hindered accordingly. Especially important—since this was an era of not only British–Mi'kmaq and British–Wulstukwiuk treaty-making in 1760–1 but also of the longer-term working through of the ensuing relationships—is the question of the relative diplomatic and military weight wielded by either side. Was British hegemony characteristic of Planter Nova Scotia, or did Mi'kma'ki and Wulstukwiuk persist autonomously despite British imperial claims?

The earlier eighteenth-century context for addressing this question has been elaborated significantly in recent studies. Historians such as Elizabeth Mancke and William Wicken have added, respectively, new imperial and Aboriginal dimensions to the existing historiography. My own work has emphasized the limitations on imperial endeavours in the region in the seventeenth and early eighteenth centuries, while Geoffrey Plank has demonstrated the British inability to erase Acadian and Mi'kmaq distinctness even by harsh military actions. Naomi Griffiths and Maurice Basque (although presenting divergent views of Acadian political economy) have shown the sophistication of Acadian responses to imperial and Aboriginal neighbours, while Barry Moody has exposed the delicate balances that kept the pre-1749 British regime intact at Annapolis Royal. For all of these authors, imperial–colonial–Aboriginal relations were invariably complex rather than simple, and it was in response to these very complexities and balances that the possibility of coexistence could be lost or found.[4]

Yet the recent studies, for the most part, make their central contributions in periods that do not extend significantly beyond the treaty-making years 1760–1. L.F.S. Upton's older and groundbreaking work, meanwhile, covers the Mi'kmaq experience of the 1760s and 1770s in greater detail but takes an ambivalent position on the Aboriginal role at this time. Upton recognized that the Mi'kmaq "refused to admit defeat" when conducting the treaties of 1760–1, but saw this manifested in having "kept the past alive" through cultural retention rather than in any remaining control over events.[5] Indeed, the long-ago assertion of J.B. Brebner that "the conquests of Louisbourg and Canada had left the Indians absolutely at the mercy of the British," with its implication that Aboriginal relations had little further significance for the non-Native settlement history of the region, has retained a tenacious currency among historians.[6] Stephen E. Patterson, though in a more nuanced manner than Brebner, has argued similarly that the defeat of France in 1758 prompted "the Native collapse as a fighting force" and that, as a result, the treaties of 1760–1 were made in a context where the end of the French–Aboriginal alliance represented for the British "both the fulfilment of their strategy and a vindication of their 'total war' approach."[7] Daniel N. Paul, while taking a totally different view of the British military role as brutal and repressive, has also argued that by the treaty-making era of 1760–1, the Mi'kmaq posed "no real threat" to the security of the British regime.[8]

The point is a critical one. If British hegemony had indeed been consolidated conclusively by the early 1760s, whether in ways that could be characterized as crudely oppressive or strategically expedient, there are profound interpretive implications for our understanding of the treaties themselves and of the Planter era more generally. If the treaties of 1760–1 were made between a victorious empire and disempowered Aboriginal nations, then their provisions must be interpreted in the light of this imbalance. Logic could even extend to regarding them as surrenders in which any British concessions were made in a spirit of mercy towards conquered peoples. If, by contrast, the treaties were negotiated by two sides that shared a strong need to reach agreement, and to hammer out a relationship accordingly, then the articles must be understood as commitments made for that urgent and highly practical purpose.[9] If the Planters moved in during the 1760s to take over a territory pacified by British hegemony, then Nova Scotia as a colonial entity had decisively taken the place of Mi'kma'ki and Wulstukwiuk. If, by contrast, this was still debatable territory, the Planter era must be seen as one in which colonial settlement was far from central in its historical significance, and in which the process of pacification initiated by the treaties could yet take different and unpredictable directions. At a more general level still, the argument is between the notion that British imperial advance (with its twin engines of military power and colonial settlement) was ineluctable, and the competing view that the Aboriginal role remained diplomatically and militarily powerful far beyond the chronological point at which most historians have been willing to write it off.

This essay takes the latter position. Offering a re-examination of certain key elements of the evidence on the Aboriginal role *vis-à-vis* the Planters and the British imperial authorities in Nova Scotia, it seeks also to draw out the imperial implications of the Aboriginal–colonial relationship in Planter Nova Scotia. Whereas Brebner's celebrated *Neutral Yankees of Nova Scotia* (1937) attributed Nova Scotia's non-involvement in the American Revolution partly to the unscrupulous self-interest of Halifax merchants but mainly to the essential apathy of most Planters, isolated as they were from the political and ideological mainstream of North America, it is argued here that the Planters were part of a different and larger mainstream of imperial experience.[10] Far from accomplishing a pacification of Nova Scotia under British rule, the events of the 1750s and early 1760s—the expulsion of the Acadians, the British military victories of 1758–60, and the treaties of 1760–1—set the stage for a ten-year era during which Aboriginal and British pacification strategies competed, followed by a partial reconciliation which was

finally swept away only by the sudden force of numbers brought by the Loyalist migration.

Revisiting the significance of the Loyalist influx that overtook Nova Scotia during the early 1780s, in an effort to evaluate the significance of the societal conjuncture that existed in Nova Scotia before the onset of this flood of migrants, also implies a challenge to the long-established consensus that eighteenth-century northeastern North America was experiencing a colonial era until 1775, and that the American Revolution then established a new and dramatic demarcation between British North America and the United States. Rather, the Loyalist migration extended into Nova Scotia a weight of settlement that, as in many parts of what was now the northeastern United States, was incompatible with Aboriginal economies. It was not, however, the culmination of a linear or inescapable process. Prior to 1782—whether imperial officials sought to advance their cause in ways that were brutally oppressive, strategically astute, or both—colonization was limited to defined areas, and there was no inexorable advance of British power. Rather, the earlier era must be understood by identifying more complex historical patterns, and through a historiographical triumvirate in which Aboriginal, imperial, and colonial history continuously interact.[11]

The British conquest of Acadia in 1710, closely followed by the Treaty of Utrecht in 1713, was an ambiguous affair. The British established their headquarters at Annapolis Royal, and attempted with intermittent success to establish British economic interests in such forms as the Canso fisheries and merchant activities around the Bay of Fundy. However, the majority of the settler population was Acadian, and the bulk of territorial control continued to rest where it always had: in the hands of the Aboriginal nations. Environmentally, the British presence in what was now defined as Nova Scotia remained fragile. Meanwhile, the non-British peoples were environmentally well established. The Acadians, numbering some 2000 at the time of the conquest and rapidly increasing, primarily occupied the Fundy marshlands, while the Aboriginal nations utilized the much larger expanses of territory that continued to support a hunting, gathering, and fishing economy. The Aboriginal population of perhaps 4000 at the time of the conquest was numerically overtaken by the Acadians about 1720. The 400 or so British, by contrast, were confined to an enclave in Annapolis Royal, the site of European enclaves of various nationalities (French, Scottish, English) that had existed with only brief intermissions since 1605.[12]

From a global perspective, the presence of a British enclave in which a small body of military and mercantile leaders—accompanied by an only slightly larger number of their military and civilian followers—conducted their dealings with more numerous and spatially unrestrained indigenous civilizations was familiar enough, especially in Africa and Asia. In northeastern North America, however, there were other models. In southern Massachusetts and along stretches of the Connecticut, Hudson, and St Lawrence valleys, clusters of agricultural settlement had brought about fundamental environmental alterations. Certain qualifications must be made. Massachusetts, Connecticut, New York, or Canada: none was an exclusively agricultural colony. Commerce was fundamental to each, whether through the internal market economy or external trade connections with Aboriginal suppliers or overseas merchants. In New York and Canada, more so than in New England, imperial military expenditure was also a vital invisible export. A second caution is that, even as late as the mid-eighteenth century, it is important not to exaggerate the extent of agricultural development, which remained localized not only in juxtaposition with the Aboriginal lands further west, but also with the large heartland associated with the Appalachian spine of northeastern North America itself.

These qualifications made, however, European-style agriculture had long been the engine of environmental change in the areas of colonial settlement, and by the mid-eighteenth century it had combined with commerce to support large, dense, and partly urbanized non-Aboriginal populations in some parts of northeastern North America. Agricultural development had led in these areas to what Daniel Richter has rightly described as "an inexorable demand for new agricultural land—land that in one way or another had to be expropriated from its aboriginal owners."[13] Agriculture, with its land clearances and its demands for the pasturing of livestock, was also a potentially lethal threat to Aboriginal hunting-gathering economies.[14] Although eighteenth-century Europeans would have seen agricultural development at one level as a natural and beneficial use of the soil, imperial strategists were aware that it also represented an efficient means of undermining Aboriginal societies where they had become obstacles to strategic or economic ambitions. Thus, the deliberate unleashing of an agriculturally based population on Aboriginal territory was an act of profound aggression, in which environmental destruction became a tool of empire.

Yet there was at least one instance in northeastern North America where non-Aboriginal agriculture had proved compatible with an immediately neighbouring Aboriginal economy. Acadians and Mi'kmaq were different and separate peoples, between whom tensions existed. As William Wicken has shown, environmentally generated disputes tended to become more frequent over time, as the Acadian population increased.[15] Nevertheless, the confinement of Acadian environmental alterations largely to coastal marshlands meant that mutual forbearance could generally prevail. Accordingly, for more than three decades after the conquest of 1710, Nova Scotia was characterized by an internal equilibrium by which disputes among

Mi'kmaq, Acadians, and British could be accommodated with only sporadic violence. "Until 1744," one recent study has concluded, "coexistence was largely though not continuously peaceful, and negotiation the favoured safeguard against destructive frictions."[16]

Warfare between 1744 and 1748, while ultimately inconclusive, revealed both British and French imperial weaknesses in the region. Each suffered a humiliating defeat—the French with the capture of Louisbourg in 1745, the British with the crushing of a New England force at Grand Pré in 1747—and each determined to assert a more powerful imperial grip following the Treaty of Aix-la-Chapelle in 1748. The building of military installations at strategic points proceeded rapidly. While the French repossessed Louisbourg under the terms of the treaty, and set about re-fortifying it, the British established the heavily defended town of Halifax on Chebucto Bay in 1749. In seeking to counteract their chief imperial rival and mend the weaknesses that had appeared in wartime, the British envisaged an approach that would be both military and environmental. With the protection of available forces, concentrated in forts and outposts that now overlooked the principal areas of Acadian settlement, British and "Foreign Protestant" colonists would begin to clear and cultivate adjoining lands. As Elizabeth Mancke has observed, it was far from unusual in eighteenth-century British colonies in North America, outside of the older settlement colonies that ranged southward from Massachusetts, for settlement to follow the state and its military forces.[17] Yet during the ensuing years, this strategy for pacification of Nova Scotia would have to compete with a treaty-based Aboriginal strategy for a different form of pacification in which colonial settlement would be rigorously confined.

The strategic linkage between imperial objectives and Protestant European settlement in Nova Scotia was made explicit in the instructions issued to Governor Edward Cornwallis in 1749. They included a series of instructions relating to settlement that had not been issued to previous governors, in Nova Scotia or elsewhere. Cornwallis was enjoined to lay out townships not only for the convenience of settlement but also for "security...against the insults and incursions of neighboring Indians or other enemies." Land was to be set aside for military installations, and the governor was explicitly instructed to ensure that Acadian settlements were included within township boundaries, "to the end that...French inhabitants may be subjected to such rules and orders as may hereafter be made for the better ordering and governing the said townships."[18] In the short term, it was hoped, the new settlers would quickly outnumber the Acadians. In the longer term, they would not only assimilate the Acadians into a larger British and Protestant society, but would also extend into strategically selected localities of Nova Scotia the agriculturally based settlement that had proved so durable in certain other portions of northeastern North America.

The British initiative of 1749 proved successful in some respects, unsuccessful in others. Halifax itself endured, despite three years of containment by Mi'kmaq forces, Annapolis Royal remained a significant settlement, though no longer the colony's headquarters. From 1753 onwards, the Foreign Protestant settlement at Lunenburg formed the third area of British-sponsored colonization in Nova Scotia. An additional though localized military presence was effectively established in such locations as Fort Lawrence (on the Isthmus of Chignecto) and Fort Edward (at Pisiquid). Most importantly, after the outbreak of renewed hostilities between British and French in 1754, Nova Scotia based British forces played a significant role in the defeat of France in key battles for Fort Beauséjour (1755) and Louisbourg (1758), and thus in the campaigns that led to the eventual withdrawal of France as an imperial power from continental North America by the Treaty of Paris in 1763.

Even by 1758, however, the other side of the balance sheet weighed heavily against British interests in the region. Settlement efforts fell far short of expectations. Even the hastily improvised establishment of Lunenburg highlighted the absence of the planned pattern of Protestant-settled townships elsewhere. The Acadians had not been assimilated. Instead, most Acadians had been deported, starting in 1755. Although Nova Scotian military authorities put a bold face on the deportation, portraying it as an unfortunate necessity, it was in reality a defeat. As aptly characterized by Julian Gwyn, it was "an act of econocide...unparalleled in pre-1815 British colonial history," and produced "such economic devastation that it set Nova Scotia behind for perhaps at least a generation."[19] Also, despite the specific affronts offered to the Mi'kmaq by the foundation of Halifax and Lunenburg, and the destructive irregular campaigns waged by companies such as that headed by the brothers John and Joseph Gorham, there was no generalized encroachment on Aboriginal lands.[20] While years of hostilities, and the loss of French gifts and supplies after 1758, brought severe economic strain to both Mi'kmaq and Wulstukwiuk villages, the territorial basis for regeneration remained intact. Thus the supreme irony of the 1750s for the British in Nova Scotia lay in the reality that at the same time as British arms had succeeded against the French, all of the plans for what the Halifax regime had chiefly attempted to accomplish within the region—the assimilation of the Acadians and the environmental change of selected Aboriginal territories—lay in ruins.

These circumstances formed the basis for a realignment in the region that took effect between 1758 and 1761. Its two central departures lay respectively in the conclusion of the British Aboriginal treaties of 1760–1, and the renewal of efforts to recruit settlers for Nova Scotia. The treaties, while not unprecedented—previous treaties of lasting historical importance had been concluded in 1725–6, 1749, and 1752—had their origins in the consequences attending the fall of Louisbourg. For the Aboriginal leaders of the region, the withdrawal of the French enhanced the importance of the treaty relationship with the only remaining imperial presence. Trade required special attention, and this was prominently reflected in British negotiations in Halifax in early 1760 with Wulstukwiuk and Passamaquoddy representatives, at which the establishment of a system of provincially operated truckhouses was negotiated, and a specific tariff of prices for trade goods was agreed upon.[21] The truck house trade became an integral part of the Wulstukwiuk–Passamaquoddy treaty dated 23 February 1760, and similar provisions characterized each of the known texts of the several agreements made with Mi'kmaq villages later in 1760 and in the following year.[22] On the British side, the necessities were to take stock after the setbacks of the 1750s and to seek colonists in an effort to breathe new life into the endeavours of that decade. Gaining an accommodation with Aboriginal inhabitants was a prerequisite for both. The written texts of the treaties contained expressions of Aboriginal submission to the British crown that, as ever with such formulae, were open to varying interpretations. Nearer the mark was Governor Charles Lawrence, who observed to the British Board of Trade in May 1760—regarding both the Wulstukwiuk-Passamaquoddy treaty and those Mi'kmaq treaties that had been signed to that point—that "One of the Chief Articles in these treaties is that of Commerce," and that "the greatest advantage from this Article...is the friendship of these Indians."[23]

A major issue that was not directly addressed in the treaties was that of land. Although the texts of the Mi'kmaq treaties contained an Aboriginal undertaking not to "molest any of His Majesty's Subjects or their dependants in their settlements already made or to be hereafter made," no boundaries were specified, and there was no mention of Aboriginal land surrender.[24] The extent to which Nova Scotia authorities would seek to extend colonial settlement remained to be determined. As William Wicken has argued, it was undoubtedly restricted in part by the assumption that the Mi'kmaq hunting-gathering economy would remain in existence long enough to provide for a continuing fur trade.[25] Nevertheless, the tenor of concurrent recruitment efforts for New England settlers made it clear that colonization on the southern New England pattern was sought, at least in some places. The proclamations inviting settlement, issued by Lawrence on 12 October 1758 and 11 January 1759, noted that settlement would not be confined to former Acadian areas, promised that where possible each individual land grant would comprise upland as well as marsh and meadow, and took pains to portray the institutional framework as closely resembling the governance structures of New England towns and provinces.[26] Accordingly, the establishment of townships went beyond the boundaries of the former Acadian settlements both by encompassing upland acreages in township grants in former Acadian areas and by creating townships in additional areas—though, with the exception of Maugerville, these were for fishing rather than primarily agricultural settlements—that had not seen large-scale Acadian settlement.[27]

An expansion to non-Aboriginal settlement was in prospect, therefore, despite the absence of land surrender in the treaties of 1760–1. Planters who arrived in the expectation that tensions with Aboriginal inhabitants had been laid to rest would soon find out otherwise. Treaty-making continued apace until the summer of 1761, when an elaborate signing ceremony at the Governor's Farm in Halifax—attended by Mi'kmaq chiefs from the Miramichi, Shediac, Pokemouche, and Cape Breton—brought the acting governor, Jonathan Belcher, to declare that "a covenant of peace" now existed.[28] Like any covenant, however, this one had two sides. Time would tell that peace would prevail to a remarkable degree over the ensuing two decades. However, it was neither an easy peace nor one that was passively sustained by Aboriginal leaders, who proved ready and willing to use the threat of coercion to reinforce their interpretation of a treaty relationship that, in their estimation, precluded undue Planter encroachments. Apprehension of the application of Mi'kmaq and Wulstukwiuk force thereupon became a central theme of the Planter experience during the 1760s, and a central concern of successive governors of Nova Scotia.

As late as the summer of 1759, a year after the fall of Louisbourg, the ability of Aboriginal forces to inflict damage on British settlements and outposts had been graphically demonstrated. In April of that year, Governor Lawrence had reported to London on raids taking place at Lunenburg and on the Isthmus of Chignecto. Although he hoped to be able "to cover the inhabitants against these mortifying and very discouraging incursions upon them," by September he was forced to admit that matters had become even worse as a result of Aboriginal raids on land and the sea-borne activities of armed Acadian fugitives.[29] Not only did these circumstances lead to the postponement of the first Planter migrations for a year,[30] but also Lawrence ensured that initial Planter settlements were planned with defence in mind. In Horton, Cornwallis, and Falmouth townships, reported his successor Jonathan Belcher, "Pallisadoed Forts were erected in each...by order of the late Governor, with room sufficient to receive all the Inhabitants, who were formed into a Militia to join what Troops could be spar'd to oppose any attempts that might be formed against them."[31] Even so, and even after the treaty-making process was well under way, there were serious doubts about whether the protection would be adequate. The surveyor Charles Morris wrote to the Nova Scotia council from Pisiquid in June 1760 that "the want of a sufficient number of Troops at this Juncture where so many Settlements are carrying on, is not a little discouraging to the new Settlers. I am in hopes no accident will happen to make a greater number necessary."[32] Henry Alline would have agreed with Morris in every respect. The young Falmouth settler and future evangelist declared that within a short time of his family's arrival in mid-1760, "it was frequently reported, that the Indians were about rising to destroy us; and many came out among us with their faces painted, and declared that the English should not settle this country."[33]

The treaty relationship offered to the Planters a realistic possibility that Aboriginal military capacity would not be exercised, even though the limited evidence suggests that Planters themselves had little if any sense of their Aboriginal neighbours as treaty partners. Certainly Bartholomew Nocvut, a Mi'kmaw from Porcupine Cove who was severely beaten by Planters in successive incidents at Horton and Cornwallis during the summer of 1763, had no reason to think that they did.[34] Yet responsible British officials were fully conscious that Aboriginal restraint could not be taken for granted. Even though British understandings tended over time to depend on narrowing interpretations of the written texts,[35] no textual readings could obscure the necessity of reaching a stable understanding in two crucial respects: first, on the extent to which the British could be judged by their Aboriginal treaty partners to be living up to their own commitments; second, on somehow reaching a *modus vivendi* on the territorial questions with which the treaties had not dealt explicitly.

Jonathan Belcher, acting as governor after Lawrence's death in late 1760, was acutely aware of these imperatives. To the council and assembly of Nova Scotia in March 1762, Belcher praised the role of favourable trade terms in consolidating the treaty relationship, and urged that "every reasonable Method ought to be pursued for preserving this Peace inviolate, and fixing their Affections and Attachments, from the Sense and experience of Protection, Integrity and Friendship."[36] Six weeks later, he turned his attention to the land question, issuing a proclamation that reserved for the use of Aboriginal inhabitants, pending confirmation or otherwise by the Crown, lands adjoining the entire coastline from Musquodoboit to the Bay of Chaleur. Justifying the proclamation to the Board of Trade, Belcher made it clear that it stemmed from "the Pretensions of the Indians" and from his recognition that Aboriginal discontent could have "disagreeable consequences in the present Situation of Affairs."[37] The Board of Trade eventually wrote to the incoming governor, Montague Wilmot, to disavow the proclamation, although even so it emphasized that "giving disgust or dissatisfaction to the Indians" must scrupulously be avoided.[38] The proclamation belonged to an era in which the Crown itself extended far-reaching, though more general, recognition to Aboriginal territories throughout eastern North America in the Royal Proclamation of 1763, to which successive governors of Nova Scotia professed their adherence.[39] Even though the concessions specifically made in the Nova Scotia proclamation were too extensive to be received favourably in London, they offer persuasive testimony on the crucial importance attached by Belcher in the spring of 1762 to the placation of Aboriginal interests.

The summer of 1762 brought more direct evidence to bear, as perceived Aboriginal threats brought desertions from Planter settlements and disaffection in the militia. British officials were inclined to blame the crisis partly on the incitement of fugitive Acadians and partly too on the hope of French intervention in Nova

Scotia following the capture of St John's, Newfoundland, by French forces at the end of June. But it was "the threatnings of the Indians" that made it a crisis.[40] From Lunenburg in mid-July came news that "the Indians which Surround us are Certainly very Numerous, and by their Motion and Insults for the last Twenty four Hours, its more than doubtfull they are meditating an Attack."[41] Belcher took the threat seriously, cancelling orders for Lunenburg militia to march to the defence of Halifax against a possible French assault. The acting governor also observed, accurately, that "it must be presum'd that in other parts of the Weak settlements the inhabitants might be alarmed."[42] Planters from the King's County settlements of Horton, Cornwallis, Falmouth, and Newport protested the removal of their militia for duties at Fort Edward and Fort Sackville at a time when "a Considerable Body of Indians were assembled together menacing the Inhabitants with Destruction," and the Halifax council of war responded by allowing the King's County men to return home, "but to hold Themselves in Readiness to March hither at a Moments Warning."[43] By August, both Belcher and the council of war were taking note of desertions from the King's County settlements. Belcher also reported to General Jeffery Amherst that by that time the threat had been extended to Halifax, where in his view the nearby assembly of an Aboriginal force estimated at 600 strong, along with the presence in the town of several hundred captive male Acadians of military age, "should make the people in the New Settlements fear the fate of this Town [Halifax], and their own."[44]

The crisis of 1762 ended as suddenly as it had begun. By early September, Belcher believed the threat had subsided and credited "the Measures...taken for checking and dispersing the Indians."[45] The question remains whether Aboriginal forces had ever intended more than a show of force. Certainly the less-ening of the tension before the French evacuation of St John's in mid-September, and well before news of that development could have reached Nova Scotia, casts doubt on any direct connection of the summer's various events. The vulnerability of the settlers and the continuing insecurity of the British presence had, however, been clearly demonstrated. During the ensuing years, successive governors of Nova Scotia used blunt language in their efforts to make this lesson clear in London. The specific causes of concern varied from year to year. In 1763, it was the fear that reports of the exploits of Pontiac's followers might prompt "the Indians of this Province to follow their Example from the present weak condition of the several Posts."[46] In 1766, it was the possibility that the Mi'kmaq were maintaining contact with the last remaining French outpost in North America, on the island of St Pierre.[47] On some occasions specific incidents between Aboriginal and non-Aboriginal individuals prompted urgent efforts from Halifax to mollify aggrieved Wulstukwiuk or Mi'kmaq. The Aboriginal nations, thought the Nova Scotia provincial secretary in the context of a case in the St John Valley in 1766, were "ever ready to revenge injuries in the Severest Manner."[48]

Maintenance of the peace, therefore, conferred responsibilities on both sides. If responsibilities were not fulfilled, then courtesy and the credible threat of coercive force could prove to be two sides of the same coin. This explained the eagerness of Nova Scotia officials to respond positively to requests made of them in the name of the treaty relationship, whether for gifts and supplies or for support of a Roman Catholic priest.[49] It also underlay the warnings the same officials repeatedly transmitted to the Board of Trade. Governor Wilmot argued in 1764 that "the custom of giving them provisions and cloathing, has been too long established to be broke through with Safety, particularly at a time when the Settlement of this Country, and the further increase of its inhabitants depend so much on their [the Aboriginal] temper and disposition." The alternative, for Wilmot, was unthinkable: "the Indians exceed six hundred fighting Men in number, of whom a small party might carry tenor and devastation thro' a Country before the Troops cou'd have sufficient Notice to prevent the Mischief; which is always secretly concerted, and suddenly executed."[50]

Acting governor Benjamin Green warned similarly in August 1766 that "the humour and disposition of the Indians have always merited a particular attention of the Government here as the safety and Success of the Settlements depend in a great measure on the turn they shall take."[51] Green's successor as acting governor, Michael Francklin, confirmed a few weeks later that "a rupture with the Indians...would throw the Settlements into the utmost Confusion, if not totally break up the greatest part of them."[52] But it was left to the next fully appointed governor, Lord William Campbell, to use the bluntest language of all. In mid-1768, as British troops began to leave Halifax to meet the revolutionary crisis in New England, the Nova Scotia council expressed concern about the weakening of military outposts in the region, notably Fort Cumberland.[53] When Campbell arrived back in Nova Scotia in September after travels in England and New England, he wasted no time in writing to senior imperial administrators to warn that troop withdrawals would provide "cause of most uneasy Allarmes for the safety of the yet thinly Inhabited Settlements in the Interior parts of the Province," and that Nova Scotia was an "infant struggling Province" and vulnerable to Aboriginal attack.[54] Some six weeks later, he reported further to the colonial secretary, Lord Hillsborough, that "I have daily advices from...[the interior settlements] which seem to confirm my apprehensions are not groundless." Campbell then went on to set out the military balance of power succinctly: "the outposts of this Province fixt, as a Shelter and retreat for the Inhabitants settled upon the Frontiers, left destitute of Garrisons, to protect them, may be either destroyed or possessed by the Savages, a very small Number of which, would be able at this juncture to bring fire and Destruction to the very entrance of this Town [Halifax]."[55]

By early 1769, Campbell was still reaffirming to Hillsborough the vulnerability of Nova Scotia. "They are daily coming in here," he wrote of the Mi'kmaq, "and demanding provisions in such terms, as indicates their being sensible of the weak State of the Interior parts of the Province, deprived of all Military protection."[56] Yet it was noteworthy that what the governor was describing was not an attack but a request for supplies. No doubt, to judge from Campbell's description, it was made as a request that could not reasonably—or, from a British standpoint, safely—be refused. It was, however, an indication of the persistence of the treaty relationship rather than a threat to end it. From the time of the treaties' conclusion at the beginning of the 1760s, there had been a peaceful undercurrent in Aboriginal–British relationships despite the tensions that had repeatedly arisen during the initial phases of Planter settlement. It was seen in a series of episodes that can be glimpsed in the evidence. Following the assaults at Horton and Cornwallis in the summer of 1763, according to the Nova Scotia council, Mi'kmaq leaders at Cape Porcupine were "very civil and courteous," and when a prompt investigation uncovered the Planter culprits, the chiefs took the opportunity to confirm that "they would inviolably observe the Peace which they had made."[57] A military settler in the St John Valley described in 1764 how "an Indian made me a present of a Pair of horns of a small Moose."[58] Some four years later, Wulstukwiuk chiefs travelled to Halifax to meet formally with the Nova Scotia council, receiving assurances regarding the colony's continuing support of a priest in the St John Valley, the removal of specific non-Native land encroachments, and the lack of any "Restriction on your Trade."[59] Two days later, acting governor Michael Francklin wrote to Hillsborough noting that the supply of the services of the priest, Charles-François Bailly de Messein, had been seen as an unavoidable obligation, "Conformable to the provisions made them at their first making Peace."[60] The fulfilment of another promise, this one made at the Halifax meeting in 1768, was presaged in early 1769 when the Nova Scotia provincial secretary Richard Bulkeley told a St John Valley Planter that agricultural tools would be sent to the Wulstukwiuk "by the first Opportunity."[61] By late 1770, even Campbell was inclined to praise the work of Bailly and hoped that the priest might persuade a substantial number of Mi'kmaq to settle in one place near Halifax, so that "their Motions may be watched and prevented if ill designed, and in time [they may] become peaceable and Useful Subjects."[62]

The idea of settling Aboriginal inhabitants in one consolidated village was an ancient preoccupation of imperial administrators in the region, and it came no closer to fulfilment now than when promoted by French officials and missionaries at the turn of the eighteenth century. Nevertheless, its contemplation by Campbell was yet another indication that Aboriginal–British relationships had become less troubled, as the pace of Planter settlement had slackened. A report reaching London in 1773 declared, even though with some oversimplification, that "the Indians...since the French have been expell'd from the Neighbourhood of this Province...have become quiet and at present are well disposed."[63] A year later, the Yorkshire travellers John Robinson and Thomas Rispin portrayed the Aboriginal population of the region as "very expert in hunting, and excellent marksmen with the gun," but to the settlers "friendly, harmless, well-behaved."[64] In effect, the Planters—from being the provocateurs of the 1760s—had become the new Acadians of the 1770s. The number of non-Aboriginals in the region remained, even at the end of that decade, many fewer than on the eve of the Acadian deportation. Although population figures for this period are necessarily estimates based on imperfect sources, Julian Gwyn has put the population of mainland Nova Scotia (including the modern New Brunswick) at 18,000 in early 1755, including Acadians, British and British-sponsored, and Aboriginal inhabitants. The corresponding figure for 1781 was 14,000.[65] As a number of scholars have observed, the rural settlements of Planter Nova Scotia were scattered and lacked effective interconnecting routes.[66] Furthermore, Planter incursions into cleared uplands had been limited in scope, and Planter marshland agriculture retained many affinities in technique with the old Acadian forms of cultivation.[67] Thus, insofar as the Planter migration had represented a coordinated, military-inspired intervention into Aboriginal territory, and one that had intended substantial environmental change in selected locations, it had met with no greater success than had the British efforts of the 1750s. Despite the persistence of occasional tensions between settlers and Aboriginal inhabitants,[68] and of debates among Aboriginal leaders during the mid-1770s over the merits of support for the revolutionaries,[69] the Halifax regime had settled into a pattern that made it only the latest of the many imperial intrusions that the Aboriginal nations had been able to domesticate since the early seventeenth century.

The Loyalist migration, beginning in earnest in 1782, was different. Most importantly, the Loyalists arrived with crude force of numbers. At least 30,000 Loyalist refugees flooded into Nova Scotia, which from 1784 onwards was divided into the three provinces of

Nova Scotia, New Brunswick, and Cape Breton. Although they met Aboriginal resistance in some areas, ranging from Antigonish to Fredericton, this was a migration that was fully capable of filling in the valleys and the interstices of the region.[70] The Loyalists did not lack for military support, either from forces deployed to Nova Scotia for the purpose or from the presence among the settlers of disbanded Loyalist troops.[71] Yet the primary force of their transformative effect was environmental. No longer were either lack of settlement numbers or an enforceable treaty relationship containing forces. Instead, the chief constraint now was simply the limited quantity of productive agricultural land in the region. Even this was insufficient to prevent substantial encroachment on Aboriginal lands, and the severing of Aboriginal communication routes by settlement. Although in places some versions of the hunting-gathering-fishing economy were able to persist for a time, the Aboriginal nations now faced a defensive struggle that had little likelihood of success in the foreseeable future. Even the fur trade—which, as Julian Gwyn has shown, expanded greatly during the Loyalist era—became largely the preserve of poor Loyalists rather than Aboriginal hunters and trappers.[72]

Examination of settler–Aboriginal relations in Planter Nova Scotia, therefore, reveals that the Planter migration represented, in one sense, a failed military intervention. There was, of course, more to the Planter communities than just that, as there had been to the Acadian communities before them. Yet the existence of Planter Nova Scotia as an arena in which imperial outreach came into direct interplay with indigenous nations, with settlement on a scale insufficient either to conflict with imperial objectives or to undermine the environmental basis of Aboriginal society, casts the role of the Planters as being entirely distinct from the role and the experience of colonial populations in the more populous areas of the Thirteen Colonies. This does not mean that the Planter experience was less significant either historically or historiographically. Rather, the Planters participated in a pattern of interactions that was more global than conventionally North American. They were members, as Elizabeth Mancke has aptly put it, of "Another British America."[73] The imperial state was present and visible. P.J. Marshall has observed of the East India Company in the same era that, although far from establishing any imperial ascendancy in India, it had emerged as "a regional power of some consequence."[74] While events in the subcontinent were unfolding on a much larger scale, it was true in the same sense that in Nova Scotia the British state also had established itself as a regional power of some consequence. Its base was secure in Halifax, it had a lesser capacity to influence developments in the areas of rural settlement, and it had little ability to do so at all in the larger swaths of territory that lay beyond. It was unthinkable that Aboriginal inhabitants should ignore the British presence, and vice versa. Yet it was not at all clear what if any kind of ascendancy might eventually separate the two sides, and whether *Pax Britannica* or *Pax Indigena* would prevail. Ultimately, the Loyalist migration settled the question. In the process it eclipsed the treaty relationship for some 200 years, during which any active recollection of the eighteenth-century treaties persisted primarily in the Aboriginal record. The Loyalist migration also removed Nova Scotia from a globalized pattern of imperial–Aboriginal relations, and placed it in the more limited context of more closely resembling an eastern North American settlement colony.

In this context, the older questions about Planter settlement re-emerge in a newer context. Or, rather, the two traditional questions—why the Planters did not give substantial support to the American Revolution, and what made the Planters distinct from the Loyalists—coalesce into the same question. What were the characteristics of Planter Nova

Scotia that distinguished it and its colonists from the rebelling colonies and from those of their inhabitants who were protagonists on one side or the other? The over-arching answer to the question, however, can best be approached by posing a newer one that can and should be applied by historians to any and all areas of early modern northeastern North America: What were the prevailing balances among Aboriginal, imperial, and colonial interests? In Planter Nova Scotia, the simple reality was (though its implications were far from simple) that the relationship between colonists and the imperial state was not a significant *remise en question*. More urgent was the relationship between colonists and Aboriginal neighbours. Most pressing of all, here and in other areas of the world where the increasingly rambling—and, at home, ideologically disputed—empire came in contact with a seemingly infinite variety of indigenous peoples, the real question was about the future shape of relations between the imperial state and the Aboriginal societies.[75]

That Nova Scotia should be, in a sense, a laboratory for the application of such a significant global question to British North America was not new in the Planter era. The same comment can be made regarding the earlier part of the eighteenth century, as the consequences of the Conquest of 1710 unfolded.[76] The Planter era, however, was distinct in that the imperial–Aboriginal relationship was more direct than had been true as long as the Acadians and the French imperial state had been important factors in the region. On the other hand, Nova Scotia in this period had a lesser claim to uniqueness in this regard. There were now comparable conjunctures in the southern part of the continent, and the British acquisition of Florida in the 1763 Peace of Paris raised questions there that related closely to those current in Nova Scotia.[77] Affinities with more westerly cross-cultural meeting places, as examined by Richard White and

others, were less marked because of the largely non-state character of encroachments in these areas to this point.[78] Planter Nova Scotia, however, belonged to a world that did not include the heavily settled colonies of what was to become the eastern United States. As Ernest Clarke has most recently shown, the origins of some Planter settlers inclined them—in combination with controversies during the winter of 1775–6 over the removal of local militias to Halifax—to create a small revolutionary movement.[79] In reality, however, by joining the Planter migration the settlers had crossed into a sphere different from one that had spawned the rebellion. It was one in which loyalism was a possible and relevant choice, because of the crucial significance here of the imperial state as well as the more pragmatic influence of the economic and military power of Halifax, but where the revolutionary crisis further south could reasonably be seen as a local difficulty that impinged but little on the wider world of which Planter Nova Scotia formed a part.

As for the settlers themselves, the crucial historiographical flaw in so much of the analysis that flowed from the work of Brebner and his successors was that it posited a symmetrical choice for the Planters—they could be revolutionaries, they could be Loyalists, or they could avoid the choice altogether by being apathetic. In reality, however, the symmetry was absent. Active loyalism was indeed an option, but even that choice would not excuse the Planters from their more urgent involvement in working through the relationship between the state and the Aboriginal nations as embodied in the treaties and lived out in the region every day. Ironically, of course, it was the revolution that brought an end to this phase in the region's experience by prompting the flood of Loyalist refugees. This inundation swept away the characteristic patterns of Planter Nova Scotia. Now, as Loyalist scholars have shown, the imperial state had to define itself in relation to colonial rather than Aboriginal interests.[80] Colonial interests, in turn, could define themselves in isolation from increasingly marginalized Aboriginal neighbours and in a relationship with the imperial state that would shift over time, until in the mid-nineteenth century the initiative in state-building lay with colonial rather than imperial elites. None of this, however, should overshadow either the distinctness of the historical experience, or the historiographical importance, of those who lived in Mi'kma'ki/Wulstukwiuk or in Nova Scotia during the preceding era when *Pax Britannica* and *Pax Indigena* hung in the balance.

Notes

This essay was originally presented as the Charles H. Read Family Lecture in Planter Studies at Acadia University on 20 March 2003, with the title "Planter Nova Scotia: Before the Flood." I thank all those who provided comments and discussion at that time, especially Barry Moody and Jim Snowdon. I am much indebted to Elizabeth Mancke and Bill Wicken for their valuable comments on the written text, and to the four anonymous readers for *CHR*. My interest in the issues discussed in this essay was prompted in part by the experience of testifying in *Regina v. Marshall* and other legal cases, and this is one of the reasons I am grateful to have been afforded that opportunity.

1 See Viola F. Barnes, "Francis Legge, Governor of Loyalist Nova Scotia, 1773–1776," *New England Quarterly,* 4 (1931), 420–47; John Bartlet Brebner, *The Neutral Yankees of Nova Scotia: A Marginal Colony During the Revolutionary Years* (New York: Columbia University Press, 1937); Brebner, *North Atlantic Triangle: The Interplay of Canada, the United States, and Great Britain,* 2nd ed. (Toronto: McClelland and Stewart, 1966); Wilfred Brenton Kerr, *The Maritime Provinces of British North America and the American Revolution* (1941; repr., New York: Russell and Russell, 1970); Kerr, "The Merchants of Nova Scotia and the American Revolution," *Canadian Historical Review,* 13 (1932), 20–36; Kerr, "Nova Scotia in 1775–6," *Dalhousie Review,* 12 (1932–3), 97–107; R.S. Longley, "The Coming of the New England Planters to the Annapolis Valley," *Collections of the Nova Scotia Historical Society* (Halifax: Nova Scotia Historical Society, 1961), 81–101; George A. Rawlyk, *Revolution Rejected, 1775–1776* (Scarborough, ON: Prentice-Hall, 1968); Gordon Stewart and George Rawlyk, *A People Highly Favoured of God: The Nova Scotia Yankees and the American Revolution* (Toronto: Macmillan, 1972); Esther Clark Wright, *Planters and Pioneers,* 2nd ed. (Hantsport, NS: Lancelot Press, 1982).

2 Margaret Conrad, ed., *They Planted Well: New England Planters in Maritime Canada* (Fredericton: Acadiensis Press, 1988), esp. "Introduction," 9–11; Conrad, ed., *Making Adjustments: Change and Continuity in Planter Nova Scotia, 1759–1800* (Fredericton: Acadiensis Press, 1991); Conrad, ed., *Intimate Relations; Family and Community in Planter Nova Scotia, 1759–1800* (Fredericton: Acadiensis Press, 1995); Conrad and Barry Moody, eds., *Planter Links: Community and Culture in Colonial Nova Scotia* (Fredericton: Acadiensis Press, 2001).

3 Bill Wicken, "Mi'kmaq Land in Southwestern Nova Scotia, 1771–1823," in Conrad, *Making Adjustments,* 113–22.

4 See Naomi Griffiths, From *Migrant to Acadian, 1604–1755: A North American Border People* (Montreal and Kingston: McGill-Queen's University Press, 2005); Elizabeth Mancke, "Another British America: A Canadian Model for the Early Modern British Empire," *Journal of Imperial and Commonwealth History* 25 (1997), 1–36; Geoffrey Plank, *An Unsettled Conquest: The British Campaign against the Peoples of Acadia* (Philadelphia: University of Pennsylvania Press, 2001); John G. Reid, *Acadia, Maine, and New Scotland: Marginal Colonies in the Seventeenth Century* (Toronto: University of Toronto Press, 1981); John G, Reid, Maurice Basque, Elizabeth Mancke, Barry Moody, Geoffrey Plank, and William Wicken, *The "Conquest" of Acadia, 1710: Imperial, Colonial, and Aboriginal Constructions* (Toronto: University of Toronto Press, 2003); William Wicken, *Mi'kmaq Treaties on Trial: History, Land, and Donald Marshall Junior* (Toronto: University of Toronto Press, 2002).

5 L.F.S. Upton, *Micmacs and Colonists: Indian–White Relations in the Maritimes, 1713–1867* (Vancouver: UBC Press, 1979), xiii–xiv, 61–78 (quotations from xiv).

6 Brebner, *The Neutral Yankees,* 71. I should point out that, in a general essay on this period published in 1987, I took a position in broad agreement with Brebner's view. Subsequent research and reflection has convinced me otherwise. See John G, Reid, *Six Crucial Decades: Times of Change in the History of the Maritimes* (Halifax: Nimbus, 1987), 49.

7 Stephen E. Patterson, "1744–1763: Colonial Wars and Aboriginal Peoples," in *The Atlantic Region to Confederation: A History,* eds. Phillip A, Buckner and John G. Reid (Toronto and Fredericton: University of Toronto Press and Acadiensis Press, 1993), 149–50. See also Patterson, "Indian–White Relations in Nova Scotia, 1749–61: Study in Political Interaction," *Acadiensis* 23, no. 1 (Autumn 1993), esp. 54–9.

8 Daniel N. Paul, *We Were Not the Savages: A Micmac Perspective on the Collision of European and Aboriginal Civilization* (Halifax: Nimbus, 1993), 166.

9 The significance of historical interpretation in legal cases involving Aboriginal treaty rights suggests a rider to Allan Greer's persuasive recent argument for greater attention to pre-Confederation Canadian history, by illustrating that some elements of pre-Confederation history can be "useful" even in an applied sense. See Allan Greer, "Canadian History: Ancient and Modern," *Canadian Historical Review* 77 (1996), 575–90.

10 Brebner, *The Neutral Yankees of Nova Scotia,* 299, 313–14, 446–7, and passim; see also Brebner, *North Atlantic Triangle,* 55–6. Brebner's interpretations did not go unopposed, and Viola Florence Barnes in particular offered an interpretation based on transatlantic rather than continental linkages. See John C. Reid, "Viola Barnes, the Gender of History, and the North Atlantic Mind," *Acadiensis* 33, no. 1 (Autumn 2003), 3–20.

11 For recent explorations of these issues in different geographical and chronological contexts, see Emerson W. Baker and John G. Reid, "Aboriginal Power in the Early Modern Northeast: A Reappraisal," *William and Mary Quarterly,* 3rd series, 61 (2004), 77–106; and Wayne E. Lee, "Fortify, Fight, or Flee: Tuscarora and Cherokee Defensive Warfare and Military Culture Adaptation," *Journal of Military History,* 68 (2004), 713–70.

12 For population estimates, see Reid et al., *The "Conquest" of Acadia, 1710,* ix, I have excluded the Passamaquoddy and Penobscot populations of the southwestern portion of the territory claimed for Nova Scotia as being outside the areas primarily occupied by Planter-era settlers. The figure given for Annapolis Royal excludes intermittent wartime reinforcements.

13 Daniel K. Richter, "Native Peoples of North America and the Eighteenth-Century British Empire," in *The Oxford History of the British Empire, Volume 11, The Eighteenth Century,* ed. P.J. Marshall (Oxford: Oxford University Press, 1998), 348.

14 For more general discussion of the environmental role of agriculture, see William Cronon, *Changes in the Land: Indians, Colonists, and the Ecology of New England* (New York: Hill and Wang, 1983), esp. 127–56; Denys Delâge, *Bitter Feast: Amerindians and Europeans in Northeastern North America, 1600–64* (Vancouver: UBC Press, 1993), 250–8; Virginia DeJohn Anderson, "King Philip's Herds: Indians, Colonists, and the Problem of Livestock in Early New England," *William and Mary Quarterly,* 3rd series, 51 (1994), 601–24.

15 William C. Wicken, "Encounters with Tall Sails and Tall Tales: Mi'kmaq Society, 1500–1760" (PhD thesis, McGill University, 1994), 227–43.

16 Reid et al., *The "Conquest" of Acadia, 1710,* 205.

17 Mancke, "Another British America," 16–17.

18 Leonard Woods Labaree, ed., *Royal Instructions to British Colonial Governors, 1670–1776* (1935; repr., New York: Octagon Books, 1967), 2:537–42, 583–5. For more general discussion of the foundation of Halifax and its strategic antecedents, see Judith Fingard, Janet Guildford, and David Sutherland, *Halifax: The First 250 Years* (Halifax: Formac, 1999), 8–16; W.S. MacNutt, *The Atlantic Provinces: The Emergence of Colonial Society* (Toronto: McCelland and Stewart, 1965), 53–6; Patterson, "1744–1763," 127–8.

19 Julian Gwyn, *Excessive Expectations: Maritime Commerce and the Economic Development of Nova Scotia, 1740–1870* (Montreal and Kingston: McGill-Queen's University Press, 1998), 7, 27.

20 See Plank, *An Unsettled Conquest,* 126–9; Paul, *We Were Not the Savages,* 111–12; David A. Charters and Stuart R.J. Sutherland, "Joseph Goreham (Gorham)," in *Dictionary of Canadian Biography,* eds., George W. Brown et al. (Toronto: University of Toronto Press, 1966– ; hereafter DCB), 4:308–10; John David Krugler, "John Gorham," ibid., 3:260–1.

21 Minutes of Nova Scotia Council, 13, 14, 16 Feb. 1760, 124–32, vol. 188, RG1, Nova Scotia Archives and Records Management (hereafter NSARM). For a recent study that explores the socio-cultural origins of the negotiating strength of Mi'kmaq leaders, see Rosalie M. Francis, "The Mi'kmaq Nation and the Embodiment of Political Ideologies: Mi'kmaq, Protocol and Treaty Negotiations of the Eighteenth Century" (master's thesis, Saint Mary's University, 2003).

22 Treaty of Peace and Friendship, 23 Feb. 1760, Great Britain, fols. 18–31, CO217/18, Public Record Office (hereafter PRO); Wicken, *Ni'kmaq Treaties on Trial*, 196–202.

23 Lawrence to Board of Trade. 11 May 1760, fols. 59–60, CO217/17, PRO.

24 Treaty of Peace and Friendship with LaHave Mi'kmaq, 10 Mar. 1760, no. 37, vol. 19071, Additional Manuscripts, Andrew Brown Papers, British Library.

25 Wicken, *Mi'kmaq Treaties on Trial*, 203–9.

26 Proclamation, 12 Oct. 1758, fol. 311, CO217/16, PRO; Proclamation, 11 Jan. 1759, fol. 315, CO217/16, PRO.

27 See Jean Daigle and Robert LeBlanc, "Acadian Deportation and Return," and Graeme Wynn and Debra McNabb, "Pre-Loyalist Nova Scotia," in *Historical Atlas of Canada, Volume I, From the Beginning to 1800,* ed. R. Cole Harris, cartographer/designer Geoffrey J. Matthews (Toronto: University of Toronto Press, 1987), plates 30, 31. The townships not in areas of substantial earlier Acadian settlement were those of Barrington, Chester, Liverpool, Maugerville, and Yarmouth, while the other townships included upland as well as marshland allocations.

28 Record of Governor's Farm Ceremony, 25 June 1761, fols. 277–83, CO217/18, PRO.

29 Lawrence to Board of Trade, 20 April, 20 Sept. 1759, fols. 317–18, 322, CO217/16, PRO.

30 Minutes of Nova Scotia Council, 16 July 1759, 88–90, vol. 188, RG1, NSARM.

31 Belcher to Board of Trade, 12 Dec. 1760, fol. 81, CO217/18, PRO.

32 Minutes of Nova Scotia Council, 5 June 1760, 149, vol. 188, RG1, NSARM. Morris's letter, recorded in the minutes, was written on 1 June 1760.

33 James Beverley and Barry Moody, eds., *The Life and Journal of the Rev. Mr. Henry Alline* (Hantsport, NS: Lancelot Press, 1982), 33; see also J.M. Bumsted, *Henry Alline, 1748–1784* (Toronto: University of Toronto Press, 1971), 9–10.

34 Minutes of Nova Scotia Council, 8 Aug. 1763, 395–8, vol. 188, RG1, NSARM.

35 Wicken, *Mi'kmaq Treaties on Trial,* 221–2.

36 Belcher to Council and Assembly, 23 Mar. 1762. fol. 31, CO217/19, PRO.

37 Proclamation, 4 May 1762, fols. 27–8, CO217/19, PRO; Belcher to Board of Trade, 2 July 1762, fols. 22–3, CO217/19, PRO.

38 Board of Trade to Montague Wilmot, fols. 194–5, CO218/6, PRO.

39 Wilmot to Board of Trade, 28 January 1764, fol. 7, CO217/21, PRO; Michael Francklin to Lord Shelburne, 10 Nov. 1766, fol. 4, CO217/22, PRO. For the text of the Royal Proclamation of 1763, see *Report of the Public Archives for the Year 1918* (Ottawa: King's Printer, 1920), 323–9.

40 Belcher to Board of Trade, 7 Sept. 1762, fols. 70–9, CO217/19, PRO.

41 Sebastian Zouberbuhler, John Creighton, and Leonard Christopher Rudolf to Belcher, 15 July 1762, fol. 118, CO217/19, PRO; Memorial of Principal Inhabitants of Lunenburg, 15 July 1782, fol. 120, CO217/19, PRO.

42 Letter of Belcher, 17 July 1762, fol. 116, CO217/19, PRO.

43 Petition of King's County Inhabitants [July 1762], no. 10, Brown Transcripts, vol. 284, RG1, NSARM; Minutes of Council of War, 21 July 1762, 11–12. vol. 188A, RG1, NSARM.

44 Minutes of Council of War, 11 Aug. 1762, 18–19, vol. 188A, RG1, NSARM; Belcher to Amherst, 12 Aug. 1762, fols. 103–4, CO217/43, PRO.

45 Belcher to Board of Trade, 7 Sept. 1762, fols. 70–9, CO217/19, PRO.

46 Richard Bulkeley to William Forster, 28 July 1763, 51, vol. 136, RG1, NSARM.

47 Michael Francklin to [Sir Hugh Palliser], 11 Sept. 1766, fol. 80, CO217/44, PRO; Palliser to Francklin, 16 Oct. 1766, fols. 81–3, CO217/44, PRO.

48 Richard Bulkeley to John Anderson, Jeremiah Mears, Francis Peabody, and James Simonds, 20 Dec. 1766 101–2, vol. 136, RG1, NSARM.

49 See, for example, Wilmot to Board of Trade, 10 Dec. 1763, fols. 356–7, CO217/20, PRO.

50 Wilmot to Board of Trade, 24 June 1764, fol. 193, CO217/21, PRO.

51 Green to Board of Trade, 24 Aug. 1766, fols. 262–3, CO217/21, PRO.

52 Francklin to Board of Trade, 3 Sept. 1766, fol. 345, CO217/21, PRO.

53 Minutes of Nova Scotia Council, 11 July 1768, 104–5, vol. 189, RG1, NSARM.

54 Campbell to Lord Hillsborough, 12 Sept. 1768, fols. 245–6, CO217/45, PRO; Campbell to Lord Barrington, 12 Sept. 1768, fol. 251, CO217/45, PRO. See also Francis A. Coghlan. "Lord William Campbell," in *Dictionary of Canadian Biography hair,* eds. George W. Brown et al. (Toronto: University of Toronto Press, 1966–) 4:131–2.

55 Campbell to Lord Hillsborough, 25 Oct. 1768, fols. 272–3, CO217/45, PRO.

56 Campbell to Lord Hillsborough, 13 Jan. 1769, fol. 112, CO217/25, PRO.

57 Minutes of Nova Scotia Council, 8, 11, 22 Aug. 1763, 395–407, vol. 188, RG1, NSARM.

58 Beamsley Glasier to [Saint John River Society], 14 Dec. 1764, *New Brunswick Historical Society Collections* 6 (1905), 310. See also D. Murray Young, "Beamsley Perkins Glasier," 4: 299–301, DCB.

59 Minutes of Nova Scotia Council, 18 July 1768, 119–23, vol. 189, RG1, NSARM.

60 See also Claude Galarneau, "Charles-François Bailly de Messein," 4: 41–4, DCB.

61 Bulkeley to John Anderson, 139, vol. 136, RG1, NSARM.

62 Campbell to Lord Hillsborough, 22 Dec. 1770, fols. 11–12, CO217/48, PRO.

63 Report of the Present State and Condition of His Majesty's Province of Nova Scotia, 1773, fols. 19–20, CO217/50, PRO.

64 John Robinson and Thomas Rispin, *Journey through Nova-Scotia Containing a Particular Account of the Country and Its Inhabitants* (1774; repr., Sackville, NB: Ralph Pickard Bell Library, Mount Allison University, 1981), 27.

65 Gwyn, *Excessive Expectations,* 25.

66 M.W. Armstrong, "Neutrality and Religion in Revolutionary Nova Scotia," *New England Quarterly* 19 (1946), 50; Graeme Wynn, "Late Eighteenth-Century Agriculture on the Bay of Fundy Marshlands," *Acadiensis* 8, no. 2 (Spring 1979), 88. See also Campbell to Lord Shelburne, 27 Feb., 21 May 1767, 293–5, fols. 167, CO217/44, PRO.

67 Alan R. MacNeil, "The Acadian Legacy and Agricultural Development in Nova Scotia, 1760–1861," in *Farm, Factory and Fortune: New Studies in the Economic History of the Maritime Provinces,* ed. Kris Inwood (Fredericton: Acadiensis Press, 1993), 7–9; Wynn, "Late Eighteenth-Century Agriculture on the Bay of Fundy Marshlands," 80–9.

68 See L.F.S. Upton, *Micmacs and Colonists: Indian–White Relations in the Maritimes, 1713–1867* (Vancouver: UBC Press, 1979), 68–71.

69 Ibid., 72–8; Stephen Augustine, "*Lsipogtog,* 'River of Fire': A Historical Analysis" (Report to the Big Cove Band, 2003), 5–6; Ernest Clarke, *The Siege of Fort Cumberland, 1776: An Episode in the American Revolution* (Montreal and Kingston: McGill-Queen's University Press, 1995), 73–5, 82–3. My thanks to Stephen Augustine for permission to cite his unpublished report.

70 Upton, *Micmacs and Colonists,* 82–3; W.S. MacNutt, *New Brunswick: A History, 1784–1867* (Toronto: Macmillan, 1963), 78.

71 See Robert S. Allen, ed., *The Loyal Americans: The Military Role of the Loyalist Provincial Corps and Their Settlement in British North America, 1775–1784* (Ottawa: National Museum of Man/National Museums of Canada, 1983), passim.

72 Julian Gwyn, "The Mi'kmaq, Poor Settlers, and the Nova Scotia Fur Trade, 1783–1853," *Journal of the Canadian Historical Association,* New Series, 14 (2003), 65–91.

73 Mancke, "Another British America," 1–2 and passim.

74 P.J. Marshall, "The British in Asia: Trade to Dominion, 1700–1765," in *The Oxford History of the British Empire, Volume II,* ed. P.J. Marshall (Oxford: Oxford University Press, 1998), 2:505.

75 See Elizabeth Mancke, "Imperial Transitions," in *The "Conquest" of Acadia: Imperial, Colonial, and Aboriginal Constructions,* ed. John G. Reid et al., 178–202; David Armitage, *The Ideological Origins of the British Empire* (Cambridge: Cambridge University Press, 2000), 170–98.

76 Reid et al., *The Conquest of Acadia, 1710,* 208.

77 See John G. Reid, "Change and Continuity in Nova Scotia, 1758–1775," in *Making Adjustments,* ed. Conrad, 45–59; Paul E. Hoffman, *Florida's Frontiers* (Bloomington: Indiana University Press, 2002).

78 See Richard White, *The Middle Ground: Indians, Empires, and Republics in the Great Lakes Region,*

1650–1815 (New York: Cambridge University Press, 1991), 59–60.

79 Clarke, *The Siege of Fort Cumberland,* 4–44.

80 See, among other works, D.C. Bell, *Early Loyalist Saint John: The Origin of New Brunswick Politics, 1783–1786* (Fredericton: New Ireland Press, 1983); Ann Gorman Condon, *The Envy of the American States: The Loyalist Dream for New Brunswick* (Fredericton: New Ireland Press, 1984); W.G. Godfrey, "Thomas Carleton," 5: 155–63, DCB; W.G. Godfrey, "James Glenie," 5: 347–58, DCB; Neil MacKinnon, *This Unfriendly Soil: The Loyalist Experience in Nova Scotia, 1783–1791* (Kingston and Montreal: McGill-Queen's University Press, 1986).

The Family in Exile: Loyalist Social Values after the Revolution

Ann Gorman Condon

"All happy families are alike but an unhappy family is unhappy after its own fashion." Thus begins Leo Tolstoy's *Anna Karenina,* that extraordinary fictional journey into the private lives of the Russian aristocracy in the nineteenth century.[1] While modern anthropologists might gasp at Tolstoy's willingness to make such sweeping generalizations about the family, no one can deny his success in creating a vivid world of intimacy and intrigue, devotion and deceit, noble suffering and base humiliation, climaxing, of course, in the necessary self-destruction of its flawed heroine, followed by a ringing affirmation of traditional, and very Christian, family values.

Culturally, Tsarist Russia was a far different place than colonial Canada, but they did, for a short while, have one thing in common: an official ruling class. Until the mid-nineteenth century, the British North American provinces were ruled by a group of privileged officers who held their powers independently of the people they governed and reinforced their authority by elaborate social codes and extensive family connections. Indeed, so powerful and so notorious were these sets of provincial oligarchs that they are known pejoratively even to this day in the former colony of Upper Canada, now Ontario, as "The Family Compact."

Alas, thus far Canada's period of gentry rule has inspired no Tolstoyan masterpiece, no insider account of the intimate life, passions and pairings of this select group. In fact, it is both remarkable and regrettable that, for all the many treatises on the political operations of the Family Compact, we have so few accounts of its internal dynamics: its elaborate network of filiations and obligations, its shared aspirations and anxieties, and the mechanisms by which it ensured the transmission not only of property and power from generation to generation, but of a distinctive code of values.[2]

Using the new methodologies developed by family historians and the wealth of personal letters left by prominent Loyalist families (which extend in some cases through four generations), I have begun a research project aimed at discovering the personal bonds and ideals which united these people over such a long stretch of time. Eventually, I will include representative family writings from five of the British North American colonies, spread over three generations. I have started with the Maritime provinces because the Loyalist style of cultural leadership was established here so very quickly after their arrival in the 1780s and is so well chronicled in their letters to each other.

This essay represents the "first fruits" of my work, my first attempt to identify patterns and

---

Ann Gorman Condon, "The Family in Exile: Loyalist Social Values after the Revolution," in Margaret Conrad, ed., *Intimate Relations: Family and Community in Planter Nova Scotia* (Fredericton: Acadiensis Press, 1995), 42–53.

figures in this very complex material, based mainly on the Jarvis Papers and Robinson Papers in the New Brunswick Museum and the Bliss Papers in the Public Archives of Nova Scotia. Unfortunately editorial constraints will not permit me to explore the wealth of material in these letters fully, but let me at least hint at the tone and atmosphere of family life among the Loyalist grandees by quoting three sets of love letters from prominent Loyalists to their wives.

My first example is a letter from Edward Winslow, the unfailingly gallant, but perpetually impoverished, Massachusetts Loyalist, to his wife Mary. The two had married before the revolutionary war and she accompanied him on his circuitous flight pattern after 1775—from Boston, to Halifax, to New York City, to Annapolis, Nova Scotia, and finally, ten years later, to their permanent abode in Kingsclear, New Brunswick. Throughout this long hegira, Mary managed the family household which at times included the first eight of their 11 children, Edward's elderly parents and his two spinster sisters. The letter I quote was written in 1784, while Edward was in Halifax, looking, as always, for a profitable job, and apparently aware that his lonely, overburdened wife could use some cheering up. Winslow starts off with trumpets blaring:

> what do I care whether it's the fashion for men to write long letters to their wives or not.... In matters where my own feelings are concerned I will not be shackled by any of the rules which bind the generality of mankind.... I cannot enjoy a pleasure equal to that of writing to you, and that's sufficient for writing. If other men do not experience the same sensation they have not the same degree of affection.

He then launches into a hilarious description of the fashionable ladies of Halifax and, with mock pity, bemoans the fact that the immensity of False-Tops False Curls, monstrous Caps. Grease, Filth of various kinds, Jewels, painted paper and trinkets, hide and deform heads of Hair that in their natural state are really beautiful. Rouge & other dirt cover cheeks and faces that without would be tolerable, whilst the unfortunate neck and breasts remain open to the inclemency of the weather & the view of the World....

But his Mary, he notes, is the exact opposite: "From 16 years old to the present time you have literally set your Cap at no creature on earth but me. Regardless of Fashion you have only endeavoured by uniform cleanliness to make yourself desirable in my eyes." After declaring his continuing love for her, Winslow closes by saying he still hopes that she will be able once more to enter the world of fashion and elegance.[3]

My second example is a series of letters from Beverley Robinson, the dashing young military officer from New York. Beverley had married Nancy Barclay during the war, and he proved, in New Brunswick, to be a bit of a martinet. Even though Nancy had abandoned a comfortable home in New York City for a refugee farm on the Nashwaaksis River, and had borne 11 children during their marriage, Beverley cannot resist chastising her for "laziness" and negligence. In one 1799 letter, he gave her elaborate instructions on the proper way to cool down and curry horses, and then proceeded to remind her to wrap his doughnuts securely so they will remain moist. The last batch were so dry he could not eat them![4]

Yet the petty irritations of married life did not undermine Beverley's devotion to his wife. For example, when he heard that Nancy was worried about losing her attractiveness now that she was forced to wear spectacles, Robinson rushed to reassure her with this stunning declaration:

...my present feelings have nothing to do with the respectability of your appearance, no madam my imagination is not confined to the age of 45 but wanders back to those days of yore when you was all youth and beauty I all ardour and affection...you are and shall be my beloved and adored mistress and as such only I will cherish the recollection of you....[5]

A year later on their twenty-second wedding anniversary Beverley acknowledged, with exquisite sensitivity, that although many changes had taken place since "the day that gave my Nancy to me, I can truly say that she is dearer to me now than when I received her with the rapture of a Bridegroom...."[6]

My final example concerns Jonathan Bliss. A crusty, 47-year-old bachelor when he came to New Brunswick, Bliss had spent the revolutionary war in England, enjoying, to the full, the pleasures of London and Bristol. He came to New Brunswick for sake of a job, but candidly admitted that he was too old, too spoiled by England to appreciate such a new country, however promising.[7] Bliss performed his duties as Attorney General in a minimal sort of way and amused himself by writing political poetry. In 1789, after much deliberation, he decided to take a wife. He returned to his American home in Massachusetts and married the daughter of the richest man in Worcester County. She was Mary Worthington, a woman in her late 20s, and thus a full 20 years younger than Bliss. Her letters to her husband make it clear that she embodied the ideal of female grace and submissiveness so cherished by people in the eighteenth century.[8]

Unexpectedly, passionately, Jonathan Bliss fell in love with his young wife. She and the four sons she bore became the enchanted centre of his life. In his letters to Mary, this aging, cynical lawyer resorted to baby talk. He confessed to her that she had made him the "happiest man in New Brunswick"—but ruined him for living alone. Mary was more deferential and demure in her responses to this older man, but she did assure Bliss that his companionship supplied all the love and support she once drew from family and friends. When Mary died in 1799 delivering their fifth child, Bliss was crushed. He would never remarry, and for both Jonathan and their sons, her memory would profoundly shape their ideals of womanhood and of happiness.[9]

It seems to me that, on the surface at least, these are remarkable letters—delicate, witty, warmly demonstrative. They suggest deep mutual concern and enduring affection, the ideal of "companionate marriage" which Lawrence Stone has described so forcefully for the English gentry of the eighteenth century and which Bernard Bailyn finds so powerfully at work within the family of Thomas Hutchinson in colonial Massachusetts. It is an ideal, according to Richard Sennett, which calls for detachment and careful control in public roles, but a warm, expressive, supportive behaviour among one's intimates.[10]

Yet how are we, citizens of the late twentieth century, living as we do in the "Age of Deconstruction," to interpret these letters? Do we take them at face value? Or do we look for evasions, masks and ambiguities, which subvert and undermine the highly polished surface? These are some of the questions I am pursuing through the thousands of Loyalist family letters still available in our public archives. My goal is to uncover the inner workings of power and intimacy among the people known universally in Canadian history as The Family Compact. As for the all-important question of interpretation, my strategy is to pursue a dual track: to try to appreciate at full value the depth of feeling and mutual dependency radiating through these letters, and at the same time to recognize that these statements were also calculated performances, survival measures and personal defences against an undeserved fate and a relentlessly cruel world.[11]

Rather than digress into methodology, I would like to use the balance of this essay to describe the three major conclusions which I have reached at this stage in my research. I hope this will provide a concrete sense of the richness of the material contained in these Loyalists letters, as well as practical examples of my interpretive strategy.

First, it seems abundantly clear from the written sources that, for the Loyalist refugees, the family was the most important institution in their lives. Despite occasional attempts by historians (including myself) to embroider Loyalist life during their years in the Maritime provinces, the fact remains that these colonial gentry found their new physical environment forbidding and its public life totally lacking in beauty or grandeur. Even those Loyalists who came with money, servants and prestigious public posts found their new homes strange and alienating.[12]

Since there was little hope of returning to America, and neither their Christian beliefs nor their self-respect would permit them to give in to despair, these displaced people threw their energies into their immediate families—the one area of life they could control and also the one area capable of positive response. Within the day-to-day life of their families, within the houses so carefully constructed and tastefully furnished, they could reenact their days of glory. They could organize little entertainments for friends according to the remembered standards of colonial Boston and New York; they could dress in silks and velvets and dancing shoes; they could exchange gossip and wit and observe the courtesies of a world far removed from the frontier. In such ways, private life became far more important than the crude tedium of public affairs.

Second, the fact that the Loyalists were exiles, not simply immigrants, had important psychological repercussions. The mentality of exile has been described many times by novelists and essayists in our century. Indeed, exile has come to be the salient fact of modern existence. Put simply, exiles are rootless, mutilated people, who live two lives simultaneously: first, their ordinary life which they find dull, even repul-sive; and second, their imagined life—their dreams, memories and feelings of nostalgia which are full of warmth, vitality and success. In a remarkable essay, "The Mind of Winter," the literary critic, Edward Said, notes how many outstanding chess players, novelists, poets and adventurers in the twentieth century are exiles—people to whom the imaginary life is much more important than the real world.[13]

The personal letters of the Loyalists provide multiple diverse glimpses into the imaginary world which they cherished during long exile in the Maritimes. And what were its contents? The answer is obvious: it was filled with remembered moments of glory and power in colonial America! It was the world painted so magnificently by John Singleton Copley and described most recently by Richard Bushman.[14] It was a world of refinement, taste and elegance—a world where men were so confident of their authority in both society and the family that they chose to display the feminine side of their nature in their portraits. Hence the silk stockings, ruffled shirts and velvet suits worn by Copley's subjects. Hence the private, domestic backdrops of sinuously carved furniture and bookcases full of the bound books which signified a man of taste. Their wives' appearance complemented the men's. Although their dresses and jewels were dazzling, their faces were those of the hostess—gentle, attentive, welcoming. Despite their elaborate garb, there was nothing worldly about these women. They were domestic creatures—decorative, dependent, nurturing of husbands and guests. Their pride came from domestic accomplishment—a piece of needlework, a fine table, an appealing bowl of fruit. Their personal world did not extend beyond the front door.[15]

These prescribed male and female roles were reenacted in their letters as they doubtless were in the actual homes of the Loyalists. In fact, the extraordinary charm and grace of the Loyalist letters were quite deliberate, expressing affirmations of their cultural ideals. Although fewer in number, the women's letters were as lively and extroverted as the men's. And they were cheerful, often deliberately so, for it was clearly against the common code for either men or women to complain about their fate. Unfortunately, we have no extant letters written by Edward Winslow's wife Mary. We do know that she was very upset when her husband decided to send their son Murray, aged 12, to military school in England. This could suggest that she had already experienced too many separations in her life. Otherwise, she seems to have borne her fate bravely and silently.[16]

Few letters from Beverley Robinson's wife Nancy have survived, but from her husband's comments it seems that she fell into a depression after moving with her 11 children to the howling wilderness. The fascinating response to her melancholy was that several members of her family—not only her husband, but her mother, her son and her brother—began writing letters urging Nancy to carry on and bear her burdens stoically.[17]

Jonathan Bliss's wife Mary wrote letters regularly to her family and her husband, many of which survive. They are marked by delicate sensitivity and a humorous vein of self-mockery. Clearly, Mary, too, went through a difficult emotional period during at least one New Brunswick winter. After admitting to her sister that she felt a certain loneliness while her husband was away on business, Mary blamed herself for her low spirits—not her four young children, nor her absent husband, nor the piercing cold. She ended this confessional letter by telling her sister not to worry, for she had just written out two pages of resolutions to improve herself and now felt much better![18]

It is notable that all letters from Loyalist women to men contained an apology for the "stupidity" of their letters, ascribed usually either to their allegedly poor handwriting or to the scattered nature of their thoughts. Although the letters themselves do not bear out this harsh judgment, it seems to have been an unwritten rule among these Loyalists that women must openly and repeatedly acknowledge their inferiority to men. Some historians call this trait "learned helplessness," but I find it more significant. Although they were encouraged to tease and flirt with the men of their circle, like other eighteenth-century women, Loyalist women did defer to male superiority—men's education and worldly knowledge. This seems to have been fundamental to the marriage bargain, an essential part of the reciprocal, complementary roles they performed as husband and wife. In accepting this deference, men implicitly agreed to protect and cherish such "stupid" but lovable creatures.

Third, the letters suggest that Loyalist children were deeply affected by their parents' history, and the most talented devoted a significant portion of their lives to redeeming their parents' fate by achieving great distinction in their professional lives. The impact of Loyalist values on their *redeemer children* is without doubt the most important finding of my research thus far. These children were raised with enormous affection and care, but also with firm discipline and fond expectations. Children were expected to carry the torch—maintain the codes of manner and dress and use their talents to bring honour to family.[19] Among the numerous examples available, consider the case of Henry Bliss. Perhaps the most talented of all the Loyalist sons, Bliss was educated at King's College, Nova Scotia, and the Inner Temple in London. He emerged laden with academic prizes, good looks and acclaimed charm. Bliss chose to settle in London where he painstakingly established a reputation as a distinguished lawyer, ran for Parliament, and, in his private moments, wrote at least seven historical dramas in iambic pentameter, exalting Loyalist principles. Although he considered these verse plays to be the most important aspect of his productive life, they were anachronistic to English tastes and failed utterly to win Bliss any notice, much less any commercial success. Admittedly discouraged, Bliss nonetheless continued writing such plays to the end of his life, in order to affirm the parental code and his own unrealized sense of destiny.[20]

The lives of Edward and Maria Jarvis illustrate a similar pattern of frustrated idealism. He was the English-educated son of Loyalist merchant Munson Jarvis and she, the daughter of a prominent medical man in Saint John. Soon after their marriage they lived for four years in the British colony of Malta, where Edward held an appointment as a law officer, and they both enjoyed the elaborate social life of the colony's rulers. Eventually, Edward's appointment as Chief Justice of Prince Edward Island permitted the Jarvises and their growing family to return to North America. They were dismayed, however, by the dull, "bumpkin" life on the Island. In consequence, the two expended both their health and their limited fortune building a grand house—"Mount Edward"—near Charlottetown and giving heroic entertainments in order to expose the local population to the best British standards. Maria's exertions produced a heart condition, and she died soon after the house was finished. The disconsolate Edward remained heavily in debt for the rest of his life, and confessed to his brother that he was so short of funds he felt he could not comment on his children's choice of marriage partners, even though he disapproved! Such were the links between financial power and patriarchal authority.[21]

A variation on second-generation experience was that of William Bliss, son of Jonathan and brother to Henry. After English legal training, William returned to Halifax to marry the richest bride in that city, Sarah Ann Armstrong, the adopted daughter of his father's childhood friend, Loyalist Sampson Salter Blowers. Within a decade William's connections enabled him to get appointed to the Nova Scotia Supreme Court. But despite this great honour, his very comfortable life, and apparently happy family, William worried ceaselessly in his letters to his brothers that he had sold out, taken the easy road, instead of seeking fame by pursuing the law in London or risking his all on a literary career.[22]

The preoccupation of these Loyalist children with their parents' world—their lifelong efforts to redeem and vindicate the parental sacrifice—meant that they, too, lived a great deal of their existence in the "floating world" of the imagination. Unlike the sons of ordinary immigrants, they had difficulty sinking roots in the local Canadian soil, committing themselves to the realities of time and place. In 1825 Henry Bliss recognized the disadvantages of this outlook and told William that he was considering returning to New Brunswick and marrying a local beauty:

> To marry a local girl will give me some connexion in the country, some friends. I mean some common interests with others; and I shall find somebody to sympathize with me, or seem to do it. That is just what our family has always wanted. We have been alone and unconnected with all the society in which we lived; and had any of us stumbled how the world would have trod on us! But then our situation...had its advantages for when their daughters whored, or their sons got drunk, it touched not us.... I sometimes regret that Father did not take a different side, or that the side he did take was not more successful in the American Revolution. We should now have been great Yankees at Boston—full of money and self conceit.... But then I might never have seen Kew...nor the inside of the Louvre...nor the Pont du Gard, nor so much of this beautiful Earth. No I am well content with my destiny. How can people doubt that God is good.[23]

This introspective, ambivalent letter, written at the age of 27, perfectly captures the dilemma of second-generation Loyalists—their cosmopolitan outlook, coupled with a severe, often crippling detachment from ordinary life. Only with the third generation do we find Loyalist heirs rooting themselves in the local soil, identifying with its landscape and people, including even the Protestant dissenting sects who once represented the antithesis of all the Loyalist gentry stood for.[24] Moreover, their obsession with Loyalist sacrifice lessened. It is true that genealogy became a hobby with the third generation, as did commemorating their ancestors in local churches and cemeteries, but such activities were not an unpaid debt, haunting their waking hours. As well, obsession with family life diminished. Relations between husbands and wives of the third generation were far more relaxed and informal, but also more separate. Husbands spent much of their leisure time in clubs or hunting camps or militia musters. This apparent preference for the exclusive company of males was a new development, an assertion of a type of "rugged" masculine identity which their grandfathers deliberately avoided.[25] Likewise, the third generation of Loyalist wives and mothers became more civic minded, more involved in such reform movements as temperance, public health and religious education. Their children were increasingly sent off early to boarding school where the girls were permitted to study an academic curriculum and even aspire to university by the end of the century, while the boys' training emphasized military drill from school days onward.[26]

As an inevitable part of this evolution, Loyalist elegance, Loyalist exclusivity and Loyalist intensity gradually dissolved. Although their grandchildren certainly respected their ancestors, they themselves had become Canadians and Victorians. In the words of the great conservative historian William L. Morton, grace had been transformed into respectability.[27]

Thus the special Loyalist culture—the special circumstances produced by the exile experience—seems to have lasted two generations at most. What we need to define is how it shaped, and perhaps even transformed English Canada in general and Planter society in particular. It is a striking fact that the rampant individualism that seized American culture in the nineteenth century—the exaltation of success, of the loner, the wilderness and even of violence—never took hold of nineteenth-century Canadian culture.[28] On the contrary, group loyalties to the community and the family, a cordial acceptance of the complementarity of the sexes, a strong emphasis on public duty as well as an equal insistence on the sheer joy of human companionship: all were values which the Loyalists brought with them from colonial America and kept vividly alive through most of the nineteenth century. Philosophically, these exiles were Aristotelians rather than Platonists, Arcadians rather than Utopians. Surely their dominance for 75 years left a residue which requires definition. Indeed, it seems singularly unfortunate that the ruling historical metaphor for the Loyalist contribution to Canadian culture is Northrop Frye's "the garrison mentality." Without denying the elements of arrogance and paranoia in the Loyalist personality, we must also recognize the social virtues of wit, learning, style and profound human solidarity. Sustained exploration of their private papers may bring both the positive and negative aspects of the Loyalist legacy into proper balance.

Notes

1 Leo Tolstoy, *Anna Karenina* (Rosemary Edmunds, tr., London, 1954), 13.

2 The *Jalna* series of Mazo de la Roche is, I believe, the closest fictional attempt to recreate the private life of Ontario's landed gentry but, unlike Tolstoy's novel, the *Jalna* novels are set in the period after the gentry's fall from political power and are essentially a romantic rejection of modern industrial Canada, not a depiction of the gentry in its years of power. More salient are several recent scholarly studies of Loyalist women. Especially noteworthy are Katherine McKenna, "Options for Elite Women in Early Upper

Canadian Society: The Case of the Powell Family," in J.K. Johnson and Bruce G. Wilson, eds., *Historical Essays on Upper Canada; New Perspectives* (Ottawa, 1989), 401–24, and her recently published book, *A Life of Propriety: Anne Murray Powell and Her Family* (Kingston and Montreal, 1994), as well as Janice Potter-MacKinnon, *While Women Only Wept: Loyalist Refugee Women in Eastern Ontario* (Montreal and Kingston, 1993). Also valuable are three doctoral studies: Robin Burns, "The First Elite of Toronto: An Examination of the Genesis, Consolidation, and Duration of Power in an Emerging Colonial Society," Ph.D. thesis, University of Western Ontario, 1975; Robert L. Fraser, "Like Eden in Her Summer Dress: Gentry, Economy and Society, Upper Canada, 1812–1840," Ph.D. thesis, University of Toronto, 1979; Beatrice Spence Ross, "Adaptation in Exile; Loyalist Women in Nova Scotia after the American Revolution," Ph.D. thesis, Cornell University, 1981. My study, *The Envy of the American States: The Loyalist Dream for New Brunswick* (Fredericton, 1984) deals briefly with family life.

3 Edward Winslow to his Wife, W.O. Raymond, ed., *The Winslow Papers* (Saint John, N.B., 1901), 225–27.

4 Beverley Robinson to Nancy Robinson, 21 November 1799, Robinson Family Papers, New Brunswick Museum.

5 Ibid., 11 November 1799.

6 Ibid., 20 January 1800.

7 Jonathan Bliss to S.S. Blowers, 19 September 1786, Bliss Family Papers, Public Archives of Nova Scotia, [PANS].

8 Phillip Buckner, "Jonathan Bliss," *Dictionary of Canadian Biography,* VI (Toronto, 1987), 74–6. Thomas Vincent, "The Image and Function of Women in the Poetry of Affection in Eighteenth-Century Maritime Canada," in Margaret Conrad, ed., *Making Adjustments: Change and Continuity in Planter Nova Scotia, 1759–1800* (Fredericton, 1991), 234–46.

9 Jno. Bliss to Mary Bliss, 4 June 1792 and Mary Bliss to Jno. Bliss, 23 July 1792, Bliss Papers, PANS. The story of the devotion of the Bliss men to Mary Worthington Bliss has never been written, but can be traced through the family papers.

10 Lawrence Stone, *The Family, Sex and Marriage in England 1500–1800* (New York, 1977); Bernard Bailyn, *The Ordeal of Thomas Hutchinson* (Cambridge, Mass., 1974); Richard Sennett, *The Fall of Public Man* (New York, 1977), 98–107. For a fine survey of recent scholarship on the family in Europe and North America, see Tamara K. Hareven, "The History of the Family and the Complexity of Social Change," *American Historical Review,* 96 (1991), 95–124.

11 In developing my interpretive approach I have been especially influenced by the work of the French philosopher Paul Ricouer. For an explanation of this methodology see my "The Celestial World of Jonathan Odell: Symbolic Unities within a Disparate Artifact Collection," in Gerald L. Pocius, ed., *Living in a Material World: Canadian and American Approaches to Material Culture* (St. John's, 1992), 192–226. I find the recent effort by Edward Said to develop a "contrapuntal" approach to historical experience an equally rich, if less systematic attempt to capture both the pure and impure elements of literary texts within a single conceptual framework. See *Culture and Imperialism* (New York, 1993).

12 Neil MacKinnon captures this estrangement especially well in *This Unfriendly Soil: The Loyalist Experience in Nova Scotia, 1783–1791* (Kingston, 1986).

13 Edward Said, "The Mind of Winter: Reflections on Life in Exile," *Harper's,* 269 (1984), 49–55. For a subtle exploration of the imaginary worlds of exiled writers Joseph Conrad and Vladimir Nabokov, amongst others, see Michael Seidel, *Exile and the Narrative Imagination* (New Haven, 1987).

14 Richard L. Bushman, *The Refinement of America: Persons, Houses, Cities* (New York, 1992).

15 Margaret Doody, "Vibrations," *London Review of Books,* 5 August 1993, 13–14.

16 Edward Winslow to his wife Mary, 15 September 1784, *Winslow Papers.*

17 Beverley Robinson, Jr. to Anna Robinson, 29 October [1799?] and Thomas Barclay to Beverley Robinson, 1 November 1799, Robinson Papers.

18 Mary Bliss to Frances Ames, 13 February 1797, Bliss Papers, PANS.

19 The best book on parent-child relations for this period is Philip G. Greven, *The Protestant Temperament: Patterns of Child-Rearing, Religious Experience and the Self in Early America* (New York, 1977). Equally insightful is a three-generation study of Virginia families within almost the same time frame as this essay on Loyalist families: Jan Lewis, *The Pursuit of Happiness: Family and Values in Jefferson's Virginia* (New York, 1985).

20 Bertis Sutton, "The Expression of Second-Generation Loyalist Sentiment in the Verse Dramas of Henry Bliss," *Nova Scotia Historical Review,* 13, 1 (1993), 43–77.

21 Anna Maria Jarvis to Caroline Boyd, 6 March 1832; E.J. Jarvis to William Jarvis, 4 August 1835 and 30 January 1837; E.J. Jarvis to Mrs. William Jarvis, 21 September 1849, Jarvis Papers, New Brunswick Museum. J.M. Bumsted and H.T. Holman, "Edward James Jarvis," *Dictionary of Canadian Biography*, VIII (Toronto, 1985), 428–30.

22 William Bliss to Henry Bliss, 18 May 1828, Bliss Papers, PANS.

23 Henry Bliss to William Bliss, Marseilles, 7 January 1825, Bliss Papers, PANS.

24 See for example, Ann Gorman Condon, ed., "'The Young Robin Hood Society': A Political Satire by Edward Winslow," *Acadiensis*, XV (1986), 120–43.

25 W.L. Morton, "Victorian Canada," in W.L. Morton, ed., *The Shield of Achilles: Aspects of Canada in the Victorian Age* (Toronto, 1968), 311–33. For the equivalent development in the United States, see E. Anthony Rotundo, *American Manhood: Transformations in Masculinity from the Revolution to the Modern Era* (New York, 1993).

26 These impressionistic findings are based on my reading of the letters of William Jarvis, Jr. and his two wives and children in the 1860s and 1870s, Jarvis Papers.

27 Morton, "Victorian Canada."

28 Alexis de Tocqueville was the first to recognize these traits in volume II of his *Democracy in America* (New York, 1957). For modern interpretations, see Richard Slotkin's trilogy: *Regeneration through Violence: The Mythology of the American Frontier, 1600–1860* (New York, 1973); *The Fatal Environment: The Myth of the Frontier in the Age of Industrialization, 1800–1890* (New York, 1985); and *Gunfighter Nation: The Mythology of the Frontier in Twentieth Century America* (New York, 1992). For the Canadian comparison, see Marcia B. Kline, *Beyond the Land Itself: Views of Nature in Canada and the United States* (Cambridge, Mass., 1970).

The Security Danger, 1793–1798

F. MURRAY GREENWOOD

Lower Canada twice experienced severe security crises in the years 1793–7. Both featured plans by revolutionary France to invade the colony—undercover activity by enemy agents (foreign and domestic) or "emissaries" in the jargon of the times; and serious province-wide rioting, which revealed the grave difficulties of maintaining order in the days before professional police. Both also featured paranoid alarm—the "garrison mentality"—among the English élite of merchants, seigneurs, professionals, and government officials, including judges. The garrison mentality in turn resulted in draconian security legislation and a manipulation of the courts.

The External Danger, 1793–1794

Citizen Edmond Genêt, appointed as French minister to the United States, was nothing if not an optimist. This young Girondist ambassador revelled in his instructions to press the Americans for a joint expedition to unite the "beautiful star of Canada" to the "American constellation."[1] When President Washington declared neutrality on 23 April 1793, Genêt enthusiastically reinterpreted his mission. To bring the truth of regenerated Frenchmen to

their brothers, to help them escape from British oppression, the minister wrote in June, would be his crowning glory. Using New York as the base, Genêt soon established a powder magazine, arsenal, and barracks and recruited an irregular army of about twenty-five hundred (mainly American adventurers and Irish and French residents of the city). He also hoped to recruit Vermont frontiersmen for an attack down the Richelieu River and to make use of the French West Indian fleet, then at anchor in New York. At one stage, this irrepressible young man intended using these fifteen or so ships to destroy British fishing stations in Newfoundland, recapture St Pierre and Miquelon, burn Halifax, seize the fur convoy from Hudson Bay, liberate the Canadiens, destroy the Nassau base of British privateers, and capture New Orleans from Spain. All this would succeed, he thought, because of the surprise factor!

A kindred spirit, Henri Mezière, who in May 1793 had walked from Montreal to Philadelphia to offer his services to the French minister, assisted in formulating Genêt's Canadian policy. Mezière soon prepared a memorandum on Canada, revealing a mind where enthusiasm made short work of facts.[2] But Genêt used Mezière's ideas and some of his own to draft an inflammatory document entitled *Les*

F. Murray Greenwood, "The Security Danger, 1793-1798," in F. Murray Greenwood, *Legacies of Fear: Law and Politics in Quebec in the Era of the French Revolution* (Toronto: The Osgoode Society, 1993), 76–103. Reprinted with permission of the publisher.

Français libres à leurs frères les Canadiens, which attributed the callous abandonment of Canada at the Conquest to the evil Bourbons, outlined the revolutionary paradise, and promised that enlightened France would help her former subjects to find it should they rebel.[3] The pamphlet dealt with such arcane subjects as free trade, the royal veto on legislation, an elected clergy, civilizing missions to the Indians, and careers open to talent, as well as more understandable matters such as the abolition of clerical tithes, corvées, and other seigneurial rights, establishment of a republic and political independence in alliance with France and the United States. By late summer Mezière, ensconced at Lake Champlain in upper New York State, sent Jacques Rousse, an expatriate Canadien, into Lower Canada with 350 copies of *Les Français libres* and a variety of other propaganda. In February 1794 Rousse reported that he had circulated the pamphlet, together with copies of revolutionary songs, American newspapers, a Justification of Louis's execution, and Thomas Paine's democratic *Rights of Man,* in all parishes of the province. He had made contact with local sympathizers who agreed to ensure Canadiens would not take up arms if France attacked.[4]

By October 1793 Genêt had toned down his strategic extravaganza, dropping the southern campaign and the visit to Quebec. The officers of the French fleet at New York considered even this scheme excessive and after a council of war at sea, sailed back to France. Thus disappeared Genêt's only realistic weapon to test the effect his emissaries were having on the Canadiens. Thus disappeared, too, Henri Mezière who had been attached to the admiral as Genêt's political officer. The minister himself retired from his duties in February 1794, choosing to avoid a Jacobin guillotine by remaining as a gentleman farmer in the United States.

Rousse had made disciples, especially in the cities. The main francophile agitators in Montreal were one Jean-Baptiste Colombe, who

read aloud *Les Français libres* outside a church door; Canadien François Duclos of Eagle Island, a former lieutenant in the American revolutionary army; carpenter Stephen Storey, of American origin; and a tailor named Costille.[5] Duclos had allegedly publicized the coming French-American attack, predicted its success since the Canadiens preferred French rule, and gloried in the prospect of a redistribution of wealth through plunder. Storey had pledged his support for the invasion, boasting he would "then mark out the Judges and Justices and Mr. Thomas Walker the Lawyer." Storey was also in cahoots with Costille, who had been busy circulating copies of *Les Français libres* and telling listeners that six hundred armed men and women north of Mount Royal had risen and were ready to assist the invasion.

In January and February of 1794 Rousse had spent about five weeks in Quebec's working-class suburb of St Jean, exhorting all not to take up arms against the American and French liberators. Some listened. Jean La Cosse, a wigmaker turned pedlar, carried the message to many parts of the colony. Tinsmith Augustin Lavau of St Jean made copies of the *Les Français libres* for circulation and read the document to illiterate *confrères.* He also worked effectively to undermine martial spirit in the Quebec militia. Joiner Louis Dumontier (from the Upper Town) did the same, citing thirty-four years of oppression, and exhorted visiting habitant relatives and friends they must not support the British militarily. Alexandre Menut, who kept a popular tavern, spread the word to artisans, workers, and farmers living near the city, claiming that the invincible French would give Canada a proper constitution. Revolutionary meetings, composed mainly of artisans, were held that winter and spring of 1794 in the St Jean house of roofer Louis Fluet. Of the dozen or so Quebec residents implicated as subversives and identifiable by occupation in depositions or voluntary examinations (out of about twenty in all), ten were artisans or labourers and two were shopkeepers. Genêt was clearly stimulating some response among the working people of the capital. The idea of not bearing arms fell on fertile soil.[6]

In his speech closing the first session of the legislature in May 1793, Lieutenant-Governor Clarke had referred to the war as a nasty but far-off event and expressed confidence in the "loyalty and faithful attachment of his majesty's subjects of the province." No particular legislation seemed to be immediately required.[7] The government confined its propaganda to partially subsidizing John Neilson's product ion of an engraved illustration (with a short propaganda text) of Louis XVI about to be guillotined. This cool assessment of the colony's security situation remained the norm for several months not only in official circles but among the English élite generally.

The reasons for calm are easily found. Until the autumn there was no evidence that France intended an attack on the colony nor that French undercover agents had entered it. The United States had declared its neutrality and during these months France suffered a number of serious reverses, particularly the outbreak of formidable royalist insurrections in La Vendée on the west coast. Such setbacks encouraged the English élite to conclude that the war would shortly be won, with John Richardson deducing that "the Game will soon be up with those Monsters of iniquity—the National Convention."[8]

Towards the end of 1793 and in the first months of 1794 that calm confidence turned into serious concern. This was stimulated principally by well-grounded suspicions that Citizen Genêt was planning an invasion of the Canadas and had sent agents in to circulate written propaganda and tamper with the people. The first indication of the new climate was the treatment of General Galbaud, deposed governor of Saint-Domingo (Haiti), his aide-de-camp, and a French sergeant who entered the colony as supposed refugees in September 1793. On Clarke's orders the three men were arrested and escorted to Quebec as prisoners of war. Galbaud and his aide eventually escaped to the United States, while the sergeant was sent to Britain. Clarke and Dorchester, who resumed his governorship in late September, believed the visitors were agents of Genêt. While at Montreal Galbaud and the sergeant were thought to have spread revolutionary principles and to have attempted to establish clubs among the working people. The governor reported that labourers, artisans, and even some middle-class youth provided a ready audience for "modern French principles." By October, English Montrealers, worried about the departure of the Royal Navy's West Indies and North American Squadron, became so suspicious of revolutionary intrigues that most of Mezière's friends were afraid to write to him.[9]

In November the government mobilized its "public relations" resources against the enemy. Chief Justice Smith warned the grand jury of the perils inherent in French "Levelism" or "Equality of Property," urging it to hunt out the seditious. A Dorchester proclamation which referred to insidious alien enemies lurking in the province, ordered everyone, in and out of authority, to inform on any person attempting to "excite Discontent...[or] lessen the Affections of His Majesty's...Subjects." Bishop Jean-François Hubert's circular letter worried that rural residents, "struck by the name *French,* would not know how to behave" if the fleet arrived. Priests must teach their parishioners that modern Frenchmen had murdered their virtuous Sovereign and given way to a spirit of "irreligion...of anarchy, of parricide."[10] Two bills dealing with security followed these propaganda initiatives during the 1794 legislative session. One gave the government tighter control over the militia. The other, known as the Alien Act, provided means of keeping foreigners under close surveillance, subjecting them to summary deportation whenever the governor saw fit, and suspended habeas corpus for political offences. But before these bills even reached the statute book the province experienced its first popular disturbances of the war.

The Riots of 1794

The first sign of popular unrest occurred in April shortly after the Montreal Quarter Sessions condemned a canoeman named Joseph Leveillé to the pillory for having obtained advances from two rival fur-trading firms. A Canadien crowd, chiefly voyageurs to the Indian country, prevented execution of the sentence by hurling the pillory into the St Lawrence River and threatening to storm the prison. These developments so unnerved the magistrate, merchant Joseph Frobisher, that he promised to intercede with Lord Dorchester for a pardon. The sheriff, finding it prudent not to attempt to carry out the sentence again, released the prisoner some days later. Four arrested ringleaders were soon bailed and no one, it seems, was ever punished for the incident. The government eventually decided, in the circumstances, to issue a pardon to Leveillé.[11] Although a modest affair, the canoemen's rising and its aftermath were to play a significant role during the militia riots which broke out a month later.

In anticipation of war with the United States over the western posts, Lord Dorchester called for the selection by lot of two thousand unmarried militiamen for active service on the frontier. This was certainly a risky proceeding. The État Major of the Trois-Rivières District did not exaggerate in 1790 when it claimed that habitant heads of household would rather give up half their possessions than see their sons drafted for military service.[12] Probably, the 1790s farmers would have defended the province against invasion by Americans (uncomplicated by French involvement) if the invasion had been actual and service confined to the province.[13]

Dorchester's order of 5 May met intense resistance throughout the colony. The English contingents, to be sure, hastened to the flag, but a mere seventeen of the 222 Canadien companies were willing to comply. While a few companies which refused would have accepted the more traditional direct order to muster and march, the vast majority made it clear they would take up arms under no circumstances whatever, believing "that should they ballot... they would thereby be enlisted as [regular] soldiers [or sailors] and sent to the West Indies, or out of the Province, and subject to military discipline." In some places stories flew about that service would be for life or that the British were embarking on a second Acadian deportation: conscription order would follow conscription order until "the country loses all its people."[14]

Other motives can be detected. Stories circulated in Quebec that the militia order had been concocted by half-pay officers (mainly Canadien seigneurs) for base monetary reasons. Attorney General Monk found that the operation of the seigneurial system had stiffened resistance. As he reported to Henry Dundas, secretary of state, the illegal exactions of the seigneurs were compared by French agents "to the Kingly Government of France" and farmers' grievances fomented "to the utmost, as the best means of detaching" them from loyalty and inducing them to "aid a Revolution."[15]

Many in the colony believed that French troops would soon appear, with or without the Americans. Evidence, including the militia returns made by the États Major following the riots, indicates the working people were generally loath to shed the blood of kin. The Duc de La Rochefoucauld-Liancourt learned from some British officers who had been stationed in Lower Canada during the balloting that resisters had often shouted words to the effect that if it "were [really] against the Americans we would march no doubt to defend our country, but these are Frenchmen who are coming and we won't march. How could we fight against our brothers?"[16]

Resistance faded by the end of May, though actual and rumoured disturbances continued sporadically through the summer. The riots had not approached insurrection, nor had they required troops for their suppression. But much talk of violence, dangerous assemblies of the disgruntled, and rhetoric which sounded sympathetic to revolutionary France had surfaced.

Violence, threatened and actual, flared in many rural parishes, but most dramatically at Charlesbourg, a village just north of Quebec. For several days and nights up to three hundred habitants, armed with muskets, pikes, pitchforks, and hunting knives, formed patrols to defend themselves against an expected armed attack of city folk bent on enforcing conscription. Some of the farmers, by their own sworn admission, also thought this might prove a good time to bash "les Anglais."[17] The idea of patrols had been initiated by mob oratory outside the captain's residence, when habitants Jerome Bédard, Pierre Chartré, and Charles Garnaud threatened those who did not join in defending the community. Armed resistance, they claimed, was justified in the name of the people "who are above any King."[18] These farmer-revolutionaries warned any who might not support the popular cause that the people would have to "kill and disembowel all those...cowards" and "mount their heads on pike-ends." Threats of house and barn burning were commonplace near Charlesbourg that May and, according to Monk, so were boasts by the locals that "they have no occasion for the clergy nor confession." In other rural areas near the capital, curés who attempted to ensure the militiamen did their duty were often threatened with physical injury.[19]

In the District of Montreal an armed mob of perhaps five hundred assembled in early June at Côte des Neiges to resist the militia order. According to Sheriff Edward Gray, these people,

mainly farmers, had met for mutual defence in the belief that "the Military were ordered to go into that part of the Country to disarm the inhabitants & force them away from their families." When in due course the troops did not appear the crowd had "dispersed without committing Any Act of Violence." Shortly after this incident Jonathan Sewell reported that the whole District, was in "a state of allmost [sic] universal and alarming disaffection." Such was popular hatred of the authorities that the Canadien magistrates in the city refused to prosecute offenders against the militia laws. If the English justices alone had to do the job, the result could well be disastrous.[20]

On the heels of Sewell's pessimistic opinion came another from Michel Eustache-Gaspard-Alain Chartier de Lotbinière, pro-government Speaker of the Assembly, seigneur of Vaudreuil, Rigaud, and Lotbinière, who habitually kept a close political watch on the farmers of his neighbourhood northwest of Montreal. The heads of families still believed that government intended "to conscript their children for life, that it wants to send them to the Caribbean islands or to England and...they will never see them again." The farmers contended that the authorities "had not punished those who threw the pillory into the river" during the Leveillé riots or those who had revolted at Côte des Neiges. Therefore, they too, if united, would escape punishment for preventing their children becoming soldiers. Lotbinière insisted the government take no precipitate action, but only make examples of indisputable ringleaders at a time when it was certain of obedience. Otherwise, there would be "a violent, flare-up, a considerable insurrection and perhaps the loss of the colony."

Chartier de Lotbinière's letter encouraged Lord Dorchester's policy of extreme caution. Although punishing the rioters was important, the timing was wrong—foreign and domestic emissaries of France might stimulate serious rioting which could get out of control—especially if the United States declared war. As a result, no special commissions were issued for the speedy trial of political offenders, and the arrest of the ringleaders at Côte des Neiges was delayed until September. Dorchester put the best face on matters when he informed Dundas that the "course of justice is advancing cautiously and with circumspection, to preserve if possible the Laws from again being insulted and to avoid all occasion of violence."[21]

Popular Unrest, 1796–1797

FRENCH INTRIGUES

The Jacobin Committee of Public Safety, seeing France desperately dependent upon the United States for grain supplies, wished to prevent any diplomatic rupture between the two republics. Thus the new minister, Jean-Antoine-Joseph Fauchet, was instructed to drop Genêt's expeditionary projects and as a result took little interest in the Canadiens.[22] Only after the Directory took power in November 1795 was the policy of conquering Lower Canada revived.

In 1796–7 the French government again interested itself in liberating Lower Canada. Paris officials of the Directory, the French minister to the United States, Pierre-Auguste Adet, his subordinates, and the near-bankrupt "Green Mountain Boy," Vermont land speculator and soldier of fortune Ira Allen, worked out various plans of invasion.[23] This was part of a grandiose political strategy to encircle the rear of the United States. After Jay's Treaty of 1794, Paris viewed it as a renegade republic allied to the enemy, providing Britain with food. Louisiana would be restored to France by Spain—now an ally—and British North America would be conquered. By controlling the Mississippi and the St Lawrence, France could dismember the frontier areas of the American union. The end result envisaged two puppet regimes under French hegemony, "United (or in some versions 'New')

Columbia" in the north and the United States in the south. A host of other benefits was anticipated from the conquest of British North America, and France would finally fulfil its obligation to forsaken nationals, who were assumed to be yearning for liberty. As J.-A.-B. Rozier, French consul at New York, put it, France "having become free, will hasten to repair the crimes of its tyrants; she will never remain dead to the cries of her new world children who hold out their arms, begging for her help."

The main provisions of the official invasion plan can be reconstructed from a report drafted by the French foreign minister Charles-Maurice de Talleyrand, in 1798[24] and memoranda prepared for the Directory by Ira Allen in the late spring or early summer of 1796.[25] The French government agreed to finance the purchase of twenty thousand muskets and bayonets and two dozen light artillery pieces, worth in all 500,000 livres (about £25,000). A transport fleet carrying three or four thousand French regulars and accompanied by two ships of the line and four or five frigates would reach Halifax in August 1797, attempt to take the town, and capture the British merchant fleet from Lower Canada. It would then proceed to join up with Allen's forces near Quebec City. Simultaneously with the naval attack on Halifax the Vermont irregulars would capture St Jean, assisted by armed men previously infiltrated into the area on one of Allen's timber rafts. From there Allen and his men would proceed to Quebec, on the way raising the Canadiens whose francophile political sentiments would meanwhile have been cultivated by emissaries. The combined forces would have no trouble in taking Quebec and then forcing the remaining enemy troops out of British North America.

From other sources additional elements of strategy can be reconstructed. French agents would contact the Indians in Upper Canada to ensure their neutrality, or if needed, participation. Serious consideration was given to a diversionary attack on Upper Canada by way of the

Mississippi, likely consisting of American frontiersmen, Indians, and French and Spanish troops. Almost certainly a body of Allen's forces and perhaps some from the New York side of the St Lawrence were to attack Montreal. The fleet, it appears, was to stop temporarily at a point near Kamouraska, east of Quebec, where proclamations would be distributed to agents for circulation among the Canadiens. The terms of these proclamations were to include a call to armed insurrection, a guarantee of private property and freedom of religion, a prohibition of violence except against persons in arms against the Republic, the promise of prompt payment in cash for goods and services, the abolition of the tithe and seigneurial dues, and the establishment in former British North America of New or United Columbia.

To expedite matters, Adet and his subordinates sent numerous agents into Lower Canada to sound out Canadien opinion, distribute propaganda, recruit sympathizers, and obtain military intelligence. About mid-September 1796 two engineering officers in the Armée française d'outre-mer (French Overseas Army) named De Millière—a general—and Ianson established a base in upper New York State on the Canadian border to gather information and organize a spy network. Ianson left for Paris shortly after. Later in September De Millière sent two Canadiens into the colony: Montreal tailors Jean-Baptiste Louisineau and Joseph Ducalvet.[26] Both were commissioned as second lieutenants. Crossing the border openly near St Jean on 27 September with inflammatory addresses signed by Adet and blank army commissions stitched into Ducalvet's breeches, they held a meeting the next day with sympathizers. Government officials apparently identified only three persons attending that meeting: Jean-Baptiste Bizette of Côte des Neiges and Ducalvet's uncle and grandfather Étienne and Joseph Girard dit Provençale, both gardeners in the employ of the Seminary of St Sulpice.

Ducalvet also attempted distribution of literature promising liberation from British slavery by France, denouncing the forced labour required by the recently passed Road Act, outlining the advantages of the Revolution, and predicting that the cry of "Vive la République" would soon be heard throughout the province.

Ducalvet quit the province at the end of September leaving his own commission behind at his uncle's. About two months later Richardson, having intercepted a letter requesting its return, organized a fictitious correspondence and misinformation campaign designed to entice Ducalvet to return home from his refuge in Vermont. Warned off at the last moment, the tailor-spy went underground and later attempts by Robert Liston, British minister to the United States, to have him extradited fell on deaf ears. The sentiments expressed in the intercepted letter gave government officials something to ponder long after he had disappeared: Ducalvet was ecstatic, he wrote, that the Canadiens in general entertained "the best principles of liberty" and wanted all his relatives to know that "I will have the pleasure of seeing them in the spring when we shall make the English dance the *carmagnole*. Vive la liberté."[27]

By the end of 1796 Citizen Adet must have been supremely confident that the invasion plan would succeed. That summer the British blockade of the French navy at Brest had proved porous and the discontent of the Canadiens with their lot had been manifest in a bitterly contested election. In the autumn his spies had brought him roseate predictions of success—and not surprisingly, since the colony had then experienced the most violent unrest since the war had begun.

THE ELECTION OF 1796

This little studied election took place in a period of economic depression. A modest wheat crop of 1794 had been followed in 1795 by the worst harvest of the decade, producing only between one-third and one-half that of the year before. Marginal farmers faced starvation or charity. Inflation hit the urban dwellers hard with the price of wheat, flour, oats, beef, butter, and eggs steeply rising in 1796. Shortages were so severe that the government proclaimed an embargo on the export of foodstuffs despite lobbying by the leading mercantile houses. As Osgoode explained to the under secretary of state in early August, "From the disposition of the minds of the people much was to be apprehended had anything in the shape of Provisions been suffer [*sic*] to go out of the province."[28] Seventeen ninety-six was indeed a painful year for the great majority of Canadiens.

The election results indicate a general alienation from the policies of government, including those of the Assembly. Dozens of habitants, artisans, and labourers, for example, had been arrested in 1794 and resentment lingered on two years later.[29] The consumption taxes—new duties on wines, spirits, coffee, salt, tobacco, and sugar—of 1795 must have been unpopular, as the traveller La Rochefoucauld-Liancourt claimed.[30] The Engagés Act of 1796 would have been resented, particularly in the Montreal region. This statute, responding to longstanding complaints of merchants by criminalizing what had been mainly a civil law field,[31] compelled canoemen, batteauxmen, guides, and winterers to enter into notarial deeds, and authorized summary imprisonment of those who did not fulfil their contracts without provable cause. But the issues which probably sparked the most resentment among working people were the failure of the Lower House to reform the seigneurial regime in 1795 and the passage of the Road Act in 1796.

Early in the 1795 session Philippe de Rocheblave moved to have the Committee of the Whole House inquire into the "legal or customary rates of...rentes and other...burthens on...concessions [of lands] before the conquest,

compared with what have been exacted since." Jean-Antoine Panet, wanting to stimulate popular opinion, moved in amendment that the committee be empowered to sit anywhere in the province and to subpoena witnesses or papers as it saw fit. The amendment was overwhelmingly defeated and the main motion was submerged in lengthy discussions of tenure in general. It came to nothing. Undoubtedly these manoeuvers strongly contributed to the almost universal unpopularity of the Canadien seigneurs.[32] Their standing sank further during the session of 1795–6.

In response to demands from Montreal merchants, Quebec magistrates and members of his own class, seigneur Gabriel-Elzéar Taschereau, highways commissioner for the District of Quebec, introduced a bill in November 1795 to improve the deplorable state of the roads. The *parti canadien* strenuously opposed it by moving that the bill be printed for public information, by withdrawing from the House so that proceedings were suspended for want of a quorum, and by arguing that the forced labour imposed on the people established a dangerous precedent justifying the enactment of land taxation. All these efforts failed and the bill became law on 7 May.[33]

The Road Act of 1796 was obviously designed in the interests of the urban upper classes, rural seigneurs, and those speculators hoping to open up crown waste lands for settlement. Unprecedented, unpaid corvées abounded. The District highway commissioners and locally elected overseers (a novelty) could require the joint labour—up to twelve days a year—of the neighbouring residents to open or repair roads through difficult terrain or unsettled areas, including unconceded seigneurial and crown lands. Roads leading to the seigneurs' grist mills were to be divided into fourteen equal parts, of which one was to be maintained by the seigneur and thirteen by the habitant heads of household. The repair of the streets in Montreal and

Quebec was the responsibility of all males, eighteen to sixty, who resided in the cities or adjacent rural areas. Thus the farmer could be forced to work not only on the roads in his parish but also on the city streets he seldom used except in going to market. In the French and early British regimes the obligations of rural owners and occupiers were largely confined to maintaining the roads adjacent to their lands. Under the new act, those who could afford to do so were permitted to offer a payment in lieu of any imposed statutory labour.

The electoral campaign clearly featured many appeals against social and political authority—much more so than in 1792. A letter from "A Good Citizen," printed by the semi-official *Quebec Gazette,* castigated the anarchy being fostered by opposition candidates: "Bad Men" who were attempting "to raise themselves and serve their own private interests." These social *parvenus* were doing everything possible to persuade "the unthinking, that a certain class of their fellow citizens, who...wisely oppose *their aims,* can triumph over the laws of the Country, and betray the people who may entrust them with the important Guard over *Public Liberty.*"[34] Alienation ran so deep in some places that the voters returned members who had been imprisoned for seditious offences or on suspicion of high treason, such as master shipwright John Black, illiterate farmer and Charlesbourg rioter Louis Paquet (Quebec County) and Quebec merchant Nicolas Dorion (Devon). Quebec tavernkeeper Alexandre Menut (Cornwallis) had been described as a subversive by two deponents.[35] There may well have been other cases, for Osgoode commented that such was the spirit of the people that "any Person who had been accused was sure of being elected."

The election results dealt a devastating blow to the colony's political and social élites, as they immediately perceived.[36] One statistic alone tells much of the tale: seventeen of the Canadiens elected in 1792 had been justices of the peace; in 1796 one Canadien magistrate ran successfully. It is true that the English contingent in the house almost maintained its numbers, dropping from sixteen at dissolution to fifteen, but this figure is highly misleading.[37] The real turnaround, though, occurred in the social rank of the elected Canadiens.

In 1792 the electorate had chosen about fourteen Canadiens of the seigneurial class—all but one in rural constituencies and only three considered safe for the government. In 1796 just three of this class succeeded—two of them in safe seats, and one, oppositionist de Rocheblave in Surrey. The big winners came from the Canadien bourgeoisie, whose numbers increased from about seventeen after the first election to twenty-three, four years later. The working people raised their representation from two to four in 1792 to nine in 1796. Typically, the newly elected and re-elected Canadiens from the middle class were professionals and shopkeepers far removed from the upper reaches of the middle ranks. Lawyer Bédard was the son of a baker, while notary-surveyor Joseph Papineau's father had been a cooper. Two seigneurs of the noblesse had held Dorchester County at dissolution; now the constituency would be represented by Charles Bégin, a tavernkeeper at Pointe-Lévi, and Alexandre Dumas, a bankrupt merchant turned notary.[38]

There is evidence of strong anti-government feelings held by Canadien voters and of the demise of the bourgeois alliance. Obscure notary Joseph Planté and shopkeeper François Huot, son of a farmer, bested De Bonne (Hampshire). In Surrey the sycophantic, "patriotic" schoolteacher Louis Labadie (who expended much energy in the years 1793–8 attempting to inculcate a reverence for British rule into his fellow countrymen) was decisively defeated by de Rocheblave and Olivier Durocher, son of a rural doctor and a committed follower of Papineau. Incumbent Judge James Walker, abandoned by Papineau, his 1792 running mate lost Montreal

County to merchant Jean-Marie Ducharme and law student Étienne Guy. Walker's brother Thomas, a lawyer, was beaten in Montreal West when his co-candidate, merchant Pierre Foretier, formerly of the Canadien Reform Committee, withdrew from the race in favour of Papineau and his cousin Denis Viger, a carpenter. Overall, the *parti canadien* won and the government clearly lost the election. In the 1797 legislative session, Executive councillor John Young (Quebec, Lower Town) was defeated as proposed Speaker by a vote of twenty-seven to fourteen, with Panet winning a second poll, twenty-nine to twelve. Soon government supporters failed to block debate on amendments to the Road Act.[39]

THE ROAD ACT RIOTS

On 26 August 1796 Quebeckers and inhabitants from the adjacent countryside were summoned to repair the city's streets. Cheered on by rowdy spectators, including many who had paid to avoid their statutory labour, the conscripted workers took the wheels off their carts, gave three cheers, and went off. Four or five ringleaders were seized and taken to the jail, in Osgoode's words "notwithstanding the menaces of 500 Women." This broke the resistance and those summoned the next day and thereafter went submissively to work. To the authorities that vigorous, early enforcement of the law entirely solved any problem of discontent in the District.[40] They had grossly underestimated the general detestation of the act.

What would prove to be far worse troubles broke out in Montreal a few doors from Ducalvet's revolutionary meeting, at a time when Ducalvet was still in the province and when his sympathizers were attempting to circulate the address with its reference to the Road Act as symbolic of Canadien oppression.[41] Late in September one Luc Berthelot, who lived on Mount Royal, was fined for following the general pattern of refusing to labour or pay. On

2 October constable Jacob Marston tried to arrest him. Five or six men in Berthelot's house, egged on by his fiery wife, Scholastique Mathieu, battered Marston. According to Sewell, the constable was "happy to escape with his life." Berthelot was arrested but, as the attorney general described the scene, "he had not been in the Sheriff's Custody above five minutes when he was forcibly and most violently rescued by a mob in the *Place d'Armes*."

Anarchy loomed. Activists in and about Montreal planned a mass protest meeting, dispatching couriers to advertise it, and encourage continued resistance to the act. Many habitants of the Longueuil area on the south shore urged their neighbours to withhold all foodstuffs from the Montreal market in order to provoke, as one of them urged, "un petit revolte" in the city. At the church in L'Assomption the farmers walked out of a sermon, after a parishioner warned the curé to remain "within the Sphere of your Clerical Duty" and not "interfere in Politicks." In Pointe-aux-Trembles and Point Claire the massacre of the English became a topic of tavern oratory. Killing the most vigilant English magistrates was talked of in the city.

Sometime shortly after the Berthelot rescue the Montreal magistrates Bench, prompted especially by the Canadien justices, agreed with a citizens' delegation that enforcement of the act should be suspended for a few days until the governor responded to a request to summon the legislature for an emergency session. The magistrates claimed that for the time being enforcement was beyond their means: "Emissaries have been dispersed through the different parishes to foment the general dissatisfaction...[which has] risen to such a pitch of popular Frenzy as to render...the Civil Power insufficient to compel obedience." The governor refused to compromise, ordering the magistrates to compel obedience to the law. This they found difficult in the extreme. On 24 October the unlucky Marston, attempting to levy a fine on one Latour, a ringleader in the "free

Berthelot movement," failed when Latour and several friends threatened musket fire. The justices thereupon suspended all further efforts to enforce the act.

In early October startling news reached the colony. The previous August, French Admiral Richery, with seven battleships and some frigates, had escaped the British blockade at Brest and sailed to Newfoundland. In September the fleet destroyed some houses, fishing boats, and stores at Bay Bulls before returning home. Rumours flew in Lower Canada that St John's was taken, Halifax seriously threatened and, most certainly, the admiral would soon be ascending the St Lawrence to free his former countrymen.[42] These developments "produced a Sensation throughout this Province," as Prescott put it, with people everywhere excitedly speculating on the likely reaction of the Canadiens, particularly those in the distant parishes along the lower St Lawrence.[43] While it is difficult to gauge the popular response, it was sufficiently francophile to alarm the governor and the chief justice.[44] Coadjutor Bishop Pierre Denaut, then in Longueuil (where mass protest assemblies and starvation plots were commonplace), was also pessimistic: "The news from Quebec of a French invasion...has given joy to the greater number... We are approaching...a revolution similar to the one in France...[That one] history tells us was begun by a mob of inflamed women; what then is not to be feared from men who have lost their heads."[45] Richery's appearance, the apparent welcome he would receive if he did attack, and the impotence of the civil power in Montreal convinced the government that determined action was vital.

Sewell was sent to Montreal with a new commission of the peace. Two Canadien magistrates were dismissed and a number of hardliners, such as John Richardson, added to the Bench. Sewell offered justiceships to two popular politicians of the area: Joseph Perineault, MPP for Huntingdon, and Joseph Papineau.

The latter had taken a prominent role in the resistance from the beginning, acting as adviser to many who were drafted for road duty. Refusing to labour or pay, not only had he headed the delegation of citizens who convinced the magistrates to suspend enforcement but had promised the people that Canadien members of the Assembly would effect the repeal of the offending statute. Papineau had also helped spread the idea that the Road Act was illegal— on the not unreasonable ground that the Legislative Council had only numbered thirteen during the session, two short of the mandatory minimum established by the Constitutional Act. Neither MPP agreed to serve. Back in Quebec, Sewell reported that Papineau had told him there would be serious trouble, perhaps even rebellion, if any Canadien blood were spilled and the government could have peace only if all fines were remitted and all attempts at implementation ceased.

General Prescott counter-attacked. On 30 October the government issued an order-in-council under the authority of the Alien Act.[46] After an obligatory recital of French wickedness, the order directed all Frenchmen who had entered the colony since 1 May 1794 to depart within twenty days. This initiative, accompanied by a proclamation urging reports on seditious conversations, instructed the magistrates to make appropriate arrests.[47] Again Bishop Hubert's resources were called upon. On 5 November 1796 he denounced the latest French intrigues as manifested by the riots, supported the measures of 30 October, and instructed his priests to emphasize that the faithful owed allegiance to George III, must obey laws punctually, and put aside any spirit of "rebellion and independence" which had "worked such sad havoc [among us] these last few years."[48]

To reinforce the capital and probably to avoid looting, virtually all the gunpowder in the king's magazines at St Jean, Chambly, and Montreal was sent to Quebec. Prescott also dispatched two regiments to Montreal which, according to Sewell, restored the "Consequence of the Magistrates and gave Energy to their Proceedings." One such energetic proceeding was to serve an order on Papineau to perform his road duty or be fined. Accompanied by a huge crowd of retainers, the accused submitted a farfetched argument based on his supposed parliamentary privileges. After Papineau's subsequent conviction, fine, and humbling, resistance to the enforcement of the Road Act crumbled in the Montreal region.

During these troubles the Quebec District had remained overtly passive, except for an incident in the suburb of St Roch. There, in October, a meeting of the Road Act overseers ended in rioting. A magistrate who attempted to disperse the crowd was assaulted and threatened with his life. Arrests restored order—but only temporarily. Rumours circulated that the elected overseers had been granted unlimited powers of oppression and were about to impose the dreaded class-based land tax of old France known as the *taille*.[49] Despite Bishop Hubert's admonitions, violence again flared, this time in St Joseph-de-Pointe-Lévi, across the river from the capital. In January angry farmers re-enacted scenes from the Stamp Act riots and the recent Whisky Rebellion in upper Pennsylvania by compelling overseers to renounce their offices. The ringleaders, arrested some days later, were being escorted to the city by two sheriff's officers, when eight habitants with bludgeons effected their rescue, informing the officers to forget about arrests, since "we have three hundred men in arms ready to support our Determination." Prescott responded by sending more than a hundred troops with two field guns to Pointe-Lévi, an action sufficient to frighten most of the rioters against whom warrants had been issued to surrender voluntarily.[50]

The Road Act riots were over, but for some months the habitants remained surly about road

duty and the statute continued as an explosive political issue.

Analysis and Evaluation of the Threats to Lower Canada

THE EXTERNAL THREAT

The external threat to Lower Canada from 1793 to 1798 was imaginary as it turned out, and modest even if the French had ordered a naval invasion and had recruited and dispatched an irregular army to proceed down the Richelieu. President Washington had immediately declared neutrality, despite the festering sore of Britain's retention of the western posts. After Jay's Treaty in 1794 the United States became an undeclared ally of Great Britain. True, the French-Irish-Vermont irregulars might have escaped American vigilance and been able to enter the colony through the frontier woods. But lack of discipline and the lure of plunder would have reduced greatly their military worth. The British naval blockade at Brest was generally effective, even though the French fleet did occasionally escape it.

Only once did senior officials of the French government, absorbed by more urgent priorities in Europe and well aware of the difficulties involved, plan an invasion. Genêt's farcical attempts had not been authorized by Paris and partly for that reason were rejected by the French West Indian fleet at New York. The attack force projected for August 1797 might conceivably have reached the colony, but the plan had been undermined months before. In December 1796 Ira Allen and his cargo of munitions, sailing from Ostend to New York aboard the ironically named *Olive Branch,* had been captured on the high seas by a British man-of-war. Allen spent much of the remainder of his life vainly attempting to convince a sceptical imperial government that he entertained no hostile intentions against the Canadas.[51] With the seizure of the *Olive Branch* the Directory lost interest in the idea of invading Lower Canada, not regaining it even when the British navy experienced serious mutinies in the spring of 1797.[52] No final decision to abandon the idea, however, was taken and French officials in the United States continued for several months to assume an attack might be made.

Had a French fleet landed a few thousand marines in Lower Canada, would the attack have succeeded? Although the British would have had the decided advantage of fighting defensively, the colony's means of protection were far from overwhelming. The Canadien militia could not be counted on. Regular troop strength in the Canadas during these years varied from about 2,600 to 3,500 all ranks.[53] This was hardly sufficient protection for the lower colony, let alone the vast exposed frontier of Upper Canada. Not surprisingly, the desperate need for reinforcements was an anxious *leitmotif* of official correspondence.[54] Nor were the regular soldiers entirely reliable. The proximity of the American border often proved an irresistible temptation for men subjected to the harsh discipline and Spartan conditions of eighteenth-century military service. In the winter of 1792–3, for example, a planned mutiny followed by mass desertion in Prince Edward's regiment at Quebec was barely averted at the eleventh hour by the arrest of the ringleaders.[55] Desertion was a recurrent lament of military commanders throughout the war.[56] Still, it seemed unlikely that three to four thousand French marines could easily have defeated about an equal number of British troops (supported by English militia) in defensive positions—unless, of course, there was a Canadien insurrection.

Contemporary expert opinions during the period, such as those of David Alexander Grant and the Comte de Maulevrier (both former army officers) and General John Graves Simcoe,

Lieutenant-Governor of Upper Canada, agreed that the colony was highly vulnerable to French invasion.[57] Prescott estimated that with the troops at his disposal there was almost no chance of winning if the smallest French attacking force landed and if the Canadiens, as was likely, responded by rising in arms.[58] As these pessimistic opinions were based on a common and crucial assumption: that the working people of Lower Canada would rise *en masse* to aid the French. Was this likely?

LOYALTY OF THE URBAN WORKERS

To incite a revolt in the cities, French agents and their local sympathizers could try to exploit four themes: inflation and consumer taxes in the years 1793–7; the attractiveness of the principles for which revolutionary France stood; pure ethnic prejudice; and resentment of the well-to-do. This last theme owed its existence to the fact that the annual income of Canadien seigneur-officials and those English in the higher reaches of the public service was often over twenty times that of unskilled labourers lucky enough to be employed for the whole year. The immense wealth of the leading merchants was apparent to all. Simon McTavish, for example, left an estate valued at more than £125,000 and James McGill's was comparable. The higher economic status of the English is reflected in the fact that they occupied almost 45 per cent of the single-family dwellings in Quebec's Upper and Lower towns, although amounting to only slightly more than 20 per cent of the population of those two districts in the city.

Several reforms introduced by the French Revolution, moreover, had the potential to generate positive response among Canadien urban workers: careers open to talent, the Declaration of the Rights of Man, *fraternité,* the abolition of hereditary titles, the entry of the sansculotte into politics, stringent price-fixing (1793) and the elimination of food conscription taxes in the

French capital (1791). How did the working districts of Montreal and Quebec perceive these changes and other news from France?

Artisans and labourers had been exposed to pro-French propaganda, and not only by *Les Français libres* which had some circulation. Those who could read had been taught by the newspapers from 1789 to late 1792 that the heroic doings in France were to be applauded. Others learned the same by word of mouth from literate artisans or those people working for the Canadien committees for constitutional reform. Montreal's Société des Patriotes was very active from 1790 to 1792 and in September of the next year Galbaud's revolutionary doctrines had some impact. In Quebec the few middle-class radicals such as Dumas, Alexandre Menut, Nicolas Dorion, Dr O'Connor, and Bezeau attempted to spread their message among urban working people.

One cannot discount, either, sympathy for France (largely of a non-ideological nature) which was manifest in these years. Rousse, an intelligent spy who made balanced judgments, reported to Mezière in September 1793 that "Nothing is so common, even in the country, as the cry of *Vivent les Français*! 'We hope to see our brothers,' the townspeople tell the peasants, and these, as if they feared that what was said was intended to tease them, reply: 'But is it really true that we shall see *Nos bonnes gens*,' and tears of regret furrow the cheeks of the old people."[59] Bits of proof support Rousse's assessment. Lévesque's shout of "vivent les Français" at the Quebec parade in May 1794 must have been made with confidence that his fellow militiamen would be responsive. Adet's agents Ducalvet and David McLane operated in Montreal without being informed on by Canadiens. More incredibly, Rousse spent about five weeks doing undercover work in Quebec's St Jean suburb without disclosure to the authorities.

The potential disloyalty of the urban workers should not, however, be exaggerated. Early approval of the French Revolution circulated easily. But from late 1792 the newspapers were full of critical comment emphasizing atrocities. Rousse reported in September 1793 that Mezière's friends had not yet distributed *Les Français libres*, "for, as they observed, with a people wholly plunged in the dense shadows of ignorance and slavery, it is not fitting to suddenly...shine the Sun of Liberty at noon."[60]

While resentment of the well-to-do, ethnic hostility, and a sentimental regard for France certainly existed, it is not clear how influential these feelings were. Emotional attachment to France was not nearly as deep among the younger generation (particularly if they had attended school) as among those who had been born in New France. Dumontier's rage over thirty-four years of injustice under the British was not shared by his apprentices. When Dumontier's teenage son, then studying at the Quebec Seminary, dared suggest that Lower Canada had the mildest of governments and on another occasion praised Prince Edward for his success in the Caribbean theatre, he was told to shut up by his father.[61] Although there were men in the cities prepared to risk punishment by working for revolutionary France, their numbers were very small. In 1794, after exhaustive investigations, including the use of an agent provocateur, the authorities were able to implicate only about ten Canadien workers of Quebec who had furthered the aim of Genêt, Mezière, and Rousse.[62] And at the time the city and its immediate environs included more than five hundred male Canadien artisans and skilled or semi-skilled labourers, exclusive of domestic servants.[63] Evidently few urban workers would have risked much to assist revolutionary France if it invaded the colony.

HABITANT LOYALTY

A fundamental point to be borne in mind when assessing the habitants' loyalty in this period is their strong resistance to propaganda. Most could not, of course, read *Les Français libres* or Adet's pamphlet of September 1796, and minatory local élites restricted rural circulation. In 1793–4 and 1796 distributors on horseback were often forced to throw copies through open windows and gallop off and the government discovered but one instance of *Les Français libres* being read publicly after divine service. During the Road Act riots the authorities traced Adet's tract to only ten recipients, all of whom claimed to have immediately burned them.[64]

Revolutionary agents and sympathizers from the cities undoubtedly tried to communicate orally a vision of the modern French paradise, but there is no reason to believe they were effective. Occasional francophile slogans emerged in the countryside at times of popular unrest. In 1794 a few habitants at Charlesbourg talked of popular sovereignty and heads on pikes, while during the election of 1796 two young hotheads from the south shore east of Quebec were arrested after shouting "vive la liberté, we are from the National Convention [of France] and will smash every thing in our way." Such examples are very rare and are not representative. Monk, it is true, remarked in 1794 that many farmers had come to refer to *Les Français libres* ironically as "le Catechisme."[65] Since the principles of 1789 were not of obvious relevance to them, this was likely a bemused comment on zealots spreading the new mysteries with the same as those who purveyed the old.

Careers open to talent in the public service could have made no appeal to farmers whose main aim in life was to find farms for their sons, a goal often realized in the 1790s. The free trade argument of the physiocrats would have been understandable to few rural dwellers, while popular sovereignty, republicanism, abolition of the royal veto, and an elected clergy were ideas alien to those who had known only monarchy and whose daily life was infused by the hierarchical authority of the family, the church, the militia, and the seigneurial system. Significantly, too,

during the militia riots a number of habitants in the Quebec District thought they were justified in resisting an order which they had been told came from the illegitimate Assembly and not the king.[66] As late as 1838—after three decades of liberal democratic agitation—many a habitant wanted to make Louis-Joseph Papineau king.[67]

Some revolutionary promises had appeal, particularly the abolition of seigneurial dues and tithes. In January 1794 Alexander Fraser, half-pay officer, seigneur of Beauchamp just southeast of the capital, remarked in alarm that talk of the coming American-French invasion had induced his *censitaires* to expect a quick end to their obligatory payments: "they have got into their heads, that their friends the New Englanders has [sic] joined the trench, and they are to be a free people, and have no rent, nor nothing to pay, such was the opinion of the greatest part of the inhabitants...here." Shortly after the 1796 election Osgoode commented that several successful candidates had promised their constituents "to abolish all Rents and all Tithes." At the time when Richery's fleet was expected and the Road Act riots were in full sway, the chief justice returned to the theme. Ignorance among the common people was so general and profound, he wrote, "they firmly believe that...under French or American Government they should be exempted from the Payment of both Tythes & Rent."[68]

This assessment by Osgoode should not be taken at face value. Of the dozens of depositions, voluntary examinations, government reports, and other extant documents bearing directly on the militia and Road Act riots none refers to abolition as a factor motivating rural rioters. The social and political situation perhaps explains why.

The Canadien farmers of the late eighteenth and early nineteenth centuries shrewdly protected their interests. Dogged, skilful litigators in disputes with the clergy over tithes, pew rentals, location of churches, or other parochial matters, they were adept at nullifying, at least temporarily, laws they considered oppressive. Letting lands recover their fertility in alternating fallow years in the 1780s and 1790s, rather than engage in the toil of clearing, rotating crops, and fertilizing was arguably intelligent. Detailed alimentary pensions (in kind) exacted by parents as they turned over the family farms to inheriting sons often exceeded notarial shrewdness.[69] And it was intelligent, also, to ignore the promptings of the legislature, the government, and an assortment of experts, from 1790 on, to invest in the growth of hemp—a crop difficult to cultivate and not assured of an imperial market.

Those farmers who thought about the elimination of seigneurial dues may have wondered what would happen to the vast amounts of unconceded land. If these were to be retained by the seigneurs as private property or auctioned off (as had occurred in France with regard to confiscated real estate) how would they obtain lands for their sons a cheaply as before? In 1791, during a highly publicized conflict in the old Legislative Council over a change in tenure,[70] prominent Canadiens—senior clergy, seigneurs, bourgeoisie (including seven to ten members of the city's reforming Canadien Committee)—defended the interests of the farmers. The latter were represented as utterly opposed to outright ownership of land and, despite the abuses, favourable to the seigneurial regime, which provided them with the valuable "right...of obliging him [the seigneur] to grant lands 'at easy rates.'"[71] The Canadien élite was nearly united in favour of the existing land law, as reformed to prevent abuse. This included members of the *parti canadien,* who became the political mentors of the farmers in the years 1794 to 1797.[72]

The potential security danger in the countryside lay not only in the operation of the seigneurial system, but also in the farmers' anglophobia and their resistance to pro-British propaganda. The farmers' anglophobia was manifest in many ways: their aversion to "scientific" agriculture, willingness to believe stories that their new masters were capable of almost any oppression and so on. A particularly telling example occurred during the general election of 1792 in Quebec County. Seigneur Louis de Salaberry won easily. The real contest was for the second seat, with the margin extremely close between lawyer Berthelot d'Artigny and clerk of the peace David Lynd, a reformer. According to depositions sworn to by resident farmers, Jean-Antoine Panet campaigned vigorously for his *confrère.* After mass he announced, outside the Charlesbourg church that "if he could get Mr. Berthelot into the House of Assembly they would trample the English underfoot." The next day Panet addressed a crowd saying "my friends, you must elect a man of law, Mr. Berthelot, to join me; we are a hundred against one and if you put him with me, we will throttle the English." When the polls closed a few days later with Lynd slightly ahead, Berthelot's supporters (some of whom had not voted) almost precipitated a riot. Only a patriotic appeal to king, constitution, and ethnic harmony delivered by de Salaberry's close friend, Prince Edward, defused the tension.[73]

During the early war years the Lower Canadian government financed publications designed to show Canadiens the manifold evils perpetrated by their former countrymen. Among them were two Burkean assaults on abstract reasoning. These made no impact whatsoever among the farmers.[74] But the local notables did try to teach the simple facts about the outrages in the old mother country. Philippe-Joseph Aubert de Gaspé recalled his parents assembling their habitants to explain the sufferings of the French royal family—for whom the farmers retained a warm affection—as constantly reported in the newspapers. On each occasion the listeners "would shake their heads, maintaining that it was all a fiction invented by the English."[75] Several contemporaries substantiate de Gaspé's recollection. Count Colbert de Maulevrier, a French emigré visitor in 1798, has left perhaps the most graphic and persuasive description of habitant opinion. Their ignorance was such, he wrote, that few

> want to believe in the death of the King of France. He's hidden, they say, and he will reappear; he has the power to make himself invisible. In general they don't want to hear a word about the Revolution's atrocities. The good French people—or as they say OUR FATHERS—aren't capable of that. These are lies that English spread for a purpose. Some priests who have tried to speak to them about the Revolution and the crimes it has spawned, have become suspect in their eyes.[76]

THE LOYAL ASSOCIATION CAMPAIGN, 1794

The idea for this campaign, originating with Attorney General Monk, was to identify the disaffected, teach the Canadiens about the horrors of revolution, and discourage agitators who might be inclined to violence when the militia rioters were brought to trial.[77] Parent associations (under the patronage of Lord Dorchester) in Quebec, Trois-Rivières, and Montreal circulated declarations execrating revolutionary France and eulogizing Britain. Citizens could prove "loyalty" by signing or affixing their marks to these manifestos. English merchants and government officials largely controlled urban associations, but Canadien seigneurs, priests nominated by Hubert, and middle-class men such as Papineau and Panet played an active role. Working through the curés, resident seigneurs, and the Canadien MPPs, the parent societies attempted to organize associations in the rural parishes. The local notables were instructed to collect signatures to the Quebec Association's 1794 declaration of thanksgiving for British rule and to set straight the ignorant

who were presumably guided to adopt those anarchistic opinions which had desolated France. The newspapers gave the campaign enormous publicity and the local notables of all varieties gave it every support. Several curés delivered speeches explaining the divine right of kings, and contrasting the benefits of British rule with the dark days of Intendant Bigot—no confiscation of grain, no military service outside the St Lawrence valley, protection of religion, and a free constitution.

Initially in the countryside there was opposition to signing. Over fifteen letters indicate that the early efforts of the priests were unsuccessful in varying degrees. The reasons for refusal were not often articulated but it is likely that illiterate farmers feared putting their mark to a written document which might impose onerous obligations (such as hypothecs or compulsory military service). In the County of Warwick the farmers feared that signatures would make them soldiers to fight in foreign lands, that the French, if they became the new "maîtres," wouldn't approve, and that priests would say anything to please the government even if it meant throwing the people away. Explanations by the local élites that the militia law generally prohibited out-of-province service,[78] that the document bound signers to nothing specific, and that the consequences of refusal could be severe, contained the opposition.

About two-thirds of potential endorsers province-wide actually signed the declaration. Rural area signatures were proportionally lower than the overall average, but allowance must be made for the fact that many live-in adult sons of farmers did not sign, on the ground that the head of household alone made political decisions. The Montreal Association even claimed the Canadien working people would defend the province against revolutionary France, while the Quebec organization asserted that the "ignorant and deluded part of the community" now understood that unspeakable atrocities inevitably flowed from modern French principles. These claims are not convincing. The minatory atmosphere of the campaign—lists kept of non-signers; habitants, labourers, and artisans in jail or threatened with imprisonment; the vocal and united local élites—ensured that most heads of farming households would subscribe to the declaration. Neither did the signatures or marks prove the signers believed what was in the document. Over sixty letters from rural loyal associations have been preserved, but only one clearly indicates that the farmers had any glimmering of the atrocities occurring in France, then at the height of the terror.[79] That they had not bound themselves to remain politically docile or obedient to law was made clear two years later, when the Road Act riots erupted.

As such contemporaries as Monk and De Bonne noticed, the 1790s riots were instances of a longstanding tradition in French Canada, known as "rebellion à justice," that is, rioting or threatening violence to prevent enforcement of the law. That tradition, which had come into being by the early 1700s, helps explain the 1837 rebellion. It would endure at least until 1850, if not up to the conscription crises of the two world wars. The important point here is that the working people could be goaded to riot, but only in a defensive way. They would not storm the prisons in 1794 or starve Montreal in 1796.

THE RIOTS AND REVOLUTIONARY FRANCE

Limited though the riots were, one wonders if they could be attributed to the machinations of revolutionary France. The answer is mixed but mainly negative. Rousse and the Canadiens working to further his aims helped stimulate the militia riots in and around the cities by spreading word that the French would attack, urging Canadiens not to fight their brothers, and presenting conscription as a malign English plot. But this is not to suggest that sympathizers with revolutionary France could bring people to riot

at will. The issue was tailor-made for agitators, given habitant detestation of militia service (especially at or near sowing time) and the government's failure to explain the law. Without any effort by francophiles whatever, resistance would likely have been widespread—it occurred all over the province, beyond areas accessible to the urban-based sympathizers. With regard to the Road Act riots, the evidence is ambiguous. The first disturbances, in August 1796, occurred before emissaries were sent into the colony and it is highly unlikely Ducalvet and those he recruited would have advocated rioting in the Montreal area. Some agitators believed they were fostering the interests of France, but detailed proof is lacking. In any case, they again had a tailor-made issue (*corvées* in or shortly after the harvest period, failure of the government to explain the law) and again refusal to work was general throughout the colony.

The evidence makes it abundantly clear that the disturbances were not initiated by French diplomatic officials in the United States. The militia riots began about three months after Genêt had left office and when his successor, Citizen Fauchet, was following instructions from the Jacobin Committee of Public Safety not to become involved in subverting Lower Canadian government. In the fall of 1796 it would have been the height of folly for French officials to have fostered rioting or insurrection. The naval attack was projected for the next summer and early provocation would have resulted in British reinforcements and/or discouragement on the part of potential supporters. Ambassador Liston, who kept a close eye on happenings in the French embassy at Philadelphia, informed Prescott in January 1797 of "the great Anxiety discovered [revealed] by Mr. Adet and his Associates here (on hearing of the Disturbance that took place at Montreal respecting the High Roads) lest an Insurrection should break out before their Plans were brought to maturity."[80]

THE EXTENT OF THE DANGER

If French forces had invaded the colony, they would probably not have received widespread support. Revolutionary ideals remained foreign to Canadiens and working people were without educated leaders. Despite a general pro-French feeling and a general expectation of invasion at some time, working Canadiens did not prepare to aid their former countrymen. No cache of arms and no domestic plans for a rising were ever found by the Lower Canadian authorities. The working people normally did not inform on emissaries operating for France, but no coherent underground of known sympathizers, accumulating intelligence and prepared to help spies, was ever constructed.

The popular response, of course, would have depended partly on circumstances. French atrocities against the clergy, refusal to pay for provisions, or treatment of the Canadiens as country bumpkins would quickly have turned opinion against the invaders. Had the government at Quebec foolishly attempted general conscription, the result would surely have been disastrous for it too. Such extreme cases aside, I think the common response would have been a prudent neutrality in action (a least until the military issue was no longer in serious doubt),

with the manifestation of national sentiment in favour of the French extending only to non-military aid, such as provisions and military intelligence. This was the opinion of emigré Jules Le Fer, a spy employed by the government at Quebec in the summer of 1798. Le Fer spent many weeks incognito in the towns and countryside gathering information for his report. According to Governor Prescott, Le Fer found the Canadiens

> in general (he had not indeed found any Exceptions) very desirous that this Country should be regained by France: but he had not discovered that they had made any actual Arrangements for lending the French any regular Assistance in arms: and although their Wishes were very strong in Favour of France he did not think it likely, so far as he could discover, that any very considerable Number would join the French in Arms immediately...[but] that the generality of them would be disposed to be mere lookers on at the first, while Matters might remain doubtful; but should the French succeed so far as to make themselves [potential] Masters of the Country in a short time...the Canadians would then join them in great Numbers.[81]

The English élite, alas, did not see it in that balanced way.

Notes

1 *AHAR* 2 (1903), 201–11 (trans.). For Genêt's Canadian policy see his correspondence in ibid. and in the Genêt Papers, LOC and the relevant dispatches of George Hammond (British Minister to the United States) in FO5, MG16, vol. 1, NAC. Useful secondary studies in print are Link, *Democratic-Republican Societies,* 141–4; Williamson, *Vermont in Quandary,* ch. 14; De Conde, *Entangling Alliance,* ch. 3; Wade, "Quebec and the French Revolution of 1789."

2 "Observations sur l'etat actuel de Canada," c. 12 June 1793, LOC/France, vol. 37. For a full treatment of Mezière's assistance to Genêt, see Wade, "Quebec and the French Revolution."

3 Printed in Michel Brunet, "La Revolution française sur les bords du Saint-Laurent," *RHAF* 11 (1957–8), 158–62.

4 Mezière to Genêt, 20 Sept. 1793, LOC/France, vol. 38. According to Mezière, Jacques Rousse had emigrated to the United States in 1777 and in 1789 had opened an inn on Lake Champlain near the Quebec–New York border (now Rouse's Point). While Mezière spelled his last name "Rous," the innkeeper spelled it "Rousse": Rousse to Genêt, 13 Feb. 1794, ibid., suppl. vol. 28.

5 See Monk to Dorchester, 12 July 1794, with enclosed deposition, CO42, vol. 101; *Quebec*

Gazette, 18 Sept. 1794; Monk to Dorchester, 2 Oct. 1794, Q series, vol. 69.

6 This paragraph is based on depositions/voluntary examinations found in CO42, vol. 100, 16–22, 361–5; CO42, vol. 101, 19–26; Records of the King's Bench, 1794.

7 9 May 1793, quoted in Christie, *A History,* I: 140–1.

8 Richardson to Porteous, 15 Sept. 1793, Richardson Letters. See also same to same, 29 June 1793, 15 Aug. 1793, ibid.; Morrison to——, 2 May 1793, Lindsay-Morrison Papers; Clarke to Simcoe, 6 June 1793, Cruikshank, *Simcoe Papers,* I: 349; Joseph Chew to Alexander McKee, Montreal, 3 July 1793, ibid., 375.

9 Dorchester to Dundas, 23 Oct. 1793, CO42, vol. 97. See also *Quebec Gazette,* 20 Oct. 1793; Mezière to Genêt, 20 Sept. 1793, LOC/France, vol. 38, pt. 3; "Jon Charles" to Mezière, 24 Oct. 1793, ibid., supp. vol. 28.

10 *Quebec Gazette* (both languages), 7 Nov. 1793; 26 Nov. 1793, *RNAC* (1921), 23–4; Nov. 1793, Têtu and Gagnon, *Mandements,* II: 471–3 (trans.).

11 Sheriff Edward Cray to Attorney General James Monk, 9 June 1794, CO42, vol. 100; J. Reid to same, 12 June 1794, ibid.; T.A. Coffin to James McGill, 21 July 1794, "Civil Secretary's Letter Books, 1788–1829," RG7, G15C, vol. 2, NAC.

12 To François Baby, 24 Sept. 1790, Collection Baby, vol. 46.

13 "Abstract of the Returns of the Commanding Officers of the Militia of the Province of Lower Canada" (1794), S series, vol. 59, pp. 19,035–47; Campbell, *Travels,* 316; John Richardson to Ryland, 21 Sept. 1801, S series, vol. 74.

14 Monk to Dorchester, 29 May 1794, CO42, vol. 100; same to Dundas, 30 May 1794, ibid.; and see also Francis de Maistre to Philip Ruiter, May 1794, Ruiter Family Papers; Militia Returns, 1794, *passim;* James McGill's address to the Montreal Quarter Sessions, *Quebec Gazette,* 24 July 1794; Dorchester to Dundas, 25 May 1794, CO42, vol. 101; Chartier de Lotbinière to Sewell, 25 June 1794, Sewell Papers, vol. 3; deposition of Jean-Baptiste Leclair, 29 May 1794, CO42, vol. 100, 10–11 (re opinion in Charlesbourg and Jeune Lorette, trans.).

15 6 June 1794, CO42, vol. 100; see also Osgoode to Simcoe, 7 Sept. 1794, Simcoe Papers, Series 4, vol. 5.

16 La Rochefoucauld-Liancourt, *Voyage,* II: 183 (trans.). See also Monk to Dundas, 17 June 1794, CO42, vol. 100; Militia Returns 1794, *passim.;* A. Fraser to M. Fraser, 12 Jan. 1794, papiers Fraser. Fifteen Canadien residents from Laprairie, who instructed the French consul at New York (1795) about the colony's defences and offered their military services, claimed the people were saying with a single voice they "will defend the English against all their enemies except the French, because they will never take arms against their fathers, their brothers or their relations": edited and printed in Brunet, "Les Canadiens et la France revolutionnaire," 474–5 (trans.). Internal evidence suggests the letter was written between August and December 1795.

17 Monk to Dorchester, 29, 31 May 1794, CO42, vol. 100; deposition of three Charlesbourg habitants, 29 May 1794, ibid. (pp. 10–15); depositions of habitants Louis Paquet et al., 23 Dec. 1794, S series, vol. 61, pp. 19,519–20.

18 Marginal note in Monk's handwriting on a deposition of Jean-Baptiste Leclair, 29 May 1794, CO42, vol. 100 (p. 11). See also Monk's "State of the Prosecutions in His Majesty's Court of King's Bench. November Term 1794," CO42, vol. 101.

19 Monk to Dorchester, 29 May 1794, CO42, vol. 100 (p. 5); same to Dundas, 30 May 1794, ibid, (p. 323), deposition of habitant Louis Savard, 29 May 1794, ibid. (pp. 14–15).

20 Gray to Monk, 9 June 1794, CO42, vol. 100 (pp. 355–6); Monk to Dorchester, 18 June 1794, ibid. (paraphrasing Sewell).

21 De Lotbinière to Sewell, 25 June 1794, Sewell Papers, vol. 3 (trans.); Monk to Dorchester, 18 June, CO42, vol. 100, (Monk cited Sewell and Judge James Walker to bolster the case for caution); Dorchester to Dundas, 21 June 1794, CO42, ibid.

22 "Orders of the Committee of Public Safety" (trans.), 15 Nov. 1793, *AHAR* 2 (1903), 290–3; Robert Liston (British minister to the United States) to Prescott, 28 Nov. 1796, *RNAC* (1891), 62; De Conde, *Entangling Alliance,* ch. 12.

23 For French sources on the Directory's policy towards North America during this period see its instructions to General Perignon (French negotiator at Madrid), 16 Mar. 1796, *AHR* (1897), 667–71 and to the proposed minister to the United States, 6 Aug. 1796, *AHAR* 2 (1903), 938; memorandum by Louis-Pierre Anguetil (official in the Foreign Ministry) to the Directory, 1 Nov. 1796, Corr. Pol. Angleterre, vol. 590 (88–98), Archives des affaires étrangères, Paris, France; George Duruy ed. and Charles E. Roche, trans., *Memoirs of Barras,* 4 vols. (London: Osgoode, McIlvaine 1895–6), II: 203;

the correspondence of Adet and Létombe in *AHAR* 2 (1903); Consul de Launay (Philadelphia), "Mémoire: apercus politiques sur les États-Unis et la Canada," 4 May 1796, LOC/France, Mém. et Doc., Ang., vol. 2; Consul J.-B. Rozier (New York), "Mémoire sur le Canada," 8 June 1797, "Mémoires et Documents, Angleterre." These sources are usefully supplemented by British diplomatic intelligence reports. See, e.g., Liston to Grenville, 18 Nov. 1796, FO5, vol. 14, NAC; same to Prescott, 28 Nov. 1796 *RNAC* (1891), 62–3.

24 Printed in translation with a covering letter from Talleyrand to the Directory, 30 Aug. 1798, in Wilbur, *Ira Allen,* II: 191–8.

25 A resumé of Allen's proposals, prepared by an official in the French Foreign Ministry, has been printed in translation by Jeanne A. Ojala, "Ira Allen and the French Directory, 1796: Plans for the Creation of the Republic of United Columbia," *William and Mary Quarterly* 36 (1979), 442–8. Copies of Allen's proposals are held in the Allen Family Papers, Box 30, Bailey/Howe Library, University of Vermont, Burlington, Vermont. A useful context is provided by J. Kevin Graffagnino, "'Twenty Thousand Muskets!!!': Ira Allen and the Olive Branch Affair, 1796–1800" *William and Mary Quarterly* 48 (1991), 409. Graffagnino notes that France was in part motivated by a desire to avenge Britain's support for a French royalist invasion at Queberon in the summer of 1791.

26 Unless otherwise specified, the activities of De Millière, Hanson, Louisineau, and Ducalvet are based on the following sources: Sewell to Prescott, 28 Oct. 1796, Sewell Papers, vol. 10; same to Executive Council, 30 Oct. 1796, *RNAC* (1891), 59; William Stanton to Colonel Barnes, 18 Nov. 1796, ibid., 60–1; Richardson to Sewell, 8, 12 Dec. 1796, 19, 23 Jan., 6 Feb. (twice), 13 Feb. 1797, Sewell Papers, vol. 3; Liston to Prescott, 23, 28 Mar., 4 May 1797, Prescott Papers, vol. 11; Sewell's report to Prescott (12 May 1797) on the Road Act riots and his calendar of cases (hereafter Sewell's report and calendar), *RNAC* (1891), 73–8.

27 Trans. A copy of the letter (10 Nov. 1796) may be found in CO42, vol. 108, 128.

28 Minutes of the Executive Council, 26 Aug.–7 Sept. 1795, Lower Canada State Book B; proclamation of 9 Sept. 1795, *RNAC* (1921), 30–1; Osgoode to John King, 3 Aug. 1796, CO42, vol. 22; Ouellet, *Economic and Social History,* 663–5.

29 Osgoode to Simcoe, 7 July 1796 Osgoode Letters, 151.

30 SLC 1795, c. 8, 9; La Rochefoucauld-Liancourt, *Voyage,* II: 185. The working people often smoked (although most habitants grew their own tobacco), were notorious consumers of rum, and used quantities of brandy on special occasions. Salt, of course, was essential for the preservation of meat.

31 SLC 1796, c. 10. The main mischiefs addressed were canoemen etc. failing to appear for departure or deserting en route. In most cases they would have received money in advance; see also the petition of the Montreal merchants in *JHALC,* 1795–6, 20 Jan. 1796. For the longstanding nature of the problem see *Montreal Gazette,* 24 Dec. 1789.

32 *JHALC,* 1795, 21, 23, Jan., 23 Feb., 5, 23 Mar., 15, 21 Apr.; Osgoode to Simcoe, 30 Jan. 1795, Osgoode Letters, 91; same to Burland, 27 Oct. 1795, CO42, vol. 22; *The Times—Du Cours du Tems,* 9 Feb. 1795 (letter of "Modestus").

33 *JHALC,* 1795–6, *passim;* Fleming, *Political Annals,* 23–4; SLC 1796, c. 9.

34 *Quebec Gazette,* 23 June 1796 (emphasis in the original). Master shipwright John Black, then down on his luck, advertised himself to the voters of Quebec County (the city and surrounding country area) as a reliable fellow who had never "reposed on the downy couch of luxurious opulence": ibid., 16 June 1796.

35 *DCB,* vol. 5, 83; Osgoode to Simcoe, 7 July 1796, Osgoode Letters, 151; Monk to Dundas, 6 Aug. 1794, CO42, vol. 100. Black was indicted for sedition and Paquet for high treason. Neither was tried. Dorion appears to have been imprisoned on suspicion of high treason. He was not indicted. It is not certain whether Menut had been actually imprisoned: see deposition of Augustin Lavau, 27 May 1794 and Jean-Baptiste Vocel dit Belhumeur, 29 May 1794, CO42, vol. 100 (16–19 [with a note on Menut in Monk's handwriting [p. 18]).

36 Osgoode to Simcoe, 7 July 1796, Osgoode Letters, 151; Prescott to Portland, 3 Sept. 1796, CO42, vol. 107.

37 Five of the English members-elect had run in safe government seats and another two may have been returned because of manipulation by the government-appointed returning officer: unsuccessful petition from electors of Buckinghamshire (*JHALC,* 1797, 18 Feb.) against the election of G.W. Allsopp and John Craigie. Black had been perceived as an oppositionist by many Canadien voters in Quebec County (Osgoode to Simcoe, 7 July 1796, Osgoode Letters, 151; Young to Ryland, 9 June 1798, CO42, vol. 111). The election of Dr James Fisher in Northumberland

was due to peculiar local circumstances and Fisher's adroit manoeuvering to ostensibly join himself to Pierre Bédard of the *parti canadien* as a running mate. Northumberland had significant numbers of Scottish settlers although they were rapidly becoming Canadienized. Fisher himself was a Scot who enjoyed the support of Colonel John Nairne. Bédard may have gone along with the ticket so as not to risk alienating Nairne and losing Scots-Canadien votes. Another factor helping Fisher was that his five opponents (excluding Bédard) were Canadiens. See Fisher to Nairne, 8 July 1796, Nairne Papers, vol. 3.

38 RG4, B28, vol. 70, NAC; *DCB,* vol. 5, 276.

39 *JHALC,* 1797, 24 Jan. 15 Feb. 1797.

40 Osgoode to John King, 3 Aug. 1796, postscript dated 27 Aug. 1796, CO42, vol. 22; same to ——, 13 Oct. 1796, ibid.; Sewell to Foucher, *3* Oct. 1796, Sewell Papers, vol. 9.

41 The principal sources relied on for the Road Act riots are references given in the preceding note and the following: Montreal Magistrates to Prescott, 6, 13 Oct 1796, S series, vol. 64, and CO42, vol. 108; Osgoode to —— King, 14 Nov. 1796, CO42, vol. 22; Isaac Winslow Clarke to William Dummer Powell, 15 Nov. 1796, W.D. Powell Papers, vol. B30; Attorney General Sewell to Prescott, 28 Oct. 1796, Sewell Papers, vol. 10; same to Executive Council, 30 Oct. 1796, *RNAC* (1891), 58–60; Sewell's report and calendar.

42 Gerald S. Graham, *Empire of the North Atlantic* (Toronto: University of Toronto Press, 1950), 226–7. The first official indication of the news reaching Lower Canada appears to be Prescott to Prince Edward, 3 Oct. 1796, Prescott Papers, vol. 25. See also Samuel Willard to Luke Knowlton, 8 Nov. 1796, Knowlton Family Papers; Henry Cull to James Dale, 23 Nov. 1796, Cull Papers.

43 Prescott to Portland, 28 Oct. 1796, CO42, vol. 108; *R. v. David Maclane* [sic] (1796), 26 St. Tr. 721 at 786 (per George Pyke, counsel for the defence).

44 Prescott to Lt.-Col. Brownrigg, 25 Oct. 1796, Prescott Papers, vol. 26; same to Major-General Delaney, 14 Aug. 1797, ibid.; Osgoode to ——, 13 Oct. 1796, CO42, vol. 22.

45 Denaut to Plessis, 18 Oct. 1796, AAQ, Cartable, Evéques de Québec, II (trans.). See also Louis Labadie's address to the habitants of Verchères, 15 Nov. 1796, *Quebec Gazette,* 5 Jan. 1797.

46 SLC 1794, c. 5 as continued/amended by SLC 1795, c. 11 and SLC 1796, c. 8.

47 *RNAC* (1913), 45–6.

48 Têtu and Gagnon, *Mandements,* II: 501–2.

49 Address of Judge P.-A. De Bonne to prisoners convicted of Road Act offences, 3 Apr. 1797; *Quebec Gazette,* 6 Apr. 1797; Jacques Vallée, ed., *Tocqueville au Bas-Canada* (Montreal: Editions du Jour 1973), 175.

50 Gaspard de Lanaudière to his wife, 30 Jan. 1797, Collection Baby, vol. 12; J. George Forth to Peter Russell, 2 Feb. 1797, Russell Papers, AO. Forth was an army officer, then stationed at Montreal.

51 Burt, *United States, Great Britain and British North America,* 171; Webster, "Napoleon and Canada," *passim;* same, "Ira Allen in Paris, 1800, Planning a Canadian Revolution," *CHAR* (1963), 74. The *Olive Branch* was an American ship.

52 Talleyrand to the Directory, 30 Aug. 1798, in Wilbur, *Ira Allen,* II: 191–8; Bryant, *Years of Endurance,* ch. 9.

53 Dorchester to Dundas, 25 Oct. 1793, CO42, vol. 97; "State of the Troops in North America etc.," enclosed in same to same, 6 Aug. 1794, CO42, vol. 100; "State of the Troops in North America," 8 Nov. 1796, Prescott Papers, vol. 15. According to the last document the total troops in British North America numbered 6,163.

54 See, for example, Monk to Dundas, 30 May 1794, CO42, vol. 100; Osgoode to ——, 13 Oct. 1796, CO42, vol. 22; Prescott to Portland, 22 Aug. 1798, CO42, vol. 111.

55 ——, "Canadian Letters: description of a tour thro' the provinces of Lower and Upper Canada in the course of the years 1792 and '93," *Canadian Antiquarian and Numismatic Journal* 3rd series, 9 (1912), 90; *Quebec Gazette,* 28 Mar. 1793.

56 See La Rochefoucauld-Liancourt, *Voyage,* II: 152–3; Prescott to Prince Edward, 4 Oct. 1797, Prescott Papers, Series 2; Commander-in-Chief Peter Hunter to the Duke of York, 24 Dec. 1800, C series, vol. 1209.

57 Grant to Simon McTavish, 10 July 1794, Collection Baby, vol. 11; Maulevrier, *Voyage,* 66; Simcoe to Portland, 11 Dec. 1796, Cruikshank and Hunter, *Correspondence of the Honourable Peter Russell,* I: 104–5. According to Maulevrier, Richery could have taken the colony with ease, if he had been able to disembark six thousand troops.

58 Prescott to Portland, 22 Aug. 1798, CO42, vol. 111.

59 Ibid.

60 Mezière to Genêt, 20 Sept. 1793, trans. taken from Wade, "Quebec and the French Revolution of 1789," 356.

61 Depositions of Alexis Monjeon and Richard Corbin, 11 June 1794, CO42, vol. 100.

62 James Monk, "State of Prosecutions in His Majesty's Court of King's Bench. November Term 1794," CO42, vol. 101. Of these, seven were indicted (one convicted, two acquitted, four continued and later released).

63 Plessis, "Les dénombrements de Québec," *RANQ* (1948–9), 3. I have treated carters and sailors as semi-skilled workers.

64 Sewell to Prescott, 28 Oct. 1796, Sewell Papers, vol. 10; Monk to Dorchester, 18 June 1794, CO42, vol. 100; Prescott to Liston, 2, 10 Feb. 1797, Prescott Papers, vol. 13; Richardson to Sewell, 13 Feb. 1797, Sewell Papers, vol. 3.

65 Pierre-Ignace Aubert de Gaspé Sr. to ———, 7 July 1796, *BRH* 42 (1936), 379 (trans.); Monk to Dorchester, 25 May 1794, CO42, vol. 101.

66 See the depositions of François Le Droit dit Perche, 25 May 1794, CO42, vol. 101 and Jean-Baptiste Leclair, 29 May 1794, CO42, vol. 100.

67 Robert Sellar, *The Histories of the County of Huntingdon and of the Seigniories of Chateauguay and Beauharnois* (Huntingdon: Canadian Gleaner 1888), 528; Fernand Ouellet, "Les insurrections de 1837–38; un phenomene social" in his *Eléments d'histoire sociale du Bas-Canada* (Montréal: Hurtubise HMH, Ltée 1972), 366–7.

68 Fraser to M. Fraser, Beauchamp, 12 Jan. 1794, papiers Fraser; Osgoode to John King, 3 Aug. 1796, CO42, vol. 22; same to ———, 13 Oct. 1796, ibid.

69 Greer, *Peasant, Lord, and Merchant*, 79.

70 *Quebec Gazette*, 24 Mar.–28 Apr. 1791; Tremaine, *Imprints*, nos. 696, 702, 708; Upton, *Loyal Whig*, 187–9, 197–8.

71 See *Quebec-Gazette*, 18 Dec. 1788, 24 Mar.–7 Apr. 1791.

72 It is noteworthy too that in the three known petitions of complaint emanating from the farmers in the 1790s (Longueuil, 1793; Berthier, 1794; Dorchester 1799 [*JHALC*, 1799, 29 Apr.]) the relief sought was not tenure change but elimination of seigneurial abuses.

73 See depositions of farmer Jean-Marie Renaud et al. and of farmer Louis Paquet, both 23 Dec. 1794, S series, vol. 61; *Quebec Gazette*, 5 July 1792; Tousignant, "La premiere campagne electorale," 142–3. For evidence of other ethnic appeals see James Morrison to ———, 5 Jan. 1792, Lindsay-Morrison Papers; Dumas, *Discours;* Monk to Dundas, 30 May 1794, CO42, vol. 100.

74 Galarneau, *L'Opinion canadienne*, 294. For the lack of impact through published propaganda, see *The Times–Du Cours du Tems,* 4 Aug. 1794; Prescott to Liston, 14 May 1798, CO42, vol. 110.

75 De Gaspé, *Mémoires,* 91. See also Galarneau, *L'Opinion canadienne*, 330.

76 Maulevrier, *Voyage,* 66. See also Gerrard to ———, 25 Apr. 1793, Collection Baby, vol. 11; La Rochefoucauld-Liancourt, *Voyage,* II: 209–10; Louis Labadie to John Neilson, 4 May 1797, Neilson Collection, vol. 1; Liston to Grenville, 2 Apr. 1798, FO5, vol. 22.

77 Dorchester to Dundas, 12 July 1794 (with enclosure), CO42, vol. 99; S series, vols. 58–60 (letters from the associations); circular letter of the Quebec Association, CO42, vol. 100, (p. 369); circular letter of the Montreal Association, 5 July 1794, *RANQ* (1948–9), 258–9; James McGill (Montreal President) to Dorchester, 6 Nov. 1794, ibid., 272; *Quebec Gazette, Montreal Gazette,* and *The Times–Du Cours du Tems* for July–Aug. 1794; Tremaine, *Imprints,* nos. 892–7.

78 The recently passed Militia Act (SLC 1794, c. 4) prohibited service outside the colony, except to assist Upper Canada should it actually be invaded or to undermine an imminent attack on Lower Canada.

79 S series, vols. 58–60, exception in vol. 58, 18917–8.

80 Liston to Prescott, 15 Jan. 1797, Prescott Papers, vol. 11.

81 Prescott to Portland, 1 Oct. 1798, CO42, vol. 111.

"Cool Calculators": Brock's Militia

GEORGE SHEPPARD

Despite the increased tempo of military preparations during 1812, most colonists still believed that war would somehow be avoided. Prideaux Selby, the receiver-general of the province, wrote to a friend in April 1812 that the British forces were acting "as if war was expected, but my own opinion is that all Jonathan's blustering will end in nothing of that sort."[1] It would seem that years of incessant rumours of impending conflict had made the inhabitants of Upper Canada somewhat complacent. A correspondent to the *St David's Spectator* would later recall that although "relations with our neighbours were very gloomy," most Upper Canadians were simply "not apprehensive of war" and the commencement of hostilities was a "totally unexpected...subject of wonder."[2] Thus, when the news reached York on 27 June that the long-dreaded event actually had occurred, the villagers appeared to be in a state of shock. Eli Playter, a farmer who lived north of the capital, rushed to the garrison and "found all York in alarm, everyone's countenance wore the mark of surprise."[3]

Isaac Brock was not startled by the news. Since April increasing numbers of "armed men in coloured clothes" had gathered on the opposite shore, and early in May he received a secret dispatch from Sir George Prevost advising that he "consider war as inevitable." The message went on to warn that hostilities would commence by July at the latest.[4] This information

confirmed Brock's belief that the course of military preparations he had embarked upon the previous autumn had been the right one. At that time he had arranged to improve the fortifications at the various garrisons and had made plans to place his militia forces in a state of readiness. Brock considered those plans to be of prime importance since, in his opinion, the "active and efficient aid" of at least a portion of the population would be necessary if the colony was to be defended successfully.[5]

The Militia acts of Upper and Lower Canada dated from June 1793, when fears that the United States was intent on attacking the British colonies prompted the governments in those provinces to pass legislation allowing for the creation of official local defence forces.[6] In Upper Canada, John Graves Simcoe was the author of the colony's first Militia Act, and its governing principle was near-universal liability for service. All able-bodied men between the ages of sixteen and fifty were required to attend authorized militia parades or pay fines ranging from two to eight dollars an offence. The first muster in 1793, however, only produced an enrolment of 4213 men. Alarmed by the small turnout, the authorities amended the Militia Act the next year so that men up to the age of sixty were liable for service. From 1794 until 1812 the Militia Act of Upper Canada remained relatively unchanged.[7] The basic militia unit was the company, and each was to consist of between twenty

George Sheppard, "'Cool Calculators': Brock's Militia," in *Plunder, Profit, and Paroles: A Social History of the War of 1812 in Upper Canada* (Montreal: McGill-Queen's University Press, 1994), 40–67.

and fifty privates and three officers (a captain, a lieutenant, and an ensign). Regiments consisted of eight to ten companies, in other words 160 to 500 privates, commanded by one colonel, one lieutenant-colonel, one major, one adjutant, and one quartermaster. Officers and men were expected to bring to every muster their own firearms and at least six rounds of ammunition. Quakers, Mennonites, and Tunkers were excused from service but were required to pay twenty shillings a year in peacetime, and £5 a year in wartime, for that privilege.[8]

Brock was concerned that the annual musters had failed to prepare men for actual combat. The parades, usually held on 4 June every year, were looked upon by the men as an opportunity to socialize and by the authorities as a chance to engage in military census-taking. Brock's concern about the utility of the Militia Act was grounded in fact. By 1805, for instance, only 200 of the province's 8600 militiamen had received any genuine training.[9] To remedy this situation, Brock wanted to revamp the old law so that at least a portion of the militia had proper instruction in military matters. He also thought new regulations dealing with discipline and training were required. Though there were "many wise and salutory provisions" in the old act, Brock felt there were too few means of enforcing them.[10] When he addressed the provincial legislature in February 1812 he requested that the House of Assembly add an oath of abjuration to the Militia Act. He felt that the number of Americans in the province who openly professed that they would never fight against their former country made this amendment necessary. Under the proposed legislation, each militiaman would be required not only to pledge allegiance to the king but also to take an oath abjuring every foreign power. Yet many representatives, especially those born in the United States, refused to support the bill. Aware that an oath of abjuration would eliminate any pretext for claiming neutrality, they voted against the

measure and managed to have it laid aside. According to Michael Smith, an American Baptist preacher in Upper Canada at that time, the assemblymen were only following the wishes of their constituents. Smith also believed that passage of the bill would have led to a rebellion by American settlers.[11]

Brock's request for legislation to suspend Habeas Corpus for a period of eighteen months met a similar fate. Had he been granted that power, Brock could have arrested and detained without trial anyone he felt was endangering the public peace. A majority of assemblymen, however, believed that the measure was unnecessary. They reasoned that hostilities would probably be avoided and that in any case the province had managed to survive over two decades without such radical legislation. In addition to this "dread of arming Government" with extraordinary powers, the American element in the Assembly was cognizant that Brock sought the change in order to "keep the numerous body of Americans in a proper state of subordination."[12]

Brock had better luck with the amendments to the Militia Act that dealt with organization, training, and discipline. The new legislation increased the size of militia companies from fifty to one hundred men. The old regulation, which stipulated that companies could not exceed fifty men, had offered a means for some settlers to escape attendance at musters. Apparently a number of Upper Canadians had approached the wording of the Militia Act as they would any contract, and their "sharp" business sense had uncovered a loophole. When their officers attempted to force them out, they replied that their company's fifty-man limit had already been met. Ralfe Clench complained that these absentees even managed to avoid paying any fines because local magistrates agreed with this strict interpretation of the law.[13]

The new regulations also called for the creation of two "flank companies" from every battalion. These forces were to be deployed on the sides, or "flanks," of a body of regular troops and each company was to consist of up to one hundred volunteers willing to undergo training as often as six times a month. Should the number of enlisted men fall short of one hundred, a ballot system would be employed to draft the remainder from those men under forty years of age who had failed to volunteer. To ensure that balloting was kept to a minimum, various inducements were offered to those men willing to enlist of their own free will. Flank volunteers were exempt from both statute labour and jury duty, and from personal arrest on any civil process. Widows and children of flank members killed on active duty were promised annual pensions of five pounds provincial currency, while disabled veterans would receive nine pounds a year.[14]

The amendments meant that a larger proportion of the nearly 13,000 militiamen in the province would be better prepared for war.[15] Under it, one-third of the eligible men under forty, totalling some 1800 recruits, would at least have a smattering of proper training. Over time that number would increase, since provisions had been made for new recruits to replace one-third of the flank members at regular intervals. The remaining men under forty, and those up to sixty years of age, would continue in "sedentary battalions" and were only to be called upon if absolutely necessary. With 1800 partially trained militiamen, and about 11,000 more or less untrained, Brock believed a successful defence of the province might be possible. Moreover, to ensure greater compliance with military decisions, all militiamen were now required to take an oath of allegiance if asked to do so. Members of both flank companies and the sedentary battalions were also subject to trial by court martial for misbehaviour. A new scale of fines and jail sentences was created so that a refusal to follow lawful orders would now prove costly.[16] Although pleased with these changes to the Militia Act, Brock was less than satisfied that the Assembly had limited the duration of these amendments to

the end of the current parliamentary session. Having failed to acquire either the oath of abjuration or the suspension of Habeas Corpus, he was forced to accept this limitation rather than come away from the session empty-handed.

While Brock issued orders directing the various districts to establish flank companies, Joseph Willcocks did his best to discredit the new system. In the pages of his Niagara newspaper, Willcocks announced that all members of the provincial militia would be forced to train at least six days a month. The *Kingston Gazette,* in contrast, pointed out that only flank volunteers were liable to train so often and that it was highly unlikely this would be necessary. The editor expressed surprise that a member of the provincial legislature could be "so base, so wicked" as to spread lies that would only lead to increased disaffection.[17] To counter Willcocks's campaign, Brock released circulars to the various colonial newspapers which explained why flank companies were needed and which stressed the benefits of volunteering. These bands of "Loyal, Brave and Respectable Young Men" would serve only as a supplementary force to the British army.[18] Should an emergency arise, the authorities would have at their disposal a group of men able to assist regular troops, who were expected to do most of the fighting. Such explanations seemed to work. After a tour of the Niagara region in early May, Brock reported that an "almost unanimous disposition to serve is daily manifested." He felt that all the flank companies could be completed shortly if arms and accoutrements were sent from Montreal.[19]

What Brock failed to appreciate was that the eagerness to enlist in the flank companies was not proof that Upper Canadians were anxious to fight. Since most inhabitants thought war was unlikely, the volunteers looked upon enlistment quite differently from Brock. For most, enlistment meant only that they acquired exemptions from statute labour, jury duty, and personal arrest for small debts. There was, however, another incentive to peacetime service in the militia. In a new colony, where marks of distinction were rare, service in the elite flank units of the militia could enhance one's status. A few serious social climbers even went so far as to purchase their own swords to brandish over the heads of their subordinates.[20]

In addition to the militia forces, Brock also had a group of volunteers gathered primarily from the eastern portion of the province. A proposal to raise a corps of volunteers from among the Scots of the Glengarry region had first been made after the *Chesapeake* incident in 1807 when a confrontation between a British warship and an American frigate nearly led to a full-scale conflict. Although not considered feasible at that time, the same proposal was understandably greeted with greater interest by Brock in 1811. He petitioned the British government to offer land grants and cash bounties to those volunteers willing to join the Glengarry Light Infantry Fencible Corps, led by Captain "Red George" Macdonell.[21] By May 1812 some four hundred "fine, young men" said to be "chiefly Scotch" in origin, were training at a camp near Three Rivers. The regiment was not made up solely of Upper Canadians, however, and recruiting parties went as far afield as Prince Edward Island in search of volunteers. Sir George Prevost believed that the recruiting had proved successful because of the "zeal of the Officers," who also received bounties for each private enlisted, and because the promised land grants had proven to be "a powerful Auxiliary."[22]

After the declaration of war, the regulations dealing with those "auxiliaries" underwent a change. From then on, privates who joined only for the duration of the American conflict were given four guineas bounty but were not entitled to land grants. Individuals willing to guarantee their services for three years, or until a general peace was declared in Europe, received slightly more money and were promised a one-hundred-acre farm. The change, therefore, meant that in

order to acquire a land grant, volunteers also had to be willing to serve overseas. But these more demanding terms did not seem to hamper recruitment, and over 700 men eventually enlisted in 1812. Unfortunately for "Red George," some signed up only to receive the cash bounty and then disappeared. Thomas Armstrong, for instance, enlisted early in May at Kingston but was still missing in June. Apparently he was one of thirty-six men who had deserted after being awarded a bounty, and another thirty left after they reached headquarters. It was later discovered that five of those deserters were already wanted for similar incidents with other regular units.[23] A soldier who served with the British army in Upper Canada later recalled that once enrolled in the ranks, the "military ardor of the young Glengarrians had evaporated like the morning dew." Donald McLeod also noted that the high rate of desertions forced future recruiting parties to be far less selective. Eventually the Fencible companies "were soon filled up with runaway sailors, English, Irish, Dutch, Americans, Canadians, and a sprinkling of Africans, with a considerable portion of broken-down raftsmen."[24]

There were also problems meeting the quotas established for the militia flank companies. Recruitment of volunteers had been limited by shortages of rations and weapons, and only in the Niagara and Home districts were the flank companies well established. At the end of April some 700 men had been embodied but, with the arrival of the confidential dispatch in May warning that war was imminent, Brock decided to call out the 1800 men which the new Militia Act permitted. On 15 May he ordered the flank companies to begin training as often as the law allowed.[25] Brock then approached the Executive Council to supplement the incentives offered to flank-company volunteers. Four days after calling out the companies, he suggested that the Council request from the prince regent that militiamen be granted "UE" status if killed or wounded on active service. Following Brock's advice that "immediate disclosure" of this request was necessary, the adjutant-general of the militia, Eneas Shaw, announced a few days later that the government was seeking a "portion of the Waste lands of the Crown" for such individuals.[26]

In addition to recruitment difficulties, the militia suffered from problems dealing with training and discipline. Militiamen were expected to bring their own arms to training sessions, but some were too poor to afford weapons and others claimed to have lost those supplied by the government. Between 1795 and 1812 several thousand muskets were given to the militiamen of the province, but when Brock attempted to account for those weapons he found most were "lost to the service."[27] Since such a valuable item was not likely to be accidentally misplaced, it was probable that many inhabitants had sold the weapons for a profit. To prevent the "disappearances of guns so common in the past," Brock directed that all government-supplied arms were to be stored in depots after each day's training.[28] Although this procedure might have reduced the number of incidents, it did not prevent all weapons from going astray. In June 1812 Abraham Nelles, a captain of one of the Fourth Lincoln flank companies, reported that seven of his men had still managed to misplace their muskets.[29]

The policy of storing guns nightly also had been prompted by the uncertain loyalties of the Upper Canadian populace. Earlier in the year Brock had noticed that some of the "most dubious characters" in the province had expressed a desire to acquire arms from the government.[30] It was probably for that reason that Brock had also decided to create the flank companies. Not only would flank members be better trained than their fellow militiamen, but it was expected that the majority would be volunteers who, unlike unwilling conscripts, could be relied on to act properly. Sir George Prevost was convinced that only about a third of the militia in Upper Canada was loyal enough to be entrusted with arms.[31] The new militia system, which limited access to the king's stores, was a reflection of the suspicions and doubts that plagued the fragmented society of Upper Canada.

Meanwhile, the mistrust that existed between British and American Upper Canadians caused problems for Robert Nichol. Brock had appointed Nichol to the command of one of the Norfolk flank regiments, but on taking up his post, the men refused to follow Nichol's orders. Apparently his junior officers, because of some personal animosity, had spread rumours about him; among others, it was alleged that he believed no American should ever be trusted. Try as he might, Nichol could not erase the impression created by such gossip. After printing and distributing handbills denying the charge, he still found that the men refused to recognize his authority. "My wish is to *command* a regiment," complained Nichol to a superior, "and *not to be* the *leader* of a mob."[32] Problems between the officers and men of the Norfolk militia undoubtedly played a part in Nichol's being offered the full-time post of quartermaster general of the militia. The Scottish merchant, concerned as always about the effect such public duty would have on his private interests, at first refused the offer. But Brock persisted and eventually the "clever little Scotsman" was persuaded. His decision to undergo such "a great personal sacrifice" was made easier when Brock reminded him that the "British government was never backward in rewarding faithful and meritorious service."[33]

On the eve of war, therefore, Brock's situation had improved only slightly. The new militia system was well suited to provincial conditions and would eventually provide a portion of the male population with the skills needed for military operations. All the same, shortages of both money and recruits had hampered the complete implementation of the plan, and the province was still far from secure against invasion.

Moreover, no assurances could be given about the loyalties of the large American element in the population. Worse still, even members of the British and Loyalist communities appeared to need added inducements to ensure their support. Members of the Six Nations also appeared to be indifferent. As a result, one could not blame Brock for having "no great confidence in the majority" of the provincial population.[34] Despite that realistic assessment, even he was surprised by how passively the inhabitants responded to the invasion of their province.

News of the outbreak of hostilities between the United States and Great Britain first reached General Brock on 24 June, but he decided against immediately informing the population of this development.[35] He reasoned that the information would eventually spread throughout Upper Canada anyway, and he was determined to use the interim period to his best advantage. He quickly ordered both the British regulars and the militia flank companies in the Niagara region to assemble and march to Fort George. Members of the flank companies were told only that muskets were to be acquired at the garrison and they were then to be sent home. According to Michael Smith, the volunteers "obeyed with cheerfulness," having no idea that war had already been declared.[36] This little act of deception served its purpose. Before they realized what was happening, some nine hundred militiamen reported for duty and found themselves distributed among the four posts along the Niagara frontier. Not surprisingly, when the real situation was made apparent to the men there were many expressions of dissatisfaction. Brock attempted to mollify the militia by announcing on 2 July that they would be entitled to the same pay and provisions as regular troops, but few seemed impressed by this offer. The next day Brock admitted to Prevost that the original cheerful disposition of the Upper Canadians had been replaced by "a spirit of impatience."[37]

Though his trick had brought the militia out, Brock's actions also meant that the volunteers had not been given the opportunity to bring blankets and other necessary equipment. Since the men were expected to supply their own kits, they demanded pay to buy the required items. When this was not given, the men began to desert. On 4 July 1812 Brock warned that if this behaviour continued, the enemy would soon "destroy and lay waste to the province."[38] That stern message appeared to have little effect, however, since the number of desertions continued to mount. To reduce the number of absentees, Brock announced on 10 July that half the men could return to their homes, but only if they left their muskets behind.[39] Of those who remained on duty, Brock was sure most would leave anyway once the harvest began in spite of the £20 fine for desertion. That possibility worried Brock immensely. Although many of the militiamen appeared willing to defend their own property, Brock felt that the majority were "either indifferent to what is passing, or so completely American as to rejoice in a change of government." Had he had a greater number of regulars at his disposal, Brock believed the population would offer its support more readily. As things stood, however, most were content to wait out events. Trying to put the best light on the situation, Brock reminded Prevost that such "cool calculators" were numerous in every society.[40]

The British were no more successful in acquiring Indian support. The New York Six Nations had adopted a position of neutrality at a council held at Buffalo on 6 July. Emissaries were then sent to their Canadian counterparts urging them to follow the same course. Previously, Brock had called on the Grand River settlements to send all their warriors to Fort George. To Brock's disgust only one hundred men of "that fickle race" appeared, and these only for a few days. Brock thought he might yet win their support, but he was sure that the crown would have to "sacrifice some money to gain them over."[41] For that purpose Joseph Willcocks, who was known to the Six Nations, was approached to serve as intermediary and he eventually achieved a good deal of success on this mission. In the meantime, the Canadian Six Nations returned the answer to the deputation from their American brothers: "We know not your disputes... We do not want to fight...but if you come to take our land, we are determined to defend ourselves."[42] Those were sentiments with which Upper Canadians of every background appeared to agree.

Meanwhile, without the support of the Six Nations and with half his trained Niagara militia on leave, Brock received word that Brigadier-General William Hull had entered western Upper Canada on 11 July. After arriving in the province, the American commander issued his proclamation asking the inhabitants to exchange British tyranny for "Civil and Religious Liberty and their necessary result—individual and general prosperity." He went on to request that the men remain at home, and he warned that any white man found fighting at the side of an Indian would be put to death. That last provision was designed to discourage the use of native warriors by the British. Tales of horrible atrocities had left many Americans, including Hull, with a considerable fear of the Indian style of fighting. News of the proclamation soon spread throughout the province, but the effect of this warning, while impressive, was not exactly what Hull had intended. A number of American settlers in Upper Canada were offended by the tone of the offer and upset by its terms. According to Smith, few of the inhabitants of the province considered themselves subjects of a tyrannical government. If they had, they would have crossed back over the border. Nonetheless, they did not wish to fight for either side in the contest; Smith said that originally many had decided they would run to the American lines and surrender when battles occurred. The threat of giving no quarter to

anyone found fighting beside an Indian, however, would have made that ploy suicidal. Smith explained that the Upper Canadians were angry because they "were well assured that Hull knew every man in Canada to be under the controul of government, and that they were obliged to bear arms...and that they could not prevent the Indians from marching with them." As to Hull's "friendly advice" about staying home and remaining neutral, most would have done so if circumstances had permitted. "This proposal they would willingly have acceded to," Smith believed, "for they dreaded the war with their whole souls."[43]

The decision to remain at home was made easier if no strong British garrison was nearby. In the western regions, where there were few regulars, the proclamation "operated very powerfully on our Militia," reported Colonel Matthew Elliot of the First Essex. Nor should it be forgotten that the American offer promised greater prosperity and guaranteed the protection of private property if citizens remained neutral. For a people dedicated to improving their economic circumstances, these were powerful incentives to obey Hull's directions. Some months later an American spy reported to Major-General Van Rensselaer that the proclamation worked primarily because there was "a security for private property contained in it."[44]

In an attempt to limit the effect of Hull's proclamation, Brock countered with one of his own only ten days later. To those who thought that the economic prospects of the colony would improve under American control, Brock explained that the "unequalled prosperity" already enjoyed by the province was a product of government expenditure and access to British markets. Brock also warned the American element in the province that the United States actually intended to give Canada back to France after the war was over. Instead of enjoying American liberty, Upper Canadians would find themselves "slaves to the Despot" Napoleon. Finally, Brock reminded all inhabitants, including those who had never taken the oath of allegiance, to resist any American appeal for assistance. As "Canadian Freeholders," every citizen owed allegiance to Britain. Those who failed to heed this advice did so at their own peril, Brock warned, since Britain would eventually win the war.[45]

A recent occurrence added an air of plausibility to that statement. In the early hours of 17 July, a small British force from St Joseph Island captured the American post at Michilimackinac. The victory was bloodless, as the American forces surrendered after being caught completely by surprise. Having never been informed by their own forces that war had been declared, the Americans at ichilimackinac were not prepared to fight when Captain Charles Roberts and his redcoats appeared at the gates. The capture of this small post proved to be of monumental significance to the British war effort. For the western Indians, such as the Miami, Shawnee, Ottawa, and Delaware, it was proof that their old ally Britain was determined to defeat the Americans. As a result, hundreds of western warriors were now committed to the British cause.[46]

Encouraged by the success at Michilimackinac, Brock began preparations to regain control of the territory occupied by Hull's forces. On 22 July he ordered all militia furloughs cancelled. Colonel Thomas Talbot was directed to assemble the two hundred members of the flank companies of the Oxford, Norfolk, and Middlesex regiments at Moraviantown. Brock assumed that the one thousand Western militiamen, many of whom were French Canadian and not recent American arrivals, could offer a spirited defence until Talbot's London militia joined them. In combination with a force of Indian volunteers expected to number at least 150, and with the regular troops from that region, Brock thought he could force Hull to retreat. In this expectation, however, he was to be sorely disappointed.[47]

Those militiamen directly in Hull's path had originally assembled at Sandwich "with as much promptitude as could be expected."[48] On hearing of Hull's generous offer of protection for the property of neutrals, however, the majority of Essex and Kent militiamen left their posts and returned to their homes. The remainder retreated to Fort Amherstburg with some three hundred regulars of the 41st Regiment on 10 July 1812.[49] Three days later Lieutenant-Colonel T.B. St George reported to Brock that the retreat to Amherstburg had been prompted by the militia, which was "in such a state as to be totally inefficient in the field." Even after leaving Sandwich the local men continued to desert, and St George noted they were "going off in such numbers" that half the men had left in only a few days. The desertion of more than five hundred Western militiamen meant that Brock's front-line defences were too weak to offer resistance to the invaders.[50]

At that point Brock turned to the men of the London District, but here he had even less luck. Colonel Talbot had managed to assemble the militia from the Long Point region and they set out for Moraviantown, but along the way the whole force, except for a handful of officers, mutinied and turned back.[51] The number of other volunteers from the London District was described as "very small," and Charles Askin said on 21 July 1812 that only fifty Grand River Indians appeared willing to fight the invaders.[52] Brock reported that the other four hundred warriors, after hearing from emissaries sent by General Hull, had determined to "sit quietly in the midst of war." He also noted that the refusal of the Six Nations to follow the British standard had produced a "domino effect" among their white neighbours. Some militiamen claimed they could not leave their families and property so long as the "fickle" natives remained behind.[53]

Not only had most western Upper Canadians refused to follow orders, but one group had even decided to aid the invaders. The most prominent members of that disloyal body, Ebenezer Allan, Andrew Westbrook, and Simon

Zelotes Watson, had crossed over to the American camp and offered to form a cavalry unit to help distribute copies of Hull's proclamation. Allan had served as a spy for the British during the revolutionary war, but in 1783 he had been imprisoned for ten months by his superiors who suspected that he was acting as a double agent. Nonetheless, after the war he moved to Upper Canada and in 1798 he received 2000 acres as a reduced officer. Allan proved to be a particularly "fractious misfit" and, after numerous disputes with neighbours, he was again arrested in 1806. This second jail term may have soured Allan's views towards the British government. One of his biographers has noted that his "allegiance to higher authority was never strong" anyway and that he was "primarily motivated by self-interest."[54]

Watson and Westbrook had both quarrelled with Thomas Talbot over business matters. Apparently Watson had sought to enter into a partnership with the colonel to settle immigrants, but the deal was never formalized and the two men had nearly come to blows over this misunderstanding. Brock remarked that Watson had paraded as far as Westminster Township in the London District distributing news of Hull's offer while at the same time vowing "bitter vengeance against the first characters of the province."[55] For his part, it seems Westbrook had quarrelled with Talbot about a number of issues in the past and he may have harboured a grievance over not being appointed an officer in the local militia.[56] His decision to support Hull in 1812, however, was probably related to more immediate concerns over property losses. A successful blacksmith, Westbrook was described as a "large, red-haired, rough featured man" who had managed to acquire land in four townships. According to Captain Daniel Springer, Westbrook had publicly declared he would not take up arms against Hull's force because "he had too much at stake."[57] Whatever Watson and Westbrook's motivations were for their actions, they could at least take some pride in knowing that they had succeeded in acquiring more followers than their old enemy. While Talbot's men deserted to their farms, Brock noted that Watson and Westbrook managed to gather about fifty individuals to assist in spreading word of the American offer.[58]

Reports of these events unnerved Brock. Though aware that most inhabitants desired to avoid war at all costs, the numerous desertions and evidence of widespread treasonous activity surprised him. "The population, although I had no great confidence in the majority," he informed Prevost on 28 July, "is worse than I expected to find it." Such an opinion is understandable. The Essex and Kent militia had done nothing to impede Hull's progress. The London area militia appeared equally unreliable, although Brock had previously placed great store in the loyalty of the settlers in that region. To prevent the "impending ruin of the country," he had determined two days earlier to go west himself and drive the enemy from the province.[59] Before embarking on such an expedition, however, Brock required a greater degree of control over the militia forces and population of the province. To acquire that power, he gathered together the members of the new sixth parliament for an emergency session on 28 July 1812.

During his speech at the Assembly's introductory session, Brock found himself offering contradictory messages about the state of the province. He claimed that the number of disaffected was few and that the militia had responded to the recent American invasion with conduct "worthy of the King whom they serve."[60] Yet his renewed request that Habeas Corpus be suspended and that more rigorous laws be enacted to deal with militia desertions revealed that the province was as threatened from within as it was from without. Aware that his speech would be published in colonial newspapers, Brock tried to put the best light on the situation, although that meant distorting the truth. Only a few days later, for example, he would admit to the Executive Council in a private session that the militia was in a "perfect state of insubordination." His purpose in addressing the Assembly had been to acquire a partial suspension of the Habeas Corpus Act. Once that was accomplished, Brock intended to begin wholesale prosecutions and he hoped the arrests would "restrain the general population from treasonable adherence to the enemy."[61] By lying to the Assembly, however, Brock had undercut his case for wider powers. Although most members of the legislature had surely heard rumours about the situation in western Upper Canada, Brock's speech offered them a way out of a difficult situation.

It seems that almost all of the assemblymen were convinced that the province would soon become part of the United States. In what they perceived to be the waning moments of British power in the colony, none wished to offend prospective American masters by offering Brock everything he wanted. Therefore, instead of authorizing a declaration of martial law, the assemblymen agreed only to amend certain aspects of the Militia Act. They spent the next eight days discussing the repeal of the 1807 School Act. In Brock's opinion those men had abandoned the "honest fulfillment of their duty" to avoid "incurring the indignation of the Enemy." Knowing that little further would be gained from the session, he prorogued the Assembly on 5 August 1812 after it had voted £10,000 for the militia.[62] For their part, the assemblymen were angered by Brock's actions and on 5 August they issued an address to the people of Upper Canada explaining the legislation adopted during the last session. They noted that "owing to the loyalty of the great body of the people," there was no need for a declaration of martial law. They also observed that the changes to the Militia Act permitted the use of very strict discipline. New regulations made it a crime to sell or barter arms and equipment, to counsel others not to appear for duty, and even to use disrespectful language against the royal family. Moreover, court martials were now empowered to deliver death sentences for desertion to the enemy and for fomenting mutiny or desertion.[63]

Of course, Brock had sought more than changes to the Militia Act, and this experience with the Assembly marked the lowest point in his career as leader of Upper Canada. The day after the Assembly began proceedings, Brock informed a fellow officer, Edward Baynes, that his situation was "most critical, not from anything the enemy can do, but from the disposition of the people—the population, believe me, is essentially bad—a full belief possess them all that this Province must inevitably succumb— this prepossession is fatal to every exertion. Legislators, magistrates, militia officers, all have imbibed this idea.... Most of the people have lost all confidence. I however, speak loud and look big." But that bravado had turned to desperation as the session dragged on without any movement on the question of wider powers for the executive. Eventually, as he later admitted to Prevost, Brock considered declaring martial law on his own authority but was warned that, if he did so, the whole of the provincial militia would disperse.[64]

After deciding to prorogue the legislature, however, Brock appeared reinvigorated. W.D. Powell remarked that after taking that step, Brock immediately "proceeded to the Barracks and harrangued the militia." Apparently this tirade impressed a number of the York militiamen. Several hundred volunteered that same day for service in any part of the province, and Brock selected 100 men and ordered them to march to Long Point. A further 150 militiamen from the Home and Niagara districts eventually followed that first group of volunteers. In this manner over the next two weeks, Brock managed to assemble a motley force for the relief of Amherstburg. He detached just over 300 regulars from the Niagara frontier and eventually acquired 600 native allies, including a handful of Six Nations warriors. He also managed to assemble 400 militiamen, including 150 from the London and Western districts; altogether, the British relief force totalled just over 1300 men.[65]

On 13 August Brock's force reached Amherstburg, only to find that the Americans, after surviving food shortages and outbreaks of disease, had retreated to their own shore. Although outnumbered two to one by the Americans, Brock decided to cross the Detroit River in pursuit of Hull's army. To fool the enemy into believing that the British force was much stronger than it actually was, the militia were supplied with the red jackets usually worn by regular soldiers. Before launching this audacious attack, Brock warned the Americans that the Amerindian warriors attached to his force would "be beyond control the moment the contest commences."[66] This announcement must have been chilling to Detroit's defenders since even British soldiers who served with the native volunteers were frightened by their appearance. Thomas Verchères recalled that the warriors afforded an "extraordinary spectacle," with bodies covered in red or blue clay, or tattooed black and white from head to foot. He described the scene as "horrifying beyond expression" and said watching the assembly of warriors made him feel as if he were "standing at the entrance to hell."[67] Hull, who was also deathly afraid of the Amerindians, heeded the British warning and surrendered Fort Detroit without firing a shot. Brock's gamble had paid off and, when later accused of being reckless, he countered by arguing "that the State of the Province admitted of nothing but desperate remedies." Yet he also denied that the unconditional surrender of the numerically superior enemy had been a matter of luck, preferring instead to see it as a product of the "cool calculation of the *pours* and *contres*."[68]

The 400 volunteers who followed Brock to Detroit, however, constituted only about 7 per cent of the 5850 militiamen eligible for service in the Home, Niagara, London, and Western districts. If the 500 men who remained on duty on the Niagara frontier are added to that number, about 85 per cent of the militiamen from those areas are still not accounted for, although the authorities had called out both the flank companies and the sedentary battalions in those districts. Where had the rest of the "Spartan Band" gone? Almost all, it seems, had returned quietly to their farms or had never left them in the first place.[69]

Most of the militia in the London and Western districts had simply returned home after Hull issued his proclamation, and many of their officers had quickly followed suit. On his arrival at Amherstburg, Brock had issued a general order expressing his discontent over the numerous desertions that had taken place during the last few weeks. Instead of fining deserters, however, Brock only asked commanding officers to transmit the names of those few militiamen who had remained faithful so "that immediate measures may be taken to discharge their arrears of pay."[70] A court of enquiry, appointed by Brock after the capture of Detroit, recommended that ten officers of the Essex and Kent militias be removed from their positions. But the court also announced that there were many others "to whom no share of blame can justly attach."[71] With no realistic means of punishing the hundreds of deserters in that region, it seems the British authorities were forced to settle for the token chastisement of a few of the most prominent offenders.

In the Niagara District, those who had been granted leave to attend to their farms early in July had refused, almost to a man, to return to their posts when called for by Brock. That left only 500 members of the Lincoln flank companies on duty, and many of them served very reluctantly. Colonel Christopher Myers, in charge of the district after Brock's departure for Amherstburg on 5 August, reported that "desertion to their homes is rather prevalent among them."[72] It seems likely that had no regular forces been present in central and eastern Upper Canada, militiamen in those areas, like the citizen-soldiers in the Western District, would have dispersed completely. For instance, a muster roll for Lieutenant Eli Playter's militia company during the month of August reveals that the men of the Home District were quite anxious to avoid service. Although by law the company could contain up to one hundred men fit for duty, the corps never reached half that total in August. Apparently one of the men had only recently discovered that he was near-sighted and therefore ineligible for duty. Beside another man's name was the notation "delirious," while others were simply classified as "deserters." Interestingly, Playter seems to have differentiated between those men who had left the ranks and two men who were listed as "gone to the States."[73] This would seem to imply that, at least for Playter, deserters were those who had returned to their farms and might yet be forced back on duty. Whether that was true or not, the muster roll for Playter's company illustrates how a fighting unit could quickly become a "paper force."

In the Niagara and Home districts, however, refusal to attend a militia summons could lead to arrest and imprisonment at the hands of British regulars. For that reason many individuals evidently decided to follow the path chosen by Playter's two men. The *Buffalo Gazette* and other American newspapers carried regular articles detailing the "escapes" made by "native born citizens of the United States."[74] Donald McLeod, a British soldier who served in the colony during the war, remarked that hundreds of people "escaped to the United States to avoid being drafted in the militia" at this time. It seems that most of those who chose to cross over were young tradesmen with little stake in Upper Canada. Those Americans with large holdings were more inclined to remain and guard their property, although the fear of military service induced a number of them to leave as well. An official list

of landowners in the province who abandoned their farms during the war to flee south contains 336 names.[75]

In view of the behaviour of most Upper Canadians, it is scarcely surprising that Brock considered the men actually willing to do their duty to be particularly deserving of praise. After his western expedition he wrote to the earl of Liverpool in August 1812 about the exploits of his "little Band" of regulars, Indians, and militia. Brock claimed that he had never "witnessed greater cheerfulness and constancy" among any other troops. That attitude apparently proved infectious. Later, Brock told his brothers that other inhabitants had been inspired with confidence by the recent successes, and he noted that the whole situation of the province was "of late much improved."[76] Because of that change he now felt sure he could repeat the experience in the eastern region of the province. Within days of his victory at Detroit, Brock was making plans to attack the American posts along the Niagara River.

But on his arrival at Fort George on 22 August he discovered that Sir George Prevost had negotiated a temporary armistice five days before.[77] Since the militia were anxious to deal with their crops, Brock announced on 26 August that four-fifths of the flank members would be granted indefinite furloughs. Before being sent home, the men were warned that they should be prepared to return at a moment's notice. He then directed that general inspections of the Home, Niagara, and London militias take place weekly. At these drills the officers were expected to call upon the men to take the oath of allegiance and to note the names of those who refused. Some officials apparently went beyond these instructions and jailed men who declined to repeat the pledge. "Many took the oath," observed Smith, "rather than suffer this."[78] Of course, not all officers acted this way, and those who ordered colonists disarmed and jailed without proper recourse to the law were described by McLeod as "insolent, cruel, and oppressive" men.[79]

Brock was in a position to grant furloughs, not only because of Prevost's armistice, but also because he had finally acquired the support of the Grand River Six Nations. The warriors had originally stood back because they feared that the contest might lead to a fratricidal struggle. The Iroquois were afraid they might end up fighting members of the New York Six Nations and most, therefore, simply chose to ignore Brock's first appeals. Apparently the recent British victories, and the offer of "good wages to engage in the war," had led the Indians to reconsider their position of neutrality.[80] By 7 September some three hundred warriors had arrived in the Niagara District. Aside from frightening the American soldiers, however, Brock feared he would get "no essential service from this degenerate race." At the same time, he noted that the warriors appeared "ashamed of themselves" and had promised "to whipe away the disgrace into which they have fallen by their late conduct."[81]

Unfortunately for Brock, those flank members who remained on active duty seemed to share none of the determination now evinced by the Six Nations warriors. Although only 20 per cent of the militia were required to remain on duty, their officers were hard pressed to keep even that small number. On 21 September deserters were informed that Brock was willing to overlook their offence if they returned voluntarily. As the problem increased, however, Brock realized that the indifference of the majority of the inhabitants made a successful defence of the province increasingly unlikely. "I am quite anxious for this state of warfare to end," he wrote his brothers on 18 September, "I scarcely can think the people will suffer it to continue."[82]

On 13 October the war between Britain and the United States came to an end for Major-General Isaac Brock. At Queenston, on the Upper Canadian side of the Niagara River, he lost his life attempting to halt the second invasion of the colony by American troops. The next day his successor, Sir Roger Hale Sheaffe,

managed to drive back the invaders, but not without loss of life on both sides. British dead, aside from twelve regulars, included two York militiamen and five Six Nations warriors. A further thirty-one York and Lincoln militiamen were wounded. Compared with casualty rates for battles in Europe, however, the losses at Queenston Heights were modest. A little over one month before, for example, Napoleon's army of 130,000 soldiers engaged a Russian force at the Battle of Borodino where casualties on both sides totalled over 70,000.[83]

Historians have sometimes said that the Battle of Queenston Heights was a turning point for Upper Canadian morale. C.P. Stacey, for instance, saw it as a "victory which further raised the spirits of the people of Upper Canada."[84] Yet an examination of the subsequent actions of the provincial militia reveals that the mood and behaviour of the inhabitants remained fundamentally unchanged. Immediately after the battle, Sheaffe called out both the flank companies and the sedentary battalions in the London, Niagara, and Home districts. This action, designed to bring together a force of 5000 men, was considered necessary in the face of further American invasions.[85] A majority of the inhabitants, however, were unwilling to answer that call. A British soldier who served in the colony during the war said that at this time hundreds of colonists "absolutely declined doing any kind of duty, civil or military, under the colonial authorities."[86] If caught, of course, shirkers could be jailed, and some chose to avoid punishment by leaving their homes. In Whitchurch Township, north of York, some seventy men chose to hide out in the woods rather than serve in their units. By December 1812, when Smith passed through the region, more than three hundred rebels had banded together. At that time Smith spotted a fifty-man contingent walking brazenly "on the main road, with Fife and drum beating for volunteers, crying Huzza for Madison."[87]

The republican sympathies of the Whitchurch rebels, and their determination to endure life away from their farms, certainly set them apart from other Upper Canadians. Most men in the province who managed to avoid service never abandoned their cozy farms for caves in the countryside. The experiences of Eli Playter with his militia company were probably typical. His diary describes the situation after the Third York regiment was once again called into service: "17th [October] I waited for the Men's coming till late the P.M. not more than ½ the company appeared…18th went early to some of the peoples Houses but they kept out of the way—I was much vexed at their conduct." Eventually Playter managed to gather about twenty men together. They set out for York, where two-thirds were excused and seven were balloted for service at the Niagara front.[88]

In addition to running off to the bush, or just lying low until their commanding officers had given up in frustration, Upper Canadians also avoided militia service through other means. Owing to recent amendments to the Militia Act, those with enough money could employ substitutes. Previously, the militia regulations had required draftees to appear for service whenever a partial call of the militia occurred. As of 5 August 1812, however, a draftee was permitted to send an able-bodied man in his place.[89] For a number of reasons, the use of substitutions, although a time-honoured and acceptable practice in most armed forces, was not as common in Upper Canada as one might expect. Since substitution was never permitted during a general call of the militia, the original draftee was still liable for service in the unlikely event that the whole regiment was called out. Also, it seems that it was exceedingly difficult to entice anyone to take the job. Those lucky enough to find a willing candidate were forced to barter away valuable items—such as a yoke of steer or as much as £50 cash—in exchange for a year's service.[90] For some Upper Canadian confidence artists, these transactions proved to be both profitable and relatively risk free. Philip Philips, for instance, deserted from the Third York militia only days after he took the place of William Shaw.[91]

As a traditional and respectable means of avoiding service, substitution was obviously a preferred method of steering clear of the fighting, but other legal means were also available. Amendments to the Militia Act passed by the Assembly in August had created a host of newly exempt occupations. According to the revised regulations, the following people now joined religious groups such as Tunkers, Quakers, and Mennonites in being excused from duty: "The Judges of the court of Kings bench, the Clergy, the Members of the Legislative and Executive Councils and their respective Officers… His Majestys Attorney General, Solicitor General, the Secretary of the Province…as well as all Magistrates, Sheriffs, Coroners, Halfpay Officers, Physicians, Surgeons, the Masters of Schools, ferrymen and one miller to every Grist Mill." Of course, the assemblymen thought it wise to include exemptions for themselves, at least "for the time being."[92]

If by some misfortune a well-to-do colonist did not qualify for an exemption or was unable to find a substitute, he could choose to remove himself from danger by simply ignoring the call and paying any fine that was levied. It has been estimated that in peacetime a farmer with thirty to forty acres cleared could expect a gross annual income of at least £110. During the war, however, inflationary pressures meant farmers' gross incomes doubled, and this prospective prosperity was a tremendous incentive to avoid militia duty. Since calls for service often came at harvest time and the largest fine that could be levied against a militia deserter in 1812 was only £20, risking punishment was often worthwhile.[93] Job Lodor, from the London District, admitted after the war that he "always procured a substitute when his tour of duty came" except when a general call for the militia was made. When that occurred, he would merely "go home & secure his many goods & property" and then await a fine. Of course, those who wished to avoid paying fines could also leave the province. That was the course chosen by Samuel Sherwood, who departed for Lower Canada as soon as war was declared. Sherwood, the son of a prominent Loyalist and a former member of the Assembly for Grenville, was apparently anxious about remaining in a region where the militia was "liable to be called out en masse." He therefore decided to go east to a safer area until hostilities had ceased.[94]

Some militia officers shielded their friends and relatives from serving by sending ineligible replacements in their stead. One such case involved Philip Lang, a private in the First York militia, who was described as being "lame an[d] sick better than two years." Nonetheless, Lang was balloted and sent to the garrison at the capital as part of the quota of men from the First York militia. His commanding officer, Captain James Mustard, was told by a superior: "Do not for the future have any man or men drafted for Actual Service that you know is sick or anyway not fit." Lieutenant-Colonel Graham went on to explain that such deception was "great trouble to me and a disappointment to the Public Service."[95] It also seems that a good number of settlers avoided militia service by simply announcing that they were Americans and, therefore, could not be forced to fight against their fellow countrymen. Brock had sought an oath of abjuration in February precisely because he foresaw that some inhabitants would take this position, but the refusal of the Assembly to pass the measure meant that the issue remained unresolved throughout the summer and it was not until 9 November that steps were finally taken to eliminate the practice. On that date, Sheaffe issued a proclamation directing the "divers Persons" claiming exemptions because of American citizenship to appear before boards that had been established in every district. Those who could prove they were Americans were to be given passports and escorted to the border. Any American who failed to appear before such a board by 1 January 1813 was warned that he would be considered an "enemy Alien" and was therefore "liable to be treated as a Prisoner of War, or a Spy."[96]

Declaring oneself an American, and therefore a noncombatant, sometimes proved risky even before Sheaffe announced his program of deportation. Some of those who had refused to take the oath of allegiance in August had been arrested and jailed for that refusal. Donald McLeod recalled that after hostilities had broken out, those Americans suspected of being disloyal were disarmed "and strictly watched."[97] Others were harassed by militiamen or British regulars who "thought it hard and unreasonable that they must bear all the burden and danger of war." Some Indian warriors, if they came across a "Yankee" who refused to serve, would threaten to kill him. According to Smith, the Indians sometimes made good on their threats.[98] In the end, however, a number of Americans who continued to refuse to fight were permitted to remain in the country even after reporting to the alien boards. Despite all Sheaffe's tough talk, it quickly became apparent that some well-established gentlemen who had purchased land and had never taken the oath of allegiance would be ruined by this order. For that reason, Sheaffe allowed such men to remain in the province under a "modified allegiance, or security of good conduct."[99] Other Americans, who it was felt knew too much about the defences of Upper Canada to be sent back to the United States, were also granted permission to remain in the colony.[100]

Whether they remained at home through legal or illegal means, or left their farms for Lower Canada, the United States, or the backwoods, the majority of Upper Canadians managed to avoid service in the militia. After the

Battle of Queenston Heights on 13 October, Sheaffe had summoned 5000 colonists to duty on the front lines, but on 24 October the paymaster recorded the presence of only 846 militia officers and privates in the Niagara peninsula.[101] Instead of increasing as time passed, the number of men on duty actually declined and, as another Canadian winter set in, the British authorities knew they would be faced with the difficult task of trying to keep even that small contingent on duty.

In addition to worsening weather, the British forces were experiencing problems with logistics. Although Sheaffe had ordered out 5000 men, he had neither the rations nor the equipment to feed and house additional soldiers. On 3 November he informed Prevost that the militia on the frontier was "in a very destitute state with respect to clothing, and in all regards bedding and barrack comforts in general." Not surprisingly, Sheaffe also went on to report that such conditions were prompting desertions. Ten days later he announced that the "many absentees" would not be punished if they returned voluntarily. The next day he sweetened the offer by promising to supply trousers, shoes, and jackets to flank members free of charge. Even men absent without leave could receive these items providing they returned "voluntarily and without delay."[102]

Other steps were also taken to reduce the number of absentees and to entice men back to duty. To help in uncovering desertions, officers commanding militia units were ordered to institute three roll calls a day. They were also instructed to establish squads comprising "a trusty sergeant and a file of men" to search for and apprehend any deserters.[103] Finally, a local resident, Samuel Street, Sr, was appointed as paymaster to the militia forces. It seems that the official formerly employed by the regular forces had often ignored the calls of the militia for pay and this, in turn, caused much dissatisfaction.[104] Several weeks after implementing this program, Sheaffe was able to report that the combined

policy of bribes, strict discipline, coercion, and prompt payment had worked. On 23 November he informed Prevost that the number of militia in the field had increased recently and he was pleased to report that the men "continue generally, to evince the best disposition."[105]

Sheaffe's appraisal of the morale of the militia was optimistic. It was clear that miserable camp conditions were taking an enormous toll. The combination of inadequate hygiene and the lack of basic camp equipment, such as tents, blankets, and kettles, made disease the principal killer of Upper Canadians in the first year of the war. James Mann, a surgeon who served on the American side of the lines, reported that soldiers in nearby New York were struck by waves of different diseases. From July to September most men suffered from dysentery, diarrhoea, and fevers but, once winter arrived, there were also outbreaks of measles and severe pneumonia. The same sort of conditions existed on the British side, with predictable results. Pension lists record the deaths of only three members of the provincial militia during battles at Queenston and Fort Erie in late 1812. Disease, however, accounted for at least forty-six casualties among men on duty. As winter progressed, so too did the number of deaths from disease. The two men who died in September were followed by five the next month, and by eleven in November. Finally, in December, a minimum of twenty-eight militiamen died from diseases contracted while on duty.[106]

The large concentration of untrained men and dangerous weapons also ensured that accidents were commonplace. On 27 September 1812 Brock was forced to issue a general order reminding Upper Canadians to guard against "careless negligence" in the handling of weapons. He informed the militiamen that no greater military offence could be committed than the reckless use of firearms or the "willful waste" of ammunition. Nonetheless, at his own headquarters four days later, Brock was forced

TABLE 1 | LINCOLN MILITIA SERVICE, 1812

	30 Nov.	4 Dec.	11 Dec.
Captain Crook's Lincoln Flank Company			
Active	32	23	15
Ill	18	14	15
AWOL	31	44	51
Total	81	81	81
Captain Macklem's Lincoln Flank Company			
Active	40	27	15
Ill	6	7	7
AWOL	8	20	32
Total	54	54	54

Source: AO, Abraham Nelles Papers, Field Reports, 1812–14. These designations are a simplified version of the various systems of notation used at that time. "Active" includes "Present and Fit" or "Present under Arms," those on leave or on duty elsewhere. "Ill" includes sick at home, in hospital, or in barracks. The "AWOL," or absent without leave, designation was at times noted explicitly, but sometimes had to be determined by eliminating other designations from the original total.

to specifically forbid the "practice of individuals firing in the swamp or any other place within the neighbourhood" of Fort George. Such activities had predictable results. Pension lists record four militia casualties from accidents between September and December 1812. It would appear that at this point in the war colonists were more likely to be wounded by their comrades than by the enemy.[107]

Hungry, cold, fearful of becoming sick or injured, and worried about their families, it is hardly surprising that Upper Canadians simply walked away from the war. After all, most considered it none of their affair in the first place. Surviving muster rolls of two flank companies from the fall campaign of 1812 reveal the course of action adopted by most militiamen (see table 1). In less than two weeks, Crook and Macklem found themselves with more men absent without leave than on duty. The situation seems to have prevailed throughout the district. Captain Applegarth's flank company of the Second York militia had only three men present and fit for duty on 11 December.[108]

In their anxiety to return home, a number of deserters may have unwittingly spread the diseases ravaging the men at the front. Militia officer William Hamilton Merritt wrote to his fiancée in the United States on 8 December 1812: "You cannot conceive the state our frontier is in. Not a woman to be seen and you, I hope, hardly know that war exists. I am sorry to say that we have had a very sickly season, many young men have died through fatigue, and fifty people from the 10 and 12 Mile Creek with a fever which is equal to a plague."[109] Apparently even some Upper Canadians who managed to remain at home found they could not escape the wider effects of the war.

The muster rolls represented in table 1 suggest that most men seemed unconcerned about the possibility of court martial, and it appears that the desire to get away from careless and diseased comrades was greater than the fear of potential punishment. The leniency with which both Brock and Sheaffe had dealt with previous instances of mass desertion no doubt helped foster that attitude. Thus, when permission to leave was not forthcoming, the men took matters into their own hands. For Sheaffe this action represented a threat to his authority as commander of the forces in Upper Canada. Faced with the complete collapse of the militia defence system, Sheaffe was forced into action. On 11 December he dismissed almost all the militia, and five days later he allowed most of the remaining flank members to return home.[110]

The expedient of letting the men return home when it appeared they were all going to go anyway had been resorted to already by Brock in July. When Sheaffe confronted the same problem he was wise enough to perceive that nothing could be done to halt the numerous desertions. These militiamen were not hardened regular soldiers but settlers with families to care for and farms to tend. Dragging the men back to the field would only have made the British army unpopular; besides, the effort was not likely to work for long. There was also another benefit to the granting of a general leave. By adding official sanction to what had occurred, Sheaffe saved face since he at least maintained the appearance of being in control of the situation.

Sheaffe could consider himself lucky in one respect. On the opposite shore, General Alexander Smith was experiencing even greater difficulty with the New York militiamen. Their refusal to cross the Niagara River had led to the American defeat at the Battle of Queenston Heights. After that loss, the men began to desert in great numbers. The New York *Evening Post* reported on 11 November 1812 that the militia companies along the Niagara River were "dwindling to mere skeletons."[111] By the end of November the remaining men had mutinied and then "disembodied themselves." According to one witness, later taken prisoner by the British, the militiamen responsible for this mutiny declared that the Upper Canadians "were brothers and sisters, with whom they had always been at peace." Determined to keep matters that way, the American mutineers posted a

$200 reward for Smith's head and then left for their farms.[112]

On the British side of the border there was also little enthusiasm for the war. Robert Nichol believed that the situation of the province had changed for the worse since Brock's death. "Confidence seems to have vanished from the land," he informed Colonel Talbot, "and a gloomy despondency has taken its place." One individual who refused to submit to the general miasma of depression was John Strachan. Reports of the frightful conditions at the front already had alarmed some members of the colonial elite and, on 22 November 1812, they met at York for the purpose of raising funds to buy supplies for the militiamen still on duty. Strachan chaired the meeting and told those in attendance that it was their duty "to comfort those who are fighting our battles."[113] By the end of the evening the Loyal and Patriotic Society of Upper Canada had been formed. A proposal to restrict voting rights in the organization to those who had paid a £10 fee was rejected and that privilege was instead automatically granted to members of the Executive and Legislative councils and, not surprisingly, to clergymen of the Church of England. Apparently, a good deal of resentment still existed over the Assembly's refusal to assist Brock, and only the speaker of the House was granted voting rights.[114]

Rather than simply assist active militiamen, the new society agreed to fund a number of projects. Families in distress because of the war were to be offered relief, and disabled militiamen were also considered fit objects for the society's bounty. The group even decided to award medals to those men who had distinguished themselves while on service. Aware that desertion was rampant at the front, the directors announced they would withhold medals from any "militiaman or soldier who has been or shall be convicted of desertion or absenting himself from duty." Of course, few of the directors themselves were on active service, chiefly because they had been lucky enough to have acquired exemptions. Chief Justice Thomas Scott was too old for militia service, but most of the other directors were under sixty years of age. Thomas Ridout was fifty-eight, William Powell had just celebrated his fifty-seventh birthday, and Alexander Wood was only forty. John Strachan, who was thirty-four years of age when he founded the society, later remarked that everywhere in the province "inhabitants rejoiced" to see those "who were exempted from their age or situation" coming forward to "comfort those who were called out." Although ostensibly designed to assist war sufferers, the society also served another purpose. It allowed Strachan and the other members of the colonial establishment to claim later that they had taken an "active part in the war" even though most of them never left the comfort of their homes.[115]

Avoidance of militia duty was the norm for Upper Canadian males throughout the struggle. Despite the high number of desertions during the first part of the war, participation in the militia actually reached a peak before Brock's death in October 1812. One researcher who has examined the postwar "cult of Brock worship"

thinks that Upper Canadians idolized the British officer because they thought he was "merely a striking specimen of the men he led."[116] Yet Isaac Brock died less than four months after hostilities had commenced, and the war would rage for more than two years after his death. The victory at Michilimackinac had been gained without his direct participation, and the capture of Detroit was as much a product of Hull's cowardice as it was a result of careful planning on Brock's part. Why, then, was he chosen as an object for praise and raised to near demigod status by Upper Canadians? To answer that question one need only examine the conduct of the colonists after 1812. While the level of militia participation was certainly low before Brock's death, it dwindled even further in the months that followed. In contrast to this pitiful record, the dismal display of the first four months of the war appeared positively remarkable. Years later, writers would focus on Brock and the first few weeks of the conflict because there was at least a grain of truth to the claim that large numbers of Upper Canadians had responded with "unwearied exertions" when called to arms by their "immortal" leader.[117]

Notes

1 Selby quoted in Ermatinger, *The Talbot Regime,* 47.

2 *St David's Spectator* quoted in *Kingston Gazette,* 11 May 1816, 2.

3 AO, Eli Playter Diary, 27 June 1812, 397.

4 NA, RG 8, C Series, British Military Documents (hereafter NA, RG 8, C Series), volume 675, Brock to Prevost, 22 April 1812, 3; CO42/146, Barclay to Prevost, 5 May 1812, 209.

5 NA, CO42/352, Brock to Prevost, 3 December 1811, 55.

6 Hitsman, *Safeguarding Canada,* 57. There were unofficial militia musters prior to the passage of the 1793 act.

7 HPL, Jones, "The Militia," 3–4.

8 *Documentary History,* "Militia Law of 1808," 3:3–18.

9 HPL, Jones, "The Militia," 5.

10 NA, CO42/352, Brock to Prevost, 3 December 1811, 58–9.

11 Ibid., Brock to Liverpool, 23 March 1812, 8; Smith, *A Geographical View,* 80–1.

12 *Documentary History,* Brock to Prevost, 25 February 1812, 3:43.

13 Ibid., "An Act to Amend the Militia Act," 6 March 1812, 4:5–11, NA, UCS, vol. 14, 1811, Clenche to Shaw, 8 June 1811, 5456.

14 *Documentary History,* "An Act to Amend the Militia Act," 6 March 1812, 4:5–11.

15 NA, UCS, vol. 13, 4 June 1811 Militia Return, 5437. Altogether the militia numbered 12,801 in 1811. That was an increase of 924 from 1810 and,

therefore, it is safe to assume that by 1812 the total was at least 13,000.

16 *Documentary History,* "An Act to Amend the Militia Act," 6 March 1812, 4:5–11.

17 *Kingston Gazette,* 24 March 1812, 3.

18 Ibid., 19 May 1812, 2.

19 NA, CO42/146, Brock to Prevost, 16 May 1812, 215.

20 At least three militia officers submitted claims for the loss of swords and belts; NA, RG 19, E5 (a), Board of Claims, Thomas Humberstone, claim 443; Nathaniel Bell, claim 467; Eli Playter, claim 1328. One historian has noted that officers sometimes purchased other items including special uniforms; Johnson, *Becoming Prominent,* 71–9.

21 Stanley, *Canada's Soldiers,* 146; NA, UCS, Edward Baynes's Notice, 22 February 1812, 5990.

22 NA, CO42/146, Prevost to Liverpool, 26 May 1812, 205.

23 For Armstrong see *Kingston Gazette,* 26 May 1812, 205; information on recruits and desertions is in Cruikshank, "Records of...The Glengarry Light Infantry," 13.

24 McLeod, *A Brief Review of the Settlement of Upper Canada,* 41.

25 Brock to Prevost, 22 April 1812, quoted in HPL, Jones, "The Militia," 7–8. Prevost discussed the 15 May call in NA, CO42/146, Prevost to Liverpool, 9 June 1812, 237.

26 NA, CO42/352, Brock to Executive Council, 19 May 1812, 101; Eneas Shaw circular, 23 May 1812, 103.

27 *Documentary History,* Brock to Prevost, 11 December 1811, 3:25–6; NA, UCS, vol. 13, 4 June 1811 Militia Return, 5437. The return lists only 1926 weapons brought by the 12,801 men.

28 *Kingston Gazette,* 19 May 1812, 2.

29 AO, Abraham Nelles Papers, June memorandum.

30 NA, CO42/352, Brock to Liverpool, 23 March 1812, 9.

31 NA, CO42/146, Prevost to Liverpool, 18 May 1812, 197.

32 *Documentary History,* Nichol to Glegg, March 1812, 3:15.

33 The description of Nichol is from Scott, *John Graves Simcoe,* 206, while his philosophy on government work is from NA, CO42/352, Nichol to Halton, 25 April 1811, 31. Brock's assurance is in Cruikshank, "Sketch," 22.

34 *Documentary History,* Brock to Prevost, 28 July 1812, 4:148–9.

35 Richardson, *Richardson's War of 1812,* 11.

36 Smith, *A Geographical View,* 81.

37 The pay offer is in NA, RG 9 UCM, IB3, vol. 1, General Orders, 1812–16, 2 July 1812, 58. *Documentary History,* Brock to Prevost, 3 July 1812, 3:97, discusses the attitudes of the men.

38 *Documentary History,* Militia General Order, 1 July 1812 3:97–8.

39 NA, RG 9 UCM, General Orders, vol. 2, 1811–21, 4 July 1812, 8; 10 July 1812, 12.

40 *Documentary History,* Brock to Prevost, 12 July 1812, 3:65.

41 Stanley, "The Significance of Six Nations Participation," 218; *Documentary History,* Brock to Prevost, 3 July 1812, 97.

42 Stanley, "The Indians in the War of 1812," 155–6.

43 NA, CO42/352, "Hull's Proclamation," 12 July 1812, 122; Smith, *A Geographical View,* 82–3.

44 Stanley, "The Contribution of the Canadian Militia," in *After Tippecanoe,* 33; *Documentary History,* spy to Van Rensselaer, 16 September 1812, 3:268.

45 NA, CO42/352, "Brock's Proclamation," 22 July 1812, 124.

46 Stanley, *The War of 1812,* 6–7; Stanley, "The Indians in the War of 1812," 150–2.

47 NA, RC 9 UCM, IB3, vol. 2, General Orders, 1811–21, 22 July 1812, 17; *Documentary History,* Militia General Order, 22 July 1812, 3:138.

48 NA, C.676, Elliot to Claus, 15 July 1812, in Stanley, "The Contribution of the Canadian Militia," 33.

49 NA, CO42/147, Prevost to Liverpool, 30 July 1812, 31–2, St George to Brock, 15 July 1812; CO42/352, Brock to Liverpool, 29 August 1812, 105.

50 T.B. St George to Brock, 15 July 1812, in *Documents Relating to the Invasion of Canada,* 61.

51 *The John Askin Papers,* Charles Askin's Journal, 24 July to 12 September 1812, 713.

52 AO, Percy Band Collection, no. 238, G. Hamilton to A. Hamilton, August 1812; no. 237, Charles Askin to A. Hamilton, 21 July 1812.

53 NA, CO42/352, Brock to Liverpool, 29 August 1812, 105.

54 "Ebeneezer Allan," *Dictionary of Canadian Biography,* 5:13–15.

55 Ermatinger, *The Talbot Regime,* 44–6, discusses the failed partnership, *Documentary History,* Brock to Prevost, 26 July 1812, 3:145–6.

56 "Andrew Westbrook," *Dictionary of Canadian Biography,* 6:808–9, notes the business deals between Talbot and others. In his fictional work *Westbrook the Outlaw; Or the Avenging Wolf,* 1, John Richardson said that Westbrook harboured a grievance over being refused a militia commission.

57 Springer to Brock, 23 July 1812, in *Documents Relating to the Invasion of Canada,* 85–6.

58 *Documentary History,* Brock to Prevost, 26 July 181, 3:45–6.

59 Ibid., Brock to Prevost, 28 July 1812, 3:148–9; Brock to Prevost, 26 July 1812, 3:145–6.

60 NA, CO42/352, Assembly Reply, 27 July 1812, 115.

61 Ibid., Executive Council Minutes, 3 August 1812, 109.

62 Ibid., Assembly Reply, 27 July 1812, 115; Brock to Liverpool, 29 August 1812, 105.

63 The address is in York *Gazette,* 5 September 1812, 2; and the new regulations in *Kingston Gazette,* 19 December 1812, 4; 26 December 1812, 4.

64 *Documentary History,* Brock to Baynes, 29 July 1812, 3:152–3; Brock to Prevost, 28 July 1812, 3:148–9.

65 NA, MG 23, H14, vol. 3, W.D. Powell Papers, "First Days in Canada," 1058. The composition of the force is discussed in NA, CO42/352, Brock to Liverpool, 29 August 1812, 105; and Stanley, *The War of 1812,* 106–7.

66 Stacey, "The Defence of Upper Canada," in *The Defended Border,* 18; Verchères in *War on the Detroit,* 107.

67 Verchères, *War on the Detroit,* 107.

68 NA, CO42/353, Brock to Brothers, 3 September 1812, 226.

69 NA, UCS, vol. 13, 4 June 1811 Militia Return, 5437. The militia of those four districts amounted to 5850 men in 1811. These calculations are an overestimate of the proportion of active men, since the total number of militiamen would have increased over the previous twelve months.

70 NA, RG 9 UCM, IB3, vol. 2, General Orders, 14 August 1812, 22.

71 *Documentary History,* Militia General Order, 18 August 1812, 3:188–9; Militia General Order, 23 January 1813, 5:46–7.

72 Ibid., Myers to Prevost, 17 August 1812, 3:185–6.

73 AO, Eli Playter Diary, August Muster Roll, 401–2.

74 *Documentary History, Buffalo Gazette,* 11 August 1812, 3:170; New York *Gazette,* 24 July 1812, 3:127.

75 McLeod, *A Brief Review of the Settlement of Upper Canada,* 44; Cruikshank, "A Study of Disaffection in Upper Canada," in *The Defended Border,* 223.

76 NA, CO42/352, Brock to Liverpool, 29 August 1812, 105; CO42/353, Brock to Brothers, 3 September 1812, 226.

77 Cruikshank, "The Battle of Queenston Heights," in *The Defended Border,* 22.

78 *Documentary History,* Militia General Order; 26 August 1812, 3:212–13; Smith, *A Geographical View,* 92.

79 McLeod, *A Brief Review of the Settlement of Upper Canada,* 44.

80 Smith, *A Geographical View,* 82.

81 *Documentary History,* Brock to Prevost, 7 September 1812, 3:243.

82 Ibid., Militia General Order, 21 September 1812, 3:285. NA, CO42/353, Brock to Brothers, 18 September 1812, 227.

83 *Kingston Gazette,* 31 October 1812, 3; *Documentary History,* Return of Casualties, 13 October 1812, 4:73; Brett, *The Wars of Napoleon,* 115–16.

84 Stacey, "The Defence of Upper Canada," in *The Defended Border,* 19.

85 Smith, *A Geographical View,* 90.

86 McLeod, *A Brief Review of the Settlement of Upper Canada,* 42.

87 This group is discussed in Smith, *A Geographical View,* 90, and *Documentary History, Baltimore Whig,* 5 June 1813, 5:269.

88 AO, Playter Diary, October 1812, 405.

89 York *Gazette,* 10 October 1812, 2.

90 For examples of substitution and costs see AO, Abraham Nelles Papers, John Frennett's Deposition, 11 September 1812; NA, Upper Canada RG 5, A1, UCS, Traitors and Treason, vol. 6, 6646; CO42/355, Baynes to Prevost, 18 June 1814, 404.

91 The Philips case is in AO, Military Records, Miscellaneous no. 5, Cameron's Company, 3d York, 1812.

92 *Kingston Gazette,* 9 January 1813, 3.

93 Peacetime figures for gross income are from Russell, *Attitudes to Social Structure,* 21, 75. Assumptions

about wartime incomes are based on prices of goods sold to the commissariat; see chapter 6.

94 NA, RG 19, E5 (a), Board of Claims for War Losses, vol. 3735, file 3, claim 116, Job Lodor testimony. *The Constitutional History of Canada, 1791–1818,* Drummond to Bathurst, 27 February 1816.

95 AO, Captain James Mustard Papers, 26 March 1813.

96 *Kingston Gazette,* 1 December 1812, 2.

97 Cruikshank, "A Study of Disaffection in Upper Canada," in *The Defended Border,* 210; McLeod, *A Brief Review of the Settlement of Upper Canada,* 50.

98 Smith, *A Geographical View,* 90.

99 *Kingston Gazette,* 1 December 1812, 2.

100 Cruikshank, "A Study of Disaffection in Upper Canada," in *The Defended Border,* 212.

101 HPL, Special Collections, "Estimate of Sums Wanted," 25 September to 24 October 1812.

102 *Documentary History,* Sheaffe to Prevost, 3 November 1812, 4:176; Militia General Order, 13 November 1812, 4:207–8; Militia General Order, 14 November 1812, 4:211–12.

103 Ibid., Militia General Order, 28 October 1812, 4:169.

104 Ibid., District General Order; 29 October 1812, 4:170.

105 NA, CO42/354, Sheaffe to Prevost, 23 November 1812, 5.

106 Mann, *Medical Sketches,* 1. Battle casualties were determined from pension lists published in the *Niagara Spectator,* 11 December 1817. Since pensions were granted to widows or orphans, the pension lists did not include the names of single men who died on duty. For example, at least two other militiamen died in battle in late 1812 according to lists in CO42/354, Sheaffe to Prevost. Return of Casualties, 30 November 1812, 16.

107 NA, RG 9 UCM, IB3, vol. 2, General Orders, 1811–21, District General Order, 27 September 1812, 30; *Documentary History,* District General Order, 1 October 1812, 4:27; *Niagara Spectator,* 11 December 1817.

108 AO, Abraham Nelles Papers, Field Reports 1812–14. The experiences of Crook, Macklem, and Applegarth were shared by other commanders. Captain Hatt's flank company had 35 men fit for duty on 30 November 1812 but only 26 by 11 December. Abraham Nelles's company had 53 present on 24 November but only 38 six days later.

109 *Documentary History,* Merritt to Pendergrast, 8 December 1812, 4:4.

110 Ibid., Shaw to Talbot, 11 December 1812, 296; Militia General Order, 16 December 1812, 324; NA, CO42/352, Sheaffe to Bathurst, 31 December 1812, 176.

111 *Documentary History,* New York *Evening Post,* 11 November 1812, 4:179–80.

112 Ibid., Bill Sherman's statement; David Harvey's statement, 3 December 1812, 4:247–9.

113 Ibid., Nichol to Talbot, 18 December 1812, 327; Robinson, *The Life of John Beverley Robinson,* 61.

114 AO, Strachan Papers, draft constitution, 15 December 1812.

115 Ibid., society history, 1813?; Spragge, *The John Strachan Letterbook,* Strachan to Stewart, winter 1814, 58.

116 Walden, "Isaac Brock: Man and Myth," iii. The deification of Brock began as early as 1813 when John Rolph informed a friend that the former administrator was a man "who ardently loved the country and whom every lisping child would follow into the field." NA, MG 24, J48, J.W. Whittaker Papers, 1813.

117 AO, Strachan Papers, society history, 1813?

Unfair Masters and Rascally Servants?

Labour Relations among Bourgeois, Clerks and Voyageurs in the Montreal Fur Trade, 1780–1821

CAROLYN PODRUCHNY

The history of working peoples in the fur trade has recently become a subject of concentrated interest. The publication of Edith Burley's *Servants of the Honourable Country,* which explores the master and servant relationship between Orkney workers and Hudson's Bay Company (HBC) officers stands as an important development in focussing attention squarely on the workers themselves, and demonstrates the extent of their power through insubordination and resistance.[1] A general pattern of master and servant relations existed among most fur trade companies and their labour forces which was similar to other 18th-century labour contexts. Servants signed a contract for several years, agreeing to be obedient and loyal to their master in exchange for food, shelter, and wages.[2] However, labour relations were highly influenced by local conditions. The personality of individual masters, the availability of food resources, the difficulty of work, and the cultural conventions of the labour force all affected the nature of the master-servant relationship. As many fur trade scholars have contended, there was never just one fur trade: it varied tremendously in different contexts.[3] The same can be said of labour relations in the fur trade. Process

and flexibility were dominant characteristics in the relationships between masters and servants.

French Canadian *voyageurs*[4] working in various Montréal-based fur trade companies developed a distinct culture which emerged in the early 18th century and lasted to the mid-19th century. During the most active period of the Montréal trade, the labour force grew from 500 men in the 1780s, to over 2000 by the time the North West Company (NWC) merged with the HBC in 1821. As voyageurs travelled from their homes in Lower Canada to the Native interior, they underwent continuous transformations in identity and their culture came to be shaped by liminality.[5] Voyageur culture was also structured by masculinity. The cluster of values that permeated voyageur culture and became markers of the ideal man included being tough, daring, risk-taking, hardworking, jovial, and carefree.[6] The voyageurs made direct links between their work and their gendered identity as men. This was a means in which to ground themselves in their passage out of French Canadian society as adolescents, and into the adult world of the exotic and dangerous *pays d'en haut* or "Indian country" where they had to become courageous and tough adventurers. Their masculine identity was influenced by their

Carolyn Podruchny, "Unfair Masters and Rascally Servants? Labour Relations among Bourgeois, Clerks and Voyageurs in the Montreal Fur Trade, 1780–1821," *Labour/Le Travail* 43 (Spring 1999): 43–70. © Canadian Committee on Labour History. Reprinted with the permission of CCLH.

French Canadian peasant and Catholic upbringing, the Native peoples they met in the interior, and of course the hegemonic rule of their masters. Although many voyageurs became freemen (independently trading and living off the land)[7] and joined Native families or emerging métis communities,[8] their occupational culture remained distinct from these groups. Voyageur culture was also different from that of other labour forces, such as the Kahnawake Iroquois, and Orcadians. The men from these groups did not often work together, and language barriers prevented close communication.

As the fur trade in North America varied tremendously during its long history and expansive presence, it is not surprising that its paternalistic structure also varied tremendously.[9] Patterns between regions and among different companies changed over time. Fur trade historian Jennifer Brown contends that the managers of Montréal companies had greater difficulty in controlling their servants than did the HBC officers. The more fortunate HBC officers could rely on the London committee to lay down the standard rules of conduct which served as a basis for governing their men's behaviour. The Montréal companies not only lacked this central disciplining influence, but they also had further obstacles with which to contend. Discipline was not easy to administer while voyageurs traded *en derouine* (out on their own among Native peoples), or on long journeys requiring their support and assistance. Brown goes on to assert that not only were Montréal masters outnumbered by French Canadian voyageurs, but:

> they also generally lacked the vertical social integration that helped to hold the Hudson's Bay men together. Differences of status, without the mitigating prospect of promotion, and of ethnic background meant that relations between the two groups were often characterized more by opposition, bargaining, and counter-bargaining, than by solidarity. In addition, the French Canadians could draw on a

long tradition of independent behaviour, social and sexual, in the Indian country.[10]

The particular form of paternalism in the post-Conquest Montréal fur trade was shaped by the high degree of control exercised by voyageurs in the labour system. Flexibility in contracts, frequent labour shortages, and continual re-postings gave the voyageurs bargaining power. Voyageurs' power was also augmented by isolation which increased their masters' dependence on them.

Burley challenges Brown's characterization of the HBC workforce as more rigidly controlled and less independent than the French Canadian voyageurs. She contends the Orcadians opposed and bargained with their masters like the voyageurs.[11] Although the culture of voyageurs was distinct from other fur trade labourers, all engaged in similar types of resistance and agency. These correlations are worth serious note, but the fractured nature of the sources prevents scholars from arguing convincingly that voyageurs were either more or less independent and "rascally" than other fur trade labourers. The partners and clerks in the NWC did not keep detailed or consistent reports of their activities at fur trade posts, and they commented less on the behaviour of their men. It is thus difficult to compare quantitatively the extent to which voyageurs and other fur trade labourers resisted the rule of their masters. This paper instead focuses on the nature and patterns of voyageur and master relations, providing comparisons with other fur trade labourers where possible.

After the 1763 conquest of New France, the fur trade operating out of Montréal reorganized under the direction of Scottish, English, American, and a few French Canadian managers who called themselves *bourgeois*.[12] These companies, which eventually merged into the NWC, hired French Canadian men mainly from parishes around Montréal and Trois-Rivières to transport goods and furs from Montréal to the North American interior during the summer months.

They were also hired to work year-round at the company posts and handled trading with Native peoples. There is no question that the job of voyageurs was difficult. They performed near miraculous feats of transporting goods and furs over immense distances and undertook challenging canoe routes. Work at the interior posts was easier than that on the summer canoe brigades, but voyageurs were responsible for a tremendous range of duties, which included construction, artisan crafts, hunting, fishing, and trading. Threats to voyageurs' well-being, including starvation and physically debilitating overwork, came mostly from the harsh environment, but hostile Native peoples and cruel masters could contribute to the misery. Despite the harsh working and living conditions, voyageurs developed a reputation as strong, capable, and cheerful, although sometimes unreliable, servants. The writings of the bourgeois and clerks working in the trade reveal a deep admiration for their skill and effectiveness as workers, and a tolerance for petty theft and minor insolence.[13] This article concerns itself with two questions: why did voyageurs put up with their tough lot without overt revolt, and what was the substance of the relationship between voyageurs and their masters? Because voyageurs were primarily non-literate and left little record of their experiences, we must rely on the writings of a diverse group of literate outsiders, including the powerful fur trade partners, lowly clerks, and assorted travellers to the north-west interior. A close and extensive examination reveals a complex network of accommodation and resistance in the master and servant relationship. This article maps out some patterns in the period from 1780 to 1821, which was the height of competition between trade companies and the expansion into the interior.

The Montréal fur trade labour system was organized around indentured servitude, paternalism, and cultural hegemony. The fur trade managers and clerks acted as paternal masters directing the labour of voyageurs. Voyageurs signed a legal contract, or *engagement,* which established the framework for the paternal relationship. The principal tenet of the contract dictated that servants obey their masters in exchange for board and wages. Voyageurs and their masters, however, interpreted the contract differently in particular contexts. Their diverging and situational "readings" of the legal contract led to the emergence of a "social contract" which constituted the actual working relationship between the two groups. The "social contract" was expressed in the customs which came to characterize the fur trade workplace and the dialogue between servants and masters over acceptable working conditions. Masters tried to enforce obedience, loyalty, and hard work among voyageurs, while the voyageurs struggled to ensure that their working conditions were fair and comfortable, and that masters fully met their paternal obligations. Voyageurs exercised relative cultural autonomy on the job, and often controlled the workpace and scope of their duties. Their masters, however, maintained ultimate authority by exercising their right to hire and fire voyageurs and by successfully profiting in the trade.

Although masters and servants can be understood as constituting two loose but distinct "classes" within the fur trade, it is important to be aware of the ranges within each class in terms of power, authority, and duty. Some masters were junior clerks, bound in a paternal relationship with senior clerks and partners. These clerks were paid a smaller annual salary than senior bourgeois, and did not hold shares in the partnerships which made up the Montréal fur trading companies. Partners were granted voting privileges in business meetings, in addition to their company shares and higher salaries.[14] *Engagés* also had varying status. At the bottom were seasonally employed summer men, referred to as *mangeurs du lard,* or Porkeaters, who paddled between Montréal and the Great Lakes. Wintering *engagés,* or *hommes du nord,* who paddled canoes to and worked at the interior posts, scorned these greenhorns. Within the canoe, paddlers called middlemen or *milieu,* were subject to the authority of the foreman and steersman, or *devant* and *gouvernail,* who usually acted as canoe and brigade leaders. Some estimates suggest that these *bouts* could earn from one third to five times as much as paddlers.[15] Interpreters and guides, paid usually twice or three times as much as other *engagés,* also assumed more authority by their greater wealth and knowledge.[16]

Although the ethnic divisions did not entirely follow occupational lines, the Montréal bourgeois became more and more British after the 1763 Conquest, while the voyageurs were primarily French Canadians. British discrimination against French Canadians, and fellow-feeling among voyageurs contributed to the social distance between masters and servants. Voyageurs lived within a different cultural ethos than that of the bourgeois, one which emphasized independence, strength, courage, and cultural adaptation rather than profit, obedience, and cultural supremacy. These different frames of reference distanced voyageurs from their masters, and frequently impeded harmonious workplace relations. Despite the range of roles within each group, the division between bourgeois and voyageur, or master and servant, served as a basic social organization of the fur trade.[17] Class, ethnic, and cultural differences operated in conjunction to create a paternalistic and hegemonic labour system.

Masters and servants accepted their positions as rulers and ruled. Voyageurs could challenge the substance and boundaries of their jobs and loyalty to their masters without contesting the fundamental power dynamics. Voyageurs' acceptance of their masters' domination was based on a deeply held belief in the legitimacy of paternalism. Voyageurs certainly became discontented, resisted their masters' authority, and sometimes revolted, but it was outside of their conception of the world to challenge the hegemonic culture.[18] Thus, the structure of cultural

hegemony was not inconsistent with the presence of labour strife. Although voyageurs participated in the formulation of the master and servant relationship, they challenged the terms of their employment and contracts without fundamentally challenging their position in the power relationship. Voyageurs, clerks and bourgeois engaged in a dialogue of accommodation and confrontation as a means of constructing a workable relationship.[19] To assert the power and agency of the voyageurs does not deny the framework of subordination; rather it looks within it. Hegemony did not envelop the lives of the voyageurs and prevent them from defending their own modes of work, play, and rituals. Hegemony offered, in the words of E.P. Thompson, writing of the 18th-century English plebians, a "bare architecture of a structure of relations of domination and subordination, but within that architectural tracery many different scenes could be set and different dramas enacted."[20]

What "scenes of rule" were enacted in the north-west fur trade? The mutuality intrinsic to paternalism and hegemony governed social relations and made up the substance of the "social contract" between the bourgeois and voyageurs in the north west. Each party accepted their roles and responsibilities in the master and servant relationship, but they pressed the boundaries, and tried to shape the relationship to best suit their desires and needs. The difficulty masters encountered in enforcing authority, and the precariousness of survival meant they had to be particularly responsive to their servants. Part of hegemony involved appearances.[21] Masters often engaged in self-consciousness public theatre, while voyageurs offered their own form of counter-theatre. Through this means of communication masters and servants came to accept common ideas of the way things should work. The formula laid out in the labour contracts served as the crux from which both parties tried to digress. In the "social contract," or "ritual theatre," masters attempted to evade their provision of welfare, and the voyageurs tried to ease the strain of their work and to control aspects of the workplace. A dialogue of resistance and accommodation kept the paternalistic relationship fluid and flexible, which was crucial to its resilience. Paternalistic hegemony was constantly being negotiated and, in the fur trade, management authority never came close to being absolute or ubiquitous.

Because the NWC and XY Company (the second most significant of the Montréal companies, hereafter XYC) were co-proprietorships, contracts were made in the names of the various firms or individuals comprising the shareholders and joint partnerships. No engagements were issued specifically in the name of the NWC or XYC, as all of the outfitting was carried out by shareholder partners and firms.[22] The labour contracts of all partnerships, both within and outside of the NWC, however, were remarkably similar. Contracts reveal voyageurs' names, parishes of origin, destinations in the north west, job positions, lengths of term, and salaries. The language of most contracts underscored the paternal nature of the relationship, requiring voyageurs to obey their masters, to work responsibly and carefully, to be honest and well-behaved, to aid the bourgeois in making a profit, and to remain in the service. For example, a contract form for the firm McTavish, McGillivrays & Co., and Pierre de Rocheblave, Ecuïer clearly instructs the *engagé*:

> to take good and proper care, while on routes, and to return to the said places, the merchandise, provisions, furs, utensils, and all the things necessary for the voyage; to serve, obey and to faithfully carry out all [orders] of the said Bourgeois, or all others who represent the Bourgeois, which are required by the present contract, he lawfully and honestly commands, to make his profit, avoid misfortune, warn him if you know of danger; and generally do all that a good and loyal servant must and is obliged to do, without doing any particular

> trading; do not leave or quit the said service, under the pain carried by the laws of this Province, and the loss of your wages.[23]

Masters were bound to pay the voyageurs' wages and provide them with equipment. The substance of the equipment, and the provision of food and welfare for the *engagé*, were rarely specified in contracts, and thus provided one of the few places for obvious negotiation between the masters and servants.[24] Custom came to dictate that equipment consisted of one blanket, one shirt, and one pair of trousers.[25]

In order to enforce the terms of the legal contracts, bourgeois tried to regulate their servants through legal and state sanctions. In January 1778, an official of the NWC sent a memorandum to Governor Guy Carleton asking him "that it be published before the Traders and their Servants that the latter must strictly conform to their agreements, which should absolutely be in writing or printed, and before witnesses if possible, as many disputes arise from want of order in this particular." The memorandum goes on to ask that men be held to pay their debts with money or service and that traders hiring men already engaged to another company should purchase their contracts.[26] Lower Canadian law eventually recognized the legality of notarial fur trade contracts, and a 1796 ordinance forbade *engagés* to transgress the terms or desert the service.[27] In Lower Canada, the legislature empowered Justices of the Peace (JPS) to create and oversee the rules and regulations for master and servant relations.[28]

Bourgeois on occasion turned to the law to enforce the terms of the contract. Voyageurs were charged with breaking contracts, mainly for deserting, rather than for insolence or disobedience.[29] The files of the Court of Quarter Sessions in the District of Montréal reveal a range of cases: voyageurs accepted wages from one employer while already working for another, they obtained advance wages without appearing for the job, and they deserted the service.[30] Cases of voyageur desertion and theft can also be found in the records of the Montréal civil court.[31] In 1803, the British government passed the Canada Jurisdiction Act by which criminal offenses committed in the "Indian territories" could be tried in Lower Canada, and the five JPs named were all prominent fur trade bourgeois, although the court's power remained limited.[32] It is difficult to determine the effectiveness of court action to control workers, especially since prosecution rates have not survived in most of the records. Presumably the bourgeois would not continue to press charges if their efforts did not pay off. Yet pressing charges against voyageurs did not seem to deter them from continuing to desert, cheat contract terms, and steal from their employers.

Other efforts to control workers included cooperation between companies to limit contract-jumping and blacklisting deserters. In 1800 NWC officer William McGillivray wrote to Thomas Forsyth of Forsyth, Ogilvy and McKenzie:

> I agree with you that protecting Deserters would be a dangerous Practice and very pernicious to the Trade and fully sensible of this when any Man belonging to People opposed to The North West Company have happened to come to our Forts, we have told the Master of such to come for them and that they should not be in any way wise prevented from taking them back.

McGillivray assured Forsyth that he was not protecting one of their deserters and had told his master to come and claim him. He went on to discuss the case of the NWC *engagé*, Poudriés, who was allowed to return to Montréal because of ill health on the understanding that he was to pay his debt in Montréal or return to the north west to serve out his time. McGillivray explained that when the NWC discovered that Poudriés

engaged himself to Forsyth, Ogilvy & McKenzie they attempted to arrest him. McGillivray accused Forsyth of protecting him, and requested that he be returned to NWC service or that his debt be paid, continuing:

> With regard to paying advances made to Men I wish to be explicit, we have alwise made it a practice and will continue so to do to pay every shilling that Men whom we hire may acknowl-edge to their former Master such Men being free on the Ground. We hire no Men who owe their Descent considering this a principle not to be deviated from in determining to adhere strictly to it we cannot allow others to treat us in a different manner - if a Man was Free at the Point au Chapeau we do not consider him at liberty to hire until he has gone to it.[33]

McGillivray decided to purchase voyageurs' engagements from their previous masters rather than paying their wages, and warned other fur trade companies against hiring any deserters.[34] The other fur trade companies soon followed suit.[35]

Voyageurs occasionally took their employ-ing masters to court, most often to sue for wages.[36] Cases of this kind were widespread in all sorts of labour contracts in New France and Lower Canada, so it is not surprising that voyageurs followed suit. However, servants were not usually successful in claiming wages for jobs which they had deserted, or where they had dis-obeyed their masters.[37] The colonial government and legal system supported fur trade labour con-tracts, but the contracts were difficult to enforce because of the limits of the policing and justice systems in the north west. Masters thus relied more on the "social contract" which they were constantly negotiating with their servants.

Masters and voyageurs had different views of their "social contract," which frequently resulted in rocky negotiations. They agreed that servants were supposed to obey their masters' requirements to trade successfully in exchange for fair board and wages. Their divergent readings of "the deal" were based on different ideas of what was fair. Establishing a mutual understanding of obligations was easier if servants respected their masters. Servants respected those masters whom they regarded as tough but evenhanded.

How did masters command and maintain their authority? In many historic circumstances, masters turned to physical might or the law as a principal vehicle for hegemony. But at the height of fur trade competition, the arm of the law was short and the high value of labour discouraged masters from physically intimidating their workers. Masters relied on paternalistic authority as an accepted ideology to justify and bolster their might. The ideology was expressed in the "theatre of daily rule."[38] Bourgeois and clerks imposed their authority believing that they were superior and were obliged to control their inferior servants. Masters also contributed to a dominant public discourse of their superiority, or enacted the "theatre of rule" in material ways. They ensured their access to more and better food, fancier clothing, and better sleeping conditions than voyageurs.[39] Further in the interior, away from the larger fur trade administrative centres, bourgeois and clerks had to rely on inexpensive symbols and actions to enforce their authority. Carefully maintained social isolation, differential work roles, control over scarce resources, reputation, and ability all symbolized masters' authority.[40]

Differentiation in work roles was very apparent in travel. Bourgeois were usually passengers aboard canoes, and only helped their men paddle and portage in cases of extreme jeopardy. At times the rituals of travel situated bourgeois at the head of a great procession. In his reminiscences of a fur trading career, Alexander Ross described how the light canoe, used for transporting men and mail quickly through the interior, clearly positioned the bourgeois as a social superior:

The bourgeois is carried on board his canoe upon the back of some sturdy fellow generally appointed for this purpose. He seats himself on a convenient mattress, somewhat low in the centre of his canoe; his gun by his side, his little cherubs fondling around him, and his faithful spaniel lying at his feet. No sooner is he at his ease, than his pipe is presented by his attendant, and he then begins smoking, while his silken banner undulates over the stern of his painted vessel.[41]

HBC surveyor Philip Turnor, both envied and criticized that the NWC

give Men which never saw an Indian One Hundred Pounds pr Annum, his Feather Bed carried in the Canoe, his Tent which is exceedingly good, pitched for him, his Bed made and he and his girl carried in and out of the Canoe and when in the Canoe never touches a Paddle unless for his own pleasure all of these indulgences.[42]

At posts, bourgeois and clerks did not participate in the vigorous round of activities which kept the post functioning smoothly, such as constructing and maintaining houses, building furniture, sleighs and canoes, gathering firewood, hunting, and preparing food. Rather, these masters kept accounts, managed the wares and provisions, and initiated trade with Native peoples.

Bourgeois and clerks were encouraged to keep a distance from their labourers. Junior clerks in particular, whose authority in isolated wintering posts was threatened by experienced labourers, had to establish firm lines of control. When the NWC clerk George Gordon was still a novice, he received advice from a senior clerk, George Moffatt, to be independent, confident, very involved in the trade, and

Mixt. very seldom with the Men, rather retire within yourself, than make them your companions—I do not wish to insinuate that you should be haughty—on the contrary—affability with them at times, may get You esteme, while the observance of a proper distance, will command respect, and procure from them ready obedience to you orders.[43]

In 1807, John McDonald of Garth was sent out as a novice to take over the NWC's Red River Department which was notorious for its corruption and difficult men. A French Canadian interpreter, who had long been in the district managing to secure great authority among voyageurs and Native peoples, had to be reminded by McDonald: "you are to act under me, you have no business to think, it is for me to do so and not for you, you are to obey."[44]

Probably the greatest challenges the bourgeois and clerks faced in asserting authority and controlling workers came from the circumstance of the fur trade itself—the great distances along fur trade routes and between posts, and the difficulties of transportation and communication. The arduous job of traversing an unfamiliar and inhospitable terrain led to frequent accidents. The incomplete nature of the sources obscures any measurement of mortality rates, but the writings of the bourgeois are filled with literally hundreds of cases of trading parties losing their way along routes, injuring themselves or perishing in canoeing accidents, being attacked by bears, and starving, to name a few of the mishaps.[45]

Masters and voyageurs dealt with the danger which infused the fur trade in a particular way. Both social groups idealized strength, toughness, and fortitude. Voyageurs competed with each other to perform awesome feats of dexterity and endurance.[46] They played rough and risk-taking games and tried to push themselves beyond their limits. In doing so, they tried to distract themselves from, and desensitize themselves to the risks inherent in fur trading and the deaths, accidents, and illnesses around them. Rather than being overwhelmed by the danger and tragedy, they made a virtue of necessity and flaunted their indifference. By incorporating manly violence and aggression into daily life, in their competitions and brawling, men could toughen themselves for the challenges of their jobs.[47] For example, in August of 1794, the Athabasca brigade raced the Fort George brigade from the south side to the north side of Lake Winnipeg. Duncan McGillivray, in charge of the Fort George crew, explained that

> The Athabasca Men piqued themselves on a Superiority they were supposed to have over the other bands of the North for expeditions marching [canoeing], and ridiculed our men *a la facon du Nord* for pretending to dispute a point that universally decided in *their* favor.

Despite the fact that the Fort George crew was more heavily loaded than the Athabasca crew, the two groups were evenly matched. They pressed on for 48 hours before agreeing to call a truce and set up camp on shore. Not surprisingly, McGillivray was delighted with their progress.[48] During a return trip to Montréal in 1815, John McDonald's crew of Canadians raced McGillivray's crew of Iroquois all day. The Canadians allowed the Iroquois to pull ahead at the start of the day, but they raced past them in the evening.[49]

Bourgeois encouraged the "rugged" ethos of the voyageurs, which conveniently suited their agenda for quick, efficient, and profitable fur trade operations.[50] In some instances, bourgeois had to remind voyageurs of their manly pride in skill and endurance. During a particularly difficult journey, Alexander Mackenzie began to hear murmurs of discontent. The desire to turn back increased when one of the canoes was lost in a stretch of rapids. In order to encourage them to continue, Mackenzie

> brought to their recollection, that I did not deceive them, and that they were made

acquainted with the difficulties and dangers they must expect to encounter, before they engaged to accompany me. I also urged the honour of conquering disasters, and the disgrace that would attend them on their return home, without having attained the object of the expedition. Nor did I fail to mention the courage and resolution which was the peculiar boast of the North men; and that I depended on them, at that moment, for the maintenance of their character....my harangue produced the desired effect, and a very general assent appeared to go wherever I should lead the way.[51]

Whether or not Mackenzie's "harangue produced the desired effect," it seems clear that both bourgeois and voyageurs valued the strength and courage required to paddle farther into the north west.

Accommodation among voyageurs, clerks and bourgeois made up part of the master and servant relationship. They worked closely for long periods of time, often shared living quarters, and faced many calamities and adventures together. As many disputes were caused by shortages of provisions, the surest way in which bourgeois and clerks could ensure loyalty was to provide plenty of good food for their men. Bourgeois and clerks fostered accommodation by meeting other paternal duties, such as attempting to protect their men from dangers in the workplace, providing medicines, and treating men with respect. Masters also solidified their hegemony through generosity and kindness, reminiscent of a kind of feudal largesse. Extra rations of alcohol and food, known as *regales,* were provided on significant occasions, such as settling accounts and signing new engagements.[52] Routine "rewards," such as the customary provision of drams at portages, were also incorporated into the more tedious aspects of fur trade work.[53] Sometimes masters' generosity was self-interested. When McKay gave his men moose skin to make themselves shoes, mit-

tens, and blankets to last them through the winter, he warned them that "we have a strong opposition to contend with this year" and that they must be ready to go at a moment's notice.[54] His gifts no doubt consolidated his authority, but they also helped the voyageurs to perform their duties more effectively.

Despite these points of accommodation, harmony in the workplace was continually under stress as voyageur resistance to master authority characterized labour relations in the fur trade. Voyageurs' discontents focused on such unsuitable working and living conditions as poor rations, or unreasonable demands by masters. Voyageurs turned to strategies such as complaining to their bourgeois and attempting to bargain for better working conditions to highlight their concerns and initiate change. Like the Orcadians working for the HBC, individual action was a more common form of worker resistance than was organized collective protest.[55]

Complaining by the voyageurs became a form of "counter-theatre," which contested bourgeois hegemonic prerogatives. Just as the bourgeois often asserted their hegemony in a theatrical style, especially with canoe processions, the voyageurs also asserted their presence by "a theatre of threat and sedition."[56] In one illuminating example in the summer of 1804, while trying to travel through low water and marshes, Duncan Cameron's men ceaselessly complained about the miserable conditions and difficulty of the work. They cursed themselves as "Blockheads" for coming to "this Infernal Part of the Country," as they called it, damning the mud, damning the lack of clean water to quench their thirst, and damning the first person who chose that route. Cameron tried to be patient and cheerful with them, as he knew that complaining was their custom.[57] Voyageurs sometimes chose to limit the theatre of resistance to a small, and perhaps more effective scale by complaining to their bourgeois in private, so that they would not appear weak in front of the other men. During a difficult trip from Kaministiquia to Pembina, Alexander Henry the Younger commented that little or nothing was said during the day when the men had "a certain shame or bashfulness about complaining openly," but at night everyone came to complain about bad canoes, ineffective co-workers, and shortages of gum, wattap, and grease.[58] Often voyageurs restricted their complaining in front of their bourgeois to avoid losing favour. If they approached the bourgeois or clerk individually with strategic concerns, their demands were more likely to be met than if they openly abused their masters for unspecified grievances.[59]

When labour was scarce, men often bargained for better wages, both individually and in groups. In a large and organized show of resistance in the summer 1803, men at Kaministiquia refused to work unless they received a higher salary.[60] However, these types of group efforts to increase wages were more rare than the relatively common occurrence of men trying to individually bargain for better remuneration or conditions. Daniel Sutherland of the XYC instructed his recruiting agent in Montréal, St. Valur Mailloux, to refuse demands made by a couple of *engagés* for higher wages, and to appease the men with small presents. One *engagé* named Cartier caused turmoil by telling the XYC wintering partners that Mailloux was hiring men at significantly higher wages and by asking for his pay to be increased to that amount. Sutherland became angry with Mailloux, warning him "Always [offer more to] oarsman and steersman, but never exceed the price that I told you for going and coming [paid to the paddlers]."[61] Voyageurs could refuse to do tasks outside the normal range of their duties without extra pay as a means of increasing their wages.[62] They also frequently demanded better working conditions. Most often their concerns centred on safety, and they could refuse to take unreasonable risks.[63] Men with valued skills and knowledge, such as interpreters and guides, were in the best position

to bargain for better working conditions and more pay.[64] Because fur trade labour was frequently scarce, and the mortality rate was high, skilled men were valued. Masters often overlooked servant transgressions and met servant demands in an effort to maintain their services.

Voyageurs also attempted to deceive their masters by pretending to be ill, or by lying about resources and Native peoples in the area to evade work. It is difficult to judge the extent to which voyageurs tried to trick their masters, especially when they were successful. However, hints of this practice, and suspicions of bourgeois and clerks emerge frequently in fur trade journals, suggesting that the practice was widespread. In December 1818, stationed near the Dauphin River, George Nelson became frustrated with one of his men, Welles, who frequently sneaked in "holiday" time by travelling slowly or claiming to be lost.[65] Less suspecting bourgeois probably did not catch the "dirty tricks" more careful voyageurs played on them regularly. Some masters, however, questioned their men's dubious actions and sent out "spies" to ensure that voyageurs were working honestly.[66] Other deceptions were of a more serious nature. Alexander Mackenzie was suspicious that his interpreters were not telling prospective Native trading partners what Mackenzie intended, which could have serious repercussions for the trade.[67]

When efforts to deceive their masters were frustrated, voyageurs could become sullen and indolent, working slowly and ineffectively, and even openly defying bourgeois orders. In one case in the fall 1800, while trying to set out from Fort Chipewyan, James Porter had to threaten to seize the wages of a man who refused to embark. When the voyageur reluctantly complied he swore that the devil should take him for submitting to the bourgeois.[68] More serious breaches of the master and servant contract included stealing provisions from cargo. Though Edward Umphreville kept up a constant watch over the merchandise in his canoes, a father and son managed to steal a nine gallon keg of mixed liquor.[69] George Nelson described the pilfering of provisions as routine.[70] Men also sometimes stole provisions to give extra food to their girlfriends or wives.[71] For the Orcadians working in the HBC service, Burley characterizes this type of counter-theatre—working ineffectively and deceiving masters—as both a neglect of duty and as an attempt to control the work process.[72] The same applies to the voyageurs.

One area of particular unease between voyageurs and masters was the issue of voyageurs freetrading with Native peoples. Unlike the HBC, the Montréal fur trading companies did not prohibit voyageurs from trading with Native peoples on the side to augment their income; some masters even expected them to do so as long as they did not abuse the privilege.[73] However, masters were often upset to find their men trading with Native peoples, because they wanted to concentrate the profit into their company's hands, and considered freetrading as "contrary to the established rules of the trade and the general practice among the natives."[74] In an 1803 trial over trading jurisdiction, John Charles Stuart, a NWC clerk, testified that when any men brought skins from the wintering grounds for the purpose of trading on their private account, "it was by a Special Favour" granted by their bourgeois, supported in the clause "Part de pactons" in their contracts. Although the practice was customary, the bourgeois retained the right to grant or refuse it.[75] After the 1804 merger of the XYC and NWC, the bourgeois decided to restrict private trade to increase profitability in the newly reformed company. Any man caught with more than two buffalo robes or two dressed skins, or one of each, would be fined 50 livres NW currency, and any employee caught trafficking with "petty traders or Montréal men" would forfeit his wages. The bourgeois were able to enforce this new restriction because the merger had created a surplus of men, so that employment became tenuous, and

many voyageurs were concerned that their contracts would not be renewed.[76] In the minutes of the 1806 annual meeting, NWC partners agreed to ban men from bringing furs out of the interior in order to discourage petty trading.[77]

Voyageurs sometimes moved out of the "counter-theatre of daily resistance" to engage in "swift, direct action" against their masters' rule. Deserting the service was an outright breach of the master and servant contract.[78] Desertion should not be viewed as the single and straightforward phenomenon of voyageurs quitting their jobs. Rather, voyageurs deserted for a variety of purposes. Temporary desertions could provide a form of vacation, a ploy for renegotiating terms of employment, and a means of shopping for a better job. Men deserted when they were ill and needed time to recuperate.[79] Men also deserted when they thought their lives might be in danger, as was the case in March 1805, when servants of both the NWC and XYC ran off from the fishery at Lac La Pluie because they feared the Native people there wanted to kill them.[80] Voyageurs felt they could desert because they had a clear notion of their rights as workers which was instilled by the reciprocal obligations of paternalism. This may be one of the more significant differences between Orcadians working for the HBC and the voyageurs. Orcadians did not desert very often because of the lack of "desirable places to go." Orcadians would most often desert to NWC posts, while voyageurs more often became freemen, joined Native families, or returned to the St. Lawrence valley.[81]

As part of the continual negotiation of the master and servant "social contract," bourgeois and clerks responded to voyageurs' counter-theatre with intense performances of authority. They disciplined their men for transgressions of the master and servant contract, and sought to encourage voyageur obedience. Servant privileges, such as the provision of regales or sale of liquor might be curtailed or denied.[82] Bourgeois and clerks also frequently humiliated and intimidated their men. In one case during a journey to the Peace River in summer 1793, Alexander Mackenzie was confronted with a man who refused to embark in the canoe. He wrote:

> This being the first example of absolute disobedience which had yet appeared during the course of our expedition, I should not have passed it over without taking some very severe means to prevent a repetition of it; but as he had the general character of a simple fellow, among his companions, and had been frightened out of what little sense he possessed, by our late dangers, I rather preferred to consider him as an object of ridicule and contempt for his pusillanimous behaviour; though, in fact, he was a very useful, active, and laborious man.[83]

He also confronted the chief canoe maker during the same trip about his laziness and bad attitude. Mackenzie described the man as mortified at being singled out.[84] This kind of ritualized public shaming reinforced masculine ideals of effectiveness and skill. On an expedition to the Missouri in 1805, one of Larocque's men wished to remain with Charles McKenzie's party. Larocque became angry and told the man his courage failed him like an old woman, which threw the man into a violent fit of anger.[85] On occasion, a voyageur could be whipped for delinquency,[86] and bourgeois and clerks sometimes used the fear of starvation as a means of asserting authority over their men.[87]

In cases of severe dereliction, bourgeois could take the liberty of firing their employees.[88] In some cases, voyageurs were happy to be let go because they desired to become freemen. Nelson fired Joseph Constant, for example, for his "fits of ill humour without cause and Constant went on to become a prosperous independent trader."[89] However, it was a very serious matter when voyageurs decided to quit. Bourgeois and clerks made efforts to recoup deserters, and could punish them with confinement.[90]

The usual difficulties of the weather, accidents, and the constant challenge of the strenuous work could lead to high levels of stress and to anxieties among bourgeois, clerks, and voyageurs. Voyageurs' blunders, lost and broken equipment, and voyageur insolence often exacerbated tensions.[91] Alexander Henry the Younger grew frustrated with one of his men named Desmarrais for not protecting the buffalo he shot from wolves. He grumbled:

> My servant is such a careless, indolent fellow that I cannot trust the storehouse to his care. I made to-day a complete overhaul, and found everything in the greatest confusion; I had no idea matters were so bad as I found them.... Like most of his countrymen, he is much more interested for himself than for his employer.[92]

On rare occasions violence punctuated the generalized tension of master-servant relations in the fur trade. Mutual resentments could lead to brawls between the masters and servants.[93]

More typically tensions in the master and servant relationship were expressed in nastiness and unfairness, rather than violence. Motivated by the desire to save money and gain the maximum benefit from their workers, bourgeois pushed their men to work hard, which could result in ill will. Most serious cases of ill will and injustice concerned bourgeois selling goods to voyageurs at inflated prices and encouraging voyageurs to go into debt as soon as they entered fur trade service. It is difficult to find many instances of "bad faith" in bourgeois writings, as they would not likely dwell on their cruelty as masters, nor reveal their unfair tricks. However, travellers, critics of fur trade companies, and disgruntled employees provide clues. The French Duke de La Rouchefoucault Liancourt, travelling through North America in the late eighteenth century, commented that the NWC encouraged vice among their men by paying them in merchandise, especially luxuries and rum, so that none of them ever earned a decent wage.[94] Lord Selkirk, certainly no fan of the NWC, criticized the bourgeois further for exploiting their men, pointing out that *engagés* often left their French Canadian families in distress, and were unable to provide for them because the cost of goods in the interior was double or triple the price in Lower Canada, and men were usually paid in goods rather than cash. The NWC saved further costs on men's wages by encouraging addiction to alcohol, and then paying wages in rum at inflated prices. The Company placed no ceiling on its men's credit, so that many of them fell deeply into debt.[95]

Despite Selkirk's obvious bias against the NWC, he was not alone in his misgivings about Montréal fur trade company labour practices. As a new clerk in the XYC, George Nelson was instructed to provide any trade goods his men might ask for, and to encourage them to take up their wages in any of the trade goods on board the canoe. Nelson was initially uneasy with this mode of dealing,

> for thought I what is there more unnatural, than to try to the get the wages a poor man for a few quarts of rum, some flour & sugar, a few half fathoms of tobacco, & but verly little Goods who comes to pass a few of his best years in this rascally & unnatural Country to try to get a little money so as to settle himself happily among the rest of his friends & relations.

Eventually Nelson came to justify his participation in this system of exploitation because he felt that the men would ruin themselves anyway, and that most of them were disobedient "blackguards" for whom slavery was too good.[96] Nelson was also surprised that these men could live such a carefree existence while deeply in debt and with few material possessions.[97] His comment reveals one of the deep cultural fissures between masters and servants.

Voyageur responses to the cruelty of bourgeois and clerks could reach intense heights in the ongoing counter-theatre of resistance. Ill will between servants and masters could impede work. Sometimes the tensions were so strong that voyageurs refused to share the fruits of their hunting and fishing with their masters.[98] The more outrageous instances of masters abusing servants could lead to collective resistance among the voyageurs in the form of strikes or mass desertion. When a voyageur named Joseph Leveillé was condemned by the Montréal Quarter Sessions to the pillory for having accepted the wages of two rival fur-trading firms in 1794, a riot ensued. A group made up largely of voyageurs hurled the pillory into the St. Lawrence River and threatened to storm the prison. The prisoner was eventually released and no one was punished for the incident.[99] Voyageurs seemed to have developed a reputation for mob belligerence in Lower Canada. Attorney general Jonathan Sewell warned in a 1795 letter to Lieutenant Colonel Beckworth that officers in Lower Canada should be given greater discretionary power to counter the "riotous inclinations" of the people, especially of the "lawless band" of voyageurs.[100]

Instances of mass riots or collective resistance were not unknown in New France and Lower Canada. However, the small population, diffuse work settings, and not too unreasonable seigneurial dues usually restricted expressions of discontent to individual desertions or localized conflicts.[101] Yet, the instances of collective action could have created a precedent and memory for future mass protest.[102] On occasion voyageurs deserted en masse during cargo transports or exploration missions. In these cases men worked closely in large groups doing essentially the same difficult and dangerous tasks. Communication, the development of a common attitude to work, and camaraderie fostered a collective consciousness and encouraged collective action. In the summer of 1794 a Montréal brigade at Lac La

Pluie attempted to strike for higher wages. Duncan McGillivray explained:

> A few discontented persons in their Band, wishing to do as much mischief as possible assembled their companions together several times on the Voyage Outward & represented to them how much their Interest suffered by the passive obedience to the will of their masters, when their utility to the Company, might insure them not only of better treatment, but of any other conditions which they would prescribe with Spirit & Resolution.

When they arrived at Lac La Pluie the brigade demanded higher wages and threatened to return to Montréal without the cargo. The bourgeois initially prevailed upon a few of the men to abandon the strike. Soon after most of the men went back to work, and the ringleaders were sent to Montréal in disgrace.[103]

Efforts at collective action in the north west did not always end in failure. In his third expedition to the Missouri Country in fall 1805 and winter 1806, Charles McKenzie's crew of four men deserted. They had been lodged with Black Cat, a chief in a Mandan Village, who summoned McKenzie to his tent to inform McKenzie of their desertion. The men had traded away all of their property to Native people and intended to do the same with McKenzie's property, but Black Cat secured it. When McKenzie declared he would punish his men, Black Cat warned that the Native people would defend the voyageurs. When McKenzie tried to persuade the men to return to service, they would not yield.[104] Men who spent their winters in the *pays d'en haut* became a skilled and highly valued labour force and felt entitled to fair working conditions; they were not afraid to work together to pressure the bourgeois.[105]

Despite the occasions of mass actions, voyageurs more often acted individually than collectively. Their most powerful bargaining tool in labour relations was the option of desertion. The decision to desert could be caused by any number of poor working conditions, such as bad food, an unfair master, and difficult journeys. Voyageurs used desertion often as a means of improving their working conditions rather than quitting their jobs. Although bourgeois took voyageurs to court for deserting their contracts, the measure had little effect as voyageurs continued to desert anyway. The option to desert acted as a safety valve, relieving pressure from the master and servant relationship. If voyageurs were very unhappy with their master, they could leave to work for another company, return to Lower Canada, or become freemen. This safety valve worked against a collective voyageur consciousness. Collective action was also hindered because voyageurs valued independence.[106] They left farms where feudal relationships prevailed to enter into contracted servitude, but part of their pull to the north west may have been the promise of a more independent way of life than that on the Lower Canadian farm. Voyageurs idealized freemen and many chose this path, becoming independent hunters and petty traders, living primarily off the land with their Native Families.[107]

Some permanent deserters maintained a casual relationship with fur trading companies, serving the occasional limited contract, or selling furs and provisions. One man, Brunet, was forced to desert because his Native wife insisted on it. He rejoined the company under a freer contract. His wife began again to pressure him to desert the company and live with her Natives relatives.[108] Another man named Vivier decided to quit his contract in November 1798 because he could not stand living with Native people, as he was ordered to do by his bourgeois, John Thomson:

> he says that he cannot live any longer with them & that all the devils in Hell cannot make him return, & that he prefers marching all Winter from one Fort to another rather than Live any Longer with them.

Thomson refused to give him provisions or equipment because in the fall he had provided him with enough to pass the winter. Thomson was frustrated with his behaviour all season, as he had refused to return to the fort when ordered. Vivier had become so disenchanted with the trade that he offered his wife and child to another voyageur, so he could return to Lower Canada, but his wife protested. Thomson finally agreed to provide him with ammunition, tobacco and an axe on credit, and Vivier left the post. It is unclear whether he remained with his Native family. A month and a half later Vivier returned to the post, and appeared to take up work again.[109] Voyageurs may have returned to work for fur trade companies because they could not find enough to eat, or desired the protection that a post provided. Fear of starvation and the dangers of the north west may have discouraged voyageurs from deserting in the first place. In one case, Alexander Henry the Younger came across a pond where André Garreau, a NWC deserter, had been killed in 1801 with five Mandans by a Swiss party.[110]

Although it is difficult to quantify the occurrence of turbulence and accommodation in the relations between masters and servants, negotiations over acceptable labour conditions dominated the north-west fur trade. Masters controlled the workforce by ensuring that all men immediately became indebted to their company, and by being the sole providers of European goods in the interior. Masters also capitalized on the risk-taking and tough masculine ethos to encourage a profitable work pace. However, their best way to maintain order was to impress their men with their personal authority which was garnered by a strong manner, bravery, and effectiveness. Formal symbols, such as dress, ritual celebrations, access to better provisions, and a lighter work load reminded voyageurs of the superior status and power of their bourgeois. This "theatre of daily rule" helped to lay out the substance of the hegemonic structure of paternal authority. Masters also turned to the courts to prosecute their men for breaches of contract, and attempted to cooperate with other companies to regulate the workforce, but these methods were far from successful in controlling their voyageurs. The "social contract" overshadowed the legal contract between masters and servants, establishing an effective working relationship that was key to ensuring a well-functioning trade and high profits.

In turn, voyageurs asserted their cultural autonomy and resisted master authority. Their "counter-theatre" shaped the working environment. Voyageurs generally had very high performance standards for work, which were bolstered by masculine ideals of strength, endurance, and risk-taking. Nonetheless, voyageurs created a space to continually challenge the expectations of their masters, in part through their complaining. They also set their own pace, demanded adequate and even generous diets, refused to work in bad weather, and frequently worked to rule. When masters made unreasonable demands or failed to provide adequate provisions, voyageurs responded by working more slowly, becoming insolent, and occasionally freetrading and stealing provisions. More extreme expressions of discontent included turning to the Lower Canadian courts for justice, but, like the bourgeois and clerks, voyageurs found that their demands were better met by challenging the social, rather than the legal, contract. Their strongest bargaining tool proved to be deserting the service, which they sometimes did *en masse*. Overall, voyageurs acted more individually than collectively, as the option to desert the service acted more as a safety valve against the development of a collective voyageur consciousness.

The master and servant relationship was thus a fragile balance, constantly being negotiated. Ruling-class domination was an on-going process where the degree of legitimation was always uneven and the creation of counterhegemonies remained a live option. E.P. Thompson's emphasis on theatre and the symbolic expression of hegemony ring true for the voyageurs and bourgeois, whose power struggles were as often about respect and authority as about decent wages and provisions.[111] The difficult working conditions, regular fear of starvation, and absence of a police force positioned labour mediation in the forefront of the trade and strengthened the symbolic power of the "theatre of daily rule." The "social contract" between the masters and servants overshadowed their legal contract, and determined the day-to-day relations between the two groups. Frequently, accommodation allowed the fur trade to run smoothly, and voyageurs and bosses cooperated, especially in the face of external threats. Yet just as often, labour disputes and power struggles characterized the trade.

Notes

1   Edith I. Burley, *Servants of the Honourable Company: Work, Discipline, and Conflict in the Hudson's Bay Company, 1770–1879* (Toronto, New York and Oxford: Oxford University Press 1997); Philip Goldring first began to compile information on labourers in *Papers on the Labour System of the Hudson's Bay Company, 1821–1900,* Volume I, Manuscript Report Series, no. 362, Parks Canada, (Ottawa: Ministry of Supply and Services 1979). Also see Ron C. Bourgeault, "The Indian, the Métis and the Fur Trade: Class, Sexism and Racism in the Transition from 'Communism' to Capitalism," *Studies in Political Economy: A Socialist Review,* 12 (Fall 1983), 45–80 and Glen Makahonuk, "Wage-Labour in the Northwest Fur Trade Economy, 1760–1849," *Saskatchewan History,* 41 (Winter 1988), 1–17.

2   For a brief report of master and servant law in a colonial setting see Douglas Hay and Paul Craven, "Master and Servant in England and the Empire: A Comparative Study," *Labour/Le Travail,* 31 (Spring 1993), 175–84.

3   Daniel Francis and Toby Morantz, *Partners in Furs: A History of the Fur Trade in Eastern James Bay, 1600–1870* (Montréal and Kingston: McGill-Queen's University Press), 167.

4   Louise Dechêne uses the term *voyageur* to identify the small-scale independent fur traders, working alone or in small groups, with some financial backing from merchants, from the late 17th century to the mid-18th century. Louise Dechêne, *Habitants and Merchants in Seventeenth-Century Montreal,* trans. Liana Vardi, (Montréal: McGill-Queen's University Press 1992), 94. Later, the term came to be used more widely to refer to contracted labourers, or *engagés.* I use the term *voyageur* interchangeably with *engagé,* servant, and worker.

5   The term "liminal" is used by cultural anthropologists to mean interstitial, implying both margins and thresholds, and a transitional state. The concept was first suggested by Arnold van Gennep in his work *The rites of passage,* trans. by Monika B. Vizedom and Gabrielle L. Caffee, (London: Routledge and Kegan Paul 1909). The concept was further developed by Victor Turner, *The Ritual Process: Structure and Anti-Structure* (Chicago: Aldine, 1969), 94–5 and *Blazing the Trail: Way Marks in the Exploration of Symbols* (Tucson: University of Arizona Press 1992), 48–51. For a theoretical discussion and cross cultural comparisons of *communitas* or the development of community in liminal spaces see Turner, *The Ritual Process,* 96–7, 125–30 and *Blazing the Trail,* 58–61.

6   My understanding of masculinity as a category for historical analysis is informed by Joan Scott, "Gender: A Useful Category of Historical Analysis," *American Historical Review,* 91 (December 1986), 1053–75 and R.W. Connell, *Masculinities* (Berkeley and Los Angeles: University of California Press 1995), 67–92.

7   John E. Foster, "Wintering, the Outsider Adult Male and the Ethnogenesis of the Western Plains Métis," *Prairie Forum,* 19, 1 (Spring 1994), 1–13.

8   See Jacqueline Peterson and Jennifer S.H. Brown, eds., *The New Peoples: Being and Becoming Métis in North America* (Winnipeg: University of Manitoba Press 1985) and Gerhard J. Ens, *Homeland to Hinterland: The Changing Worlds of the Red River Métis in the Nineteenth Century* (Toronto: University of Toronto Press 1997).

9   See Palmer, *Working-Class Experience,* 41–51.

10 Brown, *Strangers in Blood,* 88.

11 Burley, *Servants of the Honourable Company,* 15–16.

12 The term "bourgeois" was used in 18th- and 19th-century Canada to refer to the Montreal fur trade merchants and managers, which included company partners and all but the most junior clerks.

13 For a representative example see W. Kaye Lamb, ed., *Sixteen Years in Indian Country: The Journal of Daniel Williams Harmon, 1800–1816* (Toronto: The MacMillan Company of Canada 1957), 197–98.

14 Toronto, Ontario Archives (hereafter OA), North West Company Collection (hereafter NWCC), MU 2199, Box 4, No. 1 (photostat of original), "An Account of the Athabasca Indians by a Partner of the North West Company, 1795," revised 4 May 1840 (Forms part of the manuscript entitled "Some Account of the North West Company," by Roderick McKenzie, director of the North West Company. Original at McGill Rare Books (hereafter MRB), Masson Collection (hereafter MC), C.18, Microfilm reel #22. Photostat can also be found at National Archives of Canada (hereafter NAC), MC, MG19 C1, Vol. 55, Microfilm reel #C-15640); 51.

15 George Heriot, *Travels Through the Canadas, Containing a Description of the Picturesque Scenery on Some of the Rivers and Lakes; with an Account of the Productions, Commerce, and Inhabitants of those Provinces* (Philadelphia: M. Carey 1813), 254; and MRB, MC, C.27, Microfilm reel #13, Roderick McKenzie, Letters Inward [all the letters are from W. Ferdinand Wentzel, Forks, McKenzie River], 1807–1824, pp. 3, 23.

16 "An Account of the Athabasca Indians by a Partner of the North West Company, 1795," p. 51; and Alexander Mackenzie, Esq., "A General History of the Fur Trade from Canada to the North-West," *Voyages from Montréal on the River St. Laurence through the Continent of North America to the Frozen and Pacific Oceans in the Years 1789 and 1793 with a Preliminary Account of the Rise, Progress, and Present State of the Fur Trade of that Country,* (London: R. Noble, Old Bailey 1801), 34.

17 Brown, *Strangers in Blood* 35, 45–8. Also see E.P. Thompson's discussion of "patricians" and "plebs" in *Customs in Common: Studies in Traditional Popular Culture* (New York: The New Press 1993), 16–17.

18 For a discussion on cultural hegemony and the consent of the masses to be ruled, see T. J. Jackson Lears, "The Concept of Cultural Hegemony: Problems and Possibilities," *American Historical Review,* 90 (June 1985), 567–593.

19 Edith Burley also found that the relationship between masters and servants in the HBC was constantly subject to negotiation. Burley, *Servants of the Honourable Company,* 110–11.

20 Thompson, *Customs in Common,* 85–6.

21 This is suggested by Thompson, *Customs in Common,* 45–6.

22 Lawrence M. Lande, *The Development of the Voyageur Contract (1686–1821)* (Montréal: McLennan Library, McGill University 1989), 41.

23 Winnipeg, Provincial Archives of Manitoba (hereafter PAM), Fort William Collection (hereafter FWC), MG1 C1; fo. 33, contract form for McTavish, McGillivrays & Co. My translation.

24 For examples see Joseph Defont's 1809 contract with the North West Company, PAM, FWC, MG1 C1, fo. 32–1 and the contract of Louis Santier of St. Eustache with Parker, Gerrard, Ogilvy, & Co. as a *milieu* to transport goods between Montréal and Michilimackinac, 21 Avril [*sic*] 1802, NAC, MG19 A51.

25 Mackenzie, "A General History," 34.

26 NAC, Haldimand Papers, "Memorandum for Sir Guy Carleton," 20 January 1778, cited by Harold Adams Innis, *The Fur Trade in Canada* (Toronto: University of Toronto Press 1956, first published in 1930), 221.

27 *Ordinances and Acts of Quebec and Lower Canada,* 36 George III, chpt. 10, 7 May 1796.

28 Grace Laing Hogg and Gwen Shulman, "Wage Disputes and the Courts in Montreal, 1816–1835," in Donald Fyson, Colin M. Coates and Kathryn Harvey, eds., *Class, Gender and the Law in Eighteenth- and Nineteenth-Century Quebec: Sources and Perspectives* (Montréal: Montréal History Group 1993), 129.

29 For one example see Montréal, McCord Museum of Canadian History, North West Company Papers, M17607, M17614, Deposition of Basil Dubois, 21 June 1798, and Complaint of Samuel Gerrard, of the firm of Parker, Gerrard and Ogilvie against Basil Dubois.

30 Montréal, Archives nationales de Québec, dépôt de Montréal (hereafter ANQM), Court of Quarter Sessions of the District of Montréal, TL32 S1 SS1, Robert Aird vs. Joseph Boucher, 1 April 1785, JP Pierre Foretier; Atkinson Patterson vs. Jean-Baptiste Desloriers dit Laplante, 21 April 1798, JP Thomas Forsyth; and Angus Sharrest for McGillivray & Co. vs. Joseph Papin of St. Sulpice, 14 June 1810, JP J-M Mondelet. These cases were compiled by Don Fyson as part of a one in five sample of the whole series.

31 ANQM, Cours des plaidoyers communs du district de Montréal (hereafter CPCM), Cour du samedi (matières civiles superieurs), TL16 S4/00005, pp. 37, 27 mars 1784, JPs Hertelle De Rouville and Edward Southouse; and TL16 S4/00002, no page numbers, 2 Avril 1778, JPs Hertelle De Rouville and Edward Southouse.

32 The JPs were William McGillivray, Duncan McGillivray, Sir Alexander Mackenzie, Roderick McKenzie, and John Ogilvy. Marjorie Wilkins Campbell, The *North West Company* (Toronto: MacMillan Company of Canada 1957), 136–7.

33 NAC, North West Company Letterbook, 1798–1800 (hereafter NWCL), MG19 B1, vol. 1, p. 131, William McGillivray to Thomas Forsyth, Esq., Grand Portage, 30 June 1800.

34 NAC, NWCL, MG19 B1, vol. 1, pp. 152–3, William McGillivray to McTavish, Frobisher and Company, Grand Portage, 28 July 1800.

35 NAC, Letterbook of Sir Alexander McKenzie and Company, kept by Daniel Sutherland (hereafter LAMC), p. 40, D. Sutherland to Henry Harou, 15 May 1803.

36 ANQM, CPCM, Cour du vendredi (matières civiles inferieurs), TL16 S3/00001, p. 41, 314–25, 3 juillet 1770 and 3 juillet 1778, JPs Hertelle De Rouville and Edward Southouse; and TL16 S3/00008, no page numbers, 13 janvier 1786, JPs Hertelle De Rouville and Edward Southouse, 6 octobre 1786 (followed by several other entries later in the month), JPs John Fraser, Edward Southouse and Hertelle De Rouville, and 27 octobre 1786, JPs Edward Southouse and Hertelle De Rouville; and Eliot Coues, ed. *New Light on the Early History of the Greater Northwest: The Manuscript Journals of Alexander Henry* (Minneapolis: Ross and Haines 1897), vol. 2, 860–1, Sunday, 27 March 1814.

37 Hogg and Shulman, "Wage Disputes and the Courts in Montréal" 128, 132, 135–40, 141–3.

38 Thompson, *Customs in Common,* 43, 45–6.

39 Elizabeth Vibert, *Traders' Tales: Narratives of Cultural Encounters in the Columbia Plateau, 1807–1846* (Norman and London: University of Oklahoma Press 1997), 110–12.

40 James Scott Hamilton, "Fur Trade Social Inequality and the Role of Non-Verbal Communication," Ph.D. Thesis, Simon Fraser University, 1990, 138, 261–3.

41 Alexander Ross, *Fur Hunters of the Far West; A Narrative of Adventures in Oregon and the Rocky Mountains* (London: Smith, Elder and Co. 1855), 1: 301–2.

42 J.B. Tyrrell, ed. *Journals of Samuel Hearne and Philip Turnor* (Toronto: Champlain Society 1934), Journal III, "A Journal of the most remarkable Transactions and Occurrences from York Fort to Cumberland House, and from said House to York Fort from 9th Septr 1778 to 15th Septr 1779 by Mr Philip Turnor," 15 July 1779, 252.

43 OA, George Gordon Papers, MU 1146G, Moffatt, Fort William, to George Gordon, Monontagué, 25 July 1809. See also Hamilton, "Fur Trade Social Inequality," 135–6. Burley found a similar pattern in the HBC, Burley, *Servants of the Honourable Company,* 122–3.

44 NAC, Autobiographical Notes of John McDonald of Garth, 1791–1815, written in 1859, photostat, MG19 A17, pp. 119–21. The original can be found at MRB, MS 406, and a typescript can be found at the OA, MU 1763.

45 For a few examples of becoming lost see MRB, MC, C.8, microfilm reel #14, Alexander McKenzie, Journal of Great Bear Lake, 18–26 June 1806, p. 20; MRB, MC, Journal of John MacDonell, Assiniboines-Rivière qu'Appelle, 1793–95, Thursday, 13 March 1794 and Monday, 8 December 1794, pp. 11, 22; and OA, Company of Temiscamingue, Microfilm #MS65, Donald McKay, Journal from January 1805 to June 1806, Thursday, 12 September 1805, p. 32 (I added page numbers). For examples of canoeing accidents see NAC, MC, MG19 C1, vol. 1, microfilm reel #C-15638, Charles Chaboillez, "Journal for the Year 1797," Wednesday, 16, 19 and 31 August 1797, pp. 4, 6; NAC, MC, MG19 C1, vol. 4, Microfilm reel #C-15638, William McGillivray, "Rat River Fort Near Rivière Malique...," 9 September 1789 to 13 June 1790 (written transcript precedes original on reel, both badly damaged), pp. 73–4; and NAC, MC, MG19 C1, vol. 8, Microfilm reel #C-15638, W. Ferdinand Wentzel, "A Journal kept at the Grand River, Winter 1804 & 1805," 9 October 1804, p. 9. On bear attacks see Toronto, Metropolitan Reference Library, Baldwin Room (hereafter MRL BR), S13, George Nelson's Journal "No. 7," describing the Lake Winnipeg district in 1812, written as a reminiscence, pp. 283–4; NAC, MG19 A17, Autobiographical Notes of John McDonald of Garth, 1791–1815, written in 1859 (photostat), pp. 54–5, 65–6; and "First Journal of Simon Fraser from April 12th to July 18th, 1806," Appendix B, *Public Archives Report for 1929,* pp. 109–45, (transcript from a copy at University of California at Berkeley, Bancroft Collection, Pacific Coast Mss., Series C, No. 16; copy also at NAC,

MG19 A9, Simon Fraser Collection, vol. 4; originals at the Provincial Archives of British Columbia), Sunday 13 July 1806, pp. 143–4. On starvation see MRB, MC, C.24, Microfilm reel #2, Archibald Norman McLeod, Journal kept at Alexandria, 1800, Thursday, 19 February 1801, p. 22; NAC, MG19 A14, Microfilm reel #M-130, John Stuart, Journal kept at North West Company Rocky Mountain House, 1805–6 (original at Provincial Archives of British Columbia), Saturday, 1 February 1806, p. 20; and MRL BR, S13, George Nelson's Journal "No. 5," June 1807–October 1809, written as a reminiscence, dated 7 February 1851, pp. 209–10.

46 Coues, ed., *New Light,* 1: 11 August 1800, pp. 30–1; MRL BR, S13, George Nelson's diary of events on a journey from Cumberland House to Fort William, part in code, 3 June–11 July 1822 (notes taken from a transcription made by Sylvia Van Kirk); Tuesday, 9 July 1822; ibid., Nelson's diary of events on a journey from Fort William to Cumberland House, 21 July–22 August 1822 (notes taken from a transcription made by Sylvia Van Kirk); Monday, 19 August 1822; and Alexander Ross, *Fur Hunters of the Far West: A Narrative of Adventures in Oregon and the Rocky Mountains* (London: Smith, Elder and Co. 1855), II: 236–7.

47 Elliot J. Gorn describes this pattern as well in "Gouge and Bite, Pull hair and Scratch: The Social Significance of Fighting in the Southern Backcountry," *American Historical Review,* 90 (Feb. 1985), 18–43.

48 Arthur S. Morton, ed., *The Journal of Duncan McGillivray of the North West Company at Fort George on the Saskatchewan, 1794–5* (Toronto: The MacMillan Company of Canada Limited 1929), 11.

49 NAC, Autobiographical Notes of John McDonald of Garth, 215.

50 In a different case, Gunther Peck found that middle class commentators condemned miners' penchant for risk-taking in late 19th century Nevada. Gunther Peck, "Manly Gambles: The Politics of Risk on the Comstock Lode, 1860–1880," *Journal of Social History,* 26 (Summer 1993), 701–23.

51 See entries Friday, 31 May 1793 and Thursday, 13 June 1793, Mackenzie, *Voyages from Montréal,* 285, 295–6, 322–6.

52 For examples see Coues, ed., *New Light,* vol. 1, 10, 243, 23 July 1800 and 6 May 1804; Lamb, ed., *Sixteen Years,* 105, Sunday, 19 July 1807; and Ross Cox, *Adventures on the Columbia River* (New York: J. & J. Harper 1832), 304–5, 19 September 1817.

53 For examples see NAC, MC, MG19 C1, vol. 1, microfilm reel #C-15638, p. 3, Friday, 11 August 1797, Charles Chaboillez, "Journal for the Year 1797"; NAC, MC, MG19 C1, vol. 9, Microfilm reel #C-15638, p. 16, Unidentified North West Company Wintering Partner, "Journal for 1805 & 6, Cross Lake," Sunday, 10 November 1805; MRB, MC, C.1, microfilm reel #55, p. 66, Duncan Cameron, "The Nipigon Country," with extracts from his journal in the Nipigon, 1804–5, (also found in the OA, photostat, MU 2198 Box 3, Item 3; and in triplicate typescript, MU 2200, Box 5 (a–c)); and Mackenzie, *Voyages from Montréal,* 325, Thursday, 13 June 1793.

54 Approximately 20 June 1807, described in TMRL, BR, S13, p. 186, George Nelson's Journal "No. 5," June 1807–October 1809, written as a reminiscence, dated 7 February 1851.

55 Burley, *Servants of the Honourable Company,* 118–20.

56 E.P. Thompson, *Customs in Common,* 67.

57 Cameron, "The Nipigon Country," 38–39.

58 Coues, ed. *New Light,* 1: 247–8, 28 July 1804.

59 A blacksmith named Philip earned the wrath of his bourgeois, McKay, when he abused him both behind his back and to his face. Nelson, Journal "No. 5," 2 (labelled p. 186). George Nelson felt pressured by the continual complaints made by his men about their rations. He worried that his men were spreading discontent among each other and preferred them to approach him directly with their concerns. Nelson, "A Daily Memoranda," p. 8, Friday, 10 February 1815.

60 Mentioned in Coues, ed., *New Light,* 1: 247, 1 July 1804.

61 NAC, LAMC, 1802–9, vol. 1, MG19 A7, pp. 18–19, 25–26, D. Sutherland to Monsr. St. Valur Mailloux, Montréal, 10 November 1802, 29 November 1802, and 20 December 1802, (originals in the Seminaire de Quebec). My translation.

62 For one example of men demanding their pay be doubled for extra duties see Chaboillez, "Journal for the Year 1797," 49, Tuesday, 20 March 1798.

63 MRB, MC, C.27, Microfilm reel #13, p. 2, Athabasca Department, Great Slave Lake, W.F. Wentzel to Roderick McKenzie, Letters Inward, 1807–1824, 5 April 1819.

64 NAC, MC, MG19 C1, vol. 3, microfilm reel #C-15638, pp. 8–15, François-Antoine Larocque, "Missouri Journal, Winter 1804–5"; and Nelson, "A Daily Memoranda," pp. 30–2, Saturday, 8 April 1815.

65 See entries Monday, 2 November 1818, and from Tuesday, 1 December 1818 to Wednesday, 30 December 1818, OA, MU 842, pp. 10–11, 18–23, Diary of George Nelson, in the service of the North West Company at Tête au Brochet, 1818–19.

66 NAC, MC, MG19 C1, vol. 15, Microfilm reel #C-15638, p. 7, Fragment of a journal, attributed to W. Ferdinand Wentzel, kept during an expedition from 13 June to 20 August 1800, Friday, 26 June 1800.

67 MRB, MC, C.8, microfilm reel #14, p. 125, Alexander Mackenzie, Journal of Great Bear Lake, March 1806.

68 On trip from Athabasca to the McKenzie River, NAC, MC, MG19 C1, vol. 6, Microfilm reel #C-15638, p. 50, James Porter, Journal kept at Slave Lake, 18 February 1800 to 14 February 1801, 29 September 1800. Porter quotes the man as saying "Si Je avait Point des gages que le Diable ma aport si vous ma Soucier Embarker." See also John Thompson, who records that this man, named Bernier, gave further trouble to Porter on the trip. Thompson's interpretation of Bernier's swearing is "swearing the Devel myte take him if he had stirred a Step." See entries Monday, 29 September 1800 to Saturday, 4 September 1800, MRB, MC, C.26, Microfilm reel #15, pp. 1–2, John Thompson, "Journal, Mackenzies River alias Rocky Mountain, 1800–1."

69 OA, NWCC, MU 2199, p. 8, photostat of original, Edward Umfreville, "Journal of a Passage in a Canoe from Pais Plat in Lake Superior to Portage de L'Isle in Rivière Ouinipique," June to July 1784, Wednesday, 23 June 1784. Forms part of the manuscript entitled "Some Account of the North West Company," by Roderick McKenzie, director of the North West Company. Typescripts can be found also in the OA, NWCC, MU 2200, Box 5, Nos. 2 (a), (b), and (c). Photostats and typescripts can also be found in NAC, MC, vol. 55, Microfilm reel #C-15640; the MRB, MC, C.17; and the MHS, P1571. For other examples of theft see MRB, MC, C.24, Microfilm reel #2, p. 5, Archibald Norman McLeod, Journal kept at Alexandria, 1800, Friday, 28 November 1800; OA, Angus Mackintosh Papers; MU 1956, Box 4, pp. 2–3, Journal from Michilimackinac to Montréal via the French River, summer 1813, 16 July 1813; and NAC, MC, MG19 C1, vol. 2, microfilm reel # C-15638, p. 10, Michel Curot, "Journal, Folle Avoine, Riviere Jaune, Pour 1803 & 1804," Lundi, 11 octobre 1803.

70 TMRL, BR, S13, p. 9, George Nelson's Journal "No. 1," written as a reminiscence, describing a journey from Montréal to Grand Portage, and at Folle Avoine, 27 April 1802–April 1803 (a typescript

can also be found in the George Nelson Papers of the TMRL, BR).

71 Coues, ed., New Light, 1: 25, 6 August 1800.

72 Burley, Servants of the Honourable Company, 139–44.

73 Mackenzie, "A General History," 34. On the HBC prohibition of private trading see Burley, Servants of the Honourable Company, 24–25. However, Burley suggests that the lack of reporting on this offense may indicate that the officers tacitly allowed their men to do so (144–52).

74 Described by Ross, Fur Hunters, 1: 159.

75 MHS, GLNP, Folder 7, P791, p. 2, NWC Letters, 1798–1816, Dominique Rousseau and Joseph Bailley v. Duncan McGillivray, (originals from the Judicial Archives of Montréal).

76 Campbell, The North West Company, 155.

77 Wallace, W. Stewart, ed., Documents Relating to the North West Company (Toronto: Champlain Society 1934), Minutes of the Meetings of the NWC at Grand Portage and Fort William, 1801–7, with Supplementary Agreements (originals in Montréal, Sulpician Library, Baby Collection), 216, 15 July 1806.

78 For an example see MRB, MC, C. 7, microfilm reel #4, p. 4, Journal of John MacDonell, Assiniboines-Riviere qu'Appelle, 1793–95, (typescript copy in NAC, MC, MG 19 C1, vol. 54, microfilm reel #C-15640), 5 December 1793 to 6 December 1793.

79 McLeod, Journal kept at Alexandria, p. 40, Saturday, 30 May 1801; and "The Diary of John Macdonell" in Charles M. Gates, ed., Five Fur Traders of the Northwest (St. Paul: Minnesota Historical Society 1965), 72, 1 June 1793.

80 "The Diary of Hugh Faries" in Gates, ed., Five Fur Traders, 233–34, Monday, 25 March 1805.

81 Burley, Servants of the Honourable Company, 153–4.

82 For example, see McLeod, Journal kept at Alexandria, 15, Friday, 2 January 1801.

83 Mackenzie, Voyages from Montréal, 329, Saturday, 15 June 1793.

84 passim, pp. 373–4, Saturday, 29 June 1793.

85 MRB, MC, C.12, Microfilm reel #6, p. 41, Charles McKenzie, "Some Account of the Missouri Indians in the years 1804, 5, 6 & 7," addressed to Roderick McKenzie, 1809. Photostat and typescript copies can be found in NAC, MC, MG19 C1, vol. 59, Microfilm reel #C-15640 and OA, NWCC, MU2204, vol. 3 and MU2200 Box 5-4 (a), and the account is published by W. Raymond Wood and

Thomas D. Thiessen, eds., *Early Fur Trade on the Northern Plains: Canadian Traders Among the Mandan and Hidatsa Indians, 1738–1818; The narratives of John Macdonell, David Thompson, François-Antoine Larocque, and Charles McKenzie* (Norman: University of Oklahoma Press 1985).

86 For one example see McLeod, Journal kept at Alexandria, Saturday, 22 November 1800.

87 Nelson, Journal No. 1, p. 43, Saturday, 17 November 1809.

88 Nelson, "A Daily Memoranda," 8, Friday, 10 February 1815; and "The Diary of Hugh Faries," p. 235, Tuesday, 2 April 1805.

89 TMRL, BR S13, pp. 14–15, George Nelson's Coded Journal, 17 April–20 October 1821, entitled "A continuation of My Journal at Moose Lake," (notes made by Sylvia Van Kirk), Thursday, 10 May 1821. Constant had been threatening to desert the service for years, and he did make arrangements with another bourgeois, William Connolly, to leave the service. ibid., Thursdays, 10 and 24 May 1821, pp. 14–15, 20.

90 "The Diary of Hugh Faries," p. 206, Sunday, 26 August 1804.

91 Coues, ed., *New Light,* 1: 114, 9 October 1800.

92 *passim,* pp. 99–100, 18–19 September 1800.

93 Cox, *Adventures,* 166–7.

94 *Voyages dans l'Amerique par la Rouchefoucould Liancourt,* Vol. II, 225, Paris, An. 7.; cited by Thomas Douglas, Earl of Selkirk, *A Sketch of the British Fur Trade in North America; with Observations Relative to the North-West Company of Montréal,* 2nd edition (London: James Ridgway 1816), 36–7.

95 Selkirk, *A Sketch of the British Fur Trade,* 32–47.

96 Nelson, Journal, 13 July 1803–25 June 1804, 1–2, 34, Friday, 15 July 1803.

97 TMRL, BR, S13, pp. 7–9, George Nelson, Tête au Brochet, to his parents, 8 December 1811.

98 Nelson, "A Daily Memoranda," pp. 17–18, 40–1, Thursday, 9 March 1815, Tuesday, 23 May 1815 and Wednesday, 24 May 1815.

99 NAC, "Civil Secretary's Letter Books, 1788–1829," RG7, G15C, vol. 2, CO42, vol. 100, Sheriff Edward Gray to Attorney General James Monk, 9 June 1794; J. Reid to same, 12 June 1794; T.A. Coffin to James McGill, 21 July 1794; cited by

F. Murray Greenwood, *Legacies of Fear: Law and Politics in Quebec in the Era of the French Revolution* (Toronto: University of Toronto Press 1993), 80, 285.

100 NAC, Jonathan Sewell Papers, MG23 GII10, vol. 9, pp. 4613–14, Jonathan Sewell to Lieutenant Colonel Beckworth, 28 July 1795. Donald Fyson brought this reference to my attention.

101 Terence Crowley, "'Thunder Gusts': Popular Disturbances in Early French Canada," *Canadian Historical Association Historical Papers* (1979), 11–31; and Jean-Pierre Hardy et David-Thiery Ruddel, *Les Apprentis Artisans à Québec, 1660–1815* (Québec: Les Presses de L'Université du Québec 1977), 74–80.

102 Jean-Pierre Wallot, *Un Québec qui Bougeait: trame socio-politique du Québec au tournant du XIXe siècle* (Montréal: Boréal 1973), 266–7.

103 Morton, ed., *The Journal of Duncan McGillivray,* 6–7.

104 Charles McKenzie, "Some Account of the Missouri Indians," 72, 77–8.

105 MRB, MC, C.5, Microfilm reel #5, abridged version on Microfilm reel #6, pp. 75, 79, Alexander Henry the Younger, travels in the Red River Department, 1806, Saturday, 26 July 1806 and Thursday, 7 August 1806.

106 Alexander Ross, *Fur Hunters of the Far West; A Narrative of Adventures in the Oregon and Rocky Mountains,* 2 vols. (London: Smith, Elder and Co. 1855), II: 236–237.

107 Toronto; Metropolitan Reference Library; Baldwin Room; S13; George Nelson, Tête au Brochet, to his parents, 8 December 1811; pp. 9–11; and Ross, *Fur Hunters of the Far West,* 1: 291–93.

108 Nelson, Journal, 13 July 1803–25 June 1804, pp. 22–3, Monday, 31 January 1804, Monday, 14 February 1804, Tuesday, 15 February 1804, and Thursday, 17 February 1804.

109 NAC, MC, MG19 C1, vol. 7, Microfilm reel #C-15638, pp. 19–24, John Thomson, "A Journal kept at Grand Marais ou Rivière Rouge, 1798," Sunday, 18 November 1798, Monday, 19 November 1798, Tuesday, 20 November 1798, and Friday, 4 January 1799.

110 Henry, Travels in the Red River Department, p. 50, Wednesday, 23 July 1806.

111 Thompson, *Customs in Common,* 74–5.

Voices of Smallpox around the Strait of Georgia

Cole Harris

Well, it's a good thing to study these things back, you know. Like the way the people died off. (Jimmy Peters, Chawathil, 1986)[1]

The old Indians grow quite pathetic sometimes when they touch upon this subject. They believe their race is doomed to die out and disappear. They point to the sites of their once populous villages, and then to the handful of people that constitute the tribe of today, and shake their heads and sigh. (Charles Hill-Tout, 1904)[2]

Demographic collapse, in short, led to widespread settlement discontinuity. To grasp the implications of such discontinuity, one must imagine what almost total depopulation would mean in Italy or Spain ca. 1500—silent villages, decaying cities, fields lying waste, orchards overgrown with brush. (Karl W. Butzer, 1992)[3]

It is now clear that Europeans carried diseases wherever they went in the Western Hemisphere, and that among genetically similar peoples with no immunity to introduced viruses and bacteria, the results were catastrophic.[4] In the century or so after Columbus, the population of the Western Hemisphere fell by some 90 per cent according to current estimates.[5] For all the tyrannies of conquerors and colonists, diseases apparently had far more telling demographic effects.

In British Columbia, little enough is known about contact-related disease and depopulation. Whites have told other stories, ethnographers have encouraged Native informants to describe "traditional" ways, and the few recorded Native accounts of disease have been treated as myths. Today, as political debates about Native government and land claims intensify, and as appeals proceed through the courts, questions of disease and depopulation are explicitly repoliticized— which does not make listening easier.[6] For a society preoccupied with numbers, scale, and progress, more people imply fuller, more controlled occupation of land. Thus, it has been in the interest of non-Natives to suggest small pre- or early-contact Native populations, and in the interest of Natives to suggest much larger ones. A disinterested position may not exist. Yet there are Native accounts of disease, many of them long pre-dating current political and legal calculations, as well as numerous references to disease by white explorers and traders.

In this article, I consider Coast Salish accounts of pre-contact smallpox around the Strait of Georgia, the body of water between southern Vancouver Island and the mainland, and in adjacent parts of Puget Sound and the lower Fraser Valley (map 1). Even today there may be more smallpox stories in circulation, or fragments of stories partly remembered, but these are the ones that have been recorded and made public. A comparison of these Native stories with early white accounts suggests that, in different ways and from different vantage points, they describe the same events. From this insight, coupled with information from the Plains, I conclude that smallpox reached the Strait of Georgia in 1782 and that its effects were devastating. I then consider whether useful estimates of immediate pre-smallpox population are possible, and end by asking why this epidemic has been so invisible: What does it mean that whites have lived for several generations alongside the Coast Salish without understanding—without apparently wanting to understand—that Native people had been decimated by smallpox before Vancouver and Galiano sailed into the Strait of Juan de Fuca?

Although the introduction of smallpox to the Strait of Georgia was part of a hemispheric tragedy, there is no simple line from the Caribbean at the end of the fifteenth century to the Northwest Coast at the end of the eighteenth. The course, effects, and social construction of disease were different in different places. The Strait of Georgia and the larger Northwest Coast have their own stories to tell, to which I come as a geographer mindful of another geographer's adage that one cannot know a place very well without locating its people.[7] To enquire where people lived in what is now southern British Columbia at the beginning of the nineteenth century is to encounter smallpox; ongoing continental debates about disease, depopulation, and the contact process; and the politics of land in contemporary British Columbia.

Surviving Native accounts of the arrival of smallpox are scattered and fragmentary. The great late-nineteenth- and early-twentieth-century ethnographers of Northwest Coast cultures did not work among the Coast Salish; the major ethnographic collections of stories do not come from these peoples. Nor did the ethnographers have pre- and early-contact diseases in mind and,

therefore, they did not ask questions that would have elicited information about them. Generation after generation of the elderly died, cultures changed, and, eventually, oral traditions thinned. What is left are a number of short references and, condensed and often rephrased, a few whole accounts. All the material cited here has been written down, and it is impossible to reconstruct the circumstances of the stories or the intentions of the tellers. Often an account has been translated by one person, and then recorded in summary form by another. In Jan Vansina's phrase, they are "mutilated messages" that present every opportunity for misunderstanding.[8] And yet, these surviving fragments are powerful and generally consistent with each other.

Erna Gunther, writing on the Clallam (south coast of the Strait of Juan de Fuca), and Homer Barnett, writing on the Coast Salish of British Columbia, either heard no stories about early epidemics or did not record them.[9] Wilson Duff, writing on the Stó:lō (along the lower Fraser well above its mouth), considered that early epidemics probably had reached the Stó:lō, but had no information about them.[10] On the other hand, W.W. Elmendorf, ethnographer of the Twana (Hood Canal in Puget Sound), learned that his informants' grandparents "lived at times of disastrous epidemics." The most severe, he was told, was very early, "perhaps about 1800," and came from the south via the lower Chehalis; "from the Twana it passed north to the Klallam and peoples on southern Vancouver Island."[11] Wayne Suttles, writing on the Lummi (northeastern Puget Sound), reported that according to "Native tradition" smallpox arrived before Vancouver in 1792; "several villages were completely wiped out, while all suffered losses."[12]

Other accounts are fuller, though somewhat filtered by white constructions. In the mid-1890s a Vancouver woman, Ellen Webber, asked the Kwantlen about a large unoccupied midden approximately a quarter of a mile long,

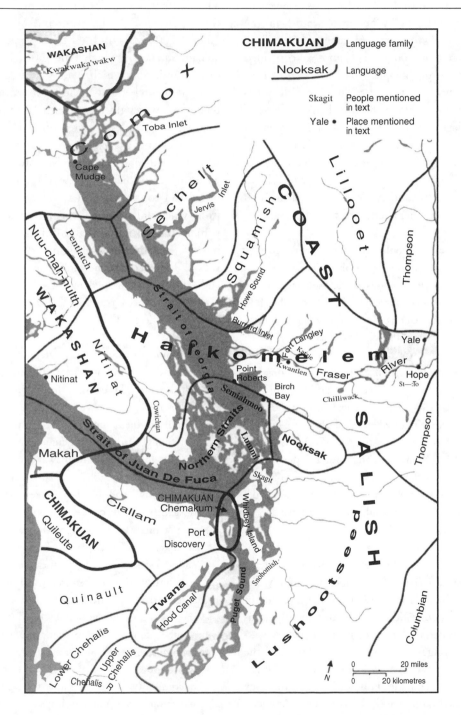

100 feet wide, and, at its centre, some twenty feet deep along the north bank of the Fraser River, twenty-four miles from its mouth. She published her findings "as they were given to me" (but largely in her own words) in the *American Antiquarian.* Apparently, the village was more than 600 years old and had contained 600 prosperous people. Attacks from the north had always been fended off, usually with stones piled in cairns along the river bank in front of the village.[13] But one year the raiders came in such numbers that their canoes blackened the river. Even so, the Kwantlen defended their village ferociously. The river ran red with blood. Then, as a Kwantlen victory seemed assured, some of their enemy attacked from the rear.

> Now all was confusion. Many were killed, and many women were taken slaves. A few escaped to the woods, where they remained in hiding two or three days. Then, with the children, they came out, and with sad hearts they laid away their dead... But misfortune followed the little band of survivors. In the swamp, near the village lived a fearful dragon with saucer-like eyes of fire and breath of steam. The village was apparently regaining its former strength when this dragon awoke and breathed upon the children. Where his breath touched them sores broke out and they burned with the heat, and they died to feed this monster. And so the village was deserted, and never again would the Indians live on that spot.[14]

Almost until Webber's day, people "remembered and respected the dragon," and when passing the swamp, crossed to the other side of the river and paddled softly and silently so as not to waken it. "Accursed is the one who awakens the dragon, he and all his people; for the sore-sickness will surely be their punishment."[15]

In 1896, Charles Hill-Tout, former theology student at Oxford and then master of an Anglican college in Vancouver, visited the Squamish "through the kindness of the Roman Catholic bishop" to record their history and cosmology.[16] The chiefs produced "the old historian of the tribe." This was Mulks, decrepit, blind, and "about 100 years old." Mulks spoke only archaic Squamish, which Hill-Tout could not understand, and which Mulks uttered "in a loud, high-pitched key" that his Squamish listeners followed with rapt attention. Every ten minutes or so, the translator offered a precis, but not even a fifth, Hill-Tout estimated, of what the old man had said. The story began with the creation of the world out of the water, and continued with accounts of a flood from which only one couple survived, and of a winter that did not end and during which all but two, a man and his daughter, died of starvation. In each case the land was re-peopled, and "the people learned to forget the terrible punishment the Great Spirit had sent upon their forefathers." Then,

> one salmon season the fish were found to be covered with running sores and blotches, which rendered them unfit for food. But as the people depended very largely upon these salmon for their winter's food supply, they were obliged to catch and cure them as best they could, and store them away for food. They put off eating them till no other food was available, and then began a terrible time of sickness and distress. A dreadful skin disease, loathsome to look upon, broke out upon all alike. None were spared. Men, women and children sickened, took the disease and died in agony by hundreds, so that when the spring arrived and fresh food was procurable, there was scarcely a person left of all their numbers to get it. Camp after camp, village after village, was left desolate. The remains of which, said the old man, in answer to my queries on this head, are found today in the old camp sites or midden-heaps over which

the forest has been growing for so many generations. Little by little the remnant left by the disease grew into a nation once more, and when the first white men sailed up the Squamish in their big boats, the tribe was strong and numerous again.[17]

In 1936, Old Pierre, then about seventy-five years old, told the ethnographer Diamond Jenness a very similar story, though more influenced by the missionaries.[18] Old Pierre, a Katzie, lived along the Pitt River, a tributary of the lower Fraser two days' paddle from the Squamish. The time came, he said, when the land was "overcrowded." When people "gathered at the Fraser River to fish, the smoke from their morning fires covered the country with a pall of smoke." Then the "Lord Above" sent rain that fell until most of the mountains were covered and most people had drowned. After the flood, the population multiplied again and "the Lord Above...saw that once more they were too numerous in the land." "Then in the third month (October) of a certain year snow began to fall." Soon every house was buried. Nine months passed "before the snow melted completely from the house-tops." Half the people died of starvation. A third time the population grew, and then came smallpox. Old Pierre's account is the most explicit surviving pre-contact description of the disease around the Strait of Georgia.

After many generations the people again multiplied until for the third time the smoke of their fires floated over the valley like a dense fog. Then news reached them from the east that a great sickness was travelling over the land, a sickness than no medicine could cure, and no person escape. Terrified, they held council with one another and decided to send their wives, with half the children, to their parents' homes, so that every adult might die in the place where he or she was raised. Then the wind carried the smallpox sickness among them. Some crawled away

into the woods to die; many died in their homes. Altogether about three-quarters of the Indians perished.

My great-grandfather happened to be roaming in the mountains at this period, for his wife had recently given birth to twins, and, according to custom, both parents and children had to remain in isolation for several months. The children were just beginning to walk when he returned to his village at the entrance to Pitt Lake, knowing nothing of the calamity that had overtaken its inhabitants. All his kinsmen and relatives lay dead inside their homes; only in one house did there survive a baby boy, who was vainly sucking at its dead mother's breast. They rescued the child, burned all the houses, together with the corpses that lay inside them, and built a new home for themselves several miles away.

If you dig today on the site of any of the old villages you will uncover countless bones, the remains of the Indians who perished during this epidemic of smallpox. Not many years later Europeans appeared on the Fraser, and their coming ushered in a new era.[19]

Farther upriver, among the Stó:lō, echoes of similar events linger to this day. Albert Louis heard of a flood before the whites came, then smallpox. "It killed, oh, half the Indians all around the Fraser River there."[20] Dan Milo, almost 100 years old in 1962, spoke of a village (Kilgard) where everyone died save one boy who settled down with a girl who was the only survivor from a village nearby.[21] In the village of Sxwoxwiymelh ("a lot of people died at once"), according to Susan Peters, twenty-five to thirty people died each day and were buried in one of the larger pit houses.[22] Patrick Charlie said that everyone there died of smallpox, and that the houses were burned down.[23] In 1986,

Jimmy Peters, who grew up after World War I in the village of Yale at the foot of the Fraser Canyon, remembered elders who tried to keep children away from the houses collapsed on the dead and the burial grounds, and the children who, curious and uncomprehending, sneaked off there anyway.

> Things that the old timers did years ago, we're not supposed to touch it even kickwillie houses. And where they were buried. A lot of them died in that place. And just buried in there... Chickenpox, smallpox, killed them all off. And they just died there. And we're not supposed to go there and touch them. A lot of times we used to go up there and dig out and see what they used to use years back. Like rock bowls, or rock knives, wood chisels, you know. But they'd tell me. "Don't you go there. Somedays, some nights you'll dream about that, and you might not live long," he says. They're too sacred. You leave them there. You're not supposed to touch anything that they owned years back.[24]

Sometime in the 1920s, Ayessic, chief at Hope, a village fifty kilometres below Yale on the Fraser, told the antiquarian and collector C.F. Newcombe about the first whites to descend the river. "News came from above... that men of different race were coming." Troubled, "the people came together and it was decided to try to please the newcomers." After they had painted their bodies "with red fungus paint (soquat)," messengers were sent to invite the strangers at Big Canyon "to come down." "They found them there camping with a number of boxes and packs which were thought to hold smallpox or miracle medicine."[25]

In the 1960s, fisherman Nick Stevens, living at the mouth of the river, remembered his Native grandfather's account of smallpox among the Cowichan on Saltspring Island. There, "according to the stories handed down," smallpox came on the south wind, and the people could not get "the clean north wind to blow the foul disease away." The south wind blew all winter "until most of the tribe were dead and there were too few left to bury their bodies." The survivors took the corpses to a small island near Fulford Harbour, "placing their remains in crevices in the rocks, covering them with flat stones." When, as boys, Stevens and his brother found a skull on this island, their grandfather flew into a rage. "Take it back where you found it, he roared. It will bring us bad luck."[26] In a slightly different category is *Indians of Skagit County* (1972), by Martin Sampson, a Swinomish chief. Relying partly on oral tradition, Sampson describes a "first epidemic in the 1700s," which he identifies as smallpox, that killed a great many coastal people but did not reach the upper Skagit.[27]

Ample ground exists for disagreement about the meaning of these fragments. They may not all refer to the same epidemic, their dating would be expected to be uncertain, some of their elements (for example, floods) recur in stories told in many cultures, and some of their analytical categories are anachronistic introductions. At the same time, many point to an eighteenth-century epidemic, and two have an explicit chronological marker: the epidemic preceded whites. Descriptions of the disease fit smallpox, though measles is probably not excluded. Yet these fragments, coming from many different performance situations, appear to describe the same event and are broadly congruent with other evidence from outside the oral tradition.

The European record of the lands and peoples around the Strait of Georgia begins in 1790 when the Spaniard Manuel Quimper sailed through the Strait of Juan de Fuca as far as the San Juan Islands. Encountering small numbers of Natives almost everywhere he went, Quimper estimated there were 500 people in the strait, and 1,000 at its southwestern entrance near

Nunez Gaona (Neah Bay). Some of these people, he thought, had been drawn from the outer coast by the great quantities of "seeds"—possibly camas—available in the strait.[28] The next year, the commander at Nootka, Francisco Eliza, continued the Spanish survey through most of El Gran Canal de Nuestra Sra del Rosario (the Strait of Georgia). Again, he saw many people at the entrance to the Strait of Juan de Fuca, and mentioned Native settlements here and there around the Gran Canal del Rosario. Along the south shore of the Strait of Juan de Fuca, Natives "from outside" came from time to time "to trade boys"; at the edge of all the beaches were "skeletons fastened to poles."[29] The next year, both British (Vancouver) and Spanish (Galiano, Valdes) expeditions circumnavigated Vancouver Island, surveying and mapping as they went.

The Spanish wrote appreciatively about the Natives, but offered few comments on Native settlements or numbers. They found both deserted and inhabited villages in the Gulf Islands, and inhabited villages near rivers at the head of some inlets and at several other places. Beyond Johnstone Strait, on the northeast coast of Vancouver Island, the Nuchaimuses (Nimpkish) were a "populous tribe."[30]

The British, who had more officers and a little more time than the Spaniards, and who were more inclined to treat Natives as objects for investigation, provided a good deal more information. Reaching the southeastern end of the Strait of Juan de Fuca, Vancouver began to find deserted villages, and human skeletons "promiscuously scattered about the beach, in great numbers." After local surveys in the ships' boats, similar reports came back from his officers; it seemed, Vancouver wrote, as if "the environs of Port Discovery were a general cemetery for the whole of the surrounding country." In some deserted villages, "the habitations had now fallen into decay; their inside, as well as a small surrounding space that appeared to have been formerly occupied, were overrun with weeds." There were also "lawns" on eminences fronting the sea, which Vancouver thought might have been sites of former villages; in a few, the framework of houses remained. In Vancouver's mind, "each of the deserted villages was nearly, if not quite, equal to contain all the scattered inhabitants we saw."[31] As the expedition continued into Puget Sound, more of the same was found.

> During this Expedition we saw a great many deserted Villages, some of them of very great extent and capable of holding many human Inhabitants—the Planks were taken away, but the Rafters stood perfect, the size of many a good deal surprized us, being much larger in girth than the Discovery's Main mast. A Human face was cut on most of them, and some were carved to resemble the head of a Bear or Wolf—The largest of the Villages I should imagine had not been inhabited for five or six years, as brambles and bushes were growing up a considerable height.[32]

In a "favoured" land that was "most grateful to the eye,"[33] there were not many people. "We saw only the few natives which are mentioned, silence prevailed everywhere, the feathered race, as if unable to endure the absence of man, had also utterly deserted this place."

The expedition continued northward, finding more deserted villages along the eastern shore of the Strait of Georgia. At Birch Bay, there was "a very large Village now overgrown with a thick crop of Nettles and bushes."[34] There were deserted villages in Burrard Inlet, Howe Sound, and Jervis Inlet, and only occasional "small parties of Indians either hunting or fishing [that] avoided us as much as possible."[35] Farther north, Toba Inlet "was nearly destitute of inhabitants," though there was a deserted but well-fortified village that "seemed so skillfully contrived and so firmly and well executed as rendered it difficult to consider the work of the untutored tribes we had been accustomed to meet."[36] Only as the expedition got well into and through Johnstone Strait did it encounter a country that was "infinitely more populous than the shores of the gulf of Georgia."[37]

While Vancouver considered that deserted villages and numerous human skeletons "do not amount to a direct proof of the extensive depopulation they indicate,"[38] he and his officers thought that the lands around Puget Sound and the Strait of Georgia recently had been severely depopulated.[39] Archibald Menzies, the expedition's botanist, estimated that "the inhabitants of this extensive Country [apparently Puget Sound] did not appear to us on making every allowance of computation from the different Villages and strolling parties that were met with to exceed one thousand in all, a number indeed too small for such a fine territory."[40] Puget gave the same figure.[41] All agreed that the cause or causes of depopulation could not be established, but variously speculated that they might have been disease, warfare, or population movements associated with seasonal hunting and fishing and with the maritime fur trade on the outer coast.

Disease

Captain Vancouver reported near Port Discovery that "Several of their stoutest men had been seen perfectly naked, and contrary to what might have been expected of rude nations habituated to warfare their skins were mostly unblemished by scars, excepting such as the smallpox seemed to have occasioned, a disease which there is great reason to believe is very fatal amongst them."[42] Farther south, in Hood Canal, he recognized "one man, who suffered very much from the small pox. This deplorable disease is not only common, but it is greatly to be apprehended is very fatal amongst them, as its indelible marks were seen on many; and several had lost the sight of one eye, which was

remarked to be generally the left, owing most likely to the virulent effects of this baneful disorder."[43] Later, near Whidbey Island, Vancouver reported that Peter Puget had met some very unwelcoming Indians: "In their persons they seemed more robust than the generality of the inhabitants; most of them had lost their right eye, and were much pitted with the small pox."[44] Puget himself wrote: "the Small pox most have had, and most terribly pitted they are; indeed many have lost their Eyes and no Doubt it has raged with uncommon Inveteracy among them but we never saw any Scars with wounds, a most convincing proof in my Mind of their peaceable Disposition."[45] The Spaniards did not report signs of smallpox.

The next Europeans in the region were the American overland explorers, Lewis and Clark. Near the mouth of the Willamette, a few miles from the present-day city of Portland, they found the remains of "a very large village."

> I endeavored to obtain from those people the situation of their nation, if scattered or what had become of the natives who must have peopled this great town. an old man who appeared of some note among them and father to my guide brought forward a woman who was badly marked with the Small Pox and made signs that they all died with the disorder which marked her face, and which she was very near dieing with when a girl. from the age of this woman this Distructive disorder I judge must have been about 28 or 30 years past, and about the time the Clatsops inform us that this disorder raged in their towns and distroyed their nation.[46]

A year later, David Thompson wrote from Kootenay House in the Rocky Mountain Trench:

> These people the Kootenaes were once numerous, but being continually at war with

Nations more powerful and far better armed than themselves, they diminished continually, 'till at length the Small Pox almost entirely rooted them out, leaving them only about 40 Families, and now they may count about 50 Families of 6 & 7 to a Family.[47]

On the lower Columbia three years later, he was asked: "is it true that the white men...have brought with them the Small Pox to destroy us...is this true and are we all soon to die."[48] Descending the Fraser River in 1808, Simon Fraser mentioned smallpox once: "the small pox was in the camp [a Native village some 200 kilometres from the mouth of the Fraser River] and several natives were marked with it."[49] Fur trader Ross Cox, who spent two months at the mouth of the Columbia River in 1814, said that the Natives remembered smallpox with "a superstitious dread."[50] John Work, a member of a Hudson's Bay Company (HBC) expedition sent from the Columbia in 1824 to explore the lower Fraser River, noted that an old chief near the mouth of the Fraser seemed to be marked with smallpox.[51] The next year, Scottish botanist John Scouler visited the Strait of Georgia in a HBC ship and saw an elderly, pockmarked Native in the retinue of Cowichan Chief Chapea at Point Roberts, just south of the Fraser's mouth. Scouler had seen no other direct evidence of smallpox on the Northwest Coast.

> The rarity of such an occurrence at once indicated the fatality of the disease and the dread they entertain of it. This epidemic broke out among them in 17_ and soon depopulated the eastern coast of America, and those on the Columbia were not secure behind the Rocky Mountains and the ravages of the disease were only bounded by the Pacific Ocean. The Cheenooks to the present time speak of it with horror, and are exceedingly anxious to obtain that medicine which protects the whites; meaning vaccination. Such is the

dread of this disease that when about to plunder the tribes of the interior, they have been deterred by the threat of disseminating smallpox among them.[52]

Three years later, the HBC established Fort Langley on the lower Fraser. In the fort journal (1827–30) and in the correspondence associated with the fort's early years, physical evidence of smallpox is not mentioned.[53]

Raiding

At the time of the Fort Langley journal, the peoples around Georgia Strait and Puget Sound lived in terror of raids from the Yaclewtas (Lequiltok), a Kwakwa̱ka'wakw people from northern Vancouver Island. Armed with muskets obtained directly or indirectly from Nawitte, a centre of the maritime fur trade at the northern end of Vancouver Island, the Lequiltok killed or captured many Coast Salish people in the 1820s. The fact that the Vancouver journals mention fortified villages and beacons, possibly watchtowers, "so frequently erected in the more southerly parts of New Georgia," and that there is abundant archeological evidence of fortified, pre-contact sites around the Strait of Georgia implies that raiding had been common before 1792.[54] The many Native accounts of these raids are difficult to date, but in the Kwantlen story reported by Ellen Webber, a raid from the north was followed by smallpox, which in turn was followed by the coming of whites. Myron Eells, a missionary in Puget Sound, reported a story, which he probably heard sometime between 1875 and 1879, of a pitched and apparently pre-contact battle near Victoria between warriors from most of the Puget Sound tribes and "the British Columbia Indians" (probably the Lequiltok). The British Columbia Indians won, and "only a few of the defeated Indians ever lived to return;

in some cases only three or four of a tribe."[55] There can be little doubt that raiding was widespread in the region before 1792, with often drastic local effects. Whether raiding could lay waste to a region as large as the lands around Puget Sound and the Strait of Georgia, especially before 1792 when few if any raiders had firearms, is another matter.

Population Movements

Twentieth-century ethnographies of people such as the Clallam (Gunther), Twana (Elmendorf), and Lummi (Suttles)—all of whom occupied territories where the Vancouver expedition found many deserted villages—describe seasonal migrations.[56] Early in the spring, people left coastal winter villages in small groups to fish, dig clams, gather edible plants, and hunt along nearby coasts. The Lummi went to the eastern San Juan Islands to dig camas and clams, fish for spring salmon and halibut, and hunt; the Twana dispersed around the shores of Hood Canal. Some old people usually remained in the winter village where, through the spring and summer, groups returned intermittently and briefly to leave dried fish or roots. In late July, some eastern Clallam went to Hood Canal to take dog salmon. In September, most Lummi gathered at fishing weirs a short distance up the Nooksack River. Such seasonal rounds did not take most people far from their winter village or the coast. The Twana named the shores of Hood Canal in great detail and the interior very sparsely. To be sure, the ethnographies describe early-nineteenth-century practices that, it has been argued recently, were even more local in the 1790s.[57] In either case, almost everyone who wintered around Puget Sound and the Strait of Georgia would have been scattered in small groups along the coast fairly near their winter villages when the Vancouver expedition passed through.

John Scouler was the first to suggest that a failure to understand the Native seasonal round was "the cause of the mistake into which the very accurate C.[aptain] Vancouver fell, concerning the apparent depopulation of the coast."[58] Scouler himself thought, incorrectly, that Natives "retreat to the interior of the country" from the end of September to the beginning of April, and then returned to the coast where, by Scouler's own logic, Vancouver should have found them. There is no evidence that Native seasonal rounds took people away in May and June from the coastlines that Vancouver and his officers explored and mapped.

Another possibility, however, is raised in the journals: that peoples from these inland waters had moved to the outer coast to trade directly with Europeans. If they had, there is no record of it in the ethnographies. Nor would peoples along or en route to the outer coast readily make room for intruding traders, much less for entire communities. The characteristic continental pattern of the fur trade is the opposite; groups well placed to trade directly with Europeans sought to monopolize such contacts by keeping others away.[59]

Native oral traditions and the texts of European explorers and traders provide different and largely independent records of late-eighteenth-century disease and depopulation around the Strait of Georgia. Besides their distinct cultural contexts, the two accounts are differently positioned in relation to the events they describe. The one grows out of the intimacy of experience and the shifting nature of oral tradition; the other out of the curiosity and ignorance of outsiders and the durability of writing. Yet the contents of one set of accounts seem to be broadly reproduced in the contents of the other. The two sets are mutually reinforcing and undoubtedly address the same horrendous event: late pre-contact depopulation around the Strait of Georgia and Puget Sound caused principally by smallpox.

This outbreak of smallpox was part of a pandemic that started in central Mexico in 1779 and quickly spread.[60] In 1780 and 1781, it devastated the Guatemalan Highlands; a decade later, it reached southern Chile, enabling the Spaniards to expand into an area they had been unable to conquer for 250 years.[61] Smallpox was in the New Mexican pueblos in 1780 and from there, transported indirectly by horse, diffused rapidly northward to affect all groups on the northern Plains. By early 1782, it reached the forest Cree north and west of Lake Manitoba.[62] From there it soon reached the Chipewyans. According to David Thompson, who was on the Plains a few years later, "From the Chipeways it extended over all the Indians of the forest to its northward extremity and by the [Dakota] Sioux over all the Indians of the Plains and crossed the Rocky Mountains."[63] The same epidemic affected groups around the Great Lakes. Thompson, who estimated that half to three-fifths of the peoples on the northern Plains died, talked with an Orcadian employee of the HBC who had witnessed the devastation: stinking tents in which all were dead, bodies eaten by wolves and dogs, "survivors in such a state of despair and despondence that they could hardly converse with us." "The countries were in a manner depopulated."[64] Twenty-three years later, when Lewis and Clark reached the middle Missouri, they found the "fallen down earth of the houses," and the scattered bones of men and animals in empty villages.[65]

An elderly man at Fort Cumberland on the North Saskatchewan River told Thompson that a war party of Nahathaway (Upper Churchill and Saskatchewan River Cree) Indians had contracted the disease from the Snake (Shoshone).[66] William Tomison, the trader at Cumberland House on the North Saskatchewan River, understood that the disease had reached the Shoshone from the Spaniards.[67] Certainly, smallpox was among the Shoshone in 1781. From a major rendezvous in southwestern Wyoming, the Shoshone traded with the Flathead, Nez Perce, Walla Walla, and various peoples along the Snake River.[68] Any of these trading connections could have brought smallpox to the lower Columbia. So could parties of Flatheads, Pend d'Oreille, Nez Perce, and others who crossed the Rockies to hunt and raid along the upper Missouri.[69] In 1840, Asa Smith, a Congregational missionary, reported that smallpox had reached the Nez Perce sixty or seventy years earlier by this means, with "very few surviving the attack of the disease."[70] In 1829, HBC trader John Work reported "a dreadful visitation of smallpox" on the Columbia Plateau near Fort Colvile that, he estimated, had occurred fifty or sixty years earlier. Jesuit missionary Gregory Mengarini reported smallpox among the Flathead at about the same time.[71]

It is clear, as Scouler reported in 1825, that smallpox reached the lower Columbia from the east. Ross Cox, on the Columbia a decade earlier, drew on the same body of common knowledge.

> The disease first proceeded from the banks of the Missouri. It travelled with destructive rapidity as far north as Athabasca and the slaves of Great Slave Lake, crossed the Rocky Mountains at the sources of the Missouri, and having fastened its deadly venom on the Snake Indians [Shoshone], spread its devastating course to the northward and westward, until its frightful progress was arrested by the Pacific Ocean.[72]

So, in the 1840s, did John Dunn, another fur trader. Smallpox, he said, "had nearly dispeopled the whole of the northern continent of its native inhabitants."[73] Breaking out "between the sources of the Missouri and the Mississippi...it spread its devastations northward as far as Athabasca, and the three horns of the Great Slave Lake; and westward across the Rocky Mountains to a short distance along the shores of the north Pacific... Numbers of tribes were totally swept away; or reduced to a few scattered and powerless individuals. The remnants of many others united; and formed a new and heterogeneous union."[74]

As James Mooney suggested years ago, diffusion from this direction probably dates smallpox's arrival along the lower Columbia to 1782.[75] From the lower Columbia, the disease spread north, probably via the Cowlitz and lower Chehalis rivers, to Puget Sound; in 1782–3, it struck most if not all the peoples around Puget Sound and Georgia Strait.[76] The epidemic extended as far north as Nitinat on the west coast of Vancouver Island, to perhaps Cape Mudge on the east coast of Vancouver Island, and up the Fraser River well into the canyon (map 2).[77] It may have stopped because it struck in winter; devastated populations may no longer have been infectious when mobility increased in the spring. The mortality rate will never be known, but given evidence from the Plains that this was hemorrhagic smallpox, and the dense, previously unaffected populations it encountered on the West Coast, Old Pierre's estimate of three-quarters may well be conservative.[78]

In my view, and contrary to Robert Boyd,[79] who has recently and usefully reopened the study of epidemics on the Northwest Coast, there was not a second smallpox epidemic in Puget Sound and around the Strait of Georgia in 1801. Boyd's evidence for a second epidemic about 1801—Elmendorf's informants, Old Pierre, Fraser's report—is consistent with a single epidemic in 1782. Moreover, visible evidence of smallpox was rare by the mid-1820s. Ross Cox, at Fort George in 1812 and for several years thereafter, reported that those bearing traces of smallpox were "nearly extinct."[80] John Scouler saw only one such face during a year on the lower Columbia and the Northwest Coast in the 1820s; John Work saw one pockmarked face on the Fraser River in 1824.[81] HBC traders, who usually reported evidence of smallpox, did not

mention smallpox in the Fort Langley journal (1827–30) or in fort correspondence because they saw no trace of it; this suggests a particularly high mortality rate in 1782 among affected children, or that the peoples who came to trade and fish along the lower Fraser had not brought the elderly with them. Had there been a smallpox epidemic in 1801, evidence would still have been abundantly at hand in the 1820s, and would have been reported.

In a sense, however, Boyd is right about the limited coastal range of "the epidemic of 1801," though his map approximately describes the epidemic of 1782. Smallpox had appeared among the Tlingit in the 1770s, but, as pointed out below, there is no evidence that there was a coastwide epidemic in 1775. There certainly was in 1862, but this time government officials and missionaries had vaccinated most of the Coast Salish, few of whom died.[82]

MAP 2 | APPROXIMATE DISTRIBUTION OF SMALLPOX, 1782

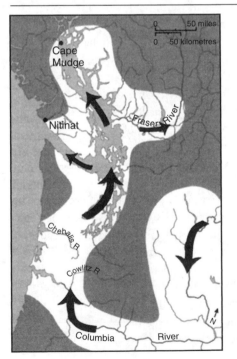

It might now appear possible to estimate the regional population just prior to smallpox, especially as Archibald McDonald, chief trader at Fort Langley, compiled a census of the peoples around Puget Sound and the Strait of Georgia in 1830.[83] Positing a sexually balanced population and a normal age distribution after 1782, no ecological constraints on population growth, and cultural pressure to build up the population (therefore, high birth rates), it would seem possible to work back from 1830 to an estimate of the population just after the epidemic. This figure multiplied by the rate of population loss in 1782 would yield the pre-epidemic population. However, it is not known whether other European diseases reached the region soon after 1782 (gonorrhea came with the traders to Fort Langley in 1827, but may already have reached the area). It is not known whether raiding was a major demographic factor, though in this period there is reason to think it was. The mortality rates for 1782 are only estimates. The census of 1830 is very approximate. And so on. No solid ground exists anywhere.

Other approaches to estimating pre-contact populations are not more promising.[84] It hardly seems possible, in this region of great ecological variety, general abundance, and occasional dearth, to usefully estimate the ecological carrying capacity for peoples of late-eighteenth-century Coast Salishan technology. Perhaps it can only be said that, given a mild, humid climate, the resources of river and sea, and the capacity of migrating salmon to transfer a portion of the food chain of the whole north Pacific Ocean to local fishing sites, there was more non-agricultural food on the Northwest Coast than anywhere else on the continent, and perhaps more in and around the lower Fraser River than elsewhere on the Northwest Coast. Nor, given the methodological problems of inferring population density from archeological evidence, can archeology readily provide reliable estimates.[85] If the diseases that shortly followed smallpox were

known (they are not), medical predictions of rates of infection and mortality could be made. The rate of population decline around the Strait of Georgia inferred from the nineteenth-century censuses (1830, 1839, 1852, 1876, 1877, 1881) could be projected back to 1780, but this takes no account of the disastrous first effects of European infectious diseases. In short, none of these approaches suggests a calculation or a research strategy that might be expected to yield a fairly reliable estimate of the pre-smallpox population around the Strait of Georgia.

I return, therefore, to opinions from the past. Captain Vancouver and his officers thought the region was depopulated. Thirty-five years later, HBC traders at Fort Langley were amazed at the numbers of people about. Canoes passed up and down river "by Hundreds," or "in great numbers."[86] In 1828, 550 canoes of Cowichan and 200 of Squamish came down from the Fraser Canyon. A three-quarter-mile-long Cowichan fishing village sat on the south bank of Lulu Island,[87] and a Nanaimo village, only somewhat smaller, was a few miles below the fort. Often, from the trader's perspective, "a great many Indians" were hanging around.[88] Archibald McDonald, chief trader at Fort Langley, noted "The Indian population in this part of the world is very great."[89]

The census he submitted in 1830 reported Native men around the Strait of Georgia, Puget Sound, and along the lower Fraser River. It had been made "by repeated examination of the Indians themselves," and particularly, for Fraser populations, of Sopitchin, a chief from a village at the foot of the Fraser Canyon. McDonald was surprised at the high figures in the canyon. But as he had seen many people there in 1828, when descending the river with Governor Simpson, and as he knew Sopitchin's estimates for the lower Fraser to be reliable, he was inclined to accept them. This census, combined with the 1835 census of the Kwakwaka'wakw by HBC trader W.F. Tolmie, yields a map—the indirect product of two HBC traders and several Native chiefs—of the distribution of population from the foot of Puget Sound to the northeastern end of Vancouver Island in the 1830s (map 3).[90]

Although the map omits some peoples altogether, its general patterns are clear. There were dense populations in the Fraser Canyon and in parts of Queen Charlotte Sound. Elsewhere, the numbers were modest. Along the lower Fraser River, a rich source of food, there were few winter residents.[91] Most of the peoples the traders commented on came to the river seasonally from around the strait. Around Puget Sound, the region that had so charmed Vancouver and his officers and in which there was such a quantity and diversity of accessible foods, the population was less than 2,500, well above Menzies' and Puget's estimates of 1,000, but still small in so favoured an area.[92] The map is what, in hindsight, it could only be: an approximate picture of populations that had recovered somewhat from a devastating smallpox epidemic fifty years before. Estimates of population density are relative. For HBC traders accustomed to sparse boreal populations, there were a lot of people around; for those who knew what the population had been, there were few.

In the Native memory, there was a time when the land was densely settled. Even before the flood, according to Old Pierre, "Families settled on the mountains, on the plains, and on the sea-shore, wherever they could find food, for the land was overcrowded." After recovering from the flood, the people were again "too numerous on the land."[93] According to Bob Joe, a Stó:lō, the population in the Chilliwack area was formerly "a thousand to one, comparing the population today."[94] Agnes Kelly said there had been "thousands" of people nearby at Agassiz.[95] More substantial is an inventory of former Stó:lō and Southern Thompson villages from which a map of winter villages from Koia'um in the north (where Fraser saw evidence of smallpox in 1808) to just below the

modern city of Chilliwack can be prepared (map 4).[96] The data in the inventory are largely from ethnographic sources, collected over the years and supplemented by archeological site surveys. Although the map has been prepared cautiously, it is uncertain whether all village sites were occupied each winter; if they were not, then the map probably exaggerates the density of late-eighteenth-century winter settlement along this stretch of the Fraser River.

Yet the village map is intriguing, especially when considered in relation to data from the 1830 census (map 5). The distribution of population in 1830 does not correspond to the earlier distribution of villages. The Chilliwack River, along which, apparently, there had been some twenty-five villages, was largely deserted in 1830. Calculations are tempting. If the average population of a village was 150 people, then before the smallpox epidemic at least 15,000 people inhabited the area. There are obvious ambiguities, but it seems clear that this section of the Fraser River once supported far more people than indicated in the census of 1830, or than white settlers and ethnographers have supposed.

The demographic outlines of the fifty years after 1780 around the Strait of Georgia and Puget Sound are, I think, fairly clear. A large, dense, and probably demographically quite unstable population was devastated by smallpox in the winter of 1781–2 or 1782–3.[97] The great majority of the people died. Although recovery was retarded by Lequiltok raiding and, perhaps, by other European diseases, the regional population had risen substantially by 1830, but not nearly to its pre-smallpox level.

Depopulation created vacuums that drew in surrounding people. Groups, for example, that had been unable to live on the Fraser River could now do so. The evidence is unclear, but some surviving Katzie may have moved out of the Pitt River to settle on the Fraser; surviving upriver Chilliwack may have moved down to the rich sloughs on the Fraser floodplain.[98] It is

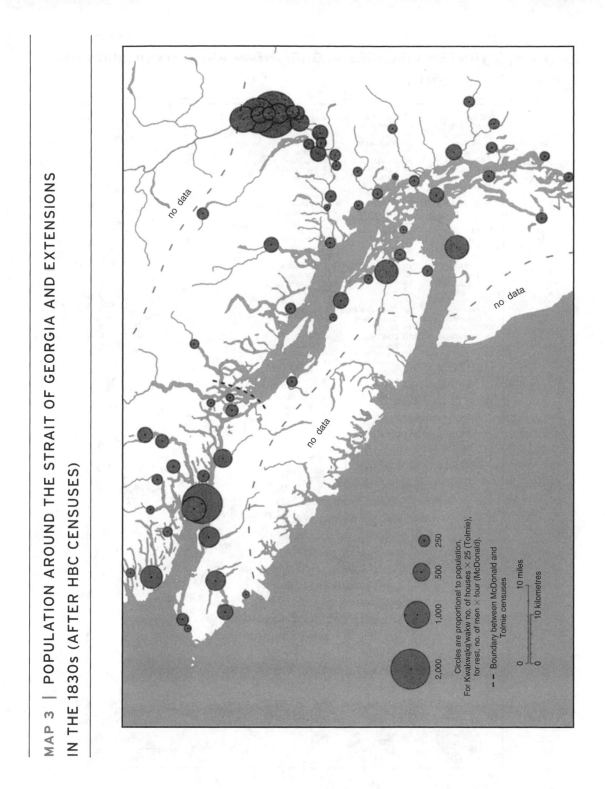

no data

no data

no data

250
500
1,000
2,000

Circles are proportional to population.
For Kwakwaka'wakw no. of houses × 25 (Tolmie),
for rest, no. of men × four (McDonald).

- - - Boundary between McDonald and
Tolmie censuses

0   10 miles
0   10 kilometres

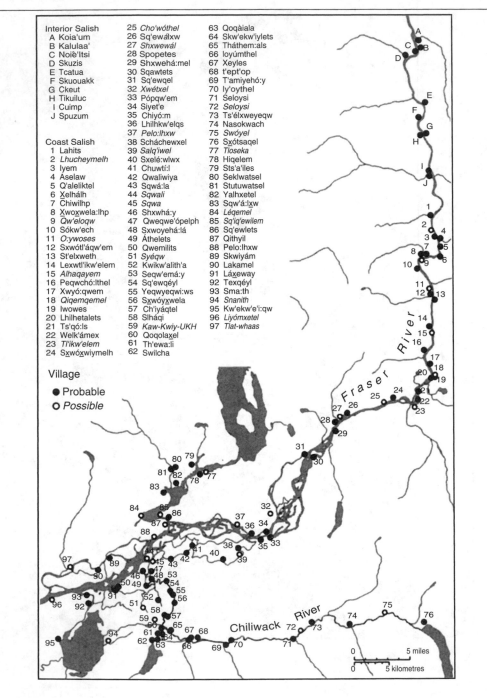

Interior Salish
A Koia'um
B Kalulaa'
C Noiè'ltsi
D Skuzis
E Tcatua
F Skuouakk
G Ckeut
H Tikuiluc
I Cuimp
J Spuzum

Coast Salish
1 Lahits
2 *Lhucheymelh*
3 Iyem
4 Aselaw
5 Q'aleliktel
6 X̱elhálh
7 Chiwilhp
8 X̱wox̱wela:lhp
9 *Qw'eloqw*
10 Sókw'ech
11 *O:ywoses*
12 Sx̱wótl'áqw'em
13 St'elxweth
14 Lexwtl'ikw'elem
15 *Alhaqayem*
16 Peqwchó:lthel
17 Xwyó:qwem
18 *Qiqemqemel*
19 Iwowes
20 Lhilhetalets
21 Ts'qó:ls
22 Welk'ámex
23 Tl'ikw'elem
24 Sx̱wóx̱wiymelh

25 *Cho'wóthel*
26 Sq'ewálxw
27 *Shxwewál*
28 Spopetes
29 Shxwehá:mel
30 Sqawtets
31 Sq'ewqel
32 *Xwétxel*
33 Pópqw'em
34 Siyet'e
35 Chiyó:m
36 Lhilhkw'elqs
37 *Pelo:lhxw*
38 Scháchewxel
39 *Salq'iwel*
40 Sxelé:wlwx
41 Chuwtí:l
42 Qwaliwiya
43 *Sqwá:la*
44 *Sqwali*
45 *Sqwa*
46 Shxwhá:y
47 Qweqwe'ópelph
48 Sxwoyehá:lá
49 Áthelets
50 Qwemilits
51 *Syéqw*
52 Kwikw'alith'a
53 Seqw'emá:y
54 Sq'ewqéyl
55 Yeqwyeqwi:ws
56 Sx̱wóyx̱wela
57 Ch'iyáqtel
58 Slháqi
59 *Kaw-Kwiy-UKH*
60 Qoqolax̱el
61 Th'ewa:li
62 Swilcha

63 Qoqàiala
64 Skw'ekw'iylets
65 Tháthem:als
66 Ioyúmthel
67 Xeyles
68 t'ept'op
69 T'amiyehó:y
70 Iy'oythel
71 Seloysi
72 Seloysi
73 Ts'élxweyeqw
74 Nasokwach
75 Swóyel
76 Sx̱ótsaqel
77 Tloseka
78 Hiqelem
79 Sts'a'iles
80 Seklwatsel
81 Stutuwatsel
82 Yalhxetel
83 Sqw'á:lx̱w
84 Léqemel
85 Sq'iq'ewilem
86 Sq'ewlets
87 Qithyil
88 Pelo:lhxw
89 Skwiyám
90 Lakamel
91 Láx̱eway
92 Texqéyl
93 Sma:th
94 Snanith
95 Kw'ekw'e'i:qw
96 Liyómxetel
97 Tlat-whaas

Village

● Probable
○ *Possible*

MAP 5 | SMAISE TO WHEE Y KUM, 1830 (AFTER HBC CENSUS)

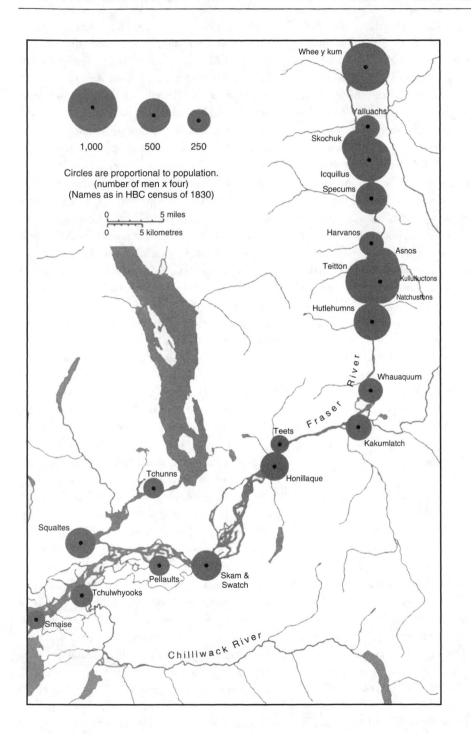

Whee y kum

Yalluachs

Skochuk

Icquillus

Specums

Harvanos

Asnos

Teitton

Kullulluctons

Natchustons

Hutlehumns

Whauaquum

Fraser River

Teets

Kakumlatch

Tchunns

Honillaque

Squaltes

Pellaults

Skam & Swatch

Tchulwhyooks

Smaise

Chilliwack River

1,000   500   250

Circles are proportional to population.
(number of men x four)
(Names as in HBC census of 1830)

0   5 miles

0   5 kilometres

quite possible—there is no evidence one way or another—that space opened on the lower Fraser at this time for the Cowichan and Nanaimo fishing villages reported in the 1820s. The people in Mud Bay, just south of the Fraser, were wiped out, and the Semiahmoo moved northward, occupying this territory. Similar relocations occurred on the San Juan Islands and on the south coast of Vancouver Island.[99] More generally, depopulation contributed to interregional political instability as the depleted Coast Salish became more vulnerable to Lequiltok raiding.[100] In the longer run, the Coast Salish, once the most numerous people on the Northwest Coast, became relatively invisible in their own territory. Other peoples came to exemplify Northwest Coast culture both to the outside world and to the newcomers in the towns and countrysides that emerged around Puget Sound and the Strait of Georgia. The relative neglect of the Coast Salish has partly to do with urbanization patterns; the particular secrecy with which the Coast Salish treated their stories, songs, and ceremonies; and the influence of Franz Boas. But it has also to do with early, profound depopulation. As the Swinomish chief Martin Sampson put it, the whites encountered "a people trying to recover from a devastating blow."[101]

How is it that the smallpox epidemic of 1782 is not part of the lore of modern British Columbia, especially as it was identified, quite precisely, more than eighty years ago? In a short piece on the Native population of North America published in the *Bulletin* of the Bureau of American Ethnology in 1910, James Mooney concluded that smallpox had reached the Pacific from the Plains in 1782; and in his considerably elaborated survey, published posthumously in 1928, he suggested that this epidemic was "very destructive throughout southern British Columbia."[102] Yet as late as 1964, the anthropologist Wilson Duff, in *The*

Indian History of British Columbia, used HBC and Dominion censuses to calculate that 70,000 people lived in what is now British Columbia in 1835.[103] Although Duff knew that there had been smallpox among the Tlingit, Haida, and Coast Tsimshian, and suspected it in the south, his estimate of the pre-contact population of British Columbia—"at least 80,000 and probably somewhat more"—largely discounted smallpox as a demographic influence. Most earlier ethnographers ignored the possibility of pre- or early-contact epidemics of infectious European diseases; as late as 1965, Philip Drucker thought "the first devastating smallpox epidemic probably occurred in the middle 1830s."[104] Among contemporary scholars, Robin Fisher doubts much of the evidence for early smallpox.[105] James Gibson has spelled out the archival case for smallpox among the Tlingit and adjacent peoples in 1835–8,[106] and, as noted above, Robert Boyd has argued an important, if jumbled, case for smallpox epidemics in 1775 and 1801. Overall, academic scholarship has approached with great hesitation the idea that Native societies were decimated by disease just before or soon after Europeans arrived on the Northwest Coast.

But why this hesitation? The question has wide ramifications, and I can only sketch components of an answer.

It is important to recognize that the early-contact Northwest Coast does not have a common epidemiological history, unlike the Plains where, with the advent of the horse, diseases could be carried quickly over great distances. On the coast, people lived geographically circumscribed lives, travelling to local or regional resource procurement and trading sites, but not, until the establishment of Fort Victoria, drawn into contact with most other coastal peoples. When smallpox broke out in Victoria in 1862 and nervous officials sent Natives home, a mechanism was at hand as never before for the diffusion of smallpox throughout the length and breadth of the Northwest Coast. Smallpox had broken out among the Tlingit in the 1770s, and had reached the lower Columbia from the east in 1782, but the two outbreaks were unconnected. Cook saw no signs of smallpox at Nootka in 1778, nor did the Spaniards in 1789–92. Nor did the maritime fur traders. Smallpox was neither there nor, from the evidence, anywhere else on the west coast of Vancouver Island north of Nitinat in the late eighteenth century.[107] Nor had it reached the northeast coast of the island. In 1841, Governor Simpson, travelling through Johnstone Strait in the HBC steamer the *Beaver,* found that the Quakeolths (Kwagulths, Kwakwaka'wakw) "had been exempted from the smallpox," a conclusion supported by the Vancouver journals and by Robert Galois's recent study of Kwakwaka'wakw settlement.[108]

To grossly simplify the geography of early-contact disease, there were, at least, three broad, epidemiological regions along the Northwest Coast: the Alaskan panhandle and north coastal British Columbia; the west coast of Vancouver Island and around Queen Charlotte Sound and Johnstone Strait; and the Strait of Georgia to the Columbia River. If a common coastal pattern is assumed, then argument about different findings in different locations obscures both the complex geography of depopulation and particular demographic disasters, such as the smallpox epidemic of 1782–3. Eventually, 100 years or more after contact, the demographic effects of introduced diseases among different populations may everywhere have been much the same—those who missed smallpox in 1782 succumbing, they or their progeny, to later European introductions—but, if this were so, there were many different local histories of depopulation.

Until the last generation, estimates of particular pre-contact populations, and therefore of particular epidemics and depopulations have been approached within the widely held assumption that the contact population of North America (north of the Rio Grande) was about one million. Mooney divided his 1910 estimate of 1,150,000 people as follows: United States: 846,000, Canada: 220,000, Alaska: 72,000, Greenland: 10,000.[109] In his more elaborated estimates, he "conservatively" estimated the pre-contact population of British Columbia at 86,000.[110] There were no other careful continental estimates. The influential Berkeley anthropologist, Alfred Kroeber, writing in 1939, thought that "until a new, equally systematic survey has been done, Mooney's figures should be accepted in total, though in Kroeber's view they were "too high rather than too low" and would probably "shrink to around 900,000, possibly somewhat farther." Moreover, for Kroeber "the outstanding fact [about Mooney's figures] is the exceptional density on the Pacific coast."[111] This powerful orthodoxy survived well into the 1960s and beyond. Therefore, if early censuses pointed to a Native population in British Columbia in the 1830s of about 70,000 (and if this was an "exceptional density" in a country with a contact population of 220,000), pre-contact totals could not have been much higher. Such was the box in which Wilson Duff and Philip Drucker found themselves. Given Mooney's, then Kroeber's, assumptions about Canadian and continental populations, there was not much demographic space for contact diseases on the Northwest Coast.

Nor, in a sense, was there ethnographic space. Salvage ethnography in the style of Franz Boas assumed traditional Native cultures yielding to modern Western cultures without much of interest between. Therefore, ethnographers in quest of the former sought out elderly people with good memories, and wrote down as much of what they were told as possible, capturing, they believed, vanishing traditional ways. When field notes were worked up into books, an academic datum plane was created: traditional Northwest Coast culture. If the ethnographers asked their questions at the end of the nineteenth or early in the twentieth century, as many of them did, their informants remembered and described early- to mid-nineteenth-century societies. This was the slice of time that ethnography transformed into timeless traditional culture.

Smallpox and other contact diseases posed two basic challenges to such procedures. First, they raised the possibility that informants' memories did not quite reach the traditional world. If smallpox and other diseases had disrupted societies before the most elderly informants remembered them, then traditional societies were simply out of ethnographic range. Ethnographic notebooks contained information about societies that were already somewhat transformed. Second, and even more telling, the concept of pre- or early-contact epidemics introduced the idea of time and began, however crudely, to situate Native people historically. Native societies before and after a devastating smallpox epidemic could not, presumably, be quite the same. In short, the farther back in time epidemics were pushed, along with the concept of change associated with them, the more the epidemics interfered with the idea of traditional culture, and the more impetus they gave to the idea of history. At the very least, the Eurocentrism inherent in the assumption that Native cultures were static would give way to another Eurocentrism: that Native history began with a devastating European introduction. Beyond this was another assumption: that Native societies changed like any others, and generated multiple histories in which epidemics were embedded; yet the ethnographers' view of Native culture was far more static, and deflected them from any serious consideration of pre- and early-contact epidemics along the Northwest Coast.

More generally, the idea of disease-induced depopulation runs counter to the long-held conviction that Europeans brought enlightenment and civilization to savage peoples.[112] It turns the story of the contact process away from the rhetorics of progress and salvation and towards the numbing recognition of catastrophe. Progress wrestled from the wilderness by hard, manly work and registered by expanding settlements and populations is suddenly qualified by population losses. The rhetoric of development begins to pale. The Western idea of property, coupled with an expanding world economy, appears as an agent of destruction as much as of creation. A linear view of progress fails. It becomes harder to believe that European goods and a European God had rescued Native peoples from want and ignorance. Ideologies and values that trans-Atlantic expansion had so powerfully reinforced lose authority. The whole European engagement with a New World, which was not new after all, begins to appear in a different light.

These sober thoughts were not what modern British Columbians or other recent North Americans, proud of their achievements and intent on their futures, wanted to hear. It was far more convenient to think that the Native population had always been small, and that those who remained would soon die off. In the late nineteenth and early twentieth centuries, as railways were built, speculations proliferated, boosterism filled the air, and Native populations dwindled, there was ample ground to think that both were true. By this time, most Natives lived on reserves as wards of the state, segregated from the mainstream of white society. To all intents and purposes they had become invisible, and their pasts, reduced to curious fragments in museums, were even more so. An immigrant, racist white society was not interested in such pasts, scholarship was blinkered, and only a few elderly Natives told stories that were easily construed as myths.

Now, some of the constraints are lifting. Hemispheric and continental pre-Columbian population estimates are far higher than in

Mooney's or Kroeber's day; in this light, there is now room to consider that there may have been many more people in British Columbia than what seemed possible only a few years ago. Native peoples have not died out, and the continuing vitality of Native societies, coupled with their growing political and academic influence, has considerably undermined the salvage ethnographers' bipolar model of culture. The broad critique of meta-theory, positivist science, and one-point perspective, sustained over the last generation, has encouraged scholarship to articulate the long-hidden or suppressed accounts of relatively powerless people: women, ethnic minorities, peasants, refugees, as well as Natives.[113] In addition, archival sources are more accessible. For all these reasons, it is easier now than it was even a short generation ago to discern infectious diseases in early-contact British Columbia.

The picture that emerges is hardly surprising. Native people in the province were not spared what Natives in the rest of the continent and hemisphere experienced. In the century or so after the first arrival of European infectious diseases, Native populations throughout the Western Hemisphere commonly declined by some 90 per cent. In all probability, that was the magnitude of population decline in British Columbia. If so, then the population of the province on the eve of the first epidemics was well over 200,000 people, of whom more than 50,000 lived around the Strait of Georgia and up the Fraser River to the limit of Coast Salish territory.[114] If population decline was in the order of 95 per cent, then these figures are doubled.

In southern British Columbia, the process of disease-related depopulation probably began with the smallpox epidemic of 1782.[115] Eventually, in recurring epidemics over approximately a century, smallpox visited all Native groups in the province, some several times. However, smallpox was only the most spectacular of a complex of European infectious diseases that together were far more devastating than any one of them. The eventual result, everywhere, was severe depopulation at precisely the time that changing technologies of transportation and communication brought more and more of the resources of the northwestern corner of North America within reach of the capitalist world economy. Here was an almost empty land, so it seemed, for the taking, and the means of marketing many of its resources. Such was the underlying geographical basis of the bonanza that awaited immigrants to British Columbia.

Passing through the province by train just before World War I, Rupert Brooke, a poet as English as the ancient village of Grantchester where he lived, missed the dead and "the friendly presence of ghosts." Mountain breezes, he said, "have nothing to remember and everything to promise." This was a stranger's conceit. Jimmy Peters, who poked as a lad in the graves of his ancestors, knew otherwise. So did Charles Hill-Tout, who listened to Mulks, the old Squamish historian, and the Scowlitz elders who believed "their race is doomed to die out and disappear." Brooke was travelling through a profound settlement discontinuity, measured not, as it would have been in Europe, by decaying cities, wasted fields, and overgrown orchards, but by the abandonment of countless seasonal settlement sites, the unnaming and renaming of the land, and the belief of some that their world was coming to an end, and of others that it was opening towards a prosperous future.

Notes

Earlier drafts of this chapter greatly benefitted from comments by Karl Butzer, Daniel Clayton, Julie Cruikshank, Jody Decker, Robert Galois, Averill Groeneveld-Meijer, Richard Inglis, Grant Keddie, Shirley Leon, George Lovell, Richard Mackie, Sonny McHalsie, Daniel Marshall, Bruce Miller, Gordon Mohs, Matthew Sparke, and Wayne Suttles. Republished with permission and with some additions from *Ethnohistory* 41, 4 (1994):593–626.

1 Jimmy Peters, interview by Gordon Mohs and Sonny McHalsie, 29 September 1986, Stó:lō Heritage, book 11(A), Oral History Stó:lō Tribal Council, Sardis. This study owes much of its initial impetus to comments by Ruben Ware in *A Stó:lō Bibliography* (Sardis 1983), and to the remarkable collection of research materials in the Coqualeetza Resource Centre.

2 Charles Hill-Tout, "Ethnological Report on the Stseelis [Chehalis] and Skaulits [Scowlitz] Tribes of the Halkomelem Division of the Salish of British Columbia," *Journal of the Royal Anthropological Institute* 34 (July–December 1904), reprinted in Ralph Maud, ed., *The Mainland Halkomelem,* vol. 3 of *The Salish People: The Local Contribution of Charles Hill-Tout* (Vancouver 1978), 100.

3 Karl W. Butzer, "The Americas before and after 1492: An Introduction to Current Geographical Research," *Annals, Association of American Geographers* 82, 3 (1992):352.

4 On the medical implications of genetic similarity, see Francis L. Black, "Why Did They Die?" *Science* 258 (11 December 1992):1, 739–40.

5 For current estimates and reviews of estimates, see William Denevan, "Native American Populations in 1492: Recent Research and Revised Hemispheric Estimate," in William Denevan, ed., *The Native Population of the Americas in 1492,* 2nd ed. (Madison 1992), xvii–xxxviii, and Douglas H. Ubelaker, "North American Indian Population Size: Changing Perspectives," in J.W. Verano and D.H. Ubelaker, eds., *Disease and Demography in the Americas* (Washington 1992), 169–78.

6 The most contested judgment is *Delgamuukw et al.* v. *The Queen, Reasons for Judgment,* Supreme Court of British Columbia, 8 March 1991.

7 Glenn Trewartha, "A Case for Population Geography," *Annals, Association of American Geographers* 43 (June 1953):71–97.

8 Jan Vansina, *Oral Tradition as History* (Madison 1985), 83.

9 Erna Gunther, *Klallam Ethnology,* University of Washington Publications in Anthropology, vol. 1, no. 5 (Washington 1927), 171–314; Homer Barnett, *The Coast Salish of British Columbia* (Eugene 1955).

10 Wilson Duff, *The Upper Stalo Indians of the Fraser River of B.C.,* Anthropology in British Columbia, Memoir no. 1 (Victoria 1952).

11 W.W. Elmendorf, *The Structure of Twana Culture,* Washington State University Research Studies 28 (3), Monographic Supplement 2 (Pullman, WA, 1960), 272.

12 Wayne Suttles, "Post-Contact Culture Change among the Lummi Indians," *British Columbia Historical Quarterly* 18, 1–2 (1954):42.

13 By "Hydahs" in this story, but Haida do not appear to have been on the south coast before 1853. These raiders were probably Lequiltok, southern Kwakwa̱ka'wakw peoples.

14 E.C. Webber, "An Old Kwanthum Village—Its People and Its Fall," *American Antiquarian* 21 (September–October 1899):309–14. The dragon, presumably, is Ellen Webber's invention.

15 ER. Webber, "A Kwantlum Battle," *Museum and Art Notes* 6, 3 (September 1931):119.

16 C. Hill-Tout, "Notes on the Cosmogony and History of the Squamish Indians of British Columbia," *Transactions, Royal Society of Canada* 2, 3 (1897): Section II, reprinted in R. Maud, ed., *The Squamish and the Lillooet,* vol. 2 of *The Salish People,* 22. Franz Boas collected a somewhat similar Squamish story about a sequence of disasters caused by fire, flood, and finally smallpox and winter: "Later Qa' is sent the smallpox and one winter with deep snow to the people as punishment for their wickedness." Cited in "Indian Legends of the North Pacific Coast of America Collected by Franz Boas," ts., translated by Deitrich Bertz for the BC Indian Languages Project, 1977, 92, Special Collections, UBC Library. T.P.O. Menzies, curator of the Vancouver City Museum, heard a version of Mulk's story from Chief George in North Vancouver in June 1934, folder 5, vol. 44, add. mss. 1,077, Newcombe Family Papers, BCARS.

17 Maud, *The Salish People,* vol. 2, 22.

18 Diamond Jenness, *The Faith of a Coast Salish Indian,* Anthropology in British Columbia, Memoir no. 3 (Victoria 1955).

19 Ibid., 34.

20 Albert Louie, interview by Oliver Wells, 28 July 1965, in "Stó:lō Villages, Encampments and Settlements," Stó:lō Tribal Council (1987), 160.

21 Oliver Wells, *The Chilliwack and Their Neighbours* (Vancouver 1987), 40. Albert Louie told much the same story (see previous note).

22 Wells, "Stó:lō Villages, Encampments and Settlements."

23 Patrick Charlie, interview by Wilson Duff, Yale, summer 1950, Stalo Notebook 1, BCARS.

24 Jimmy Peters, interview by Gordon Mohs and Sonny McHalsie, 29 September 1986, Stó:lō Heritage, book 11(A), Oral History Stó:lō Tribal Council, Sardis.

25 Series II, ethnological vol. 44, folder 1, add. mss. 1,077, Newcombe Family Papers, BCARS.

26 "Are All Fishermen Superstitious?" *Fisherman* (20 March 1964):15.

27 Martin Sampson, *Indians of Skagit County,* Skagit County Historical Series no. 2, Skagit County Historical Society (Mount Vernon, WA, 1972):25.

28 "Quimper's Journal," in H.R. Wagner, ed., *Spanish Explorations in the Strait of Juan de Fuca* (Santa Ana 1933), 129–32.

29 "Extract of the Navigation Made by the Pilot Don Juan Pantoja," in Wagner, ed., *Spanish Explorations,* 185–8.

30 "Voyage of the Sutil and Mexicana," in Wagner, ed., *Spanish Explorations,* esp. 254, 289, 293. On the Spanish route through Johnstone Strait, see Robert Galois, *Kwakwaka'wakw Settlements 1775–1920: A Geographical Survey* (Vancouver 1995).

31 W. Kaye Lamb, ed., *A Voyage of Discovery to the North Pacific Ocean and Round the World, 1791–1795,* Hakluyt Society (London 1984), 2, 516–17, 538.

32 T. Manby Journal, December 1790–June 1793, 43, William Robertson Coe Collection, Yale University; photocopy in box 1, W. Kaye Lamb Papers, Special Collections, UBC Library.

33 Puget Journal, adm. 55, 27, 133–4, Public Record Office, London.

34 James Johnstone Log Book, 2 January 1792, 20 May 1792, 176, photocopy in box 4, W Kaye Lamb Papers. This point was obviously discussed. Archibald Menzies, the expedition's botanist, put it this way: "In this excursion...we saw only the few natives I have already mentioned, silence and solitude seemed to prevail over this fine and extensive country, even the feathered race, as if unable to endure the stillness that pervaded everywhere had in great measure abandoned it and were therefore very scarce." C.F. Newcombe, ed., *Menzies' Journal of Vancouver's Voyage, April–October, 1792* (Victoria 1923), 40.

35 Newcombe, ed., *Menzies' Journal,* 53.

36 T. Manby Journal, 12 June 1792.

37 Lamb, ed., *Voyage of Discovery,* 603–4.

38 Ibid., 613.

39 Ibid., 538.

40 Newcombe, ed., *Menzies' Journal,* 49.

41 Puget Journal, 133–4.

42 Lamb, ed., *Voyage of Discovery,* 540.

43 Ibid., 528.

44 Ibid., 559.

45 Puget Journal, 34.

46 R.G. Thwaites, ed., *Original Journals of the Lewis and Clark Expedition, 1804–1806,* vol. 4. (New York 1905), 240–1.

47 Barbara Belyea, ed., *Columbia Journals: David Thompson* (Montreal and Kingston 1994), 70.

48 Richard Glover, ed., *Thompson's Narrative, 1774–1812* (Toronto 1962), 367.

49 W. Kaye Lamb, ed., *The Letters and Journals of Simon Fraser, 1806–1808* (Toronto 1960), 94.

50 Ross Cox, *Adventures on the Columbia River,* vol. 1 (London 1831), 314.

51 John Work's Journal, 18 November 1824–30 December 1824, A/B/40/W89.2A, BCARS.

52 "Dr. John Scouler's Journal of a Voyage to N.W. America," *Quarterly of the Oregon Historical Society* 6 (June 1905):303–4.

53 Fort Langley Journal, 27 June 1827–30 July 1830, BCARS.

54 Lamb, ed., *Voyage of Discovery,* 603. For example, Donald H. Mitchell, "Excavations at Two Trench Embankments in the Gulf of Georgia Region," *Syesis* 1, 1 and 2 December 1968):29–46, and Gary Coupland, "Warfare and Social Complexity on the Northwest Coast," in D.C. Tkaczuk and B.C. Vivian, eds., *Cultures in Conflict: Current Archaeological Perspectives,* University of Calgary

Archaeological Association (Calgary 1989), 205–41. Defensive sites began to be built around the Strait of Georgia about 1,000 years ago, and some were maintained into the nineteenth century; personal communication, Grant Keddie, archaeologist at the Royal British Columbia Museum.

55 Myron Eells, *The Indians of Puget Sound: The Notebooks of Myron Eells* (Seattle 1985), 24.

56 Erna Gunther, *Klallam Ethnology*, esp. 195, 196, 214; W.W. Elmendorf, *The Structure of Twana Culture*, esp. 260–4; Wayne Suttles, "Post-Contact Culture," esp. 53–4.

57 The ethnographic record has been taken to describe pre-contact patterns of settlement and seasonal migration. However, Richard Inglis and James Haggarty recently argued that on the west coast of Vancouver Island, the pre-contact settlement pattern was one of many small villages, each occupied by a house group that depended on very local resources; "Pacific Rim National Park Ethnographic History," microfiche report series 257, Parks, Environment Canada, 1986.

58 "Dr. John Scouler's Journal," 198.

59 A tendency that can be observed from the earliest days of the St. Lawrence fur trade. See, for example, R. Cole Harris, ed., *From the Beginning to 1800,* vol. 1 of *Historical Atlas of Canada* (Toronto 1987), 84 and plate 35.

60 Ann F. Ramenofsky, *Vectors of Death: The Archaeology of European Contact* (Albuquerque 1987), 130; H.F. Dobyns, "Estimating Aboriginal American Population: An Appraisal of Techniques with a New Hemispheric Estimate," *Current Anthropology 7* (1966):395–416.

61 W. George Lovell, *Conquest and Survival in Colonial Guatemala: A Historical Geography of the Cuchumatán Highlands, 1500–1821* (Montreal 1992), 154–7; Fernando Casanuava, "Smallpox and War in Southern Chile in the Late 18th Century," in N.D. Cook and W.G. Lovell, eds., *Secret Judgments of God* (Norman, OK, 1992), 183–212.

62 S.F. Cook, "Smallpox in Spanish and Mexican California, 1770–1845," *Bulletin of the History of Medicine* 7 (1939):153–94; Marc Simmons, "New Mexico's Smallpox Epidemic of 1780–1781," *New Mexico Historical Review* 41 (1966):319–26; Arthur J. Ray, *Indians in the Fur Trade: Their Role as Hunters, Trappers and Middlemen in the Lands Southwest of Hudson Bay, 1660–1870* (Toronto 1974), 105–8; Jody F. Decker, "Tracing Historical Diffusion Patterns: The Case of the 1780–1782 Smallpox Epidemic among the Indians of Western Canada," *Native Studies Review* 4, 1 and 2

(1988):1–24; and Jody F. Decker, "Depopulation of the Northern Plains Natives," *Social Science and Medicine* 33, 4 (1991):38–96.

63 Glover, ed., *Thompson's Narrative,* 236.

64 Ibid., 235–6.

65 R.G. Thwaites, ed., *Original Journals,* vol. 1, 202; cited in Ramenofsky, *Vectors of Death,* 128–9. Lewis and Clark were told that "smallpox destroyed the greater part of the [Mandan] nation and reduced them to one large village and Some Small ones, all the nations before this maladey was afraid of them, after they were reduced the Seaux and other Indians waged war, and Killed a great many, and they moved up the Missourie"; see Thwaites, ed., *Original Journals,* vol., 1, 220.

66 Glover, ed., *Thompson's Narrative,* 49.

67 Decker, "Tracing Historical Diffusion Patterns," 12.

68 William R. Swagerty, "Indian Trade in the Trans-Mississippi West to 1870," in Wilcomb E. Washburn, ed., *Handbook of North American Indians, Vol. 4, History of Indian-White Relations* (Washington, DC, 1988), 352.

69 Clark Wissler, "Material Culture of the Blackfoot Indians," *Anthropological Papers of the American Museum of Natural History* 5, 1 (1910):13.

70 The quotes from Smith and Work are cited in Robert Boyd, "The Introduction of Infectious Diseases among the Indians of the Pacific Northwest, 1774–1874," PhD diss., University of Washington, 1985, 78–80.

71 Gregory Mengarini, *Recollections of the Flathead Mission* (Glendale, CA, 1977), 193–4.

72 Cox, *Adventures on the Columbia,* vol. 1, 312–13.

73 John Dunn, *The Oregon Territory and the British North American Fur Trade* (Philadelphia 1845), 84–5.

74 Ibid.

75 James Mooney, "Population," *Bureau of American Ethnology Bulletin* 30 (1910).

76 Elmendorf was told that the disease came from the Lower Chehalis River via the Satsop people; see *The Structure of Twana Culture,* 272.

77 John Hoskins, "John Hoskins' Narrative of the Second Voyage of the *Columbia,*" in F.W. Howay, ed., *Voyages of the "Columbia" to the Northwest Coast, 1787–1790 and 1790–1793* (Boston 1941), 196; John Boit, "John Boit's Log of the Second Voyage of the *Columbia,*" in Howay, ed. *Voyages of the "Columbia,"* 371. The estimate of diffusion northward in the Strait of Georgia is approximate. it accords generally with Vancouver's observations

in 1792 and with George Simpson's in 1841 that the Qwakeolths had never been affected by smallpox. Sir George Simpson, *Narrative of a Journey around the World during the Years 1841 and 1842,* 2 vols. (London 1847), 1, 189.

78 Decker, "Tracing Historical Diffusion Patterns," 16–17.

79 Robert Boyd, "The Introduction of Infectious Diseases," 71–111, and "Demographic History, 1774–1874," 137–8, in Wayne Suttles, ed., *Northwest Coast,* vol. 7 of *Handbook of North American Indians* (Washington, DC, 1990). Boyd has recently defended his interpretation against the argument presented here. See "Commentary on Early Contact-Era Smallpox in the Pacific Northwest," *Ethnohistory* 43, 2 (1996):307–28.

80 Cox, *Adventures on the Columbia,* vol. 1, 314.

81 Even on the Columbia as early as 1814, pock-marked faces were becoming uncommon; Ross Cox noted that "the vestiges...were still visible on the countenances of the elderly men and women." Ibid., vol.1, 312.

82 It was reported that Roman Catholic missionaries vaccinated "upward of 12,000 Indians on the Lower Fraser" (see *New Westminster Columbian,* 29 April 1863), and that government officials vaccinated some 1,200 Natives at Lytton (*New Westminster Columbian,* 25 June 1862). A few Natives along the Harrison River and at Douglas contracted the disease, but there was no epidemic along the lower Fraser at this time. Beyond Lytton, the picture was very different.

83 Archibald McDonald to HBC Governor and Council, Northern Department of Rupert's Land, 25 February 1830, HBCA microfilm reel 3M53, D.4/123, fos. 66–72; and printed, with minor errors of transcription, in Mary K. Cullen, "The History of Fort Langley, 1827–96," *Canadian Historic Sites: Occasional Papers in Archaeology and History,* vol. 20 (Ottawa 1979), 82–9.

84 For a survey of methodologies of population reconstruction, see Noble David Cook, *Demographic Collapse, Indian Peru, 1520–1620,* vol. 1, (Cambridge 1981).

85 Ramenofsky, *Vectors of Death,* is a brave attempt. See also Cook, *Demographic Collapse.*

86 Fort Langley Journal, 20 and 27 July 1828.

87 John Work's Journal, 19 December 1824.

88 Such comments abound in the Fort Langley Journal.

89 McDonald to the HBC Governor and Council, 25 February 1830.

90 William F. Tolmie, *The Journals of William Fraser Tolmie, Physician and Fur Trader* (Vancouver 1963), 317–20.

91 Michael Kew, "Salmon Availability, Technology, and Cultural Adaptation in the Fraser River Watershed," in Brian Hayden, ed., *A Complex Culture of the British Columbia Plateau: Traditional Stl'atl'imx Resource Use* (Vancouver 1992).

92 This figure includes all coastal peoples listed south of the Fraser River around Puget Sound as far as, but not including, the Clallam. The census total is 570 men, a figure I have multiplied by five. This may be approximately the territory for which Puget and Menzies provided estimates.

93 Jenness, *The Faith of a Coast Salish Indian,* 33.

94 Bob Joe, interview by Oliver Wells, 8 February 1962, in Wells, *The Chilliwacks and Their Neighbours,* 54.

95 Agnes Kelly, interview by Gordon Mohs, 7 July 1986, Stó:lō Heritage, book 11(A), Oral History Stó:lō Tribal Council, Sardis.

96 The Southern Thompson villages (Tuckquiome to Spuzzum) are based largely on inventories compiled by James Teit, Charles Hill-Tout, and Gilbert M. Sproat. See Cole Harris, "The Fraser Canyon Encountered," *BC Studies* 94 (summer 1992):5–28. The Stó:lō villages are based on "Stó:lō Villages, Encampments and Settlements" an inventory prepared by Gordon Mohs and Sonny McHalsie for the Stó:lō Tribal Council, and derived from site-by-site considerations of available ethnographic and archeological evidence.

97 A dense non-agricultural population living close to the technical/ecological limit of the food supply appears to be vulnerable to sudden catastrophes or "die-offs." See Ester Boserup, "Environment, Population, and Technology in Primitive Societies," in Donald Worster, ed., *The Ends of the Earth: Perspectives on Modern Environmental History* (New York 1988), and Ezra B.W. Zubrow, *Prehistoric Carrying Capacity: A Model* (Menlo Park, CA, 1975). The many stories about a succession of disasters and depopulations should not be dismissed as myth.

98 All these movements are poorly understood, and their connections to smallpox-related depopulations are open to debate. On the Katzie: Wayne Suttles, *Katzie Ethnographic Notes,* Anthropology in British Columbia, Memoir 2 (Victoria 1955), 8–11; on the Chilliwack: Wilson Duff, *The Upper Stalo Indians,* 43–5; on the Semiahmoo: Wayne Suttles, "Economic Life of the Coast Salish of Haro and Rosario Straits," PhD diss., University of Washington, 1951, 29.

99   Suttles, "Post-Contact Culture Change," 42–3.

100 Galois, *Kwakwaka'wakw Settlement Sites,* Introduction and Section D. In the 1920s, Diamond Jenness learned that smallpox had decimated the Saanich Indians of southeastern Vancouver Island about 1780, and had crippled their resistance to enemy raids; see "The Sanitch Indians of Vancouver Island," ts., 56, n.d., BCARS. I thank Daniel Clayton for bringing this reference to my attention.

101 Sampson, *Indians of Skagit County,* 1.

102 James Mooney, *The Aboriginal Population of America North of Mexico,* Smithsonian Miscellaneous Collection, vol. 80, no. 7 (Washington, DC, 1928). For a discussion of the basis of Mooney's calculations, see Douglas H. Ubelaker, "The Sources and Methodology for Mooney's Estimates of North American Indian Populations," in Denevan, ed., *The Native Population of the Americas,* 243–92.

103 Wilson Duff, *The Impact of the White Man,* vol. 1 of *The Indian History of British Columbia,* Anthropology in British Columbia, Memoir no. 5 (Victoria 1964), 39, 44.

104 Philip Drucker, *Cultures of the North Pacific Coast* (San Francisco 1965), 188–9.

105 Robin Fisher, *Contact and Conflict: Indian-European Relations in British Columbia, 1774–1890* (Vancouver 1977), 22–3.

106 James R. Gibson, "Smallpox on the Northwest Coast, 1835–1838," *BC Studies* 56 (winter 1982–3): 61–81.

107 Except possibly in Quatsino Sound, where there is an enigmatic and isolated reference to disease and death. See E. Curtis, *The Kwakiutl,* vol. 10 of *The North American Indian* (Cambridge, MA, 1915; reprinted facs. ed., New York 1970), 305.

108 Simpson, *Narrative of a Journey,* 189; Galois, *Kwakwaka'wakw Settlements.*

109 Mooney, "The Aboriginal Population," 286–7.

110 Ibid.

111 AL. Kroeber, *Cultural and Natural Areas of Native North America,* vol. 38, 4th ed. (Berkeley 1963 [1939]), 132, 134.

112 A good introduction to the literature on these questions is Daniel T. Reff, *Disease Depopulation and Cultural Change in Northwestern New Spain, 1518–1764* (Salt Lake City 1991), ch. 1.

113 One example is the relationship between the striking work of the subaltern historian on the dispossessed in India and the spate of recent attempts to articulate Native voice in the Americas. See Ranajit Guha and Gayatri Chakravorty Spivak, eds., *Selected Subaltern Studies* (New York 1988).

114 The census of Canada lists the Native population of British Columbia as follows: 1881: 25,661; 1901: 25,488; 1911: 20,134; 1921: 22,377. None of these figures should be taken as more than a low-side approximation, but, altogether, they are the most accurate available representation of the Native population of the province a little more than a century after contact. If the population had declined by 90 to 95 per cent during these years, then its pre-contact level was in the 200,000 to 400,000 range. The estimate for the Coast Salish is derived from the nominal 1881 census, District 187, Division 7 and District 189, Division A2. Counting people on the non-Native as well as the Native rolls, there were 5,452 Coast Salish around the Strait of Georgia in 1881, a figure which is then assumed to be roughly 5 to 10 per cent of the pre-epidemic population.

115 Henry Dobyns, *Their Number Became Thinned: Native American Population Dynamics in Eastern North America* (Knoxville 1983), has argued for a hemispheric smallpox pandemic in the 1520s, but Reff's work (note 112) on northwestern Mexico and the southwestern US provides, I think, compelling evidence against a sixteenth-century pandemic in the northern Cordilera. However, the case has been argued; see Sarah Campbell, "Post-Columbian Culture History in the Northern Columbia Plateau: AD 1500–1900," PhD diss., University of Washington, 1989.

Maturing Colonial Societies, 1815–1867

The British North American colonies went their separate ways between 1815 and 1867, but they drew closer in culture and values. As population expanded in the Atlantic region and the Canadas, colonial politicians demanded a larger measure of self-government. In the old Northwest territories, a vast area dominated by the Hudson's Bay Company, agricultural settlements first supplemented and eventually supplanted the fur trade as the *raison d'être* for the European presence in areas still overwhelmingly populated by First Nations.

Historians sometimes paint the movement toward self-government in this period as inevitable, part of an inexorable move toward democracy in the Western world. Certainly, the colonists had reasons to congratulate themselves on their successes. In February 1848, Nova Scotia became the first colony in the British Empire to achieve "responsible government"; that is, a government in which the executive council (what would later be called a cabinet), enjoyed the confidence of the majority of the members of the elected Assembly. Later that year, the United Province of Canada, formed by the British-imposed union of Upper and Lower Canada in 1841, also achieved responsible government, and the remaining three Atlantic colonies had won the same victory by 1855.

As the readings in Part 4 suggest, the achievement of responsible government involved popular struggles and, in the Canadas, outright rebellion. Although the political changes ushered in during this period gave more political control to the colonies, democracy was severely circumscribed. The vote was largely limited to male property-holders of European ethnicity, leaving women and Natives, as well as the colonial poor of all backgrounds, without a formal political voice. Government priorities reflected the concerns of those who held the franchise, often completely ignoring the interests of the disenfranchised.

In their discussion of "the land question" on Prince Edward Island, Rusty Bitterman and Margaret McCallum explore the three main ideologies that divided British North Americans: conservatism, liberalism, and egalitarianism. Conservatives extolled a hierarchical society which, in the case of PEI, meant a society in which a relatively small number of landowners could dispose of the land as they wished. For them, land ownership was a sacred right, even if that meant that owners left land idle for generations so that its value could continue to rise. Liberals promoted economic development. Although they often favoured a political democracy in which all or most male citizens might vote, they felt that the role of the legislature was not to support economic equality but to support policies that would encourage economic growth. So, for example, they supported land taxes that would raise money for roads and other infrastructure, and a partial "escheat" (expropriation) of large landholdings, as long as the escheat was limited to landlords who had failed to promote settlement and economic development. In the liberal world view, land was a commodity to be made available for investment and settlement. By contrast, the egalitarians wanted a full escheat of lands because they wanted to create a society in which all men not only voted but also owned a relatively equal share of land.

Newfoundland was the last of the Atlantic colonies to receive representative government (1832). Having resisted the creation of a settler-colony in Newfoundland, Great Britain was in no hurry to grant representative government even when the colony's population expanded rapidly in the early nineteenth century. In his article, Jerry Bannister demonstrates that public pressure, initiated by the merchant elite, but eventually joined by the colony's general population, forced Britain's hand in 1832. As in other colonies, settlers criticized the arbitrary laws imposed by Britain and the insensitive way that appointed governors administered the colony.

The outbreak of rebellions in Upper and Lower Canada represented a major challenge to the old colonial system. As Jean-Marie Fecteau explains in his article on the use of martial law during the crisis in Lower Canada, British authorities were prepared to suspend the rule of law not only to crush open revolt, but also to impose a "cure" to political deadlock that resulted from *patriote* control of the elected assembly. Such a violation of political rights, he argues, was "essentially a political coup in the guise of a state emergency" because authorities saw in the *patriote* demands a plan for ethnic domination. Since the ethnic factor was less evident in the rebellion in Upper Canada, martial law was not so brutally exercised there, but both colonies were forced to submit to the union of Upper and Lower Canada, which was designed to ensure that "British" ethnicity and power prevailed.

Power relations in colonial society were also gendered. Patriarchy, the control of men over women, and older men over younger men, was embedded both in the customs of the colonists and in the law of the land. In her article on homeless Montreal women, Mary Anne Poutanen uses court records to provide a vivid picture of the hard lives and early, cruel, unnecessary deaths that many of them experienced. At the same time, she stresses that these were not women without social agency. Within the confines of their common destitution, they formed friendships that allowed them to work together—generally in the sex trade—to look after each other's children, and to pursue leisure activities together. They often resisted the authorities together as well. Many of these women also formed bonds with marginalized men, including but not restricted to men with whom they co-habited.

Similar social bonds existed for both women and men in land owning families. Catharine Anne Wilson examines the popularity in Upper Canada of work bees where neighbours helped one another by contributing their labour to get a farm started or to build a house or barn. Everyone in the community had a role to play with age, gender, wealth, and skills determining what each person's contribution would be. This was not a form of charity or selflessness. Rather it was a recognition that one farm family could not perform all the necessary tasks required to insure its survival. With hired labour too expensive for most small

farmers to afford in required amounts, an exchange of neighbours' labour proved a substitute. Mutual aid in the form of bees benefited all members of small communities in the pioneer period.

The communities that Wilson describes were largely homogeneous ethnically. By contrast, Adele Perry describes settlements on the west coast in which racism and class prejudices played a fundamental role in creating and sustaining social stratification. Her research raises fundamental questions about the extent to which the "frontier" was, as some historians suggest, the inspiration for democratic ideas. Frontier theorists sometimes claim that the process of carving out new settlements in the North American environment made settlers less likely to allow the old European class system to become entrenched in their communities. Perry suggests that this claim cannot be sustained. As she observes, the discourse of colonial promoters regarding desirable settlers revealed a great deal about the class, gender, and race prejudices that had been transplanted from Britain to the colonial frontier, where settlement was fast replacing the fur trade in the years preceding British Columbia's entry into Confederation in 1871.

In his article, Lorne Hammond describes the resilience of the Hudson's Bay Company in the face of changing conditions. Competition from other companies, the dynamics of wildlife demography, and changes in fashion were factors that company officials managed with considerable dexterity. When, for example, silk replaced beaver as the fashion in Europe, the company shifted its focus to other fur bearing animals, such as marten, and experimented with new uses for beaver skins. White settlement in the traditional fur-bearing territories in the later nineteenth-century challenged the authority of the Hudson's Bay Company, the lifestyle of the Natives, and the survival of indigenous wildlife. While the impact on both Natives and wildlife was devastating, the profits-driven fur-trading company adapted and survived into the twenty-first century.

When Private Rights Become Public Wrongs: Property and the State in Prince Edward Island in the 1830s

RUSTY BITTERMANN AND MARGARET MCCALLUM

In the 1830s, existing state structures and property relations were profoundly questioned in all of the British North American colonies. In the colonies that became Quebec and Ontario, concerns about land distribution and development were central to what historians call the rebellions in the Canadas. Similar concerns informed public debate in the Maritime colonies of Nova Scotia, New Brunswick, and Prince Edward Island.[1]

This chapter explores some of the ideas about land and public policy that had emerged on Prince Edward Island by the 1830s and examines fundamental differences in the visions articulated by various participants in the discussion. In so doing, it focuses on differences that have to some extent been obscured in subsequent historical treatments of the land question on Prince Edward Island. Some of those who were prominent in the debate saw land as a commodity and land policy as an adjunct to economic development, while others argued for systems of land distribution that would create and maintain the social structure they considered appropriate. Those who saw land as the basis of the social

structure differed on what that social structure should be, but they shared the belief that it was the state's responsibility to ensure that land law and policy provided the foundation for their particular visions.

In the wake of the violence and unrest in the Canadas in the fall of 1837, the imperial government appointed Lord Durham as Governor General of British North America and commissioned him to inquire into and adjust all questions respecting the form and administration of the civil government of the Canadas. In this capacity, Lord Durham appointed Charles Buller as commissioner to examine the past and present methods of disposing of Crown lands in British North America, including those on Prince Edward Island. Pending the outcome of the inquiry, he requested the colonial governors to refrain from further alienation of Crown lands.

Durham's interest in the management and distribution of Crown lands, and his decision to request a moratorium on further grants pending the inquiry was in keeping with the position of those who stressed the significance of land policy to growth and development. In Durham's view,

Rusty Bittermann and Margaret McCallum, "When Private Rights Become Public Wrongs: Property and the State in Prince Edward Island in the 1830s." Reprinted with permission of the Publisher from *Despotic Dominion: Property Rights in British Settler Societies* by McLaren, John, A.R. Buck, and Nancy E. Wright, eds. © University of British Columbia Press 2005. All rights reserved by the Publisher.

land resources, properly managed, would foster rapid and efficient economic development in the colonies. Meanwhile, the inadequacy of existing state policy was evident in the quantity of granted land that was still in a wilderness state. Extensive tracts of unsettled land—"waste" land—suggested problems and perhaps the need for state intervention to redress this squandering of economic resources.

This concern with economic progress, and with the state's role in guiding it, informed Durham's instructions to the colonial governors regarding Crown lands. To "preserve the public property for the most effectual attainment of a great public purpose"—that is, economic development—the state needed to reconsider questions of land management and property rights in the colonies.[2] In this, Durham echoed the developmental position that leading members of the Island's business community had been advancing throughout the second quarter of the nineteenth century.[3]

Earlier imperial decisions, however, grounded as they were in different priorities and a different vision of the role of land policy in establishing the appropriate social order, created impediments to pursuit of the developmental agenda. In 1763, by the Treaty of Paris, France transferred sovereignty over Prince Edward Island (then known as Île St.-Jean) to the British. There was considerable speculative interest in the distribution of lands in the new colony, as most of the Island's 1.4 million acres had agricultural potential and included some of the best soils in the region.

After considering several proposals for developing the colony, the imperial government divided the Island into sixty-seven lots, or townships, of about twenty thousand acres each and distributed these in large grants, often granting an entire township to one individual. No provision was made to accommodate the small number of Acadians who had not been deported following Britain's military victory over the French, nor were any lands reserved for the Mi'kmaq who lived either permanently or seasonally on the Island.[4]

Island land policy focused on attracting new settlers and promoting the fishery. Grants were conditional on the grantees settling their lands within ten years with one foreign Protestant for every two hundred acres and subject to payment of quitrents ranging from two to six shillings per hundred acres. The grants provided as well for reserves of land along the shore to facilitate the fishery. The Crown also reserved to itself one landlocked lot, as well as land for county seats in the three counties—King's, Queen's, and Prince—and land within each lot for the support of religion and education.

For the most part, then, government officials on Prince Edward Island, unlike those in other British North American colonies, were deprived at the outset of the opportunities available from the management or distribution of extensive Crown lands. Instead, almost the whole of the Island's land base had been alienated in a single day, in an attempt to construct a colonial society modeled on the hierarchical agrarian order of pre-industrial Britain, with great proprietors who would populate their estates with lease-holders.[5]

At the time, imperial policy makers did not see a conflict between this social goal and economic development; indeed, Island proprietors were required by the terms of their grants to promote settlement. Nonetheless, central to these imperial decisions were conservative social and political objectives that differed from those advocated by Lord Durham or by Islanders who saw things as he did. Thus, when Island proprietors perceived threats to their property rights, they responded not only with claims about their contribution to the economic development of the Island, but with vehement arguments about the state's responsibility to uphold the "sacred rights of property" and to support a landed elite against demands for democracy and constraints on their power.

A third vision of the goals of land policy and of the role of the state in determining the relationship between land distribution and social structure emerged as settlers began to respond to the proprietorial system fostered by imperial land policies. In the 1830s, a popular challenge that came to be known as the Escheat movement criticized the hierarchical social vision of the proprietors and called on the state to ensure that colonial lands were used to sustain a society in which producers would be able to enjoy the fruits of their labour. Unlike the conservative vision that informed the imperial land policies of 1767, Escheat leaders and their rural constituents envisaged an egalitarian society of small, "independent" freeholders. Although they had some sympathy for the economic development plans promoted by business leaders, they differed from them in their insistence that the state's first concern was to secure the well-being of an independent citizenry through appropriate land distribution policies.[6]

This chapter examines these conflicting perspectives and their social basis, focusing primarily on the differences between those who considered land policy part of a developmental agenda and those who conceptualized land ownership as fundamental to an egalitarian, agrarian vision. It considers these differences in particular as they are revealed in the consideration of two main land policy initiatives of the 1830s: a tax on wilderness lands and the possibility of an escheat of proprietorial grants. Although the policies and vision, of those advocating a position similar to Durham's appear to have triumphed in the formal political arena by the early 1840s, proponents of the alternative democratic agrarian vision created an enduring legacy.

Prince Edward Island was not the only British North American colony in which the crown made large land grants. Less than two years before the imperial government granted away most of Prince Edward Island in a single day, the government in Nova Scotia (which then included the area that is now New Brunswick) distributed more than twice that amount of land in large grants over the course of seventeen days, although this largesse did not dispose of all the colony's Crown lands. The terms of the grants, like those later on Prince Edward Island, required proprietors to pay quitrents and settle their lands. But there were important differences.

Land distribution in Nova Scotia occurred within a policy framework established by the imperial authorities, but the government in Halifax determined the grantees and the terms of their grants. In Prince Edward Island, these decisions were made in the United Kingdom before the Island was constituted as a separate colony. As well, in Nova Scotia, with its longer history of British rule and colonial land policy, effective legislation facilitating the escheat of Crown grants was in place before 1760.[7] Nova Scotia thus provided a model for using escheat as a way for the state to enhance its control of land policy.

In the early years of Prince Edward Island's history as a British colony, escheat seemed applicable there, too. In Nova Scotia, extensive escheats provided the government with land for the thousands of Loyalist refugees who came to the colony during and after the American Revolution. In Prince Edward Island's general election of 1790, some candidates advocated similar escheat initiatives and the redistribution of proprietorial land in small tracts to actual settlers. Their initiatives, which appear to have been framed in terms of an agrarian republican vision, came to naught.[8] In 1816, the Island's governor, Charles Douglass Smith, acting for the most part independently of the PEI legislature, began proceedings that culminated in 1818 in the escheat of two townships: Lot 55, in King's County, on the southeast coast; and Lot 15, a point of land in Prince County jutting out into the Northumberland Strait, to the west of Bedeque Bay. He also instituted a policy of vigorous enforcement of quitrents.[9]

With both policies, Smith's main aim was to enhance government revenues; he did not intend to alter the colony's proprietorial system. Indeed, he explicitly recognized the need for the state to sustain landlords against democratic levelers who were agitating the "question of an Agrarian Law."[10] The Colonial Office, however, put an end to Smith's plans to escheat more lots and, in what the proprietors viewed as a major victory, announced revisions to the original conditions regarding payment of quitrents and bringing in settlers. When Smith moved again to enforce payment of quitrents, proprietors lobbied successfully for his removal from office, and he was replaced in 1824 by Colonel John Ready.[11] Despite the lack of support for escheat proceedings from the Colonial Office, some Islanders urged voters in the 1824 election campaign to inquire of candidates whether they supported an escheat and to vote only for those who would commit themselves to using an escheat to make proprietorial lands available in small grants to Island farmers.[12]

By the late 1820s, the distribution of Island land had become both more complex and more concentrated than in the original distribution of 1767. Ownership of most of the original sixty-seven townships had changed through subdivision among heirs, transfers of large estates to new proprietors, or sales of small holdings to freeholders. For many townships, it was difficult to establish an unbroken and undisputed chain of title forward from the original Crown grants, a situation that created enormous problems for tenants who faced demands for rent from people whose titles they could not verify.[13] But it is possible to provide a general picture of land distribution and tenure.

At the top of the hierarchy were roughly a dozen and a half Great Proprietors, holding estates of one or more townships; that is, twenty thousand acres or more. The six largest estates each contained the better part of four townships. Most of the Great Proprietors were absentee owners living in the United Kingdom, and many were well connected with imperial policy makers. Those holding smaller estates of less than a township were more likely to be Island residents than were the Great Proprietors. If the entire proprietorial class is defined as those who claimed ownership of five hundred or more acres, it is likely that slightly more than half of the proprietors were Island residents in the 1830s. And despite the often-repeated characterization of the land question as one between landlords and tenants, there was yet another class of landowners. About a third of the Island's rural population were small freeholders, owning in total about one-fifth of the Island. Total population in the 1830s exceeded thirty thousand.[14]

Among tenants, too, there was diversity in terms of land tenures and material circumstances. Squatters and leaseholders without written contracts, or tenants at will—perhaps one-third of the Island's tenants—were vulnerable to eviction at the proprietors' will. Tenants with written leases had some security against arbitrary termination of their tenancy, but if they fell behind in their rent payments, the landlord could evict them and seize their personal property to collect the arrears. Leases for wilderness lands often had graduated rents whereby tenants paid little or no rent for the first few years of farm making, with full rents, usually of one shilling per acre, payable only in the fifth or sixth year of the lease. For capital-poor emigrants, who began to arrive in increasing numbers after the Napoleonic Wars, such terms seemed attractive. Rents seemed low in comparison to the United Kingdom, and also in comparison to spending from half a pound to a pound per acre to buy land. But turning wilderness into productive farms consumed prodigious labour, money and time, and by the 1830s, many tenants were deeply in debt. Even if all went well and tenants were able to make enough from their farming efforts to support themselves and pay the landlord, at the end of the lease term it was the landlord and not the tenants who would reap the benefit of the improvements—the cleared fields, the fences, the houses and barns, and the investments of time and effort to drain and improve the soil. Although long leases, such as those for 999 years, gave the tenant some security for the value of the improvements, long leases were by no means standard on the Island.[15]

By the 1830s, then, there were divisions within Island society, as well as the more often-noted division between residents and absentees. The interests of tenants and their supporters in the countryside were at some points congruent and at some points collided with the interests of the emerging commercial and professional class, who hoped to reap economic and social benefits from taking a leadership role in Island development.

George Dalrymple was one of this group. A Scottish-born immigrant to Prince Edward Island in the early 1820s, Dalrymple employed the advantages of his education, capital, energy, and marriage to the daughter of a resident proprietor to establish himself as a successful business person and strong proponent of the use of state resources to facilitate economic development. An apothecary by trade, Dalrymple opened the Island's first carding mill and also served as a land agent. Regarding "political reform as a natural extension of his commitment to progress," in 1828 he obtained a seat in the Island legislature in an uncontested by-election for King's County, promising to support agricultural improvement and tenant relief. He was defeated in the 1830 election, but regained a seat in the House in a by-election called when the results were disputed and set aside.[16] For the Island to advance, Dalrymple urged his fellow Islanders they needed "to keep pace with the prevailing spirit of the age" and review local laws and institutions to see whether they required "reformation or improvement."[17]

On some questions, then, tenants and tenant supporters could unite with small freeholders and with the Island's commercial and professional class. Road construction, a central item in the develop-mental agenda, was supported across the Island, as rural residents looked forward to easier communication with their neighbours and improved access to markets, as well as to the possibility of earning cash from roadwork or from selling supplies to road crews.[18] But in the latter part of the decade, falling exports, part of a cyclical downturn in the Atlantic economy reduced the money available for imports, with a consequent reduction in government revenue, which, apart from an imperial grant for officials' salaries, was derived almost wholly from import tariffs. Quitrents, the other possible source of revenue, went to the Crown rather than to the colonial Assembly and often went unpaid, so the House of Assembly and Legislative Council cooperated to pass acts to substitute a land tax in place of the quitrents and to provide that the costs of new roads would be assessed against the owners of the lands to be benefited by the roads. This legislation had the support of Governor Ready, who had helped to build a political coalition to pursue colonial development, but it met with opposition in the United Kingdom, both from the imperial authorities, who would lose control of some revenue, and from the Great Proprietors, on whom the land, tax and road assessments would fall most heavily.[19] When the death of George IV in 1830 dissolved the legislature, the tax and assessment bills were still awaiting royal assent.[20]

The ensuing fall election provided an opportunity for widespread discussion of the means and goals of developmental policies. With scant evidence of what was said on the hustings or in public gatherings and private homes in town and country, it is difficult to determine whether candidates support for improvement won voters favour, although those who had voted for the Assembly's developmental legislation thought it useful to advertise that fact in the election campaign.[21] While the election of 1830 brought many new faces to the thirteenth Assembly, the legislators initially continued to focus on economic progress and improvement and to press for royal assent to the land tax bill and the roads bill.[22]

In January 1832, a new Assembly member brought a more comprehensive and radical approach to the question of land policy and the role of the state. William Cooper, of Bay Fortune, in King's County, was elected in a bitterly contested by-election in July 1831 after placing fifth in the previous year's contest for the four King's County Assembly seats. Having campaigned under the banner of "Our country's freedom and farmers' rights," Cooper provided only qualified support for the politics of progress.[23] In his view, developmental policies ignored the primary concerns of the rural population: "I have always heard that those great proprietary Grants were the only grievances in the country, and though a great deal has been said, there is nothing done in it yet."[24] With his election, escheat gained a strong advocate in the Assembly and began to emerge as a political movement, as well as a legal strategy in the struggle to redistribute land from the few to the many.

Cooper's activities in promoting escheat as a means to a more egalitarian distribution of land can be seen as an extension of the role he had played for his rural community as a land agent. Cooper settled on Prince Edward Island after more than twenty years at sea with the British navy and as a sea captain. A literate and well-read man in his mid-thirties, he became the land agent for Lord Townshend, absentee owner of Lot 56, in King's County, toward the east end of the Island. The previous agent had been killed in 1819 by a tenant while attempting to seize the tenant's horse to collect on arrears of rent. Yet Cooper was able to take over as Townshend's land agent and gain the respect and support of the tenantry. The explanation for this may lie in Cooper's conception of the obligations as well as the rights of a landlord. Some years after he met with Townshend to receive his instructions, Cooper recollected that Townshend's primary concern was to settle his sparsely populated estate and to have his agent "ensure the kind treatment of his tenantry."[25]

During his employment as Townshend's land agent, Cooper substantially increased the numbers of tenants on the estate. He arranged for the construction of a grist mill, found markets for local goods, and accepted payment of rents in labour, timber, or agricultural goods. In 1825, he organized construction of a brigantine, *Hackmatack,* for sale abroad, as a way "to make a remittance" to Lord Townshend.

These projects were in keeping with the ideals of the older hierarchical agrarian order that had provided a model for British land policy on the Island. Cooper's vision of the landlord-tenant relationship as involving mutual rights and obligations, along with his presence as a resident of the estate and the services he provided as local peacemaker, doctor, and sustainer of those in need, earned him the loyalty of the tenants.

Townshend, however, seems to have become increasingly concerned about immediate returns from his properties, and Cooper was dismissed and replaced by an agent residing in Charlottetown. As his relationship with Townshend deteriorated, Cooper was required to take personal responsibility for debts incurred in ventures undertaken to develop Townshend's estate. With Townshend's repudiation of Cooper's understanding of the landlord's responsibilities, Cooper became a critic of landlordism on the Island.[26] Proprietors, he charged, had turned their backs on the "people they ought to support and cherish" and were not fulfilling their part of the social contract.[27]

Within two weeks of Cooper's taking his seat, the Assembly, on a motion sponsored by George Dalrymple, created a committee to inquire into "whether any and what lots or townships on this Island are liable to escheat."[28] Dalrymple and Cooper were both on the committee, along with Charles Binns, a Charlottetown lawyer and business person; Thomas Owens, a land agent and merchant involved in the shipbuilding industry; and John Brecken, from a wealthy Loyalist merchant family that provided banking services for many in the colony prior to establishment of the Bank of North America.[29] After hearing testimony—including discussion of the escheat proceedings of 1818—and inquiring into the history of the land question in the colony, the committee recommended that the Assembly petition Governor Aretas Young, who had replaced John Ready in the fall of 1831, to establish a court of escheat and pass the legislation necessary to provide for its operation. Both recommendations received the approval of the majority, with the only dissenting votes cast by two members who were resident landlords.[30]

Presumably on the basis of his motion initiating discussion of escheat, Dalrymple is identified by at least one historian as part of the nucleus of what became the Escheat Party.[31] For Dalrymple, though, escheat was not a step toward eliminating landlordism and redistributing Island land among actual settlers. Instead, Dalrymple and the majority in the Assembly hoped their advocacy of escheat proceedings would secure rural votes while channelling demands for land reform into support for their developmental agenda. Indeed, Dalrymple carefully differentiated his position from the more radical proposals that were circulating in the countryside, assuring the Assembly that he maintained "a sacred regard" for the rights of private property and that he strongly opposed "any visionary scheme being carried into execution."[32]

Rather than a dramatic redistribution of land rights that would lay the basis for an egalitarian agrarian order, what the majority approved in 1832 was a selective escheat of the least developed estates on the Island. Townships with significant numbers of tenants, squatters, or freeholders would be exempt from escheat, even if the number of settlers was not what had been stipulated by the Crown. Thus, most landlords and their local land agents would face no threat to their places in the Island economy and society. The majority in the Assembly viewed the court of escheat as a means of removing

obstacles to the colony's advancement; however, the obstacle that most concerned them was not the proprietorial system itself, but the large tracts of land that remained in a wilderness state, unavailable for incoming settlers and generating no revenue for the Island's treasury. The title of their legislation, *An Act to Encourage the Settlement and Improvement of Lands in This Island and to Regulate the Proceedings of a Court of Escheats Therein,*[33] spoke of the imperatives of growth and development. A selective escheat would remove the non-improving proprietors who held land for speculative gains and blocked the path to prosperity, leading to new investment, improved trade, and "the introduction of emigrants and thereby the cultivation of the soil."[34] A selective escheat also offered something to the Island's small freeholders, who wanted more land for themselves and their children. No doubt it would also provide opportunities for Islanders with capital to achieve prominence and profits as landowners and developers, as well as further employment for land agents. Binns and Owen could thus, without any inconsistency, support Dalrymple in his call for a court of escheat while promoting land development companies such as the New Brunswick Land Company.[35]

Cooper, alone among the eighteen members of the thirteenth Assembly, articulated a different motivation for escheat and different criteria for determining what lots should be treated this way. He advocated the broadest possible escheat, in order to extinguish leasehold tenure throughout the colony and to transfer ownership of proprietorial estates to the tenants and squatters who worked them. While providing support for Dalrymple's escheat legislation in his first speech in the Assembly, Cooper also issued a resounding call for the state to take a hand in constructing a just social order. None of the catchwords and objectives of the majority in the Assembly—prosperity, progress, improvement, economic growth and development, and immigration—

figured in his speech. A general escheat was necessary, Cooper asserted, to secure "the people's rights" and, most fundamentally to achieve "justice." The word "justice" appears ten times in his two-thousand-word speech.

Drawing from a labour theory of value, Cooper argued that an unjust land system denied rural people the rights to the value they created, "for there cannot be a greater power given to one man over another than the right of a landlord over poor tenants." Charging that many Island proprietors neither settled others on their estates nor occupied and used the land themselves, Cooper suggested that they regarded landownership as a means of exploitation. "It was not the lands they wanted, but by holding the land to have a claim on the labour of their fellow subjects, who had equal rights with themselves." The proprietors' land grants, however, could not give them the right to exploit others, because "the King owes justice and mercy to all his subjects." "Property," Cooper maintained, "is the labour of man." The Island's rural settlers had "wasted their youth in clearing lands for others...planted their labour where the forest grew, [and] made a garden in the wilderness," yet they were vulnerable to the exactions of landlords whose only claim to their farms and improvements rested on a dubious title sustained by the proprietors' "favour and power" with the imperial authorities.[36] As Cooper said in a later speech, "skins of written parchment and patches of wax can give no title to the *few* to enslave and starve the *many*."[37]

Moving beyond discussion of the legal basis for an escheat in the unfulfilled conditions of the eighteenth-century grants, Cooper based his call for an escheat in a more general discussion of justice and property rights. Drawing from diverse sources, Cooper presented a cogent justification of state intervention to secure an appropriate distribution of land, arguing that concentration of land in the hands of a few owners was a threat to the well-being of the colony. Accumulation of wealth, and especially of land, was dangerous to the polity, whether it occurred through political favours and corruption or through participation in the market economy. Citing classical precedents, Cooper defended the thinking of those who had designed the Roman agrarian laws that established limits on the amount of land that any individual might hold. Similar measures were necessary on Prince Edward Island to preserve "the liberties of the people."

Anticipating the arguments of those who would oppose restrictions on landownership, Cooper responded that limits on accumulation of wealth were necessary to secure justice for all and legitimacy for the state. Just restrictions were both "the security of the people" and "the bulwark of and support of Government; and what applies to one class of mankind, applies to all."[38] Cooper emphasized his democratic views in a later speech, arguing that the "majority of mankind must have an interest in the soil" if they are to "support and defend" their country's laws, which are no more than "the *arbitrary will* of the majority of the people." The consequences of an unjust land policy, argued Cooper, could be seen in Ireland: rule by "bullets and bayonets" rather than by consent.[39]

Sentiments such as these were anathema to the majority of the thirteenth Assembly. Conservatives condemned them as subversive, and even those such as Dalrymple, who thought of themselves as being in the British Reform tradition, balked at such a complete rethinking of the relationship between economic and political liberty. Nonetheless, despite their differing objectives, rhetoric, and program, Cooper and the majority in the thirteenth Assembly could agree on some matters. The call for a selective escheat and Cooper's call for a general escheat were rooted in a similar understanding of the Island's history. There was broad agreement that the original grantees, rather than fulfilling the conditions in their grants, had disposed of their land at bargain prices to speculators and thus had no just claims on the Crown. Yet, through persistently misrepresenting their circumstances at the Colonial Office, the proprietors had deceived the imperial authorities into granting them concessions and blocking the efforts of the Island legislature to remedy a great public wrong.[40]

The proprietors' lobby was indeed powerful, and perhaps perfidious. In September 1832, Governor Young ordered the publication of a dispatch from Lord Goderich, the Colonial Secretary, explaining that the imperial authorities would not permit the establishment of a court of escheat. Indeed, Goderich advised Islanders to give up any idea that an escheat would result in the redistribution of lands to those who occupied them or the opening up of new lands for free Crown grants. Free grants were a thing of the past; should there be an escheat, those occupying lands that reverted to the Crown would have to pay their present rents to the state.[41]

Records that are now public confirm that the Assembly was correct in attributing imperial resistance to its land initiatives to landlords' lobbying efforts. Goderich's dispatch was the product of extensive lobbying at the Colonial Office, orchestrated primarily by David and Robert Stewart, Island landlords who lived in the Bloomsbury district of London. The Stewarts were involved in estate management in the British Isles. They had begun to invest heavily in Island lands in the early 1830s and were in the final stages of assembling a holding of around 100,000 acres when Cooper made his escheat speech.[42] Publication of this speech in the Charlottetown *Royal Gazette,* coupled with news of the House of Assembly's land question initiatives, prompted the Stewarts, and other Island proprietors who followed developments in the colony, to register their concerns with the Colonial Office.[43] The Stewarts helped to draft a collective memorial to Lord Goderich opposing the legislature's escheat initiative, and this in turn generated the Goderich dispatch, which

Young ordered to be published in Island papers.[44]

More importantly, the Stewarts helped to establish a permanent organization to coordinate collective landlord action. The Prince Edward Island Association officially came into being in 1834 and operated out of the Stewarts' London residence.[45] Reflecting an older tradition of Island landlords working together to petition the imperial government when they believed their property interests were at stake,[46] this group was the formal expression of the one that had begun working together earlier in the 1830s as the Island legislature began to take a more activist role on land issues.

The Prince Edward Island Association focused on monitoring developments on the Island and developing effective landlord appeals to the Colonial Office. To this end, the organization cultivated the membership and assistance of leading members of British society who owned Island estates, including the sixth Earl of Selkirk; Andrew Colvile; Lord Townshend; Lord Montgomery; Lord Melville; the Earl of Westmorland; George Seymour, sergeant-at-arms to the House of Lords; Henry Winchester, mayor of London in the mid-1830s and a member of Parliament; and Laurence Sulivan, Deputy Secretary of War.[47]

The Island Assembly responded to Lord Goderich's dispatch by asserting, in a petition to the King, that the dispatch was yet another example of the effect of proprietorial influence. The proprietors, the petition stated, had "contrived by means of false statements" concocted for "the most sordid motive" to defeat the efforts to resolve the land question.[48] Having confirmed its dedication to its rural constituents with this strident protest, the majority in the Assembly returned to business as usual. Some no doubt privately heaved a great sigh of relief.[49]

When the Assembly met again in 1833, Joseph Pope, leader of the conservative forces, was ready with a land tax scheme that he said would "answer the end of an escheat."[50] Pope was part of a large, Plymouth-based mercantile family that had become involved in Prince Edward Island's timber trade after the Napoleonic Wars. By the early 1830s, he had charge of his family's extensive operations in and about Bedeque, in Prince County, as well as being the most prominent merchant west of Charlottetown. He was also a land agent for an absentee American proprietor.[51]

Pope's bill, which passed in the Assembly and the Legislative Council, provided for a land tax of four shillings and six pence per hundred acres of township land, to come into effect in the fall of 1837 with the expiration of the current land tax. This bill drew on Lord Goderich's dispatch, which had suggested that the imperial government would look favourably on a land tax, even one that taxed settled and unsettled lands at an equal rate, thereby providing an incentive for developing or selling lands held for speculative purposes.[52] Nonetheless, the imperial government again reserved assent, in part to allow the proprietors a chance to express their objections.[53] Cooper attempted to keep the escheat issue to the forefront with a motion to send a delegate to the United Kingdom to speak to the matter, but his motion was defeated.[54]

While Cooper had been pressing for a general escheat in the thirteenth Assembly, tenants and their supporters in the countryside were resisting the power of their landlords more directly.[55] They were also organizing to ensure the election of more Escheat supporters in the general elections held in the late fall of 1834. King's County voters returned Cooper to the House of Assembly and also elected another strong Escheator in John Lelacheur of Murray Harbour. Lelacheur was a native of Guernsey who had emigrated to Prince Edward Island in 1806. A cooper by trade, he was, like many of those who became leaders in the Escheat movement, a labouring tenant farmer. The other

two candidates elected from King's County, Peter Maccallum of St. Peter's Bay and Daniel Brenan, a prominent Irish Catholic and Charlottetown merchant who had represented King's County in the Assembly since 1830, were more equivocal in their support for escheat.[56] In Queen's County, the only person who openly supported a general escheat was defeated; Dalrymple was the most reform-minded of the four successful candidates.[57]

In the weeks before the Assembly met, rural residents of King's County prepared a petition with 1,400 signatures, reiterating the arguments for a general escheat: the proprietors had forfeited their claim to ownership by their failure to meet the conditions in the original grants, and the tenants had earned the right to the land by the labour invested in it. Short leases and high rents would permit landlords to harvest the labour of others and appropriate improvements they had not had any part in creating. If freehold grants were no longer Crown policy, the petitioners expressed their willingness to become the King's tenants and pay rent to the Crown.[58]

The King's County petition and the support it garnered from some in the Assembly provided the leverage to place escheat at the centre of debate. With Cooper's backing, Daniel Brenan moved to establish a committee to investigate the land question. It recommended a general escheat, based on a strict interpretation of the terms of the original grants, and supported the recommendation with detailed historical, economic, and legal argument.[59]

In moving beyond the selective escheat that had gained majority support in the thirteenth Assembly, the committee forced a clarification of the lines of division between those who sought a way to open wilderness lands for investment and settlement and those who called for a general escheat to secure a more just social order. Pope, who, had supported the 1832 *Escheat Act* because it was framed on "equitable principles," said that a general escheat would be "an act of dishonesty."[60]

Yet, from the perspective of much of the rural population, it was the proprietors who were dishonest. Belief in the need to reform the land system so that honest workers could keep what their work created was central to the Escheat movement. Commercial and industrial men such as Dalrymple and Pope concerned themselves with investment, growth, and business prosperity. They sought to construct an environment in which their ventures would thrive. The leasehold system was not in itself a structural obstacle to their goals, though landlords who failed to develop their holdings could be. Land reform was important to them primarily because the unrest in the countryside threatened their political and economic power. Indeed, many Island entrepreneurs derived income and labour from the proprietorial system.[61] With a partial escheat policy, they could appear to be addressing rural concerns while pursuing their developmental program, but the rise of the Escheat movement undercut their support in the countryside. Beyond this, they feared that the Escheat attack on landlordism could develop into a broader assault on capitalist values. The "progress of improvement in the colony" was threatened, they argued, by rural politicians raising "hopes of agrarian law."[62]

On the immediate issue, the advocates of developmental policies prevailed. With Dalrymple casting the deciding vote, the Assembly determined to send an address, rather than a delegation, as the Escheat supporters had wanted, to argue their cause in the United Kingdom. The address the Assembly adopted spoke generally of the need to establish a court of escheat and deal with other political grievances.[63] Although the majority could block Assembly support for a general escheat, their own program was stymied by the proprietors' influence in the Colonial Office, as was made evident by dispatches presented to the Assembly announcing that neither the 1832 escheat bill nor the 1833 land tax bill would receive royal assent.[64]

When the Assembly reconvened early in 1836, it learned that its address of the previous year had not been forwarded to the Colonial Office.[65] Sustained by another petition from his constituents, Cooper called again for a committee to inquire into the land question.[66] Pope responded in words that left no doubt about his politics. Again avowing his support for "an equitable escheat," he rejected the arguments of the petitioners, declaring many among them to be "the very scum of society," who saw in a general escheat a way to get "a share of the spoil."[67] Again, Pope offered a land tax as a substitute. And Cooper opposed any such measure, because it undermined the escheat argument by implicitly acknowledging the validity of proprietorial titles.[68]

The differences between supporters of a selective escheat and a general escheat were aired again when the Assembly debated a new address for the Colonial Office. The address submitted by the committee responsible for drafting it focused on the need for a general escheat and the creation of an "impartial tribunal" to inquire into the rights of the Island's tenantry. The address that was finally adopted, by a margin of one vote, was an alternative address proposed by Pope. It called for a court of escheat to determine whether any lands were subject to escheat and to confirm the grants of those who "may be found deserving of your Majesty's most gracious consideration under the indulgences granted by your Majesty's Royal predecessors." Such a step was necessary, the address suggested, to allay agitation in the countryside on the land question, which was causing land values to depreciate, "by exciting doubts in the minds of many persons respecting the Titles to Lands, preventing men of capital from settling in the country, and retarding the transaction of public business in the Legislature, to the serious detriment of the prosperity and welfare of the Island at large."[69]

The seeming dismissal of the escheat program by the imperial authorities and the majority in the Assembly provoked further agitation in the countryside, with public meetings to express support for a general escheat and an end to landlordism, wide circulation of newspaper reports of Escheat resolutions, and distribution of Escheat pamphlets. In a pamphlet published in the summer of 1836, Cooper elaborated on the wrongs of the proprietorial system, beginning with the contrast between an older, organic society and current norms:

> In the old fashioned times the lands were considered to be for the use of the people, to give them employment and subsistence, to raise and maintain a hardy race for the support and defense of the country—but, according to the improved system, the land is not for the use of the people, but for the proprietor...and when the present inhabitants are removed [to clear the way for more profitable uses of the land], there will be no more complaints against proprietors, because the people who were deceived and deprived of the lands they have taken out of the wilderness will be either buried or removed.[70]

Despite the strength of the support for a general escheat in the countryside, the new Colonial Secretary, Lord Glenelg, again rejected even the weak escheat proposal in Pope's address, arguing that it would be impossible to determine whether the settlement conditions had been fulfilled. Consistent with the reasoning and rhetoric of development, Glenelg identified as the main concern "the uncultivated state of the Island by reason of want of settlers" and suggested that this could be remedied by the introduction of a land tax that would penalize speculation. He helpfully provided a statute from Upper Canada to serve as a model.[71]

John Harvey, who arrived in the Island in August 1836 to take up his post as the new governor, was entirely in agreement with Glenelg's position and sought ways to neutralize the leaders of the escheat movement and to quell the continuing agitation in the countryside. To this end, he determined to punish the three Assemblymen from King's County—William Cooper, John Lelacheur, and John Macintosh—for their part in a mass Escheat meeting held at Hay River, on Lot 43, King's County, in December 1836.[72]

Most controversial among the resolutions passed at the meeting were those calling for refusal to pay rent and resistance to landlords' efforts to use the legal process to collect arrears. Turning the arguments of Escheat's opponents against them, the resolutions argued that it was the proprietary system that was "subversive of the sacred right of property" because it robbed settlers of what rightfully belonged to them. To pay rent, when proprietors and their allies in the government violated all standards of justice, would be "to foster oppression and reward crime." Those present resolved "by the honour and dignity of the King and British nation—by the rights of men to the fruits of their labour" and "by justice and equity" to "preserve from the distress of such landlords the fruits of our industry."[73]

Like their contemporaries in the Canadas, Escheators defended their actions with appeals to British justice,[74] but, in Harvey's view, the resolutions passed at the meeting were seditious. At the governor's suggestion, the majority in the Assembly passed a motion condemning the three men for their disloyalty and their "false and scandalous libel" on the Assembly in suggesting that the majority's rejection of a general escheat in 1836 might be related to the positions some members held as land agents. When the three refused to apologize in the terms required—terms that Assembly member Peter Maccallum condemned as something that no "independent honest man [could] submit to"— they were found in contempt and committed to the care of the sergeant-at-arms. And there they stayed for the remainder of the 1837 session and the entire 1838 one—deprived of their salaries, their right to take part in the proceedings and debates, and their freedom of movement while the Assembly was in session.[75]

Harvey believed his actions had "settled *forever*" the question of escheat, which in his view was what obstructed the Island's prosperity.[76] With the advocates of a general escheat out of their way, Harvey's supporters in the Assembly quickly moved forward with their plans to facilitate capitalist development. Commenting on the desirability of new initiatives, Dalrymple argued that there was now no possibility for even a selective escheat, given the wild claims made by some concerning a general escheat and the "imprudent means" resorted to in advocating their cause.[77] Instead, the Assembly passed a new land tax act that it hoped would survive the proprietors' complaints to the Colonial Office. Based on Glenelg's suggestion, the legislation provided for a tax of four shillings per hundred acres on uncultivated lands and half that on properties under cultivation.[78]

Such policies, however, did not address the concerns of much of the Island's rural population, who continued to believe in the justice of their claim to the land they needed to provide livelihoods for their families. Unrest in the countryside stemmed from unjust social and economic relations, not from the colony's economic backwardness and the lack of tenants on proprietors' undeveloped lands. As an Escheat petition of April 1837 put it, there were already "a sufficient number of inhabitants under the yoke of tenancy" and the "oppression" of landlordism.[79] Dismantling the Escheat movement required dealing with these beliefs, and with the contention that the state had a role to play in ensuring that concentration of landownership did not become the means whereby a few could oppress the majority.

Harvey attempted to do this in his published correspondence on the Hay River matter. Noting that tenants needed to heed those offering "sounder and kinder advice," the governor asserted that the problems tenants faced were essentially private ones, involving contracts with which the state could not interfere.[80] In a dispatch received and published on the Island in June 1837, Glenelg advanced similar views on the demarcation between public and private issues, suggesting that the state could intervene only as a "mediator" between the tenants and the landlords.[81]

Despite such public expressions of liberal thought, prescient government officials recognized that they could not let events unfold entirely in accordance with economic forces and existing property laws. Cooper had observed in 1833 that objection to the proprietorial system was so great, and social distress so grievous, that soon the state's laws would be enforceable only with bullet and bayonet—a note that became increasingly apt as the decade unfolded. Glenelg's statement that the government had a role to play as mediator between landlords and tenants was a shift away from the view that the terms in which tenants gained access to land was solely a private, contractual matter. It was also consistent with a similar shift in Harvey's thinking as he moved from instructing tenants to appeal to their landlords for leniency to making his own appeal to the proprietors for better terms for their tenants.[82] In June 1837, as Harvey prepared to leave Prince Edward Island to become governor of New Brunswick, he was willing to advocate even more state intervention. His final communications to the Colonial Office requested imperial support for the land tax act and authorization for the new governor to convene a court of escheat to escheat lots that had not been adequately settled as of 1826. In Harvey's view, nothing less would bring peace to the Island.[83]

By mid-1837, the Colonial Office was concerned about growing agrarian radicalism across British North America. By that winter, the authorities had to deploy the military in Upper and Lower Canada to quell armed rebellion. In late October 1837, before the outbreak of fighting, Patriote leaders in Lower Canada, addressing a rally of four thousand people, spoke of the day when they would be free from the oppression they suffered and from the burden of rents and tithes. They spoke too of the parallel struggle in Prince Edward Island.[84] In the winter of 1838, knowing of the fighting and the repression in the Canadas, Cooper, Lelacheur, and Macintosh, still confined in the care of the sergeant-at-arms, appealed to their supporters to be patient and warned them not to let themselves be driven into "open insurrection." Better to "suffer themselves to be stripped of every article they possess, rather than attempt any resistance, which would have no other effect than to expose their dwellings to desolation and themselves to all the honors of military execution."[85] With the announcement of Lord Durham's mission, Escheat leaders prepared to send a delegation to Quebec to present their view of what the Island needed.

John Lelacheur was chosen to represent the Escheat position.[86] In his testimony before Durham's Commission on Crown Lands and Emigration, he described how the proprietors had failed to fulfil the conditions of their grants and had used their influence with the Colonial Office to prevent passage of either escheat legislation or a tax on wild lands. Both Sir Charles Fitzroy, who had replaced Harvey as the Island's governor, and Robert Hodgson, the Island's attorney general, were provided by the commission with a transcript of Lelacheur's testimony, and neither disputed its accuracy with respect to the disposal of Crown lands. They differed, however, in their responses to a question about the cause of the Island's "slow progress and lack of cultivation." Lelacheur attributed responsibility to "the exorbitant terms demanded by the proprietors of land, which have deterred individuals from taking land, and have driven away many also who had come to the Island for the purpose

of settlement." In private conversations with Durham and his officials, Lelacheur urged the establishment of a court of escheat. Fitzroy and Hodgson suggested in their testimony that the landlords needed to offer the tenants better terms, including longer leases, and recommended a tax on wilderness lands, with the money to be spent on public works such as roads and bridges for the improvement of the Island. Hodgson also suggested that the government should purchase proprietorial lands, if they could be obtained for a reasonable price, and resell them to settlers.[87]

In his report, Lord Durham adopted the view of Island history presented by John Lelacheur. He did not, however, advocate escheat as a solution, despite the observation in the report on public lands that escheat, although not generally expedient or just, might be warranted in Prince Edward Island, "where the Provincial Government has never desisted from endeavours, which have been unhappily defeated by the exercise of powers vested in the Home Government, to enforce the performance of the conditions, or, in default, to resume the land."[88] Instead, Lord Durham recommended, as he did for the other colonies, a tax on wild lands to encourage speculators to develop their properties or to sell them. Indeed, Durham gave himself credit for securing royal assent for the land tax act passed by the PEI Assembly in 1837, which he described in his report as "*intended* to remove the abuse that has so long retarded the prosperity of this Colony."[89] The words were no doubt carefully chosen. In response to a query from Lord Glenelg, the Colonial Secretary, on the question of escheat in Prince Edward Island, Durham had recommended approval of the land tax act while expressing doubt that it would prove "a sufficient remedy for the evil in question."[90]

The doubts were justified. Governor Harvey had assumed that, with his support, the Island's leading commercial and professional men could carry a program that would undercut the appeal of escheat in the countryside. Fitzroy tried the same strategy, with the same lack of success. In the election in November of 1838, supporters of what was now recognizable as the Escheat Party gained a majority of seats in the Assembly. Yet the Escheators' control of the Assembly was not enough to secure imperial agreement to a general escheat. Their petitions for a redress of agrarian grievances went unheeded, and their legislative initiatives were blocked in the United Kingdom or by the colony's Legislative Council, to which Fitzroy had appointed some of those, including Dalrymple, who lost their Assembly seats in the 1838 Escheat election victory.[91] In the elections held in 1842, the new governor, Vere Huntley, like Fitzroy before him, lent his support to the anti-Escheat forces and they regained control of the Assembly, although not a monopoly on setting the political agenda.[92]

The defeat of Escheat as a political party did not end the struggle against the leasehold system and its concentration of land in the hands of a few Great Proprietors. The Escheat movement amplified, focused, and honed the conceptions and aspirations of much of the rural population, giving them a vision of a more just society and a historical, constitutional, and moral analysis that justified their efforts to realize that vision on Prince Edward Island. The Escheat vision, however, clashed with a vision of progress that subordinated claims of justice and democracy to the pursuit of economic growth and improvement and assigned to the state the role of protecting individual accumulation and providing necessary infrastructure. In the late 1820s and 1830s, Dalrymple and those who

thought like him had emerged as the favoured forces guiding the pace and direction of change in Island life. Their vision of the way forward increasingly dominated the formulation of questions and the range of legitimate responses in the public arena. Having seized the initiative, they actively sought to restructure Island affairs in keeping with the social and economic changes they observed elsewhere in the Atlantic world.

The Escheat movement challenged the view of progress promoted by Dalrymple and his colleagues, as well as the claims of proprietors that the state should enforce their sacred right to do as they wanted with their property. Despite the paucity of immediate legislative achievements, the Escheat movement succeeded in placing an alternative vision at the centre of political debate and popular resistance, and this vision sustained the long struggle to end landlordism on the Island. The Escheat challenge to the legitimacy of the landlords' claims shaped Islanders' ideas about their history and provided a strong argument for restricting private rights to prevent public wrongs.[93] Widespread support for the view that proprietors had forfeited their estates helped justify the legislation enacted in 1875 to force proprietors who owned more than five hundred acres to sell their holdings to the government for resale to the actual occupiers, with the proprietors' compensation to be determined by a tripartite tribunal.[94] Current restrictions on the amount of Island land that any individual can own show the continuing force of the Escheators' belief in the dangers of too much land in too few hands.[95]

Notes

1 The similarities were grounded in part in the activities of a cast of British and colonial developers who promoted corporate initiatives to control economic development in all three colonies. Daniel Samson's "Industrial Colonization: The Colonial Context of the General Mining Association, Nova Scotia, 1825–1842" (1999) 29 *Acadiensis* 1, details the con-

nections among some of these developers and explores their ideology. See too Ivan J. Saunders, "The New Brunswick and Nova Scotia Land Company and the Settlement of Stanley, New Brunswick" (MA thesis, University of New Brunswick, 1969), for consideration of a scheme that, but for the emergence of the Escheat movement on Prince Edward Island, would have included Island lands as well, including those of some of the company's promoters.

2 C.P. Lucas, ed., *Lord Durham's Report on the Affairs of British North America,* vol. 2 (Oxford: Clarendon Press, 1912) at 3–5, 203–8, and vol. 3 at 29–33 [Lucas, *Lord Durham's Report*]; quoted text, instructions, from Lord Durham to the Lieutenant-Governors of Her Majesty's Colonies in North America (30 June 1838) in vol. 3 at 33.

3 For discussion of similar agendas elsewhere in the region, see J. Murray Beck, *Politics of Nova Scotia,* vol. 1 (Tantallon, NS: Four East Publications, 1985) at 86–99; W.S. MacNutt, *The Atlantic Provinces: The Emergence of Colonial Society, 1712–1857* (Toronto; McClelland and Stewart, 1965) at 193–208; T.W. Acheson, "The Great Merchant and Economic Development in St. John, 1820–1850" (1979) 8 *Acadiensis* 3.

4 One recent study has suggested that there were perhaps 200 Mi'kmaq and 200 Acadians on the Island in 1767. See J.M. Bumsted, *Land, Settlement, and Politics on Eighteenth-Century Prince Edward Island* (Montreal and Kingston: McGill–Queen's University Press, 1987) at 25. Earle Lockerby estimates that a third of the Acadians of Prince Edward Island escaped deportation, either by remaining in the colony or fleeing to the mainland. See Earle Lockerby, "The Deportation of the Acadians from Île-St. Jean, 1758" (1998) 27 *Acadiensis* 45 at 79.

5 Bumsted, ibid. at 417.

6 For a full discussion of the popular movement that advanced these ideas, see Rusty Bittermann, "Escheat! Rural Protest on Prince Edward Island, 1832–42" (PhD dissertation, University of New Brunswick, 1991). In this chapter, "Escheat" refers to the movement and its program and "escheat" to the legal proceedings necessary for the Crown to retake grants for failure to fulfil the conditions in them. For accounts of anti-landlord struggles elsewhere in North America, see Richard Maxwell Brown, "Back Country Rebellions and the Homestead Ethic in America, 1740–1799" in R.M. Brown and D.E. Fehrenbacher, eds., *Tradition, Conflict and Modernization: Perspectives on the American Revolution* (New York: Academic Press, 1977) at 73–98; Edward Countryman, "'Out of the Bounds of the Law': Northern Land Rioters in the Eighteenth Century" in Alfred E Young, ed., *The American Revolution: Explorations in the History of American Radicalism* (DeKalb: Northern Illinois University Press, 1976) at 36–91; Alan Taylor, *Liberty Men and Great Proprietors: The Revolutionary settlement on the Maine Frontier,*

1760–1820 (Chapel Hill: University of North Carolina Press, 1990); Reeve Huston, *Land and Freedom: Rural Society, Popular Protest, and Party Politics in Antebellum New York* (New York: Oxford University Press, 2000); Eldridge H. Pendleton, "The New York Anti-Rent Controversy, 1830–1860" (PhD dissertation, University of Virginia, 1974); Thomas Summerhill, The Farmers' Republic: Agrarian Protest and the Capitalist Transformation of Upstate New York, 1840–1900" (PhD dissertation, University of California, San Diego, 1993). There was an anti-landlord element to "les troubles" in Lower Canada (Quebec) in 1837–38, although the commutation of seigneurial tenure to freehold tenure had more to do with increasing the commercial opportunities to landowners than with limiting the power of landlords, See Allan Greer, *The Patriots and the People: The Rebellion of 1837 in Lower Canada* (Toronto: University of Toronto Press, 1993) at 24, 35–38, 148–49, c. 9; Fernand Ouellet, *Economic and Social History of Quebec, 1760–1850: Structures and Conjunctures* (Toronto: Gage, 1980); Tom Johnson, "Perceptions of Property: The Social and Historical Imagination of Quebec's Legal Elite, 1836–1856" (SJD thesis, University of Wisconsin, 1989); Tom Johnson, "In a Manner of Speaking: Towards a Reconstitution of Property in Mid-19th-Century Quebec" (1987) 32 McGill L.J. 636.

7 Margaret Ells, "Clearing the Decks for the Loyalists" in *Annual Report* (Ottawa: Canadian Historical Association, 1993) at 50; Joshua Mauger Grant, Public Archives of Nova Scotia, Nova Scotia Land Grant Book, Old Book 6 at 545, Reel 13036; Neil MacKinnon, *This Unfriendly Soil: The Loyalist Experience in Nova Scotia, 1783–1791* (Montreal and Kingston: McGill-Queen's University Press, 1986) at 13–15; New Brunswick "Escheat Book" and "Escheats [1785], Surrenders, etc., 1785," Provincial Archives of New Brunswick (PANB), Dept. of Natural Resources: Crown Lands RS 107/RNA/C/9/3/3-4.

8 Hill memorandum, [n.d.] Colonial Office Papers (CO) 226/17/110.

9 *Prince Edward Island Gazette* (Charlottetown) (19 January and 14 March 1818); Smith to Bathurst (15 February 1818) CO 226/34/20–22; 15 March 1818 (ibid. at 31).

10 Smith to Bathurst (13 September 1814) CO 226/29/82.

11 *Prince Edward Island Gazette* (8 August 1818); [?] to Cambridge (21 March 1823) CO 226/39/420; Requisition to Sheriff, CO 226/41/64–65; Smith to

Bathurst (3 November 1823) CO 226/39/153–56; P.A. Buckner, "Charles Douglass Smith" in *Dictionary of Canadian Biography*, vol. 8 (Toronto: University of Toronto Press, 1985) at 823–27.

12 *Prince Edward Island Register* (Charlottetown) (4 December 1824).

13 Legislation requiring landlords to register their titles in the Island's Registry Office was rejected by the Colonial Office. See *An Act to Require Landlords, or Claimants of Rents, to Put the Titles by Which They Claim upon Record, in the Proper Offices of Record in This Island*, S.P.E.I. 1832, c 12.

14 List of Island proprietors and their holdings, submitted to the Colonial Office by Governor Ready in 1830, CO 226/47/166–68; George Seymour, "Journal of Tour of Canada and the United States" (1840), entry for 8 September, Warwick County Record Office (WCRO), Seymour of Ragley Papers, CR 114A/380. Distinctions between absentee and resident proprietors are blurred when proprietors maintained more than one residence and family members moved back and forth across the Atlantic.

15 Rent Books, Public Archives of Prince Edward Island (PAPEI), RG 15; *Minutes of Evidence Taken Under the Direction of a General Commission of Inquiry for Crown Lands and Emigration Appointed...by...the Earl of Durham* (Quebec: Fisher and Kemble, 1839), "Prince Edward Island," Robert Hodgson at 7–8, and T.H. Haviland at 10–11 [*Minutes of Evidence*].

16 M. Brook Taylor, "George Dalrymple" in *Dictionary of Canadian Biography*, vol. 8 (Toronto: University of Toronto Press, 1985) at 197–98.

17 *Royal Gazette* (Charlottetown) (15 January 1833).

18 For a discussion of the significance of investments in roads to the Island's agricultural economy see Fade Goff to Hay (15 July 1828) CO 226/45/332–38.

19 Petition of the House of Assembly (18 March 1825) CO 226/42/45–46; PEI, *Journals of the House of Assembly* [*JHA*] (1828) at 139; Ready to Hay (4 February 1829) CO 226/46/162–64; Ready to Murray (7 January 1829) CO 226/46/7–9. For Ready's position on an emerging politics of development, see Ready to Hay (2 June 1829) CO 226/46/85–90. See also Elinor Vass "John Ready" in *Dictionary of Canadian Biography*, vol. 7 (Toronto: University of Toronto Press, 1988) at 740–43.

20 The road assessment legislation received royal assent late in 1830, but the land tax act had to wait until 1833.

21 *Royal Gazette* (28 September and 5 October 1830).

22 *JHA* (1831) 19 April at 36, 49.

23 *JHA* (1832), app. A, "Proceedings of the Committee of Privileges and Elections," at 6.

24 *Royal Gazette* (15 February 1831).

25 Cooper to "the Committee appointed to report upon Mr. Waller's letters" (16 December 1837) CO 226/56/185; Adele Townshend, "Drama at Abell's Cape" (1979) 6 (Spring/Summer) *Island Magazine* 33. For insight into the character of the young Townshend, see *Frank Mildmay*, a novel by British naval officer Captain Marryat, an officer on board a frigate that Townshend commanded in British North American waters.

26 "Report of a Select Committee of the Inhabitants of Lot or Township Number 56 in Prince Edward Island. Submitted to the Inhabitants at a Public Meeting the 16th January 1838," CO 226/56/177–88. For an alternative reading of Cooper's change of position, see Harry Baglole, "William Cooper" in *Dictionary of Canadian Biography*, vol. 9 (Toronto: University of Toronto Press, 1976) at 155–58; "William Cooper of Sailor's Hope" (1979) (Fall–Winter) *Island Magazine* 3; "The Legacy of William Cooper" (1988) 3 *Cooper Review* 16.

27 *British American* (Charlottetown) (13 April 1833).

28 *Royal Gazette* (7 February 1832).

29 M. Brook Taylor, "Charles Binns" in *Dictionary of Canadian Biography*, vol. 8 (Toronto: University of Toronto Press, 1988) at 76–77; Harry Holman, "John Brecken" in *Dictionary of Canadian Biography*, vol. 7 (Toronto: University of Toronto Press, 1988) at 103–4.

30 *JHA* (1832), 12–13 March at 80–84; 22–23 March at 100–3.

31 F.W.P. Bolger, "The Demise of Quit Rents and Escheat, 1824–1842" in F.W.P. Bolger, ed., *Canada's Smallest Province: A History of PEI* (Halifax: Nimbus Publishing, 1991) at 104.

32 *Royal Gazette* (7 February 1832).

33 S.P.E.I. 1832, c. 19.

34 *Royal Gazette* (7 February and 3 April 1832). Critics charged that legislation providing for the sale of lands reserved to the Crown as glebe lands had favoured speculators rather than occupants, and that the primary purchasers, and beneficiaries were government officers. See *Colonial Herald* (Charlottetown) (29 December 1838).

35 "Petition of the Inhabitants of Prince Edward Island," CO 226/56/159–60; Edward Jarvis, Charles Binns, Thomas Owen, John Brecken, and Daniel Brenan to Bainbridge (11 October 1831), *JHA* (1832), app. C at 25.

36 "Mr. Cooper's speech on the escheat question" *Royal Gazette* (3 April 1832). The count includes "injustice" as well as "justice." For another speech in which Cooper reiterated and elaborated on these themes, see *Royal Gazette* (8 March 1836).

37 *British American* (13 April 1833).

38 *Royal Gazette* (3 April 1832). Cooper believed that Roman agrarian law limited an individual's landholding to 500 acres. Actually, the measure used was in Roman units, not acres, and was probably closer to 330 acres. If Escheators were familiar with more recent calls for an agrarian law in France, they may have considered it impolitic to cite them. See R.B. Rose, "The Red Scare of the 1790s: The French Revolution and the 'Agrarian Law'" (1984) 103 Past and Present 113.

39 *British American* (13 April 1833).

40 *JHA* (1833) 24 January at 36–39. As already noted, the concessions secured by the proprietors included relaxing the settlement terms in the original grants. In 1816, Lord Bathurst, the Colonial Secretary, extended the deadline for meeting the requirement to establish 100 settlers per township to 1826 (the original deadline had been 1777) and removed the requirement that settlers be foreign Protestants. See *Prince Edward Island Gazette* (8 August 1818).

41 *Royal Gazette* (11 September 1832).

42 David Stewart to Lt. Col. Sorell (9 January 1832), David Stewart to Thomas Farrer (5 April 1833), Robert Stewart Letterbooks, PAPEI Ms. 2316/1/85–86.

43 Robert Stewart to Andrew Colvile (15 May 1832), Robert Stewart to Edward Worrell (15 May 1832), Robert Stewart Letterbooks, PAPEI Ms. 2316/1/119–20.

44 "Memorial of the Undersigned Proprietors," CO 226/49/274–83.

45 *Royal Gazette* (4 November 1834); Robert Stewart Letterbooks, PAPEI Ms. 2316/2/10–12.

46 Hutchinson to Captain Seymour (22 October 1814), Correspondence, Seymour of Ragley Papers, WCRO, CR 114 A/563/1; "At a meeting of the Proprietors of Lands..." (5 March 1824) CO 226/41/268–70.

47 Robert Stewart Letterbooks, PAPEI Ms. 2316.

48 *JHA* (1833), 28 March at 108–10; *Royal Gazette* (2 April 1833).

49 Robert Stewart, a proprietor resident in London and a major organizer of the proprietorial lobby, noted seeing a letter sent to the United Kingdom by a member of the Prince Edward Island Assembly arguing that the *Escheat Act* was unjust and should be opposed by proprietors and rejected by the imperial government, although he had supported it in the Assembly. Such admission of duplicity raises the question of whether the protest is any more genuine than the support, but at the very least suggests that some played both sides and may explain the lack of vigour in the thirteenth Assembly's pursuit of a court of escheat. Robert Stewart to John Lawson (6 August 1833), Robert Stewart Letterbooks, PAPEI Ms. 2316/1/277–84.

50 *British American* (13 April 1833).

51 Harry Holman, "Joseph Pope" in *Dictionary of Canadian Biography*, vol. 7 (Toronto: University of Toronto Press, 1990) at 855–58.

52 *JHA* (1833), 25 March at 93; 6 April at 126–27; *An Act to Provide for the Civil Establishment of the Colony*, S.P.E.I. 1833, C. 39. Revenues from the current land tax, due to expire in 1837, were intended to fund the construction of government buildings.

53 Robert Stewart to Andrew Colvile (23 May 1833), Robert Stewart Letterbooks, PAPEI Ms. 2316/1/254; 31 May 1833, *ibid.* at 255–56; "The humble memorial of the undersigned and others..." (14 September 1833) CO 226/50/321–24.

54 *Royal Gazette* (9 April 1833).

55 Rusty Bittermann, "Women and the Escheat Movement: The Politics of Everyday Life" in Suzanne Morton and Janet Guildford, eds., *Separate Spheres: The World of Women in the 19th-Century Maritimes* (Fredericton, NB: Acadiensis Press, 1994) at 23–38.

56 *Minutes of Evidence, supra* note 15, "Prince Edward Island," John Lelacheur at 1; *The History of Delaware County, Iowa* (Chicago: Western Historical Co., n.d.) at 630; Ian Ross Robertson, "Daniel Brenan" in *Dictionary of Canadian Biography*, vol. 10 (Toronto: University of Toronto Press, 1972) at 90. Robertson errs in stating that Brenan acted against the Escheators "as a staunch Tory" in the Assembly. Although he disagreed with Cooper and other Escheat leaders on a number of occasions in the 1830s, he was a reformer rather than a Tory, and at times worked with Cooper, Lelacheur, and other advocates of radical reform of the proprietorial system. For his 1830 election speech calling for "radical reform," see *Royal*

Gazette (12 October 1830). For an example of his role as an ally of Escheators in the first session of the thirteenth Assembly, see *Royal Gazette* (10 February 1835). See also Brenan's description of himself as "one of the staunchest Reformers in Prince Edward Island," *Prince Edward Island Times* (Charlottetown) (10 May 1836).

57 *Royal Gazette* (16 December 1834).

58 *Royal Gazette* (13 January 1835); *JHA* (1835), 6 February at 25–27.

59 *JHA* (1835) 6 February at 27; 6 March at 77; *Royal Gazette* (31 March 1835).

60 *Royal Gazette* (31 March 1835).

61 Some tenants paid their rents by working on roads, clearing land, performing agricultural labour, and constructing buildings for their landlords. Lord Selkirk's agent, William Douse, had as many as eighty tenants at a time working to pay their rents. Others worked in the shipyards under similar arrangements. See, for instance, *Abstract of the Proceedings of the Land Commissioners' Court* (Charlottetown: *The Protestant,* 1862) at 129, 226–27; Douse to Colvile (31 July 1838 and 22 January 1839), Selkirk Papers, National Archives of Canada, MG 191/E1/74/19206–7 and 19372.

62 Satiricus, Letter to the Editor, *Royal Gazette* (19 April 1836).

63 *Royal Gazette* (31 March and 5 May 1835); *JHA* (1835) at 146–47.

64 Stanley to Young (28 May 1834) CO 227/8/23–6; *JHA* (1835), 1st Session, 26 January at 20; 2nd Session, 1 May at 11.

65 *JHA* (1836) at 21.

66 *JHA* (1836), 12 February at 26; *Royal Gazette* (16 February 1836).

67 *Royal Gazette,* ibid.

68 *Royal Gazette* (23 February and 1 March 1836).

69 *JHA* (1836), 9 April at 92–97.

70 William Cooper, *Legislative and Other Proceedings on the Expediency of Appointing a Court of Escheats in Prince Edward Island* (Charlottetown: J.D. Hazard, 1836) at 93.

71 *Royal Gazette* (18 October 1836).

72 Macintosh was elected to the Assembly in a by-election when Brenan resigned to take a government job. Peter Maccallum, the other King's County representative, was present at the Hay River meeting but was exempted from accusations and punishment because he had publicly opposed the most radical resolutions,

See Cooper to T.H. Haviland (24 January 1837) in *Royal Gazette* (7 February 1837).

73 *Royal Gazette* (10 January 1837).

74 Greer, *supra* note 6 at 121; C. Reade and R.J. Stagg, eds., *The Rebellion of 1837 in Upper Canada: A Collection of Documents* (Ottawa: Champlain Society, 1985).

75 Harvey to Grey (23 May 1836) CO 226/53/151–53; Harvey to Glenelg (5 September 1836) CO 226/53/165–66; Harvey to Glenelg (16 October 1835) CO 226/53/216–17; Harvey to Glenelg (26 January 1837) CO 226/54/26; T.H. Haviland to Gentlemen (12 January 1837) in *Royal Gazette* (7 February and 21 February 1837); *Royal Gazette* (30 January 1838).

76 Harvey to Taylor (7 February 1837), Harvey Letterbooks, RG 1, PANB R.S. 344/B/1/76.

77 *Royal Gazette* (14 February 1837).

78 *JHA* (1837) at 44, 97, 111–13, 121, 145; *Royal Gazette* (4 April and 18 April 1837); *An Act for Levying an Assessment on All Lands in This Island,* S.P.E.I. 1837, c. 31.

79 *Royal Gazette* (25 April 1837).

80 *Royal Gazette* (7 February 1837).

81 *Royal Gazette* (20 June 1837).

82 Harvey to Glenelg (24 January 1837) CO 226/54/15–19 and 62–64; Harvey Letterbooks RG 1, PANB R.S. 344/B/1/99.

83 Harvey to Glenelg (May 1837) CO 226/54/134–38.

84 Fernand Ouellet, *Lower Canada 1791–1840: Social Change and Nationalism,* trans. Patricia Claxton (Toronto: McClelland and Stewart, 1980) at 293–97.

85 *Colonial Herald* (24 February and 14 April 1838).

86 *Royal Gazette* (3 July and 4 September 1838).

87 *Minutes of Evidence, supra* note 15, "Prince Edward Island," John Lelacheur, Sir Charles Fitzroy, and Robert Hodgson at 1–9; *Colonial Herald* (17 October 1838).

88 "Report on Public Lands and Emigration from Charles Buller, 2 November 1838" in Lucas, *Lord Durham's Report,* vol. 3, *supra* note 2 at 82.

89 Lucas, *Lord Durham's Report,* vol. 1, *supra* note 2 at 199–200 [emphasis added]. Charles Buller, in "Sketch of Lord Durham's Mission to Canada in 1838" in Lucas, *Lord Durham's Report,* vol. 3, *supra* note 2 at 369, credits Durham with resolving the problem of proprietary abuses on Prince Edward

Island by securing "the Royal Assent to a law of escheat; and if Prince Edward's Island should hereafter prosper, it will be mainly owing to this interposition on his part." Chester New, presumably relying on Buller, repeats the error. See *Lord Durham: A Biography of John George Lambton, First Earl of Durham* (Oxford: Clarendon Press, 1929) at 486.

90 Durham to Glenelg (8 October 1838) in *Report and Despatches of the Earl of Durham, Her Majesty's High Commissioner and Governor-General of Canada* (London: Charles Wood, 1839) at 374.

91 *Royal Gazette* (5 March 1839).

92 *Royal Gazette* (19 July 1842); Huntley "Construction of the House of Assembly" (13 August 1843) CO 226/64/30.

93 For a brief account of the steps leading to the resolution of the land question in 1875, and an examination of the arguments that were employed against the proprietorial system in the 1860s and 1870s, see Margaret E. McCallum, "The Sacred Rights of Property: Title, Entitlement, and the Land Question in Nineteenth-Century Prince Edward Island" in G. Blaine Baker and Jim Phillips, eds., *Essays in the History of Canadian Law, Volume 8: In Honour of R.C.B. Risk* (Toronto: Osgoode Society of Canadian Legal History, 1999) at 358–97.

94 *Land Purchase Act,* S.P.E.I. 1875, c. 32. Up to 1,000 acres were exempt from sale if the proprietors occupied the land themselves.

95 *Prince Edward Island Lands Protection Act,* S.P.E.I. 1982, c. 16, set an upper limit of 1,000 acres on aggregate land holdings for an individual and 3,000 acres for a corporation. It also prohibited non-residents and corporations (apart from incorporated farming operations owned by resident farmers) from acquiring more than 10 acres in total and more than five chains of shore frontage unless they obtained a permit from the government. Amendments reduced these amounts to 5 acres in total and 165 feet of shore frontage. Section 1.1., added to the legislation in 1998, states: "The purpose of this Act is to provide for the regulation of property rights in Prince Edward Island, especially the amount of land that may be held by a person or corporation. This Act has been enacted in the recognition that Prince Edward Island faces singular challenges with regard to property rights as a result of several circumstances, including (a) historical difficulties with absentee land owners, and the consequent problems faced by the inhabitants of Prince Edward Island in governing their own affairs, both public and private."

The Campaign for Representative Government in Newfoundland

JERRY BANNISTER

The reform movement preceding the grant of representative government in 1832 has figured prominently in the writing of Newfoundland history. The traditional school of thought—which was established by D.W. Prowse and reached its apogee with A.H. McLintock—placed the reformers at the head of a colonial struggle to break the yoke of naval governors and absentee merchants responsible for the island's backward development.[1] In the first serious challenge to this orthodoxy, Keith Matthews asserted that the grant of representative government in 1832 marked simply the inevitable success of a colonial elite's ambition. As recent immigrants from Ireland and England, the reformers were merely following political currents in Britain, and they imposed a nationalist ideology which bore little relation to circumstances in the colony.[2] Matthews' thesis has been criticized by Patrick O'Flaherty, who maintains that the reform movement comprised a series of hard-fought battles against long-established injustices. According to O'Flaherty, reformers such as Patrick Morris and William Carson were responding to a legitimate sense of local grievance caused by systemic inequities suffered under naval rule.[3] In an analysis of how the reform movement shaped economic policy, Sean Cadigan has argued that while the reformers did respond to some local issues, they were a small mercantile and professional elite who based their ideas largely upon British-shaped gentry aspirations.[4] And in a recent study of sectarianism, John Greene claims that local disputes over religion formed the driving force of the reform movement. The campaign for representative government was the means by which Irish Catholics fought for their civil rights against a reactionary Protestant elite.[5]

This article offers an alternative interpretation of the rise of the reform movement and the fall of naval government. It argues that far from being inevitable, the demise of naval government, which had dominated Newfoundland since the mid-eighteenth century, came only after a protracted political campaign. Though the surrogate courts were abolished in 1824, the basic structure of naval rule remained intact until the grant of a local legislature in 1832. The first phase of the reform movement, which was dominated by Irish Catholics, repeatedly appealed for an end to naval government, but their efforts met with limited success in the face of opposition

Jerry Bannister, "The Campaign for Representative Government in Newfoundland," *Journal of the Canadian Historical Association*, New Series, 5 (1999): 19–40.

from both merchants and government officials. The pivotal factor in the campaign for representative government was the formation of a broad-based coalition in 1828, when concerns over taxation brought together leading members of the Catholic and Protestant communities. In London the reformers overcame the imperial government's intransigence through a strategy designed to gain support in Parliament and to undermine the Colonial Office. Analysis of local meetings and petitions, as well as parliamentary debates, also indicates that the press played a crucial role in the reform movement's ability to embrace disparate socio-economic interests. The newspaper press worked to maintain the necessary image of unity and respectability, and it provided essential political momentum throughout the 1820s and early 1830s.

The movement in favour of reforming the island's legal system was part of a broader wave of political upheaval throughout the British Isles in the early nineteenth century. British and Irish reformers campaigned for an end to slavery, public whippings, and other practices deemed contrary to the natural rights of man. Irish politicians worked particularly hard to persuade the British government to repeal the penal laws affecting Roman Catholics.[6] Reformers in St. John's drew upon this larger cultural milieu to formulate their demands for an end to naval government, but the impact of events and trends in Britain and Ireland on the course of reform in Newfoundland can easily be exaggerated. The Colonial Office remained wary of bestowing legislative authority on British possessions, and prior to 1828 public opinion in Newfoundland was divided on the question of reform. Merchants remained generally opposed to the campaign for representative government until they became convinced that it was in their immediate economic interests. The struggle for an elected assembly had long-term ramifications for the development

of both nationalism and democracy, as it created a political culture which persisted well into the twentieth century.

The Origins of the Reform Movement

Despite the evident strength of the naval government in the early nineteenth century, beneath the political surface surged forces that threatened the entire system of governance. The decade after the peace of 1815 witnessed the advent of bourgeois culture in St. John's. The roots of this social transformation grew out of the island's remarkable economic development during the French Revolutionary and Napoleonic Wars. As Newfoundland became a populous colony with a resident fishery, incipient political institutions emerged, such as the Society of Merchants and the Benevolent Irish Society.[7] Accompanying these organizations was a momentous development: the first local printing press. Operating under licence from the naval governor, in 1807 John Ryan began the *Royal Gazette,* a weekly paper published in St. John's devoted largely to government notices, official proclamations, and mercantile advertisements.[8] Although Ryan could initially publish only materials approved by the governor's office, the appearance of a local press marked a formative stage in the monitoring of state power. For the first time, the court calendar and the outcome of trials were published, providing a basis of accountability that far outstripped the traditional forms of communication. Under Sir Francis Forbes, Chief Justice of Newfoundland from 1817 to 1822, the judiciary also took a much more active role in upholding property rights and checking abuses by local officials.[9] The press facilitated this process by creating a *public* space in which the bourgeoisie could fix its place in the social environment, identify its local interests, and promote its own particular causes.[10] Early demands for reform had come primarily from St. John's merchants. The Society of Merchants petitioned repeatedly for advantages in trade, vowing to defend the colonists' rights secured by the British constitution. A significant challenge to the governor's authority emerged in 1811, when local merchants organized meetings to discuss grievances over a statute authorizing the lease of ships' rooms as private property.[11] In the island's first protest pamphlet, William Carson openly criticized the seizure of common property without the inhabitants' consent.[12] Carson's next tract warned the government not to insult the rights of Britons living in Newfoundland. The colonists deserved, he concluded, "what is unquestionably their right, a civil Government, consisting of a resident Governor, a Senate House, and House of Assembly."[13] From its beginnings, reform rhetoric identified social progress closely with the attainment of formal institutions comparable to other colonies and the constitutional rights granted to all British subjects. By 1820 the press contained newspapers that were clearly independent of the naval government. St. John's had two major papers—the pro-reform *Public Ledger* and the *Mercantile Journal*—and a third, the pro-Catholic *Newfoundlander,* appeared in 1827.[14] Newfoundland had lagged behind colonies such as Upper Canada in the early development of an independent press, but the public debates in St. John's were now as lively as those taking place in York.[15] Policies of the naval government were for the first time subjected to potentially critical public evaluation; the governor's office could no longer monopolize the process of political legitimization. Freedom of speech, which had emerged in England the previous century, eventually became a pivotal factor in the eventual downfall of the naval government. The press did not invent political opposition but rather revolutionized its means of expression.

Cause Célèbres and the Campaign against Naval Justice

In 1820 Newfoundland witnessed one of the most important *cause célèbres* in its history. The affair centred on the cases of two Conception Bay fishermen, James Lundrigan and Philip Butler, who were publicly whipped after receiving default judgements in surrogate court for outstanding debts. In 1818 Lundrigan had borrowed around £13 from a local supplier and, when the surrogate court met the following year, the merchant brought an action to recover the debt. The court ruled against the fisherman, whose property was attached, but Lundrigan and his wife, Sarah, successfully resisted efforts to take possession of their house. Summoned to appear before a surrogate court in July 1820, Lundrigan refused on the grounds that he had to go fishing to feed his hungry family. Arrested during the night, he was taken to a naval vessel, charged the next day with contempt of court and resisting arrest, and sentenced to receive thirty-six lashes on his bare back. Lundrigan, who was an epileptic, collapsed after fourteen lashes, and a surgeon stepped in to stop the whipping. The court ordered Lundrigan to relinquish his house and assets to his creditor, thereby evicting his wife and four children. Philip Butler's case, which took place the next day, followed a similar course. An indebted fisherman, Butler was sentenced to receive thirty-six lashes for contempt of court (he was given twelve), and he and his family were also evicted from their home. Supported by a group of reformers in St. John's, both Lundrigan and Butler took actions of trespass for assault and false imprisonment against the presiding surrogate judges in the Newfoundland Supreme Court.[16]

The reformers turned the cases of Lundrigan and Butler into a serious political issue. In 1820 they convened a meeting to protest against the cruel punishments inflicted for minor offenses.[17] Chaired by Patrick Morris, the meeting included many of the leaders of the Catholic community who formed the backbone of Newfoundland's reform movement.[18] The fact that Lundrigan and Butler were Irish only served to underscore the deep concerns among Catholics over the island's legal system.[19] Determined to win their place in the circles of power, middle-class Catholics also supported the campaign to repeal the religious penal laws. A committee was appointed to draft a petition to London: in addition to detailing the flaws in the surrogate system, the petition linked the need for a civil judiciary directly to the absence of local legislature. Stressing the reformers' patriotism and allegiance to the king, it appealed for all the rights and privileges granted to subjects in other British colonies.[20]

As had happened during the fishing admiral's controversy a century earlier, political protest involved manoeuvres on both sides of the Atlantic. After presenting memorials for legal reform to Governor Hamilton, the committee sent a representative, William Dawe, to convey its petition to the British parliament. Dawe also carried letters asking Lord Holland, who led a circle of liberal Whigs, and the prominent reform advocate Sir James Mackintosh, to represent the reform committee's interests.[21] When the House of Commons considered the petition in May 1821, Mackintosh asserted that he knew of "no other colony which more required the constant vigilance of a local assembly than Newfoundland." He took particular aim at the naval regime:

> The courts in question were called Surrogate Courts; the judges were principally composed of officers of the navy. Punishment for contempt was, he admitted, resorted to by courts of justice in England; but he believed the use of the lash

in such cases was altogether unknown in this county; it was, however, the ordinary mode of punishment adopted in Newfoundland.[22]

As to the root of the problem, Mackintosh charged:

> The mode of proceeding in these floating courts was not regulated by the common law of England, so much as the discipline and practice of the navy. The system was a bad one, but was, he believed, the remains of a system which was still worse.[23]

The British government admitted that the island's judiciary required an overhaul, but warned of the problems associated with colonial assemblies. The Colonial Office had, in fact, already informed Governor Hamilton that it had no intention of granting Newfoundland a legislative assembly.[24]

Undaunted, the St. John's reformers organized a public meeting to place their case before a wider audience. Held in August 1821, the meeting established the principal arguments for representative government. Patrick Morris recounted how the island's long history of oppression under English merchants and naval officers had produced a legal system unequaled in the annals of despotic nations. Not only did the absence of a properly-constituted civil judiciary deny settlers recourse to British justice, but backward laws also prohibited exploitation of the island's agricultural resources and thus retarded economic development. The absence of electoral representation deprived Newfoundlanders of their constitutional birthrights as British subjects. Newfoundland was left to endure taxation without representation, while its revenues were ample to support a legislature. The committee concluded that all these problems were, at bottom, caused by the want of an elected assembly.[25]

History, Politics, and Law Reform

The public outcry against the surrogate courts marked only the first salvo in a larger struggle against the naval government. Reformers incessantly attacked naval government as arbitrary, outmoded, and incompetent. In doing so, they not only drew on previous writers, such as Chief Justice John Reeves, but they also crafted their own version of Newfoundland history. Like most other nationalist movements, the St. John's reformers constructed a cultural memory of oppression as a basis on which to mount attacks on the status quo.[26] For example, William Carson asserted with biting sarcasm that the island's legal problems stretched back to its earliest settlers:

> The inhabitants appear to have been considered, either as a race of savages untamable by civilization, and which could not be re-trained by any regular code of laws, or as Angels descended immediately from Heaven, pure and perfect, possessing minds which did not require instruction, and passion that needed not the control of terrestrious [sic] institutions.[27]

And, in a lengthy speech devoted largely to Newfoundland history, Patrick Morris offered a similarly harsh appraisal:

> Here, Gentlemen, a system of Government was established for this country unequaled in the annals of the most despotic nations, and a system better calculated to oppress and barbarize a country, was never framed by the perverted ingenuity of man. Under this authority the most wanton acts of violence were committed—the houses and property of the Inhabitants and Planters were burnt and destroyed, and every other means were resorted to, to drive them from the land of their birth, or their extirpate

them altogether. It is scarcely creditable at the period we live in, that such a state of things could exist in a country calling itself civilized.[28]

In essence, Newfoundland under naval government had failed the test of civilized society.

The fervor in St. John's reached new heights with the publication of an anonymous pamphlet which detailed the history of legal abuses culminating in the whipping of Lundrigan and Butler. On the problem of finding the cause of this "maladministration of justice," it contended:

> [I]t is easy to comprehend that portion that must be of widely spreading magnitude, when it is considered that every new squadron of ships of war, and every single ship that arrives on the station, in their commanding officers, furnishes a new set of itinerant judges, who, under every disqualification for the office, save the authority which they derive under the commission of the Governor, are dispersed along the coasts of the island to exercise the functions of judges, in criminal as well as civil causes, in the surrogate and sessions courts.

The indictment of the naval government did not end there:

> When to the numberless errors in judgment, inevitably incident to such judges, and the consequent injuries to the rights of parties, are superadded the intemperate and unlawful finings, imprisonments, and floggings which they have inflicted; it becomes to a reflecting mind, a matter of surprise, how the moral relations of society have been held together, amid the heart-burnings and resentments which such a system of judicature must inevitably generate.[29]

For three generations, official correspondence and printed accounts had portrayed the naval governor and the surrogate system as the very bastion of English justice in Newfoundland.

Within the space of a few years, however, the reform press had savaged the navy's reputation.

By taking this approach, the reformers were following a well-established pattern—as Eric Hobsbawm has argued, the process of inventing a tailor-made history has been a key ingredient of most successful nationalist movements—and the only exceptional aspect of this rhetoric is the degree to which Newfoundland historians have accepted such polemics at face value.[30]

Constitutional Reform, 1824–26

In 1824 the reformers scored their first major victory. The British government introduced a bill that appeared to signal the dismantling of the naval government. The Judicature Act abolished the surrogate courts and provided for a charter of incorporation to make town bylaws.[31] With the end of the surrogate courts, the island had shed one of the principal features of naval government. Having sat as judges since the seventeenth century, naval officers in Newfoundland finally lost their prerogative to administer law. A second statute passed in 1824 finally repealed King William's Act.[32] In 1825 the British government issued a Royal Charter which authorized the creation of a revamped Supreme Court and a system of Circuit Courts.[33] Captain Thomas Cochrane, the island's new governor, was also instructed to appoint a council to aid and assist his administration. The governorship became a civil appointment, no longer under the Admiralty's control, and Newfoundland was nominally recognized as an official colony.[34] When Cochrane arrived in St. John's, he received a warm reception and was lauded in the local press. In January 1826 he presided over an elaborate public ceremony to mark the opening of the newly-constituted Supreme Court. With the streets jammed with onlookers, a long procession

of officials and dignitaries marched from the governor's residence to the court house; an officer in the parade displayed the Royal Charter as salutes were fired by an honour guard and a warship in the harbour; and, to mark the occasion, the Governor pardoned and released most of the prisoners from jail.[35]

The Royal Charter altered the island's judiciary but did not transform its basic mode of governance. Although Newfoundland was now a colony with a civil governor, many aspects of naval rule persisted under Governor Cochrane's tenure. Like most of the earlier naval governors, Cochrane was a relatively young career officer with good political connections. He had attained the rank of captain at the age of seventeen, and then served in the West Indian and North American squadrons before receiving his Newfoundland appointment. Still a captain when he assumed the governorship at the age of thirty-six, Cochrane was a martinet who treasured pomp and circumstance.[36] In a report to the Colonial Office, he affirmed, "I am persuaded from what I have heard of the people that a governor ought to go among them with all the attributes of consequence and authority belonging to the situation to ensure him that respect they are not over anxious to observe to those placed over them."[37] Not only was Cochrane himself little different from his predecessors, but the powers he enjoyed under the Judicature Act were not much different from those wielded under the old regime. Added to the system of colonial government was a council—it comprised the chief justice, two assistant judges, and the commander of the army garrison—but this was merely an advisory body, appointed by the governor and effectively under his control.[38] Like generations of naval officers before him, Cochrane was left to govern Newfoundland as best he saw fit, without the encumbrance of an elected assembly.

In early 1826 Governor Cochrane moved to implement his instructions from the Colonial Office. He held meetings with merchants and prominent reformers in order to discuss the creation of a town council in St. John's. The proposals called for a mayor and fifteen-member council, with a franchise of £10 freehold property or £20 annual leasehold.[39] However, this initiative abruptly ground to a halt when a bloc of leading merchants opposed the plans for reform.[40] While Cochrane preferred the majority's view, he left the Colonial Office to determine the "species of government" best suited to the colony. Cochrane did recommend an *ad valorem* duty as a means to raise revenue in the colony.[41] In a September 1826 report James Stephen, legal advisor to the Colonial Office, proposed a legislative council for the colony as an alternative to "the many inconveniences" attended by an assembly, but the British government decided to wait until Cochrane clarified the situation in Newfoundland.[42] In November 1826 Cochrane informed Lord Bathurst that the populace remained heavily divided on the question of local government.[43] Moreover, Henry Winton, editor of the pro-reform Public Ledger, conceded that the colony seemed unprepared for a local assembly. "The truth is," Winton wrote, "that we want a few practical lessons...before we can venture from our political leading-strings."[44] Merchants in St. John's had never fully backed the early reform movement: with a conservative faction publicly objecting to the establishment of a town council, the split between conservative and reformist parties inhibited further political change. By mid-1827 representative government still appeared to be a rather distant goal.

To keep the campaign for a local legislature alive, the reformers clung to their crusade against the naval government. These polemics were no longer restricted to anonymous pamphlets and letters to the editor. In 1827 Patrick Morris launched a full broadside against the evils of the old regime:

> The government of Newfoundland by the
> Admirals of the British fleet exhibits examples

of the danger of placing uncontrolled power in the hands of any man or set of men, and affords melancholy proofs that English gentlemen—the representatives of a constitutional king—of the highest rank in the truly honourable profession to which they belonged—did, in the exercise of power, act more like Persian satraps or Turkish bashaws than men who, it is to be supposed, were well read in the constitutional history of their country.[45]

The reformers kept invoking this argument as long as it boosted their cause. By doing so, naval government entered the realm of caricature and legend, alongside the fishing admirals, to form one of the core myths of Newfoundland nationalism. By the time Judge Prowse published his seminal history of the island, the eighteenth-century had become a dark age of anarchy.[46]

Taxation without Representation: Making a Political Coalition

The proposals for new taxes quickly provoked St. John's merchants into political action. In October 1827 the Chamber of Commerce petitioned against the import duty "with painful apprehension" of the effects on the depressed fish trade.[47] After Cochrane forwarded the petition to London, George Robinson, a partner with Thomas Brooking and the Tory M.P. for Worcester, voiced the merchants' concerns in an interview with the Colonial Secretary, William Huskisson. The free importation of fishery supplies had long been a mercantile tenet, but Huskisson reportedly justified the new duty on the grounds that the colony now had "to pay its own expenses."[48] Robinson then took action in Parliament and, on 30 May 1828, asked the government to postpone Newfoundland's grant for civil expenditure until it investigated Governor

Cochrane's financial management. With the five-year term of the Judicature Act soon to expire, Robinson demanded a select committee to inquire into the state of Newfoundland.[49] In August 1828 the Chamber of Commerce, led by Thomas Brooking, publicly denounced the import duty as a grave threat to the fishery.[50] In a form of political protest, merchant vessels sailing to St. John's refused to carry the mail in order to prevent Cochrane from receiving instructions on the new tax.[51] The Newfoundland case reflects T.W. Acheson's model of Saint John's merchants: though often fractured, merchant interests could unite rapidly when threatened with increased taxation.[52]

In the meantime the question of Newfoundland's governance surfaced in the English press. In an April 1828 pamphlet Patrick Morris entreated the government to grant the neglected colony a local legislature. He argued that those merchants who resisted the reform movement were "vainly putting forth their paralyzed arms to arrest the progress of justice and civilization—they have all the *will* to keep us in bondage and barbarism; but, thank God, they have not the *power*." "Newfoundland will no longer be a plantation of Poole," Morris declared, "and her people will no longer be their slaves."[53] Although the surrogate courts had already been abolished, the island's naval government remained a principal target: "The absurd, and ridiculous, and often unjust and arbitrary proceedings of the surrogates are well known.... I have seen so many acts of cruelty and oppression committed at Newfoundland under the authority and pretense of summary justice, that I lose all patience even at the very mention of its being established."[54] He also insisted that Newfoundland possessed the elements necessary for representative government: a population of sufficient education and property, an environment able to support agriculture, and the means to raise adequate revenues. The pamphlet drew a rejoinder from a writer in Poole who attacked

Morris' flagrant distortions, rejected notions that the island could sustain a viable agriculture, and termed the possible benefits of a local assembly too slender to alter existing policy.[55] A review of Morris' pamphlet in the *Sphynx* nevertheless lauded the triumphant refutation of the view of Newfoundland as a country too undeveloped for a local legislature.[56] In Newfoundland these exchanges received extensive coverage and editorial comment in local newspapers.[57]

The Newfoundland papers went much further than simply reporting on debates in England. With the creation of a bourgeois public sphere in St. John's, the press exerted a formative influence on political discourse.[58] In a series of editorials, the newspapers published by John Shea and Henry Winton soon transformed concerns over the proposed import duty into a cogent argument for representative government. When John Shea reported the duty in 1827, he noted the economic implications but then continued: "such a tax on a colony like ours, without representation, would be a direct violation of the pledge given by the Government to the Colonies after the American Revolutionary War."[59] That pledge was the Declaratory of 1778, which stated that the King and Parliament of Great Britain would not directly impose any duty or tax on any British colony, except for the regulation of commerce, in which case the funds could be allocated only for the internal use of the colony.[60] In April 1828, Shea appealed for the duty not to be "exacted from us upon the principle of 'taxation without representation.'"[61] A letter by "Mercator," published in the *Public Ledger* in December 1827, argued: "taxation without representation is contrary to the express promise of Great Britain to her colonies, and to the spirit of the British Laws."[62] Henry Winton claimed that he did not object to the duty itself, but to the absence of the "*right* to collect and appropriate the sums so raised." He concluded: "a new and very powerful argument arises out of this subject to confirm the necessity of introducing a change in the government of this country."[63] Three days later Winton warned that under the present system the tax would be imposed "while the people remain relatively unconscious of the indirect burthens" imposed on them.[64] The press repeatedly urged the public to unite and act upon these grievances. Upon hearing that the government intended to use the duty to pay for new public buildings, Winton warned of dire consequences if the colonists could not "agree to solicit that the appropriation of the money so exacted may be placed within their own control."[65] An editorial in the *Newfoundlander* also affirmed that the time had arrived "when the most active steps should be taken to endeavour to obtain for the people a voice in the appropriation" of the any duties.[66] In August 1828 the Public Ledger called for a public meeting of "qualified" individuals to recommend changes to the colony's government.[67] During the fall of 1828 Winton encouraged a gentlemanly discussion and asked that "former prejudices and prepossessions upon the subject be thoroughly forgotten."[68] A letter from "Atomus" called for public meetings to discuss the issues and "to sooth down all angry feelings and conflicting sentiments." The letter held that "on the present occasion, I consider the great object of *all* should be—UNANIMITY."[69] Finally, on 18 November 1828 Winton reported that objections to a local legislature had abated: "upon *that* important question," he declared, "no obstacles are likely now to be raised."[70]

In early December 1828 the local papers printed an announcement for a meeting to discuss both the proposed import duty and the question of a legislative assembly. Strongly endorsed by Shea and Winton, the meeting marked a watershed in the colony's reform movement.[71] The list of signatures on the notice and the subsequent petition for an assembly reveals that many of the leading merchants who had opposed a charter of incorporation in 1826, such as Benjamin Bowring, Robert Alsop, James McBride, Robert Brown, and John Brine, now

publicly supported the campaign for representative government.[72] Most importantly, the campaign for representative government received backing from the leadership of both the Irish Catholic community and the Protestant mercantile interests. Representing firms which would be directly affected by the new import duty, the leaders of the Chamber of Commerce—Thomas Brooking, John Dunscombe, William Thomas, and Newman Hoyles—became heavily involved in the campaign for a local legislature.[73] The Roman Catholic Church maintained excellent relations with the Protestant elite, and the lay leadership of the Irish community remained committed to political reform.[74] Tensions loomed beneath the political surface, but the apparent harmony between the Protestant and Catholic communities persisted largely because Catholics saw a colonial legislature as a means to acquire religious rights.[75] Driven by different impulses, then, the colony's two main factions came together in a coalition to work for a local assembly.

The data contained in the petitions of the 1820s reveal that political participation was not wholly restricted to a small colonial elite. The February 1826 petition against a charter of incorporation listed an occupation for each signature and provides a rough indication of the social range of political involvement in St. John's: of the 172 residents on the list, just over a quarter belonged to the elite, about forty per cent were from the middling ranks, and almost a third were artisans (table 1). A comparison of the 1829 memorial with data on an earlier petition reveals significant political involvement among the middling and working classes of St. John's. While the vast majority of identities on the 1829 memorial remain unknown, the list did contain a number of planters, shopkeepers, and artisans. The non-elite names that could be positively identified included several coopers and sailmakers, as well as a baker, wheelwright, carpenter, smith and shoemaker.[76]

TABLE 1 | POLITICAL PARTICIPATION IN ST. JOHN'S, 1826

Occupation	Number of Signatories	Percentage of Total Signatories
Merchant	40	
Land Proprietor	2	
Landowner	3	28%
Gentleman	3	
Notary Public	2	
Surgeon	2	
Apothecary	1	
Shopkeeper	13	
Planter	32	
Farmer	8	41%
Fish Culler	6	
Innkeeper	2	
Spirit Dealer	3	
Schoolmaster	1	
Watchmaker	3	
Cabinet Maker	1	
Cooper	6	
Wheelwright	1	
Mason	2	
Smith	4	
Tailor	2	31%
Sailmaker	3	
Carpenter	19	
Shoemaker	5	
Painter	1	
Baker	3	
Butcher	3	

Source: PANL, CO 194/72, p. 158, Cochrane to Bathurst, 27 May 1826, enclosure 7.

The public sphere in St. John's appears to have been largely a male preserve. Six women signed the 1826 petition: Elizabeth McLean and Jane Dameral, both described as landholders in Riverhead; Ann Curtice, who was listed as a farmer; Mary Ann McCalman and Ann Matthews, both Water Street Shopkeepers; and Emily Hill, who signed for her husband, Nathaniel, an innkeeper. Yet only one woman, Anastasia McCarthy, was among the 498 signatories to the 1829 petition. The level of women's participation in the reform movement seems to have been lower than in New Brunswick, where women were significantly involved in petitions for political reform.[77] As in Prince Edward Island, women in nineteenth-century Newfoundland were largely excluded from the public arena of formal politics, though this did not extend to the informal politics which suffused rural communities.[78] Patriarchy was, as Sean Cadigan argues, actively supported by the naval government, which took a dim view of women who overstepped their roles as obedient wives and virtuous mothers.[79] Reformers may have attacked the system of naval government as unjust, but they also viewed women through the lens of their domestic responsibilities. For example, when Patrick Morris argued that Newfoundlanders had a strong moral character, he quoted at length from Lewis Anspach's *History of Newfoundland*:

> [T]he natives, of both sexes, are equally remark-able for their ingenuity and industry; the women, besides the very valuable assistance which they afford during the season for curing and drying fish, generally understand the whole process of preparing the wool from the fleece, and of manufacturing it, by knitting it into stockings, caps, socks, and mittens. Their worsted stockings are strong, and well calculated for the climate. *The women are also characterized by a steady attention to their domestic duties, and correctness of conduct in every point of view.*[80]

Like their counterparts in other British colonies, the reformers employed gendered language to construct arguments for political rights.[81] In reacting to a perceived violation of political rights, William Carson argued that "as Men, as British Subjects they hoped for better treatment."[82]

The reform movement encompassed a variety of arguments and political traditions as it evolved in a dynamic colonial environment. The situation in Newfoundland was far from unique: virtually every colony throughout British North America experienced similar political debates in the 1820s and 1830s, particularly over the twin issues of revenue and representation.[83] As elsewhere in the Empire, the reformers used language similar to trends in Britain, but the Newfoundland reform movement did not develop solely through the importation of British reform ideology. Evidence of a vibrant public discussion in St. John's contradicts Keith Matthews' assertion that the relative harmony after 1828 was the result of an ascendancy of a pro-reform elite of recent immigrants who imposed their own agenda on Newfoundland politics.[84] By the 1820s the burgeoning public debate in St. John's inhibited the political hegemony of a single clique. Fueled by anxieties over import duties, the reform movement had transformed into a fairly broad-based coalition united against "taxation without representation." And with the renewed drive for a local assembly came a nativist voice. In a June 1828 editorial John Shea commented sarcastically that it was "very kind of John Bull, truly, to allow us potatoes and salt *duty free*."[85] Moreover, Henry Winton argued in October 1828 that Newfoundland "must be under the legislation of a body of men who are resident in the colony."[86] A letter from "A Native" opposed a local legislature and the influence of those with "no stake in the country."[87] In response to such concerns, William Thomas later asserted during a public meeting:

> I am not a native of this island, Sir, but my father was, and my children are natives. I have resided here nearly 30 years, and I look to this

island as the future residence of myself and my family. To Newfoundland I am indebted for the property I possess... I am, therefore, attached by strong ties to Newfoundland.[88]

By protesting the proposed tax in 1828, Thomas was protecting his Newfoundland property.

The meeting to discuss taxation and representation, held 18 December 1828 in St. John's, had some dissension but ended in unanimity. It began with a brief conference, dominated entirely by merchants, which resolved to petition against any import duty. William Carson then began the meeting on a local assembly by stressing the need to end the colony's oppression, but the issue of taxation dictated the ensuing discussion. Several merchants noted that if the government went ahead with the duty, then the colony needed a voice in its appropriation. Thomas Bennett reportedly declared: "if they did not tax us, there would be no necessity for the institution of a House of Assembly," and he called for an adjournment until the tax became official. William Thomas maintained the need for a legislature but also said he was "no enthusiast" about the island's agricultural potential. Chaired by William Carson, the committee appointed to prepare a petition included members from both the older reform movement, notably Patrick Doyle, and the mercha nt elite, represented by William Thomas.[89] The resulting petition stressed the colony's economic development and argued that compared to other colonies the island deserved, and could financially support, its own legislature.[90] It also argued that the new import duty was unconstitutional because it contravened the Declaratory Act of 1778, which the reformers again quoted at length.[91] In taking this course, they were following a well established tradition in contemporary reformist rhetoric.[92]

Yet in spite of its recent growth, the reform movement met with little success throughout 1829–30. Governor Cochrane had already advised the Colonial Office to oppose the agitation for reform and to extend the Judicature Act for another year.[93] In February 1829 a report from the Poole merchants urged the government to repeal the provisions for local government in the colony.[94] Despite repeated attempts, George Robinson failed to persuade the government to form a Parliamentary committee of inquiry on Newfoundland.[95] The *Public Ledger* lamented that the petitions had "failed to become the subject of serious deliberation by the government."[96] Cochrane reported in late 1829 that the planned duty on imports continued to generate considerable excitement: "Unfortunately, as the various memorials in the Colonial Office will show you, there is mixed up with the question of taxation, that of colonial representation." He explained that "while one party pray to avert taxation because they cannot bear it, another entreat a legislature on the ground that they are equal to provide for their own expenses." In order to placate the agitators Cochrane recommended a "work popular in its character," i.e., road construction, funded from the new tax.[97]

A series of letters in the local press nevertheless formed a renewed political exchange which kept the question of a local legislature in front of the St. John's public. In the first of a series of letters, "Peregrinus" pleaded that "without the fostering aide of a local legislature, it is vain to talk of the improvement of the colony." Yet other letters by "Peregrinus" adopted the language on taxation and proclaimed: "*Taxation* and *representation* are inseparately united: God hath joined them; no British Parliament can separate them; to endeavour to do so is to stab our vitals." In response to "Peregrinus," "Hospes" questioned the "bare assertion" that a legislature assisting agriculture would cure all the colony's ills. "Quis" countered with a call for unity—"He who is not for us is against us"—and cited the *probable* good brought by a legislature. Finally, "Hospes" warned of merchant domination, stressed that all of the people should have a vote, and added a very perceptive comment on "Peregrinus": "Your writings are like a Jack-of-all-trades shop."[98]

On 15 September 1830 the reformers held a public meeting to discuss solely the issue of a colonial assembly. As a sign of the reform movement's growth, the meeting took place on the military parade ground in St. John's. The day before the meeting Winton repeated rumours that a cabal of merchants had resolved to support a town council instead of an assembly.[99] Though the report proved unfounded, it illustrated the tensions within the reform movement. Open opposition later appeared when an editorial in the *Royal Gazette* argued that Newfoundland could not afford a local legislature.[100] The meeting nevertheless went smoothly; in an apparent effort to represent the two main factions of the reform coalition, the Public Ledger printed the addresses given by William Thomas and John Kent, a new leader of the Catholic community.[101] Thomas reiterated the threat of import duties and, referring to the current gossip, asked rhetorically, "would a Town Council put a stop to this tax?" Kent argued that Newfoundland needed a legislature to ensure its economic development, and concluded that "the lovers of freedom...will support our cause." He also stressed that the political discussions enjoyed "a nearer approach to unity than at any previous period."[102]

The meeting then appointed a committee, chaired by William Thomas, to prepare a petition for a local legislature and to arrange for a delegation to present it to the British government.[103] Led by Thomas Brooking, the delegation arrived in London in December 1830 to find a new Whig government; after conferring with George Robinson, Brooking arranged for an interview with the King. On Christmas Eve they presented the petition, signed by over two thousand residents, to the Colonial Secretary, Lord Goderich. While Goderich affirmed the importance of Newfoundland, he neither voiced an opinion on the question of local government nor committed the government to any action.[104] The delegation in London nonetheless believed that the meetings had boosted their cause. When news of the interviews reached Newfoundland the *Public Ledger* observed that "the present government are likely to coincide with the views of the inhabitants."[105] During a meeting of the Benevolent Irish Society in St. John's, the gathering toasted the triumphant efforts of the reformers. Amid the cheers William Carson proclaimed there was every reason to expect that the authorities would grant a local legislature and thereby supply the constitutional rights needed to "consummate our happiness."[106]

Colonial Politics in London

Despite such optimism, the drive for representative government soon bogged down again. In June 1831 Lord Howick, the Under-Secretary for the Colonies, reaffirmed the official policy that local conditions prevented the establishment of a legislative assembly: the island's society had not developed sufficiently to support electoral politics.[107] While Howick's pronouncement met with astonishment in Newfoundland, it accorded with the broader trends throughout this period. The Whig administration's commitment to political reform in Britain did not necessarily extend to the colonies. Both Cabinet and Parliament typically paid little attention to colonial affairs, particularly during the intense debates over the Reform bill in 1831–32. Lord Howick, who wielded the real power in colonial affairs, remained ambivalent towards demands for colonial self-government. Within the Colonial Office, R.W. Hay's tenure as Permanent Under-Secretary epitomized conservatism.[108] Perhaps most importantly, the reform movement had failed to neutralize Governor Cochrane's influence. In April 1831 Cochrane advised the Colonial Office against making any major changes to the existing political system.[109] Instead of an assembly he recommended the creation of a legislative council to enact laws for the internal government of the island.[110] And in July 1831 the Colonial Office informed Cochrane that the arguments against granting a local legislature were "so strong as to render it unlikely that the government will adopt such a measure."[111]

Meanwhile George Robinson struggled to keep the colonial reform movement alive in London. In July 1831 he again opposed the annual grant to Newfoundland on the grounds that the absence of a local assembly rendered its expenditure unaccountable. Robinson then quickly advanced three arguments for granting the colony a local legislature: the colony's economic development necessitated a local assembly; the Newfoundland people only wanted the legitimate right to control their own affairs; and the grant of a local legislature would eliminate the colony's cost to the British government.[112] When Howick defended the government's policy, Robinson responded:

> The people of Newfoundland have instructed me to say, that if you will grant them a local legislature they will not again ask for money. Here, then, is an inducement to alter the present system, under which it is impossible for you to tell what you pay for it.[113]

Though Robinson was chided for his "coarse game," a number of M.P.'s took the bait and voiced their indignation over the colony's financial mismanagement. By tapping into a theme which would draw an immediate response, Robinson reignited the case for a local legislature.[114]

When news of the debate reached Newfoundland, it revitalized the local reform movement. On 29 September 1831 the reform committee convened an open meeting in St. John's to discuss its next course of action. The application to hold a public assembly reveals that the coalition of the mercantile elite and Catholic reformers was still holding: Brooking, Thomas, Row and Bennett signed alongside Morris, Kent, Doyle, Beck and, of course, Carson.[115] Held on the parade ground in St. John's, the open meeting attracted a cross-section of the population. Henry Winton reported that the assembly involved "disreputable personalities" and declined to print speeches that served "simply to amuse the public."[116] Unfortunately, when the working people become visible, contemporary sources silence their voices. We can only conclude that, first, the "lower orders" were present in sufficient numbers to attract attention (and disapproval) and, second, some reform speakers were targeting a popular audience. In order to project a respectable image of the reform movement, Winton later printed a speech given by William Row. Row's address noted that while "but one opinion prevailed" on the issue of local government, it remained "highly important that this unanimity should continue, as on it must greatly depend the final success of our efforts."[117]

The meeting's other leading speeches reinforced the reform movement's established themes. William Thomas focused on the question of taxation and the need for an assembly to control the colony's revenue. John Kent concluded his appeal for a local assembly by noting that "the press—the index of public feeling, the mirror of the people's mind—loudly proclaims its necessity."[118] Carson and Morris then commented on the great strides made by the reform movement in the long struggle to overcome the colony's oppression. The meeting observed "with a degree of satisfaction the admission made in the House of Commons...that the wealth and intelligence of the people of Newfoundland have entitled them to have a direct control in the management of their own affairs." However, in an apparent contradiction, the next resolution noted that "the depressed condition of our trade and fisheries, and the infant state of our agriculture, absolutely require the fostering care and encouragement of a local legislature."[119] Yet the reformers had no difficulty with this paradox, for an eclectic mix of arguments characterized the discourse surrounding the campaign for local government. The themes of poverty and prosperity became intertwined into a vision of a local assembly as the ultimate panacea for the colony.[120]

As the St. John's reformers observed the growth of the campaign for a legislature, they increasingly discussed the issue of participation from outport communities.[121] The outports had in fact petitioned for reform as early as 1821, and in Conception Bay Robert Pack was an early proponent of a colonial legislature.[122] In 1829 the *Conception Bay Mercury* strongly endorsed a local assembly as a vehicle for improvement.[123] A letter from "An Out-Harbour Man" asked Winton to specify the reformers' plans for the operation of a local legislature.[124] But an organized campaign for a local legislature only emerged in the outports in 1831. Attached to the recent St. John's memorial were petitions from Carbonear, Port de Grave, Old Perlican, and Brigus. The texts massed population and trade statistics to illustrate rural economic development to prove that St. John's was not the colony's only town of importance.[125] Nonetheless, meetings held in Burin and St. Mary's underscored the depressed state of the fishery and, as the St. Mary's meeting noted, the hope for "practical and beneficial results" from a local legislature.[126] In 1831–32 the island endured a particularly harsh winter which saw outbreaks of looting for food.[127]

Unknown to those in Newfoundland, however, George Robinson had already pulled off a pivotal manoeuvre in the House of Commons. After consulting with Joseph Hume, Robinson introduced a motion concerning Newfoundland in the House of Commons at a time shrewdly calculated to achieve maximum publicity. On 13 September 1831, the evening reserved for the third reading of the Reform Bill, Robinson interrupted the proceedings to state that the government's neglect of Newfoundland had compelled him to speak on a local subject. After reading the colony's petitions he launched into three arguments for the establishment of a local legislature. First, he cited the colony's extensive trade and large population relative to other colonies with representative government. Second, Robinson argued that the government's financial mismanagement caused the fishery's state of great embarrassment and distress. Finally, Robinson referred to the practical difficulties entailed with Parliament's "meddling with the details of colonial legislation." Robinson concluded with a motion for an address to the Crown asking for a local assembly similar to the other North American colonies and in accordance with the principles of the British Constitution.[128]

In response Lord Howick complained of the embarrassment caused by the timing of Robinson's motion. Howick nevertheless went quickly onto the offensive and noted that a meeting of Poole merchants had declared against the establishment of a local assembly. He reiterated the government's position that Newfoundland's uneven development made it "practically impossible to have an assembly really representing the...inhabitants of the island."[129] Following some discussion Joseph Hume declared that any further delay in the establishment of a local legislature would be "extremely prejudicial" to the interests of both the island's populace and the British government. He then advanced in rapid succession three distinct arguments in favour of a local legislature:

What is it that 80,000 or 90,000 British subjects ask for? It is that [1] they may be relieved from the arbitrary sway of an individual, and that they may be allowed to manage their own affairs; and, when they ask for this, they undertake [2] to relieve this country from every portion of the expense which has hitherto been incurred in the government of Newfoundland.... But let expense be what it may, I contend that [3] it is impossible for any body of men in Downing-street properly and satisfactorily to govern a distant and populace colony like that of Newfoundland.

Next, Hume targeted the neglect of the colonists' civil rights: "The present government profess to be guided by liberal principles—let us see if they will act upon them." Hume placed the onus squarely on the government and, therefore, transformed the issue of Newfoundland's governance into a question of the credibility of the Grey administration's commitment to reform.[130]

Lord Althorp, the Chancellor of the Exchequer, responded by recommending a committee of inquiry as the proper forum to discuss the colony's government. But with Hume's support, Robinson's motion quickly excited interest in the crowded House. Henry Labouchere, a prominent Whig and an acquaintance of Lord Howick, declared that Althorp's suggestion was inadequate because Robinson's motion concerned an issue too important for a committee.[131] Labouchere argued that Newfoundland deserved a constitution "founded upon those broad principles of British liberty which have been extended to the other colonies."[132] Forced on the defensive, Lord Howick professed that he had merely noted the difficulties entailed with giving Newfoundland an assembly. Howick's defense met with a barrage of reform rhetoric in which Daniel O'Connell argued that the "great principles of liberty" should govern colonial issues. Robinson then declared that he would withdraw his motion if the govern-

ment guaranteed to appoint a committee of inquiry on Newfoundland. In response Lord Althorp stated cryptically that the government would "give to that colony as much freedom and independence as shall be considered consistent with its own prosperity and security."[133]

In October 1831 Governor Cochrane travelled to London for consultations at the Colonial Office. According to later testimony Cochrane believed that the interviews had gone well.[134] Yet Lord Howick had already instructed James Stephen to report on the type of legislature suited for the colony. Released on 19 December 1831, Stephens' report recommended a blended assembly, which would include elected representatives and officials appointed by the Governor. Emphasizing the problems which bicameral legislatures had wrought in other colonies, Stephen claimed that a single legislative body, like the one established in Demerara, would engender greater harmony and help to balance the colony's political factions.[135] On 22 December 1831 Thomas Brooking arrived in London and had a meeting with Lord Holland early in the new year. Pleased with the interview, Brooking informed William Thomas of his progress and mentioned a rumour, which was probably accurate, that the government had already made a decision regarding Newfoundland.[136] Finally, on 25 January 1832 Goderich told Brooking during a private meeting that the government had resolved to grant the colony a local legislature. Lord Howick also wrote a letter of congratulation to Robinson which claimed that the government had resisted making any promises simply out of anxiety not to raise false hopes.[137] After more than a decade of struggle, the Newfoundland reform movement had at last achieved its ultimate goal. Parliament passed legislation confirming the powers of the new assembly, and the first elections were scheduled for the autumn of 1832.[138]

Conclusion

A number of factors shaped the development of local opposition to naval government. The reform movement developed through a symbiotic process in which an inherited political culture interacted with colonial conditions. When the reformers dealt with local issues, such as the structure of the justice system, they viewed representative institutions as the proper solution to local problems. The colony's mercantile elite initially opposed the reform movement, and then publicly divided over the question of local government, but the Chamber of Commerce nevertheless maintained effective leadership of the St. John's merchant community. During the 1820s a bourgeois public sphere emerged in St John's and acted as a forum for reformist ideas. Although some people from outside the St. John's elite appear to have been involved in the reform movement's activities, the local press worked diligently to maintain an image of respectability. Following established imperial policies, the Governor and the British government both opposed granting Newfoundland a legislative assembly.

Public opinion in St. John's evolved in a dynamic colonial environment into an eclectic yet cohesive collection of arguments. While William Carson employed a sharp common rhetoric based on notions of the rights of British subjects, Patrick Morris relied on the emotive imagery of persecution suffered under despotic fishing admirals and naval governors. Carson and Morris both advanced a model of economic development in which a local assembly appeared as the key to prosperity. Reform rhetoric was never uniform, as a variety of notions permeated the malleable body of the campaign against naval rule. During the Lundrigan affair, reformers marshalled arguments of the rule of law, for example, while the view of an assembly as a panacea appeared in later petitions from rural communities. The various rhetorical strands within the reform movement came together during the 1828 crisis over taxation.

After 1828 merchant-driven concerns over fiscal responsibility, and a nativist voice for local control of government, joined the public discussion. In effect, the campaign for representative government had become all things to all people.

Although one cannot pinpoint a single direct cause for the grant of an assembly in 1832, three developments were pivotal. First, in 1828 a proposed duty on imports prompted the Chamber of Commerce to mount a political protest against government policies. The colony's leading merchants soon became actively involved in the reform movement, and this led to the formation in 1828 of a viable political coalition. Second, through a series of editorials and public letters the local press sponsored a vigorous campaign against "taxation without representation." Active participants in the reform movement, Henry Winton and John Shea pushed for public meetings and a united campaign for a legislative assembly. Third, George Robinson represented the reformers' case in Parliament and, arguing that a local legislature would eliminate the colony's cost to the British government, obtained the backing of Joseph Hume. In September 1831 Robinson managed in a shrewdly timed motion in the House of Commons to make Newfoundland's governance a public litmus-test of the Whigs' liberalism. Forced to pledge a committee of inquiry, the Grey administration commissioned a Colonial Office report and, in a move that avoided further embarrassment, granted Newfoundland representative government.

The final element behind the success of the campaign for a local legislature was its ability to avoid divisive issues. The reformers were able to use diverse and sometimes contradictory arguments because their movement focused on a single, simple goal: the achievement of an elected assembly. Contentious issues surrounding how actually to govern the colony remained largely outside the political discussion. With the advent of electoral politics, however, the struggle for power within Newfoundland had only just begun. The coalition of interests which had held together since 1828 came apart at the seams soon after the first local elections; for the next three decades bitter sectarian factionalism dominated Newfoundland politics.[139] The establishment of representative government had marked the end of an era in the island's history. Although colonial governments continued to rely periodically on warships to help maintain law and order, the last vestiges of naval government had been swept away, as the Royal Navy became merely an ancillary to civilian rule.[140]

Notes

This article is a revised version of a paper which originally appeared in the *Journal of the Canadian Historical Association* in 1994. For their comments on earlier versions of this paper, I thank Melvin Baker, Sean Cadigan, Jane Errington, Allan Greer, and Jim Phillips. I also gratefully acknowledge the research funding provided by the Institute of Social and Economic Research at Memorial University and the Social Sciences and Humanities Research Council of Canada.

1 D.W. Prowse, *A History of Newfoundland from the English, Colonial, and Foreign Records* (Belleville, Ontario: Mika Studio, 1972 reprint of 1895 ed.); A.H. McLintock, *The Establishment of Constitutional Government in Newfoundland, 1783–1832: A Study of Retarded Colonisation* (London: Longmans, Green, 1941). For reviews of liberal historiography, see George Story, *People of the Landwash: Essays on Newfoundland and Labrador.* Melvin Baker, Helen Peters, and Shannon Ryan, eds. (St. John's: Harry Cuff, 1997), pp. 77–101 & 116–28; Peter Neary, "The Writing of Newfoundland History," in J.K. Hiller and P. Neary, eds., *Newfoundland in the Nineteenth and Twentieth Centuries: Essays in Interpretations* (Toronto, 1980), pp. 3–13; Olaf U. Janzen, "Newfoundland and the International Fishery," in M. Brook Taylor, ed., *Canadian History: A Reader's Guide, Volume 1: Beginnings to Confederation* (Toronto: University of Toronto Press, 1994), pp. 280–324; James K. Hiller, "Is Atlantic Canadian History Possible?," *Acadiensis* 30, 1 (Autumn 2000), pp. 16–22.

2 Keith Matthews, "Historical Fence Building: A Critique of the Historiography of Newfoundland," *Newfoundland Quarterly* 74 (April 1978): pp. 21–9; Keith Matthews, "The Class of '32: St. John's Reformers on the Eve of Representative Government," 6, 2 (1977), pp. 80–94; Keith Matthews, *Lectures on the History of Newfoundland, 1500–1830* (St. John's: Breakwater Press, 1988), ch. 30.

3 Patrick O'Flaherty, "The Seeds of Reform: Newfoundland, 1800–18," *Journal of Canadian Studies* 23 (Fall 1988), pp. 39–56; Patrick O'Flaherty, "Government in Newfoundland Before 1832: The Context of Reform," *Newfoundland Quarterly* 23 (October 1988), pp. 26–30; Patrick O'Flaherty, *Old Newfoundland: A History to 1843* (St. John's: Long Beach Press, 1999). O'Flaherty also probed the writings of Carson and Morris in *The Rock Observed: Studies in the Literature of Newfoundland* (Toronto: University of Toronto Press, 1979), pp. 49–71.

4 Sean Cadigan, "Economic and Social Relations of Production on the Northeast-coast of Newfoundland, with Special Reference to Conception Bay, 1785–1855." (PhD thesis, Memorial University, 1991), pp. 108–11, 179, 190, 326–7, 318–21; Sean Cadigan, "The Staple Model Reconsidered: The Case of Agricultural Policy in Northeast Newfoundland, 1785–1855," *Acadiensis* 21 (Spring 1992), pp. 54–9; Sean Cadigan, *Hope and Deception in Conception Bay: Merchant-Settler Relations in Newfoundland, 1785–1855* (Toronto: University of Toronto Press, 1995).

5 John P. Greene, *Between Damnation and Starvation: Priests and Merchants in Newfoundland Politics, 1745–1855* (Montreal & Kingston: McGill-Queen's University Press, 1999), chs. 1–4.

6 For overviews of the political environment in contemporary Britain and Ireland, see Linda Colley, *Britons: Forging the Nation, 1707–1837* (New Haven: Yale University Press, 1992), ch. 8; R.F. Foster, "Ascendancy and Union," in R.F. Foster, ed., *The Oxford History of Ireland* (Oxford: Oxford University Press, 1992), pp. 134–73.

7 In 1815 the island's population was over 40,000, and Irish Catholics comprised a large majority in St. John's. On the socio-economic transformation during the Napoleonic Wars, see Shannon Ryan, "Fishery to Colony: A Newfoundland Watershed, 1793–1815," in P.A. Buckner and David Frank, eds., *The Acadiensis Reader, Volume One: Atlantic Canada Before Confederation* (Second edition, Fredericton, 1990), pp. 138–56.

8 Patrick O'Flaherty, "John Ryan," *Dictionary of Canadian Biography* (14 vols. to date, Toronto: University of Toronto Press, 1966–), vol. 7, pp. 151–6 [hereafter *DCB*].

9 Patrick O'Flaherty, "Sir Francis Forbes," *DCB*, vol. 7, pp. 301–04; Bruce Kercher, "Law Reports from a Non-Colony and a Penal Colony: The Australian Manuscript Decisions of Sir Francis Forbes as Chief Justice of Newfoundland," *Dalhousie Law Journal* 19, 2 (Fall 1996), pp. 417–24.

10 On the creation of a public sphere generally, see Jurgen Habermas, *The Structural Transformation of the Public Sphere: An Inquiry into a Category of Bourgeois Society*. Thomas Burger, trans. (Cambridge, Mass.: Massachusetts Institute of Technology Press, 1991), esp. pp. 19–26; Craig Calhoun, "Hambermas and the Public Sphere," in C. Calhoun, ed., *Habermas and the Public Sphere* (Cambridge, Mass.: Massachusetts Institute of Technology, 1992), pp. 2–41. On the cultural impact of the growth of a local press, see Robert Darnton, *The Kiss of Lamourette: Reflections in Cultural History* (New York: Norton, 1990), chs. 7–9.

11 The Act 51 Geo. III, c. 45 (1811) empowered the governor to tender building lots for thirty-year leases. See Prowse, *History of Newfoundland*, p. 386; Sean Cadigan, "The Role of the Fishing Ships' Rooms Controversy in the Rose of a Local Bourgeoisie: St. John's, Newfoundland, 1775–1812." (Unpublished paper, Centre for Newfoundland Studies, 1992.)

12 William Carson, *A Letter to the Members of Parliament of the United Kingdom* (Greenock: W. Scott, 1812), pp. 3–4. In 1808 Carson emigrated from Scotland to St. John's, where he worked as a medical doctor: over the next thirty years he remained at the heart of colonial politics and the edge of agitation for reform. See Patrick O'Flaherty, "William Carson," *DCB*, vol. 7, pp. 151–56.

13 William Carson, *Reasons for Colonizing the Island of Newfoundland* (Greenock: W. Scott, 1813), pp. 3–4, 6–8, 12–13, 24–6.

14 Suzanne Ellison, *Historical Directory of Newfoundland and Labrador Newspapers, 1806–1996* (St. John's: Memorial University, 1997), pp. 108–16 & 132–33.

15 For an incisive analysis of the role of the press in fostering public opinion, see Jeffrey McNairn, *The Capacity to Judge: Public Opinion and Deliberative Democracy in Upper Canada, 1791–1854* (Toronto: University of Toronto Press, 2000), esp. chs. 3–4.

16 Patrick O'Flaherty, "James Lundrigan," *DCB*, vol. 6, pp. 409–11.

17 Anon., *A Report of Certain Proceedings of the Inhabitants of the Town of Saint John, in the island of Newfoundland, with the view to obtain a REFORM of the LAWS, more particularly in the mode of their administration, and an INDEPENDENT LEGISLATURE* (St. John's: Printed by Lewis Ryan, 1821), esp. pp. iv, 10–11.

18 Morris had emigrated from Ireland in 1804, entered the mercantile trade, and soon became a prominent public figure. See John Mannion, "Patrick Morris," *DCB*, vol. 7, pp. 623–34.

19 *Report of Certain Proceedings*, p. 11. Eight of the thirteen men appointed to the committee were Roman Catholics. See John Mannion, "Henry Shea," *DCB*, vol. 6, pp. 709–11; Derek Bussy, "Patrick Doyle," *DCB*, vol. 8, pp. 234–35; O'Flaherty, "Seeds of Reform," p. 43.

20 *Report of Certain Proceedings*, pp. 12–13, 19–20.

21 The Newfoundland reformers were thereby able to capitalize on political trends in contemporary England. See Richard R. Follett, *Evangelicalism, Penal Theory, and the Politics of Criminal Law Reform in England, 1808–30* (New York: Palgrave, 2001), ch. 8.

22 *Parliamentary Debates*, New Series, vol. 5 (28 May 1821), pp. 1015–16; *Journals of the House of Commons*, vol. 76 (1821), p. 388.

23 Ibid.

24 On 17 May 1821 Governor Hamilton forwarded this letter to the reform committee. See *Report of Certain Proceedings*, pp. 31–2.

25 *Report of Certain Proceedings*, pp. 40–62.

26 See E.J. Hobsbawm, *Nations and Nationalism since 1780: Programme, Myth, Reality* (2nd ed. Cambridge: Cambridge University Press, 1992), ch. 1; Benedict Anderson, *Imagined Communities: Reflections on the Origins and Spread of Nationalism* (2nd ed. New York: Verso, 1991), ch. 9.

27 Carson, *Reasons for Colonizing Newfoundland*, p. 13.

28 *Report of Certain Proceedings*, pp. 43–44.

29 Anon., *Observations on the Present State of Newfoundland, in reference to its Courts of Justice* (London: A. Hancock, 1823), p. 2. The pamphlet was addressed to Lord Bathurst, the Colonial Secretary, and signed by "Britannicus."

30 Eric Hobsbawm, *On History* (London: Abacus, 1997), ch. 21.

31 5 Geo. IV, c. 67 (1824). The Judicature Act was limited to a five-year term. Two other acts passed in 1824 also revised aspects of the island's legal system: the Fisheries Act (5 Geo. IV, c. 51), and the Marriage Act (5 Geo. IV, c. 68).

32 5 Geo. IV, c. 51, s. 1 (1824). I thank Patrick O'Flaherty for kindly providing the statutory reference to the repeal of King William's Act.

33 The 1825 Royal Charter, which was promulgated on 2 January 1826, was printed in Henry Winton, ed., *Select Cases from the Records of the Supreme Court of Newfoundland* (St. John's: Henry Winton, 1829), pp. 559–74.

34 O'Flaherty, *Old Newfoundland*, pp. 139–40. As O'Flaherty points out, the fact that the statutes of 1824 referred to Newfoundland as a *colony* may have awarded a type of official colonial status, but they bestowed only piecemeal reforms.

35 *Mercantile Journal*, 5 January & 2 March 1826.

36 Frederic F. Thompson, "Sir Thomas John Cochrane," *DCB*, vol. 10, pp. 178–80. On Cochrane's administration, see Gertrude Gunn, *Political History of Newfoundland*, ch. 1; O'Flaherty, *Old Newfoundland*, ch. 7; Cadigan, *Merchant-Settler Relations*, ch. 5.

37 Cochrane to Wilmot Horton, 29 July 1825, as quoted in McLintock, *Establishment of Constitutional Government*, p. 164.

38 Christopher English, "From Fishing Schooner to Colony: The Legal Development of Newfoundland, 1791–1832," in L. Knafla and S. Binnie, eds., *Law, Society, and the State: Essays in Modern Legal History* (Toronto: University of Toronto Press, 1995), pp. 85–88; O'Flaherty, *Old Newfoundland*, p. 141.

39 *Mercantile Journal*, 9 February 1826. See also Melvin Baker, "The Government of St. John's, Newfoundland, 1800–1921" (Ph.D. thesis, University of Western Ontario, 1980), pp. 30–5.

40 Provincial Archives of Newfoundland and Labrador [PANL], Colonial Office Papers, series 194 [CO 194], vol. 72, p. 158, Cochrane to Bathurst 27 May 1826, enclosures 1–7.

41 PANL, CO 194/72, pp. 160–3, Cochrane to Bathurst, 27 May 1826. In March 1827 the government asked Parliament to consider new duties on imports into Newfoundland. See *Journals of the House of Commons* 82 (1826–7), p. 359.

42 PANL, CO 194/73, pp. 158–62, Stephen to Wilmot Horton, 16 September 1826. A prominent figure in formulating Colonial Office policy, Stephen disdained partisan politics and stressed expediency over public opinion. See Phillip Buckner, "The Colonial Office in British North America, 1801–50," *DCB*, vol. 8, pp. xxx–xxxiv; A.G.L. Shaw, "James Stephen and Colonial Policy," *Journal of Imperial and Commonwealth History* 20, 1 (January 1992), pp. 11–34.

43 PANL, CO 194/72, pp. 332–3, Cochrane to Bathurst, 17 November 1826.

44 See editorial in *Public Ledger* (St. John's), 18 May 1827. After emigrating from England, Henry Winton founded (with Alexander Haire) the *Public Ledger* in 1820. See Patrick O'Flaherty, "Henry Winton," *DCB*, vol. 7, pp. 947–50.

45 Patrick Morris, *Remarks on the State of Society, Religion, Morals, and Education at Newfoundland* (London: A. Hancock, 1827), p. 10.

46 See O'Flaherty, *Studies in the Literature of Newfoundland*, ch. 4.

47 PANL, CO 194/78, pp. 131–4, Memorial of the St. John's Chamber of Commerce to Lord Bathurst, 9 October 1827. Thomas Brooking registered his opposition to oppose the duty in a letter to the local press. See the *Public Ledger*, 27 November 1827.

48 The proposed 2.5% duty covered all imported items except salt and potatoes; the government also planned new taxes on wine and spirits. See the editorial in the *Public Ledger*, 22 April 1828.

49 A transcript of the debate appears in the *Public Ledger*, 18 July 1828. Robinson's attack singled out the Governor's mansion which, paid out of unauthorized bills, had swelled beyond original estimates. The Colonial Office had already censured Cochrane for financial mismanagement: see McLintock, *Establishment of Constitutional Government*, p. 165.

50 Thomas Brooking succeeded Newman Hoyles as president of the Chamber of Commerce for 1828, and John Dunscombe and William Thomas were elected vice-presidents. All four men had supported the proposal for a charter of incorporation. As leading Protestant merchants they each served as grand jury foremen and leaders of local philanthropic societies. See *Royal Gazette*, 19 August 1828; Keith Matthews, "Thomas Brooking," *DCB*, vol. 9, pp. 84–6; Keith Matthews, *Profiles of Water Street Merchants* (St. John's: Memorial University, 1980).

51 PANL, CO 194/76, p. 385, Cochrane to Murray, 14 December 1828.

52 T.W. Acheson, *Saint John: the Making of a Colonial Urban Community* (Toronto: University of Toronto Press, 1985), pp. 55–9, 66.

53 Patrick Morris, Arguments to Prove the Necessity of Granting Newfoundland a Constitutional Government (London: Hunt and Clarke, 1828), pp. 11–12.

54 Ibid., pp. 27–28.

55 J. Bristow, *Brief Remarks on a Pamphlet entitled*

"Arguments to Prove the Necessity of Granting to Newfoundland a Constitutional Government" (Poole: Moore and Sydenham, 1828), pp. 8–15, 19, 28.

56 The column was reprinted in the *Newfoundlander,* 2 October 1828.

57 The *Newfoundlander* reprinted Morris' pamphlets in extracts over several weeks from 23 February to 19 March 1828. In the *Public Ledger,* 25 August 1828, Henry Winton termed Morris' pamphlet "decidedly the best yet," and, on 29 August, Winton offered a critique of Bristow's essay.

58 The son of the reformer Henry Shea, John Shea established the *Newfoundlander* in 1827. See Mannion, "Henry Shea," *DCB,* vol. 6, p. 711.

59 *Newfoundlander,* 21 November 1827.

60 18 Geo. III, c. 12 (1778). This statute is referred to as either the "Colonial Tax Repeal Act" or the "Declaratory Act." On the evolution of the constitutional argument against "taxation without representation," see Bernard Bailyn, *The Ideological Origins of the American Revolution* (2nd ed., Cambridge, Mass.: Harvard University Press, 1992), esp. pp. 209–21.

61 In June 1828 Shea also questioned whether the new tax would be used to build "a new gaol, infirmary, work-house, treadmill...to improve our morals." See *Newfoundlander,* 9 April 1828, 19 June 1828.

62 *Public Ledger,* 25 December 1827.

63 *Public Ledger,* 22 April 1828.

64 *Public Ledger,* 25 April 1828.

65 *Public Ledger,* 17 June 1828. See also the editorial for 18 July 1828. In an 18 April 1828 editorial Winton had complained that the "Demon of Discord has attended our meetings."

66 *Newfoundlander,* 19 June 1828.

67 *Public Ledger,* 19 August 1828.

68 *Public Ledger,* 7 October 1828. See also the editorials on 3 & 24 October.

69 *Public Ledger,* 7 October 1828. "Atomus" declared in favour of a legislature but called for a "fair" discussion of all the options.

70 *Public Ledger,* 18 November 1828. The press played a similar role in other reform movements: see, for example, Linda Colley, *Britons: Forging the Nation, 1707–1837* (New Haven: Yale University Press, 1992), pp. 342–43; Carol Wilton, "'A Firebrand amongst the People': The Durham Meetings and Popular Politics in Upper Canada," *Canadian Historical Review* 85 (September 1994), p. 356.

71 Dated 1 December 1828, the notice requested the High Sheriff to convene a public meeting "for the purpose of taking into consideration the necessity of petitioning Parliament against any further imposts or duties upon imports or new duties upon exports, and the expediency of praying that His Majesty's Government will grant a Constitutional Legislative Government to this island." While Winton noted the announcement with "peculiar satisfaction," John Shea called for "a firm and unanimous appeal to the British Legislature." Both men signed the 1829 petition. See *Public Ledger,* 2 December 1828; *Newfoundlander,* 4 December 1828.

72 See PANL, CO 194/79, pp. 299–303, "Petition for a Legislative Government, 1 January 1829"; PANL, CO 194/72, p. 158 Cochrane to Bathurst, 27 May 1826, enclosure 7, "Memorial Against a Charter of Incorporation, 23 February 1826." Among the 498 signatories were several prominent figures: William B. Row, a merchant and lawyer; Edward Kielly, a Catholic surgeon; and John Ryan, the publisher of the *Royal Gazette.*

73 Imported items reported for sale 2 December 1828 in the *Public Ledger* include: tea (William Thomas); wine (Robinson and Brooking); rum and molasses (John Dunscombe); flour and beef (Brown, Hoyles).

74 John Edward FitzGerald, "Conflict and Culture in Irish-Newfoundland Roman Catholicism, 1829–1850" (PhD thesis, University of Ottawa, 1997), ch. 2; John Edward FitzGerald, "Michael Anthony Fleming and Ultramontanism in Irish-Newfoundland Roman Catholicism, 1829–1850," *CCHA Historical Studies* 64 (1998), pp. 27–44.

75 See Raymond Lahey, "Thomas Scallan," *DCB,* vol. 6, pp. 690–694; Raymond Lahey, "Catholicism and Colonial Policy in Newfoundland, 1779–1845," in T. Murphy and G. Stortz, eds., *Creed and Culture: The Place of English-Speaking Catholics in Canadian Society, 1750–1930* (Montreal and Kingston: McGill-Queen's University Press), pp. 50–1, 65–8; O'Flaherty, "Government in Newfoundland Before 1832," p. 30. Except for Morris, who was living in Ireland, the leaders of the older reform movement—notably Doyle, Shea, Hogan and Beck—were active in 1828. Laurence O'Brien, a Catholic merchant and later a prominent politician, was a recent addition.

76 By matching the signatures from the 1829 petition with those from the 1826 memorial, I was able to identify nineteen non-elite signatories: one cooper, one fish culler, one baker, one painter, three sailmakers, one smith, two planters, one carpenter, two spirit dealers, one shopkeeper, three coopers,

one innkeeper, and one wheelwright. See PANL, CO 194/79, pp. 299–303, Petition for a Legislative Government, 1 January 1829; CO 194/72, p. 158, Cochrane to Bathurst 27 May 1826, enclosure 7, Memorial Against a Charter of Incorporation, 23 February 1826.

77 Gail Campbell, "Disenfranchised But Not Quiescent: Women Petitioners in New Brunswick in the Mid-19th Century," in Janet Guildford and Suzanne Morton, eds., *Separate Spheres: Women's Worlds in the 19ᵗʰ-Century Maritimes* (Fredericton: Acadiensis Press, 1994), pp. 39–66.

78 Rusty Bittermann, "Women and the Escheat Movement," in Guildford and Morton, eds., *Separate Spheres,* pp. 23–38. On the informal regulation of gender in rural Newfoundland, see Willeen Keough, "The Riddle of Peggy Mountain: Regulation of Irish Women's Sexuality on the Southern Avalon, 1750–1860," *Acadiensis* 31, 2 (Spring 2002), pp. 38–70.

79 Sean Cadigan, "Whipping Them into Shape: State Refinement of Patriarchy among Conception Bay Fishing Families, 1787–1825," in C. McGrath, B. Neis, and M. Porter, eds., *Their Lives and Times: Women in Newfoundland and Labrador: A Collage* (St. John's: Killick Press, 1995), pp. 48–58.

80 Patrick Morris, *Remarks on the State of Society, Religion, Morals and Education at Newfoundland* (London: A. Hancock, 1827), pp. 13–14. Original italics.

81 Cecelia Morgan, *Public Men and Virtuous Women: The Gendered Languages of Religion and Politics in Upper Canada, 1791–1850* (Toronto: University of Toronto Press, 1996); Allan Greer, *The Patriots and the People: The Rebellion of 1837 in Rural Lower Canada* (Toronto: University of Toronto Press, 1993), ch. 7.

82 Carson, *Letter to the Members of Parliament,* p. 4.

83 There is not space here to discuss the historiography but see, *inter alia,* J. Murray Beck, *Joseph Howe, volume I: Conservative Reformer, 1804–1848* (Kingston & Montreal: McGill-Queen's University Press, 1982), esp. chs. 17–19; Rosemary Ommer, "The 1830s: Adapting Their Institutions to Their Desires," in Phillip Buckner and John Reid, eds., *The Atlantic Region to Confederation: A History* (Toronto: University of Toronto Press, 1994), pp. 300–01; Rusty Bittermann, "Agrarian Protest and Cultural Transfer: Irish Emigrants and the Escheat Movement on Prince Edward Island," in Tom Power, ed., *The Irish in Atlantic Canada* (Fredericton: Acadiensis Press, 1991), pp. 96–106; Peter Burroughs, *The Canadian Crisis and British Colonial Policy, 1828–1841* (Toronto: Macmillan, 1979); Paul

Romney, "From the Types Riot to the Rebellion: Elite Ideology, Anti-Legal Sentiment, Political Violence, and the Rule of Law in Upper Canada," *Ontario History* 79 (1987), pp. 113–44; Allan Greer, "Historical Roots of Canadian Democracy," *Journal of Canadian Studies* 34, 1 (Spring 1999), pp. 7–26.

84 See Matthews, "Class of '32," pp. 80–94.

85 *Newfoundlander,* 19 June 1828.

86 Winton later attacked John Kent for not being resident in the colony long enough to sit in the Assembly. See *Public Ledger,* 3 October 1828, 18 September 1832.

87 *Royal Gazette,* 5 October 1830.

88 *Public Ledger,* 17 September 1831.

89 *Public Ledger,* 19 December 1828; *Newfoundlander,* 25 December 1828.

90 *Public Ledger,* 23 January 1829.

91 *Public Ledger,* 20 January 1829.

92 See Frederick Madden, ed., *Select Documents on the Constitutional History of the British Empire and Commonwealth, Volume III: Imperial Reconstruction, 1763–1840* (Westport: Greenwood Press, 1987), section B; John Belcham, "Republicanism, Popular Constitutionalism and the Radical Platform in early Nineteenth-Century England," *Social History* 6 (January 1981), pp. 1–32.

93 PANL, CO 194/78, p. 39, Cochrane to Murray, 13 December 1828.

94 PANL, CO 194/79, pp. 128–31, Bristow to Murray, 26 February 1826, enclosure, "Report of the Committee of Merchants Engaged in the Newfoundland Fishery at the Port of Poole." The report called for the repeal of section 35 of 5 Geo. IV cap. 67 (1824).

95 *Parliamentary Debates* 5 (6/7/13 April 1829), pp. 463, 533–5, 714; *Parliamentary Debates* 14 (11 May 1830), pp. 580–1.

96 *Public Ledger,* 12 May 1829.

97 PANL, CO 194/78, pp. 241–60, Cochrane to Murray, 11 December 1829. Cochrane also advised the government to add bread, flour, peas, and grain to the list of items exempted from the import duty.

98 The letters appear in *Public Ledger,* 13/23/30 July 1830 and 4/13/17 August 1830.

99 *Public Ledger,* 14 September 1830.

100 *Royal Gazette,* 28 September 1830. It is doubtful whether Ryan had written the editorial; Patrick O'Flaherty has suggested that the author was perhaps

John Collier Withers. See Patrick O'Flaherty, "John Ryan," *DCB,* vol. 7, p. 765.

101 A nephew of Patrick Morris, Kent came to Newfoundland in 1820 and began working as a commission agent and auctioneer. Often compared to William Lyon Mackenzie, Kent was a combative populist who espoused democratic principles. See P.B. Waite, "John Kent," *DCB,* vol. 10, pp. 398–400.

102 *Public Ledger,* 17 September 1830. The emphasis on unity also characterized public reform meetings in Upper Canada. See Wilton, "The Durham Meetings and Popular Politics in Upper Canada," p. 356.

103 The committee consisted of Protestant merchants and lawyers (Thomas, Bennett, Row, Job and Bland), Catholic reformers (Doyle and Shea), a representative from Harbour Grace, and William Carson. See *Public Ledger,* 17 September 1830.

104 *Public Ledger,* 18 March 1831, letter from the delegation to William Thomas, 29 December 1830. The paper reprinted all of the reform committee's correspondence.

105 *Public Ledger,* 15 March 1831.

106 *Public Ledger,* 25 March 1831.

107 *Parliamentary Debates,* 3rd series, 4 (27 June 1831), pp. 359–60.

108 P.A. Buckner, *The Transition to Responsible Government: British Policy in British North America, 1815–1850* (Westport, Conn.: Greenwood Press, 1985), pp. 15–18, 151, 294; C.A. Bayly, *Imperial Meridian: The British Empire and the World, 1780–1830* (London: Longman, 1989), pp. 194–5, 209; Peter Burroughs, "Liberal, Paternalist or Cassandra?: Earl Grey as a Critic of Colonial Self-Government," *Journal of Imperial and Commonwealth History* 18 (1990), pp. 33–5.

109 PANL, CO 194/81, pp. 73–81, Cochrane to Goderich, 14 April 1831.

110 PANL, CO 194/81, pp. 111–23, Cochrane to Goderich, 4 May 1831.

111 Hay to Cochrane, 6 July 1831, as quoted in McLintock, *Establishment of Constitutional Government in Newfoundland,* p. 182.

112 *Parliamentary Debates* 5 (25 July 1831), p. 283. The debate was also reprinted in the *Public Ledger,* 6 September 1831.

113 *Public Ledger,* 6 September 1831.

114 See *Parliamentary Debates* 5 (25 July 1831), pp. 288–9. On the cost of the colonies as an important political issue, see Bayly, *Imperial Meridian,* pp. 194–5.

115 *Newfoundlander,* 6 October 1831.

116 *Public Ledger,* 30 September 1831.

117 *Public Ledger,* 7 October 1831.

118 *Newfoundlander,* 6 October 1831.

119 *Public Ledger,* 30 September 1831.

120 The *Public Ledger* reprinted the petition to the Crown and Parliament on 7 October 1831.

121 Henry Winton noted that it was "gratifying to perceive that the inhabitants of the outports are unanimous in their desire to obtain the same object." See *Public Ledger,* 11 October 1831.

122 In 1821 Parliament considered a petition from Ferryland on the Lundrigan affair. See *Journals of the House of Commons* 76 (1821), p. 388. On Robert Pack's reform activities, see Keith Matthews, "Robert Pack," *DCB,* vol. 8, p. 674.

123 An editorial argued that if the island acquired a local legislature than "we have no hesitation in saying, that in five years its labours would be productive of incalculable advantage." See the *Conception Bay Mercury* (Harbour Grace), 21 August 1829.

124 *Public Ledger,* 24 September 1830.

125 *Journals of the House of Commons* 87 (1831–32), pp. 171–2, 298. The Harbour Grace and Carbonear petitions originated from meetings held 4 October 1831. A public meeting on 28 October 1831 had approved the memorial from Brigus. See *Public Ledger,* 12/21/18 October 1831, 18 November 1831.

126 The meetings occurred in Burin on 9 November 1831 and in St. Mary's on 6 December 1831. See *Public Ledger,* 13, 27 January 1832.

127 Cadigan, "Staple Model Reconsidered," p. 59.

128 *Parliamentary Debates* 6 (13 September 1831), pp. 1377–378. The *Public Ledger* printed a transcript on 15 November 1831. Hume admitted during the ensuing debate that he had offered advice to Robinson, and the quality of Robinson's address suggests substantial preparation and outside assistance.

129 Ibid.

130 *Parliamentary Debates* 6 (13 September 1831), pp. 1381–84. Hume's endorsement was important because he acted as a liaison between the Grey administration and the radicals on the fringe of the Whig party. During the crisis over the Reform Bill in 1831, the Whigs needed all the support they could muster. For a synopsis of the political situation in

England, see Richard Brown, *Revolution, Radicalism and Reform: England, 1780–1846* (Cambridge: Cambridge University Press, 2000), ch. 4.

131 Labouchere had visited the Canadas in 1824, served on the select committee of 1828, and led the circle of Whigs with whom Howick studied in 1830. See Buckner, *Transition to Responsible Government,* pp. 149, 255.

132 *Parliamentary Debates* 6 (13 September 1831), pp. 1381–84.

133 Ibid.

134 Gunn, *Political History of Newfoundland,* p. 11.

135 The report recommended that the Newfoundland Governor be given the same commission and instructions as the Governor of Nova Scotia, with the added instruction to ask the assembly to pass a bill incorporating a council. Stephens' report is reprinted in McLintock, *Establishment of Constitutional Government,* pp. 207–10. On the use of different legislative models in imperial policy, see J.M. Ward, *Colonial Self-Government: The British Experience* (London: MacMillan, 1976), esp. pp. 126–28.

136 *Public Ledger,* 2 March 1832, letter from Brooking to Thomas, 5 January 1832.

137 *Public Ledger,* 27 March 1832, letter from Brooking to Thomas, 25 January, and letter from Howick to Robinson, 25 January 1832.

138 2-3 William IV, c. 78 (1832).

139 After 1832 Winton became a harsh critic of the political influence of the Roman Catholic Church. In an episode which marked the violent sectarian conflict of the 1830s, Henry Winton was violently attacked in 1835 by a group of masked men, presumed to be Irish Catholics, and had his face and ears brutally mutilated. Two years later the *Public Ledger* urged the government to revoke representative government in Newfoundland, and in 1842 the elected assembly was amalgamated with an appointed council. See Patrick O'Flaherty, "Henry David Winton," *DCB,* vol. 8, pp. 467–70; Patrick O'Flaherty, "The Road to Saddle Hill," *Newfoundland Quarterly* 89, 3 (July 1995), pp. 21–26; Linda Little, "Collective Action in Outport Newfoundland: A Case Study from the 1830s," *Labour/Le Travail* 26 (Fall 1990), pp. 7–35.

140 On the use of warships in assistance of civil authority, see O'Flaherty, *Old Newfoundland,* pp. 164–78.

"This Ultimate Resource": Martial Law and State Repression in Lower Canada, 1837–8

Jean-Marie Fecteau

If the soldier and the judge should sit both on one bench, the drum would drown the voice of the crier. (Sir Edward Coke, 1628)[1]

It is superfluous to state with what caution and reserve this ultimate resource should be resorted to, and that it ought to be confined within the narrowest limit which the necessity of the case would admit. But if unhappily the case shall arise in any part of Lower Canada, in which the protection of the loyal and peaceful subjects of the Crown may require the adoption of this extreme measure, it must not be declined. (Colonial Secretary Lord Glenelg, 1837)[2]

Nor shall I regret that I have wielded these despotic powers in a manner which, as an Englishman, I am anxious to declare utterly inconsistent with the British constitution, until I learn what are the constitutional principles that remain in force when a whole constitution is suspended; what principles of the British constitution holds good in a country where the people's money is taken without the people's consent, where representative government is annihilated, where martial law has been the law of the land, and where the trial by jury exists only to defeat

the ends of justice, and to provoke the righteous scorn and indignation of the community. (Lord Durham, 1838)[3]

Since Max Weber, if not before, the relationship between law and collective violence has been studied mainly in terms of *legality*, where the law is seen as one of the preferred means of controlling violence. The latter is confined by law to the formal and pre-established context of permitted relationships, with the state holding a monopoly on "legitimate" violence. The advent of democratic societies only served to confirm and systematize this tendency by associating the power of the state with the expression of popular will. Of course, there remains the question of a potential conflict between the will of political representatives or that of the state, on the one hand, and the fundamental rules and values of the society, on the other.[4] But what happens when the very organizing principle of a society is the object of questioning, along with the rules that flow from it? What happens when the ruled rise up against the rulers and, by their violent and radical actions, render inoperable the existing

---

Jean-Marie Fecteau, "'This Ultimate Resource': Martial Law and State Repression in Lower Canada, 1837–8," in F. Murray Greenwood and Barry Wright, eds., *Canadian State Trials,* vol. 2, pages 207–47. Copyright © 2002 University of Toronto Press Incorporated. Reprinted with permission of the publisher.

legal system, including the traditional modes of preserving the established "order"? In such a situation, law dissolves into, or is confused with, violence. Or else the law is reborn in terms dictated by the victors.

Towards the end of the eighteenth and during the first half of the nineteenth century, most Western societies experienced this "revolutionary" situation before falling under the shadow of a well-policed and decidedly militarized liberal order.[5] At the very moment when the concept of the right to revolt sprang from considerations on natural law, there also developed what might be called a legal economy of emergency measures. This implied a reflection on the means of intervention, ranging from riot control to martial law, available to authorities in times of insurrection. In such a context, distinctions among law, power, and politics became very much blurred. As this article will show, the imposition of martial law during the rebellions of 1837–8 in Lower Canada was no exception.

Legality, Social Disruption, and Martial Law

THE BRITISH EXAMPLE

It has often been said that the English Revolution of the seventeenth century represented less a fundamental change in the established order than a radical redistribution of power among the existing elites. What resulted was a delicate balance between royal power and the power of the dominant classes in civil society—the merchants and gentry. Critical to maintaining this balance was the establishment of a series of safeguards protecting the British subject against the arbitrary use of royal power. Thus, the idea of a "balanced constitution" implies not only a division of powers and a close regulation of the relationships between different branches of government. It is also grounded in the idea that the rights of the subject are not limited to the mere regulation of interactions among individuals (civil and criminal law) under the paternal eye of the sovereign. Rather, these rights are an integral part of a "constitution" which regulates the relationship between the subject and the sovereign.[6]

Over the course of the seventeenth century, the English Parliament led the way in instituting a set of legal measures designed to express more clearly the protections accorded to subjects. In particular, two measures were central to this process of formally recognizing the subject's basic legal rights. First, the 1679 statute on habeas corpus provided protection against arbitrary imprisonment.[7] This protection, in turn, was linked to the universal right to due process as well as to the tempering of judicial power by the consolidation of that of juries.

These rights were further consolidated by limitations placed on the king's powers to use military force. Thus, the Petition of Right (1628) stipulated that, "by the Great Charter and other laws of the realm, no man ought to be judged to death but by the laws established in the realm, either by the customs of the realm or Acts of Parliament."[8] Also, the sovereign lost all power to impose martial law on the territory of England during peacetime.[9] Later, the Bill of Rights (1689) stated that "the pretended power of suspending of laws, or the execution of laws, by regal authority, without consent of parliament, is illegal."[10] Henceforth, the maintenance of a permanent army on English soil fell under the control of Parliament. The latter passed a collection of laws regulating the armed forces, beginning with the first Mutiny Act of 1689[11] and followed by the military regulations contained in the Articles of War.

Consequently, from the end of the seventeenth century, the English monarch enjoyed much more limited prerogatives than his European counterparts when it came to intervening in cases of civil insurrection.[12] The consolidation of the powers of the justice of the peace—notably in the Riot Act of 1714[13]—completed the establishment of a system for dealing with social disturbances which was founded on a delicate balance among the rights of the subject, the powers of local elites and those of Parliament, and the royal prerogative. Parliament, elected by the elites, played a pivotal role as both the defender of "English liberties" and an instrument of state power. This flexible mode of regulation, founded on the rule of law and respect for the rights of the subject, proved to be remarkably effective.[14] Of course, the monarch retained, for times of extreme emergency, that ultimate tool of repression: the regular army. However, the suppression of the Duke of Monmouth's revolt in 1685 "proved to be the last instance of unfettered martial law in England."[15]

At the end of the eighteenth century, a rising tide of demands for democratic reforms began to threaten this increasingly fragile balance. Incidents of popular protest, such as the Wilkes Riots at the end of the 1760s,[16] were among the warning signs. They questioned both the legitimacy of Parliament as the defender of the rights of the subject and the capacity of the justice system to ensure that those rights were respected. From this moment onward, authorities had recourse to a panoply of statutory and legal measures: Lord Mansfield's clarification of the jurisprudence surrounding the intervention of the army during riots;[17] the extension of the definitions of treason and sedition in the 1790s when the repression of democratic initiatives could at least appear to be legal; and, in moments of deeper crisis, suspensions of habeas corpus (May 1794 to July 1795, April 1798 to March 1801, and again in 1817).[18]

But the periodic suspension of the fundamental rights of the British subject (habeas corpus) also reflected deeper structural changes in social relations brought about by the transition to industrial capitalism. A system founded on the ad hoc intervention of

authorities lacking any real professional expertise was quickly being rendered obsolete. Justices of the peace were increasingly turning to the regular army for help in suppressing riots,[19] thereby showing the extent to which the traditional tools of civil intervention had become overwhelmed. The necessary adjustments came in the form of a fundamental reform of the entire system for maintaining civil order, notably through changes to the criminal law, the creation of a prison system, and the establishment of a new police force.[20] It is remarkable that, given the revolutions which shook other Western societies at the time, the social and political troubles in Britain between 1780 and 1850 were suppressed without having to supplant civil and judicial authorities with military power.[21]

EXTREME CASES: MARTIAL LAW IN THE COLONIES AND DEPENDENCIES

At home, then, British authorities could do without their own version of the continental procedures for declaring states of siege. However, things were not the same in the British colonies and dependencies. Here, recourse to martial law not only was frequent but periodically became a veritable mode of governance.

As I have shown, in Britain martial law was unthinkable except in extreme situations, when the courts were incapable of functioning normally. In fact, there emerged out of the Petition of Right of 1628 and the Bill of Rights of 1689 a relatively clear definition of the parameters within which martial law could be imposed:

- martial law could not be invoked to justify any abridgement of the jurisdiction of the common law courts save in time of war within the realm; and

- a time of war for this purpose could be said to exist only where the common law courts had ceased to function.

Again, as the law developed, further principles were established:

- whether a time of war existed or not was determined solely by the functioning or non-functioning of the ordinary courts;

- the crown enjoyed no prerogative to declare a state of martial law, and, if a question arose as to whether a time of war existed, that could be determined only by the courts, either during or after the conflict; and

- the existence of a state of martial law did not render legal those acts, such as the carrying out of the death sentence by the military authorities, which were illegal at common law: it merely constituted an acknowledgment that *durante bello* the civil courts were incapable of interfering.[22]

In fact, from the end of the eighteenth to the end of the nineteenth century, British legal thought and jurisprudence would maintain this restrictive interpretation of martial law. Thus, the tradition established by Edward Coke, Matthew Hale, and William Blackstone was followed and strengthened, while recourse to martial law was increasingly confined to the logic of emergency and inevitability.[23] From this perspective, the threat posed by important social disturbances, up to and including insurrection, does not justify the imposition of an exceptional *legal* order. The power to meet force with force, established in common law,[24] appears more than sufficient to justify any necessary repression, as long as the courts can, retroactively, sanction any unjustifiable abuses of power or other arbitrary actions committed during the suppression of an insurrection. One question clearly addressed by this "liberal" vision of martial law is that of what powers are reasonable and what measures are acceptable in times of insurrection. Another, equally important, is that of the acceptable *duration* of exceptional measures, with respect not merely to the repression of the disturbance but also to the punishments meted out to those responsible: "The King may punish his subjects by martial law during such insurrection of rebellion, but not after it is suppressed."[25]

However, if the legal *theory* underlying martial law became increasingly clear during the nineteenth century, such was not the case with the *practice* of martial law. In the British colonies and dependencies, "necessity" often took the form not only of open rebellion but also of the practical impossibility of respecting British legal norms. In this context, British power had to circumvent the various legal restrictions placed on martial law by jurisprudence and legal thought. It is important to recognize that all of these restrictions touched on *executive* power and its use of the army. In fact, on the periphery, the crown could normally count on relatively compliant legislatures, prepared to pass specific legislation rendering legal any measure deemed necessary. Ireland set the pattern: first, the local legislature and then, after union, the British Parliament repeatedly passed laws permitting the imposition of martial law. These laws not only affirmed royal prerogative in the matter but also protected individuals who applied the measure against subsequent legal action from those affected by it.[26]

At work here was a systematization of extrajudicial procedures in the British colonies and dependencies. There is a striking contrast between the extreme caution exercised by authorities at home and the often brutal measures taken to deal with civil disturbances in lands under British domination. In fact, in the colonies in general, the imposition of martial law became, from the start of the nineteenth century, a familiar form of dealing with civil disturbances. Thus, martial law was imposed in Barbados in 1805 and 1816; in Guyana (Demerara) in 1823; in Upper and Lower Canada in 1837–9; in Ceylon in 1848; in Cephalonia (Ionian Islands) in 1849; in the

Cape Colony in 1835, 1849–51, and 1859; in Saint Vincent in 1863; and in Jamaica in 1831–2 and 1865. Of course, these actions were complemented by a much more frequent use of less severe exceptional measures, such as the suspension of habeas corpus.

These legal developments would soon be heralded by W.E. Finlason. The author of one of the few nineteenth-century legal works dealing specifically with martial law, Finlason showed himself from the start to be sensitive not only to the practical pressures facing authorities dealing with a rebellion, but also to the way British rules of procedure constituted an obstacle to efficient action:

> It is obvious that one of the perils we incur as the price we pay for free constitution, is the constant insecurity of those who have the courage to act in defence of law and order on occasion of riot or insurrection. It is true that in theory, at all events, the law is plain and clear; upon *paper* it is so, but in practice it is perilous, as these and subsequent events show...our system of criminal prosecution is essentially *popular;* it is the grand jury who, at common law, present or indict, and though they are composed of a *superior* class of the people, still they are of the people, and likely, more or less, to share any strong popular excitement.[27]

This explains why Finlason, going against the dominant jurisprudence of the time, was careful to affirm the primacy of royal prerogative in such matters. Furthermore, he showed particular sensitivity to the challenges posed by the imposition of British order on foreign "races":

> The important point to be observed is, that the more the Common Law is supposed to be extended to a colony in right of English blood and descent, the more it must be considered to be in favour of and for the protection of those subjects of English descent, whose birthright it is presumed peculiarly to be. So that this theory, which has lately been proclaimed upon such high authority, only makes the clearer the power of a governor to proclaim martial law for the protection of the subjects of English descent whenever really required for their protection; as in cases of a really dangerous rebellion of those of a different, perhaps hostile, race.[28]

The fact is that the maintenance of order in British colonies and dependencies reflected an entirely different logic from that which prevailed in the mother country. This "colonial" logic concerned the very legitimacy of British power in times of revolution.

THE RIGHT TO REVOLT

As the rough British equivalent of the state of siege, martial law proved to be one of the preferred weapons in fighting against movements for colonial autonomy.[29] To move beyond the nineteenth-century legal parameters of the measure, it is important to understand how martial law was also—if not primarily—the product of a particular *political* dynamic. The arrival of the "Age of Revolution," to use Eric Hobsbawm's phrase, signalled a fundamental disruption in the nature and uses of public power. The demand for democracy implied that the principle of legitimacy, no longer based on allegiance to a dynasty, increasingly meant fidelity to the homeland. An essential continuity was being established between the individual citizen and the democratic state, validated by elections and the principle of majority rule and framed within the narrow confines of the nation. The delicate "balance" of powers among established elites was giving way to an ideal of government where the "people" were at once the source and the target of power. The principle validating this new power was neither legal tradition nor dynastic inheritance, but a mandate periodically granted to representatives by the popular majority. This legitimacy, resting on the "free will" of the citizen, certainly gave the state the power to repress brutally, in the name of the majority, expressions of political dissidence. But the same legitimacy also made possible a situation where the majority, or those who claimed to speak for it, could claim to have lost confidence in the government.

This explains why the arrival of the modern democratic state coincided with a debate on the right to revolt. In other words, disobedience now had a "legal" justification in cases where the exercise of official power proved to be arbitrary. The origins of such a justification can be traced to Grotius: "The Right to war may be conceded against a King who, possessing only part of the sovereign power, seeks to possess himself of the part that does not belong to him...Whoever possesses a part of the sovereign power must...possess the right to defend it. In this case...the King may even lose his part of the sovereign power by right of war."[30] Thus, during the Glorious Revolution, the people's "right to resist" the arbitrary use of power was supported by Algernon Sidney and John Locke in the name of natural law and that of a justice which transcended the formal authority of the king.[31] In a society faced with authorities' attacks against "rights" of the people and the open collusion of the courts, rebellion becomes the ultimate recourse in demanding a legal order superior to that of the authorities who happen to be in place, or even an effective antidote against those who would manipulate the power of the people to their own ends.

This demand lies at the origins of all the great revolutions which marked the end of the eighteenth and the beginning of the nineteenth century. The right to revolt was articulated by American patriots[32] and enshrined in the French constitution of 1793.[33] In fact, in the absence of all authority above that of the elected powers, it

can be understood as the only recourse against the possible excesses of executive power. Such claims would fade away only with the decline of ideas surrounding natural law during the nineteenth century and with the development of the power of the courts to interpret constitutions along the American model.

Of course, in the colonial context, the new relationship of legitimacy at the root of popular rights took on the form of demands for political self-determination. In other words, in the colonies and dependencies, democratic thought would develop primarily along the lines of colonial autonomy. From this perspective, the use of martial law had the advantage of short-circuiting popular resistance by giving unlimited powers to imperial authorities. This temporary putting aside of the rule of law, an expedient that English courts considered with great suspicion throughout the nineteenth century, was in fact an extremely useful means of exercising power when the goal was not to suppress revolt but to quash demands which might lead to the mobilization of large populations hitherto kept in a state of submission. Ultimately, Finlason was right: foreign "races" were not worthy of the protections granted to British subjects. Lower Canadians would learn this lesson at their own expense.

Martial Law and the Lower Canadian Rebellions of 1837–8

Recent historiography relating to the rebellions in Lower Canada has prompted an important reinterpretation of those events. Different studies have underlined the sincerity and breadth of demands for democracy[34] while providing a deeper and more subtle understanding of the different forces present in the colony.[35] These trends have contributed to a reading of the rebellions which looks beyond socio-economic, ideological, and cultural determinants towards the analysis of an essentially political event, with all the implications of that term.[36]

A substantial degree of temporal and spatial unity has traditionally been attributed to the rebellions. Thus, historians have presented the events leading from the Russell Resolutions in March 1837 to the seemingly inevitable conclusion marked by the Act of Union as a tragic yet coherent drama. But I would argue that to understand the events, as well as the role of martial law, it is essential to distinguish between *two* specific moments within a larger and complex process which completely redefined political reality.[37] In other words, the uses of martial law during the winter of 1837–8 had little to do with the implementation of that measure during the winter of 1838–9. In the interim, relationships of political power were fundamentally altered in such a way that the meaning which should be given to the repression of the "second" rebellion is fundamentally different from that which should be given to the first. It is therefore necessary to take a closer look at these two individual moments.

ARBITRARY POWER AS REACTION

In reality, the events commonly referred to as the "rebellion" of 1837 consisted of the brutal military repression of the major centres of political and legal dissent which had developed in the countryside surrounding Montreal. In essence, there were a series of pre-emptive strikes designed to nip an anticipated insurrection in the bud. The armed resistance of peasant militias in response to military invasion ultimately provided the justification for the imposition of martial law.

To a great extent, martial law was not a response to a real military threat. Rather, it proved a convenient means of dealing with political deadlock in the short term. When Governor Gosford proclaimed martial law on 5 December 1837, two weeks had already passed since the "rebels" had been crushed at Saint Charles. The combined forces of the regular army and loyalist volunteer militias ensured that the remaining *patriote* stronghold at Saint-Eustache would meet the same fate on 14 December.

Lacking organization, leadership, and arms, the *patriotes* never posed a serious military challenge. However, in the countryside surrounding Montreal, they did succeed in establishing a widespread system of civil disobedience. The *patriote* strategy, beginning in the summer of 1837, was clear and remarkably effective: mobilize the peasant masses with local assemblies, culminating in the "Assemblée des Six-Comtés" held at Saint-Charles on 23–24 October 1837, which in turn was to lead to a national convention.[38] Meanwhile, in several counties, militia captains and justices of the peace opposed to the *patriotes* were replaced by individuals more sympathetic to popular demands. It was this loss of political and judicial control, potentially leading to open violence, which forced a hesitant Gosford to turn to martial law. From the end of October, the governor recognized the efficiency of the Patriots' actions: "Having for their object the superseding of the ordinary administration of justice, by the establishment of a species of tribunal over which magistrates elected by the people are to preside, for the adjustment of differences and the trial of causes, and the organization of volunteer companies of militia, under the command of officers elected by militia men, who are to be drilled in the management of firearms, which, with the other accoutrements, the permanent committee pledges itself to provide for those corps that distinguish themselves by their good order and discipline."[39]

These mobilization tactics rendered irrelevant the judicial apparatus in the countryside, a fact that Gosford had begun to recognize in September.[40] With no hope of cooperation from the House of Assembly, which had been dissolved in August, the executive had few legal means at its disposal for dealing with the situation.[41] Faced with this state of political and legal deadlock, Gosford quickly turned to considering more extreme measures: "Unless some extraordinary powers be immediately placed in the hands of the local Executive, such as that of suspending the *habeas corpus,* and declaring martial law over the whole or parts of the province, the tide of sedition cannot be stemmed but by resort to active military operations; an alternative which I cannot contemplate without the most painful reluctance."[42]

Martial law was endorsed by the Executive Council a few days later (see app. D, L.C. doc.1a). By early December, the colonial secretary, Lord Glenelg reluctantly agreed with this solution: "The first and highest prerogative and duty of the Crown is the protection of those who maintain their allegiance against the enemies of order and peace. To repress by arms any insurrection or rebellion to which the civil power cannot be successfully opposed, is therefore a legitimate exercise of the royal authority; and, in the attainment of this object, the proclamation of martial law may become indispensable."[43] In fact, what set events in motion were the military engagements at Saint-Denis and Saint-Charles on 23 and 25 November. On 27 November, the Court of Sessions of the Peace for Montreal, in special session, implored Governor Gosford to place the district under martial law.[44]

Unsure of the legality of a proclamation of martial law, Gosford had requested, on 21 November, the opinion of attorney general Charles Ogden and Solicitor General Michael O'Sullivan. Their answer was received on 30 November. Ogden and O'Sullivan began by referring to the opinion of the first attorney general after the Conquest, George Suckling, who had expressed doubts regarding the governor's right to implement martial law.[45] They put more stress, however, on the Irish laws of 1799 and 1833 whose preambles, as we have already seen,[46] proclaimed that martial law was a matter of royal prerogative. According to the Lower Canadian jurists, this prerogative was de facto extended to colonial governors. Consequently, they informed Gosford that he was entirely within his legal powers in proclaiming martial law without the approval of the assembly.[47]

Gosford would wait for more than a week after receiving the news. Ultimately, what forced his hand appears to have been an injunction issued by the magistrates of Montreal on 5 December:

> Resolved, that in the opinion of this meeting, the turbulent and disaffected persons who have incited the peasantry to rebel against Her Majesty's Government have been led on and encouraged in their career of crime by a firm belief that, whatever might be their political offences, they would not be declared guilty by any jury impannelled in the ordinary course of law; that the great mass of the population in this district having been engaged in aiding and abetting the late treasonable attempt, a fair and impartial verdict cannot be expected from a jury taken indiscriminately from the legally-qualified inhabitants...Resolved...that the only effectual mode of...arresting the progress of crime and of social disorganization, is to place this district under martial law.[48]

The magistrates' arguments were essentially about the paralysis of the province's judicial apparatus. Martial law was thus presented as a means of overcoming this problem rather than as a temporary exceptional measure aimed at suppressing an open rebellion. Lacking any alternatives, Gosford resigned himself to the need for martial law and proclaimed the measure that very night.

Gosford's hesitation is revealing. It shows how, in the absence of any political authority capable of legitimizing recourse to exceptional measures, martial law presents itself as a last resort in the face of an impending crisis, ensuring the relative stability of key institutions *while waiting* for an eventual conclusion. Thus, martial law is perceived as an eminently temporary measure, carefully linked to the intensity of the crisis and adjusted to its rhythm. Gosford expressed his views on the matter to Glenelg in the following terms: "It is with the most painful regret I now acquaint your Lordship that from the aspect of affairs in that district, and the subsequent proceedings of the insurgents, I found that I could no longer abstain from a resort to the only measure left untried of maintaining therein the royal authority, and restoring order. Accordingly I last night issued...a Proclamation...subjecting the district of Montreal to martial law."[49]

Gosford's departure and his replacement by Colborne signalled the final defeat of the former's policy of conciliation. It coincided with a troubled period during which authorities in London hesitated to act while exploring different scenarios for resolving the crisis. Ultimately, they decided to name Lord Durham as governor general of the British North American colonies. But, while he was appointed on 15 January 1838, Durham would wait four months before taking up his position in Lower Canada.

Meanwhile, Colborne saw in martial law a convenient means of preventing a resurgence of the rebellion. Once again, the uses of martial law had little to do with an actual emergency. The measure simply ensured that the executive would have the means to intervene rapidly in any future troubles without relying on slow and cumbersome legal procedures. However, in Lower Canada, maintaining such a regime for any considerable length of time faced a major obstacle: there was no political authority ready to sanction military intervention in civil affairs, nor even to

protect those responsible for implementing martial law from potential legal reprisals. As early as 5 January 1838, Gosford had asked the colonial secretary "whether whilst legislating for the affairs of the province, it would not be expedient to pass some bill of indemnity to place all recent proceedings beyond the reach of...ill-disposed parties."[50] On 17 March, it was Colborne's turn to show his concern after taking over the reigns of power. An overenthusiastic military regime had arrested, "beyond the law probably," the editors of the *Quotidienne* and the *Courrier canadien*. Colborne therefore hoped that "Her Majesty's Government will think it right to recommend the adoption of measures to prevent my being prosecuted by the factious party, or by individuals who have been checked in their career of mischief, when the Proclamation authorizing Martial Law is withdrawn."[51]

But it was not merely the arbitrary and exceptional measures taken to maintain order that were poorly protected by a legally fragile system of martial law.[52] Distressed authorities soon realized that the exceptional regime they had hastily put in place could not even guarantee that those implicated in the late rebellion would be punished. As early as 12 March 1838, during the March sessions of the Court of King's Bench in Montreal, Judge Jean-Roch Rolland had sidestepped martial law by issuing a writ of habeas corpus for three individuals imprisoned in September 1837: Toussaint Peltier, Côme-Séraphin Cherrier, and Denis-Benjamin Viger.[53]

An even greater challenge than keeping rebels imprisoned until trial was that of ensuring they would receive an appropriate punishment.[54] As early as 5 January, Gosford had decided that "some examples, selecting the most notorious and prominent characters in the revolt, must be made." But since juries were notoriously unreliable when it came to convicting prisoners, "the only course for effecting this is by trial by Court Martial; I really, at this moment, do not see any other mode by which the ends of justice can be arrived at."[55] Meanwhile, Lord Glenelg cautioned against resorting "to this measure without the most conclusive evidence of the inadequacy of any milder remedy to meet the existing evil."[56]

The future of these initiatives was further placed in doubt by an opinion of the law officers of the crown in Lower Canada, issued on 24 January 1838. Ogden and O'Sullivan declared that the establishment of a court martial was illegal since the period of open insurrection had passed and there was no impediment to the operation of the regular courts. They further stated that the Irish precedent of 1799, mentioned above, indicated that the involvement of the House of Assembly was necessary for such a project. As Canadian juries clearly could not be relied upon,[57] and a new session of the Lower Canadian legislature was out of the question, imperial legislative intervention was necessary.[58] On 19 February, Lord Glenelg instructed an uncertain Colborne as to the procedure to follow in the face of what the latter considered to be a "most embarrassing question":[59]

> With regard to the persons who have been apprehended for political offences and are now in confinement, Her Majesty's Government desire that such of them as you may not think it right at once to liberate should not be brought to trial, unless they can be tried by the ordinary tribunals of the country. In case, therefore, a reference to the ordinary tribunals should not, in your judgment, be yet advisable, a law ought to be passed for the suspension of the *Habeas Corpus* Act, which will enable you to detain such persons in prison till the arrival of Lord Durham. You will propose to the council this measure, if, for the reason I have stated, or for any other reason, you may think it expedient. You will thus be enabled immediately to revoke the proclamation of martial law in the district of Montreal, if still in force.[60]

In the end, the solution to this legal dilemma had to come from the British Parliament. In fact, on 10 February, Parliament had passed a law replacing the Lower Canadian legislature with a Special Council appointed by the governor. As examined in Stephen Watt's essay[...], the council passed a series of measures from mid-April 1838 onwards shoring up the legality of actions taken since the end of the 1837 rebellion, suspending habeas corpus and offering legal protection to anyone who had aided in repressing the rebellion. By 27 April, Colborne felt secure enough to suspend martial law.[61]

The imposition of martial law in 1837 fits perfectly with the pattern of emergency measures taken in British colonies at that time. It had been implemented as a measure of last resort, though not primarily as a response to the threat of an armed uprising. Rather, it met the urgent necessity of overcoming the political and judicial deadlock caused by popular support for the demands of political radicals. Gosford's hesitation and his cautious approach—historians have no reason to suspect his good faith—highlight the specific context in which the loss of political legitimacy on the part of the authorities and the danger it posed for a loyal minority forced ill-prepared authorities to deal with matters one at a time, beginning with the most urgent. In this case, far from constituting the centerpiece of a comprehensive program for relieving the tensions exacerbated by the rebellion, martial law serves to underline the weakness and confusion of the authorities.[62]

The clearly improvised manner in which martial law was imposed, the law officers' rejection of the idea of taking advantage of the state of emergency to dispose of prisoners by means of court martial, the issuing of a writ of habeas corpus by a judge of the Court of King's bench while martial law was supposedly in force: these were all indications of the weak and shaky foundations supporting the regime of martial law in Lower Canada. In fact, the colony needed a political alternative much more than further means of repression. It was precisely as part of this search for a way out of a deep political crisis that imperial authorities placed the fate of Lower Canada in the hands of a liberal and enlightened "despot": Lord Durham.

THE DURHAM INTERLUDE: ARBITRARY POWER AS A CURE

When Lord Durham finally landed at Quebec on 27 May 1838, charged with sorting out the colonial imbroglio, local authorities were well protected from judicial actions. However, the fate of some 140 prisoners still remained to be settled.

Durham was aware of the importance of his mission. The imperial government had given him both its full support and sweeping powers, including that of granting pardons for murder and treason without British approval. Even before he arrived, he was aware of the intensity of the political crisis, rendered worse by increasingly profound ethnic rivalries. His brief visit to Canada would be spent not only dealing with the aftermath of the first rebellion but also laying the foundations of a solution to the conflict which had ground political life in the colony to a halt.

Much has been written about Durham's mission, and my goal here is not to undertake a detailed examination of this literature. In fact, the historiography has mainly described Durham's mission as an interlude of peacemaking between two uprisings. It was an attempt, which would soon prove futile, to resolve the Canadian constitutional deadlock. However, it is also important to understand how Durham's "reign" was merely the continuation, under a new form and to new ends, of the arbitrary exercise of power. British authorities saw in their fiery and pretentious governor a referee who would not be caught up in the partisan fray, and

they gave him the proconsular powers necessary to stand above local rivalries, not to mention local laws.[63] But the intention was for Durham's despotism to be an enlightened one, oriented to reconciliation and pacification.

Thus, he began by replacing the existing Special Council with one composed of members of his entourage. Also, the British military presence, as well as that of volunteer militias, would not diminish during his stay. Finally, his freedom of action was secured by maintaining the suspension of habeas corpus, which would remain in effect until 24 August.[64] It is in the context of this great freedom of action, where the governor was handed a tremendous degree of autonomy, that the brutal end to Durham's mission can be best understood.

In fact, from the moment of Durham's arrival, the Colonial Office expressed its desire that conciliation and respect for the law might be guiding principles in pacifying the province:

> Even if it might be right to resort ultimately to any form of trial unknown to the constitution, it would at least be improper to do so without having ascertained by actual experiment that the usual forms are unequal to the occasion...The utmost lenity, compatible with public safety, should be exercised towards the insurgents...It is a principle supported, in our opinion, by considerations, not only of humanity, which cannot in such cases be admitted as the exclusive test of right conduct,[65] but also of true policy in reference to the future well-being of the Canadas...There should be no further deviation from the established modes of legal procedure...You will therefore bring them to trial, in the usual manner, before the courts of justice as at present constituted for the trial of criminal offences in the province.[66]

But in spite of these clear and unflinching instructions, Durham, after a month in the colony, refused to test the Lower Canadian judicial apparatus: "If a trial took place, there existed the danger of an acquittal, which would have been considered as a triumph (and naturally) by the disaffected, and would have produced the worst consequences. On the other hand, even if a conviction was obtained, the excitement of the proceedings, the exposure of the acts of treason and disaffection, and the revival of the whole question, would have again reopened and inflamed all those party animosities, the calming of which was an indispensable preliminary to the final settlement of Canadian affairs."[67]

Durham had, on the previous day (28 June), passed the famous ordinance exiling to Bermuda eight prisoners who had admitted to their role in the rebellion,[68] a decision that he presented to imperial authorities as a *fait accompli.* These prisoners were prohibited from returning to Lower Canada, on penalty of death, as were a certain number of *patriotes* accused of high treason who had not yet been apprehended.[69] The same day, the governor proclaimed a general amnesty for those accused or suspected of high treason as a result of their participation in the rebellion, with the exception of those named in the Bermuda Ordinance.[70]

In fact, even in openly dispensing clemency, Durham found himself resorting to exceptional and arbitrary measures. Not only had he carefully avoided all regular legal procedures, but he had exiled the prisoners to a colony over which he had no jurisdiction. Furthermore, by threatening the exiles with summary execution if they were to return to Lower Canada, he went against the most fundamental principles of British justice, specifically the assurance of legal protection and the right to due process for any person accused of any crime.[71]

Given that the province had remained remarkably calm during the summer, Durham's dramatic actions opened him up to criticism. Lord Brougham's strong indictment of the ordinance in the House of Lords in August 1838 was organized around a denunciation of the flagrant use of arbitrary legal power in a period of relative social peace. Placed in a difficult situation, the British government disallowed the ordinance and, adding insult to injury, proceeded to *indemnify* Durham against any legal proceedings related to the matter.[72]

From this moment onward, Durham's mission seemed destined to fail, a failure the governor would attribute to weakness on the part of the British government, in the face of the opposition:

> Upon two things alone could I chiefly rely for ultimate success. The first was, the great extent of the legal powers conferred upon me, enhanced as they had been morally by the universal expression in England of satisfaction at my having undertaken to exercise them. The second was the impression, which prevailed throughout these colonies, that I might reckon with perfect confidence on the undeviating approval and support of the members of Her Majesty's Government, with most of whom I had been so long and intimately connected, as well by personal friendship as by political relation. By the proceedings in question I was deprived of these, the only, but all-sufficient grounds of confidence in my own exertions... The moral authority of my government, the *prestige,* if I may so speak, of power, once imagined to be so great, and of a supposed unbounded influence with Her Majesty's Government, was gone, apparently for ever.[73]

For Durham, both the sweeping powers he had been granted and his personal prestige were essential for the success of his mission. Indeed, his at times enthusiastic reception by all parties in the colony was a product of his reputation for *neutrality*. Yet, from the moment when Durham began to take sides in the political conflict rocking the colony, and his partisan views became known to the principal political actors, the very possibility of "conciliation" evaporated. In fact, Durham quickly came to two fundamental "conclusions": first, that behind demands for democratic reforms strictly ethnic conflict was at play; second, that as a consequence of the prevailing ethnic conflict, the essential condition for a resolution to the crisis was the disappearance of French institutions and the integration of the French majority into exclusively British institutions.[74] His evaluation of the crisis in Lower Canada, provided in a letter of 9 August 1838, was already very clear and explicit. Deploring the blindness of those Americans who supported the *patriotes* in their demands, Durham stated:

> [The Americans] believe...that the majority in Lower Canada has contended for the maintenance of popular rights, and that arbitrary government is the aim of the minority. The mistake is easily accounted for: it is only on the spot that one learns how the subject of strife in Lower Canada has been a question of nationality; everywhere else, the false professions and designations employed by both parties, combined with the plain fact that the contest has been between a majority and a minority, is apt to mislead the inquirer, by keeping out of view the distinction of races... They have misunderstood the case. They have fallen into the not uncommon mistake of confounding means with ends. Believing that the means employed by the Canadians, in the Assembly, were constitutional and popular, and seeing that the British, being in a minority, necessarily clung to the local executive and the imperial authority; above all, regardless of the accident (for so it may be termed with respect to the question of nationality) by which the Canadians happen to constitute a

majority, Americans have supposed that the object of both parties in the colony were of the same nature respectively, as to the means on which each party has relied.[75]

Thus, all possible measures had to be taken to counteract this "accidental" (!) majority.[76] In fact, Durham finished by admitting that the policy of clemency, evident in both the fateful ordinance of 28 June and the general amnesty of the same day, was merely a means of making French Canadians more amenable to the necessary anglicization of their institutions: "I had made up my mind, it was evident, to the necessity of rendering the institutions of this province thoroughly British... As to the past, I proclaimed forgiveness and oblivion; as to the future, British institutions; as to the present, security against the disaffected... Since the different parts of the whole scheme of policy were intimately blended with and dependent on each other, the destruction of one portion of it affects all the rest."[77]

In his proclamation of 9 October, the governor announced the disallowance of the June ordinance and, in a rash act, openly blamed the imperial government. At the same time, he finally clearly stated to the entire colony what he had in mind for its future: "My aim was to elevate the Province of Canada to a thoroughly British character, to link its people to the sovereignty of Britain, by making them all participators in those high privileges, conducive at once to freedom and order, which have long been the glory of Englishmen. I hoped to confer on an united people a more extensive enjoyment of free and responsible government, and to merge the petty jealousies of a small community, and the odious animosities of origin, in the higher feelings of a nobler and more comprehensive nationality."[78] To their dismay, Canadian Reformers discovered that Durham, without really having consulted them, had adopted the position of the most radical elements in the

British party.[79] Even if, at this time, the governor still seemed open to a political solution in the form of a confederation—rather than a union—of Upper and Lower Canada, Durham's attitude effectively rendered impossible any conciliation of the different factions in the province.

Durham's now obsolete "benevolence" revealed the arbitrary nature of his power. In fact, Durham was conscious of the fact that the success of his mission depended not only on his power and his prestige but also on the *exceptional and despotic* nature of his power: "The government of these provinces requires something more than a knowledge of the common and statute law of England. Though the object of wise and benevolent statesmen should be to establish the great principles of the British constitution and the English law in this province, it must not be supposed that this is yet done... My acts have been despotic, because my delegated authority was despotic".[80]

Thus, it is important to understand that what I have called the Durham "interlude" was in no way an oasis of legality lying between two periods of open repression. Durham's "reign" was an exceptional regime. Specifically, arbitrary power was justified not by the necessity of repressing an armed uprising but as a form of armed neutrality with the aim of imposing peace on the warring parties. From the moment that London's delegate strayed from his symbolic image as impartial referee in order to support one of the parties, the justification for that arbitrary power had partially disappeared.[81] This is why Durham increasingly felt the need to justify the extent of the powers which had been granted to him, and notably the way these powers seemed so out of place in a British regime. In fact, the persistent political deadlock made the exercise of these powers (openly denounced by Lord Brougham in the House of Lords in August) increasingly delicate. This is why, when the colonial secretary suggested tempering the effects of the disallowance of the June ordinance by suspending habeas corpus in the colony, Durham suddenly rediscovered the reflexes of an English radical:

> To me, my Lord it appears that men's notions of right and freedom would be much more shocked at such an universal violation of every man's dearest rights, than by any summary process adopted for the punishment of the undeniable guilt of a few. I do not say that there are no circumstances under which I would consent to a suspension of the habeas corpus; I should not hesitate to adopt it in any emergency in which the notoriety of a general outbreak, or of a general purpose of insurrection, might render it advisable that a Government should be for a while armed with the power of arresting the objects of its suspicion, without brining them to immediate trial. But I see no necessity on account of any existing evil in this province, for taking such a step now... I cannot think it justifiable to take away the franchises of a whole people in order to punish a few known and dangerous individuals; or to guard against the misconduct of 23 men, by enveloping them in a general forfeiture of personal liberty.[82]

Thus, from September 1838, the political conditions for the eventual success of Durham's mission rapidly dissolved. Worse still, he also faced increasingly formidable legal challenges. That same month, during their trial at the Court of King's Bench of Montreal, Amable Daunais, François Nicolas, and two others were acquitted for the murder of Joseph Armand Chartrand, committed during the 1837 rebellion.[83] Durham concluded that "it is now certain that no jury but a French Canadian could have been empanelled, and that the acquittal of one and all would have been certain, however strong the evidence of their guilt."[84] Moreover, in October, during a request of habeas corpus before the judges of the Court of King's Bench of Quebec in favour of Firmin Moreau, arrested under the police ordinance passed by the Special Council, Judge Elzéar Bédard issued a minority opinion that the ordinance was invalid, since it modified the British law on vagabonds, while the law creating the Special Council prohibited it from modifying laws passed by the British Parliament. A particularly outraged Durham wrote to London:

> Mr. Bédard was fortunately overruled by the other judges, and no mischief resulted in the particular case before the court; but that mischief has been done, which must result from the public declaration of the illegality of the acts of the only legislative authority in the country, on the part of one of the judges of the highest court; whilst still greater mischief must result from this opinion being grounded on a view which restricts the legislative authority of the province within limits so absurdly narrow; and the greatest evil of all is, that...his opinion is unfortunately backed by those of many of the speakers in both Houses of Parliament, in the late debates on the ordinance.[85]

Thus, in early fall, as a vexed and sickly Durham prepared his definitive departure from the colony, and in the midst of rumours of agitation in the Canadian countryside, the return of a quasi-military regime was envisaged: "The indications of mischief are so numerous and so urgent, that it is no longer possible to conceal, or advisable to attempt concealing, the consciousness of danger entertained by the Government: its only course is openly and resolutely to proclaim and avert that danger. The early adoption of these measures of military precaution...will in all probability produce a state of things in which the present exasperation of parties will be aggravated by fresh causes of irritation; but these are evils which must be borne, if we mean to provide, as far as is in our

power, for the retention of the two Canadas."[86]

Durham departed from Quebec on 1 November. Two days later the second Lower Canadian rebellion began.

ARBITRARY POWER AS POLITICS

The circumstances surrounding the implementation of exceptional measures during the second rebellion had little to do with the situation that prevailed during the first.

First of all, the second uprising itself took on an entirely different form. Unlike the first, there appears to have been a significant degree of advanced planning. A secret society, the *Frères Chasseurs,* provided coordination for the *patriotes'* actions. The symbolic use of oaths and the systematic use of secrecy—characteristic of early nineteenth-century clandestine nationalist organizations[87]—allowed, in theory at least, some degree of concerted action. But the lack of external support and the difficulty, if not the impossibility, of organizing a mass movement with neither arms nor a permanent military organization ensured that what was planned as a major armed uprising was doomed to failure. Thus, the rebellion of 1838 consisted of a series of isolated skirmishes, involving clashes between the *patriotes* and volunteer loyalist militias.

The *patriotes'* preferred form of organization contributed to a profound sense of paranoia, especially in the countryside surrounding Montreal.[88] Having suffered through the events of 1837 and exasperated by Durham's failure, the most radical members of the English-speaking minority saw in the agitated context of early November the opportunity to use the second rebellion as a pretext for action.

Indeed, the speed with which the second rebellion was repressed is revealing. On 3 November, news was received of a few *Chasseur* mobilizations around Montreal. Colborne declared martial law the very next day. During the days that followed, the Special Council, in a mood of furious repression, passed a series of eleven ordinances abolishing, for all intents and purposes, the normal operation of criminal law in the colony.[89]

A few days earlier, on 26 October 1838, Colonial Secretary Lord Glenelg had joined Durham in denouncing the ineffectiveness of the regular Lower Canadian courts. He proposed the organization of special courts as a *preventative* measure:

> Where trial by jury has excited the righteous scorn and indignation of the community, it cannot be difficult to form tribunals more impartial and more competent than the existing juries... It would not be safe to postpone the formation of such tribunals until a new insurrection may happen to break out, for the same objections which induced Her Majesty's Government to reject the proposition to subject the prisoners charged with being concerned in the late revolt to new tribunals, constituted after the commission of the offences, would again apply. Men would complain that they were tried by an *ex post facto* law. While, therefore, the power of detention and imprisonment, without trial, may well be reserved for a period of emergency, of which your Lordship will be the judge, it is the desire of Her Majesty's Government that you should at once prepare and propose to the Special Council an Ordinance for constituting tribunals, by which future rebels or murderers may be tried. The leaders and agents of insurrection will thus be forewarned, and cannot justly complain if they are made amenable for their crimes.[90]

But the Special Council was one step ahead of the Colonial Office and its clear instructions. In fact, an ordinance had already been passed instituting the very retroactive measures the British government wished to avoid at all costs.[91] Colborne did his best to justify the situation: "The sudden renewal of the revolt has exposed the local government to the embarrassments and serious difficulties which it encountered last year, in regard to bringing to justice offenders guilty of treason and murder... The progress of the insurrection had been rapid extensive, and as the prisoners, most of whom had been taken with arm in their hands, were hourly increasing, it was necessary to legislate not prospectively only, but for the punishment of offences already committed."[92]

But Colborne really had no reason to be worried. British authorities had effectively given him carte blanche: "You may rely on the unequivocal sanction and firm support of the ministers of the Crown, in any further proceedings which, in the exercise of your powers as administrator of the Government, you may take for defeating intrigues against the public peace and the royal authority, even though these intrigues should be conducted in such a manner as not to render the authors of them, amenable to the legal tribunals in the ordinary course of law."[93] Indeed, one of the most striking characteristics of the measures taken by Lower Canadian authorities to suppress the second rebellion was the wholehearted support they received from their British government. This included legal representatives, who would systematically rely on a broad interpretation of the Special Council's powers in order to justify the measures taken.[94] The council even took it upon itself to exonerate retroactively all those implicated in the repression by voting two separate ordinances granting legal immunity, covering the periods from 1 November to 21 December 1838 and from 21 December to 13 April 1839.[95]

Under these circumstances, the repression faced by the rebels was virtually unrestrained. During the few days that the second uprising lasted, 753 persons were arrested in the District of Montreal alone. Beginning on 28 November, a court martial was established which would continue sitting until 8 May 1839. During that time, it would try 106 prisoners, 72 of whom were acquitted and 99 sentenced to death. Twelve were executed, 58 deported to Australia, and 27 granted a conditional release.[96]

A striking characteristic of this second wave of repression was the vigorous legal challenges it faced. In fact, the example was set from above. On 21 November 1838, at Quebec, Court of Queen's Bench judges Philippe Panet and Elzéar Bédard issued a writ of habeas corpus for John Teed, who was suspected of treason. This act directly contradicted the Special Council ordinance of 8 November authorizing the imprisonment of persons accused of treason. In their decision, the judges claimed that the Special Council had overstepped its authority in passing such an ordinance, given the terms of the imperial law creating the legislative body.[97] Soon afterwards, on 6 December, the assistant judge of Trois-Rivières, Joseph-Remi Vallières de Saint-Réal, relying on the same interpretation, issued a writ of habeas corpus for Celestin Houde.[98] The position taken by these three judges threatened to sweep away all of the exceptional measures instituted by the Special Council's legislation. Thus, authorities were quick to seek the opinion of other judges and that of the crown law officers. Their response, with the exception of Rolland, affirmed the legality of the Special Council ordinances, claiming that the three judges had wrongly interpreted the restrictions contained in the imperial act creating the council.[99] As a result, Panet and Bédard were suspended. Vallières de Saint-Réal suffered the same fate on 27 December. Finally, on 25 January 1839, British jurists rendered an opinion confirming the council's powers in such matters.[100]

In any case, legal resistance came mainly from the principal victims of repression themselves. Thus, Denis-Benjamin Viger, imprisoned on 4 November along with Louis-Hippolyte La Fontaine and Charles Mondelet, refused to post bail and demanded a regular trial. He would remain in prison until May 1840.[101] Meanwhile, those prisoners who faced the court martial, on the advice of lawyers Lewis Drummond and Aaron Hart, decided to contest the jurisdiction of the court. They insisted that "the offence or offences with which they stand charged, are cognizable only by a jury of the country, and that, by the mode of trial, and the means resorted to upon the present occasion, they are deprived of all constitutional means of defence."[102] Once again, the legal opinion of J. Campbell and R.W. Rolfe, law officers of the crown, confirming the legality of the Special Council ordinance constituting the court martial was decisive.[103]

In the face of such an unequivocal endorsement of the Special Council's powers, the only remaining course of action was to appeal to higher legal authorities. On 14 February 1839 La Fontaine and Mondelet, with the help of a radical MP, laid a petition before the House of Commons solemnly protesting against the arbitrary arrests and the exceptional measures introduced by the Special Council:

> They, with several other persons, were forcibly torn from their families...by persons calling themselves the agents of Government, and dragged to prison by her Majesty's troops, without any warrant, without any accusation against them and, as they believed, with the knowledge or by the orders of Sir John Colborne... It was publicly believed, that a carte blanche had been given to many persons, to denounce as traitors any of her Majesty's subjects in the colony, thus furnishing to enmity an opportunity of wreaking its revengeful feelings on the liberty of the subject... The country was under military and despotic rule, of a nature to drive the population of these provinces to despair, and of which the object appeared to be to destroy their institutions and their language, and drive them from their country.[104]

Of course, legal resistance ultimately proved futile. For what was at work was not the suppression of a rebellion but a brutal reorganization of power relations in the colony, in the guise of the restoration of order. One is struck, for example, by the brief, even abrupt justifications for repression to be found in the correspondence between colonial authorities and their British masters. Long gone were Gosford's hesitations and Durham's long and verbose declarations of principle. Examples had to be made and deterrence was the principal goal, as Colborne explained:

> Convinced...that the safety of both provinces depends on the firmness and unhesitating decision of the executive government, and persuaded that the insurgents were in a great degree encouraged in the second revolt by the recollection of past impunity and the hope of future amnesty, and receiving daily proof of the infatuation by which a large portion of the population have been drawn into a belief in the impotence of justice, I feel that severe examples have become indispensable, and it only remains for me seriously to consider how the cause of public justice can be vindicated with the least possible sacrifice of human life.[105]

A visitor from Europe did a good job of summing up the situation in Canada at the time: "[The English] have been thinking of nothing ever since [the second insurrection] but avenging *imagined* cruelties, and guarding against *apprehended* dangers."[106]

In fact, there were few who could not perceive what was really going on. Even Pierre de Rocheblave, a member of Colborne's Special Council and long-standing enemy of the *patriotes* who had lent a hand in the repressive measures adopted in November, would soon lose all illusions. In February he undertook the presidency of the Association loyale canadienne, a political association whose published manifesto deplored

> les prétentions injustes de cette faction de nos co-sujets d'origine Britannique qui, dans le but avoué de ravir à la majorité des habitants de ce pays toute influence constitutionnelle, profite avec ardeur de la fausse position où nous ont placés les déplorables tentatives d'un petit nombre de nos compatriotes égarés, pour attaquer nos institutions avec acharnement et mauvaise foi... Les événements déplorables qui viennent de se passer ont fait triompher la faction qu'il était essentiel de contenir; elle s'empare aujourd'hui de fautes isolées pour les rendre générales, et obtenir par là le renversement de toutes les institutions que nous tenons de la capitulation et de la bienveillance de feu Notre Auguste Monarque George III, de Glorieuse mémoire.[107]

Perhaps never before had martial law been used so openly and over such a long period of time to crush opposition to what was essentially a political coup in the guise of a state of emergency. Thus, Colborne maintained martial law in force in the District of Montreal until 24 August 1839.[108]

General Conclusions

From the end of the eighteenth century, colonial elites in the Canadas found various ways of using the law as a means of exercising their political will and guaranteeing their political power. However, a specifically *British* process of colonial expansion, with the American example ever-present as an alternative path of political development, demanded that a somewhat milder version of those constitutional rights which had been at the heart of the British political system since the seventeenth century also be transplanted into the colonial context.[109] Consequently, with the rise of democratic demands in the colonies, political battles frequently spilled over into the legal domain. To a certain extent, formal legal procedure and the complex ritual of legal conflict obscured the underlying political questions. Nevertheless, it was on the field of law that the battle between the supporters of "order" and those of the "people" took place:

> The criminal courts must be seen as arenas of struggle dominated, but by no means controlled, by the ruling alliance... While helping to facilitate and legitimize the repression, the law was also a limited instrument. Those subject to the proceedings could utilize the formal claims of the law to contest the repression... The use of sedition laws highlighted the tension between the rule of law and discretionary authority, played out in arguments about executive influence over prosecutions, the jury, and judiciary. These rule-of-law claims were not obscure legal technicalities confined to the specialist participants. They were expressions of established British constitutional principles, part and parcel of the rights and liberties of all subjects. The popular appeal of those subject to the prosecutions was that the government had deprived the public of the full benefits of the British constitution.[110]

The legal process at issue here turned on the jury. This was the crack through which popular grievances could eventually affect the process, to the extent that the "peers" who decided guilt or innocence, or the fate of a civil action, had the opportunity to influence directly the administration of justice. This is why "jury control" was such a sensitive and fundamental question in England and, a fortiori, in the colonies.[111]

As in Upper Canada—and perhaps even more so, given that it was a conquered colony—there developed in Lower Canada a precocious and widespread version of judicial authoritarianism. Greenwood has rightly insisted on the predominance of "Baconian" judges[112] in the colony, always ready to come to the aid of authorities. Here, too, there developed a local oligarchy that controlled the economic and political life of the colony, ready to take whatever exceptional legal measures were necessary to stem the tide of democracy. Paul Romney's harsh portrayal of Upper Canada is perfectly relevant to its neighbour: "Upper Canada did not possess what it was meant to possess: a constitution that was, in spirit if not in the letter, an 'image and transcript' of the English. It lacked such a constitution because the colonial administrative elite, whose duty it was to govern the colony in conformity with the precepts of the English constitution, had betrayed their trust as imperial agents by cultivating a political creed, and nurturing a political mood, that were incompatible with that duty."[113]

But an important difference needs to be underlined. In contrast to Upper Canada, where conservative forces periodically scored important electoral victories, the democratic opposition in Lower Canada quickly and decisively took control of the elected assembly. Furthermore, this opposition increasingly relied on the support of the province's francophone majority (as well as a good portion of American immigrants to the Eastern Townships and of Catholic Irish immigrants). Even if the vast British immigration beginning in the 1820s provided the ruling oligarchy with a degree of popular support, they were never able to control the "peasantry" as their Upper Canadian counterparts succeeded periodically in doing. Meanwhile, the rural French-Canadian majority, increasingly conscious of its power, was able to express its political demands in the language of democratic rights characteristic of their century. With time, the conservative elites' sense of isolation only increased as Lower Canadian demands for colonial autonomy were increasingly framed in terms hostile to British institutions. From the mid-1830s onward, they entered a state of what might be called hysteric paranoia, seeing in the *patriote*'s demands for democracy a plan for ethnic domination[114] by a population which they had always considered ignorant and easily manipulated. Thus, it became possible to read the Lower Canadian crisis as a *parody* of democracy, as an illicit and crafty use of the "privileges" granted to British subjects.

In this situation, the criteria for legitimacy could be turned upside down: the democratic farce left a threatened minority with no choice but to resort to the arbitrary use of power, justified by urgency and the enormity of the threat.[115] The rebellions of 1837 and 1838 represent two stages in the development of this political dynamic. They also underline how the Special Council proved indispensable in the exercise of this arbitrary power.

But the rebellions also reveal a side of the *law* which is little understood, especially in the age of liberal democracy and legality. The law I am referring to does not present itself as an ideology, and even less as an instrument for mediating social tensions. Rather, with the establishment of a formal rule of law, it becomes the veil behind which arbitrary power may be exercised. Martial law allows us to see past this veil. Viewed by legal scholars as a last resort in cases where the law is incapable of regulating society, as an indication of the legal void temporarily filled by military force, martial law in the Lower Canadian context became an administrative façade for an excess of order and legislation, a protective umbrella for a frustrated minority which unexpectedly found itself with an opportunity to remake a politically paralysed society. In exceptional circumstances where the fabric of society is irrevocably torn, law can also be the thin coat of legality applied to the naked use of force, a sort of legal make-up covering the arbitrary use of power which jurists can only passively ratify, leaving no room for resistance, except perhaps for the vain protests of a Denis-Benjamin Viger, a Charles Mondelet, or a Louis-Hyppolite La Fontaine.

Canadian democracy, also born of this logic whereby arbitrary power is cloaked in necessity, continues to feel its effects. But for the legal historian, martial law teaches a difficult lesson. Sometimes, in law, the exception does not confirm the rule. Rather, it establishes an entirely new order.

Notes

This essay is based on my article "Mesures d'exception et règle de droit: Les conditions d'application de la loi martiale au Québec lors des Rébellions de 1837–1838," *McGill Law Journal*, 32:3 (July 1987), 465–95, which has been completely revised with new research and analysis. I am indebted to Jean-Paul Bernard and the late F. Murray Greenwood for their comments on this version, as well as Steven Watt for his fine translation.

1 Sir Edward Coke, *Commons,* 1628, 2: 549.

2 Glenelg to Colborne, 6 Dec. 1837, *British Parliamentary Papers: Colonial Canada (1837–1838),* vol. 9, 114 (hereafter *Parliamentary Papers*).

3 Durham to Glenelg, 28 Sept. 1838, ibid., 193–4.

4 This corresponds to what Romney calls the contradiction between constitutionalism and legalism. Paul Romney, "From Constitutionalism to Legalism: Trial by Jury, Responsible Government, and the Rule of Law in the Canadian Political Culture," *Law and History Review,* 7:1 (spring 1989), 121–74.

5 Michael Mann, *The Sources of Social Power,* Vol. II: *The Rise of Classes and Nation-States, 1760–1914* (New York: Cambridge University Press 1993).

6 Dicey does a good job of capturing this relational logic—between the individual and political authority—which lies at the heart of the phenomenon: "The right to personal freedom or the right to free expression of opinion...may be looked upon

from two points of view. They may be considered simply parts of private or, it may be, of criminal law. But in so far as these rights hold good against the governing body in the state, or in other words, in so far as these rights determine the relation of individual citizens towards the executive, they are part, and a most important part, of the law of the constitution...Whereas under many foreign constitutions the rights of individuals flow or appear to flow, from the articles of the constitution, in England the law of the constitution is the result, not the source, of the rights of individuals." A.V. Dicey, *Introduction to the Study of the Law of the Constitution* (London: Macmillan 1860; repr. 1920) 280–2.

7 "An Act for the Better Securing the Liberty of the Subject, and for Prevention of Imprisonment beyond Seas" (U.K.) 31 Charles II (1679), c.2.

8 Cited by W.E. Finlason, *A Review of the Authorities as to the Repression of Riot and Rebellion* (London: Stevens and Sons, 1868), 52.

9 A report to the Privy Council dating from the end of the seventeenth century clearly explained the implications of this restriction in peacetime: "Martial law to be granted only at the advice of the Council, and that in times of dangerous stirs, and the same to be called in when the stirs shall be appeased; for now the common law hath force in most parts of the realm. The trial of malefactors by the ordinary way of 12 men is a thing that doth greatly content the people." Ronan Keane, "'The Will of the General': Martial Law in Ireland, 1535–1924," *Irish Jurist*, 25–7 (1990–2), 150–80.

10 "An Act for Declaring the Rights and Liberties of the Subject, and Settling the Succession of the Crown" (U.K.) 1 Will. and Mary II (1688), c.2, art.1(1).

11 "An Act for Punishing Officers and Soldiers Who Shall Mutiny or Desert their Majesties Service, to Continue till November, 1689, and No Longer" (U.K.) 1 Will. and Mary I (1688), c.5.

12 It is important to note that this restriction applies only to the executive and not to Parliament itself: "During the course of the war parliament was to impose measures of martial law more draconian by far than anything the king has ever attempted." Lindsay Boynton, "Martial Law and the Petition of Right," *EHR*, 79 (1964), 282.

13 1 Geo. I, st.2, c.5. See Gerald R. Williams, "The King's Peace: Riot in Its Historical Perspective," *Utah Law Review*, 6:2 (summer 1971), 240–58.

14 The classic explanation of this system of regulation, founded on the ideology of the rule of law, remains that of Douglas Hay, "Property, Authority and the Criminal Law," D. Hay et al., eds., *Albion's Fatal Tree: Crime and Society in 18th-Century England* (New York: Pantheon Books 1974), 17–64.

15 Ian Steele, "Governors or Generals? A Note on Martial Law and the Revolution of 1689," *William and Mary Quarterly*, 46:2 (1989), 304–14.

16 Georges Rudé, *Wilkes and Liberty: A Social Study* (London: Lawrence and Wishart 1983). See also W.E. Shelton, *English Hunger and Industrial Disorders* (London: Macmillan 1973); J. Brewer et J. Styles, ed., *An Ungovernable People: The English and Their Law in the 17th and 18th Centuries* (New Brunswick, NJ: Rutgers University Press 1980).

17 Steven C. Greer, "Military Intervention in Civil Disturbances: The Legal Basis Reconsidered," *Public Law* (1983), 573–99.

18 See Clive Emsley, "An Aspect of Pitt's 'Terror': Prosecutions for Sedition during the 1790s," *Social History* 6:2 (May 1981), 155–84, and F. Murray Greenwood's useful overview, "Judges and Treason Law in Lower Canada, England, and the United States during the French Revolution," in Greenwood and B. Wright, eds., *Canadian State Trials: Volume One: Law, Politics and Security Measures, 1608–1837* (Toronto: University of Toronto Press 1996), 241 (hereafter *Canadian State Trials I*).

19 Léon Radzinowicz, *A History of English Criminal Law and Its Administration from 1750*, vol. 4 (London: Stevens and Sons 1968). 115–57. The 1831 Bristol riots serve as a particularly good illustration of this phenomenon.

20 On these different points, see John Jacob Tobias, *Crime and Police in England, 1700–1900* (London: Gill and Macmillan 1979), 117–84; Randall E. McGowen, "The Image of Justice and Reform of the Criminal Law in Early 19th-Century England," *Buffalo Law Review*, 32 (winter 1983), 89–126; and Michael Ignatieff, *A Just Measure of Pain: The Penitentiary in the Industrial Revolution, 1750–1850* (New York: Pantheon Books 1978).

21 The Chartist troubles at the end of the 1830s and in the 1840s serve as a good example of the prudent application of measures for civil repression. On this subject, see Léon Radzinowicz, "New Departures in Maintaining Public Order in the Face of Chartist Disturbances," *Cambridge Law Journal*, 19 (April 1960), 51–80.

22 Ronan Keane, "'The Will of the General,'" 158.

23 "The whole drift of English legal thinking [is] towards banishing martial law from the confines of law properly understood—to say, in effect, as the Duke of Wellington had said, that it [is] 'no law at all.'" Charles Townshend, "Martial Law: Legal and Administrative Problems of Civil Emergency in Britain and the Empire, 1800–1940," *Historical Journal,* 25 (1982), 172. Also relevant here is A.V. Dicey's famous remark: "'Martial law,' in the proper sense of that term, in which it means the suspension of ordinary law and the temporary government of a country or parts of it by military tribunals, is unknown to the law of England." Dicey, *Law of the Constitution,* 283.

24 This was also the position of the great jurist Mansfield, at the end of the eighteenth century. See Greer, "Military Intervention in Civil Disturbances," 581–5. Essentially, the urgency of the situation alone cannot justify recourse to an exceptional legal order: "When martial law is proclaimed under circumstances of assumed necessity, the proclamation must be regarded as the statement of an existing fact, rather than the legal creation of that fact." Cushing, attorney general of the United States, opinion of 7/2/1857, cited in William Forsyth, *Cases and Opinions on Constitutional Law* (London: Steven and Haynes, 1869), 209.

25 Hale, *Analysis of the Law,* cited in Forsyth, ibid. See also Lord Chief Justice Cockburn, charge to the grand jury in *R. v. Lyre:* "If it be true that you can apply martial law for the purpose of suppressing rebellion, it is equally certain that you cannot bring men to trial for treason under martial law after a rebellion has been suppressed." Ibid., 213.

26 See especially "An Act for the Suppression of the Rebellion Which Still Unhappily Exists within This Kingdom, and for the Protection of the Persons and Properties of His Majesty's Faithful Subjects within the Same" (Ireland), 39 Geo. III (1799), c.11; "An Act for the Suppression of Rebellion in Ireland, and for the Protection of the Persons and Property of His Majesty's Faithful Subjects there" (U.K.), 43 Geo. III (1803), c.117; "An Act for the More Effectual Suppression of Local Disturbances and Dangerous Associations in Ireland" (U.K.), 3 and 4 Will. IV (1833), c.40. This last example (art.40) "provided...that nothing in this Act contained shall be construed to take away, abridge, or diminish...the undoubted prerogative of His Majesty, for the Public Safety, to resort to the Exercise of Martial Law against open Enemies or Traitors..."

27 Finlason, *Review,* 5–6. As the following discussion will show, this link between the need to maintain order and the unpredictability of juries was fundamental.

28 Ibid., 120–1.

29 For an early example, see Jean-Marie Fecteau and Douglas Hay, "'Government by Will and Pleasure, Instead of Law': Military Justice and the Legal System in Quebec, 1775–1783," in Greenwood and Wright, eds., *Canadian State Trials I,* 129–71.

30 Grotius, *De Jure Belli* (1625) cited in Jonathan Scott, "The Law of War: Grotius, Sidney, Locke and the Political Theory of Rebellion," *History of Political Thought,* 13:4 (winter 1992), 580.

31 "For Locke...the right to resist was not a political but a natural right," ibid., 582.

32 J.P. Reid, "In a Defensive Rage: The Uses of the Mob, the Justification in Law, and the Coming of the American Revolution," *New York University Law Review,* 49 (December 1974), 1043–91. "Unsuccessful rebellions indeed generally establish the encroachments on the rights of the people who have produced them. [Rebellion] is a medicine necessary for the sound health of government." Jefferson to Madison, 30 Jan. 1787, cited in Harris C. Mirkin, "Rebellion, Revolution and the Constitution: Thomas Jefferson's Theory of Civil Disobedience," *American Studies,* 13:2 (1972), 61–74.

33 "Quand le gouvernement viole les droits du peuple, l'insurrection est, pour le peuple et pour chaque portion du peuple, le plus sacré des droits et le plus indispensable des devoirs," Constitution de l'An I de la République (1793), article 35 in Jacques Godechot, ed., *Les constitutions de la France depuis 1789* (Paris: Garnier-Flammarion 1970), 83.

34 Allan Greer, *The Patriots and the People: The Rebellion of 1837 in Rural Lower Canada* (Toronto: University of Toronto Press 1993); Allan Greer, "1837–1838: Rebellion Reconsidered," *CHR,* 76:1 (1995), 2–18.

35 Elinor Kyte Senior, *Redcoats and Patriotes: the Rebellions in Lower-Canada, 1837–38* (Stittsville, Ont.: National Museums of Canada 1985); Steven Watt, "Authoritarianism, Constitutionalism and the Special Council of Lower Canada, 1838–1841" (M.A. thesis, McGill University 1997); Brian Young, "Class Realignment and the Transformation of Lower-Canada, 1815–1866," in Allan Greer and Ian Radforth, eds., *Colonial Leviathan. State Formation in Mid-19th Century Canada* (Toronto: University of Toronto Press 1992), 50–63.

36 Jean-Marie Fecteau, "Lendemains de défaite: les rébellions comme histoire et mémoire," Jean-Paul Bernard, ed., *Bulletin d'histoire politique,* 7:1 (fall 1998), 19–28.

37 Here, I take up an idea expressed by Jean-Paul Bernard. See *The Rebellions of 1837 and 1838 in Lower Canada* (Ottawa: Canadian Historical Association 1996).

38 See Jean-Paul Bernard, ed., *Assemblées publiques resolutions et déclarations de 1837–1838* (Montreal: VLB Éditeur 1988). The mobilization strategy based on large assemblies was directly inspired by the experience of the American Revolution. It was also adopted by the Chartists in England. The best work on the relationship between the peasantry and democracy in Lower Canada is Greer, *The Patriots and the People.*

39 Gosford to Glenelg, 12 Oct. 1837, *British Parliamentary Papers,* vol. 9, 72.

40 "The great difficulty of procuring strict trial evidence for bringing home, in a court of justice, to the parties concerned the charges that might be founded on the proceedings had at these meetings, added to the questionable policy of political prosecutions, especially at a time like the present, when the minds of a portion of the jury summoned to try the offence would probably be poisoned by the misrepresentations and efforts of the disaffected, have as yet prevented any resort to the court of law for the punishment of those implicated in such proceedings." Gosford to Glenelg, 9 Sept. 1837, ibid., 56.

41 A report of the Executive Council from 20 October reflects this feeling of helplessness: "There is no hope, under existing circumstances, to re-establish the equilibrium between the component parts of the constitution without the intervention of the Imperial Parliament...It becomes absolutely necessary that the Executive Government should be made independent of the house of Assembly, and enabled to carry on the government of the province without the assistance of the legislative body...The commission of the peace is inefficient, inasmuch as several parts of the country are without magistrates and that in the towns there is a general want of that activity which is necessary to meet the emergency of the times." "Report of a Committee of the Whole Council," 20 Oct. 1837, ibid., 91.

42 Gosford to Glenelg, 6 Nov. 1837, ibid., 104. See also Report of the Executive Council, 20 November 1837 in app. D, L.C. doc.1a.

43 Glenelg to Colborne, 6 Dec. 1837, ibid., 114.

44 Court of Special Sessions of the Peace, 27 November 1837, ibid., 137. Justice of the peace Denis-Benjamin Viger expressed his dissent, while judges Guy and Castonguay abstained.

45 Suckling's interpretation relies on a strict interpretation of the Petition of Right of 1628: "There is...however after all that has been said a disagreeable kind of obscurity still remaining in the subject which I confess myself unable to remove nor do I think it a matter entirely without doubt that the King can in any case whatever, even in case of an invasion or a rebellion, establish Martial Law by his single authority in England, or delegate power of doing so to his Governor or Governors in Council in the American Colonies, seeing that the prohibition of the issuing of Commissions to exercise Martial Law in the famous Petition of Right above mentioned is expressed in these very general words which contain no exception whatever." Cited in Ogden and O'Sullivan to Civil Secretary S. Walcott, 30 Nov. 1837, *RPAC,* CO 42/274/147.

46 See n. 26.

47 Ibid., 147–53. Note how the articles of the imperial acts cited in support of their legal opinion are *declaratory.* That is to say, they preserve a prerogative believed to exist *already.* Also, the principle that, for any proclamation of martial law, a state of war must be such that the regular courts cannot sit, was interpreted very loosely by Lower Canadian jurists. The mere incapacity to deliver the court's warrants was deemed sufficient to meet this requirement: "The functions of the ordinary legal tribunals may be considered as having virtually ceased. For although the Courts of Justice may sit with perfect security in the city of Montreal, we can hardly name any part of this district in which process of any description could be served or writs executed by the ministry of Civil Officer." Ibid., 153.

48 Court of Special Sessions of the Peace, 5 Dec. 1837, in *Parliamentary Papers,* vol. 9, 141. The justices of the peace also cited the danger of an invasion by rebels who had taken refuge in the United States. In fact, the next day, eighty *patriotes* attempted an invasion from the United States, but they were intercepted at Moore's Corner, near the border, by volunteer militiamen.

49 Gosford to Glenelg, 6 Dec. 1837, ibid., 140. The instructions to Colborne, who was charged with putting martial law into effect, were also explicit as to the need to do so with prudence and discretion: "...In all cases wherein the unlimited power with which you are now invested can be exercised in

cooperation with, or in subordination to, the ordinary laws of the land, and that in all cases where from local circumstances, or from a prompt return to their allegiance, the deluded inhabitants of any part of that district display an honest contrition for their past offences, you will revert at once to the assistance of the civil authorities, and impress upon a misguided people the conviction that Her Majesty's Government in this Province is equally prompt to pardon the repentant and punish the incorrigible." S. Walcott, civil secretary, to Colborne, 5 December 1837, ibid., 140–1.

50 Gosford to Glenelg, 5 Jan. 1838, *RPAC*, CO 42/279/18. Glenelg had also already considered granting retroactive legal protection for all acts committed under this special regime: "Reposing the utmost confidence in your prudence, Her Majesty's Government are fully prepared to assume to themselves the responsibility of instructing you to employ it, should you be deliberately convinced that the occasion imperatively demands it. They will, with confidence look to Parliament for your indemnity and their own." Glenelg to Colborne, 6 Dec. 1837, *Parliamentary Papers,* vol. 9, 114.

51 Colborne to Glenelg, 17 March 1838, *RPAC*, CO 42/280/196.

52 A curious incident from February 1838 highlights the fragility of arguments justifying martial law in Lower Canada. Governor Colborne issued a proclamation declaring a day of prayers and thanksgiving in honour of the ascension of Queen Victoria. Notably, the proclamation celebrated the fact that the rebellion had been brought under control, "thus virtually, as it may be supposed, discontinuing the Act declaring Martial law." However, Colborne had to issue another proclamation on 27 February, announcing the continuation of martial law! On this strange series of events, see the letter from Colborne to Glenelg, 28 Feb. 1838, and the proclamation of 27 Feb. 1838, in *Parliamentary Papers,* vol. 9 (1838), 200.

53 For the story of these legal procedures, see O'Sullivan's letter to Civil Secretary Rowan on 17 March 1838, in ibid., 198–9. The prisoners had requested that their trial be held during the session. O'Sullivan noted that, "if the judges should decide that martial law, as declared by the last mentioned proclamation, is not in force, I cannot help reflecting upon the disagreeable situation in which His Excellency may be placed." On this subject, see also *Le Canadien,* 30 April 1838.

54 While martial law was in force, 515 suspects were arrested, of whom 340 were released on bail before

5 April, and about thirty others after that date. See Gérard Filteau, *Histoire des patriotes* (Montreal: Aurore 1975), 389.

55 See Gosford to Glenelg, 5 January 1838, *RPAC*, CO 42/279/ 7.

56 Glenelg to Colborne, 6 Jan. 1838, *Parliamentary Papers,* vol. 10, 20.

57 The crown law officers deplored the excessive democratization of the procedure nominating juries under the law of 1832: "This change let in upon the administration of criminal justice, an honest but illiterate peasantry. This was found to conduce materially to the increase of popular power and to further ends of the disaffected...It must be obvious considering the widespread of the recent Rebellion whose ramifications have extended throughout the whole Province, that every person accused of political offence could only be brought to trial with the certainty of an anticipated acquittal." Ogden and O'Sullivan to Captain Goldie, 24 Jan. 1838, *RPAC*, CO 42/280/67.

58 Ibid., 62. Note how, for the authors of this report, the uprising was not the act of a few agitators but that of an entire population. Their angry description of the influence of the *patriote* leadership is revealing: "These men have for years past ruled the peasantry of the country as they pleased, and still possess the confidence of their deluded constituents and of several of their fellow members," Ibid., 68.

59 Colborne to Gosford, 24 Jan. 1838, *RPAC*, CO 42/280/67.

60 Glenelg to Colborne, 19 Feb. 1838, *Parliamentary Papers,* vol. 10, 1–2.

61 The full titles and range of the Special Council ordinances can be found in app. D, L.C. doc.3.

62 Hesitant British authorities would wait four months after the first rebellion to suspend the constitution. This highlights a situation where the *patriotes* had the initiative and where the social forces likely to offer resistance to them—poorly supported by a governor (Gosford) dedicated to conciliation—did not have the political means to react. On this point, see Philip A. Buckner, *The Transition to Responsible Government: British Policy in British North America, 1815–1850* (Westport, Conn.: Greenwood Press 1985).

63 "With the extensive executive power, reform credibility, immunity to local pressures, and a facility for critical inquiry, Durham was the pragmatic solution of the part of imperial administrators increasingly conscious

of, and concerned about, the compact's manoeuver-ings." Barry Wright, "Ideological Dimensions," 157.

64 To be more precise, the Special Council ordinance passed in April suspended habeas corpus only for prisoners taken during the rebellion.

65 On this point, Durham would show a much stronger attachment to humanitarian principles. He later explained his approach to Lieutenant-Governor Arthur, speaking with respect to the Upper Canadian rebels: "Where severity is advisable, the moment of the commission of the crime seems to be the only one in which it is possible to apply it. When an insurrection is suppressed, when the offender is helpless, the recollection of the crime weakened by the lapse of time and the horror of the impending punishment alone vivid, the common feelings of humanity render it impossible to use the severity which would previously have been allowable." Durham to Arthur, 18 Sept. 1838, *Parliamentary Papers,* vol. 10, 172.

66 Glenelg to Durham, 21 April 1838, ibid., 29.

67 Durham to Glenelg, 29 June 1838, ibid., 128. In April, Colborne had begun expressing the same opinion: "None of the prisoners can, I fear, be brought before the ordinary tribunals of the province with justice to the community at large." Colborne to Glenelg, 9 April 1838, ibid., 102.

68 The text of this confession can be found in [John Stuart Mill], "Lord Durham's Return," *Westminster Review,* 32 (1838), 249.

69 "An Ordinance to Provide for the Security of the Province of Lower Canada," *SLC* (Special Council, 2nd session), 2 Vic. (1838), c.1.

70 Proclamation of 28 June 1838, *Parliamentary Papers,* vol. 10, 128.

71 The ordinance stated that once these persons entered the province, they "shall in such case be deemed and taken to be guilty of high treason, and shall on conviction of being found at large or com-ing within the said province...suffer death accord-ingly." Clearly, any trial was to be concerned strictly with the presence of the rebels in Lower Canada, and not an accusation of high treason.

72 "An Act for Indemnifying Those Who Have Issued or Acted under Certain Parts of a Certain Ordinance Made under Colour of an Act Passed in the Present Session of Parliament, Intituled An Act to Make Temporary Provision for the Government of Lower Canada" (U.K.) 2 Vic. (1838), c.112.

73 Durham to Glenelg, 25 Sept. 1838, *Parliamentary Papers,* vol. 10, 182.

74 It appears fairly certain that the governor was leaning to these conclusions well before his arrival in the colony, as the words of his friend and secretary Buller would suggest: "Lord Durham from the first took a far sounder view of the matter: he saw what narrow and mischievous spirit worked at the bottom of all the acts of the French-Canadians; and while he was prepared to do the individuals full justice, and justice with mercy, he had made up his mind that no quarter should be shown to the absurd pretensions of race, and that he must throw himself on the support of the British feelings, and aim at making Canada thoroughly British." Charles Buller, cited in Chester New, *Lord Durham's Mission to Canada* (Toronto: McClelland and Stewart, [1929] 1963), 50. See also Ged Martin, "Le Rapport Durham et les origines du gouvernement responsable au Canada," *Bulletin d'histoire politique,* 6:3 (spring-summer 1998), 37.

75 Durham to Glenelg, 9 Aug. 1838, ibid., 155.

76 Clearly, Durham is speaking in terms of an *ethnic* majority. Despite the denials of a certain historio-graphical tradition (see especially Janet Ajzenstat, *The Political Thought of Lord Durham* [Montreal: McGill-Queen's University Press 1988]), the ethnic dimension was at the heart of Durham's thought, in line with the position of the British party in Lower Canada. It is also by referring to the ethnic charac-ter of political demands that Durham had a pretext for negating the principal of the democratic major-ity. In fact, appeals to ethnic solidarity constituted one of the major themes in the constitutionalist dis-course of the period. On this point, see Richard La Rue, "Allégeance et origine: contribution à l'anaylse de la crise politique au Bas-Canada," *Revue d'his-toire de l'Amérique française,* 44:4 (spring 1991), 529–48.

77 Durham to Glenelg, 28 Sept. 1838, *Parliamentary Papers,* vol. 10, 189.

78 Proclamation of 9 Oct. 1838, ibid., 207.

79 Moreover, in August, Durham had named Adam Thom, ex-columnist of the Montreal *Herald* and sworn enemy of French institutions, as commis-sioner on municipal institutions.

80 Durham to Glenelg, 28 Sept. 1838, *Parliamentary Papers,* vol. 10, 193.

81 At the same moment, in England, this same idea was clearly articulated by John Stuart Mill: "In itself ...the dictatorship which has been assumed, and of which lord Durham is the immediate depositary, admits of justification. But if it shall prove to have been assumed only to remove the obstacles which the constitution of the House of Assembly has of

late years opposed to the previously uncontrolled sway of a rapacious faction; if because the majority of the people, when they had the power over the Assembly, did not use it to our liking, we mean to remedy this inconvenience by taking the power from them and giving it to a minority; if we have set aside their constitution in order to confiscate the privileges of the old inhabitants for the benefit of a small proportion of foreigners and new settlers; then will a stain rest upon the British name, to be effaced only on the day when all that is now done shall be undone," [John Stuart Mill], "Radical Party and Canada," *Westminster Review,* 28 (1837), 529.

82 Durham to Glenelg, 28 Sept. 1838, ibid., 192. It is important to remember that, although habeas corpus was suspended during the entire summer of 1838, the suspension applied only to those implicated in the 1837 rebellion. The day before the period of suspension was to expire, Durham also passed an ordinance permitting the continued imprisonment of those prisoners who had not signed a promise to keep the peace: *SLC* (Special Council, 2nd session), 2 Vic. (1838), c.3.

83 Chartrand had been executed for treason following a summary trial organized by the rebels. On the trial, see F. Murray Greenwood, "The Chartrand Murder Trial: Rebellion and Repression in Lower Canada, 1837–1839," *Criminal Justice History,* 5 (1984), 129–59.

84 Durham to Glenelg, 12 Sept. 1838, *Parliamentary Papers,* vol. 10, 165. The jury deliberated only for a half-hour before returning a verdict of not guilty based, to the dismay and indignation of the solicitor general, "upon the grounds (and they were the only grounds urged in the defence) that pending a rebellion in which they took a part, the victim had been a spy and enemy to his country, and as such deservedly put to death by the sentence of his fellow-countrymen." C.R. Ogden to c.Buller, 19 Sept. 1838, ibid., 174.

85 Durham to Glenelg, 20 Oct. 1838, ibid., 220 Durham makes reference to the August 1838 opinion of Judge Denman in the House of Lords, according to which the Follett amendment rendered inoperable Durham's ordinance providing for the deportation of political prisoners without a conviction. See U.K., HC, *Parliamentary Debates,* 3rd series, vol. 44, col. 1162.

86 Durham to Glenelg, 20 Oct. 1838, *Parliamentary Papers,* vol. 10, 221.

87 The Italian Carbonari provide a good example. On the question of secret societies in the context of Lower Canadian politics, see Jean-Marie Fecteau, "Les dangers du secret: Note sur l'État canadien et les sociétés secrètes au milieu du 19e siècle," *Canadian Journal of Law and Society,* 6 (1991), 91–112.

88 Durham had already painted a tragic picture of the situation: "Terrified by signs of this formidable and mysterious organization, and sometimes by secret menaces or warnings of murder and massacre, the loyal inhabitants of the country quit their exposed and isolated habitations, and either at first seek refuge in the towns or at once secure their safety by quitting the British dominions." Durham to Glenelg 20 Oct. 1838 *Parliamentary Papers,* vol. 10, 222.

89 For a complete list of Special Council security legislation, see app. D, L.C. doc.3.

90 Lord Glenelg to Durham, 26 Oct. 1838, *Parliamentary Papers,* vol. 10, 79.

91 Thus, the "Ordinance for the Suppression of the Rebellion Which Unhappily Exists within This Province of Lower Canada," already cited, was retroactive to 1 Nov. 1838. This was a harsher version of the recent British law, "An Act for the More Effectual Suppression of Local Disturbances and Dangerous Associations in Ireland" (U.K.), 3 and 4 Will. IL (1833), c.40. Furthermore, the ordinance could be applied regardless of "whether the ordinary courts of justice shall or shall not at such time be open." *SLC* (Special Council, 3rd session), 2 Vic. (1838), c.3, art.1.

92 Colborne to Glenelg, 19 Dec. 1838, *Parliamentary Papers,* vol. 10, 273.

93 Glenelg to Colborne, 19 Nov. 1838, ibid., 86.

94 The brutal haste with which the Special Council removed all obstacles to repression sometimes pushed it to extremes that raised the eyebrows of even the most tolerant British jurists. Such was the case of the "Ordinance to Declare that the Second Chapter of the Statutes of the Parliament of England, Passed in the Thirty-first Year of the Reign of King Charles the Second, Is Not, Nor Has Ever Been, in Force in This Province, and for Other Purposes," *SLC* (Special Council, 3rd session), 2 Vic. (1838), c.51. This ordinance invalidated all writs of habeas corpus issued by the Court of King's Bench under the "Act for the Better Securing of the Liberty of the Subject, and for Prevention of Imprisonments beyond the Seas" (U.K.) 31 Charles 2 (1678), c.2. The crown law officers had to underline, in polite terms, that the Special Council did not have the power to rewrite the province's legal history. The ordinance

was immediately disallowed: *SLC* (Special Council, 4th session), 2 Vic. (1838), c.51; see also the letter from J. Campbell and R.W. Rolfe to Colonial Secretary Lord Glenelg, 6 Feb. 1839, in *RPAC, CO* 42/300/260–1.

95 *SLC* (Special Council, 3rd session), 2 Vic. (1838), c.14; (Special Council, 4th session), 2 Vic. (1839), c.66.

96 For an analysis of the proceedings of this court martial, see F. Murray Greenwood, "L'insurrection appréhendée et l'administration de la justice au Canada," *Revue d'histoire de l'Amérique française,* 34 (June 1980), 57–94; F. Murray Greenwood, "The General Court Martial of 1838–1839 in Lower Canada: An Abuse of Justice," in W. Wesley Pue and Barry Wright, eds., *Canadian Perspective on Law and Society—Issues in Legal History* (Ottawa: Carleton University press 1988), 249–90.

97 The judgment was published *in extenso* in *Le Canadien* (23 Nov. 1838), and the lawyer's arguments in the Quebec *Gazette* (26 Nov. 1838). As mentioned (see n.92), Judge Bédard had already given the same opinion in October.

98 Judgment published in *Le Canadien* (10 Dec. 1838).

99 See the opinions of Chief Justice J. Stuart, and judges M. O'Sullivan, G. Pyke, and S. Gale, 7 Dec. 1838, *RPAC, CO* 42/281/479; the opinion of Attorney General C.R. Ogden, 27 Dec. 1838, ibid., 487; the opinion of Solicitor General A. Stuart, 23 Dec. 1838, ibid., 489. Only Judge Rolland abstained from responding to the government's request. However, in January 1839 he refused to grant a request for a writ of habeas corpus. See Colborne to Glenelg, 21 Jan. 1839, ibid., vol. 293, 86. Finally, On 11 Feb. 1839, judges Stuart and Bowen reiterated their opinions in refusing a similar request on behalf of J. Teed, reversing the decision of judges Panet and Bédard. See the wording of the judgment in the Quebec *Gazette* (18 Feb. 1839).

100 J. Campbell and R.M. Rolfe to Glenelg, 25 Jan. 1839, *RPAC, CO* 42/300/240–3.

101 On the "Viger Affair," see G. Parizeau, *La vie studieuse et obstinée de Denis-Benjamin Viger* (Montreal: Fides 1980), 70–8; letter from governor Colborne to Colonial Secretary Marquis of Normanby, 6 May 1839, *Parliamentary Papers,* vol. 13, 65; Colborne to Normanby, 20 May 1839, ibid., vol. 11, 86–7; Colborne to Russell, 18 Oct. 1839, ibid., 153–5.

102 "Protêt de Joseph Narcisse Cardinal *et al.,* 28 novembre 1838," *Report of the State Trials before a General Court Martial Held at Montreal in*

1839–9, vol. 1 (Montreal: Armour and Ramsay 1839) 17 at 77.

103 "Joint Opinion of the Attorney and Solicitor General," J. Campbell and R.W. Rolfe, 22 Jan. 1839, in William Forsyth, *Cases and Opinions,* 205.

104 U.K., HL *Parliamentary Debates,* 3rd series, vol. 45, col. 353–4. The petition was presented but no debate followed.

105 Colborne to Glenelg, 19 Dec. 1838, *Parliamentary Papers,* vol. 10, 275. Two days earlier, Joseph Cardinal and Joseph Duguet had been executed. The other executions would take place much later (18 January: Pierre Decoigne, François Hamelin, Joseph Robert, and Ambroise Sanguinet; 15 February: Chevalier de Lorimtier, Charles Hindenlang, Pierre Narbonne, François Nicolas, Charles Sanguinet, and Amable Daunais).

106 Cited by Greenwood, "The Chartrand Murder," 150.

107 Association loyale canadienne, "Déclaration des rues et motifs de l'Association Loyale Canadienne du District de Montréal," Montreal, 1 Feb. 1838.

108 In the District of Saint-Francis, martial law was imposed on 16 Nov. 1838 and lifted by proclamation on 16 April 1839.

109 "Equality before the law, due process, and an independent judiciary were the essence of Whig constitutionalism." Paul Romney, "From the Types Riot to the Rebellion: Elite Ideology, Anti-legal Sentiment, Political Violence, and the Rule of Law in Upper Canada," *OH,* 79:2 (1987), 134.

110 Barry Wright, "Sedition in Upper Canada: Contested Legality," *Labour/Le Travail,* 29 (1992), 49 and 56.

111 On this question, see Douglas Hay, "The Class Composition of the Palladium of Liberty: Trial Jurors in the Eighteenth Century," in James S. Cockburn and Thomas A. Green, eds., *Twelve Good Men and True: The Criminal Trial Jury in England, 1200–1800* (Princeton, NJ Princeton University Press 1988) 305–57; Barry Wright, "Sedition in Upper Canada"; and Paul Romney, "From Constitutionalism to Legalism."

112 "Baconianism" is in opposition to the legal tradition of the autonomous judge, exemplified by Coke, See F. Murray Greenwood, *Legacies of Fear: Law and Politics in Quebec in the Era of the French Revolution* (Toronto: Osgoode Society/University of Toronto Press 1993). A study of the behaviour of judges and the legal struggles in the period following that covered by Greenwood is sadly lacking

and greatly hinders an understanding of Lower Canadian political history from 1815 to 1840.

113 Romney, "From the Types Riot," 139.

114 Of course, I refer here to an ultra-conservative fringe of the anglophone minority. The "Constitutional" movement, loyal to Great Britain, also contained a more democratic faction, represented most notably by John Neilson. But this faction would soon be overtaken as political struggle became increasingly radicalized. It had virtually disappeared by the time of the rebellions. On this point, see Steven Watt, "Authoritarianism, Constitutionalism and the Special Council," and Michael McCulloch, "The Death of Whiggery: Lower-Canadian British Constitutionalism and the tentation de l'histoire parallèle," *Journal of the Canadian Historical Association,* 2 (1991), 195–213.

115 Such a backwards reading, portraying the *patriotes* as deceitful and the British elites as the precursors of a democratic future, would, of course, have a rich future in Canadian historiography.

Bonds of Friendship, Kinship, and Community: Gender, Homelessness, and Mutual Aid in Early-Nineteenth-Century Montreal

MARY ANNE POUTANEN

Vagrant women in Montreal lived large parts of their lives on the streets, in squares and green spaces such as the Champs de Mars, in the fields and farms that surrounded the city, and in public buildings, including courts, prisons, and taverns. They navigated public space alone, in couples, or in groups with kin, friends, and casual acquaintances. To persevere in a hostile environment, they established bonds of mutual dependence, often in moments of need. These did not always ensure survival but helped to get them through a day, a night, or a season. Such bonds were linked to a wide range of behaviours that suggest intimacy, warmth, and love, on the one hand, and tension, anger, and mere tolerance, on the other. The variable habitats and diverse relationships amongst the homeless challenge historians' understanding of familial relationships as rooted in domestic and private, rather than public, space.

Most social historians who study communities, kinship, and family use historical sources that locate men, women, and children within dwellings. The census, in particular, lends a sense of permanency to people's assignations to a particular place and to the social relationships captured within it. Feminist historians insist on the importance of examining how reproduction occurred within families by highlighting women's prominence as bearers of the next generation and as those primarily responsible for a range of tasks that ensured that family members were sheltered clothed and fed. Family historians envision the family at the heart of some of the most intense ties of emotion. In contrast, historians of the criminal-justice system usually ignore the family, focusing their attention on crimes, criminal processes, sentencing patterns or the intent of the court system. This chapter applies some of the questions of family and community studies to the lives of a particular group within the criminal-justice system: vagrant women arrested in Montreal between 1810 and 1842. Not only did few of these women have access to permanent shelter of their own, but the very act of securing food and clothing was likely to involve them in crime or in some form of charity. As criminalized subjects, these women appear bereft of friendship, kinship, and community, yet they were not without emotional ties.

This study explores the complex inventory of relationships that vagrant women established for themselves and their dependants as they sought to secure the daily requirements of shelter, food, warmth, and emotional support and comfort in a world characterized by danger, poverty, homelessness, hunger, cold, and social ostracism. Their range of choices was limited. Yet these vagrant women's alliances and survival strategies explicitly underscore their agency and reveal both their vulnerability and tenacity. The pursuit of subsistence brought vagrant women into contact with a cast of characters facing similar challenges. First, as nonrespectable poor, they had difficulty securing charitable aid. As women alone, free of the influence and discipline of a father or husband, they presented a threat to a disciplined and orderly society. Second, their questionable liaisons, drinking habits, and proximity to vice brought them increasingly under public scrutiny as bourgeois attitudes about respectability became hegemonic. Third, the task of seeking out the necessities of life brought them together in a common purpose. Impressions of these relationships of kinship, friendship, and solidarity can be discerned in the historical documents that their misdemeanours generated.

Early-nineteenth-century Montreal criminal-court records and police registers provide valuable clues to a range of bonds that vagrant women established. Police arrested and charged Montreal women with at least 2,528 incidents of vagrancy in the period under study. The act of coming before a justice of the peace to face a charge of vagrancy meant that the event was formally inscribed in a deposition. Yet the relationships between female vagrants arrested together were not always explicit. Teasing them out is

challenging. The court clerk often recorded only basic information in the deposition or used printed forms, filling in only the name of the accused. Other sources, especially affidavits, contain further pieces of information that offer insights into vagrant women's lives and the complex and ambiguous relationships that they established with the women and men who shared their world.

The chapter begins with an examination of how vagrant women made use of public space in their daily search to find food, shelter, and security and how their movements reveal the permeability and improvisational nature of public and private spheres as well as the blurred divisions between everyday life and the criminal underworld. It then explores the diverse bonds that female vagrants developed as members of communities of women, as single parents, and as relatives. The chapter concludes with an analysis of the kinds of relationships that they established with the men with whom they shared public space.

Urban Space, the Culture of Vagrancy, and the Search for Food, Shelter, and Security

Early-nineteenth-century Montreal was a dynamic urban centre. The economy was undergoing transformations that would culminate in an industrial revolution later in the century. The rebellions, the suspension of democratic government, and the British army and local militia's brutal conclusion to the armed revolt led to dramatic political restructuring in the 1840s. The city's population expanded as Canadien(ne)s migrated from the countryside and immigrants arrived in ships from the British Isles or travelled overland from the United States. By 1832 non-francophones were the majority in the city.[1]

Thus a significant proportion of Montrealers lived together without having long-standing ties to one another, the neighbourhoods, or the community. Many immigrants forged new relations when kin were absent or when they could no longer access them.

Men and women of different social and ethnic groups clustered in the city streets, squares, and green spaces as they conducted business, shopped, socialized, and promenaded. Beggars demanded alms, peddlers sold merchandise, basket-women hawked produce, mothers performed household chores with the assistance of their children, prostitutes solicited, and vagrants loitered. Carters and caleche drivers queued up at stations along thoroughfares waiting for customers. The streets were extensions of cramped households, serving as "the drawing-room of the poor,"[2] where people lived "in full view of someone else's gaze."[3] Historian William Atherton compared mid-nineteenth-century Montreal to a primitive village: elderly men sat at their doorsteps "to gossip with passing friends and often the family would be found there of an evening."[4]

Montrealers traversed the old city with its grey stone buildings and tin roofs on wooden sidewalks along narrow streets, dodging ankle-deep mud, animal refuse, and puddles of water. Commissioners' Street was "covered with heaps of rubbish, stagnant pools, deep ruts, and in some places half covered with logs of timber."[5] The wider streets of the suburbs were hardly an improvement. In summer unpaved streets turned to dust, and in rainy weather to mud. Sherbrooke Street was passable only in daylight during the spring and autumn. Warm air carried the stench of rotting animal carcasses, unwashed market stalls, accumulated garbage, and open privies. In winter city streets were covered with snow and ice, in some places as much as two to three feet thick.

Vagrant women lived their lives within this cacophonic and tumultuous public space in an "improvisational, hand-to-mouth subsistence."[6] There they worked—usually in the sex trade—consumed food and alcohol, played, argued, courted, fought, and slept "rough." They moved through the city, congregating in the old town around the waterfront near the barracks and behind it in the Champs de Mars. Vagrants wandered in and out of unlit neighbourhoods and potentially dangerous pathways and alleyways as well as in and around abandoned houses and vacant lots. They traversed the suburbs and gathered at some of the farms, fields, and orchards on the edge of town to search for food and refuge and to solicit clients. Female vagrants also frequented drinking establishments in disreputable, unsafe areas of the city: the low tippling houses along the waterfront that catered to thirsty and randy sailors, who disembarked from the fleets of foreign ships visiting the port after long ocean voyages; the cellars under the public markets reputed to be the haunt of soldiers and thieves;[7] or the wooden sheds along the Lachine Canal that were favoured by Irish workers. There was also Capital Street, situated near the old market, where keepers carried on a brisk business dispensing drinks to visitors who patronized the eighteen taverns that festooned the street.[8] This street and its notorious taverns became the subject of a petition for their closure in 1816.[9]

Cast at the midpoint between the deserving poor and a criminal brotherhood,[10] vagrants were accused of fomenting many of society's ills and blamed for everything from corrupting the city's youth to unsolved robberies. Newspaper editors repeatedly warned Montrealers to beware of unrepentant vagrants who roamed the city streets: "As the criminal term closed at the end of last week, the usual clearing out of the jail took place. Our citizens ought, therefore, to be on the watch against the depredations of the incorrigible vagabonds now at liberty. Some robberies have recently occurred, and have no doubt been affected by these perpetual inmates of our prison."[11] The offence of vagrancy was constructed out of a fear of disorder and contributed to the growing power of a centralized state. Used against suspicious persons, it was not, Linda Kerber contends, about what a person had done—since similar behaviour had no legal consequences for property owners—but about what she appeared to be. Thus homeless women were assumed to be idle and therefore susceptible to the charge of vagrancy.[12]

Criminal-court records reveal that vagrant women pinched bread from unattended carts, food from market stalls, and small objects wherever they could for their own consumption or to convert into cash or payment in kind at pawnshops, at taverns near the city's wharves, where fences worked, or at local brothels.[13] In this way, Montreal vagrants moved between the criminal underworld—made up of a network of pawnshops, lodging houses, brothels, taverns, and other public buildings—and everyday street life. Many of the women were implicated in a street culture of dishonest activity. Grand jurors may have had vagrants to mind when they expressed alarm about Montreal women's growing role in larceny: "in present circumstances even women are emboldened to associate with the leading thieves; and having first cheered them forward to the general plunder of the Country, they next play the part of receivers of stolen goods and the procurers of false witnesses."[14]

The threat of hunger, malnutrition, and hypothermia—owing to chronic exposure to cold—coupled with neglect, illness, and lack of medical attention meant that living "rough" was gruelling, dangerous, and at times life-threatening. Homeless women sought shelter in public buildings, abandoned houses, outhouses, and farm buildings, moving from place to place as circumstances changed. In mid-November 1835 Appoline St-Germain and fellow streetwalker Emily McIntosh found refuge in a hayloft.[15] A few years later, she and Mary Milligan, Mary Ann Smith, Sarah Mitchell,

Edward Lawrence, John Leines, and Joseph Charpentier erected their own shelter in the heart of the old city. Police arrested them at their campsite in a vacant lot on St. Paul Street. The city brewer, George Bourne, labelled them vagrants "of the worst description." Despite their attempt to create a refuge, they were deemed homeless and unemployed.[16] Some of those who could afford to pay rent lived alone; Adélaide Menard leased a room in a house on St. Paul Street, where she was accused of admitting men into her lodgings through a window.[17] Others shared living space in single rooms in multifamily dwellings, in cellars below the Ste-Anne Market, in small apartments, or in run-down wooden houses, or they moved between the brothel and the street.

When police raided Ellen McConvey and Patrick Thomas' bawdy house on 21 April 1841, prostitute Margaret Delany was permitted to stay behind to attend to her five children, who lived there with her.[18] A week later, Delany's search for shelter took her and her children to a city police station, where she requested overnight lodging. This incident suggests that brothel-keepers provided a home for sex trade workers and their children, who would otherwise be left homeless. While the sources say little about who looked after the children, brothel residents more than likely shared child-care responsibilities. Undoubtedly, women like Margaret Delany who lived in city bawdy houses were expected to work. Brothel-keepers did not dispense charity. Lucie Rolland, who operated one of Montreal's most prominent houses of prostitution, denounced Emilie Blanchard to a justice of the peace as insane and a vagrant.[19] The worlds of the brothel and of the street therefore intersected: prostitutes solicited in the streets to entice men to the brothels where they worked, and streetwalkers and clients searched for uninhabited buildings, where they remained until forced out by the authorities. Elizabeth Austin, Elmire Perrault, and two soldiers broke into an abandoned house belonging to notary Pierre Beaudry; police removed them from the house a few days later and arrested the women after Beaudry complained to a justice of the peace.[20]

Others turned to the few existing private philanthropic institutions founded by genteel women to aid "nonrespectable" women. In 1831 the widow Mcdonell, otherwise known as Agathe Henriette Latour, opened the Penitent Females' Refuge, or Magdalen Asylum, which was supported financially by both public grants and private donations in a building located at the entrance to the St. Antoine suburb. The primary goal of the refuge was to rehabilitate the sexual behaviour of prostitutes and to train them for domestic service. In 1836 it was forced to close because of inadequate government financial support and disinterest in its continued operation on the part of the general population.[21] Most other charities refused to help vagrant women. The House of Industry, which opened in 1819, offered care only to Montreal's "respectable poor." Denying assistance to the disreputable is hardly surprising given that elites managed the city's charities. Janice Harvey's study of nineteenth-century Protestant benevolence in Montreal reveals that the policies of charitable institutions reflected the biases of their benefactors more than the needs of the poor and thus served as a form of social regulation.[22] The urgency for food and shelter notwithstanding, vagrant women were disqualified because of their notoriety. By 1821 this institution had failed to attract even the industrious poor.[23] For many of them, the House of Industry resembled an institution of terror from which they feared that they would never be released.[24] The historian Lynn Hollen Lees found that in England the vast majority of the urban poor avoided draconian state-run institutions that had been designed with them in mind. The indigent sought other solutions to their homelessness and poverty, turning to relatives and neighbours for help, resorting to pawn shops, obtaining credit, stealing, and begging.[25] In Ireland, during the same period, workhouses were both feared and loathed. John O'Connor's study of this institution shows that during the potato famine, the Irish preferred immigration and the uncertainty of surviving the so-called coffin ships to remaining in Ireland, where the alternatives were either confinement, chronic hunger, malnutrition, susceptibility to fatal diseases in local workhouses, or death from starvation.[26]

A comparison of the names of the women listed in the registers of the Grey Nuns, Sisters of Providence, and the Montreal Ladies' Benevolent Society as charity recipients with the names of those arrested for vagrancy reveals that few vagrants received assistance.[27] That the Montreal Ladies' Benevolent Society divided women into respectable and nonrespectable served as a major barrier to aid for those deemed disreputable. In this period, as bourgeois women carved out intermediate spaces for their activities, the Ladies' Benevolent Society did not expand either physically or ideologically to accommodate female vagrants. Rather, the organization provided poor women who were above reproach with employment, food, clothing, fuel, and sometimes rent money. The names of those judged unworthy were apparently made public in order to prevent their dependence upon the magnanimity of others and to force them either to work or to leave the city.[28] Presumably, these same charitable women worried that Montrealers would be duped into giving alms to those whom they had appraised as undeserving.

In light of the narrow range of alternatives open to them, homeless women frequently sought overnight lodging at the local police station or confinement in prison during the coldest months. After a number of female vagrants were released from prison in January 1836, four of them requested reincarceration due to inclement weather. When the justice of the peace refused, they broke several courthouse windows and were promptly rearrested and returned to prison.[29] Police also apprehended women whom they believed were in danger of perishing from hypothermia, hunger, and disease.[30] Magdeleine McDonald was one such vagrant. Four watchmen escorted her to the watch house in late December 1836. Police discovered McDonald, apparently in an alarming state, intoxicated in an inn near Ste-Anne's Market during a winter storm.[31] The common jail also served as a refuge for the dying. Martha Hyers, a single, illiterate, black woman with an eight-year history of prostitution and vagrancy, was well acquainted with this institution. For the last five years of her life, Dr. Arnoldi treated her for a variety of ailments associated with undernourishment and recurrent exposure to cold and for venereal disease each time she was imprisoned. During her last arrest in November 1841, Hyers languished in jail before succumbing to illness resulting from chronic hypothermia and neglect.[32] Prison officials sometimes sought longer periods of incarceration for homeless women who had not completed treatment for medical conditions or who did not have adequate clothing during stormy weather.

Release from this "social service" sometimes had tragic consequences. In December 1841, for example, the warden of the prison discharged a homeless woman. Police discovered her soon after, inebriated and lying in a court-yard with her clothes frozen to the ground and her legs and ankles frost-bitten. She was immediately readmitted to jail for medical treatment of her blackened and swollen extremities.[33] Vagrant women died from hypothermia: in 1825 one woman succumbed to "want" and cold near one of the city's public roads.[34] These deaths did not sit well with some Montrealers. Exasperated by the demise of a woman in Notre Dame Street, the editor of the *Montreal Herald* recommended that the old jail be opened as a refuge for the homeless: "our streets swarm with drunkards, and, now that winter is setting in without a home to shelter them, to die in the

streets is their inevitable doom."[35] Thus incarceration served as an important resource that vagrant women could access and depend upon as an alternative to sleeping "rough" on the street. In this way, like their British counterparts, they obfuscated "the divide between life inside and their own communities outside."[36]

In Montreal both the common jail and house of corrections were overcrowded, vermin-ridden, and foul-smelling at any time during the year. In summer the buildings were suffocating owing to poor ventilation, and in winter they were cold because of deficient heat. Inadequately dressed prisoners suffered the frigid air and snow that penetrated prison wards through broken windowpanes. Some slept on the floor and others on straw beds with only a thin blanket for cover. To stay warm, women huddled together in small rooms. Prisoners subsisted on bread and water during the week; meat was added to a watery broth on Sundays and holidays.[37] That homeless women turned to these abhorrent, inadequate facilities speaks to their utter destitution.[38] Marcela Aranguiz's examination of male vagrancy in Montreal confirms that the practice of seeking shelter at police stations and prisons continued well into the twentieth century and long after the establishment of refuges and a house of industry for the homeless.[39] Members of an 1842 grand jury understood that for many homeless vagrants, the door between the prison and the street was a revolving one: "she finds every door shut against her, she is compelled to remain in the streets surrounded by temptation without any means to support or a friend to care for her, she is closely watched by the police and is speedily thrust back again to the house of corrections for two months more, and thus her wretched days are spent alternately, between the streets and imprisonment."[40]

Of the more than twenty-five hundred arrests for vagrancy between 1810 and 1842, most involved single, Irish women apprehended once or twice during this time. This reflects the precariousness of their situation as recent immigrants to British North America. The public was well aware of the hardships that newcomers faced. An editorial in a local newspaper indicated that "[poor emigrants] are wandering about our streets, sunk in the lowest state of misery and want."[41] Margaret Hazette's dilemma, as a recent arrival to Montreal from Ireland, poignantly exemplified the predicament of others in similar circumstances. She suggested to the policeman who had arrested her that, unable to find work, she was "in danger of getting into improper courses."[42] Without the means to purchase food and shelter, many of the women temporarily tried to eke out a living on the streets until new opportunities arose or they could develop a contingency plan.

In contrast, a small number of women were repeatedly arrested for vagrancy-related offences. They account for two-thirds of the arrests. Their demographic characteristics were similar to those of all vagrant women: the majority were nonfrancophone and single, and a tenth were married or widowed. Some turned to street prostitution to provide for themselves and their children; some suffered from chronic alcoholism and homelessness. The police, who knew these women well, subjected them to repeated incarceration in large part due to their visibility and to their reputations. The widow Bridget Howe was arrested at least twenty-nine times for being a vagrant. She died at age twenty-six in the common jail after having spent most of her last six years there. The coroner deemed that her death was hastened by disease, destitution, and alcoholism.[43]

Among such repeat offenders, arrests for public-order offences far outnumbered those for other crimes, demonstrating the state's preoccupation with regulating public space.[44] Between 1838 and 1842, for example, the constabulary and night watch, the foremost representatives of the state, apprehended women most frequently for vagrancy, keeping disorderly houses, and streetwalking and for being loose, idle, and disorderly. These general categories, however, concealed a range of activities. Most vagrant women were soliciting at the time of their arrests; others were loitering, uttering obscenities, homeless, drunk, damaging property, or making threats. A smaller number of the vagrancy charges stemmed from indictable offences such as larceny, assault, and extortion. Similarly, Parisian policemen targeted vagrants whom they perceived as dangerous: "a population which drifted in and out of begging, prostitution and crime was more threatening and more difficult to control on account of its mobility and its ability to associate freely and easily."[45]

By 1840 Montreal's population had reached approximately forty thousand. It was becoming increasingly difficult for city constables to identify vagrants. An incident in September 1840 is especially telling. When Constable Denis Dowde failed to recognize a vagrant, the inspector of the police, P.E. Leclerc, ordered that the chief constables parade all incarcerated vagrants in front of the men each morning before they were dismissed from duty. Furthermore, Leclerc threatened to discharge policemen from the force in the future if they were unable to identify city vagrants.[46] Thus Inspector Leclerc not only attached an identity to vagrants that transcended their present state of homelessness, but also permanently delegated them to the ranks of those homeless who would henceforth be regulated by the police. This paternalism meant that vagrancy became an identity rather than an action. As long as the police knew them personally, it was not a transitory identity.

It was customary for vagrants to gather in the common land around the city, reputed as a place where homeless people could live.[47] The priests' farm, which was located below the mountain near the city, was a particularly popular site for soldiers and vagrant men and women to congregate. There they ate from the extensive gardens and orchards and milked cows pasturing in nearby fields. The farm was supposed to serve the Sulpicians and their students as a "place of recreation, to where, during the summer time, all the members of the establishment, superiors and pupils, resorted once a week."[48] To the chagrin of the Catholic authorities, it was also a place of amusement of another sort—as was a windmill, presumably on the outskirts of the city, where Constable Julien Martineau arrested John Lally and seven vagrant women, all of whom were drinking there together.[49] In Montreal proper, certain green spaces served purposes never intended by urban planners. For instance, the Champ de Mars in the old town was a military ground and a popular promenade for the city's elites during the day and a site of streetwalking and solicitation at night. Vagrants also congregated in the streets and taverns around the military barracks, where soldiers provided them with a source of money in exchange for sex.

City notables were preoccupied with and tormented by the belief that popular-class men and women participated in an array of illicit activities that were hidden by the cover of darkness. From their perspective, night camouflaged the criminal intentions of men such as Edmund Lund, a convicted criminal who reputedly disguised himself by wearing women's clothing, as well as the illicit activities of women such as an unidentified female who, a stranger to the city, apparently wandered the streets at night dressed in men's clothing. When she became ill and was placed under the care of a physician, her gender came to light.[50] Darkness was also seen to obscure "debauchery."

Street lights were supposed to create a safer city. The western part of St. Paul Street in the old city had been lit at dusk since 1815, and here, though not in most of Montreal's streets and roadways, constables and watchmen patrolled regularly, keeping an eye on the businesses of the commercial elite and regulating the sex trade

carried on near the old market. Paradoxically, this "safe zone" left vagrant women more prone to arrest and opened up new possibilities to male ramblers drawn to sites of leisure in search of sexual pleasure.[51] Mary Crechetelli's encounter with Lieutenant John Deacon of the 23rd Regiment of Foot provides a glimpse into the convoluted and perilous street choreography between a prostitute and a rambler. While allegedly walking home at dusk, Crechetelli described being approached by Deacon, who, after paying particular attention to her face when she neared a street lamp in the old city, pursued her until the Haymarket. There he grabbed her by the neck and asked her where she was going. As they passed in front of the mess hall, Deacon invited Crechetelli in, but she refused. He then followed her to Ste-Anne's Market and took from her a bundle of clothes, whereupon she accompanied him to his room, where he attempted, in Crechetelli's own words, "to have charnel [sic] connection with me but he could not succeed from my resistance." Deacon persevered, they had sex, he offered her money, but she refused and soon after left taking with her only a part of the bundle. When Crechetelli returned later to retrieve the rest of her belongings, Deacon accused her of stealing his watch. Although she was charged and the item was retrieved from her residence, she was later found not guilty.[52]

The ritual between prostitute and client could be played out in light and darkness with similar consequences, as the following example illustrates. While John West ran an errand for his master in the St. Lawrence suburbs, he "fell in" with Marguerite Miron and agreed to buy her a drink. By the time he returned to his employer's home that evening, the door was locked, and West, supposedly not wanting to disturb the family, decided to sleep in an outbuilding. Miron, who was accompanied by a male friend, allegedly followed West to the building, where they asked him for more liquor. West told them that he had no money and even suggested to Miron that she search his body to verify it. After they left, West discovered that his silver watch was missing and complained to the police. At court to face a larceny charge, Miron told the presiding justices of the peace and members of the jury that she had furnished sex to West at his request and that he had given her his watch in lieu of money. Although West denied Miron's rendering of events, the jury did not believe him and found her not guilty of larceny.[53] Street lights also functioned to cast a moral light upon "indecency." Notwithstanding the symbolism of Betsey Dunn and François Neau having sexual intercourse under a street light on Notre Dame Street, the illumination of the act made it easy for watchman Antoine Gospel to arrest Dunn for vagrancy.[54] The spotlight on Neau's participation in the act did not lead to his prosecution.

Solidarity among Vagrant Women

Women created a network of female solidarity and forged relationships with men in similar situations as they faced the worst features of vagrancy: competition for food and shelter, for alcohol, and for clients, the illicit nature of their activities, and living "rough" on city streets in a culture of danger arising from both their work and their leisure. In this section I will explore the ways that groups of vagrants lived together outside a physical household. Could, as Anthony Vidler claims, the streets be considered the "dwelling of the outcast poor"?[55]

Female vagrants ambled through urban spaces in groups made up of friends and relatives. Together they sought leisure and the daily necessities of food and shelter, worked in the sex trade, solicited, and were arrested.[56] They also appeared in court and were confined to prison collectively, and in this way, they shared large

parts of their lives. Vagrant women were instrumental in recruiting friends and relatives into the sex trade. Depositions reveal sisters and mothers and daughters working together in the trade. Magdeleine McDonald, who became a well-known prostitute, was from Quebec City. Her family name was Poliquin, but she had informally taken the name of her stepfather, Jean McDonald, when her mother remarried. In 1818, pregnant and a minor, she had married Germain Couture. Her firstborn, Magdeleine, was followed by six more children, three of whom died in infancy. We lose track of the Couture family until the birth of a stillborn baby in Montreal in 1831. Seven years later, Germain was dead, and the two Magdeleines, the widow and her eldest daughter, were working and wandering the streets together. They were arrested in brothels and on city streets. Between 1838 and 1842, police apprehended Magdeleine Couture at least twenty-seven times for prostitution and vagrancy. In all likelihood it was her widowed mother who had initiated her daughter into the sex trade.

Group members sometimes shared the same ethnicity. Police constables arrested a party of Irish women, Mary Burnet, Catharine Morrison, Mrs. Bland, and widow Catharine Raigan, because they had been living together for several months in an abandoned building at the corner of Hospital and St. Alexis Streets. A neighbour, lawyer Peter Rossiter, complained that the house, belonging to merchant Benjamin Demers, had been deemed unfit for human habitation.[57] Other women banded together in mixed groups. Adelaide St-André, Henriette Hamelle, and Peggy Dollar regularly assembled on the Papineau Road, where they solicited men, according to a city butcher by the name of Charles Picard.[58]

These women formed female bonds of mutual dependency that were critical to their survival in ways similar to the "radical community of women" that historian Maria Luddy argues existed among the "wrens of the Curragh."[59] Her study of these women who lived as camp followers on the margins of society near the Curragh army camp in county Kildare in Ireland—prostitutes, vagrants, ex-convicts, and alcoholics—is based on a book written in 1867 by journalist James Greenwood, who went to the wrens to observe and interview these women. Although he described their relationships as familial, Luddy rejects his notion of "family" on the basis that the structure was neither nuclear nor extended and therefore did not fit the Victorian ideal of family organization. She proposes instead that this group of outcast women formed a radical community. Their lives, she contends, were organized around women and children to the exclusion of men. She also draws a rather fascinating parallel between their lives and the convent life of nuns. Vagrant women in Halifax exhibited a solidarity akin to Montreal's female vagabonds. In the face of challenging life circumstances and without the support of men, they lived, worked, drank, and went to court and prison together. Upon release from incarceration, they regrouped to persevere once again on the city streets and nearby green spaces.[60]

In Montreal vagrant women shared whatever resources they had, be it food, shelter, or drink. Ann Crawley, Eliza Ferguson, Eliza Martin, Eliza Taylor, and Mary Mahoney loitered together at the St-Gabriel farm, where they could procure, albeit illegally, shelter and sustenance. They slept in farm buildings, searched for food in surrounding fields and orchards, and milked the cows together.[61] In the city proper, Adelaide St-André and Betsy Lafranchise stole ten loaves of bread from baker John Tassie when he left his cart unattended to deliver bread to customers.[62] Sharing resources had tragic results for some of the women. When prison authorities freed Mary Ann Bothwell and Ann Grimes from the common jail in January 1841, Bothwell used a cheque that she had found to procure liquor for the two of them. On Victoria Road, while under the influence of alcohol, Bothwell lay down on a snow bank, fell asleep, and froze to death.[63]

Living and working together could reduce the risk of aggression or allow women to help each other if violence erupted. When Antoine Dubord-Latourelle rented a portion of his house that he occupied on Sanguinet Street to two widows, he got more than he bargained for. According to Dubord-Latourelle, the two women "debauched his son Charles Dubord dit Latourelle and then kicked him out of their house."[64] The widows Chartrand and Shiller probably understood that there was safety in numbers. Mary Burk, who had accumulated a number of arrests for vagrancy, rented a room in James Robinson's house on Commissioners' Street. When she witnessed him attacking his wife, she went to the police to accuse him of spousal abuse.[65] Vagrant women also fought with those who endeavoured to steal what little they had. Police arrested Antoine Delaunay and his wife Louise Corbeille for petty larceny after they pinched a hat belonging to Marguerite Bleau as she strolled along a street in the Ste-Anne suburb; their attempts to snatch her coat as well failed because Bleau put up such an ardent struggle to keep the coat, an essential piece of clothing in Montreal in late December.[66]

Many women resorted to unlawful means to provide for themselves and others; some were literally sisters in crime. Félicité and Marguerite Bleau worked together as street and brothel prostitutes and occasionally as thieves. In 1839 they confessed to having stolen bank notes from an intoxicated American visitor. Working in tandem, Marguerite enticed him to Angélique Paré's bawdy house, where her sister, Félicité, had sex with him. Together they pinched his money.[67] Within a year of this caper, police arrested them several more times for vagrancy[68] until Marguerite died of tuberculosis during her last incarceration.[69]

Following her sister's death, Félicité Bleau turned to a group of vagrants for companionship. In May 1841 police arrested her and fellow associates Amable Berthier, Augustine Squire, Louise Wagner, Mary Fob, Catharine Murphy, and Mary Dear in a farmer's field on the outskirts of the city.[70] The membership of these groups changed as women died, were arrested and incarcerated, or found alternative shelter and other means to survive. In March 1840 police apprehended Susan Smith along with Maria Reeves, Esther Hewitt, and Susan Murray.[71] Two months later Smith was rearrested, this time with Ellen Lee and Elizabeth Austin.[72]

The bonds that these women formed with each other were undoubtedly complex. As Marilynn Wood Hill has suggested regarding the relationships between New York City prostitutes, these were likely characterized by competition, jealousy, and antagonism, on the one hand, and by female solidarity, on the other. Prostitutes "assumed an emotional centrality in each others' lives, which often led to deep, mutual friendships characterized by strong female bonding and a special sense of solidarity."[73] As I have argued elsewhere, vagrant women in Montreal, like their popular-class and working-class sisters who slandered, threatened, and assaulted their neighbours, also resorted to violence with one another. In February 1827 Catherine Ryan and Sarah Singleton accused fellow vagrants Margaret Perigord and Eliza Robertson of violently assaulting them and stealing Ryan's large red shawl and a plume of black feathers while they were out "strolling" around eight o'clock in the evening near the Bonsecour church in the old city.[74] In another incident, Margaret McGinnis assaulted Elizabeth Reid, wife of John Ross, in her courtyard and attempted to stab her thirteen-year-old son, James Ross. When Reid tried to protect her son, Margaret's sister, Grace, struck Reid with a shovel, wounding her on the head.[75] Struggles

to find food, shelter, drink, and clients, in addition to the illicit nature of their activities and the danger associated with work and leisure, produced tensions and conflict.[76] Whatever sparked a brawl between Jane Hicks, Emélie Gauthier, and Eliza Lewis will probably never be known. High Constable Benjamin Delisle apprehended them at the old market for disturbing the peace by fighting and quarrelling with each other.[77] Their lives were filled with what Françoise Barret-Ducrocq has called "a history made up of contrasts: of impudence and morality, cynicism and tenderness, and cruelty and generosity."[78]

Some were mothers who roamed the streets with their children in circumstances comparable to those of eighteenth-century London, where the homeless included widows and their offspring as well as abandoned married women with young children and infants.[79] One unidentified Montreal woman, in a state of utter destitution, homelessness, and without any means of support, took refuge with her six children in an outbuilding belonging to a Mr. Lloyd.[80] Similarly, Mary Ann Day and her young child were homeless when police arrested them on a wintery Montreal street in January.[81] Others had shelter but roamed the streets in search either of drink or of nourishment for their families. In the process of going door to door to sell clothing that she had stolen from Martin Duval, Jane Hicks confessed to Josephte McFarlane that she had nothing to eat and needed money to buy food for her children.[82] Within a month of this incident, police apprehended Hicks for prostitution. Margaret Delany, whom we met earlier, was a well-known street prostitute when she sought shelter at the police station for herself and her five children in April 1841.[83] A few months later she was released due to her advanced stage of pregnancy: the authorities thought that the prison was an unfit place to give birth.[84] We have no idea what happened to her children, but without waged work and as their sole parent, Margaret Delany tried to keep them with her despite the family's impoverishment. Marguerite Matin also took her son with her to the house of corrections, where she was recommitted for vagrancy.[85]

Historian Luise White contends that women turned to streetwalking because it allowed families to stay together.[86] Yet some deserted their children. In 1831 Julie-Archange Daigneau left her four daughters, Marie Elmire, Archange, Marie Henriette, and Caroline, with her husband, Jean Dérouin, and moved out of their family home. Daigneau had been pregnant and a minor when she married Dérouin in June 1821. Their four daughters were born within the first seven years of marriage. What propelled Daigneau out of the marital bed is not clear. Dérouin claimed that she had simply abandoned him and her children for a life on the streets.[87] A year after she left, he died, presumably in the cholera epidemic. She remained on the streets. What happened to her four daughters, the youngest of whom was only four years old when her father died, is not known. In contrast, the Love family—Andrew, Francis, Matthew, and Maria—survived in the streets precisely because they stayed together and when necessary even served jail time together.[88]

Historians have alluded to family-like relationships existing between groups of vagrants. John Gillis' reconstruction of past families is useful when considering vagrants, for he reminds us that the "house did not occupy the same place in the temporal or spatial imagination that the modern home does. It was a place of the moment, neither anticipating the future nor recalling the past."[89] He argues that the elasticity of the family and the permeability of family relations has allowed the family unit a certain flexibility in meeting the new demands of economic and social transformations and in creating new forms. Most adults before the nineteenth century lived some of their lives in someone else's home or in temporary shelters. They were not

considered homeless but could be part of another household or were "at home" in the fields, markets, streets, local taverns, and in front of the hearths of others. Home thus differed from the increasingly sentimental bourgeois depiction.[90] Similar family solidarity has been noted by historian Judith Fingard among Halifax's mid-nineteenth-century underclass. There a small number of families routinely turned to public asylums and prisons to pass the winter months or find refuge. They also sought admission to the poorhouse during episodes of illness or when aging made it difficult to live on the streets, or they came there to die.[91] A similar use of institutions by families has been described for European cities.[92]

Relationships with Men

Montreal court records and police registers reveal something about the bonds that these women formed with other women in the same situation as themselves as well as about family ties between sisters and mothers and children. In their daily jaunts in public, vagrant women also encountered a variety of men—police constables and watchmen, soldiers, sailors, labourers, artisans, and other vagrant men—with whom they formed relationships. Some men provided female vagrants with protection, shared whatever money, alcohol, and food they had, or scavenged for food and searched for shelter with them. Victoria E. Bynum's study of poor women in the American South reveals that some of them were willing to forsake their reputations in order to establish relationships with "nonrespectable" men in exchange for physical and economic security. In North Carolina, she argues, the rigid colour barrier did not deter women from entering into interracial relationships even though they had to relinquish their status in white society. "At the price of utter condemnation by white society [they] gained greater physical protection—something outcast poor women generally lacked—by crossing the color line."[93]

In Montreal Mary Kelly was impoverished, homeless, and separated from her husband, who had been incarcerated in the city jail, when she found lodging, of a sort, with a vagrant man. His hut, on the beach where he squatted, was "so imperfectly constructed as to be pervious to wind and rain and hardly to deserve the name of a shelter." When she died from hypothermia and malnutrition, her corpse was described as "reduced to the last degree of meagerness and emaciation." Her male companion, profoundly distraught by Mary Kelly's death, was discovered tearfully lamenting her demise.[94] Vagrant women cultivated an array of relationships with men in their leisure and in their working lives. These ranged from the casual to the intimate. They shared poverty and straddled the fine line between criminal activity and self-help. Given the number of the women who were prostitutes, many of these men likely profited from their remuneration in the sex trade. The role that the men played in the business side of street prostitution is unclear. Nevertheless, some of these men and women surely provided sexual and emotional comfort and solace to each other in ways not unlike that furnished in families, especially if they were estranged from their own kin. For others sex was more likely coerced or endured in exchange for a meal, a drink, or security. Thus vagrant women interacted with men as clients, as spouses (legally married or cohabiting), or as protectors in relationships that could be exploitative, combative, congenial, or mutually beneficial.[95]

Historians are beginning to identify such unofficial relationships in a range of times and places. Bronislaw Geremek suggests that people who lived on the margins of society in late medieval Paris forged relationships based on the similarity of their lives, their mobility, and the regularity of meeting the same companions in

their favourite haunts.[96] "For people without hearth or home, the inn provided a haven: not lodgings, but a place to pass the time, a special sort of family circle."[97] Arlette Farge's examination of Paris' criminal court records reveals that men and women who were members of gangs in Paris were often lovers and that some of the women were passed from one man to another. Moreover, both vagrant couples and homeless family members, including siblings, cousins, and nephews, roamed the city streets and green spaces sticking "together for survival through thick and thin."[98] In Montreal married couples were sometimes arrested and charged with vagrancy: police apprehended both Catharine Hicks and her husband Michael Riley for vagrancy;[99] and Louis Bonin and Henriette Mercier were detained by Constable Adelphe Delisle after they created a disturbance in the street.[100] Biddy Noah and Patrick Hanley were not married. They cohabited in a wooden shed—police elected to call it a den of thieves—where men and women gathered to drink.[101] Thomas Rawdon, a shoemaker and proprietor of a house on Williams Street, complained to a justice of the peace that Hugh McLaughlin and Catherine Clarke lived there together outside the bonds of marriage. Clarke, it seems, was already married to Ambroise Nugent.[102]

Cohabiting couples sometimes encountered moral censure from family members and neighbours. William Lemon, Henri Latreille, and Marie-Anne Labonne wanted one Charbonneau and his lover Véronique Fleury arrested for vagrancy because "in keeping Véronique Fleury at home with him, Charbonneau would cause a huge scandal."[103] Similarly, labourer Charles Leclerc asked that police apprehend his daughter and her lover following an argument that he had with Alexis Dumont over her wellbeing. They were, he argued, homeless and "roamed the streets like vagrants."[104] As the brother of brothel-keeper Angélique Leclerc, Charles could appreciate the perils of notoriety. Presumably, he worried about his daughter's welfare as well as his inability to control her behaviour.

Some vagrant women established bonds with soldiers that took the form of long-term, intimate relationships, similar to those that Judith Fingard has described between soldiers and street prostitutes and between soldiers and abandoned wives in Halifax. A number of soldiers' wives who were economically dependent upon their husbands became unofficial wives of replacement soldiers when regiments departed, leaving wives behind.[105] Others turned to prostitution after their spouses' departure. Catharine Daly, who was married to a British soldier of the 37th Regiment, was living in Montreal when he deserted her after being garrisoned at Kingston in Upper Canada. She was arrested for street prostitution some time later.[106] Similarly, when Elizabeth Thomson succumbed to hypothermia and alcohol poisoning, her husband, a soldier of the 10th Regiment, was not present to claim the body or to organize her burial. Funeral arrangements were left to the high constable.[107]

City streets contracted and expanded with soldiers who came to Montreal during episodes of conflict. Such was the case during the War of 1812 and again in 1837 and 1838 when military troops were transferred to Lower Canada to repress the rebellions that were taking place in the region around the city. Soldiers were quartered at the Quebec Barracks in the old town. More than a thousand soldiers lived there at any one time between 1839 and 1854. Most were single or separated from their wives. Historian Elinor Senior contends that only 6 percent of the British soldiers were permitted army rations and barrack lodgings for their families. Most could not afford the cost of transporting their families to Canada, nor support them at their own expense. A soldier wishing to marry had to obtain permission from the captain of his company, who apparently inquired into the charac-ter of the woman before passing the request for marriage on to the commanding officer, who made the final decision.[108]

Many of these soldiers turned to street prostitutes for intimate relations. Prostitutes likely served as informal cultural ambassadors of the city, advising new arrivals about where they could find suitable taverns and leisure activities in Montreal.[109] Catharine Raigan, the widow of soldier Daniel Burke, rented a room in a house near the soldiers' barracks for this purpose.[110] She and other female vagrants depended upon these soldiers as an important source of income. While they received money for their services, some stole from the soldiers when the opportunity arose. They also benefitted from protection against the physical abuse of other men. These paradoxical liaisons were fraught with danger and required extraordinary shrewdness on the part of the women if they were to remain safe. One streetwalker was assaulted so badly by a soldier in front of the home of Justice of the Peace Moses Judah Hayes that the doorstep was "saturated with blood." She and a few companions had been in the company of a group of soldiers in the old town when the incident occurred.[111] Tension management, which historians have argued was part of women's work in the home, was especially important in such difficult life situations.[112] The three prostitutes who accompanied thirty soldiers to Mr. Brechenridge's garden and orchard must have been especially adept at defusing a potentially violent situation. Police officers sent to the site to arrest the women refused in light of the circumstances.[113]

Soldiers who might have domineered vagrant women also used intimidation to prevent their companions' arrests. Subconstable James McGough must have been unnerved by a group of soldiers who rescued a vagrant woman whom he had arrested. In the melee, the female prisoner lost a shawl, which Subconstable John Kinch brought to the station house when he reported the incident.[114] Farmer Pierre Parent also learned how menacing soldiers could be when he complained to police that soldiers and vagrant women regularly stole apples from his orchard. The large number of soldiers who had gathered on his property repelled the constabulary by their threats and acts of violence.[115] Constable Jeremie knew just how dangerous it was to intervene in situations involving soldiers. A soldier stabbed him with a bayonet after he and a group of policemen tried to eject soldiers and vagrant women from a barn on the banks of the Lachine Canal.[116]

Soldiers, popular-class men, and male vagrants resented and resisted the police's interference in their accustomed use of public space; they rescued prisoners, intervened in police matters, and taunted and assaulted them. The constabulary responded to these threats, insults, and assaults by making their own formal complaints to the city's justices of the peace.[117] The ambiguity of such relationships has been noted by Donald Fyson for Montreal and by Bill Bramwell for nineteenth-century Birmingham. In Birmingham, too, police intervention in popular-class street life—informal assembly, loitering, noisy private quarrels, and boisterous drunken behaviour—was unpopular. Men and women were defiant and hostile to this intervention in what were not considered criminal matters, so much so that they assaulted policemen and rescued their prisoners.[118]

Vagrant women also interfered in matters between soldiers, vagrant men, and the police and participated in a variety of illegal activities in ways that speak to their mutual dependence. Emelie Millette smuggled tools into the prison to help Benjamin Johnson break out.[119] This suggests that in Montreal, as in Paris, vagrant women who were paramours of thieves were expected to help them escape from prison if they were incarcerated. They may also have played an important role of influence and support as "repositories of precious information."[120] Some misdemeanours involved furnishing alcoholic beverages for men under dubious circumstances: Margaret Kane was apprehended after supplying liquor to soldiers who were on duty.[121] Emilie Masson smuggled liquor into court to give to the vagrants Belotte and Fournelle, who were at the time prisoners in the dock. They became so intoxicated that they caused a disturbance in the court, so police arrested Masson. The presiding justice of the peace sentenced her to spend the remainder of the session in jail.[122]

At times police arrested women for vagrancy even though they were accessories to crimes of larceny, desertion, or fraud. Jennet L'Huissier was apprehended for hiding Charles Mitchell, who, while on the lam for fraud, had entrusted her with a considerable amount of money that he had obtained illegally. According to Mitchell, "she was much attached to him and the only woman with whom he had been since he was in the country."[123] Female vagrants also helped men to perpetrate violent crimes such as highway robbery. Betsey Robertson and Eliza Martin allegedly accosted pedlar James Smith while he was walking on the Champs de Mars. When he first refused to give up his money to two soldiers, Robertson and Martin pinned him to the ground, rifled his pockets, and took a purse containing bank flutes and money.[124] Police detained Mary Molloy and charged her with vagrancy for enticing a soldier to desert. Both Molloy and soldier John Hunter had managed to travel as far as Laprairie before they were apprehended.[125] Since deserting soldiers had to keep ahead of the authorities in order to avoid arrest, their illicit status encouraged a dependence upon their female companions. A party of constables from the west and east stations was organized to proceed to Griffin's farm to scour the woods and arrest all vagrants and soldiers "who by their tattered and other suspicious appearances may be considered deserters."[126]

Vagrant women took stock of opportunities and constraints in order to manoeuvre around oppressive circumstances and formed relationships with women and men who were often in similar situations. Together they struggled to survive on the margins of city life. And in this way, they persevered until other prospects materialized. They established bonds of mutual dependence to help get them through a day, a night, or a season.

Conclusion

In early-nineteenth-century Montreal, female vagrants inhabited a harsh, illicit, and dangerous world. They did so with sisters, mothers, children, and other kin, sometimes in communities of women and at other times in the company of male vagrants and soldiers. Whatever the constellation, they formed mutually dependent relationships in order to search for shelter, food, comfort, and protection. Consistently mindful of the risk of injury both at work and at leisure, they navigated public space in groups to reduce the danger. Branded nonrespectable poor, the choices that they could make were limited, but by sharing resources and by resorting to prostitution and to illegal means to find food and shelter, some managed. The competition for clients, food, and shelter, aggravated by hunger, cold, alcohol abuse, and illness, bred antagonism between vagrants. It also led to a female network of assistance. Some formed complex alliances with men in similar situations, walking a fine line between the danger of abuse and their desire for emotional and physical security. Occupying the same urban spaces, contending with the same abject poverty, and trying to solve problems of survival on a daily basis, vagrant women and men forged unique relationships.

There is no place for sentimentality when considering how vagrant women found the means to "rough it" on the streets. Mothers sought food and shelter for their children; friends and relatives looked after each other. Vagrants formed communities of women with whom they could share resources and services. Although some women provided men with sex, solace, and the potential for emotional relationships, while these men in turn furnished protection, money, and the same potential for intimacy, sex was also something to be put up with in order to survive. The manner in which these women lived demonstrates the futility of making hard divisions between family and work, public and private, and dwellings and the street.

Notes

I would like to thank Tamara Myers and Bettina Bradbury for their critique of this chapter.

1 Jean-Claude Robert, *Atlas historique de Montréal* (Montreal: Editions Libre Expression. 1994), 79.

2 Jules Vallès, *La Rue à Londres* (1866; reprint, Paris, 1951), quoted in Françoise Barret-Ducrocq, *Love in the Time of Victoria: Sexuality and Desire among Working-Class Men and Women in Nineteenth-Century London* (New York: Penguin, 1991), 9.

3 Arlette Farge, *Fragile Lives: Violence, Power and Solidarity in Eighteenth-Century Paris* (Cambridge, MA: Harvard University Press, 1993), 11.

4 William Henry Atherton, *Montreal, 1535–1914*, vol. 2, *Under British Rule, 1760–1914* (Montreal: S.J. Clarke, 1914), 131.

5 *Montreal Herald,* 17 May 1817.

6 Linda Woodbridge, *Vagrancy, Homelessness, and English Renaissance Literature* (Chicago: University of Illinois Press, 2001), 6.

7 Archives nationales du Québec à Montréal (hereafter ANQM), E17, TL3O S1 SS11, Presentment of the Grand Jury, 18 January 1840.

8 Donald Fyson, "Eating in the City: Diet and Provisioning in Early Nineteenth-Century Montreal," MA thesis, Department of History, McGill University, 1989, 89.

9 Petition by widow Joseph Perrault, *Journal of Lower Canada House of Assembly* 25, 21 (February 1816): 298–302.

10 Woodbridge, *Vagrancy,* 4.

11   *Montreal Gazette,* 15 September 1835.

12   What signified the appearance of self-support varied according to race as well as to gender. Linda K. Kerber, *No Constitutional Right to Be Ladies: Women and the Obligations of Citizenship* (New York: Hill and Wang, 1998), 51–55.

13   Police arrested Elisabeth Degane and her daughters, Catherine and Emilie, on at least four occasions for receiving stolen goods. ANQM, E17, TL32 S1 SS1, Indictment of Isabelle Marcotte and Joseph Moses, 18 August 1824; indictment of Catherine Marcotte, 27 August 1824; Deposition of James Benny, 14 October 1826; and Deposition of Marguerite Boisjolie and F-X Mareille, 18 October 1826.

14   ANQM, E17, TL30 S1 SS11, Presentment of the Grand Jury, 2 October 1825.

15   ANQM, E17, TL32 S1 SS1, Deposition of Henry Herbert, 18 November 1835.

16   ANQM, E17, TL32 S1 SS1, Deposition of George Bourne, 21 June 1838.

17   ANQM, E17, TL32 S1 SS1, Deposition of Thomas Quinn and Thomas Busby, 10 July 1824.

18   Library and Archives Canada (LAC), RG4 B 14, Police Registers no. 34, 21 April 1841.

19   ANQM, E17, TL32 S1 SS1, Deposition of Lucie Rolland, 10 July 1824.

20   ANQM, E17, TL32 S1 SS1, Deposition of Pierre Beaudry, 27 July 1839.

21   *Montreal Gazette,* 21 July 1836.

22   Janice Harvey, "Dealing with 'the Destitute and the Wretched': The Protestant House of Industry and Refuge in Nineteenth-Century Montreal," *Journal of the Canadian Historical Association* (2001): 73–94 at 74.

23   ANQM, E17, TL32 S1 SS1, Presentment of the Grand Jury, 19 January 1821.

24   ANQM, E17, TL32 S1 SS1, Presentment of the Grand Jury, 19 January 1821. *Journal of the Lower Canada House of Assembly,* 15 February 1823.

25   Lynn Hollen Lees, *The Solidarities of Strangers: The English Poor Laws and the People, 1700–1948* (Cambridge and New York: Cambridge University Press, 1998), 37, 71.

26   John O'Connor, *The Workhouses of Ireland: The Fate of Ireland's Poor* (Dublin: Anvil Books, 1995), 165.

27   The small number of these women who received assistance were usually widows, and in some cases their children or spouses, and had distanced themselves sufficiently in time from prostitution. See Mary Anne Poutanen, "'To Indulge Their Carnal Appetites': Prostitution in Early Nineteenth-Century Montreal, 1810–1842," PhD thesis, Department of History, Université de Montréal, 1996, 93–94.

28   *Montreal Gazette,* 5 October 1833.

29   *Montreal Gazette,* 23 January 1836.

30   Between 1810 and 1836 at least seventy-one homeless women were apprehended as a measure to protect them from death due to starvation and hypothermia, a further feature of the violence associated with living on the streets. In 1837, the court introduced printed forms, so information of this sort is no longer obtainable from court records after this date. Police registers disclose that the practice of providing shelter to vagrants continued throughout the late 1830s and early 1840s.

31   LAC, RG4 B 14, Police Registers no. 38, 18 December 1836.

32   ANQM, E17, TL32 S26 SS1, Coroner's Report, 25 November 1841.

33   *Montreal Transcript,* 21 December 1841,

34   ANQM, E17, TL32 S26 SS1, Coroner's Report, 25 October 1825.

35   Reprinted in the *Montreal Gazette,* 22 October 1836.

36   Lucia Zedner, *Women, Crime, and Custody in Victorian England* (New York: Oxford University Press, 1991), 5.

37   Poutanen, "'To Indulge Their Carnal Appetites,'" 302–4.

38   Judith Fingard's description of the Halifax prison, with its heated wards, clean bedding, and nourishing food, provides a contrast to its Montreal equivalent. *The Dark Side of Life in Victorian Halifax* (Porters Lake, NS: Pottersfield Press, 1989), 48–55.

39   Marcela Aranguiz, *Vagabonds et sans abris à Montréal: Perception et prise en charge de l'errance, 1840–1925* (Montreal: Regroupement des chercheurs et chercheures en histoire des travailleurs et travailleuses du Québec [RCHTQJ], 2000).

40   ANQM, E17, TL32 S1 SS1, Presentment of the Grand Jury, 19 January 1842.

41   *Montreal Herald,* 19 December 1818.

42   ANQM, E17, TL32 S1 SS1, Calendar of the House of Correction, 21 January 1826.

43   ANQM, E17, TL32 S26 SS1, Coroner's Report, 21 July 1843.

44 No criminal statistics were kept by authorities during this period. Donald Fyson's study of offences brought before the justices of the peace reveal that 4 percent of the cases between 1810 and 1830 at quarter sessions involved public order; 40 percent of convictions at weekly sessions concerned public order for the years 1810 to 1829. Donald Fyson, "Criminal Justice, Civil Society and the Local State: The Justices of the Peace in the District of Montreal, 1764–1830," PhD thesis, Department of History, Université de Montréal, 1995, 288. My examination of the police court registers for the years 1838 to 1842 shows that of the 16,680 cases coming before the magistrates, nearly three-quarters of the charges pertained to public-order infractions. The quarter or so other cases involved crimes such as assault and battery, larceny, and desertion. Of the 3,457 women charged with public-order offences, more than half (54 percent) were arrested for being "vagrants, loitering, loose, idle, and disorderly, and streetwalkers." Poutanen, "'To Indulge Their Carnal Appetites,'" 200–2.

45 Farge, *Fragile Lives,* 138.

46 LAC, RG4 B 14, Police Registers no. 31, 3 September 1940.

47 Fingard, *The Dark Side of Life,* 39–40.

48 Joseph Bouchette, *A Topographical Description of the Province of Lower Canada, with Remarks upon Upper Canada and on the Relative Connexion of Both Provinces with the USA* (London: W. Faden, 1815), 161.

49 ANQM, E17, TL32 S1 SS1, Deposition of Julien Martineau, 5 October 1833.

50 *Montreal Herald,* 20 May 1820.

51 It was no coincidence that land had been set aside next door to the Collège de Montréal for a proposed house of correction. Joseph Bouchette, *A Topographical Description,* 38–39; Jane Rendell, "Displaying Sexuality: Gendered Identities and the Early Nineteenth-Century Street," in *Images of the Street: Planning, Identity and Control in Public Space,* ed. Nicholas R. Fyfe, 75–91 (New York: Routledge, 1998), 79.

52 ANQM, E17, TL32 S1 SS1, Deposition of John Deacon, 17 January 1842.

53 *Montreal Herald,* 2 September 1826.

54 ANQM, E17, TL32 S1 SS1, Deposition of Antoine Gospel, 30 November 1829.

55 Anthony Vidler, "The Scenes of the Street: Transformations in Ideal and Reality, 1750–1871," in *On Streets,* ed. Standford Anderson, 29–111 (Cambridge, MA: MIT Press, 1978), 73.

56 I analyzed the number of streetwalkers who were arrested alone, in pairs, and in groups between 1810 and 1836. Seventy percent of these women were arrested with others. After 1836 the courts adopted printed forms that accommodated the name of only one woman per document, making it impossible to extend the analysis beyond 1836.

57 ANQM, E17, TL32 S1 SS1, Deposition of Peter N. Rossiter, 10 July 1838.

58 ANQM, E17, TL32 S1 SS1, Deposition of Charles Picard, 16 June 1836.

59 Maria Luddy, "An Outcast Community: The 'Wrens of the Curragh,'" *Women's History Review* 1, 3 (1992): 341–55.

60 Fingard, *The Dark Side of Life,* 113.

61 LAC, RG4 B 14, Police Registers no. 59, 15 June 1842.

62 ANQM, E17, TL32 S1 SS1, Deposition of John Tassie, Quarter Session Documents, 27 November 1835.

63 ANQM, E17, TL32 S26 SS1, Coroner's Report, 2 February 1841.

64 ANQM, E17, TL32 S1 SS1, Deposition of Antoine Dubord dit Latourelle, 19 November 1841.

65 ANQM, E17, TL32 S1 SSI, Deposition of Mary Burk, 3 September 1832.

66 ANQM, E17, TL32 S1 SS1, Deposition of Marguerite Bleau, 29 December 1836; and Indictment, 10 January 1837.

67 ANQM, E17, TL32 S1 SS1, Deposition of Elizabeth Gallagher, 18 February 1839.

68 LAC, RG4 B 14, Police Registers no. 55, 9 May 1840 and 6 June 1840.

69 ANQM, E17, TL32 S26 SS1, Coroner's Report, 1 December 1840.

70 LAC, RG4 B 14, Police Registers no. 59, 26 May 1841.

71 LAC, RG4 B 14, Police Registers no. 55, 9 March 1840.

72 LAC, RG4 B 14, Police Registers no. 55, 2 May 1840.

73 Marilynn Wood Hill, *Their Sisters' Keepers: Prostitution in New York City, 1830–1870* (Los Angeles: University of California Press, 1993), 296–97.

74 ANQM, E17, TL32 S1 SS1, Deposition of Catherine Ryan, 16 February 1827.

75 ANQM, E17, TL32 S1 SS1, Deposition of Elizabeth Reid, 1 December 1828.

76 See Mary Anne Poutanen, "Images du danger dans les archives judiciaires: Comprendre la violence et la vagabondage dans un centre urbain du début du 19e siècle, Montréal, 1810–1842," *Revue d'histoire de l'Amérique française* 55 (Winter 2002): 381–405.

77 ANQM, E17, TL32 S1 SS1, Deposition of Benjamin Delisle, 31 October 1831.

78 Barret-Ducrocq, *Love in the Time of Victoria,* 183.

79 Nicholas Rogers, "Policing the Poor in Eighteenth-Century London: The Vagrancy Laws and Their Administration," *Histoire sociale/Social History* 24 (May 1991): 127–47 at 135.

80 LAC, RG4 B 14, Police Registers no. 61, 22 October 1840.

81 ANQM, E17, TL32 S1 SS1, Deposition of Phillip Ryan, 22 January 1842.

82 ANQM, E17, TL32 S1 SS1, Deposition of Josephte McFarlane, 5 January 1831.

83 LAC, RG4 B 14, Police Registers no. 34, 27 April 1841.

84 ANQM, E17, TL32 S1 SS1, Deposition of William Harris, 15 June 1841.

85 ANQM, E17, TL32 S1 SS11, Quarter Sessions Register, 30 October 1815.

86 Luise White, "Prostitutes, Reformers, and Historians," *Criminal Justice History* 6 (1985): 206–11.

87 ANQM, E17, TL32 S1 SS1, Deposition of Jean Dérouin, 26 October 1831.

88 ANQM, E17, TL32 S1 SS1, Deposition of Thomas Adams, 8 November 1840.

89 John R. Cults, *A World of Their Own Making: Myth, Ritual, and the Quest for Family Values* (Cambridge, MA: Harvard University Press, 1996), 37.

90 Ibid., 36–39.

91 Fingard, *The Dark Side of Life,* 77–85.

92 Joachim Schlör, *Nights in the Big City: Paris, Berlin, London, 1840–1930* (London: Reaktion Books, 1998), 148–49.

93 Victoria E. Bynum, *Unruly Women: The Politics of Social and Sexual Control in the Old South* (Chapel Hill: University of North Carolina Press, 1992), 93.

94 *Montreal Herald,* 9 October 1821.

95 Wood Hill, *Their Sisters' Keepers,* 292.

96 Bronislaw Geremek, *The Margins of Society in Late Medieval Paris* (Cambridge and New York: Cambridge University Press, 1987).

97 Ibid., 278.

98 Farge, *Fragile Lives,* 154–56.

99 ANQM, E17, TL32 S1 SS1, Deposition of Joseph Auger, 8 May 1833.

100 ANQM, E17, TL32 S1 SS1, Deposition of Adelphe Delisle, 21 July 1824.

101 ANQM, E17, TL32 S1 SS1, Deposition of Henry Lesperance, 9 November 1833.

102 ANQM, E17, TL32 S1 SS1, Deposition of Thomas Rawdon, 28 June 1841.

103 ANQM, E17, TL32 S1 SS1, Deposition of William Lemon, Henri Latreille, and Marie-Anne Labonne, 24 April 1815.

104 ANQM, E17, TL32 S1 SS1, Deposition of Charles Leclerc 26 July 1825.

105 Fingard, *The Dark Side of Life,* 98.

106 ANQM, E17, TL32 S1 SS1, Deposition of James King, 2 July 1824.

107 *Montreal Gazette,* 11 November 1816.

108 Elinor K. Senior, *British Regulars in Montreal: An Imperial Garrison, 1832–1854* (Montreal: McGill-Queen's University Press, 1981), 148–49.

109 A number of tavern-keepers encouraged prostitutes to congregate in their establishments as a way to attract customers, For example, Chief Constable Fitzpatrick accused Nolan Millette of harbouring prostitutes in his tavern "for the accommodation of soldiers," LAC, RG4 B 14, Police Registers no. 64, 11 April 1842.

110 ANQM, E17, TL32 S1 SS1, Deposition of Thomas Earl and Mary Fraser, 11 March 1841.

111 ANQM, E17, TL32 S1 SS1, Deposition of Moses Judah Hayes, 11 December 1841.

112 Bettina Bradbury, *Working Families: Age, Gender, and Daily Survival in Industrializing Montreal* (Toronto: McClelland and Stewart, 1993), 178–80.

113 LAC, RG4 B 14, Police Registers no. 33, 27 May 1840.

114 LAC, RG4 B 14, Police Registers no. 64, 8 December 1841.

115 LAC, RG4 B 14, Police Registers no. 58, 19 September 1839.

116 LAC, RG4 B 14, Police Registers no. 38, 29 September 1839.

117 Allan Greer, "The Birth of the Police in Canada," in *Colonial Leviathan: State Formation in*

Mid-Nineteenth-Century Canada, ed. Allan Greer and Ian Radforth, 17–49 (Toronto: University of Toronto Press, 1992), 25; Fyson, "Criminal Justice, Civil Society and the Local State," 307–8; Poutanen, "Images du danger," 397.

118 Fyson, "Criminal Justice, Civil Society and the Local State"; Bill Bramwell, "Public Space and Local Communities: The Example of Birmingham, 1840–1880," in *Urbanising Britain: Essays on Class and Community in the Nineteenth Century,* ed. Gerry Kearns and Charles W.J. Withers, 31–54 (Cambridge and New York: Cambridge University Press, 1992), 43.

119 *Montreal Gazette,* 2 November 1826.

120 Farge, *Fragile Lives,* 161–62.

121 LAC, RG4 B 14, Police Registers no. 34, 13 June 1841.

122 *Montreal Gazette,* 27 February 1834.

123 ANQM, E17, TL32 S1 SS1, Deposition of Jennet L'Huissier, 7 May 1841.

124 ANQM, E17, TL32 S1 SS1, Deposition of James Smith, 8 September 1829.

125 ANQM, E17, TL32 S1 SS1, Deposition of William McKay, 8 July 1824.

126 LAC, RG4 B 14, Police Registers no. 31, 7 August 1841.

Reciprocal Work Bees and the Meaning of Neighbourhood

CATHARINE ANNE WILSON

The reciprocal work "bee" deserves to be understood as a vital and characteristic element of nineteenth-century rural Ontario. It was as much a part of Ontario folk culture as the potlatch was for West Coast Natives, and much more common than the charivari.[1] The bee was an integral part of the farm economy and an important social resource. Through reciprocal work, individual farm families who lacked self-sufficiency in labour and skills were given a measure of insurance against hard times while they established and maintained a workable farm unit. The bee was also a key component in the structuring, operation, and definition of neighbourhood.

The study of reciprocal work bees takes us directly into the construct and concept of neighbourhood. Neighbourhood is not generally understood as part of the larger social system, but tends to be treated peripherally in relation to such categories as class, ethnicity, and gender, if it is not ignored entirely.[2] As such, a disjunction exists between the family unit and the wider world. By examining the structure and process of reciprocal work bees, we reach a deeper understanding of the relationship between the individual, the family, and the larger social order. Neighbourhood, however, is a nebulous idea. Most commonly it is recognized as comprising people at a certain time who live near each other. In this article it goes beyond this spatial and temporal definition to include interaction, process,

and a sense of belonging.[3] In the nineteenth century, neighbourhood was not just the people who lived near you but the basis for economic activity, social support, and the organization of day-to-day living. Though some settlements may have been made up of independent and isolated families that kept to themselves, or tightly knit groups united by ethnicity and religion, others used the bee to develop highly effective networks of interaction. At the bee, people from diverse cultural backgrounds came together and were incorporated according to their genealogy, wealth, age, gender, and skills. Thus the bee helped to create a structural and cognitive order in the neighbourhood. Like the potlatch, it was not only an economic and social exchange but also a process through which shared values and a collective identity were created and communicated. Like the charivari, the bee was a mechanism of social integration identifying those who belonged and those who did not. As such, neighbourhood might, but did not necessarily, include the generosity and kindness that came with "neighbourliness."

This study offers a different perspective of the bee. Too often it has been eulogized as the epitome of the selfless communal ideal. Whether seen through the eyes of storytellers and journalists who lament the passing of the "old rural values" of community, kindliness, and generosity or academics with their own laments, the bee has come to symbolize and celebrate the

Catharine Anne Wilson, "Reciprocal Work Bees and the Meaning of Neighbourhood," *Canadian Historical Review* 82, 3 (September 2001): 431–64. Reprinted with permission of the University of Toronto Press Incorporated (www.utp. journals.com).

good old days of neighbourliness in an age of growing individualism and commercialism. Rural sociologists and anthropologists, often coming from a background of the urban/folk continuum, view the decline of cooperative labour as part of the larger process of modernization and individualization of society. Marxist historians view reciprocal labour as evidence of the moral economy and the antithesis to capitalistic farming systems. Feminist historians depict cooperative labour such as the quilting bee as part of the female world of support, equality, mutual dependency, and deep affection—values not duly appreciated in a male culture of independence and competition.[4] By examining how the bee actually functioned in an economic and social sense in the nineteenth century, we can better understand how the rural neighbourhood emerged, how informal labour markets were part of the social whole, and how the bee fit into the broader culture of Ontario. The bee was not the simple embodiment of a selfless communal ideal; it was a complex and sometimes paradoxical phenomenon that played an important role in a rural society of private property and social hierarchy.

"Busy as Bees"

What settlers called a "bee" was a neighbourly gathering where people worked together industriously with the bustle of bees in a hive.[5] Bees occurred with regularity and frequency throughout the calendar year in early Ontario. In the spring, bees were called for raising houses and barns, shearing sheep, picking the burrs from fleece, ploughing and dragging the land for planting, and piling logs to clear the land. In the hot, dry days of summer, farm folk gathered together at bees to clean water courses, mow and cradle hay, shell peas, and cut grain. Once the busy harvest season slowed down, a new round of bees began.

There were bees for spreading manure, husking corn, ploughing fields, picking and peeling apples, and hunting squirrels and pigeons. Fanning and threshing bees were often held in the barn in the winter months. This was also the time when neighbourhoods turned their energies to processing clothing and food. Bees for butchering livestock, plucking fowl, spinning wool, and sewing quilts and carpets enlivened the long winter months, and sawing and chopping bees kept the family warm and ready for the next round of clearing and building in the spring.[6]

Though bees were not daily or even universal events, many farm families found their year liberally sprinkled with such occasions. The fall could be a particularly busy beeing time. In a period of ten days in September 1869, the Michie family of Reach Township went to a cradling bee, a raking bee, a threshing bee, a quilting bee, a dunging bee, and two binding bees.[7] On occasion, double-bees were held, where, for example, the men might have a chopping bee while the women quilted, or a quilting during the day was followed by a paring bee in the evening. Indeed, Susanna Moodie, who was no fan of such occasions, complained that "people in the woods have a craze for giving and going to bees, and run to them with as much eagerness as a peasant runs to a racecourse or a fair."[8] This was particularly true of the early settlement days when clearing and building were at their height. Then "the call of the woodman, the falling timber, the merry 'Yo-heave' of the Raising Bee, could...be heard on every side," and the fires from logging bees lit up the whole sky at night.[9] As settlement moved inland, so too did beeing activity. Well into the twentieth century, barn-raising bees were still being held in Temiskaming District, "Ontario's New Frontier."[10] By then, in the older more established parts of the province, bees, in general, were declining in number. The logging and raising bees of the early settlement days had given over to threshing and silo-filling bees of a more intensive mixed-farming system. Bees, therefore, were an integral part of the farming year and the social calendar of many Ontario farm families well into the twentieth century.

"The Still Bee Gathers No Honey": The Economics of the Bee

Reciprocal work was typical of all agricultural communities, but especially frontier areas where land was readily available and capital and labour were in short supply. In early Ontario, few settlers had cash with which to hire labourers. With land readily available, labourers were costly and hard to come by, especially in the backwoods.[11] Most families, particularly those with young children, were simply unable to perform all the tasks themselves without assistance from neighbours. This was especially true of chopping, logging, and building, which required special skills and immense physical strength. As cultivated acreages increased, it was also true for certain periods of the year such as harvest time, when work demands reached their peak and time was of the essence. By holding a bee, individual farming families who were not self-sufficient in terms of meeting the demands of peak labour periods in the year or possessing all the skills and equipment required to establish a home and farm could attain those ends. The bee was, in effect, an informal labour exchange, part of the hidden economy overlooked by census takers and economic historians. It was a forum for labour in a variety of ways. It served to concentrate labour for those events requiring large numbers. It provided families with extra labour in emergencies that might never be fully repaid. But, most often,

it simply redistributed labour over time so that families had more at certain times in the year, in their personal settlement history, or in their life course, a debt that was then fully repaid at a later date.

The beeing phenomenon, therefore, was an essential part of the farm economy. Through reciprocal labour, the farm family was able to create capital. It was also better able to cope with risks. With a low standard of living, no insurance, and the possibility of sudden and unexpected calamities, it was essential to be on good terms with your neighbours. This was especially true in newly settled areas where population was highly dispersed and kin networks were not yet established. If your barn burnt, your fields were flooded, or your husband was killed, you needed to be able to rely on reciprocal aid rather than face these disasters on your own. If you were not part of this neighbourhood exchange system, the backwoods could be a frightening, risky, even hostile place.[12]

Certain jobs required the calling of a bee for reasons of economy and efficiency. Clearing land—chopping, logging, burning, and fencing—could be done by hired labour before mid-century for £3–£4 currency per acre.[13] Most settlers, cash-poor, knew this cost was an imprudent way to spend what little money they had. The goal was to clear enough land as soon as possible for a self-sustaining farm (about 30 to 50 cleared acres). Achieving this aim on one's own was a task that took nearly a lifetime, as the average clearing rate was 1.23–1.55 acres a year.[14] By the time a man was ready to plant the first acre he had cleared, it had already begun to grow over with weeds. Settlers were anxious to meet the cleared acreage required of settlement duties (5 cleared acres in the first year), make their farm self-sustaining, and get in their field crops by early September. Besides being time-consuming, clearing the land was extremely strenuous and dangerous work requiring considerable but rare skill with the axe. It was almost imperative to call a bee for hoisting and manoeuvring the heavy logs into piles to burn. In a single day, a bee of twenty men with five yoke of oxen could log 5 acres (a whole field), the cost being plenty of whiskey, some simple food, and work in return.[15] Likewise, erecting log buildings was a job requiring the strength and skill of more than one or two people. Time was of the essence, for families needed shelter from the cold, and barns needed to be ready to house crops and livestock come the fall. It took about sixteen men and four yoke of oxen to hoist up and connect the heavy logs of a house or barn. According to the Emigration Questionnaire conducted in 1840–1, to hire labour to erect a simple one-room log hut cost from £4–£15 currency. Such a price was prohibitive for most settlers. As respondents from the Canada Company District and Bathurst pointed out, the usual custom was for neighbours to call a bee, which cost only meat and drink estimated to be about £2 currency.[16]

Other bees were called because the chores were time-consuming and monotonous and needed to be accomplished with greater speed than one family could muster. Harvesting provided one such example. Winter wheat ripened just before barley and often overlapped with it, making the harvest a particularly busy time. Labourers were hard to find, and to hire a harvester cost five to six shillings currency per day.[17] By inviting eight neighbours to a threshing bee, 250 bushels could be hauled in while good weather prevailed, then threshed and made ready for market.[18] Once fanning mills and then threshing machines began being hired by the hour or the day, households could maximize their financial investment by calling a bee to bring back loads of grain as quickly as possible. Bees also made more efficient use of time in the production of household goods. Ill-prepared

for the onslaught of winter, new settlers knitted and wove yarn to keep large families warm outside in the bracing cold and cozy inside when the fires grew low. Sewing, knitting, and spinning in the volumes required was tedious, time-consuming, and labour-intensive work best done in the daylight. These hours, however, were just when children and chores demanded attention. As much as 60 yards of linen could be manufactured at one bee, seventeen scanes of woollen yarn spun, or an entire quilt quilted.[19] Moreover, some jobs, such as husking corn or peeling apples, were simply so mind-numbing and irksome that the competitive spirit and sociability of the bee were needed to spur people on to work to their full potential. At these bees, partying and working were easily and happily combined.

Disasters such as illness, irregular rains, late occupancy of a farm, or enforced absence often meant that a backlog of work accumulated. Bees might be called to help a sick neighbour harvest a crop or cut a winter supply of wood.[20] This kind of bee was a form of charity and was functionally distinct from the more routine annual work bees. Belonging to a regular circle of reciprocal labour was a source of insurance. There was considerable security in knowing that many people owed you favours and that you could call upon them in time of need.

In this manner, reciprocal work furthered the economic growth of individual families, the community, and the province. As Doug McCalla asserts in his economic history of Upper Canada: "If the provincial economy must be summarized in terms of a single, pre-eminent product, the farms themselves were its chief accomplishment."[21] Clearing land and erecting farm buildings were the most important elements in this extensive growth and capital creation. In the process of creating farms, reciprocal work bees made families structurally dependent on their neighbours. Such patterns of dependence may have created neighbourhoods that were self-sufficient even when individual farmers were not.[22] Furthermore, bees helped to create the basic physical infrastructure of community life, as they were frequently called to erect mills, churches, and schools.[23]

Bees were also an important part of the exchange economy of early Ontario. A tendency exists for scholars of nineteenth-century Ontario to place too much emphasis on wheat exports and, thus, the importance of cash in the economy. The economy was much more complex, involving a system of exchange that included not only cash but also the barter of goods that the family produced and the credit that settlers extended to neighbours and received in return. Indeed, anything that "earned credit in the local economy...would help to sustain farm making."[24] Certainly the giving and receiving of labour as found in the custom of bees was a part of this exchange system.

Like most significant interaction, an accounting process was at work. It may have been subtle and hidden beneath the rhetoric of neighbourliness, but it was present nevertheless. Participation was part of an exchange of labour, skills, equipment, information, hospitality, and good will. Reciprocal work operated much like a bank, in which all made their deposits and were then entitled to make their withdrawals or acquire small loans. One could even attain personal credit for the contributions made by ancestors or close relatives. It was possible to borrow and then abscond, but most settled families probably contributed and received in equal quantities. Was beeing, however, viewed by the participants as a business transaction or, in an attempt to make sense of this phenomenon, are we projecting our twentieth-century capitalist values on the past? The farm diaries do not clarify the mentality at work. On the one hand, the researcher senses that farmers who did not trust a mental system of checks and balances began their diaries as a way of keeping track of bees and other forms of reciprocal labour. Bees were frequently recorded and clearly identified as such. Walter Beatty, near Brockville, carefully noted the participant, the location, and the type of bee his family attended. For example, on 18 September 1849 his entry reads, "Jock goes to George Toes Dung Bee." Return labour was just as carefully accounted. For example, on 24 May 1849 he wrote, "Thomas Davis sent his horses and son to Plow."[25] When W.F. Munro gave advice to farmers on calculating their costs in the backwoods, he reminded them to "take into account the 'bees.'"[26] It was clearly not as strict an accounting, however, as we might expect. When costs were itemized, they were rarely given in monetary terms, but were generally a day's work for a day's work. But the rule had to be flexible. Inequalities were bound to exist—someone would have a bigger field to harvest, a smaller pile of wood to chop. A family raising a frame barn and having seventy people at the bee would not be expected to attend seventy bees in return. The major players might be repaid with labour, the skilled framer paid cash, and the others paid with the feast and frolic that followed. Clearly they did not have a strict accounting, but it was understood that the same effort would be returned and, in the end, a redistribution of skills, equipment, labour, and hospitality would occur.[27]

Reciprocal work, therefore, played an integral role in the exchange economy, assisting individual farm families to establish a workable farm unit and insure against hard times. In this manner, it contributed to the extensive growth of the larger provincial economy.

"He That Handles Honey Shall Feel It Cling to His Fingers": The Influence of Association

Beyond contributing to the economic structure of neighbourhood, the bee was a social resource.

In the early settlement period, with a scarcity of religious and educational institutions and with kin networks stretching back generations, this factor was especially important. The need to cooperate brought people of diverse backgrounds and potentially divisive lines of affiliation together. The bee provided the mechanism for social integration and bonding. Each and every individual raising or quilting can be viewed as an interaction episode where patterns of association and meaning were confirmed and sometimes initiated or reshaped.[28] By participating and abiding by the rules as they were understood, people of various ages, classes, genders, skills, and experiences were incorporated into the group.

A code of behaviour developed regarding communal labour that extended beyond a mere accounting system to encompass social relations. Those giving advice to new settlers urged them to take heed that every favour conferred required a return favour. As Catharine Parr Traill, a leading authority on life in the backwoods, told her readers, "It is, in fact regarded in the light of a debt of honour; you cannot be forced to attend a bee in return, but no one that can does refuse, unless from urgent reasons; and if you do not find it possible to attend in person you may send a substitute in a servant or in cattle, if you have a yoke." Though this might be an inconvenience, this "debt of gratitude ought to be cheerfully repaid."[29] This generalized reciprocity, "I'll help you with something later," implied a certain degree of trust and closeness. The request to return the effort at another bee could be met in three ways: accept it, discharge the debt later, and reinforce the bonds; accept to return the favour in another form, maybe discharge the debt, and reinforce the bonds; or refuse to attend, renege on your repayment, and risk breaking the social bond. Few risked exclusion from the system altogether because alienating your neighbours could be costly financially and socially.[30]

Because of this obligatory reciprocity, work groups could become highly stable among a core of persistent farmers, or even last for a generation or more.[31] It was unlikely that all labour obligations would be repaid in the same season, but they might linger for years, cementing and lengthening the lines of obligation, especially among people who shared the same values of hard work, neighbourliness, and trust. The stability of the group was essential to mutual aid. As such, the self-interest of individual families conjoined with the shared interests of the neighbourhood.

Constant social contact and mutual dependency did not necessarily imply deep affection, as work groups could be torn asunder by a serious accident or quarrels between families. Tensions simmering beneath the surface of neighbourhood life frequently erupted at bees, especially those where whiskey was liberally served. Patrick Dunigan, for example, who had accused a neighbour of stealing his valuable oak tree, was stripped and tortured with hot irons by his neighbours at a bee. Hatred between Patrick Farrell and James Donnelly Sr over possession of 50 acres culminated at a bee in June 1857 when Donnelly killed Farrell with a handspike.[32] Such violence, even verbal disagreements, acquired significance in the rumour mill. Someone drunk, disorderly, uncooperative, or insulting was clearly breaking the code of neighbourliness and was a nuisance, if not a serious liability, to completing the job efficiently and without incident. Such behaviour not only threatened life and property but also jeopardized the working relationship of the group. That person was apt to be ostracized.

In this manner, the bee was a way of asserting community identity and belonging: one either adhered to the shared values of hard work and neighbourliness and belonged or was left out. For example, two young Englishmen who considered themselves above assisting at a logging bee in Douro Township in the 1830s were ridiculed with laughter.[33] In another case, Thomas Niblock, who had gained the reputation of not paying his debts on time and disparaging his neighbours' company, was not included in the beeing circle in Delaware and had to hire men to help him clear and harvest.[34] So important was a "neighbourly" attitude that responsible, cheerful, and generous effort even took precedence over the actual quality of the work done. The neighbourly quilter was still asked to a quilting even if her stitches were uneven. Sloppy work could always be ripped out and replaced at a later date; a fissure of friendly relations was more difficult, time-consuming, and costly to repair.[35]

Besides the cheerful repayment of labour, hospitality was an integral part of the exchange and one of the most valued virtues of the social code. Just what constituted appropriate, neighbourly hospitality changed over time. In the early days of sparse settlement and rough ways, hospitality took the form of simple food, entertainment, and plenty of whiskey. Whiskey, in particular, was the measure of hospitality. Commentators were quick to point out in the 1820s that you simply could not raise a barn without it.[36] Generally it took sixteen men to raise a building, and five gallons of whiskey was the recommended store to have on hand.[37] An inexperienced grog-boss, as at Moodie's bee, inadvertently wreaked havoc by being too generous too early in the day. Susanna Moodie's "vicious and drunken" guests stayed on after the logging bee with their "unhallowed revelry, profane songs and blasphemous swearing," and left her to pick up the broken glasses, cups, and strewn remnants of the feast. Not surprisingly, Susanna condemned bees as being "noisy, riotous drunken meetings, often terminating in violent quarrels, sometimes even bloodshed."[38] Concern over the accidents, quarrels, expense of provisions, and damage to property occasioned by such drinking brought about a contest between the whiskey supporters on the one side

and the evangelicals and temperance advocates on the other in many communities. Evangelicals and temperance advocates met with considerable resistance in their attempt to redefine traditional patterns of hospitality as sinful. For example, a Waterdown man wishing to raise a sawmill without whiskey had to send to the Indian mission on the Credit before he could obtain willing men.[39] In another case, men turned out to a raising in Nissouri Township, but once the foundation was laid, refused to raise the barn unless whiskey was served. When no whiskey appeared, the men left.[40] At times resistance could take a nasty turn. For example, when Thomas Brown, who had previously been part of a gang of young men who caroused at any bee within riding distance, took the pledge, he became a target of ridicule. When he next attended a bee and refused to drink, whiskey was forcibly poured down his throat and he was beaten.[41] By the 1870s, however, as the farming population became more established, older, and respectable, and as evangelicalism gained converts, strong drink was either not offered or limited to moderate amounts after the job was done.[42] Though hospitality continued to be a vital component of the exchange, elaborate meals and entertainment replaced generous quantities of whiskey.

By reciprocating in the appropriate fashion through hospitality and labour, people demonstrated their support for reciprocal labour and the shared values that supported it. In so doing, they became or continued to be part of the neighbourhood. This process of incorporation worked to integrate newcomers and established settlers, young and old, rich and poor, women and men not as equals, but with clearly defined identities within the larger group. Though Catharine Parr Traill viewed the coming together of the educated gentleman, the poor artisan, the soldier, the independent settler, and the labourer in one common cause as the "equalizing system of America," it was neither so romantic nor so revolutionary. Although the bee publicly identified people as belonging, it also established, confirmed, and renegotiated their status in the rural hierarchy, whether that standing was based on experience, skills, age, class, or gender.

Bees constituted a rite of passage for new settlers, a time when they were incorporated into the group values and understandings that could make them into useful and valued members of the neighbourhood. Reciprocal labour tied new and established families together. On the one hand, established farmers who expanded their operations needed additional labour. On the other hand, new settlers relied on more experienced settlers for their skill, equipment, advice, and any older children they could spare.[43] When Mr Sinclair arrived in Howard Township (Kent Co.) in the 1830s, for example, he had a neighbour accompany him to summon the locals to his raising. As newcomer, he had no outstanding favours to call upon, no reputation established as a trustworthy and hard worker, and therefore needed William Anderson to provide an introduction. With no house of his own, and his wife sick with lake fever, Sinclair had to rely on another neighbour to assist in preparing for the feast and festivities that followed. In repaying all these favours in the customary way, the Sinclair family could establish its claim to membership in the neighbourhood and the rights and responsibilities that status conferred.[44]

The bee, like the farm operation itself, incorporated people of all ages into its service while publicly acknowledging their status within the group. The very young and the very old, for example, were relegated to the sidelines to watch, cheer, and pass judgement. Those able to participate in the work were given responsibilities according to their perceived capabilities and talents. It was standard practice, for example, for dangerous, strenuous work, such as raising or logging, to get experienced young men. Though an older man might shout the orders to "heave ho," only someone with a "steady head and active body" could go out on a beam.[45] On several occasions while raising barns, seasoned men had let a bent slip and someone had been killed.[46] Novices, therefore, had to be kept away from dangerous work. In John Geikie's account of a logging bee at his father's farm in the 1830s or 1840s, John and his brother (who were under fifteen years of age) were allowed only to watch on the sidelines and do the "lighter parts of the business." They lopped off branches, made piles of brush, brought the men pails of water, and kept the animals out of danger of falling trees. The men did the chopping and the "wild work" of rolling the logs together.[47] As power saws and threshing machines were introduced later in the century, the specialized knowledge required to run the machines and ownership of this technology reinforced the age-based social hierarchy. Boys, or men past their prime, were limited to carrying the logs and pitching blocks at the sawing bee, or pitching grain at the threshing bee. Only experienced, active men in their prime could take their place next to the saw blade or the threshing machine. When a worker was considered to be too old to be trusted with the serious or dangerous work, the meaning of his aging was publicly recognized, his status altered, and he was relegated to the sidelines.[48]

The bee also incorporated people of different classes. Gentlemen farmers such as the Langtons, the Stricklands, and the Moodies invited the educated gentleman, the independent settler, the tenant farmer, and the poor labourer alike to join together in common cause. That such a meeting of classes and temporary laying aside of differences was invariably cause for comment suggests that people were well aware of the social hierarchy. After raising their house in 1833, Traill concluded that, "In spite of the difference of rank among those that assisted at the bee, the greatest possible harmony prevailed."[49] Such patterns of dependence cutting across classes did not lessen inequality. As scholars studying festive labour in primitive societies have observed, the exchange was not always between equals and was, in fact, a way of reinforcing or establishing one's place in the social hierarchy.[50]

Gentlemen farmers admitted that bees, especially raisings, were essential and unavoidable. They participated in reciprocal labour, but took pains when possible to distance themselves from the lower classes and express their superiority. Both could be achieved in a number of ways. Usually the host was the work boss when a bee was convened, but where inequality between the host and workers was great, the host hired a foreman. John Thomson, a retired half-pay officer who held several properties in the Orillia area, did so when he ordered his hired hand to invite neighbours and Natives, procure supplies, and conduct the raising. It was only when workers threatened to leave because of rain and poor preparation that Thomson got involved and set about cajoling and flattering them to stay for another day.[51]

A typical way to use the bee to express one's place in the social hierarchy was through conspicuous giving; to serve a lavish feast and throw a better party than most participants could afford. Settlers expected the well-to-do to throw a good bee. To live in a commodious frame house and serve your guests only pork and peas outside was not meeting the code of hospitality. It was a challenge for most settlers to acquire and prepare enough simple fare for their guests, given the primitive storage and cooking facilities of early settlement life, but they were all expected to do their best, even if it turned out to be a very modest affair. At the Sinclairs' raising in 1831, for example, the men sat on the beams, ate bread, butter, and meat, and drank water and whiskey. They had no plates, only their pocket knives.[52] In contrast, the Stewarts, gentlemen farmers in Douro Township, threw a splendid affair at their raising. The guests sat down in the kitchen and parlour to a feast of roast pig, boiled and roast mutton, fish pie, mutton pie, ham, potatoes and a variety of vegetables, followed by puddings and tarts. In the afternoon, when rain broke up the work, tea and cakes were served. Guests were entertained by a pianist throughout the afternoon, danced to fiddle music throughout the evening, and, at eleven, sat down to another feast of a wide variety of meat, desserts, and decanters of currant cordial. Dancing continued thereafter, and everyone was bedded down for the night under buffalo robes and bear skins. At the end of it all, Frances Stewart was able to look back in satisfaction and conclude, "Altogether it looked very respectable."[53] The Stewarts had succeeded in meeting their guests and their own expectations of fitting hospitality, given their station in life, and had confirmed their position of superiority in the neighbourhood.

On such occasions it was expected that the host would at least temporarily cast aside class differences and condescend to rub shoulders with his workers. Such had been expected of the landed class in the Old World at festive occasions.[54] It was the host's way of demonstrating his good will, mutual respect, generosity of spirit, and appreciation towards workers. These were integral parts of the concept of hospitality and necessary components of a continuing social relationship. When a well-to-do host was not forthcoming, guests might demand festivities fitting his station. For example, when an owner of 500 acres called a raising, but hadn't planned any entertainment, a large group of young women cornered him during the proceedings and forced him to consider how the evening should be spent.[55] When the host succumbed, dancing and games were organized. Likewise, after rain postponed John Thomson's raising, he and two gentlemen friends retired to his dining room while the remaining workers were relegated to the kitchen for the rest of the day. This division caused "some envious feelings among certain yankiefied personages" of what Thomson called the "no-Gent" class. To keep the workers satisfied and willing to stay overnight, Thomson and his friends had to be "mixed up among them" as they did all they could "to do away with any bad impression."[56] Thereafter, Thomson resumed his distance.

In the months that followed, Thomson, like other gentlemen, paid his return labour not by attending what was deemed an "odious gathering," but by sending his hired hands or a yoke of oxen.[57] The gentleman class participated in reciprocal labour only as long as it was necessary. As an ex-settler flatly stated, "A gentleman...has no business with it—the idle riff-raff are they who will surely come, getting drunk, eating up all your pork and flour, and fighting like Irishmen."[58] John Langton considered establishing a gentleman's logging association to avoid bees altogether, and Moodie simply stopped going or even sending anyone or anything in his place.[59] Clearly the bee was not the democratizing agent it was sometimes characterized to be.

The bee incorporated people of different age, background, and gender. The view of farm men as commercialists working alone for exchange and profit, while women worked together building neighbourhood and kin ties, needs further examination.[60] The study of bees suggests that both men and women were part of the world of mutuality. Reciprocal work has generally been viewed from the separate spheres ideology. A tendency exists to see logging, raising, and threshing bees as purely male events, and as examples of a "male community" from which women were excluded.[61] In contrast, feminist scholars have viewed quiltings and other forms of female reciprocity as part of a "female community" of empathy, spirituality, support, and non-hierarchical arrangements.[62] Scholars now recognize, however, that gender is best understood as a relational system. Through the interaction of men and women, the meaning of gender is created, reinforced, and transformed. More attention is now given to the construction of gender in everyday experience and in settings where men and women operate together. Scholars of rural communities recognize that, unlike urban men and women, who were increasingly defined by their differences from one another, rural men and women continued to share many of "the tasks which produced their income and sustained their families."[63] Bees viewed as interaction episodes are exceptionally good opportunities to examine men and women working together, because this form of reciprocal work rarely occurred without the participation of both sexes.

Men were the principle actors in reciprocal labour that involved physical strength and danger. They also exchanged labour among themselves. Women were the principle actors in reciprocal labour that involved the preparation of clothing and food. They also exchanged labour among themselves. Rarely did men and women exchange labour with each other. Beyond these significant differences there was much commonality. Both men and women were involved in bees for the capital development of their farming operation (cleared fields, buildings, household goods), for market (grain, fowl, cloth), and for basic family sustenance (food and clothing). A successful bee—where work was done well, no incidents occurred, and guests were pleased with the hospitality—required the participation of both men and women. Their work, responsibilities, and space intersected at various points throughout the event. Even though they were main actors in different kinds of bees, men and women shared the values and experience of diligence, skill, competition, hierarchical working structures, and neighbourliness. Gender, nevertheless, was an essential variable in understanding their lives.

Logging bees were substantively about men and the rituals of manliness. The loggers formed gangs in different parts of the field and competed to see who would finish logging their section first. It was very strenuous work shifting and heaping logs. In the hottest days of summer, the hours were dreadfully long, the logs terribly heavy, the work tiring and dirty, the grog foul tasting and plentiful. It took physical stamina to last the day. It took bravery to run the risk of breaking a leg or losing one's life. And it took a great deal of self-control to keep a clear head. As Munro explained in *Backwoods Life,* logging was what "tries a man's mettle."[64] Just to participate as a main actor (one who rolled and piled the logs) was a mark of one's prowess. Being allowed to drive the oxen marked the beginning of manhood, and, by participating and observing, boys soon learned what was expected of them once they graduated to the status of main actors. Strength, speed, and energy were all valued, and skill was deeply appreciated and critically evaluated. Lives were at stake. Save for the skill of a good axeman, a tree might fall on man or beast. Men gained and lost reputations at these events as the strongest, the fastest, or the most skilful. Such identities were created in the heat of work and confirmed in the competitive sports that often followed. As Geikie recounted after attending a logging bee in Bidport Township in the 1830s, there was much bragging about chopping prowess, much comparison between men regarding their skills, and much laughing at those who had accidents or used inferior equipment.[65] Heavy drinking, smoking, and fights were part of the equation too, though the "rough back countryman" style of manhood exhibited by Monaghan, who attended Moodie's bee on a hot July day in 1834 "in his glory, prepared to work or fight," gradually lost favour to the more morally upright male who was esteemed for his strength, skill, stamina—and his self-restraint.[66]

Women played a supporting role at bees where men held centre stage and were a valued audience. As anthropologists who study spectacles argue, the role of spectator is not passive or neutral, as spectacles require exchange between actors and audience.[67] At barn raisings, for example, women cheered the men on as they competed to see which team raised their side

first. As Russel Clifton recalled from his barn-raising youth, he was often one of the first lads to ride up with the bent, and "usually there was some girl among the women that I hoped would worry about my falling."[68] Even at logging bees, the dirtiest and roughest events of all, women might participate as spectators. For example, Anne Langton and her kitchen helpers walked down and took "a view of the black and busy scene" at their logging.[69] At hunting bees, women swarmed the fields, supporting their teams by bringing the hunters provisions and relieving them of their game.[70] In the exchange, men and women confirmed their own and each other's gendered identities. To defy these identities was to court disapproval.[71]

Even more important than their valued role as spectators was women's role in preparing and executing the feast and festivities; these were essential components of any successful bee, the first instalment in the pay-back system, and an integral part in developing the farm.[72] Women were indispensable in this capacity. If a family could not supply enough female labour itself, additional women were hired or, more commonly, neighbouring women gave their labour, crockery, cooking utensils, and, on occasion, their kitchens, with the understanding that they would receive help in return.[73] It was hard work. For most women, even with help, it took two to three days to prepare the house and food, in order to set out what was considered "a respectable table" and to make room for the dancing or games that followed. Great activity then ensued on the day of the event, with cooking, keeping the fires going, serving food, minding children, and being the cheerful hostess.[74] Once the festivities were over, the clean-up began.

In a sense, the role of actor and spectator were reversed at the feast, as the hostess took centre stage. As fictional accounts portrayed it, "supper was the great event to which all things moved at bees."[75] Considerable pressure existed for women to perform. Isabella Bishop concluded in *The Englishwoman in America* (1856) that the "good humour of her guests depends on the quantity and quality of her viands."[76] Being hostess to a bee gave women a rare occasion to exhibit themselves, their skills, and their homes. Though men might eat with a "take what you have and you won't want fashion," they nevertheless took stock of the meal. In their accounts of bees, men carefully and, if the host, proudly itemized the menu and often evaluated the hostess. Wilkie, for example, after attending a chopping bee, noted that Mrs Webb "provident dame had busied herself to some purpose."[77] Women, however, were the most exacting critics when it came to the meal. As men competed with and assessed each other while logging, women evaluated each other at the feast. As Stan Cross recalled of his parents barn raising, senior women eagerly offered their assistance so that they could "see first-hand how my mother, who was one of their peers, would approach such an undertaking especially with three babies in tow."[78] So great was the competition and the pressure to prepare a fine feast that M.E. Graham, in an article entitled "Food for Bees," urged Ontario farm women not to give themselves "dyspepsia preparing bountiful, fancy and varied threshing feasts." She went on to say, "I know for truth that we simply cook that we may equal or excel the other woman in the neighbourhood."[79] A lot was at stake, for the quality of the hospitality could determine the family's reputation and its continuing membership in the ring of reciprocity. It was only after the feast and the festivities were over and the guests had gone away happy that the host and hostess could relax and congratulate themselves on having held a successful event.

The quilting was the female counterpart of the male logging bee. As men were the central actors at a logging bee and women played a supporting role, the reverse was true of quiltings. It was an event organized and held by and for women which combined work with socializing. For days the hostess prepared the house and the food for the event, made arrangements for the children, and pieced scraps together to form the top of the quilt. Whereas a general call might be sent out for a barn raising, women were individually invited to a quilting. The guests would secure the top, wool, and backing to a frame, quilt it, and remove it from the frame, ready for use, in the same day. To be invited to a quilting generally meant you were not only a member of a particular social circle but also accomplished in sewing skills. Whereas men were esteemed for their strength, stamina, and bravery, women were praised for their detail and dexterity. The good seamstress sewed fast, short, even stitches and wasted no thread. The hostess was evaluated on her hospitality, and the artistry and skill exhibited by her quilt top. As experienced men took the lead at loggings, experienced women took the lead at quiltings and were known as the "queen bees." Young girls learned how to sew from their mothers and grandmothers on doll quilts. Once they were experienced enough, they would be invited to participate in their first bee. In this manner, quilting skills were passed down through the generations, reaffirming the female role and female connectedness.[80]

Usually we think of the quilting bee as a female-only affair, but in the nineteenth century, though women held centre stage, men played significant supporting roles. When young women were present, the hostess, who controlled the social space of the marriage market, invited young men too.[81] A.C. Currie, a young bachelor in Niagara, got invited to several quilting bees over the winter of 1841. Sometimes he had two a week.[82] While the women sat around the quilting frame, the men, under the supervision of the queen bees, would sit on the sidelines and aid by threading needles, chatting, and flirting. As spectators, they were to appreciate the women's domestic skills and social charms; as supporting actors, they were to mingle with the young women at the "frolic" of charades, dancing, singing, and flirtations that usually followed. Such flirtations at apple paring and corn husking bees, where men and women participated as equals, took priority over the actual work accomplished, at least in the retelling. At paring bees, men might peel apples and throw them to the women, who cored, quartered, and strung them. Once the old folks retired for the evening, the young people kissed, danced, and played all sorts of games. Wilkie excitedly recounted his experiences at such a bee when, alone in a moonlit room, amid much whispering and gentle tittering, a game of forfeit ensued and he found himself holding a "bonnie lass" on each knee.[83] In this manner, bees provided an opportunity for courtship under the supervision of the community.

At the bee, one's identity was confirmed within the neighbourhood. Though people might work together in harmony like bees in a hive, they took their place within a non-egalitarian and differentiated group. While initiating, reshaping, and confirming patterns of association between individuals, the bee also served a variety of functions for the neighbourhood as a whole. One contemporary deemed it to be "the fete, the club, the ball, the town-hall, the labour convention of the whole community."[84]

"The Bee-line"

Another layer of understanding about the operation of neighbourhood emerges when we stop in time and space and analyze one family's beeing experience over a number of years. Besides confirming the economic and social importance of bees, the action-structure of one family and its neighbourhood in a spatial and interactive sense is revealed. We are able to describe how several overlapping "working" networks existed at once. This layering is in part a reflection of the second point revealed by this method of analysis. As the entire family was drawn into beeing, the main actors brought their own social networks and social space to bear on the beeing network that developed, so that each family had its own patterns of exchange that were peculiar to them. We can see the neighbourhood not only as a static diagram of interaction but also as a dynamic process that was perpetuated, recreated, and modified as the main actors changed.

Lucy Middaugh of Mountain Township (Dundas County) was nearly sixty-two years of age when she made her first entry on 1 May 1884 into the diary that has been used for this analysis.[85] Over the next four years she kept a daily account of the social and economic activities of the household. Lucy was known by her friends for possessing an unusual "ability in the affairs of domestic life" and for practising "a thrift and economy which was indeed commendable."[86] Certainly her diary reflects an economy with words, but such a terse style was not unusual in the era. Her diary recording was not a journey of self-discovery, but a simple record of events—usually one-line entries—of the lives of her family and neighbourhood. Bees and other events—births, deaths, visits—were recorded as a matter of fact, not described or evaluated.

Two generations before Lucy, the Middaughs had come to Canada in 1778 from New York state and settled in Matilda Township in Dundas County. As lots in the front townships filled up, the next generation pushed north into the neighbouring township of Mountain. Lucy's father-in-law purchased lot 2, concession 6, in Mountain Township in 1824. In 1845 he died and left the farm and a one-storey frame house to his son John and his new wife, Lucy. By the time Lucy started making entries in her diary, most of her eleven children had grown up. Over the diary years, Lucy's household contained her husband, John, who was suffering from dropsy and would die two years into the diary, and her second son,

Charles, age thirty-seven, and his wife, Min, who ran the farm and remained childless. Besides the old and young couples, Lucy's twenty-three-year-old daughter, Tory, was at home, as was her twenty-year-old son, Ezra, who temporarily returned home from California for nearly two years. Their farm and community were well beyond the pioneer stage and were typical of the established farming community of that era. They had 250 acres, of which 130 were improved. They raised a wide variety of field crops and livestock, had five stables, and several horse-drawn vehicles.[87] Situated midway on the Clark Road, between the villages of South Mountain and South Gower, they were surrounded by other farm families in similar circumstances. Like other farms, reciprocal labour was important to the Middaugh household. Of the six people in the house, only old John, owing to his illness, was not an active participant at bees. Other members regularly exchanged labour with neighbours and went to an average of eight bees a year. After family members had attended five bees in one month in the fall of 1884, Lucy dryly commented, "more Bees than Honey." But the Middaughs had been going to bees for decades, even generations, and, by the 1880s, it was an integral part of their household economy and a key component in the structuring, operation, and definition of their neighbourhood.

The Middaughs partook of bees at what might be considered three tiers of networks defined according to the intensity of the relationship—such as the degree of interaction, visiting, and swapping labour. Those in the first tier were their immediate neighbours—the Beggs, Clarks, Christies, and VanAllens. All were established families who had resided on the road for two or three generations and were cultivating over 80 acres.[88] They were households at the same stage in the life cycle who had kitchens full of grown children to spare for labour. These were the kind of families most apt to continue to engage in reciprocal labour long after the exigencies of early

settlement were over.[89] Indeed, a tradition of reciprocity that had been established by the older generations at least forty years earlier was now being continued by the younger generation. The VanAllens, Christies, Beggs, and Clarks had all exchanged labour with each other in the 1840s. In fact, the VanAllens' and Clarks' relationship with the Middaughs extended back to 1803, when the original settlers had arrived in Matilda Township.[90] Old Lucy still visited the Christies, but most of the coming and going both for work and for socializing was now between the younger generation. Hardly a day went by that family life wasn't punctuated by a visit to the neighbours, someone coming to help Charles, or Lucy visiting the sick.

In this first tier of beeing, physical distance, not kin, was the overriding cohesive ingredient. Elizabeth Clark was John Middaugh's sister, and their children worked together as cousins. No kin relationship existed, however, with the other families, nor were they bound together by religion or ethnicity. The VanAllens across the road were German Methodists like the Middaughs, but the Beggs and Christies next door were Irish and Scottish Presbyterians. A mixture of propinquity—being able to drive horses and machinery without expending too much time or energy—and trust born from years of living next door tied these people together in mutual dependency. As in other parts of the world, neighbourhood was the primary unit for reciprocal work and, by mid-century, that often meant all those on a concession line.[91] Propinquity, therefore, overrode the connections of kin that might have pulled people together and the differences of religion and ethnicity that might have driven them apart.

The Middaughs' neighbourhood extended, though with less intensity, to a second tier of families whose homes could be reached by travelling through the fields. The Smiths and the Frasers, though located one concession north of the Middaughs, abutted onto the back of the Middaugh farm. Three generations of the

Smiths had lived there, and the original settlers had done business with old John Middaugh as far back as 1828. The current generation had several young women of Tory's age and they did much visiting. The Frasers were long-time friends of Lucy and John. Their families had known each other as far back as 1803, and Tory was friends with their daughter. The Workmans' lived on the concession south of the Middaughs and were old friends. This second tier also included Alex Hyndman and his family, who had settled in the area before 1829 and were the furthest away at 5 kilometres to the northeast. As Alex had married Lucy's daughter, and he and Charles were of similar age and interests, much generalized helping and sharing occurred between the two families. The economically vital beeing group was, therefore, coterminous with farms on either side and those reachable by walking through the fields—in short, the geographic neighbourhood. It extended beyond this immediate group in the first and second tier to include only close relatives such as the Hyndmans.

Beyond the second tier of beeing was a third tier that really must not be included within the regular and economically vital group of reciprocal labour or the neighbourhood. The Middaughs were occasionally invited to bees at the Colemans, Frumes, and Ratherfords, who lived farther away to the northwest in the Township of South Gower, about an hour away by horse and buggy. As less visiting occurred with these families, the social connections are less clear. The Frumes, German Methodists, may have known the Middaughs in their Matilda Township days, and the Ratherfords had worked for old John in the 1850s. Indeed, this third tier suggests that bees sometimes extended beyond the immediate neighbourhood and provided the opportunity to meet new people. In this case, they were quilting and paring bees, which were often used for the courting opportuni-

ties they afforded, and, not surprisingly, it was the young, unmarried, Tory and Ezra who were usually invited or sent.

Though the entire Middaugh family, save for old John, were involved in the beeing network, not everyone participated equally. Charles, as household head and heir to the family farm, was arguably the most important participant, who had the most to gain or lose. He participated in raisings, wood bees, and ploughing bees at farms where a long-standing relationship existed dating back to his grandfather's era. These were families who had lived there for over a generation, were neighbours or relatives, and within the first two tiers of networks. It was important to send the most able member and household head to show commitment to and respect for these primary working relationships. In attending the bees himself, Charles also confirmed his status within the family and the neighbourhood. In contrast, his younger, unmarried brother Ezra, who was home temporarily with no real roots anymore in the community, went to only two raisings and a paring bee, something Charles would not even be expected to attend. Charles, therefore, was very important in maintaining the family's place in the local social and economic network and in maintaining the stability that was essential for effective reciprocal labour to function.

One is struck, however, by how important women were as principal actors too—and not just in supplying food for the festivities. Over the diary years, Charles and Ezra attended a combined total of fourteen bees, while the women in the house—Tory, Min, and Lucy—attended a combined total of sixteen bees. As the woman in charge of the household, Min found time to attend only four bees. Lucy, though still winning first prizes at the fair for her quilts, attended only two quilting bees, where she had women her age for company. Her neighbourhood role had become one of visiting the sick on behalf of the family. Tory, however, was central to the beeing network and nearly as important as Charles. She attended quiltings, parings, rag-rug bees, and a raising—that one at her sister's place. She rarely went to the Beggs, a neighbouring household of five young men. Instead, her activity was focused on neighbours with young women her age, friends, co-religionists, and relatives further away. Here the difference with Charles ended, as Tory travelled just as far and as often as Charles as family representative. As long as Tory lived at home, then, she made a valuable contribution to the family and the neighbourhood. While Charles seems to have maintained the essential, immediate, and long-term connections necessary to his and the family's future on the farm, Tory contributed to these ties and expanded the family's contacts in neighbouring townships. This network was important for the marriage market and for those children who would have to move beyond the farm to make new homes. Both Charles and Tory partook of the world of mutuality, working in groups that used and strengthened the ties born of geography and genealogy. Their "working" neighbourhood, built on generations of relationships, also helped shape their future opportunities.

This analysis of the Middaugh family's beeing experience reveals the complexity of the configuration of neighbourhood and the agency of its actors. Overlapping "working" neighbourhoods had existed for generations and were modified as the main actors changed. The persistence of the beeing network over the generations was, in part, because these families were social equals with similar demands on their labour supply. In this way a relative degree of equality was built into the exchange. Immediate neighbours of long-standing acquaintance made up the core of the working group, with relatives being important, though less so. Individual members of the family participated, and they all

played a particular role according to their position within the family, their perceived future in the community, and their commitment to it.

"To Bee or Not to Bee"

What the bee actually meant to participants can only be judged from their actions and the evaluations they have left. Contemporary accounts repeatedly revealed that if a bee functioned well—the job got done, money was saved, people had fun and knew their place— the communal effort was applauded. Participants, however, were well aware of the exchange system that underlay this event and were reluctant to depict reciprocal work as selfless behaviour.[92] They knew that both the communal and the individual ethic were in operation. While selfish ambition and the man who did not do his share were clearly frowned upon, individual gain had an acknowledged place in the system. The barn raising, for example, was a momentous achievement in an individual family's measure of material success. It symbolized not only their reasons for emigrating and their years of saving and planning but also their material wealth, social improvement, and independence. Indeed, private property and individual ownership were never in question. Though people agreed to share their labour, tools, and time, it was always clear whose field had been logged, whose cattle would use the newly raised barn, and who could sleep under the quilt. Most participants would have been baffled to find twentieth-century writers casting the bee as the embodiment of the selfless communal ideal and the polar opposite of the capitalistic spirit of individualism and material gain. Instead, most farm families understood that work was a commodity and also a means to foster neighbourly relations. Their lively networks of reciprocal labour fostered both individual prosperity and mutual reliance. This social reality flies in the face of a number of dichotomies that have been developed by scholars, such as use versus exchange, sufficiency versus commercialization, and the moral economy versus the market economy.[93] That reciprocal work often resulted in a warm sense of generosity, belonging, and security within a larger community was an important by-product deeply appreciated by people at the time and lamented later when lost. When given the opportunity to be released from the constraints of scarce labour and capital, however, many people chose to leave the obligations and inconvenience of cooperative work behind for other ways over which they had greater control.

The main complaints levelled against bees had to do with managing people. Cooperation is not easy. As with any kind of communal work, industrious workers had to share with the idle, and individual decisions were constrained by the decisions of the group. One common complaint was that it was difficult to control the workers. Some came with the attitude that the host was lucky to have them and they drank and ate heartily while leaving little in the way of quality workmanship. Farmers felt they had more control over their workers and the quality of work if they hired labourers. Furthermore, bees could be costly if the work was shoddy, yet the host was bound to feast and entertain the workers. After her logging bee had gone wrong, Susanna Moodie went out of her way to declare, "I am certain, in our case, had we hired with the money expended in providing for the bee, two or three industrious, hard-working men, we should have got through twice as much work, and have had it done well, and have been the gainers in the end."[94] The main disadvantage with the bee was being called upon at an inconvenient time for return work. Just when a farmer needed to

seed or harvest his own fields, he was called upon by others to work theirs.[95]

Given the difficulties in managing people, it is not surprising that once other viable alternatives arose, bees declined. Bees persisted in remote areas where hired labour was hard to find and the price of labour was high. They also continued to operate in situations such as the Middaughs' where persistent farm families of similar status had a tradition of reciprocal work firmly established. In other populous and longer settled areas, however, where farmers were expanding their operations and entering into a cash economy, it was more convenient to hire workers, and the cash payment— an immediate reciprocity—took into consideration the quality and quantity of the work done.[96] Farmers were then free of the obligations of reciprocal labour and could attend to their own farms and according to their own schedule. The growing availability of cash and hired labour removed the necessity of relying on bees.

Technology was not as central as some have argued in the decline of bees.[97] The introduction at mid-century of patented iron apple peelers, the self-raking reaper, and, later, cross-cut saws reduced the need for bees by cutting the time and labour needed in processing apples, harvesting, and sawing.[98] Some of the new technology, such as threshing machines in the 1880s and later silo-filling equipment, did not alter the tradition of collective work, but was often cooperatively owned and operated. Threshing bees and silo-filling bees continued well into the twentieth century. Only after the First World War, with the introduction of combines and tractors, was one man able to do the work that had previously taken a neighbourhood.[99]

The need for bees also declined with the rise of more formal strategies for security and new forms of entertainment. Insurance companies offering compensation for damage done by fire, fraternal orders offering sickness and death benefits, and eventually the welfare state all played their part in reducing the effect of hard times and families' reliance on traditional networks of neighbourhood support.[100] Furthermore, bees now competed with lodge meetings, Sunday school picnics, school concerts, and agricultural fairs for the visiting and courtship opportunities they provided.

As the economics, technology, and social aspects of farm life changed, bees slowly became a thing of the past.

Conclusion

Though often idealized as the epitome of the selfless communal ideal, participants in bees behaved as though there was no inherent or insurmountable conflict between individual and communal goals. Both men and women participated in reciprocal labour using the ties born of geography and genealogy to build their resources, increase their own productivity, and shape their future opportunities. Through this sharing, many individual farm families were able to acquire the extra labour, skills, and equipment necessary for capital improvements, so that profitable farming could proceed. Such structural dependence on neighbours reduced the risk of life in the backwoods. Many people found that, through reciprocal work, they could succeed individually and that it was in their own material and social interests to be neighbourly. The network of labour exchange, in effect, produced individual prosperity and mutual reliance. In the process, neighbourhoods were created that could be defined by their spatial dimension, membership, shared values, and collective identity. Such neighbourhoods were dynamic entities, with fluid patterns of interaction particular to each family and responsive to the social networks and social space that individual participants brought to bear on the network as it developed. Finally, though the bee facilitated neighbourhood and often neighbourliness, it did so in a way that incorporated differences in class, age, gender, and skill and acknowledged the importance of private property and social hierarchy.

Notes

I would like to thank my research assistants, Karen Kennedy and James Calnan. The helpful comments of my colleagues Terry Crowley, Kris Inwood, Jamie Snell, and Richard Reid on earlier versions of this article are greatly appreciated. A version of this article was presented at the 2001 annual meeting of the Canadian Historical Association in Quebec City.

1 Bryan D. Palmer, "Discordant Music: Charivaris and Whitecapping in Nineteenth-Century North America," *Labour/Le Travail* 3 (1978): 5–62; Allan Greer, "From Folklore to Revolution: Charivaris and the Lower Canadian Rebellion of 1837," and Tina Loo, "Dan Cranmer's Potlatch," both in Tina Loo and Lorna R. McLean, eds., *Historical Perspectives on Law and Society in Canada* (Mississauga: Copp Clark Longman 1994), 35–55, 219 53; and Pauline Greenhill, "Welcome and Unwelcome Visitors: Shivarees and the Political Economy of Rural-Urban Interaction in Southern Ontario," *Journal of Ritual Studies* 3, 1 (1989).

2 Studies such as those done by Bradbury, Parr, and Marks come close to examining neighbourhood, but still link families only with the larger urban area and economy and bypass the neighbourhood as a unit of analysis. See Bettina Bradbury, *Working Families: Age, Gender and Daily Survival in Industrializing Montreal* (Toronto: McClelland & Stewart 1993); Joy Parr, *The Gender of Breadwinners* (Toronto: University of Toronto Press 1990); and Lynne Marks, *Revivals and Roller Rinks: Religion, Leisure, and Identity in Late-Nineteenth-Century Small-Town Ontario* (Toronto: University of Toronto Press 1996). So far the study of neighbourhood has been

the preserve of sociologists. For example, for the study of neighbourhood helping exchanges in modern Toronto, see Barry Wellman, "The Community Question," *American Journal of Sociology* 84 (1979): 1201–31.

3 A vast literature exists on community. For the most recent overview of this literature in a Canadian context, see John Walsh and Stephen High, "Re-thinking the Concept of Community," *Histoire Sociale* 23 (Nov. 1999): 255–73. In what follows I have borrowed my approach from economists, ethnographers, and cultural historians. Many of my ideas coalesced in the community studies seminar I co-taught as part of the Tri-University Doctoral Program. Although I cannot benefit from direct questioning and observation of those actually involved in bees, some of the sources left provide something similar to the ethnographer's notebook in that they record people doing things. I have interpreted these actions as statements. The most reliable evidence for rendering the facts are diaries and farm accounts. Bees were carefully recorded as a way of keeping accounts of work owing and as noteworthy social events. Settlers' guides often presented the "how-to" of holding a bee because of its necessity in the backwoods and because of its central importance as an entry point into community life. Somewhat less reliable, but still very valuable, are the numerous travellers' accounts, memoirs, and late nineteenth-century settlement histories. Bees appear in these sources with regularity as they were memorable events. These stories are usually based on the author's direct memory of events, what they heard from others, or what they thought possible.

4 For an example of an anthropologist, see Solon T. Kimball, "Rural Social Organization and Co-operative Labour," *American Journal of Sociology* 55 (1949): 38–49; for a Marxist interpretation, see James A. Henretta, "Families and Farms: Mentalité in Pre-industrial America," *William and Mary Quarterly*, series 3, 35, 4 (1978): 3–32; and for a feminist interpretation, see Marjorie Kaethler and Susan D. Shantz, *Quilts of Waterloo County* (Waterloo: Johanns Graphics 1990), and Nancy Grey Osterud, *Bonds of Community: The Lives of Farm Women in 19th Century New York* (Ithaca: Cornell University Press 1991).

5 Samuel Strickland, *Twenty-Seven Years in Canada West*, vol. 1 (1853; Edmonton: Hurtig Publishers 1972), 35; Martin Doyle, *Hints on Emigration to Upper Canada* (Dublin: Curry 1832), 61; and George Easton, *Travels in America* (Glasgow: John S., Marr & Sons 1871), 89. John MacDougall

noted that the term was not derived from the work habits of bees, but from a word from Ancient Saxon days when danger brought people together for defence, *Rural Life in Canada* (1913; Toronto: University of Toronto Press 1973), 132. Such forms of reciprocal labour were part of an established tradition from the Old World. Peasants in Norway, Ireland, Scotland, and elsewhere had long used reciprocal work to erect buildings, harvest produce, and create cloth. In South America a distinction was drawn between exchange labour and festive labour. Charles Erasmus, "Culture Structure and Process: The Occurrence and Disappearance of Reciprocal Farm Labor," *Southwestern Journal of Anthropology* 12 (1956): 445–6. Exchange labour usually included about ten people who regularly exchanged a day's work for a day's work. Festive labour could include more than one hundred people. The obligation to reciprocate was not so great, but the host was to provide extraordinary food and festivities. No such clear distinction was drawn by settlers in Ontario. Both the big barn raisings that drew large numbers and the smaller occasions when groups of neighbours regularly got together to exchange labour were called bees.

6 Queen's University Archives, Walter Beatty Papers, Walter Beatty Diary, 1838–92, box 3057; ibid., Ewan Ross Papers, John MacGregor Diary, 1877–83, series 3, binder 94, no. 2504; ibid., Ewan Ross Papers, James Cameron Diaries, 1854–1902, series 3, binders 25–33, no. 2504; Lucy Middaugh Diary, 1884–87, private possession of Jean Wilson; John Tigert Diaries, 1888–1902, private possession of Tigert family; Joseph Abbott Diary, 1819, reprinted in his *Emigrant to North America* (Montreal: Lovell & Gibson 1843); and James O'Mara, "The Seasonal Round of Gentry Farmers in Early Ontario," *Canadian Papers in Rural History* 2 (1980): 103–12.

7 Cited in W.H. Graham, *Greenbank* (Peterborough, Ont.: Broadview Press 1988), 249.

8 Susanna Moodie, *Roughing It in the Bush* (1852; Toronto: McClelland & Stewart 1962), 156.

9 James M. Young, *Reminiscences of the Early History of Galt and the Settlement of Dumfries* (Toronto: Hunter, Rose & Co. 1880), 43; and Strickland, *Twenty-Seven Years*, 1: 97.

10 "A New Ontario Raising," *Farmer's Advocate* 47 (8 Feb. 1912): 222.

11 For the most comprehensive study of rural labour in nineteenth-century Ontario, see Terry Crowley, "Rural Labour," in Paul Craven, ed., *Labouring*

Lives: Work and Workers in Nineteenth-Century Ontario (Toronto: University of Toronto Press 1995), 13–102. For frontier labour, see Daniel Vickers, "Working the Fields in a Developing Economy: Essex County, Mass., 1630–1675," in Stephen Innes, ed., *Work and Labor in Early America* (Chapel Hill: University of North Carolina Press 1988), 60.

12 Immigrant guidebook writers were well aware of the necessity of reducing risk in the backwoods and urged their readers to take part in bees. See William Hutton, *Canada: Its Present Condition, Prospects, and Resources Fully Described for the Information of Intending Emigrants* (London 1854), 42–3; Catharine Parr Traill, *The Backwoods of Canada* (1836; Toronto: McClelland & Stewart 1929), 121; and Easton, *Travels in America,* 90–3, 168.

13 National Archives of Canada (NA), Emigration Questionnaire, 1840–1, RG 1, B21, vol. 1; Doyle, *Hints on Emigration,* 48, 65; Abbott, *The Emigrant to North America,* 113; Easton, *Travels in America,* 90; Traill, *Backwoods of Canada,* 52–3; George Henry Hume, *Canada as It Is* (New York: Stodart 1832), 13, 135; and Alexander Carlisle Buchanan Sr, *Emigration Practically Considered* (London: Colburn 1828), 5.

14 Peter Russell, "Upper Canada: A Poor Man's Country? Some Statistical Evidence," *Canadian Papers in Rural History* 3 (1982): 136, 144.

15 W.F. Munro, *The Backwoods' Life* (1869; Shelburne: The Free Press 1910), 55; John C. Geikie, ed., *Adventures in Canada: Or Life in the Woods* (Philadelphia: Porter & Coates 1882), 40; and Strickland, *Twenty-Seven Years,* 1: 97.

16 Barns usually cost a bit less. For the cost of hiring labour for such purposes, see Emigration Questionnaire, 1840–1; Edward Allan Talbot, *Five Years' Residence in the Canadas* (London: Longman, Hurst, Rees, Orme, Brown & Green 1824), 189–90; and Hutton, *Canada,* 78. For the cost and popularity of holding a bee, see Emigration Questionnaire; see also Frederick Widder, *Information for Intending Emigrants of All Classes to Upper Canada* (Toronto: Scobie & Balfour 1850), 4; and University of Guelph Archives, Dougall Family Papers, 1844–69, Henry Dougall to Brother, 26 July 1852.

17 Emigration Questionnaire; Hutton, *Canada,* 11; Doyle, *Hints on Emigration,* 49.

18 Isabella L. Bishop, *The Englishwoman in America* (London: W. Clowes & Sons 1856), 202–3, 206.

19 MacGregor Diary, 15 Nov. 1878; and Canniff Haight, *Country Life in Canada Fifty Years Ago* (Toronto: Hunter, Rose & Co. 1885), 214.

20 Louis Tivy, *Your Loving Anna: Letters from the Ontario Frontier* (Toronto: University of Toronto Press 1972), 87.

21 Doug McCalla, *Planting the Province: The Economic History of Upper Canada, 1784–1870* (Toronto: University of Toronto Press 1993), 243. Starting in 1819, the value of cleared land was considered to be five times that of uncultivated land. Ibid., 28–9, 69–70, 106.

22 McCalla makes this point regarding credit, *Planting the Province,* 69.

23 Young, *Reminiscences,* 88–9; Thomas Need, *Six Years in the Bush* (London: Simplein, Marshall & Co. 1838), 96 .

24 McCalla, *Planting the Province,* 82, 146.

25 Beatty Diary; see also Tigert Diary and Middaugh Diary. Some anthropologists have interpreted the potlatch as a system of credit or a return on an interest-bearing investment. Loo, "Dan Cranmer's Potlatch," 231.

26 Munro, *Backwoods Life,* 38.

27 A day's work for a day's work was generally the custom throughout North and South America. See Basil Hall, *Travels in North America, in the Years 1827–1828* (Edinburgh: Cadell & Co. 1829), 311–12; and Erasmus, "Culture Structure and Process," 445. For what happened when inequalities existed, see Erasmus, "Culture Structure," 447; and Kimball, "Rural Social Organization," 42. See also Peter G. Mewett, "Associational Categories and the Social Location of Relationships in a Lewis Crofting Community," in Anthony P. Cohen, ed., *Belonging* (Manchester: Manchester University Press 1982), 103. Mewett distinguishes between balanced reciprocity (return work at the same type of job) and generalized reciprocity (just helping out with anything later), 112–13.

28 I first came across the use of "interaction episode" as an analytical tool in Rhys Isaac's *The Transformation of Virginia* (Chapel Hill: University of North Carolina Press 1982), chap. "A Discourse on the Method." My thanks to Richard Reid for drawing my attention to this work. The concept is borrowed from ethnographers and begins with the premise that society is not primarily a material entity, but must be understood as the dynamic product of the activities of its members, a product that is shaped by the images participants have of

their own and others' performances. Interaction episodes or dramatic events such as the bee are like knots of encounter in the ongoing social life and are suspended in the threads of continuing relationships. The visual image is like knots in lacework. By studying the converging threads and their nodal events we can better understand the structure, action, and meaning of society. Another useful model is to view the interaction episode as a stage play.

29 Traill, *Backwoods of Canada,* 122.

30 Contemporary writers urged new settlers to repay the favour: Hall, *Travels,* 312; Talbot, *Five Years' Residence,* 69; Doyle, *Hints on Emigration,* 45. See also Paul Voisey, *Vulcan: The Making of a Prairie Community* (Toronto: University of Toronto Press 1988), 147; and Jane Marie Pederson, *Between Memory and Reality: Family and Community in Rural Wisconsin, 1870–1970* (Madison: University of Wisconsin Press 1992), 154.

31 Kimball, "Rural Social Organization," 47; Erasmus, "Culture Structure and Process," 447; and Anthony Buckley, "Neighbourliness—Myth and History," *Oral History* 11, 1 (1983): 49.

32 *Globe,* 10 Sept. 1880, 6, and 6 Feb. 1880, 1. For other examples, see Ray Fazakas, *The Donnelly Album* (Toronto: Macmillan of Canada 1977), 10–14. For a similar tension between a local social order that stressed harmony and the undercurrent of violence brought on by frontier conditions, see Susan Lewthwaite, "Violence, Law, and Community in Rural Upper Canada," in Jim Phillips, Tina Loo, and Susan Lewthwaite, eds., *Essays in the History of Canadian Law* (Toronto: University of Toronto Press 1994), 353–86. Successful work groups could manage disputes by avoiding direct confrontation; they resorted to gossip instead. To avoid recriminations they made the host responsible for decisions involving risk. See Mewett, "Associational Categories," 112, 116.

33 James Logan, *Notes of a Journey Through Canada* (Edinburgh: Fraser & Co. 1838), 46.

34 NA, Niblock Letters, MG 24, I80, microfilm A-304, Thomas Niblock to Edward Niblock, 27 Jan. 1850. For those who broke the code and were considered divergent or outsiders, see Kimball, "Rural Social Organization," 41; and Conrad M. Arensberg and Solon T. Kimball, *Family and Community in Ireland* (Cambridge Mass: Harvard University Press 1948), chap. 12.

35 Interview with quilters at a quilting bee, Martin House, Doon Village, 1 July 1996.

36 Thomas Brush Brown, *Autobiography of Thomas Brush Brown (1804–1894)* (private printing by Isabel Grace Wilson, 1967, available at the Oxford County Library), 17–18. For the importance of whiskey and hospitality, see also David Wilkie, *Sketches of a Summer Trip to New York and the Canadas* (Edinburgh: J. Anderson Jr & A. Hill 1837), 173, 176–7; Hall, *Travels,* 2: 311; Young, *Reminiscences,* 61; Strickland, *Twenty-Seven Years,* 1: 37; and William Thompson, *A Tradesman's Travels in the United States and Canada the Years 1840, 41 and 42* (Edinburgh: Oliver & Boyd 1842), 103.

37 Patrick Shirreff, *A Tour through North America* (Edinburgh: Oliver & Boyd 1835), 125. For the usual amount of whiskey per man, see Rev. T. Sockett, ed., *Emigration: Letters from Sussex Emigrants* (London: Phillips, Petworth and Longman & Co. 1833), 28; and Centennial Museum, Judicial Records, Peterboro County, Peterborough, MG–8–2V, Inquest of Charles Danford, Smith Township, Accession No. 71–007, box 5, 1876, no. 30.

38 Moodie, *Roughing It,* 156–62; and also Wilkie, *Sketches,* 176; Patrick Shirreff, *A Tour,* 125.

39 Emily Weaver, *Story of the Counties of Ontario* (Toronto: Bell & Cockburn 1913), 165; and Pederson, *Between Memory and Reality,* 142, 217, 219.

40 Brown, *Autobiography,* 25.

41 Ibid., 23–4.

42 Charles Marshall, *The Canadian Dominion* (London: Longmans, Green 1871), 63; see also Easton, *Travels in America,* 169.

43 Doyle, *Hints on Emigration,* 60–1.

44 Alexander Sinclair, *Pioneer Reminiscences* (Toronto: Warwick Bros & Rutter 1898), 11–12.

45 Frances Browne Stewart, *Our Forest Home* (1889; Montreal: Gazette Printing 1902), 174, 177; and *Canada Farmer* 2, 9 (15 Nov. 1870).

46 Trent University Archives, Court Records of the United Counties of Northumberland & Durham, Coroners' Inquests, Inquest of James Hill, 84-020, Series E, box 49; and Judicial Records Peterboro County, Inquest of Charles Danford. A bent was made of two posts connected with a beam. It was laid on the foundation and then raised to form the frame of the barn.

47 Geikie, *Adventure in Canada,* 40–4, 47–8; see also Logan, *Notes of a Journey,* 45.

48 Jim Brown, "Memories of Work Bees," *Up the Gatineau!* 21 (1995): 9; and Royce MacGillivray,

The Slopes of the Andes: Four Essays on the Rural Myth in Ontario (Belleville: Mika Publishing 1990), 90.

49 Traill, *The Backwoods,* 135; see also Moodie, *Roughing It,* 156; and Logan, *Notes of a Journey,* 46.

50 Erasmus, "Culture Structure and Process," 458.

51 Archives of Ontario, John Thomson Diary, MU-846, Part 2, 22–4 April 1834. This was done elsewhere as well; see Erasmus, "Culture Structure and Process," 448.

52 Sinclair, *Pioneer Reminiscences,* 12; see also Wilkie, *Sketches,* 177; and Strickland, *Twenty-Seven Years,* 35–6.

53 Stewart, *Our Forest Home,* 174–6.

54 Catharine Anne Wilson, *A New Lease on Life* (Montreal and Kingston: McGill-Queen's University Press 1994), 110.

55 *Canada Farmer* 2, 9 (15 Nov. 1870).

56 Thomson Diary, 22–4 April 1834.

57 For example, see Thomson Diary, July, Oct. and Nov. 1833, and June 1834. John Langton and Moodie sent their hired men to bees also. Anne Langton, *A Gentlewoman in Upper Canada* (Toronto: Clarke Irwin 1964), 167; and Moodie, *Roughing It,* 162.

58 Ex-Settler, *Canada in the Years 1832, 1833 and 1834* (Dublin: Hardy 1835), 115.

59 Langton, *A Gentlewoman,* 166; and Moodie, *Roughing It,* 162.

60 Nancy Osterud goes further than most historians in understanding the rural family and community as gendered relationships. While she acknowledges that men participated in cooperative work, she still tends to see men as part of the commercial world and argues that women were the ones who sustained cooperative relations. In fact, she goes as far as to argue that women advocated a model of interdependence as an alternative to male dominance and capitalist social relations. She states that women used mutuality as a strategy of empowerment. Osterud, *Bonds of Community.*

61 John Mack Faragher, *Women and Men on the Overland Trail* (New Haven: Yale University Press 1979), 112 and 116.

62 Carroll Smith-Rosenberg, "The Female World of Love and Ritual: Relations between Women in Nineteenth-Century America," *Journal of Women in Culture and Society* 1, 1 (1875): 1–29; Kaethler and Shantz, *Quilts of Waterloo County,* 12; Ruth Schwartz Cowan, *More Work for Mother* (New York: Basic Book Publishers 1983), 112.

63 For gender as a relational system, see Joan W. Scott, "Women's History," in Peter Burke, ed., *New Perspectives on Historical Writing* (University Park: Pennsylvania State University Press 1995); and for rural communities, see Pederson, *Between Memory and Reality;* Osterud, *Bonds of Community;* and Royden Loewen, *Family, Church, and Market: The Mennonite Community in the Old and the New Worlds, 1850–1930* (Toronto: University of Toronto Press 1993).

64 Munro, *Backwoods Life,* 55.

65 Geikie, *Adventures in Canada,* 41–3.

66 Moodie, *Roughing It,* 158; and for similar accounts of logging bees, see Logan, *Notes on a Journey,* 45; William Johnston, *Pioneers of Blanchard* (Toronto: William Briggs 1899), 188–9, 227; and Wilkie, *Sketches,* 174–5. See also Mark Carnes and C. Griffen, eds., *Meanings for Manhood* (Chicago: University of Chicago Press 1990); and Pederson, *Between Memory and Reality,* 142–3.

67 Bonnie Huskins, "The Ceremonial Space of Women: Public Processions in Victorian Saint John and Halifax," in Janet Guildford and Susanne Morton, eds, *Separate Sphere: Women's Worlds in the 19th Century Maritimes* (Fredericton: Acadiensis Press 1994), 147.

68 Cited in West Oxford Women's Institute, *The Axe and the Wheel: A History of West Oxford Township* (Tillsonburg: Otter Publishing 1974), 17.

69 Langton, *A Gentlewoman,* 94.

70 Abbott, *The Emigrant,* 42.

71 An extreme, but nonetheless suggestive, case occurred in 1918 when a young Quebec girl dressed in male attire participated in a log-driving bee, and, when exposed, was sentenced to two years at the Portsmouth Penitentiary in Kingston. Original 11 June 1918, reprinted in the *Toronto Star,* 19 May 1992.

72 Elizabeth Jane Errington, *Wives and Mothers, School Mistresses and Scullery Maids: Working Women in Upper Canada, 1790–1840* (Montreal and Kingston: McGill-Queen's University Press 1995), 96.

73 Catharine Parr Traill, *The Female Emigrant's Guide and Hints on Canadian Housekeeping* (Toronto: MacLear 1854), 40; Sinclair, *Pioneer Reminiscences,* 12; Geikie, *Adventures in Canada,* 44.

74 Munro, *Backwoods' Life,* 55; Stewart, *Our Forest Home,* 172–6; Wilkie, *Sketches,* 176–8; Bishop, *The Englishwoman,* 205–6; Tivy, *Your Loving Anna,* 89.

75 Ralph Connor, *The Man from Glengarry* (Toronto: The Westminster Co. 1901), 211.

76 Bishop, *The Englishwoman,* 205–6.

77 Wilkie, *Sketches,* 176.

78 Stan Cross, "The Raising," *Up the Gatineau!* 21 (1995): 7.

79 M.E. Graham, "Food for Bees," *The Farming World* 18 (11 Sept. 1900): 104.

80 Strickland, *Twenty-Seven Years,* 2: 295–6; Thompson, *Tradesman's Travels,* 37; and for a wool-picking bee that was similarly arranged, see Munro, *Backwoods' Life,* 57.

81 Peter Ward, "Courtship and Social Space in Nineteenth-Century English Canada," *Canadian Historical Review* 68 1 (1987): 35–62.

82 University of Western Ontario, Regional Collection, William Leslie Papers, box 4178, A.C. Currie to Richard Leslie, 25 December 1841; and see also Strickland, *Twenty-Seven Years,* 2: 296; Munro, *Backwoods' Life,* 57; and Thompson, *Tradesman's Travels,* 37.

83 Wilkie, *Sketches,* 182–6; and see also Haight, *Country Life,* 67–8; Geikie, *Adventures in Canada,* 326–7; Traill, *Female Emigrant's Guide,* 75; and Gavin Hamilton Green, *The Old Log House* (Goderich: Signal-Star Press 1948), 109.

84 Marshall, *Canadian Dominion,* 62

85 Middaugh Diary. The people mentioned in the diary have all been matched with the 1871 manuscript census; *Historical Atlas of the Counties of Leeds and Grenville* (1861; Belleville: Mika Publishing 1973); and *Illustrated Historical Atlas of Stormont Dundas and Glengarry Counties, Ontario* (1879; Belleville: Mika Silk Screening 1972). I would like to thank my mother, Mrs Jean Wilson, the great-granddaughter of Lucy, for treasuring our family heirlooms and assisting me in reconstructing the family relationships. The value of using farm womens' diaries is amply revealed in Laurel Ulrich's Pulitzer Prize-winning book *A Midwife's Tale: The Life of Martha Ballard, Based on Her Diary, 1785–1812* (New York: Vintage Books 1990); Royden Loewen, "'The Children, the Cows, My Dear Man and My Sister': The Transplanted Lives of Mennonite Farm Women," *Canadian Historical Review* 73, 3 (1992): 344–73; and Ward, "Courtship and Social Space," 35–62.

86 Obituary of Lucy Middaugh, in the private possession of Mrs Jean Wilson.

87 1871 Agricultural Census for Mountain Township.

88 Ibid.; Land Registry Abstract for Concession 6, Mountain Township; St Andrew's United Church, Hallville, Ontario Centennial Anniversary 1834–1934 brochure.

89 Munro talks about the importance of grown children in his *Backwoods' Life,* 56. See also Erasmus, "Culture Structure and Process," 456; Kimball, "Rural Social Organization," 41; and Buckley, "Neighbourliness," 50. Fay E. Dudden, in another context, notes that it was often the neighbourhood youth that was shared. *Serving Women: Household Service in Nineteenth-Century America* (Middletown, Conn.: Wesleyan University Press 1983), chap. 1.

90 Farm/store ledger of John Middaugh, 1816–1850s, in private possession of Mrs Jean Wilson; and J. Smyth Carter, *The Story of Dundas* (1905; Belleville: Mika Publishing 1973), 449–63.

91 Mewett, "Association Categories," 110–11; Munro, *Backwoods' Life,* 29; and Sinclair, *Pioneer Reminiscences,* 11.

92 Doyle, *Hints on Emigration,* 61–2; and Traill, *The Backwoods,* 122.

93 See Stephen Innes for his insightful discussion of the need for greater caution when using such dichotomies to describe the past. "John Smith's Vision," in Stephen Innes, ed., *Work and Labour in Early America,* 36–40.

94 Moodie, *Roughing It,* 13; see also the Diary of William Proudfoot, 12 June 1833, cited in Edwin Guillet, *Pioneer Days in Upper Canada* (1933; Toronto: University of Toronto Press 1975), 127; and Ex-Settler, *Canada,* 115.

95 John J.E. Linton, *The Life of a Backwoodsman; or, Particulars of the Emigrant's Situation in Settling on the Wild Land of Canada* (London: Marchant Singer & Co. 1843), 14; Langton, *Gentlewoman,* 155, 166; *Canada Farmer* 2, 12 (12 Dec. 1870); Traill, *Backwoods,* 122. For a scholarly discussion of the problems associated with bees or other forms of cooperative work, see Erasmus, "Culture Structure and Process," 456–61; Cowan, *More Work for Mother,* 117; Pederson, *Between Memory and Reality,* 149.

96 Traill, *Backwoods,* 121; and Strickland, *Twenty-Seven Years,* 1: 37.

97 Kimball, in "Rural Social Organization," 42, places significant weight on technology as a factor in the decline of cooperative labour. Erasmus disagrees, placing more emphasis on the growth of a money economy and on more intensive agriculture that makes cooperative work inconvenient

and inefficient in terms of the costs and quality of work done. "Culture Structure and Process," 456. See also Pederson, *Between Memory and Reality*, 154–5.

98 *Farmer's Advocate* 59 (10 April 1924): 548; McCalla, *Planting the Province*, 225; and Lois Russell, *Everyday Life in Colonial Canada* (London: B.T. Batsford 1973), 90.

99 Pederson, *Between Memory and Reality*, 151–4.

100 McCalla, *Planting the Province*, 161; Mewett, "Associational Categories," and James E. Taylor Calnan, "'A Home Not Made with Hands': National Voluntary Associations and Local Community in Prince Edward County, Ontario, at the Turn of the 20th Century" (PhD dissertation, University of Guelph 1999).

Hardy Backwoodsmen, Wholesome Women, and Steady Families:

Immigration and the Construction of a White Society in Colonial British Columbia, 1849–1871

ADELE PERRY

Who was in and who was out? One of the primary ways in which mid-nineteenth-century British Columbians negotiated inclusions and exclusions was through the practice and discourse of immigration. Immigration derived its social and political significance from its double ability to dispossess local peoples and establish a settler-society in their stead. The settler society this process sought to build was explicitly racialized and deeply gendered. In seeking "hardy backwoodsmen," colonial promoters encouraged men committed to hard work, steadiness, and rural life; in demanding "wholesome women," they sought women who would simultaneously serve as beacons of imperial society and constrain the excesses of white men; in courting "steady families," they pursued stable units that would exemplify the virtues of the same-race, nuclear family. Together, "hardy backwoodsmen, wholesome women and steady families" were constructed as the immigrants able to transform British Columbia into the stable settler society of imperialists' dreams.

Studies of the flow of people between Europe and the Americas in the "Great Migration Era" have tended to leave a blind spot, namely their disinterest in interrogating the politicized character of nineteenth-century "new world" migration.[1] When people left Europe for the Americas or Australia, they did not simply move into large, empty spaces. Instead, they participated in a process of colonization in which Aboriginal dispossession and settler migration were irreparably linked. As Daiva Staisulis and Nira Yuval-Davis argue, migration is one of the chief ways in which settler societies constitute themselves.[2] For individuals and families, migration was probably motivated primarily by straightforward social and economic needs, but the overarching structure of imperialism transformed these needs into imperial acts.[3] Immigration sometimes troubled and sometimes nourished the politics of empire. In either case, it cannot be separated from them.

A better acknowledgement of the connections between migration and imperialism necessitates a return to an older phase in the writing of Canadian history, albeit with newly

---

Adele Perry, "Hardy Backwoodsmen, Wholesome Women, and Steady Families: Immigration and the Construction of a White Society in Colonial British Columbia, 1849–1871" in *Histoire sociale/Social History*, Vol. 33, no.66 (November 2000): 343–360.

critical eyes. The past two decades have witnessed an increasing emphasis on the social experience of immigrant peoples to Canada. Historians have rejected earlier studies in which "immigration was acknowledged as a key ingredient in transcontinental nation-building but the immigrants were largely ignored or relegated to cameo appearances."[4] They have embraced the vantage point of the immigrant instead of the policy-maker and analysed how these people, like women and the working class, were active agents who shaped their own history. This historiographic shift is premised on a needed critique of histories that artificially isolate the powerful from both the cause and effect of their authority. An unintended and less useful consequence of changing historiographic imperatives has been to detach the process of migration from its larger political context. Instead of treating the political and social history of immigration as distinct processes, historians need to reckon with the profound ties that connect the politician with the peasant and the policy-maker with the people.

Acknowledging these ties is crucial to understanding white settler colonies like British Columbia. The significance of immigration in colonial contexts derives from its central position in the very business of imperialism. Settler societies aim simultaneously to dispossess Aboriginal peoples and to replace them with relatively homogeneous settler populations, and immigration is one of the tools that has allowed them to do so. Colonies of settlement are distinguished from other kinds of colonies chiefly by their reproductive and gendered character. That colonizers *settle* implies more than residence. It denotes a reproductive regime dependent on the presence of settler women who literally reproduce the colony. Immigration must therefore provide more than non-Aboriginal bodies. Ideally, it must provide the right kind of bodies, those suited to building a white settler colony.

These connections between immigration, empire, and gender came together in mid-nineteenth-century British Columbia in an especially revealing way. Its society was the product of three sometimes conflicting imperial intentions: the fur trade, the gold rush, and the British tradition of settler colonies. North America's northern Pacific coast and the Columbia Plateau were densely populated by linguistically, culturally, and politically diverse First Nations people reliant on foraging, hunting, and fishing. The Hudson's Bay Company (HBC) began trading with local peoples in the late eighteenth century, and formal colonial authority was established in 1849 when Vancouver Island was made a British colony.

The discovery of gold on the mainland's Fraser River in 1858 precipitated the creation of a mainland colony called British Columbia. It was, according to imperial opinion, destined to be a major colony of settlement. "[N]ever did a colony in its infancy present a more satisfactory appearance," remarked one Anglican cleric. By 1866 and 1867, however, "those who once entertained most extravagant expectations began to despond."[5] Imperial downsizing followed despondency. In 1866 the two colonies were merged, retaining the name of British Columbia, and in July 1871 British Columbia joined Canada as a province, bringing the colonial period to a close.

These shifts in political form reflected widespread disappointment in British Columbia's performance as a settler colony. "The high tide of immigration expected never reached the Colony," explained Governor Frederick Seymour, "and the ebb proved much stronger than anticipated."[6] To be sure, the population expanded: there were fewer than 1,000 settlers in 1855 and over 10,000 in 1871. But the settler population never rivalled the Aboriginal one, which, despite massive depopulation wrought by smallpox, likely hovered around the 45,000 mark in the early 1870s.[7]

Settler British Columbia did not grow as quickly as imperial observers hoped it would, nor did it grow in the way they had hoped. The periphery, like the metropole, defied pretences of ethnic and racial homogeneity.[8] For a supposed white settler colony, British Columbia was not very white: Chinese, African-American, Latino, and Kanaka (Hawaiian) settlers were a significant presence. Jews and continental Europeans pressed operative definitions of whiteness, and Americans unsettled the colony's claims to Britishness. In 1861 the local official for Douglas, a small gold-rush town on the mainland, enumerated 97 Chinese, 40 Americans, 20 Mexicans, 17 Europeans, and 6 "coloured" people. They dwelled amongst "About 700 Natives."[9] "It would have been difficult to find in one place a greater mixture of different nationalities," wrote German mathematician Carl Friesach after visiting Yale, another small mining town. "Americans were undoubtably [sic] in the majority—California, especially had sent a larger contingent. Then followed Germans, French, and Chinese. Next came Italians, Spaniards, Poles, etc," he noted.[10]

The special plurality that characterized resource towns helped shape the entire colony. American missionary Matthew Macfie found Victoria, the capital city, a small and alarmingly cosmopolitan place in the early 1860s:

> Though containing at present an average of only 5,000 or 6,000 inhabitants, one cannot pass along the principal thoroughfares without meeting representatives of almost every tribe and nationality under heaven. Within a limited space may be seen—of Europeans, Russians, Austrians, Poles, Hungarians, Italians, Danes, Swedes, French, Germans, Spaniards, Swiss, Scotch, English and Irish; of Africans, Negroes from the United States and the West Indies; of Asiatics, Lascars and Chinamen; of Americans, Indians, Mexicans, Chilanoes, and citizens of the North American Republic; and of Polynesians, Malays from the Sandwich Islands [Hawaii].[11]

Macfie's fevered attempt to classify this population perhaps speaks more to his own discomfort with the mutability of racial boundaries, but it is not surprising that this discomfort was triggered in British Columbia. The diversity fostered by the gold rushes of the early colonial days diminished but never disappeared. When British Columbia entered Canadian confederation in 1871, its settler society was constituted, according to one probably conservative count, by 8,576 whites, 1,548 Chinese, and 462 Africans.[12]

That British Columbia's settlers were overwhelmingly male further suggested its failure to fit the norms of a white settler colony. While the female proportion ebbed and flowed over the colonial period, it never exceeded a high of 35 per cent of the white society and reached lows of 5 per cent.[13] Imperial discourse that accorded white women a special role as harbingers of empire rendered this demographic problem a political one. A popular emigration guide by "A Returned Digger," like so many others, despaired of what to do with a society so lacking in women. "The great curse of the colony," he explained, "is the absence of women. I doubt if there was one woman to a hundred men twelve months ago. I am quite sure that now, when I am writing, there must be at least two hundred men to every woman."[14] In colonial discourse, the continuing demographic dominance of First Nations people, the plurality of settler society, and its prevailing masculinity became irreparably intertwined, a three-part symbol of British Columbia's departure from dominant social norms and expectations.

Colonial promoters—a term I apply to a loose collection of journalists, politicians, officials, missionaries, and self-appointed do-gooders—looked to immigration to address the smallness, diversity, and masculinity of settler British Columbia and to render it a prosperous and respectable settler colony. They attributed the colony's lamentable imperial performance to the sparseness of its settler society. The *British*

Columbian newspaper argued that the colony's poor showing stemmed from its underpopulation, "because we have only a mere handful of population, a few thousand people living upon one another."[15] The colony lacked white population of nearly every description. The Victoria press noted,

> If we enter our churches, they want worshippers; our school houses want scholars; our streets and highways want pedestrians and vehicles; our merchants want trade; our traders want customers; our steamboats want passengers and freight; our workshops want workmen; our fertile valleys want farmers; our gold and silver mines want miners; in short, the two Colonies want population.[16]

While the colony had resources, wrote the *Cariboo Sentinel,* "without a population a country may remain forever a barren wilderness, dotted here and there with a few fisherman's huts and a few miners' and lumberman's cabins, and known only to the world as an inhospitable and poverty-stricken place."[17]

If colonial promoters suggested that British Columbia's ills stemmed from the sparseness of the white population, they had a related and almost boundless faith in the political potential of white bodies to make it a successful colonial enterprise. Even the most shameless boosters, however, recognized that British Columbia's distance from centres of white population meant that active state intervention was required for mass immigration to occur. If they wanted a white population, they would have to work for it, bidding it to come hither, assisting its passage, and supporting it on arrival. "To have our country filled up we must not only assist people to reach our shores, but we must show them the way to earn a living after they get here," wrote the *Colonist* in 1866.[18] The intervention of both the local and colonial state was required. "What right has the most remote of the British

Colonies to expect immigration without even *asking for it,*" agreed the New Westminster press, "to say nothing of *assisting* it?"[19]

Colonial promoters' demands for immigration were part and parcel of a programme of asserting white supremacy in British Columbia. Himani Bannerji has recently dubbed immigration a "euphemistic expression for racist labour and citizenship policies."[20] In colonial British Columbia the process worked to exclude First Nations migrants and to minimize non-white settlers. It was difficult, although hardly impossible, to argue for the removal of First Nations with local and obvious territorial claims. Those from distant territories were easy targets for settlers committed to visions of racial segregation. The city of Victoria worked hard to control and limit the presence of the so-called Northern Tribes—people from the coastal societies of the Nisga'a, Hieltsuk, Nexalk, Kwakwaka'wakw, Tlingit, and especially the wealthy and politically powerful Haida and Tsimshian—who made annual spring visits to Victoria for trade, wage work, and festivity. In 1859 a police constable found 2,235 Northern peoples, the bulk of them probably Haida and Tsimshian, living on the outskirts of Victoria.[21] As annually as they arrived, local burghers demanded their eviction. The language they used to stigmatize Northern peoples invoked the overlapping discourses of morality, criminality, and gender that have often been used to identify and marginalize immigrant groups. "Vagrancy, filth, disease, drunkenness, larceny, maiming, murder, prostitution, in a multiplied form, are the invariable results of an annual visit from the Northern Tribes," raged the *Colonist.* "We unhesitantly declare for stopping the immigration."[22]

Those who defended the rights of Northern peoples to visit Victoria—and, by implication, their status as legitimate immigrants and thus colonial citizens—relied on another staple of immigration discourse, namely the argument that the Northern peoples' presence, however unpalatable, was sweetened by their cheap labour. When settlers demanded that Northern peoples be forcibly evicted, missionary William Duncan argued that "the driving-away policy is contrary to the interests of our Colony, which needs at least the labor of the Indians." He referred those who doubted the local need for Aboriginal labour to "the kitchens and nurseries, the fields and gardens around Victoria."[23] Governor James Douglas proposed schemes of moral and social regulation as an alternative to eviction, arguing that Northern peoples' willingness to serve as a colonial labour force made them valuable to whites. "[I]t is hardly creditable to the civilization of the nineteenth century, that so especial an element of health, as labour of the cheapest description should be, in a manner, banished from the Colony," he explained.[24]

The sweat and toil of the Northern peoples ultimately failed to buy them a legitimate role in settler Victoria. Those who wanted racial segregation of colonial space were bolstered and legitimated by the apocalyptic smallpox epidemic of 1862, when Northern peoples were repeatedly and forcibly evicted from Victoria, a process later condoned and organized by public health legislation.[25] A brand of settler imperialism premised on the removal and containment of local peoples ultimately won out over the version that positioned them as subservient labourers for the ruling minority. Historians need to broaden our understanding of migration to account for the plurality and movement of the so-called old world and to make room for the migrations of Aboriginal North America. Doing so complicates our analysis of migration and lays bare the extent to which immigration functioned as a mechanism of inclusion and exclusion.

That this process worked to include whites and exclude others is confirmed by the experience of settlers of Asian and African extraction. Douglas—himself an archetypal hybrid figure, hailing from a "creole" mother and a Scottish father and having married the half-Cree Amelia Connolly—encouraged the migration of mainly middle-class African Americans associated with the Pioneer Society of San Francisco in 1858. Other settlers did not share his enthusiasm. Despite the African Americans' apparent fit with the colony's putative values of hard work, Protestantism, and respectability, their sizable presence in Victoria was regarded by many white people as a problem. Whether Victoria would replicate or challenge American-style segregation in her churches, theatres, and saloons was a significant item of debate until the black population began to disperse in the mid-1860s.[26]

It was Chinese immigration that created the most ambivalence among British Columbia's white commentators. Representations of Chinese men celebrated industriousness and sometimes located them on the colonists' side of the local imperial divide. The Grand Jury of Cayoosh (later Lillooet) told the Governor in 1860 that Chinese settlers were a benefit to white traders and the government alike. The jury further requested that the state acknowledge the Chinese as settlers, asking that they "afford them every due protection to prevent their being driven away, wither by attacks from Indians or otherwise."[27]

More often Chinese men were positioned as undesirable immigrants who would imperil rather than bolster colonialism. The *Cariboo Sentinel* argued that Chinese men should not be colonists for a variety of reasons, all indicating their fundamental difference and many invoking explicitly gendered images. The Chinese, the newspaper argued, were "aliens not merely in nationality, but in habits, religion"; they never became "good citizens" or served on juries or fire companies; they never married or settled outside China and were "more apt to create immorality than otherwise"; they dealt "entirely with their own countrymen"; they hoarded their money and evaded taxes; and, lastly, they were, ironically for immigrants, "inimical to immigration."[28] No restrictions were imposed on

Chinese immigration, although colonists debated ways—prominent among them being a miner's licence fee levied on Chinese men alone—designed to regulate their place within settler society.[29] Such discussions anticipated the highly organized, pervasive, and vociferous attacks on Chinese people that began later in the nineteenth century and continue to shape contemporary life and politics.[30]

The role of immigration to colonial British Columbia was thus an explicitly racial one. The "'bone, muscle, and intellect,' that is required here," explained the Victoria press plainly, "differs materially from the Indian or the African. It is Caucasian—Anglo-Saxon bone, muscle, and intellect we want."[31] Class, and the politics of respectability that so often went with it, also helped determine who would be included and who excluded. Not all white people were created equal. British Columbia's colonial promoters did not want convicts, although one, tellingly, was willing to tolerate juvenile offenders as long as they were placed on First Nations settlements.[32] When the Colonial Office inquired about the emigration of distressed Lancashire mill operatives, local officials were similarly unreceptive. Douglas replied that "this Colony offers but a poor field for destitute immigrants," warning that "instead of improving their condition, it is to be feared, that by emigrating in great numbers to this Colony, they would only be involved in a more hopeless state of distress and poverty."[33] British Columbia's officials were ultimately as fearful of organized immigration's class implications—of the shovelling out of paupers—as were others in British North America.

Immigration to this settler colony was an issue of race and class, and also very much one of gender. British Columbia's colonial failure was linked, in critics' minds, not only to the smallness and diversity of the settler society but also to the failure of increasingly hegemonic gender norms to take root there. British Columbia was home to a small, highly mobile handful of settler men living amongst a large Aboriginal society. This particular demography fostered a rough, vibrant homosocial culture created by and for young men and the widespread practice of white-Aboriginal domestic and conjugal relationships. Immigration was sought as a corrective for both. When promoters called for immigration, they called for a process that would address the society's perceived gendered deficiencies as well as its racial peculiarities.

Three gendered images dominated discussions of immigration. First, the hardy backwoodsman—a steady, hard-working man willing to meet the difficulties of colonial life and permanently settle in British Columbia—shaped discussions of men and migration. The hypothetical hardy backwoodsman was constructed in contrast to the rough gold miners who so pervaded the colony. British Columbia had two major gold rushes—the Fraser River Gold Rush of 1858 and the Cariboo Gold Rush of 1862–1863—and a host of smaller ones. Waves of young, footloose men disillusioned with the false promises of capitalist, industrial society were attracted by each strike of gold. Prevailing discourse understood these men as wandering, immoral, and anti-social. George Grant, secretary of a surveying party, argued that the gold rushes brought "not an emigration of sober, steady householders, whose aim was to establish homes, and live by their own industry, but of fever-hearted adventurers from all parts of the world,—men without a country and without a home."[34]

Miners' inadequacies as colonists became axiomatic in popular colonial discourse. "It must be admitted that a very considerable section of our population is composed of adventurers, who, having been attracted to our shores by our gold, feel little or no interest in the permanent success of the Colony," wrote the *British Columbian*.[35] For British Columbia to fulfil its imperial potential, hardy backwoodsmen would have to replace the wandering miners. In 1859

Douglas told the Colonial Office, "The mining population are proverbially migratory and unsettled in their habits, seldom engaging in any other than their own absorbing pursuits, and therefore, it is he who tills the soil, the industrious farmer, who must clear the forest, bring the land into cultivation, and build up the permanent interests and prosperity of the Colony."[36]

The hardy backwoodsman stood in contrast not only to the wandering miner, but to another masculine drain on the colonial enterprise, the "croaker." This term, along with grumbler, was applied to men deemed unable to weather the difficulties of colonial life. Whether an erstwhile son of wealth or an urban loafer, the croaker was flummoxed by the realities of pioneering and proceeded to complain instead of work. Gilbert Malcolm Sproat, a sawmill owner, magistrate, amateur anthropologist, and promoter of immigration, described the croakers:

> [C]ertain persons came into the country who had a strong desire to make a living without taking off their coats—a desire which could not be gratified. The friends of these persons at home sent them money, which they put into silly investments. They rode to the diggings, and road [sic] back again. They hung, like mendicants, round the doors of the Government offices. They croaked in the streets, spent their time idly in bar-rooms, and finally disappeared.[37]

Here, the language of class is put to work in the service of gender and race: the croaker is idle and delicate, bearing the mark of both femininity and bourgeois laxity. The local press argued a similar position. Some settlers, one paper argued, "only remain to croak and whine for a season, and eventually, like sickly lambs or untimely fruit, unequal to the task of combatting [sic] and overcoming the hardships and privations incident to all new countries, drop off to their native land."[38] The test of manliness

these "sickly lambs" fail is thus generated by the specificities of the colonial context.

This was a test that the hardy backwoodsman passed. Just as they repelled the weak, colonies were thought to attract the most manly of British men who stood in contrast not only to their less rugged fellows, but to the indigenous men they alternately feminized or feared.[39] "As a rule," commented the local press, "it is the most energetic, hardy, manly, self reliant of her sons who first people her Colonies."[40] Ideal male immigrants were hard-working, disciplined, and predisposed to rural life. The new colony, argued a supporter in 1860, "does not want the idle, the profligate, and sickly."[41] The hardy backwoodsman embraced diligent labour, especially agricultural labour, just as the gold miner rejected it. His single state meant that he was able to devote himself fully to labour, to define himself as an entirely economic being. One much-reprinted emigration guide advised, "A family is a burden till a man is established."[42]

The discourse of the hardy backwoodsman both reflected and masked single men's economic significance to a colony materially tied to resource extraction. Despite the significance of Aboriginal people to British Columbia's wage-labour force, employers persisted in seeking non-Native miners and farmers and believed, in keeping with the Anglo-American world, that only men could fulfil these roles. That a work force of single men was literally reproduced elsewhere spared the colony the costs of maintaining and creating labour in the next generation.[43] Labour-force politics reinforced the prevailing gendered patterns of immigration and ensured that single men formed the overwhelming majority of independent immigrants. They also comprised a surprising percentage of assisted ones. Between 1849 and 1852 the HBC imported over 400 people, 250 of whom were adult men mainly destined to labour on Island farms.[44] The search for hardy backwoodsmen persisted throughout the colonial period. A proposed 1864 Vancouver Island scheme put "farm labourers" alongside "unmarried female domestic servants" and "married couples" as people whose passages should be subsidized.[45]

Yet single men, hardy or otherwise, constituted an ambivalent force for colonial promoters. Sproat thought that their tendency to wander made them a waste of public funds.[46] More fundamentally, imperial regimes were consistently troubled by the large numbers of working-class men assigned responsibility for practically enforcing them.[47] White soldiers, miners, and farmers frequently failed to meet standards of racial distance and superiority set by imperial masters. Racial concerns about young, footloose men in colonial contexts were also gendered concerns. Colonial promoters were disturbed by how regularly white men formed relationships and families with local women. Settler men who opted to remain single were also a worry. Increasingly in the mid-nineteenth century the domestic family was constructed as a necessary component of adult life. To be rendered a responsible colonial citizen who was appropriately distanced from local peoples, the hardy backwoodsman needed a wholesome woman.

The scarcity of white women in British Columbia became, along with the smallness of the settler population, axiomatic for the colony's condition. As I have argued elsewhere, white women were constructed as "fair ones of a purer caste"[48] with three related roles in the local colonial project. White women would first compel white men to reject the rough homosocial culture of the backwoods in favour of normative standards of masculinity, respectability, and permanence. "Women! women! women! are the great want," wrote aristocrat Harry Verney from London. "The normal state is man with a help meet for him, and if something is not soon done, either by the Imperial or Colonial Government, or by some philanthropists at home, I know not what will become of us. Poor man goes sadly down hill if

he remains long without the supporting influence of women."[49] White women were considered to be men's collective better half, as the only force capable of ensuring their proper behaviour. Such a discourse accorded them a role, albeit a limited one, as agents in both imperialism and immigration.

White women would secondly address shortages in the local labour market and relieve overpopulation in Britain. That the supposed need for domestic servants and wives in British Columbia neatly matched fears of "surplus women" in Britain gave calls for female immigration a special efficacy. A female immigration to British Columbia, wrote one observer, "would be as great a boon to the colony as I am sure it would be to many of the underpaid, under-fed, and over-worked women who drag out a weary existence in the dismal back streets and alleys of the metropolis."[50] Immigration was thus invoked as a mechanism for simultaneously resolving the different crises of gender that troubled the metropole and the periphery.

White women's third service to the colonial project was the explicitly racial one of discouraging mixed-race sexual, domestic, and conjugal relationships. As white men's "natural" objects of desire, they would draw men away from the temptations of Aboriginal women and, in doing so, shore up the colonial project as a whole. "That many of the native women are cleanly, industrious, and faithful, we do not pretend to deny," wrote New Westminster's *Mainland Guardian*, "but, we regret to to [sic] say, they are the exceptions. With the increase of our white female population, we look for new life in our agricultural pursuits and we hope that every inducement will be offered to healthy industrious women, who are desirous of finding good husbands and comfortable homes, in this province, to come out to us."[51] This discourse was premised on the construction of white women as uplifting and on the representation of First Nations women as base and threatening that circulated throughout colonial British Columbia.

In these ways, the discourse of wholesome women emphasized the political utility of ordinary, working-class women above those who held an official role in the colonial project like missionaries' or officials' wives. Their contribution lay not in independent action, but rather in their ability to transform plebeian men. Such a discourse imbued women migrants with an agency less often acknowledged in historiography. At any rate, the sheer ideological weight of the conviction that a society lacking white women could not be a moral or even adequate one provided the motivation necessary to orchestrate immigration schemes in 1862, 1863, and 1870. Organized as joint efforts of the local elite, missionaries, and British feminists, these immigration campaigns are remembered in popular lore as the "brideships," as colony- (and, later, nation-) building enterprises. Together, the *Tynemouth, Robert Lowe,* and *Alpha* carried roughly a hundred women, largely teenagers from working-class and sometimes indigent backgrounds. They were putatively destined to be domestic servants, but popular discourse ensured that their real destiny lay in the marriage market. As wives of miners and farmers, colonial promoters hoped, these wholesome women would render British Columbia's fragile colonial project a stable one.[52]

The young working-class women produced by these female immigration schemes ultimately unsettled the colonial project rather than securing it. Instead of behaving as beacons of imperial rectitude, the immigrants acted like the young, working-class women that they were. Colonial promoters were deeply disappointed. By the close of the colonial period, their faith in the political usefulness of white female migration was profoundly shaken. In 1872 Sproat looked back on his experience with three separate female immigration efforts, commenting, "How to send single women to Victoria safely across the continent, and through San Francisco, is a problem which I

cheerfully hand over for solution to those who are more experienced in the management of that sex than I am."[53] The fundamental problem with white female migration, he argued, was that *single* women were necessarily a moral problem. "The very delicate and difficult question of introducing single unmarried women into British Columbia might be partly solved by sending out a few, in charge of the heads of families—the women being from the same district as the families, and thus having an addition[al] guard for their self-respect," he argued.[54]

Wholesome women, much like hardy backwoodsmen, challenged the colonial project at the same time as they bolstered it. The enthusiasm for white female migration was always tempered and eventually overwhelmed by the conviction that single women, like men, were a dangerous population that could only be properly contained by families. After the disasters of the assisted female migration efforts of 1862 and 1863, the "steady family" gained a special cachet in pro-immigration discourse that would only increase after the 20 servant-women transported on the *Alpha* in 1870 proved, like their predecessors, a disappointment to those who so sought their importation. The Female Immigration Board that oversaw this scheme recommended that the colonial government abandon the project of female immigration and shift its monies and attentions to the "assisted passages of Families, and relatives of Farmers, Mechanics, and others settled in this Colony."[55] In pledging their support for the importation of families, and not single women, members of the board endorsed the stable family as the best kind of immigration for the colony.

They were not alone in suggesting that same-race domestic families would be the best base for a settler society and thus the best immigrants. Families simultaneously constrained young women and encouraged men to be permanent and diligent settlers. The *Victoria Press* argued, "The very class which we want above all others is the married agriculturist—the man whose social circumstances will bring him to the soil, and make him a permanent as well as productive inhabitant."[56] Sproat agreed, writing that "the married farmer with modest means, and accustomed to work in the fields, is the best kind of immigrant for British Columbia."[57] The HBC supported family migration when it imported 36 married colliers to work Nanaimo's coalfields.[58] That the Colonial Office shared this familial ideal is suggested by its willingness to pay for the passage of the wives and families of the Royal Engineers, the soldier-settlers sent to enforce British claims to the mainland.[59] On rare occasions the colonial government subsidized the migration of individual families,[60] but more often used land law to buttress domestic family formation. In Vancouver Island, nuclear family formation was encouraged by laws that gave white men an additional 50 acres of free land if they were married and 10 more acres for each child under the age of 10.[61]

The overlap between immigration discourse and immigration practice was usually indirect. These demands for hardy backwoodsmen, wholesome women, and steady families were rarely parlayed into concrete action. Immigration was what colonial pundits always wanted and never got. In referring to immigrants as "mythical beings," politician John Sebastian Helmcken astutely recognized the somewhat hypnotic role immigration played in colonial discourse.[62] The mythic rather than actual character of immigration to colonial British Columbia was not for lack of heated rhetoric or wild scheming. Colonial promoters held mass meetings, struck committees, wrote passionate letters, and developed plans for using immigration to secure their imperial fortunes.[63] With the exception of the 20 servant women carried on the *Alpha* in 1870, however, the colonial government's immigration efforts were largely confined to the cheap and discursive: they subsidized mail, explored territory, printed essays, and hired lecturers to regale the masses of various urban centres. In 1861, for instance, British Columbia created an exhibit for the World's Fair designed to prove to "struggling, hard worked Englishmen how easily a livelihood may be earned here."[64]

The modesty of these efforts deeply disappointed those who considered immigration key to imperial success. They complained bitterly about the local government's apparent inability to organize immigration. In 1864 the mainland press commented that, excepting "fifty pounds paid to a parson at Lillooet for an Essay," the colony had "not yet expended a single dollar" on immigration.[65] Five years later, the same newspaper despaired that there was not one person responsible for immigration "[a]mongst the army of officials who absorb the revenue of the Colony."[66]

If British Columbia's local government was unable, its imperial masters were unwilling. The Colonial Office argued that, given its location, British Columbia could only reasonably expect emigrants from the Australasian colonies, not from Britain, and repeatedly announced that it had no intention of ever assisting emigration to the colony.[67] When pestered to subsidize steam communication, Colonial Office staff made it clear that they lacked the requisite political will. "When this Country was supposed to be overpeopled, there was the appearance of a domestic object in schemes for using the proceeds of English taxes to encourage emigration. But that state of things has long ceased to exist," one noted.[68] Domestic issues like overpopulation fuelled the various assisted emigration schemes of the 1830s and 1840s and would again motivate major emigration schemes in the *fin de siècle*. These efforts ground to a near halt when popular economic fortunes bettered and events like New Zealand's Maori Wars and the Indian Rebellion of 1857 challenged British faith in the imperial project.

Whether in London, Victoria, or New Westminster, many doubted British Columbia's ability to attract settlers, but only a few challenged its need for a large white population. In 1861 the *Victoria Press* argued that mass immigration was an impractical goal cooked up by those unaccustomed to colonial labour, race politics, and labour relations. "It may suit a number of lackadaisical beings who are entirely unfitted for Colonial, or in fact any practical useful life, to be enabled to obtain, by a superabundant supply of immigrants, civilized *servants* at the same price they now pay for Indians," the press wrote.[69] Yet those who questioned the merits or feasibility of mass white immigration never captured the mainstream of public discourse. Ultimately, British Columbia's apparent inability to attract white and especially British immigrants served not as a reason for challenging the viability of colonialism, but rather as a rationale for the colony's entry into Canadian confederation.[70] If British Columbia could not use immigration to become a stable settler colony in its own right, it would try to do so as a Canadian province. That British Columbia finally registered a white majority in the first census taken after confederation suggests that this strategy was effective. With continuing depopulation of First Nations and the arrival of the transcontinental railroad in 1886—that tangible technology of both capital and nation and conveyor of migrants *par excellence*—British Columbia

would begin to look increasingly like a textbook white settler colony, but it would continue to be haunted by a spectre of hybridity that was, in the final analysis, more nurtured by immigration than vanquished by it.

British Columbia's colonial pundits spilled much ink on the topic of immigration. They did so because immigration was central to their effort to transform British Columbia into a white settler colony. For them, immigration was a mechanism of inclusion and exclusion, one that would marginalize First Nations people, minimize non-white settlers, and nurture white migration. It would do so in explicitly gendered ways that reflected the importance of gender to the construction of a settler society. In newspapers, government reports, and colonial circles, they called for the immigration of white, preferably British immigrants who would fit into three gendered models: the hardy backwoodsman, the wholesome woman, and the steady family. This discourse reflected a minority's aspirations rather than a society's social experience. However constant and blustery the pro-immigration discourse, British Columbia's settler society would continue to be small, dominated by men, and relatively diverse until the Canadian Pacific Railway integrated the province into more continental patterns of demography and settlement. Immigration was indeed a tool for negotiating exclusions and inclusions, but not always in predictable ways.

Notes

Adele Perry is assistant professor in the Department of History at St. Paul's College, University of Manitoba. This article is drawn from *On the Edge of Empire: Gender, Race, and the Making of British Columbia, 1849–1871* (Toronto: University of Toronto Press, 2001). She would like to thank the organizers of the conference "Recasting European and Canadian History" for their contributions to this paper.

1 See, for instance, Bernard Bailyn, *The Peopling of British North America: An Introduction* (New York: Knopf, 1986). For a revealing example, see the explicit definition of Ontario's Leeds and Landsdowne townships as "empty" in Donald Harman Akenson,

The Irish in Ontario: A Study in Rural History (Montreal and Kingston: McGill-Queen's University Press, 1984), p. 55.

2 Daiva Staisulis and Nira Yuval-Davis, "Introduction: Beyond Dichotomies—Gender, Race, Ethnicity and

Class in Settler Societies," in Staisulis and Yuval-Davis, eds., *Unsettling Settler Societies: Articulations of Gender, Race, Ethnicity and Class* (London: Sage, 1995).

3   On this point in a later period, see Stephen Constantine, "Introduction: Empire Migration and Imperial Harmony," in Constantine, ed., *Emigrants and Empire: British Settlement in the Dominions Between the Wars* (Manchester: Manchester University Press, 1990). See also Rita S. Krandis, ed., *Imperial Objects: Essays on Victorian Women's Emigration and the Unauthorized Imperial Experience* (New York: Twayne, 1998).

4   On this shift, see Franca Iacovetta, "Manly Militants, Cohesive Communities, and Defiant Domestics: Writing about Immigrants in Canadian Historical Scholarship," *Labour/Le Travail*, vol. 36 (Fall 1995), p. 221. Also see Iacovetta with Paula Draper and Robert Vantresca, "Preface," in Iacovetta, Draper, and Vantresca, eds., *A Nation of Immigrants: Women, Workers, and Communities in Canadian History, 1840s–1960s* (Toronto: University of Toronto Press, 1998).

5   Henry Wright, *Nineteenth Annual Report of the Missions of the Church of England in British Columbia for the Year 1877* (London: Rivingtons, 1878), pp. 16–17.

6   British Columbia Archives (hereafter BCA), GR 1486, mflm B-1442, Great Britain, Colonial Office, British Columbia Original Correspondence (hereafter CO 60), CO 60/32, Frederick Seymour to Duke of Buckingham and Chandos, March 17, 1868.

7   All population figures from colonial British Columbia are at best guesses. These are from British Columbia, *Report of the Hon. H.L. Langevin, C.B., Minister of Public Works* (Ottawa: I.B. Taylor, 1872), p. 22; and Edward Mallandaine, *First Victoria Directory, Third [Fourth] Issues, and British Columbia Guide* (Victoria: Mallandaine, 1871), pp. 94–95. Also see R. Cole Harris and John Warkentin, *Canada Before Confederation: A Study in Historical Geography* (Ottawa: Carleton University Press, 1991), chap. 7.

8   Antoinette Burton, *At the Heart of the Empire: Indians and the Colonial Encounter in Late-Victorian Britain* (Berkeley: University of California Press, 1998).

9   BCA, "Colonial Correspondence," GR 1372, mflm B-1330, file 620/16, John Bowles Gaggin to W.A. G. Young, April 3, 1861.

10   Carl Friesach, "Extracts from *Ein Ausflug nach Britisch-Columbien in Jahre 1858*," in E.E. Delavault and Isabel McInnes, trans., "Two Narratives of the Fraser River Gold Rush," *British Columbia Historical Quarterly*, vol. 1 (July 1941), p. 227.

11   Matthew Macfie, *Vancouver Island and British Columbia: Their History, Resources and Prospects* (London: Longman, Green, Longman, Roberts & Green, 1865), pp. 378–379.

12   British Columbia, *Report of the Hon. H.L. Langevin*, p. 22.

13   On this, see Adele Perry, *On the Edge of Empire: Gender, Race, and the Making of British Columbia, 1849–1871* (Toronto: University of Toronto Press, 2000), chap. 1.

14   A Returned Digger, *The Newly Discovered Gold Fields of British Columbia* (London: Darton and Hodge, 1862, 8th ed.), p. 7.

15   "Our Great Want," *British Columbian*, January 9, 1869.

16   "Our Wants," *British Colonist*, June 5, 1861.

17   "Emigration," *Cariboo Sentinel*, June 18, 1868.

18   "Assisted Immigration," *British Colonist*, December 11, 1866.

19   "Population, Population," *British Columbian*, May 29, 1869.

20   Himani Bannerji, *On the Dark Side of the Nation: Essays on Multiculturalism, Nationalism and Gender* (Toronto: Canadian Scholars' Press, 2000), p. 4.

21   "Our Indian Population," *Weekly Victoria Gazette*, April 28, 1859.

22   "Invasion of the Northern Indians," *British Colonist*, April 18, 1861.

23   Wm. Duncan, "The Indian Question," *British Colonist*, July 4, 1861. On Aboriginal wage labour, see John Lutz, "After the Fur Trade: Aboriginal Wage Labour in Nineteenth-Century British Columbia," *Journal of the Canadian Historical Association* (1992), pp. 69–94.

24   National Archives of Canada (hereafter NAC), Great Britain, Colonial Office Correspondence, Vancouver Island (hereafter CO 305). CO 305/10, mflm B-238, James Douglas to Sir Edward Bulwer Lytton, May 25, 1859.

25   See Perry, *On the Edge*, chap. 5.

26   For an argument for black migration to Vancouver Island, see Mary A. Shadd, *A Plea for Emigration; or, Notes of Canada West, in its Moral, Social, and Political Aspect With Suggestions Respecting Mexico, West Indies, and Vancouver Island, for the Information of Colored Emigrants* (Detroit: George W. Pattison, 1842), pp. 43–44. On black people in Victoria society, see Irene Genevieve Marie Zaffaroni, "The Great Chain of Being: Racism and Imperialism in Colonial Victoria, 1858–1871"

(MA thesis, University of Victoria, 1987), chap. 4; Crawford Killian, *Go Do Some Great Thing: The Black Pioneers of British Columbia* (Vancouver: Douglas and McIntyre, 1978).

27 NAC, CO 60/8, MG 11, mflm B-83, "Address of the Grand Jury at Cayoosh to Governor Douglas," in James Douglas to Duke of Newcastle, October 9, 1860.

28 "Our Chinese Population," *Cariboo Sentinel,* May 16, 1867.

29 See, for an explanation of why they were impracticable, NAC, CO 63/3, mflm B-1489, "Speech of His Honor the Officer Administering the Government at the Opening of the Legislative Council," *British Columbia Government Gazette.*

30 On this, see Kay Anderson, *Vancouver's Chinatown: Racial Discourse in Canada, 1875–1980* (Montreal and Kingston: McGill-Queen's University Press, 1991); Patricia E. Roy, *A White Man's Province: British Columbia Politicians and Chinese and Japanese Immigrants, 1858–1914* (Vancouver: University of British Columbia Press, 1989).

31 "Indian vs. White Labor," *British Colonist,* February 19, 1861.

32 "Convict labour," *British Columbian,* January 11, 1865; "Juvenile Offenders—Colonization," *British Columbian,* May 30, 1869.

33 NAC, CO 305/20, MG 11, mflm B-244, and CO 60/16, MG 11, mflm B-89, James Douglas to the Duke of Newcastle, July 14, 1863.

34 George M. Grant, *Ocean to Ocean: Sandford Fleming's Expedition Through Canada in 1872* (Toronto: James Campbell & Son, 1873), p. 308. Also see Adele Perry, "Bachelors in the Backwoods: White Men and Homosocial Culture in Up-Country British Columbia, 1858–1871," in R.W. Sandwell, ed., *Beyond City Limits: Rural History in British Columbia* (Vancouver: University of British Columbia Press, 1998).

35 "Arterial Highways," *British Columbian,* January 2, 1862.

36 NAC, CO 60/4, MG 11, mflm B-80, James Douglas to Edward Bulwer Lytton, July 11, 1859.

37 Gilbert Malcolm Sproat, *British Columbia: Information for Emigrants* (London: Agent General for the Province, 1873), p. 4.

38 "The Soil of British Columbia," *British Columbian,* February 3, 1863.

39 On masculinity and colonization, see Mrinalini Sinha, *Colonial Masculinity: The "Manly Englishman"* and the "Effeminate Bengali" in the Late Nineteenth Century* (Manchester: Manchester University Press, 1995); Elizabeth Vibert, *Traders' Tales: Narratives of Cultural Encounters on the Plateau, 1807–1846* (Norman: University of Oklahoma Press, 1997).

40 "The Colonial Policy of Great Britain," *British Colonist,* May 2, 1863.

41 "Testimonial to D.G.F. MacDonald, Esq., C.E.," *Weekly Victoria Gazette,* January 30, 1860.

42 A Returned Digger, *The Newly Discovered Gold Fields,* p. 8.

43 This is dealt with, to some extent, in Alicja Muszynski, *Cheap Wage Labour: Race and Gender in the Fisheries of British Columbia* (Montreal and Kingston: McGill-Queen's University Press, 1996). Muszynski, however, discusses the economics of the single male immigrant as unique to Chinese men, when in fact most non-Natives lacked co-resident families.

44 University of British Columbia Library (hereafter UBCL), CO 305/3, mflm R288, A. Colville to John Packington, November 24, 1852, p. 1.

45 British Library, BS 72/1, "England, Emigration Commissioners," *Colonization Circular,* no. 25, 1866 (London, Groombridge and Sons), p. 8.

46 BCA, Add Mss 257, file 3, Gilbert Malcolm Sproat to Lieutenant Governor, "Memo re European Immigration into B.C.," November 3, 1871.

47 See, for instance, Kenneth Ballhatchet, *Race, Sex and Class under the Raj: Imperial Attitudes and Policies and their Critics, 1783–1905* (London: Werdenfeld and Nicholson, 1980), chap. 5.

48 One of the Disappointed, untitled piece in the *British Columbian,* June 7, 1862; Adele Perry, "'Fair Ones of a Pure Caste': White Women and Colonialism in Nineteenth-Century British Columbia," *Feminist Studies,* vol. 23, no. 3 (Fall 1997), pp. 501–524.

49 "Sir Harry Verney Upon British Columbia," *British Columbian,* August 20, 1862.

50 A.D.G., "British Columbia: To the Editor of the Times," *London Times,* January 1, 1862.

51 "Immigration," *Mainland Guardian,* February 9, 1871.

52 See Perry, *On the Edge,* chaps. 6–7, for an analysis of female immigration to British Columbia.

53 BCA, GR 419, box 10, file 1872/1, British Columbia, Attorney General, "Documents," G.M.S., "Memorandum on Immigration, Oct 1972," pp. 95–96.

54 BCA, GR 419, box 10, file 1872/1, "Attorney General Documents," G.M. Sproat, "Memorandum of a few Suggestions for opening the business of emigration to British Columbia, referred to as Memo C. in a letter of G.M. Sproat to the Honourable the Provincial Secretary, dated 29th August 1972," pp. 4–5.

55 BCA, GR 1372, mflm B-1314, file 955/23, "Colonial Correspondence," Wm. Pearse, John Robson, W.J. MacDonald to Colonial Secretary, July 12, 1870; E.G.A., "The Immigration Board," *British Colonist,* June 24, 1870.

56 "The Overland Route," *Victoria Press,* March 16, 1862.

57 BCA, GR 419, box 10, file 1872/1, British Columbia, "Papers Related to Immigration, 1972," G.M.S., "Memorandum on Immigration, Oct 1872."

58 BCA, Add mss E/B/M91A, Andrew Muir, "Private Diary," November 9, 1848—August 5, 1850 [transcript]; Add mss A/C/20.1/N15, James Douglas—Joseph William McKay, "Nanaimo Correspondence, August 1852–September 1853" [transcript].

59 NAC, MG 11, CO 60/9, mflm B-83, G.C. Lewis to James Douglas, August 11, 1860, draft reply, in James Douglas to the Duke of Newcastle, May 12, 1860.

60 See, for instance, James E. Hendrickson, ed., *Journals of the Colonial Legislatures of the Colonies of Vancouver Island and British Columbia, 1851–1871,* vol. 1: *Journals of the Council, Executive Council, and Legislative Council of Vancouver Island, 1851–1866* (Victoria: Provincial Archives of British Columbia, 1980), pp. 133–134.

61 "The New Land Proclamation for Vancouver Island," *British Colonist,* March 8, 1861; "Salt Spring Island," *Victoria Press,* November 10, 1861; Macfie, *Vancouver Island and British Columbia*, p. 205.

62 "Legislative Council," *British Colonist,* February 4, 1869.

63 See examples in Hendrickson, ed., *Journals of the Colonial Legislatures,* vol. 2: *Journals of the House of Assembly, Vancouver Island, 1856–1863,* vol. 3: *Journals of the House of Assembly, Vancouver Island, 1863–1866,* and vol. 4: *Journals of the Executive Council, 1864–1871, and of the Legislative Council, 1864–1866, of British Columbia.*

64 "Industrial Exhibition Circular," *British Columbian,* May 30, 1861.

65 "Emigration," *British Columbian,* June 15, 1864.

66 "What Shall We Do With Them?" *British Columbian,* June 4, 1869.

67 NAC, MG 11, CO 60/5, mflm B-81, T.W.C. Murdoch and Frederic Rogers to Herman Merivale, April 28, 1859; mflm 69.303, Great Britain, House of Commons, Parliamentary Papers, vol. 38 (1863); no. 430, "Emigration: Number of Emigrants who left the United Kingdom for the *United States, British North America,* the several colonies of *Australasia, South Africa,* and other Places respectively; distinguishing, as far as practicable, the Native Country of the Emigrants, 1860–1863," mflm 69.303, p. 7.

68 NAC, MG 11, CO 60/14, mflm B-87, H.M. [Herman Merivale], April 8, note *en verso,* in T.W.C. Murdoch to Frederic Rogers, March 31, 1862.

69 "The Immigration Bubble," *Victoria Press,* July 27, 1861.

70 BCA, GR 1486, CO 60/29, mflm B-1440, Frederick Seymour to Duke of Buckingham and Chandos, September 24, 1867.

Marketing Wildlife: The Hudson's Bay Company and the Pacific Northwest, 1821–49

Lorne Hammond

Wildlife is an aspect of the fur trade that has received little attention in the literature, yet animals were the foundation of the trade.[1] Their presence lured trapper and trader, and the demographic fluctuations of wildlife, along with characteristics of different species, marketing, and the vagaries of fashion, were unpredictable variables of the business. This paper, although drawn from a fur trade case study in the Pacific Northwest, fits within a wider context. In the Pacific Northwest, as in many other parts of the world, commerce was the first external agent in the exploration and assignment of values and utility to wildlife. Commerce predated scientific inquiry, European settlement, the legislative process, and the cultural influence of the writer and painter.

One influential force in the field of commerce was the Hudson's Bay Company (HBC), a group with a managerial structure that distinguished it from other fur trade companies. It was a company whose management was hierarchical, an arrangement complicated by distance since its headquarters were in London, England. Major HBC shareholders were represented by a governor, deputy governor, and committee. These individuals communicated their wishes about company operations in North America to George Simpson, the North American governor. Simpson had responsibility to provide the committee with detailed annual letters on conditions in each department and post within the districts under his control. The people in each department who were responsible for major posts were called chief factors. Chief traders and clerks ran the smaller posts. Coordinating this system involved complex supply lines and frequent communication via services such as the express canoe, which took only passengers and mail. Evidence suggests that this bureaucratic structure conditioned responses to managing and standardizing wildlife as products.[2]

In 1821 HBC merged with its competitor, the North West Company of Montreal, and gained significant new territory. This new area was designated the Columbia Department and it produced 8 percent of the 18.5 million hides and pelts exported from North America from 1821 to 1849.[3] As map 1 shows, the Columbia Department included the northern interior posts of New Caledonia and much of present-day British Columbia, Oregon, and Washington. The latter two were jointly occupied with the United States under a temporary agreement regarding the disputed boundaries and ownership of the

---

Lorne Hammond, "Marketing Wildlife: The Hudson's Bay Company and the Pacific Northwest, 1821–49," *Forest and Conservation History* 37, 1 (January 1993): 14–25. Reprinted by permission of the Forest History Society, Inc., Durham, NC (www.forest.history.org).

MAP 1 POSTS AND ROUTES OF THE COLUMBIA
DEPARTMENT, 1825-50

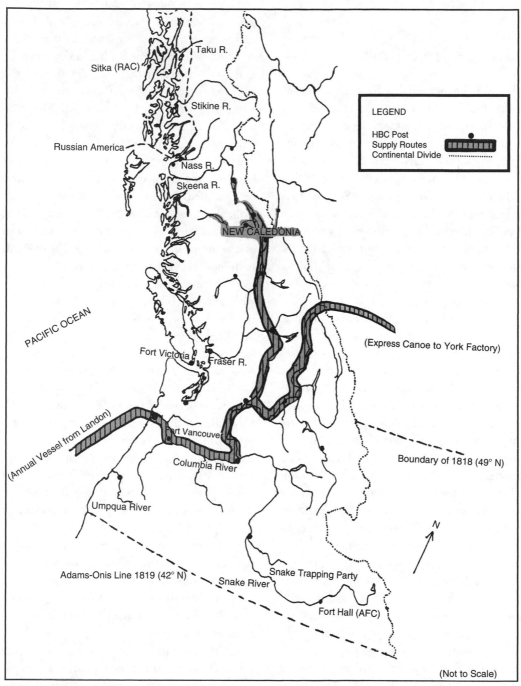

Taku R.

Sitka (RAC)

Stikine R.

Russian America

Nass R.

Skeena R.

NEW CALEDONIA

PACIFIC OCEAN

Fort Victoria Fraser R.

(Express Canoe to York Factory)

(Annual Vessel from London)

Port Vancouver

Columbia River

Boundary of 1818 (49° N)

Umpqua River

Adams-Onis Line 1819 (42° N) Snake River Snake Trapping Party

Fort Hall (AFC)

LEGEND

HBC Post
Supply Routes
Continental Divide

(Not to Scale)

Map provided by the author.

Oregon Territory, that land north of the Adams-Onis line of 1819 and west of the continental divide.

Nature's Inventory

Although it was not the first fur trading company in the Pacific Northwest, the Hudson's Bay Company was the largest and the most successful. The company's rapid expansion into the region during the years 1821–49 offers a good picture of the process of assessing wildlife as a product. When Governor George Simpson took his first tour of the Columbia Department in 1824–25, diversification in trapping and hunting the region's wildlife was just beginning. He reported on the commercial potential of wildlife, such as the mountain goat.[4] As an experiment Simpson joined his voyageurs in citing the first two he saw; he described them as "tough." From then on there was a regular flow of potential products from the hinterland posts to London, from grizzly bears to the small hoary marmot. In 1826 he issued instructions to have sample skin and horns of a mountain goat saved for a naturalist, but the first specimens went to London for a determination of their commercial potential. In 1825 Chief Factor John McLoughlin forwarded samples of swan skins and sturgeon's bladders from his post on the Columbia River at Fort Vancouver "to know what they are worth." Seventeen years later he was still sending samples, including "oulachan oil," spermaceti (a wax found in the head cavities and blubber of the sperm whale), "sea horse teeth" (walrus tusks), and sea lion hides as possible products "for trial in the English market."[5]

Once these samples reached London, the company sought informed opinions as to their relative quality, value, market, and potential competitors. Some items were sold at auction so that buyer response could be evaluated. The auction served to process market information, a means of introducing potential new products as "odd lots" on a test basis.[6] For example, wolf and wolverine appeared first in the HBC catalogs as "Sundries," but as demand increased they were sold as distinct categories of fur.

Beaver pelts for the felt hat industry are the most well-known item HBC supplied to the European market, but the company also imported a large variety of other wildlife products. Fur hats, muffs, cuffs, collars, and coats were only part of the trade. There were military contracts for bear skins; cutlers bought deer horns or stag horns for pen knife handles; and dentists used "sea horse teeth" (walrus tusks) to make dentures.[7] Castoreum, from the glands of beaver, sold as a scent lure for beaver traps and as a component in medicinal preparations and perfumes.[8] Isinglass, a pure gelatin extracted from the sturgeon's float bladder, helped clarify wine and beer. Feathers, such as the down of the trumpeter swan, sold for powder puffs.

Establishing a demand among the public for a wildlife product was difficult. Ross Cox, who traded in the Pacific Northwest before the Hudson's Bay Company, recalled how fickle the market for bearskins had been. At one point, he remembered, the North West Company found itself with a glut of bearskins and no buyers. So the company had a "hammercloth" made up, with a coat of arms in silver, and gave it to a British prince. It hung below the driver's seat on the front of his coach, covering the toolbox and advertising the rank of the coach's occupant. As the company had hoped, the bearskin was a fashion hit when it was shown at the king's next levee. Within three weeks the North West Company's warehouse was empty.[9] This and other lessons demonstrated the benefits of subtle promotion.

Although HBC's exploration of nature was primarily a commercial enterprise, the company's endeavors also promoted increased scientific knowledge. Hudson's Bay Company maintained a small museum of natural history in London and assisted institutions, artists, and scientists in their research. John Richardson, a prominent natural historian, was one such scientist.[10] His observations on wildlife illustrate the ways in which scientific study of an animal could conflict with its identity as a commercial product.

Richardson became involved in a disagreement about the red fox that reveals the company's competing interest for a recognizable and easily promoted product despite contrary opinions from scientists. The color of individuals in a litter of the red fox is determined by a single pair of genes. Individuals may be born a color other than red, similar to the occurrence of different colors of hair among the children in a family. Generic variations in color are further complicated by age, region, and climate.[11] The cross phase is a grayish-brown coat with dark black markings down the spine and across the shoulders. The silver is actually black with a white-tipped tail and silver frosting effect produced by the outer hairs of the coat. Silver is the most highly valued phase, partly because it is almost unknown in the European red fox.[12]

The silver fox was a mysterious animal, and market prices, thriving on mystery, reflected that. A prime silver fox sold for about forty dollars, half the price of a good sea otter. For HBC to insure a continuing supply of silver fox furs, it had to bow to the caprice of genetic variations within litters and accept less valuable color phases as well. Refusing pelts of the other color phases would discourage fox trapping generally and therefore reduce the number of silver foxes trapped. Thus the genetic characteristics of the red fox created constraints both on commercial harvesting and on marketing.

Although the fur trade industry preferred to distinguish between the color phases as if they were separate forms of fox, the scientific community had a different opinion. In 1829 Richardson commented on red and cross foxes: "I am inclined to adhere to the opinion of the Indians in considering the Cross Fox of the fur traders to be a mere variety of the Red Fox, as I found on inquiry that the gradations of colour between characteristic specimens of the Cross and Red Fox are so small, that the hunters are often in doubt with respect to the proper denomination of a skin, and I was frequently told 'This is not a cross fox yet, but it is becoming so.'"[13]

There is a middle ground between the cross and red fox in their aesthetic variations, as twentieth century biologist Alexander William Francis Banfield noted. He commented that differing perceptions of color phases are the result of "selective pelting, and variation in the identification of the cross fox."[14] Certain pelts could therefore be graded subjectively either as cross or red fox at the trading post or during preparation for auction. Richardson disagreed with the distinction made by fur traders, although he was admittedly uncertain about how the color variations occurred. But it was in the industry's best interest to ignore the opinion of scientific observers as well as Native People, and benefit from the flexibility of choosing the label for distinguishable but similar products.

The Hudson's Bay Company disagreed both with Richardson and Native People over the nature of another animal—the bear. The 1825 returns for the Columbia Department distinguished among three forms of bear skins: black, brown, and grizzly. The common black bear has several color phases other than black, including cinnamon, honey, white, and blue. The bears of the interior of the Pacific Northwest were evenly divided between cinnamon-brown and black phases. Richardson noted that the perceptions of fur traders about the species differed from that of the Native People: "The Cinnamon Bear of the Fur Traders is considered by the Indians to be an accidental variety of this species [black bear], and they are borne out in this opinion by the quality of the fur, which is equally fine with that of the Black Bear."[15] For the bear, like the fox, color phase characteristics constrained the supply of wildlife but aided in establishing product identity.

Competitive Strategies

Other species of wildlife arrived on the market more as a result of competitive strategy than on the merits of the product. Faced with competition from American trapping parties, especially in the Snake River basin of the disputed Oregon Territory, HBC responded by employing its own parties, in part as protection of what it viewed as its territory. These parties of Metis and Iroquois trappers worked constantly as the company engaged in a rigorous extirpation of beaver and river otters, creating "a fur desert" or a "cordon sanitaire" to destroy any inducement to American trappers and traders.[16] American traders were regarded as precursors of their government's colonization policy, drawn to the area by the economics of the wildlife resource. As Governor Simpson explained, "The greatest and best protection we can have from opposition is keeping the country closely hunted as the first step that the American Government will take towards Colonization is through their Indian Traders and if the country becomes exhausted in Fur bearing animals they can have no inducement to proceed thither."[17] The result was not a competition for Native trade but direct ecological warfare.

The Snake River party bypassed trade with Native communities and moved directly into harvesting the resource, as did other trapping parties working on the Umpqua River and in California's Buena Ventura Valley. Both the American and Hudson's Bay Company trapping parties quickly realized that an early arrival at the trapping grounds was critical to the spring hunt. Until 1824 Snake River beaver had been trapped only from June through August, yielding a harvest of inferior summer pelts.[18] In 1825 spring hunts began, which not only collected the more valuable winter coats but also moved the hunt into the reproduction cycle of the beaver. Beavers mate in January and February and give birth between late April and the end of June.[19]

Harvesting intensity increased when first a fall hunt and then year-long trapping expeditions were instituted. In 1825 the Snake River party reorganized for this competition; Simpson commented that "the country is a rich preserve of Beaver and which for political reasons we should destroy as early as possible."[20] However, despite the Snake River party's specialized purpose (beaver comprised 67 percent of its returns) and strategic value, it collected only 10 percent of the Columbia's 443,010 beaver pelts from 1825 to 1849. The party's 43,113 beaver pelts were far fewer than the 132,000 taken within New Caledonia's sustainable harvesting system, one based on beaver ponds owned by individual Native families. But as part of the battle for control of the Oregon Territory, the symbolic and political value of those furs was more important than their economic value.

The fur traders also fought an ecological war with a natural predator.[21] The Hudson's Bay Company viewed competition from predators such as wolves as destructive to the company's interest. The attitude both of Simpson and the HBC governing committee in London toward predators is clearly documented and reflects a consensus among most senior members of the fur trade. In 1822 the committee instructed Simpson that wolves on the plains should be hunted in the summer and their hides prepared for use as leather: "If the wolves are not destroyed they will either kill or drive away the Buffalo; it is therefore desirable to destroy them, if the skins will pay for the expenses it will also be the means of employing the Indians."[22]

In the Columbia annual fur returns, the first entry for wolves appears for the outfit of

1827 when five wolves were traded. By 1830 the number of wolf pelts had climbed to 69, and in 1831 as the company began exercising control over its expanded network of posts, the number was 468. In 1833, responding to Simpson's report of wolves preying on the cattle of the Red River Colony, the governor and committee went further, issuing these instructions concerning controlling wolves: "[S]ending re your request 'two ounces of Strychnine' which is considered the most powerful agent for destroying wild animals (it is used in the East Indies for killing Tigers and Leopards)...three or four grains are a sufficient dose for a full grown beast; the best way to apply it is to make an incision in a piece of flesh in which the Strychnine should be inserted, and to place the bait in situations that the animals frequent."[23]

In 1839 McLoughlin requested poison for the company farms in the Pacific Northwest and for general sale to settlers. The committee replied by sending "a small quantity of Strychnine made up in dozes [sic] for the destruction of Wolves; it should be inserted in pieces of raw meat placed in such situations that the shepherd's dogs may not have access to them, and the native people should be encouraged by high prices for the skins to destroy wolves at all seasons."[24]

Although the Columbia Department wolf kill reached a high of 1,653 in 1847, it fell to only 76 in 1853. Whether they were poisoned to protect domestic cattle, or hunted down by parties of Native People, settlers, or individual trappers, it is clear that from the company's perspective wolves were a threat to its operations. Their instructions about how to deal with wolves also reveal a much larger process: the exchange of information concerning large predators among companies operating in different parts of the world. The wolf became a product in the fur trade only as a means of insuring and underwriting its extermination.

Another animal, the highly prized land or river otter, had a role as currency, paid to the Russians in exchange for a lease. Under the terms of the 1840 Hamburg Agreement between the Hudson's Bay Company and the Russian American Company (RAC), two thousand Columbia river otter were taken to Sitka, Alaska, to pay the RAC for the use of the Alaskan panhandle. The lease contained a provision for a further three thousand otter to be traded at the Hudson's Bay Company's option. Total otter exports from North America declined from 1840 to 1847 by roughly the amount of the lease. Despite the cost of bringing extra skins over the Rocky Mountains to Sitka, and the delay caused by taking payment in bills of exchange drawn on St. Petersburg, the Hudson's Bay Company believed it had a bargain. It calculated the actual cost of leasing the Alaskan panhandle for one year at the equivalent of a middle level manager's annual salary.[25] The RAC also benefited because, unlike the Hudson's Bay Company, it had official access to the lucrative Chinese market. HBC continued to use otter instead of cash to make the lease payment until 1856.

Wildlife Cycles and Markets

In the preceding cases the Hudson's Bay Company exercised active control over which animals it chose to pursue and present as products. Having decided to supply a form of wildlife, the company often found itself mediating between the forces of nature and the vagaries of the market. Two factors created the greatest difficulties: the seemingly separate worlds of wildlife demography and fashion. The company's ability to buffet these forces varied, depending on which species were involved. With lynx and muskrat the Hudson's Bay Company was successful in minimizing the impact of wildlife demography on the marketplace.

Although the dynamics of wildlife demography are still not fully understood, trappers and sportsmen have long recognized the existence of wildlife cycles. There are various theories about why these cycles exist, ranging from the cycles of sunspot activity to a combination of ultraviolet radiation and malnutrition to periodic epidemics. Current debate focuses on intricate mathematical probability equations. Lloyd Keith has commented on the evolution of this discussion:

> Theories and hypotheses confound the natural-history literature. Most are untested and as a result unanimity is lacking on many aspects of animal-population cycles. For thirty-odd years these periods of abundance and scarcity have been passed off as resulting from chance alone; lacking sufficient precision or amplitude to be acceptable; being so multifactorial as to defy appraisal; and eventually regarded as phenomena easily reduced to ridicule. Not all attitudes are disparaging or skeptical. There are zealots in the field of biology who see cycles in virtually all tabulations of natural and social interactions. From the production of pig iron to tent caterpillars, and from ozone quantity to Nile floods, cycles have been regarded as the skeletons or the souls of numerical data.[26]

Nevertheless, Keith has concluded that there is a "ten-year cycle," a regular but imprecise fluctuation for several forms of grouse, the snowshoe rabbit, and its predator, the lynx. There is also evidence for such a cycle in the fox, the muskrat, and its predator, the mink.[27] These demographic fluctuations of the animals on which the fur trade depended threatened the stability of the market, but they also provided the Hudson's Bay Company with opportunities for speculation.

The lynx and the muskrat provide two examples of how the company responded to wildlife cycles. These species were wildcards in the marketplace because of their periodic sudden and massive population explosions. High spring water levels or low winter water levels exaggerated the muskrat's reproductive cycle, the former causing an increase in population and the latter a decrease. The lynx's cycle was dependent on the increase of its food source, the snowshoe rabbit.[28] Although the lynx was never a particularly popular fur, its rapid increases tended to flood the market and undercut prices for cats in general.[29]

The muskrat (referred to within the trade as "the rat"), a seemingly insignificant marsh dweller sold in the marketplace as the musquash, had a large impact on the fur trade. In the wild, like the beaver it seeks shallow water where it feeds on roots and grasses. Unlike the beaver, it can have several litters in a year, resulting in dramatic population fluctuations.[30] These population fluctuations meant a periodic flooding of the market, which occurred in 1828 and 1834 when over one million muskrat skins arrived at auction in London, The muskrat's demographic cycle profoundly influenced the market because it could be used as a cheaper substitute for more expensive furs, especially in hat making. Muskrat sold for between three and thirteen pence each, depending on supply. By contrast, beaver sold for seventeen to thirty-two shillings per pound.

Although the company realized the increases were part of a recurring pattern, they could not predict the onset of the cycles. Their experience taught them how long peaks would last and what caused them to end. To support beaver prices the company repeatedly used private export contracts to divert muskrat surpluses from the London market. The one million skins taken in the cycle year of 1829 threatened the trade's stability, but the company knew this increase would have limited duration and be followed by an equally drastic collapse in population. They reacted by limiting the importation and paying close attention to demographics. Governor Simpson wrote to the committee that "it is evident that the importation of next year will be small compared with that of the present, owing to a mortality which has seized the tribe [muskrats] in several parts of the Country, we beg leave to suggest that a part only be exposed to sale this year, and the remainder held until the following, when 'tis probable they will command better prices."[31]

A large increase in lynx and muskrat shipped in 1839 drew this reaction: "We do not wish that more than half the quantities shipped...this year, but that the surplus be laid aside for shipment the following season by which time those animals will in all probability become scarce as we rarely find they continue numerous three years in succession."[32]

The bottom of these cycles was equally important to the company's position in the market. After such a "crash" the wholesalers in the industry, anticipating a shortage, rushed to take control of the previous excess. Simpson wrote in 1831 that he suspected that the heavy buying by Astor's fur company was such a speculation: "It is in the anticipation of such scarcity Messrs. Astor & Company have purchased so largely, not for immediate consumption, as we have reason to believe they were at the time this purchase was made large holders of the American Fur Company's Musquash, but on speculation with a view to benefit by the demand which the probable scarcity will occasion, And as this falling off in quantity must increase the prices for all description we have not thought it advisable to destroy the small inferior skins."[33] The Hudson's Bay Company had little or no control over the entry of American muskrat onto the London market or to markets on the European continent. One example of how swings in muskrat population created competition based on speculative opportunities was the 1834 adjustment HBC made to its shipping schedule.[34] In response to the American Fur Company's entry into the English market that

year, HBC changed its transportation schedule to beat the arrival of American furs.[35]

Muskrat returns were also the subject of speculation by smaller dealers and houses. When an 1824 contract for a large sale to an American house fell through "on a flimsy pretext," the committee consoled itself with the knowledge that consumers would be forced to buy on the English market.[36] Then the following year, as a condition of the sale of 150,000 skins to Henry Carey & Co. of New York, the skins were not to be resold on the English market. When this contract felt through, the company reminded Carey that he was liable for any loss incurred in reselling the skins.[37] Again, in the 1840s, the large numbers of muskrat harvested prompted the company to restrict the succeeding year's imports. Glut continued to be a problem for the trade; in 1846 one American dealer alone brought 600,000 skins into the English market.[38] So, although historians such as John Galbraith stress the element of competition between British and American fur traders on the frontier, these divisions were not as clear in the marketplace, where furs moved back and forth through private contracts and speculative practices.[39]

The muskrat cycle also created problems for the departments and posts in North America. The large numbers of easily trapped muskrat drained posts of their inventories of trade goods during the first year of a high cycle and created an ongoing inventory problem thereafter: "The immense trade made for two or three successive years in the article of Rats was the cause of the increased demands from all parts of the country for goods, which led to the overstock we now have of many articles. This overstock will however be carried off by the outfits of next and the following years...."[40]

Overall, the system was self-regulating and able to absorb muskrat surpluses, whose roughly three-year cycle was known to the traders. The large numbers of muskrat disrupted the marketplace, but the company had a series of responses that could be implemented either in London or at the shipping depot. Although speculation on the cycles could be lucrative, HBC adapted to muskrat demography as it attempted to create an orderly system of business and left most of the speculation to others.

The beaver was one species for which HBC tried to develop a unique long-term strategy of conservation and resource management. This plan was part of an attempt to gain a competitive edge in the marketplace. Unlike the muskrat, the demographic problem presented by the beaver was one of declining population, particularly east of the Rockies, due to overtrapping and epidemics such as tularemia. Of all the species harvested, beaver was the main focus in the trade. Exploration, competition, and management of beaver stocks was foremost in shaping the managerial policy of the Hudson's Bay Company.[41] The company's expansion into the Columbia Department in the 1820s was part of a drive to conserve and replenish the depleted stocks east of the Rockies by relying on new sources for the market in the Columbia Department.

An Effort at Conservation

The company engaged in one of North America's earliest conservation experiments using those districts in which it had undisputed possession. The policy's strength lay in the advantage that the company's size and market longevity gave it. The policy's weakness lay in the assumption that market demand would continue unchanged. The conservation policy was also difficult to implement because of the Incentive system that comprised part of the company's managerial organization. The wintering partner system of the North West Company, linking salaries and pensions to the success of the concern, was adopted by HBC in 1821 and carried with it a liability: it encouraged a personal profit motive and a frontier machismo.

Through conservation strategies, the company tried to combine the advantage of scale of operation with monopoly control over the "nursing" or "recruiting" of beaver stocks. This tactic enabled HBC to supply sufficient beaver to "meet extended consumption and secure to the Company the entire control of the Trade, as [in] the countries exposed to opposition the expenses are so heavy that those who now pursue it will not then be able to meet us in the home market."[42] If the plan had succeeded it would have meant the end of the Columbia Department's frontier competition "and at once put an end to opposition in those Countries where we have no exclusive privilege, as the high prices of Beaver alone enables the small Traders to continue."[43]

The committee supplied Simpson with a mathematical argument for the Northern Council that showed the benefit of this policy over a seven-year period in a hypothetical district. If the district produced 1,200 pelts annually without depleting stocks, this would yield 8,400 pelts for export. If the conservation policy were implemented, restricting the harvest to 400 pelts for each of the first two years, 600 the following, 800 the next, 2,800 in the fifth year, 14,000 in the sixth, and 20,000 in the seventh year, the total harvest would be 39,000 pelts with 38,800 animals remaining in the district.[44] The committee acknowledged that this model was optimistic, but even with a 50 percent error the benefit was clear: they would be able to bring to market twice the volume of fur. Even at half the going price this plan would squeeze their competitors, who faced the same outfitting costs as HBC for trade goods.[45]

Arthur Ray has attributed the failure of this conservation strategy to opposition by American, Metis and Native trappers. Ray has argued that on the prairies "without a monopoly it was not possible to manage the fur trade on an ecologically sound basis since the primary suppliers of fur pelts, the Indians, did not really support the Hudson's Bay Company's conservation programme."[46] But the conservation strategy faltered due to a structural flaw in the company; ingrained habits and a related system of prestige could not be easily changed in practice. In the past the company and other traders judged individual traders according to the size of returns they generated, and their pensions were tied to past profits. Under the conservation policy, Simpson stated, "We must judge of their talents by the quality alone not the quantity."[47] Convincing the HBC commissioned officers and traders in council to agree to decrease the returns was one thing. Putting the changes into practice was another: "Many of them give it their best attention, while a few, who either cannot or will not understand either their own interests or the interests of the country and native people, give it but very little attention. They all, however, while assembled here, talk of the subject as if fully convinced of its importance, and make fair promises of giving it their best support, but I fear that many of them lose sight of it before they reach their wintering grounds."[48]

In 1841 Simpson, faced with an accelerating decline of beaver stocks throughout the districts, placed the blame on the commissioned gentlemen: "All our endeavours I am sorry to say, have been fruitless, owing very much in my opinion to the disinclination of many Gentlemen in charge of Districts & posts, to occasion a reduction in the returns, even as a measure of preservation to the country, from an over anxiety as to the appearance of turning their charges to profitable account, and in some cases perhaps, from a mistaken notion that by curtailing the returns they were injuring their own immediate interests."[49] Few traders were willing to sacrifice their short-term income in order to benefit their successors or, although they would not say it in council, the company's long-term position. Although Ray's argument is

correct, it ignores what Simpson clearly viewed as managerial resistance, structurally rooted in the profit system of the company.

The company understood that it was not possible to increase the consumption of beaver in Europe unless there was a material drop in price. Until it could achieve this, the company restricted importation in an effort to maintain the high prices needed to subsidize conservation. In 1830, a decade before the beaver market collapsed, the committee told Simpson:

> It is more profitable to keep the importation moderate until the animals become so numerous as to enable you to double the importation, which then might be sold so cheap as to force a larger consumption either by means of exportation or by making Hats so cheap as to induce a larger class of the people of this Country to use Beaver hats. We consider the effect on the market this year, holds out the strongest inducement to preserve in the plan of nursing the Country, as it shews that such an increase of quantity as has been made this year only diminishes Profits, and that it would have been better if the animals had been allowed to live and multiply.[50]

The policy was a calculated gamble, given the declining number of American trapping parties in the Columbia in the late 1830s and their problems obtaining financing to bring supplies from St. Louis. For a time it appeared to be working, but the company had underestimated the extent to which both beaver populations had declined and consumer preference had changed as silk hats grew in popularity. The slow reaction of the Hudson's Bay Company to the erosion of its traditional markets resulted from the company's reluctance to abandon a policy that would have worked in a static market.

In the Columbia Department, most of which was not under the conservation policy, production grew rapidly. Simpson's production target was 20,000 beaver pelts a year, a number reached in 1831 and surpassed by the peak of 28,949 pelts in 1833. Beaver production hovered between 18,000 and 21,000 until 1844 when it dropped to 10,812. Production rallied for two or three years and then dipped to 5,991 in 1850. Columbia district beaver production falls into two main periods: 1826–43 (the years of Simpson/ McLoughlin management) and the declining years after 1844. Production dropped before the political settlement of the Oregon Boundary, the turning point in political interpretations of the company's fortunes. The cause of this drop had more to do with European fashion than with political events in North America.

Death of a Hat

Beaver, the historic staple of the fur trade, suffered a serious collapse in the marketplace. During the 1840s the silk hat, symbolic of changing culture in the age of machinery and steam, caught consumers' attention and sense of fashion. The first blow to the market occurred in the Columbia auction on 31 August 1842. Hudson's Bay Company Secretary William Smith, forwarding catalogs of the sale to James Keith in Lachine, Quebec, wrote that demand for beaver had fallen off considerably because of the silk hat's popularity.[51] In their spring letter to George Simpson the committee wrote: "From an extraordinary freak of fashion, the article [beaver], moreover, has of late fallen much into disuse in hat making, silk hats being principally worn at present; the consequence is that its value has greatly decreased in the market, as will be seen by the accompanying sales catalogues. This depression however is but temporary, as no doubt exists that beaver hats will soon again come into more general use, when of course an amendment may be expected in the price.... The martens on the other hand, as

you will observe by the late sales, have commanded very high prices."[52]

The committee was wrong, and beaver prices began to plummet at auction after auction. While the Colombia furs were being prepared for auction in the warehouse, the male population of London was turning out for the summer promenade dressed like Prince Albert in the new silk fashion. Prices even continued to drop after an effort by HBC to carefully present "best Beaver" at the August 1843 auction.[53] The committee wrote to McLoughlin that "the continually decreasing price, when considered in connexion with a constantly decreasing supply, holds out no cheering prospect for the future, unless the tide of fashion change, and the consumption of Beaver in the manufacture of hats become more general than it has been for some time past. We hope that the low price may have some effect in bringing about an alteration in the public taste, but no hope of this must lead us to neglect any means, by which our great expences may be safely curtailed...doubly so when prices are declining and returns annually diminishing."[54]

Prices dropped further at the January auction. In March 1845 the committee told Simpson that prices probably would continue to fall. Rather than publicly accept reduced bids, the bulk of the furs were returned to the warehouse while the company searched without success for a discreet private buyer with whom they could clear the total inventory. By 1845 the silk hat was firmly established both in England and on the Continent. The committee described the situation in a letter to Simpson: "The best description of which [silk hats] may be purchased at retail shops in London about fifty percent cheaper than the first quality beaver hat."[55] Wildlife demography came into play the next year. The 1846 market was inundated with muskrat from the United States, a beaver substitute. Having lost the higher-priced market and unable to compete with muskrat prices for the lower market, the company finally conceded that a revival of the product was very unlikely.

Meanwhile, the warehouse inventory of unsold beaver pelts continued to grow. Auction catalogs show that the Columbia auction, which usually included a selection of lots from the two previous years, grew to a backlog that included unsold beaver from five separate years. In 1847 the company could delay no longer and cleared the inventory at whatever price was necessary to remove it.[56] Beaver, which sold for thirty to thirty-five shillings per pound in 1821, sold for three to four shillings. HBC began to consider alternate uses for the pelt: "We are not without hope that great cheapness may have the effect of forcing the article into consumption in some form or other, as the ingenuity of purchasers will naturally be stimulated to the means of applying it to new purposes."[57]

Beaver was no longer a viable product, and the company began to experiment with methods that could make it one again. The experiments undertaken were ingenious. Using a new process, they shaved and dyed pelts to resemble fur seals, an operation also used later during the seal fur vogue of 1890–1910. The skins exhibited in 1847 at the annual Leipzig Fair, in the German state of Saxony, evoked little response from the fur industry; many fashionable furs, including marten, went unsold. By 1847 the price of a beaver hat had dropped to that of a silk hat, but consumer response was still negligible.[58]

The company continued to experiment, preparing one thousand fully dressed and dyed beaver pelts to be sold as "fur," a novel use for the pelt that had never before been attempted. The marketplace was Canada, but only five hundred pelts were sent because of production problems. Further eroding the market, several London fur dealers who were aware of the company's plans sent earlier shipments. In another attempt to rally the market, unsold stock was sent to dealers in the United States where the beaver hat was still in use; a shipment also went to China, with disappointing results. After these attempts, the 1849 importation from North America was severely restricted to twenty thousand skins, formerly the average output of the Columbia Department alone. The beaver, slowly gaining acceptance as a "fur," ceased to be important to the European hat industry.[59]

The Hudson's Bay Company's plans for market dominance had failed due to a combination of wildlife demography and European fashions. However, the company gained experience in experimenting with and promoting alternate uses for its products, and in knowing when to cut its losses. At the same time, HBC was turning to the promotion of a "new" product, drawn from their inventory of wildlife. While the steady decrease in the price of beaver made company officials such as Archibald Barclay gloomy, there was consolation in the corresponding increase in the value of the marten. The marten's value was strong, but the best evidence of its importance is found in the tremendous volume produced. During the experimentation with beaver as a fur, Warehouse Keeper Edward Taylor expressed concern that large quantities of beaver, contrasted with the smaller numbers of marten, might cause the market for both to collapse. Another member of the company, Edward Roberts, told Simpson: "The fur is beautiful and when dyed looks as well as sea otter.... I showed a specimen to Nicholay the Queen's furrier, who has a high opinion of the fur and thinks it likely to come into extensive use for trimmings, and also for muffs, and does not think it will come into competition with Marten, so as in any way to affect the value of that article which our friend Taylor is very much afraid of."[60] Ever aware that sales depended on the perception of distinctly separate products, the company sought to maintain this separation even down to the level of a fur becoming a cuff on a garment.

Before 1838 the marten received only passing notice in the discussions of auction trends. Then increased demand pushed prices steadily upward. The declining population cycles of the Columbia Department's marten and lynx in 1839–40 stimulated prices further. Simpson considered the declines only temporary: "By the knowledge which has been acquired by experience, of the habits of these latter animals, however, there is every reason to believe that this diminution in their numbers is merely temporary, arising either from migration to other quarters, or from disease, but that as soon as these causes shall be removed, they will become as plentiful as formerly, and assist in retrieving the present unpromising aspect of affairs in this district."[61]

The decreased supply reduced the furriers' inventories, and prices continued to climb. By 1843 demand was again strong, and prices began to set new levels as they attracted speculative buyers. Increased prices in 1844 more than matched the losses incurred by declining beaver stocks. The Columbia posts encouraged trappers to switch from beaver to marten and other small furs. The committee proposed new incentives to offset the losses that beaver was taking in the marketplace: "Beaver has again fallen in price, but, as a stimulus to exertion in hunting martens, lynxes, musquash and all other furs, increased prices may be offered, as we can afford to be liberal in that way, inasmuch as all those furs are at present much in demand and have advanced, musquash as much as 40 percent on the price of last year, as you will perceive by the catalogues."[62]

The Columbia Department board of management received instructions to concentrate on marten in the fall of 1846 as the company benefited from high prices. The increased supply was not large enough to flood the market the way muskrat, rabbit, and lynx frequently did. Marten returns from the department increased rapidly after 1846. Almost 45 percent of all the marten harvested in the Columbia Department from 1825 to 1849 were taken in the following three years. This increased harvest of Columbia marten points toward a rapid response to the market by Native trappers. The company used its experience with the population cycles of other species to play the market as closely as possible. HBC cautioned in the fall of 1847 that imports from the northern department should not be so excessive as to weaken prices.[63]

New Caledonia's fur-based economy responded quickly to new markets due to the flexibility of its species mix. Because of low demand and the bottom of the marten's demographic cycle, in 1840 only 1,251 pelts came to market. The 1845 production was 7,383, reaching a high of 9,586 in 1846 before declining to a low of 2,652 in 1849. The taking of so many marten, while clearly a response to market forces, also represents the coincidence of high prices with a demographic upswing. Unlike the muskrat, which had a low market value and a high demographic peak, the marten did not exist in sufficient numbers to cause a price collapse. The large numbers traded represent the response of Native trappers to its increased value.

This change in the trade must have had structural and cultural implications for Native Peoples living in New Caledonia. Were depleted family-tenure beaver ponds abandoned in the search for a more valuable and, in the marten's case, more mobile commodity?[64] The region's species mix, rich both in marten and lynx, allowed New Caledonia to shift easily from one staple fur to another. The New Caledonia cyclical peak in marten matched the changing market's preference for the fur. Unlike the muskrat, the size of the marten population was easily absorbed by the market. However, the marten soon began one of its endemic declines. James Douglas, in charge of the Columbia Department in 1847, commented:

A heavy decline in Beaver and Martens. The former apart from the measles, which also severely afflicted the natives of the District wherein the Steam vessel carries on trade, was partly the effect of the reduction in prices; the decrease in the latter is either caused by want of exertion in the hunters, on which is more probable it arises from a scarcity of the animal producing that valuable fur. From the great abundance of martens for some years past, in all parts of the Indian Country, and the general decline which we notice with regret—this year, at all the Marten Posts in this District it is feared that we are on the eve of one of those fluctuations to which the Marten trade independently of hunting is almost periodically subject, and if so there will be a further decline in the returns of that fur next year and for some years after, until from some unknown cause they again multiply and reappear in their native forests in the utmost abundance.[65]

The decline in marten was not serious enough to create problems for the company. Douglas noted that marten probably would rebound at the end of three years in the same manner as the muskrat.

The market and the post had shifted from the traditional staple fur to the marten. In time other small furs, such as the mink, would become substitutes for the marten.[66] After intervening in the management of business at all levels in order to survive the crisis, the committee returned by 1850 to its traditional role in the daily routine of directing the system of trade. Districts that over-trapped or had too many low-grade or damaged marten in their returns were reprimanded. The staff at posts responded to the demands of the buyers of the new staple: they stopped the practice of cutting paws from marten pelts that caused a shilling depreciation in the value of the skin; pale martens were no longer classed as damaged but as high quality because of their end purpose as trimming and collars. Native trappers followed the

price incentives and brought in small furs instead of the beaver. The committee remarked about the Columbia Department that "from the abundance of small furs and the increased industry of the natives, we are inclined to look with greater hope to the future."[67] Daily operations of the company continued much as they had when the product was beaver. An early naval visitor to Fort Victoria in 1848 commented in a letter to the London *Times* that the beaver had "hardly any value now."[68] A fundamental change had taken place in the upper levels of the company. The balanced symbiotic relationships of the company with its trappers and European buyers had shifted in favor of the marketplace.

Conclusion

The Hudson's Bay Company succeeded in establishing a centralized system to the fur trade, smoothing demographic bumps, improving quality and shipping methods, and establishing recognizable products. It survived the unexpected collapse of its historic and traditional market, the felt hat industry, because of the biological and ecological diversity of the wildlife harvest gathered by its network of posts. Information about markets and wildlife became the predominant feature of company operations as the process of deciding to restrict imports or to redirect trappers became more efficient. It learned that if one product could be abandoned after so many years, then the adoption of an entirely new group of products was conceivable.[69]

There is evidence in trade leaflets of a gradual shift in organizational mentality. The oldest leaflet (1799) shows animals in descending order of value. Mid-century leaflets alphabetize the lists to a certain extent. Beaver still heads the list, before bear or badger, despite its declining economic importance, but mythical terms such as "sea horse teeth" give way to the more familiar "walrus tusks." By 1870 all animals appear alphabetically, badger before beaver, reflecting a systemized inventory.[70]

The implications for the wildlife of this case study are difficult to assess. The emphasis on smaller furs meant a wider incursion into the river-forest ecosystem. There is evidence of complex interactions between species and within specific populations that even now are only vaguely understood. None of the Pacific Northwest's more than sixty forms of wildlife recorded in HBC records are extinct. Most have declined because of habitat loss, a loss not directly attributable to the fur trade.

To the fur trade, wildlife was a harvest. Nature provided a collection of potential products, each containing characteristics that influenced how it could be offered as a product. A primary feature of the fur trade management was mediating between demographic fluctuations and the world of fashion and markets. It was not wildlife management in the twentieth-century conception, but in this nineteenth-century interest in conservation and wildlife cycles there is a curious resonance with subsequent efforts. In our focus on the fur trade, we know much about traders and Natives, but very little about what drove the global market for wildlife.

Notes

The author thanks Peter Baskerville and Chad Gaffield for their support and the Hudson's Bay Company for permission to quote from their archives; he gratefully acknowledges funding from the Social Sciences and Humanities Research Council of Canada and the Graduate School of the University of Ottawa. A draft of this paper was presented at the American Society for Environmental History conference in Houston, Texas, with the aid of Thomas Dunlap and Keir Sterling.

1 Most fur trade literature makes passing reference to wildlife and then moves immediately to European-Native trade relations. The literature that does address animals is concerned with wildlife as an aspect of Native culture, such as Calvin Martin's *Keepers of the Game: Indian-Animal Relationships and the Fur Trade* (Berkeley: University of California Press, 1978), the rebuttal by Shepard Krech III. *Indians, Animals, and the Fur Trade: A Critique of Keepers of the Game* (Athens: University of Georgia Press, 1981), or Adrian Tanner's *Bringing Home Animals: Religious Ideology and Mode of Production of the Mistassini Cree Hunters* (New York: St. Martin's Press, 1979).

There are many discussions of wildlife in the literature of environmental history, although the fur trade is strangely missing from Alfred W. Crosby's pivotal *Ecological Imperialism: The Biological Expansion of Europe, 900–1900* (Cambridge, England: Cambridge University Press, 1986). See Christine and Robert Prescott-Allen, *The First Resource: Wild Species in the North American Economy* (New Haven, Connecticut: Yale University Press, 1986); Thomas R. Dunlap, *Saving America's Wildlife* (Princeton, New Jersey: Princeton University Press, 1988); Peter Matthiessen, *Wildlife in America* (New

York: Viking, 1987); Lisa Mighetto, *Wild Animals and American Environmental Ethics* (Tucson: University of Arizona Press, 1991); Farley Mowat, *Sea of Slaughter* (Toronto, Ontario: McClelland and Stewart, 1984); and Morgan Sherwood, *Big Game in Alaska: A History of Wildlife and People* (New Haven, Connecticut: Yale University Press, 1981).

2 How this differed from other more flexible and locally controlled companies, such as the individual trapper of the Rocky Mountain rendezvous or the merchants of the St. Louis fur trade, is important. Fur trade historiography suffers from political and archival compartmentalization. Canadian scholars, including this author, rely primarily on the papers of the Hudson's Bay Company. For the researcher, the recent microfilm publication of the *Papers of the St. Louis Fur Trade* (Bethesda, Maryland: University Publications of America, 1992) offers an opportunity for a comparative study. The papers include an introduction by William R. Swagerty and an essay by Janet Lecompte.

3 This is based on a statistical examination of fur importation handbills. The error between these estimated shipments and a ledger kept by James Douglas for each trading year showed an average 4 percent difference in the annual shipments from

1825–49. Unless otherwise noted all figures cited come from a series of databases constructed by the author (these are mainframe codebook-based datafiles run under SAS, SPSS, and Paradox statistical analysis packages). One contained the annual fur returns of wildlife traded each year at the posts of the Columbia Department. It was based on James Douglas, *Fur Trade Returns for Columbia and New Caledonia Districts, 1825–1857*. Provincial Archives of British Columbia, Victoria, British Columbia (hereafter PABC), A/B/20V3. For a full analysis of the James Douglas ledger see Lorne Hammond, "Studies in Documents: Historians, Archival Technology, and Business Ledgers," *Archivaria* 28 (Summer 1989): 120–25. Another database contains the figures published in fur importation handbills listing North American fur imports to London, *Fur Trade Importation Book, 1799–1912*, Hudson's Bay Company Archives, Series I, Winnipeg, Manitoba (hereafter HBCA), A.53/1. The third is a listing of sales of Columbia wildlife drawn from the Warehouse Keeper's annotated auction catalog, Auction Catalogues of Fur Produce, HBCA, A.54.

4 George Simpson to the Governor, Deputy Governor, and Committee, 10 March 1825, HBCA, D.4/88, Para. 20; Frederick Merlk, *Fur Trade and Empire: George Simpson's Journal* (Cambridge, Massachusetts: Belknap Press, 1968), pp. 32–33.

5 John McLoughlin to the Governor, Deputy Governor, and Committee, 6 October 1825, Para. 49, in *The Letters of John McLoughlin: From Fort Vancouver to the Governor and Committee, First Series, 1825–38* (London, England: Hudson's Bay Record Society [HBRS], 1941), p. 16; John McLoughlin to the Governor, Deputy Governor, and Committee, 31 October 1842, Para. 20, in *The Letters of John McLoughlin: From Fort Vancouver to the Governor and Committee, Second Series, 1839–1844* (London, England: HBRS, 1943), p. 81.

6 James R. Beringer, *The Control Revolution: Technology and Economic Origins of the Information Society* (Cambridge, Massachusetts: Harvard University Press, 1986), pp. 144–55.

7 Governor, Deputy Governor, and Committee to Simpson, 11 March 1825, HBCA, A.6/21, Para. 23. Earlier in 1825 the denture market was overstocked because of Greenland fisheries activity.

8 Robin F. Wells, "Castoreum and Steel Traps in Eastern North America," *American Anthropologist* 74 (June 1972): 479–83; "Castoreum," *The Museum of the Fur Trade Quarterly* 8 (Spring 1972): 1–5.

9 Ross Cox, *The Columbia River, or Scenes and Adventures During A Residence of Six Years On the Western Side of the Rocky Mountains Among Various Tribes Hitherto Unknown: Together With A Journey Across the American Continent* (Norman: University of Oklahoma Press, 1957), p. 243.

10 John Richardson documented plants, lichens, birds, mammals, and fish during John Franklin's arctic expeditions between 1819 and 1827. His lasting achievement is the multivolume *Fauna Boreali-Americana; Or the Zoology of the Northern Parts of British America: Containing Descriptions of the Objects of Natural History Collected on the Late Northern Land Expeditions, Under Command of Captain Sir John Franklin, R.N.* (New York: Arno Press, 1974); *Arctic Ordeal: The Journal of John Richardson, Surgeon-Naturalist with Franklin* (Montreal, Quebec: McGill-Queen's University Press, 1984); C. Stuart Houston, "John Richardson—First Naturalist in the Northwest," *Beaver* (November 1984): 10–15.

11 In the Columbia Department from 1820–49 the average proportions were: red phase 58 percent (8,402 pelts), cross phase 31 percent (4,430), and silver phase 11 percent (1,608 pelts). See also the discussion between naturalists John Bradbury and Thomas Nuttall in James P. Ronda, *Astoria and Empire* (Lincoln: University of Nebraska Press, 1990), pp. 133, 316–20; and M. Novak, J.A. Baker, M.E. Obbard and B. Malloch, eds., *Wild Furbearer Management and Conservation in Northern America* (Toronto, Ontario: Ministry of Natural Resources, 1987), p. 751.

12 John Richardson cites A. de Capell Brooke as noting that only three or four silver foxes were taken annually on the Lofoten Islands of Norway and that they are not found elsewhere. Richardson, *Fauna Boreali-Americana*, p. 94. In "Platinum Mutations in Norwegian Silver Foxes," *Journal of Heredity* 30 (June 1939): 226–34, Otto L. Mohr and Per Tuff say that much of Norwegian stock is imported from Canada.

13 Richardson, *Fauna Boreali-Americana*, p. 93.

14 Alexander William Francis Banfield, *Mammals of Canada* (Toronto, Ontario: National Museum of Natural Sciences, University of Toronto Press, 1974), p. 299.

15 Richardson, *Fauna Boreali-Americana*, p. 15.

16 E.E. Rich, ed., *Peter Skene Ogden's Snake Country Journals, 1824–1825 and 1825–1826.* (London, England: HBRS, 1950); K.G. Davies, ed., *Peter Skene Ogden's Snake Country Journal, 1826–27* (London,

England: HBRS. 1961); Glyndwr Williams, ed., *Peter Skene Ogden's Snake Country Journals, 1827–28 and 1828–29* (London, England: HBRS, 1971).

17 George Simpson to John McLoughlin, 9 July 1827, HBCA, D.4/90, Para. 6.

18 Peter Skene Ogden to the Governor, Chief Factors, and Chief Traders 10 October 1826, in Merk, *Fur Trader and Empire,* p. 285.

19 Banfield, *Mammals of Canada,* p. 161.

20 Simpson to the Governor, Deputy Governor, and Committee, 10 March 1825, HBCA,. D.4/88, Para. 26.

21 For a discussion of a attitudes toward wolves in America after 1880 see Dunlap, *Saving America's Wildlife.*

22 Governor, Deputy Governor, and Committee to Simpson, 27 February 1822, HBCA,. A.6/20, Para. 48.

23 Governor, Deputy Governor, and Committee to Simpson, 7 June 1833,. HBCA, A.6/23. Para. 40.

24 Pelly, Colvile, and Simpson to McLoughlin, 31 December 1839, in *Letters of John McLoughlin, Second Series, 1839–1844,* p. 164n.

25 From 1827–37 the average price for a river otter was 18 shillings 11 pence (18/11), less 1/5 for insurance and other charges from the Columbia Landing warehouse. This left 17/6 as the average worth. The R.A.C. agreed to pay 23/- each, for a 5/6 profit on each to the HBC. The additional three thousand otters from the Northern Department had an average value of 26/5, less the 1/5 charge, leaving a net average value of 25/-. The R.A.C. agreed to pay 312/- each, giving HBC a 7/- profit on each skin. Although the Panhandle cost £1,750 (2,000 x 17/6) a year, the hidden profit on the Columbia otters was £550 (2,000 x 5/6) and £1,050 on the Northern Department otters (3,000 x 7/-), making the cost only £150. "Memorandum," HBCA, F.29/2, fo. 182. The conversion rate for 1840–50 was four dollars to the pound where there were currency shortages, such as in the West.

26 Lloyd Keith places the origins of the field at a conference held in July 1931 on the Matamek River in Labrador under the patronage of Copley Amory of Boston. Lloyd B. Keith, *Wildlife's Ten-Year Cycle* (Madison: University of Wisconsin Press, 1963), p. vii.

27 Keith, *Wildlife's Ten-Year Cycle.* For related work on the fluctuation of muskrats see Paul L. Errington,

Muskrat Populations (Ames: Iowa State University Press, 1963), pp. 522–38.

28 For the scientific literature see Charles S. Elton, "Periodic Fluctuations in the Numbers of Animals: Their Causes and Effects," *Journal of the Society for Experimental Biology* 1 (October 1924): 119–63; "Plague and the Regulation of Numbers in Wild Animals," *Journal of Hygiene* 24 (October 1925): 138–63; "The Ten-Year Cycle in Numbers of the Lynx in Canada," *Journal of Animal Ecology* 2 (November 1942): 215–44; *The Ecology of Invasions by Animals and Plants* (London, England: Methuen, 1958); Charles S. and Mary Nicholson, "Fluctuations in Numbers of the Muskrat (*Ondatra Zibethica*) in Canada," *Journal of Animal Ecology* 2 (May 1942): 96–126.

29 Ian McTaggart Cowan, "The Fur Trade and the Fur Cycle: 1825–1857," *British Columbia Historical Quarterly* 2 (January 1938): 19–30, points out that figures for the lynx are slightly confused because they do not distinguish between the more southern bob-cat, a generalist predator with alternate food sources, and the true lynx, a specialist predator whose numbers fluctuate in direct response to its prey, the snow-shoe rabbit. However, the composite totals for the two show the lynx had demographic peaks in the returns of 1829–30, 1837–40, and 1848–50.

30 There is a relationship between the latitude of a muskrat population and the number of litters as well as the number of young per litter. Muskrat in Louisiana may have three to six litters a year with an average of 2.4 young in each litter, while muskrat in northern Canada may have only two litters but each averaging 7.1 young. Banfield, *Mammals of Canada,* pp. 198–99. See also David J. Wishart, *The Fur Trade of the American West, 1807–1840: A Geographical Synthesis,* (Lincoln: University of Nebraska Press, 1979), p. 36.

31 Simpson to the Governor, Deputy Governor, and Committee, 30 June 1829, HBCA, D.4/96,.

32 Governor, Deputy Governor, and Committee to Simpson, 4 March 1840, HBCA, A.6/25, Para. 23.

33 Simpson to the Governor, Deputy Governor, and Committee, 18 July 1831, HBCA, D.4/98, Para. 5. Astor had approached the company about contracting for muskrat in 1827, but the company wanted a guarantee that he would take seventy thousand to one hundred thousand a year an a fixed price for five to seven years. This was a dangerous contract given the fluctuations. See William Smith to George Simpson, 30 May 1827, HBCA, A.6/21.

34 The 1835 total import of 1,111,646 muskrats came to a market that had been paying 95 pence per skin, so the total value of the stock was $44,000. But the prices given for the 1837 shipment of 838,549 skins was 3 pence each, for a book value of $10,000. This demonstrates the failure of the market to absorb these quantities. HBCA, A.54.

35 Governor, Deputy Governor, and Committee to Simpson, 5 March 1834, HBCA, A.6 23, Para. 28.

36 Governor, Deputy Governor, and Committee to Simpson, 2 June 1824, HBCA, A.6/20, Para. 54.

37 Due to the depressed market the committee decided to bend on the issue and accepted $300 compensation for the loss when the muskrats were resold. William Smith to Henry Carey & Co., 16 June 1825, 1 February 1826, and 12 June 1826, HBCA, A.6/21.

38 Archibald Barclay to George Simpson, 3 February 1846, HBCA, A.6/27.

39 John S. Galbraith, *The Hudson's Bay Company as an Imperial Factor* (New York: Octagon Books, 1977); Mary E. Wheeler, "Empires in Conflict and Cooperation: The 'Bostonians' and the Russian-American Company," *Pacific Historical Review* 40 (November 1971): 419–41; Frank E. Ross, "The Retreat of the Hudson's Bay Company in the Pacific North West," *Canadian Historical Review* 18 (September 1937): 262–80; Herman J. Deutsch. "Economic Imperialism in the Early Pacific Northwest," *Pacific Historical Review* 9 (December 1940): 377–88.

40 Simpson to the Governor, Deputy Governor, and Committee, 10 August 1832, HBCA, D.4/99, Para. 3.

41 The idea of managing beaver stocks is old. An early North American reference to the idea is a letter of Jesuit Father Paul le Jeune dated 28 August 1636. Reuben Gold Thwaits, ed., *The Jesuit Relations and Allied Documents* (New York: Pageant Book Company, 1959), 9: 165–67.

42 Simpson to the Governor, Deputy Governor, and Committee, 10 July 1828, HBCA, D.4/92, Para. 9.

43 Governor, Deputy Governor, and Committee to Simpson, 16 January 1828, HBCA, A.6/21), Para. 10.

44 Governor, Deputy Governor, and Committee to Simpson, 23 February 1826, HBCA, A.6/21, Para. 36.

45 Governor, Deputy Governor, and Committee to Simpson, 25 October 1832, HBCA, A.6/22, Para. 14.

46 Arthur J. Ray, "Some Conservation Schemes of the Hudson's Bay Company, 1821–50: An Examination of the Problems of Resource Management in the Fur Trade," *Journal of Historical Geography* 1 (January 1975): 58. Any monopoly HBC had developed was only in isolated areas because the company had difficulty getting cooperation even from its own staff. The number of furs brought in influenced not only an individual's prestige but calculation of his pension.

47 Simpson to the Governor, Deputy Governor, and Committee, 20 August 1826, HBCA, D.4/89, Para. 30.

48 Simpson to the Governor, Deputy Governor, and Committee, 10 August 1832. HBCA, D.4/99, Para. 27.

49 Simpson to the Governor, Deputy Governor, and Committee, 20 June 1841, HBCA, D.4/99, Para. 31.

50 Governor, Deputy Governor, and Committee to Simpson. 3 March 1830, HBCA, A.622, Para. 2.

51 William Smith to James Keith, 3 September 1842, HBCA, A.6/26.

52 Governor, Deputy Governor, and Committee to Simpson, 1 April 1843, HBCA, A.6/26, Para. 23.

53 Archibald Barclay to James Keith, 4 September 1843, HBCA, A.6/26.

54 Governor, Deputy Governor, and Committee to John McLoughlin, 27 September 1843, HBCA, A.6/26, Para. 9.

55 Governor, Deputy Governor, and Committee to Simpson, 11 Match 1845, HBCA, A.6/26, Para. 3.

56 Auction, 1 September 1847, HBCA, A.54/182.

57 Governor, Deputy Governor, and Committee to Chief Factors Peter Skene Ogden, James Douglas, and John Work, 8 September 1848, HBCA, A.6/27, Para. 2.

58 Governor, Deputy Governor, and Committee to Simpson, 5 June 1847, HBCA, A.6/27, Para. 6; Governor, Deputy Governor, and Committee to Simpson, 7 April 1847, HBCA, A.6/27, Para. 3.

59 Governor, Deputy Governor, and Committee to Simpson. 5 April 1848, HBCA, A.6/27, Para. 4, 5, 7; Governor, Deputy Governor, and Committee to Simpson, 4 April 1849, HBCA, A.6/28, Para. 4.

60 Edward Roberts to Simpson, 3 February 1846, HBCA, D.5/16, fos. 168–69, cited in Caroline Skynner, "History of the Beaver and Beaver Hat," unpublished paper, HBCA, PP. 1984–7, p. 27.

61 Simpson to the Governor, Deputy Governor, and Committee, 25 November 1841, HBCA, D.4/110, Para. 7.

62 Governor, Deputy Governor, and Committee to Simpson, 11 March 1845, HBCA, A.6/26, Para. 3.

63 Governor, Deputy Governor, and Committee to Simpson, 18 September, 1847, HBCA,.A 6/27.

64 Ian McTaggart Cowan, in "The Fur Trade and the Fur Cycle: 1825–1857," *British Columbia Historical Quarterly* 2 (January 1938): 27, states that the marten and the lynx both undergo mass movements after the decline of a rabbit cycle.

65 Board of Management to the Governor, Deputy Governor, and Committee, 6 November 1847, *Fort Victoria Letters, 1846–1851,* ed. Hartwell Bowsfield (Winnipeg, Manitoba: HBRS, 1979), p. 23; James Douglas to Archibald Barclay, 23 July 1851, *Fort Victoria Letters*, pp. 200–201.

66 "Mink and Musquash will no doubt rise...as those who cannot afford to pay a high price for Martens will content themselves with inferior furs of the same class," Archibald Barclay to George Simpson, 28 December 1849, HBCA, A.6/28.

67 Governor, Deputy Governor, and Committee to Chief Factors Peter Skene Ogden, James Douglas, and John Work, Fort Vancouver, 8 September 1848. HBCA,.A.6/27, Para. 3.

68 "North West Coast—Visit at H.M.S. *Constance of*" *Times*, (London), 4 May 1849, p. 7.

69 For a discussion on non-fur trade economic activities see Richard S. Mackie, "Colonial Land, Indian Labour and Company Capital: The Economy of Vancouver Island, 1849–1858" (M.A. thesis, University of Victoria, 1984).

70 The concept is drawn loosely from Robert Darnton's examination of class through a description of a parade in pre-industrial France. See Robert Darnton, "A Bourgeois Puts His World In Order: The City As A Text," in *The Great Cat Massacre and Other Episodes in French Cultural History* (New York: Vintage Books., 1985), pp. 106–143., See also Keith Thomas, *Man and the Natural World: Changing Attitudes in England 1500–1800* (London, England: Allen Lane, 1983). All examples used here are drawn from Fur Trade Importation Book, 1799–1912 HBCA, A.53/71.

PART V

Industrializing Canada, 1840–1867

Between 1840 and 1867, the British North American colonies experienced dramatic changes at all levels: economic, political, social, and cultural. These changes were symbolized by Great Britain's adoption of free trade in 1846, the introduction of responsible government in Nova Scotia and the United Canadas in 1848, the controversy over public schooling, and the growing support for separation of church and state.

In this period the Industrial Revolution, characterized by steam power, railways, and factories, was the catalyst for many of the changes taking place. Industrial capitalism not only transformed the nature of work and the relationship between labour and capital, it also quickened the pace of communications, encouraged new political arrangements, and inspired nationalist movements in Europe and the Americas.

By the mid-nineteenth century, business leaders, professionals, and politicians in the British North American colonies began to dream of a nation from sea to sea, bound together by political institutions adapted from their British heritage. Despite widespread opposition to the idea, the promoters of Confederation were successful. A new nation called Canada, made up of New Brunswick, Nova Scotia, Ontario, and Quebec, came into being on 1 July 1867. By 1880 boundaries had expanded to include Prince Edward Island, Rupert's Land, British Columbia, and the Arctic, making Canada the second-largest nation in the world.

The dizzying pace of change affected everyone. In small villages, community leaders lobbied for a railway line, parsons and priests warned against the dangers of the new secular order, and schooling became an experience in the lives of virtually every child. Families debated the merits of public schooling and in many colonies found themselves taxed to pay for such a system whether they supported it or not. Whatever one's position on how schools should be sustained, few could deny that literacy had become the key to survival in the new industrial order. As Claudette Knight shows in the first article

in this section, black residents in Canada West were eager for their children to be educated but encountered deep-seated prejudices when they tried to send their children to public schools. Despite the misgivings of the Superintendent of Education, Egerton Ryerson, the Separate Schools Act of 1859 made provision for segregated schools in what became the province of Ontario. It was, Knight argues, a "reasonable response" for racist whites who opposed integrated schooling and for black residents who demanded access to the advantages that education could bring.

The educational system extolled the social values and social hierarchy that the emerging industrial order embodied. It was joined by the expanding newspaper industry in propagating ideas that defended inequalities among the sexes and social classes in British North America. Cecilia Morgan's article focuses on the newspapers' use of sentimental fiction as well as distorted reporting both to justify the existence of large-scale destitution next to vast wealth and an ideology of separate spheres in which middle-class women and men were to play very different roles in society. In the melodramatic stories in the press, well-heeled women motivated by Christian piety helped individual poor women to improve their lives, providing them with charity if they were poor because of bad luck and with an example of moral behaviour if they were poor because of allegedly sinful habits. In this way, as Morgan writes, "gender was displayed to stablilize and contain class inequalities." The press generally reinforced racism and sexism, presenting stereotypical images of blacks and ridiculing supporters of greater rights for women, such as the right to vote (female suffrage). By contrast, Morgan notes, the *Provincial Freeman,* a Canada West (Ontario) newspaper published by Mary Ann Shadd, a black immigrant from the United States, provided positive images of blacks and defended suffragists.

If black British North Americans had few defenders against stereotypes outside the pages of the *Provincial Freeman,* Native peoples were even less defended. The authorities and the press alike attributed most problems faced by Native peoples to the supposed primitivism of these peoples. When it came to suicides, for example, there was little recognition of the variability of its frequency from First Nation to First Nation and little rational discussion of the causes of suicides. When suicides occurred, particularly among women, the colonial masters of British North America used these tragedies to justify their conquest of Native lands. After all, they argued, societies in which women occasionally did away with themselves were uncivilized societies. Lesley Erickson tries to recover the Native voice regarding suicides so that we get an understanding of Natives' views on the causes of suicide in the pre-contact period and the changes that occurred in the frequency and causes of suicide as Native peoples increasingly lost their lands and livelihoods.

While Native peoples and black British North Americans had the least power and wealth in British North America, it was hardly the case that all white settlers enjoyed equal social privileges. Women were denied the vote and while increasing numbers of men voted, state institutions evolved in ways that reinforced differences in social class and status. Bruce Curtis studies the efforts by the government of the United Province of Canada (Ontario and Quebec) to deal with a potential cholera outbreak in the period just before Confederation. They named doctors to a Central Board of Health, which established detailed regulations for local boards of health. Curtis concludes: "The scare's durable relevance to the formation of the Canadian state lies in the practical attempts it spawned to extend projects for the organization of surveillance, the centralization of knowledge, the consolidation of expertise, and the government of conduct."

The supposed benefits of centralization caused many British North Americans to consider political union of the eastern colonies and territorial expansion to the Pacific. Was this not an obvious way to maximize upon the spectacular advances associated with the Industrial Revolution and offer the promise of a better life for everyone? Among the imagined benefits were railways, new agricultural frontiers, an end to sectarian and political bickering, and greater material comfort. The Civil War in the United States (1861–1865), anti-imperialist sentiment in the British Colonial Office, and political deadlock in the United Canadas furthered this aim by creating a crisis atmosphere in which the idea of colonial union became increasingly attractive. The Fathers of Confederation and their imperial and corporate backers prevailed in 1867, with the result that the views advanced by the opponents of Confederation are often treated dismissively or ignored entirely. Ged Martin takes a careful look at what the anti-Confederates had to say, concluding that while they lost the battle, they at least won some of the arguments.

Black Parents Speak: Education in Mid-Nineteenth-Century Canada West

Claudette Knight

During the mid-nineteenth century, many black residents of Canada West were ardent advocates of public education for their children. Government policy officially supported black access to public education, although local white prejudice often limited its scope. Some black children attended common schools regularly, but others were denied public education or were forced to enroll in separate schools. Despite the increasing regulation and centralization of education during this period, local white opposition to integrated schooling ultimately shaped the policy that governed black students and, in some circumstances, was ultimately more powerful than the law.

Black parents seeking education opportunities amid anti-integrationist white communities resorted to a variety of strategies to combat local prejudice. Appeals to local officials, letters of protest to government education officers, and civil suits were initiated by black parents committed to educating their children. These initiatives not only document the history of black access to education in mid-nineteenth-century Canada West, but also serve as an important social barometer.

> I'm on my way to Canada
> That cold and distant land
> The dire effects of slavery
> I can no longer stand —

> Farewell, old master,
> Don't come after me.
> I'm on my way to Canada
> Where coloured men are free.[1]

This excerpt from George Clark's song, "The Free Slave," depicts Canada as a desirable refuge from the indignities and injustice suffered by American blacks under slavery. During the mid-nineteenth century, especially between 1850 and 1860, Canada West received a substantial influx of American blacks. The enslaved and the free sought to enjoy the freedom, equality, and justice that they were denied in the United States. According to Robin Winks, blacks migrating from the United States prior to the 1830s were generally well received in Canada West. During this period the number of blacks in Canada West was relatively small, and cheap labour was needed in many frontier communities to fell trees, lay roads, cut ties, and introduce tobacco farming.

After 1840 several significant changes altered these conditions. First, during the 1840s blacks faced increased competition from Irish immigrants, who were equally willing to embrace physically demanding, low-wage work, and whose skin colour was less likely to create social opposition. Secondly, as the availability of cheap land declined, blacks tended to drift towards towns where racial and real or

---

Claudette Knight, "Black Parents Speak: Education in Mid-Nineteenth-Century Canada West," *Ontario History* 89, 4 (December 1997): 269–284.

imagined social differences would be more easily observed. Finally, and perhaps most significantly, the number of black fugitives fleeing to Canada West increased substantially after the passage of the Fugitive Slave Act in 1850. This act required all Americans to assist in the recapture and return of fugitive slaves, regardless of whether these blacks had obtained freedom in the northern states. Prior to September 1850, ten thousand blacks lived in Canada West; ten years later, this figure had increased to between thirty and thirty-five thousand.[2]

Initially, black fugitives tended to settle near the border in order to farm in regions most geographically familiar. Lack of funds and easy return access to the United States also determined that small groups settled in Welland, St. Catharines, Colchester, Windsor, Amherstburg, London, Chatham, and Dresden. Settlement occurred more slowly in Toronto, Oro, and the Queen's Bush. It is not surprising that later arrivals tended to settle in these regions where the small, established black communities could provide assistance to incoming fugitives.

Employment opportunities for the fugitives varied in Canada West, but most were farmers. Nevertheless, during the 1830s and 1840s many waiters in hotels near Niagara Falls were black, while others were employed on road construction or hired themselves out as field hands in Oro, and a small number operated their own small businesses in various towns. Some worked as brakemen on the Great Western Railway, made rope, were fishermen, or laboured in brickyards and slaughterhouses. Black women worked on farms and as servants. Despite the opportunities and prosperity enjoyed by some of these fugitives, the majority struggled financially, were often poorly prepared for the winter months, and many suffered from consumption.[3]

Proscriptions placed on black education in both northern and southern states meant that most black fugitives were illiterate. Blacks residing in the free states were often barred from public schools or forced to attend separate schools. Educating blacks was illegal in all slave states except Kentucky. A Virginia state representative summarized southern white sentiment: "We have as far as possible closed every avenue by which light may enter their minds...if we could extinguish the capacity to see the light our work would be completed."[4]

Despite their restricted access to education in the United States, once in Canada West black fugitives eagerly sought access to public schools. Many believed that the popular myth of black inferiority would be quickly destroyed when blacks gained educational opportunities. Educated blacks would undermine racist ideology, obtain superior employment, and gain voting privileges. On 22 October 1851, three black abolitionists (Henry Bibb, John Fisher, and James Tinsely) summarized the importance of education in their *Address to the Coloured Inhabitants of North America*:

> As we value education as being one of the most important items connected with our destiny, and it is more dreaded by the slaveholders than bowie-knives or pistols, we therefore recommend that there should be no time or opportunity lost in educating people of colour. Let there be put into the hands of the refugee as soon as he crosses Mason's and Dixon's Line, the Spelling Book. Teach him to read and write intelligibly, and the slaveholder won't have him on the plantation among his slaves. It is emphatically the most effectual protection to personal or political liberty with which the human family can be armed.[5]

Recognizing the value of education, blacks sought to enroll their children in Canada West's common schools. Susan Houston and Alison Prentice state that black children, like their white peers, attended schools "when and where they could."[6] Local prejudice of varying intensity resulted in the segregation of black youth. The exclusion of many black children from public schools was not inconsistent with the aims of the elites who promoted centralized education in Canada West. Furthermore, the success of white opposition to integrated schooling reflected the inability of government officials to wholly usurp educational authority from local communities.

The School Act of 1816 provided for the establishment of schools by property owners. These local citizens were permitted to construct a school, hire a teacher, and select trustees; during this period the schools provided basic literacy for their communities. The nature of public education in Canada West was altered throughout the latter half of the nineteenth century by elite Upper Canadians who sought to wrest educational authority from local communities. These elites were not concerned with economic or social mobility for the lower classes; instead, they sought to inculcate the attitudes and values that would respect their power and authority to rule. Bruce Curtis contends that these elite school promoters "consistently stressed both the necessity and beauty of class differences and of the social subordination of women."[7] It is not unreasonable to suggest that education reformers seeking to maintain class divisions in the white community would also have preferred Canada West's black community to maintain its inferior status.

The creation of the office of the superintendent of schools, legislated in the School Act of 1841, launched the beginning of centralized education in Canada West. School acts introduced between 1843 and 1871 resulted in a significant increase in the number of public schools and a serious erosion of local control over schooling. The educational bureaucracy expanded its power through increased regulation and the appointment of regional and central education officials. Whereas the pace of bureaucracy was rapid in Canada West, the actual authority of education officials to implement school policy emerged more slowly. For example, the School

Act of 1841 provided for the superintendent of education to inspect common schools, manage the provincial school funds and distribute funds to district councils, and create and publicize plans to improve the education system. It did not, however, legislate power to enforce new school policies. Furthermore, the superintendent of education technically had no power to resolve local educational disputes.

In 1844 Egerton Ryerson, a well-known Methodist minister and former principal of Victoria College, accepted the position of superintendent of education of common schools in Canada West. To support policy development and funding responsibilities, this office expanded to include collecting educational data, resolving educational disputes, and discouraging "inappropriate behaviour." Despite the wide range of administrative responsibilities, the superintendent's power to enforce school policy was limited to withholding school funds from uncooperative communities. Egerton Ryerson was passionately committed to the development and expansion of schooling in Canada West. He sought the successful training of youth whose Christian values and developed mind and body would ensure political and moral order. It is likely that Ryerson's commitment to the expansion of Canada West's education system created a reluctance to withhold funding from disobedient school districts; his vision of a vast and regulated school system was dependent on the increase, not decline, of functioning public schools.

Before 1850, whites often used "creative" strategies to deny blacks their legal right to attend common schools; for example, they would gerrymander school districts or declare that local common schools were private. As a last resort, white parents would simply remove their children from the common school, which invariably closed due to the reduction in attendance. In a response to the exclusion of black youth from common schools, several black women established separate schools. In 1851 Mary Bibb opened a school for black children in her home, eventually expanding to a larger building. Similarly, in 1856 Amelia Freeman operated a grammar school for Chatham blacks. Between 1851 and 1853 Mary Ann Shadd, partially under the auspices of the American Missionary Association, operated a school in Windsor and eventually joined Amelia Freeman in the teaching and management of the Chatham Separate School. By providing independent education for black children, these black teachers made a valuable contribution to their communities, but their schools were plagued by financial difficulties. Since black communities were often small and relatively poor, funding was meagre. Enrolments varied and school grants, which were based on attendance, suffered as a result.[8]

Although much of black education in Canada West took place in separate schools, integrated schooling was accepted in some regions. In the late 1830s white children attended the renowned "black" school in Brantford. Similarly, the excellent reputation of the Buxton school, in the black settlement of Kent County, as well as the Church of England's Mission School, founded in London in 1854, attracted both black and white students. Even though the residents in larger, more socially heterogeneous communities such as Toronto and Hamilton were not wholly committed to racial integration, these urban centres did have some integrated schools. Prentice and Houston suggest that the central administration of these common schools, combined with teachers, trustees, and politicians who were committed to racial integration, were important components that permitted and supported integrated schooling.[9]

The voices of individuals who did not gain access to public schools are difficult for the historian to detect. Fortunately, letters written to education officials between 1840 and 1860 provide some indication of the history of black access to education. These letters articulate parents' tenacity and commitment to public education

and illuminate the opposition mounted by their prejudiced white neighbours. Despite laws that granted equal citizenship, racism was a component that circumscribed black life in Canada West.

One of the earliest available records of the black struggle for access to education was a petition to Governor General Charles Metcalfe from Hamilton's community. In a letter dated 15 October 1843, these parents protested that although they paid taxes, their children were denied access to local common schools. They had emigrated to Canada to escape racism in the United States believing that "there was not a man to be known by his colour under the British flag." Yet they encountered verbal and physical abuse from their white neighbours. The local police board, whose members were also the public school trustees, refused to protect their access to education. The letter concludes apologetically: "[We are] sorry to annoy you by allowing this thing, but we are grieved much, we are imposed on much, and if it please your excellency to attend to this grievance."[10]

Charles Metcalfe's office responded immediately to this petition. On 19 October 1843, it sought additional information from George Tiffany, president of the Hamilton Board of Police, about the number of black children in Hamilton, the attitudes of whites toward blacks attending the public schools, and requested a summary of police action concerning black education. Tiffany's response confirmed that racism was prevalent in the Hamilton community. He concluded that the Board of Trustees should not yield to prejudice, but "should enforce the law without distinction of colour...a firm stand will eventually destroy prejudice."[11] It appears that these board officials chose to ignore the plight of their black neighbours until queries from Metcalfe's office prompted them to reverse their discriminatory enrolment practices. As a result of their parents' petition, black children gained access to Hamilton's common schools.

Similar circumstances existed in Amherstburg in 1846, but the outcome here was not so favourable. The Reverend Isaac Rice, a white Presbyterian missionary, wrote a letter on behalf of the black citizens of Amherstburg on 23 January 1846. Addressed to the Reverend Alexander McNab, the former acting superintendent of education, the letter complained that black children were barred from the common school by prejudiced whites. These white residents stated that, rather than send their children "to school with niggers, they will cut their children's heads off and throw them in the road side ditch." The letter asserted that Amherstburg's black students, children of tax-paying parents, deserved access to the public school. Nonetheless, the school trustees and white residents falsely claimed that the school was private and barred black students. The white teacher's response to black children was to "turn them out doors."[12]

Egerton Ryerson responded promptly to the concerns of the Amherstburg residents. Before replying, he sought additional information from Robert Peden, Amherstburg's former education superintendent. In a letter of 23 February 1846, Robert Peden concurred with the black residents' assessment of their exclusion from educational opportunities. Peden had attempted unsuccessfully to assuage these black parents by creating a separate school, but they had adamantly rejected segregated education.[13]

Ryerson's response to Amherstburg's black community was sympathetic: "the exclusion of your children from the school was at variance with the letter and spirit of the law, and the ground of exclusion is at variance with the principles and spirit of British institutions, which deprive no human beings of any benefit which they can confer on account of the colour of their skin." Unfortunately the affirmation of black citizens' rights as British citizens was the extent of Ryerson's assistance. He acknowledged the recent election of Amherstburg school trustees and concluded that he "trusts that a sufficient

remedy will be provided against the recurrence of the inquiries of which you complain."[14]

Although Egerton Ryerson's written response to the residents of Hamilton and Amherstburg was of little tangible use, he was not wholly insincere in the sympathy that he expressed. Ryerson was committed to educational opportunities for all children, but he was unwilling to jeopardize his burgeoning universal common school program by directly confronting racist opponents to integrated schooling. Instead he opted for an indirect resolution. Recognizing the possible destabilizing effects of attempting to compel local whites to accept integrated schooling, Egerton Ryerson chose to push for legislation aimed at ensuring that all black children had educational opportunities. The School Act of 1850 included a provision for the creation of separate schools for blacks which would permit any group of five black families to ask local trustees to establish a school for their children. Theoretically, this legislation was to provide an option for black parents seeking education for their children, and it was in fact used by some black communities. But racist whites also used it to establish separate schools for blacks who did not want segregated education. In the 1859 School Act, Egerton Ryerson encouraged more active separation by legislating that any "12 or more heads of families, Protestant or Negro, could open their own institutions and receive apportionments from the common school fund."[15] Again, this provision was problematic because white school supporters interpreted it as a legitimate way of barring black youth from local common schools and forcing them to establish their own schools. As a result, many black children were excluded from local common schools, and those who did not have access to separate schools received no education at all.

The School Act of 1850 received mixed reviews from Canada West's black residents. Despite the misuse of the separate school provision by some white school supporters, this legislation was welcomed in several black communities. Separate schools were established in Amherstburg, Chatham, Colchester, and Windsor and these parents embraced the opportunity for their children to learn on their own terms protected from prejudice.[16] Other blacks were passionately opposed to this legislation because it often prevented access to a superior common school, and they believed that such segregation encouraged racism. In the March 1857 edition of the *Provincial Freeman,* black editor H.F. Douglas condemned religious and educational segregation: "Separate schools and churches are nuisances that should be abated as soon as possible, they are dark and hateful relics of Yankee Negrophobia." It is difficult for the historian to determine whether the overall effect of the 1850 School Act was favourable or detrimental to black children. Clearly, the existence of separate schooling remained a contentious issue in Canada West's black community. Nonetheless, it is probable that black advocates, on both sides of the debate, were governed by a belief in the value of education and a commitment to uplifting the black race.

On 12 December 1851, black residents of Simcoe questioned the intent of the 1850 School Act. The community petitioned Egerton Ryerson because their children were denied access to the local common schools. Their letter stated that school trustees and teachers excluded black students even though their parents paid municipal taxes. These parents had "no desire for separate schools" and requested Ryerson's assistance since they had attempted by "every possible means" to gain access to the public schools. They were particularly distressed because their poverty eliminated the prospect of private tutoring: "We are poor and can't provide education for our kids." Aware of the provision for separate schools, the Simcoe residents requested a specific interpretation of the law: did they have the right to attend the public schools with their white neighbours?[17]

Again, Ryerson's response expressed his dismay and sympathy for the Simcoe residents: "I deeply grieve the painful circumstances which you state." He cited the 1850 act to prove that black children enjoyed the same rights and privileges as their white peers unless their parents chose separate schooling. If black parents did not establish separate schools they "have the same right of access for their children as the parent of any other children residing in the section." He advised the Simcoe parents to pursue legal action. He suggested they should sue the school trustees for denying their children the right to education. Egerton Ryerson's final remarks compassionately reaffirmed Simcoe blacks' rights and privileges as British citizens, declaring that it was a "deplorable calamity to be denied access to education...more especially for those who are seeking it...who have been greatly wronged and oppressed in a neighbouring country and who are assured of all the rights and privileges of British subjects in this country, which ought not be infected with the spirit any more than it is cursed with the curse of slavery."[18]

The battle to gain access to public schools in Canada West continued in Camden Township, Kent County. In November 1852 Dennis Hill, a black resident, wrote to Ryerson asking: "Is it presumptuous to expect my eleven year old be educated with whites?" White residents had denied Hill's son access to the public school for "no crime other than skin a few shades darker." Hill sought Ryerson's advice because he "refused to allow his children to grow up in ignorance." He was particularly angry because he had significant landholdings and paid more taxes than most of his white neighbours. Hill was further incensed by white school trustees who barred local black children yet invited white students from other districts to attend the Camden Common School.

Ryerson's response was again supportive in emphasizing his disgust at yet another case of injustice. "It is mean beyond expression as well as unjust for the Trustees and other supporters of the school to levy and receive taxes from you," he wrote, "for the education of their children and then refuse admission to yours." He again cited the 1850 School Act, highlighting black students' fundamental right to public education unless a separate school had been established for their benefit. Ryerson advised Hill to prosecute for damages.[19]

Letters concerning black access to education were not exclusively written by black parents. The provincial education office received several letters from white school supporters who were frustrated by their black neighbours' determined efforts to gain access to Canada West's common schools. In 1856 James Douglas, the school superintendent of West Flamborough, Wentworth County, sought Ryerson's advice on segregated schooling. In his letter he outlined the ongoing racial conflict that threatened the survival of the local common school. West Flamborough school trustees demanded that their public school teacher physically separate black and white students in the classroom. This action provoked the wrath of a black parent who disrupted classroom proceedings in his attempt to eliminate this segregation. Superintendent Douglas summarized the anti-black sentiment that dominated his township: "old Canadian families are unwilling to allow their children to sit promiscuously with Negroes and Mulattos."[20] James Douglas feared that his school would soon close because white parents would withdraw their children unless black students were relegated to a separate area of the classroom.

Discrimination against black students was also the topic of Samuel Atkinson's letter of 29 December 1856 to Ryerson. This school trustee from Malden, Essex County, explained that a separate school established for black students had fallen into disuse, and black parents were seeking admission to the local common school. Atkinson was firmly opposed to integrated schooling. He stated that "a mixed school with them [blacks] at present cannot be had!" Again, school closure would result if black parents persisted in their efforts to gain access to the public school because white parents would refuse to send their children to the school. Certain that the black residents would continue to "push themselves on us," Atkinson advocated the legitimacy of rejecting blacks from public schools. Ryerson responded immediately and succinctly. "The Trustees," he wrote, "are not required by law to admit into the public school the children of persons, whether Roman Catholic or coloured people for whom a separate school has been established. Should the persons for whom a Separate School has been established not keep open the Separate School they do not thereby acquire a right to send their children to the public school."[21] It is probable that Malden's black children received no education following Ryerson's decision that supported their exclusion from the local common school.

The persistence of black citizens in seeking public education was also a source of aggravation for white residents of the township of Harwich, Kent County. In March 1862, Duncan Campbell, a white school trustee, wrote to Ryerson asserting that blacks did not request separate schools because they rarely possessed the funds to maintain these institutions. As a result of the attendance of eight black students in the local common school, fifty white children had been withdrawn because "the white people are determined that they shall not send their children to any school while the coloured people have the privilege of sending their children." Anger at his inability to relegate blacks to a separate school had led him to resign as a school trustee, a position that he had held for ten years. Harwich school trustees corroborated his testimony, stating that their black neighbours had "never contributed to the support of our school as there is not one of them who owns a single foot of land." Legally unable to exclude blacks from the classroom, the

Harwich trustees proposed the construction of a connecting classroom in order to segregate black and white students.[22]

The struggle to gain access to common schools was also seen in Dresden, Kent County. In January 1852 William Newman informed Ryerson, on the behalf of his black neighbours, that he needed clarification of the 1850 Common Schools Act. These black citizens frankly inquired if "the spirit of the law was to aid Blacks or the prejudice against colour?"[23] As Dresden's black children were denied access to the common school, they were forced to attend a separate school seven miles away. Exasperated by the inequity of contributing taxes towards the Dresden Common School, these citizens asked whether "the law was intended to give blacks the same rights as whites?"

An incident in Windsor showed that although Egerton Ryerson was committed to the education of black children, he was resigned to the racism that relegated blacks to separate schools. In February 1859, Clayborn Harris wrote to a barrister, William Horton, on behalf of the blacks in Windsor who sought legal assistance to enable their children to attend the local common school. Confident in their rights and privileges as British subjects, their letter asked: "Shall the Trustees use government money to support a prejudice of one class of Her Majesty's subjects against another?"[24]

All levels of Windsor's educational hierarchy had united to exclude black students from the public school. The local school administration refused to teach or admit these students. The regional superintendent of education stated that he was subordinate to the trustees and "consequently he, too, must reject Black students." These white officials provided blacks with a separate school, described as a "16 by 24 feet coop," in order to satisfy their black neighbours' desire for education. Windsor blacks were adamantly opposed to separate education. They believed that segregated schooling provided inferior education and thus defied British principles of equity and justice. The "idea of us asking for a separate school when it will debar us from all the higher branches of literature," Clayborn Harris wrote, "would be like cutting off our noses to spite our faces...We as a people feel to love British Law and will ever defend it, but we shall equally stand up for all the rights that the law provides for us, otherwise we would be unworthy of the rights that we are guaranteed." Harris concluded his letter to Horton by suggesting that Superintendent Ryerson might provide some valuable assistance. The postscript remarked that black residents of Sandwich encountered similar injustices. Their children were barred from the local common school and forced to attend a separate school four miles from their homes.

In addition to retaining William Horton, the black residents of Windsor wrote to Egerton Ryerson themselves. These parents were willing to abide by the laws of their new homeland, but were angered by the "use of the general Government as a means of fostering for a moment that hydra-headed monster [prejudice] at the cost of any class either on account of complexion or religion." Their letter addressed the fundamental legislative obstacle encountered by blacks pursuing public education after 1850: "Have they [school trustees] power to decide without our request according to Section 19 that the coloured children shall go in a separate school?" William Horton also wrote to Ryerson on the behalf of his clients. He stated that he had advised Windsor's black parents to seek separate education, but that they were either unwilling or unable to accept his suggestion. Unable to advance an alternative, Horton requested Ryerson's advice.[25]

Ryerson came to the point quickly in replying that if no separate school had been established, black children had the right to attend the local common school. It seems that an increased awareness of the strength of local racism led Ryerson to qualify his view: "If however public feeling is very strongly expressed against such a course it may be expedient with the consent of the parties concerned to establish a Separate School under the section quoted by you [section 19], but it is very undesirable that such a prejudice be sustained."[26] In 1862 a separate schoolhouse was constructed for Windsor's black community. Defeated in their attempt to gain access to the local common school, these black parents probably resigned themselves to segregated education.

Petitioning Superintendent Ryerson was clearly not an effective strategy for black parents seeking integrated education. Although Ryerson supported principles of equity and justice for blacks, he reluctantly concluded that "the prejudice and feelings of people are stronger than the law."[27] Perhaps it was the recognition of the education system's inability to overcome white racism that prompted several black parents to pursue legal action. Between 1855 and 1864 four cases concerning black access to public education were resolved in Canada West's civil courts. The justices presiding over these legal disputes acknowledged the prejudice that restricted black children's education. Nonetheless, they were firmly committed to the education of black youth, either through integrated or segregated schooling.

The first case occurred in 1855 when a black man named Washington prosecuted the school trustees of Charlotteville. The plaintiff's son, Solomon Washington, was barred from the local common school, yet there was no separate school in the district. Previously, this child had attended the common school and his father had been assessed and billed for school tax. Mr. Washington continued to pay school taxes despite his son's exclusion from the school. The Charlotteville school trustees defended their actions by stating that Solomon Washington had exhibited poor behaviour when he attended the school. In 1850 two of the school trustees

had altered the boundaries of the school district so as to exclude Washington's fifty acres of land, and had instructed the local school teacher to bar Solomon Washington because his attendance promoted conflict and the potential dissolution of the school. These trustees used the new school boundaries to legitimize their expulsion of the black student from school.

John Beverley Robinson, the chief justice of Upper Canada from 1830 to 1862, presided over this case. Robinson's ruling favoured Washington. He declared the case to be a clear example of gerrymandering. He was particularly concerned that, due to the lack of a local separate school, Solomon Washington had been denied access to public education. Robinson's concluding comments acknowledged that the formation of the School Act of 1850 was predicated on an acceptance of racism, but he believed that prejudice should not wholly deny black children their right to education. "The legislation," he found, "does seem to have meant, though reluctantly, to give way so far to any prejudice that may exist in the minds of white inhabitants as to allow the establishment of separate schools for the coloured people, if thought expedient, but not to shut them out from the only public schools that do exist, by leaving it discretionary in the school trustees to deny them arbitrarily, when they have no other school to go to."[28]

Washington's legal triumph over the Charlotteville school trustees was financially debilitating. The defendants possessed no property that could be sold and Washington was forced to sell his farm to pay for legal expenses. *Washington* v. *Trustees of Charlotteville* established a precedent rendering gerrymandering of school districts illegal and unacceptable, especially if there was no proximate separate school.[29] The issue of segregated education surfaced again in *Dennis Hill* v. *The School Trustees of Camden and Zone*. Failing in his attempt to elicit a solution from Ryerson in 1852, Dennis Hill resorted to legal action in 1855. On several occasions he had requested permission to send his two sons to the local common school. The school trustees, both individually and collectively, had refused to admit Hill's sons because they were black. Dennis Hill was particularly distressed because there was no proximate separate school and his children received no public education.

Contrary to Dennis Hill's testimony, the school trustees of Camden alleged that a separate school, located at the British American Institute, had been established for the exclusive benefit of black residents under a bylaw passed in 1850. One of the defendants explicitly stated that the establishment of the separate school was a direct response to the prejudice displayed by white residents.

Chief Justice Robinson's decision favoured the Camden school trustees. He concluded that the "legislature did not intend at that time that separate schools should be resorted to or not according to the choice of the persons in whose behalf they have been established, by which I understand not only the applicants of the school, but those individuals belonging to the class of persons in whose behalf they have been established." In addition to ruling that black children must attend separate schools in their district, Robinson identified the prejudice that supported segregated schooling:

> We are of the opinion that separate schools for coloured people were authorized, as the defendants have suggested, out of deference to the prejudice of the white population, prejudices which the Legislature evidently, from the language they used, disapproved of and regretted and which arise, perhaps not so much from the mere difference of colour, as from the apprehension that the coloured people, many of whom have lately escaped from a state of slavery, may be, in respect to morals and habits, unfortunately worse trained than the white children are in general, and that their children might suffer from the effect of the example.[30]

Robinson's ruling suggests that white racism fuelled the legislation for separate schools. His theory that white prejudice arises not from race but from substandard morals and behaviour exhibited by blacks may have some validity. Certainly, life in Canada West must have been considerably different from slavery in the American South. Many of the blacks in Canada West, however, had not recently escaped plantation slavery. Several writers, including Mary Ann Shadd, Benjamin Drew, Henry Bibb, and Samuel Gridley Howe, stressed the high moral standards and temperance exhibited by blacks. It is most likely that white prejudice stemmed from a variety of sources, including "mere difference of colour."

In 1861 gerrymandering was again at issue in the case of Simmons and the Corporation of the Township of Chatham. Simmons, a black parent, prosecuted the local school trustees who had established a school section according to the presence of black inhabitants. Chatham's School District No. 1 was vaguely defined and fluctuating because it included "every lot or parcel of land occupied, or which shall be occupied by any coloured person in front of the said township." By establishing a separate school in this manner, Chatham school trustees compelled all black residents to attend this school regardless of their proximity to the school. Their exclusionary objectives were addressed in Chief Justice Robinson's ruling. Identifying the trustees' attempt to deny all blacks access to local common schools, Robinson quashed the bylaw responsible for School District No. 1. He concluded that Chatham's school districts were "not intelligibly confined,...uncertain in nature and do not give the school section any limits that can be said to [be] ascertained or known at any point in time."[31]

In 1864, George Stewart, of Sandwich, Essex County, successfully prosecuted local school trustees for refusing to admit his daughter Lively to the local common school. This black parent requested permission to send his child to the common school on several occasions, but his requests were rejected by school trustees because "he and his daughter were coloured people." Despite Lively's exclusion from the school, George Stewart regularly paid school taxes. The Sandwich East school trustees attempted to justify Lively Stewart's exclusion from school by stating that a separate school had been established at the request of local blacks. The trustees also alleged that George Stewart had not been taxed to support the common school. Although a separate school had been established by the Refugee Home Society, financial difficulties had forced its closure in 1861.

Chief Justice William Draper's ruling favouring Stewart was predicated on his belief in the immutability of black children's right to receive public education. He concluded that "coloured people are not to be excluded from the ordinary common schools if there be no separate school established and in operation for their use. The creation of a separate school suspends but does not annul those privileges [conferred by the common school act], and when the separate school ceases to exist the rights revive." Draper awarded Lively Stewart the right to attend the Sandwich East common school, but his judgment recognized the prejudice that motivated the school trustees. "We do not question the sincerity of those who state their apprehension of the consequences of allowing coloured children to enter the common schools," his judgment read, "but this is an argument against the law itself, if it can have any weight. The law does give such a right, subject to certain defined exceptions. The existence of these exceptions is not proved in this case."[32]

Canada West's black community continued to seek access to public schools until the outbreak of the American Civil War. The war launched a massive exodus of blacks back to their homeland. By 1865 approximately three-quarters of Canada West's black community had returned to the United States.[33] A desire to renew family ties and friendships, as well as to participate in the civil war and reconstruction, are plausible explanations for their departure. However, white racism in Canada was also a catalyst as William Henry Bradley, a black Dresden resident, accurately and succinctly summarized:

> There is a great deal of prejudice here. Statements have been made that coloured people wished for separate schools; some did ask for them and they have been established, although many coloured people have prayed against them as an infringement of their rights. Still we have more freedom here than in the United States, as far as the government guarantees...There are many respectable coloured people moving in, but I have not much hope of a better state of things. Public sentiment will move a mountain of laws.[34]

The history of black education in mid-nineteenth century Canada West establishes the presence of racism in the formation of Ontario's public education system. Although unpalatable to modern sensibilities, the introduction of segregated education in Canada West seems to have been a reasonable response to blacks who sought educational opportunities for their children and racist whites who opposed integrated schooling. Separate schools gradually fell into disuse during the 1890s, but the 1859 Separate Schools Act remained until 1964. Nonetheless, even today black parents struggle against the more subtle racism in academic curricula and the assessment of student ability. It is likely that the tradition of active concern for educational rights, initiated by black parents in the mid-nineteenth century and currently exhibited by blacks, will continue to influence the development of Ontario's education system.

Notes

I am indebted to Professor Ian Radforth and *Ontario History* for their faith and invaluable criticism. Many thanks to Guy and my family for providing constructive criticism and encouragement throughout the evolution of this manuscript.

1 Quoted in Daniel Hill, *The Freedom Seekers: Blacks in Early Canada* (Agincourt: The Book Society of Canada Limited, 1981), 25.

2 Robin Winks, *The Blacks in Canada* (Montreal: McGill-Queen's University Press, 1980), 142–44. James Walker, *The History of Blacks in Canada* (Quebec: Government Publications, 1980), 55. Alison Prentice and Susan Houston, *Schooling and Scholars in Nineteenth-Century Ontario* (Toronto: University of Toronto Press, 1988), 298.

3 Winks, *Blacks in Canada,* 144, 246.

4 Jason Silverman and Donna Gillie, "Pursuit of Knowledge under Difficulties: Education and the Fugitive Slave in Canada," *Ontario History* 74 (1982), 95. See also Donald G. Simpson, "Negroes in Ontario from Early Times to 1870" (Ph.D. diss, University of Western Ontario, 1971), 26–29.

5 "Address to the Coloured Inhabitants of North America," in Peter C. Ripley, ed., *The Black Abolitionist Papers, Volume II, 1830–1865* (Chapel Hill and London: The University of North Carolina Press, 1986), 173.

6 Prentice and Houston, *Schooling and Scholars,* 299.

7 Bruce Curtis, *Building the Educational State: Canada West, 1836–1871* (London: The Falmer Press, 1988), 13–15. See also 54–56, 102, 115.

8 Prentice and Houston, *Schooling and Scholars,* 299. See Afua Cooper, "Black Women and Work in Nineteenth Century Canada West: Black Woman Teacher Mary Bibb," in Peggy Bristow, ed., *We're Rooted Here and They Can't Pull Us Up* (Toronto: University of Toronto Press, 1994), 144, 155, and Walker, *Blacks in Canada,* 65.

9 Prentice and Houston, *Schooling and Scholars,* 301.

10 Public Archives of Ontario, Incoming General Correspondence 1842–1871 [hereafter RG2 C6C], petition, People of Hamilton to Charles Metcalf, 15 October 1843.

11 Public Archives of Ontario, Outgoing General Correspondence 1842–1860 [hereafter RG2 C1], Robert Murray to George Tiffany, 19 October 1843. RG2 C6C, George Tiffany to Robert Murray, 9 November 1843. Silverman and Gillie, "Pursuit of Knowledge," 99.

12 RG2 C6C, Isaac Rice to Reverend Alexander McNab, 23 January 1846.

13 RG2 C6C, Robert Peden to Egerton Ryerson, 23 February 1846.

14 RG2 C1, Egerton Ryerson to Isaac Rice, 5 March 1846.

15 Winks, *Blacks in Canada,* 368, 370. Simpson, "Negroes in Ontario," 498–500. Cooper, "Black Woman Teacher," 148.

16 Walker, *Blacks in Canada,* 61.

17 RG2 C6C, Coloured Inhabitants of Simcoe County to Egerton Ryerson, 12 December 1851.

18 RG2 C1, Egerton Ryerson to R. Henderson, 17 December 1851.

19 RG2 C6C, Dennis Hill to Egerton Ryerson, 22 November 1852. RG2 C1, Egerton Ryerson to Dennis Hill, 30 November 1852.

20 RG2 C6C, James Douglas to Egerton Ryerson, 3 February 1856.

21 Ibid., Samuel Atkinson to Egerton Ryerson, 29 December 1856. RG2 C1, Egerton Ryerson to Samuel Atkinson, 29 January 1857.

22 RG2 C6C, Duncan Campbell to Egerton Ryerson, 14 March 1862; Harwich School Trustees to Egerton Ryerson, 17 March 1862.

23 Ibid., William Newman to Egerton Ryerson, 13 January 1852.

24 Ibid., Clayborn Harris to William Horton, 15 February 1859.

25 Ibid., Committee for the Coloured People of Windsor to Egerton Ryerson, 2 March 1859; William Horton to Egerton Ryerson, 16 February 1859.

26 RG2 C1, Egerton Ryerson to William Horton, 21 February 1859. Silverman and Gillie, "Pursuit of Knowledge," 103.

27 Quoted in Winks, *Blacks in Canada,* 112.

28 Report of the Cases Decided in the Court of Queen's Bench, Vol. II (Toronto: Harry Rowsell, 1854), *Washington* v. *Charlotteville,* 569–70.

29 Robin Winks, "Negro Education in Ontario and Nova Scotia," *Canadian Historical Review* 50, 175.

30 Court of Queen's Bench, Vol. 11, *Dennis Hill* v. *The School Trustees of Camden and Zone,* 574, 575–78.

31 Ibid., Vol. 21, *In The Matter of Simmons* v. *The Corporation of the Township of Chatham,* 75–79.

32 Ibid., Vol. 22, *Re Stewart* v. *Sandwich East School Trustees,* 636–38.

33 Winks, *Blacks in Canada,* 61.

34 William Henry Bradley, in Benjamin Drew, *A North-Side View of Slavery* (New York: John P. Jeweth, 1856), 312.

"Better Than Diamonds": Sentimental Strategies and Middle-Class Culture in Canada West

CECILIA MORGAN

On a cold winter's day in a large city, so the story goes, a little girl had a chance encounter with a beautiful rich woman in front of a jeweller's store. The child was taking slippers for "spangling" back to her mother who did piece-work in the garret where they lived; she had slipped on the ice in front of the store. She wore no shoes and her clothes were thread-bare rags. Her father, she told the lady, was dead, her baby brother was ill, and her mother bound shoes. The pair she held in her hand had to be finished by tonight or there would be no more work and, moreover, her mother had no money to buy milk for the sick baby. Her listener, upon seeing the name stamped on the shoe, flushed and then turned pale; the child's story brought tears to her eyes but she went into the store without offering her any money and as she left the store the narrator tells us that the glitter of a diamond pin could be seen. The child, in the meantime, returned home to a "small, dark room" with only a candle, a scanty fire and a little piece of bread. After hearing her prayers and folding her "tenderly to her bosom," her mother told her that the angels would always take care of her and returned to her sewing. The child dreamt of

"warm stockings, and new shoes." Did her mother dream of a "bright room, and gorgeous clothing, and a table loaded with all that was good and nice...of a pleasant cottage, and of one who had dearly loved her, and whose strong arms had kept want and trouble from her and her babes, but who could never come back?" If she did entertain such fantasies, she also put her trust in God and asked for his forgiveness.

As the mother drifted off to sleep over the fine slipper, the door opened softly and someone ("was it an angel?") entered, leaving behind soft, warm blankets draped over the girl, a blazing fire, a huge loaf, fresh milk, and, taking the unfinished slipper from the mother's hand, a bag of gold. In a "voice like music," the beneficent intruder said "Blessed thy God, who is the God of the fatherless and the widow," and departed, murmuring "Better than diamonds! Better than diamonds!" The mother awoke, saw the transformation and with "clasped hands and streaming eyes," blessed God for sending an angel. Leaving the garret, the narrator then takes the reader to a ballroom, with bright lights, music, flowers, dancing, happy faces and beautiful women in rich dresses and jewels. But only one

Cecilia Morgan, "'Better Than Diamonds' Sentimental Strategies and Middle-Class Culture in Canada West," *Journal of Canadian Studies* 32, 4 (1998): 125–148. Reprinted with permission of the University of Toronto Press Incorporated (www.utp.journals.com).

woman truly stood out from the crowd, wearing a simple white dress with only a rose-bud on her bosom. Her voice, we are told, was "like the sweet sound of a silver lute"; she had no spangled slippers to wear but the "divine beauty of holiness had so glorified her face" that the narrator felt "she was indeed an angel of God."[1]

"Better Than Diamonds" was by no means an unusual story in the canon of mid-Victorian sentimental fiction. The cast of characters (the pathetic yet brave widow and her family, especially the innocent child who was the catalyst for the beneficent anonymous donor's actions); the large, impersonal city, whose anonymity could allow it to be either London or New York; the themes of hard work, bad fortune (especially the absent father), maternal self-sacrifice, trust in providence and virtue rewarded through the medium of feminine benevolence were all to be found in fiction published in newspapers, periodicals and popular novels. As a number of historians of middle-class formation in Britain and America have pointed out, the tropes and rhetorical strategies of sentimental fiction were more than marketing devices deployed by middle-class writers eager to capture a reading audience. Sentimentality itself was a cultural tool that helped provide the middle classes with a framework for envisioning and regulating the relations of gender, class and race within the British and American bourgeoisie. This framework helped to divorce the so-called public realm of political life from the private world of affections, masking and obscuring the relations of power and contestation that shaped and linked home, market, nation-state and imperial power.[2]

Some Canadian historians have explored these issues, but middle-class cultural configurations in Ontario during the mid-nineteenth-century have yet to receive the sustained attention given to developments in Britain and the United States.[3] Furthermore, with a few notable exceptions, historians of this period have

not deployed gender as an analytical category and Canadian gender historians have not displayed much interest in mid-nineteenth-century Ontario. Yet by examining a selection of newspapers, including some that were well-known and politically influential, some from smaller centres, and one which represented the distinctive racial minority perspective of Black Canadians, it is possible to explore this facet of middle-class cultural development and to examine how it was imbued with relations of gender and race. In the pages of the press members of the colonial middle class both were presented with—particularly through the medium of literature imported from Britain and America—and participated in their own moral self-fashioning. To be sure, the kinds of developments that were underway in metropolitan and provincial urban centres in England and the United States were both slower to occur in Canada West, and smaller in scale (the result of a much smaller population grouped in smaller configurations). The province's colonial status also makes it difficult to delineate neatly the process of class formation and to point to the possibly arbitrary moment when a middle class was wholly formed. Discourses surrounding class formation, developed in Britain and America and spread through the medium of the press and fiction, may have borne little relation to material conditions in many areas of Canada West.[4] As in other national contexts during this period, the delineations of private and public were mapped out and usually (albeit not inevitably) coded as female and male, providing readers with a blueprint for the organization of colonial society.[5] These discursive configurations drew strength and meanings from each other, belying bourgeois attempts to insist on a social and political landscape irredeemably bifurcated by these divisions.

By the early 1850s the British colony of Upper Canada (renamed Canada West in 1841 after its legislative union with Lower Canada/Canada East) had undergone a number of significant shifts. Developments heralded by historians as shaping and signifying the emergence of the middle class included the attainment of responsible government, the expansion of the state in areas from banking and transportation to education, the growth of commercial and, on a smaller scale, manufacturing enterprises, an increase of immigration into urban centres and the development of voluntary societies. The province's middle class was not as widespread as it would be later in the nineteenth century, and it was fragmentated by regional, political, religious and occupational differences.[6] But within the pages of the press, itself a bourgeois institution, dialogues were conducted between writers and readers on the nature of middle-class identities, moral virtues and self-representation.[7]

The sentimental and, to a lesser extent, melodramatic, narratives and rhetorical devices of articles such as "Better Than Diamonds" (printed in the *Niagara Mail* in 1853) permeated both fictional and factual writings in the press. They provided authors with convenient modes of explaining and justifying social, political and economic changes. By valorizing the individual woman's or man's feelings and emotions, particularly humanitarian impulses; by evoking similar feelings in the spectator and reader; by placing sentiment upon a higher moral plain than unfeeling logic and rationality; by enacting sentimentality upon men's and, in particular, women's bodies through signs such as tears, sighs, groans and sobs; by fetishizing innocence, particularly children's; and by linking these elements in familial relations middle-class writers explained themselves and pronounced upon the character and activities of others. The rescue and redemption of workers, Native peoples, the sexually "deviant" and unbelievers whose presence was so often necessary to sentimental narratives were also crucial in the formation of middle-class identity; so too was a tendency to deny the power relations that framed encounters between them and Anglo-Canadian bourgeois men and women. Finally,

gender relations were defined by middle-class commentators to elide or efface inequities of class or colonial expansion. A few authors, however, contested and provided alternative meanings of mid-century cultural and social developments; not all Upper Canadians believed in the power of "rescuing angels."

Bourgeois Families and Fashionable Temptations

The strength of maternal love, considered to be an extremely powerful and entirely natural emotion, was a theme addressed in fictional pieces run by the Methodist newspaper, the *Christian Guardian*. "The Governor and the Mother," narrated by the president of Emory College, told of an encounter between the state's governor and the mother of a man condemned to death.[8] Set at the narrator's residence on the school's graduation day, the story reached its climax when she fell to her knees and begged the governor for pity, a sight that moved men (including the narrator) to tears. Lifting her, he repeated his refusal to pardon her son, whereupon a cross between a sigh and a groan came from her heart, "an indescribable out-breathing of all that is eloquent in grief and melting in sorrow." All fell silent, and the president's home, "so lately the scene of mirth, was like the court of death." In a passage evoking the prisoner's walk to the scaffold, she then rose, "tremblingly advanced," but on the last porch step "cast a melting look," made one last verbal appeal, and sank to the floor. This last entreaty had the desired effect, presumably, for upon rising and leaving she was followed by the governor.

Sentiment worked through and was enacted on the bodies of both women and men: the fainting, beseeching mother who, having walked 65 miles, prostrated herself before the masculine, upright body of the governor, and also the male spectators who were moved to tears as, it was hoped, would be the reader. As well, the unnamed female protagonist was defined entirely by maternity; she had no other function or relationship to her audience. She was also the only woman in the otherwise masculine enclave of an institution of higher learning closed to women. The governor was presented in contrast as a dispassionate representative of the (masculine) public and the state, who was charged with the powers of life and death. He was not, however, impervious to the ties of affection and domesticity.[9]

Sentimental appeals based on selfless maternity evoked the highest moral values, possessing a rationality, logic and sincerity superseding the supposedly logical reasoning of courtrooms and juries. In this context, a woman's body could be deployed in ways that transgressed the boundaries of genteel femininity and that would be deemed disorderly in other contexts. A woman crying out, weeping copious tears, flinging herself on the floor and displaying physical abandon in public were forms of physical expression that had earlier been decried by conservative commentators as symptoms of social and political anarchy. By the 1850s, they had also fallen in disfavour with many colonial evangelicals.[10] While sentimentality permitted certain physical displays of emotion for both women and men it also channeled these displays, demarcating and patrolling the boundaries between appropriate and inappropriate behaviours.

Relations between mothers and sons were a recurring theme in the fiction run by newspapers such as the *Guardian*. In "The Factory Boy," the nine-year-old hero has promised his dying mother that he would look after his younger siblings. He kept his promise and extended his care to his workmates' and neighbours' spiritual well-being. When he died prematurely in an industrial accident the streets were filled with mourners, his funeral was a

sight rarely seen and his dirge was "the uncontrollable groans of a heart-stricken multitude." Here the power of maternal affection and Christian piety were visibly intertwined. The dying body of the mother helped to trigger and set in motion true religion, realized at the story's climax in the damaged—yet redeeming—body of the son. His life and death also triggered emotional, physically manifested responses from the community.[11] Furthermore, as in "Better Than Diamonds," gender was deployed to stabilize and contain class inequalities, effacing them by drawing the reader's attention to domesticity rather than to poverty or dangerous working conditions.[12]

While the beseeching bodies of mothers were enlisted in the struggle against immorality and irreligion, many religious writers emphasized the paternal authority of fathers and husbands. Men were urged to take an active role in religion, particularly in overseeing and guiding the religious practices of their households through family prayers. The lesson of didactic fiction such as "Family Prayers" was clear: "May heads of households consider well their responsibilities and train their children in the ways of duty of religion, and teach them a reverence for all the sacred ordinances of religious worship."[13] Those who did not fulfil these duties might see their wives and children enticed by the seduction of the ballroom, an ever-present danger in a society which, according to Egerton Ryerson, was undergoing a "too worldly, sensual, dancing epidemic at present." Balls were held to celebrate everything and anything, from the opening of lying-in hospitals to the arrival of a new governor.[14] Not only were such environments conducive to displays of physical abandonment—in themselves suggestive of sexual immorality—they also encouraged girls and young women to fritter away their time on frivolous accomplishments, rather than learning useful household skills that would win them sober and sensible husbands. In such writers' moral economy, a notable shift had occurred in the definition of "feminine" arts and crafts. The decorative and "modern" had replaced the long-standing utilitarian traditions of spinning, plain-sewing, knitting, straw plaiting, baking, brewing and animal husbandry. The result did little to improve colonial social and economic conditions. Fashion, frivolity, urbanity and possibly irreligion were signified by crochet hooks and embroidery, in contrast to the more useful tools of agrarian womanhood, the knitting needle and spinning wheel.[15]

Even writers who did not couch their critiques of bourgeois society in such nostalgic terms believed that over-indulgence in fashion was contrary to women's well-being. Middle-class aspirations to fashionable respectability sacrificed a more natural environment and imposed restrictions of dress and movement on women and children.[16] The victimized wife, a favourite image of temperance literature, also appeared in such satires of middle-class pretensions as "Pipkin's Ideas of Family Retrenchment," in which Mr Pipkin's fondness for expensive suits, horses, and wining and dining his male friends was conducted at the expense of his wife's and children's domestic comfort.[17]

Women could become victims in other ways, as the *Globe* told its readers in its 1855 tales of threats by sexual predators to the virtue of the city's young, single women. Such tales were not new: earlier in the century the Upper Canadian press had run cautionary stories of young women who had been betrayed and abandoned by duplicitous men.[18] Yet George Brown's revelations about the existence of Toronto brothels and their owners' need for young women's virginity elaborated upon earlier imagery, giving it specific local meanings and also pointing to a new sexual villain: the prostitute/madam. In its coverage of police raids on Toronto brothels, the paper constructed a world

of "dissolute women," where male sexual desire might ultimately underpin the ruin of young girls, but women themselves were often the agents of their unhappy fates. "A Disorderly House" recounted the story of a 15-year-old girl enticed into a house of "ill fame" on Duchess street by a "set of dissolute women." Two officers were immediately dispatched to the address, where they found a number of women of all ages, a few of them drunk, lying on the floor and reclining on "bundles of rags."[19] In contrast to the scenes of middle-class domesticity that papers such as the *Globe* liked to describe, the house was sparsely furnished, with boxes for seats, an old bedstead, potatoes (possibly a hint that these women were Irish), a looking-glass and whiskey (symbolic of the vanity and moral weaknesses that had led to these women's downfall). Seven women were arrested and each given a month's hard labour.[20]

The problem did not end with their incarceration, however, for one month later the paper announced that the young daughter of a respectable tradesman had vanished. Private information led the police to a house on the west side of Victoria Street that had for some time been suspected of "harbouring disorderly females." The girl had apparently met a woman on the street who had lured her into the place "under the most specious promises"; she was now, the paper was happy to report, back at home with her parents.[21] To discuss the probable increase in prostitution during the mid-nineteenth-century growth, social commentary used melodramatic languages and narrative conventions encoded with images of women either as helpless innocents or as hardened madams who contributed to the innocents' social and moral ruin. Sexually predatory men might be understood to lurk behind the women who lay on bundles of rags, but the men who occupied centre stage in these tales were the Toronto police, the rescuers of young girls. These men represented the order of law and the state that was instrumental in restoring these girls to the safety of their families.

The Toronto police were not the only saviours in scripts of sexual danger. The city's Magdalen Asylum's *Report* of 1855 relied on many of the same rhetorical devices as the *Globe*'s warnings, but it also deployed sentimental imagery in its tale of rescues and reformations. While the asylum's managing board consisted of eight men, including two ministers and men who were active in Toronto's voluntary societies, such as James Lesslie and G.W. Allan, the institution was also served by a 31-member ladies' committee with surnames such as Baldwin, Dunlop, Robinson and Lesslie. This group performed one of the asylum's most important activities: "the periodic visits of the ladies to Jail." From that institution the asylum gathered in its outcasts. Using the language of Christian love alongside the tropes of women's victimization and the lady who would uplift them, the report stated that the committee's members were "gratefully received" by those they visited, despite hearts hardened by licentiousness. When appeals were made to Christian love and the gospels were heeded, "many a weeping eye has given testimony that the springs of sensibility had not wholly been dried up in that moral descent." The asylum housed three women in a "hopeful condition" and had sent one to hospital, where she had recently died in hope of religion; six women had gone into service, four to their friends and three to the House of Industry. To be sure, these figures were small in comparison with rescue work in New York City but, nevertheless, the asylum performed a valuable service. The women in it were friendless and were "watched for by those monster criminals who keep houses of infamy and live by the ruin and death of women" (there were, the committee believed, at least 10 such houses in Toronto). The "most wicked artifices are being constantly employed to supply them with victims": young, innocent girls, particularly those who were new to the city and looking for work,

were enticed to these places and then ruined.[22] As we have seen, this story would be all too familiar to the paper's readers, although the villains of this piece—the monster criminals—were not given a gender-specific identity, unlike the hardened madams of the other articles. And, in the asylum's narrative of rescue and uplift, these unfortunates were saved by other women, by middle-class, respectable "ladies," not by representatives of the nineteenth-century state.

This choice of melodramatic narrative was not entirely new, nor was it confined to mid-nineteenth-century Ontario. These pieces were not just reflecting or describing a social evil in Toronto; instead, they were part of widespread Anglo-American discourses on commercialized sexuality.[23] Moreover, while the rescue and redemption of Toronto's fallen women by their moral sisters may have provided readers with the satisfaction of a morally uplifting ending to the narrative, sentimentality was never the only language used by the colonial press to represent gender relations and, in particular, womanhood. Other kinds of femininity and other kinds of women were delineated by writers' portraits that differed in many ways from the heroine of "Better Than Diamonds," the Daughters of Temperance, or the virtuous rescuers of the Magdalen Asylum's penitent inhabitants. The records of convictions from the Lincoln and Welland county courts, for example, presented women as both plaintiffs and defendants: Harriet Allan prosecuted Jane Kirkland for assault and damage, Bridget Welsh charged Charles Blake for assault and battery, and Elizabeth Madden took Judy McNamara to court for a breach of a bylaw.[24] Four years later, "Bloody Affray" recounted the story of two women of Hibbert Township who came to blows over a man whom both claimed as their husband. Ellen Doyle was arrested for attacking Mrs Dougherty when the two met in the woods; Doyle cut her husband's first wife's throat with a razor, slashing her "sinews, veins, and windpipe." Although Mrs Dougherty was not expected to live, she apparently had won the fight and received an apology from Doyle. The latter was a "fearful spectacle" upon her arrest, "being covered with wounds and her clothes saturated with blood."[25] The press treated this encounter with morbid fascination suggesting that such behaviour was not commonly found amongst women and that such women were decidedly not ladies.

Beyond even the maternal redemption offered by middle-class women of the Magdalen Asylum's voluntary committee, Ellen Doyle was deemed fit only for the punitive, paternalistic hand of the colonial state. For the readers of such pieces she served as a warning and reminder of the limits of sentimentality's power to regulate behaviour and character, but she also highlighted the need for such regulation in the first place, inspiring readers to re-examine and re-evaluate their character and, perhaps, to congratulate themselves on their moral distance from the Ellen Doyles of the colony.

Racial Redemption

Working-class prostitutes were one of many groups perceived by the colonial middle class to need rescue and salvation. For religious writers, the transformation of the potentially unruly bodies of Native peoples through Christianity was one of the triumphs of both revealed religion and the sentimental ethos. Children were particularly popular in sentimental writing and Native children delivered especially poignant messages in obituaries. For example the obituary of nine-year-old Ellen Hess, the daughter of Sampson, a Mohawk chief, told of her youthful piety and its effect on her family. Ellen, a student at the local mission school from the age of four, had woken her father with her praying a few nights before her death. Ellen "clapped her hands in seeming

joyful emotion" in the "agonies of death," despite being "speechless."[26] Ellen's physical condition—the reasons for her death—is left unmentioned and is not important. Rather, the reader should be impressed, and presumably moved to tears by the power of religious faith, manifested upon her child's body, to transcend the "agonies of death" and become an instrument of her race's conversion.[27] The effect of the Gospel on her parents, both in family worship and in sustaining Ellen in her last days, raised the "writer's bowed head and drooping spirits" (many aspects of mission work at the Grand River were disheartening and discouraging) with "results that may swell the celestial choir."

If Ellen Hess's death might be represented as a sentimental spectacle that transcended "race, class, and gender boundaries,"[28] the *Guardian*'s depiction of a camp meeting held at the Saugeen reserve near Lake Huron went even further in demonstrating how reformed characters and morals might be written on Native bodies for the edification of a non-Native audience. The meeting was attended by Indians from Port Sarnia, Beausoeil and Nawash, "A Lover of Camp Meetings" told the readers; some were pagans but most were "under the influence of Christianity." During the evening exercises, led by the Methodist missionary Conrad Van Dusen, "as the ground became illuminated by the surrounding fires the scene became truly impressive." A hymn of divine praise was "swelled forth by those whose manly voices in other years had joined to sing the song of war." Now, "instead of brandished weapons and tomahawks reeking with the gore of human victims, whose bloody scalps of conquered foes lie scattered on the ground, or piled in heaps, or hung in show; we see the bended knee, we hear the humble prayer of supplication deep." This shift in Native masculinity was not lost on the writer, who went on in praise: "Christianity, most blessed, what changes hast thou wrought, yes what a trophy is here. Shall not heaven itself rejoice, and angels bright, their harps retune, of shining gold, to sing the praises of God and also to the Lamb."[29]

Clearly juxtaposed in this passage were elements that had previously signified Native manhood to many colonists—war-chants, weapons, blood and, especially, scalps—with those that now signalled Native men's identity: hymns, prayers, bent knees, and, above all, the subjugation of their bodies before a greater power. Instead of garnering the "trophies" of war, Native men now offered themselves as trophies to God, supposedly accepting both Christianity and white civilization. This passage was a particularly telling construction of the scene, because the Saugeen band had just been pressured to sign a treaty with the Canadian government surrendering their lands in the Bruce peninsula for non-Native settlement.[30] To be sure, four months earlier Van Dusen had protested the government's treatment of the Saugeen, pointing out to the Guardian's readers that they were still waiting for the fulfilment of "verbal promises" made at the signing of the treaty.[31] Yet evangelicals also hoped for the transformation of gender relations in Native communities, and the eradication of the warrior and hunter was a critical aspect of such changes.

Native men's bodies and morals—indeed, their entire culture—were thus seen as malleable, transmuted and liberated of necessity for their own and their race's salvation. Colonial abolitionist rhetoric argued that the bodies of black men were not so much in need of an essential transformation as of a liberation that would restore the "innate" masculine dignity taken from them by slavery. In the pages of George Brown's Globe a number of rhetorical strategies were deployed to raise sympathy for the abolitionist cause, but a recurring figure was the black man whose masculine self-respect and honour had been affronted—although not erased—by the degradation of slavery.

According to the Globe, the abolition of slavery would bring about a "glorious era" when all will be free and "the negro...wakes to liberty" and "sleeps in peace." "Read the great charter on his brow / I am a man a brother now!"[32] It was not, as pro-slavery writers argued, any natural moral failing or character defect that had led slaves into their present condition. In "Beauties of Practical Republicanism," Brown castigated Northern politicians who supported the 1850 Fugitive Slave Bill: "(should not) the heroism of these poor negroes, who died rather than go back to life-bondage of mind and body, sink into utter bombast the shedding of blood in resistance of a tea-tax?"[33]

Brown felt obliged to spend a considerable amount of editorial ink defending both fugitives and free Blacks from attacks on their characters and customs. A number of his readers agreed with his arguments.[34] "Pro-Slavery in a Church!" sent to the Globe by "An Observor [sic]" recounted an event that had recently occurred at a local Wesleyan church. A "fine, intelligent-looking, respectable and well-dressed lad" had been denied entry into a pew by his white companion's father; according to the writer the boy was "at least three-fifths to five-eights African." "The fine little fellow evidently felt this outrage upon his humanity, by retaining his hold of the door; and fixing his full, expressive eye, sparkling with indignation, which proved to be no other than a derisive look." He was pointed to a side seat but other members of the congregation, realizing what had just occurred, reacted with indignation and contempt. A gentleman "beckoned the little man" to his own seat and shared his scripture with him, inviting "his noble hand to press the same page with his own, thus sharing the sacred morsel together." The gentleman experienced happiness for having helped heal a "wounded spirit," the boy was made to feel welcome, and the congregation expressed its approval of the deed. "An Observor [sic]" suggested, this incident might possibly have been motivated by class differences as well as racial prejudice, citing the growth of the invidious practice of using pews to classify congregations. The writer was indignant that such behaviour could occur in Canada; the colony's religious and philanthropic institutions, as well as its British constitution, should have guaranteed that Upper Canadians would not harbour "pro-slavery" sentiments.[35]

While the protagonist of this piece was a child and, like Ellen Hess, could be used to demonstrate the power of abolitionist sentiment, the foreshadowing of his manhood—"the little man," the "fine little fellow"—was meant to evoke not tears but righteous anger. Of course the image of the black child's and the white man's hands united in religious worship might bring forth a satisfied sigh directly from the reader's heart. In this tale, prejudice and bigotry were acknowledged, but they were personified as an immoral individual's aberration. The writer's point was that racist behaviour was not inherent in colonial structures and institutions. Instead, such conduct stemmed from one person's lack of enlightenment and humanitarian feeling. Racial prejudice thus could be countered by Upper Canadian political and social institutions and, even more importantly, by the moral suasion—expressed by the meeting of the hands—of those who took action to shame such individuals.

Self-Made Men and "National" Identities

Anti-slavery rhetoric was deployed not only when the fates of Native peoples and Blacks were at stake. Certainly it helped illuminate the plight of and raise sympathy for these particular groups; it suggested that their differences from those of European descent had been artificially imposed by cultural, socio-economic and political forces. The trope of liberation from servitude was also deployed when distinctions needed to be drawn between Upper Canada and the United States or when the encroachments of the Catholic church were perceived as threatening the freedom of Upper Canadians. The language of anti-slavery was used to reinforce the colony's link to Britain and the imperial power's traditions of constitutional and religious freedoms (particularly those of Protestant churches). Much of this rhetoric was organized around the figure of the free, British and Protestant man who had a history of combating tyranny and absolutism. He would protect Upper Canadian liberties against slave-catchers, priests and republican demagogues; he would also bring Native peoples under his protection and closer to his position. As an ideal to be worked towards (although never completely attained) by men of other races and a protector of the helpless and weak (especially women and children of all races and classes), in these discourses masculine integrity and morality was meant to complement the rescuing angels of sentimental fiction. Such a man was not, though, expected to emanate from a state of nature. His character was the product of years of careful maternal tutelage, followed by self-regulation and control as he entered the workplace and became a responsible member of civil society.

Both religious literature and secular writings on moral conduct were aimed at elevating male and female behaviour through the medium of masculine self-improvement. To reassure readers worried about their own humble origins "Self-Made Men" compiled a list of famous men's backgrounds. The writer informed those from more elevated homes that self-made men were not to be scorned; instead, they should be admired and emulated for their ability to take control over their fates.[36] In temperance literature men were urged to embrace sobriety most importantly because it created domestic prosperity and happiness, and gave the opportunity to become a more knowledgeable, orderly and productive citizen. Such virtues could be demonstrated as a Son of Temperance, membership in that demanded public and visual manifestations of masculine morality in temperance parades and meetings. While men shared streets and platforms with middle-class women, who might appear as both supporters of the cause and as Daughters of Temperance, nevertheless it was the men, by and large, who spoke at temperance gatherings and marched in processions.[37]

The lessons in moral sagacity and self-control learned from pious mothers, writers on self-improvement and temperance advocates were also used in the political realm, where a number of journalists and politicians held up the symbol of the "public man." The image developed during the 1840s political debates over the meanings of *party* in Canada West. The anxieties that surrounded the rise of political parties in the early 1840s may have dissipated by the early 1850s, but political figures were still identified as needing moral guidance—particularly those men who had succumbed to populist rhetoric.[38] While Brown's initial opposition to the Clear Grit movement would give way to an alliance with them in the mid-1850s, in the early years of the decade the *Globe*'s editor not only "flatly rejected the Clear Grit program," he also charged its supporters with political immorality.[39] Many political figures, in Brown's opinion, did not measure up to the moral standards of the "public man" and sacrificed "manly independence" for sycophancy, falsehood and manipulation of colonial politics for personal gain.[40] The *Globe* instructed its readers on how public men might identify and attain political morality: their private lives must be governed by the same moral standards as the public realm (particularly concerning sexual conduct); they must adhere to patriotic principles, the foundation of political principle and public service; they must be prepared to submit to the people's

never-ending surveillance and judgment. The colony possessed many public men who could serve their country, "whose principles are sound, and motives pure." This is no time to trifle, Brown warned his readers, for "vile things have lately been done in high places," a hint of political nefariousness that might have been aimed at either Francis Hincks or Brown's conservative enemy, Sir Alan McNab.[41]

To be sure, there was no essential connection between the people, Upper Canadian farmers and Upper Canadian men, no explicit reason why this language should be understood as only pertaining to male voters. Yet political affairs had by this point been *officially* defined as a masculine realm: the electorate and its representatives were male (and predominantly white and middle-class); public offices were held by men; public political demonstrations, such as banquets and meetings, were either attended only by men or directed by them. These writings reiterated that a clearly defined code of male morality in political life was needed.[42] The electorate could not assume that men in political life would naturally know how to conduct themselves in an ethical and moral fashion, no more than youths and young men could be assumed to possess the knowledge needed to avoid the moral perils of the workplace or tavern. Once such a moral framework had been defined, it was essential that men's conduct be carefully scrutinized for its adherence to this code. A public man could remain so only if nothing in his life was secretive or subject to private interests. The temptations of political life were particularly alluring because of the power that public men supposedly wielded, above all the power to dispense patronage, an essential element of nineteenth-century Ontario politics.[43] Brown's position was not held by all: as Paul Romney has argued, Brown and Hincks and their supporters represented differing perspectives on the meanings of political morality. Brown's beliefs reflected Lockean theories of representative government in which public officials were trustees empowered by the public to act for the social good, not their own. Other political figures, such as John Beverley Robinson, argued that public men's moral obligations did not preclude the use of political office to enrich their private life: public office was a piece of property bought by those of high rank, whose social and political standing entitled them to all of its fruits.[44]

Concerns over morality in public life were not limited to men who ran for office. Attacks on Catholics, many published by the *Globe,* often focussed on the tyranny of ultramontanism (whereby a foreign, unelected power made decisions that affected the liberties of British subjects). They also suggested that men who obeyed the Catholic church had renounced their manly independence to bow to Rome's despotism, and were no better than slaves. With its suggestion that Catholic clerics (and their political supporters) were unmanly and effeminate, some of this rhetoric was redolent of 1820s and 1830s reform attacks on churchmen who took money from the state.[45] But attacks on bishops and priests in the previous decades had targeted them as parasites and sycophants because of their financial relationship to the state (whether Anglican or, after 1833, Methodist); the articles of the 1850s were much more clearly focussed on the Catholic Church and its effect on British manhood.[46]

Devotion to Rome was depicted as unmanning men. It denied them their independent status as adult men free of hidden entanglements, and it robbed them of political virtue and morality, because they no longer possessed the free will to act according to their consciences. Such men were the antithesis of public men because they were bound by secret, hidden ties, no longer able to act in an unencumbered fashion for the good of all. Other articles warned Upper Canadians of the growing power of the Catholic church both abroad and in British North America, and the sorry state of countries dominated by the Church, where politicians' subservience to priests had perverted political and social relations, and was a lesson of what might happen if it went unchecked.[47] To be sure, Canada West differed from Spain because of the colony's history of resistance to absolutism by loyal Protestant men. But without their continued vigilance, the Catholic church might be able to dupe and enslave their fellow colonists. In addition to overtly political attacks on the Catholic church, some fiction also relied on the cruelty of the Catholic church as a central theme. Its despotism took the form of indignities inflicted upon the bodies of young men by absolutist priests who believed themselves exempt from the laws of the French state.[48]

In other contexts, women's moral integrity was directly threatened by the Church in countries where national identity had been subsumed under religious obedience. "Woman's Liberty and Virtue—Nunneries," published in the *Canadian Son of Temperance and Literary Gem* in 1853, described widespread sexual immorality in Lyons, a city that housed a large number of priests and nuns. Unmarried, and therefore flouting both divine and natural law, these men and women were "worldly minded" people with vast amounts of time on their hands, who the writer deduced, must be engaged in enormous vice. Other examples of sexual promiscuity within the Catholic church included Tudor monasteries and the Spanish inquisition, whose members had corrupted and ruined 62 young women, keeping them secluded in the priests' apartments. The author also claimed to have personally witnessed in Rome the suicide of an abbess, who ran frantically from her convent's gates and jumped into the Tiber. Filled with remorse, she had drowned herself to escape memories of a dissolute life. The writer also alluded to Maria Monk, stating that charges of vicious practices had also been proved "many years ago in Montreal.[49] Although it is unclear whether Monk's tales ever caused the furor in Upper Canada that they raised in America and Lower Canada, the frequent allusions to her in political and religious commentaries suggest that her story was well-known.[50]

Cautionary tales about other countries might also be laced with a strong dose of xenophobia, suggesting, for example, that the French background of Lyons' citizens predisposed them to lasciviousness. But the newspapers' position on foreigners and their customs was more complex than simple condemnation. As events in the Crimea began to draw journalists' attention in the early 1850s, articles on Turkey supported Turkish resistance to Russian aggression and applauded the reform efforts of certain Turkish leaders. In contrast to the despotism of the Catholic church and her effeminate priests and supporters, Turkey had produced men such as Reschid Pacha, the minister of Foreign Affairs. Though a "Mussulman," he "was not unacquainted with the superior influence of Christian civilizations," having spent time in England and France studying their "opinions, science, and customs." A reformer of the Turkish penal code and tax laws, Pacha will "ultimately prove a great benefactor." A description of his appearance stressed the qualities that garnered Western admiration: a man of medium height with a robust frame, dark face, regular features and a short beard (which "distinguishes him from the Orientals"), and "black and brilliant eyes," the minister's "physiognomy and attitude exhibit that reserve, that dignified calmness, which characterize the Turkish race." A man of few words and simple manners who usually refrained from wearing his "many decorations," Pacha was a man who loved his family, showed kindness and affection towards them, and joined in his children's sports. Altogether, Reschid Pacha was "a favourable specimen of the Ottoman character."[51]

In "The Late Sultana of Turkey," run by the *Canadian Son of Temperance* in 1853, the theme of Christian enlightenment was coupled with unabashed fascination with Oriental sexual practices. Born into a Christian family, the Sultana had been kidnapped as a child (her father had died fighting for her protection) and sold to Kosref Pacha. Her beauty moved Pacha to educate her for the imperial seraglio which she entered at the age of 17. A favourite of Sultan Mahmoud, she bore a son who succeeded his father. The Sultana, however, did not forget her Christian origins, for she used her enormous influence over her son to protect Christians in Turkey. She monitored the Turkish courts to ensure that justice was being done, gave aid to the sick and needy, built and endowed both the only Turkish civil hospital in Constantinople and a free school, and maintained many public fountains. The Sultana also was involved in a number of commercial interests.[52] Her activities suggested a much greater freedom and range of public activism than the more popular image of women cloistered in harems with little or no contact with the outside world (although as a favourite and a Christian the Sultana certainly differed from other women of the seraglio). Unlike other writings on women in Muslim countries, this article did not argue that polygamy was automatically dissolute and destructive of women's morality. In fact, the Sultana could be held up as a more inspiring female image than nuns, who were also women cut off from the outside world, but who, because they had not become wives and mothers, had degenerated into enormous vice.

Other newspapers applauded Turkish resistance to Russian encroachments, at times portraying Turkey as a land of enlightened developments (such as the Sultan's abolition of the slave trade). Russia, in turn, was depicted as a land where serfdom was still practised, and as a country whose leaders were driven by the need to expand its borders through military conquest.[53] Although articles about Turkey attempted to portray it as a country besieged by a despotic power (hardly surprising given Canada's support for Turkey through the colony's British connection), Orientalist discourse was woven into these character sketches. An "Orient" unexposed to the civilizing influence of the West (particularly that of British men) was a place of cruelty, luxury and tyranny. Pacha, while undoubtedly a Turkish man, had seen first-hand the benefits of Western values and was thus an exception amongst his countrymen. Unlike the stereotypical figure of the Turkish ruler, whose private life consisted of uncontrolled sexuality with a number of women, this "favourable specimen" was an eager participant in family life. While the article on Reschid Pacha was on one level about Turkey, it was placed next to a piece that described Irish riots in Lower Canada, where violence committed by criminals had frightened Lower Canadian Protestants into acquiescence to Catholic demands. The effect was to contrast Pacha, the enlightened "Mussulman," with those who continued to be duped and seduced by Catholicism.[54]

While Pacha was a useful symbol, his masculinity—and his apparent conformity to some western standards of manliness—made him a less compelling figure than the Christianized Sultana. As Joanna De Groot has argued, "women were presented as the *means* for imagining or finding out about the Orient."[55] Like Pacha, the Sultana could be compared to so-called Christian women with the intent to expose the hypocrisy of the latter's religion. But the piece on the Sultana also depended on the implicit comparison to the non-Christian women who remained behind the seraglio's walls. While absent from the article itself, they underscored the unusual position of the Sultana, who was much closer to the heroines of colonial fiction and prose, particularly in her philanthropic activities. In other contexts, the image of the secluded woman was deployed strategically to undermine opposition to Upper Canadian women's activities. The author of

"Union of Daughters in Canada," for example, responded to criticisms that the Daughters of Temperance took women out of the private sphere. Such critics would veil women, like the "Turkish ladies of Constantinople" who were forced to look at the world through barred windows.[56] While Turkish society and its leaders might be portrayed as worthy of support and sympathy, this was in no small part due to the Western perception that Turkey had learnt valuable lessons from Christian society and was struggling to Westernize or, as in the case of the Sultana, to retain Christian traits. In the articles consulted here, Turkey was defined as a site of geographical, political and cultural liminality, where both east and west might be found, and whose culture and tradition were mediated by the reforming influence of Western practices and beliefs. Turkish society was thus depicted as exemplary in its attempts to throw off habits and customs that had enslaved Turkish women and corrupted Turkish men. But Turkey could easily return to such practices and the vigilance of its leaders—as well as the gaze of Western writers—was essential if such backsliding was to be avoided. Turkey might serve as a reminder of what Upper Canadians had achieved through their own moral efforts and the practices of institutions such as the Christian church, the colonial state and the middle-class family; like Ellen Doyle, it could also stand as a warning to Upper Canadians who took such safeguards for granted.

Sentiment and the *Provincial Freeman*

Black Upper Canadians' formations of race, gender and class have received even less attention from historians than those of their white contemporaries.[57] The pages of the *Provincial Freeman* provide some hints for future research by historians. While not the first anti-slavery paper in the province, the *Freeman* was the first Upper Canadian paper to be co-founded and edited by a black woman, Mary Ann Shadd.[58] The *Freeman* emphasised "the elevation of the coloured people" through self-help. Some writers believed that elevation should create a black middle class. Moses argued that the African-Canadian community did not really need more labourers (although he hastened to assure his readers that all labour was inherently respectable). Instead, Blacks in Canada should set their sights on becoming doctors, lawyers, school-teachers and merchants. They must educate themselves and their children, and with that end in mind, young men and women should form literary and debating societies. Such strategies may seem to replicate merely those of the white colonial middle class, particularly when coupled with the paper's emphasis on respectability through temperance. But we should also consider the differences that a history of slavery might make to narratives of racial and class uplift for, as Evelyn Brooks Higginbotham has argued, "racial meanings were never internalized by Blacks and whites in an identical way."[59] Shadd and other black writers supported black integration with whites, vehemently denounced those who opposed racial amalgamation as friends of slavery, and pointed to areas of the colony where Blacks and whites co-existed happily. But they also insisted that Blacks must take responsibility for their own fate. They hoped that whites (particularly white Upper Canadians whose connection to Britain would inspire them) would support their endeavours but, given the histories of racism and slavery in Anglo-American communities, many writers in the *Freeman* stressed that Blacks must develop their own strengths as individuals and as a community. They could not rely solely on the goodwill of British men and women to perform their work for them.

Because of this insistence on self-sufficiency, and because the paper also appealed to a Black audience, the language of the *Freeman* did not rely as heavily or exclusively on images of victimization as did anti-slavery rhetoric in the *Globe*. One writer insisted that not all Blacks in Canada West came as fugitives who had to earn respectability in the eyes of whites. "Our Free Colored Emigrants" compared the position of this group to fugitive men and women who arrived in Upper Canada, "hunted" and destitute, and who therefore were given help and welcomed. Free Blacks from the northern United States "who know the value of pounds, shillings and pence—who ha[ve] attended to [their] business without the 'anxious care' of a master" were not given the same reception, however, although they were progressive, enterprising and "go onward, planning, improving, accumulating and enlarging." While free Blacks might feel less welcome than fugitives, they should play an essential role in the Black community. As "a class of men not in service to any man, they must, by common consent, take a position in which they can cheer on the weaker brethren who have just emerged from oppression; and as the bone and sinew of a powerful and increasing class they will...help to shape the destiny of this continent."[60]

The *Freeman's* conception of gender relations also differed significantly from that of other papers. Instead of the ridicule and fear apparent in other Toronto papers when the American women's rights movement was discussed, Lucy Stone's Toronto lecture was described enthusiastically. Stone, Shadd informed her readers, had a reputation as a talented woman and orator; even in Toronto, with its "strong attachment to antiquated notions respecting woman and her sphere so prevalent," she was greeted with patience and much applause. The St Lawrence Hall was packed and there were no shouts of brigadier or virago. Shadd was disappointed, however, that so few "coloured people seized upon the occasion to learn lessons of practical wisdom." Shadd's own support for women's suffrage influenced her treatment of Stone; the *Freeman* was one of the very few papers consulted here to accept women's right to speak *for* their rights in public. In its pages Lucy Stone thus appears as a very different figure than in other papers published in the colony.[61]

Upon her resignation from the paper's editorship in 1855, Shadd wrote an Adieu to her readers that acknowledged the "difficulties, and...obstacles such as we feel confident few, if any, females have had to contend against in the same business, except the sister who shared our labors [sic] for awhile." And "to colored women, we have a word—we have 'broken the editorial ice,' whether willingly or not, for your class in America; so go to Editing, as many of you as are willing, and able, and as soon as you may, if you think you are ready." Women who did not feel ready, Shadd wrote, should assist in other ways, by subscribing to the paper and encouraging their neighbours to do the same.[62] Shadd's comment about facing obstacles unknown to other women in journalism suggests that the configurations of race and gender might have very different meanings for African-Canadian women.[63]

While much work remains to be done on black women's *and* men's understandings of white womanhood in nineteenth-century Ontario, the *Freeman* suggests that may have differed significantly from the image of the inherent beneficence and moral superiority of white women conveyed by evangelical writers. In the *Globe*'s coverage of the address written by the Toronto Ladies' Association for Relief of Destitute Coloured Fugitives, the paper spoke of the usefulness of female influence, particularly within the family and in education.[64] The *Freeman* commended the appeal of white British women abolitionists who had called upon their American counterparts to work for the abolition of slavery.[65] But, as an article taken from "Lloyd's Newspaper" pointed out, American women had

responded with an extraordinarily bad grace, so much so that their letter might have been written by a man. "We cannot mistake the masculine stride that distends the petticoats," wrote the author of "Mrs America answers Mrs England." Even if the response was the work of women, they "pucker their mouths, and with a prolonged, laborious, curtsey" beg English women to look to the behaviour of their own menfolk in India, Africa, China, and Ireland and towards the British working class. "With a truly feminine self-denial they swallow their indignation; put down the rising heart with a strong hand, and proceed with the catalogue. Sisters in America are so sisterly towards sisters of Stafford House!"[66] There was little here to suggest women's elevated morality or natural propensity to help the oppressed and downtrodden.

At times white women were directly implicated in the viciousness of slavery, as slaveholders themselves. Such was the lesson of "Slavery in Baltimore," which recounted the cruel treatment of slaves by rich owners. One particularly wealthy woman was notorious for her inhumanity. Her coachman died of frostbite after being kept outside on her carriage in bitter weathers; another slave, who escaped after similar treatment, was caught by the woman's son and made to run for 16 miles; yet another woman was left crippled after falling from a third-story window (she had fallen asleep while washing windows as the result of being deprived of rest as a punishment). "Such is the system as administered by the rich, the fashionable, and the aristocratic," concluded the writer.[67] The viciousness of this woman might be attributed to her class for, as we have seen, middle-class writers often targeted men and women of the aristocracy for their callousness towards the poor. The writer did not suggest that her womanly nature or maternal feeling might mitigate or soften her contempt for the human beings whom she owned and who served her.

Middle-class sentimentality was deployed to reify definitions of private and public and to exalt the middle-class family as the epitome of harmonious relations, yet at times the trajectory taken by sentimental rhetoric undermined apparently monolithic meanings and challenged the seeming confinement of middle-class white women to home and hearth. These women's voluntary efforts often deployed the kinds of rhetoric discussed above, shaping their work in temperance, religious fundraising and similar efforts within the public realm of Upper Canadian society.[68] None of this work, to be sure, enjoyed the same access to formal institutions and their prestige as the labours of men's organizations. Yet such women's willingness and ability to mobilize the languages of sympathy, sensibility and domesticity begs further exploration from historians of Ontario's middle class, of colonialism, and of the women's movement of the late-nineteenth century.[69]

At present it is difficult to determine, given the lack of research in this area, to what extent and in what ways these discourses shaped the subjectivities and identities of individual middle-class men and women; it also remains to be seen how these languages were contested and debated within the public realm of moral and social reform. As Bruce Curtis has pointed out, British and American school reformers vigorously opposed fiction because

of its focus on experience and appeal to emotion. In their eyes, sentimental fiction also lacked rationality and self-discipline; readers constantly bombarded with pitiful tales would become hardened to real-life instances of suffering and would refuse to participate in philanthropic endeavours, thus precipitating working-class revolt.[70] Yet in the public pages of the colony's press, sentimental images of middle-class domesticity were a critical component of the language of bourgeois formation in nineteenth-century Ontario, justifying women's supposed confinement to the home because of their positions as wives and mothers; they also legitimated the individual woman's tears and the subjectivity that produced them. This language of feelings and affection reached beyond the individual to justify the mobilization of middle-class men and especially women, producing a consciousness that went beyond tears to the moral indignation underpinning moral and social reform movements of the late nineteenth century. The contradictions that existed in mid-nineteenth-century, middle-class sentimental rhetoric may have supplied middle-class women later in the century with the scripts that allowed them to enact the roles of rescuing angels—with results that were contradictory for both themselves and for those deemed in need of salvation.

Notes

I would like to thank Paul Deslandes, Steven Heathorn and Tori Smith for their comments on an earlier version of this piece. I would also like to thank the *Journal of Canadian Studies* anonymous reviewers for their very helpful and perceptive comments and suggestions.

1 "Better Than Diamonds," *Niagara Chronicle* 11 March 1853.

2 For discussions of such literature and sentimental thought in general, see Ann Douglas, The *Feminization of American Culture* (New York: Knopf, 1977); Shirley Samuels ed., *The Culture of Sentiment: Race, Gender, and Sentimentality in* *Nineteenth-Century America* (New York: Oxford University Press, 1992); G.J. Barker-Benfield, *The Culture of Sensibility: Sex and Society in Eighteenth-Century England* (Chicago: University of Chicago Press, 1992).

3 In the case of Canada West (present-day Ontario), work on the development of the middle class has

focussed on political and economic themes; see, for example David G. Burley, *A Particular Condition in Life: Self-Employment and Social Mobility in Mid-Victorian Brantford, Ontario* (Montreal and Kingston: McGill-Queen's University Press, 1994). For examinations of social and cultural formation, see work in the history of education particularly Bruce Curtis, *True Government by Choice Men? Inspection, Education, and State Formation in Canada West* (Toronto: University of Toronto Press, 1992); Bruce Curtis, *Building the Educational State: Canada West, 1836–1871* (London, Ont.: Althouse Press, 1988); Alison Prentice, "The Public Instructor: Ryerson and the Role of the Public School Administrator," *Egerton Ryerson and His Times,* eds. N. McDonald and A. Chaiton (Toronto: Macmillan, 1978) 129–57; Robert Lanning, *The National Album: Collective Biography and the Formation of the Canadian Middle Class* (Ottawa: Carleton University Press, 1996).

4 For a discussion of Anne Langton's "re-evaluation of class and gender self" brought about by her changed physical circumstances, see Helen E.H. Smith and Lisa M. Sullivan, "Now that I know how to manage: Work and Identity in the Journals of Anne Langton," *Ontario History* LXXXVII.3 (September 1995): 253–70. Furthermore, I would suggest that class formation is never complete and set—that as much as we can identify a clearly discernible group, discourses and practices that we might call middle class, as historians we must also be attentive to class formation as an ongoing process.

5 See, for example, Leonore Davidoff and Catherine Hall, *Family Fortunes: Men and Women of the British Middle Class, 1780–1850* (Chicago: University of Chicago Press, 1987).

6 Many aspects of this process are discussed in Allan Greer and Ian Radforth eds., *Colonial Leviathan: State Formation in Mid-Nineteenth-Century Canada* (Toronto: University of Toronto Press, 1992).

7 See Benedict Anderson, *Imagined Communities: Reflections on the Origins and Spread of Nationalism* (London: Verso, 1991) especially chapter three; also Jürgen Habermas, *The Structural Transformation of the Public Sphere: An Inquiry into a Category of Bourgeois Society,* trans. Thomas Burger and Frederick Lawrence (Cambridge MA: MIT Press, 1989) 59–67.

8 The press of both Upper Canada and Canada West often ran literature that originated in both the English and the American press. Our knowledge of circulation figures and readership of the colonial press is limited for this period, although W.H. Kesterton has argued that the number of newspapers grew from one in 1813 to 114 by 1853. The little that is known about subscription rates suggests that these publications were supported by a relatively small group, although the political impact of the press was far greater. Moreover, the number of subscribers also does not tell us much about total numbers of readers, since papers were likely passed around and read aloud. See W.E. Kesterton, *A History of Journalism in Canada* (Toronto: McClelland & Stewart, 1967) 11–44; Paul Rutherford, *The Making of the Canadian Media* (Toronto: McGraw-Hill Ryerson, 1978).

9 "The Governor and the Mother," *Christian Guardian,* 17 September 1851.

10 See Neil Semple, "The Quest for the Kingdom: Aspects of Protestant Revivalism in Nineteenth-Century Ontario," *Old Ontario: Essays in Honour of J.M.S. Careless,* eds. David Keane and Colin Read (Toronto: Dundurn Press, 1990) 95–117.

11 "The Factory Boy," *Christian Guardian,* 21 May 1851; see also "A Mother's Prayer," *Christian Guardian,* 13 June 1855.

12 Amy Schrager Lang, "Class and the Strategies of Sympathy," *The Culture of Sentiment,* 128–42.

13 "Family Worship," by Veritas, *Christian Guardian,* 17 January 1855.

14 See the articles in the *Christian Guardian:* "The Dancing Season," "Dancing Among Professing Christians," 26 March 1851; "Dancing Among Professing Christians," 2 April 1851; "Dancing," 19 October 1853; "Revivals and Dancing Schools," 13 April 1853; "Shall Christians Dance?" 13 July 1853.

15 "The County Fair," *Niagara Mail,* 31 October 1855. See also "English Women in the Country," *Globe,* 3 April 1851; "A Word About the Plates in Books of Fashion," *Niagara Chronicle,* 21 August 1851.

16 Eliza Cook, "Best Rooms," *Canadian Son of Temperance,* 26 February 1851. This piece was also run by the *Globe,* 18 January 1851. See also "Woman Temperance," *Canadian Son of Temperance,* 8 February 1853; Fanny Fern, "Pipkin's Ideas of Family Retrenchment," *Canadian Son of Temperance,* 9 August 1853; Fanny Fern, "The Invalid Wife," *Provincial Freeman,* 27 May 1853. Similar pieces by anonymous authors were "Female Prudishness," *Provincial Freeman,* 20 January 1855 and "Miss Biffin the Limbless Lady," *Canadian Son of Temperance,* 15 November 1853. For Fanny Fern (Sarah Payson

Willis), one of the most outspoken critics of antebellum domesticity, see Mary P. Ryan, *The Empire of the Mother: American Writing about Domesticity 1830–1860* (New York and London: Harrington Park Press, 1982) 118 and 123. Lauren Berlant, "The Female Woman: Fanny Fern and the Form of Sentiment," *The Culture of Sentiment,* 265–82.

17 Fanny Fern, "Pipkin's Ideas of Family Retrenchment," *Canadian Son of Temperance,* 9 August 1953.

18 See Cecilia Morgan, *Public Men and Virtuous Women: The Gendered Languages of Religion and Politics in Upper Canada, 1791–1850* (Toronto: University of Toronto Press, 1996) 143–5.

19 Precisely how they knew of the incident was not made clear, an absence of information that suggested the panoptic power of the force's surveillance and their knowledge of the city.

20 "A Disorderly rouse," *Globe,* 3 March 1855.

21 "Heartless Deception," *Globe,* 6 April 1855. See also "Society for the Protection of Young Females," *Globe,* 4 September 1853.

22 "The Magdalen Asylum—Annual Meeting," *Globe,* 28 May 1855.

23 See, for example, Anna Clark, "Queen Caroline and the Sexual Politics of Popular Culture in London, 1820," *Representations* 31 (Summer 1990): 47–68; Judith R. Walkowitz, *City of Dreadful Delight: Narratives of Sexual Danger in Late-Victorian London* (Chicago: University of Chicago, 1992); Karen Dubinsky, *Improper Advances: Rape and Hetero-Sexual Conflict in Ontario, 1880–1920* (Chicago: University of Chicago, 1993). Although he does not focus on gender or sexuality, in "Law and Ideology: The Toronto Police Court 1850–80," Paul Craven notes the use of melodramatic language in police court reporting (David Flaherty ed., *Essays in the History of Canadian Law,* Volume II, [Toronto: University of Toronto Press, 1983] 248–307).

24 "Schedules of Convictions," *Niagara Chronicle,* 4 December 1851.

25 "Bloody Affray," *Niagara Mail,* 13 June 1855; see also "Frailty Thy Name is Woman," which was coverage of a similar clash (with less horrific results) between two women in Allegheny, New York (*Niagara Chronicle,* 26 August 1853).

26 A.W. Sickles, "Biographical," by *Christian Guardian,* 9 February 1853.

27 See Neil Semple, "The Nuture and Admonition of the Lord: Nineteenth-Century Canadian Methodism's

Response to 'Childhood'," *Histoire sociale/Social History* 27 (May 1981): 257–75.

28 Samuels, "Introduction," *The Culture of Sentiment,* 3–8.

29 "Saugeen Camp Meeting," *Christian Guardian,* 4 October 1855. The "Lover" continued in this tone, describing the arrival of a party of white Christians from the nearby town of Southampton.

30 For a discussion of this treaty, see Donald B. Smith, *Sacred Feathers: The Reverend Peter Jones (Kahkewaquonaby) and the Missisauga Indians* (Toronto: University of Toronto Press, 1987) 225; also Peter S. Schmalz, *The Ojibwa of Southern Ontario* (Toronto: University of Toronto Press, 1991) 143–44.

31 C. Van Dusen, "The Saugeen Indian Affairs," *Christian Guardian,* 25 July 1855; also "Rama and Orillia Missions," 2 April 1851; "The Indian's Illustration," 23 March 1853.

32 "Slavery Not So Bad as People Think!" *Globe;* 11 March 1851. For a discussion of anti-slavery in Ontario, see Allan P. Stouffer, *The Light of Nature and the Law of God: Antislavery in Ontario 1833–1877* (Montreal and Kingston: McGill-Queen's University Press, 1992).

33 "Beauties of Practical Republicanism," *Globe,* 11 January 1851. This piece should also be read as a warning to those Clear Grits who admired American political culture of its moral consequences.

34 See, for example, "The Elgin Association," and "A Host of Negroes," 25 September 1851; "Anti-Slavery Society in Hamilton," *Globe,* 22 March 1853.

35 "Pro-Slavery in a Church!" *Globe,* 24 September 1853; see also "Slave Decoys at St. Catharines," *Globe,* 1 September 1855.

36 "Self Made Men," *Globe,* 9 August 1851. See also "Romance and Tragedy," *Globe,* 18 February 1851 (a warning to self-made men of the vicsisitudes of commerce) and "A Dark Chapter from the Diary of a Law Clerk," *Niagara Chronicle,* 15 July 1853. Much greater optimism was shown in the *Niagara Mail's* discussion of "The Farmer of Upper Canada," 1 August 1855. For a discussion of this phenomenon on Canadian writings, see Allan Smith, "The Myth of the Self-Made Man in English Canada, 1850–1914," Canadian *Historical Review* LIX.2 (1978): 189–219.

37 See, for example, *Canadian Son of Temperance,* 26 February 1851 and 11 March 1851; "A Voice from the North," 22 July 1851; "Don Mills Soiree," 29 November 1851; "Oshawa Cadets," 19 April

1853; "Great National Jubilee of the Sons of Temperance," *Canadian Son of Temperance,* 10 June 1851; "Mimico Soiree on 2nd April 1851," *Canadian Son of Temperance,* 8 April 1851; "Woman and Temperance," *Canadian Son of Temperance,* 8 February 1853; "Mimico Soiree on 2nd April 1851," *Canadian Son of Temperance,* 8 April 1851. See also "Movement of Cadets in Lincoln" 19 April 1853; "Miss Naylor's Address," 8 April 1851; *Canadian Son of Temperance,* 11 March and 13 May 1851. For a discussion of women's role in temperance, see Jan Noel, *Canada Dry: Temperance Crusades Before Confederation* (Toronto: University of Toronto Press, 1995) especially chapter 7, "Mothers of the Millennium."

38 The emergence of the Clear Grit movement was an important part of this shift. Influenced by conceptions of American-style popular democracy, this group of men (many from the western area of the province) who challenged Robert Baldwin's liberal ministry have been described as left-wing: supporters of an elective constitution, the abolition of property qualifications for members of the legislature, fixed biennial parliaments and representation by population. The Clear Grit platform also called for "free trade and direct taxation, the abolition of the Courts of Chancery and Common Pleas, the secularization of the reserves, and even Canadian control of external policy." For a discussion of the Clear Grits, see J.M.S. Careless, *The Union of the Canadas: The Growth of Canadian Institutions, 1841–1857* (Toronto: McClelland & Stewart, 1967) 166–69; also his "Introduction" to *The Pre-Confederation Premiers: Ontario Government Leaders, 1841–1867* (Toronto: University of Toronto Press, 1980) 9–11. Careless, *The Union of the Canadas* 169; see also *The Pre-Confederation Premiers* 9–10.

39 Careless, *The Union of the Canadas,* 169; see also *The Pre-Confederation Premiers,* 9–10.

40 Brown's targets ranged from Malcolm Cameron, a wealthy lumber merchant from Sarnia who in 1850 had resigned his position as assistant commissioner of Public Works in Baldwin's cabinet in order to ally with the Clear Grits, to Francis Hincks, Baldwin's successor as western leader in the coalition government, and his supporters. See "The Sarnia Dinner," *Globe,* 16 July 1853; "Mr Vansittart," *Globe,* 9 August 1853.

41 "The Morality of Public Men," *Globe,* 1 October 1855. Brown was not alone in his suspicions of political power. See, for example, "The Patronage of the Canadian Executive," run by the *Canadian Son of Temperance and Literary Garland* in 1854, which lamented both government corruption and the

behaviour of the Canadian electorate in the province's cities: the "vicious arid unprincipled men" such as the Orange Lodge agitator Ogle Gowan who had stirred up the urban electorate (particularly through the use of free liquor). Furthermore, the executive's abuse of power had also brought about widespread corruption, particularly in their use of patronage appointments (country court judges, sheriffs, registrars, postmasters, coroners and customs officials) with a resulting deterioration in political morality ("The Patronage of the Canadian Electorate," *Canadian Son of Temperance and Literary Garland,* 30 September 1854). For discussions of the political events that highlighted Brown's enmity towards Hincks, see Paul Romney, "'The Ten Thousand Pound Job': Political Corruption, Equitable Jurisdiction, and the Public Interest in Upper Canada, 1852–6," *Essays in the History of Canadian Law,* Volume II, 143–99; also George A. Davison, "The Hincks–Brown Rivalry and the Politics of Scandal," *Ontario History* LXXXI.2 (June 1989): 129–51.

42 Morgan, *Public Men and Virtuous Women,* Chapters II and V.

43 S.J.R. Noel, "Canada West," *Patrons, Clients, Brokers: Ontario Society and Politics, 1791–1896* (Toronto: University of Toronto Press, 1990).

44 Romney 183; see also Davison 141–6.

45 See, for example, "The Roman Organ," *Globe,* 1 July 1851; "William Lyon Mackenzie on Endowments," *Globe,* 30 April 1853.

46 J.R. Miller, "Anti-Catholicism in Canada: From the British Conquest to the Great War," *Creed and Culture: The Place of English-Speaking Catholics in Canadian Society, 1750–1930,* eds. Terence Murphy and Gerald Stortz (Montreal and Kingston: McGill-Queen's University Press, 1993) 25–28. As Miller points out, not only was the church seen as intervening in the husband-wife relation, it was also perceived as a particularly misogynistic religion that denigrated marriage through its insistence on priestly celibacy and "destroyed the family by brutalizing and corrupting its heart, the wife and mother" (34–35). Later in the century, as J.R. Miller has argued, attacks on the church often focussed on the confessional and its potential to disrupt familial harmony by replacing a husband's authority with that of the priest.

47 See, for example, "The Liberality of Priestcraft," *Globe,* 24 September 1853; "Letter from Peter Prayer," 9 August 1853; "Mariolatry," 18 June 1855; also the *Globe*'s editorial for 4 September 1853, which discussed mob attacks on Protestant

evangelicals in Ireland that had been instigated by priests. See also Miller 35, for a discussion of the use of these examples of Catholic domination.

48 This was the fate of "The Last De Boufflers," a young French nobleman of the late-seventeenth century, whose unjust corporal punishment by Jesuits (whose college he attended) led to his death from shame (*Niagara Chronicle,* 28 January 1853). The virtue and superior morality of Protestant women, however, might be enlisted in resisting Catholicism occasionally. "Transubstantiation" told the story of a clever Protestant woman who had married a Catholic on the condition that he did not try to convert her but was constantly harangued by his priest, who refused to respect her religion and made repeated visits attempting to instill "popish notions," particularly that of transubstantiation. She held fast, though, and continued to resist his efforts, outsmarting him until he stopped bothering her ("Transubstantiation," *Canadian Son of Temperance,* 9 December 1854). Miller has pointed out that transubstantiation was a favourite target of anti-Catholics (32).

49 "Woman's Liberty and Virtue—Nunneries," *Canadian Son of Temperance,* 5 October 1853; see also "The Beast Biting, with Intent to Kill," *Christian Guardian,* 4 December 1855.

50 See, for example, "Lecture to Wives," *Canadian Son of Temperance,* 9 December 1853. For an analysis of the gendered dimensions of Monk's tale, see Maureen McCarthy, "Maria Monk: The Construction of an Escaped Nun," paper presented to the Canadian Historical Association's 73rd annual conference, Calgary, June 1994.

51 "Reschid Pacha," *Globe,* 2 August 1853. A very similar piece was "Abdul Mejid, the Sultan of the Ottoman Empire," *Canadian Son of Temperance,* 25 October 1854.

52 "The Late Sultana of Turkey," *Canadian Son of Temperance,* 23 August 1854.

53 "The Organization of the Empire," *Niagara Mail,* 3 October 1855; "Serfdom in Russia," *Niagara Mail,* 17 October 1855; "Abolition of the Slave Trade in Turkey," *Niagara Mail,* 3 January 1855.

54 As Edward Said has reminded us, Orientalist discourse was also about European, or in this specific case British, culture (*Orientalism* [New York: Vintage, 1979] 2–3 and 12).

55 Joanna De Groot, 'Sex' and 'Race': the Construction of Language and Image in the Nineteenth Century," *Sexuality and Subordination: Interdisciplinary Studies of Gender in the Nineteenth*

Century, eds. Susan Mendus and Jane Rendall (New York: Routledge, 1989) 89–128, 105.

56 "Union of Daughters in Canada," *Canadian Son of Temperance,* 10 June 1851.

57 Although see, for example, Robin Winks, *The Blacks in Canada* (New Haven: Yale University Press, 1971); C. Peter Ripley, *The Black Abolitionist Papers, Vol. 2, Canada, 1830–1865* (Chapel Hill: University of North Carolina Press, 1986); Peggy Bristow, Dionne Brand, Linda Carty, Afua P. Cooper, Sylvia Hamilton and Adrienne Shadd, *"We're Rooted Here and They Can't Pull Us Up": Essays in African Canadian Women's History* (Toronto: University of Toronto Press, 1994); Shirley J. Yee, "Gender Ideology and Black Women as Community-Builders in Ontario, 1850–70," *Canadian Historical Review* LXXV (March 1994): 53–73.

58 Shadd, a member of a free black family from Delaware, had come to Canada in 1850, settling in Windsor and opening a school with money from the American Missionary Association. She quickly became involved in anti-slavery societies and in 1852 published *A Plea for Emigration,* which offered information on Canada West to African-Americans who wanted to move north. A year later Shadd founded the *Freeman,* inviting a prominent member of the African-Canadian community, Samuel Ringgold Ward, to serve as editor. But it appears that this was a task Ward performed in name only, for in 1854 when the paper moved to Toronto for one year Ward's name no longer appeared on the masthead. Shadd continued to edit the paper with the help of her sister, Amelia, until 1855, just before she returned to southwestern Ontario to set up business in Chatham. The Reverend William Newman became the *Freeman's* editor, with Shadd devoting herself to the business of selling subscriptions and lecturing throughout the United States. She returned there in 1863 and, apart from visits to Canada in 1866 and 1881, spent the rest of her life in the United States. See Peggy Bristow, "Black Women in Buxton and Chatham, 1850–1865," *"We're Rooted Here,"* 69–142, 105–122. See also Jim Bearden and Linda Jean Butler, *Shadd: The Life and Times of Mary Shadd Cary* (Toronto: NC Press, 1977). For Ward, the son of escaped slaves who had been a Congregational minister, teacher, temperance activist, and editor in New York state, and who was a fundraiser and lecturer for the Anti-Slavery Society of Canada, see Stouffer 201–29.

59 Evelyn Brooks Higginbotham, "African-American Women's History and the Metalanguage of Race," *Signs* 17.2 (Winter 1992): 251–74.

60 *Provincial Freeman,* 24 April 1853. See also the *Freeman*'s editorial, "Introductory," 24 March 1853 and "Our Tour," 23 July 1854. At times the archetypal slave might be constructed as male. See "The Maroons," *Provincial Freeman,* 12 May 1855, for the story of Freme, the captive son of an African chief.

61 "Lectures," *Provincial Freeman,* 17 March 1855.

62 "Adieu," *Provincial Freeman,* 30 June 1855.

63 These differences are a theme addressed throughout Jacqueline Jones, *Labour of Love, Labour of Sorrow: Black Women, Work and the Family, From Slavery to the Present* (New York: Vintage Books, 1985).

64 "American Slavery," *Globe,* 11 January 1853. Brown also commended the ladies for not sweetening the truth, expressing it in plain speech.

65 This appeal was apparently sponsored by the Duchess of Sutherland; see Stouffer, 125–26.

66 "Mrs. America answers Mrs. England," *Provincial Freeman,* 24 March 1853.

67 "Slavery in Baltimore," *Provincial Freeman,* 30 June 1855.

68 "Knox Church Bazaar," *Globe,* 1 January 1851; "Soirees! Soirees! Soirees!" *Canadian Son of Temperance,* 19 April 1853; "The Women's Convention," *Canadian Son of Temperance,* 27 September 1853.

69 While work on women's participation in reform and suffrage has examined the relations of class and, to some extent, race to these movements, the lack of a historiography for earlier decades of the nineteenth century makes it difficult to assess continuities and changes. See Linda Kealey ed., *A Not Unreasonable Claim: Women and Reform in Canada, 1880s–1920* (Toronto: The Women's Press, 1979); Mariana Valverde, *The Age of Light, Soap, and Water: Moral Reform in English Canada, 1885–1925* (Toronto: McClelland & Stewart, 1991).

70 Bruce Curtis, "The Speller Expelled: Disciplining the Common Reader in Canada West," *Canadian Review of Sociology and Anthropology* 22. 3 (1985): 346–68, 357–8, 362.

Constructed and Contested Truths: Aboriginal Suicide, Law, and Colonialism in the Canadian West(s), 1823–1927

LESLEY ERICKSON

In *The Amazing Death of Calf Shirt,* Hugh Dempsey recounts the oral history of a suicide at the Kainai (Blood) Reserve in southern Alberta: "Sometimes even Low Horn could not help. In 1894, a woman named Only a Flower became despondent and wandered away from the camps. When a young boy found her hanging from a cottonwood tree, he rushed to the medicine man's house for help. Low Horn went to the site to cut her down, but there was nothing he could do for the unfortunate woman."[1] Only a Flower's death occurred at a significant moment in Kainaiwa history when Department of Indian Affairs (DIA) agents and physicians campaigned to decrease the influence of medicine men by vilifying and ridiculing Aboriginal healing methods. The journalist who covered the incident, however, chose to focus on the investigation, emphasizing that the inquest on "the body of Black Antelope's squaw" had been attended by a government-appointed coroner and six white jurymen who arrived at a verdict of "suicide while temporarily insane."[2] In his annual report, the Indian agent abbreviated the incident further: "The births numbered seventy-one during the year, while the deaths amounted to eighty-eight...the latter including the suicide of a woman by hanging and the accidental death of a girl by drowning."[3] Contrary to the evidence, he concluded that the Kainaiwa were in "fairly good" health that year.

In contrast to the Indian agent's casual dismissal of Only a Flower's death, the Royal Commission on Aboriginal Peoples reported in 1995 that status Indians in contemporary Canada suffer a suicide rate three times the total national average, while adolescents are five to six times more likely to commit suicide than their non-Aboriginal age-group peers.[4] The commission concluded that Aboriginal suicide was an outward expression of the "cultural stress" that accompanied Canada's colonial relations with First Nations.[5] While the correlation between colonialism and Aboriginal suicide remains unchallenged, psychologists Christopher Lalonde and Michael Chandler, focusing on British Columbia, have demonstrated that suicide rates can vary dramatically from First Nation to First Nation. Arguing that there is no monolithic "suicidal indigene," they established that 90 per cent of youth suicides between 1987 and 1992 occurred in only 10 per cent of bands, while half of the province's 198 bands had not experienced a single youth suicide in six years.[6] Similarly, anthropologist Ronald

Lesley Erickson, "Constructed and Contested Truths: Aboriginal Suicide, Law, and Colonialism in the Canadian West(s), 1823–1927," *Canadian Historical Review* 86, 4 (December 2005): 595–618. Reprinted with permission of the University of Toronto Press Incorporated (www.utp.journals.com).

Niezen has noted that although many academics and activists use official statistics to construct social pathologies in Aboriginal communities as the legacies of colonialism, "solid connections between dispossession and depression are difficult to establish."[7] His observation may explain why the history of Aboriginal suicide in Canada has been limited to passing references, much speculation, and a case study.[8]

Drawing upon a wide array of sources from British Columbia and the Prairies, this article traces these connections by exploring how representations of Aboriginal suicide and coroners' investigations into cases of unnatural death created the "suicidal indigene" and legitimated his and her dispossession and regulation between 1823 and 1927. As Only a Flower's case illustrates, Aboriginal peoples and newcomers attached multiple, contested meanings to cases of self-directed violence in colonial settings. A rereading of nineteenth-century narrative accounts of life and travel in the region reveals that representations of Aboriginal suicide played an integral, but overlooked, role in evolutionary anthropology, which constructed race, British-Canadian identity, and modernity in Britain and North America.[9] Fur traders, explorers, and amateur anthropologists offered tales of Aboriginal women hanging themselves on the margins of Empire as evidence that Aboriginal culture was primitive, irrational, and doomed to extinction.[10] According to Aboriginal guides and shamans, however, these narratives not only misrepresented attitudes toward suicide that were diverse, complex, and undergoing transformation, they constructed as normative behaviour that was either unsanctioned or (as Lalonde and Chandler suggest) confined to segments of select Aboriginal communities.

These trends escalated in the 1870s when the West entered Confederation and officials, settlers, and journalists attached new, sometimes conflicting, layers of meaning to Aboriginal suicide within the imposed and resisted structure of the coroner's inquest. In her study of coroners' investigations of prostitute deaths in turn-of-the-century British Columbia, historian Susan Johnston observes, "The bodies of the dead can be read as texts which invoke multiple interpretations and meanings."[11] When the body of the dead was "Indian," coroners' inquests became "contact zones" within an intricate web of surveillance that encouraged colonial agents to define deaths as suicides by drawing upon "shared social meanings" or "common sense ideas" about circumstances that "typically" culminated in Aboriginal suicide.[12] Local newspapers, inquest collections for British Columbia and Alberta, DIA reports and correspondence, and North-West Mounted Police (NWMP) investigations contain references to only sixty-seven cases of Aboriginal suicide between 1872 and 1937. Despite their rarity and confinement to select Aboriginal communities, these cases garnered intense scrutiny by government officials, police investigators, and journalists. In many cases, the imposed structure of the inquest permitted government officials, jurors, and journalists to manipulate investigations and media accounts of suicide (now defined by Canadian law as a crime) to provide concrete proof that Aboriginal peoples were in need of further "protection," regulation, and surveillance because they were pathologically drunken, criminal, and suicidal.[13]

As a growing number of scholars argue, however, imposed colonial procedures also provided Aboriginal peoples with the opportunity to contest negative stereotypes and the government policies that promoted their emergence.[14] Speaking of the traumatic impact that the loss of land, lives, and freedom was having on some community members, Aboriginal witnesses (sometimes with police cooperation) disclosed how variables like age, gender, marriage, mental illness, and the adoption of Christianity were influencing suicide patterns and responses to colonialism. In 1921, when a juryman asked a member of the Yale band in British Columbia, why his friend, the son of a chief, had taken his own life, he responded, "He used to say they stoped [sic] the fishing and they stopped the hunting. I am poor and I am going to starve."[15] Although Aboriginal witnesses frequently inscribed the suicide's body with their critiques of colonialism, the state invested inquest proceedings with the majesty of law,[16] legitimating stereotypical, colonial constructions of Aboriginal suicide that continue to inform discussions of the issue in contemporary Canada.

Suicide and Evolutionary Anthropology

In August 1905, a journalist with the *Edmonton Bulletin,* reporting on the return of a steamer from northern Alberta, wrote, "The captain remarked that the Indians were acquiring the ways of the white man...one of them committed suicide by shooting himself with his rifle this winter. It is the first case of suicide he has ever heard of among the Indians."[17] Historical geographer Cole Harris defines colonialism as "a culture of domination, a set of values that infused European thought and letters; led Europeans confidently out into the world; stereotyped non-Europeans as the obverse, the negative counterpart, of civilized Europeans; and created moral justification for appropriating non-European lands and reshaping non-European cultures."[18] The belief that suicide was anathema to pre-contact Aboriginal culture was integral to colonial discourse. Early nineteenth-century traders and explorers believed that the "stoic Indian" had suffered bouts of deprivation that had immunized him against normal human pain and suffering.[19] Functionalist anthropologists likewise envisaged pre-contact societies as inherently cohesive. When Sebald Steinmetz and Edward Westermarck undertook the first cross-cultural explorations of suicide in 1894 and 1908, they hoped to prove that the "noble savage" was exempt from the evolutionary hubris that had corrupted "civilized man." They found, however, that suicide was not exclusive to "civilization."[20]

In fact, fur traders, travellers, and amateur historians had long commented upon the phenomenon of suicidal women in the North American West. Tales of Nlaka'pamux (Thompson), Stl'atl'imx (Lilloet), and Dakota (Sioux) women hanging themselves in the wilderness were central to narratives that constructed Aboriginal women as "squaw drudges," or irrational beasts of burden, in primitive polygamous societies. In his 1832 narrative of the Columbia River Expedition, for instance, fur trader Ross Cox argued that sterility drew women of the Upper Fraser River (Nlaka'pamux and Stl'atl'imx) into prostitution. Sickness and excessive labour, he added, produced a depression of the spirits that compelled them to suicide: "We saw the bodies of several of these wretched beings, who had hanged themselves from trees in sequestered parts of the wood."[21] Visiting the same area in the 1840s, Irish-Canadian painter Paul Kane reported that two sisters, married to the same man, had hanged themselves in the woods unbeknownst to each other.[22] Twenty years later, the Anglican missionary Rev. Robert C. Lundin Brown, working among the Stl'atl'imx, reported that the number of young women killing themselves in British Columbia—for "contemptibly trivial" reasons—was incredible.[23]

Newcomers to the Great Plains likewise interpreted female suicide as a primitive, irrational response to arranged marriages and polygamy. Following his expedition to Dakota territory, English botanist John Bradbury reported in 1817 that the situation of Aboriginal women was so dire that they destroyed their female children and committed suicide.[24] In 1823, explorers James Edward Colhoun, Stephen Long, and William Keating similarly recounted the tale of Winona, a Dakota woman who committed suicide by jumping from a cliff when her family negotiated (against her wishes) marriage to an elderly, distinguished warrior.[25] When Edward Duffield Neill wrote *Dahkotah Land and Dahkotah Life* fifty years later, he included a chapter, "The Hardships of Dahkotah Females," wherein Dakota women were driven to suicide by their parents and husbands' whims: "Uncultivated and made to do the labour of beasts, when they are desperate, they act more like infuriated brutes than creatures of reason."[26] As Glenda Riley has noted, the perceived connection between Aboriginal marriage law and suicide provided raw material for hundreds of fictionalized, romanticized stories of the West.[27]

Suicide by Aboriginal women fascinated newcomers because they linked it to "primitive" marriage "customs" and practices; the phenomenon also contravened separate spheres ideology, which constructed suicide as predominantly masculine behaviour. Armed with new English and American statistics that "proved" that men were more susceptible, William Knighton argued in 1881 that women clung tenaciously to life because their subsumption within the family and inherent religiosity gave them a larger measure of "that hope that springs eternal." Those few who did commit suicide fell neatly into the stereotype of the fallen woman who preferred death to loss of innocence. By the end of the century, functional sociologists interpreted female suicides as rare acts committed by irrational individuals, while the male suicide rate became a barometer of "civilization," modernity, and national economic well-being.[28] Tales of suicidal women on the margins of Empire, consequently, fit neatly into late nineteenth-century, social Darwinian representations of the primitive, "vanishing Indian." In 1895, the curator of ethnology at the Smithsonian wrote, "Even in the animal world, any species that would

pollute the fountain and destroy the very foundation of life or in which females committed suicide must speedily disappear."[29]

Given these assumptions, few newcomers recognized that Aboriginal people's attitudes towards suicide were diverse, complex, and undergoing transformation, For instance, James Teit, an ethnographer who lived with and married into the Nlaka'pamux, was atypically interested in women's experiences and discussed suicide in *The Thompson Indians of British Columbia* (1900).[30] Observing that suicide was common in the 1890s among women suffering from shame, remorse, or quarrels with relatives, Teit explored the phenomenon's historical and cultural underpinnings. Elders advised him that female suicide had once been associated with touching marriages; however, the Nlaka'pamux had ceased these courting practices by the 1860s. Prior to the gold rush, young men wishing to marry could touch their intended with an arrow at culturally sanctioned times and events. The touch (considered a proposal that could be accepted or rejected by the girl's parents) initiated formal courting. Elders agreed that women occasionally committed suicide out of shame or anger: some had touched a man, but met with rejection, while parents forced others into unwanted marriages. Suicide, however, was not exclusive to women: Nlaka'pamux men who wished to test their guardian spirits' ability to return them to life would occasionally take their own lives.[31] Nor was it sanctioned behaviour: shamans agreed that the suicide's soul never made it to the land of souls.[32]

Although Nlaka'pamux Elders contested and complicated colonial discourses on Aboriginal suicide, Teit explained the suicides of the 1890s by observing simply, "The belief that they are doomed to extinction seems to have a depressing effect on some of the Indians."[33] An Anglican missionary stationed at Lytton between 1867 and 1883 likewise observed that suicide in Nlaka'pamux communities was complex and undergoing transformation, but then proceeded to interpret it within the framework of evolutionary anthropology. Given the power of shaming in Nlaka'pamux society, the Rev. John Booth Good feared that the acceptance of monogamy by Christian converts would have an adverse effect on wives turned away because the action branded them unchaste. Booth predicted that prostitution and suicide would accompany the progress of "civilization."[34]

On the Great Plains, suicide patterns and beliefs were likewise more complex than non-Aboriginal preoccupations with the status of women, arranged marriages, and polygamy suggested. John West, an Anglican missionary stationed at Red River in the early 1820s, noted that Cree and Saulteaux women occasionally committed suicide to nurse and accompany the spirit of a deceased child to the otherworld.[35] Similarly, Dakota Elders in the 1880s disclosed that women were known to have hanged themselves upon the death of a favoured child; the custom waned in the 1850s, however.[36] Finally, although Kainai elders recounted to Beverly Hungry Wolf that suicide had been "not uncommon" among young women married to older men with many wives, cultural anthropologist Alan Klein argues that polygamy itself became a notable feature of Blackfoot political economy only with colonialism and the buffalo-robe trade.[37]

As was the case in Nlaka'pamux culture, suicide by women was a serious transgression in plains societies. In the 1820s, Stephen Long and William Keating's Dakota guide, Wazecota, explained that the souls of the dead travelled to Wanare-tebe, the dwelling place of souls. In order to reunite with friends, family, and ancestors, however, the soul had to pass over a sharp rock. Those who fell entered the region of the evil spirit, where they were doomed to chop wood and carry water for eternity. Women who had violated their chastity, committed infanticide, or hanged themselves were most likely to enter this

realm. The latter, he continued, "are said to go to the regions of the wicked, dragging after them the tree to which they are suspended.... for this reason they always suspend themselves to as small a tree as can possibly sustain their weight."[38] Assiniboine guides related similar beliefs to Alexander Henry and David Thompson. Explaining that the soul had to cross a river to get to the land of Eth'tom-E, the guides recounted that a hideous red bull would force the guilty to tumble headlong into the river: Female suicides were "the most miserable wretches of the earth."[39]

The figure of the suicidal Aboriginal woman fit neatly into European and North American narratives written for popular, metropolitan audiences seeking evidence of primitive man. Written by men who used male elders, shamans, and guides as informants, these tales represented but a fragment of the complex, diverse behaviour patterns and belief systems in the region. For instance, evidence suggests that all plains warrior societies—with various degrees of institutionalization—had traditions of "masked" suicide whereby the family and band sanctioned voluntary death in battle as an acceptable and honourable way for an elderly, ill, or grief-stricken warrior to die. If the warrior died in battle, he would gain prestige in the tribe's collective memory; if he failed, he would be ridiculed. Anthropologist Karin Andriolo argues that masked suicide mitigated surplus alienation for the individual within cultures that evaluated self-killing by hanging negatively and considered it a characteristically feminine form of behaviour.[40] As was the case in the Pacific Northwest, evidence of suicide by Aboriginal men rarely found its way into popular narratives because it contested dominant, evolutionary models that constructed suicide as a masculine behaviour particular to "modern" civilizations. With Confederation, this trend would change as officials, juries, and journalists attached new layers of meaning to Aboriginal suicide within the imposed structures of the Indian Act and the inquest.

Constructing Aboriginal Pathologies

In May 1881, a journalist reported that a "Penelecot" man, arrested for drunkenness, had hanged himself in the Nanaimo jail. Allegedly, the cook had raised an alarm, but no officers were present to aid the prisoner. Officer Drake deposed at the inquest that he had arrested the deceased—who appeared to be "quite rational"—in the morning and left him alone in a cell that afternoon.[41] Although the incident could have opened a public inquiry on jail conditions, the treatment of Aboriginal prisoners, or police practice (indeed, the jury recommended that officers always be in charge of prisoners), the article's follow-up focused on the character of the deceased: "It is now stated that the Indian who hung himself in the Nanaimo jail was a bad character. The Indians were very generally afraid of him, but now say that he has been mixed up in several murders."[42]

Historian John Lutz has argued that state surveillance of Aboriginal peoples made colonization and the extension of settlement possible.[43] As Qual-ah-que-ah's case illustrates, coroners' inquests—and the newspaper accounts they generated—created and reproduced knowledge about Aboriginal peoples and cultures for consumption by white settlers, government officials, and legal authorities bent on unsettling them. When British Columbia and the North-West Territories (Alberta and Saskatchewan) entered Confederation, the federal government assumed responsibility for "Indians"; the revised and consolidated 1876 Indian Act constituted a comprehensive program for naming, defining, and providing surveillance of Aboriginal peoples. By designating "Indians" as a special class of persons legally dependent on the Crown, legislators consigned them to a "legal never-never land."[44] Legislation defined Indians as British subjects, but made

them wards of the state—a status they shared with children, felons, and the insane. As Lutz argues, the state "pathologized" Aboriginal peoples by blurring the line between "Indians" and "criminals"; it criminalized behaviour (like drinking or selling alcohol) carried out routinely by non-Aboriginals. Furthermore, Indian agents acted as justices of the peace for Indian Act offences, presiding over summary trials in special courts.[45]

Coroners' inquests and police investigations of suicide were one more thread in an intricate web of surveillance. Provincial governments designated local physicians who were British citizens as coroners, working on the assumption that these men had the expertise required to fulfill the office's judicial and medical functions. When a physician, police officer, Indian agent, or concerned citizen reported a sudden or unnatural death, coroners (at their discretion) could either conduct an inquiry or order the summons of six local citizens to act as jurymen at a formal inquest. After viewing the body, the jury heard depositions and rendered a verdict.[46] If the jury concluded that the death was a suicide, it chose between three verdicts: *felo de se,* felonious self-murder; *non compos mentis,* temporary insanity; or insufficient evidence as to state of mind.[47] The evidence suggests that when coroners, police, government officials, and juries considered the evidence and judged the state of mind of the deceased, their investigations and verdicts were governed variously by colonial constructions of Aboriginal suicide, political expediency, and public policy.

Given prevailing discourses on the "vanishing Indian," officials could be remarkably indifferent to the death of reserve residents. Indian agents rarely mentioned suicide in annual reports, and police investigators cited instances of coroners being unwilling to travel to reserves.[48] In May 1920, the Alberta Provincial Police received a report of a hanging at the Hobbema Reserve. When the investigating officer phoned Dr. Stevenson to proceed to the scene, he discovered that the coroner was away on business. A second coroner informed the police that he was too ill to travel. Advised to proceed alone, the officer arrived at the reserve and discovered that the majority of residents were away attending a local pageant. The deceased's body had been hanging unattended in the heat for more than a week. Although the second coroner promised to catch the next train, he never arrived. In the absence of a coroner, the Indian agent advised a department physician to examine the body. When the physician declared the death a suicide, Officer Cowey advised the coroners to conduct a proper investigation. Upon their refusal, he travelled to Wetaskiwin to present the case to Stevenson. Based on the testimony of two Aboriginal witnesses who had informed Cowey that the deceased, a nineteen-year-old unmarried youth, had been "acting strangely of late," Stevenson accepted the agency physician's verdict and ordered an immediate burial.[49]

Working closely with Aboriginal scouts and witnesses, police investigators produced evidence that contradicted the Indian agents' interpretations. In March 1904, the Kainai Reserve agent reported to the commissioner that Clay-Bank-Foot shot his wife and himself "under the influence of a condition of despondency not uncommon to the Indian mind, this being the fourth case of the sort occurring on this reserve within the memory of the writer."[50] However, the investigating officer reported that the Kainaiwa believed that Clay-Bank-Foot's behaviour stemmed from depression brought on by chronic tuberculosis. The deceased allegedly believed that his wife had been unfaithful during his stay at the Roman Catholic hospital at Stand Off. Despite his fears, the couple moved into a shack together upon his release. At the scene, Indian scouts found no signs of foul play and reported that all signs indicated a deliberate murder-suicide—the carefully arranged contents of the shack, the fully clothed condition of the bodies on the bed, the deceased's papers pinned to the wall.[51]

Unlike police investigators, DIA officials concentrated on turning suicide cases in the department's favour. In 1893, Indian Commissioner Hayter Reed reported to Deputy Superintendent General Lawrence Vankoughnet that an Oak River Sioux woman in southern Manitoba had hanged herself because her husband took two more wives. Although Reed dismissed the woman's actions as a "jealous fit," Vankoughnet advised him to see to her children's care: "It would be well, *considering the character of the father*...to get them if of proper age into some Industrial School where they will be properly cared for and trained."[52] Similarly, in 1937 the Cote Reserve (Saulteaux) agent lamented that alcohol had not played a role in a recent triple murder-suicide in southern Saskatchewan: "Although the Cote Indians are rather noted for their drinking of intoxicants, this had nothing to do with the case in question. If no other good results for the other Indians in this case, it has at least shown them the evil results of an uncontrollable temper."[53]

Because evidence of alcohol abuse led to criminal charges and resonated with settler perceptions of Aboriginal suicide, police, jurors, and journalists likewise fixated on the issue. When a resident of the Piikani (Peigan) Reserve in southern Alberta allegedly committed suicide after murdering his wife, son, and another man in 1907, the coroner claimed that suicide was "too evident" since he found rye whiskey at the scene and the deceased had recently lost a wife and child. Sergeant J.S. Piper concurred, expressing the belief that no man would take his son's life unless crazed with drink or insane. Piper's assumption reflected the colonial myth that Aboriginal peoples—constructed as racially and physically inferior—did not have the same tolerance for alcohol as non-Aboriginals.[54] While the murder-suicide case was built on little more than circumstantial evidence, the Indian commissioner advised the agent, "Although the tragedy seems self-explanatory, an effort should be made to discover whether whisky constituted a factor in bringing it about, and if so, to discover and punish the parties or parties who supplied it."[55]

While alcohol played a role in only 15 per cent of reported cases, jurors subjected most Aboriginal witnesses to intense questioning regarding the drinking habits of their friends and loved ones, In June 1875, the death of "Indian Maggie" resulted in an inquest at New Westminster, British Columbia. The deceased's husband alleged that he had been in town the previous night buying shingles; when he returned home, his wife accused him of being unfaithful. Later that evening, a married couple living with him found Maggie hanging from a tree. In response to questioning, the husband denied that he, or any members of his household, had been drinking. Night watchman William Moresby corroborated the husband's deposition, disclosing that he found no liquor on the premises.[56] Ten years later, two members of the North Arm Fraser River Band likewise deposed that their stepfather had not been drinking when he hanged himself at New Westminster; he was, in fact, elderly, blind, and infirm.[57] When a Tlatlasikwala woman allegedly poisoned herself near Alert Bay in 1909, her husband testified that they had recently quarrelled over money and separated. Although the ownership of wages appeared to be at issue, the coroner and juror focused their questions on whether the husband had purchased liquor. He responded, "I did not buy a case of whiskey in town. I do not drink."[58]

Journalists reflected and enhanced jurors' biases and assumptions by recording only those cases where alcohol placed a role or, when it did not, exaggerating or manipulating the evidence to fit prevailing stereotypes of the "drunken" or "criminal Indian." In October 1890, the *Victoria Daily Colonist* reported that an Indian man, suffering from temporary insanity induced by alcohol, committed suicide. A contributor to the same edition wrote, "It is much to be regretted that the Canadian Indian who has been long in contact with civilization is not a very interesting specimen of the genus 'homo.'" Indians, the author continued, had few recognized virtues: Most were addicted to vice, and only a few appeared to be intelligent or communicative.[59] A non-Aboriginal visitor to the Lekwammen Reserve had reported the suicide to the authorities. Claiming that he had witnessed excess drinking there, the informant named the deceased as the party responsible for the debauch. An investigating officer failed to find evidence of "drunken Indians" on the date in question, however.[60]

Prairie journalists similarly manipulated the evidence. When a Secwepemc (Shuswap) man, visiting Alberta from British Columbia, jumped from the roof of a Calgary hotel in 1921, the newspaper contradicted inquest findings by reporting, "The police officer who found the body stated that he detected a strong odor of liquor on the dead man."[61] Four years later, the *Lethbridge Herald* similarly slanted the evidence when it reported that a Montana Blackfoot, "deciding that life held nothing for him...hanged himself from a Canadian Pacific Railway bridge." The deceased, the article continued, had been an "on and off inmate of the provincial jail."[62] Although the article created the impression that the deceased was a hardened criminal, witnesses testified that the police and Indian agent had arrested and convicted him for trespassing on the Kainai Reserve each time he visited friends and family.[63]

The process of inquest and inquiry not only permitted non-Aboriginal government officials, jurymen, and journalists to impose their own interpretations of suicide on Aboriginal communities, it allowed jurors to pass judgment on the deceased. By the late nineteenth century, juries rarely used the *felo de se* verdict of exclusion to punish the deceased posthumously, yet seven Aboriginal men and women suffered the label in British Columbia between 1871 and 1937. Although British legislators abolished traditional common law penalties for suicide (like confiscation of property) prior to Confederation, it remained a crime, and self-murder verdicts carried considerable social stigma.[64] The condemned men included one who allegedly got drunk and stole a pair of boots, one who tried to kill his wife and a police officer, and another who allegedly practised Indian medicine.[65] All three women were Cowichan of Vancouver Island who hanged themselves only months after giving birth—one also threatened to leave her husband.[66] Jurymen perhaps used *felo de se* verdicts to express strong disapproval of practices that threatened the construction of a liberal, Christian order and patriarchal conceptions of marriage and motherhood. In addition, two of the Cowichan cases involved female witnesses who tried to revive the deceased by blowing into her ears. Occurring in the 1890s, these verdicts likely enhanced campaigns, led by missionaries and physicians, to discredit Aboriginal healing practices.[67] In all cases, the meaning that non-Aboriginal jurors attached to Aboriginal suicides rarely corresponded with the testimonials of their friends, family, and neighbours.

Contesting Truths in the Contact Zone

The stereotypes that emerged out of coroners' inquests and inquiries not only legitimated increased state regulation and surveillance of Aboriginal peoples, it also disguised colonialism's impact on suicide patterns in certain Aboriginal communities. In 1879, Edgar Dewdney, Indian commissioner for the North-West Territories, kept a journal of his travels in the region. At Blackfoot Crossing he recorded,

"From French & Father Scollen heard awful tales of the state of Indians. They have been selling their horses for a mere song, eating gophers, mice, Badgers & for the first time have hunted the Antelope & nearly killed them all off. One woman came to French and said she must have food for her children...if not she we go off and hang herself." When Dewdney visited Isapomuxika's (Crowfoot's) camp, another woman informed French, "If I can't get any food for my two children I must kill myself. I live only for them & I can't bear to see them starve."[68] Although they were less direct, police reports and inquest depositions also contain Aboriginal people's critiques of and active resistance to the loss of lives, land, and freedom that accompanied colonization.

On the Canadian Prairies, the disappearance of the buffalo in the 1870s, the treaty process, and resettlement on reserves ushered in two decades of widespread suffering, destitution, and starvation. The Metis military defeat during the 1885 Rebellion also signalled a new direction in Canadian Indian policy: Its architect, Hayter Reed, sought to dismantle the "tribal" system by promoting individualism through "the policy of the Bible and the plough." Missionary-run residential and industrial schools would promote "aggressive civilization" by severing the ties that bound children to the customs and traditions of their parents, while a ban on all forms of cultural and religious ceremonies (notably, the potlatch and Sun Dance) would destroy "communist" perceptions of property. Significantly, although Canadian courts accepted the legality of Aboriginal marriages (but not divorce) in 1867, Indian Act provisions and unofficial DIA policies encouraged agents to discourage practices that fell outside of monogamy and life-long union by cutting off male and female "offenders" from treaty payments and rations.[69]

Within a cultural milieu characterized by confinement and surveillance, warrior societies could no longer sustain the tradition of voluntary death in battle. The available evidence suggests that only a few women, including Only a Flower, hanged themselves on the Great Plains in the early reserve period.[70] By contrast, possibly the first recorded, "unmasked" incident of a man attempting to commit suicide occurred in 1885 when Kapapamahehakwew (Wandering Spirit), Mistahimaskwa's (Big Bear) war chief, stabbed himself in the chest to avoid punishment following surrender.[71] After pleading "guilty" to murder, Kapapamahehakwew told a reporter "that he had always been a friend of the white man until last spring, and that he had been a great warrior fighting the Blackfeet until the white men came into the country."[72] Although a priest baptized Kapapamahehakwew, the prisoner sought assurances that the guards would remove his shackles prior to hanging because he feared they would accompany him to the afterlife.[73] Kapapamahehakwew's attempted suicide marked a turning point in the history of suicide on the Prairies. Two-thirds of the twenty-two suicides collected for analysis involved men from Great Plains warrior societies. Although the tradition of masked suicide was no longer sustainable, culturally patterned behaviours persisted: With the exception of a few who hanged themselves in prison, the majority of men chose death by firearm.

Subtexts of resistance to unfair police practices and government policies run throughout police and coroners' investigations of these cases. In September 1894, the NWMP commissioner reported that "Peigan Mike" had shot himself while awaiting trial for horse theft at Pincher Creek. Police investigators learned later that, contrary to procedure, officers had forced the prisoner to work as a cook assistant rather than relocating him to district gaol following committal. A constable informed Superintendent Steele that he had locked Peigan Mike into a cell each evening, but admitted that physicians had condemned the cell four years ago. Prior to his death, Peigan

Mike told police that his mother had forced him to sell the horse for food. He also informed the police that he would rather die than suffer the indignities of imprisonment. The local paper reported simply and inaccurately that the prisoner had been awaiting trial for "killing cattle" and had "managed to get a hold of a revolver."[74]

Sun Calf, a Siksika (Blackfoot) man sentenced to three years at Stony Mountain Penitentiary for horse theft, echoed Peigan Mike's sentiments following his escape and recapture on the Piikani Reserve in June 1905. When the police promised his return to prison, Sun Calf attempted suicide by puncturing his arm with a needle. He later informed the NWMP that his conviction and sentence had been unjust and that "he would cut his throat rather than go back to Stony Mountain" where, he argued, conditions were so deplorable he contracted tuberculosis.[75] When Tail Feathers, a Kainai scout with the NWMP, shot himself in 1907, the investigation likewise revealed subtexts of resistance to Canadian criminal justice. Kainai witnesses deposed that Tail Feathers had become enraged when a local justice of the peace sentenced a man found guilty of sexually assaulting his wife to only one month in prison. The scout, they continued, also believed that the Kainaiwa detested and distrusted him because he worked for the police and that the NWMP had cheated him of rations. Only Chief deposed that he last saw Tail Feathers riding towards the house of his wife's rapist "chanting the old song the Indians used when starting on the war path."[76]

While members of the Siksika Nation connected suicide to state surveillance, legal regulation, and the loss of freedom that accompanied colonialism, Aboriginal witnesses more generally associated it with the moral uncertainty and confusion that accompanied government and missionary attempts to impose monogamous, Christian marriages. Over 90 per cent of the suicides examined involved not adolescents, but young to middle-aged married men and women. In 40 per cent of cases, Aboriginal witnesses cited domestic disputes as the precipitating cause. As the earlier example involving the Oak River Sioux woman suggests, a husband or wife's acceptance or rejection of Christian marriage could precipitate disagreements that culminated in suicide or murder. In 1887, a member of the Little Black Bear Band of the File Hills Agency (Cree) shot his wife, then himself, following a dispute. Family and friends testified that the husband had left the reserve with another woman; in his absence, the wife returned to her father's tent. When the husband returned and demanded that the wife return to him, she turned to the Indian agent for advice. Although witnesses provided a clear narrative of events leading up to the murder-suicide, the coroner's jury found that Mes-Kan-achs had committed murder-suicide for "no known reason."[77]

In British Columbia, where women accounted for 40 per cent of all reported cases, Aboriginal witnesses likewise connected suicide to the confusion in gender roles and marital relationships that accompanied colonialism. In 1891, a Saanich witness deposed at an inquest into the death of "Loxin Bill" that the deceased was his son whom he had not seen for two years. The deceased's sister-in-law, a Semiahmoo widow, testified that she had refused to marry the deceased until a Catholic priest arrived to perform the ceremony. Loxin Bill and his sister-in-law belonged to Coast Salish cultures, where parents arranged marriages, wives lived in their husband's village, and widows married a brother-in-law upon their husband's death.[78] In this case, when the widow refused her brother-in-law's proposal, he went into the woods where he was found "hanging by his gaily coloured yarn belt to the limb of a little maple."[79] When a Cowichan woman hanged herself in October 1902, witnesses likewise cited uncertainty regarding her

marital status as a key motivating factor. Thomas, her husband by Aboriginal law, deposed that he and his wife had been preparing to marry in a church when family members forbade it because Thomas's first wife, by Christian marriage, was still alive. When Thomas told his wife that he would ask the priest if they could marry legally, she started to cry, fearing "they would bring my first wife back."[80]

Aboriginal testimony at the inquests into the suicide deaths mentioned by Teit likewise bore out Booth's predictions that colonialism would have an adverse effect on women. Three Nlaka'pamux women at the Nicola reserves committed suicide in the brief period between 1891 and 1900. Their cases coincided with mass British settlement, which abruptly ended female out-migration and the cross-cultural sexual relationships that had characterized the gold-rush era. Historical geographer Nadine Schuurman argues that the advent of colonial administration, missionaries, and disease increased women's physical labour and hardships.[81] In 1891, "Indian Frank" testified that his wife, Tell:whiliks, had committed suicide following a domestic dispute. According to the husband, Tell:whiliks had accused him of giving her a venereal disease; when he denied it, she confessed to carnal relations with another, When Frank left to confront the man in question, Tell:whiliks hanged herself in the woods. Frank admitted that he had been living with the deceased for two years, but had not married her in a church. When asked by a juryman to explain his wife's actions, Frank responded, "All the young Indian women hang themselves when they feel bad over men." A male friend corroborated his testimony.[82] Martin Shuta likewise represented his wife's behaviour as "customary" when she hanged herself in 1897. Residents of the Nicola Lake Reserve, the Shutas married according to Aboriginal law in

1882 and within the church ten years later. On the day in question, Shuta came home from the fields to discover his wife having "criminal connections" with his brother. When Shuta told his wife that the act was bad, owing to their Christian marriage, she claimed that his brother had forced her. Martin did not believe his wife and assured the jury that shame, remorse, and heartsickness had motivated his wife's actions: "Suicide by hanging is an Indian custom among women, when in trouble."[83]

Nlaka'pamux men perhaps represented these suicides as "traditional" because of the method chosen; they may also have been playing to non-Aboriginal perceptions to avoid trouble from a legal system they feared. Female Nlaka'pamux witnesses more freely connected the suicides to changes that accompanied colonialism. Martin Shuta's sister, for instance, testified that her sister-in-law had been labouring unhappily in the fields on the morning of her death and had suffered the deaths of three children since her marriage.[84] When Agnes, a resident of the Coldwater Reserve, committed suicide in May 1900, her sister likewise testified that her status as an unmarried woman with an illegitimate child motivated her decision.[85] Whereas the Nlaka'pamux had once viewed suicide as an option for women shamed during the rituals of courtship, within the imposed structures of colonialism it became a last desperate option for women caught on the boundary between two cultures.

Conclusion

In January 1876, a Skxwúmish man, identified as "Lazy Jim," testified that he, "Indian Ginger," and another man had attended a dance near their home at Burrard Inlet after drinking two glasses of gin. Ginger's sister informed the court that her brother threatened to hang himself later that night. Suspecting that

it was only the alcohol talking, she took the rope from her brother and went to bed. The next morning, a neighbour discovered Ginger hanging in a deserted building. The jury passed a verdict of "suicide" with insufficient evidence as to state of mind. According to Ginger's friend, however, the deceased would often get drunk and threaten to kill himself because he did not know where his father was buried.[86]

As sociologist Jack Douglas argues, police officers, relatives, coroners, jurors, and the suicides themselves draw upon commonsense ideas or "shared social meanings" about the circumstances and motives that "typically" culminate in suicide.[87] When white settlers in colonial societies met to determine the cause of death of Aboriginal peoples like Only a Flower and "Indian Ginger," the shared social meanings they drew upon were constructed visions that had developed over a century of cultural contact. Although nineteenth-century anthropologists had assumed that suicide was a phenomenon unique to "civilized," capitalistic societies, European travellers, fur traders, and missionaries recorded instances of its feminine form in pre- and early-contact cultures. When viewed through a lens clouded by European gender norms, Aboriginal suicide fell neatly into the colonizers' perceptions of Indigenous peoples as primitive, irrational, and doomed to extinction. With the advent of federal administration and the Indian Act, settlers, journalists, and colonial agents added new layers of meaning to Aboriginal suicide. The non-Aboriginal men who met to judge "Indian Ginger's" suicide concentrated on alcohol as a motivating factor and, consequently, failed to take seriously "Lazy Jim's" belief that the deceased's behaviour stemmed from unresolved grief over the loss of his father—and the links to the cultural community that his father represented.

As "Indian Ginger's" example illustrates, the case files collected by police investigators and coroners contain subtexts of resistance to the stereotype of the "suicidal Indian" and to the loss of lives, land, and freedom that accompanied colonialism that have only recently entered public discourse on Aboriginal suicide in Canada. Some Aboriginal witnesses contested the assumption that substance abuse or conflicts with the law were the motivating cause of their friend or loved one's death; others directly linked substance abuse and suicide to the regulation, death, poverty, and confusion in gender roles and marital relationships that accompanied colonialism. While it is impossible to mistake the connections between dispossession, depression, and suicide contained in many of these testimonies, depositions by Aboriginal witnesses indicate that variables like age, marital status, religion, gender, and mental illness influenced responses to colonialism *within* Aboriginal communities. As Christopher Lalonde and Michael Chandler argue, the myth of the "suicidal Aboriginal," constructed in the nineteenth and early twentieth centuries, cloaked the realities of intra-community variability.

If coroners' inquest depositions truly reflect the "realities" of suicidal behaviour within Aboriginal communities, then the historical record also supports Lalonde and Chandler's finding that suicide rates vary dramatically from community to community. Although some First Nations bands and tribes like the Cowichan, Nlaka'pamux, and Siksika experienced suicide "clusters" in the early reserve period, the trend waned by the First World War. In British Columbia, only five status Indians committed suicide between 1910 and 1937; in Alberta, six did so between 1910 and 1927. Significantly, only two of the pre-Second World War suicides examined involved adolescents. Despite their rarity, these cases helped to construct the "suicidal," "drunken," and "criminal" Indian in the settler imagination and to legitimate increased regulation and surveillance of reserve populations. Lalonde and Chandler's contemporary research has revealed a strong correlation between cultural continuity and suicide: Communities with self-government, control of land, band-controlled schools, community-controlled health services, cultural facilities, and control of police and fire services are significantly less at risk.

The historical record reveals that the state's usurpation of the process by which Aboriginal peoples defined and mediated suicidal behaviour—and the conflicts that precipitated it—contributed to the cultural trauma that accompanied colonialism. The inquest process promoted myths and stereotypes that have disguised the need for in-depth studies of suicide in specific First Nations communities. In addition, the internalization of these stereotypes by subsequent generations of Aboriginal children has likely contributed to escalating rates of adolescent suicide in certain First Nations communities since the Second World War.[88]

Notes

I would like to thank John Weaver and the editors and reviewers of the *Canadian Historical Review* for insightful suggestions and comments on earlier drafts of this article, and the SSHRC for supporting the research on which it is based.

1 Hugh Dempsey, *The Amazing Death of Calf Shirt and Other Blackfoot Stories* (Norman: University of Oklahoma Press, 1994), 44.

2 "Aboriginal Woman Suicides," *Macleod Gazette*, 20 July 1894.

3 James Wilson, Blood Agency, 8 Aug. 1895, "Annual Report of the Department of Indian Affairs for the Year Ended 30 June 1895," *Sessional Papers* (hereafter cited as *SP*), 1896, p. 75.

4 Section 35 of the Constitution Act, 1982, used the generic term *aboriginal* to refer to Indian, Inuit, and Metis peoples. The term *Aboriginal* is used throughout this paper, but the suicide cases examined involved only victims defined as "status Indian" under the 1876 Indian Act.

5 Royal Commission on Aboriginal Peoples, *Choosing Life: Special Report on Suicide among Aboriginal People* (Ottawa: Minister of Supply and Services Canada, 1995). Cathrena Primrose Narcisse critically reviews the abundant literature on Aboriginal suicide in contemporary Canada in "The Social Construction of Aboriginal Suicide" (master's thesis, Simon Fraser University, 1994). Anthropologist Peter Carstens interprets Aboriginal suicide as a *latent* function of the reserve system in "An Essay on Suicide and Disease in Canadian Indian Reserves: Bringing Durkheim Back In," *Canadian Journal of Native Studies* 29 (2000): 309–45.

6 M.J. Chandler and C.E. Lalonde, "Cultural Continuity as a Hedge against Suicide in Canada's First Nations," *Transcultural Psychiatry* 35, no. 2 (1998): 193–211.

7 Ronald Niezen, *Spirit Wars: Native North American Religions in the Age of Nation Building* (Berkeley and Los Angeles: University of California Press, 2000), 117.

8 Two recent historical studies of Aboriginal health and colonialism either make no mention of suicide or discuss it briefly in connection with residential schools: Mary-Ellen Kelm, *Colonizing Bodies: Aboriginal Health and Healing in British Columbia, 1900–50* (Vancouver: UBC Press, 1998), 74, 78, 177, and Maureen K. Lux, *Disease, Medicine, and Canadian Plains Native People, 1880–1940* (Toronto: University of Toronto Press, 2001). Similarly, major texts on Native–newcomer relations often end with discussions of Canada's escalating Aboriginal suicide rate, while the suicide rate among contemporary adolescents has likewise added fuel to the debate on residential schools: Olive Dickason, *Canada's First Nations: A History of Founding Peoples from Earliest Times* (Toronto: McClelland and Stewart, 1992), 418, and David Napier, "Sins of the Fathers: The Legacy of Indian Residential Schools," *Anglican Journal* 126 (2000): 1–16. Elizabeth Furniss explores the suicide of a residential school student in *Victims of Benevolence: Discipline and Death at the Williams Lake Residential School* (Williams Lake: Cariboo Tribal Council, 1992).

9 In *Women and Indians on the Frontier, 1825–1915* (Albuquerque: University of New Mexico Press, 1984), 74, 78, Glenda Riley notes briefly the important role that tales of suicide played in constructing Aboriginal women as beasts of burden in primitive societies. Although they do not address suicide specifically, (post)colonial historians, influenced by the work of Edward Said and Homi Bhabha, have likewise traced the manipulation of women's/cultural imagery and the construction of race in western Canada: Edward Said, *Culture and Imperialism* (New York: Vintage Books, 1994); Homi Bhabha, "Of Mimicry and Man: The Ambivalence of Colonial Discourse," in *Tensions of Empire: Colonial Cultures in a Bourgeois World*, ed. Frederick Cooper and Ann Laura Stoler (Berkeley and Los Angeles: University of California Press, 1997), 152–62; Jo-Anne Fiske, "Pocahontas's Granddaughters: Spiritual Transition and Tradition of Carrier Women of British Columbia," *Ethnohistory* 43 (1996): 663–81; Elizabeth Vibert, *Traders' Tales: Narratives of Cultural Encounters in the Columbia Plateau, 1807–1846* (Norman: University of Oklahoma Press, 1997); Sarah Carter, *Capturing Women: The Manipulation of Cultural Imagery in Canada's Prairie West* (Montreal and Kingston: McGill-Queen's University Press, 1997); Kim Greenwell, "Picturing 'Civilization': Missionary Narratives and the Margins of Mimicry," *BC Studies* 135 (2002): 3–45; Carol J. Williams, *Framing the West: Race, Gender, and the Photographic Frontier in the Pacific Northwest* (Oxford: Oxford University Press, 2003).

10 Robert F. Berkhofer, *The White Man's Indian* (New York: Alfred A. Knopf, 1978), and Daniel Francis, *The Imaginary Indian: The Image of the Indian in Canadian Culture* (Vancouver: Arsenal Pulp, 1992), discuss evolutionary anthropology and the "vanishing Indian." Anne McClintock explores the colonial figure in literature "made mad through the intersection of her race and sexuality" in *Double Crossings: Madness, Sexuality, and Imperialism* (Vancouver: Ronsdale, 2001).

11 Susan J. Johnston, "Twice Slain: Female Sex-Trade Workers and Suicide in British Columbia, 1870–1920," *Journal of the Canadian Historical Association* [new series] 5 (1994): 147. Following the lead of cultural anthropologists and historians and ethnomethodologists in the field of sociology, Johnston foregoes attaching meaning to suicide statistics (the traditional focus of Durkheimian positivists) and instead studies the meanings attached to suicide in a given culture at a given time: Jack D. Douglas, *The Social Meaning of Suicide* (Princeton, NJ: Princeton University Press, 1967), chaps. 9–13; Clifford Geertz, "Religion as a Cultural System," in *Anthropological Approaches to the Study of Religion*, ed. Michael Banton (New York: Praeger, 1966), 7–9; and Michael MacDonald and Terence R. Murphy, *Sleepless Souls: Suicide in Early Modern England* (Oxford: Oxford University Press, 1990). Victor Bailey discusses the debate between

ethnomethodologists and Durkheimian positivists in *"This Rash Act": Suicide across the Life Cycle in the Victorian City* (Stanford, CA: Stanford University Press, 1998), chap. 1.

12 Douglas, *Social Meaning of Suicide,* chaps. 9–13. In *Imperial Eyes: Travel Writing and Transculturation* (New York: Routledge, 1992), 4, Mary Louise Pratt defines contact zones as "social spaces where disparate cultures meet, dash, and grapple with each other, often in highly asymmetrical relations of domination and subordination."

13 Scholars have examined the role of alcohol consumption in colonial discourse and how alcohol laws "criminalized the colonized": Mimi Ajzenstadt, "Racializing Prohibitions: Alcohol Laws and Racial/Ethnic Minorities in British Columbia, 1871–1927," in *Regulating Lives: Historical Essays on the State, Society, the Individual, and the Law,* ed. John McLaren, Robert Menzies, and Dorothy E. Chunn (Vancouver: UBC Press, 2002), 97–119; Bonnie Duran, "Indigenous versus Colonial Discourse: Alcohol and American Indian Identity," in *Dressing in Feathers: The Construction of the Indian in American Popular Culture,* ed. S. Elizabeth Bird (Boulder, CO: Westview, 1996), 111–28; Renisa Mawani, "In Between and Out of Place: Mixed-Race Identity, Liquor, and the Law in British Columbia, 1850–1913," in *Race, Space, and the Law: Unmapping a White Settler Society*, ed. Sherene H. Razack (Toronto: Between the Lines, 2002), 47–70; Joan Sangster, "Criminalizing the Colonized: Ontario Native Women Confront the Criminal Justice System, 1920–1960," *Canadian Historical Review* 80 (1999): 32–60.

14 Robin Brownlie and Mary-Ellen Kelm explore the ethical and legal ramifications of historical studies on law and colonialism that emphasize resistance and agency and underplay the real, damaging effects of state regulation and colonialism: "Desperately Seeking Absolution: Native Agency as Colonialist Alibi?" *Canadian Historical Review* 75 (1994): 543–57. Recent studies that address the issue of resistance and representation while recognizing the coercive effects of colonialism and state regulation in western Canada include: Paige Raibmon, "Theatres of Contact: The Kwakwaka'wakw Meet Colonialism in British Columbia and at the Chicago World's Fair," *Canadian Historical Review* 81 (2000): 157–90; Peter Geller, "'Hudson's Bay Company Indians': Images of Native People and the Red River Pageant, 1920," in *Dressing in Feathers,* 65–78.

15 Inquest 1921/116, reel B2407, GR1327, British Columbia Attorney General, Inquisitions

1872–1937, British Columbia Archives (hereafter cited as BCA). The British Columbia Freedom of Information and Protection of Privacy Act prohibits certain information pertaining to inquests and inquiries after 1910 from being made public. The names of the deceased, if used, have been changed, and file identification numbers do not correspond to those of the Attorney General.

16 Johnston, "Twice Slain," 149.

17 "An Indian Suicided," *Edmonton Bulletin,* 2 Aug. 1905.

18 Cole Harris, *Making Native Space: Colonialism, Resistance, and Reserves in British Columbia* (Vancouver: UBC Press, 2002), xxiv.

19 James Edward Colhoun, Stephen Long, and William Keating, *Narrative of an Expedition to the Source of St Peter's River, Lake Winnipeck, Lake of the Woods* (Philadelphia: H.C. Carey and I. Lea, 1824), 138.

20 S.R. Steinmetz, "Suicide among Primitive Peoples," *American Anthropologist* 7 (1894): 53–60; Edward Westermarck, "Suicide: A Chapter in Comparative Ethics," *Sociological Review* 1 (1908): 12–33.

21 Ross Cox, *Adventures on the Columbian River* (New York: J. & J. Harper, 1832), 325.

22 Paul Kane, *Wanderings of an Artist* (London: Longman, Brown, Green, Longman, and Roberts, 1859), 310.

23 R.C. Lundin Brown, *Klatsassin, and Other Reminiscences of Missionary Life in British Columbia* (London: Society for Promoting Christian Knowledge, 1873), 34.

24 John Bradbury, *Travels in the Interior of America* (1817; repr., Ann Arbor: University Microfilms, 1966), 89.

25 Colhoun, Long, Keating, *Narrative,* 227, 230, 234.

26 Edward Duffield Neill, *Dahkotah Land and Dahkotah Life* (Philadelphia and Chicago: J.B. Lippincott; S.C. Griggs, 1859), 83; George Bird Grinnell similarly recounts incidents of suicide among young women in *Blackfoot Lodge Tales* (1892; repr., Lincoln: University of Nebraska Press, 2003), 216.

27 Riley, *Women and Indians,* 75, 78.

28 William Knighton, "Suicidal Mania," *Littel's Living Age,* 5 Feb. 1881, 430, quoted in Howard I. Kushner, "Women and Suicide in Historical Perspective," in *Feminist Research Methods: Exemplary Readings in the Social Sciences* (Boulder, CO: Westview, 1990), 193–6, and "Suicide,

Gender, and the Fear of Modernity in Nineteenth-Century Medical and Social Thought," *Journal of Social History* 26, no. 3 (1993): 461–90.

29 Otis T. Mason, *Women's Share in Primitive Culture* (London and New York: Macmillan, 1895), 276.

30 Nadine Schuurman, "Contesting Patriarchies: Nlaka'pamux and Stl'atl'imx Women and Colonialism in Nineteenth-Century British Columbia," *Gender, Place, and Culture: A Journal of Feminist Geography* 5 (1998): 141–58.

31 James Alexander Teit and Franz Boaz, *The Thompson Indians of British Columbia* (New York: American Museum of Natural History, 1900), 324–5.

32 Ibid., 358–9.

33 Ibid.

34 Brett Christophers, *Positioning the Missionary: John Booth Good and the Confluence of Cultures in Nineteenth-Century British Columbia* (Vancouver: UBC Press, 1998), 130.

35 John West, *The Substance of a Journal during a Residence at the Red River Colony, British North America* (London: L.B. Sicley, 1824), 141.

36 Henry C. Yarrow, *A Further Contribution to the study of the Mortuary Customs of the North American Indians* (Washington, DC: Smithsonian Institution, 1881), 109.

37 Beverly Hungry Wolf, *The Ways of My Grandmothers* (New York: Quill, 1982), 27; Alan M. Klein, "The Political Economy of Gender: A Nineteenth-Century Plains Case Study," in *The Hidden Half: Studies of Plains Indian Women,* ed. Patricia Albers and Beatrice Medicine (Washington, DC: University Press of America, 1983), 143–73 and "The Plains Truth about the Fur Trade: The Impact of Colonialism on Plains Indian Women," *Dialectical Anthropology* 7, no. 4 (1983): 308–9.

38 Colhoun, Long, and Keating, *Narrative,* 394, 293.

39 Alexander Henry and David Thompson, *Henry and Thompson Journals* (New York: F. Harper, 1897), 2: 521.

40 Karn R. Andriolo, "Masked Suicide and Culture," in *The Relevance of Culture,* ed. Morris Freilich (New York: Morris Freilich; Bergin and Garvey Publishers, 1989), 173–4; George Grinnell, "Early Blackfoot History," *American Anthropologist* [old series] 5, no. 2 (1892): 153–64.

41 "Suicide at the Jail," *Nanaimo Free Press,* 28 May 1881.

42 "Bad Character," *Nanaimo Free Press,* 29 May 1881; Coroners' Inquiries/Inquests, vol. 3, 1865/1937, 1881, GR0431, British Columbia Attorney General, BCA.

43 John Lutz, "Relating to the Country: The Lekwammen and the Extension of European Settlement," in *Beyond the City Limits: Rural History in British Columbia,* ed. Ruth Sandwell (Vancouver: UBC Press, 1999), 18.

44 Sydney L. Harring, *White Man's Law: Native People in Nineteenth-Century Canadian Jurisprudence* (Toronto: University of Toronto Press, 1998), 262.

45 Ibid., 263–4; Lutz, "Relating to the Country," 23; Indian Act, 1894, 57 & 58, c. 32, s. 8.

46 Johnston, "Twice Slain," 149; Coroners' Act 1885, *Statutes of the Province of British Columbia;* An Act Respecting Coroners, *Statutes of Alberta,* 1906, c. 15.

47 Bailey, *"This Rash Act,"* 65–6.

48 W.L. Reynolds, Indian agent, File Hills, 13 Aug. 1888, Annual Report of the DIA for the Year Ended 31 Dec. 1888, *SP* (1889), 65; Harry Guillod, agent, West Coast, Victoria, 11 Aug. 1891, DIA Annual Report for the Year Ended 1891, *SP* (1892), 118.

49 J.N. Cowey, Crime Report, Alberta Provincial Police, Wetaskiwin Detachment, 12 May 1920, file Cor-184, box 12, Coroners' Inquiries, acc. 68.261, Attorney General, Provincial Archives of Alberta (hereafter cited as PAA).

50 R.N. Wilson, Indian agent, Blood Agency, to Indian commissioner, Winnipeg, 24 Mar. 1904, file 19103-3, pt. 1, vol. 7468, reel C-14768, RG 10, Department of Indian Affairs (hereafter cited as DIA), Library and Archives Canada (hereafter cited as LAC).

51 P.C.A. Primrose, Macleod, Crime Report, "D" Division, 23 Mar. 1904, series A-1, file 373-04, vol. 274, RG 18, Royal Canadian Mounted Police (RCMP), LAC.

52 Deputy superintendent general to Indian commissioner, DIA, 10 Apr. 1898, file 99752, vol. 3900, reel C-10196, RG 10, LAC.

53 Report of J.P.B. Ostrender, Indian agent, Dec. 1937, file 1911 7-2, vol. 7469, reel C 147 69, RG 10, LAC; "Three Slain on Reserve in Saskatchewan," *Ottawa Evening Citizen,* 29 Nov. 1937.

54 J.S. Piper, Crime Report, "D" Division, Macleod, 25 Oct. 1907, file HG-681-K-1, F-2, vol. 3229, RG 18, LAC; Geoffrey York discusses the colonial myth of Aboriginal alcohol consumption in *The Dispossessed: Life and Death in Native Canada* (Toronto: Lester and Orpen Dennys, 1989), 188.

55 David Laird, Indian commissioner, to agent, Peigan Reserve, 20 Nov. 1907, file 19116-2, pt. 1, vol. 7469, RG 10, LAC.

56 Indian Maggie, 1875, vol. 1, GR 0431, BCA.

57 File 11/86, reel B2372, GR 1327, BCA.

58 File 170/09, reel B2384, GR 1327, BCA.

59 "A Verdict of Suicide" and "The Canadian Indian," *Victoria Daily Colonist*, 17 Oct. 1890.

60 File 56/90, reel B2373, GR 1327, BCA.

61 "Jumps from Fire Escape of Local Hotel to Death," *Calgary Herald*, 30 Sept. 1921; file 1554, box 28, Coroners' Inquests, acc. 67.172, PAA.

62 "Indian Found Dead: Appears To Be a Case of Suicide," *Lethbridge Herald*, 24 Dec. 1925.

63 Vol. 2, file Cor-168, box 11, acc. 68.261, PAA.

64 Bailey, *"This Rash Act,"* 69.

65 Cold Chuck Joe, G-P, file 1876, vol. 1, GR 0431, BCA; "Suicide," *Mainland Guardian,* 27 Sept. 1876; Indian John, file 11/86, reel B02372, GR 1327, BCA; "Suicide," *Mainland Guardian,* 28 Apr. 1886; Auchilla, file 44/95, reel B2375, GR 1327, BCA; Indian Edward, file 47/02, reel B02379, GR 1327, BCA.

66 Qual-i-ah, K-W, file 1877-2, vol. 2, GR 0431, BCA; Se-nel-e-air, file 52/94, reel B0237, GR 1327, BCA; Josephine, file 83/96, reel B02375, GR 1327, BCA.

67 Kelm, *Colonizing Bodies,* 92–3, 158–9.

68 Hugh A. Dempsey, ed., "The Starvation Year: *Edgar Dewdney's Diary for 1879*," pt. 1, *Alberta History,* 31 (1983): 9. Thanks to Sarah Carter for this reference.

69 Indian Act, 1894, 57 & 58, c. 32, s. 4. For literature that discusses government attempts to create patriarchal, bourgeois families, see Jean Barman, "Taming Aboriginal Sexuality: Gender, Power, and Race in British Columbia, 1850–1900," *BC Studies* 115–116 (1997–98): 237–66; Sarah Carter, "Complicated and Clouded: The Federal Administration of Marriage and Divorce among the First Nations of Western Canada, 1887–1906," in *Unsettled Pasts: Reconceiving the West through Women's History,* ed., Sarah Carter, Lesley Erickson, Patricia Roome, and Char Smith (Calgary, AB: University of Calgary Press, 2005); Julia V. Emberley, "The Bourgeois Family, Aboriginal Women, and Colonial Governance in Canada," *Signs* 27 (2001): 59–85: Pamela White, "Restructuring the Domestic Sphere: Prairie Indian Women on Reserves: Image, Ideology, and State Policy, 1880–1930" (PhD diss, McGill University, 1987).

70 DIA Annual Report, 1888, *SP* (1889), 65; "Indian Woman Suicides," *Lethbridge News,* 28 July 1904.

71 *Saskatchewan Herald,* 26 Oct. 1885.

72 Ibid., 30 Nov. 1885.

73 B-1, vol. 1421, 196A, Capital Case Files, RG 13, Department of Justice, LAC.

74 File 679-94, vol. 98, A-1, RCMP, RG 18, LAC; *Macleod Gazette,* 5 Oct. and 14 Sept. 1894.

75 P.C.H. Primrose, superintendent, "D" Division, Macleod, Crime Report, 9 July 1905, series A-1, file 550-05, vol. 301, RG 18, RCMP, LAC.

76 Corporal C.B. Miles, Stand-Off, to Officer Commanding NWMP, Macleod, 4 Oct. 1907, A-1, file 615-07, vol. 343, RG 18, RCMP, LAC; Inspector J.W.S. Grant, Crime Report, Macleod, 5 Oct. 1907; "Trusted Indian Scout Suicides," *Montreal Daily Star,* 14 Oct. 1907.

77 "Murder-Suicide at File Hills," *Regina Leader,* 19 July 1887; file 41151, vol. 3784, reel C-10192, DIA, RG 10, LAC; file 501-1887, vol. 1083, B-1, RCMP, RG 18, LAC.

78 Homer G. Barnett, *The Coast Salish of British Columbia* (Eugene: University of Oregon Press, 1955), 250.

79 File 92/91, reel B2373 GR 1327, BCA; "A Curious Mistake," *Victoria Daily Colonist,* 7 Nov. 1891.

80 File 103/02, reel B2379, GR 1327, BCA.

81 Schuurman, "Contesting Patriarchies," 141–59.

82 File 82/91, reel B2373, GR 1327, BCA.

83 File 162/97, reel B02376, GR 1327, BCA.

84 Ibid.

85 File 50/180, reel B02378, GR 1327, BCA.

86 File 1876, G-P, vol. 1, GR 0431, BCA.

87 Bailey, *"This Rash Act,"* 23; Douglas, *Social Meaning of Suicide,* chaps. 9–13.

88 For studies that connect Indigenous suicide to internalized oppression, see Paulo Freire, *Pedagogy of the Oppressed* (New York: Seabury, 1960); Lisa M. Poupart, "The Familiar Face of Genocide: Internalized Oppression among American Indians," *Hypatia* 18 (2003): 86–100; Maria YellowHorse BraveHeart and Lemyra DeBruyn, "The American Indian Holocaust: Healing Historical Unresolved Grief," *American Indian and Alaska Native Mental Health Research: Journal of the National Centre* 8 (1998): 60–82.

Social Investment in Medical Forms: The 1866 Cholera Scare and Beyond

Bruce Curtis

The nineteenth-century cholera epidemics continue to attract interest across the disciplines. Although cholera had been endemic to the Indian subcontinent for a considerable period, to the point where pilgrims were said to make offerings to a cholera deity, in the early 1800s the disease spread around the world in a series of pandemics which have been linked to the ecological havoc wreaked by British imperialism in India and to the accelerated movement of commodities and human beings coincident with the growth of the capitalist world economy. Cholera reached England in 1817 and swept through British North America in 1832, 1849, and 1854–5. Canadian mortality was last seriously affected in the 1850s, that of England and the United States in 1866, and that of parts of continental Europe, such as the city of Hamburg, in 1892. Other parts of the world were affected well into the twentieth century and, recently, the disease has been resurgent.[1]

Cholera usually appeared in the European shipping ports or in the Caribbean islands in the fall or winter months preceding its arrival in British North America. In the fall of 1865, cholera was declared to be present in continental Europe, and in the early months of 1866 it was reported in Guadeloupe and Martinique. News of its presence in those places provoked a major panic in the Canadas, heightened dramatically by reports of the arrival of the immigrant ship *England* at Halifax in early April with Asiatic cholera aboard. A ship from the same company was reported to have arrived at New York the same week with further cases.[2]

This article documents the extensive preventive public health measures undertaken by a group of Canadian public servants and medical practitioners, led especially by the fundamentalist Catholic doctor Joseph-Charles Taché, deputy minister of agriculture and statistics, to meet the threat of epidemic cholera. Taché and the others attempted to forge a new set of social alliances that would tie together central and local government bodies, doctors, shipping companies, reputable local observers, and residents of the country as a whole in the pursuit of a wide-ranging project of reform. The object was to make Canada into a healthy place, and Canadians into people who would conduct themselves in keeping with the rules of good health. Taché and his allies attempted to define health—and the rules of conduct to achieve it.

Extensive powers under the Public Health Act of 1849, together with the climate of fear generated by the cholera scare, created a conjuncture whereby existing social arrangements

Bruce Curtis, "Social Investment in Medical Forms: The 1866 Cholera Scare and Beyond," *Canadian Historical Review* 81, 3 (2000): 347–379. Reprinted with permission of the University of Toronto Press Incorporated (www.utpjournals.com).

and patterns of conduct could be problematized and targeted for reform. The cholera scare was an occasion for activists to attempt to define the boundaries of a new domain of intervention—namely, the public health—and to codify relations and practices within it. The state system was expanded dramatically, if briefly, in the face of the cholera threat, and the boundaries between public and private, or between the interests of society in health and the liberties of individuals, were redrawn. A select group of doctors, appointed by order in council in the absence of parliamentary debate or discussion, formulated detailed regulations to be followed by municipal governments and individual citizens. The group commanded extraordinary police powers and conducted an extensive public information campaign. Although cholera did not in fact reach epidemic proportions in Canada in 1866, an examination of the scare allows us to investigate such matters as the contemporary state of medical knowledge, the administrative capacities of the state system on the eve of the Confederation, and the mid-Victorian practice of social medicine in a crisis situation.

With the notable exception of the early work of Heather MacDougall, the 1866 cholera scare has been seen in Canadian literature as an anti-climax. There were no dramatic scenes of death on a large scale, and the Public Health Act was not renewed at the end of its six-month term. MacDougall, by contrast, drawing on the English literature on the "nineteenth-century revolution in government," in which the trio composed of the "Sanitary Idea," the "Educational Idea," and the "Inspective Function" influenced the course of state formation, argued that the 1866 scare had durable consequences on public health in Toronto. It put sanitary matters on the local government agenda and markedly increased public awareness of these matters. City council passed a detailed public health bylaw and cre-

ated the logistical arrangements necessary for a targeting of health matters. The cholera scare also stimulated the growth of a local sanitary movement. Although a period of lassitude followed the non-appearance of cholera, arrangements put in place in 1866 could be revived in the event of later public health crises.[3]

My investigation of conditions in Kingston and Montreal suggests that the level of activity which accompanied the scare in Toronto took place in these two cities as well, although in Montreal the push for reform was organized more formally in groups such as the 1866 Association sanitaire.[4] Further research into the many other municipalities in which boards of health were formed in 1866 is needed to make a more systematic assessment of the long-term consequences of the measures taken to meet the crisis. Still, that three of the country's largest cities saw the emergence of public health movements in the wake of the 1866 scare suggests that a more detailed investigation may be rewarding.

This article will focus particularly on the activities of the central government, for the rules, regulations, and advice offered by the Central Board of Health framed local health initiatives, and the provisions for quarantine and medical inspection of immigrant shipping were seen as the first line of defence against the disease. Before investigating the mobilization of the Canadian state system and discussing projects pursued in the 1866 cholera scare, however, I will examine some of the ways the phenomenon of the cholera has been taken up in the scholarly literature and provide further contextualization of Canadian events.

Cholera and the Social Question

The palpable terror inspired by the cholera in nineteenth-century Europe and America was not a measure of its importance among contemporary causes of mortality and morbidity. In England, for instance, it killed considerably fewer people than did scarlatina, yellow fever, or even smallpox, and malaria was probably more serious in the Canadas. However, its mysterious and dramatic spread, its ability to kill people in apparent good health without warning in less than a day, its tendency to ignore social distinctions, and the coincidence of the nineteenth-century epidemics with urbanization and rapid social, political, and economic change all combined to make cholera a privileged object of administration and investigation. It is no exaggeration to assert that in some years of the 1860s, people in the Canadas participated in a "cholera culture," for the disease was present in science, politics, administration, trade and commerce, religion, music, and poetry.

Cholera played an important role in the general development of the sciences of both social observation and social/medical administration. In Paris, according to François Delaporte, the 1832 epidemic led to the development and extension of practices of sanitary surveillance, the emergence of what he called "political medicine," and the proliferation of discourses about moral hygiene. The legitimacy of public health initiatives as such was bolstered by the inability of clinicians to locate the site or agent of the disease and the impotence of therapeutics to cure it. Catherine Kudlick goes so far as to suggest that the 1832 Parisian epidemic had a formative influence on the class identity of an urban bourgeoisie confronted by the rage of a population convinced that plague had been inflicted on it consciously as punishment for its revolutionary activities or as a means of reducing the supply of labour power.[5]

Mary Poovey has stressed the importance of investigations into social conditions in Manchester, conducted in the wake of the 1832 epidemic by the young Dr James Kay (later Sir James Kay-Shuttleworth), in drawing connections between the individual body and the social body. Kay, a founding member of the Manchester Statistical Society, contributed to the formation of a style of social observation that proved remarkably influential and durable. The fear and misery provoked by the cholera sent him out into the working-class neighbourhoods; and his study of them publicized the centrality of the "social question," the conditions of reproduction of the new industrial working class, to public health.[6]

From 1849 onwards in England, attempts to deal with the disease led to the convening of "consensus conferences" at which doctors and administrators sought to determine cholera's nosology. They hoped to define the measures required to prevent its spread and to cure its victims. But consensus proved to be elusive. As early as 1849, for instance, John Snow had published his claim that the disease reproduced itself in its victims' intestines and was transmitted to others through the accidental ingestion of a victim's evacuations, typically in polluted water.[7] Snow's analysis was not considered to be definitive. While William Farr of the General Register Office, for instance, thought Snow's hypothesis promising, he was more enticed by his own demonstration that mortality from cholera in the 1849 London epidemic was inversely proportional to the height of victims' residences above the Thames. This demonstration tended to reinforce an anti-contagionist analysis, in which the disease was held to be spread by the miasmas given off by the decay and putrefaction of human, animal, and vegetable waste. The notoriously polluted Thames was a prime source of miasmatic contamination. At the same time, a wide variety of competing interpretations—humoral, telluric, electric, atmospheric, ozonic, and so on—continued to coexist.

Snow's position was reinforced in 1855 by studies of comparative mortality rates among people living in the same London streets who drank water coming from different water companies. Those drinking water from the Thames tidal basin, heavily polluted with sewage, had a mortality rate from cholera about four times that of those drinking from an unpolluted source. In the same decade, microscopic investigations led to the conclusion that the evacuations of cholera victims contained a specific organic entity.

None of these arguments was definitive, and many people found the idea that the human body could contain living organisms capable of producing disease repugnant in principle. The proposition that a microscopic entity could cause the dramatic effects associated with cholera seemed incredible. Most European and American doctors, it has been suggested, combined propositions from different cholera theories in their practice, despite the rigidly ideological support for the miasmatic view proposed by such figures as Edwin Chadwick and Florence Nightingale.[8]

For those interested in the reform of public health in nineteenth-century Europe and America, the miasmatic, anti-contagionist, or sanitarian view was particularly congenial, as Perry Williams's interesting study of the English Ladies' National Association for the Diffusion of Sanitary Knowledge, founded in 1857, suggests.[9] The adoption of the Chadwickian formula "all disease is smell" democratized medical expertise in the middle classes, making it possible for anyone with a sense of smell to identify causes of ill health. Broad consensus in favour of practical sanitary measures, such as the emptying of privy pits and cesspools and the improvement of drainage and water supply, was relatively easy to achieve, even in the absence of precise clinical knowledge.

Moreover, Williams suggests, anti-contagionist approaches meshed well with relations of class and gender domination in England. They authorized men in the dominant classes to struggle inside state institutions for the reform of social infrastructures, while authorizing women in the same classes to undertake home visitation in working-class districts to teach the poor how they might live. Sanitarianism tended to transform the health question into a matter of education and morality, distancing it from the distribution of social resources. Still, calls for the provision of urban infrastructure had the potential to make public health questions into questions of political economy.

The organization studied by Williams was close to the National Association for the Promotion of Social Science, which tended to see the "social question" as susceptible to scientific solution through systematic observation and intervention based on a knowledge of the "facts." In the domain of health, such a solution was sought through "totalizing" initiatives, such as the construction of statistical profiles of mortality, and through individualizing techniques focused on teaching people the arts of healthy living.[10] In short, until the increasing acceptance of Robert Koch's 1884 isolation of the *vibrio cholerae* displaced the locus of medical expertise from the noses of the bourgeoisie towards the microbiological laboratory, the nosology of cholera was characterized by a fertile uncertainty that sustained many different social interventions in the name of health.[11]

Instances of scientific uncertainty have been especially interesting to those working in the field of social studies of scientific knowledge. Uncertainty creates opportunities for world making. Faced with uncertainty (scientific, but also social uncertainty more generally), strategically located groups and individuals may attempt to configure the unknown in keeping with their own interests and projects, enlisting allies in networks of support to sustain their positions.[12]

The 1866 Canadian cholera scare was a moment of particularly compelling uncertainty. Government administrators, politicians, newspaper editors, doctors, and others did not know whether cholera would reach Canada. They did not even know what cholera was exactly or how best to deal with it. Yet the government was under intense pressure to act quickly and decisively. It fell to Joseph-Charles Taché and the doctors associated with him in the Central Board of Health to define the nature of the crisis and to take appropriate steps in consequence. For Taché, this was a set of opportunities not to be missed, an occasion both to extend initiatives for the production of social statistics and to install his own fundamentalist conception of Catholic morality as the art of healthy living.[13]

Canadian public health legislation was based on similar British law, and, from the 1840s on, Canadians drew upon the information from expert "consensus" conferences on cholera convened by the imperial government. In the 1830s, French authorities had distributed pamphlets containing public health advice, which may also have influenced Canadian officials. As in the United States and Britain, the Canadian government relied heavily on quarantine as a first line of defence. What was unusual in Canadian terms in the 1866 scare was the alacrity with which both preventive measures were taken and social expertise was attributed to medical doctors. Also unusual was the stimulus given to attempts to capture and reconfigure first, social relations in statistical forms, and, second, personal comportment in keeping with newly formulated rules of good health.

The First Reports

On 1 April 1865 Doctor R.L. MacDonnell of Montreal wrote to the minister of agriculture to warn him of the apparent danger posed by the presence of infectious disease in European ports. MacDonnell, a member of the Central Board of Health in 1849,[14] reminded the minister that it was he who had predicted the arrival of the 1847 typhus epidemic and that, on that occasion, no one had paid him any heed until the first great wave of famine immigration reached the country. As a result, there had been insufficient accommodation for the sick at the Grosse Isle quarantine station. The sick and the healthy had remained confined together in close quarters on the immigrant ships, which had been undersupplied with the necessities of life. A great many people had died, and epidemic fever soon spread to all the Canadian cities.

MacDonnell cited articles he had seen in the English medical journal the *Lancet* to bolster his claims that typhus had reached epidemic proportions in the ports of Glasgow and Liverpool. He pressed the minister to determine the ports of embarkation of passengers for Canada and to take immediate steps for the organization of a more extensive quarantine at Grosse Isle. Copies of his letter were sent to Taché, as deputy minister of agriculture, and to superintendant A. Von Iffland of Grosse Isle.[15]

This foretaste of medical panic soon amounted to nothing. The evidence offered by MacDonnell was not considered sufficiently alarming to provoke any extraordinary measures for the reception of immigrants. The arrangements at Grosse Isle, designed by the chief emigrant agent, A.C. Buchanan, remained unchanged. Perhaps Buchanan was still congratulating himself on a recent British imperial survey of colonial arrangements for the reception of immigrants which had given the Canadas an excellent rating.[16] In any case, the 1865 immigration season proved to be unexceptional.

Still, the immigration officers were on the alert. They tried to take action against the captain of the *President Harbitz* of Bergen, who did not stop at Grosse Isle and claimed ignorance of the regulations. They were alarmed that other captains followed suit, and complained that there were insufficient copies of immigration regulations intended for distribution by the river pilots to foreign captains. The brigue *B.L. George* was subjected to disinfection, although it seemed clean, because there had been three deaths from yellow fever on board. The *Glorian* was detained, even though as a former man o'war it was exempt from the provisions of the Passenger Act, when Von Iffland discovered four sailors on board suffering from smallpox. Buchanan warned Taché of a loophole in the law concerning the medical inspection of actual or former military ships.[17]

Immigration officials had a heightened awareness of the dangers posed by cholera. In his 1865 annual report on the Grosse Isle station, Von Iffland claimed that he had organized his hospital in anticipation of the disease. He repeated a warning about the danger posed by several ships that had not stopped for inspection. He stressed that the statements of ships' captains about their passengers' health could not be trusted. Several captains had sworn that their crews were in excellent health, but a medical inspection had revealed otherwise. Von Iffland sent to Ottawa a copy of the report of the Imperial Cholera Commissioners describing the conditions for the propagation of cholera, and also criticized the 1849 Public Health Act. In his view, the act contained only reactive measures, while cholera demanded preventive sanitary initiatives.[18]

Towards the end of 1865 the press in Canada began to carry more and more alarming reports of the presence of cholera in Europe. In January 1866 the news spread that the disease was epidemic in the Caribbean. Editors predicted it would arrive on the American continent in April or May and would "then travel northward with the rapidity of a prairie fire, increasing in intensity day by day with the heat of the sun."[19] City and village residents were increasingly uneasy. In Toronto, on 14 February, the university medical faculty met with the municipal Board of Health to consider steps to meet the threat. On 26 February the editor of the Hamilton *Spectator*

announced to his readers that "the dread pestilence, cholera, which wasteth at noonday, is now knocking at our very doors for admission, and experience sufficiently teaches all who will heed the lessons of the past, that this city cannot escape the unwelcome visitant. To prepare for it in the fullest sense and minutest particular is but the commonest wisdom. By all means have your cellars, alleyways, out-houses, gardens, yards, cisterns and wells thoroughly cleansed. An ounce of preventative is better than a pound of cure."[20] Hamilton City Council moved quickly to take coercive measures, establishing a Board of Health and placing two officers of police at its disposal. Citizens were instructed to proceed without delay to clean up the city.[21]

In Kingston, on 14 February, the mayor issued a proclamation under the municipal health bylaw instructing residents that "all Yards, Cellars, Stables, Outhouses and other Buildings and Enclosures, Lanes or Alleys, shall be thoroughly cleansed of all Filth, Dirt, Nuisance Soil, or other Impurities, by the owners or persons occupying the same Before the 15th Day of March, Proximo." The chief of police and his constables were collectively named municipal health officers and charged with supervising the cleansing of all cess pools and privy pits. Those refusing to cooperate were subject to a fine of 20 shillings. The mayor also declared that pigs and slaughterhouses were banned from within city limits effective 1 March. The filth collected by cleaning the city was to be deposited on the channel ice in front of Point Frederick. On 15 February Kingston doctors assembled to consider preventive measures against cholera.[22]

Similar initiatives were taken by other colonial municipalities. In Montreal Dr J.-P. Rottot, described in the press as "l'une des sommités médicales dans cette ville," a founding member of the Canadian Medical Association, gave a public lecture at the Institut-Médical on 1 February to explain the essential nature of the cholera. The disease attacked "le principe vital" and spread by means of dangerous miasmas. It originated in India, where it had been caused by "l'habitude des Indiens de jetter leurs morts dans le Gange." Without explaining how such miasmas managed to make it to Canada, Rottot reported that in London, England, the municipality had created a commission of medical experts who travelled throughout the city to "prévenir le fléau par des prescriptions hygiéniques. ou du moins l'arrêter dès ses débuts. On assure que cette commission eut les plus grands succès."[23]

At the Montreal City Council on 3 February, the medical committee charged with matters of vaccination warned that cholera would arrive in the city in the spring and proposed "que l'on ordonne au commencement d'avril une inspection générale et soignée de toute la ville, que les quartiers soient divisés en sous-districts, à chacun desquels sera assigné un comité de visiteurs dont l'un au moins sera médécin."[24] Three weeks later, council received a petition from a citizens' group urging "la nécessité pressante de faire et de mettre en vigueur les règlements sanitaires qui pourront assurer les vidanges complètes de tous les puisards et fosses d'aisance dans les limites de la ville, avant la fin de l'hiver; l'enlèvement, aussitôt après la cessation de la gelée, de toutes les ordures qui se trouvent à la surface des cours, des ruelles et des autres localités; la mise à blanc des chaux des murs et clôtures de toutes les cours et enclos; l'absence de tous les dépôts d'ordures et d'immondices, et les vidanges de tous les privés dans les cours, des puisards et des canaux à découvert et exposés en plein air."[25] Le Pays claimed to speak for the city's doctors in criticizing as completely inadequate the corporation's proposal to have a single medical officer of health, despite the defence offered by M. Devlin, chairman of the health committee, that the city would choose a bilingual doctor and that he would have ten police officers at his disposal to inspect people's yards. "On a compris à Ottawa l'inefficacité de la mesure montréalaise," declared the paper, "puisse notre conseil de ville le comprendre à son tour."[26]

While the municipal government struggled over the form of its sanitary organization with some members demanding the creation of a board of health and others supporting the nomination of a single medical officer of health, the press and citizens' groups were increasingly alarmed. A delegation of bakers petitioned for the formulation of regulations to govern them in case of an epidemic. Letter writers to the newspapers denounced the members of the city's health committee as stupid and wasteful. The committee was suggesting that holes be drilled in the harbour ice and that the contents of the city's privies and cess pools be dumped into them. One correspondent declaimed, "et ce sont des hommes d'une pareille intelligence qu'on nomme pour veiller à la santé publique! Leur place serait plutôt dans un asile d'aliénés." On 7 April the chief of police in Montreal published an ordinance regulating the disposal of waste and the cleansing of the city.[27]

Pressure was mounting on the central government in Ottawa to proclaim the Public Health Act. The initiatives of the urban councils, such as in Kingston, were probably illegal since they sought legitimacy in the act, which came into force only for a renewable six-month period on proclamation. The city clerk from London, Canada West, demanded rapid government action to prevent an epidemic, and similar demands came from a variety of localities. From Ancaster, Canada West, for instance, James Wilson wrote in March requesting an immediate proclamation of the Public Health Act and the creation of local boards of health, "as we have a large floating population here connected with the factories, and as we have no municipal functions as a village and the near proximity to Hamilton and Dundas makes it more urgent that we act early in the matter."[28]

Central Government Initiatives

Fearing a repetition of the scenes of horror witnessed by the country in 1832, 1849, and 1854–5. the government acted early. In cabinet on 20 February 1866, Thomas D'Arcy McGee, the minister of agriculture, who was responsible for immigration and quarantine, won approval for the proclamation of the Public Health Act and the creation of the Central Board of Health. His deputy, Joseph-Charles Taché, drafted a pamphlet entitled *Memorandum on Cholera,* which contained practical advice for dealing with cholera, and arranged for the Queen's printer to typeset the Public Health Act, which was to be included in the pamphlet, in readiness for a rapid press run.[29] A group of medical doctors, soon to be appointed to the Central Board of Health, was summoned to Ottawa for a national cholera conference on 17 March. In the meantime, McGee proposed to cabinet that the government import 10,000 pounds of lime to be distributed by the Board of Health as a disinfectant to the Quebec Marine and Emigrant Hospital and throughout the colony.[30]

The March medical conference in Ottawa lasted about ten days. It was an innovative event in which eight doctors, with MacDonnell in the chair and Taché as "reporter," considered the existing store of knowledge about the nature of cholera, its mode of transmission, and the preventive and therapeutic measures to be adopted in dealing with it. The participants spent part of their time going through Taché's draft pamphlet paragraph by paragraph, approving it for publication, before moving on to the formulation of a set of public health regulations.[31]

The *Memorandum* was a remarkable document. Given a lack of consensus around the nosology of the cholera, Taché blended contagionist, anti-contagionist, and humoral approaches in his suggestions for how people should deal with the threat of epidemic. Sanitary remedies and precautions tended to dominate, since William Marsden, the leading Canadian contagionist, was not among those invited to the conference. But the practical advice Taché offered to citizens about what they should do and how they should live to protect themselves from disease was meant to hold good even if cholera did not arrive. His ostensibly medical advice in fact moved easily from the medical to the moral. Taché also insisted repeatedly that only regular medical doctors should be allowed to treat cholera. He urged individuals and local government bodies to observe all conditions in their localities carefully should the disease appear.[32]

The publication and widespread distribution of the *Memorandum* was one element in a three-pronged official attack on the threat of cholera. The other elements concerned, first, the reorganization of immigration regulations and arrangements, and, second, the initiatives taken by the Central Board of Health, including the elaboration of detailed regulations to be followed by local boards of health and the publication of advice in various forms to colonial residents.

The Immigration Apparatus

Immigration and quarantine arrangements were under the supervision of the minister of agriculture and statistics and did not depend for their operation on the proclamation of the Public Health Act. Given claims that it was England's quarantine system that spared that country from cholera after 1866, Canadian quarantine regulations are of particular interest.[33]

D'Arcy McGee's memorandum on quarantine and immigration received cabinet approval, and new quarantine regulations were proclaimed and published in the official *Gazette* on 9 April 1866. These regulations attempted to close loopholes in past practice by covering all ships—those carrying freight and passengers; those in ballast, if they came from outside the colony; and Canadian tugs that had had foreign ships in tow. All were to report to Grosse Isle for inspection, with a further inspection to be conducted at the Port of Quebec. The river pilots were made responsible for distributing copies of the regulations to all masters of vessels, and for bringing vessels to anchor off Grosse Isle. On arrival off the station, they were to fly the ship's national flag at full mast, unless there was sickness aboard, in which case they were to fly it at half mast.

The medical personnel at Grosse Isle would inspect each ship and make a determination about its condition and its passengers' health, taking such sanitary precautions as they felt to be necessary. Most probably through the systematizing influence of Joseph-Charles Taché, the determination of the medical condition of ships was now to be made with the help of a questionnaire and records were to be kept. Medical officers were required to ask ships' captains a series of eleven questions and to record and preserve the answers. The port physicians at Quebec were to ask a similar set of questions and again record the answers. Clearly, the occasion was used to generate more than information about the threat of cholera.

Although apparently anodyne to modern observers, questionnaires—like lists of rules, regulations, and memoranda—are crucial instruments and sites for investment in forms. Indeed, the statement itself is deceptively mundane: social relations may seem to be invested in forms in the sense that certain communicable dimensions of them are translated into entities on a written schedule, known as a form. But investment, in the sense employed in social studies of scientific knowledge, is a concept richer in signification than this statement suggests. It means investment

in the economic sense of the expenditure of resources, especially expenditure directed towards those elementary forms that subtend human practice, such as the creation and maintenance of systems of time discipline, weights and measures, quality standards, or professional codes of conduct. It also carries the related meanings of laying hold of or seizing (armies at war invest enemy positions), and of investiture: clothing in a particular garb and enduing with particular attributes or qualities. Laurent Thévenot writes of ways of categorizing things and relations so that the protocols to be followed in dealing with them may be determined.[34]

It is through investment in forms that projects seek to render human conduct stable, predictable, and open to scrutiny. It is through investment in forms that objects real or imagined are identified and defined in ways that render them susceptible to practical intervention. Formalization, argues Pierre Bourdieu, allows one to move "from a logic which is immersed in the particular case to a logic independent of the individual case." Successful investments in forms create "that constancy which ensures calculability over and above individual variations and temporal fluctuations."[35]

Investment in forms identifies objects of intervention in bounded domains so they may be seized and ordered according to some protocol. The posing of a series of questions to ships' captains was an attempt to determine the medical attributes with which their vessels should be endued so they could be inserted appropriately into the quarantine apparatus. Attempts to come to grips with the cholera threat stimulated other and more general attempts to invest social relations in statistical forms—Taché's central mandate as the official in charge of the Canadian statistical apparatus.[36]

At Grosse Isle station, captains were to identify themselves, their vessels, and their ports and dates of departure. They were to state what cargo they carried and where it had been loaded, the points they had touched en route to Canada, and whether fever had been present in any of them. They were to report the number of persons on board at sailing and to give an account of disease and deaths during the voyage, with causes for these deaths. The medical officer was to inquire into the identity of any other ships with which they had communicated while in transit, before noting the presence of any lunatic, idiotic, deaf, dumb, blind, or infirm persons unaccompanied by persons able to support them. If a captain's manner or answers roused the medical officer's suspicions, he had full power to demand access to the ship's log and any other records.[37]

The medical officers at Grosse Isle were granted extensive powers under the regulations. They could give a ship a "clean bill of health" and allow it to proceed. They could cause passengers found to be ill to disembark and detain them in isolation in the island hospital. Or they could cause all passengers on a ship where there had been infectious disease, or where it was in an unsanitary condition, to spend time in quarantine on the island. They could disinfect ships before allowing them to continue their voyage, or they could place ships in quarantine and detain them off the island until they considered them to be in a healthy condition. They could destroy offending items of baggage. Captains allowed to proceed who had left some of their passengers on the island were required to post a bond to cover their onward passage to Quebec, as well as an amount per diem to cover the cost of their care for the number of days the medical officer estimated they must remain.

The second line of defence was the inspection at the Port of Quebec. Here the inspecting physician would again question captains about outbreaks of disease on the voyage from Grosse Isle and detain those ships where disease was present. The previous regulatory investment of a ship was to be verified by the captain's producing the licence or passport granted to it at the station. Ships that made it to port and were found to harbour infectious disease were immediately to raise a yellow flag, and all commerce and intercourse with them were to cease. Ships found to be in a healthy condition were allowed to continue into inland commerce.

The new immigration regulations also dealt with the personnel at Grosse Isle and their powers. The station was to be under the supervision of a medical superintendent aided by such officers as the government might choose to name. The superintendent or his deputy was to be a justice of the peace with a jurisdiction extending for a mile in all directions around the island, and he was given extensive powers to regulate the movement of ships' passengers. No one was to have any intercourse or communication with the island except under licence from the superintendent. The regulations also included an explicit prohibition of venality, declaring that the superintendent was to ensure that all "persons within the same limits are fairly dealt with and subjected to no imposition nor exacting of rewards from the paid officers and employees of the Station."[38]

The quarantine apparatus was soon extended farther to the east. In early May, while fears of an epidemic were still intense, the Department of Agriculture received a resolution of the county council, a grand jury presentment, and a petition bearing the names of about three hundred men from New Carlisle calling for the establishment of a board of health and a permanent quarantine station at that place. The petitioners claimed that a local captain had died of cholera and, since their port was 600 miles from Grosse Isle, they had no protection through its quarantine arrangements. On 8 May the government announced the appointment of a medical officer for the inspection of ships at New Carlisle. Those ships found to contain infectious disease would be ordered to quarantine at Grosse Isle. Similarly, residents of Gaspé sought the establishment of a quarantine station because many ships landed there to deal with the customs officers.[39]

The steamship companies involved in the transatlantic trade, one of which was subsidized by the government as the official mail carrier, were particularly incensed by the delays occasioned by the stop at Grosse Isle. Despite an initial suggestion in his *Memorandum* that the government might be willing to consider exempting steamers from the regulations if they carried a ship's physician executed sanitary measures, and were reported free of disease at Father's Point (where the river pilots embarked), Taché informed Allan Brothers on 13 April that their vessels would be subject to the regulations. He suggested that, to speed matters up, they should announce their arrival off Grosse Isle by firing a cannon.[40]

Hugh Allan, whose company was notorious for its high fares, protested that it was useless to fire a cannon: no one would hear it if the wind was in the wrong direction, and, in any case, the inspecting physicians would not board vessels between dusk and dawn. Since his ships were bound to carry a physician under the Passenger Act, Allan argued that they should be allowed to proceed to Quebec without stopping if the physician reported at Father's Point that there was no sickness aboard. When Taché was unresponsive to this suggestion, Allan proposed that the government put an inspecting physician of its own aboard at Father's Point who would be authorized to allow healthy ships to continue to Quebec. Other complaints addressed the requirement of a second inspection at the Port of Quebec: the companies claimed there was not enough space off the port for all ships to wait, and that inspection was useless here because many ships unloaded between Grosse Isle and the port.[41]

On 8 May the regulations were amended to avoid congestion at Quebec by allowing ships with a clean bill of health to await inspection anywhere in the river from the Isle d'Orléans to Sillery. Inspection regulations were also relaxed

for the government mail contractor. A medical inspector would board the mail steamers at Father's Point and travel on them to Quebec. If they were free from disease en route, they were exempted from stopping at Grosse Isle. If disease was discovered, the quarantine regulations would apply to them. It seems, however, that the physician appointed, a Dr Taschereau, conducted his inspection only at Father's Point, and Taché and Buchanan were alarmed when the *Peruvian* made port on 18 June after there had been two deaths at sea. The deaths were not from cholera, but Taschereau should have sent the ship to Grosse Isle. Buchanan expressed his concern that this loophole in the *cordon sanitaire* would cause public alarm.[42]

Although the mail contractor received preferential treatment, both Taché and the Central Board of Health remained adamant that all other steamers be subject to the quarantine regulations. Allan Brothers protested again at the end of July that two of their Glasgow steamers had been forced to wait off the immigration station from 8 o'clock in the evening until the following morning for inspection, while it was now clear that no cholera cases would reach Canada from England or Ireland. They criticized the continuing application of the regulations to their vessels when the danger was posed by communication with the American states, against which the quarantine apparatus was impotent. Taché refused to budge and noted that all his department's inland agents, as well as all customs officials, had strict instructions to report any cases of cholera by telegram to Ottawa immediately.[43]

Grosse Isle in the 1866 Season

The Grosse Isle station was opened in the last week of April 1866. The requirement to board and inspect every vessel under the new immigration regulations led superintendent Von Iffland to demand the engagement of two new boatmen and two medical assistants. He had already hired an infirmier for the hospital, and claimed he would have to board as many as 140 or 150 vessels a day at the height of the spring and fall shipping seasons. In anticipation of deaths at the station, the government subsidized the expenses of resident Catholic and Anglican chaplains and dispatched two young medical assistants, Doctors Lachaine and Montizambert, to the station on 12 May. However, it quickly became apparent that while there was much work to do, Von Iffland's estimates of traffic were exaggerated.[44]

Between the opening of the station and 16 May, 124 ships were inspected. Although sixty people were in the island hospital, most of them with measles, there was no sign of cholera. Von Iffland used Frederick Montizambert as his boarding officer, a duty he described as "requiring strong health, and muscular activity," while Lachaine, being "of a weaker temperament," was left to attend to the hospital patients. Buchanan, the chief emigrant agent, reported that 2421 people were landed at Quebec in the first half of May and there had been no sign of sickness at sea on any of the ships carrying them.[45]

On 23 May Von Iffland reported that 237 vessels had been inspected, but there was still no sign of cholera. The most common form of illness discovered was syphilis and venereal disease among the members of the ships' crews. Congestion was caused on the island by the ruling of the Central Board of Health that passengers who had suffered from measles or diarrhoea during their ocean passage should debark to recover their strength before proceeding inland, as well as by the quarantine of other passengers for whom captains were required to post a bond. Given that the Ottawa Cholera Conference had concluded that cholera was usually preceded by a condition involving diarrhoea called Cholerine, which might or might not pass without becoming cholera, the requirement that those affected debark at the station was a reasonable precaution. By mid-June, however, when a total of 489 ships had been inspected, Von Iffland was calling for a bi-weekly steamer service between the station and Quebec to take off the healthy.[46]

Although Von Iffland's weekly reports provide a thorough account of immigrant arrivals at the station and of admissions to the island hospital, they quickly took on a routine character as no sign of epidemic disease troubled the work of inspection and quarantine. He did, however, lose his infirmier to typhus contracted in the island hospital in mid-July. He was forced to defend his management against claims that there was free commerce between the station and the surrounding district, and he complained of the ragged equipment and uniforms of his boatmen and their low pay. Still, fears of a public health crisis proved unfounded. In June, Von Iffland ceased giving information about all the ships he inspected, and reported only on passenger vessels.[47]

With no cholera epidemic in the shipping season, the Grosse Isle station closed as usual in the first week of November 1866. Von Iffland's team had inspected 956 vessels, 172 of them passenger ships, and 271 people had been admitted to the island hospital—the most serious cases being from typhus, smallpox, and measles. Between the arrival of the passenger steamer *Hibernian* on 1 May and that of the *Nova Scotian* on 14 November, 28,648 people debarked at Quebec, and there was a total of ten reported deaths at the quarantine station. Buchanan noted that although the "extreme vigilance" used in "enforcing a rigorous quarantine" on the St Lawrence shipping placed his department in a position of financial deficit, the expense incurred was worthwhile because it had "calmed the public mind."[48]

The Central Board of Health

The Public Health Act of 1849 (12 Vic., c. 8) was an emergency measure granting extensive temporary powers to a centrally appointed board of health, including the power to instruct local boards of health. Municipal governments were required to appoint a local board of health within two days of being petitioned to do so by ten resident householders, although the central government could also proclaim geographical limits to the operation of the act and, perhaps, also specify places where local boards were to be organized. In 1866, fear of the epidemic led to the organization of boards of health in at least thirty-eight municipalities in Canada East and fourteen in Canada West.[49]

The Public Health Act empowered the Central Board of Health to issue such regulations as it saw fit to provide for the cleansing and disinfecting of places, the removal of nuisances and the burying of bodies, and the dispensing of medicine and the provision of medical assistance. The central board could require local boards at their own expense to remove inhabitants of infected dwellings from their houses and to lodge them elsewhere as long as the act was in effect. On their own account, any two of the three members of a local board of health were given extensive police powers to enter any place in which they believed a person had died from an epidemic disease, or which they believed to be in a "filthy or degraded condition," and to enforce their orders on the inhabitants, if necessary with the assistance of a constable. Anyone disobeying any order under the act was liable to a fine or imprisonment, and the central board's regulations were to be in effect as soon as they appeared in the Canada *Gazette*.

In the name of public health in times of crisis, the government was prepared to abrogate individual liberties of property, privacy, and movement while specifying regulations for the conduct of individuals in relation to themselves and others. This is not to argue that the public and its health were simply artifacts of the cholera scare. Nonetheless, the contours of a domain of public health were specified and delimited in part through practical attempts to define and engage the mysterious threat posed by the cholera. The scare was thus an important site for state formation. It was implicated in the specification of a new domain of rule, and in the shaping of instruments and practices for operations within that domain. In practical administrative terms, investing the cholera through medical forms led to the construction of new health-focused relations between central and local authorities, to attempts to extend practices of inspection, even into a formerly "private" realm, and to further attempts at the standardization and centralization of knowledge. Preparing for the cholera propelled novel attempts at moral regulation through ideological initiatives that aimed at influencing common sense and personal habits, and at extending the authority and social leadership of state-sanctioned experts. From another point of view, attempts to deal with the threat of cholera sustained a novel articulation of the technologies of domination (that is, objectification, discipline, and meaning-making) with the technologies of self-formation (living according to the rules of health) characteristic of the liberal, "governmental" state.[50]

The Public Health Act left much of the detail of regulation to the administrative discretion of the Central Board of Health, although the permanent Quebec City Health Act (12 Vic., c. 116), passed in the same parliamentary session, provides a clearer view of how far government was prepared to go to root out potential sources of disease. Regulations under the Quebec act were to be superseded by those of the Central Board in cases where the Public Health Act was proclaimed. Still, the urban legislation attempted to make it possible to construct an effective and regular *cordon sanitaire* around the main colonial port of entry.

"An Act to provide for the health of the City of Quebec" exempted the regulations of the city Board of Health from central government approval, protected its health officers from prosecution for executing the board's regulations, and relaxed the conditions under which the board could prosecute citizens. The authority of the urban board extended to virtually all matters deemed injurious to health in the city, the surrounding area, and on board vessels in the harbour. On the strength of a warrant from a justice of the peace, during the day time two members of the board could enlist such police assistance as they required to inspect any place they considered to pose a threat to health and order the inhabitants at their own expense to remove the threat in question. They could seize and destroy unwholesome food. If contagious or epidemic disease existed in the city, the board as a whole could limit the number of persons allowed in any building. Other provisions allowed the health board or the city council to remove infected prisoners from the gaol and to regulate the rag trade. The Quebec City Health Act also contained a reporting clause requiring all city doctors to report cases of infectious disease in a manner specified by city council on pain of a £5 fine.

Preliminary steps for the appointment of a Central Board of Health and the proclamation of the Public Health Act were taken on 20 February 1866, before the Ottawa cholera conference. The conference rose on or about 30 March, and the act was proclaimed and cabinet approval granted for the nomination of members of the board at the beginning of the second week of April. In an effort to save expense, D'Arcy McGee arranged matters so that the five Ottawa members of the board, Doctors Taché, J.C. Beaubien, J.A. Grant, Hamnett Hill, and E. Vancortland, would be a quorum for routine

business and they alone would be paid for their services. Hill and Grant were elected vice-president and secretary, respectively, at the board's first meeting, with R.L. MacDonnell of Montreal as president. The other members provided the board with connections to the main colonial towns and cities: C.S. Badeau in Three Rivers, J.E. Landry in Quebec, J.R. Dickson in Kingston, W.T. Aikins in Toronto, J.D. Macdonald in Hamilton, and Charles Moore in London. At precisely the same period when regular doctors were extending their agitations for legal professional recognition, they found themselves placed to exercise leadership in a major social panic.[51]

It was 28 April, however, before the board met for the first time, and while the regulations it formulated to be followed by local boards of health received cabinet approval on 3 May, it was 8 May, almost a month after widespread reports of cholera on the ship *England* at Halifax, before the regulations were gazetted. Many municipalities had organized boards of health immediately on proclamation of the Public Health Act, but these bodies lacked authority to act in the absence of regulations from the central board. Thus the Kingston nominee to the central board, John Dickson, pointed out in his letter of acceptance to the provincial secretary on 20 April that the new Board of Health formed in his city after the proclamation of the act "determined to commence a house to house visitation at once, and enforce the provisions of the Health Act, but, they find that they have not any inherent power in themselves, but derive it all from the Central Board and consequently they are powerless to enforce any sanitary measures until such time as the Central Board will meet." Similarly from Cobourg on 26 April, Dr James Beatty complained in a petition to the governor general that "no 'Regulations' have been issued and our civic authorities are left without power to enforce any sanitary measures while the best season for doing so is passing away and from time to time is heard rumours of the approach of the dreaded pestilence."[52]

The board was under pressure to formulate its regulations quickly, not least because, as Beatty implied, the weather was warming up and, according to the prevalent sanitary interpretation, it was dangerous to disturb piles of filth and excrement in hot weather, for they would then release volatile miasmatic vapours into the atmosphere. As it turned out, the board's regulations were a close copy of the main administrative measures recommended in Taché's *Memorandum on Cholera*.

There were twenty published regulations, eleven of them dealing with the treatment of "nuisances." Local officers were required to supervise the cleaning of streets and highways, the emptying of privy pits and cess pools, the disinfecting and draining of open sewers and stagnant water, and the removal of industrial by-products and raw materials. Drains were to be properly trapped and directed away from water supplies, which local authorities should ensure to be clean and abundant. The sale of rotten, green, or out-of-season meat, fish, and fruit was to be forbidden, as was the sale of rags and used clothing, both in markets and by hawkers working from door to door. The health officers should exercise a close inspection over the state of the toilets in steamers, railway cars, and railway stations, and livestock cars were to be cleaned outside the limits of municipalities. Wherever possible, underdrainage was to be provided for all stables, cow-sheds, and privies that lacked it. These regulations were to be followed whether or not cholera declared itself, and they spoke to the dominant anti-contagionist interpretation of disease transmission.

Other measures embodied contagionist assumptions. The local health inspectors were to prevent overcrowding in public transport and in other places such as hotels and lodging houses. If cholera broke out, they were to ban fairs, races, theatrical performances, and circuses and were to enforce early closing regulations on taverns and other public venues. Provision was to be made for the isolation of victims of the disease. The major cities were required to establish cholera hospitals, where those afflicted could receive separate treatment, and also separate medical dispensaries for the distribution, especially to the poor, of food, clothing, bedding, and medicine. Refuges were to be provided for convalescent poor citizens whom the medical officers might find it necessary to remove in the event of "some focus or hot-bed of pestilence being formed in overcrowded lodgings visited by the disease." Finally, the local officers were to inspect dwellings in which there had been cholera cases and to enforce the removal of the victims' evacuations and the disinfection of their clothing and bedding.

The remaining regulations contained rudimentary reporting provisions. "Every city or town of some importance" was to appoint one or more medical officers of health to carry out the regulations, and they were to report to the local boards of health. In turn, the regulations concluded, "everything which may become a subject of sufficient importance or of more than ordinary difficulty is to be reported to the Central Board of Health, in order that they may be dealt with by further Regulations."[53]

The mix of contagionist and anti-contagionist precautions in the board's regulations speaks to the reigning medical common sense, but what was missing from them initially was any serious investment of the domain of public health in statistical forms, although an outline plan for information-gathering had been discussed at the cholera conference.[54] The board was now at the centre of a skeleton network of health actors and had its own activists in the main cities, often on local boards of health, but its capacity to specify what was to be observed and how such observations should be carried out was rudimentary at first.

The board quickly undertook a public information campaign that went beyond the distribution of Taché's *Memorandum*. As an immediate measure before publishing its regulations, the board informed the press that "considering it prudent that the public should be supplied with a remedy to be used in the diarrhoea preceding cholera, until the service of a physician can be procured," the remedy contained in "the Medical Field Companion, so generally used in the British army in India, may be safely employed." The recipe was given: "oil of aniseed, oil of cajeput, and oil of juniper, of each half a drachm; sulphuric ether, half an ounce; strong sulphuric acid, ten drops; tincture of cinnamon, two ounces. Mix," as well as the "Dose:—Ten drops, in a table spoonful of water, every quarter of an hour, until relief is obtained, or medical services procured." Local pharmacists were quick to advertise their ability to supply the official remedy.[55]

Even before the board's first meeting, Taché announced the proclamation of the Public Health Act and sent copies to county clerks in Canada West and mayors in Canada East. In early May he sent copies of the quarantine and public health regulations to individual doctors directly. The board also sent its regulations to the Catholic bishops of Montreal and Toronto, with a plea for their distribution to parish priests.[56]

Early in its mandate, the board supplemented the call for regular reports from local bodies, contained in its regulations, by instructing boards of health to provide monthly returns of mortality and daily returns of mortality from cholera. Many of the local boards were lax in reporting. With increasing reports of cholera in the United States, the board in July distributed a circular urging municipalities "to exercise every precaution in carrying out those sanitary measures requisite to stay the spread of disease."

Most of the board's fifty-one reported meetings were said to be taken up with routine communications with local bodies and with discussions of possible signs of the appearance of cholera. Still, the board attempted to exercise strict control over matters in the main communication corridor with the European continent. As we have seen, it urged a lengthened quarantine period at Grosse Isle for victims of measles and diarrhoea, but it also insisted on the separation of the ill from the healthy on the island and criticized the quality of the provisions furnished there. It attacked the prevailing practice of passengers being landed on the wharves at Quebec to await inland passage, arguing that immigrants should be picked up directly from Grosse Isle, and it attempted to reform overcrowded conditions on river steamers plying between Quebec and Montreal. It pointed to needed improvements for the reception of arriving immigrants at inland points.

The board attempted to monitor the health of troops garrisoned at Quebec, and made a number of regulations and recommendations for the police of the town. It opposed intramural burying for those not possessing vaults, and urged prohibition of the coffins of cholera victims through the centre of the city. It warned against large congregations of people generally, and attempted to have the races on the Plains of Abraham cancelled. At the board's invitation, the military surgeon Dr Blatherwick wrote a circular letter to American boards of health in an effort to chart the progress of the disease there.[57]

Although it never issued them and copies seem not to have survived, Dr MacDonnell reported that the board had prepared forms for the collection of statistical information, as Taché had recommended in his *Memorandum*. In MacDonnell's words:

> Being fully impressed with the utility of collecting Statistics, should the epidemic invade our shores, the Board after mature discussion adopted blank forms for the collection of such Statistics, intending to have them printed and distributed,

and to be filled up by health officers, medical men, clergymen and other persons connected with the service of the sick. Those forms, however, have neither been distributed nor even printed, because the Board in order to avoid creating unnecessary fears on the one hand and useless expenditure on the other, had determined to wait until the moment of absolute need, which happily did not come.[58]

The board was prepared to invest the disease formally, if the occasion had presented itself.

The End of the Scare

If the disease that killed people on the ship *England* off Halifax in April 1866 was cholera, it was successfully contained by quarantine and did not make its way up the St Lawrence. The Central Board of Health delivered a report on its activities in early November, as the Public Health Act was about to expire, pointing out that the disease was still active in Europe and America, where it was "travelling from city to city...not spreading much, but fatal in the majority of cases. Under such circumstances the probability is that the epidemic will have its influence more or less localized in warm climates during the winter, to travel north with the re-appearance of the mild season." That Canada would be affected in the next year seemed "more than probable." Still, the preparations made had already "contributed to materially improve the sanitary conditions of the country; although there is ample room still left for further improvements."

For the following season, the government returned to the less stringent quarantine regulations in effect in 1865, although this fact was not publicized and was intended as an accommodation for the steamship companies.[59] Von Iffland, the anti-contagionist Grosse Isle superintendent, was soon to retire, and contagionist interpretations of cholera were bolstered by their official endorsement by the Colonial Office. However, the disease did not reappear in epidemic form in Canada.[60]

Although a Canadian cholera epidemic did not take place in 1866, it is not appropriate to see this scare as a non-event or as an anti-climax to earlier epidemics: Unlike earlier appearances of cholera, strategically located state servants acted quickly in this instance to take preventive measures. Led by Joseph-Charles Taché, and in spite of the excitement provoked by Fenianism, the government acted to convoke a conference of experts to define the nature of the crisis it faced and the measures required to combat it. Medical doctors, themselves struggling to consolidate their professional status and independence, found themselves in command of extraordinary powers to regulate individual and collective liberties and to specify rules for the conduct of conduct at the levels of the police of towns and individual comportment. Despite the inability of medical experts to define the fundamental nature of cholera, its agent, or a reliable therapeutics, a new network of social-medical activists was formed that connected medical experts on the Central Board of Health with agents in the colonial cities and in many towns and villages. The board attempted to enrol the Catholic clergy, shipping companies, newspaper editors, and local government officials in order to invest the domain of health, and the central government commanded others of its agents to exercise medical vigilance.

The cholera scare took place on the eve of a marked extension of Canadian state sovereignty. Yet the scare's durable relevance to the formation of the Canadian state lies in the practical attempts it spawned to extend projects for the organization of surveillance, the centralization of knowledge, the consolidation of expertise, and the government of conduct. Both Heather MacDougall's work on Toronto and my own investigations of Hamilton, Kingston, and Montreal suggest that the 1866 scare not only provoked a dramatically heightened short-term effort at urban sanitation but also stimulated public health activists in more wide-ranging projects of municipal sanitary reform. The evidence suggests that we should be extremely sceptical of claims that urban infrastructural development had no connection to public health matters.[61] The central board's account of its own activities reported a more formal project for the statistical investment of the new domain of public health, at the same time as the 1866 scare underlined the relatively underdeveloped statistical capacities of the central government in health matters.

It is at least reasonable to postulate that Taché's experience of the capacities and limitations of the Canadian state system, faced with a social-medical crisis in 1866, shaped his ongoing efforts at the creation of resources for a national statistical appropriation of social relations. After Confederation, for instance, he consulted repeatedly with John Costley. Nova Scotia's registrar general, about the possibilities of basing a uniform national system of civil registration on the Nova Scotia model and he encouraged Costley to draft a plan for a more general national statistical system. Taché's 1871 census was the first to include a separate schedule for a nominal return of deaths in the preceding year, including a statement of cause of death.[62]

More enticing still is Taché's abortive attempt at a sanitary census of Canadian cities, originally intended for the summer of 1871, delayed until 1872 by the work involved in census compilation and the necessity of defending the 1871 census against attacks, and then abandoned as Taché and John Lowe attempted to deal with the controversy generated by the 1872 re-enumeration of Montreal.[63] The sanitary census would have re-mobilized and expanded the network of medical activists whose formation was stimulated by the 1866 cholera scare.

The project apparently originated from Doctors A. Larocque and P. Carpenter of Montreal, both of whom were founding members of the Association sanitaire organized in 1866, with Larocque also serving as a long-time Montreal public health officer renowned for his initiatives in the field of public hygiene. Carpenter had been instrumental in insisting that regular statistics of births and deaths, containing for the latter a note of age and cause, be kept by the health committee in Montreal, and the practice may have influenced Taché's 1871 census schedules. The Association sanitaire had a direct conduit to agriculture and statistics in its secretary, George Weaver, the 1871 Montreal census commissioner and census staff officer, who was a close acquaintance of John Lowe, the secretary to agriculture and statistics from 1870. The fragmentary surviving correspondence suggests that Larocque and Carpenter were able to relate death rates to the sanitary condition of wards in Montreal by 1870, and Carpenter had been publishing comparative infant mortality rates for Montreal and other cities for some years. Indeed, his claims that Montreal's inferior sanitary arrangements caused its death rates to be much higher than those in Glasgow or London were hotly contested.[64]

The connections between the sanitary census project and the reactions to the cholera scare via the Association sanitaire are solid. The census project got as far as the drafting of both the sanitary reporting schedules and a supporting memorandum, likely destined for cabinet consideration. The rough draft of the "Proposed Schedule for Sanitary Census, to be taken in the Five Principal Cities of Canada" contained nineteen heads dealing with housing conditions. The schedule identified houses by street number, described whether or not they fronted on a street, called for the number of inmates, the number of bedrooms and living rooms with their approximate size, the condition of the walls and ceiling, and the presence or absence of through ventilation. Two columns were headed "How Drained" and "Smell at Drain," and the schedule sought a return of the condition of the cellar, the number and condition of separate privies or water closets, the condition of the yard, and the presence of disease in the building. A second schedule, the "Sanitary Schedule of Streets," sought the street name, a description of its elevation, average breadth, its surface material and condition, a statement of how it was drained, whether there were "Gully Holes," what was its "Smell," and finally a calculation of the proportion of the lots that were vacant, a description of house styles, and any additional remarks.

The schedules make it obvious that this initiative was situated on anti-contagionist terrain, with its repeated references to drains, open spaces, elevation, and ventilation. The draft memorandum supporting the project reinforced sanitarian arguments. Its general claim, however, was that Canadian cities were the sites of unnecessarily high rates of infant mortality, and that English practice had demonstrated the value of statistical investigation as a resource for combatting this problem.[65]

In sum, then, the 1866 cholera scare not only encouraged the formation of local sanitary and public health movements, but also led to serious attempts to invest the emerging domain of public health in statistical forms. Such investments were fundamental to intervention in the name of health, a key site for state-forming initiatives.

Notes

Research for this paper was supported by the Social Sciences and Humanities Research Council of Canada. I wish to thank Josée Lecomte, Erin Mills, and Emma Whelan for research assistance.

1 David Arnold, *Colonizing the Body: State Medicine and Epidemic Disease in Nineteenth-Century India* (Berkeley: University of California Press 1993); Geoffrey Bilson, *A Darkened House: Cholera in Nineteenth-Century Canada* (Toronto: University of Toronto Press 1980); François Delaporte, *Disease and Civilization: The Cholera in Paris, 1832* (Cambridge. Mass.: MIT Press 1986); Richard J. Evans, *Death in Hamburg: Society and Politics in the Cholera Years, 1830–1910* (Oxford: Clarendon Press 1987); C.M. Godfrey, *The Cholera Epidemics in Upper Canada, 1832–1866* (Toronto: Seccombe House 1968); Anne Hardy, "Cholera, Quarantine and the English Preventive System, 1850–1895," *Medical History* 37 (1993): 250–69; Catherine J. Kudlick, *Cholera in Post-Revolutionary Paris: A Cultural History* (Berkeley: University of California Press 1996); W. Luckin, "The Final Catastrophe: Cholera in London, 1866," *Medical History* 21 (1977): 32–42; V. Prashad, "Native Dirt/Imperial Ordure: The Cholera of 1832 and the Morbid Resolutions of Modernity," *Journal of Historical Sociology* 7 (1994): 243–60; Charles E. Rosenberg, *The Cholera Years: The United States in 1832, 1849, and 1866* (Chicago: University of Chicago Press 1962); Walter Sendzik, "The 1832 Cholera Epidemic: A Study in State Formation" (MA thesis, McGill University 1998).

2 It is impossible to say with any certainty how many, if any, deaths from cholera took place in 1866, although one authoritative source has claimed that "North America was not spared" from the disease in that year; see Kenneth F. Kiple, ed., *The Cambridge World History of Human Disease* (Cambridge: Cambridge University Press 1993), 527–8. Death and illness in Canada were not invested in stable medical/statistical forms until after 1921, and 1866 was not a census year, so even the dubious death-reporting practices of enumerators are unavailable; see Jacalyn Duffin, "Census versus Medical Daybooks: A Comparison of Two Sources on Mortality in Nineteenth-Century Ontario," *Continuity and Change* 12, 2 (1997): 199–219; George Emery, *Facts of Life: The Social Construction of Vital Statistics in Ontario, 1869–1952* (Montreal and Kingston: McGill-Queen's University Press 1993). There were certainly reports of cholera on the *England*, but the contemporary press also claimed that, despite the holding of the passengers on board

ship in quarantine, the disease had disappeared in a few days; see, for instance, *Le Pays,* 17 and 21 April 1866.

3 See Heather MacDougall, "Public Health and the 'Sanitary Ideal' in Toronto, 1866–1890," in W. Mitchinson and J. McGinnis. eds., *Essays in the History of Canadian Medicine,* (Toronto: McClelland & Stewart 1988), 62–87; City of Toronto, *By-Law 431, Relative to the Board of Health: Practical Remarks to Citizens, Domestic Sanitary Regulations and Treatment of Cholera* (Toronto: Leader Press 1866).

4 See, for instance, the report in *Le Pays,* 19 April 1866.

5 Delaporte, *Disease and Civilization;* Kudlick, *Cholera in Post-Revolutionary Paris.*

6 Mary Poovey, "Curing the 'Social Body' in 1832: James Phillips Kay and the Irish in Manchester," *Gender and History* 5, 2 (1993): 196–211; and *Making a Social Body* (Chicago: University of Chicago Press 1995); also, T.S. Ashton, *Economic and Social Investigations in Manchester, 1833–1933: A Centenary History of the Manchester Statistical Society* (1934; Brighton: Harvester Press 1977); R.J.W. Selleck, *James Kay-Shuttleworth: Journey of an Outsider* (Essex: Woburn Press 1994). Frederick Engels, *The Condition of the Working Class in England* (1844; New York: International 1974), draws heavily on Kay.

7 John Snow, *On the Mode of Communication of Cholera,* 2nd ed. (London: John Churchill 1855).

8 See John M. Eyler, *Victorian Social Medicine: The Ideas and Methods of William Farr* (Baltimore: Johns Hopkins University Press 1979); Samuel Finer, *The Life and Times of Sir Edwin Chadwick* (1952; New York: Barnes and Noble 1970); Margaret Pelling, *Cholera, Fever and English Medicine, 1825–1865* (Oxford: Oxford University Press 1978); F.B. Smith, *Florence Nightingale: Reputation and Power* (London: Croom Helm 1982).

9 Perry Williams, "The Laws of Health: Women, Medicine and Sanitary Reform, 1850–1890," in Marina Benjamin, ed., *Science and Sensibility: Gender and Scientific Enquiry 1780–1945* (Oxford: Basil Blackwell 1991), 60–88.

10 Cholera is thus an interesting site for Foucauldian-inspired investigations of "governmentality." See G. Burchell et al., eds., *The Foucault Effect: Studies in Governmentality* (Chicago: University of Chicago Press 1993).

11 The isolation of the agent would later be attributed to Filippo Pacini in 1854. Evans, *Death in Hamburg,* 264–80, shows that Koch had the political backing needed to sustain a bacteriological interpretation.

12 See, for example, Michel Callon, "Some Elements of a Sociology of Translation: Domestication of the Scallops and the Fishermen of St. Brieuc Bay," in John Law, ed., *Power, Action and Belief: A New Sociology of Knowledge* (London: Routledge 1988), 197–233; Michel Callon and John Law, "On Interests and Their Transformation: Enrolment and Counter-Enrolment," *Social Studies of Science* 12 (1982): 615–25, and "On the Construction of Sociotechnical Networks: Content and Context Revisited," *Knowledge and Society* 8 (1989): 57–83; and Laurent Thévenot, "Rules and Implements: Investment in Forms," *Social Science Information* 23, 1 (1984): 1–45.

13 For more on Taché's biography, see Jean-Guy Nadeau, "Joseph-Charles Taché," *Dictionary of Canadian Biography,* vol. 12 (Toronto: University of Toronto Press 1990), 1012–16; Evelyn Bossé, *Joseph-Charles Taché: Un grand représantant de l'élite canadienne-française* (Québec: Éditions Garneau 1971). For an examination of Taché's *Memorandum* as a fundamentalist Catholic propaganda sheet, see B. Curtis, "La moralité miasmatique: le *Mémoire sur le Choléra* de Joseph-Charles Taché," paper presented to the Canadian History of Medicine Association, Sherbrooke, 1999.

14 See Canada *Gazette,* 9 June 1849. The first General Board of Health was composed of doctors and other men of substance—Wolfred Nelson, Olivier Berthelet, William Workman, John James Day, Moses J. Hayes, Guillaume Deschambault, and Robert Levy MacDonnell—with Doctor Aaron H. David as secretary. MacDonnell sought his pay in a petition of 21 June 1850. See Legislative Assembly of Canada, *Journals.*

15 National Archives of Canada (NA), RG 17, 4, MacDonnell to McGee, 1 April 1865; RG 17, AI 2, Taché to MacDonnell, 4 April 1865.

16 NA, RG 7, G1 157, Newcastle to Monck, 6 April 1864. According to the survey, "the Canadian institutions are the only ones which are subjected to a special body of general inspectors properly qualified and devoted to their business." At the time, Taché was chair of the Board of Prison and Asylum Inspectors, which inspected the quarantine station and the Marine and Emigrant Hospital. NA, RG 17, 4, Buchanan to Taché, 21 April 1865.

17 NA, RG17, 5, Buchanan to Taché, 18, 19 July 1865. The sailors claimed to have been innoculated. Von Iffland treated them with "the celebrated herb sent to me on last Saturday by a Mr Lindsay Lighthouse Keeper of 'Isle Verte' and it seems to have acted to all appearance with good effect...It is called 'Sabots de la Vierge.'"; NA, RG 17, 6, Lindsay to Taché, 26 July and 1 Aug. 1865, Von Iffland to Taché, 24 Aug. 1865, and Roy to McGee, 21 Sept. 1865.

18 NA, RG 17, 6, Von Iffland to Taché, 15 Nov. (with 19 Oct.) 1865. For more on Von Iffland, aptly called by his patients "va renifler," since he was a committed sanitarian and an odd choice for the management of contagion, see M.=J. Ahern and Georges Ahern, *Useful Notes on the History of Medicine in Lower Canada from the Founding of Quebec to the Beginning of the 19th Century* (Quebec: Privately published 1923), 555–7; and Jacques Bernier, *La médecine au Québec. Naissance et évolution d'une profession* (Québec: Les Presses de l'université Laval 1989), passim.

19 "The Cholera," Kingston *British Whig*, 6 Feb. 1866.

20 For Toronto, see Hamilton *Spectator*, 12 Feb. 1866; for the quotation, see ibid., 26 Feb. 1866; for more on events in Toronto, including the meeting mentioned, see MacDougall, "Public Health," 67.

21 *Spectator*, 16 March 1866. The editor hoped the installation of the government at Ottawa would incite it to take sanitary measures.

22 *British Whig*, 17 Feb. 1866.

23 *Le Pays*, 1 Feb. 1866.

24 Ibid., 6 Feb. 1866.

25 Ibid., 22 Feb. 1866.

26 Ibid., 1, 6, 15 March 1866.

27 Ibid., 24, 29 March, 7 April 1866.

28 NA, RG 17, 9, petition of S. Abbott, 7 March 1866; James Wilson to McDougall. 17 March 1866; RG 17, AI 2, Taché to City Clerk, London, 13 March 1866; Taché to W.W.F. Tinsdale, Ancaster, 28 March 1866.

29 NA, RG 1, E7 66, and RG 17, 8, 20 Feb. 1866; RG 17, AI 1, Taché to J.G. Moylan, *Canadian Freeman*, 28 Feb. 1866.

30 NA, RG 17, AI 2, for the invitations. Taché to doctors, 8 March 1866; for the lime, RG 1, E7 66, 10 March 1866.

31 *British Whig*, 21 and 30 March 1866; *Memorandum on Cholera, Adopted at a Medical Conference Held in the Bureau of Agriculture, in March, 1866* (Ottawa: Bureau of Agriculture and Statistics 1866).

32 See Curtis, "La moralité miasmatique," and, for Marsden, Bernier, *La médecine au Québec,* passim. Note that Marsden, with an international reputation as a quarantine expert, was invited repeatedly to consult with the American government about such measures, but not the Canadian. See, for instance. *British Whig,* March 1866. Marsden seems not to have figured in any of Taché's arrangements.

33 See Luckin. "The Final Catastrophe."

34 Thévenot, "Rules and implements"; as the *Shorter Oxford English Dictionary* has it, to invest means to "1...Clothe...endue (person etc. *with* qualities, insignia of office, rank etc.) 2. Lay siege to. 3. Employ...esp. for profit."

35 Pierre Bourdieu, "Codification," in *In Other Words: Essays towards a Reflexive Sociology* (Stanford: Stanford University Press 1990), 83. See also M.E. Hobart and Z.S. Schiffman, *Information Ages: Literacy, Numeracy, and the Computer Revolution* (Baltimore: Johns Hopkins University Press 1988), 11–31.

36 Space considerations preclude a more systematic examination of the implications of the politics of representation involved in forming social relations in these ways. Note the argument of Law and Whittaker that suppression of empirical variation and the simplification of objects and relations is necessary if "heterogeneous objects distributed through time and space are to be brought together in a conformable space at a particular time." John Law and John Whittaker, "On the Art of Representation: Notes on the Politics of Visualisation," in Gordon Fyfe and John Law, eds., *Picturing Power: Visual Depiction and Social Relations,* Sociological Review Monograph 35 (London: Routledge 1988), 160–83.

37 The questions are given in NA, RG 17, 9, 9 April 1866, reprinted with the regulations in the Canada *Gazette,* April 1866, 1295–8.

38 NA, RG 17, AI 2, Memorandum on Public Health and Quarantine, 1866. The regulations in draft are in RG 1, E7 66, 9 April 1866, and here McGee seeks permission not only to declare them but to be allowed to suspend them from time to time as circumstances might require.

39 NA, RG 17, 10, Theodore Robitaille, 4 May 1866; RG 17, 11, J.D. Short, 31 May 1866; Canada *Gazette,* 8 May 1866.

40 NA, RG 17, AI 2, Taché to Allan Brothers, 13 April 1866.

41 NA, RG 17, 9, Hugh Allan, 14 April 1866; RG 17, 10, Dixon to Taché, 3 May 1866; Allan Brothers, 4 May 1866; Allan & Gilmour Co., 8 May 1866.

42 NA, RG 17, 11, A.C. Buchanan, 21 June 1866.

43 NA, RG 17, 11, Allan Brothers, 31 July 1866; RG 17, AI 2, Taché to Allan Brothers, 3 Aug. 1866. "The Customs officers have been instructed by the Minister of Finance to look after the prospect of the Cholera threatening any part of our Frontier and to Telegraph to the Minister of Agriculture any occurrence which may call for action."

44 NA, RG 17, 9, Von Iffland to McGee, 17 April 1866; RG 17 10, Von Iffland to Taché, 2 May 1866; Buchanan to Taché, 7 and 12 May 1866. RG 17, AI 2, 1866, for giant for missionaries. For Montizambert's qualifications, see RG 17, 15, 9 March 1867; he had two years' training at Laval before going to Edinburgh, where he was dresser and non-resident clerk for James Syme.

45 NA, RG 17, 10, Buchanan to Taché, Von Iffland to Taché, 17 May 1866.

46 NA, RG 17, 10, Von Iffland. weekly reports, 23 May, 13 June 1866; for the Board of Health, see RG 17, 2432.

47 For complaints about contact, see NA, RG 17, 10, W. Warden, 31 May 1866; RG 17, AI 2, Taché to Von Iffland, 2 June 1866; RG 17, 10, Buchanan to Taché, enclosing Von Iffland to Buchanan, 6 June 1866, where it is noted for Taché's information that the contractor provisioning the island was approved initially by Taché's uncle Étienne-Pascal; RG 17, 11, see the weekly reports from 13 June until the station closed in the first week in November; for the death of his infirmier, 18 July 1866.

48 NA, RG 17, 14, Buchanan to Chapais, enclosing Von Iffland to Buchanan, 7 March 1867; Province of Canada, Legislative Assembly, *Sessional Papers,* 1867, no. 3, "Nine and Twentieth Annual Report of the Chief Agent for Immigration, 1866." Not including the $3200 expense of the boarding physicians, the costs for the Grosse Isle station for the year were as follows: Pay of officers' wintering party, $10,221.37; Hospital charges, $1,085.26; Cartage, $677.25; Medicines, $114.31; Furniture, stoves, &c, $836.11; Steamboat service, weekly, $2,535.19; Repairs, &c, $1,919.99; Sundries, $166.80; Printing, stationery, advertising, $589.79; Total, $18,146.07.

49 Province of Canada, Legislative Assembly, *Sessional Papers,* 1867, no. 3.

50 There seems to be little attention to public health in the Canadian state-formation literature. It is not a theme, for instance, in Allan Greer and Ian Radforth, eds., *Colonial Leviathan* (Toronto: University of Toronto Press 1992). On inspection and the centralization of knowledge, see B. Curtis, *True Government by Choice Men? Inspection, Education and State Formation in Canada West* (Toronto: University of Toronto Press 1992). On the work of domain formation and state formation, see Jacques Donzelot, *L'invention du social* (Paris: Fayard 1984);B. Curtis, "Working Past the Great Abstraction: Abrams and Foucault on the State and Government." *Les Cahiers d'histoire* 17 (1997): 9–18, and "Mapping the Social: Jacob Keefer's Educational Tour, 1845," *Journal of Canadian Studies* 28, 2 (1993): 51–68. The standard work on state formation and moral regulation is Philip Corrigan and Derek Sayer, *The Great Arch: English State Formation as Cultural Revolution* (Oxford: Basil Blackwell 1985); see also Prashad, "Native Dirt/Imperial Ordure." For the "governmental state," see Michel Foucault. "La << gouvernementalité >>," and "Méthodologie pour la connaissance du monde: comment se débarrasser du marxisme," in *Dits et écrits,* vol. 3 (Paris: Gallimiard 1996), 635–57 and 595–618, and "Technologies of the Self," in L.H. Martin et al., eds., *Technologies of the Self: A Seminar with Michel Foucault* (Amherst: University of Massachusetts Press 1988). 16–19. Thomas Osborne. "Security and Vitality: Drains, Liberalism and Power in the Nineteenth Century," in Andrew Barry et al., eds., *Foucault and Political Reason* (London: UCL Press 1996), 99–123, presents a "governmentality" take on public health; see also Mariana Valverde, *Diseases of the Will: Alcohol and the Dilemmas of Freedom* (Cambridge: Cambridge University Press 1999).

51 See R.D. Gidney and W.P.J. Millar, *Professional Gentlemen: The Professions in Nineteenth-Century Ontario,* Ontario Historical Studies Series (Toronto: University of Toronto Press 1994).

52 NA, RG 17, 1663, J. Dickson, 20 April, J. Beatty, 26 April 1866.

53 The regulations are reprinted widely in various official sources and in the press of the period; see, for instance, Canada *Gazette,* May 1866, 1738–40.

54 See Thévenot. "Rules and Implements."

55 Hamilton *Spectator,* 2 May 1866; *British Whig,* 3 May 1866. In the *British Whig* of 5 May, G.S. Hobart of the Kingston Medical Hall was advertising supplies of the remedy for sale. See also Arnold, *Colonizing the Body,* for the attempts by the British Army in India to deal with cholera.

56 NA, RG 17, AI 2, Taché to municipal officials, 12 April 1866; Taché to medical doctors, 9 May 1866.

57 NA, RG 17, 2432, for the Board's correspondence and activities.

58 Province of Canada, Legislative Assembly, *Sessional Papers,* 1867, no. 3, "Report of the Central Board of Health."

59 NA, RG 17, AI 2, Cambie to Buchanan, 27 March 1867.

60 NA, RG 17, 14, Carnarvon to Governor General, 26 Jan. 1867: RG 17, 15, Meredith to minister of agriculture, 27 March 1867.

61 The argument is strongly opposed to John S. Hagopian's position in "Debunking the Public Health Myth: Municipal Politics and Class Conflict during the Galt, Ontario, Waterworks Campaigns, 1888–1890," *Labour/Le Travail* 39 (spring 1997): 39–68, where public health concerns are held to have had no importance in campaigns for municipal infrastructure.

62 See, for example, Costley's autograph draft plan for a national statistical system in NA, RG 17, 51, Costley to Dunkin, 4 Sept. 1871.

63 For the 1872 controversy, see B. Curtis, "Expert Knowledge and the Social Imaginary: The Case of the Montreal Check Census," *Histoire sociale/Social History* 28 (Nov. 1995): 313–38.

64 See *Le Pays,* 19 April 1866; 4, 6 April 1867; and especially for Carpenter, 20 Jan. 1870.

65 NA, MG 29, E18 3. Lowe to Carpenter, 24 July, 25 Aug. 1871. Lowe's son Johnny was apparently living with the Carpenters. For the schedules, see MG 29 E18, 7, 1871–2.

The Case Against Canadian Confederation

Ged Martin

[...] A "high politics" view of Confederation would lead us to question the value of the actual arguments put forward against Confederation, since the root reason for opposition in many cases could be suspected to be resentment at not being taken aboard. At the very least, the prospect of loaves and fishes could soften the opposition of some critics of Confederation. Members of Albert J. Smith's New Brunswick ministry were prepared to take up the question in 1866, despite having been elected in 1865 to oppose it.[1] In Nova Scotia, the spectacular bolt to change sides in April 1866 was alleged to have been touched off by the suspicious decision of two anti-Confederates that others would rat first, and "we...had better get into line or we should be left out in the cold and lose all chance of obtaining good positions."[2]

The two major sources on which this paper is based are the *Confederation Debates* of 1865 in the province of Canada, and the Nova Scotia petitions of 1866 in the *British Parliamentary Papers*. The Canadian parliament had not previously printed its debates, and we may echo the lament of Dr. Joseph Blanchet, four weeks and 545 pages after discussion began on 3 February 1865, that the decision "to have the speeches of this House printed in official form certainly did no good service to the country." Yet vast as was the eventual volume, it does not necessarily do justice to the opposition case. In the early phases of the debate, there was a tendency to demand further information, for the Quebec plan required much fleshing-out of practical details on which the ministers were unforthcoming—and it was tempting to debunk the visionary orations of Macdonald and McGee by trumpeting that there was no case to answer. Luther Holton replied to the first great onslaught of explanations with the flourish that if the government's speeches "contain all that can be said in favour of this scheme, we have no fear of letting them go unanswered." As the Canadian debate was getting into its stride, so news arrived of Tilley's defeat in New Brunswick which, A.A. Dorion claimed, caused the issue "to lose much of its interest."[3] Much of the debate was taken up with members taunting each other with inconsistency, which often provoked elaborate apologetics. Some speeches were intended to drag matters out while petitions were circulated:[4] Cartier embarrassed Eric Dorion, by reading into the record a circular letter he had sent to supporters requesting them to have anti-Confederation petitions "signed as soon as possible by men, women and children."[5] Similar devices were used to produce petitions in Nova Scotia, as the governor-general, Lord Monck, and a former lieutenant-governor, the Marquess of Normanby, assured the House of Lords in 1867.[6] It is certainly hard to believe that the 210 inhabitants of the district of Port Medway who signed their names to a massive, two thousand word petition against Confederation were entirely unprompted,[7] and it may be doubted if any of the petitions emerged from the sober atmosphere

Ged Martin, "The Case Against Canadian Confederation, 1864–1867," in Ged Martin, ed., *The Causes of Canadian Confederation* (Fredericton: Acadiensis Press, 1990), 19–49.

of a political science seminar. At Yarmouth, Joseph Howe preceded a two hour assault on Confederation with "an eloquent eulogy on the character of Her Majesty Queen Victoria, as a child, a wife and mother, a queen and a widow" which was much cheered.[8] It is not surprising that in Nova Scotia opposition to Confederation became what modern American politics would term a "motherhood" issue.

There are other difficulties in accommodating the available material to the logical approach of the historian. A sound historical analysis would seek to balance arguments for and arguments against, coming to a fair and reasonable conclusion. The arguments *for* Confederation, which we normally equate with the reasons for its adoption, are clear enough and capable of neat presentation. The arguments *against* offend our sense of order. Cartier was able to have fun playing off opposites: the Montreal *Witness* warned that Protestantism in Lower Canada would be doomed by Confederation, while its deadly rival, the *True Witness,* saw it as leading to the destruction of French Canada.[9] The easy but fallacious assumption behind such debating devices is that the two strands of argument cancel each other out, whereas in reality one or the other—perhaps even both, but for different reasons—might well be entirely valid. Perhaps the real task of explanation is not to explain *why* Confederation was accepted, but *how* it managed to seize the central ground and divide the opposition to right and left.

"I do not know of any one opposed to union in the abstract," said New Brunswick's Timothy Warren Anglin. "But my impression is that the time has not arrived for any kind of union, and I will oppose it to the last."[10] This was a common theme among the critics: intercolonial union in principle, union one day, but not this union, not now.[11] As Edward Whelan put it, the critics accepted the principle of ploughing the field, but objected to destroying the daisies and field mice.[12] How sincere were

these protestations—by some, but by no means all the critics of Confederation—in favour of an eventual British North American union? Perhaps they were gestures of open-mindedness merely to win over waverers. David Reesor found it "extraordinary" that so many members of the Canadian Legislative Council spoke "strongly and emphatically against many of the resolutions" while declaring their reluctant intention to vote for the package.[13] Yet even A.A. Dorion, who went to some lengths to clear his name of the slander of having ever spoken favourably of the idea, could leave open a faint and distant possibility: "Population may extend over the wilderness that now lies between the Maritime Provinces and ourselves, and commercial intercourse may increase sufficiently to render Confederation desirable."[14] As late as August 1864, admittedly at a social occasion, Joseph Howe proclaimed: "I have always been in favour of uniting any two, three, four, or the whole five of the provinces."[15] It is not necessary to follow McGee in the full flight of his oratory, but he may have been right in thinking of the idea of Confederation as an autonomous cause of its own happening. "If we have dreamed a dream of union...it is at least worth while remarking that a dream which has been dreamed by such wise and good men, may, for aught we know or you know, have been a sort of vision—a vision foreshadowing forthcoming natural events in a clear intelligence."[16]

If some of the opponents subscribed to the idea of an eventual intercolonial union, most of the critics in the province of Canada argued that Confederation was not a solution to present difficulties, and it would itself require a far greater degree of political wisdom than was necessary to rescue the existing system. Henri Joly felt that the various provinces would meet in a confederated parliament "as on a field of battle." Christopher Dunkin referred to the airy dismissals of such warnings by ministerial supporters: "Oh! there won't be any trouble;

men are in the main sensible, and won't try to make trouble." If public men were so reasonable as to be able to work the new system, why then had the province of Canada had "four crises in two years"? In any case, even if it were accepted that Upper and Lower Canada were not living together in harmony, the answer was surely for them to work out a new system of government and not to claim that only through a wider union could they get along. Dunkin noted that in the five years between the lapsing of Galt's federation initiative in 1859 and the formation of the Grand Coalition of June 1864, "we quarrelled and fought about almost everything, but did not waste a thought or a word upon this gigantic question of the Confederation of these provinces." "Surely," Thomas Scatcherd argued, "if parties could unite as they did in June last, they could have united to prevent the difficulty complained of...without entering upon a scheme to subvert the Constitution."[17]

While some critics of Confederation admitted that the Canadian Union had its problems, others felt them to have been exaggerated. Henri Joly contrasted Taché's claim that "the country was bordering on civil strife" with the ministry's throne speech, which thanked "a beneficent Providence for the general contentment of the people of this province."[18] Joseph Perrault asked, "have we not reason to be proud of our growth since 1840, and of the fact that within the past twenty-five years, our progress, both social and material, has kept pace with that of the first nations in the world?"[19] For French Canadians, a crucial issue was whether they could indeed maintain the equal representation which the two sections of the province of Canada had in the Assembly. In 1858, Joseph Cauchon had believed that Lower Canada had enough allies in the upper province to stand firmly on its rights. By 1865, those allies were becoming fewer; the minority English-speaking representatives from Lower Canada now held

the balance of power between French Canadians and an upper province increasingly united in its demand for representation by population. The entrenchment of equal representation in the imperial act of 1840, which required a two-thirds vote to change the balance of representation, had been repealed in 1854—and replaced by a simple majority, thus opening the way to the carrying of "rep. by pop." through the sudden defection of the Lower Canadian English. From that perspective, Confederation—a negotiated scheme which gave French Canadians their own legislature—was preferable to swamping within the existing structure.[20] However, other French Canadian politicians took the threat of "rep. by pop." less seriously, dismissing it—in Joly's words—as "one of those political clap-traps which ambitious men, who can catch them no other way, set to catch the heedless multitude." Joly argued that hypocrisy was proved by the alacrity with which Upper Canada Reformers had entered the Macdonald-Sicotte administration of 1862, which agreed not to press the issue—proof that "Upper Canada is much more indifferent, and its leaders much less sincere touching this question of the representation, than they would have us believe."

Perrault went much further. In a speech presumably aimed at stoking every French Canadian fear of assimilation—it ranged from the Acadian deportation, via the history of Mauritius, to the francophobia of Lord Durham's Report—Perrault denied that Upper Canada had more people than Lower Canada at all. The "true total" of the population of Upper Canada had been "greatly exaggerated" in the census of 1861, a fraud revealed by the fact that the census figure for population under the age of one year exceeded the live births of the previous twelve months by eight thousand. Perrault also claimed that the census had under-counted the population of Lower Canada, for "our farmers have always stood in dread of the census, because they have a suspicion that it is taken with the sole object of imposing some tax, or of making some draft of men for the defence of the country." Yet, confusingly, he contended that even if Upper Canada's population did exceed that of Lower Canada, it was no more than a temporary blip, caused by Irish famine migration, which had now ceased. So too had the outward flow of French Canadians to New England, with the result that within ten years, the higher birth rate of Lower Canada would bring the two provinces back to equality of population.[21]

The core of the case against Confederation was that there was no crisis sufficient to justify so large a change. Consequently, critics largely refused to enter the trap of offering alternative solutions. "We are asked, 'what are you going to do? You must do something. Are you going to fall back to our old state of dead-lock?'" Dunkin reported, adding that whenever he heard the argument "that something must be done, I suspect that there is a plan on foot to get something very bad done." Henri Joly took the same line. "I am asked: 'If you have nothing to do with Confederation, what will you have?' I answer, we would remain as we are."[22] "Now my proposition is very simple," Joseph Howe told the people of Nova Scotia. "It is to let well enough alone."[23] Not surprisingly, the opponents of Confederation indignantly rejected the argument that they were—wittingly or otherwise—working for annexation to the United States. They replied that the campaign for Confederation itself contained the germ of an annexationist threat. Matthew Cameron, one of the few prominent Upper Canada Conservatives to oppose the scheme, warned that the delusive arguments of material gain from Confederation with the tiny Maritimes "are arguments ten-fold stronger in favour of union with the United States."[24] Nor did the danger lie simply in encouraging hopes of greater prosperity, as was shown when a moderate

Lower Canadian journal could proclaim "qu'à tous les points de vue, nos institutions, notre langue, et nos lois seront mieux protégés avec la confédération américaine qu'avec le projet de confédération de l'Amérique Britannique du Nord."[25] "Once destroy public confidence in our institutions," warned T.C. Wallbridge, "and it is impossible to predict what extremes may be resorted to."[26] Joseph Howe similarly predicted that the imposition of Confederation on unwilling provinces would lead to "undying hatreds and ultimate annexation."[27]

At first sight, it might seem surprising that the opponents of Confederation were able to escape the tactical trap of offering alternative solutions to intercolonial problems. Christopher Dunkin and Joseph Howe were on insecure ground in putting forward the far more ambitious idea of imperial federation,[28] while Tupper found that Maritime Union had no friends at all when he attempted the ploy of reviving it in 1865.[29] In the province of Canada, the demand for an alternative would have been dangerous for the cause of Confederation after its defeat in the New Brunswick election of 1865. The teleological and celebratory accounts of the textbooks stress that the Great Coalition of June 1864 was pledged "in the most earnest manner, to the negotiation for a confederation of all the British North American provinces." Less noticed is the fact that the agreement contained a fall-back position, that "failing a successful issue to such negotiations, they are prepared to pledge themselves to legislation during the next session of Parliament for the purpose of remedying existing difficulties by introducing the federal principle for Canada alone," with provision for future expansion. Minutes before the celebrated coalition deal was struck at the St Louis Hotel, Brown had still been insisting that "the Canadian federation should be constituted first." In March 1865, after the setback in New Brunswick, the coalition came close to breaking up over Brown's insistence on invoking the fall-back position. Brown pressed the issue again in the negotiations for the succession to Taché in August 1865, and forced John A. Macdonald to give formal endorsement, in the name of the new premier, Sir Narcisse Belleau, to his interpretation of the coalition deal. Brown, leader of the majority party in the majority section, could afford to be philosophical about the defeat of Confederation after the New Brunswick election: "If it fails after all legitimate means have been used, we will go on with our scheme for Canada alone."[30] For John A. Macdonald, such a solution could offer little comfort: as a Conservative, he had been dependent since 1857 upon Bleu support for his periods of office. Anything which strengthened Upper Canada and its Reform party against Lower Canada was likely to mean problems for the Conservative party. Once it seemed that New Brunswick had dropped out, Brown and his Upper Canada Reform colleagues were under pressure to deliver the small print of the coalition bargain. "The Administration could not give a pledge that they would carry the Confederation of all the provinces," A.A. Dorion reminded his former allies, "but they could pledge and did pledge themselves to bring in, in the event of the failure of that scheme, a measure for the federation of Upper and Lower Canada."[31] Far from heading a triumphant march to nationhood, Macdonald and his allies were walking a desperately narrow tightrope.

Consequently, supporters of Confederation could not afford to admit that rival schemes might be possible. Rather they were obliged to present the Quebec scheme as an immutable package, a balanced intercolonial treaty—thus denying themselves any room for manoeuvre to win over those Maritimers who objected to the terms rather than the aim of Confederation. Critics objected to being faced with the resolutions as a package. "What is the use of considering them if we cannot come to our conclusions and give them effect in the shape of amendments?" asked one Upper Canadian critic. At Quebec, Dunkin pointed out, twenty three men had sat for seventeen working days to produce "a scheme of a Constitution which they vaunt as being altogether better than that of the model republic of the United States, and even than that of the model kingdom of Great Britain."[32] William Annand of Nova Scotia thought that a scheme "matured in a few weeks, amid exhaustive festivities" could not be the best constitution possible.[33] Joseph Howe noted that the inflexibility of the Quebec scheme would be carried forward to the future: "No means are provided by which the people, should it be found defective, can improve it from time to time. Whenever a change is required they must come back to the Imperial Parliament."[34] Indeed, the Canadian people were to continue coming back to Westminster until 1982.

Coupled with resentment at the rejection of any possibility of amendment was anger at the total refusal of a popular vote on so major a constitutional change. An exasperated Hamilton paper exclaimed that if there was to be no general election on Confederation, the polling booths "may as well be turned into pig-pens, and the voters lists cut up into pipe-lighters."[35] In Nova Scotia, where petition after petition dwelt on the province's long tradition of representative and responsible government, the people of Shelburne put the issue in more fundamental and sober terms: "whilst Your Majesty's petitioners freely admit the right of their representatives in Provincial Parliament to legislate for them within reasonable limits, they cannot admit the right of such representatives to effect sudden changes, amounting to an entire subversion of the constitution, without the deliberate sanction of the people expressed at the polls." As Joseph Howe put it in more succinct and homely terms, the local legislature had "no right to violate a trust only reposed in them for four years, or in fact to sell the fee simple of a mansion of which they have but a limited lease." Even if the scheme were beneficial, which the people of Queen's County flatly doubted, "the means employed to force it upon the country without an appeal to the people, and with full knowledge of their intense dislike of the measure" were enough to discredit it.[36]

Both in Canada and the Atlantic provinces, opponents of Confederation attacked the scheme as "very costly, for the money is scattered on all sides in handfuls."[37] Simply listing the promised commitments left critics breathless with horror. Joseph Howe recounted that with a debt of $75 million, "the public men of Canada propose to purchase the territories of the Hudson's Bay Company, larger than half Europe," take over British Columbia and Vancouver Island, "provinces divided from them by an interminable wilderness," as well as absorb the Atlantic provinces, "countries severally as large as Switzerland, Sardinia, Greece, and Great Britain."[38] Dunkin similarly warned that with "a promise of everything for everybody," the scheme could only "be ambiguous, unsubstantial and unreal."[39] Others feared not disappointment but jobbery. "The proposed Constitution framed by arch jobbers is so devised as to provide for the very maximum of jobbing and corruption," Arthur Gordon assured Gladstone.[40] Unfortunately, responses to the threat of corruption depended on assessments by individuals of whether they would be victims or gainers from it. "Are the people of Nova Scotia prepared to yield up their flourishing customs revenue to a federal treasury in Canada, there to be squandered in jobbery and corruption?" asked the Yarmouth *Tribune*.[41] The people might indeed balk at the idea, but their elected representatives were perhaps open to persuasion: as Joseph Howe lamented, when John A. Macdonald "opened his confederation mousetrap he did not bait it with toasted cheese."[42] A scheme of government launched in this way could hardly bode well for the future. Christopher Dunkin warned that the representatives of each province would seek popularity back home by inching up federal subsidies or by taking special arrangements for one province as a benchmark and precedent for comparable concessions. They would prove to be "pretty good daughters of the horse-leech, and their cry will be found to be pretty often and pretty successfully—'Give, give give!'"[43] His warning can hardly be dismissed as inaccurate.

Related to the general question of cost were various predictions about the effect of Confederation on tariffs. James Currie predicted that Canada's tariff would have to rise by fifty percent to produce the necessary revenue to pay for Confederation. Other Canadian critics recognised that the province's existing tariff, which leaned towards protectionism, would have to be cut in order to meet the free-trading Maritimers half-way. This would reduce revenue at a time when more, not less, money was needed to meet increased costs. Letellier de St. Just predicted that "the deficit which that reduction of our revenue will produce will have to be filled up by the agriculture and industry of Canada" and Dunkin thought it "rather strange" that a government should propose to cut its tariff income and "at the same time, so to change our whole system as to involve ourselves in the enormous extravagances here contemplated." Dunkin felt that no plan of direct taxation could possibly meet the cost, and that the only alternative was a reckless policy of borrowing, except that "we cannot even borrow to any large amount unless under false pretences."[44] The argument that Confederation would create a larger credit base and make it easier to attract investment evidently did not convince everybody.

If Canadian critics feared the consequences of lowering the tariff at the dictation of the lower provinces, Maritimers feared even the compromise increase that Confederation seemed to imply. "Unless Canada consents to economize and curtail its expenses to a very considerable degree, which is not likely to happen," explained the Fredericton *Headquarters,* "the Lower provinces will have to raise their tariffs to that standard, as they will require a greater revenue to meet the expenses of government under the new confederation."[45] Whereas the Canadian tariff was intended to protect industry, Nova Scotia's commercial policy was aimed at fostering the province's worldwide carrying trade.[46] Thus raising the tariff would destroy trade rather than increase revenue—pointing to direct taxation which, Ambrose Shea warned, was "a point on which it is easy to alarm the masses everywhere." It certainly had that effect on Prince Edward Island, where the despairing Edward Whelan reported that it scared "the asses of country people, who can't see an inch beyond their noses."[47] A British journalist who visited Charlottetown in 1865 reported that taxation was regarded as "an evil which not only the Prince Edward Islanders, but the British colonies generally throughout North America, seem to consider as the greatest which can befall a community."[48] Historians have not been notably more sympathetic. When George Coles stated at Quebec that if Prince Edward Island surrendered control over customs and excise "she would have no revenues left with which to carry on the business of the Province," he was surely not adopting "the obstructionist tactics which were destined to characterize the Island's attitude" at the conference, but rather stating a simple fact. The province of Canada derived one third of its revenue from customs and would dominate the new political structure. Prince Edward Island raised three-quarters of its income from customs duties, and the Islanders would be a tiny minority in a British American union.[49]

Textbook explanations of the coming of Confederation assume that it was necessary for the construction of the Intercolonial Railway,

and that the Intercolonial was necessary both for defence and to give Canada a winter outlet, freeing its trade from the twin strangleholds of a frozen St Lawrence and a capriciously hostile United States. Opponents accepted neither argument and indeed found much to object to in the whole scheme. First, to reassure Maritimers who had not forgotten the Canadian bad faith of 1862, the railway project was actually written into the Quebec Resolutions, and would thus form part of the British legislation and the constitution of the Confederation—"a novelty, perhaps, that might not be found in the constitution of any country."[50] It certainly gave an unusual status to a mere railway line, the more so as its route had yet to be agreed. Arthur Gordon argued forcefully that to include such a provision in an Act of the British parliament would "be either unnecessary or unjust"—unnecessary if, as everyone assumed, the federal legislature proceeded with the scheme and "unjust if it were to have the effect of forcing on the people of British America the execution of a work which their representatives in Parliament may consider it inexpedient to undertake." In any case, such a provision "would be impossible to enforce, as no penalty could be inflicted after the passage of the Act, in the event of the subsequent neglect of its provisions by the Federal Government and Legislature."[51]

Canadian critics were less concerned by the constitutional impropriety of giving a railway the same status as peace, order and good government as by the fact that the Intercolonial would gain an advantage over their own preferred projects, especially hopes for improved communications to the Red River.[52] Suspicions were further fuelled by ministerial reluctance to say where the Intercolonial would run or how much it would cost, thus prompting the prediction that "it will be a piece of corruption from the time of the turning of the first shovelful of earth."[53] It was widely appreciated that the reason for vagueness lay in the local politics of New Brunswick, where military security pointed to a route along the thinly populated North Shore, but political expediency required a vote-pulling line up the Saint John valley, never far from the American border. Tilley attempted to offer all routes to all men, prompting the only durable piece of doggerel from the Confederation controversy: "Mr. Tilley, will you stop your puffing and blowing / And tell us which way the railway is going?"[54] The question of the cost of the Intercolonial was a sore point to Upper Canada critics of Confederation. In 1862, the Sandfield Macdonald-Sicotte ministry had withdrawn, abruptly and in an unedifying manner, from an interprovincial agreement backed by an imperial loan guarantee, by which the province of Canada undertook to pay five-twelfths of the cost of the line—which, as Henri Joly pointed out, meant that the railway could be built if required without an accompanying political union. Now Canada, with three-quarters of the population, was accepting a *pro rata* obligation to shoulder double the share envisaged in 1862. "This will involve five to seven millions of dollars of an expense more than we had any occasion for incurring," complained David Reesor, "for the other provinces were all [sic] willing to have been responsible for the rest, and there is very good reason why they should."[55] Indeed, Galt had assured Maritimers at a banquet in Halifax in September 1864, "you will get the best of the bargain." Yet, ironically, Canada's sudden outburst of generosity aroused counter-suspicions. In New Brunswick, Albert J. Smith hinted darkly that Canada must have some hidden motive for increasing the very offer it had so recently dishonoured.[56]

Fundamentally, opponents argued that the Intercolonial was no more attractive a project in 1865 than it had been when rejected in 1862. "I have not heard any reason why we should pledge our credit and resources to the construction of the Intercolonial Railway, even previous to any estimate of its cost being made,

that was not urged in 1862 when the question was before the country," A.A. Dorion asserted. William McMaster, a leading Toronto merchant, challenged the argument that the Intercolonial was "an indispensable necessity in order to secure an independent outlet to the seaboard." Rather than use the existing railways to American ports, Upper Canada merchants and millers preferred to pay warehousing, insurance and interest charges to keep wheat and flour in store through the winter months, "until the opening of the navigation." They were even less likely to use a railway to Halifax, which would be double the distance to the American winter ports. Henri Joly also doubted whether the Intercolonial could be used to send flour to the Maritimes, for "the cost of transport over five hundred miles of railway would be too great."[57]

The critics did not simply doubt whether trade could profitably flow along the Intercolonial; they also wondered whether Canada and the Maritimes were likely to have any trade at all. "Let us not...be lulled with fallacies of the great commercial advantages we shall derive from a Confederation of these provinces," intoned Eric Dorion. "We have wood, they produce it; we produce potash, and so do they."[58] "With regard to timber," said Henri Joly, "the Gulf Provinces have no more need of ours than we of theirs." Canada imported its coal direct from Britain, as ballast on returning timber ships. If that supply should ever fail, "Upper Canada will probably get its coal from the Pennsylvania mines, which are in direct communication with Lake Erie."[59] Yet, at the same time, Canadian critics could argue that free trade with the Maritimes could be achieved without "this mock Federal union," just as the provinces had enjoyed a decade of closer economic relations with the United States through the Reciprocity Treaty.[60] Not everyone shared these doubts: it was alleged that some Halifax merchants opposed Confederation precisely because they feared the competition it would bring, and it has indeed been contended that by 1874 "Central Canadian business owed its prosperity to its successful conquest of the market in the Maritimes."[61] Nonetheless, the belief that there was a prospect of major trading gains and the assumption that these would be dependent upon a political union were not held by everyone.

The critics were no more convinced by the argument that the Intercolonial was necessary for the defence of the provinces. A.A. Dorion argued that "a railway lying in some places not more than fifteen or twenty miles from the frontier, will be of no use whatever.... An enemy could destroy miles of it before it would be possible to resist him, and in time of difficulty it would be a mere trap for the troops passing along it, unless we had almost an army to keep it open." However far the Intercolonial snaked away from the American border, there was an existing stretch of the Grand Trunk "at places within twenty-six miles of the boundary of Maine," and thus easily vulnerable to American attack. Far from transporting large numbers of troops, the Intercolonial would need large forces simply to guard it. "Unless with a strong force to defend it, in a military point of view, it would be of just no use at all." In summary, the Intercolonial, centrepiece of so many textbook explanations of the causes of Confederation, was comprehensively dismissed by James L. Biggar: "Looking at it from a military point of view, it is well known that part of the proposed line would run within twenty-six miles of the American frontier, and that communication could be cut off at any moment by an American army; and that as a commercial undertaking it could never compete with the water route during the season of navigation; and in winter it would be comparatively useless on account of the depth of snow."[62]

The opponents of Confederation were unconvinced that the political union of the provinces would strengthen their defences in any way. "We do not need Confederation to give us that unity which is indispensable in all military operations—unity of headship. A commander-in-chief will direct the defence of all our provinces," argued Henri Joly. Defence had remained outside the orbit of colonial self-government until very recent times, and Canada's record on militia reform was hardly impressive. Consequently, the argument that unity meant strength is one which appeals more to the twentieth century observer than it did to contemporaries, especially when the unity proposed involved such tiny provinces. John S. Sanborn was simply bewildered. "How the people of New Brunswick could be expected to come up to Canada to defend us, and leave their own frontier unprotected," he could not comprehend. Conversely, Matthew Cameron asked why Canada should be taxed to build fortifications in the Maritimes: "Fortifications in St. John, New Brunswick, would not protect us from the foe, if the foe were to come here." Sanborn argued that if there were indeed a war with the United States, each province would be attacked from a neighboring state. "Under these circumstances, each section of the Confederation would have enough to do to attend to its own affairs." Except, contended A.A. Dorion, that New Brunswick could not defend itself, since the province's population of a quarter of a million was only one-third that of the adjoining state of Maine: "Those 250,000 Canada will have to defend, and it will have to pledge its resources for the purpose of providing means of defence along that extended line."[63]

In the Atlantic colonies, the arguments were inverted. Petitioners from Nova Scotia's Digby County were ready to rally to "the defence of their country and their flag" but were "not disposed to adopt, as a means of ensuring their more efficient defence, a union with a Province which in 1862 refused to sanction a measure involving increased outlay for the better and more elaborate organisation of their militia."[64] Joseph Howe deftly alluded to Canadian complicity in border raids by Southern sympathizers, and the resulting threats of Northern retaliation, proclaiming: "let those who provoke these controversies fight them out."[65] He objected to a system under which Nova Scotia's militia "may be ordered away to any point of the Canadian frontier."[66] Prince Edward Islanders feared that they would be "marched away to the frontiers of Upper Canada" or, as John Hamilton Gray put it with vivid bitterness, "drafted for slaughter."[67] In Newfoundland, the outspoken Charles Fox Bennett spoke of the island's young men "leaving their bones to bleach in a foreign land," a phrase which he was to refine in the 1869 election into the celebrated references to "the desert sands of Canada."[68]

In three of the four Atlantic provinces, insularity was a physical as well as a mental factor. "We are surrounded by the sea," proclaimed Joseph Howe and—what was more to the point—"within ten days' sail of the fleets and armies of England."[69] J.C. Pope of Prince Edward Island echoed Canadian critics in predicting that an American attack would make it "necessary to retain all available strength in each of the provinces for the defence of their respective territories." His emphasis differed in his confidence that local efforts would be powerfully seconded by the British navy and army.[70] Many critics argued that Confederation would actually make the defence of British North America more difficult. Henri Joly argued that there was "no need" of political union to warn "our neighbours" not to pick on a single province. The Americans were "sufficiently sharp-witted to discover, without being told it, that if they content themselves with attacking us at a single point at a time, of course they will have to meet all our strength." Perhaps, he added sarcastically, they could be persuaded to "enter into a contract, binding them to attack us at a single point only at one time—say Quebec."

More seriously, L.A. Olivier warned that if Confederation was thrust upon an unwilling population, they could not be expected to rally to the defence of their homeland with the full enthusiasm shown in earlier conflicts. Joseph Howe similarly warned that if the rights of Nova Scotians were "overridden by an arbitrary Act of Parliament, very few of them will march to defend Canada."[71]

"With Confederation, neither the number of men in the several provinces, nor the pecuniary resources now at their disposal, will be increased." The kernel of the Canadian opposition case on defence was that Confederation involved too much territory and no additional manpower. "Can you alter the geographical position of the country?," asked Benjamin Symour. "Will you have any more people or means?" "If nature were to make the necessary effort and move their territory up alongside of us, and thus make a compact mass of people, I would at once agree that it would strengthen us in a military point of view," Philip Moore ironically conceded. In reality, however, Confederation "will weaken instead of strengthen us," since "the union will give an extension of territory far greater in proportion to the number of the population than [sic] now exists in Canada." The planned massive extension into empty and inaccessible territory westward to the Pacific struck A.A. Dorion as "a burlesque" in terms of defence. In short, critics found the defence argument literally laughable: "If we could attach the territory possessed by the moon to these provinces, and obtain the assistance for our joint defence of the man who is popularly supposed to inhabit that luminary, we might derive strength from Confederation."[72]

Critics were equally unimpressed by ringing talk of a "new nationality" in British North America. "I cannot see that the Federation of these provinces has anything of a national phase in it," commented Thomas Scatcherd. "When you speak of national existence, you speak of independence; and so long as we are colonists of Great Britain we can have no national existence."[73] Some Nova Scotian petitions protested that British North America was "incapable of forming a new nationality,"[74] but the loyal people of Barrington township had an each-way bet in wanting no part of "new nationalities too feeble to stand alone, yet difficult to be controlled."[75] Their governor, Sir Richard MacDonnell,

> was unable to see in what way England would be less vulnerable through Canada or Canada less vulnerable through England when a confederated Parliament meets at Ottawa than now. There is not a foot of territory in all these hundreds of thousands of square miles which would thereby become less English than now, so long as the Queen's Representative is head of the Federation; nor is there any obligation in regard to these Provinces which now devolves upon Britain that would be diminished by their being thus huddled into one heterogeneous assemblage.[76]

In fact, critics feared that Confederation would actually provoke Americans into hostilities. Howe warned: "let this guy of 'near nationality' be set up...and every young fellow who has had a taste of the license of camp life in the United States will be tempted to have a fling at it."[77] Christopher Dunkin even expressed alarm at the tone of the Confederation debates, asking "how is the temper of the United States going to be affected...by the policy here urged on us, of what I may call hostile independent effort—effort made on our part, with the avowed object of setting ourselves up as a formidable power against them[?]" The Northern States, A.A. Dorion pointed out, had put into the field an army of 2,300,000, "as many armed men as we have men, women and children in the two Canadas." Military expenditure on any large scale would be useless and "we are not bound to ruin ourselves in anticipation of a supposed invasion which we could not repel."

Public opinion should force the Canadian press to cease its anti-American outbursts: "The best thing that Canada can do is to keep quiet, and to give no cause for war."[78] Joseph Howe agreed that British North America could never stand alone militarily against the United States, but he took the argument a stage further. "Inevitably it must succumb to the growing power of the republic. A treaty offensive and defensive with the United States, involving ultimate participation in a war with England, would be the hard terms of its recognition as a separate but not independent state."[79]

Given their overwhelming rejection of the case for Confederation as a defence measure, it is hardly surprising that this aspect of the scheme produced some of the most colourful imagery among critics. Joining with the Maritimes, said James Currie, "was like tying a small twine at the end of a long rope and saying it strengthened the whole line." Incorporating the vast Hudson's Bay Territories, said Henri Joly, would create "the outward form of a giant, but with the strength of a child."[80] John Macdonald, member for Toronto West, thought "the casting of the burden of defence upon this country is like investing a sovereign with all the outward semblance of royalty, and giving him a dollar per day to keep up the dignity of his court." Macdonald has been overshadowed by his namesake to the point of invisibility, but he had a homely touch in his comments, telling the legislators as they met for the last year in Quebec City that Confederation was like taking the engine from the Lévis ferry and using it "to propel the *Great Eastern* across the Atlantic."[81] In a far smaller town, an angry young Rouge editor denounced Confederation in less whimsical imagery. As a defence against the United States it was like being "armed with an egg-shell to stop a bullet...a wisp of straw in the way of a giant."[82] The writer's name was Wilfrid Laurier.

Studies of the opposition to Confederation within the individual provinces have tended to concentrate on the risks and disadvantages of Confederation to each community—an approach which by its nature portrays the critics as "parochial."[83] However, while the objections made on behalf of each province were naturally contradictory, they fell into a common pattern. John Simpson denied that seventeen additional MPs would be of any use to Upper Canada, while Matthew Cameron argued that if the eighty-two Upper Canadians proposed to develop the North-West, they would be outvoted by "sixty-five members from Lower Canada and forty-seven from the Lower Provinces, whose interests will be united against US."[84] By contrast, Joseph Howe warned that New Brunswick and Nova Scotia "must be a prey to the spoiler" for "having but forty-seven representatives, all told, it is apparent that the Government of the confederacy will always rest upon the overwhelming majority of 147, and that, even when close divisions and ministerial crises occur, the minority can easily be split up and played off against each other for purely Canadian purposes."[85] French Canadians challenged that assumption of a unity of purpose, doubting that "all the members from Lower Canada would make common cause on any question." Although the province was guaranteed sixty-five MPs in perpetuity, they would not all be francophones: "we shall have forty-eight members in the Federal Parliament against one hundred and forty of English origin; in other words, we shall be in a proportion of one to four. What could so weak a minority do to obtain justice?"[86] Joseph Howe evidently felt that French Canadians possessed a greater measure of political skill than Maritimers, for he warned that "as the English will split and divide, as they always do, the French members will in nine cases out of ten, be masters of the situation."[87] A.A. Dorion agreed that they "would go as a body to the Legislature, voting as one man, and caring for nothing else but the protection of their beloved institutions and law, and making government all but impossible," but he felt this a "deplorable state of things."[88]

There was little direct contact between Canada and Maritimes prior to Confederation: during a visit to Montreal in 1860, T. Heath Haviland of Prince Edward Island had encountered "the utmost difficulty" in finding "so much as a newspaper from the Lower Provinces."[89] It is therefore surprising to discover the extent of their mutual antipathy. The "plain meaning" of the Canadian ministry's desire to force through the Quebec Resolutions without amendment was "that the Lower Provinces have made out a Constitution for us and we are to adopt it," said A.A. Dorion. Voting at the Quebec Conference had been by provinces, which "made Prince Edward Island equal to Upper Canada." Dorion complained of "the humiliation of seeing the Government going on its knees and begging the little island of Prince Edward to come into this union."[90] Only by appreciating the existence of this sentiment of disdain for the Maritimes among Canadian critics can we understand why Macdonald and his colleagues had no alternative but to outface and outmanoeuvre opposition in Nova Scotia and New Brunswick. Maritimers returned the hostility. James Dingwell of Prince Edward Island thought "Canadians had not been able to manage the business of their country as we have been to manage ours; and why should we trust the management of our own affairs to people who have never been able to manage their own with satisfaction?"[91] With colourful exaggeration, Joseph Howe claimed that Canadians were "always in trouble of some sort, and two or three times in open rebellion."[92]

Despite Howe's suspicions that Lower Canadian solidarity in the federal parliament would entrench French power, hostility to Confederation in the Atlantic colonies seems to have been directed against the whole of what later became the monster of "central Canada" and was relatively free of explicit francophobia. There was a hint of it in an open letter to the British Colonial Secretary in January 1867, when a recitation of Nova Scotia's loyal service to the Empire in wars against France was followed by the waspish comment: "We are now asked to surrender it to Monsieur Cartier."[93] Although francophobia was so endemic that it was not necessary to articulate it, inter-communal flashpoints in the mid-nineteenth century were more likely to concern sectarian schooling than the politics of language. Memories of their homeland's forced unification with Britain led many Irish Catholics to oppose Confederation. If anti-Confederates had warned of the danger of French power, Irish Catholics might have concluded that Confederation could bring benefits for their Church. In any case, Acadians were as suspicious of Confederation as their anglophone neighbours, and it suited Howe to portray them as one of the contented minorities—along with Micmacs and Blacks—who had flourished under the benign institutions of an autonomous Nova Scotia.[94]

In each province, critics argued that their constituents had got the worst of the bargain. That their arguments were contradictory did not much matter, since by definition they were intended for purely local consumption, directed at those whose "mental vision"—as an impatient Halifax newspaper put it—"is bounded by Dartmouth on the one side, and Citadel Hill on the other."[95] However, claims in each province of a bad deal provoked supporters of Confederation into refutations which were seized upon by critics elsewhere as confirmation of their fears. One of the earliest public expositions of the Quebec scheme came in a major speech by Galt at Sherbrooke in November 1864. Tupper admired it, but mildly complained that it was "a little too much from the Canadian point of view to suit this meridian." From Prince Edward Island, Edward Whelan similarly warned that "in the Lower Provinces a view of the Confederation question with a very decided Canadian colouring is apt to lessen confidence in it as we barbarians

down in these lower regions are terribly doubtful and suspicious of Canadian intentions."[96] Within a few months, hard-pressed Confederates in the Maritimes had given similar hostages to the scheme's critics in the province of Canada. David Reesor read into the record extracts from Tilley's election speeches to show that politicians in the Maritimes "see the great advantage they have gained over Canada, and are not slow to set them [sic] before the people." Dorion similarly quoted Tilley and Whelan, and pictured them "chuckling over the good bargains they have made at the expense of Canada."[97]

Behind these mutual suspicions, there surely lay something deeper than the cussedness which we normally dismiss as parochialism. Even in the superheated provincial politics of the mid-nineteenth century it seems exaggerated that Cartier could have been accused of "la lâchéte la plus insigne dans la trahison la plus noire," merely for forming a coalition with George Brown, or that Prince Edward Island representatives at the Charlottetown conference were pointed out in the street as "the men who would sell their country."[98] The fact that such remarks were made suggests that the different provinces felt themselves to possess distinct social and political cultures. This was most obvious in predominantly French-speaking and Catholic Lower Canada: "Confederation is in fact a Legislative union, because upon the Federal Government is conferred the right of legislating upon those subjects which Lower Canada holds most dear."[99] The complication in Lower Canada was the existence of a minority-within-a-minority, equally suspicious of those aspects of the new constitution which guaranteed provincial autonomy under a local francophone majority. Principal Dawson of McGill thought that "scarcely anyone among the English of Lower Canada desires Confederation, except perhaps as an alternative to simple dissolution of the Union."[100] This was a case where clashing objections had a reinforcing effect, for every reassurance offered to the Lower Canada English was a confirmation of French Canadian fears.[101]

The separate identity of French Canadian society on an Anglo-Saxon continent was obvious enough. What may be less obvious is that in the Maritimes—and especially in Nova Scotia—there was as great a sense of being different from the province of Canada as modern Canadians would today feel separates themselves from their neighbours in the United States. True, Joseph Howe could welcome a party of Canadian visitors to Halifax in August 1864 with the sentiment: "I am not one of those who thank God that I am a Nova Scotian merely, for I am a Canadian as well."[102] Yet the picture which emerges from his subsequent anti-Confederation campaign is of a province not simply resentful of losing its autonomy, but fearful of being subordinated to the capricious and unattractive values of "those who live above the tide," "the administration of strangers."[103] A recurrent theme of Nova Scotian opposition was loss of its historic self-government. Behind the issue of high principle, there lay practical and local fears. The petitioners of Digby County pointed out that "while that portion of this county which borders on the sea is thickly inhabited and rapidly increasing in population and wealth, there are still considerable districts but lately reclaimed from the primaeval forest," which required grants of public money for the development of roads and bridges. They regarded "with dismay" the transfer of control over public expenditure "to a Government by which they would necessarily all be expended for widely different purposes."[104] Canada was associated with inflationary paper money and high interest rates. "Every post-master and every way office keeper is to be appointed and controlled by the Canadians."[105] Canada was as distant from Nova Scotia as Austria from Britain.[106] "You cannot...invest a village on the Ottawa with the

historic interest and associations that cluster around London," wrote Joseph Howe—and he emphatically preferred "London under the dominion of John Bull to Ottawa under the dominion of Jack Frost."[107] To the modern mind, Joseph Howe was descending to the darkest depths of petty parochialism when he proclaimed that travellers "can scarcely ride five miles in Upper Canada without being stopped by a toll bar or a toll bridge. There are but two toll-bridges in Nova Scotia and all the roads are free."[108] Yet Howe's complaint was really little different in spirit from modern Canadian concern to defend welfare and regional programmes against American allegations of unfair wage subsidies.[109]

Another theme common to the critics, whatever their regional loyalty, was rejection of both the proposed provincial governments and the confederate upper house as safeguards for their rights. "Ce n'est donc pas une confédération qui nous est proposée, mais tout simplement une Union Législative déguisée sous le nom de confédération," argued A.A. Dorion.[110] George Coles predicted that under Confederation, the legislature of Prince Edward Island "would be the laughing stock of the world," left "to legislate about dog taxes, and the running at large of swine."[111] While some critics concluded that the whole plan of union should be abandoned, others argued from similar premises that the union should be strengthened. The Halifax *Citizen* agreed that the Quebec scheme "has given these local legislatures very little to do," and predicted that they would occupy themselves in mischief, preserving local loyalties which would prevent "the fusion of the British American population in one actual indivisible nationality."[112] "One of the worst features of the Union plan proposed by Canada is, that it will leave our local legislature still in existence," lamented the Saint John *Globe,* which would have preferred to see outright unification.[113] Even the fervent anti-Confederate, T.W. Anglin, writing in the rival *Freeman,* agreed that if they had to have Confederation, "it would be better to abolish the local Legislatures at once in appearance as well as in reality."[114]

The critics were not reassured by the fact that both lieutenant-governors and members of the upper house were to be appointed by the central government. The prospect of lieutenant-governors drawn from provincial politics aroused little enthusiasm. "Let any one of our dozen or twenty most prominent Canadian politicians be named Lieutenant-Governor of Upper or of Lower Canada, would not a large and powerful class of the community...be very likely to resent the nomination as an insult?" asked Christopher Dunkin.[115] In Canada, where the legislative Council had become elective in 1856—with life members retaining their seats—there was resentment at the reintroduction of nomination, "because the Maritime Provinces are opposed to an elective Chamber, and hence we in Canada—the largest community and the most influential—must give way to them."[116] There was also resentment at the provision in the Quebec Resolutions by which the first Confederate legislative councillors would be appointed from the existing Legislative Councils (except in Prince Edward Island)—a transparent bribe to curb the opposition in the upper houses. Worse still, the first Confederate upper house was to be appointed for life, on the nomination of the existing provincial governments—with the central government not even possessing a veto. A.A. Dorion's objection was not to the principle but to the unlucky fact that most British North American governments were Conservative. "For all time to come, as far as this generation and the next are concerned, you will find the Legislative Council controlled by the influence of the present government."[117] Future appointment by the central government aroused no more enthusiasm, since as Dunkin suggested, a government might be formed in which an entire province "either is not represented, or is represented otherwise than it would wish to be." How would such a province, "out in the cold," be served when vacancies in the upper house came to be filled?[118] Macdonald and McGee may strike posterity as the visionaries of the time, but it was the dry-as-dust Dunkin who foresaw the position of Alberta in the later Trudeau years, or Quebec under Joe Clark.

The arguments of the critics of Confederation must be conceded to have been at least plausible. Why then did they fail to prevent the passage of the British North America Act in 1867? First, of course, their arguments did not pass unchallenged. Just as conventional studies of the causes of Confederation tend to underplay the opposition case, so a study of the critics necessarily distorts the debate in their favour. Indeed, arguments which high-minded posterity may find irrefutable could perhaps have produced diametrically opposite responses among contemporaries: Upper Canadian critics, in damning the Intercolonial as an irresponsible waste of money, might have convinced some Lower Canadians of its pork-barrel value.[119] Even if the opposition case against the Intercolonial Railway had been overwhelming, Confederation might still have been supported on general grounds as the most practicable solution to a range of problems. The Confederation package mattered more than the interlocking detail, and not everybody bothered with those details. Bishop Laflèche did not allow ignorance of the latter to inhibit him from pronouncing on the former: "Le projet de Confédération est tellement vaste et complexe en lui-même et dans ses détails qu'il est bien difficile de l'aborder sans en avoir auparavant faire une étude spéciale; et c'est que je n'ai point fait." What Laflèche saw was a province in which the legislative process was paralysed, where political opponents confronted each other almost like enemy camps, a state of affairs which could only end disastrously for Lower Canadians—either in "la guerre civile ou la domination du Haut-Canada dans l'Union Législative."[120] The bishop was probably wrong—at least in his fears of civil war—but could anyone be sure? In any case, even if the argument were won inside the provinces, there remained that "atmosphere of crisis" over the North American continent. "Look around you to the valley of Virginia," McGee challenged those who wanted to know why Confederation was necessary, "look around you to the mountains of Georgia, and you will find reasons as thick as blackberries."[121] Perhaps the fundamental mistake of the opponents of Confederation was to ask people to react logically to the activities of Macdonald and Cartier in the conference chamber rather than to the operations of Grant and Sherman on the battlefield. The question for explanation then becomes why it should have been intercolonial union—rather than, say, neutrality or annexation—which met the psychological need for a dramatic response to continental crisis. One explanation may be that the idea had been around for a long time, answer looking for a question. "Everybody admits that Union must take place sometime," said John A. Macdonald, "I say now is the time."[122] In seeking to account for the adoption of so vast a scheme as Canadian Confederation, historians have naturally turned to the arguments of its supporters, and have been tempted to conclude that the arguments put forward *for* Canadian Confederation equal the reasons *why* Canadian Confederation came about.

Certainly hindsight finds it easy to draw neat lines of causation linking argument to outcome: the lines may be straight, but the process itself is circular, since it identifies the winners of history as—in Morton's terms—those who sensed the currents of events. Yet we should not forget that the case against Confederation was argued as tenaciously, as eloquently and—we must assume—as sincerely as the arguments in its favour. However much historians may admire the "Fathers of Confederation," only by recognising not just the strength of opposition to Confederation but also the plausibility of some of the arguments put forward, can we begin to see that the outcome was by no means inevitable. Of course, some historians believe that posterity is not entitled to second-guess past controversies, that a century later we cannot award points to individual arguments, for or against, since we cannot make ourselves fully part of the atmosphere of the time. Yet such an attitude is tantamount to an uncritical abdication of our own judgement to each and every claim made by those who were on the winning side perhaps for reasons other than the simply intellectual. "La raison du plus fort, c'est toujours la meilleure," is not the most appropriate explanatory strategy for the historian to adopt. Hindsight may yet conclude that while the Antis lost the battle, they won at least some of the arguments.

Notes

1 Cf. A.G. Bailey, "The Basis and Persistence of Opposition to Confederation in New Brunswick," *Canadian Historical Review,* XXIII (1942), pp. 367–83 and Carl Wallace, "Albert Smith, Confederation and Reaction in New Brunswick, 1852–1882," ibid. XLIV (1963), pp. 285–312.

2 G. Patterson, "An Unexplained Incident of Confederation in Nova Scotia," *Dalhousie Review,* VII (1927), pp. 442–46.

3 *CD,* pp. 545 (Blanchet); 147 (Holton); 682 (Dorion).

4 *Life and Times,* p. 154.

5 Not reported in *CD,* but see Waite, ed., *Confederation Debates,* pp. xv–xvi.

6 *Hansard's Parliamentary Debates* (3rd series), CLXXXV, 19 February 1867, cols. 579–80, 577.

7 *British Parliamentary Papers* [cited as *BPP*], 1867, XLVIII, *Correspondence Respecting the Proposed Union of the British North American Provinces,* pp. 75–77.

8 Ibid., p. 68. Howe's tour is described in J.M. Beck, *Joseph Howe: II, The Briton Becomes Canadian 1848–1873* (Kingston, 1983), p. 201.

9 *CD,* p. 61.

10 Speech of 7 April 1866, quoted in William M. Baker, *Timothy Warren Anglin 1822–1896: Irish Catholic Canadian* (Toronto, 1977), p. 103, and see also p. 58. Anglin was editor of the Saint John

Morning Freeman. According to Creighton, Anglin was "an unsubdued ex-rebel" who "flung the full force of his abusive and mendacious journalism against Confederation" (*Road to Confederation*, p. 251, and see also p. 247). It is unlikely that Anglin took part in the Irish rising of 1848 and there is no reason to think that his journalism was unusually abusive or mendacious by contemporary standards, which were admittedly low. Thus have critics of Confederation been dismissed.

11 Similar views were expressed in the Canadian Legislative Council by James G. Currie, Bill Flint and David Reesor and in the Assembly by Christopher Dunkin, Joseph Perrault, Thomas Scatcherd and T.C. Wallbridge. *CD*, pp. 46, 164, 319, 483, 585, 749, 660.

12 Charlottetown *Examiner*, 30 January 1865, quoted in *Life and Times*, p. 186.

13 *CD*, p. 328.

14 *CD*, p. 248. In May 1860, Dorion had said that he regarded a federation of the two Canadas as "le noyau de la grande confédération des provinces de l'Amérique du nord que j'appelle de mes voeux." Quoted by Joseph Cauchon, *L'Union des Provinces de l'Amérique Britannique du Nord* (Quebec, 1865), p. 7.

15 Speech in Halifax, 13 August 1864, in J.A. Chisholm, ed., *The Speeches and Public Letters of Joseph Howe* (2 vols, Halifax, 1909), II, p. 433.

16 *CD*, p. 126.

17 *CD*, pp. 352 (Joly); 508, 485 (Dunkin); 747 (Scatcherd).

18 *CD*, p. 357.

19 *CD*, p. 586.

20 *CD*, p. 357 (Joly) and cf p. 591 (Perrault).

21 *CD*, pp. 593–95, 625–26.

22 *CD*, pp. 543 (Dunkin); 356–57 (Joly).

23 Open letter, 10 April 1866, in Chisholm, ed., *Speeches and Public Letters of Joseph Howe*, II, p. 463.

24 *CD*, p. 456.

25 *L'Ordre*, 7 June 1865, quoted in *Life and Times*, p. 147.

26 *CD*, p. 659.

27 Howe to Isaac Buchanan, 20 June 1866, in Chisholm, ed., *op. cit.*, II, p. 464. In his 1866 pamplet, *Confederation Considered in Relation to the Interests of the Empire*, Howe complained that in the New Brunswick election that year, "one half of an entirely loyal population were taught to brand the other half as disloyal." Quoted in ibid., II, p. 484.

28 Dunkin spoke about imperial federation in *CD*, p. 545, and was criticised by Frederick Haultain, MPP for Peterborough, p. 646. Howe's long-standing enthusiasm culminated in his 1866 pamphlet, *The Organisation of the Empire*, quoted in Chisholm, ed., *op. cit.*, II, pp. 492–506. Tupper savagely exploited the logical contradictions in Howe's position: within an imperial federation, Nova Scotians would be in a far more insignificant minority than within Confederation, liable to fight in bloody wars in all corners of the world, a scheme "as useless as it would be unjust and repressive." Letter in Halifax *British Colonist*, 13 December 1866, in E.M. Saunders, ed., *Life and Letters of Sir Charles Tupper* (2 vols, London, 1916), I, pp. 139–40.

29 Creighton, *Road to Confederation*, pp. 266–67.

30 Pope, ed., *op. cit.*, p. 684, and quoted by Dorion, *CD*, p. 654. See also *CD*, p. 248 (and cf. p. 657) for the negotiations after the death of Taché, Pope, ed., *op. cit.*, pp. 700–706. George Brown's letter to his wife of 8 March 1865 is quoted in Careless, *op. cit.*, II, p. 190.

31 *CD*, p. 657.

32 *CD*, pp. 155, 158 (James Aikens, MLC); 487 (Dunkin).

33 Halifax *Morning Chronicle*, 24 January 1866, quoted in *Life and Times*, p. 221. Annand used the argument, not to reject Confederation, but as a device to suggest an alternative approach. The allusion to "festivities" may have been a coded reference to a campaign of denigration directed against John A. Macdonald's intermittent bouts of drunkenness.

34 *BPP*, 1867, XLVIII, Howe, Annand and McDonald to Carnarvon, 19 January 1867, p. 13.

35 Hamilton *Times*, November 1864, quoted in *Life and Times*, p. 122. See also Bruce W. Hodgins, "Democracy and the Ontario Fathers of Confederation," in Bruce Hodgins and Robert Page, eds, *Canadian History Since Confederation: Essays and Interpretations* (2nd ed., Georgetown, Ontario, 1979), pp. 19–28.

36 *BPP*, 1867, XLVIII, *Correspondence*, pp. 70, 75; Howe et al. to Carnarvon, 19 January 1867, p. 18.

37 *CD*, p. 179 (L.A. Olivier, MLC for the Lanaudière).

38 Quoted in Chisholm, ed., *op. cit.*, II, p. 473.

39 *CD*, p. 490.

40 Gordon to Gladstone, private, 27 February 1865, in Paul Knaplund, ed., *Gladstone-Gordon Correspondence, 1851–1896* (Transactions of the American Philosophical Society, n.s., Ll, pt 4, 1961), p. 46.

41 Yarmouth *Tribune*, 9 November 1864, quoted in *Life and Times*, p. 202.

42 Speech at Dartmouth, NS, 22 May 1867, quoted in Chisholm, ed., *op. cit.*, II, p. 514.

43 *CD*, p. 520.

44 *CD*, pp. 50 (Currie); 188 (Letellier); 524 (Dunkin).

45 Fredericton *Headquarters*, 19 October 1864, quoted in Bailey, "Basis and Persistence," p. 375.

46 "We have the trade of the world now open to us on nearly equal terms, and why should we allow Canada to hamper us?," Yarmouth *Herald*, 15 December 1864, quoted in *Life and Times*, p. 202.

47 Shea to Galt, 15 December 1864 and Whelan to Galt, 17 December 1864, in Ormsby, "Letters to Galt," pp. 167, 168.

48 Charles Mackay, "A Week in Prince Edward Island," *Fortnightly Review*, V (1865), p. 147.

49 Bolger, *Prince Edward Island and Confederation*, p. 68. In 1863, while the province of Canada derived 35.95 percent of its revenue from customs, New Brunswick derived 66.12 percent, Nova Scotia 81.09 percent, Prince Edward Island 74.66 percent and Newfoundland 86.08 percent. However, in per capita yield, Canadians paid roughly double Maritimers. The figures for 1863 customs revenues (with year of population in parentheses) were: Canada (1865) £1.04; New Brunswick (1861) £0.36; Nova Scotia (1861) £0.52; Prince Edward Island (1863) £0.36; Newfoundland (1857) £0.79. (Calculated from *BPP*, 1866, LXXIII, Colonial Trade Statistics, pp. 126, 148–49. 160–61, 168, 174.) Estimated wages rates (ibid., pp. 159, 173, 181) for tradesmen in 1863 were between £0.3 and £0.4 per diem in Newfoundland, and £0.25 and £0.4 in New Brunswick, but the Prince Edward Island figure (£40 per annum) suggests that tradesmen were employed for only 100 to 160 days each year. Thus for a tradesman on Prince Edward Island supporting a wife and four children, a rise in per capita tariff yield to Canadian levels would have cost over £4 a year, or about five weeks' wages.

50 *CD*, p. 17 (Holton).

51 PRO, CO 188/143, Gordon to Cardwell, no. 23, 27 February 1865, fos 181–85, printed in *BPP*, 1867, XLVIII, *Correspondence*, pp. 88–89.

52 Article 69 of the Quebec Resolutions offered only that improved communications to the Red River "shall be prosecuted at the earliest possible period that the state of the Finances will permit." According to T.C. Wallbridge, this meant "that the North-West is hermetically sealed." *CD*, p. 453 and cf. Matthew Cameron, pp. 452–53.

53 *CD*, p. 759 (Scatcherd).

54 Fredericton *Headquarters*, 1 February 1865, quoted in Bailey, "Basis and Persistence," p. 379.

55 *CD*, pp. 356 (Joly); 164 (Reesor). The 1862 agreement involved only the two provinces of New Brunswick and Nova Scotia.

56 Wallace, "Albert Smith," p. 289. The Nova Scotian deputation to London in 1867 could "scarcely bring themselves to discuss" the Intercolonial, "so selfish and unfair at all times has been the conduct of the public men of Canada in regard to it." *BPP*, 1867, XLVIII, Howe et al. to Carnarvon, 19 January 1867, p. 8. For Galt's Halifax speech, see Edward Whelan, comp., *The Union of the British Provinces* (Charlottetown, 1865), p. 48.

57 *CD*, pp. 263 (Dorion); 230 (McMaster); 356 (Joly).

58 *CD*, p. 863, Canada took 1.11 percent of its imports from the other British North American territories, and sent them 2.2 percent of its exports. New Brunswick took 2.3 percent of its imports from Canada, to which it sent 0.87 percent of its exports. Prince Edward Island took 2.1 percent of its imports from Canada, to which it sent 0.6 percent of its exports. Newfoundland took 3.9 percent of its imports from Canada, to which it sent 0.68 percent of its exports. (Calculated from *BPP*, 1866. LXIII, *Colonial Trade Statistics*, pp. 132, 152, 170, 177.) Nova Scotia figures are less helpful, but in 1866 the province took 5.5 percent of its imports from Canada, and sent 7.15 percent of its exports (1865 figures being 3.5 percent and 4.96 percent). (Calculated from *BPP*, 1867–68, LXXI, *Colonial Trade Statistics*, p. 144.)

59 *CD*, p. 355.

60 *CD*, pp. 356 (Joly) and 528 (Dorion).

61 Halifax *Evening Reporter*, 10 December 1864, quoted in *Life and Times*, p. 208; Peter B. Waite, *Canada 1874–1896: Arduous Destiny* (Toronto, 1971), p. 76. This "conquest" of Maritime markets could not have been the result of the Intercolonial, which was not completed until 1876. In 1875, Senator A.W. McLelan of Nova Scotia described Canadian goods and produce arriving "by steamer and sail on the Gulf and by the Grand Trunk via Portland," ibid., pp. 76–77.

62 *CD*, pp. 257 (Dorion); 750 (Scatcherd): 521 (Dorion); 883 (Biggar).

63 *CD*, pp. 355 (Joly); 123 (Sanborn); 456 (Cameron); 124 (Sanborn): 256 (Dorion).

64 *BPP*, 1867, XLVIII, *Correspondence*, pp. 69–70.

65 Halifax *Morning Chronicle,* 11 January 1865, quoted in Chisholm, ed., *op. cit.,* II, p. 435 (the first of the celebrated "Botheration Scheme" letters).

66 Speech at Dartmouth, 22 May 1867, quoted in ibid., II, p. 512.

67 *Islander,* 6 January 1865 and J.H. Gray to Tupper, 7 January 1865, quoted in *Life and Times,* pp. 186, 183.

68 *Newfoundlander,* 12 January 1865, quoted in *Life and Times,* p. 167. It was alleged that in the 1869 election, Newfoundlanders were told "that their young children would be rammed into guns" by Canadians. James Hiller, "Confederation Defeated: The Newfoundland Election of 1869" in J. Hiller and P. Neary, eds, *Newfoundland in the Nineteenth and Twentieth Centuries: Essays in Reinterpretation* (Toronto, 1980), p. 83.

69 Quoted in Chisholm, ed., *op. cit.,* II, pp. 435–36.

70 Quoted in Bolger, ed., *Canada's Smallest Province,* pp. 175–76.

71 *CD,* pp. 354 (Joly); 180 (Olivier); *BPP,* 1867, XLVI-II, Howe et al. to Carnarvon, 19 January 1867, p. 7.

72 *CD,* pp. 176 (Olivier); 203 (Seymour); 229 (Moore); 263 (Dorion); 234 (John Simpson, MLC for Queen's). The Halifax *Citizen* alleged that Tupper was perfectly capable of campaigning for federation with the Moon if he thought it would divert public attention. Quoted in *Life and Times,* p. 200.

73 *CD,* p. 748. Critics dismissed appeals to Italian and German unity as proving that the spirit of the times pointed to wider unions. Henri Joly gave a list of federations which had failed (*CD,* pp. 346–48), while the imperially minded Howe likened Confederation to a handful of small states withdrawing from the North German Confederation, or "a few offshoots from Italian unity" attempting to form "an inferior confederation." *BPP,* 1867, XLVIII, Howe et al. to Carnarvon, 19 January 1867, p. 21.

74 E.g. Petition from King's, *BPP,* 1867, XLVIII, *Correspondence,* p. 67.

75 Ibid., p. 71.

76 PRO, CO 217/235, MacDonnell to Cardwell, 22 November 1865, fos 187–212.

77 Quoted in Chisholm, ed., *op. cit.,* II, p. 487.

78 *CD,* pp. 529 (Dunkin); 257 (Brome).

79 Quoted in Chisholm, ed., *op. cit.,* II, p. 489.

80 *CD,* pp. 46 (Currie); 353 (Joly). Henri Joly doubted comparisons between the Hudson's Bay Territories and European Russia, doubting that the West could ever support a large population. It may be noted that he ended his public career by serving as lieutenant-governor of British Columbia, 1900–1906. John A. Macdonald believed in 1865 that the prairies were "of no present value to Canada" which had "unoccupied land enough to absorb the immigration for many years." To open Saskatchewan would be to "drain away our youth and strength." Macdonald to E.W. Watkin, 27 March 1865, in Pope, *Memoirs,* pp. 397–98.

81 *CD,* p. 753.

82 Quoted in J. Schull, *Laurier: The First Canadian* (Toronto, 1966), p. 57.

83 Localism could also be harnessed to Confederation, influencing the kind of scheme which emerged. Elwood H. Jones, "Localism and Federalism in Upper Canada in 1865," in Bruce W. Hodgins, D. Wright and W. H. Heick, eds, *Federalism in Canada and Australia: The Early Years* (Waterloo, Ont., 1978), pp. 19–41.

84 *CD,* pp. 232 (Simpson); 452–53 (Cameron).

85 Quoted in Chisholm, ed., *op. cit.,* II, p. 490.

86 *CD,* pp. 191 (J.O. Bureau, Rouge MLC for De Lorimier); 624 (Perrault). McGee argued that in addition up to seven members from the Lower Provinces would represent largely francophone ridings. *CD,* p. 137.

87 Halifax *Morning Chronicle,* 13 January 1865, quoted in *Life and Times,* p. 212.

88 *CD,* p. 264.

89 Speech at Montreal, 28 October 1864, in Whelan, comp., *Union,* p. 115.

90 *CD,* pp. 252, 47, 656.

91 Quoted in Bolger, ed., *Canada's Smallest Province,* II, p. 177.

92 Howe to Earl Russell, 19 January 1865, quoted in Chisholm, ed., *op. cit.,* II, p. 437.

93 *BPP,* 1867, XLVIII, Howe et al. to Carnarvon, 19 January 1867, p. 16. See also ibid., p. 12 for an unsubtle reference to the Hundred Years War.

94 Ibid., p. 17. Cf. Leon Thériault, "L'Acadie, 1763–1978: Synthèse Historique" in Jean Daigle, éd., *Les Acadiens des Maritimes: Etudes Thématiques* (Moncton, 1980), pp. 63–68.

95 *Morning Chronicle,* 23 December 1864, quoted in *Life and Times,* p. 208.

96 Tupper to Galt, 13 December 1864, and Whelan to Galt, 17 December 1864, in Ormsby, "Letters," pp. 166, 168.

97 *CD,* pp. 329 (Reesor): 261 (Dorion).

98 *Le Pays,* 27 June 1864, quoted in Creighton, *Road to Confederation,* p. 78, and ibid., p. 122.

99 *CD,* p. 174, and cf. pp. 192 (Bureau) and 350 (Joly). An emotive example cited was central control of divorce proceedings.

100 Dawson to Howe, 15 November 1866, quoted in *Life and Times,* p. 135.

101 *CD,* p. 351 (Joly).

102 Speech, 13 August 1864, in Chisholm, ed., *op. cit.,* II, p. 433. Howe rose to speak at ten minutes to midnight. "Who ever heard of a public man being bound by a speech on such an occasion as that?" he asked three years later. Beck, *op. cit.,* II, p. 182. In fact, Howe spoke before the Charlottetown conference.

103 Speech at Dartmouth, 22 May 1867, in Chisholm, ed., *op. cit.,* II, p. 511.

104 *BPP,* 1867, XLVIII, *Correspondence,* pp. 69–70.

105 Dartmouth speech, Chisholm, ed., *op. cit.,* II, pp. 512, 511.

106 Port Medway petition, *BPP,* 1867, XLVIII, *Correspondence,* p. 76; Howe et al. to Carnarvon, 19 January 1867, p. 7.

107 *BPP,* 1867, XLVIII, Howe et al. to Carnarvon, 19 January 1867, p. 15. J.W. Longley, *Joseph Howe* (Toronto, 1906), p. 202, and cf. Beck, *op. cit.,* II, p. 202. The reference to "a village" was, of course, unfair, but Dunkin was concerned that the federal capital was to remain "within the jurisdiction of a subordinate province." *CD,* p. 507.

108 *BPP,* 1867, XLVIII, Howe et al. to Carnarvon, 19 January 1867, p. 17 and cf. Dartmouth speech, 22 May 1867, in Chisholm, ed., *op. cit.,* II, p. 517.

109 The Nova Scotia press, it was alleged, emphasised the less attractive aspects of Canadian life, just as modern Canadians often reflect a cataclysmic view of the United States. "Not a fight occurs, not a train runs off the track and kills one or two persons in that Province but it is blazoned forth in that press." Speech by Dr. Hamilton, *Debates and Proceedings of the House of Assembly of Nova Scotia 1865,* pp. 264–65. I am grateful to Dr. James Sturgis for this reference.

110 Dorion's anti-Confederation manifesto was widely published in 1864. Quoted in *Life and Times,* p. 142. His objection may partly have originated in an element of mistranslation: "Confederation" in English had come to be a shorthand term for a reasonably centralised form of intercolonial union, while its French equivalent continued to mean a loose alliance.

111 Quoted in Bolger, ed., *op. cit.,* p. 174.

112 Halifax *Citizen,* 19 November 1864, quoted in *Life and Times,* p. 203. The lieutenant-governor, Sir Richard MacDonnell, used the same argument a few days later in a despatch: "I do not believe that so long as the boundaries of the different Provinces are maintained and Local Legislatures and petty politics fostered, the Confederation can rise to that status, and that dignity of national feeling, which creates and maintains a national military spirit and self-reliance." PRO, CO 217/235, MacDonnell to Cardwell, 22 November 1864, fos 187–212.

113 Saint John *Daily Evening Globe,* 17 October 1864, quoted in *Life and Times,* p. 136.

114 Saint John *Freeman,* 3 November 1864, quoted in Baker, *Anglin,* p. 65. Joseph Howe also condemned the duplication of legislatures as "cumbrous and expensive." Howe to Earl Russell, 19 January 1865, in Chisholm, ed., *op. cit.,* II, p. 437.

115 *CD,* p. 504. Perrault alleged that some politicians were influenced by hopes of "being governor of one of the Federated Provinces," as did Letellier, who subsequently became a lieutenant-governor himself. *CD,* pp. 626, 188.

116 *CD,* p. 157 (James Aikins).

117 *CD,* p. 253. Dorion chose to overlook the provision in Article 14 of the Quebec Resolutions that "in such nomination due regard shall be had to the claims of the Members of Legislative Council in Opposition in each Province, so that all political parties may as nearly as possible be fairly represented."

118 *CD,* pp. 494–95. The fear was a real one for French Canadians. Cf. *CD,* p. 174 (Olivier).

119 Support for the Intercolonial might not translate into support for Confederation, as in the case of J.B. Pouliot, MPP for Témiscouata.

120 Laflèche to Boucher de Niverville, 2 March 1864, quoted in Walter Ullman, "The Quebec Bishops and Confederation," *Canadian Historical Review,* XLIII (1963), p. 218.

121 Speech at Montreal, 29 October 1864, in Whelan, comp., *op. cit.,* pp. 122–23.

122 Speech at Halifax, 12 September 1864, in ibid., p. 46.

Index

habeus corpus (*Continued*)
  suspension in Lower Canada,
    321

habitants, 186–189

Haida, 256, 387

Halifax, 144, 150, 151, 152,
  154, 155, 156

Hamburg Agreement (1840),
  403

Hawaiian islanders, 46

Henry Carey &; Co., 405

Hielstuk, 387

Hillsborough, Lord, 155

History of New France
  (Lescarbot), 43

History of Newfoundland
  (Anspach), 298

Hobsbawm, Eric, 316

House of Burgesses, 133

House of Industry, 344

Howe, Joseph, 494, 496,
  497–498, 502, 504, 506

Howick, Lord, 300–301,
  302–303

Hudson, Henry, 5

Hudson's Bay Company, 11,
  266, 267, 398–416
  archival records of,
    6, 12
  competitive strategies of,
    402–403
  conservation strategies,
    406–408
  decline of beaver market,
    408–411
  employment by, 390
  labour relations, 218–219
  merger with North West
    Company, 218, 398
  operations of, 5, 385,
    411–412
  relations with Natives, 36
  structure of, 398–399

Hull, General William,
  202–203, 206, 214

Hunt, Lynn, 7

Huron-Petuns, 84, 88

Hurons, 6, 87, 118
  see also Wabanaki
    Confederacy
  and Indian Wars, 86–88
  and Iroquois Confederacy, 6,
    58, 81
  Grand Settlement of 1701
    and, 84–85

I

Iglulingmiut. *See* Inuit of North
  Baffin

Île Royale. *See* Cape Breton
  Island

Illinois, 86, 87

immigration to British
  Columbia, 384–397
  ethnic diversity of, 386–389
  gendered patterns of,
    389–391
  social and political agenda of,
    384–394

Incas, 48

Indian Act, 461, 464
  and Inuit
  status of Natives under, 458

"Indian Ginger", 464–465

*Indian History of British
  Columbia* (Duff), 256

Indian Rebellion (1857), 393

Indians of Skagit County
  (Sampson), 244

indigenous oral histories, 4–17,
  18–30
  blended history precedents,
    14–15
  challenges and criticisms of,
    1, 5–7, 9–16, 20–23
  contemporary examples of,
    6–7, 20–21

different perspectives and histories, 4–5, 7–9
  interpersonal research meth-
    ods and, 1–2, 24–26, 27
  native participation in, 21–22
  standards, protocols and
    copyright, 15, 26–27

indigenous oral traditions
  complexities and conventions
    in, 9–13
  concept of time and, 8–9,
    11–12
  distinctiveness of, 15, 22–23,
    25–26, 27
  elements and concepts of,
    7–8
  importance of, 19
  standards, protocols and
    copyright, 15, 26–27

Industrial Revolution, 58, 418,
  419

Information Age, 58

Innu oral tradition, 8–9, 15

Intercolonial Railway, 499–501,
  507

Inuit Justice Task Force, 38

Inuit of North Baffin, 32–40
  background of, 32
  cultural decay of, 34–35,
    39–40
  environmental adaptation of,
    32–33
  historical status of, 35
  justice and governance sys-
    tems, 35–36, 38–39
  spirituality of, 36–37
  whaling and trading practices
    of, 34–35, 39–40

Irish immigrants, 420, 344
  and Confederation, 505
  and government reform in
    Newfoundland, 288–290
  vagrancy among, 345–346,
    348

Iroquois Confederacy, 77

fortifications for, 113
population (1650-1710), 44
siege of, 118

Portugal, 104

Potawatomis, 84, 87

Poundmaker (Cree chief), 25

Prescott, General, 183–184, 185, 190, 191

press
of Black immigrants, 418, 425, 444–446
and government reform in Newfoundland, 289–290, 295–300, 302, 304
moral/ political agenda of, 418, 432–452
and national identities, 440–444
and racial redemption, 438–440

Prevost, Sir George, 196, 199, 200, 201, 205, 207–209, 210

Price, Richard, 14, 15

Pricket, Abacuk, 5, 12

Prince Edward Island
see also Acadia
land policy in, 266, 268–287
opposition to Confederation, 499, 502, 503, 504, 505, 506

Prince Edward Island Association, 276

Principles of Gardening (Johnson), 48, 49

prostitution
among vagrant women, 343, 346, 347–348, 351, 352, 353
in Canada West, 436–437, 438

Protestantism, 150
in eighteenth century Montreal, 344

and government reform in Newfoundland, 288–289, 296
in Nova Scotia, 150–151
in Hawaii, 46
and land policy in Prince Edward Island, 269

Provincial Freeman, 418, 425, 444–446

Public Health Act(s), 470–471, 475, 476, 477, 482–485

Public Ledger, 290, 295, 299, 300

publication of the banns, 64–65

Q

Qitdlarssuaq, 39

Quakeolths, 257

Quakers, 197, 209

Quebec, 144
see also Lower Canada; New France
cholera epidemic, 419, 470–492

Quebec Act (1774), 144

Quebec City Health Act, 482–483

Quebec Resolutions and Confederation, 493–512

Queen Victoria, 494

Queenston Heights, Battle of, 208, 211, 213

Quimper, Manuel, 244

R

racism. *See* stereotypes and racism

Rappaport, Joanne, 14, 15

Rasmussen, Knud, 32

RCMP. *See* Royal Canadian Mounted Police (RCMP)

rebellion(s)

see also Lower Canada security threats
of 1837 (Upper and Lower Canada), 281
of Lower Canada, 317–329
by Montreal fur trade workers, 230–231
North-West (1885), 461
riots of 1794, 176–178, 187, 190

reciprocal labour. *See* work bees

reform movements. *See* escheat movement; representative government campaign in Newfoundland

Relation (Biard), 47, 53

religion. *See* Catholic Church; Christianity; Protestantism

representative government campaign in Newfoundland, 288–311
background and origins of, 288–290, 304
colonial reform movement in London, 300–303
constitutional reform, 293–294
against naval government, 290–293
summary of, 304–305
taxation without representation, 291, 296–300, 304

responsible government, 266, 418
in Newfoundland, 288–311

Richardson, John, 401

Riot Act (1714), 314

riots of 1794, 176–178, 187, 190

Rivière Sainte-Marie, 114

Road Act (1796)
purpose of, 180–181
riots, 182–184, 187, 190